463.21 LANGENSC

D0328096

WEST WYANDOTTE
KANSAS CITY KANSAS
PUBLIC LIBRARY

DEC 2 8 2006

admirador *m*, **~a** *f* admirer
campeón *m*, **-ona** *f* champion
salvapantallas *m inv* INFOR screen saver
ronquido *m* snore; **~s** *pl* snoring *sg*
enemigo 1 *adj* enemy *atr* **2** *m* enemy; **ser ~ de** *fig* be opposed to, be against
lleno *adj* full (**de** of); *pared* covered (**de** with)

---

debatir <3a> **1** *v/t* debate, discuss **2** *v/i* struggle **3** *v/r* **~se**: **~se entre la vida y la muerte** fight for one's life

División de artículo en categorías gramaticales
Entries divided into grammatical categories

---

uva *f* BOT grape; **estar de mala ~** F be in a foul mood; **tener mala ~** F be a nasty piece of work F
fiambre *m* cold cut, *Br* cold meat; P (*cadáver*) stiff P
profiláctico 1 *adj* preventive, prophylactic *fml* **2** *m* condom

Marcas de registro
Register labels

---

acomedido *adj L.Am.* obliging, helpful; **acomedirse** <3l> *v/r Méx* offer to help
residencial 1 *adj* residential **2** *f Arg*, *Chi* boarding house
sablear <1a> *v/t & v/i L.Am.* F scrounge (**a** from)

Español latinoamericano
Latin American Spanish

---

riñonera *f* fanny pack, *Br* bum bag
rotonda *f* traffic circle, *Br* roundabout

Variantes del inglés británico
British variants

D
E
F
G
H
I
J K
L
M
N
Ñ
O
P
Q
R S
T
U
V
W X
Y
Z

Langenscheidt

Pocket Spanish Dictionary

Spanish – English
English – Spanish

edited by the
Langenscheidt editorial staff

Langenscheidt

New York · Berlin · Munich · Vienna · Zurich

Neither the presence nor the absence of a des-
ignation indicating that any entered word
constitutes a trademark should be regarded as
affecting the legal status thereof.

Compiled by LEXUS
with
José A. Gálvez · Roy Russell
Jane Goldie · Peter Terrell
Monica Tamariz-Martel Mirêlis · Rafael Alarcón Gaeta
Andrew Wilkes · Stephanie Parker
Mike Gonzalez

© 2006 Langenscheidt KG, Berlin and Munich
Printed in Germany

06 07 08 09 10 5. 4. 3. 2. 1.

Preface

Here is a new dictionary of English and Spanish, a tool with some 50,000 references for those who work with the English and Spanish languages at beginner's or intermediate level.

Focusing on modern usage, the dictionary offers coverage of everyday language – and this means including vocabulary from areas such as computer use and business. English means both American and British English; Spanish means both Latin American and European Spanish.

The editors have provided a reference tool to enable the user to get straight to the translation that fits a particular context of use. Indicating words are given to identify senses. Is the *mouse* you need for your computer, for example, the same in Spanish as the *mouse* you don't want in the house? Is *flimsy* referring to furniture the same in Spanish as *flimsy* referring to an excuse? This dictionary is rich in sense distinctions like this – and in translation options tied to specific, identified senses.

Vocabulary needs grammar to back it up. So in this dictionary you'll find irregular verb forms, in both English and Spanish, irregular English plural forms, guidance on Spanish feminine endings and on prepositional usage with verbs.

Since some vocabulary items are often only clearly understood when contextualized, a large number of idiomatic phrases are given to show how the two languages correspond in particular contexts.

All in all, this is a book full of information, which will, we hope, become a valuable part of your language toolkit.

Contents

How to use the dictionary

To get the most out of your dictionary you should understand how and where to find the information you need. Whether you are yourself writing text in a foreign language or wanting to understand text that has been written in a foreign language, the following pages should help.

1. How and where do I find a word?

1.1 Spanish and English headwords. The word list for each language is arranged in alphabetical order and also gives irregular forms of verbs and nouns in their correct alphabetical order.

Sometimes you might want to look up terms made up of two separate words, for example **shooting star**, or hyphenated words, for example **absent-minded**. These words are treated as though they were a single word and their alphabetical ordering reflects this.

The only exception to this strict alphabetical ordering is made for English phrasal verbs - words like **go off**, **go out**, **go up**. These are positioned in a block directly after their main verb (in this case **go**), rather than being scattered around in alphabetical positions.

Spanish words beginning with **ch** and **ll** are positioned in their alphabetical position in letters C and L. Words beginning with **ñ** are listed after N.

1.2 Spanish feminine headwords are shown as follows:

> **abogado** *m*, **-a** *f* lawyer
> **fumador** *m*, **-a** *f* smoker
> **bailarín** *m*, **-ina** *f* dancer
> **pibe** *m*, **-a** *f Rpl* F kid F
> **edil** *m*, **~a** *f* council(l)or

The feminine forms of these headwords are: **abogada**, **fumadora**, **bailarina**, **piba** and **edila**.

When a Spanish headword has a feminine form which translates differently from the masculine form, the feminine is entered as a separate headword in alphabetical order:

> **empresaria** *f* businesswoman; **empresario** *m* businessman

1.3 Running heads

If you are looking for a Spanish or English word you can use the **running heads** printed in bold in the top corner of each page. The running head on the left tells you the *first* headword (either blue or black) on the left-hand page and the one on the right tells you the *last* headword (either blue or black) on the right-hand page.

1.4 How is the word spelt?

You can look up the spelling of a word in your dictionary in the same way as you would in a spelling dictionary. British spelling variants are marked *Br.* If just a single letter is omitted in the American spelling, this is put between round brackets:

colo(u)r – hono(u)r – travel(l)er

2. How do I split a word?

Spanish speakers find English hyphenation very difficult. All you have to do with this dictionary is look for the bold dots between syllables. These dots show you where you can split a word at the end of a line but you should avoid having just one letter before or after the hyphen as in **a•mend** or **thirst•y**. In such cases it is better to take the entire word over to the next line.

3. Swung dashes and long dashes

3.1 A swung dash (~) replaces the entire headword, when the headword is repeated within an entry:

> **face** [feɪs] **1** *n* cara *f*; ~ *to* ~ cara a cara

Here ~ *to* ~ means *face to face*.

> **rencor** *m* resentment; *guardar* ~ *a alguien* bear s.o. a grudge

Here *guardar* ~ *a alguien* means *guardar rencor a alguien*.

3.2 When a headword changes form in an entry, for example if it is put in the past tense or in the plural, then the past tense or plural ending is added to the swung dash – but only if the rest of the word doesn't change:

> **flame** [fleɪm] *n* llama *f*; *go up in* ~*s* ser pasto de las llamas
> **parch** [pɑːrtʃ] *v/t* secar; *be* ~*ed* F *of person* estar muerto de sed F

But:

> **sur•vive** [sərˈvaɪv] **1** *v/i* sobrevivir; *how are you? – I'm surviving* ¿cómo estás? – voy tirando
> **saltón** *adj*: *ojos saltones* bulging eyes

3.3 Double headwords are replaced by a single swung dash:

> **Pan•a•ma Ca'nal** *n*: *the* ~ el Canal de Panamá
> **one-track 'mind** *hum*: *have a* ~ ser un obseso

3.4 In the Spanish-English part of the dictionary, when a headword is repeated in a phrase or compound with an altered form, a long dash is used:

> **escaso** *adj* ... *-as posibilidades de* not much chance of, little chance of

Here *-as posibilidades* means *escasas posibilidades*.

4. What do the different typefaces mean?

4.1 All Spanish and English headwords and the Arabic numerals differentiating between parts of speech appear in **bold**:

> **neoyorquino 1** *adj* New York *atr* **2** *m*, **-a** New Yorker
> **splin·ter** ['splɪntər] **1** *n* astilla *f* **2** *v/i* astillarse

4.2 *Italics* are used for:

a) abbreviated grammatical labels: *adj*, *adv*, *v/i*, *v/t* etc

b) gender labels: *m*, *f*, *mpl* etc

c) all the indicating words which are the signposts pointing to the correct translation for your needs:

> **sport·y** ['spɔːrtɪ] *adj person* deportista; *clothes* deportivo
> ♦ **work out 1** *v/t problem*, *puzzle* resolver; *solution* encontrar, hallar
>   **2** *v/i at gym* hacer ejercicios; *of relationship etc* funcionar, ir bien
> **completo** *adj* complete; *autobús*, *teatro* full
> **grano** *m* grain; *de café* bean; *en la piel* pimple, spot

4.3 All phrases (examples and idioms) are given in ***secondary bold italics***:

> **sym·pa·thet·ic** [sɪmpə'θetɪk] *adj* (*showing pity*) compasivo;
> (*understanding*) comprensivo; ***be ~ toward a person / an idea***
> simpatizar con una persona / idea
> **salsa** *f* GASTR sauce; *baile* salsa; ***en su ~*** *fig* in one's element

4.4 The normal typeface is used for the translations.

4.5 If a translation is given in italics, and not in the normal typeface, this means that the translation is more of an *explanation* in the other language and that an explanation has to be given because there just is no real equivalent:

> **'walk-up** *n apartamento en un edificio sin ascensor*
> **adobera** *f Méx type of mature cheese*

5. Stress

To indicate where to put the **stress** in English words, the stress marker ' appears before the syllable on which the main stress falls:

> **mo·tif** [moʊ'tiːf] motivo *m*
> **rec·ord¹** ['rekɔːrd] *n* MUS disco *m*; SP *etc* récord *m*
> **re·cord²** [rɪ'kɔːrd] *v/t electronically* grabar; *in writing* anotar

Stress is shown either in the pronunciation or, if there is no pronunciation given, in the actual headword or compound itself:

> **'rec·ord hold·er** plusmarquista *m/f*

6. What do the various symbols and abbreviations tell you?

6.1 A solid blue diamond is used to indicate a phrasal verb:

> ♦ **call off** *v/t* (*cancel*) cancelar; *strike* desconvocar

6.2 A white diamond is used to divide up longer entries into more easily digested chunks of related bits of text:

> **de** *prp* ◊ *origen* from; ~ *Nueva York* from New York; ~ *... a* from ... to ◊ *posesión* of; *el coche* ~ *mi amigo* my friend's car ◊ *material* (made) of; *un anillo* ~ *oro* a gold ring ◊ *contenido* of; *un vaso* ~ *agua* a glass of water ◊ *cualidad*: *una mujer* ~ *20 años* a 20 year old woman ◊ *causa* with; *temblaba* ~ *miedo* she was shaking with fear ...

6.3 The abbreviation F tells you that the word or phrase is used colloquially rather than in formal contexts. The abbreviation V warns you that a word or phrase is vulgar or taboo. Words or phrases labeled P are slang. Be careful how you use these words.

These abbreviations, F, V and P, are used both for headwords and phrases (placed after) and for the translations of headwords and phrases (placed after). If there is no such label given, then the word or phrase is neutral.

6.4 A colon before an English or Spanish word or phrase means that usage is restricted to this specific example (at least as far as this dictionary's translation is concerned):

> **catch-22** [kætʃtwentɪˈtuː]: *it's a ~ situation* es como la pescadilla que se muerde la cola
> **co-au·thor** [ˈkoʊɒːθər] ... **2** *v/t*: ~ *a book* escribir un libro conjuntamente
> **decantarse** <1a> *v/r*: ~ *por* opt for

7. Does the dictionary deal with grammar too?

7.1 All English headwords are given a part of speech label:

> **tooth·less** [ˈtuːθlɪs] *adj* desdentado
> **top·ple** [ˈtɑːpl] **1** *v/i* derrumbarse **2** *v/t government* derrocar

But if a headword can only be used as a noun (in ordinary English) then no part of speech is given, since none is needed:

> **'tooth·paste** pasta *f* de dientes, dentífrico *m*

7.2 Spanish headwords have part of speech labels. Spanish gender markers are given:

> **barbacoa** *f* barbecue
> **bocazas** *m/f inv* F loudmouth F
> **budista** *m/f & adj* Buddhist

7.3 If an English translation of an Spanish adjective can only be used in front of a noun, and not after it, this is marked with *atr*:

> **bursátil** *adj* stock market *atr*
> **campestre** *adj* rural, country *atr*

7.4 If the Spanish, unlike the English, doesn't change form if used in the plural, this is marked with *inv*:

> **cortacircuitos** *m inv* circuit breaker
> **metrópolis** *f inv* metropolis

7.5 If the English, in spite of appearances, is not a plural form, this is marked with *nsg*:

> **bil·li·ards** ['bɪljərdz] *nsg* billar *m*
> **mea·sles** ['mi:zlz] *nsg* sarampión *m*

English translations are given a *pl* or *sg* label (for plural or singular) in cases where this does not match the Spanish:

> **acciones** *pl* COM stock *sg*, *Br* shares
> **entarimado** *m* (*suelo*) floorboards *pl*

7.6 Irregular English plurals are identified:

> **the·sis** ['θi:sɪs] (*pl* **theses** ['θi:si:z]) tesis *f inv*
> **thief** [θi:f] (*pl* **thieves** [θi:vz]) ladrón(-ona) *m(f)*
> **trout** [traʊt] (*pl* **trout**) trucha *f*

7.7 Words like **physics** or **media studies** have not been given a label to say if they are singular or plural for the simple reason that they can be either, depending on how they are used.

7.8 Irregular and semi-irregular verb forms are identified:

> **sim·pli·fy** ['sɪmplɪfaɪ] *v/t* (*pret & pp* **-ied**) simplificar
> **sing** [sɪŋ] *v/t & v/i* (*pret* **sang**, *pp* **sung**) cantar
> **la·bel** ['leɪbl] **1** *n* etiqueta *f* **2** *v/t* (*pret & pp* **-ed**, *Br* **-led**) bags etiquetar

7.9 Cross-references are given to tables of Spanish conjugations:

> **gemir** <3l> *v/i* moan, groan
> **esconder** <2a> **1** *v/t* hide, conceal ...

7.10 Grammatical information is provided on the prepositions you'll need in order to create complete sentences:

> **'switch·o·ver** *to new system* cambio *m* (**to** a)
> **sneer** [snɪr] **1** *n* mueca *f* desdeñosa **2** *v/i* burlarse (**at** de)
> **escindirse** <3a> *v/r* (*fragmentarse*) split (**en** into); (*segregarse*) break away (**de** from)
> **enviciarse** <1b> *v/r* get addicted (**con** to)

Abbreviations

and	&	y	electronics, electronic engineering	ELEC	electrónica, electrotecnia
see	→	véase	Spain	*Esp*	España
registered trademark	®	marca registrada	especially	*esp*	especialmente
abbreviation	*abbr*	abreviatura	euphemistic	*euph*	eufemismo
abbreviation	*abr*	abreviatura	familiar, colloquial	F	familiar
adjective	*adj*	adjetivo	feminine	*f*	femenino
adverb	*adv*	adverbio	feminine noun and adjective	*f/adj*	sustantivo femenino y adjetivo
agriculture	AGR	agricultura			
anatomy	ANAT	anatomía			
architecture	ARCHI	arquitectura	railroad	FERR	ferrocarriles
Argentina	*Arg*	Argentina	figurative	*fig*	figurativo
architecture	ARQUI	arquitectura	financial	FIN	finanzas
article	*art*	artículo	physics	FÍS	física
astronomy	AST	astronomía	formal	*fml*	formal
astrology	ASTR	astrología	photography	FOT	fotografía
attributive	*atr*	atributivo	feminine plural	*fpl*	femenino plural
motoring	AUTO	automóvil			
civil aviation	AVIA	aviación	feminine singular	*fsg*	femenino singular
biology	BIO	biología			
Bolivia	*Bol*	Bolivia	gastronomy	GASTR	gastronomía
botany	BOT	botánica	geography	GEOG	geografía
British English	*Br*	inglés británico	geology	GEOL	geología
			geometry	GEOM	geometría
Central America	*C.Am.*	América Central	grammatical	GRAM	gramática
chemistry	CHEM	química	historical	HIST	histórico
Chile	*Chi*	Chile	humorous	*hum*	humorístico
Colombia	*Col*	Colombia	IT term	INFOR	informática
commerce, business	COM	comercio	interjection	*int*	interjección
comparative	*comp*	comparativo	interrogative	*interr*	interrogativo
computers, IT term	COMPUT	informática	invariable	*inv*	invariable
			ironic	*iron*	irónico
conjunction	*conj*	conjunción	ironic	*irón*	irónico
Southern Cone	*CSur*	Cono Sur	law	JUR	jurisprudencia
sports	DEP	deporte	Latin America	*L.Am.*	América Latina
contemptuous	*desp*	despectivo	law	LAW	jurisprudencia
determiner	*det*	determinante	linguistics	LING	lingüística
Ecuador	*Ecuad*	Ecuador	literary	*lit*	literario
education (schools, universities)	EDU	educación, enseñanza (sistema escolar y universitario)	masculine	*m*	masculino
			masculine noun and adjective	*m/adj*	sustantivo masculino y adjetivo
electronics, electronic engineering	EL	electrónica, electrotecnia	nautical	MAR	navegación, marina
			mathematics	MAT	matemáticas

mathematics	MATH	matemáticas	preterite	*pret*	pretérito
medicine	MED	medicina	(past tense)		
meteorology	METEO	meteorología	pronoun	*pron*	pronombre
Mexico	*Mex*	México	preposition	*prp*	preposición
Mexico	*Méx*	México	psychology	PSI	psicología
masculine and feminine	*m/f*	masculino y femenino	psychology	PSYCH	psicología
			chemistry	QUÍM	química
masculine and feminine plural	*m/fpl*	masculino y femenino plural	radio	RAD	radio
			railroad	RAIL	ferrocarriles
military	MIL	militar	relative	*rel*	relativo
mineralogy	MIN	mineralogía	religion	REL	religión
motoring	MOT	automóvil	River Plate	*Rpl*	Río de la Plata
masculine plural	*mpl*	masculino plural	South America	*S.Am.*	América del Sur
music	MUS	música	singular	*sg*	singular
music	MÚS	música	someone	s.o.	alguien
mythology	MYTH	mitología	sports	SP	deporte
noun	*n*	sustantivo	Spain	*Span*	España
nautical	NAUT	navegación, náutica	something	*sth*	algo, alguna cosa
negative	*neg*	negativo	subjunctive	*subj*	subjuntivo
noun plural	*npl*	sustantivo plural	superlative	*sup*	superlativo
			bullfighting	TAUR	tauromaquia
noun singular	*nsg*	sustantivo singular	also	*tb*	también
			theater, theatre	TEA	teatro
ornithology	ORN	ornitología	technology	TÉC	técnica
oneself	o.s.	sí mismo	technology	TECH	técnica
popular, slang	P	popular	telecommunications	TELEC	telecomunicaciones
painting	PAINT	pintura			
Paraguay	*Parag*	Paraguay	theater	THEA	teatro
past participle	*part*	participio pasado	typography, typesetting	TIP	tipografía
Peru	*Pe*	Perú	transportation	TRANSP	transportes
pejorative	*pej*	peyorativo	television	TV	televisión
photography	PHOT	fotografía	vulgar	V	vulgar
physics	PHYS	física	auxiliary verb	*v/aux*	verbo auxiliar
painting	PINT	pintura	verb	*vb*	verbo
plural	*pl*	plural	Venezuela	*Ven*	Venezuela
politics	POL	política	intransitive verb	*v/i*	verbo intransitivo
possessive	*pos*	posesivo			
possessive	*poss*	posesivo	impersonal verb	*v/impers*	verbo impersonal
past participle	*pp*	participio pasado	reflexive verb	*v/r*	verbo reflexivo
predicative usage	*pred*	predicativo	transitive verb	*v/t*	verbo transitivo
prefix	*pref*	prefijo	West Indies	*W.I.*	Antillas
preposition	*prep*	preposición	zoology	ZO	zoología

The pronunciation of Spanish

Stress

1. If a word ends in a vowel, or in *n* or *s*, the penultimate syllable is stressed: **espada, biblioteca, hablan, telefonean, edificios**.

2. If a word ends in a consonant other than *n* or *s*, the last syllable is stressed: **dificultad, hablar, laurel, niñez**.

3. If a word is to be stressed in any way contrary to rules 1 and 2, an acute accent is written over the stressed vowel: **rubí, máquina, crímenes, carácter, continúa, autobús**.

4. **Diphthongs and syllable division.** Of the 5 vowels *a, e, o* are considered "strong" and *i* and *u* "weak":

   a) A combination of weak + strong forms a diphthong, the stress falling on the stronger element: **reina, baile, cosmonauta, tiene, bueno**.

   b) A combination of weak + weak forms a diphthong, the stress falling on the second element: **viuda, ruido**.

   c) Two strong vowels together remain two distinct syllables, the stress falling according to rules 1 and 2: **ma/estro, atra/er**.

   d) Any word having a vowel combination not stressed according to these rules has an accent: **traído, oído, baúl, río**.

Sounds

Since the pronunciation of Spanish is (unlike English) adequately represented by the spelling of words, Spanish headwords have not been given a phonetic transcription. The sounds of Spanish are described below.

The pronunciation described is primarily that of the educated Spaniard. But the main features of Latin American pronunciation are also covered.

Vowels

a As in English *father*: **paz, pata**.

e Like *e* in English *they* (but without the following sound of *y*): **grande, pelo**. A shorter sound when followed by a consonant in the same syllable, like *e* in English *get*: **España, renta**.

i Like *i* in English *machine*, though somewhat shorter: **pila, rubí**.

o As in English *November, token*: **solo, esposa**. A shorter sound when followed by a consonant in the same syllable, like *au* in English *fault* or the *a* in *fall*: **costra, bomba**.

u Like *oo* in English *food*: **pura, luna**. Silent after **q** and in **gue, gui**, unless marked with a dieresis (**antigüedad, argüir**).

y when occurring as a vowel (in the conjunction **y** or at the end of a word), is pronounced like *i*.

Diphthongs

ai like *i* in English *right*: **baile, vaina**.

ei like *ey* in English *they*: **reina, peine**.

oi like *oy* in English *boy*: **boina, oigo**.

au like *ou* in English *bout*: **causa, audacia**.

eu like the vowel sounds in English *may-you*, without the sound of the *y*: **deuda, reuma**.

Semiconsonants

i, y like *y* in English *yes*: **yerno, tiene**; in some cases in *L.Am.* this *y* is pronounced like the *s* in English *measure*: **mayo, yo**.

u like *w* in English *water*: **huevo, agua**.

Consonants

b, v These two letters represent the same value in Spanish. There are two distinct pronunciations:
  1. At the start of a word and after *m* and *n* the sound is like English *b*: **batalla, ventaja; tromba, invierno**.
  2. In all other positions the sound is what is technically a "bilabial fricative". This sound does not exist in English. Go to say a *b* but do not quite bring your lips together: **estaba, cueva, de Vigo**.

c 1. *c* before *a, o, u* or a consonant is like English *k*: **café, cobre**.
  2. *c* before *e, i* is like English *th* in *thin*: **cédula, cinco**. In *L.Am.* this is pronounced like an English *s* in *chase*.

ch like English *ch* in *church*: **mucho, chocho**.

d Three distinct pronunciations:
  1. At the start of a word and after *l* and *n*, the sound is like English *d*: **doy, aldea, conde**.
  2. Between vowels and after consonants other than *l* and *n* the sound is relaxed and approaches English *th* in *this*: **codo, guardar**; in parts of Spain it is further relaxed and even disappears, particularly in the -ado ending.
  3. In final position, this type 2 is further relaxed or omitted altogether: **usted, Madrid**.

f like English *f*: **fuero, flor**.

g Three distinct pronunciations:
  1. Before *e* and *i* it is the same as the Spanish j (below): **coger, general**.
  2. At the start of a word and after *n*, the sound is that of English *g* in *get*: **granada, rango**.
  3. In other positions the sound is like 2 above, but much softer, the *g* almost disappearing: **agua, guerra**. N.B. In the group **gue, gui** the u is silent (**guerra, guindar**) unless marked with a dieresis (**antigüedad, argüir**). In the group **gua** all letters are sounded.

h	always silent: **honor, búho**.
j	A strong guttural sound not found in English, but like the *ch* in Scots *loch*, German *Achtung*: **jota, ejercer**.
k	like English *k*: **kilogramo, ketchup**.
l	like English *l*: **león, pala**.
ll	approximating to English *lli* in *million*: **millón, calle**. In *L.Am.* like the *s* in English *measure*.
m	like English *m*: **mano, como**.
n	like English *n*: **nono, pan**; except before **v**, when the group is pronounced like *mb*: **enviar, invadir**.
ñ	approximating to English *ni* in *onion*: **paño, ñoño**.
p	like English *p*: **Pepe, copa**.
q	like English *k*; always in combination with **u**, which is silent: **que, quiosco**.
r	a single trill stronger than any *r* in English, but like Scots *r*: **caro, querer**. Somewhat relaxed in final position. Pronounced like **rr** at the start of a word and after **l, n, s**: **rata**.
rr	strongly trilled: **carro, hierro**.
s	like *s* in English *chase*: **rosa, soso**. But before **b, d**, hard **g, l, m** and **n** it is like English *s* in *rose*: **desde, mismo, asno**. Before "impure **s**" in recent loan-words, an extra *e*-sound is inserted in pronunciation: **e-sprint, e-stand**.
t	like English *t*: **patata, tope**.
v	see **b**.
w	found in a few recent loan-words only and pronounced pretty much as the English *w*, but sometimes with a very slight *g* sound before it: **whisky, windsurf**. In one exceptional case it is pronounced like an English *v* or like Spanish **b** and **v**: **wáter**.
x	like English *gs* in *big sock*: **máximo, examen**. Before a consonant like English *s* in *chase*: **extraño, mixto**.
z	like English *th* in *thin*: **zote, zumbar**. In *L.Am.* like English *s* in *chase*.

The Spanish Alphabet

a [ah]	g [Heh]	m ['emeh]	rr ['erreh]	x ['ekees]
b [beh]	h ['acheh]	n ['eneh]	s ['eseh]	y [eegree-'eh-ga]
c [theh]	i [ee]	ñ ['en-yeh]	t [teh]	z ['theh-ta]
ch [cheh]	j ['Hota]	o [oh]	u [oo]	
d [deh]	k [ka]	p [peh]	v ['ooveh]	*H is pronounced*
e [eh]	l ['eleh]	q [koo]	w ['ooveh	*as in the Scottish*
f ['ef-feh]	ll ['el-yeh]	r ['ereh]	doh-bleh]	*way of saying loch*

Written Spanish

I. Capitalization

The rules for capitalization in Spanish largely correspond to those for the English language. In contrast to English, however, adjectives derived from proper nouns are not capitalized (*americano* American, *español* Spanish).

II. Word division

Spanish words are divided according to the following rules:

1. If there is a **single consonant** between two vowels, the division is made between the first vowel and the consonant (*di-ne-ro*, *Gra-na-da*).

2. **Two consecutive consonants** may be divided (*miér-co-les*, *dis-cur-so*). If the second consonant is an *l* or *r*, however, the division comes before the two consonants (*re-gla*, *nie-bla*; *po-bre*, *ca-bra*). This also goes for ch, ll and rr (*te-cho*, *ca-lle*, *pe-rro*).

3. In the case of **three consecutive consonants** (usually including an *l* or *r*), the division comes after the first consonant (*ejem-plo*, *siem-pre*). If the second consonant is an *s*, however, the division comes after the *s* (*cons-tan-te*, *ins-ti-tu-to*).

4. In the case of **four consecutive consonants** (the second of these is usually an *s*), the division is made between the second and third consonants (*ins-tru-men-to*).

5. **Diphthongs** and **triphthongs** may not be divided (*bien*, *buey*). Vowels which are part of different syllables, however, may be divided (*frí-o*, *acre-e-dor*).

6. **Compounds**, including those formed with prefixes, are divided morphologically (*nos-otros*, *des-ali-ño*, *dis-cul-pa*).

III. Punctuation

In Spanish a comma is often placed after an adverbial phrase introducing a sentence (*sin embargo, todos los esfuerzos fueron inútiles* however, all efforts were in vain). A subsidiary clause beginning a sentence is also followed by a comma (*si tengo tiempo, lo haré* if I have time, I'll do it, **but**: *lo haré si tengo tiempo* I'll do it if I have time).

Questions and exclamations are introduced by an inverted question mark and exclamation point respectively, which immediately precedes the question or exclamation (*Dispense usted, ¿está en casa el señor Pérez?* Excuse me, is Mr. Pérez at home?; *¡Que lástima!* What a shame!).

English pronunciation

Vowels

[ɑː]	*father* [ˈfɑːðər]
[æ]	*man* [mæn]
[e]	*get* [get]
[ə]	*about* [əˈbaʊt]
[ɜː]	*absurd* [əbˈsɜːrd]
[ɪ]	*stick* [stɪk]
[iː]	*need* [niːd]
[ɒː]	*in-laws* [ˈɪnlɒːz]
[ɔː]	*more* [mɔːr]
[ʌ]	*mother* [ˈmʌðər]
[ʊ]	*book* [bʊk]
[uː]	*fruit* [fruːt]

Diphthongs

[aɪ]	*time* [taɪm]
[aʊ]	*cloud* [klaʊd]
[eɪ]	*name* [neɪm]
[ɔɪ]	*point* [pɔɪnt]
[oʊ]	*oath* [oʊθ]

Consonants

[b]	*bag* [bæg]
[d]	*dear* [dɪr]
[f]	*fall* [fɒːl]
[g]	*give* [gɪv]
[h]	*hole* [hoʊl]
[j]	*yes* [jes]
[k]	*come* [kʌm]
[l]	*land* [lænd]
[m]	*mean* [miːn]
[n]	*night* [naɪt]
[p]	*pot* [pɑːt]
[r]	*right* [raɪt]
[s]	*sun* [sʌn]
[t]	*take* [teɪk]
[v]	*vain* [veɪn]
[w]	*wait* [weɪt]
[z]	*rose* [roʊz]
[ŋ]	*bring* [brɪŋ]
[ʃ]	*she* [ʃiː]
[ʧ]	*chair* [ʧer]
[dʒ]	*join* [dʒɔɪn]
[ʒ]	*leisure* [ˈliːʒər]
[θ]	*think* [θɪŋk]
[ð]	*the* [ðə]
[ˈ]	means that the following syllable is stressed: *ability* [əˈbɪlətɪ]

A

a *prp* ◊ *dirección* to; **al este de** to the east of; **a casa** home; **ir a la cama/ al cine** go to bed/to the movies; **vamos a Bolivia** we're going to Bolivia; **voy a casa de Marta** I'm going to Marta's (house) ◊ *situación* at; **a la mesa** at the table; **al lado de** next to; **a la derecha** on the right; **al sol** in the sun; **a treinta kilómetros de Quito** thirty kilometers (*Br* kilometres) from Quito; **está a cinco kilómetros** it is five kilometers (*Br* kilometres) away ◊ *tiempo:* **¿a qué hora llegas?** what time do you arrive?; **a las tres** at three o'clock; **estamos a quince de febrero** it's February fifteenth; **a los treinta años** at the age of thirty ◊ *modo:* **a la española** the Spanish way; **a mano** by hand; **a pie** on foot; **a 50 kilómetros por hora** at fifty kilometers (*Br* kilometres) an hour ◊ *precio:* **¿a cómo** or **cuánto está?** how much is it? ◊ *objeto indirecto:* **dáselo a tu hermano** give it to your brother ◊ *objeto directo:* **vi a mi padre** I saw my father ◊ *en perífrasis verbal:* **empezar a** begin to; **jugar a las cartas** play cards; **a decir verdad** to tell the truth ◊ *para introducir pregunta:* **¿a que no lo sabes?** I bet you don't know; **a ver ...** OK ..., right ...

ábaco *m* abacus

abadía *f* abbey

abajo 1 *adv situación* below, underneath; *en edificio* downstairs; **ponlo ahí** → put it down there; **el cajón de** → siguiente the drawer below; *último* the bottom drawer ◊ *dirección: en edificio* downstairs; **cuesta** → downhill; **empuja hacia** → push down ◊ *con cantidades:* **de diez para** → ten or under, ten or

below **2** *int:* **¡**~ **los traidores!** down with the traitors!

abalanzarse <1f> *v/i* rush *o* surge forward; ~ **sobre algo/alguien** leap *o* pounce on sth/s.o.

abalear <1a> *v/t S.Am.* shoot

abandonar <1a> **1** *v/t lugar* leave; *objeto, a alguien* abandon; *a esposa, hijos* desert; *idea* give up, abandon; *actividad* give up **2** ~**se** let o.s. go; ~**se a** abandon o.s. to

abanicar <1g> **1** *v/t* fan **2** *v/r* ~**se** *v/r* fan o.s.; **abanico** *m* fan; *fig* range; ~ **eléctrico** *Méx* electric fan

abaratar <1a> *v/t* reduce or lower the price of; *precio* reduce, lower

abarcar <1g> *v/t territorio* cover; *fig* comprise, cover; *L.Am.* (*acaparar*) hoard, stockpile; **el libro abarca desde ... hasta ...** the book covers the period from ... to ...; ~ **con la vista** take in

abarrotado *adj* packed; **abarrotar** <1a> **1** *v/t lugar* pack; *L.Am.* COM buy up, stockpile **2** *v/r* ~**se** *L.Am. del mercado* become glutted; **abarrotería** *f Méx, C.Am.* grocery store, *Br* grocer's; **abarrotero** *m*, -**a** *f Méx, C.Am.* storekeeper, shopkeeper; **abarrotes** *mpl L.Am.* (*mercancías*) groceries *pl*; (**tienda de**) ~ grocery store, *Br* grocer's

abastecer <2d> **1** *v/t* supply (**de** with) **2** *v/r* ~**se** stock up (**de** *o* **con** with); **abastecimiento** *m* supply

abasto *m:* **no dan** ~ they can't cope (**con** with)

abatí *m Rpl* corn, *Br* maize; *Parag:* fermented maize drink

abatible *adj* collapsible, folding *atr*; **abatido** *adj* depressed; **abatimiento** *m* gloom; **abatir** <3a> *v/t edificio* knock *o* pull down; *árbol* cut down, fell; AVIA shoot *o* bring down; *fig*

kill; (*deprimir*) depress
abdicación *f* abdication; **abdicar** <1g> *v/t* abdicate
abdomen *m* abdomen; **abdominal** *adj* abdominal; **abdominales** *mpl* sit-ups
abecedario *m* alphabet
abedul *m* birch
abeja *f* ZO bee; **abejorro** *m* bumblebee
aberración *f* aberration
abertura *f* opening
abeto *m* fir (tree)
abiertamente *adv* openly; **abierto 1** *part* → **abrir 2** *adj tb persona* open; **está ~ a nuevas ideas** *fig* he's open to new ideas
abigarrado *adj* multicolo(u)red
abismo *m* abyss; *fig* gulf
ablandar <1a> **1** *v/t tb fig* soften **2** *v/r* **~se** soften, get softer; *fig* relent; **ablande** *m Arg* AUTO running in
abnegación *f* self-denial; **abnegado** *adj* selfless
abocado *adj* doomed; **~ al fracaso** doomed to failure, destined to fail
abochornar <1a> **1** *v/t* embarrass **2** *v/r* **~se** feel embarrassed
abogacía *f* law
abogaderas *fpl L.Am.* F (*discusiones*) arguments
abogado *m*, **-a** *f* lawyer; *en tribunal superior* attorney, *Br* barrister; **no le faltaron ~s** *fig* there were plenty of people who defended him; **abogar** <1h> *v/i*: **~ por** *alguien* defend; *algo* advocate
abolición *f* abolition; **abolir** <3a> *v/t* abolish
abollado *adj* dented; **abolladura** *f* dent; **abollar** <1a> *v/t* dent
abombado *adj S.Am.* F *comida* rotten, bad; F (*tonto*) dopey F; **abombarse** *S.Am. de comida* go off, go bad
abominable *adj* abominable; **abominar** <1a> *v/t* detest, loathe
abonado *m*, **-a** *f* subscriber; *a teléfono, gas, electricidad* customer; *a ópera, teatro* season-ticket holder;

abonar <1a> **1** *v/t* COM pay; AGR fertilize; *Méx* pay on account; **~ el terreno** *fig* sow the seeds **2** *v/r* **~se** *a espectáculo* buy a season ticket (*a* for); *a revista* take out a subscription (*a* to); **abono** *m* COM payment; AGR fertilizer; *para espectáculo, transporte* season ticket
abordar <1a> *v/t* MAR board; *tema, asunto* broach, raise; *problema* tackle, deal with; *a una persona* approach
aborigen 1 *adj* native, indigenous **2** *m/f* native
aborrecer <2d> *v/t* loathe, detest
abortar <1a> **1** *v/i* MED *espontáneamente* miscarry; *de forma provocada* have an abortion **2** *v/t plan* foil; **abortivo** *adj* abortion *atr*; **píldora -a** abortion pill; **aborto** *m espontáneo* miscarriage; *provocado* abortion; *fig* F freak F; **tener un ~** have a miscarriage
abotonar <1a> *v/t* button up
abra *f L.Am.* clearing
abrasador *adj* scorching (hot); **abrasar** <1a> **1** *v/t* burn **2** *v/i del sol* burn, scorch; *de bebida, comida* be boiling hot **3** *v/r* **~se**: **~se de sed** be parched F; **~se de calor** F be sweltering F; **~se de pasión** *lit* be aflame with passion *lit*
abrazar <1f> **1** *v/t* hug **2** *v/r* **~se** embrace; **abrazo** *m* hug; **dar un ~ a alguien** hug s.o., give s.o. a hug; **un ~ en carta** best wishes; *más íntimo* love
abrebotellas *m inv* bottle opener; **abrelatas** *m inv* can opener, *Br tb* tin opener
abreviar <1b> *v/t* shorten; *palabra* abbreviate; *texto* abridge; **abreviatura** *f* abbreviation
abridor *m* bottle opener
abrigado *adj* warmly dressed; **abrigar** <1h> **1** *v/t* wrap up; *esperanzas* hold out; *duda* entertain **2** *v/r* **~se** wrap up warm; **~se del frío** (take) shelter from the cold; **abrigo** *m* coat; (*protección*) shelter; **ropa de ~** warm clothes; **al ~ de** in the

shelter of

abril *m* April

abrir <3a; *part* **abierto**> **1** *v/t* open; *túnel* dig; *grifo* turn on; **le abrió el apetito** it gave him an appetite **2** *v/i de persona* open up; *de ventana, puerta* open; **en un ~ y cerrar de ojos** in the twinkling of an eye **3** *v/r* **~se** open; **~se a algo** *fig* open up to sth; **~se paso entre** make one's way through

abrochar <1a> **1** *v/t* do up; *cinturón de seguridad* fasten **2** *v/r* **~se** do up; *cinturón de seguridad* fasten; **tendremos que abrocharnos el cinturón** we'll have to tighten our belts

abrumador *adj* overwhelming; **abrumar** <1a> *v/t* overwhelm (*con or de* with); *abrumado de or con trabajo* snowed under with work

abrupto *adj terreno* rough; *pendiente* steep; *tono, respuesta* abrupt; *cambio* sudden

absentismo *m* absenteeism; **~ escolar** truancy

absolución *f* absolution

absolutamente *adv* absolutely; **no entendió ~ nada** he didn't understand a thing; **absolutismo** *m* absolutism; **absoluto** *adj* absolute; **en ~** not at all

absolver <2h; *part* **absuelto**> *v/t* JUR acquit; REL absolve

absorbente *adj* absorbent; **absorber** <2a> *v/t* absorb; (*consumir*) take; (*cautivar*) absorb; **absorto** *adj* absorbed (*en* in), engrossed (*en* in)

abstemio 1 *adj* teetotal **2** *m*, **-a** *f* teetotal(l)er

abstención *f* abstention; **abstenerse** <2l> *v/r* refrain (*de* from); POL abstain; **abstinencia** *f* abstinence; **síndrome de ~** MED withdrawal symptoms *pl*

abstracto *adj* abstract; **abstraerse** <2p; *part* **abstraído**> *v/r* shut o.s. off (*de* from); **abstraído 1** *adj* preocupied; **~ en algo** engrossed in sth **2** *part* → **abstraer**

absuelto *part* → **absolver**

absurdo 1 *adj* absurd **2** *m*: **es un ~ que** it's absurd that

abuchear <1a> *v/t* boo; **abucheo(s)** *m(pl)* booing *sg*, boos *pl*

abuela *f* grandmother; F *persona mayor* old lady; **¡cuéntaselo a tu ~!** F don't try to put one over on me! F, *Br* pull the other one! F; **abuelo** *m* grandfather; F *persona mayor* old man; **~s** grandparents

abultado *adj* bulging; *derrota* heavy; **abultamiento** *m* bulge; **abultar** <1a> *v/i* be bulky; **no abulta casi nada** it takes up almost no room at all

abundancia *f* abundance; **había comida en ~** there was plenty of food; **abundante** *adj* plentiful, abundant; **abundar** <1a> *v/i* be plentiful *o* abundant

aburguesarse <1a> *v/r desp* become bourgeois *o* middle class

aburrido *adj* (*que aburre*) boring; (*que se aburre*) bored; **~ de algo** bored *o* fed up F with sth; **aburrimiento** *m* boredom; **aburrir** <3a> **1** *v/t* bore **2** *v/r* **~se** get bored; **~se de algo** get bored *o* fed up F with sth; **~se como una ostra** F get bored stiff F

abusado *adj Méx* F smart, clever; **¡~!** look out!; **abusar** <1a> *v/i*: **~ de poder, confianza** abuse; *persona* take advantage of; **~ del alcohol** drink too much; **~ sexualmente de alguien** sexually abuse s.o.; **abusivo** *adj* JUR unfair; **abuso** *m* abuse; **~s** *pl* **deshonestos** indecent assault *sg*

A.C. *abr* (= **antes de Cristo**) BC (= before Christ)

acá *adv* here; **de ~ para allá** from here to there; **de entonces para ~** since then

acabado *m* finish

acabar <1a> **1** *v/t* finish **2** *v/i de persona* finish; *de función, acontecimiento* finish, end; **acabé haciéndolo yo** I ended up doing it myself; **~ con** put an end to; *caramelos* finish off; *persona* destroy; **~ de hacer algo** have just done sth; **va a ~ mal** F *persona* he'll come to no good; **esto va a ~ mal** F this is going to end badly **3** *v/r* **~se** *de actividad* finish, end; *de pan, dinero* run out; **se nos ha acabado el azúcar** we've run out of sugar; **¡se acabó!** that's that!

acacia *f* acacia

academia *f* academy; **~ de idiomas** language school; **~ militar** military academy; **académico 1** *adj* academic **2** *m,* **-a** *f* academician

acalenturarse <1a> *v/r L.Am.* (*afiebrarse*) get a temperature *o* fever

acallar <1a> *v/t tb fig* silence

acalorarse <1a> *v/r* (*enfadarse*) get worked up; (*sofocarse*) get embarrassed

acampada *f* camp; **ir de ~** go camping; **acampar** <1a> *v/i* camp

acantilado *m* cliff

acaparar <1a> *v/t* hoard, stockpile; *tiempo* take up; *interés* capture; (*monopolizar*) monopolize

acápite *m L.Am.* section; (*párrafo*) paragraph

acaramelado *adj fig* F lovey-dovey F

acariciar <1b> *v/t* caress; *perro* stroke; **~ una idea** *fig* contemplate an idea

acarrear <1a> *v/t* carry; *fig* give rise to, cause

acaso *adv* perhaps; **por si ~** just in case

acatar <1a> *v/t* comply with, obey

acatarrarse <1a> *v/r* catch a cold

acaudalado *adj* wealthy, well-off

acceder <2a> *v/i* (*ceder*) agree (**a** to), accede (**a** to) *fml*; **~ a lugar** gain access to; *cargo* accede to *fml*

accesible *adj* accessible; **acceso** *m tb* INFOR access; *de fiebre* attack, bout; *de tos* fit; **de difícil ~** inaccessible; **accesorio 1** *adj* incidental **2** *m* accessory

accidentado 1 *adj terreno, camino* rough; *viaje* eventful **2** *m,* **-a** *f* casualty; **accidental** *adj* (*no esencial*)

incidental; (*casual*) chance *atr*; **accidente** *m* accident; (*casualidad*) chance; GEOG feature; **~ de tráfico** *o* **de circulación** road traffic accident, RTA; **~ laboral** industrial accident

acción *f* action; **acciones** *pl* COM stock *sg, Br* shares; **poner en ~** put into action; **accionar** <1a> *v/t* activate; **accionista** *m/f* stockholder, *Br* shareholder

acebo *m* holly

acechar <1a> *v/t* lie in wait for; **acecho** *m:* **al ~** lying in wait

aceite *m* oil; **~ de girasol / oliva** sunflower / olive oil; **~ lubricante** lubricating oil; **aceitera** *f* TÉC oilcan; GASTR cruet; **aceitoso** *adj* oily; **aceituna** *f* olive

aceleración *f* acceleration; **acelerador** *m* accelerator; **acelerar** <1a> **1** *v/t motor* rev up; *fig* speed up; **aceleró el coche** she accelerated **2** *v/i* accelerate **3** *v/r* **~se** *L.Am.* F (*enojarse*) lose one's cool

acelgas *fpl* BOT Swiss chard *sg*

acento *m en ortografía, pronunciación* accent; (*énfasis*) stress, emphasis; **poner el ~ en** *fig* stress, emphasize; **acentuar** <1e> **1** *v/t* stress; *fig* accentuate, emphasize **2** *v/r* **~se** become more pronounced

acepción *f* sense, meaning

aceptable *adj* acceptable; **aceptación** *f* acceptance; (*éxito*) success; **aceptar** <1a> *v/t* accept

acequia *f* irrigation ditch

acera *f* sidewalk, *Br* pavement; **ser de la otra ~, ser de la ~ de enfrente** F be gay

acerca *adv:* **~ de** about

acercar <1g> **1** *v/t* bring closer; **~ a alguien a un lugar** give s.o. a ride (*Br* lift) somewhere **2** *v/r* **~se** approach; (*ir*) go; *de grupos, países* come closer together; *de fecha* draw near; **se acercó a mí** she came up to me *o* approached me; **acércate** come closer; **no te acerques a la pared** don't get close to the wall

acero *m* steel; **~ inoxldablo** stainless steel

acertado *adj comentario* apt; *elección* good, wise; **estar muy ~** be dead right; **acertar** <1k> **1** *v/t respuesta* get right; *al hacer una conjetura* guess **2** *v/i* be right; **~ con algo** get sth right

acertijo *m* riddle, puzzle

achacar <1g> *v/t* attribute (**a** to)

achantarse <1a> *v/r* F keep quiet, keep one's mouth shut F

achaque *m* ailment

achatado *adj* flattened; **achatarse** <1a> *v/r* be flattened

achicharrar <1a> *v/t* **1** burn **2** *v/r* **~se** *fig* F roast F

achinado *adj L.Am.* oriental-looking

achinero *m C.Am. vendedor* peddler

achiquitarse <1a> *v/r L.Am.* become frightened *o* scared

achisparse <1a> *v/r* F get tipsy F

acholar <1a> *v/t S.Am.* embarrass

achuchar <1a> *v/t fig* F pester, nag; **achuchón** *m* F squeeze, hug; (*empujón*) push; **le dio un ~** *desmayo* she felt faint

achuras *fpl S.Am.* variety meat *sg*, *Br* offal *sg*

aciago *adj* fateful

acicalarse <1a> *v/r* get dressed up

acidez *f* acidity; **~ de estómago** heartburn; **ácido 1** *adj tb fig* sour, acid **2** *m* acid

acierto *m idea* good idea; *respuesta* correct answer; *habilidad* skill

aclamación *f* acclaim; **aclamar** <1a> *v/t* acclaim

aclaración *f* clarification; **aclarar** <1a> **1** *v/t duda, problema* clarify, clear up; *ropa, vajilla* rinse **2** *v/i de día* break, dawn; *del tiempo* clear up **3** *v/r* **~se: ~se la voz** clear one's throat; **no me aclaro** F I don't understand; *por cansancio, ruido etc* I can't think straight

aclimatarse <1a> *v/r* acclimatize, become acclimatized

acné *m* acne

ACNUR *abr* (= **Alto Comisionado de las Naciones Unidas para los Refugiados**) UNHCR (= United Nations High Commission for Refugees)

acobardar <1a> **1** *v/t* daunt **2** *v/r* **~se** get frightened, lose one's nerve

acodarse <1a> *v/r* lean (one's elbows) (**en** on)

acogedor *adj* welcoming; *lugar* cozy, *Br* cosy; **acoger** <2c> **1** *v/t* receive; *en casa* take in; **~ con satisfacción** welcome, greet with satisfaction **2** *v/r* **~se: ~se a algo** have recourse to sth; **acogida** *f* reception; **tener buena ~** get a good reception, be well received

acojonar <1a> **1** *v/t* V (*asustar*) scare the shit out of P; (*asombrar*) knock out F, blow away P **2** *v/r* **~se** V be shit scared P

acolchado *adj Rpl* quilted; **acolchonar** <1a> *v/t Rpl* quilt

acomedido *adj L.Am.* obliging, helpful; **acomedirse** <3l> *v/r Méx* offer to help

acometer <2a> **1** *v/t* attack; *tarea, proyecto* undertake, tackle **2** *v/i* attack; **~ contra algo** attack sth

acomodado *adj* well-off; **acomodador** *m* usher; **acomodadora** *f* usherette; **acomodar** <1a> **1** *v/t* (*adaptar*) adapt; *a alguien* accommodate **2** *v/r* **~se** make o.s. comfortable; (*adaptarse*) adapt (**a** to)

acompañamiento *m* accompaniment; **acompañante** *m/f* companion; MÚS accompanist; **acompañar** <1a> *v/t* (*ir con*) go with, accompany *fml*; (*permanecer con*) keep company; MÚS, GASTR accompany; **acompaño** *m C.Am.* (*reunión*) meeting

acomplejar <1a> **1** *v/t:* **~ a alguien** give s.o. a complex **2** *v/r* **~se** get a complex

acondicionar <1a> *v/t un lugar* equip, fit out; *pelo* condition

acongojar <1a> *v/t lit* grieve *lit*, distress

aconsejable *adj* advisable; **aconsejar** <1a> *v/t* advise

acontecer <2d> *v/i* take place, occur; **acontecimiento** *m* event

acopio *m:* **hacer ~ de** gather, muster

acoplar <1a> **1** *v/t piezas* fit together **2** *v/r* **~se** *de persona* join (*a* with); *de nave espacial* dock (*a* with); *de piezas* fit together

acorazado *adj* armo(u)red

acordar <1m> **1** *v/t* agree **2** **~se** *v/r* remember; **¿te acuerdas de él?** do you remember him?; **acorde 1** *adj:* **~ con** appropriate to, in keeping with **2** *m* MÚS chord

acordeón *m* accordion; **acordeonista** *m/f* accordionist

acordonar <1a> *v/t* cordon off

acorralar <1a> *v/t tb fig* corner

acortar <1a> **1** *v/t* shorten **2** *v/i* take a short cut **3** *v/r* **~se** get shorter

acosar <1a> *v/t* hound, pursue; *con preguntas* bombard (*con* with)

acosijar <1a> *v/t Méx* badger, pester

acoso *m fig* hounding, harrassment; **~ sexual** sexual harrassment

acostar <1m> **1** *v/t* put to bed **2** *v/r* **~se** go to bed; (*tumbarse*) lie down; **~se con alguien** go to bed with s.o., sleep with s.o.

acostumbrado *adj* (*habitual*) usual; **estar ~ a algo** be used to sth; **acostumbrar** <1a> **1** *v/t* get used (*a* to) **2** *v/i:* **acostumbraba a venir a este café todas las mañanas** he used to come to this café every morning **3** *v/r* **~se** get used (*a* to); **se acostumbró a levantarse temprano** he got used to getting up early

ácrata *m/f & adj* anarchist

acre *adj olor* acrid; *crítica* biting

acrecentar <1k> **1** *v/t* increase **2** *v/r* **~se** increase, grow

acreditar <1a> **1** *v/t diplomático etc* accredit (**como** as); (*avalar*) prove; **un documento que lo acredita como el propietario** a document that is proof of his ownership **2** *v/r* **~se** acquire a good reputation

acreedor *m*, **~a** *f* creditor; **acreencia** *f L.Am.* credit

acribillar <1a> *v/t:* **~ a alguien a balazos** riddle s.o. with bullets; **~ a alguien a preguntas** bombard s.o. with questions

acrílico *m/adj* acrylic

acristalar <1a> *v/t* glaze

acróbata *m/f* acrobat; **acrobático** *adj* acrobatic; **vuelo ~** stunt flight

acta(s) *f(pl)* minutes *pl*

actitud *f* (*disposición*) attitude; (*posición*) position; **activar** <1a> *v/t* activate; (*estimular*) stimulate; **actividad** *f* activity; **activista** *m/f* POL activist; **activo 1** *adj* active; **en ~** on active service; **población -a** labo(u)r force **2** *m* COM assets *pl*

acto *m* (*acción*), TEA act; *ceremonia* ceremony; **~ sexual** sexual intercourse; **~ seguido** immediately afterward(s); **en el ~** instantly, there and then

actor *m* actor; **actriz** *f* actress

actuación *f* TEA performance; (*intervención*) intervention; **actual** *adj* present, current; **un tema muy ~** a very topical issue; **actualidad** *f* current situation; **en la ~** at present, presently; (*hoy en día*) nowadays; **~es** current affairs; **actualizar** <1f> *v/t* bring up to date, update; **actualmente** *adv* currently

actuar <1e> *v/i* (*obrar, ejercer*), TEA *adv* act; MED work, act

acuarela *f* watercolo(u)r

acuario *m* aquarium

Acuario *m/f inv* ASTR Aquarius

acuático *adj* aquatic; **deporte ~** water sport

acuchillar <1a> *v/t* stab

acuciante *adj* pressing, urgent

acudir <3a> *v/i* come; **~ a alguien** turn to s.o.; **~ a las urnas** go to the polls

acueducto *m* aqueduct

acuerdo *m* agreement; **estar de ~ con** agree with; **llegar a un ~, ponerse de ~** come to *o* reach an agreement (**con** with); **de ~ con**

algo in accordance with sth; *¡de ~!* all right!, OK!

acumulación *f* accumulation; **acumular** <1a> **1** *v/t* accumulate **2** *v/r* **~se** accumulate

acuñar <1a> *v/t* rock

acuñar <1a> *v/t monedas* mint; *término, expresión* coin

acuoso *adj* watery

acupuntura *f* acupuncture

acurrucarse <1g> *v/r* curl up

acusación *f* accusation; **acusado** *m*, **-a** *f* defendant; **acusar** <1a> *v/t* accuse (*de* of); JUR charge (*de* with); (*manifestar*) show; *~ recibo de* acknowledge receipt of; **acuse** *m*: *~ de recibo* acknowledg(e)ment

acusetas *m/f inv S.Am.* F tattletale F, *Br* tell-tale F; **acusica** *m/f* F tattletale F, *Br* tell-tale F

acústica *f* acoustics

adaptable *adj* adaptable; **adaptación** *f* adaptation; *~ cinematográfica* screen *o* movie version; **adaptador** *m* adaptor; **adaptar** <1a> **1** *v/t* adapt **2** *~se* *v/r* adapt (*a* to)

A. de C. *abr* (= *año de Cristo*) AD (= Anno Domini)

adecentar <1a> *v/t* straighten up, tidy up

adecuadamente *adv* properly; **adecuado** *adj* suitable, appropriate; **adecuar** <1d> **1** *v/t* adapt (*a* to) **2** *v/r* **~se** fit in (*a* with)

adefesio *m fig* F monstrosity F; *persona* freak F; *estar hecho un ~* look a sight

a. de J.C. *abr* (= *antes de Jesucristo*) BC (= before Christ)

adelantado *adj* advanced; *por ~* in advance; *ir ~ de un reloj* be fast; **adelantamiento** *m* AUTO passing maneuver, *Br* overtaking manoeuvre; **adelantar** <1a> **1** *v/t mover* move forward; *reloj* put forward; AUTO pass, *Br* overtake; *dinero* advance; (*conseguir*) achieve, gain **2** *v/i de un reloj* be fast; (*avanzar*) make progress, AUTO pass, *Br* overtake **3** *v/r* **~se** *mover* move forward; (*ir delante*) go on ahead; *de*

estación, cosecha be early; *de un reloj* gain; *se me adelantó* she beat me to it, she got there first; **adelante** *adv en espacio* forward; *seguir ~* carry on, keep going; *¡~!* come in; *más ~ en tiempo* later on; *de ahora or de aquí en ~* from now on; *salir ~* *fig: de persona* succeed; *de proyecto* go ahead; **adelanto** *m tb* COM advance

adelfa *f* BOT oleander

adelgazante *adj* weight-reducing, slimming *atr*; **adelgazar** <1f> **1** *v/t* lose **2** *v/i* lose weight

ademán *m* gesture; *hacer ~ de* make as if to

además 1 *adv* as well, besides **2** *prp*: *~ de* as well as

adentrarse <1a> *v/r*: *~ en territorio* penetrate; *tema* go into; **adentro 1** *adv* inside; *¡~!* get inside!; *mar ~* out to sea; *~ de L.Am.* inside **2** *mpl*: *para sus ~s* to oneself

adepto *m* follower; *fig* supporter

aderezar <1f> *v/t con especias* season; *ensalada* dress; *fig* liven up

adeudar <1a> *v/t* owe

adherente *adj* adhesive; **adherir** <3i> **1** *v/i* stick, adhere *fml* **2** *v/t* stick **3** *v/r* **~se** *a superficie* stick (*a* to), adhere (*a* to) *fml*; **~se** *a una organización* become a member of *o* join an organization; **~se** *a una idea* support an idea; **adhesivo** *m/adj* adhesive

adicción *f* addiction; *~ a las drogas* drug addiction

adicional *adj* additional

adictivo *adj* addictive; **adicto 1** *adj* addicted (*a* to); *ser ~ al régimen* be a supporter of the regime **2** *m*, **-a** *f* addict

adiestrar <1a> *v/t* train

adinerado *adj* wealthy

adiós 1 *int* goodbye, bye; *al cruzarse* hello **2** *m* goodbye; *decir ~* say goodbye (*a* to)

aditivo *m* additive

adivinanza *f* riddle; **adivinar** <1a> *v/t* guess; *de adivino* foretell

adjetivo *m* adjective

adjudicar <1g> **1** v/t award **2** v/r ~se win

adjuntar <1a> v/t enclose

adm. abr (= **administración**) admin (= administration)

administración f administration; de empresa etc management; (gobierno) administration, government; ~ **pública** civil service; **administrador** m, ~**a** f administrator; de empresa etc manager; **administrar** <1a> v/t medicamento, sacramentos administer, give; empresa run, manage; bienes manage; **administrativo 1** adj administrative **2** m, -**a** f administrative assistant

admirable adj admirable; **admiración** f admiration; **signo de ~** exclamation mark; **admirador** m, ~**a** f admirer; **admirar** <1a> **1** v/t admire; (asombrar) amaze **2** v/r ~**se** be amazed (de at o by)

admisible adj admissible; **admisión** f admission; **derecho de ~** right of admission; **admitir** <3a> v/t (aceptar) accept; (reconocer) admit

admón. abr (= **administración**) admin (= administration)

ADN abr (= **ácido desoxirribonucleico**) DNA (= deoxyribonucleic acid)

adobar <1a> v/t GASTR marinate; **adobera** f Méx type of mature cheese; **adobo** m GASTR marinade

adoctrinar <1a> v/t indoctrinate

adolecer <2d> v/t suffer (de from)

adolescencia f adolescence; **adolescente** m/f adolescent

adonde adv where

adónde interr where

adopción f adoption; **adoptar** <1a> v/t adopt; **adoptivo** adj padres adoptive; hijo adopted

adoquín m paving stone

adorable adj lovable, adorable; **adoración** f adoration; **adorar** <1a> v/t love, adore; REL worship

adormecer <2d> **1** v/t make sleepy **2** v/r ~**se** doze off; **adormidera** f BOT poppy; **adormilado** adj sleepy; **adormilarse** <1a> v/r doze off

adornar <1a> v/t decorate; **adorno** m ornament; de Navidad decoration

adosar <1a> v/t: ~ **algo a algo** put sth (up) against sth

adquirir <3i> v/t acquire; (comprar) buy; **adquisición** f acquisition; **hacer una buena ~** make a good purchase; **adquisitivo** adj: **poder ~** purchasing power

adrede adv on purpose, deliberately

adrenalina f adrenaline

aduana f customs; **aduanero 1** adj customs atr **2** m, -**a** f customs officer

aducir <3o> v/t razones, argumentos give, put forward; (alegar) claim

adueñarse <1a> v/r: ~ **de** take possession of

adulación f flattery; **adular** <1a> v/t flatter; **adulón 1** adj S.Am. fawning **2** m, -**ona** f flatterer

adultera f adulteress; **adulterar** <1a> v/t adulterate; **adulterio** m adultery; **cometer ~** commit adultery; **adúltero 1** adj adulterous **2** m adulterer

adultez f adulthood; **adulto 1** adj adult; **edad -a** adulthood **2** m, -**a** f adult

adusto adj paisaje harsh; persona stern, severe; L.Am. (inflexible) stubborn

adverbio m adverb

adversario m, -**a** f adversary, opponent; **adverso** adj adverse

advertencia f warning; **advertir** <3i> v/t warn (de about, of); (notar) notice

adyacente adj adjacent

aéreo adj air atr; vista, fotografía aerial; **compañía -a** airline

aerobic, aeróbic m aerobics

aerodinámico adj aerodynamic

aeroespacial adj aerospace atr

aerolínea f airline

aeromozo m, -**a** f L.Am. flight attendant

aeronáutico adj aeronautical

aeropuerto m airport

aerosol m aerosol

afable *adj* pleasant, affable

afamado *adj* famous

afán *m* (*esfuerzo*) effort; (*deseo*) eagerness; **sin ~ de lucro** *organización* not-for-profit, non-profit (making); **afanar** <1a> **1** *v/i C.Am.* (*ganar dinero*) make money **2** *v/t C.Am. dinero* make; *Rpl* F (*robar*) pinch F **3** *v/r ~se* make an effort

afección *f MED* complaint, condition; **afectado** *adj* (*afligido*) upset (*por* by); (*amanerado*) affected; **afectar** <1a> *v/t* (*producir efecto en*) affect; (*conmover*) upset, affect; (*fingir*) feign; **afectivo** *adj* emotional; **afecto** *m* affection; **tener ~ a alguien** be fond of s.o.; **afectuoso** *adj* affectionate

afeitada *f* shave; **afeitado** *m* shave; **afeitadora** *f* electric razor; **afeitar** <1a> **1** *v/t* shave; *barba* shave off **2** *v/r ~se* shave, have a shave

afeminado *adj* effeminate

aferrarse <1k> *v/r fig* cling (*a* to)

Afganistán Afghanistan

afianzar <1f> **1** *v/t fig* strengthen **2** *v/r ~se* become consolidated

afición *f* love (*por* of); (*pasatiempo*) pastime, hobby; **la ~** *DEP* the fans; **aficionado 1** *adj:* **ser ~ a** be interested in, *Br tb* be keen on **2** *m*, **-a** *f* enthusiast; *no profesional* amateur; **un partido de ~s** an amateur game; **aficionarse** <1a> *v/r* become interested (*a* in)

afiebrarse <1a> *v/r L.Am.* develop a fever

afilado *adj* sharp; **afilador** *m* sharpener; **afilalápices** *m inv* pencil sharpener; **afilar** <1a> **1** *v/t* sharpen; *L.Am.* F (*halagar*) flatter, butter up F; *S.Am.* (*seducir*) seduce **2** *v/r ~se* *S.Am.* F (*prepararse*) get ready

afiliarse <1a> *v/r:* **~ a un partido** become a member of a party, join a party

afinar <1a> *v/t MÚS* tune; *punta* sharpen; *fig* perfect, fine-tune

afincarse <1g> *v/r* settle

afinidad *f* affinity

afirmación *f* statement; *declaración positiva* affirmation; **afirmar** <1a> *v/t* state, declare; **afirmativo** *adj* affirmative

afligido *adj* upset; **afligir** <3c> **1** *v/t* afflict; (*apenar*) upset; *L.Am.* F (*golpear*) beat up **2** *v/r ~se* get upset

aflojar <1a> **1** *v/t nudo, tornillo* loosen; F *dinero* hand over **2** *v/i de tormenta* abate; *de viento, fiebre* drop **3** *v/r ~se* come *o* work loose

afluente *m* tributary

afmo. *abr* (= **afectísimo**): **su ~** Yours truly

afónico *adj:* **está ~** he has lost his voice

aforo *m* capacity

afortunado *adj* lucky, fortunate

afrecho *f Arg* bran

África Africa; **~ del Sur** South Africa; **africano 1** *adj* African **2** *m*, **-a** *f* African

afrodisíaco *m* aphrodisiac

afrontar <1a> *v/t* face (up to)

afuera *adv* outside; **afueras** *fpl* outskirts

agachar <1a> **1** *v/i* duck **2** *v/r ~se* bend down; (*acuclillarse*) crouch down; *L.Am.* (*rendirse*) give in

agalla *f ZO* gill; **tener ~s** F have guts F

agarrado *adj fig* F mean, stingy F; **agarrar** <1a> **1** *v/t* (*asir*) grab; *L.Am.* (*tomar*) take; *L.Am.* (*atrapar, pescar*) *resfriado* catch; *L.Am. velocidad* gather, pick up; **~ una calle** *L.Am.* go up *o* along a street **2** *v/i* (*asirse*) hold on; *de planta* take root; *L.Am. por un lugar* go; **agarró y se fue** he upped and went **3** *v/r ~se* (*asirse*) hold on; *L.Am. a golpes* get into a fight; **agarrón** *m Rpl* P (*pleito*) fight, argument; *L.Am.* (*tirón*) pull, tug

agarrotado *adj* stiff; **agarrotarse** <1a> *v/r de músculo* stiffen up; *TÉC* seize up

agasajar <1a> *v/t* fête

agazaparse <1a> *v/r* crouch (down); (*ocultarse*) hide

agencia *f* agency; **~ *inmobiliaria*** real estate office, *Br* estate agency; **~ *de viajes*** travel agency; **agenciarse** <1b> *v/t* F get hold of

agenda *f diario* diary; *programa* schedule; *de mitin* agenda

agente **1** *m* agent; **2** *m/f* agent; **~ *de cambio y bolsa*** stockbroker; **~ *de policía*** police officer

ágil *adj* agile; **agilidad** *f* agility

agilizar <1f> *v/t* speed up

agitación *f* POL unrest; **agitar** <1a> **1** *v/t* shake; *brazos, pañuelo* wave; *fig* stir up **2** *v/r* **~se** become agitated *o* worked up

aglomeración *f de gente* crowd; **aglomerar** <1a> *v/t* pile up

aglutinar <1a> *v/t fig* bring together

agobiante *adj* oppresssive; **agobiar** <1b> **1** *v/t de calor* oppress; *de problemas* get on top of, overwhelm **2** *v/r* **~se** F feel overwhelmed; **agobio** *m*: **es un ~** it's unbearable, it's a nightmare F

agolparse <1a> *v/r* crowd together

agonía *f* agony; **la espera fue una ~** the wait was unbearable; **agonizante** *adj* dying; **agonizar** <1f> *v/i de persona* be dying; *de régimen* be crumbling

agorero *adj* ominous

agosto *m* August; **hacer su ~** F make a fortune

agotado *adj* (*cansado*) exhausted, worn out; (*terminado*) exhausted; (*vendido*) sold out; **agotador** *adj* exhausting; **agotar** <1a> **1** *v/t* (*cansar*) wear out, exhaust; (*terminar*) use up, exhaust **2** *v/r* **~se** (*cansarse*) get worn out, exhaust o.s.; (*terminarse*) run out, become exhausted; (*venderse*) sell out

agraciado *adj persona* attractive

agradable *adj* pleasant, nice; **agradar** <1a> *v/i*: **me agrada la idea** *fml* I like the idea; **nos ~ía mucho que ...** *fml* we would be delighted *o* very pleased if ...

agradecer <2d> *v/t*: **~ *algo a alguien*** thank s.o. for sth; **te lo agradezco** I appreciate it; **agradecimiento** *m*

appreciation; **agrado** *m*: **ser del ~ de alguien** be to s.o.'s liking

agrandar <1a> **1** *v/t* make bigger **2** *v/r* **~se** get bigger

agrario *adj* land *atr*, agrarian; *política* agricultural

agravar <1a> **1** *v/t* make worse, aggravate **2** *v/r* **~se** get worse, deteriorate

agravio *m* offense, *Br* offence

agredir <3a> *v/t* attack, assault

agregado *m*, **-a** *f en universidad* senior lecturer; *en colegio* senior teacher; POL attaché; **~ *cultural*** cultural attaché

agregar <1h> *v/t* add

agresión *f* aggression; **agresividad** *f* aggression; **agresivo** *adj* aggressive; **agresor** *m*, **~a** *f* aggressor

agreste *adj terreno* rough; *paisaje* wild

agriarse <1b or 1c> *v/r de vino* go sour; *de carácter* become bitter

agrícola *adj* agricultural, farming *atr*; **agricultor** *m*, **~a** *f* farmer; **agricultura** *f* agriculture

agridulce *adj* bittersweet

agriera *f L.Am.* heartburn

agrietarse <1a> *v/r* crack; *de manos, labios* chap

agringarse <1h> *v/r L.Am.* become Americanized

agrio *adj fruta* sour; *disputa, carácter* bitter

agrios *mpl* BOT citrus fruit *sg*

agropecuario *adj* farming *atr*, agricultural

agrupar <1a> **1** *v/t* group, put into groups **2** *v/r* **~se** gather

agua *f* water; **~ *corriente*** running water; **~ *dulce*** fresh water; **~ *mineral*** mineral water; **~ *oxigenada*** (hydrogen) peroxide; **~ *potable*** drinking water; **es ~ pasada** it's water under the bridge; **está con el ~ al cuello** *con problemas* he's up to his neck in problems F; *con deudas* he's up to his neck in debt F; **se me hace la boca ~** it makes my mouth water; **aguas** *fpl* waters; **~ *residuales*** effluent *sg*, sewage *sg*

aguacate m BOT avocado

aguacero m downpour

aguachento adj CSur watery

aguafiestas m/f inv partypooper F, killjoy

aguaitar <1a> v/t S.Am. spy on

aguamala f S.Am. jellyfish

aguamiel f L.Am. mixture of water and honey; Méx (jugo de maguey) agave sap

aguanieve f sleet

aguantar <1a> **1** v/t un peso bear, support; respiración hold; (soportar) put up with; **no lo puedo ~** I can't stand o bear it **2** v/i hang on, hold out **3** v/r **~se** contenerse keep quiet; **me tuve que ~** conformarme I had to put up with it; **aguante** m patience; física stamina, endurance

aguar <1a> v/t fiesta spoil

aguardar <1a> **1** v/t wait for, await **2** v/i wait

aguardiente m fruit-based alcoholic spirit

aguarrás m turpentine, turps F

aguatero m, **-a** f S.Am. water-seller

agudeza f de voz, sonido high pitch; MED intensity; (perspicacia) sharpness; **~ visual** sharpsightedness

agudizar <1f> **1** v/t un sentido sharpen; **~ un problema** make a problem worse **2** v/r **~se** MED get worse; de un sentido become sharper

agudo adj acute; (afilado) sharp; sonido high-pitched; (perspicaz) sharp

agüero m omen; **ser de mal ~** be an ill omen

aguijón m ZO sting; fig spur

águila f eagle; **¿~ o sol?** Méx heads or tails?; **ser un ~** fig be very sharp; **aguilucho** m eaglet

agüita f L.Am. F (agua) water; (infusión) infusion

aguja f needle; de reloj hand; **buscar una ~ en un pajar** fig look for a needle in a haystack

agujerear <1a> **1** v/t make holes in

2 v/r **~se** develop holes; **agujero** m hole

agujetas fpl stiffness sg; **tener ~** be stiff

aquzar <1f> v/t sharpen; **~ el ingenio** sharpen one's wits; **~ el oído** prick up one's ears

ah int ah!

ahí adv there; **está por ~** it's (somewhere) over there; dando direcciones it's that way

ahijada f goddaughter; **ahijado** m godson

ahínco m effort; **trabajar con ~** work hard

ahogado adj en agua drowned; **ahogar** <1h> **1** v/t (asfixiar) suffocate; en agua drown; AUTO flood; protestas stifle **2** v/r **~se** choke; (asfixiarse) suffocate; en agua drown; AUTO flood; **~se en un vaso de agua** fig F get in a state over nothing

ahondar <1a> v/i: **~ en algo** go into sth in depth

ahora adv (en este momento) now; (pronto) in a moment; **~ mismo** right now; **por ~** for the present, for the time being; **~ bien** however; **desde ~, de ~ en adelante** from now on; **¡hasta ~!** see you soon

ahorcar <1g> **1** v/t hang **2** v/r **~se** hang o.s.

ahorita adv L.Am. (en este momento) (right) now; Méx, C.Am. (pronto) in a moment; Méx, C.Am. (hace poco) just now

ahorrar <1a> **1** v/t save; **~ algo a alguien** save s.o. (from) sth **2** v/i save (up) **3** v/r **~se** dinero save; fig spare o.s., save o.s.; **ahorro** m saving; **~s** pl savings; **caja de ~s** savings bank

ahulado m C.Am., Méx oilskin

ahumar <1a> v/t smoke

ahuyentar <1a> **1** v/t scare off o away **2** v/r **~se** L.Am. run away

AI abr (= **Amnistía Internacional**) AI (= Amnesty International)

airado adj angry

airbag m AUTO airbag

aire *m* air; **~ acondicionado** air-conditioning; **al ~ libre** in the open air; **a mi ~** in my own way; **estar en el ~** *fig* F be up in the air F; **hace mucho ~** it is very windy; **airear** <1a> *v/t tb fig* air

airoso *adj*: **salir ~ de algo** do well in sth

aislado *adj* isolated; **aislante 1** *adj* insulating, insulation *atr* **2** *m* insulator; **aislar** <1a> **1** *v/t* isolate; EL insulate **2** *v/r* **~se** cut o.s. off

ajardinado *adj* landscaped; **zona -a** area with parks and gardens

a. J.C. *abr* (= *antes de Jesucristo*) BC (= before Christ)

ajedrez *m* chess

ajeno *adj propiedad, problemas etc* someone else's; **me era totalmente ~** it was completely alien to me; **estar ~ a** be unaware of, be oblivious to; **por razones -as a nuestra voluntad** for reasons beyond our control

ajete *m* BOT young garlic

ajetreo *m* bustle

ají *m S.Am.* chili, *Br* chilli; **ajiaco** *m Col* spicy potato stew; **ajillo** *m*: **al ~** with garlic; **ajo** *m* BOT garlic; **estar** *or* **andar en el ~** F be in the know F

ajuar *m de novia* trousseau

ajustar <1a> **1** *v/t máquina etc* adjust; *tornillo* tighten; *precio* set; **~ cuentas** *fig* settle a score **2** *v/i* fit **3** *v/r* **~se** *el cinturón* tighten; **~se a algo** *fig* keep within sth; **~se a la ley** comply with the law; **ajuste** *m*: **~ de cuentas** settling of scores

ajusticiar <1b> *v/t* execute

al *prp* **a** *y art* **el**; **~ entrar** on coming in, when we/they *etc* came in

ala *f* wing; MIL flank; **~ delta** hang glider; **cortar las ~s a alguien** clip s.o.'s wings

alabanza *f* acclaim; **alabar** <1a> *v/t* praise, acclaim

alacena *f* larder

alacrán *m* ZO scorpion

alambrada *f* wire fence; **alambrar** <1a> *v/t* fence; **alambre** *m* wire; **~ de espino** *or* **de púas** barbed wire

álamo *m* BOT poplar; **~ temblón** aspen

alarde *m* show, display; **hacer ~ de** make a show of; **alardear** <1a> *v/i* show off (**de** about)

alargador *m* TÉC extension cord, *Br* extension lead; **alargar** <1h> **1** *v/t* lengthen; *prenda* let down; *en tiempo* prolong; *mano, brazo* stretch out **2** *v/r* **~se** *de sombra, día* get longer, lengthen

alarido *m* shriek; **dar ~s** shriek

alarma *f* (*mecanismo, miedo*) alarm; **dar la voz de ~** raise the alarm; **alarmante** *adj* alarming; **alarmar** <1a> **1** *v/t* alarm **2** *v/r* **~se** become alarmed

alba *f* dawn

albahaca *f* BOT basil

Albania Albania

albañil *m* bricklayer

albaricoque *m* BOT apricot

albatros *m inv* ZO albatross

albedrío *m*: **libre ~** free will

alberca *f* reservoir; *Méx* (swimming) pool

albergar <1h> *v/t* (*hospedar*) put up; (*contener*) house; *esperanzas* hold out

albergue *m* refuge, shelter; **~ juvenil** youth hostel

albino *m*, **-a** *f* albino

albóndiga *f* meatball

albornoz *m* bathrobe

alborotador *m*, **~a** *f* rioter; **alborotar** <1a> **1** *v/t* stir up; (*desordenar*) disturb **2** *v/i* make a racket **3** *v/r* **~se** get excited; (*inquietarse*) get worked up; **alboroto** *m* commotion

álbum *m* album

alcachofa *f* BOT artichoke; *de ducha* shower head

alcalde *m*, **-esa** *f* mayor

alcalino *adj* alkaline

alcance *m* reach; *de arma etc* range; *de medida* scope; *de tragedia* extent, scale; **al ~ de la mano** within reach; **¿está al ~ de tu bolsillo?** can you afford it?; **dar ~ a alguien** catch up with s.o.; **poner al ~ de alguien** put within s.o.'s reach

alcancía *f L.Am.* piggy bank

alcantarilla *f* sewer; (*sumidero*) drain

alcanzar <1f> **1** *v/t* a *alguien* catch up with; *lugar* reach, get to; *en nivel* reach; *cantidad* amount to; *objetivo* achieve **2** *v/i en altura* reach; *en cantidad* be enough; **~ a oír/ver** manage to hear/see

alcaparra *f* BOT caper

alcayata *f* hook

alcázar *m* fortress

alce *m* ZO elk

alcista *adj en bolsa* rising, bull *atr*; *tendencia* ~ upward trend

alcoba *f S.Am.* bedroom

alcohol *m* alcohol; MED rubbing alcohol, *Br* surgical spirit; ~ **de quemar** denatured alcohol, *Br* methylated spirits *sg*; **alcoholemia** *f* blood alcohol level; *prueba de* ~ drunkometer test, *Br* Breathalyzer® test; **alcohólico 1** *adj* alcoholic **2** *m*, **-a** *f* alcoholic; **alcoholismo** *m* alcoholism

alcornoque *m* BOT cork oak; *pedazo de* ~ F blockhead F

alcurnia *f* ancestry

aldea *f* (small) village

aleación *f* alloy

aleatorio *adj* random

aleccionar <1a> *v/t* instruct; (*regañar*) lecture

aledaños *mpl* surrounding area *sg*; *de ciudad* outskirts

alegador *adj L.Am.* argumentative; **alegar** <1h> **1** *v/t motivo, razón* cite; ~ *que* claim *o* allege that **2** *v/i L.Am.* (*discutir*) argue; (*quejarse*) moan, gripe

alegrar <1a> **1** *v/t* make happy; (*animar*) cheer up **2** *v/r* ~**se** cheer up; F *bebiendo* get tipsy; ~**se por alguien** be pleased for s.o. (*de* about); **alegre** *adj* (*contento*) happy; *por naturaleza* happy, cheerful; F *bebido* tipsy; **alegría** *f* happiness

alejar <1a> **1** *v/t* move away **2** *v/r* ~**se** move away (*de* from); *de situación, ámbito* get away (*de* from); *¡no te alejes mucho!* don't go too far away!

alelar <1a> *v/t* stupefy

aleluya *m & int* hallelujah

alemán 1 *m/adj* German **2** *m*, **-ana** *f persona* German; **Alemania** Germany

alentado *adj L.Am.* encouraged; **alentar** <1k> **1** *v/t* (*animar*) encourage; *esperanzas* cherish **2** *v/r* ~**se** *L.Am.* get better

alergia *f* allergy; **alérgico** *adj* allergic (*a* to)

alerta 1 *adv: estar* ~ be on the alert **2** *f* alert; *dar la* ~ raise the alarm; *poner en* ~ alert; **alertar** <1a> *v/t* alert (*de* to)

aleta *f* ZO fin; *de buzo* flipper; *de la nariz* wing

aletargarse <1h> *v/r* feel lethargic

aletear <1a> *v/i* flap one's wings

alevosía *f* treachery

alfabético *adj* alphabetical; **alfabetizar** <1f> *v/t lista etc* put into alphabetical order; ~ *a alguien* teach s.o. to read and write; **alfabeto** *m* alphabet

alfalfa *f* BOT alfalfa

alfanumérico *adj* alphanumeric

alfarero *m*, **-a** *f* potter

alfil *m* bishop

alfiler *m* pin; ~ *de gancho Arg* safety pin; *no cabe un* ~ fig F there's no room for anything else; **alfiletero** *m* (*cojín*) pincushion; (*estuche*) needlecase

alfombra *f* carpet; *más pequeña* rug; **alfombrado** *m L.Am.* carpeting, carpets *pl*; **alfombrar** <1a> *v/t* carpet; **alfombrilla** *f* mouse mat

alga *f* BOT alga; *marina* seaweed

álgebra *f* algebra

álgido *adj fig* decisive

algo 1 *pron en frases afirmativas* something; *en frases interrogativas o condicionales* anything; ~ *es* ~ it's something, it's better than nothing **2** *adv* rather, somewhat

algodón *m* cotton; *criado entre algodones* F mollycoddled, pampered

alguacil *m*, **~esa** *f* bailiff

alguien *pron en frases afirmativas*

somebody, someone; *en frases interrogativas o condicionales* anybody, anyone

algún *adj en frases afirmativas* some; *en frases interrogativas o condicionales* any; **~ día** some day

alguno 1 *adj en frases afirmativas* some; *en frases interrogativas o condicionales* any; **no la influyó de modo ~** it didn't influence her in any way; **¿has estado alguna vez en ...?** have you ever been to ...? **2** *pron*: *persona* someone, somebody; **~s opinan que ...** some people think that ...; **~ se podrá usar** *objeto* we'll be able to use some of them

alhaja *f* piece of jewel(le)ry; *fig* gem; **~s** jewelry *sg*

alhelí *m* BOT wallflower

aliado *m*, **-a** *f* ally; **alianza** *f* POL alliance; (*anillo*) wedding ring; **aliarse** <1c> *v/r* form an alliance (**con** with)

alias *m inv* alias

alicaído *adj* F down F

alicatar <1a> *v/t* tile

alicates *mpl* pliers

aliciente *m* (*estímulo*) incentive; (*atractivo*) attraction

alienar <1a> *v/t* alienate; **alienígena** *m/f* alien

aliento *m* breath; *fig* encouragement

aligerar <1a> *v/t carga* lighten; **~ el paso** quicken one's pace

alijo *m* MAR consignment

alimentación *f* (*dieta*) diet; *acción* feeding; EL power supply; **alimentar** <1a> **1** *v/t* tb TÉC, *fig* feed; EL power **2** *v/i* be nourishing **3** *v/r* **~se** feed o.s.; **~se de algo** *de persona, animal* live on sth; *de máquina* run on sth; **alimento** *m* (*comida*) food; **tiene poco ~** it has little nutritional value; **~s dietéticos** (*de régimen*) slimming aids

alineación *f* DEP line-up; **alinear** <1a> **1** *v/t* align **2** *v/r* **~se** (*ponerse en fila*) line up; POL align o.s. (**con** with)

aliñar <1a> *v/t* dress; **aliño** *m* dressing

alioli *m* GASTR garlic mayonnaise

alisar <1a> *v/t* smooth

alistarse <1a> *v/r* MIL enlist

aliviar <1b> *v/t* alleviate, relieve; **alivio** *m* relief

allá *adv de lugar* (over) there; **~ por los años veinte** back in the twenties; **más ~** further on; **más ~ de** beyond; **el más ~** the hereafter; **~ él/ella** F that's up to him/her

allanamiento *m*: **~ de morada** JUR breaking and entering; **allanar** <1a> *v/t* (*alisar*) smooth; (*aplanar*) level (out); *obstáculos* overcome

allegado *m*, **-a** *f* relation, relative

allí *adv* there; **por ~** over there; *dando direcciones* that way; **¡~ está!** there it is!

alma *f* soul; **se me cayó el ~ a los pies** F my heart sank; **llegar al ~** *conmover* move deeply; *herir* hurt deeply; **no se ve un ~** there isn't a soul to be seen; **lo siento en el ~** I am truly sorry

almacén *m* warehouse; (*tienda*) store, shop; **grandes almacenes** *pl* department store *sg*; **almacenamiento** *m* storage; **~ de datos** data storage; **almacenar** <1a> *v/t tb* INFOR store; **almacenero** *m*, **-a** *f* storekeeper, shopkeeper

almanaque *m* almanac

almeja *f* ZO clam

almenas *fpl* battlements

almendra *f* almond; **almendro** *m* almond tree

almíbar *m* syrup; **en ~** in syrup; **almibarado** *adj fig* syrupy

almidón *m* starch

almirante *m* admiral

almirez *m* mortar

almohada *f* pillow; **consultarlo con la ~** sleep on it; **almohadilla** *f* small cushion; TÉC pad; **almohadón** *m* large cushion

almorranas *fpl* piles

almorzada *f Méx* lunch; **almorzar** <1f & 1m> **1** *v/i al mediodía* have lunch; *a media mañana* have a mid-morning snack **2** *v/t*: **~ algo al**

mediodía have sth for lunch; *a media mañana* have sth as a mid-morning snack

almuerzo *m al mediodía* lunch; *a media mañana* mid-morning snack; ~ *de trabajo* working lunch

¿alo? *L.Am.* hello?

alocado 1 *adj* crazy **2** *m*, *-a f* crazy fool

áloe *m* BOT aloe

alojamiento *m* accommodations *pl*, *Br* accommodation; **alojar** <1a> **1** *v/t* accommodate **2** *v/r* ~*se* stay (*en* in); **alojo** *m L.Am.* → *alojamiento*

alondra *f* ZO lark

alopecia *f* MED alopecia

alpaca *f animal, lana* alpaca

alpargata *f Esp* espadrille

alpinismo *m* mountaineering; **alpinista** *m/f* mountaineer, climber

alpiste *m* birdseed

alquilar <1a> *v/t de usuario* rent; *de dueño* rent out; **alquiler** *m acción: de coche etc* rental; *de casa* renting; *dinero* rental, *Br tb* rent; ~ *de coches* car rental, *Br tb* car hire

alquitrán *m* tar

alrededor 1 *adv* around **2** *prp*: ~ *de* around; **alrededores** *mpl* surrounding area *sg*

alta *f* MED discharge; *dar de* ~ MED discharge; *darse de* ~ *en organismo* register

altanero *adj* arrogant

altar *m* altar; *llevar al* ~ marry

altavoz *m* loudspeaker

alteración *f* alteration; **alterar** <1a> **1** *v/t* (*cambiar*) alter; *a alguien* upset; ~ *el orden público* cause a breach of the peace **2** *v/r* ~*se* get upset (*por* because of)

altercado *m* argument, altercation *fml*

alternar <1a> **1** *v/t* alternate; ~ *el trabajo con el descanso* alternate work and study **2** *v/i* mix **3** *v/r* ~*se* alternate, take turns; **alternativa** *f* alternative; **alternativo** *adj* alternative; **alterno** *adj* alternate; *corriente -a* EL alternating current;

en días ~*s* on alternate days

Alteza *f título* Highness

altibajos *mpl* ups and downs

altillo *m* (*desván*) attic; *en armario* top (part of the) closet

altiplano *m* high plateau

altisonante *adj* high-flown

altitud *f* altitude

altivo *adj* haughty

alto[1] **1** *adj persona* tall; *precio, número, montaña* high; *-as presiones* high pressure; ~ *horno* blast furnace; *clase -a* high class; *en -a mar* on the high seas; *en voz -a* out loud **2** *adv volar, saltar* high; *hablar* ~ speak loudly; *pasar por* ~ overlook; *poner más* ~ TV, RAD turn up; *por todo lo* ~ F lavishly **3** *m* (*altura*) height; *Chi* pile

alto[2] *m* halt; (*pausa*) pause; *hacer un* ~ stop; ~ *el fuego* ceasefire; *¡~!* halt!

altoparlante *m L.Am.* loudspeaker

altozano *m* hillock

altramuz *m planta* lupin; *semilla* lupin seed

altruismo *m* altruism; **altruista** *adj* altruistic

altura *f* MAT height; MÚS pitch; AVIA altitude, height; GEOG latitude; *a estas* ~*s* by this time, by now; *estar a la* ~ *de algo* be up to sth F

alubia *f* BOT kidney bean

alucinación *f* hallucination; **alucinado** *adj* F gobsmacked F; **alucinante** *adj* F incredible

alucinar <1a> **1** *v/i* hallucinate **2** *v/t* F amaze; **alucine** *m*: *de* ~ F amazing; **alucinógeno** *m* hallucinogen

alud *m* avalanche

aludir <3a> *v/i*: ~ *a algo* allude to sth; **aludido**: *darse por* ~ take it personally

alumbrar <1a> **1** *v/t* (*dar luz a*) light (up) **2** *v/i* give off light

aluminio *m* aluminum, *Br* aluminium; *papel de* ~ aluminum (*Br* aluminium) foil

alumno *m*, *-a f* student

alusión *f* allusion (*a* to); *hacer* ~ *a* refer to, allude to

aluvión *m* barrage
alza *f* rise; **en ~** *en bolsa* rising; **alzado** *m*, **-a** *f L.Am.* insurgent; **alzar** <1f> **1** *v/t barrera, brazo* lift, raise; *precios* raise **2** *v/r* **~se** rise; **en armas** rise up; **alzo** *m C.Am.* theft
a.m. *abr* (= *ante meridiem*) a.m. (= ante meridiem)
ama *f* (*dueña*) owner; **~ de casa** housewife, homemaker; **~ de llaves** housekeeper; **~ de leche** *or* **cría** *L.Am.* wetnurse
amabilidad *f* kindness; **amable** *adj* kind (**con** to)
amaestrar <1a> *v/t* train
amago *m* threat; **hizo ~ de levantarse** she made as if to get up; **~ de infarto** minor heart attack
amainar <1a> *v/i de lluvia, viento* ease up, slacken off
amalgamar <1a> **1** *v/t fig* combine **2** *v/r* **~se** amalgamate
amamantar <1a> *v/t bebé* breastfeed; *cría* feed
amanecer **1** <2d> *v/i* get light; *de persona* wake up **2** *m* dawn
amanerado *adj* affected
amante 1 *adj* loving; **es ~ de la buena vida** he's fond of good living **2** *m/f en una relación* lover; **los ~s de la naturaleza** nature lovers
amañar <1a> *v/t* F rig F; *partido* fix F
amapola *f* BOT poppy
amar <1a> *v/t* love
amargar <1h> **1** *v/t día, ocasión* spoil; **~ a alguien** make s.o. bitter **2** *v/r* **~se** get bitter; **~se la vida** get upset; **amargo** *adj tb fig* bitter; **amargura** *f tb fig* bitterness
amarillento *adj* yellowish; **amarillo** *m/adj* yellow
amarrar <1a> *v/t L.Am.* (*atar*) tie
amasar <1a> *v/t pan* knead; *fortuna* amass
amatista *f* amethyst
amazona *f* horsewoman; **amazónico** *adj* GEOG Amazonian
Amazonas: el ~ the Amazon
ambages *mpl*: **decirlo sin ~** say it straight out
ámbar *m* amber; **el semáforo está**

en ~ the lights are yellow, *Br* the lights are at amber
ambición *f* ambition; **ambicioso** *adj* ambitious
ambidextro, ambidiestro *adj* ambidextrous
ambientador *m* air freshener; **ambiental** *adj* environmental; **ambientar** <1a> **1** *v/t película, novela* set **2** *v/r* **~se** be set; **ambiente 1** *adj*: **medio ~** environment; **temperatura ~** room temperature **2** *m* (*entorno*) environment; (*situación*) atmosphere
ambigüedad *f* ambiguity; **ambiguo** *adj* ambiguous
ámbito *m* area; (*límite*) scope
ambo *m Arg* two-piece suit
ambos, ambas 1 *adj* both **2** *pron* both (of us / you / them)
ambulancia *f* ambulance; **ambulante 1** *adj* travel(l)ing; **venta ~** peddling, hawking **2** *m/f L.Am.* (*vendedor*) street seller; **ambulatorio 1** *adj* MED out-patient *atr* **2** *m* out-patient clinic
amedrentar <1a> *v/t* terrify
amén 1 *m* amen **2** *prp*: **~ de** as well as
amenaza *f* threat; **~ de bomba** bomb scare; **amenazador** *adj* threatening; **amenazante** *adj* threatening; **amenazar** <1f> **1** *v/t* threaten (**con, de** with) **2** *v/i*: **~ con** threaten to; **amenaza tempestad** there's a storm brewing
amenizar <1f> *v/t*: **~ algo** make sth more entertaining *o* enjoyable
ameno *adj* enjoyable
América America; **~ del Norte** North America; **~ del Sur** South America; **americana** *f* American (woman); *prenda* jacket; **americano** *m/adj* American
amerizar <1f> *v/i de nave espacial* splash down
ametralladora *f* machine gun
amianto *m* MIN asbestos
amígdala *f* ANAT tonsil; **amigdalitis** *f* MED tonsillitis
amigo 1 *adj* friendly; **ser ~ de algo**

be fond of sth **2** *m*, **-a** *f* friend; *hacerse ~s* make friends

aminorar <1a> *v/t* reduce; *~ la marcha* slow down

amistad *f* friendship; *~es* friends; **amistosamente** *adv* amicably; **amistoso** *adj* friendly; *partido ~* DEP friendly (game)

amnesia *f* amnesia

amnistía *f* amnesty

amo *m* (*dueño*) owner; HIST master

amoblado *S.Am.* **1** *adj* furnished **2** *m* furniture

amodorrarse <1a> *v/r* feel sleepy

amoldarse <1a> *v/r* adapt (*a* to)

amonestación *f* warning; DEP caution; **amonestar** <1a> *v/t reñir* reprimand; DEP caution

amoníaco, amoniaco *m* ammonia

amontonar <1a> **1** *v/t* pile up **2** *v/r ~se de objetos, problemas* pile up; *de gente* crowd together

amor *m* love; *~ mío* my love, darling; *~ propio* self-respect; *por ~ al arte* fig just for the fun of it; *por ~ de Dios* for God's sake; *hacer el ~* make love; **amoral** *adj* amoral

amoratado *adj* bruised

amordazar <1f> *v/t* gag; *animal, la prensa* muzzle

amorfo *adj* shapeless

amoroso *adj* amorous

amortajar <1a> *v/t* shroud

amortiguador *m* AUTO shock absorber; **amortiguar** <1i> *v/t impacto* cushion; *sonido* muffle

amortizar <1f> *v/t* pay off; COM *bienes* charge off, *Br* write off

amotinarse <1a> *v/r* rebel

amp. *abr* (= *amperios*) amp (= amperes)

amparar <1a> **1** *v/t* protect; (*ayudar*) help **2** *v/r ~se* seek shelter (*de* from); *~se en algo* seek protection in sth; **amparo** *m* protection; (*cobijo*) shelter; *al ~ de* under the protection of

ampliación *f de casa, carretera* extension; FOT enlargement; *~ de capital* COM increase in capital; **ampliadora** *f* FOT enlarger;

ampliamente *adv* widely; **ampliar** <1c> **1** *v/t plantilla* increase; *negocio* expand; *plazo, edificio* extend; FOT enlarge **2** *v/r ~se* broaden; **amplificador** *m* amplifier; **amplificar** <1g> *v/t* amplify; **amplio** *adj casa* spacious; *gama, margen* wide; *falda* full; **amplitud** *f* breadth

ampolla *f* MED blister; (*botellita*) vial, *Br* phial; **ampolleta** *f Arg, Chi* light bulb

ampuloso *adj* pompous

amputación *f* amputation; **amputar** <1a> *v/t brazo, pierna* amputate

amueblar <1a> *v/t* furnish

amuermar <1a> *v/t* F bore

amuleto *m* charm

anabolizante *m* anabolic steroid

anacardo *m* BOT cashew

anaconda *f* ZO anaconda

anacoreta *m/f* hermit

anacrónico *adj* anachronistic

ánade *m* ZO duck

anagrama *m* anagram

anal *adj* anal

anales *mpl* annals

analfabeto **1** *adj* illiterate **2** *m*, **-a** *f* illiterate

analgésico **1** *adj* painkilling, analgesic **2** *m* painkiller, analgesic

análisis *m inv* analysis; *~ de mercado* market research; *~ de sangre* blood test; *~ de sistemas* INFOR systems analysis; **analista** *m/f* analyst; **analizar** <1f> *v/t* analyze

analogía *f* analogy; **analógico** *adj* analog, *Br* analogue; **análogo** *adj* analogous

ananá(s) *m S.Am.* BOT pineapple

anarquía *f* anarchy; **anárquico** *adj* anarchic; **anarquista** **1** *adj* anarchist *atr* **2** *m/f* anarchist

anatema *m* anathema

anatomía *f* anatomy; **anatómico** *adj* anatomical; *asiento ~* AUTO anatomically designed seat

anca *f* haunch; *~s pl de rana* GASTR frogs' legs

ancestral *adj* ancestral

ancho **1** *adj* wide, broad; *a sus -as* at

eas̱e, relaxed; **quedarse tan ~** F carry on as if nothing had happened **2** *m* width; **~ de vía** FERR gauge; **dos metros de ~** two meters (*Br* metres) wide

anchoa *f* anchovy

anchura *f* width

anciana *f* old woman; **anciano 1** *adj* old **2** *m* old man

ancla *f* MAR anchor; **anclar** <1a> *v/i* MAR anchor

andadas *fpl*: **volver a las ~** F fall back into one's old ways

andador *m para bebé* baby walker; *para anciano* walker, Zimmer®

andamio *m* scaffolding

andanzas *fpl* adventures

andar <1q> **1** *v/i* (*caminar*) walk; (*funcionar*) work; **andando** on foot; **~ bien/mal** *fig* go well/badly; **~ con cuidado** be careful; **~ en algo** (*buscar*) rummage in sth; **~ tras algo** be after sth F; **~ haciendo algo** be doing sth; **¡anda!** come on! **2** *v/t* walk **3** *v/r* **~se**: **~se con bromas** kid around F

andas *fpl*: **llevar en ~** carry on one's shoulders

andén *m* platform; *L.Am.* sidewalk, *Br* pavement

Andes *mpl* Andes

andinismo *m L.Am.* mountaineering, climbing; **andinista** *m/f L.Am.* mountaineer, climber

andino *adj* Andean

Andorra Andorra

andrajoso *adj* ragged

andurriales *mpl*: **por estos ~** F around here

anécdota *f* anecdote

anegar <1h> **1** *v/t* flood **2** *v/r* **~se de** *campo, terreno* be flooded; **~se en llanto** dissolve into tears

anemia *f* MED an(a)emia; **anémico** *adj* an(a)emic

anestesia *f* MED an(a)esthesia; **anestesiado** *adj* an(a)esthetized, under F; **anestesiar** <1b> *v/t* an(a)esthetize

anexión *f* POL annexation; **anexionar** <1a> *v/t* POL annex; **anexo**

1 *adj* attached **2** *m edificio* annex, *Br* annex(e)

anfeta F, **anfetamina** *f* MED amphetamine

anfibio *m/adj* amphibian

anfiteatro *m* TEA amphitheater, *Br* amphitheatre; *de teatro* dress circle

anfitrión *m* host; **anfitriona** *f* hostess

ánfora *f L.Am.* POL ballot box; HIST amphora

ángel *m* angel; **~ custodio** *or* **de la guarda** guardian angel; **angelical** *adj* angelic

angina *f* MED: **~s** *pl* sore throat *sg*, strep throat *sg*; **~ de pecho** angina

anglicano 1 *adj* Anglican **2** *m*, **-a** *f* Anglican; **anglicismo** *m* Anglicism; **anglófono** *adj* English-speaking; **anglosajón 1** *adj* Anglo-Saxon **2** *m*, **-ona** *f* Anglo-Saxon

angora *f* angora

angosto *adj* narrow

anguila *f* ZO eel; **angula** *f* ZO, GASTR elver

ángulo *m* MAT, *fig* angle

angustia *f* anguish; **angustiado** *adj* distraught; **angustiante** *adj* distressing; **angustiar** <1b> **1** *v/t* distress **2** *v/r* **~se** agonize (*por* over); **angustioso** *adj* agonizing

anhelar <1a> *v/t* long for; **anhelo** *m* longing, desire (*de* for)

anhídrido *m* QUÍM anhydride; **~ carbónico** carbon dioxide

anidar <1a> *v/i* nest

anilla *f* ring; **cuaderno de ~s** ring binder; **~s** *pl* DEP rings

anillo *m* ring; **te viene como ~ al dedo** F it suits you perfectly

animación *f* liveliness; *en películas* animation; **hay mucha ~** it's very lively; **animado** *adj* lively; **animador** *m* host; **~ turístico** events organizer; **animadora** *f* hostess; DEP cheerleader

animal 1 *adj* animal *atr*, *fig* stupid **2** *m tb fig* animal; **~ doméstico** *mascota* pet; *de granja* domestic animal; **animalada** *f*: **decir/hacer una ~** F say/do something nasty

animar <1a> **1** v/t cheer up; (*alentar*) encourage **2** v/r ~**se** cheer up

anímico adj mental; **estado** ~ state of mind

ánimo m spirit; (*coraje*) encouragement; **estado de** ~ state of mind; **con** ~ **de** with the intention of; **¡~!** cheer up!

animosidad f animosity

aniquilar <1a> v/t annihilate

anís m BOT aniseed; *bebida* anisette

aniversario m anniversary

ano m ANAT anus

anoche adv last night; **antes de** ~ the night before last; **anochecer** <2d> **1** v/i get dark; **anocheció** night fell, it got dark **2** m dusk

anodino adj anodyne; *fig* bland

anómalo adj anomalous

anonadar <1a> v/t: ~ **a alguien** take s.o. aback

anónimo 1 adj anonymous **2** m poison pen letter

anorak m anorak

anorexia f MED anorexia; **anoréxico** adj anorexic

anormal adj abnormal

anotar <1a> v/t note down

anquilosarse <1a> v/r get stiff

ansia f yearning; (*inquietud*) anxiousness; **ansiar** <1b> v/t yearn for, long for; **ansiedad** f anxiety; **ansioso** adj anxious; **está ~ por verlos** he's longing to see them

anta f L.Am. ZO tapir

antagonista m/f antagonist

antaño adv long ago

antártico adj Antarctic; **Antártida** Antarctica

ante[1] m suede; ZO moose; *Méx* (*postre*) egg and coconut dessert

ante[2] prp *posición* before; *dificultad* faced with; ~ **todo** above all

anteayer adv the day before yesterday

antebrazo m forearm

antecedente m precedent; ~**s penales** previous convictions; **poner a alguien en** ~**s** put s.o. in the picture; **antecesor** m, ~**a** f predecessor

antediluviano adj prehistoric *hum*

antelación f: **con** ~ in advance

antemano· **do** ~ beforehand

antena f *de radio, televisión* antenna, *Br* aerial; ZO antenna; ~ **parabólica** satellite dish

anteojos mpl binoculars

antepasado m, **-a** f ancestor

antepenúltimo adj third last

anteponer <2r> v/t: ~ **algo a algo** put sth before sth

anteproyecto m draft

anterior adj previous, former

antes 1 adv before; **cuanto** ~, **lo** **posible** as soon as possible; **poco** ~ shortly before; ~ **que nada** first of all **2** prp: ~ **de** before

antesala f lobby

antiadherente adj non-stick

antiaéreo adj anti-aircraft *atr*

antibala(s) adj bulletproof

antibelicista adj anti-war

antibiótico m antibiotic

anticiclón m anticyclone

anticipado adj *pago* advance *atr*; *elecciones* early; **por** ~ in advance; **anticipar** <1a> **1** v/t *sueldo* advance; *fecha, viaje* move up, *Br* bring forward; *información, noticias* give a preview of **2** v/r ~**se** *de suceso* come early; ~**se a alguien** get there ahead of s.o.

anticonceptivo 1 adj contraceptive *atr* **2** m contraceptive

anticongelante m antifreeze

anticonstitucional adj unconstitutional

anticuado adj antiquated; **anticuario** m antique dealer

anticuerpo m BIO antibody

antideslizante adj non-slip

antidisturbios adj: **policía** ~ riot police

antidoping adj: **control** ~ dope test, drug test

antídoto m MED antidote; *fig* cure

antifaz m mask

antiguamente adv in the past; **antigüedad** f age; *en el trabajo* length of service; ~**es** antiques; **antiguo** adj old; *del pasado remoto* ancient; *su ~ novio* her old *o* former boyfriend

antiinflamatorio *adj* MED antiinflammatory

Antillas *fpl* West Indies

antílope *m* ZO antelope

antinatural *adj* unnatural

antinuclear *adj* anti-nuclear

antioxidante *m/adj* antioxidant

antipatía *f* antipathy, dislike; **antipático** *adj* disagreeable, unpleasant

antípodas *mpl* antipodes

antirreglamentario *adj* DEP *posición* offside; *una jugada -a* a foul

antirrobo *m* AUTO antitheft device

antisemitismo *m* anti-Semitism

antiséptico *m/adj* antiseptic

antisocial *adj* antisocial

antiterrorista *adj brigada* antiterrorist; *la lucha ~* the fight against terrorism

antítesis *f inv* antithesis

antojarse <1a> *v/r: se le antojó salir* he felt like going out; *se me antoja que ...* it seems to me that ...; **antojo** *m* whim; *de embarazada* craving; *a mí ~* as I please

antología *f* anthology; *de ~ fig* F fantastic, incredible F

antonomasia *f: por ~* par excellence

antorcha *f* torch

antro *m* F dive F, dump F

antropófago *m*, **-a** *f* cannibal

antropología *f* anthropology

anual *adj* annual; **anualidad** *f* annual payment; **anualmente** *adv* yearly

anudar <1a> *v/t* knot

anular¹ <1a> *v/t* cancel; *matrimonio* annul; *gol* disallow

anular² *adj* ring-shaped; *dedo ~* ring finger

anunciante *m* COM advertiser; **anunciar** <1b> *v/t* announce; COM advertise; **anuncio** *m* announcement; (*presagio*) sign; COM advertisement; *~ luminoso* illuminated sign; *~s por palabras*, *pequeños ~s* classified advertisements

anzuelo *m* (fish) hook; *morder o tragar el ~ fig* F take the bait

añadidura *f: por ~* in addition; **añadir** <3a> *v/t* add

añejo *adj* mature

añicos *mpl: hacer ~* F smash to smithereens F

año *m* year; *~ bisiesto* leap year; *~ fiscal* fiscal year, *Br* financial year; *~ luz* light year; *~ nuevo* New Year; *¿cuándo cumples ~s?* when's your birthday?; *¿cuántos ~s tienes?* how old are you?; *a los diez ~s* at the age of ten; *los ~s veinte* the twenties

añorar <1a> *v/t* miss

aorta *f* ANAT aorta

apabullante *adj* overwhelming; **apabullar** <1a> *v/t* overwhelm

apacible *adj* mild-mannered

apaciguar <1i> **1** *v/t* pacify, calm down **2** *v/r ~se* calm down

apadrinar <1a> *v/t* be godparent to; *político* support, back; *artista etc* sponsor; *~ a la novia* give the bride away

apagado *adj fuego* out; *luz* off; *persona* dull; *color* subdued; **apagar** <1h> **1** *v/t televisor, luz* turn off; *fuego* put out **2** *v/r ~se de luz* go off; *de fuego* go out; **apagón** *m* blackout

apaisado *adj* landscape *atr*

apalabrar <1a> *v/t* agree (verbally)

apalancar <1g> **1** *v/t* lever **2** *v/r ~se* F settle

apalear <1a> *v/t* beat

apañar <1a> **1** *v/t* tidy up; *aparato* repair; *resultado* rig F, fix F; *estamos apañados* F we've had it F **2** *v/r ~se* manage; *apañárselas* manage, get by; **apaño** *m fig* F makeshift repair

aparador *m* sideboard; *Méx* (*escaparate*) shop window

aparato *m* piece of equipment; *doméstico* appliance; BIOL, ANAT system; *de partido político* machine; *~ respiratorio* respiratory system; *al ~* TELEC speaking; **aparatoso** *adj* spectacular

aparcacoches *m inv* valet; **aparcamiento** *m* parking lot, *Br* car park; *~ subterráneo* underground parking garage, *Br* underground car park;

aparcar <1g> **1** v/t park; *tema, proyecto* shelve **2** v/i park

aparearse <1a> v/r ZO mate

aparecer <2d> **1** v/i appear **2** v/r ~**se** turn up

aparejador m, ~**a** f *architectural technician*, Br quantity surveyor; **aparejo** m: ~**s** pl **de pesca** fishing gear sg

aparentar <1a> v/t pretend; **no aparenta la edad que tiene** she doesn't look her age; **aparente** adj (*evidente*) apparent; L.Am. (*fingido*) feigned; **aparentemente** adv apparently; **aparición** f appearance; (*fantasma*) apparition; **hacer su** ~ make one's appearance; **apariencia** f appearance; **en** ~ outwardly; **las ~s engañan** appearances can be deceptive

apartado m section; ~ **de correos** PO box; **apartamento** m apartment, Br flat; **apartamiento** m separation; L.Am. (*apartamento*) apartment, Br flat; **apartar** <1a> **1** v/t separate; *para después* set o put aside; *de un sitio* move away (**de** from); ~ **a alguien de hacer algo** dissuade s.o. from doing sth **2** v/r ~**se** move aside (**de** from); ~**se del tema** stray from the subject; **aparte** adv to one side; (*por separado*) separately; ~ **de** aside from, Br apart from; **punto y** ~ new paragraph

apasionado 1 adj passionate **2** m/f enthusiast; **apasionante** adj fascinating; **apasionar** <1a> v/t fascinate

apatía f apathy; **apático** adj apathetic

apdo. abr (= **apartado** (**de correos**)) PO Box (= Post Office Box)

apearse <1a> v/r get off, alight *fml*; ~ **de algo** get off sth, alight from sth *fml*

apechugar <1h> v/i: ~ **con algo** cope with sth

apego m attachment

apelación f JUR appeal; **apelar** <1a> v/t tb JUR appeal (**a** to)

apellidarse <1a> v/r: **¿cómo se apellida?** what's your/his/her surname?; **se apellida Ocaña** his/her surname is Ocaña; **apellido** m surname; ~ **de soltera** maiden name

apelmazarse <1f> v/r *de lana* get matted; *de arroz* stick together

apelotonarse <1a> v/r crowd together

apenado adj sad; L.Am. (*avergonzado*) ashamed; L.Am. (*incómodo*) embarrassed; L.Am. (*tímido*) shy; **apenar** <1a> **1** v/t sadden **2** v/r ~**se** be upset o distressed; L.Am. (*avergonzarse*) be ashamed; L.Am. (*sentir incómodo*) be embarrassed; L.Am. (*ser tímido*) be shy

apenas 1 adv hardly, scarcely **2** conj as soon as

apéndice m appendix; **apendicitis** f MED appendicitis

apercibirse <3a> v/r: ~ **de algo** notice sth

apergaminado adj fig wrinkled

aperitivo m *comida* appetizer; *bebida* aperitif

apero m *utensilio* implement; L.Am. (*arneses*) harness; ~**s de labranza** farming implements

apertura f opening; FOT aperture; POL opening up

apesadumbrado adj heavy-hearted

apestar <1a> **1** v/t stink out F **2** v/i reek (**a** of); **huele que apesta** it reeks; **apestoso** adj smelly

apetecer <2d> v/i: **me apetece ir a dar un paseo** I feel like going for a walk; **¿qué te apetece?** what do you feel like?; **apetito** m appetite; **apetitoso** adj appetizing

apiadarse <1a> v/r take pity (**de** on)

ápice m: **ni un** ~ fig not an ounce; **no ceder ni un** ~ fig not give an inch

apicultura f beekeeping

apilar <1a> v/t pile up

apiñarse <1a> v/r crowd together

apio m BOT celery

apisonadora f steamroller

aplacar <1g> v/t *hambre* satisfy; *sed* quench; *a alguien* calm down, placate *fml*

aplanar <1a> **1** v/t level, flatten; **~ las calles** C.Am., Pe hang around the streets **2** v/r **~se** fig (descorazonarse) lose heart

aplastante adj overwhelming; calor suffocating; **aplastar** <1a> v/t tb fig crush

aplaudida f L.Am. applause; **aplaudir** <3a> **1** v/i applaud, clap **2** v/t tb fig applaud; **aplauso** m round of applause

aplazamiento m de visita, viaje postponement; **aplazar** <1f> v/t visita, viaje put off, postpone; Arg fail

aplicación f application; **aplicar** <1g> **1** v/t apply; sanciones impose **2** v/r **~se** apply o.s.

aplomo m composure, aplomb fml

apocalíptico adj apocalyptic

apócrifo adj apocryphal

apodar <1a> v/t nickname, call

apoderado m COM agent; **apoderar** <1a> **1** v/t authorize **2** v/r **~se** take possession o control (**de** of)

apodo m nickname

apogeo m fig height, peak; **estar en su ~** be at its height

apolillarse <1a> v/r get moth-eaten

apolítico adj apolitical

apología f defense, Br defence

apoltronarse <1a> v/r en asiento settle down; en trabajo, rutina get into a rut

apoplejía f MED apoplexy; **ataque de ~** MED stroke

aporrear <1a> v/t pound on

aportación f contribution; COM investment; **aportar** <1a> v/t contribute; **~ pruebas** JUR provide evidence

apósito m dressing

aposta adv on purpose, deliberately; **apostar** <1m> **1** v/t bet (**por** on) **2** v/i bet; **~ por algo** opt for sth **3** v/r **~se** bet; MIL position o.s.

apóstata m/f apostate

apóstol m apostle

apóstrofe, **apóstrofo** m apostrophe

apoteosis f fig climax

apoyar <1a> **1** v/t lean (**en** against), rest (**en** against); (respaldar, confir-

mar) support **2** v/r **~se** lean (**en** on; **contra** against); en persona rely (**en** on); **¿en qué te apoyas para decir eso?** what are you basing that comment on?; **apoyo** m fig support

apreciable adj (visible) appreciable, noticeable; (considerable) considerable, substantial; **apreciar** <1b> v/t appreciate; (sentir afecto por) be fond of, think highly of; **aprecio** m respect

apremiar <1b> **1** v/t pressure, put pressure on **2** v/t: **el tiempo apremia** time is pressing

aprender <2a> **1** v/t learn **2** v/r **~se** learn; **~se algo de memoria** learn sth (off) by heart; **aprendiz** m, **~a** f apprentice, trainee; **aprendizaje** m apprenticeship

aprensión f (miedo) apprehension; (asco) squeamishness

apresar <1a> v/t nave seize; ladrón, animal catch, capture

aprestarse <1a> v/r: **~ a** get ready to

apresurar <1a> **1** v/t hurry **2** v/r **~se** hurry up; **~se a hacer algo** hurry o rush to do sth

apretado adj tight; **iban muy ~s en el coche** they were very cramped o squashed in the car; **apretar** <1k> **1** v/t botón press; (pellizcar, pinzar) squeeze; tuerca tighten; **~ el paso** quicken one's pace; **~ los puños** clench one's fists **2** v/i de ropa, zapato be too tight **3** v/r **~se** squeeze o squash together; **~se el cinturón** fig tighten one's belt; **apretón** m squeeze; **~ de manos** handshake

apretujar <1a> **1** v/t F squeeze, squash **2** v/r **~se** F squash o squeeze together

aprieto m predicament

aprisa adv quickly

aprisionar <1a> v/t fig trap

aprobación f approval; de ley passing; **aprobado** m EDU pass; **aprobar** <1m> v/t approve; comportamiento, idea approve of; exa-

men pass
apropiado *adj* appropriate, suitable;
apropiarse <1b> *v/r*: ~ *de algo*
take sth
aprovechado 1 *adj desp* opportunistic **2** *m*, **-a** *f desp* opportunist;
aprovechar <1a> **1** *v/t* take advantage of; *tiempo, espacio* make good
use of; *quiero* ~ *la ocasión para ...*
I would like to take this opportunity to ... **2** *v/i* take the opportunity
(*para* to); *¡que aproveche!* enjoy
your meal! **3** *v/r* ~*se* take advantage (*de* of)
aprovisionarse <1a> *v/r* stock up
(*de* on)
aproximadamente *adv* approximately; **aproximado** *adj* approximate; **aproximar** <1a> **1** *v/t* bring
closer **2** *v/r* ~*se* approach
aptitud *f* aptitude (*para* for), flair
(*para* for); **apto** *adj* suitable (*para*
for); *para servicio militar* fit; EDU
pass
apuesta *f* bet
apuesto *adj* handsome
apunado *adj* Pe, Bol suffering from
altitude sickness; **apunarse** <1a>
v/r S.Am. get altitude sickness
apuntador *m*, ~**a** *f* TEA prompter
apuntalar <1a> *v/t edificio* shore up;
fig prop up
apuntar <1a> **1** *v/t* (*escribir*) note
down, make a note of; TEA prompt;
en curso, para viaje etc put down (*en,
a* on; *para* for); ~ *con el dedo* point
at *o* to **2** *v/i con arma* aim **3** *v/r* ~*se*
put one's name down (*para, en o* for); *¡me apunto!* count me in!;
apunte *m* note
apuñalar <1a> *v/t* stab
apurado *adj L.Am.* (*con prisa*) in a
hurry; (*pobre*) short (of cash);
apurar <1a> **1** *v/t vaso* finish off; *a
alguien* pressure, put pressure on
2 *v/i Chi*: *no me apura* I'm not in a
hurry for it **3** *v/r* ~*se* worry; *L.Am.*
(*darse prisa*) hurry (up); **apuro** *m*
predicament, tight spot F; *vergüenza*
embarrassment; *L.Am.* rush; *me da
*~ I'm embarrassed

aquejado *adj*: *estar* ~ *de* be suffering from
aquel, aquella, aquellos, aquellas
det singular that; *plural* those
aquél, aquélla aquéllos, aquéllas
pron singular that (one); *plural*
those (ones)
aquello *pron* that
aquí *adv en el espacio* here; *en el
tiempo* now; *desde* ~ from here; *por*
~ here
árabe 1 *m/f & adj* Arab **2** *m idioma*
Arabic
Arabia Saudí Saudi Arabia
arado *m* plow, *Br* plough
arancel *m* tariff; **arancelario** *adj* tariff *atr*
arándano *m* blueberry
arandela *f* washer
araña *f* ZO spider; *lámpara* chandelier
arañar <1a> *v/t* scratch; **arañazo** *m*
scratch
arar <1a> *v/t* plow, *Br* plough
arbitraje *m* arbitration; **arbitrar**
<1a> *v/t en fútbol, boxeo* referee; *en
tenis, béisbol* umpire; *en conflicto* arbitrate; **arbitrario** *adj* arbitrary;
árbitro *m en fútbol, boxeo* referee;
en tenis, béisbol umpire; *en conflicto*
arbitrator
árbol *m* tree; ~ *genealógico* family
tree; **arboleda** *f* grove
arbusto *m* shrub, bush
arca *f* chest; ~ *de Noé* Noah's Ark
arcada *f* MED: *me provocó* ~*s* it
made me retch *o* heave F
arcaico *adj* archaic
arce *m* BOT maple
arcén *m* shoulder, *Br* hard shoulder
archidiócesis *f inv* archdiocese
archipiélago *m* archipelago
archivador *m* filing cabinet; **archivar** <1a> *v/t papeles, documentos*
file; *asunto* shelve; **archivo** *m* archive; INFOR file
arcilla *f* clay
arco *m* ARQUI arch; MÚS bow; *L.Am.*
DEP goal; ~ *iris* rainbow
arder <2a> *v/i* burn; *estar muy caliente*
be exceedingly hot; *la reunión está*

que arde F the meeting is about to erupt F

ardilla *f* ZO squirrel

ardor *m entusiasmo* fervo(u)r; **~ de estómago** heartburn

arduo *adj* arduous

área *f* area; DEP **~ de castigo** *or* **de penalty** penalty area; **~ de descanso** pull-in (at the side of the road); **~ de servicio** service area

arena *f* sand; **~s** *pl* **movedizas** quick-sand *sg*

arenga *f* morale-boosting speech; (*sermón*) harangue

arenque *m* herring

arepa *f C.Am.*, *Ven* cornmeal roll

arete *m L.Am.* joya earring

Argelia Algeria

Argentina Argentina; **argentino 1** *adj* Argentinian **2** *m*, **-a** *f* Argentinian

argolla *f L.Am.* ring

argot *m* slang

argucia *f* clever argument; **argüir** <3g> *v/t* & *v/i* argue; **argumentar** <1a> *v/t* argue; **argumento** *m razón* argument; *de libro, película etc* plot

árido *adj* arid, dry; *fig* dry

Aries *m/f inv* ASTR Aries

arisco *adj* unfriendly

aristocracia *f* aristocracy; **aristócrata** *m/f* aristocrat; **aristocrático** *adj* aristocratic

aritmética *f* arithmetic

arma *f* weapon; **~ blanca** knife; **~ de doble filo** *or* **de dos filos** *fig* two-edged sword; **~ de fuego** firearm; **alzarse en ~s** rise up in arms

armada *f* navy

armadillo *m* ZO armadillo

armado *adj* armed; **armadura** *f* armo(u)r; **armamento** *m* armaments *pl*

armar <1a> **1** *v/t* MIL arm; TÉC assemble, put together; **~ un escándalo** F kick up a fuss F, make a scene F **2** *v/r* **~se** arm o.s.; *la que se va a armar* F all hell will break loose F; **~se de valor** pluck up courage

armario *m* closet, *Br* wardrobe; **~ de cocina** cabinet, *Br* cupboard

armazón *f* skeleton, framework

armisticio *m* armistice

armonía *f* harmony; **armónica** *f* harmonica, mouth organ; **armonioso** *adj* harmonious; **armonizar** <1f> **1** *v/t* harmonize; *diferencias* reconcile **2** *v/i* **de color, estilo** blend (*con* with); *de persona* get on (*con* with)

arnés *m* harness; *para niños* leading strings *pl*, *Br* leading reins *pl*

aro *m* hoop; *L.Am.* (*pendiente*) earring; *entrar* **or** *pasar por el* **~** *fig* F bite the bullet, take the plunge

aroma *m* aroma; *de flor* scent

arpa *f* harp

arpía *f* harpy

arpón *m* harpoon

arquear <1a> *v/t espalda* arch; *cejas* raise

arqueología *f* arch(a)eology; **arqueológico** *adj* arch(a)eological; **arqueólogo** *m*, **-a** *f* arch(a)eologist

arquero *m* archer; *L.Am. en fútbol* goalkeeper

arquetipo *m* archetype

arquitectónico *adj* architectural; **arquitecto** *m*, **-a** *f* architect; **arquitectura** *f* architecture

arrabal *m* poor outlying area

arraigado *adj* entrenched; **arraigar** <1h> **1** *v/i* take root **2** *v/r* **~se de persona** settle (*en* in); *de costumbre, idea* take root

arramblar <1a> *v/t* (*destruir*) destroy

arrancar <1g> **1** *v/t planta, página* pull out; *vehículo* start (up); (*quitar*) snatch **2** *v/i de vehículo, máquina* start (up); INFOR boot (up); *Chi* (*huir*) run away **3** *v/r* **~se** *Chi* run away; **arranque** *m* AUTO starting mechanism; (*energía*) drive; (*ataque*) fit

arrasar <1a> **1** *v/t* devastate **2** *v/i* F be a big hit

arrastrar <1a> **1** *v/t por el suelo*, INFOR drag (*por* along); (*llevarse*) carry away **2** *v/i por el suelo* trail on the ground **3** *v/r* **~se** crawl; *fig*

(*humillarse*) grovel (**delante de** to);
arrastre m: **estar para el ~** *fig* F be
fit to drop F

arreada f *Rpl* round-up

arrebatar <1a> *v/t* snatch (**a** from);
arrebato m fit

arrebujarse <1a> *v/r* F wrap o.s. up;
en cama snuggle up

arreciar <1b> *v/i* get worse; *de viento*
get stronger

arrecife m reef

arredrarse <1a> *v/r* be intimidated
(**ante** by)

arreglar <1a> **1** *v/t* (*reparar*) fix, repair; (*ordenar*) tidy (up); (*solucionar*) sort out; MÚS arrange; **~
cuentas** settle up; *fig* settle scores
2 *v/r* **~se** get (o.s.) ready; *de
problema* get sorted out; (*apañarse*)
manage; **arreglárselas** manage;
arreglo m (*reparación*) repair;
(*solución*) solution; (*acuerdo*) arrangement, agreement; MÚS arrangement; **~ de cuentas** settling
of scores; **con ~ a** in accordance
with; **esto no tiene ~** there's nothing to be done

arrellanarse <1a> *v/r* settle

arremangarse <1h> *v/r* roll up one's
sleeves

arremeter <2a> *v/i*: **~ contra** charge
(at); *fig* (*criticar*) attack

arremolinarse <1a> *v/r* mill around

arrendamiento m renting; **arrendar**
<1k> *v/t L.Am.* (*dar en alquiler*) rent
(out), let; (*tomar en alquiler*) rent; **se
arrenda** for rent

arreo m *Rpl* driving, herding; (*manada*) herd

arrepentimiento m repentance;
(*cambio de opinión*) change of
heart; **arrepentirse** <3i> *v/r* be
sorry; (*cambiar de opinión*) change
one's mind; **~ de algo** regret sth

arrestar <1a> *v/t* arrest; **arresto** m
arrest

arriba 1 *adv* ◊ *situación* up; *en edificio* upstairs; **ponlo ahí ~** put it up
there; **el cajón de ~ siguiente** the
next drawer up, the drawer above;
último the top drawer; **~ del todo**

right at the top ◊ *dirección* up; *en edificio* upstairs; **sigan hacia ~** keep
going up; **me miró de ~ abajo** *fig*
she looked me up and down ◊ *con
cantidades*: **de diez para ~** ten or
above **2** *int* long live

arribeño m, **-a** f *L..Am.* uplander,
highlander

arribista m/f social climber

arriesgado *adj* adventurous; **arriesgar** <1h> **1** *v/t* risk **2** *v/r* **~se** take a
risk; **~se a hacer algo** risk doing
sth

arrimar <1a> **1** *v/t* move closer; **~ el
hombro** F pull one's weight **2** *v/r*
~se move closer (**a** to)

arrinconar <1a> *v/t* (*acorralar*) corner; *libros etc* put away; *persona*
cold-shoulder

arroba f INFOR 'at' symbol, @

arrodillarse <1a> *v/r* kneel (down)

arrogancia f arrogance; **arrogante**
adj arrogant

arrojar <1a> **1** *v/t* (*lanzar*) throw; *resultado* produce; (*vomitar*) throw up
2 *v/r* **~se** throw o.s.

arrollador *adj* overwhelming

arropar <1a> *v/t* wrap up; *fig*
protect

arrope m *Rpl, Chi, Pe* fruit syrup

arroyo m stream; **sacar a alguien
del ~** *fig* lift s.o. out of the gutter

arroz m rice; **~ con leche** rice pudding

arruga f wrinkle; **arrugar** <1h> **1** *v/t*
wrinkle; **2** *v/r* **~se** *de piel, ropa* get
wrinkled

arruinado *adj* ruined, broke F;
arruinar <1a> **1** *v/t* ruin **2** *v/r* **~se**
be ruined

arrullo m *de paloma* cooing; *para niño*
lullaby

arsenal m arsenal

arsénico m arsenic

art *abr* (= **artículo**) art. (= article)

art.° *abr* (= **artículo**) art. (= article)

arte m (*pl* f) art; **~ dramático** dramatic art; **bellas ~s** *pl* fine art *sg*;
malas ~s *pl* guile *sg*

artefacto m (*dispositivo*) device

arteria f artery

arterio(e)sclerosis f arteriosclerosis

artesana f craftswoman; **artesanía** f (handi)crafts pl; **artesano** m craftsman

Ártico zona, océano Arctic

articulación f ANAT, TÉC joint; de sonidos articulation; **artículo** m de periódico, GRAM, JUR article; COM product, item

artificial adj artificial

artillería f artillery; **~ ligera/pesada** light/heavy artillery

artilugio m aparato gadget

artimaña f trick

artista m/f artist; **artístico** adj artistic

artritis f MED arthritis

arveja f Rpl, Chi, Pe BOT pea

arzobispo m archbishop

as m tb fig ace

asa f handle

asado 1 adj roast atr **2** m roast

asalariado m, **-a** f wage earner; de empresa employee

asaltante m/f assailant; **asaltar** <1a> v/t persona attack; banco rob; **asalto** m a persona attack (**a** on); robo robbery, raid; en boxeo round

asamblea f reunión meeting; ente assembly

asar <1a> **1** v/t roast; **~ a la parrilla** broil, Br grill **2** v/r **~se** fig F be roasting F

ascender <2g> **1** v/t a empleado promote **2** v/i de precios, temperatura etc rise; de montañero climb; DEP, en trabajo be promoted (**a** to); **ascensión** f ascent; **ascenso** m de temperatura, precios rise (**de** in); de montaña ascent; DEP, en trabajo promotion; **ascensor** m elevator, Br lift

ascético adj ascetic

asco m disgust; **me da ~** I find it disgusting; **¡qué ~!** how revolting o disgusting!

ascua f ember; **estar en** or **sobre ~s** be on tenterhooks

asearse <1a> v/r wash up, Br have a wash

asediar <1b> v/t tb fig besiege; **asedio** m MIL siege, blockade; a alguien hounding

aseguradora f insurance company; **asegurar** <1a> **1** v/t (afianzar) secure; (prometer) assure; (garantizar) guarantee; COM insure **2** v/r **~se** make sure

asentamiento m settlement; **asentarse** <1k> v/r settle

asentir <3i> v/i agree (**a** to), consent (**a** to); con la cabeza nod

aseo m cleanliness; (baño) restroom, toilet

aséptico adj aseptic

asequible adj precio affordable; obra accessible

aserrar <1k> v/t saw; **aserrín** m L.Am. sawdust

asesinar <1a> v/t murder; POL assassinate; **asesinato** m murder; POL assassination; **asesino** m, **-a** f murderer; POL assassin

asesor m, **-a** f consultant, advisor, Br adviser; **~ fiscal** financial advisor (Br adviser); **~ de imagen** public relations consultant; **asesorar** <1a> v/t advise; **asesoría** f consultancy

asestar <1a> v/t golpe deal (**a** to); **me asestó una puñalada** he stabbed me

asfaltar <1a> v/t asphalt; **asfalto** m asphalt

asfixia f asphyxiation; **asfixiante** adj asphyxiating, suffocating; **asfixiar** <1b> **1** v/t asphyxiate, suffocate **2** v/r **~se** asphyxiate, suffocate

así 1 adv (de este modo) like this; (de ese modo) like that; **~ no más** S.Am. just like that; **~ pues** so; **~ que** so; **~ de grande** this big **2** conj: **~ como** al igual que while, whereas

Asia Asia

asiático 1 adj Asian **2** m, **-a** f Asian

asiduidad f frequency; **con ~** con frecuencia regularly; **asiduo** adj regular

asiento m seat; **tomar ~** take a seat

asignación f acción allocation; dinero allowance; **asignar** <1a> v/t allocate; *persona, papel* assign; **asignatura** *f* subject

asilarse <1a> *v/r* take refuge, seek asylum; **asilo** *m* home, institution; POL asylum; **~ de ancianos** old people's home

asimétrico *adj* asymmetrical

asimilar <1a> *v/t* assimilate

asimismo *adv* (*también*) also; (*igualmente*) in the same way, likewise

asistencia *f* (*ayuda*) assistance; *a lugar* attendance (**a** at); **~ en carretera** AUTO roadside assistance; **~ médica** medical care; **asistenta** *f* cleaner, cleaning woman; **asistente** *m/f* (*ayudante*) assistant; **~ social** social worker; **los ~s** those present; **asistir** <3a> **1** *v/t* help, assist **2** *v/i* be present; **~ a una boda** attend a wedding

asma *f* asthma; **asmático** *adj* asthmatic

asno *m* ZO donkey; *persona* idiot

asociación *f* association; **asociar** <1b> **1** *v/t* associate; **~ a alguien con algo** associate s.o. with sth **2** *v/r* **~se** team up (**con** with), go into partnership (**con** with); **~se a** *grupo, club* become a member of

asolar <1m> *v/t* devastate

asoleada *f:* **pegarse una ~** *Bol, Pe* sunbathe

asomar <1a> **1** *v/t* put *o* stick out **2** *v/i* show **3** *v/r* **~se** lean out; **~se a** *or* **por la ventana** lean out of the window

asombrado *adj* amazed; **asombrar** <1a> **1** *v/t* amaze, astonish **2** *v/r* **~se** be amazed *o* astonished; **asombro** *m* amazement, astonishment; **asombroso** *adj* amazing

asomo *m:* **ni por ~** no way

asorocharse <1a> *v/r* Pe, Bol get altitude sickness

aspecto *m de persona, cosa* look, appearance; (*faceta*) aspect; **tener buen ~** look good

áspero *adj superficie* rough; *sonido* harsh; *persona* abrupt

aspersor *m* sprinkler

aspiraciones *fpl* aspirations

aspirador *m,* **~a** *f* vacuum cleaner; **aspirante** *m/f a cargo* candidate (**a** for); *a título* contender (**a** for); **aspirar** <1a> **1** *v/t* suck up; *al respirar* inhale, breathe in **2** *v/i:* **~ a** aspire to

aspirina *f* aspirin

asqueado *adj* disgusted; **asquear** <1a> *v/t* disgust; **asqueroso 1** *adj* (*sucio*) filthy; (*repugnante*) revolting, disgusting **2** *m,* **-a** *f* creep

asterisco *m* asterisk

astigmatismo *m* astigmatism

astilla *f* splinter; **~s** *pl para fuego* kindling *sg;* **hacer ~s algo** *fig* smash sth to pieces

astillero *m* shipyard

astral *adj* astral

astringente *m/adj* astringent

astro *m* AST, *fig* star

astrología *f* astrology; **astrólogo** *m,* **-a** *f* astrologer

astronauta *m/f* astronaut

astronave *f* spaceship

astronomía *f* astronomy; **astronómico** *adj* astronomical; **astrónomo** *m,* **-a** *f* astronomer

astucia *f* shrewdness, astuteness

astuto *adj* shrewd, astute

asumir <3a> *v/t* assume; (*aceptar*) accept, come to terms with

asunto *m* matter; F (*relación*) affair; **~s exteriores** foreign affairs; **no es tuyo** it's none of your business

asustar <1a> **1** *v/t* frighten, scare **2** *v/r* **~se** be frightened *o* scared

atacar <1g> *v/t* attack

atajar <1a> **1** *v/t* check the spread of, contain; *L.Am. pelota* catch **2** *v/i* take a short cut; **atajo** *m L.Am.* short cut

atañer <2f> *v/i* concern

ataque *m* (*agresión*) attack; (*acceso*) fit; **~ cardíaco** *o* **al corazón** MED heart attack; **le dio un ~ de risa** she burst out laughing

atar <1a> *v/t* tie (up); *fig* tie down

atardecer <2d> **1** *v/i* get dark **2** *m* dusk

atareado *adj* busy

atascar <1g> **1** v/t block **2** v/r ~**se de cañería** get blocked; *de mecanismo* jam, stick; *al hablar* dry up; **atasco** m traffic jam

ataúd m coffin, casket

atemorizar <1f> v/t frighten

atención f attention; (*cortesía*) courtesy; *¡~!* your attention, please!; **llamar la ~ a alguien** *reñir* tell s.o. off; *por ser llamativo* attract s.o.'s attention; **prestar ~** pay attention (*a* to)

atender <2g> **1** v/t *a enfermo* look after; *en tienda* attend to, serve **2** v/i pay attention (*a* to)

atenerse <2l> v/r: ~ *a normas* abide by; *consecuencias* face, accept; **saber a qué** know where one stands

atentado m attack (*contra, a* on); ~ **terrorista** terrorist attack

atentamente adv attentively; *en carta* sincerely, *Br* Yours sincerely

atentar <1k> v/i: ~ **contra** *vida* make an attempt on; *moral etc* be contrary to

atento adj attentive; **estar ~ a algo** pay attention to sth

atenuante adj JUR extenuating; **circunstancia ~** JUR extenuating circumstance; **atenuar** <1e> v/t lessen, reduce

ateo 1 adj atheistic **2** m, **-a** f atheist

aterciopelado adj tb fig velvety

aterido adj frozen

aterrador adj frightening; **aterrar** <1a> v/t terrify

aterrizaje m AVIA landing; ~ **forzoso** *or* **de emergencia** emergency landing; **aterrizar** <1f> v/i land

aterrorizado adj terrified, petrified F; **aterrorizar** <1f> v/t terrify; (*amenazar*) terrorize

atestado adj overcrowded

atestiguar <1i> v/t JUR testify; *fig* bear witness to

atiborrarse <1a> v/r F stuff o.s. F (*de* with)

ático m *piso* top floor; *apartamento* top floor apartment (*Br* flat); (*desván*) attic

atinar <1a> v/i manage (*a* to); *no*

atinó con la respuesta correcta she couldn't come up with the right answer

atípico adj atypical

atisbo m sign

atizar <1f> v/t *fuego* poke; *pasiones* stir up; *le atizó un golpe* she hit him

Atlántico m/adj: **el** (**océano**) ~ the Atlantic (Ocean)

atlas m inv atlas

atleta m/f athlete; **atlético** adj athletic; **atletismo** m athletics

atmo. abr (= **atentísimo**): **su ~** Yours truly

atmósfera f atmosphere

atole m *Méx* flavored hot drink made with maize flour

atolladero m: **sacar a alguien del ~** fig F get s.o. out of a tight spot

atolondrado adj scatterbrained

atómico adj atomic; **átomo** m atom; **ni un ~ de** fig not an iota of

atónito adj astonished, amazed

atontar <1a> v/t make groggy *o* dopey; *de golpe* stun, daze; (*volver tonto*) turn into a zombie

atorar <1a> *L.Am.* **1** v/t *cañería etc* block (up) **2** v/r ~**se** choke; *de cañería etc* get blocked (up)

atormentar <1a> v/t torment

atornillar <1a> v/t screw on

atorrante m *Rpl*, *Chi* F bum F, *Br* tramp; (*holgazán*) layabout

atosigar <1h> v/t pester

atrabancado adj *Méx* clumsy

atracar <1g> **1** v/t *banco, tienda* hold up; *a alguien* mug; *Chi* F make out with F, neck with *Br* F **2** v/i MAR dock

atracción f attraction

atraco m *de banco, tienda* robbery; *de persona* mugging

atracón m: **darse un ~ de** stuff o.s. with F

atractivo 1 adj attractive **2** m appeal, attraction; **atraer** <2p> v/t attract

atragantarse <1a> v/r choke (*con* on); **se le ha atragantado** *fig* she can't stand *o* stomach him

atrancar <1g> **1** v/t *puerta* barricade

auto A

2 *v/r* ~**se** *fig* get stuck
atrapar <1a> *v/t* catch, trap
atrás *adv para indicar posición* at the back, behind; *para indicar movimiento* back; *años* ~ years ago *o* back; *hacia* ~ back, backwards; *quedarse* ~ get left behind; **atrasado** *adj en estudios, pago* behind (*en* in *o* with); *reloj* slow; *pueblo* backward; *ir* ~ *o un reloj* be slow; **atrasar** <1a> **1** *v/t reloj* put back; *fecha* postpone, put back **2** *v/i de reloj* lose time; **atraso** *m* backwardness; COM ~**s** arrears
atravesar <1k> *v/t* cross; (*perforar*) go through, pierce; *crisis* go through
atrevido *adj* daring; **atreverse** <2a> *v/r* dare
atribuir <3g> **1** *v/t* attribute (*a* to) **2** *v/r* ~**se** claim
atrincherarse <1a> *v/r* MIL dig o.s. in, entrench o.s.; *se atrincheró en su postura fig* he dug his heels in
atrocidad *f* atrocity
atrofiado *adj* atrophied; **atrofiarse** <1b> *v/r* atrophy
atropellar <1a> *v/t* knock down
atroz *adj* appalling, atrocious
ATS *abr* (= *ayudante técnico sanitario*) registered nurse
atte. *abr* (= *atentamente*) sincerely (yours)
atuendo *m* outfit
atufar <1a> *v/t* stink out F
atún *m* tuna (fish)
aturdido *adj* in a daze; **aturdir** <3a> **1** *v/t de golpe, noticia* stun, daze; (*confundir*) bewilder, confuse **2** *v/r* ~**se** be stunned *o* dazed; (*confundirse*) be bewildered *o* confused
aturrullar <1a> **1** *v/t* confuse **2** *v/r* ~**se** get confused
audacia *f* audacity; **audaz** *adj* daring, bold, audacious
audición *f* TEA audition; JUR hearing
audiencia *f* audience; JUR court; *índice de* ~ TV ratings *pl*
audífono *m para sordos* hearing aid
audiovisual *adj* audiovisual
auditivo *adj* auditory; *problema*

hearing *atr*
auditor *m*, ~**a** *f* auditor; **auditoría** *f* audit; **auditorio** *m* (*público*) audience; *sala* auditorium
auge *m* peak; *estar en* ~ *aumento* be enjoying a boom
augurar <1a> *v/t de persona* predict, foretell; *de indicio* augur; **augurio** *m* omen, sign; *un buen/mal* ~ a good/bad omen
aula *f* classroom; *en universidad* lecture hall, *Br* lecture theatre
aullido *m* howl
aumentar <1a> **1** *v/t* increase; *precio* increase, raise, put up **2** *v/i de precio, temperatura* rise, increase, go up; **aumento** *m de precios, temperaturas etc* rise (*de* in), increase (*de* in); *de sueldo* raise, *Br* rise; *ir en* ~ be increasing
aun *adv* even; ~ *así* even so
aún *adv en oraciones no negativas* still; *en oraciones negativas* yet; *en comparaciones* even; ~ *no* not yet
aunar <1a> *v/t* combine
aunque *conj* although, even though; + *subj* even if
auricular *m de teléfono* receiver; ~**es** headphones, earphones
aurora *f* dawn; ~ *boreal* northern lights *pl*
auscultar <1a> *v/t*: ~ *a alguien* listen to s.o.'s chest
ausencia *f de persona* absence; *no existencia* lack (*de* of); *brillaba por su* ~ he was conspicuous by his absence; **ausente** *adj* absent
auspicio *m* sponsorship; *bajo los* ~**s** *de* under the auspices of
austeridad *f* austerity; **austero** *adj* austere
austral *adj* southern
Australia Australia; **australiano** **1** *adj* Australian **2** *m*, -**a** *f* Australian
Austria Austria; **austriano 1** *adj* Austrian **2** *m*, -**a** *f* Austrian
auténtico *adj* authentic; **autentificar** <1g> *v/t* authenticate
autismo *m* autism
auto *m* JUR order; *L.Am.* AUTO car

autoadhesivo *adj* self-adhesive
autoayuda *f* self-help
autobiografía *f* autobiography
autobombo *m* F self-glorification
autobús *m* bus
autocar *m* bus
autocaravana *f* camper van
autocontrol *m* self-control
autocrítica *f* self-criticism
autóctono *adj* indigenous, native
autodefensa *f* self-defense, *Br* self-defence
autodeterminación *f* self-determination
autodidacta **1** *adj* self-taught **2** *m/f* self-taught person
autoedición *f* desktop publishing, DTP
autoescuela *f* driving school
autoestima *f* self-esteem
autoestop *m* hitchhiking; **autoestopista** *m/f* hitchhiker
autógrafo *m* autograph
automático *adj* automatic; **automatizar** <1f> *v/t* automate
automedicación *f* self-medication
automóvil *m* car, automobile; **automovilismo** *m* driving; **automovilista** *m/f* motorist
autonomía *f* autonomy; *en España* autonomous region; **autónomo** *adj* autonomous
autopista *f* freeway, *Br* motorway; **~ de la información** *or* **de la comunicación** INFOR information (super)highway
autopsia *f* post mortem, autopsy
autor *m*, **~a** *f* author; *de crimen* perpetrator
autoridad *f* authority; **autoritario** *adj* authoritarian; **autorización** *f* authority; **autorizar** <1f> *v/t* authorize
autorradio *m* car radio
autorretrato *m* self-portrait
autoservicio *m* supermarket; *restaurante* self-service restaurant
autostop *m* hitchhiking; **hacer ~** hitch(hike)
autosuficiencia *f* self-sufficiency; *desp* smugness; **autosuficiente** *adj*

self-sufficient; *desp* smug
autovía *f* divided highway, *Br* dual carriageway
auxiliar **1** *adj* auxiliary; *profesor* assistant **2** *m/f* assistant; **~ f de vuelo** stewardess, flight attendant **3** <1b> *v/t* help; **auxilio** *m* help; **primeros ~s** *pl* first aid *sg*
Av. *abr* (= **Avenida**) Ave (= Avenue)
aval *m* guarantee; **~ bancario** bank guarantee
avalancha *f* avalanche
avalar <1a> *v/t* guarantee; *fig* back
avance *m* advance
avanzado *adj* advanced; **avanzar** <1f> **1** *v/t* move forward, advance **2** *v/i* advance, move forward; MIL advance (**hacia** on); *en trabajo* make progress
avaricia *f* avarice; **avaro 1** *adj* miserly **2** *m*, **-a** *f* miser
avasallar <1a> *v/t* subjugate; **no dejes que te avasallen** *fig* don't let them push you around
Av.ᵈᵃ *abr* (= **Avenida**) Ave (= Avenue)
ave *f* bird; *S.Am.* (*pollo*) chicken; **~ de presa** *or* **de rapiña** bird of prey
avecinarse <1a> *v/r* approach
avejentar <1a> *v/t* age
avellana *f* BOT hazelnut; **avellano** *m* BOT hazel
avena *f* oats *pl*
avenida *f* avenue
avenirse <3s> *v/r* agree (**a** to)
aventajar <1a> *v/t* be ahead of
aventura *f* adventure; *riesgo* venture; *amorosa* affair; **aventurar 1** *v/t* risk; *opinión* venture **2** *v/r* **~se** venture; **~se a hacer algo** dare to do sth; **aventurero** *adj* adventurous
avergonzar <1n & 1f> **1** *v/t* (*abochornar*) embarrass; **le avergüenza algo reprensible** she's ashamed of it **2** *v/r* **~se** be ashamed (**de** of)
avería *f* TÉC fault; AUTO breakdown; **averiarse** <1c> *v/r* break down
averiguar <1i> *v/t* find out
aversión *f* aversion
avestruz *m* ZO ostrich; **del ~ política,**

B

táctica head-in-the-sand
aviación *f* aviation; MIL air force
avicultor *m*, **~a** *f* poultry farmer
avidez *f* eagerness; **ávido** *adj* eager (*de* for), avid (*de* for)
avinagrarse <1a> *v/r de vino* turn vinegary; *fig* become bitter *o* sour
avión *m* plane; *por* ~ *mandar una carta* (by) airmail; **avioneta** *f* light aircraft
avisar <1a> *v/t notificar* let know, tell; *de peligro* warn; (*llamar*) call, send for; **aviso** *m comunicación* notice; (*advertencia*) warning; *L.Am.* (*anuncio*) advertisement; *hasta nuevo* ~ until further notice; *sin previo* ~ unexpectedly, without any warning
avispa *f* ZO wasp
avivar <1a> *v/t fuego* revive; *interés* arouse
avizor *adj*: *estar ojo* ~ be alert
axila *f* armpit
axioma *m* axiom
ay *int de dolor* ow!, ouch!; *de susto* oh!
ayer *adv* yesterday; ~ *por la mañana* yesterday morning
ayuda *f* help; ~ *al desarrollo* development aid *o* assistance; **ayudante** *m/f* assistant; **ayudar** <1a> *v/t* help
ayunas: *estoy en* ~ I haven't eaten anything; **ayuno** *m* fast
ayuntamiento *m* city council, town council; *edificio* city hall
azabache *m* MIN jet
azadón *m* mattock
azafata *f* flight attendant; ~ *de congresos* hostess
azafrán *m* BOT saffron
azalea *f* BOT azalea
azar *m* fate, chance; *al* ~ at random
azorarse <1a> *v/r* be embarrassed
azotar <1a> *v/t con látigo* whip, flog; *con mano* smack; *de enfermedad, hambre* grip; *Méx puerta* slam; **azote** *m con látigo* lash; *con mano* smack; *fig* scourge; *dar un* ~ *a alguien* F smack s.o.
azotea *f* flat roof; *estar mal de la* ~ *fig* F be crazy F
azteca *m/f & adj* Aztec
azúcar *m* (*also f*) sugar; ~ *glas* confectioner's sugar, *Br* icing sugar; ~ *moreno* brown sugar; **azucarero** *m* sugar bowl
azucena *f* BOT Madonna lily
azufre *m* sulfur, *Br* sulphur
azul 1 *adj* blue; ~ *celeste* sky-blue; ~ *marino* navy(-blue) **2** *m* blue
azulejo *m* tile
azuzar <1f> *v/t*: ~ *los perros a alguien* set the dogs on s.o.; *fig* egg s.o. on

B

B.A. *abr* (= *Buenos Aires*) Buenos Aires
baba *f* drool, dribble; *se le caía la* ~ F he was drooling F (*con* over); **babear** <1a> *v/i* dribble; **babero** *m* bib
Babia *f*: *estar en* ~ be miles away
babor *m* MAR port
babosa *f* ZO slug
babosada *f L.Am.* F stupid thing to do / say; **baboso** *adj L.Am.* F stupid
baca *f* AUTO roof rack
bacalao *m* cod; *cortar el* ~ F call the shots F
bache *m* pothole; *fig* rough patch
bachicha 1 *m/f Rpl, Chi desp* wop *desp* **2** *f Méx* cigarette stub
bachillerato *m Esp* high school leaver's certificate
bacón *m* bacon

B

bacteria f bacteria
bádminton m badminton
bafle m loudspeaker
bahía f bay
bailaor m, **~a** f flamenco dancer;
bailar <1a> **1** v/i dance; *de zapato*
be loose **2** v/t dance; **se lo bailó** *Méx*
F he pinched F *o* swiped F it;
bailarín m, **-ina** f dancer; **baile** m
dance; *fiesta formal* ball; **~ de salón**
ballroom dancing; **~ de San Vito** fig
St. Vitus's dance
baja f *descenso* fall, drop; **estar de ~**
(por enfermedad) be off sick; **~s**
MIL casualties; **bajada** f fall; **bajar**
<1a> **1** v/t *voz, precio* lower; *escalera*
go down; **~ algo de arriba** get sth
down **2** v/i go down; *de intereses* fall,
drop **3** v/r **~se** get down; *de*
automóvil get out (**de** of); *de tren,*
autobús get off (**de** sth)
bajío m *L.Am.* lowland
bajo 1 *adj* low; *persona* short; **por lo ~**
at least **2** m MÚS bass; *piso* first
floor, *Br* ground floor **3** *adv cantar,*
hablar quietly, softly; *volar* low **4** *prp*
under; **tres grados ~ cero** three degrees below zero
bajón m sharp decline; **dar un ~** decline sharply, slump
bala f bullet; **como una ~** like
lightning; **ni a ~** *L.Am.* F no way;
balaceo m *L.Am.*, **balacera** f
L.Am. shooting
balada f ballad
balance m COM balance; **balancear-**
se <1a> v/r swing, sway
balanza f scales *pl*; **~ comercial** balance of trade; **~ de pagos** balance
of payments
balaustrada f balustrade
balazo m shot
balbucear <1a>, **balbucir** <3f; *defec-*
tive> **1** v/i stammer; *de niño* babble
2 v/t stammer
Balcanes *mpl* Balkans; **balcánico**
adj Balkan
balcón m balcony
baldado *adj fig* F bushed F
balde *adv*: **de ~** for nothing; **en ~** in
vain

baldosa f floor tile
balear <1a> v/t *L.Am.* shoot
Baleares *fpl* Balearic Islands;
baleárico *adj* Balearic
baleo m *L.Am.* shooting
baliza f MAR buoy
ballena f ZO whale
ballet m ballet
balneario m spa
balón m ball; **baloncesto** m basketball; **balonmano** m handball;
balonvolea m volleyball
balsa f raft; **como una ~ de aceite**
fig like a mill pond
bálsamo m balsam
baluarte m stronghold; *persona* pillar, stalwart
balumba f *L.Am.* F heap, pile; F (*rui-*
do) noise, racket F
bambolearse <1a> v/r sway
bambolla f *L.Am.* F fuss
bambú m BOT bamboo
banal *adj* banal
banana f *L.Am., Rpl, Pe, Bol* banana
banca f *actividad* banking; *conjunto*
de bancos banks *pl*; *en juego* bank;
DEP, *Méx* (*asiento*) bench
bancal m terrace; *división de terreno*
plot
bancario *adj* bank *atr*; **bancarrota** f
bankruptcy; **estar en ~** be bankrupt
banco m COM bank; *para sentarse*
bench; **~ de arena** sand bank; **~ de**
datos data bank
banda f MÚS, (*grupo*) band; *de delin-*
cuentes gang; (*cinta*) sash; *en fútbol*
touchline; **~ sonora** soundtrack;
bandada f *de pájaros* flock
bandazo m: **dar ~s** *de coche* swerve
bandeja f tray; **servir en ~** hand on a
plate
bandera f flag; (*lleno*) **hasta la ~**
packed (out); **bajar la ~** *de taxi* start
the meter running; **banderilla** f
TAUR banderilla (*dart stuck into*
bull's neck during bullfight)
bandido m, **-a** f bandit
bando m edict; *en disputa* side
bandolero m, **-a** f bandit
banjo m MÚS banjo
banquero m, **-a** f banker

banqueta *f L.Am.* stool; *L.Am.* (*acera*) sidewalk, *Br* pavement; **~ trasera** AUTO back seat

banquete *m* banquet; **~ de bodas** wedding reception

banquillo *m* JUR dock; DEP bench

bañadera *f Rpl* (*baño*) bath; **bañador** *m* swimsuit; **bañar** <1a> **1** *v/t de sol, mar* bathe; *a un niño, un enfermo* bathe, *Br* bath; GASTR coat (**con** with, **en** in) **2** *v/r* **~se** have a bath; *en el mar* go for a swim; **bañera** *f* (bath)tub, bath; **bañista** *m/f* swimmer; **baño** *m* bath; *en el mar* swim; *esp L.Am.* bathroom; TÉC plating; **~ de sangre** blood bath; **~ María** bain-marie

baptisterio *m* baptistry

baquiano *L.Am.* **1** *adj* expert *atr* **2** *m*, **-a** *f* guide

bar *m* bar

baraja *f* deck of cards

barandilla *f* handrail, banister

barata *f Méx* bargain counter; (*saldo*) sale; **baratero** *m*, **-a** *f Chi tendero* junk-shop owner; **baratija** *f* trinket; **barato** *adj* cheap

barba *f tb* BOT beard; *por* **~** F a head, per person

barbacoa *f* barbecue

barbaridad *f* barbarity; **costar una ~** cost a fortune; **decir ~es** say outrageous things; **¡qué ~!** what a thing to say / do!; **bárbaro 1** *adj* F tremendous, awesome F; **¡qué ~!** amazing!, wicked! F **2** *m*, **-a** *f* F punk F

barbería *f* barber's shop; **barbero** *m* barber

barbilla *f* chin

barbitúrico *m* barbiturate

barbo *m pescado* barbel

barca *f* boat; **barcaza** *f* MAR barge; **barco** *m* boat; *más grande* ship; **~ de vela** sailing ship

baremo *m* scale

barniz *m para madera* varnish; **barnizar** <1f> *v/t* varnish

barómetro *m* barometer

barquero *m* boatman

barquillo *m* wafer; *Méx, C.Am.* ice-cream cone

barra *f de metal, en bar* bar; *de cortinas* rod; **~ de labios** lipstick; **~ de pan** baguette; **~ espaciadora** space bar; **~ de herramientas** INFOR tool bar; **~ invertida** backslash

barraca *f* (*chabola*) shack; *de tiro* stand; *de feria* stall; *L.Am.* (*deposito*) shed; **~s** *pl L.Am.* shanty town *sg*

barracón *m* MIL barrack room

barranco *m* ravine

barrenar <1a> *v/t* drill

barrendero *m*, **-a** *f* street sweeper

barreno *m* drill hole

barreño *m* washing up bowl

barrer <2a> *v/t* sweep

barrera *f* barrier; **~ del sonido** sound barrier

barriada *f C.Am.* (*barrio marginal*) slum, shanty town

barrial *m L.Am.* bog

barricada *f* barricade

barrida *f L.Am.* sweep; *L.Am.* (*redada*) police raid

barriga *f* belly; **rascarse la ~** *fig* F sit on one's butt F; **barrigón** *adj* F pudgy F

barril *m* barrel

barrio *m* neighbo(u)rhood, area; **~ de chabolas** *Esp* shanty town; **irse al otro ~** F kick the bucket P

barro *m* mud

barroco *m/adj* baroque

barrote *m* bar

bártulos *mpl* F things, gear *sg* F

barullo *m* uproar, racket

basar <1a> **1** *v/t* base (**en** on) **2** *v/r* **~se** be based (**en** on)

báscula *f* scales

base *f* QUÍM, MAT, MIL base; **~ de datos** INFOR database; **~s de concurso** *etc* conditions; **a ~ de** by dint of; **básico** *adj* basic

basílica *f* basilica

básquetbol *m L.Am.* basketball

bastante 1 *adj* enough; *número o cantidad considerable* plenty of; **quedan ~s plazas** there are plenty of seats left **2** *adv* quite, fairly; **bebe ~** she drinks quite a lot;

B

bastar <1a> *v/i* be enough; *basta con uno* one is enough; *¡basta!* that's enough!

bastardo 1 *adj* bastard *atr* **2** *m* bastard

bastidor *m*: *entre ~es* F behind the scenes

bastión *m* bastion

basto 1 *adj* rough, coarse **2** *mpl*: *~s* (*en naipes*) suit in Spanish deck of cards

bastón *m* stick

basura *f tb fig* trash, *Br* rubbish; *cubo de la ~* trash can, *Br* rubbish bin; **basural** *m L.Am.* dump, *Br* tip; **basurero** *m* garbage collector, *Br* dustman

bata *f* robe, *Br* dressing gown; MED (white) coat; TÉC lab coat

batacazo *m* F bump

batalla *f* battle; **batallón** *m* battalion

batata *f* BOT sweet potato

bate *m* DEP bat

batería *f* MIL, EL, AUTO battery; MÚS drums, drum kit; *~ de cocina* set of pans; *aparcar en ~* AUTO parallel park

batido 1 *adj camino* well-trodden **2** *m* GASTR milkshake; **batidora** *f* mixer

batir <3a> *v/t* beat; *nata* whip; *récord* break

baúl *m* chest, trunk; *L.Am.* AUTO trunk, *Br* boot

bautismo *m* baptism, christening; *~ de fuego* baptism of fire; **bautizar** <1f> *v/t* baptize, christen; *barco* name; *vino* F water down; **bautizo** *m* baptism, christening

baya *f* berry

bayeta *f* cloth

bayoneta *f* bayonet

bayunco *adj C.Am.* P silly, stupid

baza *f en naipes* trick; *fig* trump card; *meter ~* F interfere

bazar *m* hardware and fancy goods store; *mercado* bazaar

bazo *m* ANAT spleen

bazofia *f fig* F load of trash F

beatífico *adj* beatific; **beatitud** *f* beatitude; **beato 1** *adj desp* over-

pious **2** *m*, *-a f desp* over-pious person

bebé *m* baby

bebedor *m*, *~a f* drinker; **beber** <2a> **1** *v/i & v/t* drink **2** *v/r ~se* drink up; **bebida** *f* drink

beca *f* scholarship; (*del estado*) grant

becerro *m* calf

béchamel *f* GASTR béchamel (sauce)

bedel *m* porter

beige *adj* beige

béisbol *m* baseball

belén *m* nativity scene

belga *m/f & adj* Belgian; **Bélgica** Belgium

Belice Belize

belicista *m/f* warmonger; **bélico** *adj* war *atr*; **beligerante** *adj* belligerent

bellaco *m*, *-a f Arg* rascal

belleza *f* beauty; **bello** *adj* beautiful

bellota *f* BOT acorn

bemol *m* MÚS flat; *mi ~* E flat; *tener ~es fig* F be tricky F

bencina *f* benzine; *Pe, Bol* (*gasolina*) gas, *Br* petrol

bendecir <3p> *v/t* bless; **bendición** *f* blessing; **bendito** *adj* blessed

benefactor *m adj* charitable; **beneficencia** *f* charity; **beneficiar** <1b> **1** *v/t* benefit; *Rpl ganado* slaughter **2** *v/r ~se* benefit (*de, con* from); **beneficio** *m* benefit, COM profit; *Rpl* slaughterhouse; *C.Am.* coffee-processing plant; *en ~ de* in aid of; **beneficioso** *adj* beneficial; **benéfico** *adj* charity *atr*; *función -a* charity function *o* event

beneplácito *m* approval

benévolo *adj* benevolent, kind; (*indulgente*) lenient

bengala *f* flare

benigno *adj* MED benign

benjamín *m* youngest son; **benjamina** *f* youngest daughter

beodo *adj* drunk

berberecho *m* ZO cockle

berenjena *f* BOT egg plant, *Br* aubergine; **berenjenal** *m*: *meterse en un ~ fig* F get o.s. into a jam F

bermudas *mpl, fpl* Bermuda shorts
berrear <1a> *v/i* bellow; *de niño* bawl, yell; **berrido** *m* bellow; *de niño* yell
berrinche *m* F tantrum, **coger un ~** F throw a tantrum
berro *m* BOT watercress
berza *f* BOT cabbage
besamel *f* GASTR béchamel (sauce)
besar <1a> **1** *v/t* kiss **2** *v/r* **~se** kiss; **beso** *m* kiss
bestia 1 *f* beast **2** *m/f fig* F brute F, swine F; *mujer* bitch F; **conducir a lo ~** F drive like a madman
besugo *m* ZO bream; *fig* F idiot
betún *m* shoe polish
biberón *m* baby's bottle
Biblia *f* Bible
bibliografía *f* bibliography; **biblioteca** *f* library; *mueble* bookcase; **bibliotecario** *m*, **-a** *f* librarian
bicarbonato *m*: **~ (de sodio)** bicarbonate of soda, bicarb F
bíceps *mpl* biceps
bicho *m* bug, *Br tb* creepy-crawly; *(animal)* creature; *fig* F *persona* nasty piece of work; **¿qué ~ te ha picado?** what's eating you?
bici *f* F bike; **bicicleta** *f* bicycle; *ir or montar en ~* go cycling; **~ de montaña** mountain bike
BID *abr* (= **Banco Interamericano de Desarrollo**) IADB (= Inter-American Development Bank)
bidé *m* bidet
bidón *m* drum
bien 1 *m* good; **por tu ~** for your own good; **~es** *pl* goods, property *sg*; **~es de consumo** consumer goods *o* durables; **~es inmuebles** real estate *sg* **2** *adv* well; *(muy)* very; **más ~** rather; **o ... o ...** either ... or ...; **¡está ~!** it's OK!, it's alright!; **estoy ~** I'm fine, I'm OK; **¿estás ~ aquí?** are you comfortable here?; **¡~ hecho!** well done!
bienestar *m* well-being
bienvenida *f* welcome; **dar la ~ a alguien** welcome s.o.; **bienvenido** *adj* welcome
bife *m* *Rpl* steak

bifocal *adj* bifocal
bifurcación *f* fork; *de línea férrea* junction; **bifurcarse** <1g> *v/r* fork
bigamia *f* bigamy
bigote *m* m(o)ustache; **~s de gato etc** whiskers
bikini *m* bikini
bilateral *adj* bilateral
bilingüe *adj* bilingual
bilis *f* bile; *fig* f bad mood
billar *m* billiards; **~ americano** pool
billete *m* ticket; **~ abierto** open ticket; **~ de autobús** bus ticket; **~ de banco** bill, *Br* banknote; **~ de ida, ~ sencillo** one-way ticket, *Br* single (ticket); **~ de ida y vuelta** round-trip ticket, *Br* return (ticket); **billetera** *f L.Am.*, **billetero** *m* billfold, *Br* wallet
billón *m* trillion
binario *adj* binary
bingo *m* bingo; *lugar* bingo hall
biodegradable *adj* biodegradable
biodiversidad *f* biodiversity
biografía *f* biography
biología *f* biology; **biológico** *adj* biological; *AGR* organic; **biólogo** *m*, **-a** *f* biologist
biombo *m* folding screen
biopsia *f* MED biopsy
bioquímica *f* biochemistry
bipartidismo *m* POL two-party system
biquini *m* bikini
birlar <1a> *v/t* F lift F, swipe F
birome *m* *Rpl* ballpoint (pen)
birria *f* F piece of junk F; **va hecha una ~** F she looks a real mess
bis *m* encore; **9 ~** 9A
bisabuela *f* great-grandmother; **bisabuelo** *m* great-grandfather
bisagra *f* hinge
biscote *m* rusk
bisexual *adj* bisexual
bisiesto *adj*: **año ~** leap year
bisnieta *f* great-granddaughter; **bisnieto** *m* great-grandson
bisonte *m* ZO bison
bisoñé *m* hairpiece, toupee
bisté, bistec *m* steak
bisturí *m* MED scalpel

B

bisutería f costume jewel(le)ry
bit m INFOR bit
bizco adj cross-eyed
bizcocho m sponge (cake)
blanca f persona white; MÚS half-note, Br minim; **estar sin ~** fig F be broke F; **blanco 1** adj white; (sin escrito) blank; **arma -a** knife 2 m persona white; (diana), fig target; **dar en el ~** hit the nail on the head; **ser el ~ de todas las miradas** be the center (Br centre) of attention
blando adj soft
blanquear <1a> v/t whiten; pared whitewash; dinero launder; **blanqueo** m whitewashing; **~ de dinero** money laundering; **blanquillo** m Méx egg
blasfemar <1a> v/i curse, swear; REL blaspheme; **blasfemia** f REL blasphemy
blindado adj armo(u)red; puerta reinforced; EL shielded
bloc m pad
blof m L.Am. bluff
bloque m block; POL bloc; **~ de apartamentos** apartment building, Br block of flats; **en ~** en masse; **bloquear** <1a> v/t block; DEP obstruct; (atascar) jam; MIL blockade; COM freeze; **bloqueo** m blockade
blusa f blouse
boa f ZO boa constrictor
bobada f piece of nonsense
bobina f bobbin; FOT reel, spool; EL coil
bobo 1 adj silly, foolish 2 m, -a f fool
boca f mouth; **~ a ~** mouth to mouth; **~ de metro** subway entrance; **~ abajo** face down; **~ arriba** face up; **dejar con la ~ abierta** leave open-mouthed; **se me hace la ~ agua** my mouth is watering; **bocacalle** f side street; **bocadillo** m sandwich; **bocado** m mouthful, bite; **bocana** f river mouth; **bocanada** f mouthful; de viento gust; **bocata** m F → **bocadillo**; **bocazas** m/f inv F loudmouth F
boceto m sketch
bochar <1a> v/t Rpl F en examen fail,

flunk F; Méx cold-shoulder, rebuff
bochinche m Méx uproar
bochorno m sultry weather; fig embarrassment
bocina f MAR, AUTO horn
bocio m MED goiter, Br goitre
boda f wedding
bodega f wine cellar; MAR, AVIA hold; L.Am. bar; C.Am., Pe, Bol grocery store
bodeguero m, -a f L.Am., Pe, Ven storekeeper
body m prenda body
bofetada f slap; **bofetear** <1a> v/t L.Am. slap
bofia f F cops pl F
boga f: **estar en ~** fig be in fashion
bogavante m ZO lobster
bohemio 1 adj bohemian **2** m, -a f bohemian
bohío m Cuba, Ven hut
boicot m boycott; **boicotear** <1a> v/t boycott; **boicoteo** m boycotting
boina f beret
bojote m L.Am. fig bundle
bol m bowl
bola f ball; TÉC ball bearing; de helado scoop; F (mentira) fib F; **~ de nieve** snowball; **no dar pie con ~** get everything wrong; **bolada** f L.Am. throw; (suerte) piece of luck; **bolado** m S.Am. deal; L.Am. F (mentira) fib F
boleada f Arg hunt; **boleador** m, **~a** f Méx bootblack; **boleadoras** fpl L.Am. bolas; **bolear** <1a> **1** v/i L.Am. DEP have a knockabout **2** v/t L.Am. DEP bowl; Rpl con boleadoras bring down; Méx zapatos shine **3** v/r **~se** Rpl fall; (aperarse) get embarrassed; **bolera** f bowling alley
bolero 1 m MÚS bolero **2** m/f Méx F bootblack
boleta f L.Am. ticket; L.Am. (pase) pass, permit; L.Am. (voto) ballot paper; **boletería** f L.Am. ticket office; en cine, teatro box office; **boletero** m, -a f L.Am. ticket clerk; en cine, teatro box office employee; **boletín** m bulletin, report; **~ de**

evaluación report card; **~ *meteo-rológico*** weather report; **boleto** *m L.Am.* ticket; **~ *de autobús*** *L.Am.* bus ticket; **~ *de ida y vuelta*** *L.Am.*, **~ *redondo*** *Méx* round-trip ticket; *Br* return

boliche *m* AUTO jack; *CSur* grocery store, *Br* grocer's

bólido *m fig* racing car

bolígrafo *m* ball-point pen

bolillo *m* bobbin; *Méx* bread roll; ***encaje de* ~s** handmade lace

Bolivia Bolivia; **boliviano 1** *adj* Bolivian **2** *m*, **-a** *f* Bolivian

bollo *m* bun; (*abolladura*) bump

bolo *m* pin; *C.Am.*, *Méx* christening present; **bolos** *mpl* bowling *sg*

bolsa *f* bag; COM stock exchange; *L.Am.* (*bolsillo*) pocket; **~ *de agua caliente*** hot-water bottle; **bolsero** *m*, **-a** *f Méx* F scrounger

bolsillo *m* pocket; **meterse a alguien en el ~** F win s.o. over; **bolso** *m* purse, *Br* handbag; **bolsón** *m Arg*, *Pe* traveling bag, *Br* holdall

bomba *f* bomb; TÉC pump; *S.Am.* gas station; **~ *de relojería*** time bomb; **caer como una ~** *fig* F come as a bombshell; **pasarlo ~** F have a great time

bombacha *f Arg* panties *pl*, *Br tb* knickers *pl*; **bombacho** *m*: **~s** *pl*, **pantalón ~** baggy pants *pl*

bombardear <1a> *v/t* bomb

bombero *m*, **-a** *f* firefighter; **llamar a los ~s** call the fire department

bombilla *f* light bulb; *Rpl* metal straw for the mate gourd; **bombillo** *m C.Am.*, *Pe*, *Bol* light bulb; **bombita** *f Arg* light bulb

bombo *m* MÚS bass drum; TÉC drum

bombón *m* chocolate; *fig* F babe F

bombona *f* cylinder

bonaerense 1 *adj* of Buenos Aires, Buenos Aires *atr* **2** *m/f* native of Buenos Aires

bonanza *f fig* boom, bonanza

bondad *f* goodness, kindness; **tenga la ~ de** please be so kind as to; **bondadoso** *adj* caring

bongo *m L.Am.* bongo

boniato *m* BOT sweet potato

bonito 1 *adj* pretty **2** *m* ZO tuna

bono *m* voucher; COM bond

bonsái *m* bonsai

boñiga *f* dung

boom *m* boom

boquerón *m* ZO anchovy

boquete *m* hole

boquiabierto *adj fig* F speechless

borbotón *m*: **salir a borbotones de agua** gush out; **hablaba a borbotones** *fig* it all came out in a rush; **hablar ~** burble, splutter

borda *f* MAR gunwale; **echar** *or* **tirar por la ~** throw overboard

bordado 1 *adj* embroidered **2** *m* embroidery; **bordar** <1a> *v/t* embroider; **~ *algo*** *fig* do sth brilliantly

borde¹ *adj* F rude, uncouth

borde² *m* edge; **al ~ de** *fig* on the verge *o* brink of

bordear <1a> *v/t* border; **bordillo** *m* curb, *Br* kerb

bordo *m*: **a ~** MAR, AVIA on board

borona *f* corn, *Br* maize

borrachera *f* drunkenness; **agarrar una ~** get drunk; **borrachería** *f Méx*, *Rpl* → **borrachera**; **borracho 1** *adj* drunk **2** *m*, **-a** *f* drunk

borrador *m* eraser; *de texto* draft; (*boceto*) sketch; **borrar** <1a> *v/t* erase; INFOR delete; **pizarra** clean; *recuerdo* blot out

borrasca *f* area of low pressure

borrego *m* ZO lamb; *fig*: *persona* sheep

borrico *m*, **-a** *f* donkey; *fig* dummy

borrón *m* blot; *mancha extendida* smudge; **hacer ~ y cuenta nueva** *fig* wipe the slate clean; **borroso** *adj* blurred, fuzzy

Bosnia Bosnia

bosque *m* wood; *grande* forest

bosquejo *m* sketch; *fig* outline

bostezar <1f> *v/i* yawn; **bostezo** *m* yawn

bota *f* boot; **~ *de montar*** riding boot; **ponerse las ~s** *fig* F coin it F, rake it in F; (*comer mucho*) make a pig of o.s. F

botado *L.Am.* F **1** *adj* (*barato*) dirt

cheap **2** *m*, **-a** *f* abandoned child

botana *f Méx* snack

botánica *f* botany

botar <1a> **1** *v/t* MAR launch; *pelota* bounce; *L.Am.* (*echar*) throw; *L.Am.* (*desechar*) throw out; *L.Am.* (*despedir*) fire **2** *v/i de pelota* bounce

bote *m* (*barco*) boat; *L.Am.* (*lata*) can, *Br tb* tin; (*tarro*) jar; **pegar un ~** jump; **~ de la basura** *Méx* trash can, *Br* rubbish bin; **~ salvavidas** lifeboat; **chupar del ~** *fig* F line one's pockets F; **tener a alguien en el ~** F have s.o. in one's pocket F; **de ~ en ~** packed out

botella *f* bottle

botijo *m container with a spout for drinking from*

botín *m* loot; *calzado* ankle boot

botiquín *m* medicine chest; *estuche* first-aid kit

botón *m en prenda*, TÉC button; BOT bud; **botones** *m inv en hotel* bellhop, bellboy

boutique *f* boutique

bóveda *f* vault

bovino *adj* bovine

boxeador *m*, **-a** *f* boxer; **boxear** <1a> *v/i* box; **boxeo** *m* boxing

boya *f* buoy; *de caña* float; **boyante** *adj fig* buoyant

bragas *fpl* panties, *Br tb* knickers

bragueta *f* fly

bramido *m* roar, bellow

brandy *m* brandy

branquia *f* ZO gill

brasa *f* ember; **a la ~** GASTR char-broiled, *Br* char-grilled; **brasero** *m* brazier; *eléctrico* electric heater

Brasil Brazil; **brasileño 1** *adj* Brazilian **2** *m*, **-a** *f* Brazilian

bravata *f* boast; (*amenaza*) threat

bravo *adj animal* fierce; *mar* rough, choppy; *persona* brave; *L.Am.* (*furioso*) angry; **¡~!** well done!; *en concierto etc* bravo!

bravucón *m*, **-ona** *f* F boaster, blowhard F

braza *f* breaststroke; **brazalete** *m* bracelet; (*banda*) armband; **brazo**

m arm; **~ de gitano** GASTR jelly roll, *Br* Swiss roll; **con los ~s abiertos** with open arms; **dar su ~ a torcer** give in

brebaje *m desp* concoction

brecha *f* breach; *fig* F gap; MED gash; **seguir en la ~** F hang on in there F

brécol *m* broccoli

breva *f* BOT early fig; **no caerá esa ~** *fig* F no such luck!

breve *adj* brief; **en ~** shortly; **brevedad** *f* briefness, shortness; **brevemente** *adv* briefly

brezo *m* BOT heather

bribón *m*, **-ona** *f* rascal

bricolaje *m* do-it-yourself, DIY

brigada *f* MIL brigade; *en policía* squad

brillante 1 *adj* bright; *fig* brilliant **2** *m* diamond; **brillar** <1a> *v/i fig* shine; **brillo** *m* shine; *de estrella*, *luz* brightness; **dar** or **sacar ~ a algo** polish sth

brincar <1g> *v/i* jump up and down; **brinco** *m* F leap, bound; **dar ~s** jump

brindar <1a> **1** *v/t* offer **2** *v/i* drink a toast (*por* to); **brindis** *m inv* toast

brío *m fig* verve, spirit

brisa *f* MAR breeze; **brisera** *f L.Am.* windshield, *Br* windscreen

británico 1 *adj* British **2** *m*, **-a** *f* Briton, Brit F

broca *f* TÉC drill bit

brocha *f* brush

broche *m* brooch; (*cierre*) fastener; *L.Am.* (*pinza*) clothes pin; **brocheta** *f* skewer

brócoli *m* broccoli

broma *f* joke; **en ~** as a joke; **gastar ~s** play jokes; **tomar algo a ~** take sth as a joke; **bromear** <1a> *v/i* joke; **bromista** *m/f* joker

bronca *f* F telling off F; *Méx* P fight; **armar una ~** *Méx* get into a fight; **echar ~ a alguien** F give s.o. a telling off, tell s.o. off

bronce *m* bronze; **bronceado 1** *adj* tanned **2** *m* suntan; **bronceador** *m* suntan lotion; **broncearse** <1a> *v/r* get a tan

bronquitis f MED bronchitis

brotar <1a> v/i BOT sprout, bud; fig appear, arise; **brote** m BOT shoot; MED, fig outbreak; **~s de bambú** bamboo shoots; **~s de soja** beansprouts

bruces: *caer de ~* F fall flat on one's face

bruja f witch; **brujo** m wizard

brújula f compass

bruma f mist

bruñir <3h> v/t burnish, polish; C.Am. F (*molestar*) annoy

brusco adj sharp, abrupt; *respuesta, tono* brusque, curt

Bruselas Brussels

brutalidad f brutality; **bruto 1** adj brutish; (*inculto*) ignorant; (*torpe*) clumsy; COM gross **2** m, **-a** f brute, animal

buceador m, **~a** f diver; **bucear** <1a> v/i dive; fig delve (**en** into)

bucólico adj bucolic

budista m/f & adj Buddhist

buen adj → **bueno**

buenaventura f fortune

bueno adj good; (*bondadoso*) kind; (*sabroso*) nice; *por las -as* willingly; *de -as a primeras* without warning; *ponerse ~* get well; *¡~!* well!; *¿~?* Méx hello; *-a voluntad* goodwill; *¡-as!* hello!; *~s días* good morning; *-as noches* good evening; *-as tardes* good evening

buey m ZO ox

búfalo m ZO buffalo

bufanda f scarf; fig F perk

bufete m lawyer's office

buffet m GASTR buffet

bufón m buffoon, fool

buganvilla f BOT bougainvillea

buhardilla f attic, loft

búho m ZO owl

buitre m ZO vulture

bulbo m BOT bulb

bulevar m boulevard

Bulgaria Bulgaria

bulimia f MED bulimia

bulla f din, racket; **bullicio** m

hubbub, din; (*actividad*) bustle; **bullir** <3h> v/i fig: *de sangre* boil; *de lugar* swarm, teem (**de** with)

bulo m F rumo(u)r

bulto m package; MED lump; *en superficie* bulge; (*silueta*) vague shape; (*pieza de equipaje*) piece of baggage

bumerán m boomerang

buque m ship; **~ de guerra** warship

burbuja f bubble

burdel m brothel

burdo adj rough

burgués 1 adj middle-class, bourgeois **2** m, **-esa** f middle-class person, member of the bourgeoisie

burguesía f middle class, bourgeoisie

burla f joke; (*engaño*) trick; **hacer ~ de alguien** F make fun of s.o.; **burlar** <1a> **1** v/t F get round **2** v/r **~se** make fun (**de** of)

burlete m L.Am. draft excluder, Br draught excluder

buró m bureau

burocracia f bureaucracy; **burócrata** m/f bureaucrat; **burocrático** adj bureaucratic

burrada f fig F piece of nonsense; **hay una ~** there's loads F; **costar una ~** cost a packet F

burro m ZO donkey; **no ver tres en un ~** be as blind as a bat

bursátil adj stock market atr

bus m bus

busca 1 f search; **en ~ de** in search of **2** m F pager; **buscador** m searcher; INFOR search engine; **buscapersonas** m inv pager; **buscapleitos** m/f inv F troublemaker; **buscar** <1a> v/t search for, look for

búsqueda f search

busto m bust

butaca f armchair; TEA seat

butano m butane

butifarra f type of sausage

buzo m diver

buzón m mailbox, Br postbox; **~ de voz** TELEC voicemail

byte m INFOR byte

C *abr* (= *Centígrado*) C (= Centigrade); (= *compañía*) Co. (= Company); c (= *calle*) St. (= Street); (= *capítulo*) ch. (= chapter)

cabal *adj*: **no estar en sus ~es** not be in one's right mind

cabalgar <1h> *v/i* ride

cabalgata *f* procession

caballa *f* ZO mackerel

caballada *f Rpl*: **decir / hacer una ~** say / do sth stupid

caballería *f* MIL cavalry; (*caballo*) horse

caballero 1 *adj* gentlemanly, chivalrous **2** *m hombre* gentleman, man; *hombre educado* gentleman; HIST knight; *trato* sir; (*servicio de*) **~s** *pl* men's room, gents; *en tienda de ropa* menswear; **caballeroso** *adj* gentlemanly, chivalrous

caballito *m*: **~ del diablo** ZO dragonfly; **~ de mar** ZO seahorse; **~s** *pl* carousel *sg*, merry-go-round *sg*

caballo *m* horse; *en ajedrez* knight; **~ balancín** rocking horse; **a ~ entre** halfway between; **montar** *or* **andar** *Rpl* **a ~** ride (a horse); **me gusta montar a ~** I like riding; **ir a ~** go on horseback

cabaña *f* cabin

cabaret *m* cabaret

cabecear <1a> **1** *v/i* nod **2** *v/t el balón* head; **cabecera** *f de mesa, cama* head; *de periódico* masthead; *de texto* top; **cabecero** *m de cama* headboard

cabecilla *m/f* ringleader

cabello *m* hair

caber <2m> *v/i* fit; **caben tres litros** it holds three liters *o Br* litres; **cabemos todos** there's room for all of us; **no cabe duda** *fig* there's no doubt; **no me cabe en la cabeza** I just don't understand

cabestrillo *m* MED sling

cabeza 1 *f* ANAT head; **~ de ajo** bulb of garlic; **~** (**de ganado**) head (of cattle); **~ nuclear** nuclear warhead; **el equipo a la ~** *or* **en ~** the team at the top; **por ~** per head, per person; **estar mal** *or* **no estar bien de la ~** F not be right in the head F **2** *m/f*: **~ de familia** head of the family; **~ de turco** scapegoat; **~ rapada** skinhead

cabezada *f*: **echar una ~** have a nap

cabezonería *f* pigheadedness; **cabezota 1** *adj* pig-headed **2** *m/f* pig-headed person

cabida *f* capacity; **dar ~ a** hold

cabildo *m* POL council

cabina *f* cabin; **~ telefónica** phone booth

cabizbajo *adj* dejected, downhearted

cable *m* EL cable; MAR line, rope; **echar un ~ a alguien** give s.o. a hand

cabo *m* end; GEOG cape; MAR rope; MIL corporal; **al ~ de** after; **de ~ a rabo** F from start to finish; **atar ~s** F put two and two together F; **llevar a ~** carry out

cabra *f* ZO goat; **estar como una ~** F be nuts F

cabrear <1a> **1** *v/t* P bug F **2** *v/r* **~se** P get mad F

cabriola *f*: **hacer ~s** *de niño* jump around

cabro *m Chi* boy; **~ chico** Chi baby

cabrón *m* V bastard P, son of a bitch V

caca *f* F poop F, *Br* pooh F; *cosa mala* piece of trash F; **hacer ~** poop F, *Br* do a pooh F

cacahuate *m Méx* peanut

cacahuete *m* peanut

cacalote *m C.Am., Cuba, Méx* crow

cacao *m* cocoa; *de labios* lip salve; **no**

valer un ~ *L.Am. fig* not be worth a bean F

cacatúa *f* ZO cockatoo

cacería *f* hunt

cacerola *f* pan

cachar <1a> *v/t L.Am.* (*engañar*) trick; *L.Am.* (*sorprender*) catch out; *¿me cachas? Chi* get it?

cacharro *m* pot; *Méx, C.Am.* F (*trasto*) piece of junk; *Méx, C.Am.* F *coche* junkheap; ***lavar los ~s*** *Méx, C.Am.* wash the dishes

cachas *adj*: ***estar ~*** F be a real hunk F

cachear <1a> *v/t* frisk

cachemira *f* cashmere

cachetada *f L.Am.* slap; **cachete** *m* cheek; **cachetear** <1a> *v/t L.Am.* slap

cachimba *f* pipe

cachivache *m* thing; **~s** *pl* (*cosas*) things, stuff *sg* F; (*basura*) junk *sg*

cacho *m* F bit; *Rpl* (*cuerno*) horn; *Ven, Col* F (*marijuana*) joint F; ***jugar al ~*** *Bol, Pe* play dice; ***ponerle ~s a alguien*** cheat on sb

cachondeo *m*: ***estar de ~*** F be joking; ***tomar a ~*** F take as a joke; *¡vaya ~!* F what a laugh! F

cachondo *adj* F (*caliente*) horny F; (*gracioso*) funny

cachorro *m* ZO pup

cacique *m* chief; POL *local political boss*; *fig* F tyrant

cacle *m Méx* shoe

caco *m* F thief

cactus *m inv* BOT cactus

cada *adj considerado por separado* each; *con énfasis en la totalidad* every; ***~ cosa en su sitio*** everything in its place; ***~ uno, ~ cual*** each one; ***~ vez*** every time, each time; ***~ vez más*** more and more, increasingly; ***~ tres días*** every three days; ***uno de ~ tres*** one out of every three

cadáver *m* (*dead*) body, corpse

cadena *f* chain; *de perro* leash, *Br* lead; TV channel; ***~ perpetua*** life sentence

cadencia *f* MÚS rhythm, cadence

cadera *f* hip

caducado *adj* out of date; **caducar** <1g> *v/i* expire; **caducidad** *f*: ***fecha de ~*** expiry date; *de alimentos, medicinas* use-by date

caer <2o> **1** *v/i* fall; ***me cae bien/mal*** *fig* I like / don't like him; ***dejar ~ algo*** drop sth; ***estar al ~*** be about to arrive; ***~ enfermo*** fall ill; ***~ en lunes*** fall on a Monday; *¡ahora caigo!* *fig* now I get it! **2** *v/r* ***~se*** fall (down)

café *m* coffee; (*bar*) café; ***~ con leche*** white coffee; ***~ descafeinado*** decaffeinated coffee; ***~ instantáneo*** instant coffee; ***~ solo*** black coffee; **cafeína** *f* caffeine; **cafetera** *f* coffee maker; *para servir* coffee pot; **cafetería** *f* coffee shop

cagar <1h> V **1** *v/i* have a shit P **2** *v/r* ***~se*** shit o.s. P; ***~se de miedo*** shit o.s. P

caguama *f Méx* (*tortuga*) turtle

caída *f* fall

caigo *vb* → *caer*

caimán *m* ZO alligator; *Méx, C.Am. útil* monkey wrench

Cairo: El ~ Cairo

caja *f* box; *de reloj, ordenador* case, casing; COM cash desk; *en supermercado* checkout; ***~ de ahorros*** savings bank; ***~ de cambios*** gearbox; ***~ de caudales, ~ fuerte*** safe, strongbox; ***~ de cerillas*** matchbox; ***~ de música*** music box; ***~ postal*** post office savings bank; ***~ registradora*** cash register; ***echar a alguien con ~s destempladas*** F send s.o. packing; **cajero** *m*, **-a** *f* cashier; *de banco* teller; ***~ automático*** ATM, *Br tb* cash point

cajeta *f Méx* caramel spread

cajón *m* drawer; *L.Am.* casket, coffin

cajuela *f Méx* AUTO trunk, *Br* boot

cal *f* lime

cala *f* cove

calabacín *m* BOT zucchini, *Br* courgette; **calabaza** *f* pumpkin; ***dar ~s a alguien*** *en examen* fail s.o., flunk s.o. F; *en relación* give s.o. the brush off F

calabozo *m* cell

calada *f* puff

calado *adj* soaked; **~ hasta los huesos** soaked to the skin

calamar *m* ZO squid

calambre *m* EL shock; MED cramp

calamidad *f* calamity

calaña *f desp* sort, type

calar <1a> **1** *v/t* (*mojar*) soak; *techo, tela* soak through; *persona, conjura* see through **2** *v/i de zapato* leak; *de ideas, costumbres* take root; **~ hondo en** make a big impression on 3 *v/r* **~se de motor** stall; **~se hasta los huesos** get soaked to the skin

calato *adj* Chi, Pe naked

calavera *f* skull

calcar <1g> *v/t* trace

calceta *f*: **hacer ~** knit; **calcetín** *m* sock

calcinado *adj* burnt

calcio *m* calcium

calcomanía *f* decal, *Br* transfer

calculador *adj fig* calculating; **calculadora** *f* calculator; **calcular** <1a> *v/t tb fig* calculate; **cálculo** *m* calculation; MED stone; **~ biliar** gallstone; **~ renal** kidney stone

caldear <1a> *v/t* warm up; *ánimos* inflame

caldera *f* boiler; *Rpl, Chi* kettle; **calderilla** *f* small change; **caldero** *m* (small) boiler; **caldillo** *m* Méx GASTR stock

caldo *m* GASTR stock; **~ de cultivo** *fig* breeding ground

caldoso *adj* watery

calefacción *f* heating; **~ central** central heating; **calefactor** *m* heater

calendario *m* calendar; (*programa*) schedule

caléndula *f* BOT marigold

calentador *m* heater; **~ de agua** water heater; **calentamiento** *m*: **~ global** global warming; **calentar** <1k> **1** *v/t* heat (up); **~ a alguien** *fig* provoke s.o. **2** *v/i* DEP warm up **3** *v/r* **~se** warm up; *fig: de discusión, disputa* become heated; **calentura** *f* fever

calibrar <1a> *v/t* gauge; *fig* weigh up;

calibre *m tb fig* caliber, *Br* calibre

calidad *f* quality; **~ de vida** quality of life; **en ~ de médico** as a doctor

cálido *adj tb fig* warm

caliente *adj* hot; F (*cachondo*) horny F; **en ~** in the heat of the moment

calificable *adj* gradable; **calificación** *f* description; EDU grade, *Br* mark; **calificar** <1g> *v/t* describe, label (*de* as); EDU grade, *Br* mark

caligrafía *f* calligraphy

caliza *f* limestone

callado *adj* quiet; **callar** <1a> **1** *v/i* (*dejar de hablar*) go quiet; (*guardar silencio*) be quiet, keep quiet; **¡calla!** be quiet!, shut up! **2** *v/t* silence **3** *v/r* **~se** (*dejar de hablar*) go quiet; (*guardar silencio*) be quiet, keep quiet; **~se algo** keep sth quiet

calle *f* street; DEP lane; **echar a alguien a la ~** *fig* throw s.o out onto the street; **callejón** *m* alley; **~ sin salida** blind alley; *fig* dead end

callo *m* callus; **~s** *pl* GASTR tripe *sg*

calma *f* calm; **calmante 1** *adj* soothing **2** *m* MED sedative; **calmar** <1a> **1** *v/t* calm (down) **2** *v/r* **~se** calm down

calor *m* heat; *fig* warmth; **hace mucho ~** it's very hot; **tengo ~** I'm hot; **caloría** *f* calorie

caluroso *adj* hot; *fig* warm

calva *f* bald patch

calvario *m fig* calvary

calvicie *f* baldness; **calvo 1** *adj* bald **2** *m* bald man

calzada *f* road (surface); **calzado** *m* footwear; **calzador** *m* shoe horn; **calzar** <1f> **1** *v/t zapato, bota etc* put on; *mueble, rueda* wedge **2** *v/r* **~se** *zapato, bota etc* put on

calzón *m* DEP shorts *pl*; *L.Am. de hombre* shorts *pl*, *Br* (under)pants *pl*; *L.Am. de mujer* panties *pl*, *Br tb* knickers *pl*; **calzones** *pl*; *L.Am.* shorts, *Br* (under)pants

calzoncillos *mpl* shorts, *Br* (under)pants

cama f bed; **~ de matrimonio** double bed; **hacer la ~** make the bed; **irse a la ~** go to bed

camaleón m chameleon

cámara f FOT, TV camera; (*sala*) chamber; **~ de comercio e industria** chamber of commerce and industry; **a ~ lenta** in slow motion; **~ de vídeo** video camera

camarada m/f comrade; *de trabajo* colleague, co-worker; **camaradería** f camaraderie, comradeship

camarera f waitress; **camarero** m waiter

camarógrafo m, **-a** f L.Am. camera operator

camarón m L.Am. ZO shrimp, Br prawn

camarote m MAR cabin; **camarotero** m L.Am. steward

cambalache m Arg F second-hand shop

cambiar <1b> **1** v/t change (*por* for); *compra* exchange (**por** for) **2** v/i change; **~ de lugar** change places; **~ de marcha** AUTO shift gear, Br change gear **3** v/r **~se** change; **~se de ropa** change (one's clothes); **cambio** m change; COM exchange rate; **~ climático** climate change; **~ de marchas** AUTO gear shift, Br gear change; **~ de sentido** U-turn; **a ~ de** in exchange for; **en ~** on the other hand

camelia f BOT camellia

camello 1 m ZO camel **2** m/f F (*vendedor de drogas*) pusher F, dealer

camelo m F con F; (*broma*) joke

camilla f stretcher

caminar <1a> **1** v/i walk; *fig* move; **caminando** on foot **2** v/t walk; **camino** m (*senda*) path; (*ruta*) way; **a medio ~** halfway; **de ~ a** on the way to; **por el ~** on the way; **abrirse ~** fig make one's way; **ir por buen/mal ~** fig be on the right/wrong track; **ponerse en ~** set out

camión m truck, Br tb lorry; *Méx* bus; **camionero** m, **-a** f truck driver, Br tb lorry driver; *Méx* bus driver;

camioneta f van

camisa f shirt; **camiseta** f T-shirt; **camisón** m nightdress

camorra f F fight; **armar ~** F cause trouble

campal adj: **batalla ~** pitched battle

campamento m camp

campana f bell; **~ extractora** extractor hood; **campanada** f chime; **dar la ~** cause a stir; **campanario** m bell tower

campanazo m L.Am. warning

campanilla f small bell; ANAT uvula

campante adj: **tan ~** F as calm as anything F

campaña f campaign; **~ electoral** election campaign

campechano adj down-to-earth

campeón m, **-ona** f champion; **campeonato** m championship; **de ~** F terrific F

campera f L.Am. jacket

campesino 1 adj peasant atr **2** m, **-a** f peasant; **campestre** adj rural, country atr

camping m campground, Br tb campsite

campo m field; DEP field, Br tb pitch; (*estadio*) stadium, Br tb ground; **el ~** (*área rural*) the country; **~ de batalla** battlefield; **~ de concentración** concentration camp; **~ de golf** golf course; **~ visual** MED field of vision; **a ~ traviesa, ~ a través** cross-country

campus m inv: **~ universitario** university campus

camuflaje m camouflage; **camuflar** <1a> v/t camouflage

cana f gray (Br grey) hair

Canadá Canada; **canadiense** m/f & adj Canadian

canal m channel; TRANSP canal; **canalete** m paddle; **canalizar** <1f> v/t channel

canalla m swine F, rat F

canalón m gutter

canapé m (*sofá*) couch; *para cama* base; GASTR canapé

Canarias f pl Canaries; **canario 1** adj Canary atr **2** m ZO canary

canasta f basket; *juego* canasta
cancela f (wrought-iron) gate
cancelación f cancellation; **cancelar** <1a> v/t cancel; *deuda, cuenta* settle, pay
cáncer m MED, fig cancer; **Cáncer** m/f inv ASTR Cancer; **cancerígeno** adj carcinogenic; **canceroso** adj cancerous
cancha f DEP court; *L.Am. de fútbol* field, *Br tb* pitch; **~ de tenis** tennis court; **¡~!** Rpl F gangway! F; **abrir** or **hacer ~** Rpl make room; **canchear** <1a> v/i L.Am. climb
canciller m Chancellor; *S.Am. de asuntos exteriores* Secretary of State, *Br* Foreign Minister
canción f song; **siempre la misma ~** F the same old story F
candado m padlock
candela f L.Am. fire; **¿me das ~?** have you got a light?
candelabro m candelabra; **candelero** m: **estar en el ~ de persona** be in the limelight
candente adj red-hot; *tema* topical
candidato m, **-a** f candidate; **candidatura** f candidacy
cándido adj naive; **candor** m innocence; (*franqueza*) cando(u)r
canela f cinnamon
canelones mpl GASTR cannelloni sg
cangrejo m ZO crab
canguro 1 m ZO kangaroo **2** m/f baby-sitter
caníbal 1 adj cannibal atr **2** m/f cannibal
canica f marble
caniche m poodle
canícula f dog days pl
canijo adj F puny
canilla f L.Am. faucet, *Br* tap
canillita m/f Arg newspaper vendor
canjear <1a> v/t exchange (**por** for)
canoa f canoe
canónico adj canonical; **canónigo** m canon; **canonizar** <1f> v/t canonize
cansado adj tired; **cansancio** m tiredness; **cansar** <1a> **1** v/t tire; (*aburrir*) bore **2** v/r **~se** get tired;

(*aburrirse*) get bored; **~se de algo** get tired of sth
cantante m/f singer; **cantar** <1a> **1** v/i sing; *de delincuente* squeal P **2** v/t sing **3** m: **ése es otro ~** fig that's a different story
cántaro m pitcher; **llover a ~s** F pour (down)
cantautor m, **~a** f singer-songwriter
cante m: **~ hondo** or **jondo** flamenco singing
cantera f quarry
cantidad f quantity, amount; **había ~ de** there was (pl were) a lot of
cantimplora f water bottle
cantina f canteen
canto¹ m singing; *de pájaro* song
canto² m edge; (*roca*) stone; **~ rodado** boulder; **darse con un ~ en los dientes** count o.s. lucky
canturrear <1a> v/t sing softly
canutas: **las pasé ~** F it was really tough F
caña f BOT reed; (*tallo*) stalk; *cerveza* small glass of beer; *L.Am.* straw; **muebles de ~** cane furniture; **~ de azúcar** sugar cane; **~ de pescar** fishing rod; **dar** or **meter ~ a alguien** F wind s.o. up F; **¡dale ~!** get off your butt! F
cañada f ravine; *L.Am.* (*arroyo*) stream
cáñamo m hemp; *L.Am.* marijuana plant
cañería f pipe
cañero adj L.Am. sugar-cane atr
caño m pipe; *de fuente* spout; **cañón 1** m HIST cannon; *antiaéreo, antitanque etc* gun; *de fusil* barrel; GEOG canyon **2** adj F great, fantastic F; **cañonazo** m gunshot
caoba f mahogany
caos m chaos; **caótico** adj chaotic
cap abr (= **capítulo**) ch. (= chapter)
capa f layer; *prenda* cloak; **~ de ozono** ozone layer; **~ de pintura** coat of paint
capacidad f capacity; (*aptitud*) competence; **~ de memoria/de almacenamiento** INFOR memory/ storage capacity; **capacitar** <1a>

C

v/t prepare; **~ alguien para hacer algo** qualify s.o. to do sth

capar <1a> v/t castrate

oaparazón m ZO shell

capataz m foreman; **capataza** f forewoman

capaz adj able (**de** to); **ser ~ de** be capable of

capcioso adj: **pregunta -a** trick question

capear <1a> v/t temporal weather

capellán m chaplain

capicúa adj: **número ~** reversible number

capilar 1 adj capillary atr; loción hair atr **2** m capillary

capilla f chapel; **~ ardiente** chapel of rest

capirotada f Méx type of French toast with honey, cheese, raisins etc

capital 1 adj importancia prime; **pena ~** capital punishment **2** f de país capital **3** m COM capital; **capitalismo** m capitalism; **capitalista 1** adj capitalist atr **2** m/f capitalist

capitán m captain; **capitanear** <1a> v/t captain

capitel m ARQUI capital

Capitolio m Capitol

capitulación f capitulation, surrender; (pacto) agreement; **capitular** <1a> v/i surrender, capitulate

capítulo m chapter

capó m AUTO hood, Br bonnet

capón m Rpl mutton

capota f AUTO top, Br hood

capote m cloak; MIL greatcoat; **capotera** f L.Am. coat stand

capricho m whim; **caprichoso** adj capricious

Capricornio m/f inv ASTR Capricorn

cápsula f capsule; **~ espacial** space capsule

captar <1a> v/t understand; RAD pick up; negocio take

capturar <1a> v/t capture

capucha f hood

capuchino m cappuccino

capullo m ZO cocoon; BOT bud

caqui 1 adj khaki **2** m BOT persimmon

cara f face; (expresión) look; fig nerve; **~ a algo** facing sth; **~ a ~** face to face; **de ~ a** facing; fig with regard to; **dar la ~** face the consequences; **echar algo en ~ a alguien** remind s.o. of sth; **tener ~ dura** have a nerve; **tener buena/mala ~** de comida look good/bad; de persona look well/sick; **~ o cruz** heads or tails

carabinero m GASTR (large) shrimp, Br prawn; (agente de aduana) border guard

caracol m snail; **¡~es!** wow! F; enfado damn! F; **caracola** f ZO conch

carácter m character; (naturaleza) nature; **característica** f characteristic; **característico** adj characteristic (**de** of); **caracterizar** <1f> **1** v/t characterize; TEA play (the part of) **2** v/r **-se** be characterized (**por** by)

caradura m/f F guy/woman with a nerve, Br cheeky devil F

carajillo m coffee with a shot of liquor

carajo m: **irse al ~** F go down the tubes F

caramba int wow!; enfado damn! F

carambola f billar carom, Br cannon; **por** or **de ~** F by sheer chance

caramelo m dulce candy, Br sweet; (azúcar derretida) caramel

carantoña f caress

caraqueño 1 adj of/from Caracas, Caracas atr **2** m, **-a** f native of Caracas

carátula f de disco jacket, Br tb sleeve; L.Am. de reloj face

caravana f (remolque) trailer, Br caravan; de tráfico queue of traffic, traffic jam; Méx (reverencia) bow

caray int F wow! F; enfado damn! F

carbón m coal; **carboncillo** m charcoal; **carbonizar** <1f> v/t char; **carbono** m QUÍM carbon

carburador m AUTO carburet(t)or; **carburante** m fuel

carca m/f & adj F reactionary

carcajada f laugh, guffaw; **reír a ~s** roar with laughter; **carcajearse** <1a> v/r have a good laugh (**de** at)

cárcel f prison; **carcelero** m, **-a** f

warder, jailer

carcinoma f MED carcinoma

carcoma f ZO woodworm; **carcomer** <2a> **1** v/t eat away; fig: de envidia eat away at, consume **2** v/r ~se be eaten away; **~se de** fig be consumed with

cardamomo m BOT cardamom

cardenal m REL cardinal; (hematoma) bruise

cardíaco, cardiaco adj cardiac

cardinal adj cardinal; **número** ~ cardinal number; **puntos ~es** points of the compass, cardinal points

cardiólogo m, **-a** f cardiologist

cardo m BOT thistle

carecer <2d> v/i: **~ de algo** lack sth; **carencia** f lack (**de** of); **carente** adj: **~ de** lacking in

careta f mask

carga f load; de buque cargo; MIL, EL charge; (responsabilidad) burden; **~ explosiva** explosive charge; **~ fiscal** or **impositiva** tax burden; **ser una ~ para alguien** be a burden to s.o.; **volver a la ~** return to the attack; **cargado** adj loaded (**de** with); aire stuffy; ambiente tense; café strong; **cargamento** m load; **cargante** adj F annoying

cargar <1h> **1** v/t arma, camión load; batería, acusado charge; COM charge (**en** to); L.Am. (traer) carry; **esto me carga** L.Am. P I can't stand this **2** v/i (apoyarse) rest (**sobre** on); (fastidiar) be annoying; **~ con algo** carry sth; **~ con la culpa** fig shoulder the blame; **~ contra alguien** MIL, DEP charge (at) s.o. **3** v/r **~se con peso, responsabilidad** weigh o.s. down; F (matar) bump off F; F (romper) wreck F

cargo m position; JUR charge; **alto** ~ high-ranking position; persona high-ranking official; **a ~ de la madre** in the mother's care; **está a ~ de Gómez** Gómez is in charge of it; **hacerse ~ de algo** take charge of sth

cariarse <1b> v/r decay

Caribe m Caribbean; **caribeño** adj Caribbean

caricatura f caricature; **caricaturizar** <1f> v/t caricature

caricia f caress

caridad f charity

caries f MED caries

cariño m affection, fondness; **hacer ~ a alguien** L.Am. (acariciar) caress s.o.; (abrazar) hug s.o.; **¡~!** darling!; **con** ~ with love; **cariñoso** adj affectionate

carisma m charisma; **carismático** adj charismatic

caritativo adj charitable

cariz m look; **tomar mal** ~ start to look bad

carmín m de labios lipstick

carnaval m carnival

carne f meat; de persona flesh; **~ de gallina** fig goose bumps pl, Br gooseflesh; **~ picada** ground meat, Br mince; **de ~ y hueso** flesh and blood; **sufrir algo en sus propias ~s** fig go through sth oneself

carné m → **carnet**

carnear <1a> v/t L.Am. slaughter

carnero m ram

carnet m card; **~ de conducir** driver's license, Br driving licence; **~ de identidad** identity card

carnicería f butcher's; fig carnage; **carnicero** m, **-a** f butcher

carnívoro adj carnivorous

carnoso adj fleshy

caro adj expensive, dear; **costar** ~ fig cost dear

carozo m Chi, Rpl pit

carpa f de circo big top; ZO carp; L.Am. para acampar tent; L.Am. de mercado stall

carpeta f file

carpintero m carpenter; de obra joiner; **pájaro** ~ woodpecker

carpir <3a> v/t L.Am. hoe

carraspear <1a> v/i clear one's throat; **carraspera** f hoarseness

carrera f race; EDU degree course; profesional career; **~ de armamento** arms race; **a las ~s** at top speed; **con prisas** in a rush; **hacer la ~** F de *prostituta* turn tricks F; *~s pl de coches* motor racing *sg*; **carrerilla** *f*: *tomar ~* take a run up; *decir algo de ~* reel sth off

carreta *f* cart; **carrete** *m* FOT (roll of) film; *~ de hilo* reel of thread

carretera *f* highway, (main) road; *~ de circunvalación* ring road; **carretilla** *f* wheelbarrow

carril *m* lane; *~-bici* cycle lane; *~-bus* bus lane

carrillo *m* cheek; *comer a dos ~s* F stuff oneself F

carrito *m* cart, *Br* trolley; *~ de bebé* buggy, *Br* pushchair; **carro** *m* cart; *L.Am.* car; *L.Am.* (*taxi*) taxi, cab; *~ de combate* tank; *~-patrulla L.Am.* F patrol car

carrocería *f* AUTO bodywork

carroña *f* carrion

carruaje *m* carriage

carta *f* letter; GASTR menu; (*naipe*) playing card; (*mapa*) chart; *~ certificada o registrada* registered letter; *~ urgente* special-delivery letter; *a la ~* a la carte; *dar ~ blanca a alguien* give s.o. carte blanche *o* a free hand; *poner las ~s boca arriba* *fig* put one's cards on the table; *tomar ~s en el asunto* intervene in the matter; **cartearse** <1a> *v/r* write to each other

cartel *m* poster; *estar en ~ de película, espectáculo* be on

cártel *m* cartel

cartelera *f* billboard; *de periódico* listings, entertainments section

cartera *f* wallet; (*maletín*) briefcase; COM, POL portfolio; *de colegio* knapsack, *Br* satchel; *L.Am.* purse, *Br* handbag; *mujer* mailwoman, *Br* postwoman; **carterista** *m/f* pickpocket; **cartero** *m* mailman, *Br* postman

cartílago *m* cartilage

cartilla *f* reader; *Méx* identity card; *~ de ahorros* savings book; *leerle a alguien la ~* F give s.o. a telling off F

cartógrafo *m*, **-a** *f* cartographer

cartón *m* cardboard; *de tabaco* car-

ton; *~ piedra* pap(i)er- mâché

cartuchera *f* cartridge belt; **cartucho** *m de arma* cartridge

cartulina *f* sheet of card; *~ roja* DEP red card

casa *f* house; (*hogar*) home; *en ~* at home; *como una ~* F huge F; *~ cuna* children's home; *~ de huéspedes* rooming house, *Br* boarding house; *~ matriz* head office; *~ de socorro* first aid post; *~ adosada*, *~ pareada → chalet*

casaca *f* cassock

casado *adj* married; *recién ~* newlywed; **casamiento** *m*, **-a** *f* matchmaker; **casar** <1a> **1** *v/i fig* match (up); *~ con* go with **2** *v/r* ~*se* get married; *~se con alguien* marry s.o.; *no ~se con nadie fig* refuse to compromise

cascabel *m* small bell

cascada *f* waterfall

cascado *adj voz* hoarse; F *persona* worn out F

cascanueces *m inv* nutcracker

cascar <1g> *v/t* crack; *algo quebradizo* break; *fig* F whack F; *~la* peg out F

cáscara *f de huevo* shell; *de naranja*, *limón* peel

cascarón *m* shell; *salir del ~* hatch (out)

cascarrabias *m inv* F grouch F

casco *m* helmet; *de barco* hull; (*botella vacía*) empty (bottle); *edificio* empty building; *de caballo* hoof; *de vasija* fragment; *~ urbano* urban area; *~s azules* MIL blue berets, UN peace-keeping troops

cascote *m* piece of rubble

casera *f* landlady; **casero 1** *adj* home-made; *comida -a* home cooking **2** *m* landlord

caseta *f* hut; *de feria* stall

casete *m* (*also f*) cassette

casi *adv* almost, nearly; *en frases negativas* hardly

casilla *f en formulario* box; *en tablero* square; *de correspondencia* pigeon hole; *S.Am.* post office box; *sacar a alguien de sus ~s* drive s.o. crazy

casino *m* casino

caso *m* case; **en ~ de que**, **~ de** in the event that, in case of; **hacer ~** take notice; **ser un ~** F be a real case F; **no venir al ~** be irrelevant; **en todo ~** in any case, in any event; **en el peor de los ~s** if the worst comes to the worst; **en último ~** as a last resort

caspa *f* dandruff

caspiroleta *f S.Am.* eggnog

casquillo *m* *de cartucho* case; EL *bulb* holder; *L.Am.* horseshoe

cassette *m* (*also f*) cassette; **~ virgen** blank cassette

casta *f* caste

castaña *f* chestnut; **sacar las ~s del fuego a alguien** *fig* F pull s.o.'s chestnuts out of the fire F; **castaño 1** *adj color* chestnut, brown **2** *m* chestnut (tree); *color* chestnut, brown; **ya pasa de ~ oscuro** F it's gone too far, it's beyond a joke; **castañuela** *f* castanet; **estar como unas ~s** F be over the moon F

castellano *m* (Castilian) Spanish

castidad *f* chastity

castigar <1h> *v/t* punish; **castigo** *m* punishment

castillo *m* castle; **~ de fuegos artificiales** firework display

castizo *adj* pure

casto *adj* chaste

castor *m* ZO beaver

castrar <1a> *v/t* castrate; *fig* emasculate

castrense *adj* army *atr*

casual *adj* chance *atr*; **casualidad** *f* chance, coincidence; **por** *or* **de ~** by chance

cataclismo *m* cataclysm, catastrophe

catalán 1 *adj* Catalan **2** *m*, **-ana** *f* Catalan

catalejo *m* telescope

catalizador *m* catalyst; AUTO catalytic converter; **catalizar** <1f> *v/t* catalyze

catalogar <1h> *v/t* catalog(ue); *fig* class; **catálogo** *m* catalog(ue)

catamarán *m* MAR catamaran

cataplasma *f* MED poultice; *fig: persona* bore

catapulta *f* slingshot, *Br* catapult; **catapultar** <1a> *v/t* catapult

catar <1a> *v/t* taste

catarata *f* GEOG waterfall; MED cataract

catarro *m* cold; *inflamación* catarrh

catástrofe *f* catastrophe; **catastrófico** *adj* catastrophic

cate *m* EDU F fail; **catear** <1a> *v/t* F flunk F

catecismo *m* catechism

catedral *f* cathedral; **una mentira como una ~** F a whopping great lie F

catedrático *m*, **-a** *f* EDU head of department

categoría *f* category; *social* class; *fig: de local, restaurante* class; (*estatus*) standing; **actor de primera ~** first-rate actor; **categórico** *adj* categorical

catequesis *f* catechism

catéter *m* MED catheter

catolicismo *m* (Roman) Catholicism; **católico 1** *adj* (Roman) Catholic **2** *m*, **-a** *f* (Roman) Catholic

catorce *adj* fourteen

catre *m* bed

cauce *m* riverbed; *fig* channel; **volver a su ~** *fig* get back to normal

caucho *m* rubber; *L.Am.* (*neumático*) tire, *Br* tyre

caudal *m* *de río* volume of flow; *fig* wealth

caudillo *m* leader

causa *f* cause; (*motivo*) reason; JUR lawsuit; **a ~ de** because of; **causante** *m* cause; **causar** <1a> *v/t* cause

cáustico *adj tb fig* caustic

cautela *f* caution; **cauteloso** *adj* cautious

cauterizar <1f> *v/t* cauterize

cautivar <1a> *v/t fig* captivate; **cautiverio** *m*, **cautividad** *f* captivity; **cautivo 1** *adj* captive **2** *m*, **-a** *f* captive

cauto *adj* cautious

cava *m* cava, sparkling wine

cavar <1a> *v/t* dig
caverna *f* cavern; **cavernícola** *m/f* caveman; *mujer* cavewoman
caviar *m* caviar
cavidad *f* cavity
cavilar <1a> *v/t* meditate on
cayó *vb* → **caer**
caza 1 *f* hunt; *actividad* hunting; **~ mayor/menor** big/small game; **andar a la ~ de algo/alguien** be after sth/s.o. **2** *m* AVIA fighter; **cazador** *m* hunter; **cazadora** *f* hunter; *prenda* jacket; **cazar** <1f> **1** *v/t animal* hunt; *fig: información* track down; (*pillar, captar*) catch; **~ un buen trabajo** get o.s. a good job **2** *v/i* hunt; **ir a ~** go hunting
cazo *m* saucepan; **cazuela** *f* pan; *de barro, vidrio* casserole
cazurro *adj* stubborn; (*basto*) coarse; (*lento de entender*) dense F, thick F
c.c. *abr* (= **centímetro cúbico**) c.c. (= cubic centimeter)
c/c *abr* (= **cuenta corriente**) C/A (= checking account)
CD *m* (= **disco compacto**) CD (= compact disc); *reproductor* CD-player; **CD-ROM** *m* CD-ROM
cebada *f* barley
cebar <1a> **1** *v/t* fatten; *anzuelo* bait; TÉC prime; *L.Am. mate* prepare **2** *v/r* ~**se** feed (*en* on); **~ con alguien** vent one's fury on s.o.; **cebo** *m* bait
cebolla *f* onion
cebra *f* zebra; **paso de ~** crosswalk, *Br* zebra crossing
ceceo *m* *pronunciation of 's' with 'th' sound*
cecina *f* cured meat
cedazo *m* sieve
ceder <2a> **1** *v/t* give up; (*traspasar*) transfer, cede; **~ el paso** AUTO yield, *Br* give way **2** *v/i* give way, yield; *de viento, lluvia* ease off
cedro *m* BOT cedar
cédula *f* *L.Am.* identity document
cegar <1h & 1k> *v/t* blind; *tubería* block; **ceguera** *f* tb fig blindness
ceja *f* eyebrow; **lo tiene entre ~ y ~** F

she can't stand him F
cejar <1a> *v/i* give up; **no ~ en** not let up in
celador *m*, ~**a** *f* orderly; *de cárcel* guard; *de museo* attendant
celda *f* cell
celebración *f* celebration; **celebrar** <1a> *v/t misa* celebrate; *reunión, acto oficial* hold; *fiesta* have, hold; **célebre** *adj* famous
celeste *adj* light blue, sky blue; **celestial** *adj* celestial; *fig* heavenly
celibato *m* celibacy
celo *m* zeal; (*cinta adhesiva*) Scotch® tape, *Br* Sellotape®; **en ~** ZO in heat; **~s** *pl* jealousy *sg*; **tener ~s de** be jealous of
celofán *m* cellophane
celoso *adj* jealous (*de* of)
célula *f* cell; **celular** *adj* cellular; **celulitis** *f* cellulite; **celulosa** *f* cellulose
cementerio *m* cemetery
cemento *m* cement
cena *f* dinner; *más tarde* supper
cenagoso *adj* boggy
cenar <1a> **1** *v/t*: **~ algo** have sth for dinner **2** *v/i* have dinner
cencerro *m* cowbell
cenicero *m* ashtray
ceniza *f* ash; **~s** ashes
cenit *m* AST zenith; *fig* peak
censo *m* census; **~ electoral** voting register, electoral roll
censura *f* censorship; **censurar** <1a> *v/t* censor; *tratamiento* condemn
cent *abr* (= **céntimo**) cent
centavo *m* cent
centellear <1a> *v/i* sparkle; *de estrella* twinkle
centena *f* hundred; **centenar** *m* hundred; **regalos a ~es** hundreds of gifts; **centenario 1** *adj* hundred-year-old *atr* **2** *m* centennial, *Br* centenary
centeno *m* BOT rye
centígrado *adj* centigrade; **dos grados ~s** two degrees centigrade; **centímetro** *m* centimeter, *Br* centimetre; **céntimo** *m* cent; **estar**

sin un **~** not have a red cent F
centinela *m/f* sentry; *de banda criminal* lookout
central 1 *adj* central; (*principal*) main, central **2** *f* head office; **~ atómica** *or* **nuclear** nuclear power station; **~ eléctrica** power station; **~ telefónica** telephone exchange; **~ térmica** thermal power station; **centralismo** *m* POL centralism; **centralita** *f* TELEC switchboard; **centralizar** <1f> *v/t* centralize; **centrar** <1a> **1** *v/t tb* DEP center, *Br* centre; *esfuerzos* focus (**en** on) **2** *v/r* **~se** concentrate (**en** on); **céntrico** *adj* central
centrifugar <1h> *v/t* spin
centro *m* center, *Br* centre; **~ comercial** (shopping) mall, *Br* shopping centre; **~ urbano** *en señal* town center (*Br* centre)
Centroamérica Central America; **centroamericano** *adj* Central American
ceñido *adj* tight; **ceñirse** <3h & 3l> *v/r*: **~ a algo** *fig* stick to sth
ceño *m*: **fruncir el ~** frown
cepa *f de vid* stock
cepillar <1a> **1** *v/t* brush **2** *v/r* **~se** brush; F (*comerse*) polish off F; F (*matar*) kill, knock off F; **cepillo** *m* brush; **~ de dientes** toothbrush
cera *f* wax
cerámica *f* ceramics
cerca[1] *f* fence
cerca[2] *adv* near, close; **de ~** close up; **~ de** near, close to; (*casi*) nearly
cercanía *f*: **tren de ~s** suburban train; **cercano** *adj* nearby; **~ a** close to, near to; **cercar** <1g> *v/t* surround; *con valla* fence in
cerciorarse <1a> *v/r* make sure (**de** of)
cerco *m* ring; *de puerta* frame; *L.Am.* fence; **poner ~ a** lay siege to
cerda *f animal* sow; *fig* F *persona* pig F; *de brocha* bristle; **cerdo** *m* hog, *Br* pig; *fig* F *persona* pig F
cereal *m* cereal; **~es** *pl* (breakfast) cereal *sg*
cerebro *m* ANAT brain; *fig: persona*

brains *sg*
ceremonia *f* ceremony
cereza *f* cherry; **cerezo** *m* cherry (tree)
cerilla *f* match
cernerse <2g> *v/r*: **~ sobre** *fig* hang over
cernícalo *m* ZO kestrel
cero *m* EDU zero, *Br tb* nought; *en fútbol etc* zero, *Br* nil; *en tenis* love; **bajo/sobre ~** below/above zero; **empezar desde ~** *fig* start from scratch; **vencer por tres a ~** win three-zero (*Br* nil)
cerrado *adj* closed; *persona* narrow-minded; (*tímido*) introverted; *cielo* overcast; *curva -a* tight curve
cerradura *f* lock; **ojo de la ~** keyhole; **cerrajero** *m*, **-a** *f* locksmith
cerrar <1k> **1** *v/t* close; *para siempre* close down; *tubería* block; *grifo* turn off; **~ con llave** lock **2** *v/i* close; *para siempre* close down **3** *v/r* **~se** close; *de cielo* cloud over; *de persona* shut o.s. off (**a** from); **~se de golpe** slam shut
cerrazón *f fig* narrow-mindedness
cerrero *adj L.Am. persona* rough
cerril *adj animal* wild; (*terco*) stubborn, pig-headed F; (*torpe*) F dense F
cerro *m* hill
cerrojo *m* bolt; **echar el ~** bolt the door
certamen *m* competition
certeza *f* certainty; **certidumbre** *f* certainty
certificado 1 *adj carta* registered **2** *m* certificate; **certificar** <1g> *v/t* certify; *carta* register
cerval *adj*: **miedo ~** terrible fear
cervecería *f* bar
cerveza *f* beer; **~ de barril** *or* **de presión** draft, *Br* draught (beer); **~ negra** stout; **~ rubia** lager; **fábrica de ~** brewery
cesante *adj Chi* unemployed, jobless; **dejar ~ a alguien** let s.o. go;
cesar <1a> *v/i* stop; **no ~ de hacer algo** keep on doing sth; **sin ~** nonstop

cesárea *f* MED C(a)esarean
cese *m* cessation
cesión *f* transfer
césped *m* lawn
cesta *f* basket; **~ de la compra** shopping basket; **cesto** *m* large basket
C.F. *abr* (= *Club de Fútbol*) FC (= Football Club)
cfc *abr* (= *clorofluorocarbono*) CFC (= chlorofluorocarbon)
cg. *abr* (= *centigramo*) centigram
ch/ *abr* (= *cheque*) check
chabacano *adj* vulgar, tacky F
chabola *f* shack; **barrio de ~s** shanty town
chacal *m* ZO jackal
chacarero *m*, **-a** *f* Rpl, Chi smallholder, farmer
chacha *f* F maid
chácharas *fpl* L.Am. junk *sg*, bits and pieces
chachi *adj* F great F
chacra *f* L.Am. AGR smallholding
chafar <1a> *v/t* squash; *cosa erguida* flatten; F *planes etc* ruin F
chaflán *m* corner
chal *m* shawl
chalado *adj* F crazy F (*por* about)
chalé *m* → **chalet**
chaleco *m de traje* waistcoat; *de sport* gilet, bodywarmer; **~ salvavidas** life vest; **~ antibalas** bulletproof vest
chalet *m* chalet; **~ adosado** *house sharing one or more walls with other houses*; **~ pareado** semi-detached house
chalupa *f* MAR small boat; *Méx* stuffed tortilla
chamaca *f* C.Am., *Méx* girl; **chamaco** *m* C.Am., *Méx* boy
chamarra *f* Méx (*saco*) (short) jacket
chamba *f* Méx F job
chambón *m*, **-ona** *f* Méx F clumsy idiot F
champán *m*, **champaña** *m* champagne
champiñón *m* BOT mushroom
champú *m* shampoo
chamuscar <1g> *v/t* scorch; *pelo* singe
chamusquina *f*; **oler a ~** F smell fishy F
chance 1 *m* L.Am. chance; **dame ~** let me have a go **2** *conj* Méx perhaps, maybe
chanchería *f* L.Am. pork butcher's shop; **chancho** *m* L.Am. hog, Br pig; *carne* pork
chanchullo *m* F trick, scam F
chancla *f* thong, Br flip-flop; *Méx*, C.Am. (*zapato*) slipper; **chancleta** *f* thong, Br flip-flop; S.Am. F baby girl
chándal *m* tracksuit
changa *f* Rpl odd job
chango 1 *adj* Méx F sharp, smart **2** *m*, **-a** *f* Méx monkey
chanquetes *mpl* GASTR whitebait *sg*
chantaje *m* blackmail; **hacer ~ a alguien** blackmail s.o.; **chantajear** <1a> *v/t* blackmail; **chantajista** *m/f* blackmailer
chanza *f* wisecrack
chao *int* bye
chapa *f* (*tapón*) cap; (*plancha*) sheet (of metal); (*insignia*) badge; AUTO bodywork; **chapado** *adj* plated; **~ a la antigua** old-fashioned; **~ en oro** gold-plated; **chapar** <1a> *v/t* plate; *Arg, Pe* catch
chaparro *adj* Méx small
chaparrón *m* downpour; *fig* F *de insultos* barrage
chapotear <1a> *v/i* splash
chapucero 1 *adj* shoddy, slapdash **2** *m*, **-a** *f* shoddy worker
chapurrear <1a> *v/t*: **~ el francés** speak poor French
chapuza *f* (*trabajo mal hecho*) shoddy piece of work; (*trabajo menor*) odd job
chapuzón *m* dip; **darse un ~** go for a dip
chaqué *m* morning coat; **chaqueta** *f* jacket; **~ de punto** cardigan; **chaquetero** *m*, **-a** *f* F turncoat; **chaquetón** *m* three-quarter length coat
charango *m* Pe, Bol five string guitar
charca *f* pond; **charco** *m* puddle
charcutería *f* delicatessen

charla *f* chat; *organizada* talk; **charlar** <1a> *v/i* chat; **charlatán 1** *adj* talkative **2** *m*, **-ana** *f* chatterbox

charol *m* patent leather; **zapatos de ~** patent leather shoes

charqui *m L.Am.* beef jerky

charro 1 *adj desp* garish, gaudy **2** *m Méx* (Mexican) cowboy

chasco *m* joke; *llevarse un ~* be disappointed

chasis *m inv* AUTO chassis

chasquear <1a> *v/t* click; *látigo* crack; **chasquido** *m* click; *de látigo* crack

chatarra *f* scrap

chato *adj nariz* snub; *L.Am. nivel* low

chau *int Rpl* bye

chaucha *f Rpl* French bean

chaval *m* F kid F, boy; **chavala** *f* F kid F, girl; **chavalo** *m C.Am.* F kid F, boy

che *int Rpl* hey!, look!

checar <1g> *v/t Méx* check

checo 1 *adj* Czech **2** *m*, **-a** *f* Czech

chef *m* chef

chelo *m* MÚS cello

chepa *f* F hump; *subírsele a la ~* get too familiar

cheque *m* check, *Br* cheque; **~ cruzado** crossed check (*Br* cheque); **~ sin fondos** bad check (*Br* cheque); **~ de viaje** traveler's check, *Br* traveller's cheque; **chequear** <1a> *v/t* check; *C.Am. equipaje* check (in); **chequeo** *m* MED check-up; **chequera** *f* checkbook, *Br* chequebook

chica *f* girl

chicha *f L.Am.* corn liquor; *no ser ni ~ ni limonada* F be neither one thing nor the other

chícharo *m Méx* pea

chiche 1 *adj C.Am.* F (*fácil*) easy **2** *m S.Am.* (*juguete*) toy; (*adorno*) trinket

chichera *f C.Am.* jail

chichería *f L.Am.* bar selling corn liquor

chichón *m* bump

chicle *m* chewing gum

chico 1 *adj* small, little **2** *m* boy

chifa *m Pe* Chinese restaurant; (*comida china*) Chinese food

chifla *f Méx* whistling; **chiflado** *adj* F crazy F (*por* about), nuts F (*por* about); **chiflar** <1a> **1** *v/t* boo **2** *v/i* whistle; *me chifla ...* F I'm crazy about ... F

chile *m* chilli (pepper)

Chile Chile; **chileno 1** *adj* Chilean **2** *m*, **-a** *f* Chilean

chillar <1a> *v/i* scream, shriek; *de cerdo* squeal; **chillido** *m* scream, shriek; *de cerdo* squeal; **chillón 1** *adj voz* shrill; *color* loud **2** *m*, **-ona** *f* loudmouth

chilote *m C.Am.* baby corn

chimenea *f* chimney; *de salón* fireplace

chimichurri *m Rpl* hot sauce

chimpancé *m* ZO chimpanzee

China China

china[1] *f* Chinese woman

china[2] *f piedra* small stone

chincheta *f* thumbtack, *Br* drawing pin

chinchorro *m* hammock

chinear <1a> *v/t C.Am. niños* look after

chingar <1h> *v/t Méx* V screw V, fuck V; *¡chinga tu madre!* screw you! V, fuck you! V; *no chingues* don't screw me around V

chino 1 *adj* Chinese **2** *m* Chinese man; *idioma* Chinese; *L.Am. desp* half-breed *desp*; *trabajo de ~s* F hard work; *me suena a ~* F it's all Chinese *o* double Dutch to me F

chip *m* INFOR chip

chipirón *m* baby squid

chiquilla *f* girl, kid; **chiquillo** *m* boy, kid

chirimoya *f* BOT custard apple

chiringuito *m* beach bar

chiripa *f*: *de ~* F by sheer luck

chirona *f*: *en ~* F in the can F, inside F

chirriar <1c> *v/i* squeak; **chirrido** *m* squeak

chisme *m* F bit of gossip; *objeto* doodad F, *Br* doodah F; **chismografía** *f* F gossip; **chismorrear** <1a> *v/i* F gossip; **chismoso 1** *adj*

gossip **2** *m*, **-a** *f* F gossip
chispa *f* spark; (*cantidad pequeña*) spot; *fig* F wit; **chispear** <1a> *v/i* spark, *flg* sparkle; *de lluvia* spit
chistar <1a> *v/i*: **sin ~** without saying a word
chiste *m* joke
chiva *f* L.Am. goat; C.Am., Col bus
chivarse <1a> *v/r* F rat F (**a** to); **chivato** *m*, **-a** *f* F stool pigeon F; **chivo** *m* ZO kid; C.Am., Méx wages *pl*
chocante *adj* (*sorprendente*) startling; (*que ofende*) shocking; (*extraño*) odd; L.Am. (*antipático*) unpleasant; **chocar** <1g> **1** *v/t*: **¡choca esos cinco!** P give me five! P, put it there! P **2** *v/i* crash (**con, contra** into), collide (**con** with); **~le a alguien** (*sorprender*) surprise s.o.; (*ofender*) shock s.o.; **me choca ese hombre** F that guy disgusts me; **~ con un problema** come up against a problem
chocho *adj* F senile; **estar ~ con** dote on
choclo *m* Rpl corn, Br corn on the cob
chocolate *m* chocolate; F (*hachís*) hashish, hash F; **chocolatina** *f* chocolate bar
chófer, L.Am. **chofer** *m* driver
chollo *m* F bargain
cholo *m* L.Am. half-caste *desp*
chompa *f* S.Am. jumper, sweater
chop *m* L.Am. large beer
chopo *m* BOT poplar
choque *m* collision, crash; DEP, MIL clash; MED shock
chorizo *m* chorizo (*spicy cured sausage*); F thief; Rpl (*filete*) rump steak
chorlito *m*: **cabeza de ~** F featherbrain F
chorrada *f* F piece of junk; **decir ~s** F talk garbage, Br talk rubbish
chorrear <1a> *v/i* gush out, stream; (*gotear*) drip; **chorro** *m líquido* jet, stream; *fig* stream; C.Am. faucet, Br tap
chovinista *m/f* chauvinist
choza *f* hut

chubasco *m* shower; **chubasquero** *m* raincoat
chuchería *f* knick-knack; (*golosina*) candy, Br sweet
chucho 1 *adj* C.Am. mean **2** *m* F (*perro*) mutt F, mongrel; Chi (*cárcel*) can F, prison
chueco *adj* L.Am. (*torcido*) twisted
chulería *f* bragging
chuleta *f* GASTR chop
chulo F 1 *adj* fantastic F, great F; Méx (*guapo*) attractive; (*presuntuoso*) cocky F **2** *m* pimp F
chumbera *f* C.Am. prickly pear
chumpipe *m* C.Am. turkey
chupa *f* jacket
chupado *adj* F (*delgado*) skinny F; (*fácil*) dead easy F; L.Am. F drunk; **chupar** <1a> **1** *v/t* suck; (*absorber*) soak up **2** *v/r* **~se**: **~se algo** suck sth; *fig* F put up with sth; **~se los dedos** F lick one's fingers; **chupete** *m de bebé* pacifier, Br dummy; (*sorbete*) Popsicle®, Br ice lolly
chupi *adj* F great F, fantastic F
churrasco *m* Rpl steak
churro *m* fritter; (*chapuza*) botched job
chusma *f desp* rabble *desp*
chutar <1a> *v/i* DEP shoot; **esto va que chuta** F this is working out fine; **y vas que chutas** F and that's your lot! F
chuzo *m* Chi F *persona* dead loss F; **caer ~s de punta** F pelt down F
Cía. *abr* (= **Compañía**) Co. (= Company)
ciberespacio *m* cyberspace; **cibernauta** *m/f* Internet surfer; **cibernética** *f* cybernetics
cicatriz *f* scar; **cicatrizar** <1f> scar
cíclico *adj* cyclical; **ciclismo** *m* cycling; **ciclista** *m/f* cyclist; **ciclo** *m* cycle; **de cine** season; **ciclomotor** *m* moped; **ciclón** *m* cyclone; **cicloturismo** *m* bicycle touring
ciega *f* blind woman; **ciego 1** *adj* blind; **a -as** blindly **2** *m* blind man
cielito *m* Rpl folk dance
cielo *m* sky; REL heaven; **ser un ~** be an angel F; **~ raso** ceiling

ciempiés *m inv* ZO centipede

cien *adj* a o one hundred

ciencia *f* science; **~ ficción** science fiction; **a ~ cierta** for certain, for sure; **científico 1** *adj* scientific **2** *m*, **-a** *f* scientist

ciento *pron* a o one hundred; **~s de** hundreds of; **el cinco por ~** five per cent

ciernes: en ~ *fig* potential, in the making

cierre *m* fastener; *de negocio* closure; **~ centralizado** AUTO central locking; **~ relámpago** *L.Am.* zipper, *Br* zip

cierto *adj* certain; **hasta ~ punto** up to a point; **un ~ encanto** a certain charm; **es ~** it's true; **~ día** one day; **por ~** incidentally; **estar en lo ~** be right

ciervo *m* ZO deer; **~ volante** ZO stag beetle

c.i.f. *abr* (= **costo, seguro y flete**) cif (= cost, insurance, freight)

cifra *f* figure

cigala *f* ZO crayfish

cigarra *f* ZO cicada

cigarrería *f* *L.Am.* shop selling cigarettes etc; **cigarrillo** *m* cigarette; **cigarro** *m* cigar; *L.Am.* cigarette

cigüeña *f* ZO stork

cigüeñal *m* AUTO crankshaft

cilantro *m* BOT coriander

cilindrada *f* AUTO cubic capacity; **cilíndrico** *adj* cylindrical; **cilindro** *m* cylinder

cima *f* summit; *fig* peak

cimarrón *adj* *L.Am. animal* wild; *esclavo* runaway; **mate ~** *Arg* unsweetened maté

cimentar <1k> *v/t* lay the foundations of; *fig* base (**en** on); **cimientos** *mpl* foundations

cinc *m* zinc

cincel *m* chisel

cinco 1 *adj* five **2** *m* five; **no tener ni ~** F not have a red cent F

cincuenta *adj* fifty; **cincuentón** *m* man in his fifties; **cincuentona** *f* woman in her fifties

cine *m* movies *pl*, cinema; **cineasta**

m/f film-maker; **cinéfilo** *m*, **-a** *f* movie buff; **cinematográfico** *adj* movie *atr*

cinético *adj* kinetic

cínico 1 *adj* cynical **2** *m*, **-a** *f* cynic; **cinismo** *m* cynicism

cinta *f* ribbon; *de música, vídeo* tape; **~ adhesiva** adhesive tape; **~ aislante** electrical tape, friction tape, *Br* insulating tape; **~ métrica** tape measure; **~ de vídeo** video tape

cintura *f* waist; **cinturón** *m* belt; **~ de seguridad** AUTO seatbelt

cíper *m* *Méx* zipper, *Br* zip

ciprés *m* BOT cypress

circo *m* circus

circuito *m* circuit; **corto ~** EL short circuit; **circulación** *f* movement; FIN, MED circulation; AUTO traffic; **poner en ~** put into circulation; **circular 1** *adj* circular **2** <1a> *v/i* circulate; AUTO drive, travel; *de persona* move (along); **círculo** *m* circle; **~ vicioso** vicious circle

circuncisión *f* circumcision

circundante *adj* surrounding

circunferencia *f* circumference

circunscribir <3a; *part* **circunscrito**> *v/t* limit (**a** to); **circunscripción** *f* POL electoral district, *Br* constituency

circunspecto *adj* circumspect, cautious

circunstancia *f* circumstance; **circunstancial** *adj* circumstantial

circunvalación *f*: (**carretera de**) **~** beltway, *Br* ring-road

cirio *m* candle; **armar** or **montar un ~** F kick up a fuss F

ciruela *f* plum; **~ pasa** prune

cirugía *f* surgery; **~ estética** cosmetic surgery; **cirujano** *m*, **-a** *f* surgeon

cisco *m*: **hacer ~** smash

cisne *m* ZO swan

cisterna *f* *de WC* cistern

cistitis *f* MED cystitis

cita *f* appointment; *de texto* quote, quotation; **citar** <1a> **1** *v/t* a *reunión* arrange to meet; *a juicio* summon; (*mencionar*) mention; *de texto* quote **2** *v/r* **~se** arrange to meet

citología *f* smear test

cítrico *m* citrus fruit

ciudad *f* town; *más grande* city; **~ universitaria** university campus; **ciudadano** *m*, **-a** *f* citizen

cívico *adj* civic; **civil** *adj* civil; **casarse por lo ~** have a civil wedding; **civilización** *f* civilization; **civismo** *m* civility

cizaña *f*: **sembrar** *or* **meter ~** cause trouble

cl. *abr* (= **centilitro**) cl. (= centiliter)

clamar <1a> *v/i*: **~ por algo** clamo(u)r for sth, cry out for sth; **clamor** *m* roar; *fig* clamo(u)r

clan *m* clan

clandestino *adj* POL clandestine, underground

claqué *m* tap-dancing

clara *f de huevo* white; *bebida* beer with lemonade, *Br* shandy

claraboya *f* skylight

claridad *f* light; *fig* clarity; **clarificar** <1g> *v/t* clarify

clarinete *m* clarinet

clarividente *m/f* clairvoyant

claro *adj tb fig* clear; *color* light; *(luminoso)* bright; *salsa* thin; **¡~!** of course!; **hablar ~** speak plainly

clase *f* class; *(variedad)* kind, sort; **~ particular** private class; **dar ~(s)** teach

clásico *adj* classical

clasificación *f* DEP league table; **clasificar** <1g> **1** *v/t* classify **2** *v/r* **~se** DEP qualify

claudicar <1g> *v/i* give in

claustro *m* ARQUI cloister

claustrofobia *f* claustrophobia

cláusula *f* clause

clausurar <1a> *v/t acto oficial* close; *por orden oficial* close down

clavadista *m/f Méx* diver

clavado *adj*: **ser ~ a alguien** be the spitting image of s.o. F; **clavar** <1a> **1** *v/t* stick (*en* into); *clavos, estaca* drive (*en* into); *uñas* sink (*en* into); **~ los ojos en alguien** fix one's eyes on s.o.; **~ a alguien por algo** F overcharge s.o. for sth **2** *v/r* **~se**: **~se un**

cuchillo en la mano stick a knife into one's hand

clave 1 *f* key; **en ~** in code **2** *adj (importante)* key

clavel *m* BOT carnation

clavícula *f* ANAT collarbone

clavija *f* EL pin

clavo *m de metal* nail; GASTR clove; *CSur* F *persona* dead loss F; **dar en el ~** hit the nail on the head

claxon *m* AUTO horn

clemencia *f* clemency, mercy

clementina *f* BOT clementine

clérigo *m* priest, clergyman; **clero** *m* clergy

clic *m* INFOR click; **hacer ~ en** click on

cliché *m* cliché

clienta, cliente *m/f de tienda* customer; *de empresa* client; **clientela** *f* clientele, customers *pl*

clima *m* climate; **climatizado** *adj* air-conditioned; **climatizar** <1f> *v/t* air-condition

clímax *m fig* climax

clínica *f* clinic; **clínico** *adj* clinical

clip *m para papeles* paperclip; *para el pelo* bobby pin, *Br* hairgrip

cloaca *f tb fig* sewer

clon *m* BIO clone; **clonación** *f* BIO cloning; **clonar** <1a> *v/t* clone

cloro *m* QUÍM chlorine

clóset *m L.Am.* closet, *Br* wardrobe

club *m* club; **~ náutico** yacht club

cm *abr* (= **centímetro**) cm (= centimeter)

coacción *f* coercion; **coaccionar** <1a> *v/t* coerce

coagular <1a> **1** *v/t* coagulate; *sangre* clot **2** *v/r* **~se** coagulate; *de sangre* clot; **coágulo** *m* clot

coala *m* ZO koala

coalición *f* coalition; **coaligarse** <1h> *v/r tb* POL work together, join forces

coartada *f* JUR alibi

coba *f*: **dar ~ a alguien** F soft-soap s.o.

cobarde 1 *adj* cowardly **2** *m/f* coward

cobaya *m/f* guinea pig

cobertizo *m* shed; **cobertor** *m* (*manta*) blanket; **cobertura** *f* cover; TV *etc* coverage

cobija *f L.Am.* blanket; **cobijar** <1a> **1** *v/t* give shelter to; (*acoger*) take in **2** *v/r* ~**se** take shelter; **cobijo** *m* shelter, refuge

cobra *f* ZO cobra

cobrador *m*, ~**a** *f a domicilio* collector; **cobrar** <1a> **1** *v/t* charge; *subsidio, pensión* receive; *deuda* collect; *cheque* cash; *salud, fuerzas* recover; *importancia* acquire **2** *v/i* be paid, get paid; *vas a* ~ F (*recibir un palo*) you're going to get it! F

cobre *m* copper

cobro *m* charging; *de subsidio* receipt; *de deuda* collection; *de cheque* cashing

coca *f* F *droga* coke F; *de* ~ *Méx* free

cocacho *m S.Am.* F whack on the head F

cocada *f L.Am.* coconut cookie

cocaína *f* cocaine; **cocainómano** *m*, ~**a** *f* cocaine addict

cocción *f* cooking; *en agua* boiling; *al horno* baking; **cocer** <2b & 2h> **1** *v/t* cook; *en agua* boil; *al horno* bake **2** *v/r* ~**se** cook; *en agua* boil; *al horno* bake; *fig* F *de persona* be roasting F

cochambroso *adj* F filthy

coche *m* car; *Méx* (*taxi*) cab, taxi; ~ *de caballos* horse-drawn carriage; ~ *cama* sleeping car; ~ *comedor* *L.Am.* dining car; ~ *de línea* (long-distance) bus; **cochecito** *m*: ~ *de niño* stroller, *Br* pushchair; **cochera** *f* garage; *de trenes* locomotive shed

cochina *f* sow; F *persona* pig F; **cochino 1** *adj fig* filthy, dirty; (*asqueroso*) disgusting **2** *m* hog, *Br* pig; F *persona* pig F

cocido 1 *adj* boiled **2** *m* stew

cociente *m* quotient

cocina *f habitación* kitchen; *aparato* cooker, stove; *actividad* cooking; ~ *de gas* gas cooker *o* stove; **cocinar** <1a> **1** *v/t* cook; *fig* F plot **2** *v/i* cook; **cocinero** *m*, ~**a** *f* cook

coco *m* BOT coconut; *monstruo* bogeyman F; *comer el ~ a alguien* F softsoap s.o.; *más fuerte* brainwash s.o.

cocodrilo *m* crocodile

cocoliche *m Arg* pidgin Spanish

cocotazo *m L.Am.* F whack on the head F

cocotero *m* coconut palm

cóctel *m* cocktail; ~ *Molotov* Molotov cocktail

cód *abr* (= **código**) code

codazo *m*: *darle a alguien un* ~ elbow s.o.

codearse <1a> *v/r*: ~ *con alguien* rub shoulders with s.o.

codicia *f* greed; **codiciar** <1b> *v/t* covet; **codicioso** *adj* greedy

codificado *adj* TV encrypted; **código** *m* code; ~ *de barras* COM barcode; ~ *postal* zip code, *Br* postcode

codo *m* ANAT elbow; ~ *con* ~ *fig* F side by side; *hablar por los* ~**s** F talk nineteen to the dozen F

codorniz *f* ZO quail

coeficiente *m* coefficient

coetáneo *m*, ~**a** *f* contemporary

coexistir <3a> *v/i* coexist (*con* with)

cofradía *f* fraternity; (*gremio*) guild

cofre *m de tesoro* chest; *para alhajas* jewel(le)ry box

coger <2c> **1** *v/t* (*asir*) take (hold of); *del suelo* pick up; *ladrón, enfermedad* catch; TRANSP catch, take; (*entender*) get; *L.Am.* V screw V **2** *v/i en un espacio* fit; *L.Am.* V screw V; ~ *por la primera a la derecha* take the first right **3** *v/r* ~**se** hold on (tight); ~**se** *de algo* hold on to sth

cogorza *f*: *agarrar una* ~ F get plastered F

cogote *m* F nape of the neck

cohabitar <1a> *v/i* live together, cohabit

cohecho *m* JUR bribery

coherencia *f* coherence; **coherente** *adj* coherent; *ser* ~ *con* be consistent with; **cohesión** *f* cohesion

cohete *m* rocket

cohibir <3a> *v/t* inhibit

COI *abr* (= **Comité Olímpico Internacional**) IOC (= International Olympic Committee)

coima *f L.Am.* bribe

coincidencia *f* coincidence; **coincidir** <3a> *v/i* coincide

coito *m* intercourse

cojear <1a> *v/i de persona* limp, hobble; *de mesa, silla* wobble; **cojera** *f* limp

cojín *m* cushion

cojo *adj persona* lame; *mesa, silla* wobbly

cojón *m* ∨ ball ∨

cojonudo *adj* P awesome F, brilliant

col. *abr* (= **columna**) col. (= column)

col *f* cabbage; **~ de Bruselas** Brussels sprout

cola[1] *f* (*pegamento*) glue

cola[2] *f* (*de animal*) tail; *de gente* line, *Br* queue; *L.Am.* F *de persona* butt F, *Br* bum F; **hacer ~** stand in line, *Br* queue; **estar a la ~** be in last place

colaboración *f* collaboration; **colaborador** *m*, **-a** *f* collaborator; *en periódico* contributor; **colaborar** <1a> *v/i* collaborate

colación *f*: **traer** *or* **sacar a ~** bring up

colada *f*: **hacer la ~** do the laundry *o* washing; **colado** *adj*: **estar ~ por alguien** F be nuts about s.o. F; **colador** *m* colander; *para té etc* strainer

colapsar <1a> **1** *v/t* paralyze; **~ el tráfico** bring traffic to a standstill **2** *v/r* **~se** grind to a halt; **colapso** *m* collapse; **provocar un ~ en la ciudad** bring the city to a standstill

colar <1m> **1** *v/t líquido* strain; *billete falso* pass; **~ algo por la aduana** F smuggle sth through customs **2** *v/i fig* F: **no cuela** I'm not buying it F **3** *v/r* **~se** F *en un lugar* get in; *en una fiesta* gatecrash; *en una cola* cut in line, *Br* push in

colcha *f L.Am.* bedspread; **colchón** *m* mattress; *fig* buffer; **colchoneta** *f* DEP mat; *hinchable* air bed

cole *m* F school

colección *f* collection; **coleccionar** <1a> *v/t* collect; **coleccionista** *m/f* collector; **colecta** *f* collection; **colectivero** *m*, **-a** *f Arg* bus driver; **colectivo 1** *adj* collective **2** *m L.Am.* bus; *Méx, C.Am.* taxi

colega *m/f* colleague; F pal

colegiado *m*, **-a** *f* DEP referee

colegial *m* student, schoolboy; **colegiala** *f* student, schoolgirl; **colegio** *m* school; **~ electoral** electoral college; **~ profesional** professional institute

cólera 1 *f* anger; **montar en ~** get in a rage **2** *m* MED cholera

colesterol *m* cholesterol

coleta *f* ponytail; **~s de pelo** bunches

colgado *adj*: **dejar ~ a alguien** F let s.o. down; **colgador** *m L.Am.* hanger; **colgante 1** *adj* hanging **2** *m* pendant; **colgar** <1h & 1m> **1** *v/t* hang; TELEC put down **2** *v/i* hang (**de** from); TELEC hang up **3** *v/r* **~se** hang *o.s.*; INFOR F lock up; **~se de algo** hang from sth; **~se de alguien** hang onto s.o.

colibrí *m* ZO hummingbird

cólico *m* MED colic

coliflor *f* cauliflower

colilla *f* cigarette end

colina *f* hill

colindante *adj* adjoining

colirio *m* MED eye drops *pl*

colisión *f* collision; *fig* clash; **colisionar** <1a> *v/i* collide (**con** with)

colitis *f* MED colitis

collar *m* necklace; *para animal* collar

colleras *fpl Chi* cuff links

colmar <1a> *v/t deseos, ambición etc* fulfill; **~ un vaso** fill a glass to the brim; **~ a alguien de elogios** heap praise on s.o.

colmena *f* beehive

colmillo *m* ANAT eye tooth; *de perro* fang; *de elefante, rinoceronte* tusk

colmo *m*: **¡es el ~!** this is the last straw!; **para ~** to cap it all

colocación *f* positioning, placing; (*trabajo*) position; **colocar** <1g> **1** *v/t* put, place; **~ a alguien en un trabajo** get s.o. a job **2** *v/r* **~se de**

persona position o.s.; *se colocó a mi lado* he stood next to me; *se colocaron en primer lugar* they moved into first place

colofón *m fig* culmination

Colombia Colombia; **colombiano 1** *adj* Colombian **2** *m*, **-a** *f* Colombian

Colón Columbus

colonia *f* colony; *de viviendas* subdivision, *Br* estate; *perfume* cologne; **~ de verano** summer camp; **colonial** *adj* colonial; **colonización** *f* colonization; **colonizar** <1f> *v/t* colonize

coloquial *adj* colloquial; **coloquio** *m* talk

color *m* colo(u)r; **~ café** coffee-colo(u)red; *L.Am.* brown; **colorado** *adj* red; **colorante** *m* colo(u)ring; **colorear** <1a> *v/t* colo(u)r; **colorete** *m* blusher; **colorido** *m* colo(u)rs *pl*

colosal *adj* colossal

columna *f* column; **~ vertebral** ANAT spinal column; **columnista** *m/f* columnist

columpiar <1b> **1** *v/t* swing **2** *v/r* **~se** swing; **columpio** *m* swing

colza *f* BOT rape

coma 1 *f* GRAM comma **2** *m* MED coma

comadre *f L.Am.* godmother

comadrear <1a> *v/i* F gossip

comadrona *f* midwife

comandante *m* MIL commander; *rango* major; AVIA captain

comarca *f* area

comba *f* jump rope, *Br* skipping rope; *jugar or saltar a la* **~** jump rope, *Br* skip

combate *m acción* combat; MIL engagement; DEP fight; *fuera de* **~** out of action; **combatir** <3a> *v/t & v/i* fight

combi *m Méx* minibus

combinación *f* combination; *prenda* slip; *hacer* **~** TRANSP change; **combinar** <1a> *v/t* combine

combustible *m* fuel; **combustión** *f* combustion

comedia *f* comedy; **comedianta** *f*

actress; **comediante** *m* actor

comedido *adj* moderate

comedor *m* dining room

comején *m* termite

comensal *m/f* diner

comentar <1a> *v/t* comment on; **comentario** *m* comment; **~ de texto** textual analysis; **~s** *pl* gossip *sg*; **comentarista** *m/f* commentator

comenzar <1f & 1k> *v/t* begin

comer <2a> **1** *v/t* eat; *a mediodía* have for lunch **2** *v/i* eat; *a mediodía* have lunch; *dar de* **~** *a alguien* feed s.o. **3** *v/r* **~se** *tb fig* eat up; *se comió una palabra* she missed out a word; *está para comértela* F she's really tasty F

comercial 1 *adj* commercial; *de negocios* business *atr*; *el déficit* **~** the trade deficit **2** *m/f* representative; **comercializar** <1f> *v/t* market, sell; *desp* commercialize; **comerciante** *m/f* trader; **~ al por menor** retailer; **comercio** *m actividad* trade; *local* store, shop; **~ exterior** foreign trade

comestible 1 *adj* eatable, edible **2** *m* foodstuff; **~s** *pl* food *sg*

cometa 1 *m* comet **2** *f* kite

cometer <2a> *v/t* commit; *error* make; **cometido** *m* task

comezón *f* itch

cómic *m* comic

comicios *mpl* elections *pl*

cómico 1 *adj* comical **2** *m*, **-a** *f* comedian

comida *f* (*comestibles*) food; *ocasión* meal

comienzo *m* beginning

comillas *fpl* quotation marks, inverted commas

comino *m* BOT cumin; *me importa un* **~** F I don't give a damn F

comisaría *f* precinct, *Br* police station; **comisario** *m* commissioner; *de policía* captain, *Br* superintendent; **comisión** *f* committee; *de gobierno* commission; (*recompensa*) commission

comité *m* committee

comitiva *f* retinue

como 1 adv as; **así ~** as well as; **había ~ cincuenta** there were about fifty **2** conj if; **~ si** as if; **~ no bebas vas a enfermar** if you don't drink you'll get sick; **~ no llegó, me fui solo** as o since she didn't arrive, I went by myself

cómo adv how; **¿~ estás?** how are you?; **¡~ me gusta!** I really like it; **me gusta ~ habla** I like the way he talks; **¿~ dice?** what did you say?; **¡~ no!** Méx of course!

cómoda f chest of drawers

comodidad f comfort

comodín m en naipes joker

cómodo adj comfortable

comp. abr (= **compárese**) cf (= confer)

compacto adj compact

compadecer <2d> **1** v/t feel sorry for **2** v/r **~se** feel sorry (**de** for)

compadre m L.Am. F buddy F; **compadrear** <1a> v/i Arg F brag; **compadrito** m Arg F show-off

compaginar <1a> v/t fig combine

compañero m, **-a** f companion; en una relación, en un juego partner; **~ de trabajo** coworker, colleague; **~ de clase** classmate; **compañía** f company; **hacer ~ a alguien** keep s.o. company

comparación f comparison; **en ~ con** in comparison with; **comparado** adj: **~ con** compared with; **comparar** <1a> v/t compare

comparecencia f JUR appearance; **comparecer** <2d> v/i appear

compartir <3a> v/t share (**con** with)

compás m MAT compass; MÚS rhythm; **al ~** to the beat

compasión f compassion

compatibilidad f compatibility; **compatible** adj INFOR compatible

compatriota m/f compatriot

compendio m summary

compenetrado adj: **están muy ~s** they are very much in tune with each other; **compenetrarse** <1a> v/r: **~ con alguien** reach a good understanding with s.o.

compensación f compensation;

compensar <1a> **1** v/t compensate (**por** for) **2** v/i fig be worthwhile

competencia f (habilidad) competence; entre rivales competition; (incumbencia) area of responsibility, competency; **~ desleal** unfair competition; **competente** adj competent

competición f DEP competition; **competir** <3l> v/i compete (**con** with); **competitivo** adj competitive

compilar <1a> v/t compile

compinche m/f F buddy F; desp crony F

complacencia f (placer) pleasure; (tolerancia) indulgence; **complacer** <2x> v/t please; **complaciente** adj obliging, helpful

complejidad f complexity

complejo 1 adj complex **2** m PSI complex; **~ de inferioridad** inferiority complex

complementar <1a> v/t complement; **complemento** m complement; GRAM complement, object; **~s de moda** fashion accessories

completar <1a> v/t complete; **completo** adj complete; autobús, teatro full; **por ~** completely

complicación f complication; **complicado** adj complicated; **complicar** <1g> **1** v/t complicate **2** v/r **~se** get complicated; **~se la vida** make things difficult for o.s.

cómplice m/f accomplice

complot m plot

componente m component; **componer** <2r; part **compuesto**>**1** v/t make up, comprise; sinfonía, poema etc compose; algo roto fix, mend **2** v/r **~se** be made up (**de** of); L.Am. MED get better

comportamiento m behavio(u)r; **comportarse** <1a> v/r behave

composición f composition; **compositor** m, **-a** f composer

compostura f fig composure

compota f compote

compra f acción purchase; (cosa comprada) purchase, buy; **ir de ~s** go shopping; **comprar** <1a> v/t buy, purchase; **compraventa** f buying and selling

comprender <2a> v/t understand; (*abarcar*) include; **comprensión** f understanding; *de texto, auditiva* comprehension; **comprensivo** adj understanding

compresa f sanitary napkin, Br sanitary towel; **compresión** f tb INFOR compression; **comprimido** m MED pill; **comprimir** <3a> v/t compress

comprobación f check; **comprobar** <1m> v/t check; (*darse cuenta de*) realize

comprometer <2a> **1** v/t compromise; (*obligar*) commit **2** v/r **~se** promise (**a** to); *a una causa* commit o.s.; *de novios* get engaged; **comprometido** adj committed; **estar ~ en algo** be implicated in sth; **estar ~ de novios** be engaged; **compromiso** m commitment; (*obligación*) obligation; (*acuerdo*) agreement; (*apuro*) awkward situation; **sin ~** COM without commitment; **soltero y sin ~** F footloose and fancy-free

compuesto 1 part → **componer 2** adj composed; **estar ~ de** be composed of

compulsar <1a> v/t certify; **compulsivo** adj PSI compulsive

computación f L.Am. computer science

computadora f L.Am. computer; **~ de escritorio** desktop (computer); **~ personal** personal computer; **~ portátil** laptop; **computarizar** <1f> v/t computerize

comulgar <1h> v/i take communion; **~ con alguien** (**en algo**) fig F think the same way as s.o. (on sth)

común adj common; **por lo ~** generally; **comuna** f commune; L.Am. (*población*) town

comunicación f communication; TRANSP link; **comunicado 1** adj connected; **el lugar está bien ~** the place has good transport links **2** m POL press release, communiqué;

comunicar <1g> **1** v/t TRANSP connect, link; **~ algo a alguien** inform s.o. of sth **2** v/i communicate; TELEC be busy, Br tb be engaged **3** v/r **~se** communicate

comunidad f community; **~ autónoma** autonomous region

comunión f REL communion

comunismo m Communism; **comunista** m/f & adj Communist

comunitario adj POL EU atr, Community atr

con prp with; **voy ~ ellos** I'm going with them; **pan ~ mantequilla** bread and butter; **~ todo eso** in spite of all that; **~ tal de que** provided that, as long as; **~ hacer eso** by doing that

conato m: **~ de violencia** minor outbreak of violence; **~ de incendio** small fire

cóncavo adj concave

concebir <3l> v/t conceive

conceder <2a> v/t concede; *entrevista, permiso* give; *premio* award

concejal m, **~a** f council(l)or

concentración f concentration; *de personas* gathering; **concentrar** <1a> **1** v/t concentrate **2** v/r **~se** concentrate (**en** on); *de gente* gather

concepto m concept; **en ~ de algo** COM (in payment) for sth; **bajo ningún ~** on no account

concernir <3i> v/t concern; **en lo que concierne a X** as far as X is concerned

concertar <1k> v/t *cita* arrange; *precio* agree; *esfuerzos* coordinate

concesión f concession; COM dealership; **hacer concesiones** make concessions; **concesionario** m dealer

concha f ZO shell

conchabar <1a> **1** v/t L.Am. *trabajador* hire **2** v/r **~se** F plot

conciencia f conscience; **a ~** conscientiously; **con plena ~ de** fully conscious of; **concienciar** <1b> **1** v/t: **~ a alguien de algo** make s.o. aware of sth **2** v/r **~se** realize (**de** sth); **concienzudo** adj conscientious

concierto *m* MÚS concert; *fig* agreement

conciliador *adj* conciliatory; **conciliar** <1b> *v/t* reconcile; **~ el sueño** get to sleep

conciso *adj* concise

concluir <3g> *v/t & v/i* conclude; **conclusión** *f* conclusion; **en ~** in short

concretar <1a> **1** *v/t* specify; (*hacer concreto*) realize **2** *v/r* **~se** materialize; *de esperanzas* be fulfilled; **concreto 1** *adj* specific; (*no abstracto*) concrete; **en ~** specifically **2** *m* *L.Am.* concrete

concurrencia *f* audience; *de circunstancias* combination; **concurrido** *adj* crowded; **concursante** *m/f* competitor; **concursar** <1a> *v/i* compete; **concurso** *m* competition; COM tender

conde *m* count

condecoración *f* decoration; **condecorar** <1a> *v/t* decorate

condena *f* JUR sentence; (*desaprobación*) condemnation; **condenar** <1a> *v/t* JUR sentence (*a* to); (*desaprobar*) condemn

condensación *f* condensation; **condensado** *adj* condensed; **condensar** <1a> **1** *v/t* condense; *libro* abridge **2** *v/r* **~se** condense

condesa *f* countess

condescendiente *adj* *actitud* accommodating; *desp* condescending

condición *f* condition; **a ~ de que** on condition that; **estar en condiciones de** be in a position to

condimentar <1a> flavo(u)r; **condimento** *m* seasoning

condón *m* condom

cóndor *m* ZO condor

conducir <3o> **1** *v/t* *vehículo* drive; (*dirigir*) lead (*a* to); EL, TÉC conduct **2** *v/i* drive; *de camino* lead (*a* to); **conducta** *f* conduct, behavio(u)r; **conducto** *m* pipe; *fig* channel; **por ~ de** through; **conductor** *m*, **~a** *f* driver; **~ de orquesta** *L.Am.* conductor

conduje *vb* → **conducir**

conectar <1a> *v/t* connect, link; EL connect

conejillo *m*: **~ de Indias** *tb fig* guinea pig; **conejo** *m* rabbit

conexión *f* *tb* EL connection

confabularse <1a> *v/r* plot

confección *f* making; *de vestidos* dressmaking; *de trajes* tailoring; **confeccionar** <1a> *v/t* make

confederación *f* confederation

conferencia *f* lecture; (*reunión*) conference; TELEC long-distance call; **conferenciante** *m/f* lecturer; **conferencista** *m/f* *L.Am.* lecturer; **conferir** <3i> *v/t* award

confesar <1k> **1** *v/t* REL confess; *delito* confess to, admit **2** *v/i* JUR confess **3** *v/r* **~se** confess; (*declararse*) admit to being; **confesión** *f* confession

confeti *m* confetti

confiado *adj* trusting; **confianza** *f* confidence; **~ en sí mismo** self-confidence; *de ~ persona* trustworthy; *amigo de ~* good friend; **confiar** <1c> **1** *v/t* *secreto* confide (*a* to); **~ algo a alguien** entrust s.o. with sth, entrust sth to s.o. **2** *v/i* trust (*en* in); (*estar seguro*) be confident (*en* of); **confidencia** *f* confidence; **confidencial** *adj* confidential

configuración *f* configuration; INFOR set-up, configuration; **configurar** <1a> *v/t* shape; INFOR set up, configure

confinar <1a> *v/t* confine

confirmación *f* confirmation; **confirmar** <1a> *v/t* confirm

confiscar <1g> *v/t* confiscate

confitería *f* confectioner's

confitura *f* preserve

conflagración *f* conflagration; (*guerra*) war

conflicto *m* conflict

conformarse <1a> *v/r* make do (*con* with); **conforme 1** *adj* satisfied (*con* with) **2** *prp*: **~ a** in accordance with

confortable *adj* comfortable

confrontación *f* confrontation

confundir <3a> **1** v/t confuse; (*equivocar*) mistake (*con* for) **2** v/r **~se** make a mistake; **~ de calle** get the wrong street; **confusión** f confusion; **confuso** adj confused

congelación f freezing; **~ de precios / de salarios** price / wage freeze; **congelado** adj frozen; **congelador** m freezer; **congelar** <1a> **1** v/t freeze **2** v/r **~se** freeze

congeniar <1b> v/i get on well (*con* with)

congénito adj congenital

congestión f MED congestion; **~ del tráfico** traffic congestion; **congestionar** <1a> v/t congest

congoja f anguish

congregar <1h> v/t bring together; **congresal** m/f L.Am., **congresista** m/f conference o convention delegate, conventioneer; **congreso** m conference, convention; **Congreso en EE.UU** Congress; **~ de los diputados** lower house of Spanish parliament

congrio m ZO conger eel

conjetura f conjecture

conjugar <1h> v/t GRAM conjugate; *fig* combine

conjunción f GRAM conjunction; **conjuntivitis** f MED conjunctivitis; **conjunto 1** adj joint **2** m de personas, objetos collection; de prendas outfit; MAT set; **en ~** as a whole

conllevar <1a> v/t entail

conmemorar <1a> v/t commemorate

conmigo pron with me

conmoción f shock; (*agitación*) upheaval; **conmocionar** <1a> v/t shock; **conmovedor** adj moving; **conmover** <2h> **1** v/t move **2** v/r **~se** be moved

conmutador m EL switch; L.Am. TELEC switchboard

connotación f connotation

cono m cone

conocer <2d> **1** v/t know; *por primera vez* meet; *tristeza, amor etc* experience, know; (*reconocer*) recognize; **dar a ~** make known **2** v/r **~se** know one another; *por primera vez* meet one another; *a sí mismo* know o.s.; **se conoce que** it seems that; **conocido 1** adj well-known **2** m, **-a** f acquaintance; **conocimiento** m knowledge; MED consciousness; **perder el ~** lose consciousness

conquista f conquest; **conquistar** <1a> v/t conquer; *persona* win over

consabido adj usual

consagrar <1a> **1** v/t REL consecrate; (*hacer famoso*) make famous; *vida* devote **2** v/r **~se** devote o.s. (*a* to)

consciente adj MED conscious; **~ de** aware of, conscious of

consecuencia f consequence; **a ~ de** as a result of; **en ~** consequently; **consecuente** adj consistent; **consecutivo** adj consecutive; **tres años ~s** three years in a row; **conseguir** <3l & 3d> v/t get; *objetivo* achieve

consejero m, **-a** f adviser; COM director; **consejo** m piece of advice; **~ de administración** board of directors; **~ de ministros** grupo cabinet; *reunión* cabinet meeting

consenso m consensus; **consentido** adj spoilt; **consentimiento** m consent; **consentir** <3i> **1** v/t allow; *a niño* indulge **2** v/i: **~ en algo** agree to sth

conserje m/f superintendent, Br caretaker

conserva f: **en ~** canned, Br tinned; **~s** pl canned (Br tinned) food sg; **conservación** f de alimentos preservation; de edificios, especies conservation; **conservador** adj conservative; **conservante** m preservative; **conservar** <1a> **1** v/t conserve; *alimento* preserve **2** v/r **~se** survive; **conservatorio** m conservatory

considerable adj considerable; **consideración** f consideration; **considerar** <1a> v/t consider

consigna f order; de equipaje baggage room, Br left-luggage

consigo *pron* with him/her; *(con usted, con ustedes)* with you; *(con uno)* with you, with one *fml*

consiguiente *adj* consequent; *por ~* and so, therefore

consistencia *f* consistency; **consistente** *adj* consistent; *(sólido)* solid; **consistir** <3a> *v/i* consist (*en* of)

consola *f* INFOR console

consolar <1m> *v/t* console

consolidar <1a> **1** *v/t* consolidate **2** *v/r* **~se** strengthen

consomé *m* GASTR consommé

consonancia *f*: *en ~ con* in keeping with; **consonante** *f* consonant

consorte *m/f* spouse

conspiración *f* conspiracy; **conspirar** <1a> *v/i* conspire

constancia *f* constancy; *dejar ~ de* leave a record of; **constante** *adj* constant; **constar** <1a> *v/i* be recorded; *~ de* consist of

constatación *f* verification; **constatar** <1a> *v/t* verify

constelación *f* AST constellation

consternar <1a> *v/t* dismay

constipado 1 *adj*: *estar ~* have a cold **2** *m* cold; **constiparse** <1a> *v/r* get a cold

constitución *f* constitution; **constituir** <3g> *v/t* constitute, make up; *empresa, organismo* set up

construcción *f* construction; *(edificio)* building; **construir** <3g> *v/t* build, construct

consuelo *m* consolation

cónsul *m/f* consul; **consulado** *m* consulate

consulta *f* consultation; MED local office, *Br* surgery; **consultar** <1a> *v/t* consult; **consultor** *m*, *~a f* consultant; **consultoría** *f* consultancy; **consultorio** *m* MED office, *Br* surgery

consumidor *m*, *~a f* COM consumer; **consumir** <3a> **1** *v/t* consume **2** *v/r* **~se** waste away; **consumo** *m* consumption; *de bajo ~* economical

contabilidad *f* accountancy; *llevar la ~* do the accounts; **contable** *m/f* accountant

contactar <1a> *v/i*: *~ con alguien* contact s.o.; **contacto** *m* contact; AUTO ignition; *ponerse en ~* get in touch (*con* with)

contado *adj*: *al ~* in cash; **contador 1** *m* meter **2** *m*, *~a f* L.Am. accountant

contagiar <1b> **1** *v/t*: *~ la gripe a alguien* give s.o. the flu; *nos contagió su entusiasmo* he infected us with his enthusiasm **2** *v/r* **~se** become infected; **contagioso** *adj* contagious

contaminación *f de agua etc* contamination; *de río, medio ambiente* pollution; **contaminar** <1a> *v/t* contaminate; *río, medio ambiente* pollute

contar <1m> **1** *v/t* count; *(narrar)* tell **2** *v/i* count; *~ con* count on

contemplación *f*: *sin contemplaciones* without ceremony; **contemplar** <1a> *v/t (mirar)* look at, contemplate; *posibilidad* consider

contemporáneo 1 *adj* contemporary **2** *m*, *~a f* contemporary

contenedor *m* TRANSP container; *~ de basura* dumpster, *Br* skip; *~ de vidrio* bottle bank; **contener** <2l> **1** *v/t* contain; *respiración* hold; *muchedumbre* hold back **2** *v/r* **~se** control o.s.; **contenido** *m* content

contentarse <1a> *v/r* be satisfied (*con* with); **contento** *adj (satisfecho)* pleased; *(feliz)* happy

contestación *f* answer; **contestador** *m*: *~ automático* TELEC answer machine; **contestar** <1a> **1** *v/t* answer, reply to **2** *v/i* reply (*a* to), answer (*a* sth); *de forma insolente* answer back

contexto *m* context

contigo *pron* with you

contiguo *adj* adjoining, adjacent

continental *adj* continental; **continente** *m* continent

continuación *f* continuation; *a ~ (ahora)* now; *(después)* then; **continuar** <1e> **1** *v/t* continue **2** *v/i* continue; *~ haciendo algo* continue *o* carry on doing sth; **continuidad** *f* continuity; **continuo** *adj* (*sin parar*) continuous; (*frecuente*) continual

contorno *m* outline

contra *prp* against; **en ~ de** against

contraataque *m* counterattack

contrabajo *m* double bass

contrabandista *m/f* smuggler; **contrabando** *m* contraband, smuggled goods *pl*; **acción** smuggling; **hacer ~** smuggle; **pasar algo de ~** smuggle sth in

contracción *f* contraction

contraceptivo *m/adj* contraceptive

contradecir <3p> *v/t* contradict; **contradicción** *f* contradiction; **contradictorio** *adj* contradictory

contraer <2p; *part* **contraído**> 1 *v/t* contract; *músculo* tighten; **~ matrimonio** marry 2 *v/r* **~se** contract

contraindicación *f* MED contraindication

contraluz *f*: **a ~** against the light

contrapartida *f* COM balancing entry; **como ~** *fig* in contrast

contrapeso *m* counterweight

contraposición *f*: **en ~ a** in comparison to

contraproducente *adj* counterproductive

contrariedad *f* setback; (*disgusto*) annoyance

contrario 1 *adj* contrary; *sentido* opposite; *equipo* opposing; **al ~, por el ~** on the contrary; **de lo ~** otherwise; **ser ~ a algo** be opposed to sth; **llevar la -a a alguien** contradict s.o. 2 *m*, **-a** *f* adversary, opponent

contrarreloj *f* DEP time trial

contrarrestar <1a> *v/t* counteract

contraseña *f* password

contrastar <1a> *v/t & v/i* contrast (**con** with); **contraste** *m* contrast

contratar <1a> *v/t* contract; *trabajadores* hire

contratiempo *m* setback

contrato *m* contract

contravenir <3s> *v/i* contravene

contribución *f* contribution; (*impuesto*) tax; **contribuir** <3g> *v/t*

contribute (**a** to); **contribuyente** *m/f* taxpayer

contrincante *m/f* opponent

control *m* control; (*inspección*) check; **~ remoto** remote control; **controlador** *m*, **~a** *f*: **~ aéreo** air traffic controller; **controlar** <1a> 1 *v/t* control; (*vigilar*) check 2 *v/r* **~se** control o.s.

controversia *f* controversy

contundente *adj arma* blunt; *fig*: *derrota* overwhelming; **contusión** *f* MED bruise

convalecencia *f* convalescence; **convaleciente** *m/f* convalescent

convalidar <1a> *v/t* recognize

convencer <2b> *v/t* convince

convención *f* convention; **convencional** *adj* conventional

conveniencia *f de hacer algo* advisability; **hacer algo por ~** do sth in one's own interest; **conveniente** *adj* convenient; (*útil*) useful; (*aconsejable*) advisable; **convenio** *m* agreement; **convenir** <3s> 1 *v/t* agree 2 *v/i* be advisable; **no te conviene** it's not in your interest; **~ a alguien hacer algo** be in s.o.'s interests to do sth

conventillo *m* CSur tenement

convento *m de monjes* monastery; *de monjas* convent

converger <2c> *v/i* converge

conversación *f* conversation; **conversar** <1a> *v/i* make conversation

conversión *f* conversion; **convertible** 1 *adj* COM convertible 2 *m* *L.Am.* convertible; **convertir** <3i> 1 *v/t* convert 2 *v/r* **~se**: **~se en algo** turn into sth

convexo *adj* convex

convicción *f* conviction

convidar <1a> *v/t* invite (**a** to)

convincente *adj* convincing

convivencia *f* living together; **convivir** <3a> *v/i* live together

convocar <1g> *v/t* summon; *huelga* call; *oposiciones* organize; **convocatoria** *f* announcement; *de huelga* call

convoy *m* convoy

convulsión *f* convulsion; *fig* upheaval

conyugal *adj* conjugal; **cónyuge** *m/f* spouse

coña *f*: *decir algo de* ~ say sth as a joke; *darle la* ~ *a alguien* F bug s.o. F; *¡ni de* ~*!* F no way! F

coñac *m* (*pl* ~s) brandy, cognac

coño *m* V cunt V

cooperación *f* cooperation; **cooperar** <1a> *v/i* cooperate; **cooperativa** *f* cooperative

coordinación *f* coordination; **coordinar** <1a> *v/t* coordinate

copa *f* *de vino etc* glass; DEP cup; *tomar una* ~ have a drink; ~*s* *pl* (*en naipes*) suit in Spanish deck of cards

copia *f* copy; ~ *pirata* pirate copy; **copiar** <1b> F *v/t* copy

copiloto *m/f* copilot

copioso *adj* copious

copla *f* verse; (*canción*) popular song

copo *m* flake; ~ *de nieve* snowflake; ~*s de maíz* cornflakes

copropietario *m*, **-a** *f* co-owner, joint owner

coquetear <1a> *v/i* flirt; **coquetería** *f* flirtatiousness; **coqueto** *adj* flirtatious; *lugar* pretty

coraje *m* courage; *me da* ~ *fig* F it makes me mad F; **corajudo** *adj* L.Am. brave

coral¹ *m* ZO coral

coral² *f* MÚS choir

Corán *m* Koran

coraza *f* cuirasse; ZO shell; *fig* shield

corazón *m* heart; *de fruta* core; **corazonada** *f* hunch

corbata *f* tie

corcho *m* cork

cordel *m* string

cordero *m* lamb

cordial *adj* cordial

cordillera *f* mountain range

cordón *m* cord; *de zapato* shoelace; ~ *umbilical* ANAT umbilical cord

cordura *f* sanity; (*prudencia*) good sense

Corea Korea; **coreano 1** *adj* Korean **2** *m*, **-a** *f* Korean

coreografía *f* choreography

cormorán *m* ZO cormorant

cornada *f* TAUR goring

corneja *f* ZO crow

córner *m* *en fútbol* corner (kick)

corneta *f* MIL bugle

cornisa *f* ARQUI cornice

cornudo 1 *adj* horned **2** *m* cuckold

coro *m* MÚS choir; *de espectáculo, pieza musical* chorus; *a* ~ together, in chorus

corona *f* crown; ~ *de flores* garland; **coronar** <1a> *v/t* crown; **coronario** *adj* MED coronary

coronel *m* MIL colonel

coronilla *f* ANAT crown; *estoy hasta la* ~ I've had it up to here F

corotos *mpl* L.Am. F bits and pieces

corporación *f* corporation; **corporal** *adj* placer, estética physical; *fluido* body *atr*; **corpulento** *adj* solidly built

corral *m* farmyard

correa *f* lead; *de reloj* strap

corrección *f* correction; *en el trato* correctness; **correcto** *adj* correct; (*educado*) polite

corredizo *adj* sliding; **corredor 1** *m*, **-a** *f* DEP runner; COM agent; ~ *de bolsa* stockbroker **2** *m* ARQUI corridor

corregir <3c & 3l> *v/t* correct

correlación *f* correlation

correligionario *m*, **-a** *f*: *sus ~s republicanos* his fellow republicans

correntada *f* L.Am. current; **correntoso** *adj* L.Am. fast-flowing

correo *m* mail, *Br tb* post; ~*s* *pl* post office *sg*; ~ *aéreo* airmail; ~ *electrónico* e-mail; *por* ~ by mail; *echar al* ~ mail, *Br tb* post

correr <2a> **1** *v/i* run; (*apresurarse*) rush; *de tiempo* pass; *de agua* run, flow; ~ *con los gastos* pay the expenses; *a todo* ~ at top speed **2** *v/t* run; *cortinas* draw; *mueble* slide, move; ~ *la misma suerte* suffer the same fate **3** *v/r* ~*se* move; *de tinta* run

correspondencia *f* correspondence; FERR connection (*con* with); **corresponder** <2a> *v/i*: ~ *a alguien de bienes* be for s.o., be due to s.o.; *de responsabilidad* be up to s.o.; *de asunto* concern s.o.; *a un favor* repay s.o. (*con* with); *actuar como corresponde* do the right thing; **correspondiente** *adj* corresponding; **corresponsal** *m/f* correspondent

corretear <1a> *v/i* run around

corrida *f*: ~ *de toros* bullfight; **corrido** *adj*: *decir algo de* ~ *fig* say sth parrot-fashion

corriente 1 *adj* (*actual*) current; (*común*) ordinary; ~ *y moliente* F run-of-the-mill; *estar al* ~ be up to date **2** *f* EL, *de agua* current; ~ *de aire* draft, *Br* draught

corro *m* ring

corroborar <1a> *v/t* corroborate

corroer <2za> *v/t* corrode; *fig* eat up

corromper <2a> **1** *v/t* corrupt **2** *v/r* ~*se* become corrupted

corrosión *f* corrosion; **corrosivo** *adj* corrosive; *fig* caustic

corrupción *f* decay; *fig* corruption; ~ *de menores* corruption of minors; **corrupto** *adj* corrupt

corsetería *f* lingerie store

cortacésped *m* lawnmower

cortacircuitos *m inv* circuit breaker

cortada *f L.Am.* cut; **cortado 1** *adj* cut; *calle* closed; *leche* curdled; *persona* shy; *quedarse* ~ be embarrassed **2** *m* coffee with a dash of milk; **cortar** <1a> **1** *v/t* cut; *electricidad* cut off; *calle* close **2** *v/i* cut **3** *v/r* ~*se* cut o.s.; *fig* F get embarrassed; ~*se el pelo* have one's hair cut; **cortaúñas** *m inv* nail clippers *pl*

corte[1] *m* cut; ~ *de luz* power outage; ~ *de pelo* haircut; ~ *de tráfico* F road closure; *me da* ~ F I'm embarrassed

corte[2] *f* court; *L.Am.* JUR (law) court; *las Cortes* Spanish parliament

cortejar <1a> *v/t* court

cortés *adj* courteous; **cortesía** *f*

courtesy

corteza *f de árbol* bark; *de pan* crust; *de queso* rind

cortina *f* curtain

corto *adj* short; ~ *de vista* nearsighted; *ni* ~ *ni perezoso* as bold as brass; *quedarse* ~ fall short; **cortocircuito** *m* EL short circuit

corzo *m* ZO roe deer

cosa *f* thing; *como si tal* ~ as if nothing had happened; *decir a alguien cuatro* ~*s* give s.o. a piece of one's mind; *eso es otra* ~ that's another matter; *¿qué pasa?* – *poca* ~ what's new? – nothing much

coscorrón *m* bump on the head

cosecha *f* harvest; **cosechar** <1a> *v/t* harvest; *fig* gain, win

coser <2a> *v/t* sew; *ser* ~ *y cantar* F be dead easy F

cosmético *m/adj* cosmetic

cósmico *adj* cosmic; **cosmonauta** *m/f* cosmonaut; **cosmopolita** *adj* cosmopolitan; **cosmos** *m* cosmos; **cosmovisión** *f L.Am.* world view

cosquillas *fpl*: *hacer* ~ *a alguien* tickle s.o.; *tener* ~ be ticklish; **cosquilleo** *m* tickle

costa[1] *f*: *a* ~ *de* at the expense of; *a toda* ~ at all costs

costa[2] *f* GEOG coast

costado *m* side; *por los cuatro* ~*s fig* throughout, through and through

costar <1m> **1** *v/t en dinero* cost; *trabajo, esfuerzo etc* take; *¿cuánto cuesta?* how much does it cost? **2** *v/i en dinero* cost; *me costó* it was hard work; *cueste lo que cueste* at all costs; ~ *caro fig* cost dear

Costa Rica Costa Rica; **costarricense** *m/f & adj* Costa Rican

coste *m → costo*

costear <1a> *v/t* pay for

costero *adj* coastal

costilla *f* ANAT rib; GASTR sparerib

costo *m* cost; ~ *de la vida* cost of living; **costoso** *adj* costly

costra *f* MED scab

costumbre *f* custom; *de una persona* habit; *de* ~ usual

costura f sewing; **costurear** <1a> v/t L.Am. sew

cotarro m: **manejar el ~** F be the boss F

cotejar <1a> v/t compare

cotidiano adj daily

cotilla m/f F gossip; **cotillear** <1a> v/i F gossip

cotizado adj COM quoted; fig sought-after; **cotizar** <1f> v/i pay social security, Br pay National Insurance; de acciones, bonos be listed (**a** at); ~ **en bolsa** be listed on the stock exchange

coto[1] m: ~ **de caza** hunting reserve; **poner ~ a algo** fig put a stop to sth

coto[2] m S.Am. MED goiter, Br goitre

cotorra f ZO parrot; F persona motormouth F

coyote m ZO coyote

coyuntura f situation; ANAT joint

C.P. abr (= **código postal**) zip code, Br post code

cráneo m ANAT skull, cranium

cráter m crater

creación f creation; **creador** m, ~a f creator; **crear** <1a> v/t create; empresa set up; **creativo** adj creative

crecer <2d> v/i grow; **creces** fpl: **con ~** superar by a comfortable margin; pagar with interest; **creciente** adj growing; luna waxing; **crecimiento** m growth

credencial f document

credibilidad f credibility; **crédito** m COM credit; **a ~** on credit; **no dar ~ a sus oídos / ojos** F not believe one's ears / eyes

credo m REL, fig creed; **crédulo** adj credulous; **creencia** f belief; **creer** <2e> 1 v/i believe (**en** in) 2 v/t think; (dar por cierto) believe; **no creo que esté aquí** I don't think he's here; **¡ya lo creo!** F you bet! F 3 v/r ~**se**: ~**se que ...** believe that ...; **se cree muy lista** she thinks she's very clever

crema f GASTR cream

cremallera f zipper, Br zip; TÉC rack

crematorio m crematorium

cremoso adj creamy

crepe f GASTR crêpe, pancake

crepitar <1a> v/i crackle

crepúsculo m tb fig twilight

cresta f crest

cretino m, -a f F cretin F, moron F

creyente 1 adj: **ser ~** REL believe in God 2 m REL believer

creyó vb → **creer**

cría f acción breeding; de zorro, león cub; de perro puppy; de gato kitten; de oveja lamb; **sus ~s** her young; **criada** f maid; **criado** m servant; **criar** <1c> 1 v/t niños raise, bring up; animales breed 2 v/r ~**se** grow up; **criatura** f creature; ⊢ (niño) baby, child

crimen m crime; **criminal** m/f & adj criminal

crío m, -a f F kid F

criollo 1 adj Creole 2 m, -a f Creole

cripta f crypt

crisantemo m BOT chrysanthemum

crisis f inv crisis

crismas m inv Christmas card

crispar <1a> v/t irritate; ~**le a alguien los nervios** get on s.o.'s nerves

cristal m crystal; (vidrio) glass; (lente) lens; de ventana pane; ~ **líquido** liquid crystal; **cristalizar** <1f> v/i crystallize; de idea, proyecto jell

cristianismo m Christianity; **cristiano** 1 adj Christian 2 m, -a f Christian

Cristo Christ

criterio m criterion; (juicio) judg(e)ment

crítica f criticism; **muchas ~s** a lot of criticism; **criticar** <1g> v/t criticize; **crítico** 1 adj critical 2 m, -a f critic

Croacia Croatia

crol m crawl

cromo m QUÍM chrome; (estampa) picture card, trading card

crónica f chronicle; en periódico report

crónico adj MED chronic

cronológico adj chronological

cronometrar <1a> v/t DEP time; **cronómetro** m stopwatch

croqueta *f* GASTR croquette

croquis *m inv* sketch

cross *m* DEP cross-country (running); **con motocicletas** motocross

cruce *m* cross; **de carreteras** crossroads *sg*; **~ en las líneas** TELEC crossed line

crucero *m* cruise

crucial *adj* crucial

crucificar <1g> *v/t* crucify; **crucifijo** *m* crucifix; **crucigrama** *m* crossword

crudo 1 *adj alimento* raw; *fig* harsh **2** *m* crude (oil)

cruel *adj* cruel

cruento *adj* bloody

crujiente *adj* GASTR crunchy; **crujir** <3a> *v/i* creak; *al arder* crackle; *de grava* crunch

cruz *f* cross; **Cruz Roja** Red Cross; **cruzar** <1f> **1** *v/t* cross **2** *v/r* **~se** pass one another; **~se de brazos** cross one's arms; **~se con alguien** pass s.o.

c.s.f. *abr* (= **costo, seguro, flete**) cif (= cost, insurance, freight)

cta, c.ta *abr* (= **cuenta**) A/C (= account)

cuaderno *m* notebook; EDU exercise book

cuadra *f* stable; *L.Am.* (*manzana*) block; **cuadrado 1** *adj* square **2** *m* square; **al ~** squared

cuadrilla *f* squad, team

cuadro *m* painting; (*grabado*) picture; (*tabla*) table; DEP team; **~ de mandos** *or* **de instrumentos** AUTO dashboard; **de** *or* **a ~s** checked; **cuádruple, cuadruplo** *m* quadruple

cuajada *f* GASTR curd; **cuajar** <1a> *v/i de nieve* settle; *fig: de idea, proyecto etc* come together, jell F

cuajo *m:* **de ~** by the roots

cual 1 *pron rel:* **el ~, la ~** *etc cosa* which; *persona* who; **por lo ~** (and) so **2** *adv* like

cuál *interr* which (one)

cualidad *f* quality

cualificar <1g> *v/t* qualify

cualquier *adj* any; **~ día** any day; **~**

cosa anything; **de ~ modo** *or* **forma** anyway; **cualquiera** *pron persona* anyone, anybody; *cosa* any (one); **un ~** a nobody; **¡~ lo comprende!** nobody can understand it!

cuando 1 *conj* when; *condicional* if; **~ quieras** whenever you want **2** *adv* when; **de ~ en ~** from time to time; **~ menos** at least

cuándo *interr* when

cuantía *f* amount, quantity; *fig* importance; **cuantificar** <1g> *v/t* quantify; **cuantioso** *adj* substantial

cuanto 1 *adj:* **~ dinero quieras** as much money as you want; **unos ~s chavales** a few boys **2** *pron* all, everything; **se llevó ~ podía** she took all *o* everything she could; **le dio ~ necesitaba** he gave her everything she needed; **unas ~as** a few; **todo ~** everything **3** *adv:* **~ antes, mejor** the sooner the better; **en ~** as soon as; **en ~ a** as for

cuánto 1 *interr adj* how much; *pl* how many; **¿~ café?** how much coffee?; **¿~s huevos?** how many eggs? **2** *pron* how much; *pl* how many; **¿~ necesita Vd.?** how much do you need?; **¿~s ha dicho?** how many did you say?; **¿a ~ están?** how much are they?; **¿a ~s estamos?** what's the date today? **3** *exclamaciones:* **¡cuánta gente había!** there were so many people!; **¡~ me alegro!** I'm so pleased!

cuarenta *adj* forty

Cuaresma *f* Lent

cuartear <1a> **1** *v/t* cut up, quarter **2** *v/r* **~se** crack

cuartel *m* barracks *pl*; **~ general** headquarters *pl*; **cuartelazo** *m* *L.Am.* military uprising; **cuartilla** *f* sheet of paper

cuarto 1 *adj* fourth **2** *m* (*habitación*) room; (*parte*) quarter; **~ de baño** bathroom; **~ de estar** living room; **~ de hora** quarter of an hour; **~ de kilo** quarter of a kilo; **de tres al ~** F third-rate; **las diez y ~** quarter past ten, quarter after ten; **las tres menos ~** a quarter to *o* of three

cuarzo *m* quartz

cuatro *adj* four; **~ gotas** F a few drops; **cuatrocientos** *adj* four hundred

cuba *f*: **estar como una ~** F be plastered F

Cuba *f* Cuba; **cubano 1** *adj* Cuban **2** *m*, **-a** *f* Cuban

cubierta *f* MAR deck; AUTO tire, *Br* tyre; **cubierto 1** *part* → **cubrir 2** *m* piece of cutlery; **en la mesa** place setting; **~s** *pl* cutlery *sg*

cubito *m*: **~ de hielo** ice cube; **cubo** *m* cube; *(recipiente)* bucket; **~ de la basura** *dentro* garbage can, *Br* rubbish bin; *fuera* garbage can, *Br* dustbin

cubrir <3a; *part* **cubierto**> **1** *v/t* cover *(de* with) **2** *v/r* **~se** cover o.s.

cucaracha *f* ZO cockroach

cuchara *f* spoon; **meter su ~** *L.Am.* F stick one's oar in F; **cucharada** *f* spoonful; **cucharilla** *f* teaspoon; **cucharón** *m* ladle

cuchichear <1a> *v/i* whisper

cuchilla *f* razor blade; **cuchillo** *m* knife

cuclillas: **en ~** squatting

cuco 1 *m* ZO cuckoo; **reloj de ~** cuckoo clock **2** *adj (astuto)* sharp

cucurucho *m* *de papel etc* cone; *sombrero* pointed hat

cuece *vb* → **cocer**

cuelgo *vb* → **colgar**

cuello *m* ANAT neck; *de camisa etc* collar

cuelo *vb* → **colar**

cuenca *f* GEOG basin; **cuenco** *m* bowl

cuenta *f (cálculo)* sum; *de restaurante* check, *Br* bill; COM account; **~ atrás** countdown; **~ bancaria** bank account; **~ corriente** checking account, *Br* current account; **más de la ~** too much; **caer en la ~** realize; **darse ~ de algo** realize sth; **pedir ~s a alguien** ask s.o. for an explanation; **perder la ~** lose count; **tener** *or* **tomar en ~** take into account; **corre por mi/su ~** I'll/he'll pay for it

cuentagotas *m inv* dropper

cuentakilómetros *m inv* odometer, *Br* mileometer

cuentista *m/f* story-teller; F *(mentiroso)* fibber F

cuento *m* (short) story; *(pretexto)* excuse; **~ chino** F tall story F; **venir a ~** be relevant

cuerda *f* rope; *de guitarra, violín* string; **dar ~ al reloj** wind the clock up; **dar ~ a algo** *fig* F string sth out F; **~s vocales** ANAT vocal chords

cuerdo *adj* sane; *(sensato)* sensible

cuerno *m* horn; *de caracol* feeler; **irse al ~** F fall through, be wrecked; **poner los ~s a alguien** F be unfaithful to s.o.

cuero *m* leather; *Rpl (fuete)* whip; **en ~s** F naked

cuerpo *m* body; *de policía* force; **~ diplomático** diplomatic corps *sg*; **a ~ de rey** like a king; **en ~ y alma** body and soul

cuervo *m* ZO raven, crow

cuesta *f* slope; **~ abajo** downhill; **~ arriba** uphill; **a ~s** on one's back

cuestión *f* question; *(asunto)* matter, question; **en ~ de ...** in a matter of ...; **cuestionar** <1a> *v/t* question; **cuestionario** *m* questionnaire

cueva *f* cave

cuidado *m* care; **¡~!** look out!; **andar con ~** tread carefully; **me tiene sin ~** I could *o Br* couldn't care less; **tener ~** be careful; **cuidadora** *f Méx* nursemaid; **cuidadoso** *adj* careful

cuidar <1a> **1** *v/t* look after, take care of **2** *v/i*: **~ de** look after, take care of **3** *v/r* **~se** look after o.s., take care of o.s.; **~se de hacer algo** take care to do sth

culebra *f* ZO snake

culebrón *m* TV soap

culinario *adj* cooking *atr*, culinary

culminación *f* culmination; **culminante** *adj*: **punto ~** peak, climax; **culminar** <1a> **1** *v/i* culminate *(en* in); *fig* reach a peak *o* climax **2** *v/t* finish

culo *m* ∨ ass ∨, *Br* arse ∨; F butt F, *Br* bum F; **ser ~ de mal asiento** *fig* F be restless, have ants in one's pants F

culpa f fault; **echar la ~ de algo a alguien** blame s.o. for sth; **ser por ~ de alguien** be s.o.'s fault; **tener la ~** be to blame (**de** for); **culpabilidad** f guilt; **culpable 1** adj guilty **2** m/f culprit; **culpar** <1a> v/t: ~ **a alguien de algo** blame s.o. for sth

cultivar <1a> v/t AGR grow; tierra farm; fig cultivate; **cultivo** m AGR crop; BIO culture; **culto 1** adj educated **2** m worship; **cultura** f culture; **cultural** adj cultural; **un nivel ~ muy pobre** a very poor standard of education

cumbre f tb POL summit

cumpleaños m inv birthday

cumplido m compliment; **no andarse con ~s** not stand on ceremony

cumplimentar <1k> v/t trámite carry out

cumplir <3a> **1** v/t orden carry out; promesa fulfill; condena serve; ~ **diez años** reach the age of ten, turn ten **2** v/i: ~ **con algo** carry sth out; ~ **con su deber** do one's duty; **te invita sólo por ~** he's only inviting you out of politeness **3** v/r **~se** de plazo expire

cúmulo m (montón) pile, heap

cuna f tb fig cradle

cundir <3a> v/i spread; (dar mucho de sí) go a long way

cuneta f ditch

cuñada f sister-in-law; **cuñado** m brother-in-law

cuota f share; de club, asociación fee

cupón m coupon

cúpula f dome; esp POL leadership

cura 1 m priest **2** f cure; (tratamiento) treatment; Méx, C.Am. F hangover; **tener ~** be curable; **curado** adj Méx, C.Am. F drunk; **curandero** m, **-a** f faith healer; **curar** <1a> **1** v/t tb GASTR cure; (tratar) treat; herida dress; pieles tan **2** v/i MED recover (**de** from) **3** v/r **~se** MED recover; Méx, C.Am. F get drunk

curda f: **agarrarse una ~** F get plastered F

curiosidad f curiosity; **curioso 1** adj curious; (raro) curious, odd, strange **2** m, **-a** f onlooker

curita f L.Am. Band-Aid®, Br Elastoplast®

currar <1a> v/i F work

currículum vitae m résumé, Br CV, Br curriculum vitae

curry m GASTR curry

cursi adj F persona affected

cursillo m short course

cursiva f italics pl

curso m course; ~ **a distancia** or **por correspondencia** correspondence course; **en el ~ de** in the course of

cursor m INFOR cursor

curtir <3a> v/t tan; fig harden

curva f curve; **curvo** adj curved

cúspide f de montaña summit; de fama etc height

custodia f JUR custody; **custodiar** <1b> v/t guard

cususa f C.Am. corn liquor

cutre adj F shabby, dingy

cuyo, -a adj whose

CV m resumé, Br CV

D

D. abr (= **Don**) Mr

Dª. abr (= **Doña**) Mrs

dactilar adj finger atr

dadivoso adj generous

dado¹ m dice

dado² 1 part → **dar 2** adj given; **ser ~**

a algo be given to sth **3** *conj*: **~ que** since, given that

dalia *f* BOT dahlia

daltónico *adj* colo(u)r-blind; **daltonismo** *m* colo(u)r-blindness

dama *f* lady; **~ de honor** bridesmaid; **(juego de) ~s** checkers *sg*, *Br* draughts *sg*

damasco *m* damask; *L.Am. fruta* apricot

damnificado 1 *adj* affected **2** *m*, **-a** *f* victim

danés 1 *adj* Danish **2** *m*, **-esa** *f* Dane

danza *f* dance; **danzar** <1f> *v/i* dance

dañar <1a> **1** *v/t* harm; *cosa* damage **2** *v/r* **~se** harm o.s.; *de un objeto* get damaged; **dañino** *adj* harmful; *fig* malicious; **daño** *m* harm; *a un objeto* damage; **hacer ~** hurt; **~s** *pl* damage *sg*; **~s y perjuicios** damages

dar <1r; *part* **dado**> **1** *v/t* give; *beneficio* yield; *luz* give off; *fiesta* give, have; **~ un golpe a** hit; **~ un salto/una patada/miedo** jump/kick/frighten; **el jamón me dió sed** the ham made me thirsty **2** *v/i*: **dame** give it to me, give me it; **~ a de ventana** look onto; **~ con algo** come across sth; **~ de comer a alguien** feed s.o.; **~ de beber a alguien** give s.o. something to drink; **~ de sí** *de material* stretch, give; **le dio por insultar a su madre** F she started insulting her mother; **¡qué más da!** what does it matter!; **da igual** it doesn't matter **3** *v/r* **~se** *de una situación* arise; **~se a algo** take to sth; **esto se me da bien** I'm good at this; **dárselas de algo** make o.s. out to be sth, claim to be sth

dardo *m* dart

datar <1a> *v/i*: **~ de** date from

dátil *m* BOT date

dato *m* piece of information; **~s** *pl* information *sg*, data *sg*; **~s personales** personal details

D.C. *abr* (= **después de Cristo**) AD (= Anno Domini)

dcho., dcha *abr* (= **derecho, derecha**) r (= right)

d. de J.C. *abr* (= **después de**

Jesucristo) AD (= Anno Domini)

de *prp* ◊ *origen* from; **~ Nueva York** from New York; **~ ... a** from ... to ◊ *posesión* of; **el coche ~ mi amigo** my friend's car ◊ *material* (made) of; **un anillo ~ oro** a gold ring ◊ *contenido* of; **un vaso ~ agua** a glass of water ◊ *cualidad:* **una mujer ~ 20 años** a 20 year old woman ◊ *causa* with; **temblaba ~ miedo** she was shaking with fear ◊ *hora:* **~ noche** at night, by night; **~ día** by day ◊ *en calidad de* as; **trabajar ~ albañil** work as a bricklayer ◊ *agente* by; **~ Goya** by Goya ◊ *condición* if; **~ haberlo sabido** if I'd known

dé *vb* → **dar**

deambular <1a> *v/i* wander around

debajo 1 *adv* underneath **2** *prp*: **(por) ~ de** under; **un grado por ~ de lo normal** one degree below normal

debate *m* debate, discussion; **debatir** <3a> **1** *v/t* debate, discuss **2** *v/i* struggle **3** *v/r* **~se**: **~se entre la vida y la muerte** fight for one's life

deber 1 *m* duty; **~es** *pl* homework *sg* **2** <2a> *v/t* owe **3** *v/i* *en presente* must, have to; *en pretérito* should have; *en futuro* (will) have to; *en condicional* should; **debe de tener quince años** he must be about 15 **4** *v/r* **~se**: **~se a** be due to, be caused by; **debido 1** *part* → **deber 2** *adj*: **como es ~** properly; **~ a** owing to, on account of

débil *adj* weak; **debilitar** <1a> **1** *v/t* weaken **2** *v/r* **~se** weaken, become weak; *de salud* deteriorate

debut *m* debut

década *f* decade

decadencia *f* decadence; *de un imperio* decline; **decaer** <2o; *part* **decaído**> *v/i tb fig* decline; *de rendimiento* fall off, decline; *de salud* deteriorate; **decaído 1** *part* → **decaer 2** *adj fig* depressed, down F

decantarse <1a> *v/r*: **~ por** opt for

decapitar <1a> *v/t* behead, decapitate

decenio *m* decade

decente *adj* decent

decepción *f* disappointment; **decepcionado** *adj* disappointed; **decepcionante** *adj* disappointing; **decepcionar** <1a> *v/t* disappoint

decidido 1 *part* → **decidir 2** *adj* decisive; **estar ~** be determined (**a** to); **decidir** <3a> **1** *v/t* decide **2** *v/r* **~se** make up one's mind, decide

decimal *adj* decimal *atr*; **décimo 1** *adj* tenth **2** *m de lotería* share of a lottery ticket

decir <3p; *part* **dicho**> **1** *v/t* say; (*contar*) tell; **querer ~** mean; **~ que sí** say yes; **~ que no** say no; **es ~** in other words; **no es rico, que digamos** let's say he's not rich; **¡no me digas!** you're kidding!; **¡quién lo diría!** who would believe it!; **se dice que ...** they say that ..., it's said that ... **2** *v/i*: **¡diga!, ¡dígame!** *Esp* TELEC hello

decisión *f* decision; *fig* decisiveness; **decisivo** *adj* critical, decisive

declaración *f* declaration; **~ de la renta** *o* **de impuestos** tax return; **prestar ~** JUR testify, give evidence; **declarar** <1a> **1** *v/t* state; **bienes** declare; **~ culpable** find guilty **2** *v/i* JUR give evidence **3** *v/r* **~se** declare o.s.; *de incendio* break out; **~se a alguien** declare one's love for s.o.

declinar <1a> *v/t* & *v/i* decline

declive *m fig* decline; **en ~** in decline

decodificador *m* → **descodificador**, **decodificar** <1g> *v/t* → **descodificar**

decolaje *m L.Am.* takeoff; **decolar** <1a> *v/i L.Am.* take off

decolorar <1a> *v/t* bleach

decoración *f* decoration; **decorado** *m* TEA set; **decorador** *m*, **~a** *f*: **~ (de interiores)** interior decorator; **decorar** <1a> *v/t* decorate; **decorativo** *adj* decorative

decreciente *adj* decreasing, diminishing

decrépito *adj* decrepit

decretar <1a> *v/t* order, decree; **decreto** *m* decree

dedicación *f* dedication; **dedicar** <1g> **1** *v/t* dedicate; *esfuerzo* devote **2** *v/r* **~se** devote o.s. (**a** to); **¿a qué se dedica?** what do you do (for a living)?; **dedicatoria** *f* dedication

dedillo *m*: **conocer algo al ~** F know sth like the back of one's hand; **saber algo al ~** F know sth off by heart

dedo *m* finger; **~ del pie** toe; **~ gordo** thumb; **~ índice** forefinger; **no tiene dos ~s de frente** F he doesn't have much commonsense

deducción *f* deduction; **deducir** <3o> *v/t* deduce; COM deduct

defecar <1g> *v/i* defecate

defecto *m* defect; *moral* fault; INFOR default; **defectuoso** *adj* defective, faulty

defender <2g> **1** *v/t* defend **2** *v/r* **~se** defend o.s. (**de** against); *fig* F manage, get by; **~se del frío** ward off the cold

defenestrar <1a> *v/t fig* F oust

defensa 1 *f* MIL, DEP defense, *Br* defence; *L.Am.* AUTO fender, *Br* bumper; **~s** MED defenses, *Br* defences **2** *m/f* DEP defender; **defensivo** *adj* defensive; **defensor** *m*, **~a** *f* defender, champion; JUR defense counsel, *Br* defending counsel; **~ del pueblo** *en España* ombudsman

deficiente 1 *adj* deficient; (*insatisfactorio*) inadequate **2** *m/f* handicapped person; **déficit** *m* deficit

definición *f* definition; **de alta ~** TV high definition; **definir** <3a> **1** *v/t* define **2** *v/r* **~se** come down (**por** in favor of); **definitivo** *adj* definitive; *respuesta* definite; **en ~a** all in all

deforestación *f* deforestation

deformar <1a> *v/t* distort; MED deform; **deforme** *adj* deformed

defraudar <1a> *v/t* disappoint; (*estafar*) defraud; **~ a Hacienda** evade taxes

defunción *f* death, demise *fml*

degenerar <1a> *v/i* degenerate (**en** into)

degollar <1n> *v/t* cut the throat of

degradante *adj* degrading; **degra-**

dar <1a> **1** *v/t* degrade; MIL demote; PINT gradate **2** *v/r* **~se** demean o.s.

degustar <1a> *v/t* taste

dejadez *f* slovenliness; (*negligencia*) neglect

dejar <1a> **1** *v/t* leave; (*permitir*) let, allow; (*prestar*) lend; *beneficios* yield; *déjame en la esquina* drop me at the corner; *~ para mañana* leave until tomorrow; *~ caer algo* drop sth **2** *v/i*: *~ de hacer algo* (*parar*) stop doing sth; *no deja de fastidiarme* he keeps (on) annoying me **3** *v/r* **~se** let o.s. go; *~se llevar* let o.s. be carried along

del *prp* **de** *y art* **el**

delantal *m* apron

delante *adv* in front; (*más avanzado*) ahead; (*enfrente*) opposite; *por ~* ahead; *se abrocha por ~* it does up at the front; *tener algo por ~* have sth ahead of o in front of one; *~ de* in front of; *el asiento de ~* the front seat; **delantera** *f* DEP forward line; *llevar la ~* be ahead of, lead; **delantero** *m*, **-a** *f* DEP forward

delatar <1a> *v/t*: *~ a alguien* inform on s.o.; *fig* give s.o. away

delegación *f* delegation; (*oficina*) local office; *~ de Hacienda* tax office; **delegado** *m*, **-a** *f* delegate; COM representative; **delegar** <1h> *v/t* delegate

deleitar <1a> **1** *v/t* delight **2** *v/r* **~se** take delight

deletrear <1a> *v/t* spell

delfín *m* ZO dolphin

delgado *adj* slim; *lámina, placa* thin

deliberado *adj* deliberate; **deliberar** <1a> *v/i* deliberate (*sobre* on)

delicadeza *f* gentleness; *de acabado, tallado* delicacy; (*tacto*) tact; **delicado** *adj* delicate

delicia *f* delight; *hacer las ~s de alguien* delight s.o.; **delicioso** *adj* delightful; *comida* delicious

delimitar <1a> *v/t* delimit

delincuente *m/f* criminal

delineante *m/f* draftsman, *Br* draughtsman; *mujer* draftswoman, *Br* draughtswoman; **delinear** <1a> *v/t* draft; *fig* draw up

delirar <1a> *v/i* be delirious; *¡tú deliras! fig* you must be crazy!; **delirio** *m* MED delirium; *tener ~ por el fútbol fig* be mad about soccer; *~s de grandeza* delusions of grandeur

delito *m* offense, *Br* offence

demacrado *adj* haggard

demagógico *adj* demagogic

demanda *f* demand (*de* for); JUR lawsuit, claim; **demandar** <1a> *v/t* JUR sue

demás 1 *adj* remaining **2** *adv*: *lo ~* the rest; *los ~* the rest, the others; *por lo ~* apart from that; **demasiado 1** *adj* too much; *antes de pl* too many; *-a gente* too many people; *hace ~ calor* it's too hot **2** *adv antes de adj, adv* too; *con verbo* too much

demencia *f* MED dementia; *fig* madness; *~ senil* MED senile dementia; **demencial** *adj fig* crazy, mad; **demente 1** *adj* demented, crazy **2** *m/f* mad person

democracia *f* democracy; **demócrata 1** *adj* democratic **2** *m/f* democrat; **democrático** *adj* democratic

demografía *f* demographics

demoler <2h> *v/t* demolish

demoniaco, demoníaco *adj* demonic; **demonio** *m* demon; *¡~s!* F hell! F, damn! F

demora *f* delay; *sin ~* without delay; **demorar** <1a> **1** *v/i* stay on; *L.Am.* (*tardar*) be late; *no demores* don't be long **2** *v/t* delay **3** *v/r* **~se** be delayed; *¿cuánto se demora de Concepción a Santiago?* how long does it take to get from Concepción to Santiago?

demostración *f* proof; *de método* demonstration; *de fuerza, sentimiento* show; **demostrar** <1m> *v/t* prove; (*enseñar*) demonstrate; (*mostrar*) show

denegar <1h & 1k> *v/t* refuse

denigrante *adj* degrading; *artículo* denigrating; **denigrar** <1a> *v/t* degrade; (*criticar*) denigrate

denominación f name; ~ **de origen** guarantee of quality of a wine; **denominador** m: ~ **común** fig common denominator; **denominar** <1a> **1** v/t designate **2** v/r ~**se** be called

denotar <1a> v/t show, indicate

densidad f density; **denso** adj bosque dense; fig weighty

dentadura f: ~ **postiza** false teeth pl, dentures pl; **dental** adj dental; **dentera** f: **darle** ~ **a alguien** set s.o.'s teeth on edge; **dentífrico** m toothpaste; **dentista** m/f dentist

dentro 1 adv inside; **por** ~ inside; **de** ~ from inside **2** ~ **de** en espacio in, inside; en tiempo in, within

denuncia f report; **poner una** ~ make a formal complaint; **denunciar** <1b> v/t report; fig condemn, denounce

departamento m department; L.Am. (apartamento) apartment, Br flat

depender <2a> v/i depend (**de** on); ~ **de alguien** en una jerarquía report to s.o.; **eso depende** that all depends; **dependiente 1** adj dependent **2** m, **-a** f sales clerk, Br shop assistant

depilación f hair removal; con cera waxing; con pinzas plucking; **depilar** <1a> v/t con cera wax; con pinzas pluck

deplorar <1a> v/t deplore

deportar <1a> v/t deport

deporte m sport; **deportista** m/f sportsman; mujer sportswoman

depositar <1a> v/t tb fig put, place; dinero deposit (**en** in); **depósito** m COM deposit; (almacén) store; de agua, AUTO tank; ~ **de cadáveres** morgue, Br mortuary

depravado adj depraved; **depravar** <1a> v/t deprave

depreciación f depreciation; **depreciar** <1b> **1** v/t lower the value of **2** v/r ~**se** depreciate, lose value

depredador 1 adj predatory **2** m ZO predator

depresión f MED depression; **deprimente** adj depressing; **deprimir** <3a> **1** v/t depress **2** v/r ~**se** get depressed

depuradora f purifier; **depurar** <1a> v/t purify; agua treat; POL purge

derecha f tb POL right; **la** ~ the right(-hand); **a la** ~ posición on the right; dirección to the right

derecho 1 adj lado right; (recto) straight; C.Am. fig straight, honest **2** adv straight **3** m (privilegio) right; JUR law; **del** ~ on the right side; ~ **de asilo** right to asylum; ~**s de autor** royalties; ~**s humanos** human rights; ~ **de voto** right to vote; **no hay** ~ it's not fair, it's not right; **tener** ~ **a** have a right to **4** mpl: ~**s** fees; ~**s de inscripción** registration fee sg

derechura f straightness; C.Am., Pe (suerte) luck; **en** ~ straight away

deriva f: **ir a la** ~ MAR, fig drift; **derivar** <1a> **1** v/i derive (**de** from); de barco drift **2** v/r ~**se** be derived (**de** from)

dermatólogo m, **-a** f dermatologist

derogar <1h> v/t repeal

derramar <1a> **1** v/t spill; luz, sangre shed; (esparcir) scatter **2** v/r ~**se** spill; de gente scatter; **derrame** m MED: ~ **cerebral** stroke

derrapar <1a> v/i AUTO skid

derrengado adj exhausted

derretir <3l> **1** v/t melt **2** v/r ~**se** melt; fig be besotted (**por** with)

derribar <1a> v/t edificio, persona knock down; avión shoot down; POL bring down

derrocar <1g> v/t POL overthrow

derrochador m, **-a** f spendthrift; **derrochar** <1a> v/t waste; salud, felicidad exude, burst with; **derroche** m waste

derrota f defeat; **derrotar** <1a> v/t MIL defeat; DEP beat, defeat

derruir <3g> v/t edificio demolish

derrumbar <1a> **1** v/t knock down **2** v/r ~**se** collapse, fall down; de una persona go to pieces

desabrido adj (soso) tasteless; persona surly; tiempo unpleasant

desabrochar <1a> v/t undo, unfasten

desacato m JUR contempt

desaceleración f deceleration

desacertado adj misguided

desaconsejar <1a> v/t advise against

desacreditado adj discredited; **desacreditar** <1a> v/t discredit

desactivar <1a> v/t bomba etc deactivate

desacuerdo m disagreement; **estar en ~ con** disagree with

desafiar <1c> v/t challenge; peligro defy

desafinar <1a> v/i MÚS be out of tune

desafío m challenge; al peligro defiance

desafortunado adj unfortunate, unlucky

desagradable adj unpleasant, disagreeable; **desagradar** <1a> v/i: **me desagrada tener que ...** I dislike having to ...; **desagradecido** adj ungrateful; **una tarea -a** a thankless task; **desagrado** m displeasure

desagravio m apology

desagüe m drain; acción drainage; (cañería) drainpipe

desahogar <1h> **1** v/t sentimiento vent **2** v/r ~**se** fig F let off steam F, get it out of one's system F; **desahogo** m comfort; **con ~** comfortably

desahuciar <1b> v/t: ~ **a alguien** declare s.o. terminally ill; (inquilino) evict s.o.

desairar <1a> v/t snub

desajustar <1a> v/t tornillo, pieza loosen; mecanismo, instrumento affect, throw out of balance; **desajuste** m disruption; COM imbalance

desalentar <1k> v/t discourage; **desaliento** m discouragement

desalinización f desalination

desaliñado adj slovenly

desalojar <1a> v/t ante peligro evacuate; (desahuciar) evict; (vaciar) vacate

desamparar <1a> v/t: ~ **a alguien** abandon s.o.

desangelado adj lugar soulless

desangrarse <1a> v/r bleed to death

desanimar <1a> **1** v/t discourage, dishearten **2** v/r ~**se** become discouraged o disheartened; **desánimo** m discouragement

desapacible adj nasty, unpleasant

desaparecer <2d> **1** v/i disappear, vanish **2** v/t L.Am. disappear F; **desaparecido** m, -a f L.Am.: **un ~** one of the disappeared; **desaparición** f disappearance

desapego m indifference; (distancia) distance, coolness

desapercibido adj unnoticed; **pasar ~** go unnoticed

desaprensivo adj unscrupulous

desaprobar <1m> v/t disapprove of

desaprovechar <1a> v/t oportunidad waste

desarmado adj unarmed; **desarmar** <1a> v/t MIL disarm; TÉC take to pieces, dismantle; **desarme** m MIL disarmament

desarraigo m fig rootlessness

desarreglar <1a> v/t make untidy; horario disrupt

desarrollar <1a> **1** v/t develop; tema explain; trabajo carry out **2** v/r ~**se** develop, evolve; (ocurrir) take place; **desarrollo** m development

desarticular <1a> v/t banda criminal break up; MED dislocate

desaseado adj F scruffy

desasirse <3a> v/r get free, free o.s.

desasosiego m disquiet, unease

desastre m tb fig disaster; **desastroso** adj disastrous

desatar <1a> **1** v/t untie; fig unleash **2** v/r ~**se** de animal, persona get free; de cordón come undone; fig be unleashed, break out

desatascar <1g> v/t unblock

desatender <2g> v/t neglect; (ignorar) ignore

desatino m mistake

desatornillador m esp L.Am. screwdriver; **desatornillar** <1a> v/t unscrew

desatrancar <1g> v/t *cañería* un-block

desavenencia f disagreement

desaventajado adj unfavo(u)rable

desayunar <1a> **1** v/i have break-fast **2** v/t: **~ algo** have sth for break-fast; **desayuno** m breakfast

desazón f (*ansiedad*) uneasiness, anxiety; **desazonar** <1a> v/t worry, make anxious

desbancar <1g> v/t fig displace, take the place of

desbandarse <1a> v/r disband; *de un grupo de personas* scatter

desbarajuste m mess

desbaratar <1a> *planes* ruin; *organización* disrupt

desbarrancar <1g> *L.Am.* **1** v/t push over the edge of a cliff **2** v/r **~se** go over the edge of a cliff

desbocarse <1g> v/r *de un caballo* bolt

desbordante adj *energía, entusiasmo etc* boundless; **~ de** bursting with, overflowing with; **desbordar** <1a> **1** v/t *de un río* overflow, burst; *de un multitud* break through; *de un acontecimiento* overwhelm; *fig* exceed **2** v/i overflow **3** v/r **~se** *de un río* burst its banks, overflow; *fig* get out of control

descabellado adj: **idea -a** F hare-brained idea F; **descabellar** <1a> v/t TAUR *kill with a knife-thrust in the neck*; **descabello** m *fatal knife thrust*

descafeinado adj decaffeinated; *fig* watered-down

descalabro m calamity, disaster

descalificar <1g> v/t disqualify

descalzarse <1f> v/r take one's shoes off; **descalzo** adj barefoot

descaminado adj fig misguided; **andar** or **ir ~** be on the wrong track

descamisado adj shirtless; *fig* ragged

descampado m open ground

descansar <1a> v/i rest, have a rest; **¡que descanses!** sleep well; **descansillo** m landing; **descanso** m rest; DEP half-time; TEA interval;

sin ~ without a break

descapotable m AUTO convertible

descarado adj rude, impertinent

descarga f EL, MIL discharge; *de mercancías* unloading; **descargar** <1h> v/t *arma, EL* discharge; *fig: ira etc* take out (**en, sobre** on); *mercancías* unload; *de responsabilidad, culpa* clear (**de** of)

descaro m nerve

descarriado adj: **ir ~** go astray

descarrilar <1a> v/t derail

descartar <1a> v/t rule out

descastado adj cold, uncaring

descender <2g> **1** v/i *para indicar alejamiento* go down, descend; *para indicar acercamiento* come down, descend; *fig* go down, decrease, diminish; **~ de** descend from **2** v/t *escalera* go down; *para indicar acercamiento* come down; **descendiente** **1** adj descended **2** m/f descendant; **descenso** m *de precio etc* drop; *de montaña,* AVIA descent; DEP relegation; **la prueba de ~ en esquí** the downhill (race *o* competition)

descentralizar <1f> v/t decentralize

descentrar <1a> v/t fig shake

descifrar <1a> v/t decipher; *fig* work out

descodificación f decoding; **descodificador** m decoder; **descodificar** <1g> v/t decode

descolgar <1h & 1m> **1** v/t take down; *teléfono* pick up **2** v/r **~se** *por una cuerda* lower o.s.; *de un grupo* break away

descollar <1m> v/i stand out (**sobre** among)

descolonización f decolonization

descolorido adj faded; *fig* colo(u)rless

descomponer <2r; *part* **descompuesto**> **1** v/t (*dividir*) break down; (*pudrir*) cause to decompose; *L.Am.* (*romper*) break **2** v/r **~se** (*pudrirse*) decompose, rot; TÉC break down; *Rpl* (*emocionarse*) break down (in tears); **se le descompuso la cara** he turned pale;

93   desear

descomposición f breaking down; *putrefacción* decomposition; (*diarrea*) diarrh(o)ea; **descompuesto 1** *part* → **descomponer 2** *adj alimento* rotten; *cadáver* decomposed; *persona* upset; *L.Am.* tipsy; *L.Am. máquina* broken down

descomunal *adj* huge, enormous

desconcertar <1k> v/t *a persona* disconcert

desconchado, desconchón m place where the paint is peeling; *en porcelana* chip

desconcierto m uncertainty

desconectar <1a> **1** v/t EL disconnect **2** v/i fig switch off **3** v/r ~**se** fig lose touch (*de* with)

desconfiar <1c> v/i be mistrustful (*de* of), be suspicious (*de* of)

descongelar <1a> v/t *comida* thaw, defrost; *refrigerador* defrost; *precios* unfreeze

descongestionar <1a> v/t MED clear; ~ **el tráfico** relieve traffic congestion

desconocer <2d> v/t not know; **desconocido 1** *adj* unknown **2** m, **-a** f stranger

desconsiderado *adj* inconsiderate

desconsolado *adj* inconsolable; **desconsuelo** m grief

descontado 1 *part* → **descontar 2** *adj*: **dar por** ~ take for granted; **por** ~ certainly

descontaminar <1a> v/t decontaminate

descontar <1m> v/t COM deduct, take off; fig exclude

descontento 1 *adj* dissatisfied **2** m dissatisfaction

descontrol m chaos; **descontrolarse** <1a> v/r get out of control

desconvocar <1g> v/t call off

descorazonar <1a> **1** v/t discourage **2** v/r ~**se** get discouraged

descorchar <1a> v/t *botella* uncork

descortés *adj* impolite, rude

descoserse <2a> v/r *de costura, dobladillo etc* come unstitched; *de prenda* come apart at the seams; **descosido** m: **como un** ~ F like

descoyuntar <1a> v/t dislocate

descremado *adj* skimmed

describir <3a; *part* **descrito**> v/t describe; **descripción** f description; **descrito** *part* → **describir**

descuajaringarse <1h> v/r F fall apart, fall to bits

descuartizar <1f> v/t quarter

descubierto 1 *part* → **descubrir 2** *adj* uncovered; *persona* bareheaded; *cielos* clear; *piscina* openair; **al** ~ in the open; **quedar al** ~ be exposed **3** m COM overdraft; **descubrimiento** m discovery; (*revelación*) revelation; **descubrir** <3a; *part* **descubierto**> **1** v/t discover; *poner de manifiesto* uncover, reveal; *estatua* unveil **2** v/r ~**se** take one's hat off; fig give o.s. away

descuento m discount; DEP stoppage time

descuerar <1a> v/t *L.Am.* skin; ~ **a alguien** fig tear s.o. to pieces

descuidado *adj* careless; **descuidar** <1a> **1** v/t neglect **2** v/i: ¡**descuida!** don't worry! **3** v/r ~**se** get careless; *en cuanto al aseo* let o.s. go; (*despistarse*) let one's concentration drop; **descuido** m carelessness; (*error*) mistake; (*omisión*) oversight; **en un** ~ *L.Am.* in a moment of carelessness

desde 1 *prp en el tiempo* since; *en el espacio* from; *en escala* from; ~ **1993** since 1993; ~ **hace tres días** for three days; ~ **... hasta ...** from ... to ... **2** *adv*: ~ **luego** of course; ~ **ya** *Rpl* right away

desdén m disdain, contempt; **desdeñable** *adj* contemptible; **nada** ~ far from insignificant; **desdeñar** <1a> v/t scorn

desdibujado *adj* blurred

desdichado 1 *adj* unhappy; (*sin suerte*) unlucky **2** m, **-a** f poor soul

desdoblar <1a> v/t unfold; (*dividir*) split

desear <1a> v/t wish for; *suerte etc* wish; ¿**qué desea?** what would you like?

desecar <1g> v/t dry

desechable adj disposable; **desechar** <1a> v/t (tirar) throw away; (rechazar) reject; **desechos** mpl waste sg

desembalar <1a> v/t unpack

desembarazarse <1f> v/r: **~ de** get rid of; **desembarazo** m ease

desembarcadero m MAR landing stage; **desembarcar** <1g> v/i disembark

desembocadura f mouth; **desembocar** <1g> v/i flow (**en** into); de calle come out (**en** into); de situación end (**en** in)

desembolsar <1a> v/t pay out

desembuchar <1a> v/i fig F spill the beans F, come out with it F

desempacar <1g> v/t unpack

desempaquetar <1a> v/t unwrap

desempatar <1a> v/i DEP, POL decide the winner

desempeñar <1a> v/t deber, tarea carry out; cargo hold; papel play

desempleado 1 adj unemployed **2** m, **-a** f unemployed person; **desempleo** m unemployment

desencadenar <1a> **1** v/t fig trigger **2** v/r **~se** fig be triggered

desencajarse <1a> v/r de una pieza come out; **se me ha desencajado la mandíbula** I dislocated my jaw

desencantado adj fig disenchanted (**con** with); **desencanto** m fig disillusionment

desenchufar <1a> v/t EL unplug

desenfadado adj self-assured; programa light, undemanding

desenfocado adj FOT out of focus

desenfrenado adj frenzied, hectic; **desenfreno** m frenzy

desenfundar <1a> v/t arma take out, draw

desengañarse <1a> v/r become disillusioned (**de** with); (dejar de engañarse) stop kidding o.s.; **desengaño** m disappointment

desenlace m outcome, ending

desenmascarar <1a> v/t fig unmask, expose

desenredar <1a> v/t untangle; situación confusa straighten out, sort out

desenrollar <1a> v/t unroll

desenroscar <1g> v/t unscrew

desentenderse <2g> v/r not want to know (**de** about); **desentendido** adj: **hacerse el ~** F pretend not to notice

desentonar <1a> v/i MÚS go off key; **~ con** fig clash with; **decir algo que desentona** say sth out of place

desentrañar <1a> v/t fig unravel

desenvoltura f ease; **desenvolverse** <2h; part **desenvuelto**> v/r fig cope; **desenvuelto 1** part → **desenvolver 2** adj self-confident

deseo m wish

desequilibrar <1a> v/t unbalance; **~ a alguien** throw s.o. off balance; **desequilibrio** m imbalance; **~ mental** mental instability

desertar <1a> v/i MIL desert

desértico adj desert atr; **desertización** f desertification

desertor m, **~a** f deserter

desesperación f despair; **desesperado** adj in despair; **desesperante** adj infuriating, exasperating; **desesperar** <1a> **1** v/t infuriate, exasperate **2** v/i give up hope (**de** of), despair (**de** of) **3** v/r **~se** get exasperated

desestabilizar <1f> v/t POL destabilize

desfachatez f impertinence

desfalco m embezzlement

desfallecer <2d> v/i faint

desfase m fig gap

desfavorable adj unfavo(u)rable; **desfavorecer** <2d> v/t (no ser favorable) not favo(u)r, be disadvantageous to; de ropa etc not suit

desfigurar <1a> v/t disfigure

desfiladero m ravine; **desfilar** <1a> v/i parade; **desfile** m parade; **~ de modelos** or **de modas** fashion show

desfogarse <1h> v/r fig vent one's emotions

desforestación f deforestation

desgana f loss of appetite; **con ~** fig reluctantly, half-heartedly

desgañitarse <1a> v/r F shout one's head off F

desgarbado adj F ungainly

desgarrador adj heartrending; **desgarrar** <1a> v/t tear up; fig: corazón break

desgastar <1a> v/t wear out; defensas wear down; **desgaste** m wear (and tear)

desglose m breakdown, itemization

desgracia f misfortune; suceso accident; **por ~** unfortunately; **desgraciadamente** adv unfortunately; **desgraciado 1** adj unfortunate; (miserable) wretched **2** m, -a f wretch; (sinvergüenza) swine F

desgravar <1a> **1** v/t deduct **2** v/i be tax-deductible

desguazar <1f> v/t scrap

deshabitado adj uninhabited

deshacer <2s; part **deshecho**> **1** v/t undo; maleta unpack; planes wreck, ruin; **eso los obligó a ~ todos sus planes** this forced them to cancel their plans **2** v/r **~se** de nudo de corbata, lazo etc come undone; de hielo melt; **~se de** get rid of; **deshecho 1** part → **deshacer 2** adj F anímicamente devastated F; de cansancio beat F, exhausted

desheredar <1a> v/t disinherit

deshice vb → **deshacer**

deshidratar <1a> v/t dehydrate

deshielo m thaw

deshinchar <1a> **1** v/t globo deflate, let down **2** v/r **~se** deflate, go down; fig lose heart

deshonesto adj dishonest

deshonra f dishono(u)r; **deshonroso** adj dishono(u)rable

deshora f: **a ~(s)** at the wrong time

desidia f apathy, lethargy

desierto 1 adj lugar empty, deserted; **isla -a** desert island **2** m desert

designar <1a> v/t appoint, name; lugar select; **designio** m plan

desigual adj unequal; terreno uneven, irregular; **desigualdad** f inequality

desilusión f disappointment; **desilusionado** adj disappointed; **desilusionar** <1a> **1** v/t disappoint; (quitar la ilusión) disillusion **2** v/r **~se** be disappointed; (perder la ilusión) become disillusioned

desinfectante m disinfectant; **desinfectar** <1a> v/t disinfect

desinflar <1a> **1** v/t globo, neumático let the air out of, deflate **2** v/r **~se** de neumático deflate; fig lose heart

desinformación f disinformation

desinhibir <3a> **1** v/t: **~ alguien** get rid of s.o.'s inhibitions **2** v/r **~se** lose one's inhibitions

desintegrar <1a> **1** v/t cause to disintegrate; grupo de gente break up **2** v/r **~se** disintegrate; de grupo de gente break up

desinterés m lack of interest; (generosidad) unselfishness; **desinteresado** adj unselfish

desintoxicación f detoxification; **hacer una cura de ~** go into detox F, have treatment for drug / alcohol abuse

desistir <3a> v/i give up; **tuvo que ~ de hacerlo** I had to stop doing it

deslealtad f disloyalty

desligar <1h> **1** v/t separate (de from); fig persona cut off (de from) **2** v/r **~se** fig cut o.s. off (de from)

desliz m fig F slip-up F; **deslizar** <1f> **1** v/t slide, run (por along); idea, frase slip in **2** v/i slide **3** v/r **~se** slide

deslomarse <1a> v/r fig kill o.s.

deslucido adj tarnished; colores dull, drab; **deslucir** <3f> v/t tarnish; fig spoil

deslumbrante adj dazzling; **deslumbrar** <1a> **1** v/t fig dazzle **2** v/r **~se** fig be dazzled

desmadre m F chaos

desmandarse <1a> v/r de animal break loose

desmantelar <1a> v/t fortificación, organización dismantle

desmañado adj clumsy

desmaquillar <1a> **1** v/t remove makeup from **2** v/r **~se** remove one's makeup

desmarcarse <1g> v/r DEP lose one's marker; **~ de** distance o.s. from

desmayarse <1a> v/r faint; **desmayo** m fainting fit; **sin ~** without flagging

desmedido adj excessive

desmelenarse <1a> v/r fig F let one's hair down F; (enfurecerse) hit the roof F

desmembrar <1k> v/t dismember

desmemoriado adj forgetful

desmentido m denial; **desmentir** <3i> v/t deny; a alguien contradict

desmenuzar <1f> v/t crumble up; fig break down

desmerecer <2d> **1** v/t not do justice to **2** v/i be unworthy (con of); **~ de** not stand comparison with; **no ~ de** be in no way inferior to

desmesurado adj excessive

desmilitarización f demilitarization

desmitificar <1g> v/t demystify, demythologize

desmontar <1a> **1** v/t dismantle, take apart; tienda de campaña take down **2** v/i dismount

desmoralizado adj demoralized; **desmoralizar** <1f> v/t demoralize

desmoronamiento m tb fig collapse; **desmoronarse** <1a> v/r tb fig collapse

desnatado adj skimmed

desnaturalizado adj QUÍM denatured

desnivel m unevenness; entre personas disparity; **desnivelar** <1a> v/t upset the balance of

desnucarse <1g> v/r break one's neck

desnudar <1a> **1** v/t undress; fig fleece **2** v/r **~se** undress; **desnudo** **1** adj naked; (sin decoración) bare **2** m PINT nude

desnutrición f undernourishment

desobedecer <2d> v/t disobey; **desobediencia** f disobedience; **desobediente** adj disobedient

desocupación f L.Am. unemployment; **desocupado** **1** adj apartamento vacant, empty; L.Am. sin trabajo unemployed **2** mpl: **los ~s** the unemployed; **desocupar** <1a> v/t vacate

desodorante m deodorant

desoído part → **desoír**; **desoír** <3q; part **desoído**> v/t ignore, turn a deaf ear to

desolado adj desolate; fig griefstricken, devastated; **desolar** <1m> v/t tb fig devastate

desollar <1m> v/t skin

desorbitado adj astronomical; **con ojos ~s** pop-eyed

desorden m disorder; **desordenado** adj untidy, messy F; fig disorganized; **desordenar** <1a> v/t make untidy

desorganización f lack of organization; **desorganizado** adj disorganized

desorientar <1a> **1** v/t disorient; (confundir) confuse **2** v/r **~se** get disoriented, lose one's bearings; fig get confused

despabilado adj fig bright; **despabilar** <1a> **1** v/t wake up; **¡despabila!** get your act together! **2** v/r **~se** fig get one's act together

despachar <1a> **1** v/t a persona, cliente attend to; problema sort out; (vender) sell; (enviar) send, dispatch **2** v/i meet (con with) **3** v/r **~se** F polish off F; **~se a su gusto** speak one's mind; **despacho** m office; diplomático dispatch; **~ de billetes** ticket office

despacio adv slowly; L.Am. (en voz baja) in a low voice

desparpajo m self-confidence

desparramar <1a> **1** v/t scatter; líquido spill; dinero squander **2** v/r **~se** spill; fig scatter

despavorido adj terrified

despecho m spite; **a ~ de** in spite of

despectivo adj contemptuous; GRAM pejorative

despedazar <1f> v/t tear apart

despedida f farewell; **~ de soltero**

stag party; **~ de soltera** hen party;
despedir <3l> **1** v/t see off; *emplea
do* dismiss; *perfume* give off; *de jinete*
throw **2** v/r **~se** say goodbye (**de**
to)

despegar <1h> **1** v/t remove, peel
off **2** v/i AVIA, *fig* take off **3** v/r **~se**
come unstuck (**de** from), come off
(**de** sth); *de persona* distance o.s. (**de**
from); **despegue** m AVIA, *fig* take-
off

despeinar <1a> v/t: **~ a alguien**
muss s.o.'s hair

despejado *adj cielo, cabeza* clear;
despejar <1a> **1** v/t clear; *persona*
wake up **2** v/r **~se** *de cielo* clear up;
fig wake o.s. up

despellejar <1a> v/t skin; **~ a
alguien** *fig* tear s.o. to pieces

despenalizar <1f> v/t decriminalize

despensa f larder

despeñarse <1a> v/r throw o.s. off a
cliff

desperdiciar <1b> v/t *oportunidad*
waste; **desperdicio** m waste; **~s** pl
waste sg; **no tener ~** be worthwhile

desperdigar <1h> v/t scatter

despertador m alarm (clock);
despertar <1k> **1** v/t wake, waken;
apetito whet; *sospecha* arouse;
recuerdo reawaken, trigger **2** v/i
wake up **3** v/r **~se** wake (up)

despiadado *adj* ruthless

despido m dismissal

despierto *adj* awake; *fig* bright

despilfarrar <1a> v/t squander

despistado *adj* scatterbrained; **despistarse** <1a> v/r get distracted;
despiste m distraction; **tener un ~**
become distracted

desplante m: **hacer un ~ a alguien**
fig be rude to s.o.

desplazar <1f> **1** v/t move; (*suplantar*) take over from **2** v/r **~se** travel

desplegar <1h & 1k> v/t unfold, open
out; MIL deploy; **despliegue** m MIL
deployment; **con gran ~ de** *fig* with
a great show of

desplomarse <1a> v/r collapse;
desplome m collapse

despojar <1a> **1** v/t strip (**de** of)

2 v/r **~se**: **~se de** *prenda* take off ;
despojos mpl (*restos*) left-overs;
(*desperdicios*) waste sg; *fig* spoils; *de
animal* offal sg

desposeídos mpl: **los ~** the dispos-
sessed

déspota m/f despot

despotricar <1g> v/i F rant and rave
F (**contra** about)

despreciar <1b> v/t look down on;
propuesta reject; **desprecio** m contempt; (*indiferencia*) disregard; *acto*
slight

desprender <2a> **1** v/t detach, separate; *olor* give off **2** v/r **~se** come
off; **~se de** *fig* part with; **de este
estudio se desprende que …** what
emerges from the study is that …

despreocupación f indifference;
despreocuparse <1a> v/r not
worry (**de** about)

desprestigio m loss of prestige

desprevenido *adj* unprepared; **pillar** *or L.Am.* **agarrar ~** catch un-
awares

desproporcionado *adj* dispropor-
tionate

despropósito m stupid thing

desprotegido *adj* unprotected

desprovisto *adj*: **~ de** lacking in

después *adv* (*más tarde*) afterward,
later; *seguido en orden* next; *en el
espacio* after; **yo voy ~** I'm next; **~
de** after; **~ de todo** after all; **~ de
que se vaya** after he's gone

desquiciar <1b> **1** v/t *fig* drive crazy
2 v/r **~se** *fig* lose one's mind

desquitarse <1a> v/r get one's own
back (**de** for)

desrielar <1a> v/t *Chi* derail

destacado *adj* outstanding; **destacar** <1g> **1** v/i stand out **2** v/r **~se**
stand out (**por** because of); (*ser
excelente*) be outstanding (**por**
because of)

destajo m: **a ~** piecework

destapar <1a> **1** v/t open, take the
lid off; *fig* uncover **2** v/r **~se** take
one's coat off; *en cama* kick off the
bedcovers; *fig* strip (off)

destartalado *adj vehículo, casa*

D

dilapidated

destello *m de estrella* twinkling; *de faros* gleam; *fig* brief period, moment

destemplarse <1a> *v/r fig* become unwell

desteñir <3h & 3l> **1** *v/t* discolo(u)r, fade **2** *v/r* **~se** fade

desternillante *adj* F hilarious

desterrar <1k> *v/t* exile

destiempo *m*: **a ~** at the wrong moment

destierro *m* exile

destilar <1a> *v/t* distill; *fig* exude

destinar <1a> *v/t fondos* allocate (**para** for); *a persona* post (**a** to); **destino** *m* fate; *de viaje etc* destination; *en el ejército etc* posting

destituir <3g> *v/t* dismiss

destornillador *m* screwdriver; **destornillar** <1a> *v/t* unscrew

destreza *f* skill

destrozar <1f> *v/t* destroy; *emocionalmente* shatter, devastate; **destrozos** *mpl* damage *sg*

destrucción *f* destruction; **destruir** <3g> *v/t* destroy; *(estropear)* ruin, wreck

desunir <3a> *v/t* divide

desuso *m* disuse; **caer en ~** fall into disuse

desvaído *adj color, pintura* faded

desvalido *adj* helpless; **desvalijar** <1a> *v/t* rob; *apartamento* burglarize, burgle

desván *m* attic

desvanecimiento *m* MED fainting fit

desvarío *m* delirium; **~s** ravings

desvelar <1a> **1** *v/t* keep awake; *secreto* reveal **2** *v/r* **~se** stay awake; *fig* do one's best (**por** for); **desvelo** *m* sleeplessness; **~s** efforts

desventaja *f* disadvantage

desventura *f* misfortune

desvergonzado *adj* shameless; **desvergüenza** *f* shamelessness

desvestir <3l> **1** *v/t* undress **2** *v/r* **~se** get undressed, undress

desviar <1c> **1** *v/t golpe* deflect, parry; *tráfico* divert; *río* alter the

course of; **~ la conversación** change the subject; **~ la mirada** look away; **~ a alguien del buen camino** lead s.o. astray **2** *v/r* **~se** *(girar)* turn off; *(bifurcarse)* branch off; *(apartarse)* stray (**de** from)

desvincular <1a> **1** *v/t* dissociate (**de** from) **2** *v/r* **~se** dissociate o.s. (**de** from)

desvío *m* diversion

detallar <1a> *v/t* explain in detail, give details of; COM itemize; **detalle** *m* detail; *fig* thoughtful gesture; **al ~** retail

detección *f* detection; **detectar** <1a> *v/t* detect; **detective** *m/f* detective; **~ privado** private detective; **detector** *m* detector; **~ de mentiras** lie detector

detención *f* detention; **orden de ~** arrest warrant; **detener** <2l> **1** *v/t* stop; *de policía* arrest, detain **2** *v/r* **~se** stop; **detenido 1** *adj* held up; *(minucioso)* detailed **2** *m*, **-a** *f* person under arrest; **detenimiento** *m*: **con ~** thoroughly

detentar <1a> *v/t* hold

detergente *m* detergent

deteriorar <1a> **1** *v/t* damage **2** *v/r* **~se** deteriorate; **deterioro** *m* deterioration

determinado *adj* certain; **determinar** <1a> **1** *v/t* determine **2** *v/r* **~se** decide (**a** to)

detestar <1a> *v/t* detest

detonación *f* detonation; **detonante** *m* explosive; *fig* trigger; **detonar** <1a> **1** *v/i* detonate, go off **2** *v/t* detonate, set off

detractor *m*, **~a** *f* detractor, critic

detrás *adv* behind; **por ~** at the back; *fig* behind your / his etc back; **~ de** behind; **uno ~ de otro** one after the other; **estar ~ de algo** *fig* be behind sth

detrimento *m*: **en ~ de** to the detriment of

detritus *m* detritus

detuvo *vb* → **detener**

deuda *f* debt; **estar en ~ con alguien** *fig* be in s.o.'s debt, be in-

D

debted to s.o.; **deudor** *m*, **~a** *f* debtor

devaluación *f* devaluation; **devaluar** <1e> *v/t* devalue

devanarse <1a> *v/r*: **~ los sesos** F rack one's brains F

devaneo *m* affair

devastar <1a> *v/t* devastate

devoción *f tb fig* devotion

devolver <2h; *part* **devuelto**> **1** *v/t* give back, return; *fig: visita, saludo* return; F (*vomitar*) throw up F **2** *v/r* **~se** *L.Am.* go back, return

devorar <1a> *v/t* devour

devuelto *part* → **devolver**

D.F. *abr Méx* (= **Distrito Federal**) Mexico City

dg. *abr* (= **decigramo**) decigram

di *vb* → **dar**

día *m* day; **~ de fiesta** holiday; **~ festivo** holiday; **~ hábil** *or* **laborable** work day; **poner al ~** update, bring up to date; **a los pocos ~s** a few days later; **algún ~, un ~** some day, one day; **de ~** by day, during the day; **de un ~ a** *or* **para otro** from one day to the next; **el ~ menos pensado** when you least expect it; **hace mal ~** *tiempo* it's a nasty day; **hoy en ~** nowadays; **todo el santo ~** all day long; **todos los ~s** every day; **un ~ sí y otro no** every other day; **ya es de ~** it's light already; **¡buenos ~s!** good morning

diabetes *f* diabetes; **diabético 1** *adj* diabetic **2** *m*, **-a** *f* diabetic

diablesa *f* F she-devil; **diablo** *m* devil; **un pobre ~** *fig* a poor devil; **mandar a alguien al ~** tell s.o. to go to hell; **diablura** *f* prank, lark; **diabólico** *adj* diabolical

diadema *f* tiara; *para el pelo* hairband

diáfano *adj* clear

diafragma *m* diaphragm

diagnosticar <1g> *v/t* diagnose; **diagnóstico 1** *adj* diagnostic **2** *m* diagnosis

diagonal 1 *adj* diagonal **2** *f* diagonal (line)

diagrama *m* diagram

dialecto *m* dialect

dialogar <1h> *v/i* talk (**sobre** about), discuss (**sobre** sth); (*negociar*) hold talks (**con** with); **diálogo** *m* dialog(ue)

diamante *m* diamond

diametralmente *adv*: **~ opuesto** diametrically opposed; **diámetro** *m* diameter

diana *f* MIL reveille; (*blanco*) target; *para jugar a los dardos* dartboard; (*centro de blanco*) bull's eye; **dar en la ~** *fig* hit the nail on the head

diantre *int* F hell! F

diapositiva *f* FOT slide, transparency

diariero *m*, **-a** *f Arg* newspaper vendor; **diario 1** *adj* daily **2** *m* diary; (*periódico*) newspaper; **a ~** daily

diarrea *f* MED diarrh(o)ea

dibujante *m/f* draftsman, *Br* draughtsman; *mujer* draftswoman, *Br* draughtswoman; *de viñetas* cartoonist; **dibujar** <1a> **1** *v/t* draw; *fig* describe **2** *v/r* **~se** *fig* appear; **dibujo** *m arte* drawing; *ilustración* drawing, sketch; *estampado* pattern; **~s animados** cartoons; **película de ~s animados** animation

diccionario *m* dictionary

dic.ᵉ *abr* (= **diciembre**) Dec. (= December)

dice *vb* → **decir**

díceres *mpl L.Am.* sayings

dicharachero *adj* chatty; (*gracioso*) witty

dicho 1 *part* → **decir 2** *adj* said; **~ y hecho** no sooner said than done; **mejor ~** or rather **3** *m* saying

dichoso *adj* happy; F (*maldito*) damn F

diciembre *m* December

diciendo *vb* → **decir**

dictado *m* dictation; **dictador** *m*, **~a** *f* dictator; **dictadura** *f* dictatorship

dictaminar <1a> *v/t* state

dictar <1a> *v/t* lección, texto dictate; *ley* announce; **~ sentencia** JUR pass sentence

didáctico *adj* educational

diecinueve *adj* nineteen; **dieciocho** *adj* eighteen; **dieciséis** *adj* sixteen;

adj eighteen; **dieciséis** *adj* sixteen; **diecisiete** *adj* seventeen

diente *m* tooth; **~ de ajo** clove of garlic; **~ de león** BOT dandelion; **poner los ~s largos a alguien** make s.o. jealous

diesel *m* diesel

diestro 1 *adj*: **a ~ y siniestro** *fig* F left and right **2** *m* TAUR bullfighter

dieta *f* diet; **estar a ~** be on a diet; **~s** travel(l)ing expenses; **dietético** *adj* dietary

diez *adj* ten

diezmar <1a> *v/t* decimate

difamar <1a> *v/t* slander, defame; *por escrito* libel, defame; **difamatorio** *adj* defamatory

diferencia *f* difference; **a ~ de** unlike; **con ~** *fig* by a long way; **diferenciar** <1b> **1** *v/t* differentiate **2** *v/r* **~se** differ (**de** from); **no se diferencian en nada** there's no difference at all between them; **diferente** *adj* different

diferido *adj* TV: **en ~** prerecorded

difícil *adj* difficult; **dificultad** *f* difficulty; **poner ~es** make it difficult

dificultar <1a> *v/t* hinder

difundir <3a> **1** *v/t* spread; (*programa*) broadcast **2** *v/r* **~se** spread

difunto 1 *adj* late **2** *m*, **-a** *f* deceased

difuso *adj idea, conocimientos* vague, sketchy

digerir <3i> *v/t* digest; F *noticia* take in; **digestión** *f* digestion

digital *adj* digital; **digitalizar** <1f> *v/t* INFOR digitalize; **dígito** *m* digit

dignarse <1a> *v/r* deign; **dignidad** *f* dignity; **digno** *adj* worthy; *trabajo* decent; **~ de mención** worth mentioning

digo *vb* → **decir**

digresión *f* digression

dije *vb* → **decir**

dilación *f*: **sin ~** without delay

dilapidar <1a> *v/t* waste

dilatar <1a> **1** *v/t* dilate; (*prolongar*) prolong; (*aplazar*) postpone **2** *v/i Méx* (*tardar*) be late; **no me dilato** I won't be long

dilema *m* dilemma

diligencia *f* diligence; *vehículo* stagecoach; **~s** JUR procedures, formalities; **diligente** *adj* diligent

dilucidar <1a> *v/t* clarify

diluir <3g> *v/t* dilute

diluviar <1b> *v/i* pour down; **diluvio** *m* downpour; *fig* deluge

dimensión *f* dimension; *fig* size, scale; **dimensiones** measurements

diminutivo *m* diminutive; **diminuto** *adj* tiny, diminutive

dimisión *f* resignation; **dimitir** <3a> *v/t* resign

Dinamarca Denmark

dinámico *adj fig* dynamic

dinamita *f* dynamite

dinastía *f* dynasty

dinero *m* money; **~ en efectivo**, **~ en metálico** cash

dinosaurio *m* dinosaur

dio *vb* → **dar**

Dios *m* God; **hazlo como ~ manda** do it properly; **¡~ mío!** my God!; **¡por ~!** for God's sake!; **sabe ~ lo que dijo** God knows what he said

dios *m tb fig* god; **diosa** *f* goddess

diploma *m* diploma; **diplomacia** *f* diplomacy; **diplomático 1** *adj* diplomatic **2** *m*, **-a** *f* diplomat

diputado *m*, **-a** *f* representative, *Br* Member of Parliament

dique *m* dike, *Br* dyke

dirá *vb* → **decir**

diré *vb* → **decir**

dirección *f tb* TEA, *de película* direction; COM management; POL leadership; *de coche* steering; *en carta* address; **~ en aquella ~** that way; **~ asistida** AUTO power steering; **~ de correo electrónico** e-mail address; **directiva** *f* board of directors; POL executive committee; **directivo 1** *adj* governing; COM managing **2** *m*, **-a** *f* COM manager; **directo** *adj* direct; **en ~** TV, RAD live; **director 1** *adj* leading **2** *m*, **~a** *f* manager; EDU principal, *Br* head (teacher); TEA, *de película* director; **~ de orquesta** conductor; **directriz** *f* guideline

dirigir <3c> **1** *v/t* TEA, *película* direct;

COM manage, run; MÚS conduct; ~ *una carta a* address a letter to; ~ *una pregunta a* direct a question to **2** *v/r* ~*se* make, head (*a, hacia* for)

discapacidad *f* disability; **discapacitado 1** *adj* disabled **2** *m*, -*a f* disabled person

discar <1g> *v/t L.Am.* TELEC dial

discernir <3i> *v/t* distinguish, discern

disciplina *f* discipline; **disciplinar** <1a> *v/t* discipline; **discípulo** *m*, -*a f* REL, *fig* disciple

disco *m* disk, *Br* disc; MÚS record; (*discoteca*) disco; DEP discus; ~ *compacto* compact disc; ~ *duro*, *L.Am.* ~ *rígido* INFOR hard disk

discordante *adj* discordant; **discordia** *f* discord; (*colección de discos*) record collection

discreción *f* discretion; *a* ~ *disparar* at will; *a* ~ *de* at the discretion of

discrepancia *f* discrepancy; (*desacuerdo*) disagreement; **discrepar** <1a> *v/i* disagree

discreto *adj* discreet

discriminación *f* discrimination; **discriminar** <1a> *v/t* discriminate against; (*diferenciar*) differentiate

disculpa *f* apology; **disculpar** <1a> **1** *v/t* excuse **2** *v/r* ~*se* apologize

discurrir <3a> *v/i de tiempo* pass; *de acontecimiento* pass off; (*reflexionar*) reflect (*sobre* on); **discurso** *m* speech; *de tiempo* passage, passing

discusión *f* discussion; (*disputa*) argument; **discutir** <3a> **1** *v/t* discuss **2** *v/i* argue (*sobre* about)

diseminar <1a> *v/t* scatter; *fig* spread

disentir <3i> *v/i* disagree (*de* with)

diseñador *m*, ~*a f* designer; **diseñar** <1a> *v/t* design; **diseño** *m* design; ~ *gráfico* graphic design

disfraz *m para ocultar* disguise; *para fiestas* costume, fancy dress; **disfrazarse** <1f> *v/r para ocultarse* disguise o.s. (*de* as); *para divertirse* dress up (*de* as)

disfrutar <1a> **1** *v/t* enjoy **2** *v/i* have fun, enjoy o.s.; ~ *de buena salud* be

in *o* enjoy good health

disgregarse <1h> *v/r* disintegrate

disgustar <1a> **1** *v/t* upset **2** *v/r* ~*se* get upset; **disgusto** *m*: *me causó un gran* ~ I was very upset; *llevarse un* ~ get upset; *a* ~ unwillingly

disidente *m/f* dissident

disimular <1a> **1** *v/t* disguise **2** *v/i* pretend; **disimulo** *m*: *con* ~ unobtrusively

disipar <1a> **1** *v/t duda* dispel **2** *v/r* ~*se de niebla* clear; *de duda* vanish

diskette *m* diskette, floppy (disk)

dislexia *f* dyslexia

dislocar <1g> *v/t* dislocate

disminución *f* decrease; **disminuido 2** *adj* handicapped **2** *m*, -*a f* handicapped person; ~ *físico* physically handicapped person; **disminuir** <3g> *v/t gastos, costos* reduce, cut; *velocidad* reduce **2** *v/i* decrease, diminish

disociar <1b> *v/t* separate

disolvente *m* solvent; **disolver** <1h; *part disuelto*> *v/t* dissolve; *manifestación* break up

disparada *f L.Am.*: *a la* ~ in a rush; **disparar** <1a> **1** *v/t tiro, arma* fire; *foto* take; *precios* send up **2** *v/i* shoot, fire **3** *v/r* ~*se de arma, alarma* go off; *de precios* rise dramatically, rocket F

disparatado *adj* absurd; **disparate** *m* F piece of nonsense; *es un* ~ *hacer eso* it's crazy to do that

disparo *m* shot

dispendio *m* waste

dispensar <1a> *v/t* dispense; *recibimiento* give; (*eximir*) excuse (*de* from); **dispensario** *m* MED clinic

dispersar <1a> **1** *v/t* disperse **2** *v/r* ~*se* disperse; **disperso** *adj* scattered

displicente *adj* disdainful

disponer <2r; *part dispuesto*> **1** *v/t* (*arreglar*) arrange; (*preparar*) prepare; (*ordenar*) stipulate **2** *v/i*: ~ *de algo* have sth at one's disposal **3** *v/r* ~*se* get ready (*a* to); **disponibilidad** *f* COM availability; **disponible** *adj* available; **disposición** *f* disposition; *de objetos* arrangement; **~ de ánimo** state of mind; **estar a ~ de alguien** be at s.o.'s disposal

dispositivo *m* device

dispuesto 1 *part* → **disponer 2** *adj* ready (**a** to)

disputa *f* dispute; **disputar** <1a> **1** *v/t* dispute; *partido* play **2** *v/i* argue (*sobre* about) **3** *v/r* **~se** compete for

disquería *f L.Am.* record store

disquete *m* INFOR diskette, floppy (disk); **disquetera** *f* disk drive

distancia *f* *tb fig* distance; **distanciarse** <1b> *v/r* distance o.s. (*de* from); **distante** *adj tb fig* distant; **distar** <1a> *v/i* be far (*de* from)

distinción *f* distinction; **a ~ de** unlike; **distinguido** *adj* distinguished; **distinguir** <3d> *v/t* distinguish (*de* from); (*divisar*) make out; **con un premio** hono(u)r; **distintivo** *m* emblem; MIL insignia; **distinto** *adj* different; **~s** (*varios*) several

distorsión *f* distortion

distracción *f* distraction; (*descuido*) absent-mindedness; (*diversión*) entertainment; (*pasatiempo*) pastime; **por ~** out of absent-mindedness; **distraer** <2p; *part* **distraído**> **1** *v/t* distract; **la radio la distrae** she enjoys listening to the radio **2** *v/r* **~se** get distracted; (*disfrutar*) enjoy o.s.; **distraído 1** *part* → **distraer 2** *adj* absent-minded; *temporalmente* distracted

distribución *f* COM, *de película* distribution; **distribuir** <3g> *v/t* distribute; *beneficio* share out

distrito *m* district

disturbio *m* disturbance

disuadir <3a> *v/t* dissuade; POL deter; **~ a alguien de hacer algo** dissuade s.o. from doing sth

disuelto *part* → **disolver**

disyuntiva *f* dilemma

diurético *adj* diuretic

diurno *adj* day *atr*

divagar <1h> *v/i* digress

diván *m* couch

diversidad *f* diversity

diversión *f* fun; (*pasatiempo*) pastime; **aquí no hay muchas diversiones** there's not much to do around here; **diverso** *adj* diverse; **~s** several, various

divertido *adj* funny; (*entretenido*) entertaining; **divertir** <3i> **1** *v/t* entertain **2** *v/r* **~se** have fun, enjoy o.s.

dividendo *m* dividend; **dividir** <3a> *v/t* divide

divinamente *adv fig* wonderfully; **divinidad** *f* divinity; **divino** *adj tb fig* divine

divisa *f* currency; **~s** *pl* foreign currency *sg*

divisar <1a> *v/t* make out

división *f* MAT, MIL, DEP division; **hubo ~ de opiniones** there were differences of opinion

divorciado 1 *adj* divorced **2** *m*, **-a** *f* divorcee; **divorciarse** <1b> *v/r* get divorced; **divorcio** *m* divorce

divulgación *f* spread; **divulgar** <1h> **1** *v/t* spread **2** *v/r* **~se** spread

d.J.C. *abr* (= **después de Jesucristo**) A.D. (= Anno Domini)

dl. *abr* (= **decilitro**) deciliter

dm. *abr* (= **decímetro**) decimeter

dobladillo *m* hem; **doblado** *adj* película dubbed; **doblaje** *m de película* dubbing; **doblar** <1a> **1** *v/t* fold; *cantidad* double; *película* dub; MAR round; *pierna, brazo* bend; *en una carrera* pass, *Br* overtake; **~ la esquina** go round *o* turn the corner **2** *v/i* turn; **~ a la derecha** turn right **3** *v/r* **~se** bend; *fig* give in; **doble 1** *adj* double; *nacionalidad* dual; **~ clic** *m* double click **2** *m*: **el ~** twice as much (*de* as); **el ~ de gente** twice as many people; **~s** *tenis* doubles **3** *m/f en película* double

doblegar <1h> *v/t fig*: *voluntad* break; *orgullo* humble

doblez 1 *m* fold **2** *f fig* deceit

doce *adj* twelve; **docena** *f* dozen

docente *adj* teaching *atr*

dócil *adj* docile

doctor *m*, **~a** *f* doctor; **~ honoris**

causa honorary doctor; **doctorado** m doctorate

doctrina f doctrine

documentación f documentation; *de una persona* papers; **documental** m documentary; **documento** m document; **~ nacional de identidad** national identity card

dogma m dogma

dogo m ZO mastiff

dólar m dollar

dolencia f ailment; **doler** <2h> v/t tb fig hurt; **me duele el brazo** my arm hurts; **le dolió que le mintieran** fig she was hurt that they had lied to her

dolor m tb fig pain; **~ de cabeza** headache; **~ de estómago** stomach-ache; **~ de muelas** toothache; **dolorido** adj sore, aching; fig hurt; **doloroso** adj tb fig painful

domador m, **~a** f tamer

domesticar <1g> v/t domesticate; **doméstico** 1 adj domestic, household atr 2 m, **-a** f servant

domiciliación f de sueldo credit transfer; de pagos direct billing, Br direct debit; **domicilio** m address; **repartir a ~** do home deliveries

dominante adj dominant; desp domineering; **dominar** <1a> 1 v/t dominate; idioma have a good command of 2 v/i dominate 3 v/r **~se** control o.s.

domingo m Sunday; **~ de Ramos** Palm Sunday; **dominguero** m, **-a** f F weekender, Sunday tripper; **dominical** adj Sunday atr

dominicano GEOG 1 adj Dominican 2 m, **-a** f Dominican

dominio m control; fig command; **ser del ~ público** be in the public domain

dominó m dominoes pl

don[1] m gift; **~ de gentes** way with people

don[2] m Mr; **~ Enrique** Mr Sanchez English uses the surname while Spanish uses the first name

donación f donation; **~ de sangre** blood donation; **~ de órganos** organ donation; **donante** m/f donor; **~ de sangre** blood donor; **donar** <1a> v/t sangre, órgano, dinero donate; **donativo** m donation

doncella f maid

donde 1 adv where 2 prp esp L.Am.: **fui ~ el médico** I went to the doctor's

dónde interr where; **¿de ~ eres?** where are you from?; **¿hacia ~ vas?** where are you going?

dondequiera adv wherever

doña f Mrs; **~ Estela** Mrs Sanchez English uses the surname while Spanish uses the first name

dopaje m doping

dopar <1a> v/t doping

dorada f ZO gilthead

dorado adj gold; montura gilt

dormido adj asleep; **quedarse ~** fall asleep; **dormir** <3k> 1 v/i sleep; (estar dormido) be asleep 2 v/t put to sleep; **~ a alguien** MED give s.o. a general an(a)esthetic 3 v/r **~se** go to sleep; (quedarse dormido) fall asleep; (no despertarse) oversleep; **no podía dormirme** I couldn't get to sleep; **dormitorio** m bedroom

dorso m back

dos adj two; **de ~ en ~** in twos; **los ~** both; **anda con ojo con los ~** watch out for the pair of them; **cada ~ por tres** all the time, continually

doscientos adj two hundred

dosificar <1g> v/t cut down on; **dosis** f inv dose

dotar <1a> v/t equip (de with); fondos provide (de with); cualidades endow (de with); **dote** f a novia dowry; **tener ~s para algo** have a gift for sth

doy vb → **dar**

dpto. abr (= **departamento**) dept (= department)

Dr. abr (= **Doctor**) Dr (= Doctor)

Dra. abr (= **Doctora**) Dr (= Doctor)

dragar <1h> v/t dredge

dragón m dragon; MIL dragoon

drama m drama; **dramático** adj dramatic; **arte ~** dramatic art;

dramatizar <1f> v/t dramatize
drástico adj drastic
drenaje m drainage
droga f drug; **~ de diseño** designer
drug; **drogadicto 1** adj: **una mujer
-a** a woman addicted to drugs **2** m,
-a f drug addict; **drogarse** <1h> v/r
take drugs; **drogodependencia** f
drug dependency; **droguería** f store
selling cleaning and household products
dromedario m ZO dromedary
d.to abr (= **descuento**) discount
ducha f shower; **ser una ~ de agua
fría** fig come as a shock; **ducharse**
<1a> v/r have a shower, shower
duda f doubt; **sin ~** without doubt;
poner en ~ call into question;
dudar <1a> **1** v/t doubt **2** v/i hesitate (**en** to); **dudoso** adj doubtful;
(indeciso) hesitant
duele vb → **doler**
duelo m grief; (combate) duel
duende m imp
dueño m, **-a** f owner
duermo vb → **dormir**
dulce 1 adj sweet; fig gentle **2** m
candy, Br sweet; **dulzura** f tb fig
sweetness

dumping m dumping
duna f dune
duo m MÚS duo
duodécimo adj twelfth
dúplex m duplex (apartment)
duplicado 1 adj duplicate; **por ~** in
duplicate **2** m duplicate; **duplicar**
<1g> v/t duplicate
duque m duke; **duquesa** f duchess
duración f duration; **duradero** adj
lasting; ropa, calzado hard-wear-
ing
durante prp indicando duración during; indicando período for; **~ seis
meses** for six months
durar <1a> v/i last
duraznero m L.Am. BOT peach
(tree); **durazno** m L.Am. BOT
peach
Durex® m Méx Scotch tape®, Br
Sellotape®
duro 1 adj hard; carne tough; clima,
fig harsh; **~ de oído** F hard of hearing; **ser ~ de pelar** be a tough nut to
crack **2** adv hard **3** m five peseta
coin
DVD abr (= **Disco de Vídeo Digital**)
DVD (= Digital Versatile o Video
Disc)

E

E abr (= **este**) E (= East(ern))
e conj (instead of **y** before words starting with **i, hi**) and
ebanista m cabinetmaker; **ébano** m
ebony
ebrio adj drunk
ebullición f: **punto de ~** boiling
point
eccema m eczema
echar <1a> **1** v/t (lanzar) throw;
(poner) put; de un lugar throw out;
humo give off; carta mail, Br tb post;
lo han echado del trabajo he's

been fired; **~ abajo** pull down, destroy; **~ la culpa a alguien** blame
s.o., put the blame on s.o.; **me echó
40 años** he thought I was 40 **2** v/i: **~
a** start to, begin to; **~ a correr** start o
begin to run, start running **3** v/r **~se**
(tirarse) throw o.s.; (tumbarse) lie
down; (ponerse) put on; **~se a llorar**
start o begin to cry, start crying
eclesiástico adj ecclesiastical,
church atr
eclipsar <1a> v/t eclipse; **eclipse** m
eclipse

eco *m* echo; **tener ~** *fig* make an impact

ecografía *f* (ultrasound) scan

ecología *f* ecology; **ecológico** *adj* ecological; *alimentos* organic; **ecologista** *m/f* ecologist

economato *m* co-operative store

economía *f* economy; *ciencia* economics; **~ de mercado** market economy; **~ sumergida** black economy; **económico** *adj* economic; (*barato*) economical; **economista** *m/f* economist; **economizar** <1f> *v/t* economize on, save

ecosistema *m* ecosystem

ecoturismo *m* ecotourism

ecuación *f* equation

ecuador *m* equator

Ecuador Ecuador

ecuánime *adj* (*sereno*) even-tempered; (*imparcial*) impartial

ecuatorial *adj* equatorial

ecuatoriano 1 *adj* Ecuadorean **2** *m*, **-a** *f* Ecuadorean

eczema *m* eczema

ed. *abr* (= **edición**) ed (= edition)

edad *f* age; **la Edad Media** the Middle Ages *pl*; **la tercera ~** the over 60s; **estar en la ~ del pavo** be at that awkward age; **a la ~ de** at the age of; **¿qué ~ tienes?** how old are you?

edición *f* edition

edificar <1g> *v/t* construct, build; **edificio** *m* building

edil *m*, **~a** *f* council(l)or

editar <1a> *v/t* edit; (*publicar*) publish; **editor** *m*, **~a** *f* editor; **editorial 1** *m* editorial, leading article **2** *f* publishing company *o* house, publisher

edredón *m* eiderdown

educación *f* (*crianza*) upbringing; (*modales*) manners; **~ física** physical education, PE; **educado** *adj* polite, well-mannered; **mal ~** rude, ill-mannered; **educar** <1g> *v/t* educate; (*criar*) bring up; *voz* train; **educativo** *adj* educational

edulcorante *m* sweetener

EE. UU. *abr* (= **Estados Unidos**)

US(A) (= United States (of America))

efectista *adj* theatrical, dramatic; **efectivamente** *adv* indeed; **efectivo 1** *adj* effective; **hacer ~** COM cash **2** *m*: **en ~** (in) cash; **efecto** *m* effect; **~ invernadero** greenhouse effect; **~s secundarios** side effects; **en ~** indeed; **surtir ~** take effect, work

efectuar <1e> *v/t* carry out

efervescente *adj* effervescent; *bebida* carbonated, sparkling

eficacia *f* efficiency; **eficaz** *adj* (*efectivo*) effective; (*eficiente*) efficient; **eficiencia** *f* efficiency; **eficiente** *adj* efficient

efímero *adj* ephemeral, short-lived

efusivo *adj* effusive

egipcio 1 *adj* Egyptian **2** *m*, **-a** *f* Egyptian; **Egipto** Egypt

ego *m* ego; **egocéntrico** *adj* egocentric, self-centered (*Br* -centred); **egoísmo** *m* selfishness, egoism; **egoísta 1** *adj* selfish, egoistic **2** *m/f* egoist

egresar <1a> *v/i* L.Am. *de universidad* graduate; *de colegio* graduate from high school, *Br* leave school; **egreso** *m* L.Am. graduation

eh *int para llamar atención* hey!; **¿~?** eh?

eje *m* axis; *de auto* axle; *fig* linchpin

ejecución *f* (*realización*) implementation, carrying out; *de condenado* execution; MÚS performance; **ejecutar** <1a> *v/t* (*realizar*) carry out, implement; *condenado* execute; INFOR run, execute; MÚS play, perform; **ejecutiva** *f* executive; **ejecutivo 1** *adj* executive; **el poder ~** POL the executive **2** *m* executive; **el Ejecutivo** the government

ejemplar 1 *adj* *alumno, padre etc* model *atr*, exemplary **2** *m de libro* copy; *de revista* issue; *animal, planta* specimen; **ejemplo** *m* example; **dar buen ~** set a good example; **por ~** for example

ejercer <2b> **1** *v/t cargo* practice, *Br* practise; *influencia* exert **2** *v/i de* *profesional* practice, *Br* practise; *ejerce de médico* he's a practicing (*Br* practising) doctor; **ejercicio** *m* exercise; COM fiscal year, *Br* financial year; *hacer ~* exercise; **ejercitar** <1a> **1** *v/t músculo, derecho* exercise **2** *v/r ~se* train; *~se en* practice, *Br* practise; **ejército** *m* army

ejido *m Méx* traditional rural communal farming unit

ejote *m L.Am.* green bean

el 1 *art* the **2** *pron:* **~ de ...** that of ...; **~ de Juan** Juan's; **~ más grande** the biggest (one); **~ que está ...** the one who is ...

él *pron sujeto* he; *cosa* it; *complemento* him; *cosa* it; *de ~* his

elaborar <1a> *v/t* produce, make; *metal etc* work; *plan* devise, draw up

elasticidad *f* elasticity; **elástico 1** *adj* elastic **2** *m* elastic; (*goma*) elastic band, *Br* rubber band

elección *f* choice; **eleccionario** *adj L.Am.* election *atr*, electoral; **elecciones** *fpl* election *sg*; **elector** *m* voter; **electorado** *m* electorate; **electoral** *adj* election *atr*, electoral

electricidad *f* electricity; **electricista** *m/f* electrician; **eléctrico** *adj luz, motor* electric; *aparato* electrical; **electrocutar** <1a> **1** *v/t* electrocute **2** *v/r ~se* be electrocuted, electrocute o.s.

electrodo *m* electrode

electrodoméstico *m* electrical appliance

electrón *m* electron; **electrónica** *f* electronics; **electrónico** *adj* electronic

elefante *m* ZO elephant; **~ marino** elephant seal, sea elephant

elegancia *f* elegance, stylishness; **elegante** *adj* elegant, stylish; **elegantoso** *adj L.Am.* F stylish, classy F

elegía *f* elegy

elegible *adj* eligible; **elegir** <3c & 3l> *v/t* choose; *por votación* elect

elemental *adj* (*esencial*) fundamental, essential; (*básico*) elementary,

basic; **elemento** *m* element

elevado *adj* high; *fig* elevated; **elevador** *m* hoist; *L.Am.* elevator, *Br* lift; **elevar** <1a> **1** *v/t* raise **2** *v/r ~se* rise; *de monumento* stand

eliminación *f* elimination; *de desperdicios* disposal; **eliminar** <1a> *v/t* eliminate; *desperdicios* dispose of; **eliminatoria** *f* DEP qualifying round, heat

élite *f* elite; **elitista** *adj* elitist

elixir *m* elixir; **~ bucal** mouthwash

ella *pron sujeto* she; *cosa* it; *complemento* her; *cosa* it; *de ~* her; *es de ~* it's hers

ellas *pron sujeto* they; *complemento* them; *de ~* their; *es de ~* it's theirs

ello *pron* it

ellos *pron sujeto* they; *complemento* them; *de ~* their; *es de ~* it's theirs

elocuente *adj* eloquent

elogiar <1b> *v/t* praise; **elogio** *m* praise

elote *m L.Am.* corncob; *granos* corn, *Br* sweetcorn

El Salvador El Salvador

eludir <3a> *v/t* evade, avoid

emanar <1a> **1** *v/i fml* emanate (*de* from) *fml; fig* stem (*de* from), derive (*de* from) **2** *v/t* exude, emit

emancipación *f* emancipation; **emanciparse** <1a> *v/r* become emancipated

embadurnar <1a> *v/t* smear (*de* with)

embajada *f* embassy; **embajador** *m*, **~a** *f* ambassador

embalaje *m* packing; **embalar** <1a> **1** *v/t* pack **2** *v/r ~se de persona* get excited; *el coche se embaló* the car went faster and faster; *no te embales* don't go so fast

embalse *m* reservoir

embarazada 1 *adj* pregnant **2** *f* pregnant woman; **embarazo** *m* pregnancy; *interrupción del ~* termination, abortion; **embarazoso** *adj* awkward, embarrassing

embarcación *f* vessel, craft; **embarcadero** *m* wharf; **embarcar** <1g> **1** *v/t pasajeros* board, embark; *mer-*

107 **empapar**

cancías load **2** *v/i* board, embark **3** *v/r* *~se en barco* board, embark; *en avión* board; *~se en* fig embark on

embargo *m* embargo; JUR seizure; *sin ~* however

embarque *m* boarding; *de mercancías* loading

embarrancar <1g> **1** *v/i* MAR run aground **2** *v/r* *~se* MAR run aground

embaucador 1 *adj* deceitful **2** *m*, *~a f* trickster

embeberse <2a> *v/r* get absorbed *o* engrossed (*en* in)

embelesar <1a> *v/t* captivate

embestir <3l> **1** *v/t* charge **2** *v/i* charge (*contra* at)

emblema *m* emblem

embobar <1a> *v/t* fascinate

embolarse <1a> *v/r* C.Am., Méx F get plastered F

émbolo *m* TÉC piston

embolsar <1a> **1** *v/t* pocket **2** *v/r* *~se* pocket

emborrachar <1a> **1** *v/t* make drunk, get drunk **2** *v/r* *~se* get drunk

emborronar <1a> *v/t* blot, smudge

emboscada *f* ambush

embotar <1a> *v/t* blunt

embotellamiento *m* traffic jam; **embotellar** <1a> *v/t* bottle

embrague *m* AUTO clutch

embriagar <1h> *v/t* fig intoxicate; **embriaguez** *f* intoxication

embrión *m* embryo; *en ~* in an embryonic state, in embryo

embrollo *m* tangle; fig mess, muddle

embromar <1a> *v/t* Rpl F (*molestar*) annoy

embrujar <1a> *v/t* tb fig bewitch

embrutecer <2d> **1** *v/t* brutalize **2** *v/r* *~se* become brutalized

embudo *m* funnel

embustero 1 *adj* deceitful **2** *m*, *~a f* liar

embutido *m* GASTR type of dried sausage

emergencia *f* emergency

emerger <2c> *v/i* emerge

emigración *f* emigration; **emigrante** *m* emigrant; **emigrar** <1a> *v/i* emigrate; ZO migrate

eminente *adj* eminent

emirato *m* emirate

emisario *m* emissary; **emisión** *f* emission; COM issue; RAD, TV broadcast; **emisora** *f* radio station; **emitir** <3a> *v/t calor, sonido* give out, emit; *moneda* issue; *opinión* express, give; *veredicto* deliver; RAD, TV broadcast; *voto* cast

emoción *f* emotion; *¡qué ~!* how exciting!; **emocionado** *adj* excited; **emocionante** *adj* (*excitante*) exciting; (*conmovedor*) moving; **emocionarse** <1a> *v/r* get excited; (*conmoverse*) be moved

emotivo *adj* emotional; (*conmovedor*) moving

empacar <1g> **1** *v/t* & *v/i* L.Am. pack **2** *v/r* *~se* L.Am. (*ponerse tozudo*) dig one's heels in; *tragar* devour

empacharse <1a> *v/r* F get an upset stomach (*de* from); *~ de* fig overdose on; **empacho** *m* F upset stomach; *fig* bellyful F; *sin ~* unashamedly

empadronar <1a> **1** *v/t* register **2** *v/r* *~se* register

empalagoso *adj* sickly; fig sickly sweet, cloying

empalizada *f* palisade

empalmar <1a> **1** *v/t* connect, join **2** *v/i* connect (*con* with), join up (*con* with); *de idea, conversación* run *o* follow on (*con* from)

empanada *f* pie; **empanadilla** *f* pasty; **empanar** <1a> *v/t* coat in breadcrumbs

empantanarse <1a> *v/r* become swamped *o* waterlogged; fig get bogged down

empañado *adj* misty; **empañar** <1a> **1** *v/t* steam up, mist up; fig tarnish, sully **2** *v/r* *~se de vidrio* steam up, mist up

empapado *adj* soaked, dripping wet; **empapar** <1a> **1** *v/t* soak; (*absorber*) soak up; **2** *v/r* *~se* get soaked o drenched; **~se de algo** immerse o.s. in sth

empapelar <1a> v/t wallpaper

empaque m presence; (*seriedad*) solemnity; **empaquetar** <1a> v/t pack

emparedado m sandwich

emparejar <1a> v/t personas pair off; *calcetines* match up

emparentado adj related

empastador m, **~a** f L.Am. bookbinder; **empastar** <1a> v/t muela fill; *libro* bind; **empaste** m filling

empatar <1a> v/i tie, Br draw; (*igualar*) tie the game, Br equalize; **empate** m tie, draw; **gol del ~ en** *fútbol* equalizer

empecinarse <1a> v/r get an idea into one's head; **~ en algo** insist on sth

empedernido adj inveterate, confirmed

empedrado m paving

empeine m instep

empellón m shove; **entró a empellones** he shoved his way in

empelotarse <1a> v/r L.Am. P take one's clothes off, strip off

empeñado adj (*endeudado*) in debt; **estar ~ en hacer algo** be determined to do sth; **empeñar** <1a> **1** v/t pawn **2** v/r **~se** (*endeudarse*) get into debt; (*esforzarse*) strive (**en** to), make an effort (**en** to); **~se en hacer** obstinarse insist on doing, be determined to do

empeñero Méx **1** adj determined **2** m, **-a** f determined person; **empeño** m (*obstinación*) determination; (*esfuerzo*) effort; Méx fig pawn shop; **empeñoso** adj L.Am. hardworking

empeorar <1a> **1** v/t make worse **2** v/i deteriorate, get worse

empequeñecer <2d> v/t fig diminish

emperador m emperor; *pez* swordfish; **emperatriz** f empress

emperrarse <1a> v/r F: **~ en hacer algo** have one's heart set on doing sth; **~ con algo** set one's heart on sth

empezar <1f & 1k> **1** v/t start, begin **2** v/i start, begin; **~ a hacer algo** start to do sth, start doing sth; **~ por hacer algo** start o begin by doing sth; **empiezo** m S.Am. start, beginning

empinado adj steep; **empinar** <1a> v/t raise; **~ el codo** F raise one's elbow F

empírico adj empirical

emplazamiento m site, location; JUR subpœna, summons

empleado 1 adj: **le está bien ~** it serves him right **2** m, **-a** f employee; **~a de hogar** maid; **emplear** <1a> v/t (*usar*) use; *persona* employ; **empleo** m employment; (*puesto*) job; (*uso*) use; **modo de ~** instructions for use pl, directions pl

emplomar <1a> v/t S.Am. fill

empobrecer <2d> **1** v/t impoverish, make poor **2** v/i become impoverished, become poor **3** v/r **~se** become impoverished, become poor; **empobrecimiento** m impoverishment

empollar <1a> v/i F cram F, Br swot F; **empollón** m F grind F, Br swot F

emporio m L.Am. almacén department store

empotrado adj built-in, fitted; **empotrarse** <1a> v/r crash (**contra** into)

emprendedor adj enterprising; **emprender** <2a> v/t embark on, undertake; **~la con alguien** F take it out on s.o.

empresa f company; fig venture, undertaking; **~ de trabajo temporal** temping agency; **empresaria** f businesswoman; **empresarial** adj business atr; **ciencias ~es** business studies; **empresario** m businessman

empujar <1a> v/t push; fig urge on, spur on; **empujón** m push, shove; **salían a empujones** F they were pushing and shoving their way out

empuñar <1a> v/t grasp

emular <1a> v/t emulate

emulsión f emulsion

en prp (*dentro de*) in; (*sobre*) on; **~ un mes** in a month; **~ la mesa** on the table; ~ **inglés** in English; ~ **la calle** on the street, *Br tb* in the street; ~ **casa** at home; ~ **coche/tren** by car/train

enajenación *f* JUR transfer; ~ **mental** insanity; **enajenar** <1a> *v/t* JUR transfer; (*trastornar*) drive insane

enamorado *adj* in love (*de* with); **enamorar** <1a> **1** *v/t*: *lo enamoró* she captivated him **2** *v/r* ~**se** fall in love (*de* with)

enano 1 *adj* tiny; *perro, árbol* miniature, dwarf *atr* **2** *m* dwarf; **trabajar como un** ~ *fig* F work like a dog F

enarbolar <1a> *v/t* hoist, raise

encabezamiento *m* heading; **encabezar** <1f> *v/t* head; *movimiento, revolución* lead

encabritarse <1a> *v/r de caballo* rear up

encadenar <1a> **1** *v/t* chain (up); *fig* link *o* put together **2** *v/r* ~**se** chain oneself (**a** to)

encajar <1a> **1** *v/t piezas* fit; *golpe* take **2** *v/i* fit (**en** in; **con** with); **encaje** *m* lace

encalado *m* whitewashing; **encalar** <1a> *v/t* whitewash

encallar <1a> *v/i* MAR run aground

encaminar <1a> *v/r* set off (**a** for), head (**a** for); *fig* be aimed *o* directed (**a** at)

encandilar <1a> *v/t* dazzle

encantado *adj* (*contento*) delighted; *castillo* enchanted; *¡~!* nice to meet you; **encantador** *adj* charming; **encantar** <1a> *v/t*: *me/le encanta* I love/he loves it; **encanto** *m* (*atractivo*) charm; **como por** ~ as if by magic; *eres un* ~ you're an angel

encapricharse <1a> *v/r* fall in love (*de* with)

encapuchado *adj* hooded

encaramarse <1a> *v/r* climb

encarar <1a> *v/t* approach; *desgracia etc* face up to

encarcelar <1a> *v/t* put in prison, imprison

encarecer <2d> **1** *v/t* put up the price of, make more expensive **2** *v/r* ~**se** become more expensive; *de*

precios increase, rise; **encarecidamente** *adv*: *le ruego* ~ *que ...* I beg *o* urge you to ...

encargado *m*, **-a** *f* person in charge; *de un negocio* manager; **encargar** <1h> **1** *v/t* (*pedir*) order; *le encargué que me trajera ...* I asked him to bring me ... **2** *v/r* ~**se** (*tener responsabilidad*) be in charge; *yo me encargo de la comida* I'll take care of *o* see to the food; **encargo** *m* job, errand; COM order; *¿te puedo hacer un* ~? can I ask you to do something for me?; *hecho por* ~ made to order

encariñarse <1a> *v/r*: ~ **con alguien/algo** grow fond of s.o/sth, become attached to s.o./sth

encarnado *adj* red; **encarnar** <1a> *v/t cualidad etc* embody; TEA play; **encarnizado** *adj* bitter, fierce

encarrilar <1a> *v/t fig* direct, guide

encasillar <1a> *v/t* class, classify; (*estereotipar*) pigeonhole

encasquetar <1a> *v/t gorro etc* pull down; *me lo encasquetó* F he landed me with it F

encasquillarse <1a> *v/r de arma* jam

encauzar <1f> *v/t tb fig* channel

encefalopatía *f*: ~ **espongiforme bovina** bovine spongiform encephalitis, BSE

encendedor *m* lighter; **encender** <2g> **1** *v/t fuego* light; *luz, televisión* switch on, turn on; *fig* inflame, arouse, stir up **2** *v/r* ~**se** *de luz, televisión* come on; **encendido 1** *adj luz, televisión* (switched) on; *fuego* lit; *cara* red **2** *m* AUTO ignition

encerado *m* blackboard

encerar <1a> *v/t* polish, wax

encerrar <1k> **1** *v/t* lock up, shut up; (*contener*) contain **2** *v/r* ~**se** shut o.s. up; **encerrona** *f tb fig* trap

encestar <1a> *v/i* score

encharcado *adj* flooded, waterlogged

enchicharse <1a> *v/r L.Am.* (*emborracharse*) get drunk; *Rpl* P (*enojarse*) get angry, get mad F

enchilada *f Méx* GASTR enchilada (*tortilla with a meat or cheese filling*)

enchiloso *adj C.Am., Méx* hot

enchufado *m*: **es un ~** F he has connections, he has friends in high places; **enchufar** <1a> *v/t* EL plug in; **enchufe** *m* EL *macho* plug; *hembra* socket; **tener ~** *fig* F have pull F, have connections F; **enchufismo** *m* string-pulling

encía *f* gum

enciclopedia *f* encyclop(a)edia

encierro *m protesta* sit-in; *de toros* bull running

encima *adv* on top; **~ de** on top of, on; **por ~ de** over, above; **por ~ de todo** above all; **lo ayudo, y ~ se queja** I help him and then he goes and complains; **hacer algo muy por ~** do sth very quickly; **no lo llevo ~** I haven't got it on me; **ponerse algo ~** put sth on; **encimera** *f sábana* top sheet; *Esp mostrador* worktop

encina *f* BOT holm oak

encinta *adj* pregnant

enclaustrarse <1a> *v/r fig* shut o.s. away

enclave *m* enclave

enclenque 1 *adj* sickly, weak **2** *m/f* weakling

encoger <2c> **1** *v/t* shrink; *las piernas* tuck in **2** *v/i de material* shrink **3** *v/r* **~se** *de material* shrink; *fig: de persona* be intimidated, cower; **~se de hombros** shrug (one's shoulders)

encolar <1a> *v/t* glue, stick

encolerizarse <1f> *v/r* get angry

encomienda *f L.Am.* HIST grant of land and labor by colonial authorities after the Conquest

enconado *adj* fierce, heated

encontrar <1m> **1** *v/t* find **2** *v/r* **~se** (*reunirse*) meet; (*estar*) be; **~se con alguien** meet s.o., run into s.o.; **me encuentro bien** I'm fine, I feel fine; **encontronazo** *m* smash, crash

encorvar <1a> *v/t* hunch; *estantería* cause to buckle

encrespar <1a> **1** *v/t pelo* curl; *mar* make rough *o* choppy; *fig* arouse, inflame **2** *v/r* **~se** *del mar* turn choppy; *fig* become inflamed

encrucijada *f* crossroads; *fig* dilemma

encuadernar <1a> *v/t* bind

encuadrar <1a> *v/t en marco* frame; *en grupo* include, place

encuartelar <1a> *v/t L.Am.* billet

encubierto *part → encubrir*; **encubrir** <3a; *part* **encubierto**> *v/t delincuente* harbo(u)r; *delito* cover up, conceal

encuentro *m* meeting, encounter; DEP game; **salir** *or* **ir al ~ de alguien** meet s.o., greet s.o.

encuerado *adj L.Am.* naked

encuesta *f* survey; (*sondeo*) (opinion) poll; **encuestar** <1a> *v/t* poll

encumbrarse <1a> *v/r fig* rise to the top

encurtidos *mpl* pickles

ende *adv*: **por ~** therefore, consequently

endeble *adj* weak, feeble

endémico *adj* endemic

endemoniado *adj* possessed; *fig* F terrible, awful

enderezar <1f> **1** *v/t* straighten out **2** *v/r* **~se** straighten up, stand up straight; *fig* straighten o.s. out, sort o.s out

endeudarse <1a> *v/r* get (o.s.) into debt

endiablado *adj fig* (*malo*) terrible, awful; (*difícil*) tough

endibia *f* BOT endive

endilgar <1h> *v/t*: **me lo endilgó a mí** F he landed me with it F; **~ un sermón a alguien** F lecture s.o., give s.o. a lecture

endosar <1a> *v/t* COM endorse; **me lo endosó a mí** F she landed me with it F

endrina *f* BOT sloe

endrogarse <1h> *v/r Méx, C.Am.* get into debt

endulzar <1f> *v/t* sweeten; (*suavizar*) soften

endurecer <2d> **1** *v/t* harden; *fig* toughen up **2** *v/r* **~se** harden, become harder; *fig* become harder, toughen up

enebro *m* BOT juniper

enema *m* MED enema

enemigo 1 *adj* enemy *atr* **2** *m* enemy; ***ser ~ de*** *fig* be opposed to, be against; **enemistarse** <1a> *v/r* fall out

energético *adj crisis* energy *atr*; *alimento* energy-giving; **energía** *f* energy; **~ eólica** wind power; **~ nuclear** nuclear power, nuclear energy; **~ solar** solar power, solar energy; **enérgico** *adj* energetic; *fig* forceful, strong

energúmeno *m* lunatic; ***ponerse hecho un ~*** go crazy F, blow a fuse F

ene. *abr* (= *enero*) Jan. (= January)

enero *m* January

enervar <1a> *v/t* irritate, get on the nerves of

enésimo *adj* nth; ***por -a vez*** for the umpteenth time

enfadado *adj* annoyed (**con** with); (*encolerizado*) angry (**con** with); **enfadar** <1a> **1** *v/t* (*molestar*) annoy; (*encolerizar*) make angry, anger **2** *v/r* **~se** (*molestarse*) get annoyed (**con** with); (*encolerizarse*) get angry (**con** with); **enfado** *m* (*molestia*) annoyance; (*cólera*) anger

enfangarse <1h> *v/r* get muddy; **~ en** *fig* get (o.s.) mixed up in

énfasis *m* emphasis; ***poner ~ en*** emphasize, stress; **enfático** *adj* emphatic

enfermar <1a> **1** *v/t* drive crazy **2** *v/i* get sick, *Br tb* get ill; **enfermedad** *f* illness, disease; **enfermería** *f sala* infirmary, sickbay; *carrera* nursing; **enfermero** *m*, **-a** *f* nurse; **enfermizo** *adj* unhealthy; **enfermo 1** *adj* sick, ill **2** *m*, **-a** *f* sick person; **enfermoso** *adj* L.Am. sickly, unhealthy

enfiestarse <1a> *v/r* L.Am. F party F, live it up F

enfocar <1g> *v/t cámara* focus; *imagen* get in focus; *fig: asunto* look at, consider

enfoque *m fig* approach

enfrentamiento *m* clash, confrontation; **enfrentar** <1a> **1** *v/t* confront, face up to **2** *v/r* **~se** DEP meet; **~se con alguien** confront s.o.; **~se a algo** face (up to) sth

enfrente *adv* opposite; **~ del colegio** opposite the school, across (the street) from the school

enfriar <1c> **1** *v/t vino* chill; *algo caliente* cool (down); *fig* cool **2** *v/r* **~se** (*perder calor*) cool down; (*perder demasiado calor*) get cold, go cold; *fig* cool, cool off; MED catch a cold, catch a chill

enfurecer <2d> **1** *v/t* infuriate, make furious **2** *v/r* **~se** get furious, get into a rage **enfurecido** *adj* furious, enraged

enfurruñado *adj* F sulky; **enfurruñarse** <1a> *v/r* F go into a huff F

enganchar <1a> **1** *v/t* hook; F *novia, trabajo* land **2** *v/r* **~se** (*en* on); MIL sign up, enlist; **~se a la droga** F get hooked on drugs F

engañar <1a> *v/t* deceive, cheat; (*ser infiel a*) cheat on, be unfaithful to; ***te han engañado*** you've been had **2** *v/r* **~se** (*mentirse*) deceive o.s., kid o.s. F; (*equivocarse*) be wrong; **engaño** *m* (*mentira*) deception, deceit; (*ardid*) trick

engarzar <1f> *v/t joya* set

engatusar <1a> *v/t* F sweet-talk

engendrar <1a> *v/t* father; *fig* breed, engender *fml*; **engendro** *m fig* eyesore

englobar <1a> *v/t* include, embrace *fml*

engordar <1a> **1** *v/t* put on, gain **2** *v/i de persona* put on weight, gain weight; *de comida* be fattening

engorrar <1a> *v/t Méx, W.I.* F annoy

engorroso *adj* tricky

engranaje *m* TÉC gears *pl*; *fig* machinery

engrasar <1a> *v/t* grease, lubricate; **engrase** *m* greasing, lubrication

engreído *adj* conceited

engrosar <1m> **1** *v/t* swell, increase

2 *v/i* put on weight, gain weight
engrudo *m* (flour and water) paste
engullir <3h> *v/t* bolt (down)
enhebrar <1a> *v/t* thread, string
enhiesto *adj lit persona* erect, upright; *torre, árbol* lofty
enhorabuena *f* congratulations *pl*; *dar la ~* congratulate (*por* on)
enigma *m* enigma; **enigmático** *adj* enigmatic
enjabonar <1a> *v/t* soap
enjambre *m tb fig* swarm
enjoyado *adj* bejewel(l)ed
enjuagar <1h> *v/t* rinse
enjugar <1h> *v/t deuda etc* wipe out; *líquido* mop up; *lágrimas* wipe away
enjuiciar <1b> *v/t* JUR institute proceedings against; *fig* judge
enlace *m* link, connection; *~ matrimonial* marriage
enlatar <1a> *v/t* can, *Br tb* tin
enlazar <1f> **1** *v/t* link (up), connect; *L.Am. con cuerda* rope, lasso **2** *v/i de carretera* link up (*con* with); AVIA, FERR connect (*con* with)
enloquecer <2d> **1** *v/t* drive crazy *o* mad **2** *v/i* go crazy *o* mad
enmarañar <1a> **1** *v/t pelo* tangle; *asunto* complicate, muddle **2** *v/r ~se de pelo* get tangled; *~se en algo* get entangled *o* embroiled in sth
enmarcar <1g> *v/t* frame
enmascarar <1a> *v/t* hide, disguise
enmendar <1k> **1** *v/t asunto* rectify, put right; JUR, POL amend; *~le la plana a alguien* find fault with what s.o. has done **2** *v/r ~se* mend one's ways; **enmienda** *f* POL amendment
enmicar <1g> *v/t L.Am.* laminate
enmudecer <2d> **1** *v/t* silence **2** *v/i* fall silent
ennoblecer <2d> *v/t* ennoble
enojado *adj L.Am.* angry; **enojar** <1a> **1** *v/t* (*molestar*) annoy; *L.Am.* (*encolerizar*) make angry **2** *v/r ~se L.Am.* (*molestarse*) get annoyed; (*encolerizarse*) get angry; **enojo** *m L.Am.* anger; **enojón** *adj L.Am.* irritable, touchy; **enojoso** *adj* (*delicado*) awkward; (*aburrido*) tedious,

tiresome
enorgullecer <2d> **1** *v/t* make proud, fill with pride **2** *v/r ~se* be proud (*de* of)
enorme *adj* enormous, huge
enrarecido *adj aire* rarefied; *relaciones* strained
enredadera *f* BOT creeper, climbing plant
enredar <1a> **1** *v/t* tangle, get tangled; *fig* complicate, make complicated **2** *v/i* make trouble **3** *v/r ~se* get tangled; *fig* get complicated; *~se en algo* get mixed up *o* involved in sth; **enredo** *m* tangle; (*confusión*) mess, confusion; (*intriga*) intrigue; *amoroso* affair
enrevesado *adj* complicated, involved
enriquecer <2d> **1** *v/t* make rich; *fig* enrich **2** *v/r ~se* get rich; *fig* be enriched
enrojecer <2d> **1** *v/t* turn red **2** *v/i* blush, go red
enrolarse <1a> *v/r* MIL enlist
enrollar <1a> **1** *v/t* roll up; *cable* coil; *hilo* wind; *me enrolla* F I like it, I think it's great **2** *v/r ~se* F *hablar* go on and on F; *se enrolló mucho con nosotros* (*se portó bien*) he was great to us; *¡no te enrolles!* F get to the point!; *~se con alguien fig* F neck with s.o.
enroscar <1g> **1** *v/t tornillo* screw in; *cable, cuerda* coil **2** *v/r ~se* coil up
ensaimada *f* GASTR *pastry in the form of a spiral*
ensalada *f* GASTR salad; **ensaladera** *f* salad bowl; **ensaladilla** *f*: *~ rusa* GASTR Russian salad
ensalmo *m*: *como por ~* as if by magic
ensalzar <1f> *v/t* extol, praise
ensamblar <1a> *v/t* assemble
ensanchar <1a> **1** *v/t* widen; *prenda* let out **2** *v/r ~se* widen, get wider; *de prenda* stretch
ensangrentar <1k> *v/t* stain with blood, cover with blood
ensañarse <1a> *v/r* show no mercy

(con to)

ensartar <1a> **1** v/t en hilo string; aguja thread; **ensayo** m (engañar) trick, trap **2** v/r **~se** L.Am. en discusión get involved, get caught up

ensayar <1a> v/t test, try (out); TEA rehearse; **ensayo** m TEA rehearsal; escrito essay; **~ general** dress rehearsal

enseguida adv immediately, right away

ensenada f inlet, cove

enseñanza f teaching; **~ primaria** elementary education, Br primary education; L.Am.; **~ secundaria** or **media** secondary education; **~ superior** higher education; **enseñar** <1a> v/t (dar clases) teach; (mostrar) show

ensillar <1a> v/t saddle

ensimismarse <1a> v/r become lost in thought; L.Am. F get conceited o big-headed F

ensombrecer <2d> v/t cast a shadow over

ensordecedor adj deafening

ensuciar <1b> **1** v/t (get) dirty; fig sully, tarnish **2** v/r **~se** get dirty; fig get one's hands dirty

ensueño m: **de ~** fig fairy-tale atr, dream atr

entablar <1a> v/t strike up, start

entablillar <1a> v/t splint, put in a splint

entarimado m (suelo) floorboards pl; (plataforma) stage, platform

ente m (ser) being, entity; F (persona rara) oddball F; (organización) body

entejar <1a> v/t L.Am. tile

entender <2g> **1** v/t understand; **dar a ~ a alguien** give s.o. to understand **2** v/i understand; **~ de algo** know about sth **3** v/r **~se** communicate; **a ver si nos entendemos** let's get this straight; **yo me entiendo** I know what I'm doing; **~se con alguien** get along with s.o., get on with s.o. **4** m: **a mi ~** in my opinion, to my mind; **entendido 1** adj understood; **¿~?** do you

understand?, understood?; **tengo ~ que** I gather o understand that **2** m, -a f expert, authority; **entendimiento** m understanding; (inteligencia) mind

enterado adj knowledgeable, well-informed; **estar ~ de** know about, have heard about; **darse por ~** get the message, take the hint; **enterarse** <1a> v/r find out, hear (de about); **¡para que te enteres!** F so there! F; **¡se va a enterar!** F he's in for it! F

entereza f fortitude

enternecer <2d> v/t move, touch

entero 1 adj (completo) whole, entire; (no roto) intact, undamaged; **por ~** completely, entirely **2** m (punto) point

enterrar <1k> v/t bury; **~ a todos** fig outlive everybody

entidad f entity, body

entierro m burial; (funeral) funeral

entonar <1a> **1** v/t intone, sing; fig F perk up **2** v/i sing in tune **3** v/r **~se** con bebida get tipsy

entonces adv then; **desde ~** since, since then; **por ~**, **en aquel ~** in those days, at that time

entornar <1a> v/t puerta leave ajar; ojos half close; **entorno** m environment

entorpecer <2d> v/t hold up, hinder; paso obstruct; entendimiento dull

entrada f acción entry; lugar entrance; localidad ticket; pago deposit, down payment; de comida starter; **de ~** from the outset, from the start

entrañable adj amistad close, deep; amigo close, dear; recuerdo fond; **entrañar** <1a> v/t entail, involve; **entrañas** fpl entrails

entrar <1a> **1** v/i para indicar acercamiento come in, enter; para indicar alejamiento go in, enter; caber fit; **me entró frío / sueño** I got cold / sleepy, I began to feel cold / sleepy; **no me entra en la cabeza** I can't understand it **2** v/t para indicar acercamiento bring in; para indicar *alejamiento* take in

entre *prp dos cosas, personas* between; *más de dos* among(st); *expresando cooperación* between; *la relación ~ ellos* the relationship between them; *~ nosotros* among us; *lo pagamos ~ todos* we paid for it among *o* between us

entreabierto 1 *part* → **entreabrir 2** *adj* half-open; *puerta* ajar; **entreabrir** <3a; *part* **entreabierto**> *v/t* half-open

entreacto *m* TEA interval

entrecejo *m*: *fruncir el ~* frown

entrecomillar <1a> *v/t* put in quotation marks

entrecortado *adj* *habla* halting; *respiración* difficult, labo(u)red

entrecot *m* entrecote

entredicho *m*: *poner en ~* call into question, question

entrega *f* handing over; *de mercancías* delivery; *(dedicación)* dedication, devotion; *~ a domicilio* (home) delivery; *~ de premios* prize-giving, presentation; *hacer ~ de algo a alguien* present s.o. with sth; **entregar** <1h> **1** *v/t* give, hand over; *trabajo, deberes* hand in; *mercancías* deliver; *premio* present **2** *v/r* *~se* give o.s. up; *~se a fig* devote o.s. to, dedicate o.s. to

entrelazar <1f> *v/t* interweave, intertwine

entremeses *mpl* GASTR appetizers, hors d'œuvres

entremezclar <1a> **1** *v/t* intermingle, mix **2** *v/r* *~se* intermingle, mix

entrenador *m*, *~a* *f* coach; **entrenamiento** *m* coaching; **entrenar** <1a> **1** *v/t* train **2** *v/r* *~se* train

entrepierna *f* ANAT crotch

entresacar <1g> *v/t* extract, select

entresijos *mpl* *fig* details, ins and outs F

entresuelo *m* mezzanine; TEA dress circle

entretanto *adv* meanwhile, in the meantime

entretecho *m* *Arg, Chi* attic

entretener <2l> **1** *v/t* *(divertir)* entertain, amuse; *(retrasar)* keep, detain; *(distraer)* distract **2** *v/i* be entertaining **3** *v/r* *~se* *(divertirse)* amuse o.s.; *(distraerse)* keep o.s. busy; *(retrasarse)* linger; **entretenido** *adj* *(divertido)* entertaining, enjoyable; *estar ~ ocupado* be busy; **entretenimiento** *m* entertainment, amusement

entrevero *m* *S.Am.* *(lío)* mix-up, mess; *Chi (discusión)* argument

entrevista *f* interview; **entrevistar** <1a> **1** *v/t* interview **2** *v/r* *~se*: *~se con alguien* meet (with) s.o.

entristecer <2d> **1** *v/t* sadden **2** *v/r* *~se* grow sad

entrometerse <2a> *v/r* meddle (*en* in); **entrometido 1** *part* → **entrometerse 2** *adj* meddling *atr*, interfering **3** *m* meddler, busybody

entronizar <1f> *v/t* *fig* instal(l)

entumecer <2d> **1** *v/t* numb **2** *v/r* *~se* go numb, get stiff

enturbiar <1b> *v/t* *tb fig* cloud

entusiasmado *adj* excited, delirious; **entusiasmar** <1a> *v/t* excite, make enthusiastic; **entusiasmo** *m* enthusiasm; **entusiasta 1** *adj* enthusiastic **2** *m/f* enthusiast

enumerar <1a> *v/t* list, enumerate

enunciar <1b> *v/t* state

envalentonarse <1a> *v/r* become bolder *o* more daring; *(insolentarse)* become defiant

envanecerse <2d> *v/r* become conceited *o* vain

envasar <1a> *v/t* *en botella* bottle; *en lata* can; *en paquete* pack; **envase** *m* container; *botella* (empty) bottle; *~ de cartón* carton; *~ no retornable* nonreturnable bottle

envejecer <2d> **1** *v/t* age, make look older **2** *v/i* age, grow old; **envejecimiento** *m* aging, ageing

envenenar <1a> *v/t* *tb fig* poison

envergadura *f* AVIA wingspan; MAR breadth; *fig* magnitude, importance; *de gran or mucha ~ fig* of great importance

enviado *m*, *~a* *f* POL envoy; *de un*

periódico reporter, correspondent;
~ *especial* POL special envoy; *de un
periódico* special correspondent;
enviar <1c> *v/t* send

enviciarse <1b> *v/r* get addicted
(**con** to)

envidia *f* envy, jealousy; **me da ~** I'm
envious *o* jealous; **tener ~ a alguien
de algo** envy s.o. sth; **envidiar** <1b>
v/t envy; **~ a alguien por algo** envy
s.o. sth; **envidioso** *adj* envious, jealous

envilecer <2d> **1** *v/t* degrade, debase **2** *v/r* **~se** degrade o.s., debase
o.s.

envío *m* shipment

enviudar <1c> *v/i* be widowed

envoltorio *m* wrapper; **envoltura** *f*
cover, covering; *de regalo* wrapping;
de caramelo wrapper

envolver <2h; *part* **envuelto**> **1** *v/t*
wrap (up); (*rodear*) surround, en-
velop; (*involucrar*) involve; **~ a
alguien en algo** involve s.o. in sth
2 *v/r* **~se** wrap o.s. up; **~se en** *fig* become involved in; **envuelto** *part* →
envolver

enyesado *m* plastering

enzarzarse <1f> *v/r* get involved
(**en** in)

eólico *adj* wind *atr*

épico *adj* epic

epidemia *f* epidemic

epilepsia *f* MED epilepsy

epílogo *m* epilog(ue)

episcopal *adj* episcopal

episodio *m* episode

epistolar *adj* epistolary

epitafio *m* epitaph

época *f* time, period; *parte del año*
time of year; GEOL epoch; **hacer ~**
be epoch-making

epopeya *f* epic, epic poem

equidad *f* fairness

equidistante *adj* equidistant

equilibrado *adj* well-balanced;
equilibrar <1a> *v/t* balance; **equilibrio** *m* balance; FÍS equilibrium

equino *adj* equine

equinoccio *m* equinox

equipaje *m* baggage; **~ de mano**

hand baggage

oquipamiento *m*: **~ de serie** AUTO
standard features *pl*; **equipar** <1a>
v/t equip (**con** with)

equiparar <1a> *v/t* put on a level (*a
or* **con** with); **~ algo con algo** *fig*
compare *o* liken sth to sth

equipo *m* DEP team; *accesorios*
equipment; **~ de música** *or* *de
sonido* sound system

equitación *f* riding

equitativo *adj* fair, equitable

equivalente *m/adj* equivalent; **equivaler** <2q> *v/i* be equivalent (**a**
to)

equivocación *f* mistake; **por ~** by
mistake; **equivocado** *adj* wrong;
estar ~ be wrong, be mistaken;
equivocar <1g> **1** *v/t*: **~ a alguien**
make s.o. make a mistake **2** *v/r* **~se**
make a mistake; **te has equivo-
cado** you are wrong *o* mistaken;
~se de número TELEC get the
wrong number; **equívoco 1** *adj* ambiguous, equivocal **2** *m* misunderstanding; (*error*) mistake

era *f* era

erección *f* erection

eres *vb* → **ser**

ergonómico *adj* ergonomic

erguir <3n> **1** *v/t* raise, lift; (*poner
derecho*) straighten **2** *v/r* **~se** *de persona* stand up, rise; *de edificio* rise

erial *m* uncultivated land

erigir <3c> **1** *v/t* erect **2** *v/r* **~se**: **~se
en** set o.s. up as

erizarse <1f> *v/r* *de pelo* stand on
end; **erizo** *m* ZO hedgehog; **~ de
mar** ZO sea urchin

ermita *f* chapel; **ermitaño 1** *m* ZO
hermit crab **2** *m*, **-a** *f* hermit

erogación *f* *Méx, S.Am.* expenditure,
outlay

erógeno *adj* erogenous

erosión *f* erosion; **erosionar** <1a>
v/t GEOL erode

erótico *adj* erotic; **erotismo** *m* eroti-
cism

erradicar <1g> *v/t* eradicate, wipe
out

errante *adj* wandering; **errar** <1l>

1 *v/t* miss; **~ el tiro** miss **2** *v/i* miss; **~ es humano** to err is human

equivocarse be wrong, be mistaken

errata *f* mistake, error; *de imprenta* misprint

erre *f*: **~ que ~** F doggedly, stubbornly

erróneo *adj* wrong, erroneous *fml*; **error** *m* mistake, error; **~ de cálculo** error of judg(e)ment

eructar <1a> *v/i* belch F, burp F; **eructo** *m* belch F, burp F

erudito 1 *adj* learned, erudite **2** *m* scholar

erupción *f* GEOL eruption; MED rash

esbelto *adj* slim, slender

esbozar <1f> *v/t* sketch; *idea, proyecto etc* outline; **esbozo** *m* sketch; *de idea, proyecto etc* outline

escabeche *m type of marinade*

escabroso *adj* rough; *problema* tricky; *relato* indecent

escabullirse <3h> *v/r* escape, slip away

escala *f tb* MÚS scale; AVIA stopover; **~ de cuerda** rope ladder; **~ de valores** scale of values; **a ~** to scale, life-sized

escalada *f* DEP climb, ascent; **~ de los precios** increase in prices, escalation of prices; **escalador** *m*, **~a** *f* climber; **escalafón** *m fig* ladder; **escalar** <1a> **1** *v/t* climb, scale **2** *v/i* climb

escaldar <1a> *v/t* GASTR blanch; *manos* scald

escalera *f* stairs *pl*, staircase; **~ de caracol** spiral staircase; **~ de incendios** fire escape; **~ de mano** ladder; **~ mecánica** escalator

escalfar <1a> *v/t* poach

escalofriante *adj* horrifying; **escalofrío** *m* shiver

escalón *m* step; *de escalera de mano* rung; **escalonar** <1a> *v/t en tiempo* stagger; *terreno* terrace

escalope *m* escalope

escama *f* ZO scale; *de jabón, piel* flake; **escamar** <1a> *v/t* scale, remove the scales from; *fig* make suspicious **2** *v/r* **~se** become suspicious

escamotear <1a> *v/t* (*ocultar*) hide, conceal; (*negar*) withhold

escampar <1a> *v/i* clear up, stop raining

escanciar <1b> *v/t fml* pour

escandalizar <1f> **1** *v/t* shock, scandalize **2** *v/r* **~se** be shocked; **escándalo** *m* (*asunto vergonzoso*) scandal; (*jaleo*) racket, ruckus; **armar un ~** make a scene; **escandaloso** *adj* (*vergonzoso*) scandalous, shocking; (*ruidoso*) noisy, rowdy

Escandinavia Scandinavia

escanear <1a> *v/t* scan; **escáner** *m* scanner

escaño *m* POL seat

escapar <1a> **1** *v/t* escape (*de* from); **dejar ~** *oportunidad* pass up, let slip; *suspiro* let out, give **2** *v/r* **~se** (*huir*) escape (*de* from); *de casa* run away (*de* from); **~se de situación** get out of

escaparate *m* store window

escapatoria *f*: **no tener ~** have no way out

escape *m de gas* leak; AUTO exhaust; **salir a ~** rush out

escarabajo *m* ZO beetle

escaramuza *f* skirmish

escarbadientes *m inv* toothpick; **escarbar** <1a> **1** *v/i tb fig* dig around (*en*) **2** *v/t* dig around in

escarceos *mpl* forays, dabbling *sg*; **~ amorosos** romantic *o* amorous adventures

escarcha *f* frost

escardar <1a> *v/t* hoe

escarmentar <1k> **1** *v/t* teach a lesson to **2** *v/i* learn one's lesson; **~ en cabeza ajena** learn from other people's mistakes; **escarmiento** *m* lesson; **le sirvió de ~** it taught him a lesson

escarnio *m* ridicule, derision

escarola *f* endive, escarole

escarpado *adj* sheer, steep

escarpia *f* hook

escasear <1a> *v/i* be scarce, be in short supply; **escasez** *f* shortage, scarcity; **escaso** *adj recursos* limited; **andar ~ de algo** *falto* be short of sth; **-as posibilidades de** not much chance of, little chance of; **falta un mes ~** it's barely a month away

escatimar <1a> v/t be mean with, be very sparing with; **no ~ esfuerzos** be unstinting in one's efforts, spare no effort

escayola f (plaster) cast; **escayolar** <1a> v/t put in a (plaster) cast

escena f scene; **escenario** stage; **entrar en ~** come on stage; **hacer una ~** fig make a scene; **escenario** m stage; fig scene; **escénico** adj stage atr; **escenificar** <1g> v/t stage

escepticismo m skepticism, Br scepticism; **escéptico 1** adj skeptical, Br sceptical **2** m, **-a** f skeptic, Br sceptic

escindirse <3a> v/r (fragmentarse) split (**en** into); (segregarse) break away (**de** from); **escisión** f (fragmentación) split; (segregación) break

esclarecer <2d> v/t throw o shed light on; misterio clear up; **esclarecimiento** m clarification; de misterio solving

esclavitud f slavery; **esclavizar** <1f> v/t enslave; fig tie down; **esclavo** m slave

esclerosis f MED: **~ múltiple** multiple sclerosis

escoba f broom; **escobilla** f small brush; AUTO wiper blade

escocer <2b & 2h> v/i sting, smart; **todavía escuece la derrota** he's still smarting from the defeat

escocés **1** adj Scottish **2** m Scot, Scotsman; **escocesa** f Scot, Scotswoman; **Escocia** Scotland

escoger <2c> v/t choose, select; **escogido** adj select

escolar **1** adj school atr **2** m/f student; **escolarización** f education, schooling; **~ obligatoria** compulsory education; **escolarizar** <1f> v/t educate, provide schooling for; **escolástico** adj scholarly

escollera f breakwater; **escollo** m

MAR reef; (obstáculo) hurdle, obstacle

escolta f escort **2** m/f motorista outrider; (guardaespaldas) bodyguard; **escoltar** <1a> v/t escort

escombros mpl rubble sg

esconder <2a> **1** v/t hide, conceal **2** v/r **~se** hide; **escondidas** fpl S.Am. hide-and-seek sg; **a ~** in secret, secretly; **escondite** m lugar hiding place; juego hide-and-seek; **escondrijo** m hiding place

escopeta f shotgun; **~ de aire comprimido** air gun, air rifle; **escopetado** adj: **salir ~** F shoot o dash off F; **escopetazo** m gunshot

escorbuto m scurvy

escoria f slag; desp dregs pl

Escorpio m/f inv ASTR Scorpio; **escorpión** m ZO scorpion

escotado adj low-cut; **escote** m neckline; de mujer cleavage

escotilla f MAR hatch

escozor m burning sensation, stinging; fig bitterness

escribir <3a; part **escrito**> v/t write; (deletrear) spell; **~ a mano** handwrite, write by hand; **~ a máquina** type; **escrito 1** part → **escribir 2** adj written; **por ~** in writing **3** m document; **~s** writings; **escritor** m, **~a** f writer, author; **escritorio** m desk; **artículos de ~** stationery; **escritura** f writing; JUR deed; **Sagradas Escrituras** Holy Scripture

escrúpulo m scruple; **sin ~s** unscrupulous; **escrupuloso** adj (cuidadoso) meticulous; (honrado) scrupulous; (aprensivo) fastidious

escrutar <1a> v/t scrutinize; votos count; **escrutinio** m de votos count; (inspección) scrutiny

escuadrón m squadron

escuálido adj skinny, emaciated

escucha f: **estar a la ~** be listening out; **~s pl telefónicas** wiretapping sg, Br tb phone-tapping sg; **escuchar** <1a> **1** v/t listen to; L.Am. (oír) hear **2** v/i listen

escuchimizado *adj* F puny F, scrawny F

escudarse <1a> *v/r fig* hide (*en* behind)

escudería *f* stable

escudilla *f* bowl

escudo *m arma* shield; *insignia* badge; *moneda* escudo; **~ de armas** coat of arms

escudriñar <1a> *v/t* (*mirar de lejos*) scan; (*examinar*) scrutinize

escuela *f* school; **~ de comercio** business school; **~ de idiomas** language school; **~ primaria** elementary school, *Br* primary school

escuelero 1 *adj L.Am.* school *atr* **2** *m*, **-a** *f L.Am.* (*maestro*) teacher; *Pe, Bol* (*alumno*) student

escueto *adj* succinct, concise

escuincle *m/f Méx, C.Am.* F kid

esculpir <3a> *v/t* sculpt; **escultor** *m*, **~a** *f* sculptor; **escultura** *f* sculpture

escupidera *f* spitoon; *L.Am.* chamber pot; **escupir** <3a> **1** *v/i* spit **2** *v/t* spit out; **escupitajo** *m* F gob of spit F

escurreplatos *m inv* plate rack

escurridizo *adj* slippery; *fig* evasive; **escurridor** *m* (*colador*) colander; (*escurreplatos*) plate rack; **escurrir** <3a> **1** *v/t ropa* wring out; *platos, verduras* drain **2** *v/i de platos* drain; *de ropa* drip-dry **3** *v/r* **~se** *de líquido* drain away; (*deslizarse*) slip; (*escaparse*) slip away

escusado *m* bathroom

ese, esa, esos, esas *det singular* that; *plural* those

ése, ésa, ésos, ésas *pron singular* that (one); *plural* those (ones); **le ofrecí dinero pero ni por ésas** I offered him money but even that wasn't enough; **no soy de ésos que** I'm not one of those who

esencia *f* essence; **esencial** *adj* essential

esfera *f* sphere; **~ de actividad** *fig* field *o* sphere (of activity); **esférico 1** *adj* spherical **2** *m* DEP F ball

esfinge *f* sphinx

esforzarse <1f & 1m> *v/r* make an effort, try hard; **esfuerzo** *m* effort; **hacer un ~** make an effort; **sin ~** effortlessly

esfumarse <1a> *v/r* F *tb fig* disappear

esgrima *f* fencing; **esgrimir** <3a> *v/t arma* wield; *fig: argumento* put forward, use

esguince *m* sprain

eslabón *m* link; **el ~ perdido** the missing link

eslavo 1 *adj* Slavic, Slavonic **2** *m*, **-a** *f* Slav

eslogan *m* slogan

eslora *f* length

Eslovaquia Slovakia

Eslovenia Slovenia

esmalte *m* enamel; **~ de uñas** nail polish, nail varnish

esmerado *adj* meticulous

esmeralda *f* emerald

esmerarse <1a> *v/r* take great care (*en* over)

esmerilado *adj*: **cristal ~** frosted glass

esmero *m* care; **con ~** carefully

esmirriado *adj* F skinny F, scrawny F

esmoquin *m* tuxedo, *Br* dinner jacket

esnifar <1a> *v/t* F *pegamento* sniff F; *cocaína* snort F

esnob 1 *adj* snobbish **2** *m* snob; **esnobismo** *m* snobbishness

eso *pron* that; **en ~** just then, just at that moment; **~ mismo, ~ es** that's it, that's the way; **a ~ de las dos** at around two; **por ~** that's why; **¿y ~?** why's that?; **y ~ que le dije que no se lo contara** and after I told him not to tell her

esotérico *adj* esoteric

espabilado *adj* (*listo*) bright, smart; (*vivo*) sharp, on the ball F; **espabilar** <1a> **1** *v/t* (*quitar el sueño*) wake up, revive; **lo ha espabilado** (*avivado*) she's got him to wise up **2** *v/i* (*darse prisa*) hurry up, get a move on; (*avivarse*) wise up **3** *v/r* **~se** *del sueño* wake oneself up; (*darse prisa*) hurry up, get a move on; (*avivarse*) wise up

espacial adj cohete, viaje space atr; FÍS, MAT spatial; **espaciarse** <1a> v/r become more (and more) infrequent; **espacio** m space; TV program, Br programme; **~s verdes** green spaces; **~ de tiempo** space of time; **~ vital** living space; **espacioso** adj spacious, roomy

espada f sword; **~s** pl (en naipes) suit in Spanish deck of cards; **estar entre la ~ y la pared** be between a rock and a hard place; **espadachín** m skilled swordsman

espaguetis mpl spaghetti sg

espalda f back; **a ~s de alguien** behind s.o.'s back; **de ~s a** with one's back to; **por la ~** from behind; **caerse de ~s** fall flat on one's back; **no me des la ~** don't sit with your back to me; **nadar a ~** swim backstroke; **tener cubiertas las ~s** fig keep one's back covered; **volver la ~ a alguien** fig turn one's back on s.o.; **espaldarazo** m slap on the back; (reconocimiento) recognition; **espalderas** fpl wall bars

espantajo m scarecrow; fig sight; **espantapájaros** m inv scarecrow; **espantar** <1a> 1 v/t (asustar) frighten, scare; (ahuyentar) frighten away, shoo away; F (horrorizar) horrify, appal(l) 2 v/r **~se** get frightened, get scared; F (horrorizarse) be horrified, be appal(l)ed; **espanto** m (susto) fright; L.Am. (fantasma) ghost; **nos llenó de ~** desagrado we were horrified; **¡qué ~!** how awful!; **de ~** terrible; **espantoso** adj horrific, appalling; para enfatizar terrible, dreadful; **hace un calor ~** it's terribly hot, it's incredibly hot

España Spain; **español 1** adj Spanish 2 m idioma Spanish 3 m, **-a** f Spaniard; **los ~es** the Spanish

esparadrapo m Band-Aid®, Br plaster

esparcimiento m relaxation; **esparcir** <3b> 1 v/t papeles scatter; rumor spread 2 v/r **~se** de papeles be

scattered; de rumor spread

espárrago m BOT asparagus; **~ triguero** wild asparagus; **¡vete a freír ~s!** F get lost! F

espartano adj spartan

esparto m BOT esparto grass

espasmo m spasm

espátula f spatula; en pintura palette knife

especia f spice

especial adj special; (difícil) fussy; **en ~** especially; **especialidad** f specialty, Br speciality; **especialista** m/f specialist, expert; en cine stuntman; mujer stuntwoman; **especializarse** <1f> v/r specialize (en in)

especie f BIO species; (tipo) kind, sort

especiero m spice rack

especificar <1g> v/t specify; **específico** adj specific

espectacular adj spectacular; **espectáculo** m TEA show; (escena) sight; **dar el ~** fig make a spectacle of o.s.; **espectador** m, **~a** f en cine etc member of the audience; DEP spectator; (observador) on-looker, observer

espectro m FÍS spectrum; (fantasma) ghost

especulación f speculation; **especular** <1a> v/i speculate; **especulativo** adj speculative

espejismo m mirage; **espejo** m mirror; **~ retrovisor** rear-view mirror

espeleólogo m spelunker, Br potholer

espeluznante adj horrific, horrifying

espera f wait; **sala de ~** waiting room; **en ~ de** pending; **estar a la ~ de** be waiting for; **esperanza** f hope; **~ de vida** life expectancy; **esperar** <1a> 1 v/t (aguardar) wait for; con esperanza hope; (suponer, confiar en) expect 2 v/i (aguardar) wait

esperma f sperm

espesar <1a> 1 v/t thicken 2 v/r **~se** thicken, become thick; **espeso** adj thick; *vegetación, niebla* thick, dense; **espesor** *m* thickness; **espesura** *f* dense vegetation

espía *m/f* spy; **espiar** <1c> **1** *v/t* spy on **2** *v/i* spy

espiga *f* BOT ear, spike

espina *f de planta* thorn; *de pez* bone; **~ dorsal** spine, backbone; *dar mala* **~ a alguien** F make s.o. feel uneasy

espinacas *fpl* BOT spinach *sg*

espinazo *m* spine, backbone; *doblar el* **~** *fig (trabajar mucho)* work o.s. into the ground; *(humillarse)* kowtow (*ante* to)

espinilla *f de la pierna* shin; *en la piel* pimple, spot

espinoso *adj* thorny, prickly; *fig* thorny, knotty

espionaje *m* spying, espionage

espiral **1** *adj* spiral *atr* **2** *f* spiral

espirar <1a> *v/t & v/i* exhale

espiritismo *m* spiritualism; **espíritu** *m* spirit; **espiritual** *adj* spiritual

espléndido *adj* splendid, magnificent; *(generoso)* generous; **esplendor** *m* splendo(u)r

espliego *m* lavender

espolear <1a> *v/t tb fig* spur on

espolvorear <1a> *v/t* sprinkle

esponja *f* sponge; **esponjoso** *adj bizcocho* spongy; *toalla* soft, fluffy

espónsor *m/f* sponsor; **esponsorizar** <1f> *v/t* sponsor

espontáneo *adj* spontaneous

esporádico *adj* sporadic

espora *f* BOT spore

esposa *f* wife; **esposas** *fpl (manillas)* handcuffs *pl*; **esposar** <1a> *v/t* handcuff; **esposo** *m* husband

esprint *m* sprint

espuela *f* spur

espuerta *f*: *ganar dinero a* **~s** F make money hand over fist F

espuma *f* foam; *de jabón* lather; *de cerveza* froth; **~ de afeitar** shaving foam; **~ moldeadora** styling mousse; **espumadera** *f* slotted spoon, skimmer; **espumarajo** *m* froth, foam

espumilla *f C.Am.* GASTR meringue

espumoso *adj* frothy, foamy; *caldo* sparkling

esqueje *m* cutting

esquela *f aviso* death notice, obituary

esquelético *adj* skeletal; **esqueleto** *m* skeleton; *Méx, C.Am., Pe, Bol fig* blank form; *mover o menear el* **~** F dance

esquema *m (croquis)* sketch, diagram; *(sinopsis)* outline, summary; **esquemático** *adj* schematic, diagrammatic; *resumen* simplified

esquí *m tabla* ski; *deporte* skiing; **~ de fondo** cross-country skiing; **~ náutico** *o* **acuático** waterskiing; **esquiador** *m*, **~a** *f* skier; **esquiar** <1a> *v/i* ski

esquilar <1a> *v/t* shear

esquilmar <1a> *v/t* overexploit; *a alguien* suck dry

esquina *f* corner; **esquinazo** *m Arg, Chi* serenade; *dar* **~ a alguien** F give s.o. the slip F

esquirol *m/f* strikebreaker, scab F

esquite *m C.Am., Méx* popcorn

esquivar <1a> *v/t* avoid, dodge F; **esquivo** *adj (huraño)* unsociable; *(evasivo)* shifty, evasive

esquizofrenia *f* schizophrenia; **esquizofrénico** *adj* schizophrenic

esta *det* this

está *vb → estar*

estabilidad *f* stability; **estabilizante** *m* stabilizer; **estabilizar** <1f> *v/t* stabilize; **estable** *adj* stable

establecer <2d> **1** *v/t* establish; *negocio* set up **2** *v/r* **~se** *en lugar* settle; *en profesión* set up; **establecimiento** *m* establishment

establo *m* stable

estaca *f* stake; **estacada** *f*: *dejar a alguien en la* **~** F leave s.o. in the lurch

estación *f* station; *del año* season; **~ espacial** *or* **orbital** space station; **~ de invierno** *or* **invernal** winter resort; **~ de servicio** service station; **~ de trabajo** INFOR work station; **estacional** *adj* seasonal; **estacionamiento** *m* AUTO parking; *L.Am.* parking lot, *Br* car park; **estacionar** <1a> **1** *v/t* AUTO park **2** *v/r* **~se**

stabilize; **estacionómetro** *m Méx* parking meter

estadio *m* DEP stadium

estadística *f cifra* statistic; *ciencia* statistics

estado *m* state; MED condition; ~ **civil** marital status; ~ **de guerra** state of war; **en buen** ~ in good condition; **el Estado** the State; ~ **del bienestar** welfare state; **los Estados Unidos** (**de América**) the United States (of America)

estadounidense 1 *adj* American, US *atr* **2** *m/f* American

estafa *f* swindle, cheat; **estafador** *m*, ~**a** *f* con artist F, fraudster; **estafar** <1a> *v/t* swindle, cheat (**a** out of), defraud (**a** of)

estalactita *f* stalactite; **estalagmita** *f* stalagmite

estallar <1a> *v/i* explode; *de guerra* break out; *de escándalo* break; **estalló en llanto** she burst into tears; **estallido** *m* explosion; *de guerra* outbreak

estamento *m* stratum, class

estampa *f de libro* illustration; (*aspecto*) appearance; REL prayer card; **estampado** *adj tejido* patterned; **estampar** <1a> *v/t sello* put; *tejido* print; *pasaporte* stamp; **le estampó una bofetada en la cara** F she smacked him one F

estampido *m* bang

estampilla *f L.Am.* stamp

estancado *adj agua* stagnant; *fig* at a standstill; **estancar** <1g> **1** *v/t río* dam up, block; *fig* bring to a standstill **2** *v/r* ~**se** stagnate; *fig* come to a standstill

estancia *f* stay; *Rpl* farm, ranch; **estanciero** *m*, ~**a** *f Rpl* farmer, rancher

estanco 1 *adj* watertight **2** *m shop* selling cigarettes etc

estándar *m* standard; **estandarizar** <1f> *v/t* standardize

estandarte *m* standard, banner

estanque *m* pond

estante *m* shelf; **estantería** *f* shelves *pl*; *para libros* bookcase

estaño *m* tin

estar <1p> **1** *v/i* be; **¿está Javier?** is Javier in?; ~ *haciendo algo* be doing sth; **estamos a 3 de enero** it's January 3rd; **el kilo está a cien pesetas** they're a hundred pesetas a kilo; **te está grande** it's too big for you; ~ **con alguien** agree with s.o.; (*apoyar*) support s.o.; **ahora estoy con Vd.** I'll be with you in just a moment; ~ **a bien / mal con alguien** be on good / bad terms with s.o.; ~ **de ocupación** work as, be; ~ **en algo** be working on sth; ~ **para hacer algo** be about to do sth; **no** ~ **para algo** not be in a mood for sth; ~ **por algo** be in favo(u)r of sth; **está por hacer** it hasn't been done yet; ~ **sin dinero** have no money; **¿cómo está Vd.?** how are you?; **estoy mejor** I'm (feeling) better; **¡ya estoy!** I'm ready!; **¡ya está!** that's it! **2** *v/r* ~**se** stay; ~**se quieto** keep still

estárter *m* choke

estatal *adj* state *atr*

estático *adj* static

estatua *f* statue; **estatura** *f* height; **estatutario** *adj* statutory; **estatuto** *m* statute; ~**s** articles of association; **estatus** *m* status

este¹ *m* east

este², **esta**, **estos**, **estas** *det singular* this; *plural* these

éste, **ésta**, **éstos**, **éstas** *pron singular* this (one); *plural* these (ones)

estela *f* MAR wake; AVIA, *fig* trail; **estelar** *adj* star *atr*

estepa *f* steppe

estera *f* mat

estercolero *m* dunghill, dung heap

estéreo *adj* stereo; **estereofónico** *adj* stereophonic; **estereotipo** *m* stereotype

estéril *adj* MED sterile; *trabajo, esfuerzo* futile; **esterilidad** *f* sterility; **esterilizar** <1f> *v/t tb persona* sterilize

esterilla *f* mat

esterlina *adj*: **libra** ~ pound sterling

esternón *m* breast bone, sternum

estero *m Rpl* marsh

estertor *m* death rattle

esteticista *m/f* beautician; **estético** *adj* esthetic, *Br* aesthetic

estetoscopio *m* MED stethoscope

estibador *m* stevedore

estiércol *m* dung; (*abono*) manure

estilarse <1a> *v/r* be fashionable; **estilista** *m/f* stylist; *de modas* designer; **estilo** *m* style; **al ~ de** in the style of; **algo por el ~** something like that; **son todos por el ~** they're all the same

estilográfica *f* fountain pen

estima *f* esteem, respect; **tener a alguien en mucha ~** hold s.o. in high regard *o* esteem; **estimación** *f* (*cálculo*) estimate; (*estima*) esteem, respect; **estimar** <1a> *v/t* respect, hold in high regard; **estimo conveniente que** I consider it advisable to

estimulante 1 *adj* stimulating **2** *m* stimulant; **estimular** <1a> *v/t* stimulate; (*animar*) encourage; **estímulo** *m* stimulus; (*incentivo*) incentive

estío *m lit* summertime

estipular <1a> *v/t* stipulate

estirado *adj* snooty F, stuck-up F

estirar <1a> *v/t* stretch; (*alisar*) smooth out; *dinero* stretch, make go further; **~ la pata** F kick the bucket F; **~ las piernas** stretch one's legs

estirpe *f* stock

estival *adj* summer *atr*

esto *pron* this; **~ es** that is to say; **por ~** this is why; **a todo ~** (*mientras tanto*) meanwhile; (*a propósito*) incidentally

estofa *f*: **de baja ~** *desp* low-class *desp*

estofado *adj* stewed; **estofar** <1a> *v/t* stew

estoico 1 *adj* stoic(al) **2** *m*, **-a** *f* stoic

estómago *m* stomach

estor *m* blind

estorbar <1a> **1** *v/t* (*dificultar*) hinder; **nos estorbaba** he was in our way **2** *v/i* get in the way; **estorbo** *m* hindrance, nuisance

estornino *m* ZO starling

estornudar <1a> *v/i* sneeze; **estornudo** *m* sneeze

estoy *vb* → **estar**

estrado *m* platform

estrafalario *adj* F eccentric; *ropa* outlandish

estragón *m* BOT tarragon

estragos *mpl* devastation *sg*; **causar ~ entre** wreak havoc among

estrambótico *adj* F eccentric; *ropa* outlandish

estrangular <1a> *v/t* strangle

estraperlo *m* black market; **de ~** on the black market

estratagema *f* stratagem; **estrategia** *f* strategy; **estratégico** *adj* strategic

estrato *m fig* stratum

estrechar <1a> **1** *v/t* *ropa* take in; *mano* shake; **~ entre los brazos** hug, embrace **2** *v/r* **~se** narrow, get narrower; **estrechez** *f fig* hardship; **~ de miras** narrow-mindedness; **pasar ~es** suffer hardship; **estrecho 1** *adj* narrow; (*apretado*) tight; *amistad* close; **~ de miras** narrow-minded **2** *m* strait, straits *pl*

estrella *f tb de cine etc* star; **~ fugaz** falling star, shooting star; **~ de mar** ZO starfish; **~ polar** Pole star; **estrellar** <1a> **1** *v/t* smash; **~ algo contra algo** smash sth against sth; **estrelló el coche contra un muro** he smashed the car into a wall **2** *v/r* **~se** crash (**contra** into); **estrellón** *m Pe, Bol* crash

estremecer <2d> **1** *v/t* shock, shake F **2** *v/r* **~se** shake, tremble; *de frío* shiver; *de horror* shudder

estrenar <1a> **1** *v/t ropa* wear for the first time, christen F; *objeto* try out, christen F; TEA, *película* premiere; **a ~** brand new **2** *v/r* **~se** make one's debut; **estreno** *m* TEA, *de película* premiere; *de persona* debut; **estar de ~** be wearing new clothes

estreñimiento *m* constipation

estrépito *m* noise, racket

estrés *m* stress; **estresar** <1a> *v/t*: **~**

alguien cause s.o. stress, subject s.o. to stress

estría *f en piel* stretch mark

estribar <1a> *v/i*: ~ **en** stem from, lie in

estribillo *m* chorus, refrain

estribo *m* stirrup; *perder los* ~**s** *fig* fly off the handle F

estrictez *f S.Am.* strictness; **estricto** *adj* strict

estridente *adj* shrill, strident

estrofa *f* stanza, verse

estropajo *m* scourer; **estropajoso** *adj persona* wiry; *boca* dry; *camisa* scruffy

estropeado *adj* (*averiado*) broken; **estropear** <1a> **1** *v/t aparato* break; *plan* ruin, spoil **2** *v/r* ~**se** break down; *de comida* go off, go bad; *de plan* go wrong

estructura *f* structure; **estructurar** <1a> *v/t* structure, organize

estruendo *m* racket, din

estrujar <1a> *v/t* F crumple up, scrunch up F; *trapo* wring out; *persona* squeeze, hold tightly

estuario *m* estuary

estuche *m* case, box

estuco *m* stuccowork

estudiante *m/f* student; **estudiantil** *adj* student *atr*; **estudiar** <1b> *v/t & v/i* study; **estudio** *m disciplina* study; *apartamento* studio, *Br* studio flat; *de cine, música* studio; **estudioso** *adj* studious

estufa *f* heater

estupefaciente *m* narcotic (drug); **estupefacto** *adj* stupefied, speechless

estupendo *adj* fantastic, wonderful

estupidez *f cualidad* stupidity; *acción* stupid thing; **estúpido 1** *adj* stupid **2** *m*, **-a** *f* idiot

estupor *m* astonishment, amazement; *MED* stupor

esturión *m ZO* sturgeon

estuve *vb* → *estar*

estuvo *vb* → *estar*

etapa *f* stage; *por* ~**s** in stages

etarra *m/f* member of ETA

etc *abr* (= *etcétera*) etc (= etcetera)

etcétera *m* etcetera, and so on; *y un largo* ~ *de* ... and a long list of ..., and many other ...

etéreo *adj* ethereal

eternidad *f* eternity; **eterno** *adj* eternal; *la película se me hizo* -**a** the movie seemed to go on for ever

ética *f en filosofía* ethics; *comportamiento* principles *pl*; **ético** *adj* ethical

etimología *f* etymology

Etiopía Ethiopia

etiqueta *f* label; (*protocolo*) etiquette; **etiquetar** <1a> *v/t tb fig* label

étnico *adj* ethnic

eucalipto *m* BOT eucalyptus

eucaristía *f* Eucharist

eufemismo *m* euphemism

euforia *f* euphoria; **eufórico** *adj* euphoric

euro *m* euro

eurodiputado *m*, **-a** *f* MEP, member of the European Parliament

Europa Europe

europeísta *m/f* pro-European

europeo 1 *adj* European **2** *m*, **-a** *f* European

eusquera *m/adj* Basque

eutanasia *f* euthanasia

evacuación *f* evacuation; **evacuar** <1d> *v/t* evacuate

evadir <3a> **1** *v/t* avoid; *impuestos* evade **2** *v/r* ~**se** *tb fig* escape

evaluación *f* evaluation, assessment; (*prueba*) test; **evaluar** <1e> *v/t* assess, evaluate

evangelio *m* gospel; **evangelizar** <1f> *v/t* evangelize

evaporación *f* evaporation; **evaporarse** <1a> *v/r* evaporate; *fig* F vanish into thin air

evasión *f tb fig* escape; ~ *de capitales* flight of capital; ~ *fiscal* tax evasion; **evasiva** *f* evasive reply

evento *m* event; **eventual** *adj* possible; *trabajo* casual, temporary; *en el caso* ~ *de* in the event of; **eventualidad** *f* eventuality

evidencia *f* evidence, proof; *poner*

en ~ demonstrate; ***poner a alguien en ~*** show s.o. up; **evidente** *adj* evident, clear

evitar <1a> *v/t* avoid; *(impedir)* prevent; *molestias* save; ***no puedo ~lo*** I can't help it

evocar <1g> *v/t* evoke

evolución *f* BIO evolution; *(desarrollo)* development; **evolucionar** <1a> *v/i* BIO evolve; *(desarrollar)* develop

ex 1 *pref* ex- **2** *m/f* F ex F

exabrupto *m* sharp remark

exacerbar <1a> *v/t* exacerbate, make worse; *(irritar)* exasperate

exacto *adj medida* exact, precise; *informe* accurate; *¡~!* exactly!, precisely!

exageración *f* exaggeration; **exagerado** *adj* exaggerated; **exagerar** <1a> *v/t* exaggerate

exaltación *f (alabanza)* exaltation; *(entusiasmo)* agitation, excitement; **exaltar** <1a> *v/t* excite, get worked up

examen *m* test, exam; MED examination; *(análisis)* study; ***~ de conducir*** driving test; **examinar** <1a> **1** *v/t* examine **2** *v/r* **~se** take an exam

exasperar <1a> **1** *v/t* exasperate **2** *v/r* **~se** get exasperated

excarcelar <1a> *v/t* release (from prison)

excavación *f* excavation; **excavadora** *f* digger; **excavar** <1a> *v/t* excavate; *túnel* dig

excedencia *f* extended leave of absence; **excedente 1** *adj* surplus; *empleado* on extended leave of absence **2** *m* surplus; **exceder** <2a> **1** *v/t* exceed **2** *v/r* **~se** go too far, get carried away

excelencia *f* excellence; ***Su Excelencia la señora embajadora*** Her Excellency the Ambassador; ***por ~*** par excellence; **excelente** *adj* excellent

excéntrico 1 *adj* eccentric **2** *m*, **-a** *f* eccentric

excepción *f* exception; ***a ~ de*** except for; ***sin ~*** without exception; **excepcional** *adj* exceptional; **excepto** *prp* except; **exceptuar** <1e> *v/t* except; ***exceptuando*** with the exception of, except for

excesivo *adj* excessive; **exceso** *m* excess; **~ de equipaje** excess baggage; **~ de velocidad** speeding; ***en ~*** in excess, too much

excitación *f* excitement, agitation; **excitante 1** *adj* exciting; ***una bebida ~*** a stimulant **2** *m* stimulant; **excitar** <1a> *v/t* excite; *sentimientos, sexualmente* arouse **2** *v/r* **~se** get excited; *sexualmente* become aroused

exclamación *f* exclamation; **exclamar** <1a> *v/t* exclaim

excluir <3g> *v/t* leave out *(de* of), exclude *(de* from); *posibilidad* rule out; **exclusiva** *f privilegio* exclusive rights *pl (de* to); *reportaje* exclusive; **exclusivo** *adj* exclusive

excomunión *f* excommunication

excremento *m* excrement

exculpar <1a> *v/t* exonerate

excursión *f* trip, excursion; **excursionista** *m/f* excursionist

excusa *f* excuse; **~s** apologies

excusado *m* bathroom; **excusar** <1a> *v/t* excuse

execrable *adj* abominable, execrable *fml*

exención *f* exemption; **~ fiscal** tax exemption; **exento** *adj* exempt *(de* from); **~ de impuestos** tax-exempt, tax-free

exhalación *f*: ***salir como una ~*** *fig* rush *o* dash out

exhaustivo *adj* exhaustive; **exhausto** *adj* exhausted

exhibición *f* display, demonstration; *de película* screening, showing; **exhibicionista** *m/f* exhibitionist; **exhibir** <3a> **1** *v/t* show, display; *película* screen, show; *cuadro* exhibit **2** *v/r* **~se** show o.s., let o.s. be seen

exhumar <1a> *v/t* exhume

exigencia *f* demand; **exigente** *adj* demanding; **exigir** <3c> *v/t* demand; *(requerir)* call for, demand;

le exigen mucho they ask a lot of him

exiguo *adj* meager, *Br* meagre

exiliado 1 *adj* exiled, in exile *pred* **2** *m*, **-a** *f* exile; **exiliar** <1a> **1** *v/t* exile **2** *v/r* ~**se** go into exile; **exilio** *m* exile; **en el** ~ in exile

eximir <3a> *v/t* exempt (*de* from)

existencia *f* existence; (*vida*) life; ~**s** COM supplies, stocks; **existencialista** *m/f* & *adj* existentialist; **existir** <3a> *v/i* exist; *existen muchos problemas* there are a lot of problems

éxito *m* success; ~ *de taquilla* box office hit; *tener* ~ be successful, be a success; **exitoso** *adj* successful

Exmo. *abr* (= **Excelentísimo**) Your / His Excellency

exonerar <1a> *v/t* exonerate; ~ *a alguien de algo* exempt s.o. from sth

exorbitante *adj* exorbitant

exorcista *m/f* exorcist

exótico *adj* exotic

expandir <3a> **1** *v/t* expand **2** *v/r* ~**se** expand; *de noticia* spread; **expansión** *f* expansion; (*recreo*) recreation

expatriarse <1b> *v/r* leave one's country

expectación *f* sense of anticipation; **expectativa** *f* (*esperanza*) expectation; *estar a la* ~ *de algo* be waiting for sth; ~**s** (*perspectivas*) prospects

expedición *f* expedition

expediente *m* file, dossier; (*investigación*) investigation, inquiry; ~ *académico* student record; ~ *disciplinario* disciplinary proceedings *pl*; *abrir un* ~ *a alguien* take disciplinary action against s.o.

expedir <3l> *v/t documento* issue; *mercancías* send, dispatch

expeditar <1a> *v/t L.Am.* (*apresurar*) hurry; (*concluir*) finish, conclude

expeditivo *adj* expeditious

expendedor *adj*: *máquina* ~**a** vend-

ing machine

expendio *m I. Am.* store, shop

expensas *fpl*: *a* ~ *de* at the expense of

experiencia *f* experience

experimentado *adj* experienced; **experimentar** <1a> **1** *v/t* try out, experiment with **2** *v/i* experiment (*con* on); **experimento** *m* experiment

experto 1 *adj* expert; ~ *en hacer algo* expert *o* very good at doing sth **2** *m* expert (*en* on)

expiar <1c> *v/t* expiate, atone for

expirar <1a> *v/i* expire

explanada *f* open area; *junto al mar* esplanade

explayarse <1a> *v/r* speak at length; (*desahogarse*) unburden o.s.; (*distraerse*) relax, unwind; ~ *sobre algo* expound on sth

explicación *f* explanation; **explicar** <1g> **1** *v/t* explain **2** *v/r* ~**se** (*comprender*) understand; (*hacerse comprender*) express o.s.; *no me lo explico* I can't understand it, I don't get it F

explícito *adj* explicit

explorador *m*, ~**a** *f* explorer; MIL scout; **explorar** <1a> *v/t* explore

explosión *f* explosion; ~ *demográfica* population explosion; *hacer* ~ go off, explode; **explosionar** <1a> *v/t* & *v/i* explode; **explosivo** *m/adj* explosive

explotación *f de mina, tierra* exploitation, working; *de negocio* running, operation; *de trabajador* exploitation; **explotar** <1a> **1** *v/t tierra, mina* work, exploit; *situación* take advantage of, exploit; *trabajador* exploit **2** *v/i* go off, explode; *fig* explode, blow a fuse F

expoliar <1b> *v/t* plunder, pillage

exponente *m* exponent; **exponer** <2r; *part* **expuesto**> **1** *v/t idea, teoría* set out, put forward; (*revelar*) expose; *pintura, escultura* exhibit, show; (*arriesgar*) risk **2** *v/r* ~**se**: ~**se** *a algo* (*arriesgarse*) lay o.s. open to sth

exportación *f* export; **exportar** <1a> *v/t* export

exposición *f* exhibition

expresar <1a> **1** *v/t* express **2** *v/r* ~**se** express o.s.; **expresión** *f* expression; **expresivo** *adj* expressive

expreso 1 *adj* express *atr*; **tren** ~ express (train) **2** *m* tren express (train); *café* espresso

exprimidor *m* lemon squeezer; *eléctrico* juicer; **exprimir** <3a> *v/t* squeeze; (*explotar*) exploit

ex profeso *adv* (*especialmente*) expressly; (*a propósito*) deliberately

expropiar <1b> *v/t* expropriate

expuesto *part* → **exponer**

expugnar <1a> *v/t* take by storm

expulsar <1a> *v/t* expel, throw out F; DEP expel from the game, *Br* send off; **expulsión** *f* expulsion; DEP sending off

exquisito *adj comida* delicious; (*bello*) exquisite; (*refinado*) refined

extasiarse <1c> *v/r* be enraptured, go into raptures; **éxtasis** *m tb droga* ecstasy

extender <2g> **1** *v/t brazos* stretch out; (*untar*) spread; *tela, papel* spread out; (*ampliar*) extend; **me extendió la mano** she held out her hand to me **2** *v/r* ~**se** *de campos* stretch; *de influencia* extend; (*difundirse*) spread; (*durar*) last; *explayarse* go into detail; **extendido 1** *part* → **extender 2** *adj costumbre* widespread; *brazos* outstretched; *mapa* spread out; **extensión** *f tb* TELEC extension; *superficie* expanse, area; **por** ~ by extension; **extenso** *adj* extensive, vast; *informe* lengthy, long

extenuar <1e> **1** *v/t* exhaust, tire out **2** *v/r* ~**se** exhaust o.s., tire o.s. out

exterior 1 *adj aspecto* external, outward; *capa* outer; *apartamento* overlooking the street; POL foreign; **la parte** ~ **del edificio** the exterior *o* the outside of the building **2** *m* (*fachada*) exterior, outside; *aspecto* exterior, outward appearance; **viajar al** ~ (*al extranjero*) travel abroad; **exteriorizar** <1f> *v/t* externalize

exterminar <1a> *v/t* exterminate, wipe out

externo 1 *adj aspecto* external, outward; *influencia* external, outside; *capa* outer; *deuda* foreign **2** *m*, **-a** *f* EDU *student who attends a boarding school but returns home each evening*, *Br* day boy/ girl

extinción *f*: **en peligro de** ~ in danger of extinction; **extinguidor** *m L.Am.*: ~ **(de incendios)** (fire) extinguisher; **extinguir** <3d> **1** *v/t* BIO, ZO wipe out; *fuego* extinguish, put out **2** *v/r* ~**se** BIO, ZO become extinct, die out; *de fuego* go out; *de plazo* expire; **extintor** *m* fire extinguisher

extirpar <1a> *v/t* MED remove; *vicio* eradicate, stamp out

extorsión *f* extortion; **extorsionar** <1a> *v/t* extort money from

extra 1 *adj excelente* top quality; *adicional* extra; **horas** ~ overtime; **paga** ~ extra month's pay **2** *m/f de cine* extra **3** *m gasto* additional expense

extracto *m* extract; (*resumen*) summary; GASTR, QUÍM extract, essence; ~ **de cuenta** bank statement; **extractor** *m* extractor; ~ **de humos** extractor fan

extradición *f* extradition; **extraditar** <1a> *v/t* extradite

extraer <2p> *v/t* extract, pull out; *conclusión* draw

extrajudicial *adj* out-of-court

extralimitarse <1a> *v/r* go too far, exceed one's authority

extramatrimonial *adj* extramarital

extranjería *f*: **ley de** ~ immigration laws *pl*; **extranjero 1** *adj* foreign **2** *m*, **-a** *f* foreigner; **en el** ~ abroad

extranjis: **de** ~ F on the quiet F, on the sly F

extrañar <1a> **1** *v/t L.Am.* miss **2** *v/r* ~**se** be surprised (**de** at); **extraño 1** *adj* strange, odd **2** *m*, **-a** *f* stranger

extraordinario *adj* extraordinary
extrapolar <1a> *v/t* extrapolate
extrarradio *m* outlying districts *pl*, outskirts *pl*
extraterrestre *adj* extraterrestial, alien
extravagante *adj* outrageous
extravertido *adj* extrovert
extraviar <1c> **1** *v/t* lose, mislay **2** *v/r* **~se** get lost, lose one's way
extremadamente *adv* extremely; **extremado** *adj* extreme; **extremar** <1a> *v/t* maximize

extremidad *f* end; **~es** extremities; **extremista 1** *adj* extreme **2** *m/f* POL extremist; **extremo 1** *adj* extreme **2** *m* extreme; *parte primera o última* end; *punto* point; **llegar al ~ de** reach the point of **3** *m/f*: **~ derecho/izquierdo** DEP right/left wing; **en ~** in the extreme
extrovertido *adj* extrovert
exuberante *adj* exuberant; *vegetación* lush
exultante *adj* elated
eyacular <1a> *v/t* ejaculate

F

F

fabada *f* GASTR *Asturian stew with pork sausage, bacon and beans*
fábrica *f* plant, factory; **fabricación** *f* manufacturing; **fabricante** *m* manufacturer, maker; **fabricar** <1g> *v/t* manufacture
fábula *f* fable; (*mentira*) lie; **fabuloso** *adj* fabulous, marvel(l)ous
facción *f* POL faction; **facciones** *pl* (*rasgos*) features
faceta *f* *fig* facet
facha 1 *f* look; (*cara*) face **2** *m/f desp* fascist
fachada *f* *tb fig* façade
facial *adj* facial
fácil *adj* easy; **es ~ que** it's likely that; **facilidad** *f* ease; **con ~** easily; **tener ~ para algo** have a gift for sth; **~es de pago** credit facilities, credit terms; **facilitar** <1a> *v/t* facilitate, make easier; (*hacer factible*) make possible; *medios, dinero etc* provide
factible *adj* feasible
factor *m* factor
factoría *f esp L.Am.* plant, factory
factura *f* COM invoice; *de luz, gas etc* bill; **facturación** *f* COM invoicing; (*volumen de negocio*) turnover;

AVIA check-in; **facturar** <1a> *v/t* COM invoice, bill; *volumen de negocio* turn over; AVIA check in
facultad *f* faculty; (*autoridad*) authority
faena *f* task, job; **hacer una ~ a alguien** play a dirty trick on s.o.
fagot *m* MÚS bassoon
faisán *m* ZO pheasant
faja *f* *prenda interior* girdle
fajarse <1a> *v/r Méx, Ven* F get into a fight
fajo *m* wad; *de periódicos* bundle
falacia *f* fallacy; (*engaño*) fraud
falange *f* ANAT phalange; MIL phalanx
falda *f* skirt; *de montaña* side
faldero *adj*: **perro ~** lap dog
falla *f* fault; *de fabricación* flaw; **fallar** <1a> **1** *v/i* fail; (*no acertar*) miss; *de sistema etc* go wrong; JUR find (**en favor de** for; **en contra de** against); **~ a alguien** let s.o. down **2** *v/t* JUR pronounce judg(e)ment in; *pregunta* get wrong; **~ el tiro** miss
fallecer <2d> *v/i* pass away; **fallecimiento** *m* demise
fallo *m* mistake; TÉC fault; JUR

judg(e)ment; **~ cardiaco** heart failure

falsedad *f* falseness; (*mentira*) lie; **falsificación** *f de moneda* counterfeiting; *de documentos, firma* forgery; **falsificar** <1g> *v/t moneda* counterfeit; *documento, firma* forge, falsify; **falso** *adj* false; *joyas* fake; *documento, firma* forged; **jurar en ~** commit perjury

falta *f* (*escasez*) lack, want; (*error*) mistake; (*ausencia*) absence; *en tenis* fault; *en fútbol* foul; (*tiro libre*) free kick; **hacerle ~ a alguien** foul s.o.; **~ de** lack of, shortage of; **sin ~** without fail; **buena ~ le hace** it's about time; **echar en ~ a alguien** miss s.o.; **hacer ~** be necessary

faltar <1a> *v/i* be missing; **falta una hora** there's an hour to go; **faltan 10 kilómetros** there are 10 kilometers to go; **sólo falta hacer la salsa** there's only the sauce to do; **~ a** be absent from; **~ a clase** miss class, be absent from class; **~ a alguien** be disrespectful to s.o.; **~ a su palabra** not keep one's word; **falto** *adj*: **~ de** lacking in, devoid of; **~ de recursos** short of resources

fama *f* fame; (*reputación*) reputation; **tener mala ~** have a bad reputation

familia *f* family; **sentirse como en ~** feel at home; **familiar 1** *adj* family *atr*; (*conocido*) familiar; LING colloquial **2** *m/f* relation, relative; **familiaridad** *f* familiarity; **familiarizarse** <1f> *v/r* familiarize o.s. (**con** with)

famoso 1 *adj* famous **2** *m*, **-a** *f* celebrity

fan *m/f* fan

fanático 1 *adj* fanatical **2** *m*, **-a** *f* fanatic; **fanatismo** *m* fanaticism

fanfarrón 1 *adj* boastful **2** *m*, **-ona** *f* boaster; **fanfarronear** <1a> *v/i* boast, brag

fango *m tb fig* mud

fantasear <1a> *v/i* fantasize; **fantasía** *f* fantasy; (*imaginación*) imagination; **joyas de ~** costume

jewel(l)ery; **fantasma** *m* ghost; **fantástico** *adj* fantastic

farándula *f* show business

fardar <1a> *v/i*: **~ de algo** F boast about sth, show off about sth

fardo *m* bundle

faringitis *f* MED inflammation of the pharynx, pharyngitis

fariña *f S.Am.* manioc flour, cassava

farmacéutico 1 *adj* pharmaceutical **2** *m*, **-a** *f* pharmacist, *Br* chemist; **farmacia** *f* pharmacy, *Br* chemist's; *estudios* pharmacy; **~ de guardia** 24-hour pharmacist, *Br* emergency chemist; **fármaco** *m* medicine; **farmacología** *f* pharmacology

faro *m* MAR lighthouse; AUTO headlight, headlamp; **~ antiniebla** fog light; **farol** *m* lantern; (*farola*) streetlight, streetlamp; *en juegos de cartas* bluff; **farola** *f* streetlight, streetlamp; **farolillo** *m*: **ser el ~ rojo** *fig* F be bottom of the league

farragoso *adj texto* dense

farrear <1a> *v/i L.Am.* F go out on the town F

farrista *adj L.Am.* F hard-drinking

farsa *f tb fig* farce; **farsante** *m/f* fraud, fake

fascículo *m* TIP instal(l)ment

fascinación *f* fascination; **fascinante** *adj* fascinating; **fascinar** <1a> *v/t* fascinate

fascismo *m* fascism; **fascista** *m/f* & *adj* fascist

fase *f* phase

fastidiar <1b> **1** *v/t* annoy; F (*estropear*) spoil **2** *v/r* **~se** grin and bear it; **fastidio** *m* annoyance; **¡qué ~!** what a nuisance!

fastuoso *adj* lavish

fatal 1 *adj* fatal; (*muy malo*) dreadful, awful **2** *adv* very badly

fatídico *adj* fateful

fatiga *f* tiredness, fatigue; **fatigar** <1h> **1** *v/t* tire **2** *v/r* **~se** get tired

fatuo *adj* conceited; (*necio*) fatuous

fauces *fpl* ZO jaws

fauna *f* fauna

favor *m* favo(u)r; **a ~ de** in favo(u)r of; **por ~** please; **hacer un ~** do

a favo(u)r; **favorecer** <2d> *v/t*
favo(u)r; *de ropa, color* suit;
favoritismo *m* favo(u)ritism; **favo-**
rito 1 *adj* favo(u)rite **2** *m*, **-a** *f*
favo(u)rite

fax *m* fax; **enviar un ~ a alguien** send
s.o. a fax, fax s.o.

fayuca *f Méx* smuggling; **fayuquero**
m, **-a** *f Méx* dealer in smuggled
goods

F.C. *abr* (= *Fútbol Club*) FC (= Football Club)

fdo. *abr* (= *firmado*) signed

fe *f* faith (**en** in); **~ de erratas** errata

fealdad *f* ugliness

feb. *abr* (= *febrero*) Feb. (= February)

febrero *m* February

fecal *adj* f(a)ecal

fecha *f* date; **~ límite de consumo**
best before date; **~ de nacimiento**
date of birth; **fechador** *m Chi, Méx*
postmark

fécula *f* starch

fecundación *f* fertilization; **~ in vitro**
MED in vitro fertilization; **fecundar**
<1a> *v/t* fertilize; **fecundo** *adj* fer-
tile

federación *f* federation; **federal** *adj*
federal

felicidad *f* happiness; **¡~es!** congratulations!; **felicitación** *f* letter
of congratulations; **¡felicitaciones!**
congratulations!; **felicitar** <1a> *v/t*
congratulate (**por** on)

felino *adj tb fig* feline

feliz *adj* happy; **¡~ Navidad!** Merry
Christmas!

felpa *f* towel(l)ing; **felpudo** *m* door-
mat

femenino 1 *adj* feminine; *moda,*
equipo women's **2** GRAM feminine;
femin(e)idad *f* femininity; **femi-**
nismo *m* feminism; **feminista** *m/f*
& *adj* feminist

fenomenal 1 *adj* F fantastic F, phe-
nomenal F **2** *adv*: **lo pasé ~** F I had a
fantastic time F; **fenómeno 1** *m*
phenomenon; *persona* genius **2** *adj*
F fantastic F, great F

feo 1 *adj* ugly; *fig* nasty **2** *m*: **hacer**

un ~ a alguien F snub s.o.

féretro *m* casket, coffin

feria *f* COM fair; *L.Am. (mercado)*
market; *Méx (calderilla)* small
change; **~ de muestras** trade fair;
feriado 1 *adj L.Am.*: **día ~** (public)
holiday **2** *m L.Am.* (public) holiday;
abierto ~s open on public holidays;
ferial 1 *adj*: **recinto ~** fairground
2 *m* fair

fermentación *f* fermentation; **fer-**
mentar <1a> *v/t* ferment; **fermen-**
to *m* ferment

ferocidad *f* ferocity; **feroz** *adj* fierce;
(cruel) cruel

férreo *adj tb fig* iron *atr; del ferrocarril*
rail *atr*; **ferretería** *f* hardware store;
ferrocarril *m* railroad, *Br* railway;
ferrocarrilero *m L.Am.* railroad *o*
Br railway worker; **ferroviario** *adj*
rail *atr*

ferry *m* ferry

fértil *adj* fertile; **fertilidad** *f* fertility;
fertilizante *m* fertilizer

ferviente *adj fig* fervent; **fervor** *m*
fervo(u)r

festejar <1a> *v/t persona* wine and
dine; *L.Am.* celebrate; **festejo** *m*
celebration; **~s** festivities; **festín** *m*
banquet; **festival** *m* festival; **~**
cinematográfico film festival;
festividad *f* feast; **~es** festivities;
festivo *adj* festive

fetal *adj* fetal

fetiche *m* fetish

fétido *adj* fetid

feto *m* fetus

feudal *adj* feudal; **feudo** *m fig* domain

FF. AA. *abr* (= *fuerzas armadas*)
armed forces

FF. CC. *abr* (= *ferrocarriles*) rail-
roads

fiable *adj* trustworthy; *datos, máquina*
etc reliable

fiambre *m* cold cut, *Br* cold meat; P
(cadáver) stiff P; **fiambrera** *f* lunch
pail, *Br* lunch box; **fiambrería** *f*
L.Am. delicatessen

fianza *f* deposit; JUR bail; **bajo ~** on
bail

F

fiar <1c> **1** *v/i* give credit **2** *v/r* ~**se**: ~**se de alguien** trust s.o.; **no me fío** I don't trust him/them *etc*

fiasco *m* fiasco

fibra *f en tejido, alimento* fiber, *Br* fibre; ~ **óptica** optical fiber (*Br* fibre); ~ **de vidrio** fiberglass, *Br* fibreglass; **fibroso** *adj* fibrous

ficción *f* fiction

ficha *f* file card, index card; *en juegos de mesa* counter; *en un casino* chip; *en damas* checker, *Br* draught; *en ajedrez* man, piece; TELEC token; **fichar** <1a> **1** *v/t* DEP sign; *en open a file on* **2** *v/i* DEP sign (*por* for); **fichero** *m* file cabinet, *Br* filing cabinet; INFOR file

ficticio *adj* fictitious

fidedigno *adj* reliable

fidelidad *f* fidelity

fideo *m* noodle

fiebre *f* fever; (*temperatura*) temperature; ~ **del heno** hay fever

fiel 1 *adj* faithful; (*leal*) loyal **2** *mpl*: **los** ~**es** REL the faithful *pl*

fieltro *m* felt

fiera *f* wild animal; **ponerse hecho una** ~ F go wild F; **fiero** *adj* fierce

fierro *m L.Am.* iron

fiesta *f* festival; (*reunión social*) party; (*día festivo*) public holiday; **estar de** ~ be in a party mood

fifí *m L.Am.* P *afeminado* sissy F

figura *f* figure; (*estatuilla*) figurine; (*forma*) shape; *naipes* face card, *Br* picture card; **tener buena** ~ have a good figure; **figurado** *adj* figurative; **sentido** ~ figurative sense; **figurar** <1a> **1** *v/i* appear (*en* in); **aquí figura como ...** she appears *o* is down here as ... **2** *v/r* ~**se** imagine; **¡figúrate!** just imagine!

fijar <1a> **1** *v/t* fix; *cartel* stick; *fecha, objetivo* set; *residencia* establish; *atención* focus **2** *v/r* ~**se** (*establecerse*) settle; (*prestar atención*) pay attention (*en* to); ~**se en algo** (*darse cuenta*) notice sth; **fijo** *adj* fixed; *trabajo* permanent; *fecha* definite

fila *f* line, *Br* queue; *de asientos* row; **en** ~ **india** in single file; ~**s** MIL ranks

filatelia *f* philately, stamp collecting

filete *m* GASTR fillet

filial 1 *adj* filial **2** *f* COM subsidiary

Filipinas *fpl* Philippines

film(e) *m* movie, film; **filmación** *f* filming, shooting; **filmar** <1a> *v/t* film, shoot

filo *m* edge; *de navaja* cutting edge; **al** ~ **de las siete** *fig* around 7 o'clock

filología *f* philology; ~ **hispánica** EDU Spanish language and literature; **filólogo** *m*, **-a** *f* philologist

filón *m* vein, seam; *fig* goldmine

filoso *adj* L.Am. sharp

filosofía *f* philosophy; **filosófico** *adj* philosophical; **filósofo** *m*, **-a** *f* philosopher

filtración *f* leak; **filtrar** <1a> **1** *v/t* filter; *información* leak **2** *v/r* ~**se** filter (*por* through); *de agua, información* leak; **filtro** *m* filter

fin *m* end; (*objetivo*) aim, purpose; ~ **de semana** weekend; **a** ~**es de mayo** at the end of May; **al** ~ **y al cabo** at the end of the day, after all; **en** ~ anyway

final *f/adj* final; **finalidad** *f* purpose, aim; **finalista 1** *adj*: **las dos selecciones** ~**s** the two teams that reached the final **2** *m/f* finalist; **finalización** *f* completion; **finalizado** *adj* complete; **finalizar** <1f> *v/t & v/i* end, finish; **finalmente** *adv* eventually

financiación *f* funding; **financiar** <1b> *v/t* finance, fund; **financista** *m/f L.Am.* financier; **finanzas** *fpl* finances

finca *f* (*bien inmueble*) property; *L.Am.* (*granja*) farm

fingido *adj* false; **fingir** <3c> **1** *v/t* feign *fml*; **fingió no haberlo oído** I pretended I hadn't heard **2** *v/r* ~**se**: ~**se enfermo** pretend to be ill, feign illness *fml*

finlandés 1 *adj* Finnish **2** *m*, **-esa** *f* Finn; **Finlandia** Finland

fino *adj calidad* fine; *libro, tela* thin;

(*esbelto*) slim; *modales, gusto* refined; *sentido de humor* subtle
firma *f* signature; *acto* signing; COM firm
firmamento *m* firmament
firmar <1a> *v/t* sign
firme *adj* firm; (*estable*) steady; **en ~** COM firm
fiscal 1 *adj* tax *atr*, fiscal **2** *m/f* district attorney, *Br* public prosecutor
fisgar <1h> *v/i* snoop F; **~ en algo** snoop around in sth; **fisgón** *m*, **-ona** *f* snoop; **fisgonear** <1a> *v/i* F snoop around F (**en** in)
física *f* physics; **físico 1** *adj* physical **2** *m*, **-a** *f* physicist **3** *m de una persona* physique
fisiología *f* physiology
fisión *f* fission
fisioterapeuta *m/f* physical therapist, *Br* physiotherapist; **fisioterapia** *f* physical therapy, *Br* physiotherapy
fisonomía *f* features *pl*
fisura *f* crack; MED fracture
flác(c)ido *adj* flabby
flaco *adj* thin; **punto ~** weak point
flacuchento *adj* L.Am. F skinny
flagelar <1a> *v/t* flagellate
flagrante *adj* flagrant; **en ~ delito** red-handed, in flagrante delicto
flamante *adj* (*nuevo*) brand-new
flamenco 1 *adj* MÚS flamenco **2** *m* MÚS flamenco; ZO flamingo
flan *m* crème caramel
flanco *m* flank
flaquear <1a> *v/i* weaken; *de entusiasmo* flag; **flaqueza** *f fig* weakness
flash *m* FOT flash
flato *m* MED stitch
flatulencia *f* MED flatulence
flauta *f* flute; *Méx* fried taco; **~ dulce** recorder; **~ travesera** (transverse) flute; **flautista** *m/f* flautist
flecha *f* arrow; **flechazo** *m fig* love at first sight
flecos *mpl* fringe *sg*
flema *m fig* phlegm; **flemático** *adj* phlegmatic
flemón *m* MED gumboil

flequillo *m del pelo* fringe
fletar <1a> *v/t* charter; (*embarcar*) load; **flete** *m* L.Am. freight, cost of transport; **fletero** *adj* L.Am. hire *atr*, charter *atr*
flexibilidad *f* flexibility; **flexible** *adj* flexible
flexión *f en gimnasia* push-up, *Br* press-up; *de piernas* squat; *de la voz* inflection; **flexionar** <1a> **1** *v/t* flex **2** *v/r* **~se** bend
flexo *m* desk lamp
flipar <1a> *v/i*: **le flipa el cine** P he's mad about the movies F
flirtear <1a> *v/i* flirt (**con** with)
flojera *f* L.Am. laziness; **me da ~** I can't be bothered; **flojo** *adj* loose; *café, argumento* weak; COM *actividad* slack; *novela, redacción* poor; *L.Am.* lazy
flor *f* flower; **flora** *f* flora; **florear** <1a> **1** *v/t* decorate with flowers; *Méx* (*halagar*) flatter, compliment **2** *v/i* flower, bloom; **florecer** <2d> *v/i* BOT flower, bloom; *de negocio, civilización* etc flourish; **floreciente** *adj* flourishing; **florero** *m* vase; **florista** *m/f* florist; **floristería** *f* florist's, flower shop
flota *f* fleet; **flotación** *f* flotation; **flotador** *m* float; **flotar** <1a> *v/i* float; **flote** MAR: **a ~** afloat
fluctuación *f* fluctuation; **fluctuar** <1e> *v/i* fluctuate
fluidez *f* fluidity; **fluido 1** *adj* fluid; *tráfico* free-flowing; *lenguaje* fluent **2** *m* fluid; **fluir** <3g> *v/i* flow
flujo *m* flow
fluorescente 1 *adj* fluorescent **2** *m* strip light
fluvial *adj* river *atr*
FM *abr* (= **frecuencia modulada**) FM (= frequency modulation)
FMI *abr* (= **Fondo Monetario Internacional**) IMF (= International Monetary Fund)
fobia *f* phobia
foca *f* ZO seal
foco *m* focus; TEA, TV spotlight; *de infección* center, *Br* centre; *de incendio* seat; *L.Am.* (*bombilla*)

lightbulb; *de auto* headlight; *de calle* streetlight

fofo *adj* flabby

fogata *f* bonfire; **fogoso** *adj* fiery, ardent

foie-gras *m* foie gras

folclore *m* folklore

fólico *adj*: **ácido ~** folic acid

folio *m* sheet (of paper)

folklore *m* folklore

follaje *m* foliage

folleto *m* pamphlet

follón *m* argument; (*lío*) mess; **armar un ~** kick up a fuss

fomentar <1a> *v/t* foster; COM promote; *rebelión* foment, incite; **fomento** *m* COM promotion

fonda *f* L.Am. cheap restaurant; (*pensión*) boarding house

fondear <1a> **1** *v/t* MAR anchor **2** *v/r* **~se** L.Am. get rich

fondero *m*, **-a** *f* L.Am. restaurant owner

fondista *m/f* DEP long-distance runner

fondo *m* bottom; *de sala, cuarto etc* back; *de pasillo* end; (*profundidad*) depth; PINT, FOT background; *de un museo etc* collection; COM fund; **~ de inversión** investment fund; **~ de pensiones** pension fund; **Fondo Monetario Internacional** International Monetary Fund; **~s** *pl* money *sg*, funds; **tiene buen ~** he's got a good heart; **en el ~** deep down; **tocar ~** *fig* reach bottom

fonética *f* phonetics

fontanería *f* plumbing; **fontanero** *m* plumber

footing *m* DEP jogging; **hacer ~** go jogging, jog

forastero 1 *adj* foreign **2** *m*, **-a** *f* outsider, stranger

forcejear <1a> *v/i* struggle; **forcejeo** *m* struggle

forense 1 *adj* forensic **2** *m/f* forensic scientist

forestación *f* afforestation; **forestal** *adj* forest *atr*; **forestar** <1a> *v/t* L.Am. afforest

forjar <1a> *v/t metal* forge

forma *f* form; (*apariencia*) shape; (*manera*) way; **de todas ~s** in any case, anyway; **estar en ~** be fit; **formación** *f* formation; (*entrenamiento*) training; **~ profesional** vocational training; **formal** *adj* formal; *niño* well-behaved; (*responsable*) responsible; **formalizar** <1f> *v/t* formalize; *relación* make official; **formar** <1a> **1** *v/t* form; (*educar*) educate **2** *v/r* **~se** form

formatear <1a> *v/t* INFOR format; **formato** *m* format

formidable *adj* huge; (*estupendo*) tremendous

fórmula *f* formula; **formular** <1a> *v/t teoría* formulate; *queja* make, lodge; **formulario** *m* form

fornicar <1g> *v/i* fornicate

fornido *adj* well-built

foro *m* forum

forofo *m*, **-a** *f* F fan

forrado *adj prenda* lined; *libro* covered; *fig* F loaded F

forraje *m* fodder

forrar <1a> **1** *v/t prenda* line; *libro, silla* cover **2** *v/r* **~se** F make a fortune F; **forro** *m de prenda* lining; *de libro* cover

fortalecer <2d> **1** *v/t tb fig* strengthen **2** *v/r* **~se** strengthen; **fortaleza** *f* strength of character; MIL fortress; **fortificar** <1g> *v/t* MIL fortify

fortuito *adj* chance *atr*, accidental

fortuna *f* fortune; (*suerte*) luck; **por ~** fortunately, luckily

forzar <1f & 1m> *v/t* force; (*violar*) rape; **forzoso** *adj aterrizaje* forced; **forzudo** *adj* brawny

fosa *f* pit; (*tumba*) grave; **~ común** common grave; **~s nasales** nostrils

fósforo *m* QUÍM phosphorus; L.Am. (*cerilla*) match

fósil 1 *adj* fossilized **2** *m* fossil

foso *m* ditch; TEA, MÚS pit; *de castillo* moat

foto *f* photo

fotocopia *f* photocopy; **fotocopiadora** *f* photocopier; **fotocopiar** <1a> *v/t* photocopy

fotogénico *adj* photogenic

fotografía *f* photography; **fotografiar** <1c> *v/t* photograph; **fotógrafo** *m*, **-a** *f* photographer

FP *f* (= *formación profesional*) vocational training

frac *m* tail coat

fracasado 1 *adj* unsuccessful **2** *m*, **-a** *f* loser; **fracasar** <1a> *v/i* fail; **fracaso** *m* failure

fracción *f* fraction; POL faction; **fraccionamiento** *m* L.Am. (housing) project, Br estate; **fraccionar** <1a> *v/t* break up; FIN pay in instal(l)ments

fractura *f* MED fracture; **fracturar** <1a> *v/t* MED fracture

fragancia *f* fragrance

frágil *adj* fragile

fragmentar <1a> *v/t* fragment; **fragmento** *m* fragment; *de novela, poema* excerpt, extract

fraguar <1i> *v/t* forge; *plan* devise; *complot* hatch

fraile *m* friar, monk

frambuesa *f* raspberry

francés 1 *adj* French **2** *m* Frenchman; *idioma* French; **francesa** *f* Frenchwoman; **Francia** France

franco *adj* (*sincero*) frank; (*evidente*) distinct, marked; COM free

francotirador *m* sniper

franela *f* flannel

franja *f* fringe; *de tierra* strip

franquear <1a> *v/t carta* pay the postage on; *camino, obstáculo* clear; **franqueo** *m* postage; **franqueza** *f* frankness; **franquicia** *f* (*exención*) exemption; COM franchise

frasco *m* bottle

frase *f* phrase; (*oración*) sentence; **~ hecha** set phrase

fraternal *adj* brotherly; **fraternidad** *f* brotherhood, fraternity; **fraternizar** <1f> *v/i* POL fraternize

fraude *m* fraud; **fraudulento** *adj* fraudulent

frazada *f* L.Am. blanket

frecuencia *f* frequency; **~ modulada** RAD frequency modulation; **con ~** frequently; **frecuentar** <1a> *v/t* frequent; **frecuente** *adj* frequent; (*común*) common; **frecuentemente** *adv* often, frequently

fregadero *m* sink; **fregar** <1h & 1k> *v/t platos* wash; *el suelo* mop; L.Am. F bug F; **fregón 1** *adj* annoying **2** *m* L.Am. F nuisance, pain in the neck F; **fregona** *f* mop; L.Am. F nuisance, pain in the neck F

freidora *f* deep fryer; **freidura** *f* frying; **freír** <3m; *part frito*> *v/t* fry; F (*matar*) waste P

frenada *f* esp L.Am.: **dar una ~** F slam the brakes on, hit the brakes F; **frenar** <1a> **1** *v/i* AUTO brake **2** *v/t fig* slow down; *impulsos* check; **frenazo** *m*: **pegar** *or* **dar un ~** F slam the brakes on, hit the brakes F

frenesí *m* frenzy; **frenético** *adj* frenetic

freno *m* brake; **~ de mano** parking brake, Br handbrake

frente 1 *f* forehead **2** *m* MIL, METEO front; **de ~ colisión** head-on; **de ~ al grupo** L.Am. facing the group; **hacer ~ a** face up to **3** *prp*: **~ a** opposite

fresa *f* strawberry

fresco 1 *adj* cool; *pescado etc* fresh; *persona* F fresh F, cheeky F **2** *m*, **-a** *f*: **¡eres un ~!** F you've got nerve! F, Br you've got a cheek! F **3** *m* fresh air; C.Am. fruit drink; **frescor** *m* freshness; **frescura** *f* freshness; (*frío*) coolness; *fig* nerve

fresno *m* BOT ash tree

fresón *m* strawberry

frialdad *f tb fig* coldness

fricción *f* TÉC, *fig* friction; **friccionar** <1a> *v/t* rub

friega *f* L.Am. F hassle F, drag F

frígido *adj* MED frigid; **frigorífico 1** *adj* refrigerated **2** *m* fridge

fríjol *m*, **frijol** *m* L.Am. bean

frío 1 *adj tb fig* cold **2** *m* cold; **tener ~** be cold; **friolento** L.Am., **friolero** *adj*: **es ~** he feels the cold

fritar <1a> *v/t* L.Am. fry; **frito 1** *part* → **freír 2** *adj* fried **3** *mpl*: **~s** fried

food *sg*; **fritura** *f* fried food
frívolo *adj* frivolous
frondoso *adj* leafy
frontal *adj* frontal; *ataque etc* head-on; *(delantero)* front *atr*
frontera *f* border; **fronterizo** *adj* border *atr*
frontón *m* DEP pelota; *cancha* pelota court
frotar <1a> *v/t* rub
fructífero *adj* fruitful, productive
frugal *adj persona* frugal
fruncir <3b> *v/t material* gather; **~ el ceño** frown
frustración *f* frustration; **frustrante** *adj* frustrating; **frustrar** <1a> **1** *v/t* frustrate; *plan* thwart **2** *v/r* **~se** fail
fruta *f* fruit; **frutal 1** *adj* fruit *atr* **2** *m* fruit tree; **frutería** *f* fruit store, *Br* greengrocer's
frutilla *f S.Am.* strawberry
fruto *m tb fig* fruit; *nuez, almendra etc* nut; **~s secos** nuts
fucsia *adj* fuchsia
fue *vb* → *ir, ser*
fuego *m* fire; **¿tienes ~?** do you have a light?; **~s artificiales** fireworks; **pegar** *o* **prender ~ a** set fire to
fuel(-oil) *m* fuel oil
fuelle *m* bellows *pl*
fuente *f* fountain; *recipiente* dish; *fig* source
fuera 1 *vb* → *ir, ser* **2** *adv* outside; *(en otro lugar)* away; *(en otro país)* abroad; **por ~** on the outside; **¡~!** get out! **3** *prp*: **~ de** outside; **¡sal ~ de aquí!** get out of here!; **está ~ del país** he's abroad, he's out of the country
fuero *m*: **en el ~ interno** deep down
fuerte 1 *adj* strong; *dolor* intense; *lluvia* heavy; *aumento* sharp; *ruido* loud; *fig* P incredible F **2** *adv* hard **3** *m* MIL fort; **fuerza** *f* strength; *(violencia)* force; EL power; **~ aérea** air force; **~ de voluntad** willpower; **~s armadas** armed forces; **~s de seguridad** security forces; **a ~ de ...** by (dint of)
fuese *vb* → *ir, ser*
fuete *m L.Am.* whip

fuga *f* escape; *de gas, agua* leak; **darse a la ~** flee; **fugarse** <1h> *v/r* run away; *de la cárcel* escape; **fugaz** *adj fig* fleeting; **fugitivo 1** *adj* runaway *atr* **2** *m*, **-a** *f* fugitive
fui *vb* → *ir, ser*
fuimos *vb* → *ir, ser*
fulano *m* so-and-so
fulgor *m* brightness; **fulgurante** *adj fig* dazzling
fulminante *adj* sudden; **fulminar** <1a> *v/t*: **lo fulminó un rayo** he was killed by lightning; **~ a alguien con la mirada** look daggers at s.o. F
fumador *m*, **-a** *f* smoker; **fumar** <1a> **1** *v/t* smoke **2** *v/i* smoke; **prohibido ~** no smoking **3** *v/r* **~se** smoke; **~se una clase** F skip a class F
fumigar <1h> *v/t* fumigate
función *f* purpose, function; *en el trabajo* duty; TEA performance; **en ~ de** according to; **funcional** *adj* functional; **funcionamiento** *m* working; **funcionar** <1a> *v/i* work; **no funciona** out of order; **funcionario** *m*, **-a** *f* government employee, civil servant
funda *f* cover; *de gafas* case; *de almohada* pillowcase
fundación *f* foundation; **fundador** *m*, **~a** *f* founder
fundamental *adj* fundamental; **fundamentalismo** *m* fundamentalism; **fundamentalista** *m/f* fundamentalist; **fundamentalmente** *adv* essentially; **fundamento** *m* foundation; **~s** *(nociones)* fundamentals; **fundar** <1a> **1** *v/t fig* base *(en* on) **2** *v/r* **~se** be based *(en* on)
fundición *f* smelting; *(fábrica)* foundry; **fundir** <3a> **1** *v/t hielo* melt; *metal* smelt; COM merge **2** *v/r* **~se** melt; *de bombilla* fuse; *de plomos* blow; COM merge; *L.Am. fig*: *de empresa* go under
fúnebre *adj* funeral *atr*; *fig*: *ambiente* gloomy; **funeral** *m* funeral; **funeraria** *f* funeral parlo(u)r, *Br* undertaker's
funesto *adj* disastrous

funicular *m* funicular; (*teleférico*) cable car
furcia *f* P whore P
furgón *m* van; FERR boxcar, *Br* goods van; **~ de equipajes** baggage car, *Br* luggage van; **furgoneta** *f* van
furia *f* fury; **ponerse hecho una ~** go into a fury *o* rage; **furibundo** *adj* furious; **furioso** *adj* furious; **furor** *m*: **hacer ~** *fig* be all the rage F
furtivo *adj* furtive
fuselaje *m* fuselage
fusible *m* EL fuse
fusil *m* rifle; **fusilar** <1a> *v/t* shoot; *fig* F (*plagiar*) lift F

fusión *f* FÍS fusion; COM merger; **fusionar** <1a> **1** *v/t* COM merge **2** *v/r* **~se** merge
fusta *f* riding crop
fútbol *m* soccer, *Br* football; **~ americano** football, *Br* American football; **~ sala** five-a-side soccer (*Br* football); **futbolín** *m* Foosball®, table football; **futbolista** *m/f* soccer player, *Br* footballer, *Br* football player
fútil *adj* trivial
futre *m* Chi dandy
futuro 1 *adj* future *atr* **2** *m* future; **futurólogo** *m*, **-a** *f* futurologist

G

G

g. *abr* (= **gramo(s)**) gr(s) (= gram(s))
gabardina *f prenda* raincoat; *material* gabardine
gabinete *m* (*despacho*) office; *en una casa* study; POL cabinet; *L.Am. de médico* office, *Br* surgery
gacela *f* ZO gazelle
gaceta *f* gazette
gachas *fpl* porridge *sg*
gachupín *m Méx desp* Spaniard
gacilla *f C.Am.* safety pin
gafas *fpl* glasses; **~ de sol** sunglasses
gafe 1 *adj* jinxed **2** *m* jinx **3** *m/f*: **es un ~** he's jinxed
gaita *f* MÚS bagpipes *pl*
gajes *mpl*: **~ del oficio** *irón* occupational hazard
gajo *m* segment
gala *f* gala; **traje de ~** formal dress
galante *adj* gallant
galápago *m* ZO turtle
galardonar <1a> *v/t*: **fue galardonado con ...** he was awarded ...
galaxia *f* galaxy
galería *f* gallery; **~ de arte** art gallery

Gales Wales; **galés** Welsh
galgo *m* greyhound
gallera *f* L.Am. cockpit
galleta *f* cookie, *Br* biscuit
gallina 1 *f* hen **2** *m* F chicken
gallinazo *m* L.Am. turkey buzzard
gallo *m* rooster, *Br* cock
galón *m adorno* braid; MIL stripe; *medida* gallon
galope *m* gallop
galpón *m* L.Am. large shed; *W.I.* HIST slave quarters *pl*
gama *f* range
gamba *f* ZO GASTR shrimp, *Br* prawn
gamberro *m*, **-a** *f* troublemaker
gamín *m*, **-ina** *f* Col street kid
gamo *m* ZO fallow deer
gamonal *m* Pe, Bol desp chief
gamuza *f* chamois
gana *f*: **de mala ~** unwillingly, grudgingly; **no me da la ~** I don't want to; **... me da ~s de ...** makes me want to; **tener ~s de (hacer) algo** feel like (doing) sth
ganadería *f* stockbreeding; **ganadero** *m*, **-a** *f* stockbreeder; **ganado** *m* cattle *pl*

ganador *m* winner; **ganancia** *f* profit; **ganar** <1a> **1** win; *mediante el trabajo* earn **2** *v/i mediante el trabajo* earn; (*vencer*) win; (*mejorar*) improve **3** *v/r* ~**se** earn; *a alguien* win over; ~**se la vida** earn one's living

ganchillo *m* crochet; **gancho** *m* hook; *L.Am.*, *Arg fig* F sex-appeal; **hacer ~** *L.Am.* (*ayudar*) lend a hand; **tener ~** *de un grupo, una campaña* be popular; *de una persona* have that certain something

gandul *m* lazybones *sg*; **gandulear** <1a> *v/i* F loaf around F

ganga *f* bargain

gangrena *f* MED gangrene

gángster *m* gangster

ganso *m* goose; *macho* gander

garabatear <1a> *v/i & v/t* doodle; **garabato** *m* doodle

garaje *m* garage

garantía *f* guarantee; **garantizar** <1f> *v/t* guarantee

garapiña *f Cuba, Méx* pineapple squash

garbanzo *m* BOT chickpea

garbo *m al moverse* grace

gardenia *f* BOT gardenia

garete *m*: **irse al ~** *fig* F go to pot F

garfio *m* hook

gargajo *m* piece of phlegm

garganta *f* ANAT throat; GEOG gorge; **gargantilla** *f* choker

gárgaras *fpl*: **hacer ~** gargle

garito *m* gambling den

garra *f* claw; *de ave* talon; **caer en las ~s de alguien** *fig* fall into s.o.'s clutches; **tener ~** F be compelling

garrafa *f* carafe

garrafal *adj error etc* terrible

garrapata *f* ZO tick

garrote *m palo* club, stick; *tipo de ejecución* garrotte

garúa *f L.Am.* drizzle; **garuar** <1e> *v/i L.Am.* drizzle

garzón *m Rpl* (*mesero*) waiter

garza *f* ZO heron

gas *m* gas; ~ *natural* natural gas; ~**es** *pl* MED gas *sg*, wind *sg*; **con ~** sparkling, carbonated; **sin ~** still

gasa *f* gauze

gaseosa *f* lemonade; **gasfitero** *m Pe, Bol* plumber; **gasoducto** *m* gas pipeline; **gasoil**, **gasóleo** *m* oil; *para motores* diesel; **gasolina** *f* gas, *Br* petrol; **gasolinera** *f* gas station, *Br* petrol station

gastar <1a> **1** *v/t dinero* spend; *energía, electricidad etc* use; (*llevar*) wear; (*desperdiciar*) waste; (*desgastar*) wear out; **¿qué número gastas?** what size do you take?, what size are you? **2** *v/r* ~**se** *dinero* spend; *gasolina, agua* run out of; *pila* run down; *ropa, zapatos* wear out; **gasto** *m* expense

gastronomía *f* gastronomy

gata *f* (female) cat; *Méx* servant, maid; **a ~s** F on all fours; **andar a ~s** F crawl; **gatear** <1a> *v/i* crawl

gatillo *m* trigger

gato *m* cat; AUTO jack; **aquí hay ~ encerrado** F there's something fishy going on here F; **cuatro ~s** a handful of people

gaucho *m Rpl* gaucho

gaviota *f* (sea)gull

gay 1 *adj* gay **2** *m* gay (man)

gazpacho *m* gazpacho (*cold soup made with tomatoes, peppers, garlic etc*)

gel *m* gel

gelatina *f* gelatin(e); GASTR Jell-O®, *Br* jelly

gélido *adj* icy

gema *f* gem

gemelo 1 *adj* twin *atr*; **hermano ~** twin brother **2** *mpl*: ~**s** twins; *de camisa* cuff links; (*prismáticos*) binoculars

gemido *m* moan, groan

Géminis *m/f inv* ASTR Gemini

gemir <3l> *v/i* moan, groan

gen *m* gene

genealógico *adj*: **árbol ~** family tree

generación *f* generation; **generador** *m* EL generator

general 1 *adj* general; **en ~** in general; **por lo ~** usually, generally **2** *m* general; **generalización** *f* generalization; **generalizar** <1f> **1** *v/t* spread **2** v/i generalize **3** v/r ~se spread; **generalmente** adv generally

generar <1a> v/t generate

género m (tipo) type; de literatura genre; GRAM gender; COM goods pl, merchandise

generosidad f generosity; **generoso** adj generous

genética f genetics; **genético** adj genetic

genial adj brilliant; F (estupendo) fantastic F, great F; **genialidad** f brilliance; **genio** m talento, persona genius; (carácter) temper; **tener mal ~** be bad-tempered

genital adj genital; **genitales** mpl genitals

genocidio m genocide

gente f people pl; L.Am. (persona) person

gentileza f kindness; **por ~ de** by courtesy of

gentío m crowd

genuino adj genuine, real

geografía f geography; **geográfico** adj geographical

geología f geology; **geológico** adj geological; **geólogo** m, -a f geologist

geometría f geometry; **geométrico** adj geometric(al)

geranio m BOT geranium

gerente m/f manager

geriatría f geriatrics sg

germen m germ

germinar <1a> v/i tb fig germinate

gerundio m GRAM gerund

gestación f gestation

gesticular <1a> v/i gesticulate

gestión f management; **gestiones** pl (trámites) formalities, procedure sg; **gestionar** <1a> v/t trámites take care of; negocio manage

gesto m movimiento gesture; (expresión) expression

gestoría f Esp agency offering clients help with official documents

gigante 1 adj giant atr **2** m giant

gilipollas m/f inv P jerk P

gilipollez f Esp V bullshit V

gimnasia f gymnastics; **hacer ~** do exercises; **gimnasio** m gym; **gimnasta** m/f gymnast

gimotear <1a> v/i whine, whimper

ginebra f gin

ginecólogo m, -a f gyn(a)ecologist

gin-tonic m gin and tonic, G and T F

gira f tour; **girar** <1a> **1** v/i (dar vueltas, torcer) turn; alrededor de algo revolve; fig (tratar) revolve (**en torno a** around) **2** v/t COM transfer

girasol m BOT sunflower

giro m turn; GRAM idiom; **~ postal** COM money order

gis m L.Am. chalk

gitano 1 adj gypsy atr **2** m, **-a** f gypsy

glacial adj icy; **glaciar** m glacier

glándula f ANAT gland

global adj (de todo el mundo) global; visión, resultado overall; cantidad total; **globo** m aerostático, de niño balloon; terrestre globe; **~ terráqueo** globe

gloria f glory; (delicia) delight; **estar en la ~** F be in seventh heaven; **gloriado** m Pe, Bol, Ecuad type of punch; **glorieta** f traffic circle, Br roundabout; **glorioso** adj glorious

glosario m glossary

glotón 1 adj greedy **2** m, **-ona** f glutton

glucosa f glucose

gnomo m gnome

gobernador m governor; **gobernante** m leader; **gobernar** <1k> v/t & v/i rule, govern; **gobierno** m government

goce m pleasure, enjoyment

gofre m waffle

gol m DEP goal; **goleador** m DEP (goal-)scorer

golf m DEP golf; **golfista** m/f golfer

golfo 1 m GEOG gulf **2** m, **-a** f good-for-nothing; niño little devil

Golfo de México m Gulf of Mexico

golondrina f ZO swallow

golosina f candy, Br sweet; **goloso** adj sweet-toothed

golpe m knock, blow; **~ de Estado** coup d'état; **de ~** suddenly; **no da ~** F she doesn't do a thing; **golpear**

<a1a> v/t cosa bang, hit; persona hit

goma f (caucho) rubber; (pegamento) glue; (banda elástica) rubber band; F (preservativo) condom, rubber P; C.Am. F (resaca) hangover; ~ (de borrar) eraser; ~ espuma foam rubber; gomina f hair gel; **gominola** f jelly bean

góndola f Chi bus

gong m gong

gordinflón m, -ona f F fatso F; **gordo 1** adj fat; me cae ~ F I can't stand him; se va a armar la -a all hell will break loose F **2** m, -a f fat person **3** m premio jackpot

gorila m ZO gorilla

gorjeo m de pájaro chirping, warbling; de niño gurgling

gorra f cap; de ~ F for free F

gorrino m fig pig

gorrión m ZO sparrow

gorro m cap; estar hasta el ~ de algo F be fed up to the back teeth with sth F

gorrón m, -ona f F scrounger; **gorronear** <1a> v/t & v/i F scrounge F

gota f drop; ni ~ de cerveza, leche etc not a drop; de pan not a scrap; **gotear** <1a> v/i drip; filtrarse leak; **gotera** f leak; (mancha) stain; **gotero** m MED drip; L.Am. (eye)-dropper

gozar <1f> v/i (disfrutar) enjoy o.s.; ~ de (disfrutar de) enjoy; (poseer) have, enjoy; **gozo** m (alegría) joy; (placer) pleasure

grabación f recording; **grabado** m engraving; **grabadora** f tape recorder; **grabar** <1a> v/t en vídeo, cinta etc record; PINT, fig engrave

gracia f: tener ~ (ser divertido) be funny; (tener encanto) be graceful; me hace ~ I think it's funny, it makes me laugh; no le veo la ~ I don't think it's funny; dar las ~s a alguien thank s.o.; ~s thank you

grácil adj dainty

gracioso adj funny

gradas fpl DEP stands, grandstand sg; **graderío** m stands pl

grado m degree; de buen ~ with good grace, readily

graduación f TÉC etc adjustment; de alcohol alcohol content; EDU graduation; MIL rank; **gradual** adj gradual; **gradualmente** adv gradually

graduarse <1e> v/r graduate, get one's degree

gráfica f graph; **gráfico 1** adj graphic; artes -as graphic arts **2** m MAT graph; INFOR graphic

gragea f tablet, pill

grajo m ZO rook

gramática f grammar; **gramatical** adj grammatical

gramo m gram

gran short form of **grande** before a noun

granada f BOT pomegranate; ~ de mano MIL hand grenade

granangular m wide-angle lens

granate adj dark crimson

Gran Bretaña Great Britain

grande 1 adj big; a lo ~ in style **2** m/f L.Am. (adulto) grown-up, adult; (mayor) eldest; pasarlo en ~ F have a great time; **grandeza** f greatness; **grandiosidad** f grandeur; **grandioso** adj impressive, magnificent

granel m: vender a ~ COM sell in bulk; había comida a ~ F there was loads of food F

granero m granary

granito m granite

granizada f hailstorm; **granizado** m type of soft drink made with crushed ice; **granizar** <1f> v/i hail; **granizo** m hail

granja f farm

granjearse <1a> v/r win, earn

granjero m, -a f farmer

grano m grain; de café bean; en la piel pimple, spot; ir al ~ get (straight) to the point

granuja m rascal

grapa f staple; **grapadora** f stapler; **grapar** <1a> staple

grasa f BIO, GASTR fat; lubricante, suciedad grease; **grasiento** adj greasy, oily; **graso** *adj* greasy; *carne* fatty

gratificación *f* gratification; **gratificar** <1g> *v/t* reward

gratinar <1a> *v/t* cook au gratin

gratis *adj & adv* free; **gratitud** *f* gratitude; **gratuito** *adj* free

grava *f* gravel

gravar <1a> *v/t* tax

grave *adj* serious; *tono* grave, solemn; *nota* low; *voz* deep; **estar** ~ be seriously ill; **gravedad** *f* seriousness, gravity; FÍS gravity; **gravemente** *adv* seriously

gravilla *f* grave

Grecia Greece

gremio *m* HIST guild; *fig* F (*oficio manual*) trade; (*profesión*) profession

griego 1 *adj* Greek **2** *m*, **-a** *f* Greek

grieta *f* crack

grifo 1 *adj* Méx F high **2** *m* faucet, *Br* tap; *Pe* (*gasolinera*) gas station, *Br* petrol station

grillo *m* ZO cricket

grima *f*: **me da** ~ *Esp* de ruido, material etc it sets my teeth on edge; *de algo asqueroso* it gives me the creeps F; **en** ~ *Pe* alone

gringo *m* L.Am. desp gringo desp, foreigner

gripe *f* flu, influenza; ~ **aviar** bird flu

gris *adj* gray, *Br* grey

gritar <1a> *v/t & v/i* shout, yell; **griterío** *m* shouting; **grito** *m* cry, shout; **a ~ pelado** at the top of one's voice; **pedir algo a ~s** F be crying out for sth

grosella *f* redcurrant

grosero 1 *adj* rude **2** *m*, **-a** *f* rude person; **grosor** *m* thickness

grotesco *adj* grotesque

grúa *f* crane; AUTO wrecker, *Br* breakdown truck

grueso *adj* thick; *persona* stout

grulla *f* ZO crane

grumo *m* lump

gruñido *m* grunt; *de perro* growl; **gruñir** <3h> *v/i* (*quejarse*) grumble, moan F; *de perro* growl; *de cerdo* grunt; **gruñón 1** *adj* F grumpy

2 *m*, **-ona** *f* F grouch F

grupo *m* group

gruta *f* cave; *artificial* grotto

guacamol, **guacamole** *m* guacamole

guachimán *m* Chi watchman

guacho 1 *adj* S.Am. (*sin casa*) homeless; (*huérfano*) orphaned **2** *m*, **-a** *f* S.Am. sin casa homeless person; (*huérfano*) orphan

guadaño *m* Cuba, Méx small boat

guagua *f* W.I., Ven, Canaries bus; *Pe, Bol, Chi* (*niño*) baby

guajolote *m* Méx, C.Am. turkey

guanaco 1 *adj* L.Am. F dumb F, stupid **2** *m* ZO guanaco **3** *m*, **-a** *f* persona idiot

guantazo *m* slap

guante *m* glove; **guantera** *f* AUTO glove compartment

guapo *adj* hombre handsome, good-looking; *mujer* beautiful; *S.Am.* gutsy

guaracha *f* W.I. street band

guarache → *huarache*

guarapo *m* L.Am. alcoholic drink made from sugar cane and herbs

guarda *m/f* guard; ~ **jurado** security guard

guardabosques *m/f inv* forest ranger

guardacostas *m inv* coastguard vessel

guardaespaldas *m/f inv* bodyguard

guardameta *m/f* DEP goalkeeper

guardar <1a> **1** *v/t* keep; *poner en un lugar* put (away); *recuerdo* have; *apariencias* keep up; INFOR save; ~ **silencio** remain silent, keep silent **2** *v/r* ~**se** keep; ~**se de** refrain from

guardarropa *m* checkroom, *Br* cloakroom; (*ropa, armario*) wardrobe

guardería *f* nursery

guardia 1 *f* guard; **de** ~ on duty; **bajar la** ~ *fig* lower one's guard **2** *m/f* MIL guard; (*policía*) police officer; ~ **civil** *Esp* civil guard; ~ **de seguridad** security guard; ~ **de tráfico** traffic warden

guardián 1 *adj*: **perro** ~ guard dog

2 *m*, **-ana** *f* guard; *fig* guardian

guarecer <2d> **1** *v/t* shelter **2** *v/r* **~se** shelter, take shelter (**de** from)

guarida *f* ZO den; *de personas* hideout

guarnición *f* GASTR accompaniment; MIL garrison

guaro *m* C.Am. sugar-cane liquor

guarro 1 *adj* F *sucio* filthy **2** *m tb fig* F pig

guarura *m Méx* (*guardaespaldas*) bodyguard; F (*gamberro*) thug

guasa *f L.Am.* joke; *de* **~** as a joke

guaso 1 *adj* S.Am. rude **2** *m Chi* peasant

guata *f L.Am.* F paunch

Guatemala *f* Guatemala

guatemalteco 1 *adj* Guatemalan **2** *m*, **-a** *f* Guatemalan

guatón *adj L.Am.* F pot-bellied, bigbellied

guay *int Esp* F cool F, neat F

guayaba *f L.Am.* BOT guava

guayabera *f Méx, C.Am., W.I.* loose embroidered shirt

gubernamental *adj* governmental, government *atr*

guepardo *m* ZO cheetah

güero 1 *adj Méx, C.Am.* fair, light-skinned **2** *m*, **-a** *f Méx, C.Am.* blond(e)

guerra *f* war; **~ civil** civil war; **~ fría** cold war; **~ mundial** world war; *dar* **~ a alguien** F give s.o. trouble; **guerrero 1** *adj* warlike **2** *m* warrior; **guerrilla** *f* guerillas *pl*; **guerrillero** *m* guerilla

gueto *m* ghetto

guevear *v/i → huevear*

guevón → huevón

guía 1 *m/f* guide; **~ turístico** tourist guide **2** *f libro* guide (book); **~ telefónica** or **de teléfonos** phone book; **guiar** <1c> **1** *v/t* guide **2** *v/r* **~se**: **~se por** follow

guijarro *m* pebble

guillotina *f* guillotine

güinche *m L.Am.* winch, pulley

guinda 1 *adj L.Am.* purple **2** *f fresca* morello cherry; *en dulce* glacé cherry

guindilla *f* GASTR chil(l)i

guiñar <1a> *v/t*: **le guiñó un ojo** she winked at him; **guiño** *m* wink

guión *m de película* script; GRAM *corto* hyphen; *largo* dash; **guionista** *m/f* scriptwriter

guiri *m Esp* P (light-skinned) foreigner

guirnalda *f* garland

guisante *m* pea; **guisar** <1a> *v/t* GASTR stew, casserole; **guiso** *m* GASTR stew, casserole

guitarra *f* guitar; **guitarrista** *m/f* guitarist

gula *f* gluttony

gusano *m* worm

gustar <1a> *v/i*: **me gusta viajar** I like to travel, I like travelling; **¿te gusta el ajo?** do you like garlic?; **no me gusta** I don't like it; **gusto** *m* taste; (*placer*) pleasure; **a ~** at ease; **con mucho ~** with pleasure; **de buen ~** in good taste, tasteful; **de mal ~** in bad taste, tasteless; **da ~ ...** it's a pleasure ...; **mucho** or **tanto ~** how do you do

gutural *adj* guttural

H

ha *vb → haber*

haba *f* broad bean; **en todas partes se cuecen ~s** it's the same the

world over

Habana: *La ~* Havana; **habanero** *m*, **-a** *f* citizen of Havana; **habano** *m*

hala

Havana (cigar)

haber <2k> **1** v/aux have; **hemos llegado** we've arrived; **he de levantarme pronto** I have to o I've got to get up early; **de ~lo sabido** if I'd known; **has de ver** Méx you ought to see it **2** v/impers: **hay** there is sg, there are pl; **hubo un incendio** there was a fire; **¿qué hay?**, Méx **¿qué hubo?** how's it going?, what's happening?; **hay que hacerlo** it has to be done; **no hay de qué** not at all, don't mention it; **no hay más que decir** there's nothing more to be said **3** m asset; **pago** fee; **tiene en su ~ 50.000 ptas** she's 50,000 pesetas in credit

habichuela f kidney bean

hábil adj skilled; (capaz) capable; (astuto) clever, smart; **habilidad** f skill; (capacidad) ability; (astucia) cleverness; **habilitar** <1a> v/t lugar fit out; persona authorize

habitación f room; (dormitorio) bedroom; **~ doble/individual** double/single room; **habitante** m/f inhabitant; **habitar** <1a> v/i live (**en** in); **hábitat** m habitat

hábito m tb REL habit; (práctica) knack; **colgar los ~s** fig de sacerdote give up the priesthood; **habitual 1** adj usual, regular **2** m/f regular; **habituar** <1e> **1** v/t: **~ a alguien a algo** get s.o. used to sth **2** v/r **~se: ~se a algo** get used to sth

habla f speech; **¡al ~!** TELEC speaking; **quedarse sin ~** fig be speechless; **hablada** f L.Am. piece of gossip; **~s** pl gossip sg; **hablador** adj talkative; Méx boastful; **habladurías** fpl gossip sg

hablante m/f speaker

hablar <1a> **1** v/i speak; (conversar) talk; **~ claro** fig say what one means; **~ con alguien** talk to s.o., talk with s.o.; **~ de** de libro etc be about, deal with; **~ por ~** talk for the sake of it; **¡ni ~!** no way! **2** v/r **~se** speak to one another; **no se hablan** they're not speaking (to each other)

hacendado 1 adj land-owning **2** m, **-a** f land-owner; **hacendoso** adj hardworking

hacer <2s; part **hecho**> **1** v/t (realizar) do; (elaborar, crear) make; **¡haz algo!** do something!; **~ una pregunta** ask a question; **¡qué le vamos a ~!** that's life; **no hace más que quejarse** all he does is complain; **le hicieron ir** they made him go; **tengo que ~ los deberes** I have to do my homework **2** v/i: **haces bien/mal en ir** you are doing the right/wrong thing by going; **esto hace mal** it's making me ill; **esto hará de mesa** de objeto this will do as a table; **~ como que** or **como si** act as if; **no le hace** L.Am. it doesn't matter; **se me hace qué** L.Am. it seems to me that **3** v/impers: **hace calor/frío** it's hot/cold; **hace tres días** three days ago; **hace mucho (tiempo)** a long time ago; **desde hace un año** for a year **4** v/r **~se** traje make; casa build o.s.; (cocinarse) cook; (convertirse, volverse) get, become; **~se viejo** get old; **~se de noche** get dark; **se hace tarde** it's getting late; **~se el sordo/el tonto** pretend to be deaf/stupid; **~se a algo** get used to sth; **~se con algo** get hold of sth

hacha f ax, Br axe; **ser un ~ para algo** F be brilliant at sth

hachís m hashish

hacia prp toward; **~ adelante** forward; **~ abajo** down; **~ arriba** up; **~ atrás** back(ward); **~ las cuatro** about four (o'clock)

Hacienda f ministerio Treasury Department, Br Treasury; oficina Internal Revenue Service, Br Inland Revenue

hacienda f L.Am. (granja) ranch, estate

hacinar <1a> v/t stack

hada f fairy

haga vb → **hacer**

hago vb → **hacer**

Haití Haiti

hala int come on!; sorpresa wow!

H

halagar <1h> v/t flatter; **halago** m flattery

halar <1a> v/t L.Am. haul, pull

halcón m zo falcon

halitosis f MED halitosis, bad breath

hall m hall

hallar <1a> **1** v/t find; (descubrir) discover; muerte, destino meet **2** v/r ~**se** be; (sentirse) feel; **hallazgo** m find; (descubrimiento) discovery

halógeno adj halogen

halterofilia f DEP weight-lifting

hamaca f hammock; (tumbona) deck chair; L.Am. (mecedora) rocking chair; **hamacar** <1g> v/t L.Am. swing; **hamaquear** <1a> v/t L.Am. swing

hambre f hunger; **morirse de ~** fig be starving; **pasar ~** be starving; **hambriento** adj tb fig hungry (de for); **hambruna** f famine

hamburguesa f GASTR hamburger; **hamburguesería** f hamburger bar

hampa f underworld

hámster m zo hamster

hangar m hangar

haragán m, **-ana** f shirker

harapo m rag

hardware m INFOR hardware

haré vb → **hacer**

harina f flour; **harinoso** adj floury

hartar <1a> **1** v/t: ~ **a alguien con algo** tire s.o. with sth; ~ **a alguien de algo** give s.o. too much of sth **2** v/r ~**se** get sick (de of) F, get tired (de of); (llenarse) stuff o.s. (de with); **harto 1** adj fed up F; (lleno) full (up); **había ~s pasteles** there were cakes in abundance; **hace ~ frío** L.Am. it's very cold; **estar ~ de algo** be sick of sth F, be fed up with sth F **2** adv very much; **delante del adjetivo** extremely; **me gusta ~** L.Am. F I like it a lot; **hartón 1** adj L.Am. greedy **2** m: **darse un ~ de algo** overdose on sth

has vb → **haber**

hasta 1 prp until, till; **llegó ~ Bilbao** he went as far as Bilbao; ~ **ahora** so far; ~ **aquí** up to here; **¿~ cuándo?** how long?; ~ **que** until; **¡~ luego!**

see you (later); **¡~ la vista!** see you (later) **2** adv even

hastiar <1c> v/t tire; (aburrir) bore; **hastío** m boredom

hatajo m bunch; **hato** m L.Am. bundle

hay vb → **haber**

haya 1 vb → **haber 2** f BOT beech

haz 1 m bundle; **de luz** beam **2** vb → **hacer**

hazaña f achievement

hazmerreír m fig F laughing stock

he vb → **haber**

hebilla f buckle

hechicero 1 adj bewitching, captivating **2** m sorcerer; **de tribu** witchdoctor; **hechizado** adj spellbound; **hechizar** <1f> v/t fig bewitch, captivate; **hechizo** m spell, charm

hecho 1 part → **hacer**, ~ **a mano** hand-made; **¡bien ~!** well done!; **muy ~** carne well-done **2** adj finished; **un hombre ~ y derecho** a fully grown man **3** m fact; **de ~** in fact

hectárea f hectare (10,000 sq m)

hedor m stink, stench

helada f frost; **heladera** f Rpl fridge; **heladería** f ice-cream parlo(u)r; **helado 1** adj frozen; fig icy; **quedarse ~** be stunned **2** m ice cream; **helar** <1k> **1** v/t freeze **2** v/i freeze; **anoche heló** there was a frost last night **3** v/r ~**se** tb fig freeze

helecho m BOT fern

hélice f propeller

helicóptero m helicopter

hematoma m bruise

hembra f ZO, TÉC female

hemiplejía f MED hemiplegia; **hemisferio** m hemisphere

hemofilia f MED h(a)emophilia; **hemorragia** f MED h(a)emorrhage, bleeding; **hemorroides** fpl MED h(a)emorrhoids, piles

hendidura f crack

heno m hay

hepatitis f MED hepatitis

herbicida m herbicide, weed-killer; **herboristería** f herbalist

hercúleo *adj* Herculean

heredar <1a> *v/t* inherit (*de* from); **heredera** *f* heiress; **heredero** *m* heir; **hereditario** *adj* hereditary

hereje *m* heretic

herencia *f* inheritance

herida *f* de arma wound; (*lesión*) injury; *mujer* wounded woman; *mujer lesionada* injured woman; **herido 1** *adj* de arma wounded; (*lesionado*) injured **2** *m* de bala wounded man; (*lesionado*) injured man; **herir** <3i> *v/t* con arma wound; (*lesionar*) injure; *fig* (*ofender*) hurt

hermana *f* sister; **hermanastra** *f* stepsister; **hermanastro** *m* stepbrother; **hermano** *m* brother

hermético *adj* airtight, hermetic; *fig: persona* inscrutable

hermoso *adj* beautiful

hernia *f* MED hernia

héroe *m* hero; **heroico** *adj* heroic; **heroína** *f* mujer heroine; *droga* heroin

heroinómano *m*, *-a* *f* heroin addict

herpes *m* MED herpes

herradura *f* horseshoe

herramienta *f* tool

hervidero *m* fig hotbed; **hervido** *m* S.Am. stew; **hervir** <3i> **1** *v/i* boil; *fig* swarm, seethe (*de* with) **2** *v/t* boil

heterodoxo *adj* unorthodox

heterogéneo *adj* heterogeneous

hez *f* scum, dregs *pl*

hibernar <1a> *v/i* hibernate

híbrido 1 *adj* hybrid *atr* **2** *m* hybrid

hice *vb* → **hacer**

hicimos *vb* → **hacer**

hidratante *adj* moisturizing; *crema* ~ moisturizing cream; **hidratar** <1a> *v/t* hydrate; *piel* moisturize; **hidrato** *m*: ~ *de carbono* carbohydrate

hidráulico *adj* hydraulic

hidroavión *m* seaplane

hidroeléctrico *adj* hydroelectric

hidrógeno *m* hydrogen

hiedra *f* BOT ivy

hielo *m* ice; *romper el* ~ *fig* break the ice

hiena *f* ZO hyena

hierba *f* grass; *mala* ~ weed

hlere *vb* → **herir**

hierro *m* iron

hierve *vb* → **hervir**

hígado *m* liver; *ser un* ~ *C.Am., Méx* F be a pain in the butt F

higiene *f* hygiene; **higiénico** *adj* hygienic

higo *m* BOT fig; **higuera** *f* BOT fig tree

hija *f* daughter; **hijastra** *f* stepdaughter; **hijastro** *m* stepson; **hijo** *m* son; ~*s* children *pl*; ~ *de puta* P son of a bitch V, bastard P; ~ *único* only child

hilachos *mpl* Méx rags

hilera *f* row, line

hilo *m* thread; ~ *dental* dental floss; *sin* ~*s* TELEC cordless; *colgar or pender de un* ~ *fig* hang by a thread; *perder el* ~ *fig* lose the thread

himno *m* hymn; ~ *nacional* national anthem

hincapié *m*: *hacer* ~ put special emphasis (*en* on)

hincar <1g> **1** *v/t* thrust, stick (*en* into); ~ *el diente* F sink one's teeth (*en* into) **2** *v/r* ~*se*: *~se de rodillas* kneel down

hincha *m* F fan, supporter; **hinchado** *adj* swollen; **hinchar** <1a> **1** *v/t* inflate, blow up; *Rpl* P annoy **2** *v/r* ~*se* MED swell; *fig* stuff o.s (*de* with); (*mostrarse orgulloso*) swell with pride; **hinchazón** *f* swelling

hiperactivo *adj* hyperactive

hipermercado *m* hypermarket

hipertensión *f* MED high blood pressure, hypertension

hipertexto *m* hypertext

hípico *adj* equestrian; *concurso* ~ show-jumping event; *carrera -a* horse race

hipnosis *f* hypnosis; **hipnotizar** <1f> *v/t* hypnotize

hipo *m* hiccups *pl*, hiccoughs *pl*; *quitar el* ~ F take one's breath away

hipocondríaco 1 *adj* hypochondriac **2** *m*, *-a* *f* hypochondriac

hipocresía *f* hypocrisy; **hipócrita 1** *adj* hypocritical **2** *m/f* hypocrite

H

hipódromo *m* racetrack

hipopótamo *m* ZO hippopotamus

hipoteca *f* COM mortgage; **hipotecar** <1g> *v/t* COM mortgage; *fig* compromise

hipótesis *f* hypothesis; **hipotético** *adj* hypothetical

hispánico *adj* Hispanic; **hispano 1** *adj* (*español*) Spanish; (*hispanohablante*) Spanish-speaking; *en EE.UU.* Hispanic **2** *m*, **-a** *f* (*español*) Spaniard; (*hispanohablante*) Spanish speaker; *en EE.UU.* Hispanic; **hispanohablante** *adj* Spanish-speaking

histeria *f* hysteria; **histérico** *adj* hysterical

historia *f* history; (*cuento*) story; *una ~ de drogas* F some drugs business; *déjate de ~s* F stop making excuses; **historiador** *m*, **-a** *f* historian; **historial** *m* record; **histórico** *adj* historical; (*importante*) historic; **historieta** *f* anecdote; (*viñetas*) comic strip

hito *m tb fig* milestone

hizo *vb* → **hacer**

Hnos. *abr* (= **Hermanos**) Bros (= Brothers)

hobby *m* hobby

hocico *m* snout; *de perro* muzzle

hockey *m* field hockey, *Br* hockey; *~ sobre hielo* hockey, *Br* ice hockey

hogar *m fig* home; **hogareño** *adj* home-loving

hoguera *f* bonfire

hoja *f* BOT leaf; *de papel* sheet; *de libro* page; *de cuchillo* blade; *~ de afeitar* razor blade; *~ de cálculo* INFOR spreadsheet

hojalata *f* tin

hojaldre *m* GASTR puff pastry

hojear <1a> *v/t* leaf through, flip through

hola *int* hello, hi F

Holanda Holland

holandés 1 *adj* Dutch **2** *m* Dutchman; **holandesa** *f* Dutchwoman

holding *m* holding company

holgado *adj* loose, comfortable; *estar ~ de tiempo* have time to spare

holgazán *m* idler; **holgazanear** <1a> *v/i* laze around

holgura *f* ease; *de ropa* looseness; TÉC play; *vivir con ~* live comfortably

hollín *m* soot

holocausto *m* holocaust

hombre *m* man; *el ~* (*la humanidad*) man, mankind; *~ lobo* werewolf; *~ de negocios* businessman; *~ rana* frogman; *¡claro, ~!* you bet!, sure thing!; *¡~, qué alegría!* that's great!

hombro *m* shoulder; *~ con ~* shoulder to shoulder; *encogerse de ~s* shrug (one's shoulders)

homenaje *m* homage; *rendir ~ a alguien* pay tribute to s.o.

homeopatía *f* hom(o)eopathy

homicidio *m* homicide

homogéneo *adj* homogenous

homologación *f* approval; *de título, diploma* official recognition

homólogo *m*, **-a** *f* counterpart, opposite number

homosexual *m/f & adj* homosexual

hondo *adj* deep

Honduras Honduras; **hondureño 1** *adj* Honduran **2** *m*, **-a** *f* Honduran

honesto *adj* hono(u)rable, decent

hongo *m* fungus

honor *m* hono(u)r; *en ~ a* in hono(u)r of; *hacer ~ a* live up to; *palabra de ~* word of hono(u)r

honorarios *mpl* fees

honra *f* hono(u)r; *¡a mucha ~!* I'm hono(u)red; **honradez** *f* honesty; **honrado** *adj* honest

hora *f* hour; *~s pl extraordinarias* overtime *sg*; *~ local* local time; *~ punta* rush hour; *a la ~ de ...* fig when it comes to ...; *a última ~* at the last minute; *¡ya era ~!* about time too!; *tengo ~ con el dentista* I have an appointment with the dentist; *¿qué ~ es?* what time is it?; **horario** *m* schedule, *Br* timetable; *~ comercial* business hours *pl*; *~ flexible* flextime, *Br* flexitime; *~ de trabajo* (working) hours *pl*

horca *f* gallows *pl*; **horcajadas** *fpl: a*

~ astride

horchata f drink made from tiger-nuts

horda f horde

horizontal adj horizontal; **horizonte** m horizon

hormiga f ant

hormigón m concrete; ~ **armado** reinforced concrete

hormigueo m pins and needles pl; **hormiguero** m ant hill; **la sala era un ~ de gente** the hall was swarming with people

hormona f hormone

hornilla f ring; **horno** m oven; de cerámica kiln; **alto ~** blast furnace

horóscopo m horoscope

horqueta f L.Am. de camino fork

horquilla f para pelo hairpin

horrendo adj horrendous

horrible adj horrible, dreadful; **horripilante** adj horrible; **horror** m horror (**a** of); **tener ~ a** be terrified of; **me gusta ~es** F I like it a lot; **¡qué ~!** how awful!; **horrorizar** <1f> v/t horrify; **horroroso** adj terrible; de mala calidad) dreadful; (feo) hideous

hortaliza f vegetable

hortensia f BOT hydrangea

hortera 1 F adj tacky **2** m/f F tacky person F; **horterada** f F tacky thing F; **es una ~** it's tacky F

horticultor m, **-a** f horticulturist; **horticultura** f horticulture

hosco adj sullen

hospedaje m accommodations pl, Br accommodation; **dar ~ a alguien** put s.o. up; **hospedarse** <1a> v/r stay (**en** at); **hospital** m hospital; **hospitalario** adj hospitable; MED hospital atr; **hospitalidad** f hospitality; **hospitalizar** <1f> v/t hospitalize

hostal m hostel

hostelera f landlady; **hostelería** f hotel industry; **hostelero 1** adj hotel atr **2** m landlord

hostia f REL host; P (golpe) sock F, wallop F; **¡~s!** P Christ! P

hostigar <1h> v/t pester; MIL harass; caballo whip

hostil adj hostile; **hostilidad** f hostility

hotel m hotel; **hotelero** m, **-a** f hotelier

hoy adv today; **de ~** of today; **los padres de ~** today's parents, parents today; **de ~ en adelante** from now on; **por ~** for today; **~ por ~** at the present time; **~ en día** nowadays

hoya f hole; de tumba grave; GEOG plain; S.Am. river basin; **hoyo** m hole; (depresión) hollow; **hoyuelo** m dimple

hoz f sickle

huachafo adj Pe (cursi) affected, pretentious

huarache m Méx rough sandal

huayno m Pe, Bol Andean dance rhythm

hubo vb → **haber**

hucha f money box

hueco 1 adj hollow; (vacío) empty; fig: persona shallow **2** m gap; (agujero) hole; de ascensor shaft

huele vb → **oler**

huelga f strike; **~ de celo** work-to-rule; **~ general** general strike; **~ de hambre** hunger strike; **declararse en ~, ir a la ~** go on strike; **huelguista** m/f striker

huella f mark; de animal track; **~s dactilares** finger prints

huelo vb → **oler**

huérfano 1 adj orphan atr **2** m, **-a** f orphan

huero adj fig empty; L.Am. blond

huerta f truck farm, Br market garden; **huerto** m kitchen garden; **llevar a alguien al ~** F put one over on s.o. F

huesear <1a> v/t C.Am. beg

huesillo m S.Am. sun-dried peach

hueso m bone; de fruta pit, stone; persona tough nut; Méx F cushy number F; Méx F (influencia) influence, pull F; **~ duro de roer** fig F hard nut to crack F; **estar en los ~s** be all skin and bone

huésped m/f guest

huesudo *adj* bony

huevas *fpl* roe *sg*; **huevear** <1a> *v/i Chi* P mess around F; **huevo** *m* egg; P (*testículo*) ball V; **~ duro** hard-boiled egg; **~ escalfado** poached egg; **~ frito** fried egg; **~ pasado por agua** soft-boiled egg; **~s revueltos** scrambled eggs; **un ~ de** P a load of F; **huevón** *m*, **-ona** *f Chi* P idiot; *L.Am.* F (*flojo*) idler F

huida *f* flight, escape; **huir** <3g> *v/i* flee, escape (**de** from); **~ de algo** avoid sth

hulado *m C.Am.*, *Méx* rubberized cloth; **hule** *m* oilcloth; *L.Am.* (*caucho*) rubber

humanidad *f* humanity; **~es** humanities; **humanismo** *m* humanism; **humanitario** *adj* humanitarian; **humanizar** <1f> *v/t* humanize; **humano** *adj* human

humareda *f* cloud of smoke; **humear** <1a> *v/i con humo* smoke; *con vapor* steam

humedad *f* humidity; *de una casa* damp(ness); **humedecer** <2d> *v/t* dampen; **húmedo** *adj* humid; *toalla* damp

humildad *f* humility; **humilde** *adj* humble; (*sin orgullo*) modest; *clase social* lowly; **humillación** *f* humiliation; **humillante** *adj* humiliating;

humillar <1a> *v/t* humiliate

humita *f S.Am.* meat and corn paste wrapped in leaves

humo *m* smoke; (*vapor*) steam; **tener muchos ~s** F be a real big-head F

humor *m* humo(u)r; **estar de buen / mal ~** be in a good / bad mood; **sentido del ~** sense of humo(u)r; **humorista** *m/f* humo(u)rist; (*cómico*) comedian

humus *m* GASTR hummus

hundido *adj* fig: *persona* depressed; **hundir** <3a> **1** *v/t* sink; *fig: empresa* ruin, bring down; *persona* devastate **2** *v/r* **~se** sink; *fig: de empresa* collapse; *de persona* go to pieces

húngaro 1 *adj* Hungarian **2** *m*, **-a** *f* Hungarian

Hungría Hungary

huracán *m* hurricane

huraño *adj* unsociable

hurgar <1h> **1** *v/i* rummage (**en** in) **2** *v/r* **~se**: **~se la nariz** pick one's nose

hurón *m* ZO ferret

hurtadillas *fpl*: **a ~** furtively

hurtar <1a> *v/t* steal; **hurto** *m* theft

husmear <1a> *v/i* F nose around F (**en** in)

huy *int sorpresa* wow!; *dolor* ouch!

huyo *vb* → **huir**

I

I+D *abr* (= **investigación y desarrollo**) R&D (= research and development)

iba *vb* → **ir**

ibérico *adj* Iberian; **iberoamericano** *adj* Latin American

iceberg *m* iceberg

icono *m tb* INFOR icon

ida *f* outward journey; (**billete de**) **~ y vuelta** round trip (ticket), *Br* re-

turn (ticket)

idea *f* idea; **hacerse a la ~ de que ...** get used to the idea that ...; **no tener ni ~** not have a clue; **ideal** *m/adj* ideal; **idealista 1** *adj* idealistic **2** *m/f* idealist; **idear** *v/t* <1a> think up, come up with

idéntico *adj* identical

identidad *f* identity; **identificación** *f* identification; **identificar** <1g>

1 *v/t* identify **2** *v/r* ~**se** identify o.s.
ideología *f* ideology
idílico *adj* idyllic; **idilio** *m* idyll; (*relación amorosa*) romance
idioma *m* language
idiota 1 *adj* idiotic **2** *m/f* idiot; **idiotez** *f* stupid thing to say / do
ido 1 *part* → **ir 2** *adj* (*chiflado*) nuts F; **estar** ~ be miles away F
idolatrar <1a> *v/t tb fig* worship; **ídolo** *m tb fig* idol
idóneo *adj* suitable
iglesia *f* church
ignominioso *adj* ignominious
ignorancia *f* ignorance; **ignorante** *adj* ignorant, **ignorar** <1a> *v/t* not know, not be aware of; **ignoro cómo sucedió** I don't know how it happened
igual 1 *adj* (*idéntico*) same (**a, que** as); (*proporcionado*) equal (**a** to); (*constante*) constant; **al** ~ **que** like, the same as; **me da** ~ I don't mind **2** *m/f* equal; **no tener** ~ have no equal; **igualado** *adj* even; **igualar** <1a> **1** *v/t precio, marca* equal, match; (*nivelar*) level off; ~ **algo** MAT make sth equal (**con, a** to) **2** *v/i* DEP tie the game, *Br* equalize; **igualdad** *f* equality; ~ **de oportunidades** equal opportunities; **igualitario** *adj* egalitarian; **igualmente** *adv* equally
iguana *f* ZO iguana
ilegal *adj* illegal
ilegible *adj* illegible
ilegítimo *adj* unlawful; **hijo** illegitimate
ileso *adj* unhurt
ilícito *adj* illicit
ilimitado *adj* unlimited
Ilmo. *abr* (= **ilustrísimo**) His / Your Excellency
ilógico *adj* illogical
iluminación *f* illumination; **iluminar** <1a> *v/t edificio, calle etc* light, illuminate; *monumento* light up, illuminate; *fig* light up
ilusión *f* illusion; (*deseo, esperanza*) hope; **ilusionarse** <1a> *v/r* get one's hopes up; (*entusiasmarse*) get

excited (**con** about)
ilustración *f* illustration; **ilustrar** <1a> *v/t* illustrate; (*aclarar*) explain; **ilustre** *adj* illustrious
imagen *f tb fig* image; **ser la viva** ~ **de** be the spitting image of; **imaginable** *adj* imaginable; **imaginación** *f* imagination; **imaginar** <1a> **1** *v/t* imagine **2** *v/r* ~**se** imagine; **¡ya me lo imagino!** I can just imagine it!; **imaginativo** *adj* imaginative
imán *m* magnet
imbatible *adj* unbeatable
imbécil 1 *adj* stupid **2** *m/f* idiot, imbecile; **imbecilidad** *f* stupidity; **¡qué** ~ **decir eso!** what a stupid thing to say!
imitación *f* imitation; **imitar** <1a> *v/t* imitate
impaciencia *f* impatience; **impacientar** <1a> *v/t* make impatient **2** *v/r* ~**se** lose (one's) patience; **impaciente** *adj* impatient
impactar <1a> *v/t* hit; (*impresionar*) have an impact on; **impacto** *m tb fig* impact; ~ **de bala** bullet wound; ~ **ecológico** ecological
impar *adj número* odd
imparcial *adj* impartial; **imparcialidad** *f* impartiality
impasible *adj* impassive
impávido *adj* fearless, undaunted
impecable *adj* impeccable
impedimento *m* impediment; **impedir** <3l> *v/t* prevent; (*estorbar*) impede
imperante *adj* ruling; *fig* prevailing; **imperar** <1a> *v/i* rule; *fig* prevail; **imperativo 1** *adj* GRAM imperative; *obligación* pressing **2** *m* GRAM imperative
imperdible *m* safety pin
imperdonable *adj* unpardonable, unforgivable
imperfecto *m/adj* imperfect
imperial *adj* imperial; **imperio** *m* empire; **imperioso** *adj necesidad* pressing; *persona* imperious
impermeable 1 *adj* waterproof **2** *m* raincoat
impersonal *adj* impersonal

impertérrito *adj* unperturbed, unmoved

impertinente 1 *adj* impertinent **2** *m/f*: **¡eres un ~!** you've got nerve! F, *Br* you've got a cheek! F

ímpetu *m* impetus; **impetuoso** *adj* impetuous

implacable *adj* implacable

implemento *m* implement

implicar <1g> *v/t* mean, imply; *(involucrar)* involve; *en un delito* implicate (*en* in)

implícito *adj* implicit

implorar <1a> *v/t* beg for

imponente *adj* impressive, imposing; F terrific; **imponer** <2r> **1** *v/t* impose; *miedo, respeto* inspire; *impuesto* impose, levy **2** *v/i* be imposing *o* impressive **3** *v/r* **~se** *(hacerse respetar)* assert o.s.; DEP win; *(prevalecer)* prevail; *(ser necesario)* be imperative; **~se una tarea** set o.s. a task

importación *f* import, importation; *artículo* import

importancia *f* importance; **dar ~ a** attach importance to; **darse ~** give o.s. airs; **tener ~** be important; **importante** *adj* important; **importar** <1a> *v/i* matter; **no importa** it doesn't matter; **eso a ti no te importa** that's none of your business; **¿qué importa?** what does it matter?; **¿le importa ...?** do you mind ...?; **importe** *m* amount; *(coste)* cost

importuno *adj* inopportune

imposibilitar <1a> *v/t*: **~ algo** make sth impossible, prevent sth; **imposible** *adj* impossible

impostor *m*, **~a** *f* impostor

impotencia *f* impotence, helplessness; MED impotence; **impotente** *adj* helpless, powerless, impotent; MED impotent

impreciso *adj* imprecise

impredecible *adj* unpredictable

impregnar <1a> *v/t* saturate (*de* with); TÉC impregnate (*de* with)

imprenta *f taller* printer's; *arte, técnica* printing; *máquina* printing press

imprescindible *adj* essential; *persona* indispensable

impresión *f* impression; *acto* printing; *(tirada)* print run; **la sangre le da ~** he can't stand the sight of blood; **impresionante** *adj* impressive; **impresionar** <1a> *v/t*: **~le a alguien** impress s.o.; *(conmover)* move s.o.; *(alterar)* shock s.o.; **impresionismo** *m* impressionism; **impreso** *m* form; **~s** *pl* printed matter *sg*; **impresora** *f* INFOR printer; **~ de chorro de tinta** inkjet (printer); **~ de inyección de tinta** inkjet (printer); **~ láser** laser (printer)

imprevisible *adj* unpredictable; **imprevisto 1** *adj* unforeseen, unexpected **2** *m* unexpected event

imprimir <3a> *v/t tb* INFOR print; *fig* transmit

improbable *adj* unlikely, improbable

improcedente *adj* improper

improductivo *adj* unproductive

impropio *adj* inappropriate

improvisar <1a> *v/t* improvise; **improviso** *adj*: **de ~** unexpectedly

imprudencia *f* recklessness, rashness; **imprudente** *adj* reckless, rash

impuesto *m* tax; **~ sobre el valor añadido** sales tax, *Br* value-added tax; **~ sobre la renta** income tax

impugnar <1a> *v/t* challenge

impulsar <1a> *v/t* TÉC propel; COM boost

impulsivo *adj* impulsive; **impulso** *m* impulse; *(empuje)* impetus; COM boost; *fig* urge, impulse; **tomar ~** take a run up

impunidad *f* impunity

impureza *f* impurity

imputar <1a> *v/t* attribute

inacabable *adj* endless, never-ending

inaccesible *adj* inaccessible

inaceptable *adj* unacceptable

inactivo *adj* inactive

inadaptado *adj* maladjusted

inadecuado *adj* inadequate

inadmisible *adj* inadmissible
inadvertido *adj*: **pasar ~** go unnoticed
inagotable *adj* inexhaustible
inaguantable *adj* unbearable
inalámbrico 1 *adj* TELEC cordless **2** *m* TELEC cordless telephone
inamovible *adj* immovable
inanición *f* starvation
inapreciable *adj* (*valioso*) priceless; (*insignificante*) negligible
inasequible *adj objetivo* unattainable; *precio* prohibitive
inaudito *adj* unprecedented
inauguración *f* official opening, inauguration; **inaugurar** <1a> *v/t* (*officially*) open, inaugurate
inca *m/f & adj* HIST Inca
incalculable *adj* incalculable
incalificable *adj* indescribable
incandescente *adj* incandescent
incansable *adj* tireless
incapacidad *f* disability; (*falta de capacidad*) inability; (*ineptitud*) incompetence; **incapacitar** <1a> *v/t* JUR disqualify; **incapaz** *adj* incapable (**de** of)
incautarse <1a> *v/r*: **~ de** seize
incauto *adj* unwary
incendiar <1b> **1** *v/t* set fire to **2** *v/r* **~se** burn; **incendio** *m* fire; **~ forestal** forest fire
incentivo *m* incentive
incertidumbre *f* uncertainty
incesante *adj* incessant
incesto *m* incest
incidencia *f* (*efecto*) effect; (*frecuencia*) incidence; (*incidente*) incident; **incidente** *m* incident; **incidir** <3a> *v/i*: **~ en** (*afectar*) have an effect on, affect; (*recalcar*) stress; **~ en un error** make a mistake
incienso *m* incense
incierto *m* uncertain
incineración *f de cadáver* cremation; **incinerador** *adj* incinerator; **incinerar** <1a> *v/t* incinerate; *cadáver* cremate
incipiente *adj* incipient
incitante *adj* provocative; **incitar** <1a> *v/t* incite

inclemencia *f del tiempo* inclemency
inclinación *f* inclination; *de un terreno* slope; *muestra de respeto* bow; *fig* tendency; **inclinar** <1a> **1** *v/t* tilt; **~ la cabeza** nod (one's head); **me inclina a creer que ...** it makes me think that ... **2** *v/r* **~se** bend (down); *de un terreno* slope; *desde la vertical* lean; *en señal de respeto* bow; **~se a** *fig* tend to be, to be inclined to
incluido *prp* inclusive; **incluir** <3g> *v/t* include; **inclusive** *adv* inclusive; **incluso** *adv*, *prp & conj* even
incógnita *f* unknown factor; MAT unknown (quantity); **incógnito** *adj*: **de ~** incognito
incoherente *adj* incoherent
incombustible *adj* fireproof
incomodidad *f* uncomfortableness; (*fastidio*) inconvenience; **incómodo** *adj* uncomfortable; (*fastidioso*) inconvenient
incomparable *adj* incomparable
incompatibilidad *f* incompatibility; **incompatible** *adj tb* INFOR incompatible
incompetencia *f* incompetence; **incompetente** *adj* incompetent
incompleto *adj* incomplete
incomprendido *adj* misunderstood; **incomprensible** *adj* incomprehensible
incomunicado *adj* isolated, cut off; JUR in solitary confinement
inconcebible *adj* inconceivable
incondicional *adj* unconditional; **inconexo** *adj* unconnected
inconfesable *adj* shameful
inconformista *m/f* nonconformist
inconfundible *adj* unmistakable
incongruente *adj* incongruous
inconsciencia *f* MED unconsciousness; (*desconocimiento*) lack of awareness, unawareness; (*irreflexión*) thoughtlessness; **inconsciente** *adj* MED unconscious; (*ignorante*) unaware; (*irreflexivo*) thoughtless
inconsecuente *adj* inconsistent
inconsistente *adj* flimsy, weak
inconsolable *adj* inconsolable

inconstante adj fickle

incontable adj uncountable

incontinencia f MED incontinence

incontrolable adj uncontrollable

inconveniente 1 adj (*inoportuno*) inconvenient; (*impropio*) inappropriate **2** m (*desventaja*) drawback, disadvantage; (*estorbo*) problem; **no tengo ~** I don't mind

incordiar <1b> v/t annoy; **incordio** m nuisance

incorporar <1a> **1** v/t incorporate **2** v/r **~se** sit up; **~se a** MIL join

incorrecto adj incorrect, wrong; *comportamiento* impolite; **incorregible** adj incorrigible

incorruptible adj incorruptible

incredulidad f disbelief, incredulity; **incrédulo** adj incredulous; **increíble** adj incredible

incrementar <1a> **1** v/t increase **2** v/r **~se** increase; **incremento** m growth

incriminar <1a> v/t incriminate

incruento adj bloodless

incrustar <1a> **1** v/t incrust (*de* with) **2** v/r **~se de la suciedad** become ingrained

incubación f incubation; **incubadora** f incubator; **incubar** <1a> v/t incubate

incuestionable adj unquestionable

inculcar <1g> v/t instil(l) (*en* in)

inculpar <1a> v/t JUR accuse

inculto adj ignorant, uneducated; **incultura** f ignorance, lack of education

incumbencia f responsibility, duty; **no es de mi ~** it's not my responsibility

incumplimiento m non-fulfillment (*de* of), non-compliance (*de* with); **incumplir** <3a> v/t break

incurable adj incurable

incurrir <3a> v/i: **~ en un error** make a mistake; **~ en gastos** incur costs; **incursión** f MIL raid; *fig* foray

indagar <1h> v/i investigate

indecente adj indecent; *película* obscene

indecisión f indecisiveness; **indeci-so** adj undecided; *por naturaleza* indecisive

indefenso adj defenseless, *Br* defenceless

indefinidamente adv indefinitely; **indefinido** adj (*impreciso*) vague; (*ilimitado*) indefinite

indemnización f compensation; **indemnizar** <1f> v/t compensate (*por* for)

independencia f independence; **independentismo** m POL pro-independence movement; **independiente** adj independent; **independizarse** <1f> v/r become independent

indescriptible adj indescribable

indeseable adj undesirable

indestructible adj indestructible

indeterminado adj indeterminate; (*indefinido*) indefinite

India: **la ~** India; **indiada** f L.Am. group of Indians

indicación f indication; (*señal*) sign; **indicaciones para llegar** directions; (*instrucciones*) instructions; **indicado** adj (*adecuado*) suitable; **lo más / menos ~** the best / worst thing; **hora -a** specified time; **indicador** m indicator; **indicar** <1g> v/t show, indicate; (*señalar*) point out; (*sugerir*) suggest; **índice** m index; **dedo ~** index finger; **~ de precios al consumo** consumer price index, *Br* retail price index; **indicio** m indication, sign; (*vestigio*) trace

indiferencia f indifference; **indiferente** adj indifferent; (*irrelevante*) immaterial

indígena 1 adj indigenous, native **2** m/f native

indigente adj destitute

indigestión f indigestion; **indigesto** adj indigestible

indignación f indignation; **indignado** adj indignant; **indignar** <1a> **1** v/t: **~ a alguien** make s.o. indignant **2** v/r **~se** become indignant

indigno adj unworthy (*de* of)

indio 1 adj Indian **2** m, **-a** f Indian; **hacer el ~** F clown around F, play the fool F

indirecta f insinuation; (*sugerencia*) hint

indirecto adj indirect

indiscreción f indiscretion, lack of discretion; (*declaración*) indiscreet remark; **indiscreto** adj indiscreet

indiscriminado adj indiscriminate

indiscutible adj indisputable

indispensable adj indispensable

indisponerse <2r> v/r become unwell; **~ con alguien** fall out with s.o.; **indisposición** f indisposition; **indispuesto** adj indisposed, unwell

indistinto adj forma indistinct, vague; noción vague

individual adj individual; cama, habitación single; **individualismo** m individualism; **individualista** m/f individualist; **individuo** m individual

indivisible adj indivisible

indocumentado adj: **un hombre ~** a man with no identity papers

índole f nature

indolente adj lazy

indoloro adj painless

indómito adj indomitable

Indonesia Indonesia

inducir <3o> v/t (persuadir) lead, induce (**a** to); EL induce

indudable adj undoubted; **indudablemente** adv undoubtedly

indulgente adj indulgent

indultar <1a> v/t pardon; **indulto** m pardon

indumentaria f clothing

industria f industry; (esfuerzo) industriousness, industry; **industrial** 1 adj industrial 2 m/f industrialist; **industrializar** <1f> 1 v/t industrialize 2 v/r **~se** industrialize

inédito adj unpublished; fig unprecedented

ineficacia f inefficiency; de un procedimiento ineffectiveness; **ineficaz** adj inefficient; procedimiento ineffective; **ineficiencia** f inefficiency; **ineficiente** adj inefficient

ineludible adj unavoidable

inepto 1 adj inept, incompetent **2** m, **-a** f incompetent fool

inequívoco adj unequivocal

inercia f inertia; **inerte** adj fig lifeless; FÍS inert

inesperado adj unexpected

inestabilidad f instability; **inestable** adj unstable; tiempo unsettled

inestimable adj invaluable

inevitable adj inevitable

inexacto adj inaccurate

inexcusable adj inexcusable

inexistente adj non-existent

inexperto adj inexperienced

inexplicable adj inexplicable

infalible adj infallible

infame adj vile, loathsome; (terrible) dreadful

infancia f infancy

infantería f MIL infantry

infantil adj children's atr; naturaleza childlike; desp infantile, childish

infarto m MED heart attack

infección f MED infection; **infeccioso** adj infectious; **infectar** <1a> **1** v/t infect **2** v/r **~se** become infected

infecundo adj infertile

infeliz 1 adj unhappy, miserable **2** m/f poor devil

inferior 1 adj inferior (**a** to); en el espacio lower (**a** than) **2** m/f inferior; **inferioridad** f inferiority

inferir <3i> v/t infer (**de** from); daño do, cause (**a** to)

infernal adj ruido infernal; (muy malo) diabolical

infertilidad f infertility

infestar <1a> v/t infest; (invadir) overrun

infidelidad f infidelity; **infiel 1** adj unfaithful **2** m/f unbeliever

infierno m hell

infiltrarse <1a> v/r: **~ en** infiltrate; de agua seep into

infinidad f: **~ de** countless; **infinitivo** m GRAM infinitive; **infinito 1** adj infinite **2** m infinity

inflación f COM inflation; **tasa de ~** inflation rate; **inflacionista** adj inflationary

I

inflamable *adj* flammable; **inflamación** *f* MED inflammation; **inflamar** <1a> **1** *v/t tb fig* inflame **2** *v/r* **~se** MED become inflamed

inflar <1a> **1** *v/t* inflate **2** *v/r* **~se** swell (up); *fig* F get conceited

infligir <3c> *v/t* inflict

inflexible *adj fig* inflexible

influencia *f* influence; **tener ~s** have contacts; **influenciar** <1b> *v/t* influence; **influir** <3g> *v/i*: **~ en alguien/algo** influence s.o./sth, have an influence on s.o./sth; **influjo** *m* influence; **influyente** *adj* influential

infografía *f* computer graphics *pl*

información *f* information; (*noticias*) news *sg*; **informal** *adj* informal; (*irresponsable*) unreliable; **informar** <1a> **1** *v/t* inform (*de, sobre* about) **2** *v/r* **~se** find out (*de, sobre* about); **informática** *f* information technology; **informático 1** *adj* computer *atr* **2** *m*, **-a** *f* IT specialist; **informativo 1** *adj* informative; *programa* news *atr* **2** *m* TV, RAD news *sg*; **informatizar** <1f> *v/t* computerize

informe 1 *adj* shapeless **2** *m* report; **~s** (*referencias*) references

infracción *f* offense, *Br* offence

infraestructura *f* infrastructure

in fraganti *adv* F in the act F

infrahumano *adj* subhuman

infrarrojo *adj* infra-red

infravalorar <1a> *v/t* undervalue

infrecuente *adj* infrequent

infringir <3c> *v/t* JUR infringe, violate

infructuoso *adj* fruitless

infundado *adj* unfounded, groundless

infundir <3a> *v/t* inspire; *terror* instil(l); *sospechas* arouse

infusión *f* infusion; *de tila, manzanilla* tea

ingeniarse <1b> *v/r*: **ingeniárselas para** manage to; **ingeniería** *f* engineering; **ingeniero** *m*, **-a** *f* engineer; **ingenio** *m* ingenuity; (*aparato*) device; **~ azucarero** *L.Am.* sugar refinery; **ingenioso** *adj* ingenious

ingenuidad *f* naivety; **ingenuo 1** *adj* naive **2** *m*, **-a** *f* naive person, sucker F

ingerir <3i> *v/t* swallow

Inglaterra England

ingle *f* groin

inglés 1 *adj* English **2** *m* Englishman; *idioma* English; **inglesa** *f* Englishwoman

ingrato *adj* ungrateful; *tarea* thankless

ingrediente *m* ingredient

ingresar <1a> **1** *v/i*: **~ en** *en universidad* go to; *en asociación, cuerpo* join; *en hospital* be admitted to **2** *v/t* *cheque* pay in, deposit; **ingreso** *m* entry; *en una asociación* joining; *en hospital* admission; COM deposit; **~s** *pl* income *sg*; **examen de ~** entrance exam

inhabitable *adj* uninhabitable

inhalar <1a> *v/t* inhale

inherente *adj* inherent

inhibición *f* inhibition; JUR disqualification; **inhibir** <3a> *v/t* inhibit

inhóspito *adj* inhospitable

inhumano *adj* inhuman

iniciación *f* initiation; **inicial** *f/adj* initial; **iniciar** <1b> *v/t* initiate; *curso* start, begin; **iniciativa** *f* initiative; **tomar la ~** take the initiative; **inicio** *m* start, beginning

inigualable *adj* incomparable; *precio* unbeatable

inimaginable *adj* unimaginable

inimitable *adj* inimitable

ininteligible *adj* unintelligible

ininterrumpido *adj* uninterrupted

injerencia *f* interference

injertar <1a> *v/t* graft; **injerto** *m* graft

injuriar <1b> *v/t* insult

injusticia *f* injustice; **injustificado** *adj* unjustified; **injusto** *adj* unjust

inmaculado *adj* immaculate

inmaduro *adj* immature

inmediaciones *fpl* immediate area *sg* (**de** of), vicinity *sg* (**de** of); **inmediatamente** *adv* immediately; **inmediato** *adj* immediate; **de ~**

immediately
inmejorable *adj* unbeatable
inmenso *adj* immense
inmersión *f* immersion; *de submarino* dive; **inmerso** *adj fig* immersed (**en** in)
inmigración *f* immigration; **inmigrante** *m/f* immigrant; **inmigrar** <1a> *v/i* immigrate
inminente *adj* imminent
inmiscuirse <3g> *v/r* meddle
inmobiliaria *f* realtor's office, *Br* estate agency
inmoderado *adj* excessive, immoderate
inmoral *adj* immoral; **inmoralidad** *f* immorality
inmortal *adj* immortal
inmóvil *adj persona* motionless; *vehículo* stationary; **inmovilizar** <1f> *v/t* immobilize
inmueble *m* building
inmundo *adj* filthy
inmune *adj* immune; **inmunidad** *f* MED, POL immunity; **inmunizar** <1f> *v/t* immunize
inmutarse <1a> *v/r*: **no ~** not bat an eyelid; **sin ~** without batting an eyelid
innato *adj* innate, inborn
innecesario *adj* unnecessary
innegable *adj* undeniable
innovación *f* innovation
innumerable *adj* innumerable, countless
inocencia *f* innocence; **inocente** *adj* innocent
inocuo *adj* harmless, innocuous; *película* bland
inodoro *m* toilet
inofensivo *adj* inoffensive, harmless
inoficioso *adj L.Am.* (*inútil*) useless
inolvidable *adj* unforgettable
inopia *f*: **estar en la ~** F (*distraído*) be miles away F; (*alejado de la realidad*) be on another planet F
inoportuno *adj* inopportune; (*molesto*) inconvenient
inorgánico *adj* inorganic
inoxidable *adj*: **acero ~** stainless

steel
inquietar <1a> **1** *v/t* worry **2** *v/r* **~se** worry, get worried *o* anxious; **inquietud** *f* worry, anxiety; *intelectual* interest
inquilino *m* tenant
inquisitivo *adj* inquisitive
insaciable *adj* insatiable
insatisfacción *f* dissatisfaction; **insatisfactorio** *adj* unsatisfactory; **insatisfecho** *adj* dissatisfied
inscribir <3a> **1** *v/t* (*grabar*) inscribe; *en lista, registro* register, enter; *en curso, concurso* enrol(l); **2** *v/r* **~se** *en un curso* enrol(l), register; *en un concurso* enter; **inscripción** *f* inscription; *en lista, registro* registration, entry; *en curso, concurso* enrol(l)ment, registration;
insecticida *m* insecticide; **insecto** *m* insect
inseguro *adj* insecure; *estructura* unsteady; (*peligroso*) dangerous, unsafe
inseminación *f* insemination; **~ artificial** artificial insemination
insensato *adj* foolish
insensible *adj* insensitive (**a** to)
inseparable *adj* inseparable
insertar <1a> *v/t* insert
inservible *adj* useless
insidia *f* treachery; **actuar con ~** act treacherously
insignia *f* insignia
insignificante *adj* insignificant
insinuante *adj* suggestive
insinuar <1e> **1** *v/t* insinuate **2** *v/r* **~se**: **~se a alguien** make advances to s.o.
insípido *adj* insipid
insistencia *f* insistence; **insistir** <3a> *v/i* insist; **~ en hacer algo** insist on doing sth; **~ en algo** stress sth
insociable *adj* unsociable
insolación *f* MED sunstroke
insolente *adj* insolent
insólito *adj* unusual
insolvente *adj* insolvent
insomnio *m* insomnia
insondable *adj* unfathomable

insonorizar <1f> v/t soundproof

insoportable adj unbearable, intolerable

insospechado adj unexpected

inspección f inspection; **inspeccionar** <1a> v/t inspect; **inspector** m, **~a** f inspector

inspiración f inspiration; MED inhalation; **inspirar** <1a> v/t inspire; MED inhale

instalación f acto installation; **instalaciones deportivas** sports facilities; **instalar** <1a> **1** v/t instal(l); (colocar) put; un negocio set up **2** v/r **~se en un sitio** instal(l) o.s.

instancia f JUR petition; (petición por escrito) application; **a ~s de** at the request of

instantáneo adj immediate, instantaneous; **instante** m moment, instant; **al ~** right away, immediately; **instar** <1a> v/t urge, press

instaurar <1a> v/t establish

instigar <1h> v/t incite (**a** to)

instinto m instinct

institución f institution; **instituto** m institute; Esp high school, Br secondary school; **~ de belleza** beauty salon; **~ de educación secundaria** high school, Br secondary school

instrucción f education; (formación) training; MIL drill; INFOR instruction, statement; JUR hearing; **instrucciones de uso** instructions, directions (for use); **instructor** m, **~a** f instructor; **instruido** adj educated; **instruir** <3g> v/t educate; (formar) train; JUR pleito hear

instrumental 1 adj instrumental **2** m MED instruments pl; **instrumento** m instrument; (herramienta) tool, instrument; fig tool; **~ musical** musical instrument

insubordinación f insubordination; **insubordinarse** <1a> v/r con un superior be insubordinate; (rebelarse) rebel

insuficiente 1 adj insufficient, inadequate **2** m EDU nota fail

insufrible adj insufferable

insulina f insulin

insulso adj bland, insipid

insultada f L.Am. (insultos) string of insults; **insultar** <1a> v/t insult; **insulto** m insult

insumiso m person who refuses to do military service

insuperable adj insurmountable

insurrección f insurrection

insustancial adj conferencia lightweight; estructura flimsy

intachable adj faultless

intacto adj intact; (sin tocar) untouched

integración f integration; **integral** adj complete; alimento whole; **integrar** <1a> v/t integrate; equipo make up; **íntegro** adj whole, entire; **un hombre ~** fig a man of integrity

intelectual m/f & adj intellectual

inteligencia f intelligence; **inteligente** adj intelligent; **inteligible** adj intelligible

intemperie f: **a la ~** in the open air

intempestivo adj untimely

intención f intention; **doble** or **segunda ~** ulterior motive; **intencionado** adj deliberate

intendente m Rpl military governor; (alcalde) mayor

intensidad f intensity; (fuerza) strength; **intensificar** <1g> **1** v/t intensify **2** v/r **~se** intensify; **intensivo** adj intensive; **intenso** adj intense; (fuerte) strong

intentar <1a> v/t try, attempt; **intento** m attempt, try; Méx (intención) aim

interacción f interaction; **interactivo** adj interactive

intercalar <1a> v/t insert

intercambiar <1a> v/t exchange, swap; **intercambio** m exchange, swap

interceder <2a> v/i intercede (**por** for)

interceptar <1a> v/t tb DEP intercept

intercesión f intercession

interés m tb COM interest; desp self-interest; **sin ~** interest free; **intereses** (bienes) interests; **interesante** adj interesting; **interesar** <1a> **1** v/t interest **2** v/r **~se: ~se por** take an interest in

interface m, **interfaz** f INFOR interface

interferencia f interference; **interferir** <3i> **1** v/t interfere with **2** v/i interfere (**en** in)

interino adj substitute atr, replacement atr; (provisional) provisional, acting atr

interior 1 adj interior; bolsillo inside atr; COM, POL domestic **2** m interior; DEP inside-forward; **en su ~** fig inwardly; **interiorista** m/f interior designer

interjección f GRAM interjection

interlocutor m, **~a** f speaker; **mi ~** the person I was talking to

intermediario m COM intermediary, middle-man; **intermedio 1** adj nivel intermediate; tamaño medium; calidad average, medium **2** m intermission

interminable adj interminable, endless

intermitente 1 adj intermittent **2** m AUTO turn signal, Br indicator

internacional adj international

internado m boarding school; **internarse** <1a> v/r: **~ en** go into

internauta m/f INFOR Internet user, Net surfer

Internet f INFOR Internet

interno 1 adj internal; POL domestic, internal **2** m, **-a** f EDU boarder; (preso) inmate; MED intern, Br houseman

interpelar <1a> v/t question

interplanetario adj interplanetary

interpolar <1a> v/t insert, interpolate fml

interponerse <2r> v/r intervene

interpretación f interpretation; TEA performance (**de** as); **interpretar** <1a> v/t interpret; TEA play; **intérprete** m/f interpreter

interrogación f interrogation; **signo de ~** question mark; **interrogante 1** adj questioning **2** m (also f) question; fig question mark, doubt; **interrogar** <1h> v/t question; de po-

licía interrogate, question; **interrogatorio** m questioning, interrogation

interrumpir <3a> **1** v/t interrupt; servicio suspend; reunión, vacaciones cut short, curtail **2** v/i interrupt; **interrupción** f interruption; de servicio suspension; de reunión, vacaciones curtailment; **sin ~** non-stop; **interruptor** m EL switch

intersección f intersection

intervalo m tb MÚS interval; (espacio) gap

intervención f intervention; en debate, congreso participation; en película, espectáculo appearance; MED operation; **intervenir** <3s> **1** v/i intervene; en debate, congreso take part, participate; en película, espectáculo appear **2** v/t TELEC tap; contrabando seize; MED operate on

intestino m intestine

intimar <1a> v/i (hacerse amigos) become friendly (**con** with); (tratar) mix (**con** with); **intimidad** f intimacy; (lo privado) privacy; **en la ~** in private

intimidar <1a> v/t intimidate

íntimo adj intimate; (privado) private; **somos ~s amigos** we're close friends

intolerable adj intolerable, unbearable; **intolerante** adj intolerant

intoxicación f poisoning

intranquilidad f unease; (nerviosismo) restlessness; **intranquilo** adj uneasy; (nervioso) restless

intransferible adj non-transferable

intransigente adj intransigent

intransitable adj impassable

intransitivo adj GRAM intransitive

intrascendente adj unimportant

intravenoso adj MED intravenous

intrépido adj intrepid

intriga f intrigue; de novela plot; **intrigante 1** adj scheming; (curioso) intriguing **2** m/f schemer; **intrigar** <1h> **1** v/t (interesar) intrigue **2** v/i plot, scheme

intrincado adj intricate

intrínseco adj intrinsic

introducción *f* introduction; *acción de meter* insertion; INFOR input; **introducir** <3o> **1** *v/t* introduce; *(meter)* INFOR input **2** *v/r*: **~se**: **~se en** get into; **~se en un mercado** gain access to *o* break into a market

intromisión *f* interference

introvertido *adj* introverted

intruso *m* intruder

intuición *f* intuition; **intuir** <3g> *v/t* sense; **intuitivo** *adj* intuitive

inundación *f* flood; **inundadizo** *adj* L.Am. prone to flooding; **inundar** <1a> *v/t* flood

inusitado *adj* unusual, uncommon; **inusual** *adj* unusual

inútil 1 *adj* useless; MIL unfit **2** *m/f*: **es un ~** he's useless; **inutilidad** *f* uselessness; **inutilizar** <1f> *v/t*: **~ algo** render sth useless; **inútilmente** *adv* uselessly

invadir <3a> *v/t* invade; *de un sentimiento* overcome

invalidar <1a> *v/t* invalidate; **invalidez** *f* disability; **inválido 1** *adj persona* disabled; *documento, billete* invalid **2** *m*, **-a** *f* disabled person

invasión *f* MIL invasion; **invasor** *m*, **~a** *f* invader

invencible *adj* invincible; *miedo* insurmountable

invención *f* invention; **inventar** <1a> *v/t* invent; **inventario** *m* inventory; **invento** *m* invention; **inventor** *m* inventor

invernada *f* Rpl winter pasture; **invernadero** *m* greenhouse; **invernal** *adj* winter *atr*

inverosímil *adj* unlikely

inversión *f* reversal; COM investment; **inverso** *adj* opposite; *orden* reverse; **a la -a** the other way round; **inversor** *m*, **~a** *f* investor; **invertir** <3i> *v/t* reverse; COM invest (**en** in)

invertebrado *m* invertebrate

investigación *f* investigation; EDU, TÉC research; **~ y desarrollo** research and development; **investigador** *m*, **~a** *f* researcher; **investigar** <1h> *v/t* investigate; EDU, TÉC research

inviable *adj* nonviable

invidente *m/f* blind person

invierno *m* winter

inviolable *adj* inviolable

invisible *adj* invisible

invitación *f* invitation; **invitado** *m*, **-a** *f* guest; **invitar** <1a> *v/t* invite (**a** to); *(convidar)* treat (**a** to)

invocar <1g> *v/t* invoke

involucrar <1a> *v/t* involve (**en** in)

involuntario *adj* involuntary

invulnerable *adj* invulnerable

inyección *f* MED, AUTO injection; **inyectar** <1a> *v/t tb* TÉC inject

IPC *abr* (= **índice de precios al consumo**) CPI (= consumer price index), *Br* RPI (= retail price index)

ir <3t> **1** *v/i* go (**a** to); **~ a pie** walk, go on foot; **~ en avión** fly; **¡ya voy!** I'm coming!; **~ a por algo** go and fetch sth; **~ bien/mal** go well/badly; **iba de amarillo/de uniforme** she was wearing yellow/uniform; **van dos a dos** DEP the score is two all; **¿de qué va la película?** what's the movie about?; **¡qué va!** you must be joking! F; **¡vamos!** come on!; **¡vaya!** well! **2** *v/aux*: **va a llover** it's going to rain; **ya voy comprendiendo** I'm beginning to understand; **~ para viejo** be getting old **3** *v/r* **~se** go (away), leave; **¡vete!** go away!; **¡vámonos!** let's go

ira *f* anger

Irak Iraq, Irak

Irán Iran; **iraní** *m/f & adj* Iranian

iraquí *m/f & adj* Iraqi, Iraki

iris *m inv* ANAT iris; **arco ~** rainbow

Irlanda Ireland; **irlandés 1** *adj* Irish **2** *m* Irishman; **irlandesa** *f* Irishwoman

ironía *f* irony; **irónico** *adj* ironic

irracional *adj tb* MAT irrational

irradiar <1b> *v/t* radiate; MED irradiate

irreal *adj* unreal; **irrealizable** *adj* unattainable; *proyecto* unfeasible

irreconciliable *adj* irreconcilable
irrecuperable *adj* irretrievable
irrefutable *adj* irrefutable
irregular *adj* irregular; *superficie uneven*; **irregularidad** *f* irregularity;
de superficie unevenness
irrelevante *adj* irrelevant
irremediable *adj fig* irremediable
irreparable *adj* irreparable
irreprochable *adj* irreproachable
irresistible *adj* irresistible
irrespetuoso *adj* disrespectful
irresponsable *adj* irresponsible
irreverente *adj* irreverent
irreversible *adj* irreversible
irrevocable *adj* irrevocable
irrigar <1h> *v/t* MED, AGR irrigate
irrisorio *adj* laughable, derisory
irritación *f tb* MED irritation; **irritante** *adj tb* MED irritating; **irritar** <1a>
1 *v/t tb* MED irritate **2** *v/r* ~**se** get
irritated
irrompible *adj* unbreakable

irrumpir <3a> *v/i* burst in; **irrupción**
f: *hacer ~ en* burst into
isla *f* island
islám *m* Islam; **islámico** *adj* Islamic;
islamismo *m* Islam
isleño 1 *adj* island *atr* **2** *m*, **-a** *f* is-
lander
Israel Israel; **israelí** *m/f & adj* Israeli
Italia Italy; **italiano 1** *adj* Italian **2** *m*,
-a *f* Italian
itinerario *m* itinerary
ITV *abr Esp* (= *inspección técnica
de vehículos*) *compulsory annual
test of motor vehicles of a certain age,
Br* MOT
IVA *abr* (= *impuesto sobre el valor
añadido*) *sales tax, Br* VAT (= value-
added tax)
izar <1f> *v/t* hoist
izdo., izda. *abr* (= *izquierdo, izquierda*) l (= left)
izquierda *f tb* POL left; *por la ~* on the
left; **izquierdo** *adj* left

J

J

jabalí *m* ZO wild boar
jabalina *f* javelin
jabón *m* soap; *~ de afeitar* shaving
soap; **jabonera** *f* soap dish; **jabonoso** *adj* soapy
jacinto *m* hyacinth
jactancia *f* boasting; **jactancioso**
adj boastful; **jactarse** <1a> *v/r* boast
(*de* about), brag (*de* about)
jacuzzi *m* jacuzzi®
jade *m* MIN jade
jadear <1a> *v/i* pant; **jadeo** *m* pant-
ing
jaguar *m* ZO jaguar
jalar <1a> **1** *v/t L.Am.* pull; *con esfuer-
za* haul; (*atraer*) attract; *Méx* F (*dar
aventón*) give a ride *o Br* a lift to; *¿te
jala el arte?* *Méx* do you feel drawn
to art? **2** *v/i L.Am.* pull; (*trabajar*

mucho) work hard; *Méx* F (*tener influencia*) have pull F; *~ hacia* F head
toward; *~ para la casa* F clear off
home F **3** *v/r* ~**se** *Méx* (*irse*) go,
leave; F (*emborracharse*) get plastered F
jalea *f* jelly; *~ real* royal jelly
jaleo *m* (*ruido*) racket, uproar; (*lío*)
mess, muddle; *armar ~* F kick up a
fuss F
jalón *m* pull; *dar un ~ a algo* pull sth;
de un ~ *Méx fig* in one go
jalonar *v/t fig* mark out
Jamaica Jamaica
jamás *adv* never; *~ te olvidaré* I'll
never forget you; *¿viste ~ algo así?*
did you ever see anything like it?;
nunca ~ never ever; *por siempre ~*
for ever and ever

jamón *m* ham; **~ de York** cooked ham; **~ serrano** cured ham; **¡y un ~!** F *(¡no!)* no way! F; *(¡bromeas!)* come off it! F

jangada *f S.Am.* F dirty trick

Japón Japan; **japonés 1** *adj* Japanese **2** *m*, **-esa** *f* Japanese

jaque *m* check; **~ mate** checkmate; **dar ~ a** checkmate

jaqueca *f* MED migraine

jarabe *m* syrup; *Méx* type of folk dance

jardín *m* garden; **~ botánico** botanic(al) gardens; **~ de infancia** kindergarten; **jardinería** *f* gardening; **jardinero** *m*, **-a** *f* gardener

jarra *f* pitcher, *Br* jug; **en ~s** with hands on hips; **jarro** *m* pitcher, *Br* jug; **un ~ de agua fría** *fig* a total shock, a bombshell; **jarrón** *m* vase

jauja *f*: **¡esto es ~!** this is the life!

jaula *f* cage

jauría *f* pack

jazmín *m* BOT jasmine

J.C. *abr* (= **Jesucristo**) J.C. (= Jesus Christ)

jefatura *f* headquarters; *(dirección)* leadership; **~ de policía** police headquarters; **jefe** *m*, **-a** *f* de *departamento, organización* head; *(superior)* boss; POL leader; *de tribu* chief; **~ de cocina** (head) chef; **~ de estado** head of state

jengibre *m* BOT ginger

jeque *m* sheik

jerarquía *f* hierarchy

jerez *m* sherry

jerga *f* jargon; *(argot)* slang

jeringa *f* MED syringe; **jeringuilla** *f* MED syringe; **~ desechable** or **de un solo uso** disposable syringe

jeroglífico *m* hieroglyphic; *rompecabezas* puzzle

jersey *m* sweater

Jesucristo *m* Jesus Christ; **Jesús** *m* Jesus; **¡~!** good grief!; *por estornudo* bless you!

jet 1 *m* AVIA jet **2** *f*: **~ (set)** jet set

jeta *f* F face, mug F; **¡qué ~ tiene!** F he's got nerve! F, *Br* what a cheek! F

jibia *f* ZO cuttlefish

jícara *f Méx* drinking bowl; **jícaro** *m L.Am.* BOT calabash

jilguero *m* ZO goldfinch

jilote *m C.Am.*, *Méx* young corn

jineta *f* ZO civet

jinete *m* rider; *en carrera* jockey

jirafa *f* ZO giraffe

jitomate *m Méx* tomato

JJ.OO. *abr* (= **Juegos Olímpicos**) Olympic Games

jocoso *adj* humorous, joking

joder <2a> **1** *v/i* V screw V, fuck V **2** *v/t* V *(follar)* screw V, fuck V; *(estropear)* screw up V, fuck up V; *L.Am.* *(fastidiar)* annoy, irritate; **¡~!** V fuck! V; **me jode un montón** V it really pisses me off P

jolgorio *m* F partying F

jolín *int* wow! F, jeez! F

jornada *f* (working) day; *distancia* day's journey; **media ~** half-day; **~ laboral** work day; **~ partida** split shift; **jornal** *m* day's wage; **jornalero** *m*, **-a** *f* day labo(u)rer

joroba *f* hump; *fig* pain F, drag F; **jorobado** *adj* hump-backed; *fig* F in a bad way F; **jorobar** <1a> *v/t* F *(molestar)* bug F; *planes* ruin

jorongo *m Méx* poncho

jota *f letter 'j'*; **no saber ni ~** F not have a clue F

joven 1 *adj* young **2** *m/f* young man; *mujer* young woman; **los jóvenes** young people

jovial *adj* cheerful

joya *f* jewel; *persona* gem; **~s** *pl* jewelry *sg*, *Br* jewellery *sg*; **joyería** *f* jewelry store, *Br* jeweller's; **joyero 1** *m*, **-a** *f* jewel(l)er **2** *m* jewelry (*Br* jewellery) box

juanete *m* MED bunion

jubilación *f* retirement; **~ anticipada** early retirement; **jubilado 1** *adj* retired **2** *m*, **-a** *f* retiree, *Br* pensioner; **jubilar** <1a> **1** *v/t* retire; *(desechar)* get rid of **2** *v/r* **~se** retire; *C.Am.* play hooky F, play truant; **júbilo** *m* jubilation; **jubiloso** *adj* jubilant

judaísmo *m* Judaism

judía f BOT bean; **~ verde** green bean, runner bean

judicial adj judicial

judío 1 adj Jewish **2** m, **-a** f Jew

judo m DEP judo

juego m game; acción play; por dinero gambling; (conjunto de objetos) set; **~ de azar** game of chance; **~ de café** coffee set; **~ de manos** conjuring trick; **~ de mesa** board game; **~ de rol** role-playing game; **~ de sociedad** game; **Juegos Olímpicos** Olympic Games; **estar en ~** fig be at stake; **fuera de ~** DEP offside; **hacer ~ con** go with, match

juerga f F partying F; **irse de ~** F go out on the town F, go out partying F

juergista m/f F party animal F

jueves m inv Thursday

juez m/f judge; **~ de línea** en fútbol assistant referee; en fútbol americano line judge; **jueza** f → **juez**

jugada f play, Br move; en ajedrez move; **hacerle una mala ~ a alguien** play a dirty trick on s.o.; **jugador** m, **-a** f player; **jugar** <1o> **1** v/t play **2** v/i play; con dinero gamble; **~ al baloncesto** play basketball **3** v/r **~se** risk; **~se la vida** risk one's life; **jugársela a alguien** F do the dirty on s.o. F; **jugarreta** f F dirty trick F

jugo m juice; **sacar ~ a algo** get the most out of sth; **jugoso** adj tb fig juicy

juguete m toy; **juguetear** <1a> v/i play; **juguetería** f toy store, Br toy shop

juicio m judg(e)ment; JUR trial; (sensatez) sense; (cordura) sanity; **a mi ~** in my opinion; **estar en su ~** be in one's right mind; **perder el ~** lose one's mind

julio m July

junco m BOT reed

jungla f jungle

junio m June

júnior adj tb DEP junior

junta f POL (regional) government; militar junta; COM board; (sesión) meeting; TÉC joint; **~ directiva** board of directors; **~ general anual** annual general meeting; **juntar** <1a> **1** v/t put together; gente gather together; bienes collect, accumulate **2** v/r **~se** (reunirse) meet, assemble; de pareja: empezar a salir start going out; empezar a vivir juntos move in together; de caminos, ríos meet, join; **~se con alguien** socialmente mix with s.o.; **junto 1** adj together **2** prp: **~ a** next to, near; **~ con** together with

juntura f TÉC joint

jupa f C.Am., Méx fig F head, nut F

jura f (promesa) oath; ceremonia swearing (on oath); **jurado** m JUR jury; **juramento** m oath; **bajo ~** under oath; **jurar** <1a> v/t & v/i swear; **jurídico** adj legal; **jurisdicción** f jurisdiction; **jurisprudencia** f jurisprudence

justamente adv fairly; (precisamente) precisely

justicia f justice; **la ~** (la ley) the law; **hacer ~ a** do justice to; **justificable** adj justifiable; **justificación** f tb TIP justification; **justificante** m de pago receipt; de ausencia, propiedad certificate; **justificar** <1g> v/t & tb TIP justify; mala conducta justify, excuse; **justo** adj just, fair; (exacto) right, exact; **lo ~** just enough; **¡~!** right!, exactly!

juvenil adj youthful; **juventud** f youth

juzgado 1 part → **juzgar 2** m court; **juzgar** <1h> v/t JUR try; (valorar) judge; considerar consider, judge; **a ~ por** to judge by, judging by

J

K

kárate *m* DEP karate
kayak *m* DEP kayak
ketchup *m* ketchup
kg. *abr* (= **kilogramo**) kg (= kilogram)
kilo *m* kilo; *fig* F million
kilogramo *m* kilogram, *Br* kilogramme
kilómetro *m* kilometer, *Br* kilometre

kiosco *m* kiosk
kiwi *m* BOT kiwi (fruit)
kleenex® *m* kleenex, tissue
km. *abr* (= **kilómetro**) km (= kilometer)
km./h. *abr* (= **kilómetros por hora**) kph (= kilometers per hour)
kv. *abr* (= **kilovatio**) kw (= kilowatt)

L

la 1 *art* the **2** *pron complemento directo sg* her; *a usted* you; *algo* it; **~ que está embarazada** the one who is pregnant; **~ más grande** the biggest (one); **dame ~ roja** give me the red one
laberinto *m* labyrinth, maze
labia *f*: **tener mucha ~** have the gift of the gab; **labio** *m* lip
labor *f* work; *(tarea)* task, job; **hacer ~es** do needlework; **no estar por la ~** F not be enthusiastic about the idea; **laborable** *adj*: **día ~** workday; **laboral** *adj* labo(u)r *atr*; **laboratorio** *m* laboratory, lab F; **laborioso** *adj* laborious; *persona* hardworking; **labrador** *m* farm labo(u)rer, farm worker; **labranza** *f de la tierra* cultivation; **labrar** <1a> *v/t tierra* work; *piedra* carve; **labriego** *m* farm labo(u)rer, farm worker
laca *f* lacquer; *para el cabello* hairspray; **~ de uñas** nail varnish *o*

polish
lacear <1a> *v/t Rpl* lasso
lacio *adj* limp; *pelo* lank
lacónico *adj* laconic
lacra *f* scar; *L.Am. (llaga)* sore; **la corrupción es una ~ social** corruption is a blot on society
lacre *m* sealing wax
lacrimógeno *adj fig* tear-jerking
lactancia *f* lactation; **lácteo** *adj*: **Vía Láctea** Milky Way; **productos ~s** dairy products
ladear <1a> *v/t* tilt; **ladera** *f* slope
ladino 1 *adj* cunning, sly **2** *m C.Am. Indian who has become absorbed into white culture*
lado *m* side; *(lugar)* place; **al ~** nearby; **al ~ de** beside, next to; **de ~** sideways; **ir por otro ~** go another way; **por un ~ ... por otro ~** on the one hand ... on the other hand; **hacerse a un ~** *tb fig* stand aside
ladrar <1a> *v/i* bark

ladrillo *m* brick
ladrón *m* thief
lagartija *f* ZO small lizard; **lagarto** *m* ZO lizard
lago *m* lake
lágrima *f* tear
laguna *f* lagoon; *fig* gap
laico *adj* lay
lamentable *adj* deplorable; **lamentablemente** *adv* regretfully; **lamentar** <1a> **1** *v/t* regret, be sorry about; *muerte* mourn **2** *v/r* ~se complain (*de* about); **lamento** *m* whimper; *por dolor* groan
lamer <2a> *v/t* lick
lámina *f* sheet
lámpara *f* lamp; ~ **halógena** halogen lamp; ~ **de pie** floor lamp, *Br* standard lamp; **lamparón** *m* F grease mark
lana *f* wool; *Méx* P dough F; *pura ~ virgen* pure new wool
lancha *f* launch; ~ **fueraborda** outboard
langosta *f* ZO *insecto* locust; *crustáceo* spiny lobster; **langostino** *m* ZO king prawn
languidecer <2d> *v/i* languish; **lánguido** *adj* languid
lanza *f* lance; **lanzadera** *f* shuttle; ~ **espacial** space shuttle; **lanzado 1** *adj fig* go-ahead; *es muy ~ con las chicas* he's not shy with girls **2** *part* → **lanzar**; **lanzamiento** *m* MIL, COM launch; ~ **de disco/martillo** discus/hammer (throw); ~ **de peso** shot put; **lanzar** <1f> **1** *v/t* throw; *cohete, producto* launch; *bomba* drop **2** *v/r* ~se throw o.s. (*en* into); (*precipitarse*) pounce (*sobre* on); ~se **a hacer algo** rush into doing sth
lapa *f* ZO limpet
lapicera *f Rpl, Chi* (ballpoint) pen; ~ **fuente** *L.Am.* fountain pen; **lapicero** *m* automatic pencil, *Br* propelling pencil
lápida *f* memorial stone; **lapidario** *adj* memorable
lápiz *m* pencil; ~ **de ojos** eyeliner; ~ **labial** *or* **de labios** lipstick; ~ **óptico**

light pen
lapso *m de tiempo* space, period; **lapsus** *m inv* slip; *tener un ~* have a momentary lapse
larga *f*: *poner la(s) ~(s)* put the headlights on full beam; *dar ~s a alguien* F put s.o. off; **largar** <1h> **1** *v/t* drive away **2** *v/r* ~se F clear off *o* out F; **largo 1** *adj* long; *persona* tall; *a la ~a* in the long run; *a lo ~ del día* throughout the day; *a lo ~ de la calle* along the street; *¡~!* ⊦ scram! F; *esto va para ~* this will take some time; *pasar de ~* go (straight) past **2** *m* length; **largometraje** *m* feature film; **larguero** *m* DEP crossbar
laringe *f* larynx; **laringitis** *f* MED laryngitis
larva *f* ZO larva
las 1 *art fpl* the **2** *pron complemento directo pl* them; *a ustedes* you; *llévate* <1a> *que quieras* take whichever ones you want; ~ **de ...** those of ...; ~ **de Juan** Juan's; ~ **que llevan falda** the ones *o* those that are wearing dresses
lasaña *f* GASTR lasagne
lascivo *adj* lewd
láser *m* laser; *rayo* ~ laser beam
lástima *f* pity, shame; *me da ~ no usarlo* it's a shame *o* pity not to use it; *¡qué ~!* what a pity *o* shame!; **lastimar** <1a> **1** *v/t* (*herir*) hurt **2** *v/r* ~se hurt o.s.; **lastimoso** *adj* pitiful; (*deplorable*) shameful
lastre *m* ballast; *fig* burden
lata *f* can, *Br* tb tin; *fig* F drag F, pain F; *dar la ~* F be a drag F *o* a pain F
latente *adj* latent
lateral 1 *adj* side *atr*; *cuestiones ~es* side issues **2** *m* DEP: ~ **derecho/izquierdo** right/left back
latería *f L.Am.* tin works; **latero**, **-a** *f L.Am.* tinsmith
latido *m* beat
latifundio *m* large estate
latigazo *m* lash; (*chasquido*) crack; **látigo** *m* whip
latín *m* Latin; **latino** *adj* Latin; **Latinoamérica** Latin America;

latinoamericano 1 *adj* Latin American **2** *m*, **-a** *f* Latin American

latir <3a> *v/i* beat

latitud *f* GEOG latitude

latón *m* brass

laucha *f S.Am.* mouse

laurel *m* BOT laurel; **dormirse en los ~es** *fig* rest on one's laurels

lava *f* lava

lavable *adj* washable; **lavabo** *m* washbowl; **lavada** *f L.Am.* wash; **lavado** *m* washing; **~ de cerebro** *fig* brainwashing; **lavadora** *f* washing machine; **lavamanos** *m inv L.Am.* → *lavabo*

lavanda *f* BOT lavender

lavandería *f* laundry

lavaplatos *m inv* dishwasher; *L.Am.* sink

lavar <1a> **1** *v/t* wash; **~ los platos** wash the dishes; **~ la ropa** do the laundry, *Br tb* do the washing; **~ en seco** dry-clean **2** *v/i* (*lavar los platos*) do the dishes; *de detergente* clean **3** *v/r* **~se** wash up, *Br* have a wash; **~se los dientes** brush one's teeth; **~se las manos** wash one's hands; **yo me lavo las manos** *fig* I wash my hands of it

lavarropas *m inv L.Am.* washing machine

lavavajillas *m inv líquido* dishwashing liquid, *Br* washing-up liquid; *electrodoméstico* dishwasher

laxante *m/adj* MED laxative; **laxo** *adj* relaxed; (*poco estricto*) lax

lazada *f* bow

lazarillo *m* guide; **perro ~** seeing eye dog, *Br* guide dog

lazo *m* knot; *de adorno* bow; *para atrapar animales* lasso

le *pron sg complemento indirecto* (to) him; (*a ella*) (to) her; (*a usted*) (to) you; (*a algo*) (to) it; *complemento directo* him; (*a usted*) you

leal *adj* loyal; **lealtad** *f* loyalty

lección *f* lesson; **esto te servirá de ~** that will teach him a lesson

lechar <1a> *v/t L.Am.* (*ordeñar*) milk; **leche** *f* milk; **~ condensada**

condensed milk; **~ entera** whole milk; **~ en polvo** powdered milk; **estar de mala ~** P be in a foul mood; **tener mala ~** P be out to make trouble; **lechería** *f* dairy; **lechero 1** *adj* dairy *atr* **2** *m* milkman

lecho *m tb de río* bed

lechón *m* suckling pig

lechuga *f* lettuce; **ser más fresco que una ~** F have a lot of nerve

lechuza *f* ZO barn-owl; *Cuba, Méx* P hooker F

lectivo *adj*: **día ~** school day; **lector** *m*, **-a** *f* reader; **lectura** *f* reading

leer <2e> *v/t* read

legado *m* legacy; *persona* legate

legal *adj* legal; *fig* F *persona* great F, terrific F; **legalidad** *f* legality; **legalizar** <1f> *v/t* legalize

legaña *f*: **tener ~s en los ojos** have sleep in one's eyes

legar <1h> *v/t* leave

legendario *adj* legendary

legible *adj* legible

legión *f* legion

legislación *f* legislation; **legislar** <1a> *v/i* legislate; **legislativo** *adj* legislative; **legislatura** *f cuerpo* legislature; *periodo* term of office

legitimar <1a> *v/t* justify; *documento* authenticate; **legítimo** *adj* legitimate; (*verdadero*) authentic

lego *adj* lay *atr*; *fig* ignorant

legua *f*: **se ve a la ~** *fig* F you can see it a mile off F; *hecho* it's blindingly obvious F

legumbre *f* BOT pulse

leída *f L.Am.* reading

lejanía *f* distance; **en la ~** in the distance; **lejano** *adj* distant

lejía *f* bleach

lejos 1 *adv* far, far away; **Navidad queda ~** Christmas is a long way off; **a lo ~** in the distance; **ir demasiado ~** *fig* go too far, overstep the mark; **llegar ~** *fig* go far **2** *prp*: **~ de** far from

lele *adj C.Am.* stupid

lema *m* slogan

lencería *f* lingerie

lengua f tongue; **~ materna** mother tongue; **con la ~ fuera** fig with one's tongue hanging out; **irse de la ~** let the cat out of the bag; **sacar la ~ a alguien** stick one's tongue out at s.o.; **lo tengo en la punta de la ~** it's on the tip of my tongue

lenguado m ZO sole

lenguaje m language; **~ de programación** INFOR programming language; **lenguaraz** adj foul-mouthed; **lengüeta 1** f de zapato tongue **2** adj: **ser ~** S.Am. F be a gossip

lenitivo m balm

lente f lens; **~s de contacto** contact lenses, contacts; **lentes** mpl L.Am. glasses

lenteja f BOT lentil

lentejuela f sequin

lentillas fpl contact lenses

lentitud f slowness; **lento** adj slow; **a fuego ~** on a low heat

leña f (fire)wood; **echar ~ al fuego** fig add fuel to the fire; **leñador** m woodcutter; **leño** m log

Leo m/f inv ASTR Leo

león m ZO lion; L.Am. puma; **~ marino** sealion; **leona** f lioness; **leonera** f lion's den; jaula lion's cage; Rpl, Chi fig F habitación desordenada etc pigsty F; L.Am. F para prisioneros bullpen F, Br communal cell for holding prisoners temporarily

leopardo m ZO leopard

leotardo m de gimnasta leotard; **~s** tights, Br heavy tights

lépero adj C.Am., Méx coarse

lerdo adj (torpe) slow(-witted)

les pron pl complemento indirecto (to) them; (a ustedes) (to) you; complemento directo them; (a ustedes) you

lesbiana f lesbian

lesión f injury; **lesionado** adj injured; **lesionar** <1a> v/t injure

letal adj lethal

letanía f litany

letárgico adj lethargic

letra f letter; de canción lyrics pl; **~ de cambio** COM bill of exchange; **~ de**

imprenta block capital; **~ mayúscula** capital letter; **al pie de la ~** word for word

letrero m sign

letrina f latrine

leucemia f MED leuk(a)emia

levadura f yeast

levantamiento m raising; (rebelión) rising; de embargo lifting; **levantar** <1a> **1** v/t raise; bulto lift (up); del suelo pick up; edificio, estatua put up, erect; embargo lift; **~ sospechas** arouse suspicion; **¡levanta los ánimos!** cheer up!; **~ la voz** raise one's voice **2** v/r **~se** get up; (ponerse de pie) stand up; de un edificio, una montaña rise; en rebelión rise up

levante m east

levar <1a> v/t: **~ anclas** weigh anchor

leve adj slight; sonrisa faint; **levedad** f lightness

levitar <1a> v/i levitate

léxico m lexicon

ley f law; **con todas las de la ~** fairly and squarely

leyenda f legend

leyendo vb → **leer**

leyó vb → **leer**

liana f BOT liana, creeper

liar <1c> **1** v/t tie (up); en papel wrap (up); cigarillo roll; persona confuse **2** v/r **~se** de una persona get confused; **~se a hacer algo** get tied up doing sth; **~se con alguien** F get involved with s.o.

Líbano Lebanon

libélula f ZO dragonfly

liberación f release; de un país liberation; **liberal** adj liberal; **liberalización** f liberalization; **liberalizar** <1f> v/t liberalize; **liberar** <1a> **1** v/t (set) free, release; país liberate; energía release **2** v/r **~se de algo** free o.s. of sth; **libertad** f freedom, liberty; **~ bajo fianza** JUR bail; **~ condicional** JUR probation; **dejar a alguien en ~** release s.o., let s.o. go

libertinaje m licentiousness

Libia Libya

líbido f libido
libio(-a) m/f & adj Libyan
libra f pound; **~ esterlina** pound (sterling)
Libra m/f inv ASTR Libra
librar <1a> **1** v/t free (**de** from); cheque draw; batalla fight **2** v/i: **libro los lunes** I have Mondays off **3** v/r **~se**: **~se de algo** get out of sth; **de buena nos hemos librado** F that was lucky
libre adj free; tiempo spare, free; **eres ~ de** you're free to; **librecambio** m free trade
librera f bookseller; **librería** f book store; **librero** m bookseller; L.Am. mueble bookcase; **libreta** f notebook; **~ de ahorros** bankbook, passbook; **libro** m book; **~ de bolsillo** paperback (book); **~ de cocina** cookbook, cookery book; **~ de familia** booklet recording family births, marriages and deaths; **~ de reclamaciones** complaints book
licencia f permit, license, Br licence; (permiso) permission; MIL leave; **~ (de manejar or conducir)** L.Am. driver's license, Br driving licence; **tomarse demasiadas ~s** take liberties; **licenciado** m, **-a** f graduate; **licenciar** <1b> **1** v/t MIL discharge **2** v/r **~se** graduate; MIL be discharged; **licenciatura** f EDU degree
liceo m L.Am. high school, Br secondary school
licitación f L.Am. bidding; **licitador** m, **~a** f L.Am. bidder; **licitar** <1a> v/t L.Am. en subasta bid for
lícito adj legal; (razonable) fair, reasonable
licor m liquor, Br spirits pl
licuado m Méx fruit milkshake; **licuadora** f blender; **licuar** <1d> v/t blend, liquidize
líder **1** m/f leader **2** adj leading; **liderar** <1a> v/t lead; **liderazgo** m leadership
lidia f bullfighting; **lidiar** <1b> **1** v/i fig do battle, struggle **2** v/t toro fight
liebre f ZO hare

lienzo m canvas
liga f POL, DEP league; de medias garter; **ligamento** m ANAT ligament; **ligar** <1h> **1** v/t bind; (atar) tie **2** v/i: **~ con** F pick up F
ligereza f lightness; (rapidez) speed; de movimiento agility; de carácter shallowness, superficiality; **ligero** **1** adj (de poco peso) light; (rápido) rapid, quick; movimiento agile, nimble; (leve) slight; **~ de ropa** scantily clad; **a la -a** (sin pensar) lightly, casually; **tomar algo a la -a** not take sth seriously **2** adv quickly
ligón m F: **es un ~** he's a real Don Juan F
ligue m F: **estar de ~** be on the pick-up F, Br be on the pull F
liguero m garter belt, Br suspender belt
lija f: **papel de ~** sandpaper; **lijar** <1a> v/t sand
lila f BOT lilac
lima f file; BOT lime; **~ de uñas** nail file; **limar** <1a> v/t file; fig polish
limitado **1** adj limited **2** part → **limitar**; **limitar** <1a> **1** v/t limit **2** v/i: **~ con** border on **3** v/r **~se** limit o restrict o.s. (**a** to); **límite** **1** m limit; (línea de separación) boundary; **~ de velocidad** speed limit **2** adj: **situación ~** life-threatening situation; **limítrofe** adj neighbo(u)ring
limón m lemon; **limonada** f lemonade
limosna f: **una ~, por favor** can you spare some change?
limpiabotas m/f inv bootblack
limpiacristales m inv window cleaner
limpiada f L.Am. clean
limpiamanos m inv L.Am. hand towel
limpiaparabrisas m inv AUTO windshield wiper, Br windscreen wiper
limpiar <1b> v/t clean; con un trapo wipe; fig clean up; **~ a alguien** F clean s.o. out F; **limpieza** f estado cleanliness; acto cleaning; **~ general**

spring cleaning; **~ en seco** dry-cleaning; **hacer la ~** do the cleaning; **limpio** *adj* clean; *(ordenado)* neat, tidy; *político* honest; **gana $5.000 ~s al mes** he takes home $5,000 a month; **quedarse ~** *S.Am.* F be broke F; **sacar algo en ~** *fig* make sense of sth

limusina *f* limousine

linaje *m* lineage

lince *m* ZO lynx; **ojos** *or* **vista de ~** *fig* eyes like a hawk

linchar <1a> *v/t* lynch

lindar <1a> *v/i*: **~ con algo** adjoin sth; *fig* border on sth

lindo *adj* lovely; **de lo ~** a lot, a great deal

línea *f* line; **~ aérea** airline; **mantener la ~** watch one's figure; **de primera** *fig* first-rate; **tecnología de primera ~** state-of-the art technology; **entre ~s** *fig* between the lines; **lineal** *adj* linear

linfático *adj* lymphatic

lingote *m* ingot; **~ de oro** gold bar

lingüista *m/f* linguist; **lingüística** *f* linguistics; **lingüístico** *adj* linguistic

linier *m* DEP assistant referee, linesman

lino *m* linen; BOT flax

linterna *f* flashlight, *Br* torch

lío *m* bundle; F *(desorden)* mess; F *(jaleo)* fuss; **~ amoroso** F affair; **estar hecho un ~** be all confused; **hacerse un ~** get into a muddle; **meterse en ~s** get into trouble

liposucción *f* MED liposuction

lipotimia *f* MED blackout

liquen *m* BOT lichen

liquidación *f* COM **de cuenta, deuda** settlement; *de negocio* liquidation; **~ total** clearance sale; **liquidar** <1a> *v/t* **cuenta, deuda** settle; COM **negocio** wind up, liquidate; *existencias* sell off; F *(matar)* liquidate F, bump off F; **liquidez** *f* COM liquidity; **líquido 1** *adj* liquid; COM net **2** *m* liquid

lira *f* lira

lírico *adj* lyrical

lirio *m* BOT lily

lirón *m* ZO dormouse; **dormir como un ~** *fig* F sleep like a log

lisiado 1 *adj* crippled **2** *m* cripple

liso *adj* smooth; *terreno* flat; *pelo* straight; *(sin adornos)* plain; **-a y llanamente** plainly and simply

lisonja *f* flattery

lista *f* list; **~ de boda** wedding list; **~ de espera** waiting list; **pasar ~** take the roll call, *Br* call the register; **listado** *m* INFOR printout; **listín** *m*: **~ (telefónico)** phone book

listo *adj (inteligente)* clever; *(preparado)* ready; **pasarse de ~** F try to be too smart F

listón *m* **de madera** strip; DEP bar; **poner el ~ muy alto** *fig* set very high standards

lisura *f* Rpl, Pe curse, swearword

litera *f* bunk; *de tren* couchette

literal *adj* literal; **literario** *adj* literary; **literatura** *f* literature

litigante *m/f & adj* JUR litigant; **litigar** <1h> *v/i* JUR go to litigation; **litigio** *m* lawsuit

litografía *f* lithography

litoral 1 *adj* coastal **2** *m* coast

litro *m* liter, *Br* litre

liturgia *f* REL liturgy

liviano *adj* light; *(de poca importancia)* trivial

lívido *adj* pale

llaga *f* ulcer; **poner** *or* **meter el dedo en la ~** *fig* put one's finger on it

llama *f* flame; ZO llama

llamada *f* call; *en una puerta* knock; *en timbre* ring; **~ a cobro revertido** collect call; **~ de auxilio** distress call; **llamado** *m* L.Am. call; **llamador** *m* (door) knocker; **llamamiento** *m* call; **hacer un ~ a algo** call for sth; **llamar** <1a> **1** *v/t* call; TELEC call, *Br tb* ring **2** *v/i* TELEC call, *Br tb* ring; **~ a la puerta** knock at the door; *con timbre* ring the bell; **el fútbol no me llama nada** football doesn't appeal to me in the slightest **3** *v/r* **~se** be called; **¿cómo te llamas?** what's your name?

llamarada *f* flare-up

L

llamativo *adj* eyecatching; *color* loud

llamón *adj Méx* moaning

llano 1 *adj terreno* level; *trato* natural; *persona* unassuming **2** *m* flat ground

llanta *f* wheel rim; *C.Am., Méx (neumático)* tire, *Br* tyre

llanto *m* sobbing

llanura *f* plain

llave *f* key; *para tuerca* wrench, *Br tb* spanner; **~ de contacto** AUTO ignition key; **~ inglesa** TÉC monkey wrench; **~ de paso** stop cock; **~ en mano** available for immediate occupancy; **bajo ~** under lock and key; **cerrar con ~** lock; **llavero** *m* key ring

llegada *f* arrival; **llegar** <1h> **1** *v/i* arrive; *(alcanzar)* reach; **la comida no llegó para todos** there wasn't enough food for everyone; **me llega hasta las rodillas** it comes down to my knees; **el agua me llegaba a la cintura** the water came up to my waist; **~ a saber** find out; **~ a ser** get to be; **~ a viejo** live to a ripe old age **2** *v/r* **~se**: **llégate al vecino** F run over to the neighbo(u)r's

llenar <1a> **1** *v/t* fill; *impreso* fill out *o* in **2** *v/i* be filling **3** *v/r* **~se** fill up; **me he llenado** I have had enough (to eat); **lleno** *adj* full *(de* of); *pared* covered *(de* with); **de ~** fully

llevadero *adj* bearable

llevar <1a> **1** *v/t* take; *ropa, gafas* wear; *ritmo* keep up; **~ a alguien en coche** drive s.o., take s.o. in the car; **~ dinero encima** carry money; **~ las de perder** be likely to lose; **me lleva dos años** he's two years older than me; **llevo ocho días aquí** I've been here a week; **llevo una hora esperando** I've been waiting for an hour **2** *v/i* lead (**a** to) **3** *v/r* **~se** take; *susto, sorpresa* get; **~se bien/mal** get on well/badly; **se lleva el color rojo** red is fashionable

llorar <1a> *v/i* cry, weep; **lloriquear** <1a> *v/i* snivel, whine; **lloro** *m*

weeping, crying; **llorón 1** *adj*: **ser ~** be a crybaby F **2** *m* F crybaby F

llovedera *f L.Am.*, **llovedero** *m L.Am.* rainy season

llover <2h> *v/i* rain; **llueve** it is raining

llovizna *f* drizzle; **lloviznar** <1a> *v/i* drizzle

llueve *vb* → **llover**

lluvia *f* rain; *Rpl (ducha)* shower; **~ ácida** acid rain; **lluvioso** *adj* rainy

lo 1 *art sg* the; **~ bueno** the good thing; **no sabes ~ difícil que es** you don't know how difficult it is **2** *pron sg*: *a él* him; *a usted* you; *algo* it; **~ sé** I know **3** *pron rel sg*: **~ que** what; **~ cual** which

loable *adj* praiseworthy, laudable

lobo *m* wolf; **~ marino** seal; **~ de mar** *fig* sea dog

lóbrego *adj* gloomy

lóbulo *m* lobe; **~ de la oreja** earlobe

loca *f* madwoman

locador *m S.Am.* landlord

local 1 *adj* local **2** *m* premises *pl*; **~ comercial** commercial premises *pl*; **localidad** *f* town; TEA seat; **localización** *f* location; **localizar** <1f> *v/t* locate; *incendio* contain, bring under control

loción *f* lotion

loco 1 *adj* mad, crazy; **a lo ~** F *(sin pensar)* hastily; **es para volverse ~** it's enough to drive you mad *o* crazy **2** *m* madman

locomoción *f* locomotion; **medio de ~** means of transport; **locomotora** *f* locomotive

locro *m S.Am.* stew of meat, corn and potatoes

locuaz *adj* talkative, loquacious *fml*; **locución** *f* phrase

locura *f* madness; **es una ~** it's madness

locutor *m*, **~a** *f* RAD, TV presenter; **locutorio** *m* TELEC phone booth

lodazal *m* quagmire; **lodo** *m* mud

lógica *f* logic; **lógico** *adj* logical; **logística** *f* logistics

logopeda *m/f* speech therapist

logotipo *m* logo

logrado *adj* excellent; **lograr** <1a> *v/t* achieve, *(obtener)* obtain; **~ hacer algo** manage to do sth; **~ que alguien haga algo** (manage to) get s.o. to do sth; **logrero** *m L.Am.* F profiteer; **logro** *m* achievement

loma *f L.Am.* small hill

lombriz *f*: **~ de tierra** earthworm

lomo *m* back; GASTR loin; **a ~s de burro** on a donkey

lona *f* canvas

loncha *f* slice

lonche *m L.Am.* afternoon snack; **lonchería** *f L.Am.* diner, luncheonette

londinense 1 *adj* London *atr* **2** *m/f* Londoner; **Londres** London

longaniza *f* type of dried sausage

longevidad *f* longevity; **longevo** *adj* long-lived

longitud *f* longitude; *(largo)* length; **longitudinal** *adj* longitudinal

lonja *f* **de pescado** fish market; *(loncha)* slice

loquera *f L.Am.* F shrink F; *enfermera* psychiatric nurse; **loquero** *m L.Am.* F *persona* shrink F; *enfermero* psychiatric nurse; *(manicomio)* mental hospital, funny farm F

loro *m* parrot; **estar al ~** F *(enterado)* be clued up F, be on the ball F

los *mpl* **1** *art* the **2** *pron complemento directo pl* them; *a ustedes* you; **llévate ~ que quieras** take whichever ones you want; **~ de ...** those of ...; **~ de Juan** Juan's; **~ que juegan** the ones *o* those that are playing

losa *f* flagstone

lote *m en reparto* share, part; *L.Am.* *(solar)* lot; **lotería** *f* lottery; **loto 1** *m* BOT lotus **2** *f* F lottery

loza *f* china

lozano *adj* healthy-looking

lubina *f* ZO sea bass

lubri(fi)cación *f* lubrication; **lubri(fi)cante 1** *adj* lubricating **2** *m* lubricant; **lubri(fi)car** <1g> *v/t* lubricate

lucero *m* bright star; *(Venus)* Venus

lucha *f* fight, struggle; DEP wrestling;

~ libre DEP all-in wrestling; **luchador 1** *adj* espíritu fighting **2** *m*, **-a** *f* fighter; **luchar** <1a> *v/i* fight *(por* for*)*

lúcido *adj* lucid, clear

luciérnaga *f* ZO glow-worm

lucimiento *m* *(brillo)* splendo(u)r; **le ofrece oportunidades de ~** it gives him a chance to shine

lucio *m* ZO pike

lucir <3f> **1** *v/i* shine; *L.Am. (verse bien)* look good **2** *v/t ropa, joya* wear **3** *v/r* **-se** *tb irón* excel o.s., surpass o.s.

lucrativo *adj* lucrative; **lucro** *m* profit; **afán de ~** profit-making; **sin ánimo de ~** non-profit (making), not-for-profit

ludopatía *f* compulsive gambling

luego 1 *adv* *(después)* later; *en orden, espacio* then; *L.Am. (en seguida)* right now; **~ ~** *Méx* straight away; **¡desde ~!** of course!; **¡hasta ~!** see you (later) **2** *conj* therefore; **~ que** *L.Am.* after

lugar *m* place; **~ común** cliché; **en ~ de** instead of; **en primer ~** in the first place, first(ly); **fuera de ~** out of place; **yo en tu ~** if I were you, (if I were) in your place; **dar ~ a** give rise to; **tener ~** take place

lúgubre *adj* gloomy

lujo *m* luxury; **lujoso** *adj* luxurious; **lujuria** *f* lust; **lujurioso** *adj* lecherous

lumbago *m* MED lumbago

lumbre *f* fire; **lumbrera** *f* genius; **luminoso** *adj* luminous; *lámpara, habitación* bright

luna *f* moon; *de tienda* window; *de vehículo* windshield, *Br* windscreen; **~ de miel** honeymoon; **~ llena/nueva** full/new moon; **media ~** *L.Am.* GASTR croissant; **estar en la ~** F have one's head in the clouds F; **lunar 1** *adj* lunar **2** *m en la piel* mole; **de ~es** spotted, polka-dot; **lunático** *adj* lunatic

lunes *m inv* Monday

luneta *f*: **~ térmica** AUTO heated windshield, *Br* heated windscreen

L

lunfardo *m Arg slang* used in Buenos Aires

lupa *f* magnifying glass; **mirar algo con ~** *fig* go through sth with a fine toothcomb

lustrabotas *m/f inv L.Am.* bootblack; **lustrador** *m*, **~a** *f L.Am.* bootblack; **lustrar** <1a> *v/t* polish; **lustre** *m* shine; *fig* luster, *Br* lustre; **dar ~ a** *fig* give added luster (*Br* lustre) to; **lustro** *m* period of five years; **lustroso** *adj* shiny

luto *m* mourning; **estar de ~ por alguien** be in mourning for s.o.

luxación *f MED* dislocation

luz *f* light; **~ trasera** AUTO rear light; **luces de carretera** *or* **largas** AUTO full *o* main beam headlights; **luces de cruce** *or* **cortas** AUTO dipped headlights; **~ verde** *tb fig* green light; **arrojar ~ sobre algo** *fig* shed light on s.th.; **dar a ~** give birth to; **salir a la ~** *fig* come to light; **a todas luces** evidently, clearly; **de pocas luces** *fig* F dim F, not very bright

M

m *abr* (= *metro*) m (= meter); (= *minuto*) m (= minute)

macabro 1 *adj* macabre **2** *m*, **-a** *f* ghoul

macaco *m* ZO macaque

macana *f L.Am.* billyclub, *Br* truncheon; F (*mentira*) lie, fib F; **hizo/ dijo una ~** he did/said something stupid; **¡qué ~!** *Rpl* P what a drag!; **macanear** <1a> *v/t L.Am.* (*aporrear*) beat; **macanudo** *S.Am.* F great F, fantastic F

macarra 1 *m* P pimp **2** *adj* F: **ser ~** be a bastard P

macarrones *mpl* macaroni *sg*

macedonia *f*: **~ de frutas** fruit salad

macerar <1a> *v/t* GASTR soak

maceta *f* flowerpot; **macetero** *m* flowerpot holder; *L.Am.* flowerpot

machacar <1g> *v/t* crush; *fig* thrash

machete *m* machete

machismo *m* male chauvinism; **machista 1** *adj* sexist **2** *m* sexist, male chauvinist; **macho 1** *adj* male; (*varonil*) tough; *desp* macho **2** *m* male; *apelativo* F man F, *Br* mate F; *L.Am.* (*plátano*) banana

macizo 1 *adj* solid; **estar ~** F be a

dish F **2** *m* GEOG massif; **~ de flores** flower bed

macuto *m* backpack

madeja *f* hank

madera *f* wood; **tener ~ de** have the makings of; **maderera** *f* timber merchant; **madero** *m* P cop P

madrastra *f* step-mother

madre 1 *f* mother; **~ soltera** single mother; **dar en la ~ a alguien** F hit s.o. where it hurts ; **¡me vale ~!** *Méx* V I don't give a fuck! V **2** *adj Méx*, *C.Am.* F great F, fantastic F; **madreselva** *f* BOT honeysuckle

Madrid Madrid

madriguera *f* (*agujero*) burrow; (*guarida*) *tb fig* den

madrileño 1 *adj* of/ from Madrid, Madrid *atr* **2** *m*, **-a** *f* native of Madrid

madrina *f* godmother

madrugada *f* early morning; (*amanecer*) dawn; **de ~** in the small hours; **madrugador** *m*, **~a** *f* early riser; **madrugar** <1h> *v/i L.Am.* (*quedar despierto*) stay up till the small hours; (*levantarse temprano*) get up early

madurar <1a> **1** *v/t fig*: *idea* think

through **2** *v/i de persona* mature; *de fruta* ripen; **madurez** *f mental* maturity; *edad* middle age; *de fruta* ripeness; **maduro** *adj mentalmente* mature; *de edad* middle-aged; *fruta* ripe

maestría *f* mastery; *Méx* EDU master's (degree); **maestro 1** *adj* master *atr* **2** *m*, **-a** *f* EDU teacher; MÚS maestro

mafia *f* mafia; **mafioso 1** *adj* mafia *atr* **2** *m* mafioso, gangster

magdalena *f* cupcake, *Br tb* fairy cake

magia *f tb fig* magic; **mágico** *adj* magic

magisterio *m* teaching profession; **magistrado** *m* judge; **magistral** *adj* masterly

magnanimidad *f* magnanimity; **magnánimo** *adj* magnanimous

magnate *m* magnate, tycoon

magnesio *m* magnesium

magnético *adj* magnetic

magnetofón *m* tape recorder

magnífico *adj* wonderful, magnificent

magnitud *f* magnitude

magnolia *f* BOT magnolia

mago *m tb fig* magician; *los Reyes Magos* the Three Wise Men, the Three Kings

magrear <1a> *v/t* F feel up F

Magreb Maghreb

magro *adj carne* lean

magulladura *f* bruise; **magullar** <1a> *v/t* bruise; **magullón** *m L.Am.* bruise

mahometano 1 *adj* Muslim **2** *m*, **-a** *f* Muslim

mahonesa *f* mayonnaise

maillot *m* DEP jersey

maíz *m* corn

majada *f CSur* flock of sheep

majaderear <1a> *L.Am.* F **1** *v/t* bug F **2** *v/i* keep going on F

majadería *f*: *decir / hacer una ~* say / do something stupid

majadero F **1** *adj* idiotic, stupid **2** *m*, **-a** *f* idiot

majareta *adj* F nutty F, screwy F

majestad *f* majesty; **majestuoso** *adj* majestic

majo *adj* F nice; (*bonito*) pretty

mal 1 *adj* → **malo 2** *adv* badly; *~ que bien* one way or the other; *¡menos ~!* thank goodness!; *ponerse a ~ con alguien* fall out with s.o.; *tomarse algo a ~* take sth badly **3** *m* MED illness; *el ~ menor* the lesser of two evils

malabar *m/adj*: (*juegos*) *-es pl* juggling *sg*; **malabarista** *m/f* juggler

malacrianza *f L.Am.* rudeness

malaria *f* MED malaria

malcriadez *f L.Am.* bad upbringing; **malcriado** *adj* spoilt; **malcrianza** *f L.Am.* rudeness; **malcriar** <1c> *v/t* spoil

maldad *f* evil; *es una ~ hacer eso* it's a wicked thing to do

maldecir <3p> **1** *v/i* curse; *~ de alguien* speak ill of s.o. **2** *v/t* curse; **maldición** *f* curse; **maldito** *adj* F damn F; *¡-a sea!* (god)damn it!

maleante *m/f & adj* criminal

malecón *m* breakwater

maleducado *adj* rude, bad-mannered

maleficio *m* curse; **maléfico** *adj* evil

malentendido *m* misunderstanding

malestar *m* MED discomfort; *social* unrest

maleta *f* bag, suitcase; *L.Am.* AUTO trunk, *Br* boot; *hacer la ~* pack one's bags; **maletero** *m* trunk, *Br* boot; **maletín** *m* briefcase

malévolo *adj* malevolent

maleza *f* undergrowth

malformación *f* MED malformation

malgastar <1a> *v/t* waste

malgenioso *adj Méx* bad-tempered

malhablado *adj* foul-mouthed

malhechor *m*, *~a f* criminal

malherir <3i> *v/t* hurt badly

malhumorado *adj* bad-tempered

malicia *f* (*mala intención*) malice; (*astucia*) cunning, slyness; *no tener ~* F be very naive; **malicioso** *adj* (*malintencionado*) malicious; (*astuto*) cunning, sly

maligno *adj* harmful; MED malignant

M

malinchismo *m Méx* treason

malla *f* mesh; *Rpl* swimsuit

malo 1 *adj* bad; *calidad* poor; *(enfermo)* sick, ill; **por las buenas o por las -as** whether he/she etc likes it or not; **por las -as** by force; **lo ~ es que** unfortunately; **ponerse ~** fall ill **2** *m hum* bad guy, baddy F

malogrado *adj muerto* dead before one's time; **malograr** <1a> **1** *v/t* waste; *trabajo* spoil, ruin **2** *v/r* **~se** fail; *de plan* come to nothing; *fallecer* die before one's time; *S.Am. (descomponerse)* break down; *(funcionar mal)* go wrong

maloliente *adj* stinking

malparado *adj:* **quedar** *or* **salir ~ de algo** come out badly from sth

malpensado *adj:* **ser ~** have a nasty mind

malsano *adj* unhealthy

malsonante *adj* rude

malta *f* malt

maltratar <1a> *v/t* mistreat; **maltrato** *m* abuse, harsh words *pl*

maltrecho *adj* weakened, diminished; *cosa* damaged

malva *adj* mauve

malvado *adj* evil

malversación *f:* **~ de fondos** embezzlement; **malversar** <1a> *v/t* embezzle

Malvinas: *las* **~** the Falklands, the Falkland Islands

malvivir <3a> *v/i* scrape by

mamá *f* mom, *Br* mum

mama *f* breast; **mamadera** *f L.Am.* feeding bottle

mamar <1a> *v/i* suck; **dar de ~** (breast)feed

mamarracho *m:* **vas hecho un ~** F you look a mess F

mamífero *m* mammal

mamila *f Méx* feeding bottle

mamografía *f MED* mammography

mamón 1 *adj Méx* P cocky **2** *m* P bastard P; **mamona** *f* P bitch P

mamotreto *m F libro* hefty tome

mampara *f* screen

mamporro *m* F punch

mampostería *f* masonry

maná *m fig* manna

manada *f* herd; *de lobos* pack

manantial *m* spring

manar <1a> *v/i* flow

manatí *m* ZO manatee

manaza *f:* **ser un ~s** F be ham-handed F

mancebo *m* youth

Mancha: *Canal de la* **~** English Channel

mancha *f* (dirty) mark; *de grasa, sangre etc* stain; **manchar** <1a> **1** *v/t* get dirty; *de grasa, sangre etc* stain **2** *v/r* **~se** get dirty

mancillar <1a> *v/t fig* sully

manco *adj de mano* one-handed; *de brazo* one-armed

mancornas *fpl Pe, Bol* cufflinks

mancuernas *fpl C.Am.* cufflinks

mandamás *m inv* F big shot F

mandado *m Méx, C.Am.:* **los ~s** *pl* the shopping *sg*; **mandamiento** *m* order; JUR warrant; REL commandment

mandar <1a> **1** *v/t* order; *(enviar)* send; *a mí no me manda nadie* nobody tells me what to do; **~ hacer algo** have sth done **2** *v/i* be in charge; *¿mande?* Méx can I help you?; *Méx* TELEC hallo?; *(¿cómo?)* what did you say?, excuse me?

mandarina *f* mandarin (orange)

mandatario *m* leader; *primer ~ Méx* President; **mandato** *m* order; POL mandate

mandíbula *f* ANAT jaw; *reírse a* **~ batiente** F laugh one's head off F

mandioca *f* cassava

mando *m* command; *alto* **~** high command; **~ a distancia** TV remote control; *tablero de* **~s** AUTO dashboard

mandolina *f MÚS* mandolin

mandón *adj* F bossy F

manecilla *f* hand

manejable *adj* easy to handle; *automovil* maneuverable, *Br* manoeuvrable; **manejar** <1a> **1** *v/t* handle; *máquina* operate; *L.Am.* AUTO drive **2** *v/i L.Am.* AUTO drive

3 v/r **~se** manage, get by; **manejo** m handling; *de una máquina* operation

manera f way; *esa es su ~ de ser* that's the way he is; **~s** manners; *lo hace a su ~* he does it his way; *de ~ que* so (that); *de ninguna ~* certainly not; *no hay ~ de* it is impossible to; *de todas ~s* anyway, in any case

manga f sleeve; *~ de riego* hosepipe; *en ~s de camisa* in shirtsleeves; *sin ~s* sleeveless; *sacarse algo de la ~ fig* make sth up; *traer algo en la ~* F have sth up one's sleeve

manganeso m manganese

mangar <1h> v/t P swipe F, pinch F

mangle m BOT mangrove

mango m BOT mango; *CSur* F (*dinero*) dough F, cash; *estoy sin un ~ CSur* F I'm broke F, I don't have a bean F

mangonear <1a> **1** v/i F boss people around; (*entrometerse*) meddle **2** v/t F: *~ a alguien* boss s.o. around

manguera f hose(pipe)

maní m *S.Am.* peanut

manía f (*costumbre*) habit, mania; (*antipatía*) dislike; (*obsesión*) obsession; *~ persecutoria* persecution complex; *tiene sus ~s* she has her little ways; *tener ~ a alguien* F have it in for s.o. F; **maniaco** m maniac

maniatar <1a> v/t: *~ a alguien* tie s.o.'s hands

maniático adj F fussy

manicomio m lunatic asylum

manicura f manicure; *hacerse la ~* have a manicure

manido adj fig clichéd, done to death F

manifestación f *de gente* demonstration; (*muestra*) show; (*declaración*) statement; **manifestante** m/f demonstrator; **manifestar** <1k> **1** v/t (*demostrar*) show; (*declarar*) declare, state **2** v/r **~se** demonstrate; **manifiesto 1** adj clear, manifest; *poner de ~* make clear **2** m manifesto

manigua f *W.I.* thicket, bush

manija f *L.Am.* (*asa*) handle

manillar m handlebars pl

maniobra f maneuver, *Br* manoeuvre; *hacer ~s* maneuver, *Br* manoeuvre; **maniobrar** <1a> v/i maneuver, *Br* manoeuvre

manipulación f manipulation; (*manejo*) handling; **manipular** <1a> v/t manipulate; (*manejar*) handle

maniquí 1 m dummy **2** m/f model

manirroto 1 adj extravagant **2** m, **-a** f spendthrift

manisero m, **-a** f *W.I.*, *S.Am.* peanut seller

manitas fpl: *ser un ~* be handy

manito m *Méx* pal, buddy

manivela f handle

manjar m delicacy

mano 1 f hand; *~ de obra* labo(u)r, manpower; *~ de pintura* coat of paint; *¡~s arriba!* hands up!; *a ~ derecha / izquierda* on the right / left; *atar las ~s a alguien* tie s.o.'s hands; *de segunda ~* secondhand; *echar una ~ a alguien* give s.o. a hand; *estar a ~s L.Am.* be even, be quits; *hecho a ~* handmade; *poner la ~ en el fuego fig* swear to it; *poner ~s a la obra* get down to work; *se le fue la ~ con fig* he overdid it with; *tener a ~* have to hand; *traerse algo entre ~s* be plotting sth **2** m *Méx* F pal F, buddy F

manojo m handful; *~ de llaves* bunch of keys; *~ de nervios fig* bundle of nerves

manopla f mitten

manosear <1a> v/t *fruta* handle; *persona* F grope F

manotazo m slap; **manotear** <1a> **1** v/t *Arg*, *Méx* grab **2** v/i *Arg*, *Méx* wave one's hands around

mansalva f: *a ~* in vast numbers; *bebida*, *comida* in vast amounts

mansedumbre f docility; *de persona* mildness

mansión f mansion

manso adj docile; *persona* mild

manta f blanket; *tirar de la ~ fig*

uncover the truth

manteca f fat; *Rpl* butter; **~ de cacao** cocoa butter; **~ de cerdo** lard

mantel m tablecloth; **~ individual** table mat; **mantelería** f table linen; **una ~** a set of table linen

mantención f *L.Am.* → **manutención**

mantener <2l> **1** v/t (*sujetar*) hold; *techo etc* hold up; (*preservar*) keep; *conversación, relación* have; *económicamente* support; (*afirmar*) maintain **2** v/r **~se** (*sujetarse*) be held; *económicamente* support o.s.; *en forma* keep; **mantenimiento** m maintenance; *económico* support; **gimnasia de ~** gym

mantequilla f butter; **mantequillera** f *L.Am.* butter dish

mantilla f *de bebé* shawl; **estar en ~s** *fig* F be in its infancy

mantuvo vb → **mantener**

manual m/adj manual; **manualidades** fpl handicrafts; **manubrio** m handle; *S.Am.* handlebars pl

manufacturar <1a> v/t manufacture

manuscrito **1** adj handwritten **2** m manuscript

manutención f maintenance

manzana f apple; *de casas* block; **~ de la discordia** *fig* bone of contention; **manzanilla** f camomile tea; **manzano** m apple tree

maña f skill; **darse** o **tener ~ para** be good at; **tiene muchas ~s** *L.Am.* she's got lots of tricks up her sleeve F

mañana **1** f morning; **por la ~** in the morning; **~ por la ~** tomorrow morning; **de la ~ a la noche** from morning until night; **de la noche a la ~** *fig* overnight; **esta ~** this morning; **muy de ~** very early (in the morning) **2** adv tomorrow; **pasado ~** day after tomorrow

mañanita f shawl

mañero adj *Rpl* (*animal: terco*) stubborn; (*nervioso*) skittish, nervous

mañoso adj skil(l)ful; *L.Am. animal* stubborn

mapa m map; **~ de carreteras** road map

mapache m raccoon

mapamundi m map of the world

maqueta f model

maquillador m, **~a** f make-up artist; **maquillaje** m make-up; **maquillar** <1a> **1** v/t make up **2** v/r **~se** put on one's make-up

máquina f machine; FERR locomotive; *C.Am., W.I.* car; **~ de afeitar** (electric) shaver; **~ de coser** sewing machine; **~ de fotos** camera; **~ recreativa** arcade game; **pasar algo a ~** type sth; **a toda ~** at top speed; **maquinaciones** fpl scheming sg; **maquinador** **1** adj scheming **2** m, **~a** f schemer; **maquinal** adj fig mechanical; **maquinar** <1a> v/t plot; **maquinaria** f machinery; **maquinilla** f: **~ de afeitar** razor; **~ eléctrica** electric razor; **maquinista** m/f FERR engineer, *Br* train driver

mar m (*also* f) GEOG sea; **sudaba a ~es** *fig* F the sweat was pouring off him F; **llover a ~es** *fig* F pour, bucket down F; **alta ~** high seas pl; **la ~ de bien** (*muy bien*) really well

maraca f MÚS maraca

maraña f *de hilos* tangle; (*lío*) jumble

marasmo m fig stagnation

maratón m (*also* f) marathon; **maratoniano** adj marathon atr

maravilla f marvel, wonder; BOT marigold; **de ~** marvellously, wonderfully; **a las mil ~s** marvellously, wonderfully; **maravillar** <1a> **1** v/t amaze, astonish **2** v/r **~se** be amazed o astonished (**de** at); **maravilloso** adj marvellous, wonderful

marca f mark; COM brand; **~ registrada** registered trademark; **de ~** brand-name atr; **marcador** m DEP scoreboard; **marcaje** m DEP marking; **marcapasos** m inv MED pacemaker; **marcar** <1g> v/t mark; *número de teléfono* dial; *gol* score; *res* brand; *de termómetro, contador etc* read, register

marcha f (*salida*) departure;

(*velocidad*) speed; (*avance*) progress; MIL march; AUTO gear; DEP walk; **~ atrás** AUTO reverse (gear); **a ~s forzadas** *fig* flat out; **a toda ~** at top speed; **hacer algo sobre la ~** do sth as one goes along; **ponerse en ~** get started, get going; **tener mucha ~** F be very lively

marchante *m L.Am.* regular customer

marchar <1a> **1** *v/i* (*progresar*) go; (*funcionar*) work; (*caminar*) walk; MIL march **2** *v/r* **~se** leave, go

marchitarse <1a> *v/r* wilt

marcial *adj* martial; **artes ~es** martial arts

marciano *m* Martian

marco *m moneda* mark; *de cuadro, puerta* frame; *fig* framework

marea *f* tide; **~ alta** high tide; **~ baja** low tide; **~ negra** oil slick

mareado *adj* dizzy; **marear** <1a> **1** *v/t* make feel nauseous, *Br* make feel sick; *fig* (*confundir*) confuse **2** *v/r* **~se** feel nauseous, *Br* feel sick

marejada *f* heavy sea; **maremoto** *m* tidal wave; **mareo** *m* seasickness

marfil *m* ivory

margarina *f* margarine

margarita *f* BOT daisy

margen *m tb fig* margin; **al ~ de eso** apart from that; **mantenerse al ~** keep out; **marginación** *f* marginalization; **marginal** *adj* marginal; **marginar** <1a> *v/t* marginalize

mariachi **1** *m* mariachi band **2** *m/f* mariachi player

marica *m* F fag P, *Br* poof P

maricón *m* P fag P, *Br* poof P

marido *m* husband

marihuana *f* marijuana

marimacho *m* F butch woman

marimba *f* Rpl MÚS marimba

marina *f* navy; **~ mercante** merchant navy

marinar <1a> *v/t* GASTR marinade

marinero **1** *adj* sea *atr* **2** *m* sailor; **marino** **1** *adj* *brisa* sea *atr*; *planta, animal* marine; **azul ~** navy blue **2** *m* sailor

marioneta *f tb fig* puppet

mariposa *f* butterfly

mariquita *f* ladybug, *Br* ladybird

marisco *m* seafood

marisma *f* salt marsh

marítimo *adj* maritime

marketing *m* marketing

mármol *m* marble

marmita *f* pot, pan

marmota *f*: **dormir como una ~** F sleep like a log

marqués *m* marquis; **marquesa** *f* marchioness

marquesina *f* marquee, *Br* canopy

marranada *f* F dirty trick; **marrano** **1** *adj* filthy **2** *m* hog, *Br* pig; F *persona* pig F

marras *adv*: **el ordenador de ~** the darned computer F

marrón *m/adj* brown

marroquinería *f* leather goods

Marruecos Morocco

marta *f* ZO marten

Marte *m* AST Mars

martes *m inv* Tuesday

martillero *m* *S.Am.* auctioneer; **martillo** *m* hammer; **~ neumático** pneumatic drill

martín *m*: **~ pescador** ZO kingfisher

mártir *m/f* martyr; **martirio** *m tb fig* martyrdom; **martirizar** <1f> *v/t tb fig* martyr

marzo *m* March

mas *conj* but

más **1** *adj* more **2** *adv comp* more; *sup* most; MAT plus; **~ grande/pequeño** bigger/smaller; **el ~ grande/pequeño** the largest/smallest; **trabajar ~** work harder; **~ bien** rather; **~ que**, **~ de lo que** more than; **~ o menos** more or less; **¿qué ~?** what else?; **no ~** *L.Am.* → **nomás**; **por ~ que** however much; **sin ~** without more ado; **~ lejos** further

masa *f* mass; GASTR dough; **pillar a alguien con las manos en la ~** F catch s.o. red-handed

masacrar <1a> *v/t* massacre; **masacre** *f* massacre

masaje *m* massage; **masajista** *m/f*

M

masseur; *mujer* masseuse

mascar <1g> **1** *v/t* chew **2** *v/i L.Am.* chew tobacco

máscara *f* mask; **mascarilla** *f* mask; *cosmética* face pack

mascota *f* mascot; *animal doméstico* pet

masculino *adj* masculine

mascullar <1a> *v/t* mutter

masificación *f* overcrowding

masilla *f* putty

masita *f L.Am.* small sweet cake or bun

masivo *adj* massive

masón *m* mason

masoquismo *m* masochism; **masoquista 1** *adj* masochistic **2** *m/f* masochist

máster *m* master's (degree)

masticación *f* chewing; **masticar** <1g> *v/t* chew

mástil *m* mast; *de tienda* pole

mastín *m* ZO mastiff

mastodóntico *adj* colossal, enormous

mastuerzo *m* BOT cress

masturbarse <1a> *v/r* masturbate

mata *f* bush

matadero *m* slaughterhouse; **matador** *m* TAUR matador; **matanza** *f de animales* slaughter; *de gente* slaughter, massacre; **matar** <1a> **1** *v/t* kill; *ganado* slaughter **2** *v/r* **~se** kill o.s.; *morir* be killed; **~se a trabajar** work o.s. to death; **matarratas** *m* rat poison; **matasanos** *m/f inv* F quack F

matasellos *m inv* postmark

mate 1 *adj* matt **2** *m en ajedrez* mate; *L.Am.* (*infusión*) maté

matear <1a> **1** *v/t CSur* checkmate **2** *v/i L.Am.* drink maté

matemáticas *fpl* mathematics; **matemático 1** *adj* mathematical **2** *m*, **-a** *f* mathematician

materia *f* matter; (*material*) material; (*tema*) subject; **~ prima** raw material; **en ~ de** as regards; **material** *m/adj* material; **materialismo** *m* materialism; **materializar** <1f> *v/t*: **~ algo** make sth a reality

maternal *adj* maternal

matero *m*, **-a** *f L.Am.* maté drinker

matinal *adj* morning *atr*

matiz *m de ironía* touch; *de color* shade; **matizar** <1f> *v/t comentarios* qualify

matón *m* bully; (*criminal*) thug

matorral *m* thicket

matrícula *f* AUTO license plate, *Br* numberplate; EDU enrol(l)ment, registration; **matricular** <1a> **1** *v/t* register **2** *v/r* **~se** EDU enrol(l), register

matrimonial *adj* marriage *atr*, marital; **matrimonio** *m* marriage; *boda* wedding

matriz *f* matrix; ANAT womb

matrona *f* (*comadrona*) midwife

matutino *adj* morning *atr*

maullar <1a> *v/i* miaow; **maullido** *m* miaow

mausoleo *m* mausoleum

máxima *f* maxim; **máxime** *adv* especially; **máximo** *adj* maximum

mayo *m* May

mayonesa *f* GASTR mayonnaise

mayor 1 *adj comp: en tamaño* larger, bigger; *en edad* older; *en importancia* greater; **ser ~ de edad** be an adult; **al por ~** COM wholesale **2** *adj sup*: **el ~** *en edad* the oldest *o* eldest; *en tamaño* the largest *o* biggest; *en importancia* the greatest; **los -es** adults; **la ~ parte** the majority

mayordomo *m* butler

mayoreo *m*: **vender al ~** *Méx* sell wholesale

mayoría *f* majority; **alcanzar la ~ de edad** come of age; **la ~ de** the majority of, most (of); **en la ~ de los casos** in the majority of cases, in most cases; **mayorista** *m/f* wholesaler; **mayoritario** *adj* majority *atr*

mayúscula *f* capital (letter), upper case letter

mazamorra *f S.Am.* kind of porridge made from corn

mazapán *m* marzipan

mazmorra *f* dungeon

mazo *m* mallet

mazorca *f* cob

me *pron pers complemento directo* me; *complemento indirecto* (to) me; *reflexivo* myself; ~ **dio el libro** he gave me the book, he gave the book to me

mear <1a> F **1** *v/i* pee F **2** *v/r* ~se pee o.s. F; ~se **de risa** wet o.s. (laughing) F

meca *f fig* mecca

mecachis *int* ~ blast! F

mecánica *f* mechanics; mecánico **1** *adj* mechanical **2** *m*, -a *f* mechanic; mecanismo *m* mechanism; mecanizar <1f> *v/t* mechanize; mecanografiar <1c> *v/t* type; mecanógrafo *m*, -a *f* typist

mecate *m Méx* string, cord

mecedora *f* rocking chair

mecenas *m inv* patron, sponsor

mecer <2b> **1** *v/t* rock **2** *v/r* ~se rock

mecha *f* wick; *de explosivo* fuse; *del pelo* highlight; *Méx* F fear; mechero *m* cigarette lighter; mechón *m de pelo* lock

medalla *f* medal; medallista *m/f* medal(l)ist

media *f* stocking; ~s *pl* pantyhose *pl*, *Br* tights *pl*

mediación *f* mediation; mediado *adj*: **a** ~s **de junio** in mid-June, halfway through June; mediador *m*, ~a *f* mediator; mediana *f* AUTO median strip, *Br* central reservation; mediano *adj* medium, average; medianoche *f* midnight; mediante *prp* by means of; mediar <1b> *v/i* mediate

mediático *adj* media *atr*

medicación *f* medication; medicamento *m* medicine, drug; medicina *f* medicine; medicinal *adj* medicinal; médico **1** *adj* medical **2** *m/f* doctor; ~ **de cabecera** *o* **de familia** family physician, *Br* GP, *Br* general practitioner; ~ **de urgencia** emergency doctor

medida *f* measure; *acto* measurement; *(grado)* extent; **hecho a** ~ made to measure; **a** ~ **que** as; **tomar** ~**s** *fig* take measures *o* steps

medidor *m S.Am.* meter

medieval *adj* medi(a)eval

medio **1** *adj* half, *tamaño* medium; *(de promedio)* average; **las tres y -a** half past three, three-thirty **2** *m* environment; *(centro)* middle; *(manera)* means; ~ **ambiente** environment; *por* ~ **de** by means of; **en** ~ **de** in the middle of; ~**s dinero** means, resources; ~**s de comunicación** *or* **de información** (mass) media; ~**s de transporte** means of transport **3** *adv* half; **hacer algo a -as** half do sth; **ir a -as** go halves; **día por** ~ *L.Am.* every other day; **quitar de en** ~ **algo** F move sth out of the way

medioambiental *adj* environmental

mediocre *adj* mediocre

mediodía *m* midday; **a** ~ *(a las doce)* at noon, at twelve o'clock; *(a la hora de comer)* at lunchtime

medir <3l> **1** *v/t* measure **2** *v/i*: **mide 2 metros de ancho / largo / alto** it's 2 meters *(o Br* metres) wide / long / tall

meditación *f* meditation; meditar <1a> **1** *v/t* ponder **2** *v/i* meditate

Mediterráneo *m/adj*: *(mar)* ~ Mediterranean (Sea)

médium *m/f* medium

médula *f* marrow; ~ **espinal** spinal cord; **hasta la** ~ *fig* through and through, to the core

medusa *f* ZO jellyfish

megafonía *f* public-address *o* PA system; megáfono *m* bullhorn, *Br* loud-hailer

megalomanía *f* megalomania

mejicano **1** *adj* Mexican **2** *m*, -a *f* Mexican; Méjico Mexico; *Méx DF* Mexico City

mejilla *f* cheek

mejillón *m* ZO mussel

mejor *adj comp* better; **el** ~ *sup* the best; **lo** ~ the best thing; **lo** ~ **posible** as well as possible; **a lo** ~ perhaps, maybe; **tanto** ~ all the better; mejora *f* improvement

mejorana *f* BOT marjoram

mejorar <1a> **1** *v/t* improve **2** *v/i*

M

improve; **¡que te mejores!** get well soon!; **mejoría** f improvement

mejunje m desp concoction

melancolía f melancholy; **melancólico** adj gloomy, melancholic

melena f long hair; **de león** mane

melindroso adj affected

mella f: **hacer ~ en alguien** have an effect on s.o., affect s.o.; **mellado** adj gap-toothed

mellizo 1 adj twin atr **2** m, **-a** f twin

melocotón m peach; **melocotonero** m peach tree

melodía f melody

melodrama m melodrama

melón m melon

membrana f membrane

membrillo m quince; **dulce de ~** quince jelly

memela f Méx corn tortilla

memo 1 adj F dumb **2** m, **-a** f F idiot

memorable adj memorable

memoria f tb INFOR memory; (informe) report; **de ~** by heart; **~s** (biografía) memoirs

memorizar <1f> v/t memorize

mención f: **hacer ~ de** mention; **mencionar** <1a> v/t mention

mendigar <1h> v/t beg for; **mendigo** m beggar

menear <1a> **1** v/t shake; **las caderas** sway; **~ la cola** wag its tail **2** v/r **-se** fidget

menestra f vegetable stew

mengano m, **-a** f F so-and-so F

menguante adj decreasing, diminishing; luna waning; **menguar** <1i> v/i decrease, diminish; **de la luna** wane

meningitis f MED meningitis

menopausia f MED menopause

menor adj comp less; **en tamaño** smaller; **en edad** younger; **ser ~ de edad** be a minor; **al por ~** COM retail; **el ~** sup: en tamaño the smallest; en edad the youngest; **el número ~** the lowest number

menos 1 adj en cantidad less; en número fewer **2** adv comp en cantidad less; sup en cantidad least; MAT minus; **es ~ guapa que Ana** she is

not as pretty as Ana; **tres ~ dos** three minus two; **a ~ que** unless; **al ~, por lo ~** at least; **echar de ~** miss; **eso es lo de ~** that's the least of it; **ni mucho ~** far from it; **son las dos ~ diez** it's ten of two, it's ten to two

menoscabar <1a> v/t autoridad diminish; (dañar) harm

menospreciar <1b> v/t underestimate; (desdeñar) look down on

mensaje m message; **mensajero** m courier

menstruación f menstruation; **menstruar** <1h> v/i menstruate

mensual adj monthly; **mensualidad** f monthly instal(l)ment, monthly payment; **mensualmente** adv monthly

menta f BOT mint

mental adj mental; **mentalidad** f mentality; **mentalizar** <1f> **1** v/t: **~ a alguien** make s.o. aware **2** v/r **~se** mentally prepare o.s.; **mente** f mind

mentecato 1 adj F dim **2** m F fool

mentir <3i> v/i lie; **mentira** f lie; **mentiroso 1** adj: **ser muy ~** tell a lot of lies **2** m, **-a** f liar

mentón m chin

mentor m mentor

menú m tb INFOR menu; **~ de ayuda** help menu

menudencias fpl Méx giblets; **menudeo** m L.Am. retail trade; **menudo 1** adj small; **¡-a suerte!** fig F lucky devil!; **¡-as vacaciones!** irón F some vacation!; **a ~** often **2** m L.Am. small change; **~s** GASTR giblets

meñique m/adj: (dedo) **~** little finger

meollo m fig heart

mercader m trader; **mercadería** f L.Am. merchandise; **mercadillo** m street market; **mercado** m market; **Mercado Común** Common Market; **~ negro** black market; **mercadotecnia** f marketing; **mercancía** f merchandise; **mercantil** adj commercial

merced f: **estar a ~ de alguien** be at

s.o.'s mercy

mercenario *m/adj* mercenary

mercería *f* notions *pl*, *Br* haberdashery

MERCOSUR *abr* (= *Mercado Común del Sur*) *Common Market including Argentina, Brazil, Paraguay and Uruguay*

mercurio *m* mercury

merecer <2d> *v/t* deserve; ***no ~ la pena*** it's not worth it; **merecido** *m* just deserts *pl*

merendar <1k> **1** *v/t*: ***~ algo*** have sth as an afternoon snack **2** *v/i* have an afternoon snack

merengue *m* GASTR meringue

meridiano *m/f* meridian; **meridional 1** *adj* southern **2** *m* southerner

merienda *f* afternoon snack

mérito *m* merit

merluza *f* ZO hake; ***agarrar una ~*** *fig* F get plastered F

mermar <1a> **1** *v/t* reduce **2** *v/i* diminish

mermelada *f* jam

mero 1 *adj* mere; ***el ~ jefe*** *Méx* F the big boss **2** *m* ZO grouper

merodear <1a> *v/i* loiter

mes *m* month

mesa *f* table; **~ *de centro*** coffee table; **~ *redonda*** *fig* round table; ***poner/quitar la ~*** set/clear the table; **mesera** *f* L.Am. waitress; **mesero** *m* L.Am. waiter; **meseta** *f* plateau; **mesilla, mesita** *f*: **~ (*de noche*)** night stand, *Br* bedside table

mesón *m* traditional restaurant decorated in rustic style

mestizo *m* person of mixed race

mesura *f*: ***con ~*** in moderation

meta *f* en fútbol goal; *en carrera* finishing line; *fig (objetivo)* goal, objective

metabolismo *m* metabolism

metafísica *f* metaphysics

metáfora *f* metaphor

metal *m* metal; **metálico 1** *adj* metallic **2** *m*: **en ~** (in) cash; **metalúrgico** *adj* metallurgical

metamorfosis *f inv* transformation, metamorphosis

metedura *f*: **~ *de pata*** F blunder

meteorito *m* meteorite; **meteorológico** *adj* weather *atr*, meteorological; ***pronóstico ~*** weather forecast; **meteorólogo** *m*, **-a** *f* meteorologist

meter <2a> **1** *v/t gen* put (***en*** in, into); *(involucrar)* involve (***en*** in); **~ *a alguien en un lío*** get s.o. into a mess **2** *v/r* **~se**: **~se *en algo*** get into sth; *(involucrarse)* get involved in sth, get mixed up in sth; **~se *con alguien*** pick on s.o.; **~se *de administrativo*** get a job in admin; ***¿dónde se ha metido?*** where has he got to?

meticuloso *adj* meticulous

metido *adj* involved; *L.Am.* F nosy F; ***estar muy ~ en algo*** be very involved in sth

metódico *adj* methodical; **método** *m* method

metomentodo *m/f* F busybody F

metralleta *f* sub-machine gun

métrico *adj* metric; **metro** *m medida* meter, *Br* metre; *para medir* rule; *transporte* subway, *Br* underground

metrópolis *f inv* metropolis; **metropolitano** *adj* metropolitan

mexicano 1 *adj* Mexican **2** *m*, **-a** *f* Mexican; **México** Mexico; *Méx DF* Mexico City

mezcal *m Méx* mescal

mezcla *f sustancia* mixture; *de tabaco, café etc* blend; *acto de tabaco, café etc* blending; **mezclar** <1a> **1** *v/t* mix; *tabaco, café etc* blend; **~ *a alguien en algo*** get s.o. mixed up *o* involved in sth **2** *v/r* **~se** mix; **~se *en algo*** get mixed up *o* involved in sth

mezquinar <1a> *v/t L.Am.* skimp on; **mezquino** *adj* mean

mezquita *f* mosque

mg. *abr* (= *miligramo*) mg (= milligram)

mi, mis *adj pos* my

mí *pron* me; *reflexivo* myself; ***¿y a ~ qué?*** so what?, what's it to me?

michelín *m* F spare tire, *Br* spare tyre

mico *m* ZO monkey

micro *m or f Chi* bus
microbio *m* microbe
microbús *m* minibus
microchip *m* (micro)chip
microfilm(e) *m* microfilm
micrófono *m* microphone; **~ oculto** bug
microondas *m inv* microwave
microordenador *m* microcomputer
microprocesador *m* microprocessor
microscópico *adj* microscopic; **microscopio** *m* microscope
mide *vb → medir*
miedo *m* fear (**a** of); **dar ~** be frightening; **me da ~ la oscuridad** I'm frightened of the dark; **tener ~ de que** be afraid that; **por ~ a** for fear of; **de ~** F great F, awesome F; **miedoso** *adj* timid; **¡no seas tan ~!** don't be scared!
miel *f* honey
miembro *m* member; (*extremidad*) limb, member *fml*
mientras 1 *conj* while; **~ que** whereas **2** *adv*: **~ tanto** in the meantime, meanwhile
miércoles *m inv* Wednesday
mierda *f* P shit P, crap P; **una ~ de película** a crap movie P; **¡una ~!** no way! F
miga *f de pan* crumb; **~s** crumbs; **hacer buenas/malas ~s** *fig* F get on well/badly
migraña *f* MED migraine
migratorio *adj* migratory
mijo *m* BOT millet
mil *adj* thousand
milagro *m* miracle; **de ~** miraculously, by a miracle; **milagroso** *adj* miraculous
milano *m* ZO kite
milenio *m* millennium
mili *f* F military service
milicia *f* militia
milico *m S.Am. desp* soldier
milímetro *m* millimeter, *Br* millimetre
militante *m/f & adj* militant; **militar 1** *adj* military **2** *m* soldier; **los ~es** the military **3** <1a> *v/i* POL: **~ en** be

a member of
milla *f* mile
millar *m* thousand
millón *m* million; (*mil millones*) billion; **millonario** *m* millionaire
milpa *f Méx, C.Am.* corn, *Br* maize; **terreno** cornfield, *Br* field of maize
mimar <1a> *v/t* spoil, pamper
mimbre *m* BOT willow; **muebles pl de ~** wicker furniture *sg*
mímica *f* mime; **mimo** *m* TEA mime
mimosa *f* BOT mimosa
mimoso *adj*: **ser ~** be cuddly
mina *f* MIN mine; *Rpl* F broad F, *Br* bird F; **~ antipersonal** MIL antipersonnel mine; **minar** <1a> *v/t* mine; *fig* undermine
mineral *m/adj* mineral; **minería** *f* mining; **minero 1** *adj* mining **2** *m* miner
miniatura *f* miniature
minifalda *f* miniskirt
minimizar <1f> *v/t* minimize; **mínimo 1** *adj* minimum; **como ~** at the very least **2** *m* minimum
minino *m* F puss F, pussy (cat) F
ministerio *m* POL department; **~ de Asuntos Exteriores,** *L.Am.* **~ de Relaciones Exteriores** State Department, *Br* Foreign Office; **~ de Hacienda** Treasury Department, *Br* Treasury; **~ del Interior** Department of the Interior, *Br* Home Office; **ministro** *m*, **-a** *f* minister; **~ del Interior** Secretary of the Interior, *Br* Home Secretary; **primer ~** Prime Minister
minoría *f* minority
minorista COM **1** *adj* retail *atr* **2** *m/f* retailer
minoritario *adj* minority *atr*
mintió *vb → mentir*
minucia *f* minor detail; **minucioso** *adj* meticulous, thorough
minúscula *f* small letter, lower case letter; **minúsculo** *adj* tiny, minute
minusvalía *f* disability; **minusválido 1** *adj* disabled **2** *m*, **-a** *f* disabled person; **los ~s** the disabled
minutero *m* minute hand
minuto *m* minute

mío, mía *pron* mine; **el ~/ la -a** mine

miope *adj* near-sighted, short-sighted; **miopía** *f* near-sightedness, short-sightedness

mira *f*: **con ~s a** with a view to; **mirada** *f* look; **echar una ~** take a look (**a** at); **mirador** *m* viewpoint; **mirar** <1a> **1** *v/t* look at; (*observar*) watch; *L.Am.* (*ver*) see; **¿qué miras desde aquí?** what can you see from here? **2** *v/i* look; **~ al norte** *de una ventana etc* face north; **~ por la ventana** look out of the window; **mirilla** *f* spyhole

mirlo *m* ZO blackbird

misa *f* REL mass

misántropo *m* misanthropist

miserable *adj* wretched; **miseria** *f* poverty; *fig* misery; **misericordia** *f* mercy, compassion; **mísero** *adj* wretched; *sueldo* miserable

misil *m* missile

misión *f* mission; **misionero** *m*, **-a** *f* missionary

mismo 1 *adj* same; **lo ~ que** the same as; **yo ~** I myself; **da lo ~** it doesn't matter, it's all the same; **me da lo ~** I don't care, it's all the same to me **2** *adv*: **aquí ~** right here; **ahora ~** right now, this very minute

misógino *m* misogynist

misterio *m* mystery; **misterioso** *adj* mysterious; **místico** *adj* mystic(al)

mitad *f* half; **a ~ del camino** halfway; **a ~ de la película** halfway through the movie; **a ~ de precio** half-price

mítico *adj* mythical

mitigar <1h> *v/t* mitigate; *ansiedad, dolor etc* ease

mitin *m* POL meeting

mito *m* myth; **mitología** *f* mythology

mixto *adj* mixed; *comisión* joint

mm. *abr* (= **milímetro**) mm (= millimeter)

mobiliario *m* furniture

mochila *f* backpack; **mochilero** *m*, **-a** *f* backpacker

mochuelo *m* ZO little owl

moción *f* POL motion; **~ de confianza/ censura** vote of confidence / no confidence

moco *m*: **tener ~s** have a runny nose; **mocoso** *m*, **-a** *f* F snotty-nosed kid F

moda *f* fashion; **de ~** fashionable, in fashion; **estar pasado de ~** be out of fashion

modales *mpl* manners

modalidad *f* form; DEP discipline; **~ de pago** method of payment

modelar <1a> *v/t* model; **modelismo** *m* model making; **modelo 1** *m* model **2** *m/f persona* model

módem *m* INFOR modem

moderado 1 *adj* moderate **2** *m*, **-a** *f* moderate; **moderador** *m*, **~a** *f* TV presenter; **moderar** <1a> **1** *v/t* moderate; *impulsos* control, restrain; *velocidad, gastos* reduce; *debate* chair **2** *v/r ~se* control o.s., restrain o.s.

modernización *f* modernization; **modernizar** <1f> *v/t* modernize; **moderno** *adj* modern

modestia *f* modesty; **~ aparte** though I say so myself; **modesto** *adj* modest

módico *adj precio* reasonable

modificación *f* modification; **modificar** <1g> *v/t* modify

modista *m/f* dressmaker; *diseñador* fashion designer

modo *m* way; **a ~ de** as; **de ~ que** so that; **de ningún ~** not at all; **en cierto ~** in a way *o* sense; **de todos ~s** anyway

modorra *f* drowsiness

módulo *m* module

mofarse <1a> *v/r*: **~ de** make fun of

mofeta *f* ZO skunk

mofletes *mpl* chubby cheeks

mogollón *m* F (*discusión*) argument; **~ de** F loads of F

moho *m* mo(u)ld

moisés *m inv* Moses basket

mojado *adj* (*húmedo*) damp, moist; (*empapado*) wet; **mojar** <1a> **1** *v/t* (*humedecer*) dampen, moisten; (*empapar*) wet; *galleta* dunk, dip **2** *v/r* **~se** get wet

mojigato 1 *adj* prudish **2** *m*, **-a** *f* prude

M

mojón m tb fig milestone

molar <2h> **1** v/t: *me mola ese tío* P I like the guy a lot **2** v/i P be cool F

molcajete m Méx, C.Am. (*mortero*) grinding stone

molde m mo(u)ld; *para bizcocho* (cake) tin; *romper ~s* fig break the mo(u)ld; **moldear** <1a> v/t mo(u)ld; **moldura** f ARQUI mo(u)lding

mole 1 f mass **2** m Méx mole (*spicy sauce made with chilies and tomatoes*)

molécula f molecule

moler <2h> v/t grind; *fruta* mash; *carne molida* ground meat, Br mince; *~ a alguien a palos* fig beat s.o. to a pulp

molestar <1a> **1** v/t bother, annoy; (*doler*) trouble; *no ~* do not disturb **2** v/r *~se* get upset; (*ofenderse*) take offense (Br offence) (*enojarse*) get annoyed; *~ en hacer algo* take the trouble to do sth; **molestia** f nuisance; **~s** pl MED discomfort sg; **molesto** adj annoying; (*incómodo*) inconvenient; **molestoso** adj L.Am. annoying

molido adj F bushed F

molinillo m: *~ de café* coffee grinder o mill; **molino** m mill; *~ de viento* windmill

mollera f F head; *duro de ~* F pigheaded F

molusco m ZO mollusk, Br mollusc

momento m moment; *al ~* at once; *por el ~*, *de ~* for the moment

momia f mummy; **momificar** <1g> v/t mummify

monada f: *su hija es una ~* her daughter is lovely; *¡qué ~!* how lovely!

monaguillo m altar boy

monarca m monarch; **monarquía** f monarchy

monasterio m monastery

mondadientes m inv toothpick

mondar <1a> **1** v/t peel; *árbol* prune **2** v/r *~se*: *~se de risa* F split one's sides laughing

mondongo m tripe

moneda f coin; (*divisa*) currency; **monedero** m change purse, Br purse; **monetario** adj monetary

monigote m rag doll; F (*tonto*) idiot

monitor¹ m TV, INFOR monitor

monitor² m, **~a** f (*profesor*) instructor

monja f nun; **monje** m monk

mono 1 m ZO monkey; *prenda* coveralls pl, Br boilersuit **2** adj pretty, cute

monógamo adj monogamous

monólogo m monolog(ue)

monopatín m skateboard

monopolio m monopoly; **monopolizar** <1f> v/t tb fig monopolize

monosílabo adj monosyllabic

monotonía f monotony; **monótono** adj monotonous

monovolumen m AUTO minivan, Br people carrier, MPV

monsergas fpl: *déjate de ~* F stop going on F

monstruo m monster; (*fenómeno*) phenomenon; **monstruosidad** f eyesore, monstrosity; **monstruoso** adj monstrous

monta f: *de poca ~* unimportant

montacargas m inv hoist

montada f L.Am. mounted police

montaje m TÉC assembly; *de película* editing; TEA staging; fig F con F

montante m COM total

montaña f mountain; *~ rusa* roller coaster; **montañero** m, **-a** f mountaineer; **montañismo** m mountaineering; **montañoso** adj mountainous

montaplatos m inv dumb waiter

montar <1a> **1** v/t TÉC assemble; *tienda* put up; *negocio* set up; *película* edit; *caballo* mount; *~ la guardia* mount guard **2** v/i: *~ en bicicleta* ride a bicycle; *~ a caballo* ride a horse

monte m mountain; (*bosque*) woodland

montículo m mound

montón m pile, heap; *ser del ~* fig be average, not stand out; *montones de* F piles of F, loads of F

montura *f de gafas* frame

monumento *m* monument

moño *m* bun

moqueta *f* (wall-to-wall) carpet

mora *f* BOT *de zarza* blackberry; *de morera* mulberry

morada *f* dwelling

morado *adj* purple; *pasarlas -as* F have a rough time

moral 1 *adj* moral **2** *f* (*moralidad*) morals *pl*; (*ánimo*) morale; **moraleja** *f* moral; **moralidad** *f* morality; **moralista** *m/f* moralist

moratón *m* bruise

moratoria *f* moratorium

morbo *m* ⊢ perverted kind of pleasure; **morboso** *adj* perverted

morcilla *f* blood sausage, *Br* black pudding

mordaz *adj* biting; **mordaza** *f* gag; **morder** <2h> *v/t* bite; **mordida** *f Méx* F bribe; **mordisco** *m* bite; **mordisquear** <1a> *v/t* nibble

morena *f* ZO moray eel

moreno *adj pelo, piel* dark; (*bronceado*) tanned

morera *f* BOT white mulberry tree

moretón *m L.Am.* bruise

morfina *f* morphine

morfología *f* morphology

moribundo *adj* dying

morir <3k; *part muerto*> **1** *v/i* die (*de* of); ~ *de hambre* die of hunger, starve to death **2** *v/r* ~*se* die; ~*se de fig* die of; ~*se por fig* be dying for

morisco *adj* Moorish

mormón *m* Mormon

moro 1 *adj* North African **2** *m* North African; *no hay ~s en la costa* F the coast is clear

morocho *adj S.Am. persona* dark

moronga *f C.Am., Méx* blood sausage, *Br* black pudding

morralla *f Méx* small change

morriña *f* homesickness

morro *m* ZO snout; *tener mucho ~* F have a real nerve

morrongo *m* F pussycat F

morsa *f* ZO walrus

mortaja *f* shroud; *L.Am.* cigarette paper

mortal 1 *adj* mortal; *accidente, herida* fatal; *dosis* lethal **2** *m/f* mortal; **mortalidad** *f* mortality; **mortalmente** *adv* fatally

mortero *m tb* MIL mortar

mortífero *adj* lethal; **mortificar** <1g> **1** *v/t* torment **2** *v/r* ~*se fig* distress o.s.; *Méx* (*apenarse*) be embarrassed *o* ashamed

mosaico *m* mosaic

mosca *f* fly; *por si las* ~*s* F just to be on the safe side

moscada *adj: nuez* ~ nutmeg

moscardón *m* hornet

Moscú Moscow

mosquear <1a> **1** *v/t Esp* F rile **2** *v/r* ~*se* F get hot under the collar F; (*sentir recelo*) smell a rat F

mosquitero *m* mosquito net; **mosquito** *m* mosquito

mostaza *f* mustard

mosto *m* grape juice

mostrador *m* counter; *en bar* bar; ~ *de facturación* check-in desk; **mostrar** <1m> **1** *v/t* show **2** *v/r* ~*se*: ~*se contento* seem happy

mota *f* speck; *en diseño* dot

mote *m* nickname; *S.Am.* boiled corn *o Br* maize

motel *m* motel

motín *m* mutiny; *en una cárcel* riot

motivación *f* motivation; **motivar** <1a> *v/t* motivate; **motivo** *m* motive, reason; MÚS, PINT motif; *con* ~ *de* because of

moto *f* motorcycle, motorbike; ~ *acuática o de agua* jet ski

motocicleta *f* motorcycle; **motociclismo** *m* motorcycle racing; **motociclista** *m/f* motorcyclist

motocross *m* motocross

motor *m* engine; *eléctrico* motor; **motora** *f* motorboat; **motorista** *m/f* motorcyclist

motosierra *f* chain saw

motriz *adj* motor

mover <2h> **1** *v/t* move; (*agitar*) shake; (*impulsar, incitar*) drive **2** *v/r* ~*se* move; *¡muévete!* get a move on! F, hurry up!

M

movida f F scene

móvil 1 adj mobile **2** m TELEC cellphone, Br mobile (phone); **movilidad** f mobility; **movilizar** <1f> v/t mobilize; **movimiento** m movement; COM, fig activity

moza f girl; camarera waitress; **mozo 1** adj: **en mis años ~s** in my youth **2** m boy; camarero waiter

mucama f Rpl maid; **mucamo** m Rpl servant

muchacha f girl; **muchachada** f Arg group of youngsters; **muchacho** m boy

muchedumbre f crowd

mucho 1 adj cantidad a lot of, lots of; esp neg much; **no tengo ~ dinero** I don't have much money; **~s** a lot of, lots of, many; esp neg many; **no tengo ~s amigos** I don't have many friends; **tengo ~ frío** I am very cold; **es ~ coche para mí** it's too big a car for me **2** adv a lot; esp neg much; **no me gustó ~** I didn't like it very much; **¿dura/tarda ~?** does it last/take long?; **como ~** at the most; **ni ~ menos** far from it; **por ~ que** however much **3** pron a lot, much; **~s** a lot of people, many people

muda f de ropa change of clothes; **mudanza** f de casa move; **mudarse** <1a> v/r: **~ de casa** move house; **~ de ropa** change (one's clothes)

mudo adj mute; letra silent

mueble m piece of furniture

mueca f de dolor grimace; **hacer ~s** make faces

muela f tooth; ANAT molar; **~ del juicio** wisdom tooth

muelle m TÉC spring; MAR wharf

muérdago m BOT mistletoe

muerde vb → **morder**

muere vb → **morir**

muermo m fig F boredom; **ser un ~** fig F be a drag F

muerte f death; **de mala ~** fig F lousy F, awful F; **muerto 1** part → **morir** **2** adj dead **3** m, **-a** f dead person

muestra f sample; (señal) sign; (exposición) show; **muestrario** m collection of samples

mueve vb → **mover**

mugir <3c> v/i moo

mugre f filth; **mugriento** adj filthy; **mugroso** adj dirty

mujer f woman; (esposa) wife; **mujeriego** m womanizer

mújol m ZO gray o Br grey mullet

mula f mule; Méx trash, Br rubbish

mulato m mulatto

muleta f crutch; TAUR cape

mullido adj soft

mullir <3h> v/t almohada plump up

multa f fine; **multar** <1a> v/t fine

multicine m multiscreen

multicolor adj multicolo(u)red

multilateral adj multilateral

multimedia f/adj multimedia

multimillonario m multimillionaire

multinacional f multinational

múltiple adj multiple; **multiplicación** f multiplication; **multiplicar** <1g> **1** v/t multiply **2** v/r **~se** multiply; **múltiplo** m MAT multiple

multipropiedad f timeshare

multitud f crowd; **~ de** thousands of; **multitudinario** adj mass atr

multiuso adj multipurpose

mundano adj society atr; REL wordly; **mundial 1** adj world atr **2** m: **el ~ de fútbol** the World Cup; **mundo** m world; **el otro ~** the next world; **nada del otro ~** nothing out of the ordinary; **todo el ~** everybody, everyone

munición f ammunition

municipal adj municipal; **municipio** m municipality

muñeca f doll; ANAT wrist; **muñeco** m doll; fig puppet; **~ de nieve** snowman

muñón m MED stump

mural 1 adj wall atr **2** m mural; **muralla** f de ciudad wall

murciélago m ZO bat

murga f: **dar la ~ a alguien** F bug s.o. F

murió vb → **morir**

murmullo m murmur; **murmurar** <1a> v/i hablar murmur; criticar gossip

muro m wall

musa f muse
musaraña f ZO shrew; *pensar en las ~s* F daydream
muscular adj muscular; **músculo** m muscle; **musculoso** adj muscular
museo m museum; *de pintura* art gallery
musgo m BOT moss
música f music; **musical** m/adj musical; **músico** m, **-a** f musician
musitar <1a> v/i mumble

muslo m thigh
mustio adj withered, *fig* down F
musulmán 1 adj Muslim **2** m, **-ana** f Muslim
mutilado m, **-a** f disabled person; **mutilar** <1a> v/t mutilate
mutualidad f benefit society, *Br* friendly society; **mutuo** adj mutual
muy adv very; (*demasiado*) too; *~ valorado* highly valued

N

N abr (= *norte*) N (North(ern))
nabo m **1** adj *Arg* F dumb F **2** m turnip
nácar m mother-of-pearl
nacatamal m *C.Am., Méx* meat, rice and corn in a banana leaf
nacer <2d> v/i be born; *de un huevo* hatch; *de una planta* sprout; *de un río, del sol* rise; (*surgir*) arise (*de* from); **naciente** adj *país, gobierno* newly formed; *sol* rising; **nacimiento** m birth; *de Navidad* crèche, nativity scene
nación f nation; **nacional** adj national; **nacionalidad** f nationality; **nacionalismo** m nationalism; **nacionalización** f COM nationalization; **nacionalizar** <1f> **1** v/t COM nationalize; *persona* naturalize **2** v/r *~se* become naturalized
naco m *Col* purée
nada 1 pron nothing; *no hay ~* there isn't anything; *¡~ de eso!* F you can put that idea out of your head; *~ más* nothing else; *~ menos que* no less than; *lo dices como si ~* you talk about it as if it was nothing; *¡de ~!* you're welcome, not at all; *no es ~* it's nothing **2** adv not at all; *no ha llovido ~* it hasn't rained **3** f nothingness

nadador m, **~a** f swimmer; **nadar** <1a> v/i swim
nadería f trifle
nadie pron nobody, no-one; *no había ~* there was nobody there, there wasn't anyone there
nado: *atravesar a ~* swim across
nafta f *Arg* gas(oline), *Br* petrol; **naftalina** f naphthalene
nailon m nylon
naipe m (playing) card
nalga f buttock
nana f lullaby; *Rpl* F (*abuela*) grandma
napias fpl F schnozzle *sg* F, *Br* hooter *sg* F
naranja 1 f orange; *media ~* F (*pareja*) other half **2** adj orange; **naranjada** f orangeade; **naranjo** m orange tree
narciso m BOT daffodil
narcótico m/adj narcotic; **narcotráfico** m drug trafficking
nariz f nose; *¡narices!* F nonsense!; *estar hasta las narices de algo* F be sick of sth F, be up to here with sth F; *meter las narices en algo* F stick one's nose in sth F
narración f narration; **narrador** m, **~a** f narrator; **narrar** <1a> v/t: *~ algo* tell the story of sth

nasal *adj* nasal

nata *f* cream; **~ montada** whipped cream

natación *f* swimming

natal *adj* native; **ciudad ~** city of one's birth, home town; **natalidad** *f* birthrate

natillas *fpl* custard *sg*

nativo *m*, **-a** *f* native; **nato** *adj* born

natural **1** *adj* natural; **ser ~ de** come from; **es ~** it's only natural **2** *m*: **fruta al ~** fruit in its own juice; **naturaleza** *f* nature; **naturalidad** *f* naturalness; **naturalmente** *adv* naturally; **naturista 1** *adj* nudist, naturist; **medicina** natural **2** *m/f* nudist, naturist

naufragar <1h> *v/i* be shipwrecked; *fig* fail; **naufragio** *m* shipwreck; **náufrago 1** *adj* shipwrecked **2** *m*, **-a** *f* shipwrecked person

náuseas *fpl* nausea *sg*; **nauseabundo** *adj* nauseating

náutico *adj* nautical

navaja *f* knife; **navajazo** *m* knife wound, slash; **navajero** *m*: **le asaltó un ~** he was attacked by a man with a knife

naval *adj* naval; **nave** *f* ship; *de iglesia* nave; **~ espacial** spacecraft; **navegación** *f* navigation; **~ a vela** sailing; **navegador** *m* INFOR browser; **navegante** *m/f* navigator; **navegar** <1h> **1** *v/i* sail; *por el aire, espacio* fly; **~ por la red** *or por Internet* INFOR surf the Net **2** *v/t* sail

Navidad *f* Christmas; **navideño** *adj* Christmas *atr*

navío *m* ship

nazi *m/f* & *adj* Nazi; **nazismo** *m* Nazi(i)sm

N.B. *abr* (= *nótese bien*) NB (= *nota bene*)

neblina *f* mist; **nebuloso** *adj fig* hazy, nebulous

necesario *adj* necessary; **neceser** *m* toilet kit, *Br* toilet bag; **necesidad** *f* need; (*cosa esencial*) necessity; **de primera ~** essential; **en caso de ~** if necessary; **hacer sus -es** F

relieve o.s.; **necesitado** *adj* needy; **necesitar** <1a> *v/t* need

necio *adj* brainless

necrológica *f* obituary

nefasto *adj* harmful

negación *f* negation; **de acusación** denial; **negar** <1h & 1k> **1** *v/t* acusación deny; (*no conceder*) refuse **2** *v/r* **-se** refuse (*a* to); **negativa** *f* refusal; *de acusación* denial; **negativo 1** *adj* negative **2** *m* FOT negative

negligencia *f* JUR negligence

negociable *adj* negotiable; **negociación** *f* negotiation; **negociaciones** talks; **negociador** *m*, **~a** *f* negotiator; **negociante** *m/f* businessman; *mujer* businesswoman; *desp* money-grubber; **negociar** <1b> *v/t* negotiate; **negocio** *m* business; (*trato*) deal

negra *f* black woman; MÚS quarter note, *Br* crotchet; *L.Am.* (*querida*) honey, dear; **negrita** *f* bold; **negro 1** *adj* black; **estar ~** F be furious **2** *m* black man; *L.Am.* (*querido*) honey, dear

nena *f* F little girl, kid F; **nene** *m* F little boy, kid F

nenúfar *m* BOT water lily

neocelandés *m*, **-esa** *f* New Zealander

neón *m* neon

neoyorquino **1** *adj* New York *atr* **2** *m*, **-a** *f* New Yorker

nepotismo *m* nepotism

nervio *m* ANAT nerve; **nerviosismo** *m* nervousness; **nervioso** *adj* nervous; **ponerse ~** get nervous; (*agitado*) get agitated; **poner a alguien ~** get on s.o.'s nerves

neto *adj* COM net

neumático **1** *adj* pneumatic **2** *m* AUTO tire, *Br* tyre

neumonía *f* MED pneumonia

neurocirujano *m*, **-a** *f* brain surgeon

neurólogo *m*, **-a** *f* neurologist

neurosis *f inv* neurosis; **neurótico** *adj* neurotic

neutral *adj* neutral; **neutralidad** *f* neutrality; **neutralizar** <1f> *v/t* neutralize; **neutro** *adj* neutral

nevada *f* snowfall; **nevar** <1k> *v/i* snow; **nevazón** *f* *Arg, Chi* snowstorm; **nevera** *f* refrigerator, fridge; ~ **portátil** cooler; **nevería** *f* *Méx, C.Am.* ice-cream parlo(u)r; **nevero** *m* snowdrift

nexo *m* link; GRAM connective

ni *conj* neither; ~ ... ~ neither ... nor; ~ **siquiera** not even; **no di ~ una** I made a real mess of things

Nicaragua Nicaragua; **nicaragüense** *m/f & adj* Nicaraguan

nicho *m* niche

nicotina *f* nicotine; **bajo en** ~ low in nicotine

nido *m* nest

niebla *f* fog

nieta *f* granddaughter; **nieto** *m* grandson; ~**s** grandchildren

nieva *vb* → **nevar**

nieve *f* snow; *Méx* water ice, sorbet

nihilismo *m* nihilism

nimiedad *f* triviality; **nimio** *adj* trivial

ningún *adj* → **ninguno**

ninguno *adj* no; **no hay ~a razón** there's no reason why, there isn't any reason why

niña *f* girl; *forma de cortesía* young lady; **niñato** *m*, **-a** *f* brat; **niñera** *f* nanny; **niñería** *f*: **una** ~ a childish thing; **niñez** *f* childhood; **niño 1** *adj* young; *desp* childish **2** *m* boy; *forma de cortesía* young man; ~**s** children *pl*; ~ **de pecho** infant

níquel *m* nickel

níspero *m* BOT loquat

nítido *adj* clear; *imagen* sharp

nitrógeno *m* nitrogen; **nitroglicerina** *f* nitroglycerin

nivel *m* level; *(altura)* height; ~ **del mar** sea level; ~ **de vida** standard of living; **nivelar** <1a> *v/t* level

nixtamal *m* *Méx, C.Am.* dough from which corn tortillas are made

n.º *abr* (= **número**) No. (= number)

no *adv* no; *para negar verbo* not; **no entiendo** I don't understand, I do not understand; ~ **te vayas** don't go; ~ **bien** as soon as; ~ **del todo** not

entirely; **ya** ~ not any more; ~ **más** *L.Am.* ; **nomás**; **así** ~ **más** *L.Am.* just like that; **te gusta, ¿~?** you like it, don't you?; **te ha llamado, ¿~?** he called you, didn't he?; **¿a que ~?** I bet you don't / can't etc

nobiliario *adj* noble; **noble** *m/f & adj* noble; **nobleza** *f* nobility

noche *f* night; **de** ~, **por la** ~ at night; **de la** ~ **a la mañana** *fig* overnight; **¡buenas ~s!** *saludo* good evening; *despedida* good night; **Nochebuena** *f* Christmas Eve; **nochecita** *f* *L.Am.* evening; **nochero** *m* *L.Am.* night watchman; **Nochevieja** *f* New Year's Eve

noción *f* notion

nocivo *adj* harmful

noctámbulo *m*, **-a** *f* sleepwalker; **nocturno** *adj* night *atr*; ZO nocturnal; **clase -a** evening class

nogal *m* BOT walnut

nómada 1 *adj* nomadic **2** *m/f* nomad

nomás *adv* *L.Am.* just; only; **llévaselo** ~ just take it away; ~ **llegue, te avisaré** as soon as he arrives, I'll let you know; **siga** ~ just carry on; ~ **lo vio, echó a llorar** as soon as she saw him she started to cry

nombramiento *m* appointment; **nombrar** <1a> *v/t* mention; *para un cargo* appoint; **nombre** *m* name; GRAM noun; ~ **de pila** first name; **no tener** ~ *fig* be inexcusable

nomenclatura *f* nomenclature

nomeolvides *f* *inv* BOT forget-me-not

nómina *f* pay slip; **nominal** *adj* nominal; **nominar** <1a> *v/t* nominate

non *adj* odd

nono *adj* ninth

nopal *m* *L.Am.* BOT prickly pear

nor(d)este *m* northeast

noria *f* **de agua** waterwheel; **en feria** ferris wheel

norma *f* standard; *(regla)* rule, regulation; **normal** *adj* normal; **normalidad** *f* normality; **normalizar** <1f> *v/t* standardize; **normativa** *f* rules *pl*, regulations *pl*

noroeste *m* northwest

norte *m* north

Norteamérica North America; **norteamericano 1** *adj* North American **2** *m*, **-a** *f* North American

norteño **1** *adj* northern **2** *m*, **-a** *f* northerner

Noruega Norway; **noruego 1** *adj* Norwegian **2** *m*, **-a** *f* Norwegian

nos *pron complemento directo* us; *complemento indirecto* (to) us; *reflexivo* ourselves; ~ **dio el dinero** he gave us the money, he gave the money to us

nosotros, nosotras *pron* we; *complemento* us; **ven con** ~ come with us; **somos** ~ it's us

nostalgia *f* nostalgia; *por la patria* homesickness; **nostálgico** *adj* nostalgic

nota *f tb* MÚS note; EDU grade, mark; ~ **a pie de página** footnote; **tomar** ~ **de algo** make a note of sth; **notable** *adj* remarkable, notable; **notar** <1a> *v/t* notice; (*sentir*) feel; **hacer** ~ **algo a alguien** point sth out to s.o.; **se nota que** you can tell that; **hacerse** ~ draw attention to o.s.

notaría *f* notary's office; **notario** *m*, **-a** *f* notary

noticia *f* piece of news; **en noticiario** news story, item of news; ~**s** *pl* news *sg*; **noticiario** *m* RAD, TV news *sg*

notificación *f* notification; **notificar** <1g> *v/t* notify

notorio *adj* famous, well-known

novatada *f* practical joke

novato *m*, **-a** *f* beginner, rookie F

novecientos *adj* nine hundred

novedad *f* novelty; *cosa* new thing; (*noticia*) piece of news; *acontecimiento* new development; **llegar sin** ~ arrive safely; **novedoso** *adj* novel, new; *invento* innovative; **novela** *f* novel; ~ **negra** crime novel; ~ **rosa** romantic novel; **novelista** *m/f* novelist

noveno *adj* ninth; **noventa** *adj* ninety

novia *f* girlfriend; *el día de la boda* bride; **noviazgo** *m* engagement

noviembre *m* November

novilla *f vaca* heifer; **novillada** *f bullfight featuring novice bulls*; **novillero** *m* novice (bullfighter); **novillo** *m* ZO young bull; **hacer** ~**s** F play hooky F, play truant

novio *m* boyfriend; *el día de la boda* bridegroom; **los** ~**s** the bride and groom; (*recién casados*) the newlyweds

nube *f* cloud; **estar en las** ~**s** *fig* be miles away; **estar por las** ~**s** F be incredibly expensive; **nublado 1** *adj* cloudy, overcast **2** *m* storm cloud; **nublarse** <1a> *v/r* cloud over; **nuboso** *adj* cloudy

nuca *f* nape of the neck

nuclear *adj* nuclear; **núcleo** *m* nucleus; *de problema* heart

nudillo *m* knuckle

nudista *m/f* nudist; **playa** ~ nudist beach

nudo *m* knot; **se me hace un** ~ **en la garganta** F I get a lump in my throat

nuera *f* daughter-in-law

nuestro **1** *adj pos* our **2** *pron* ours

nueva *f lit* piece of news; **nuevamente** *adv* again

Nueva York New York

Nueva Zelanda New Zealand

nueve *adj* nine

nuevo *adj* new; (*otro*) another; **de** ~ again

nuez *f* BOT walnut; ANAT Adam's apple

nulidad *f* nullity; *fig* F dead loss F; **nulo** *adj* null and void; F *persona* hopeless; (*inexistente*) nonexistent, zero

núm. *abr* (= **número**) No. (= number)

numerar <1a> *v/t* number; **numérico** *adj* numerical; **teclado** ~ numeric keypad, number pad; **número** *m* number; *de publicación* issue; *de zapato* size; ~ **complementario** *en lotería* bonus number; ~ **secreto** PIN (number); **en** ~**s rojos** *fig* in the red; **montar un** ~ F make a scene; **numeroso** *adj* numerous

numismática *f* numismatics

nunca *adv* never; ~ **jamás** *or* **más**

never again; **más que** ~ more than ever

nupcial adj wedding atr

nutria f ZO otter

nutrición f nutrition; **nutrido** adj fig

nutriente m nutrient; **nutrir** <3a> v/t nourish, fig. esperanzas cherish; **nutritivo** adj nutritious, nourishing

nylon m nylon

Ñ

ñandú m ZO rhea

ñandutí m Parag type of lace

ñapa f S.Am. extra, bonus; **le di dos de ~** I threw in an extra two

ñato adj Rpl snub-nosed

ñeque m S.Am. strength; **de ~** F gutsy

F; **tener mucho ~** F have a lot of guts F

ñoñería f feebleness F, wimpish behavio(u)r F; **ñoño 1** adj feeble F, wimpish F **2** m, **-a** f drip F, wimp F

ñu m ZO gnu

O

O abr (= **oeste**) W (= West(ern))

o conj or; **~ ... ~** either ... or; **~ sea** in other words

oasis m inv oasis

obcecación f obstinacy; **obcecarse** <1g> v/r stubbornly insist

obedecer <2d> **1** v/t obey **2** v/i obey; de una máquina respond; **~ a** fig be due to; **obediencia** f obedience; **obediente** adj obedient

obelisco m obelisk

obesidad f obesity; **obeso** adj obese

obispo m bishop

objeción f objection; **~ de conciencia** conscientious objection; **objetar** <1a> **1** v/t object; **tener algo que ~** have any objection **2** v/i become a conscientious objector

objetividad f objectivity; **objetivo 1** adj objective **2** m objective; MIL target; FOT lens

objeto m object; **con ~ de** with the

aim of

objetor m, **~a** f objector; **~ de conciencia** conscientious objector

oblícuo adj oblique, slanted

obligación f obligation, duty; COM bond; **obligar** <1h> v/t: **~ a alguien** oblige o force s.o. (**a** to); de una ley apply to s.o.; **obligatorio** adj obligatory, compulsory

obnubilar <1a> v/t cloud

oboe m MÚS oboe

obra f work; **~s** pl de construcción building work sg; en la vía pública road works; **~ de arte** work of art; **~ maestra** masterpiece; **~ de teatro** play; **obraje** m Méx butcher's; **obrar** <1a> v/i act; **obrero 1** adj working **2** m, **-a** f worker

obsceno adj obscene

obsequiar <1b> v/t: **~ a alguien con algo** present s.o. with sth; **obsequio** m gift; **obsequioso** adj attentive

observación f observation; JUR observance; **observador 1** adj observant **2** m, **~a** f observer; **observar** <1a> v/t observe; (advertir) notice, observe; (comentar) remark, observe; **observatorio** m observatory

obsesión f obsession; **obsesionar** <1a> **1** v/t obsess **2** v/r **~se** become obsessed (con with); **obsesivo** adj obsessive

obsoleto adj obsolete

obstaculizar <1f> v/t hinder, hamper; **obstáculo** m obstacle

obstante: **no ~** nevertheless

obstetra m/f obstetrician; **obstetricia** f obstetrics

obstinación f obstinacy; **obstinado** adj obstinate; **obstinarse** <1a> v/r insist (en on)

obstrucción f obstruction, blockage; **obstruir** <3g> v/t obstruct, block

obtener <2l; part obtuvo> v/t get, obtain fml

obturador m shutter

obtuvo vb → **obtener**

obvio adj obvious

oca f goose

ocasión f occasion; (oportunidad) chance, opportunity; **con ~ de** on the occasion of; **de ~** COM cut-price, bargain atr; **de segunda mano** second-hand, used; **ocasional** adj occasional; **ocasionar** <1a> v/t cause

ocaso m del sol setting; de un imperio, un poder decline

occidental 1 adj western **2** m/f Westerner; **occidente** m west

OCDE abr (= **Organización de Cooperación y Desarrollo Económico**) OECD (= Organization for Economic Cooperation and Development)

océano m ocean; **oceanógrafo** m, **-a** f oceanographer

ocelote m ZO ocelot

ochenta adj eighty; **ocho** adj eight; **ochocientos** adj eight hundred

ocio m leisure time, free time; desp idleness; **ociosear** <1a> v/i S.Am. laze around; **ocioso** adj idle

ocre m/adj ocher, Br ochre

oct.e abr (= **octubre**) Oct. (= October)

octavilla f leaflet; **octavo 1** m eighth **2** m eighth; DEP **~s de final** last 16

octógono m octagon

octubre m October

ocular adj eye atr; **oculista** m/f ophthalmologist

ocultación f concealment; **ocultar** <1a> v/t hide, conceal; **ocultismo** m occult; **oculto** adj hidden; (sobrenatural) occult

ocupación f tb MIL occupation; (actividad) activity; **ocupado** adj busy; asiento taken; **ocupante** m/f occupant; **ocupar** <1a> **1** v/t espacio take up, occupy; (habitar) live in, occupy; obreros employ; periodo de tiempo spend, occupy; MIL occupy **2** v/r **~se**: **~se de** deal with; (cuidar de) look after

ocurrencia f occurrence; (chiste) quip, funny remark; **ocurrir** <3a> v/i happen, occur; **se me ocurrió** it occurred to me, it struck me

odiar <1b> v/t hate; **odio** m hatred, hate; **odioso** adj odious, hateful

odisea f fig odyssey

odontólogo m odontologist

OEA abr (= **Organización de los Estados Americanos**) OAS (= Organization of American States)

oeste m west

ofender <2a> **1** v/t offend **2** v/r **~se** take offense (por at); **ofensa** f insult; **ofensiva** f offensive; **ofensivo** adj offensive

oferta f offer; **~ pública de adquisición** takeover bid

oficial 1 adj official **2** m/f MIL officer; **oficialista** adj L.Am. pro-government; **oficina** f office; **~ de correos** post office; **~ de empleo** employment office; **~ de turismo** tourist office; **oficinista** m/f office worker; **oficio** m trabajo trade; **oficioso** adj unofficial

ofimática f INFOR office automation

ofrecer <2d> **1** v/t offer **2** v/r **~se**

volunteer, offer one's services (*de as*); (*presentarse*) appear; *¿qué se le ofrece?* what can I do for you?'; **ofrecimiento** *m* offer; **ofrenda** *f* offering

oftalmólogo *m*, **-a** *f* ophthalmologist

ofuscar <1g> *v/t tb fig* blind

ogro *m tb fig* ogre

oída *f*: *conocer algo de ~s* have heard of sth; **oído** *m* hearing; *hacer ~s sordos* turn a deaf ear; *ser todo ~s fig* be all ears

oigo *vb* → **oír**

oír <3q> *v/t tb* JUR hear; (*escuchar*) listen to; *¡oye!* listen!, hey! F; *como quien oye llover, salió sin él* F he turned a deaf ear and went off without it

OIT *abr* (= *Organización Internacional de Trabajo*) ILO (= International Labor Organization)

ojal *m* buttonhole

ojalá *int*: *¡~!* let's hope so; *¡~ venga!* I hope he comes; *¡~ tuvieras razón!* I only hope you're right

ojeada *f* glance; *echar una ~ a alguien* glance at s.o.; **ojeras** *fpl* bags under the eyes; **ojo** *m* ANAT eye; *¡~!* F watch out!, mind! F; *~ de la cerradura* keyhole; *a ~* roughly; *andar con ~* F keep one's eyes open F; *costar un ~ de la cara* F cost an arm and a leg F; *no pegar ~* F not sleep a wink F

ojota *f C.Am.*, *Méx* sandal

okupa *m/f Esp* F squatter

ola *f* wave; *~ de calor* heat wave; *~ de frío* cold spell; **oleada** *f fig* wave, flood; **oleaje** *m* swell

óleo *m* oil; **oleoducto** *m* (oil) pipeline

oler <2i> **1** *v/i* smell (*a* of) **2** *v/t* smell **3** *v/r*: *me huelo algo fig* there's something fishy going on, I smell a rat; **olfatear** <1a> *v/t* sniff; **olfato** *m* sense of smell; *fig* nose

olimpíada, **olimpiada** *f* Olympics *pl*; **olímpico** *adj* Olympic

olisquear <1a> *v/t* sniff

oliva *f* BOT olive; **olivo** *m* olive tree

olla *f* pot; *~ exprés or a presión* pressure cooker

olmo *m* BOT elm

olor *m* smell; *agradable* scent; *~ corporal* body odo(u)r, BO; **oloroso** *adj* scented

OLP *abr* (= *Organización para la Liberación de Palestina*) PLO (= Palestine Liberation Organization)

olvidadizo *adj* forgetful; **olvidar** <1a> **1** *v/t* forget **2** *v/r* ~**se**: *~se de algo* forget sth; **olvido** *m* oblivion

ombligo *m* ANAT navel

OMC *abr* (= *Organización Mundial de Comercio*) WTO (= World Trade Organization)

omisión *f* omission; **omiso** *adj*: *hacer caso ~ de algo* ignore sth; **omitir** <3a> *v/t* omit, leave out

omnipotente *adj* omnipotent

omóplato, **omoplato** *m* ANAT shoulder blade

OMS *abr* (= *Organización Mundial de la Salud*) WHO (= World Health Organization)

once *adj* eleven

oncología *f* MED oncology

onda *f* wave; *estar en la ~* F be with it F; *¿qué ~? Méx* F what's happening? F; **ondulado** *adj* wavy; *cartón corrugado* corrugated

ONG *abr* (= *Organización no Gubernamental*) NGO (= non-governmental organization)

onomatopeya *f* onomatopœia

ONU *abr* (= *Organización de las Naciones Unidas*) UN (= United Nations)

onza *f* ounce

OPA *abr* (= *oferta pública de adquisición*) takeover bid

opaco *adj* opaque

opción *f* option, choice; (*posibilidad*) chance; **opcional** *adj* optional

OPEP *abr* (= *Organización de Países Exportadores de Petróleo*) OPEC (= Organization of Petroleum Exporting Countries)

ópera *f* MÚS opera; *~ prima* first work

operación *f* operation; **operador** *m*,

O

~a f TELEC, INFOR operator; **~ turístico** tour operator; **operar** <1a> **1** v/t MED operate on; *cambio* bring about **2** v/i operate; COM do business (**con** with) **3** v/r **~se** MED have an operation (**de** on); *de un cambio* occur; **operario** m, **-a** f operator, operative; **operativo 1** adj operational; *sistema* ~ INFOR operating system **2** m L.Am. operation

opereta f MÚS operetta

opinar <1a> **1** v/t think (**de** about) **2** v/i express an opinion; **opinión** f opinion; *la* ~ *pública* public opinion; *en mi* ~ in my opinion

opio m opium

opíparo adj sumptuous

oponente m/f opponent; **oponer** <2r; part **opuesto**> **1** v/t *resistencia* put up (**a** to), offer (**a** to); *razón, argumento* put forward (**a** against) **2** v/r **~se** be opposed (**a** to); *(manifestar oposición)* object (**a** to)

oporto m port

oportunidad f opportunity; **oportunista 1** adj opportunistic **2** m/f opportunist; **oportuno** adj timely; *momento* opportune; *respuesta, medida* suitable, appropriate

oposición f POL opposition; **oposiciones** official entrance exams

opresión f oppression; **opresor 1** adj oppressive **2** m, **-a** f oppressor; **oprimir** <3a> v/t oppress; *botón* press; *de zapatos* be too tight for

optar <1a> v/i *(elegir)* opt (**por** for); ~ **a** be in the running for; ~ **por hacer algo** opt to do sth; **optativo** adj optional

óptica f optician's; FÍS optics; *fig* point of view; **óptico 1** adj optical **2** m, **-a** f optician

optimismo m optimism; **optimista 1** adj optimistic **2** m/f optimist

optimizar <1f> v/t optimize; **óptimo** adj ideal

opuesto 1 part → **oponer 2** adj opposite; *opinión* contrary

opulencia f opulence

opuso vb → **oponer**

oquedad f cavity

oración f REL prayer; GRAM sentence

orador m, **-a** f orator; **oral** adj oral; *prueba de inglés* ~ English oral (exam)

orangután m ZO orangutan

orar <1a> v/i pray (**por** for); **oratoria** f oratory

órbita f orbit; *colocar or poner en* ~ put into orbit

orca m ZO killer whale

órdago m: **de** ~ F terrific F

orden 1 m order; ~ **del día** agenda; **por** ~ **alfabético** in alphabetical order; **poner en** ~ tidy up **2** f *(mandamiento)* order; *¡a la* ~! yes, sir; **por** ~ **de** by order of, on the orders of; **ordenado** adj tidy; **ordenador** m INFOR computer; ~ **de escritorio** desktop (computer); ~ **personal** personal computer; ~ **portátil** portable (computer), laptop; *asistido por* ~ computer aided; **ordenanza 1** f by-law **2** m office junior, gofer F; MIL orderly; **ordenar** <1a> v/t *habitación* tidy up; *alfabéticamente* arrange; *(mandar)* order

ordeñar <1a> v/t milk

ordinario adj ordinary; *desp* vulgar; **de** ~ usually, ordinarily

orégano m BOT oregano

oreja f ear; *aguzar las* ~**s** L.Am. prick one's ears up; *ver las* ~**s al lobo** fig F wake up to the danger; **orejeras** fpl earmuffs

orfanato m orphanage

orfebrería f goldsmith / silversmith work

orfelinato m orphanage

orgánico adj organic

organigrama m flow chart; *de empresa* organization chart, tree diagram

organillo m barrel organ

organismo m organism; POL agency, organization; ~ **modificado genéticamente** genetically modified organism

organización f organization; **Or-**

ganización de Cooperación y Desarrollo Económico Organization for Economic Cooperation and Development; *Organización de las Naciones Unidas* United Nations; *Organización de los Estados Americanos* Organization of American States; *Organización del Tratado del Atlántico Norte* North Atlantic Treaty Organization; *Organización de Países Exportadores de Petróleo* Organization of Petroleum Exporting Countries; *Organización Internacional de Trabajo* International Labor Organization; *Organización Mundial de Comercio* World Trade Organization; *Organización Mundial de la Salud* World Health Organization; *Organización para la Liberación de Palestina* Palestine Liberation Organization; **organizador 1** *adj* organizing **2** *m*, ~a *f* organizer; ~ *personal* personal organizer; **organizar** <1f> **1** *v/t* organize **2** *v/r* ~se *de persona* organize one's time

órgano *m* MÚS, ANAT, *fig* organ

orgasmo *m* orgasm

orgía *f* orgy

orgullo *m* pride; **orgulloso** *adj* proud (*de* of)

orientación *f* orientation; (*ayuda*) guidance; *sentido de la* ~ sense of direction; **orientador** *m*, ~a *f* counsel(l)or

oriental 1 *adj* oriental, eastern **2** *m/f* Oriental

orientar <1a> **1** *v/t* (*aconsejar*) advise; ~ *algo hacia algo* turn sth toward sth **2** *v/r* ~se get one's bearings; *de una planta* turn (*hacia* toward)

oriente *m* east; *Oriente* Orient; *Oriente Medio* Middle East; *Extremo or Lejano Oriente* Far East

orificio *m* hole; *en cuerpo* orifice

origen *m* origin; *dar* ~ *a* give rise to; **original** *m/adj* original; **originalidad** *f* originality; **originar** <1a> **1** *v/t* give rise to **2** *v/r* ~se

originate; *de un incendio* start; **originario** *adj* original; (*nativo*) native (*de* of)

orilla *f* shore; *de un río* bank

orina *f* urine; **orinal** *m* urinal; **orinar** <1a> *v/i* urinate

oriundo *adj* native (*de* to)

ornamental *adj* ornamental

ornitología *f* ornithology; **ornitólogo** *m*, **-a** *f* ornithologist

oro *m* gold; *guardar como* ~ *en paño con mucho cariño* treasure sth; *con mucho cuidado* guard sth with one's life; *prometer el* ~ *y el moro* promise the earth; *~s* (*en naipes*) suit in Spanish deck of cards

orondo *adj* fat; *fig* smug

oropéndola *f* ZO golden oriole

orquesta *f* orchestra; **orquestar** <1a> *v/t fig* orchestrate

orquídea *f* BOT orchid

ortiga *f* BOT nettle

ortodoncia *f* MED orthodontics

ortodoxo *adj* orthodox

ortografía *f* spelling

ortopédico 1 *adj* orthop(a)edic **2** *m*, **-a** *f* orthop(a)edist

oruga *f* ZO caterpillar; TÉC (*caterpillar*) track

orujo *m* liquor made from the remains of grapes

orzuelo *m* MED stye

os *pron complemento directo* you; *complemento indirecto* (to) you; *reflexivo* yourselves; ~ *lo devolveré* I'll give you it back, I'll give it back to you

osa *f* AST: *Osa Mayor* Great Bear; *Osa Menor* Little Bear

osadía *f* daring; (*descaro*) audacity

osamenta *f* bones *pl*

osar <1a> *v/i* dare

oscilación *f* oscillation; *de precios* fluctuation; **oscilar** <1a> *v/i* oscillate; *de precios* fluctuate

oscurecer <2d> **1** *v/t* darken; *logro, triunfo* overshadow **2** *v/i* get dark **3** *v/r* ~se darken; **oscuridad** *f* darkness; **oscuro** *adj* dark; *fig* obscure; *a -as* in the dark

óseo *adj* bone *atr*

osezno *m* cub

osito *m*: **~ de peluche** teddy bear; **oso** *m* bear; **~ hormiguero** anteater; **~ panda** panda; **~ polar** polar bear

ostensible *adj* obvious

ostentación *f* ostentation; **hacer ~ de** flaunt; **ostentar** <1a> *v/t* flaunt; *cargo* hold; **ostentoso** *adj* ostentatious

osteoporosis *f* MED osteoporosis

ostra *f* ZO oyster; **¡~s!** F hell! F

ostrero *m* ZO oyster-catcher

OTAN *abr* (= **Organización del Tratado del Atlántico Norte**) NATO (= North Atlantic Treaty Organization)

otitis *f* MED earache

otoño *m* fall, *Br* autumn

otorgar <1h> *v/t* award; *favor* grant

otorrino F, **otorrinolaringólogo** *m* MED ear, nose and throat *o* ENT specialist

otro 1 *adj* (*diferente*) another; *con el, la* other; **~s** other; **~s dos libros** another two books **2** *pron* (*adicional*) another (one); (*persona distinta*) someone *o* somebody else; (*cosa distinta*) another one, a different one; **~s** others; *entre ~s* among others **3** *siguiente*: **¡hasta -a!** see you soon **4** *pron recíproco*: **amar el uno a ~** love one another

ovación *f* ovation; **ovacionar** <1a> *v/t* cheer, give an ovation to

ovalado *adj* oval; **óvalo** *m* oval

ovario *m* ANAT ovary

oveja *f* sheep; **~ negra** *fig* black sheep

overol *m* Méx overalls *pl*, *Br* dungarees *pl*

ovillo *m* ball; **hacerse un ~** *fig* curl up (into a ball)

ovino 1 *adj* sheep *atr* **2** *m* sheep; **~s** sheep *pl*

OVNI *abr* (= **objeto volante no identificado**) UFO (= unidentified flying object)

ovulación *f* ovulation; **óvulo** *m* egg

oxidado *adj* rusty; **oxidar** <1a> **1** *v/t* rust **2** *v/r* **~se** rust, go rusty; **óxido** *m* QUÍM oxide; (*herrumbre*) rust; **oxigenarse** <1a> *v/r* *fig* get some fresh air; **oxígeno** *m* oxygen

oye *vb* → **oír**

oyendo *vb* → **oír**

oyente *m/f* listener

oyó *vb* → **oír**

ozono *m* ozone; **capa de ~** ozone layer

P

pabellón *m* pavilion; *edificio* block; MÚS bell; MAR flag

pachanga *f*: **ir de ~** Méx, W.I., C.Am. F go on a spree F

pachocha L.Am., **pachorra** *f* F slowness

pachucho *adj* MED F poorly

paciencia *f* patience; **paciente** *m/f* & *adj* patient

pacificador *m*, **~a** *f* peace-maker; **pacificar** <1g> *v/t* pacify; **pacífico 1** *adj* peaceful; *persona* peaceable; *el océano Pacífico* the Pacific Ocean **2** *m*: *el Pacífico* the Pacific; **pacifista 1** *adj* pacifist *atr* **2** *m/f* pacifist

paco *m*, **-a** *f* L.Am. F (*policía*) cop F

pacotilla *f*: **de ~** third-rate, lousy F; **pacotillero** *m*, **-a** *f* L.Am. street vendor

pactar <1a> **1** *v/t* agree; **~ un acuerdo** reach (an) agreement **2** *v/i* reach (an) agreement; **pacto** *m* agreement, pact

padecer <2d> **1** v/t suffer **2** v/i suffer; **~ de** have trouble with

padrastro m step-father; **padre** m father; REL Father; **de ~ y muy señor mío** terrible; **~s** parents; **¡qué ~!** *Méx* F brilliant!; **padrenuestro** m Lord's Prayer; **padrillo** m *Rpl* stallion; **padrino** m *en bautizo* godfather; (*en boda*) man who gives away the bride

padrón m register of local inhabitants

paella f GASTR paella

pág. *abr* (= **página**) p. (= page)

paga f pay; *de niño* allowance, *Br* pocket money; **pagado** adj paid

pagano adj pagan

pagar <1h> **1** v/t pay; *compra, gastos, crimen* pay for; *favor* repay; **¡me las pagarás!** you'll pay for this! **2** v/i pay; **~ a escote** F go Dutch F; **pagaré** m IOU

página f page; **~ web** web page; **~s amarillas** yellow pages

pago m payment; *Rpl* (*quinta*) piece of land; **~ al contado** or **en efectivo** payment in cash; **en ~ de** in payment for; **por estos ~s** F in this neck of the woods F

país m country; **~ en vías de desarrollo** developing country; **los Países Bajos** the Netherlands; **paisaje** m landscape; **paisano** m: **de ~** MIL in civilian clothes; *policía* in plain clothes

paja f straw; **hacerse una ~** V jerk off V; **pajar** m hayloft

pajarería f pet shop; **pajarita** f corbata bow tie; *de papel* paper bird; **pájaro** m bird; *fig* ugly customer F, nasty piece of work F; **~ carpintero** woodpecker; **matar dos ~s de un tiro** kill two birds with one stone

Pakistán Pakistan; **pakistaní** m/f & adj Pakistani

pala f spade; *raqueta* paddle; *para servir* slice; *para recoger* dustpan

palabra f tb fig word; **~ de honor** word of hono(u)r; **bajo ~** on parole; **en una ~** in a word; **tomar la ~**

speak; **palabrota** f swearword

palacete m small palace; **palaciego** adj palace atr; **palacio** m palace; **~ de deportes** sports center (*Br* centre); **~ de justicia** law courts

paladar m palate

palanca f lever; **~ de cambios** AUTO gearshift, *Br* gear lever; **tener ~** *Méx* fig F have pull F o clout F

palangana f plastic bowl for washing dishes, *Br* washing-up bowl

palanganear <1a> v/i *S.Am.* show off

palanqueta f crowbar

palco m TEA box

palenque m *L.Am.* cockpit (*in cock fighting*)

Palestina Palestine; **palestino 1** adj Palestinian **2** m, **-a** f Palestinian

palestra f arena; **salir** or **saltar a la ~** fig hit the headlines

paleta f PINT palette; TÉC trowel; **paletilla** f GASTR shoulder

paleto F **1** adj hick atr F, provincial **2** m, **-a** f hick F, *Br* yokel F

paliar <1b> v/t alleviate; *dolor* relieve; **paliativo** m/adj palliative

palidecer <2d> v/i *de persona* turn pale; **palidez** f paleness; **pálido** adj pale

palillo m *para dientes* toothpick; *para comer* chopstick

palique m: **estar de ~** F have a chat

paliza 1 f beating; (*derrota*) thrashing F, drubbing F; (*pesadez*) drag F **2** m/f F drag F

palma f palm; **dar ~s** clap (one's hands); **palmada** f pat; (*manotazo*) slap

palmar <1a> v/t: **~la** P kick the bucket F

palmera f BOT palm tree; (*dulce*) heart-shaped pastry; **palmito** m BOT palmetto; GASTR palm heart; *fig* F attractiveness

palmo m hand's breadth; **~ a ~** inch by inch

palo m *de madera etc* stick; MAR mast; *de portería* post, upright; **~ de golf** golf club; **~ mayor** MAR mainmast; **a medio ~** *L.Am.* F half-drunk; **a ~ seco** whisky straight up; **ser un ~**

P

L.Am. F be fantastic; *de tal ~ tal astilla* a chip off the old block F

paloma *f* pigeon; *blanca* dove; *~ mensajera* carrier pigeon; **palomar** *m* pigeon loft

palometa *f* ZO *pez* pompano

palomilla *f C.Am.*, *Méx* F gang

palomita *f Méx* checkmark, *Br* tick; *~s pl de maíz* popcorn *sg*

palpable *adj fig* palpable; **palpar** <1a> *v/t con las manos* feel, touch; *fig* feel

palpitación *f* palpitation; **palpitante** *adj corazón* pounding; *cuestión* burning; **palpitar** <1a> *v/i del corazón* pound; *Rpl fig* have a hunch F, have a feeling

palta *f S.Am.* BOT avocado

palto *m S.Am.* jacket

paludismo *m* MED malaria

palurdo 1 *adj* F hick *atr* F, provincial **2** *m*, *-a f* F hick F, *Br* yokel F

pamela *f* picture hat

pampa *f* GEOG pampa, prairie; *a la ~ Rpl* in the open

pamplinas *fpl* nonsense *sg*

pan *m* bread; *un ~* a loaf; *~ francés L.Am.* French bread; *~ integral* wholemeal bread; *~ de molde* sliced bread; *~ de barra* French bread; *~ rallado* breadcrumbs *pl*; *~ tostado* toast; *ser ~ comido* F be easy as pie F

pana *f* corduroy

panacea *f* panacea

panadería *f* baker's shop; **panadero** *m*, *-a f* baker

panal *m* honeycomb

Panamá Panama; *el Canal de ~* the Panama Canal; *Ciudad de ~* Panama city; **panameño 1** *adj* Panamanian **2** *m*, *-a f* Panamanian

pancarta *f* placard

panceta *f* belly pork

páncreas *m inv* ANAT

panda *m* ZO panda

pandereta *f* tambourine

pandilla *f* group; *de delincuentes* gang

panecillo *m* (bread) roll

panel *m tb grupo de personas* panel; *~ solar* solar panel

panela *f L.Am.* brown sugar loaf

panera *f* bread basket

panfleto *m* pamphlet

pánico *m* panic; *sembrar el ~* spread panic

panocha, panoja *f* ear

panoli *adj* dopey F

panorama *m* panorama; **panorámico** *adj*: *vista -a* panoramic view

panqueque *m L.Am.* pancake

pantalla *f* TV, INFOR screen; *de lámpara* shade; *pequeña ~ fig* small screen

pantalón *m*, **pantalones** *mpl* pants *pl*, *Br* trousers *pl*; *llevar los pantalones fig* F wear the pants (*Br* trousers) F

pantano *m* reservoir

panteón *m* pantheon

pantera *f* ZO panther

pantomima *f* pantomime

pantorrilla *f* ANAT calf

pantufla *f* slipper

panty *m* pantyhose *pl*, *Br* tights *pl*

panza *f de persona* belly

pañal *m* diaper, *Br* nappy

paño *m* cloth; *~ de cocina* dishtowel; **pañuelo** *m* handkerchief; *el mundo es un ~ fig* F it's a small world

papa 1 *m* Pope **2** *f L.Am.* potato

papá *m* F pop F, dad F; *~s L.Am.* parents; *Papá Noel* Santa Claus

papada *f* double chin

papagayo *m* ZO parrot

papal 1 *adj* papal **2** *m L.Am.* potato field

papalote *m Méx* kite

papanatas *m/f inv* F dope F, dimwit F

paparruchas *fpl* F baloney *sg* F

papaya *f* BOT papaya

papel *m* paper; *trozo* piece of paper; TEA, *fig* role; *~ de aluminio* foil; *~ de envolver* wrapping paper; *~ de regalo* giftwrap; *~ higiénico* toilet paper *o* tissue; *~ reciclado* recycled paper; *perder los ~es* lose control; *ser ~ mojado fig* not be worth the paper it's written on; **papelada** *f L.Am.* farce; **papeleo** *m* paperwork; **papelera** *f* wastepaper basket; **papelería** *f* stationer's

195 **parecer**

shop; **papelerío** *m L.Am.* F muddle, mess; **papeleta** *f de rifa* raffle ticket; *fig* chore; **~ de voto** ballot paper

paperas *fpl* MED mumps

papilla *f para bebés* baby food; *para enfermos* puree; *hacer* **~ a alguien** F beat s.o. to a pulp F

papista *adj*: **ser más ~ que el papa** hold extreme views

paquete *m* package, parcel; *de cigarrillos* packet; F *en moto* (pillion) passenger

Paquistán Pakistan; **paquistaní** *m/f & adj* Pakistani

par 1 *f* par; *es bella a la* **~ que inteligente** she is beautiful as well as intelligent, she is both beautiful and intelligent **2** *m* pair; *abierto de* **~ en ~** wide open; *un* **~ de** a pair of

para *prp* for ◊ *dirección* toward(s); *ir* **~** head for; *va* **~ directora** she's going to end up as manager ◊ *tiempo* for; *listo* **~ mañana** ready for tomorrow; **~ siempre** forever; *diez* **~ las ocho** *L.Am.* ten of eight, ten to eight ◊ *finalidad*: *lo hace* **~ ayudarte** he does it (in order) to help you; **~ que** so that; *¿***~ qué te marchas?** what are you leaving for?; **~ mí** for me; *lo heredó todo* **~ morir a los 30** he inherited it all, only to die at 30

parabólica *f* satellite dish

parabrisas *m inv* AUTO windshield, *Br* windscreen; **paracaídas** *m inv* parachute; **paracaidista** *m/f* parachutist; MIL paratrooper; **parachoques** *m inv* AUTO fender, *Br* bumper

parada *f* stop; **~ de autobús** bus stop; **~ de taxis** taxi rank

paradero *m* whereabouts *sg*; *L.Am.* → **parada**

parado 1 *adj* unemployed; *L.Am.* (*de pie*) standing (up); *salir bien / mal* come off well / badly **2** *m*, **-a** *f* unemployed person

paradoja *f* paradox; **paradójico** *adj* paradoxical

parador *m Esp* parador (*state-run*

luxury hotel)

parafernalia *f* F paraphernalia

parafina *f* kerosene, *Br* paraffin

paraguas *m inv* umbrella

Paraguay Paraguay; **paraguayo 1** *adj* Paraguayan **2** *m*, **-a** *f* Paraguayan

paraíso *m* paradise; **~ fiscal** tax haven

paralelismo *m* parallel; **paralelo** *m/adj* parallel

parálisis *f tb fig* paralysis; **paralítico 1** *adj* paralytic **2** *m*, **-a** *f* person who is paralyzed; **paralización** *f tb fig* paralysis; **paralizar** <1f> *v/t* MED paralyze; *actividad* bring to a halt; *país, economía* paralyze, bring to a standstill

parámetro *m* parameter

paramilitar *adj* paramilitary

parangón *m*: *sin* **~** incomparable

paranoia *f* paranoia; **paranoico 1** *adj* MED paranoid **2** *m*, **-a** *f* MED person suffering from paranoia

paranormal *adj* paranormal

parapente *m* hang glider; *actividad* hang gliding

parapeto *m* parapet

parapléjico 1 *adj* MED paraplegic **2** *m*, **-a** *f* paraplegic

parar <1a> **1** *v/t* stop; *L.Am.* (*poner de pie*) stand up **2** *v/i* stop; *en alojamiento* stay; **~ de llover** stop raining; *ir a* **~** end up **3** *v/r* **~se** stop; *L.Am.* (*ponerse de pie*) stand up

pararrayos *m inv* lightning rod

parásito *m* parasite

parcela *f* lot, *Br* plot

parchar <1a> *v/t L.Am.* patch; (*arreglar*) repair; **parche** *m* patch

parcial *adj* (*partidario*) bias(s)ed

pardo 1 *adj color* dun; *L.Am. desp* half-breed *desp*, *Br tb* half-caste *desp* **2** *m color* dun; *L.Am. desp* half-breed *desp*

parecer 1 *m* opinion, view; *al* **~** apparently **que** <2d> *v/i* seem, look; *me* **parece que** I think (that), it seems to me that; *me parece bien* it seems fine to me; *¿qué te parece?* what do you think? **3** *v/r* **~se** resemble

P

each other; **~se a alguien** resemble s.o.; **parecido 1** adj similar **2** m similarity

pared f wall; **subirse por las ~es** F hit the roof F

pareja f (conjunto de dos) pair; en una relación couple; de una persona partner; de un objeto other one

parejo adj L.Am. suelo level, even; **andar ~s** be neck and neck; **llegaron ~s** they arrived at the same time

paréntesis m inv parenthesis; fig break; **entre ~** fig by the way

pareo m wrap-around skirt

parida f P stupid thing to say / do

pariente m/f relative

paripé m: **hacer el ~** F put on an act F

parir <3a> **1** v/i give birth **2** v/t give birth to

París Paris; **parisino 1** adj Parisian **2** m, **-a** f Parisian

parka f parka

parking m parking lot, Br car park

parlamentario 1 adj parliamentary **2** m, **-a** f member of parliament; **parlamento** m parliament

parlanchín adj chatty; **parlante** m L.Am. loudspeaker

parlotear <1a> v/i chatter

parmesano m/adj Parmesan

paro m unemployment; **estar en ~** be unemployed; **~ cardíaco** cardiac arrest

parodia f parody

parpadear <1a> v/i blink; **parpadeo** m blinking; **párpado** m eye lid

parque m park; para bebé playpen; **~ de atracciones** amusement park; **~ de bomberos** fire station; **~ nacional** national park; **~ natural** nature reserve; **~ temático** theme park

parqué m → **parquet**

parquear <1a> v/t L.Am. park

parquet m parquet

parquímetro m parking meter

parra f (grape) vine

párrafo m paragraph

parranda f: **andar** or **irse de ~** F go out on the town F

parricidio m parricide

parrilla f broiler, Br grill; **a la ~** broiled, Br grilled; **parrillada** f L.Am. barbecue

párroco m parish priest; **parroquia** f REL parish; COM clientele, customers pl

parsimonia f calm

parte 1 m report; **~ meteorológico** weather report; **dar ~ a alguien** inform s.o. **2** f trozo part; JUR party; **alguna ~** somewhere; **ninguna ~** nowhere; **otra ~** somewhere else; **de ~ de** on behalf of; **en ~** partly; **en** or **por todas ~s** everywhere; **la mayor ~ de** the majority of, most of; **por otra ~** moreover; **estar de ~ de alguien** be on s.o.'s side; **formar ~ de** form part of; **tomar ~ en** take part in

participación f participation; **participante** m/f participant; **participar** <1a> **1** v/t una noticia announce **2** v/i take part (**en** in), participate (**en** in); **participio** m GRAM participle

partícula f particle

particular 1 adj clase, propiedad private; asunto personal; (específico) particular; (especial) peculiar; **en ~** in particular **2** m (persona) individual; **~es** particulars; **particularidad** f peculiarity

partida f en juego game; (remesa) consignment; documento certificate; **~ de nacimiento** birth certificate; **partidario 1** adj: **ser ~ de** be in favo(u)r of **2** m, **-a** f supporter; **partidismo** m partisanship; **partido** m POL party; DEP game; **sacar ~ de** take advantage of; **tomar ~** take sides

partir <3a> **1** v/t (dividir, repartir) split; (romper) break open, split open; (cortar) cut **2** v/i (irse) leave; **a ~ de hoy** (starting) from today; **a ~ de ahora** from now on; **~ de** fig start from **3** v/r **~se** (romperse) break; **~se de risa** F split one's sides laughing F

partitura f MÚS score

parto *m* birth; *fig* creation
parvulario *m* kindergarten
pasa *f* raisin
pasable *adj* passable
pasada *f con trapo* wipe; *de pintura* coat; *de* ~ in passing; *¡qué* ~*!* that's incredible! F; **pasadizo** *m* passage;
pasado 1 *adj tiempo* last; *el lunes* ~ last Monday; ~ *de moda* old-fashioned **2** *m* past
pasaje *m* (*billete*) ticket; MÚS, *de texto* passage; **pasajero 1** *adj* temporary; *relación* brief **2** *m*, -a *f* passenger
pasamano(s) *m* handrail
pasamontañas *m inv* balaclava (helmet)
pasaporte *m* passport
pasar <1a> **1** *v/t* pass; *el tiempo* spend; *de* ~ in passing; *¡qué* ~*!* go past; *frontera* cross; *problemas, dificultades* experience; AUTO (*adelantar*) pass, *Br* overtake; *una película* show; *para* ~ *el tiempo* (in order) to pass the time; ~ *la mano por* run one's hand through; ~*lo bien* have a good time **2** *v/i* (*suceder*) happen; *en juegos* pass; ~ *de alguien* F not want anything to do with s.o.; *paso de coger el teléfono* F I can't be bothered to pick up the phone; *pasé a visitarla* I dropped by to see her; ~ *de moda* go out of fashion; ~ *por* go by; *pasé por la tienda* I stopped off at the shop; *pasa por aquí* come this way; *dejar* ~ *oportunidad* miss; *hacerse* ~ *por* pass o.s. off as; *pasaré por tu casa* I'll drop by your house; *¡pasa!* come in; *¿qué pasa?* what's happening?, what's going on?; *¿qué te pasa?* what's the matter?; *pase lo que pase* whatever happens, come what may **3** *v/r* ~*se tb fig* go too far; *del tiempo* pass, go by; (*usar el tiempo*) spend; *de molestia, dolor* go away; ~*se al enemigo* go over to the enemy; *se le pasó llamar* he forgot to call
pasarela *f* catwalk
pasatiempo *m* pastime

Pascua *f* Easter; *¡felices* ~*s!* Merry Christmas!
pase *m tb* DEP, TAUR pass; *en el cine* showing; ~ *de modelos* fashion show
pasear <1a> **1** *v/t* take for a walk; (*exhibir*) show off **2** *v/i* walk **3** *v/r* ~*se* walk; *paseo* m walk; ~ *marítimo* seafront; *dar un* ~ go for a walk; *mandar a alguien a* ~ *fig* F tell s.o. to get lost
pasillo *m* corridor; *en avión, cine* aisle
pasión *f* passion
pasividad *f* passivity; **pasivo** *adj* passive
pasmar <1a> *v/t* amaze, astonish
paso *m* step; (*manera de andar*) walk; (*ritmo*) pace, rate; *de agua* flow; *de tráfico* movement; (*cruce*) crossing; *de tiempo* passing; (*huella*) footprint; ~ *a nivel* grade crossing, *Br* level crossing; ~ *de peatones* crosswalk, pedestrian crossing; *a este* ~ *fig* at this rate; *de* ~ on the way; *estar de* ~ be passing through
pasta *f sustancia* paste; GASTR pasta; P (*dinero*) dough P; ~ *de dientes* toothpaste; ~*s de té* type of cookie (*Br biscuit*)
pastel *m* GASTR cake; *pintura, color* pastel; **pastelería** *f* cake shop; **pastelero** *m*, -a *f* pastry cook
paste(u)rizar <1f> *v/t* pasteurize
pastilla *f* tablet; *de jabón* bar; *a toda* ~ F at top speed F, flat out F
pasto *m* (*hierba*) grass; *a todo* ~ F for all its worth F; **pastor** *m* shepherd; REL pastor; ~ *alemán* German shepherd
pata[1] *m/f Pe* F pal F, buddy F
pata[2] *f* leg; *a cuatro* ~*s* on all fours; *meter la* ~ F put one's foot in it F; *tener mala* ~ F be unlucky; **patada** *f* kick; *dar una* ~ kick; **patalear** <1a> *v/i* stamp one's feet; *fig* kick and scream
patata *f* potato; ~*s fritas de sartén* French fries, *Br* chips; *de bolsa* chips, *Br* crisps

patatús *m*: *le dio un ~* F he had a fit F

paté *m* paté

patear <1a> *v/t & v/i L.Am. de animal* kick

patentar <1a> *v/t* patent; **patente 1** *adj* clear, obvious **2** *f* patent; *L.Am.* AUTO license plate, *Br* numberplate

paternidad *f* paternity, fatherhood; **paterno** *adj* paternal

patético *adj* pitiful

patíbulo *m* scaffold

patilla *f de gafas* arm; *~s barba* sideburns

patín *m* skate; *~ (de ruedas) en línea* rollerblade®, in-line skate; **patinador** *m*, *~a f* skater; **patinaje** *m* skating; *~ artístico* figure skating; *~ sobre hielo* ice-skating; *~ sobre ruedas* roller-skating; **patinar** <1a> *v/i* skate; **patinazo** *m* skid; *fig* F blunder; *dar un ~* skid; **patinete** *m* scooter

patio *m* courtyard, patio; *~ de butacas* TEA orchestra, *Br* stalls *pl*

pato *m* ZO duck; *pagar el ~* F take the rap F, *Br* carry the can F

patojo *adj Chi* F squat

patológico *adj* pathological

patoso *adj* clumsy

patraña *f* tall story

patria *f* homeland

patriarca *m* patriarch

patrimonio *m* heritage; *~ artístico* artistic heritage

patriota *m/f* patriot; **patriótico** *adj* patriotic; **patriotismo** *m* patriotism

patrocinador *m*, *~a f* sponsor; **patrocinar** <1a> *v/t* sponsor; **patrocinio** *m* sponsorship

patrón *m* (*jefe*) boss; REL patron saint; *para costura* pattern; (*modelo*) standard; MAR skipper; **patrona** *f* (*jefa*) boss; REL patron saint; **patronal** *f* employers *pl*

patrulla *f* patrol; **patrullar** <1a> *v/t* patrol; **patrullero** *m* patrolman

paulatino *adj* gradual

pausa *f* pause; *en una actividad* break; MÚS rest; *~ publicitaria* commercial break; **pausado** *adj* slow,

deliberate

pauta *f* guideline; *marcar la ~* set the guidelines

pavimento *m* pavement, *Br* road surface

pavo 1 *adj L.Am.* F stupid **2** *m* ZO turkey; *~ real* peacock

pavonearse <1a> *v/r* boast (*de* about)

pavor *m* terror; *me da ~* it terrifies me

payada *f Rpl* improvised ballad

payador *m Rpl* gaucho singer

payasadas *fpl* antics; *hacer ~* fool *o* clown around; **payaso** *m* clown

paz *f* peace; *dejar en ~* leave alone

PC *abr* (= *Partido Comunista*) CP (= Communist Party)

P.D. *abr* (= *posdata*) PS (= postscript)

pe: *de ~ a pa* F from start to finish

peaje *m dinero, lugar* toll

peatón *m* pedestrian; **peatonal** *adj* pedestrian *atr*

pebete *m*, *-a f Rpl* F kid F

peca *f* freckle

pecado *m* sin; **pecador** *m*, *~a f* sinner; **pecaminoso** *adj* sinful

pecar <1g> *v/i* sin; *~ de ingenuo/ generoso* be very naive / generous

pecera *f* fish tank, aquarium

pecho *m* (*caja torácica*) chest; (*mama*) breast; *tomar algo a ~* take sth to heart; **pechuga** *f* GASTR breast; *L.Am. fig* (*caradura*) nerve F

pecoso *adj* freckled

pectoral *adj* ANAT pectoral

peculiar *adj* peculiar, odd; (*característico*) typical; **peculiaridad** *f* (*característica*) peculiarity

pedagogía *f* education; **pedagogo** *m*, *-a f* teacher

pedal *m* pedal; **pedalear** <1a> *v/i* pedal

pedante 1 *adj* pedantic; (*presuntuoso*) pretentious **2** *m/f* pedant; (*presuntuoso*) pretentious individual; **pedantería** *f* pedantry; (*presunción*) pretentiousness

pedazo *m* piece, bit; *~ de bruto* F

blockhead F; *hacer ~s* F smash to
bits F

pederasta *m* pederast

pedestal *m* pedestal

pediatra *m/f* p(a)ediatrician

pedicura *f* pedicure; **pedicuro** *m*, **-a**
f pedicurist, *Br* chiropodist

pedido *m* order

pedigrí *m* pedigree

pedigüeño *m*, **-a** *f person who is
always asking to borrow things,*
moocher F

pedir <3l> **1** *v/t* ask for; (*necesitar*)
need; *en bar, restaurante* order; *me
pidió que no fuera* he asked me not
to go **2** *v/i mendigar* beg; *en bar,
restaurante* order

pedo 1 *adj* drunk **2** *m* F fart F;
agarrarse un ~ F get plastered F;
tirarse or echar un ~ F fart F;
pedorreta *f* F Bronx cheer F, *Br*
raspberry F

pedrada *f* blow with a stone; *me dio
una ~ en la cabeza* he hit me over
the head with a stone; **pedregal**
m stony ground; **pedregoso** *adj*
stony

Pedro *m*: *como ~ por su casa fig* F as
if he/she owned the place

pega *f* F snag F, hitch F; *poner ~s*
raise objections; **pegadizo** *adj*
catchy; **pegado** *adj* (*adherido*)
stuck (*a* to); *estar ~ a* (*cerca de*) be
right up against; *estar ~ a alguien*
fig follow s.o. around, be s.o.'s
shadow; **pegajoso** *adj* sticky; *fig:
persona* clingy; **pegamento** *m* glue

pegar <1h> **1** *v/t* (*golpear*) hit; (*adherir*) stick, glue; *bofetada, susto, resfriado* give; *~ un grito* shout; *no me
pega la gana Méx* F I don't feel like
it **2** *v/i* (*golpear*) hit; (*adherir*) stick;
del sol beat down; (*armonizar*) go
(together) **3** *v/r ~se resfriado* catch;
acento pick up; *susto* give o.s.; *~se
un golpe/un tiro* hit/shoot o.s.; *pe-
gársela a alguien* F con s.o. F

pegatina *f* sticker

pegote *m* F (*cosa fea*) eyesore

peinado *m* hairstyle; **peinador** *m*, **-a**
f L.Am. hairdresser; **peinar** <1a>

1 *v/t tb fig* comb; *~ a alguien* comb
s.o.'s hair **2** *v/r ~se* comb one's hair;
peine *m* comb

p. ej. *abr* (= *por ejemplo*) e.g. (= ex-
empli gratia, for example)

Pekín Beijing

pela *f* F peseta

peladero *m L.Am.* vacant lot

peladilla *f* sugared almond

pelado *adj* peeled; *fig* bare; F (*sin
dinero*) broke F; **pelar** <1a> **1** *v/t
manzana, patata etc* peel; *hace un
frío que pela* F it's freezing **2** *v/r
~se* (*cortarse el pelo*) have a haircut;
Rpl F (*chismear*) gossip

pelazón *f C.Am.* backbiting

peldaño *m* step

pelea *f* fight; **pelear** <1a> **1** *v/i* fight
2 *v/r ~se* fight

pelele *m* puppet

peleón *adj* argumentative; *vino ~* F
jug wine, *Br* plonk F

peletería *f* furrier's

peliagudo *adj* tricky

pelícano *m* zo pelican

película *f* movie, film; FOT film; *~ del
Oeste* Western; *de ~* F awesome F,
fantastic F

peligrar <1a> *v/i* be at risk; **peligro**
m danger; *correr ~* be in danger;
poner en ~ endanger, put at risk;
peligroso *adj* dangerous

pelillo *m*: *¡~s a la mar fig* F let's bury
the hatchet

pelín: *un ~* F a (little) bit

pelirrojo *adj* red-haired, red-headed

pellejo *m de animal* skin, hide;
salvar el ~ fig F save one's (own)
skin F

pellizcar <1g> *v/t* pinch; **pellizco** *m*
pinch; *un buen ~* F a tidy sum F

pelma 1 *adj* annoying **2** *m/f* pain F;
pelmazo *m*, **-a** *f* F pain F

pelo *m de persona, de perro* hair; *de
animal* fur; *tiene el ~ muy largo* he
has very long hair; *a ~* F (*sin
preparación*) unprepared; *montar a
~* ride bareback; *por los ~s* F by a
whisker F, by the skin of one's teeth
F; *tomar el ~ a alguien* F pull s.o.'s
leg F

P

pelota 1 *f* ball; **~s** F nuts F, balls F; **en ~s** P stark naked; *hacer la ~ a alguien* suck up to s.o. F **2** *m/f* F creep F; **pelotazo** *m*: *rompió el cristal de un ~* he smashed the window with a ball; **pelotero** *m*, **-a** *f* L.Am. (base)ball player

pelotón *m* MIL squad; DEP bunch, pack

peluca *f* wig

peluche *m* soft toy; *oso de ~* teddy bear

peludo *adj persona* hairy; *animal* furry

peluquearse <1a> *v/r* L.Am. get one's hair cut; **peluquería** *f* hairdresser's; **peluquero** *m*, **-a** *f* hairdresser; **peluquín** *m* toupee, hairpiece

pelusa *f* fluff

pelvis *f inv* ANAT pelvis

pena *f* (*tristeza*) sadness, sorrow; (*congoja*) grief, distress; (*lástima*) pity; JUR sentence; ~ *capital* death penalty, capital punishment; ~ *de muerte* death penalty; *no vale* or *no merece la* ~ it's not worth it; *¡qué* ~*!* what a shame *o* pity!; *a duras ~s* with great difficulty; *me da* ~ L.Am. I'm ashamed; **penal** *adj* penal; *derecho* ~ criminal law; **penalidad** *f fig* hardship; **penalización** *f acción* penalization; DEP penalty; **penalizar** <1f> *v/t* penalize; **penalty** *m* DEP penalty

penca 1 *adj* Chi soft, weak **2** *f* L.Am. (*nopal*) leaf of the prickly pear plant

pendejada *f* L.Am. stupid thing to do

pendejo 1 *m* (*pelea*) fight **2** *m*, **-a** *f* L.Am. F dummy F

pendenciero *adj* troublemaker

pendiente 1 *adj* unresolved, unfinished; *cuenta* unpaid **2** *m* earring **3** *f* slope

pendón 1 *adj* swinging F **2** *m*, **-ona** *f* F swinger F

péndulo *m* pendulum

pene *m* ANAT penis

penetración *f* penetration; **penetrante** *adj mirada* penetrating; *soni-*

do piercing; *frío* bitter; *herida* deep; *análisis* incisive; **penetrar** <1a> *v/i* penetrate; (*entrar*) enter; *de un líquido* seep in

penicilina *f* penicillin

península *f* peninsula; ~ *Ibérica* Iberian Peninsula

penique *m* penny

penitencia *f* penitence; **penitenciado** *m* L.Am. prisoner, convict; **penitenciario** *adj* penitentiary *atr*, prison *atr*

penoso *adj* distressing; *trabajo* laborious

pensamiento *m* thought; BOT pansy; **pensar** <1k> **1** *v/t* think about; (*opinar*) think; *¡ni* ~ *lo!* don't even think about it **2** *v/i* think (*en* about); **pensativo** *adj* thoughtful

pensión *f hotel* rooming house, *Br* guesthouse; *dinero* pension; ~ *alimenticia* child support, *Br* maintenance; ~ *completa* American plan, *Br* full board; **pensionista** *m/f* pensioner

pentagrama *m* MÚS stave

pentatlón *m* DEP pentathlon

penúltimo *adj* penultimate

penumbra *f* half-light

penuria *f* shortage (*de* of); (*pobreza*) poverty

peña *f* crag, cliff; (*roca*) rock; F *de amigos* group, circle; **peñasco** *m* boulder; **peñón** *m*: *el Peñon de Gibraltar* the Rock of Gibraltar

peón *m en ajedrez* pawn; *trabajador* labo(u)rer

peor *adj comp* worse; *de mal en* ~ from bad to worse

pepa *f* L.Am. (*semilla*) seed; *soltar la* ~ F spill the beans

pepinillo *m* gherkin; **pepino** *m* cucumber; *me importa un* ~ F I don't give a damn F

pepita *f* pip

pequeño 1 *adj* small, little; *de* ~ when I was small *o* little **2** *m*, **-a** *f* little one

pequinés *m* ZO Pekinese, Peke F

pera *f* pear; **peral** *m* pear tree

perca *f pez* perch

percance *m* mishap

percatarse <1a> *v/r* notice; **~ de algo** notice sth

percebe *m* ZO barnacle

percepción *f* perception; COM **acto** receipt

percha *f* coat hanger; **gancho** coat hook; **perchero** *m* coat rack

percibir <3a> *v/t* perceive; COM **sueldo** receive

percusión *f* MÚS percussion

perdedor *m*, **~a** *f* loser; **perder** <2g> **1** *v/t* objeto lose; *tren, avión etc* miss; *el tiempo* waste **2** *v/i* lose; *echar a* **~** ruin; *echarse a* **~** *de alimento* go bad **3** *v/r* **~se** get lost; **perdición** *f* downfall; **pérdida** *f* loss; **perdido** *adj* lost; *ponerse* **~** get filthy

perdigón *m* pellet

perdiz *f* ZO partridge

perdón *m* pardon; REL forgiveness; *pedir* **~** say sorry, apologize; *¡~!* sorry; **perdonar** <1a> *v/t* forgive; JUR pardon; **~ algo a alguien** forgive s.o. sth; *¡perdone!* sorry; *perdone, ¿tiene hora?* excuse me, do you have the time?

perdurar <1a> *v/i* endure

perecedero *adj* perishable; **perecer** <2d> *v/i* perish

peregrinación *f* pilgrimage; **peregrinar** <1a> *v/i* go on a pilgrimage; **peregrino** *m*, **-a** *f* pilgrim

perejil *m* BOT parsley

perenne *adj* BOT perennial

perentorio *adj* (*urgente*) urgent, pressing; (*apremiante*) peremptory

pereza *f* laziness; **perezoso 1** *adj* lazy **2** *m* ZO sloth

perfección *f* perfection; *a la* **~** perfectly, to perfection; **perfeccionamiento** *m* perfecting; **perfeccionar** <1a> *v/t* perfect; **perfeccionista** *m/f* perfectionist; **perfecto** *adj* perfect

pérfido *adj* treacherous

perfil *m* profile; *de* **~** in profile, from the side

perforación *f* puncture; **perforadora** *f* punch; **perforar** <1a> *v/t* pierce;

calle dig up

perfumar <1a> *v/t* perfume; **perfume** *m* perfume; **perfumería** *f* perfume shop

pergamino *m* parchment

pergenio *m*, **-a** *f Rpl* F kid F

pericia *f* expertise

pericote *m Chi, Pe* ZO large rat

periferia *f* periphery; *de ciudad* outskirts *pl*

perilla *f* goatee; *me viene de* **~** F that'll be very useful; *tu visita me viene de* **~** F you've come at just the right time

perímetro *m* perimeter

periódico 1 *adj* periodic **2** *m* newspaper; **periodismo** *m* journalism; **periodista** *m/f* journalist; **período**, **periodo** *m* period

peripecia *f* adventure

periquete *m*: *en un* **~** F in a second, in no time F

periquito *m* ZO budgerigar

periscopio *m* periscope

perito 1 *adj* expert **2** *m*, **-a** *f* expert; COM *en seguros* loss adjuster

perjudicar <1g> *v/t* harm, damage; **perjudicial** *adj* harmful, damaging; **perjuicio** *m* harm, damage; *sin* **~** *de* without affecting

perjurio *m* perjury

perla *f* pearl; *nos vino de* **~s** F it suited us fine F

permanecer <2d> *v/i* remain, stay; **permanente 1** *adj* permanent **2** *f* perm

permeable *adj* permeable

permisible *adj* permissible; **permisivo** *adj* permissive; **permiso** *m* permission; *documento* permit; **~ de conducir** driver's license, *Br* driving licence; **~ de residencia** residence permit; *con* **~** excuse me; *estar de* **~** be on leave; **permitir** <3a> **1** *v/t* permit, allow **2** *v/r* **~se** afford; **~se el lujo de** permit o.s. the luxury of

pernicioso *adj* harmful

pernoctar <1a> *v/i* spend the night

pero 1 *conj* but **2** *m* flaw, defect; *no hay* **~s** *que valgan* no excuses

perogrullada *f* platitude

peronismo *m* Peronism; **peronista** *m/f* Peronist

perorata *f* F lecture

perpendicular *adj* perpendicular

perpetrar <1a> *v/t crimen* perpetrate, commit

perpetuar <1e> *v/t* perpetuate; **perpetuidad** *f*: **a ~** in perpetuity; **perpetuo** *adj fig* perpetual

perplejidad *f* perplexity; **perplejo** *adj* puzzled, perplexed

perra *f* dog; **el perro y la ~** the dog and the bitch; **~s** F pesetas; **perrera** *f* kennels *pl*; **perrería** *f* F dirty trick; **perrito** *m*: **~ caliente** GASTR hot dog; **perro** *m* dog; **~ callejero** stray; **~ guardián** guard dog; **~ lazarillo** seeing eye dog, *Br* guide dog; **~ pastor** sheepdog; **llevarse como el ~ y el gato** *fig* fight like cat and dog; **hace un tiempo de ~s** F the weather is lousy F

persecución *f* pursuit; (*acoso*) persecution; **perseguidor** *m*, **~a** *f* persecutor; **perseguir** <3l & 3d> *v/t* pursue; *delincuente* look for; (*molestar*) pester; (*acosar*) persecute

perseverancia *f* perseverance; **perseverar** <1a> *v/i* persevere (**en** with)

persiana *f* blind

pérsico *adj* Persian

persignarse <1a> *v/r* cross o.s.

persistente *adj* persistent; **persistir** <3a> *v/i* persist

persona *f* person; **quince ~s** fifteen people; **personaje** *m* TEA character; *famoso* celebrity; **personal** **1** *adj* personal **2** *m* personnel, staff; **personalidad** *f* personality; **personalizar** <1f> *v/t* personalize; **personificar** <1g> *v/t* personify, embody

perspectiva *f* perspective; *fig* point of view; **~s** *pl* outlook *sg*, prospects

perspicacia *f* shrewdness, perspicacity

persuadir <3a> *v/t* persuade; **persuasión** *f* persuasion; **persuasivo** *adj* persuasive

pertenecer <2d> *v/i* belong (**a** to); **pertenencias** *fpl* belongings

pértiga *f* pole; **salto con ~** DEP pole vault

pertinaz *adj* persistent; (*terco*) obstinate

pertinente *adj* relevant, pertinent

pertrechos *mpl* MIL equipment *sg*

perturbar <1a> *v/t* disturb; *reunión* disrupt

Perú Peru; **peruano 1** *adj* Peruvian **2** *m*, **-a** *f* Peruvian

perversión *f* perversion; **perverso** *adj* perverted; **pervertido** *m*, **-a** *f* pervert; **pervertir** <3i> *v/t* pervert

pesa *f para balanza* weight; DEP shot; *C.Am., W.I.* butcher's shop

pesadez *f fig* drag F

pesadilla *f* nightmare

pesado 1 *adj objeto* heavy; *libro, clase etc* tedious, boring; *trabajo* tough **2** *m*, **-a** *f* bore; **¡qué ~ es!** F he's a real pain F

pésame *m* condolences *pl*

pesar <1a> **1** *v/t* weigh **2** *v/i* be heavy; (*influir*) carry weight; *fig* weigh heavily (**sobre** on); **me pesa tener que informarle ...** I regret to have to inform you ... **3** *m* sorrow; **a ~ de** in spite of, despite

pesca *f actividad* fishing; (*peces*) fish *pl*; **pescadería** *f* fish shop; **pescadero** *m*, **-a** *f* fishmonger; **pescadilla** *f pez* whiting; **pescado** *m* GASTR fish; **pescador** *m* fisherman; **pescar** <1g> **1** *v/t un pez, resfriado etc* catch; (*intentar tomar*) fish for; *trabajo, marido etc* land F **2** *v/i* fish

pescuezo *m* neck

pese: ~ a despite

pesero *m L.Am.* minibus; *Méx* (collective) taxi

peseta *f* peseta; **pesetero** *adj* F money-grubbing F

pesimismo *m* pessimism; **pesimista 1** *adj* pessimistic **2** *m/f* pessimist

pésimo *adj sup* awful, terrible

peso *m* weight; *moneda* peso; **de ~** *fig* weighty

pesquero 1 *adj* fishing *atr* **2** *m* fishing boat

pesquisa *f* investigation

pestaña *f* eyelash; **pestañear** <1a> *v/i* flutter one's eyelashes; *sin ~* *fig* without batting an eyelid

peste *f* MED plague; F *olor* stink F; *echar ~s* F curse and swear

pesticida *m* pesticide

pestilente *adj* foul-smelling

pestillo *m* (*picaporte*) door handle; (*cerradura*) bolt

petaca *f para tabaco* tobacco pouch; *para bebida* hip flask; *C.Am.* F *insecto* ladybug, *Br* ladybird

pétalo *m* petal

petanca *f type of bowls*

petardo 1 *m* firecracker **2** *m, -a f* F nerd F

petate *m* kit bag; *L.Am.* F *en el suelo* mat

petición *f* request; *a ~ de* at the request of

petirrojo *m* ZO robin

petiso *L.Am.* **1** *m, -a f* F shorty F **2** *m* pony

peto *m* bib; *pantalón de ~* overalls *pl*, *Br* dungarees *pl*

petrificado *adj* petrified

petróleo *m* oil, petroleum; **petrolero 1** *adj* oil *atr* **2** *m* MAR oil tanker; **petrolífero** *adj* oil *atr*; **petroquímica** *f* petrochemical

petulante *adj* smug

peyorativo *adj* pejorative

pez *m* ZO fish; *~ espada* swordfish; *~ gordo* F big shot F; *estar ~ en algo* F be clueless about sth F

pezón *m* nipple

pezuña *f* ZO hoof

piadoso *adj* pious

pianista *m/f* pianist; **piano** *m* piano; *~ de cola* grand piano

piar <1c> *v/i* tweet, chirrup

PIB *abr* (= *producto interior bruto*) GDP (= gross domestic product)

pibe *m, -a f* Rpl F kid F

picada *f de serpiente* bite; *de abeja* sting; *L.Am. para comer* snacks *pl*, nibbles *pl*; *Rpl* (*camino*) path; **picadero** *m escuela* riding school;

picado 1 *adj diente* decayed; *mar* rough, choppy; *carne* ground, *Br* minced; *verdura* minced, *Br* chopped; *fig* offended **2** *m L.Am.* dive; *caer en ~ de precios* nosedive, plummet; **picadora** *f en cocina* mincer; **picadura** *f de reptil, mosquito* bite; *de avispa* sting; *tabaco* cut tobacco

picaflor *m L.Am.* ZO hummingbird; *fig* womanizer

picante 1 *adj* hot, spicy; *chiste* risqué **2** *m* hot spice

picaporte *m* door handle

picar <1g> **1** *v/t de mosquito, serpiente* bite; *de avispa* sting; *de ave* peck; *carne* grind, *Br* mince; *verdura* mince, *Br* finely chop; TAUR jab with a lance; (*molestar*) annoy; *la curiosidad* pique **2** *v/i tb fig* take the bait; *L.Am. de la comida* be hot; (*producir picor*) itch; *del sol* burn

picardía *f* (*astucia*) craftiness, slyness; (*travesura*) mischievousness; *Méx* (*taco, palabrota*) swearing, swearwords *pl*

pícaro *adj persona* crafty, sly; *comentario* mischievous

picarón *m Méx, Chi, Pe* (*buñuelo*) fritter

picatoste *m* piece of fried bread

picha *f* V prick V

pichicato *m Pe, Bol* P coke P

pichincha *f L.Am.* bargain

pichón *m L.Am.* ORN chick; F (*novato*) rookie F

Picio: *más feo que ~* F as ugly as sin F

picnic *m* (*pl ~s*) picnic

pico *m* ZO beak; F (*boca*) mouth; *de montaña* peak; *herramienta* pickax(e); *a las tres y ~* some time after three o'clock; *cerrar el ~* F shut one's mouth F

picor *m* itch

picota *f* bigarreau (*type of sweet cherry*)

picotazo *m* peck; **picotear** <1a> *v/t* peck

pido *vb* → **pedir**

pie *m* foot; *de estatua, lámpara* base; *a*

~ on foot; **de ~** standing; **no tiene ni ~s ni cabeza** it doesn't make any sense at all, I can't make head nor tail of it

piedad *f* pity; (*clemencia*) mercy

piedra *f tb* MED stone; **~ preciosa** precious stone; **quedarse de ~** *fig* F be stunned

piel *f de persona, fruta* skin; *de animal* hide, skin; (*cuero*) leather; **abrigo de ~es** fur coat

pienso[1] *vb* → **pensar**

pienso[2] *m* animal feed

pierdo *vb* → **perder**

pierna *f* leg; **dormir a ~ suelta** sleep like a log

pieza *f de un conjunto*, MÚS piece; *de aparato* part; TEA play; (*habitación*) room; **~ de recambio** spare (part); **quedarse de una ~** F be amazed

pifia *f* F (*error*) booboo F; *Chi, Pe, Rpl* defect

pigmento *m* pigment

pigmeo *m*, **-a** *f* pigmy

pijama *m* pajamas *pl*, *Br* pyjamas *pl*

pijo 1 *adj* posh 2 *m* V (*pene*) prick V 3 *m*, **-a** *f* F *persona* rich kid F

pila *f* EL battery; (*montón*) pile; (*fregadero*) sink

pilar *m tb fig* pillar

píldora *f* pill

pileta *f Rpl* sink; (*alberca*) swimming pool

pillaje *m* pillage; **pillar** <1a> *v/t* (*tomar*) seize; (*atrapar*) catch; (*atropellar*) hit; *chiste* get

pillo 1 *adj* mischievous 2 *m*, **-a** *f* rascal

pilón *m Méx*: **me dio dos de ~** he gave me two extra

pilotar <1a> *v/t* AVIA fly, pilot; AUTO drive; MAR steer; **piloto** *m* AVIA, MAR pilot; AUTO driver; EL pilot light; **~ automático** autopilot

piltrafa *f*: **~s** rags; **estar hecho una ~** *fig* be a total wreck F

pimentón *m* paprika; **pimienta** *f* pepper; **pimiento** *m* pepper; **me importa un ~** F I couldn't care less F

pimpón *m* ping-pong

PIN *m* PIN

pinar *m* pine forest

pincel *m* paintbrush

pinchadiscos *m/f* F disc jockey, DJ

pinchar <1a> **1** *v/t* prick; AUTO puncture; TELEC tap; F (*molestar*) bug F, needle F; **~le a alguien** MED give s.o. a shot **2** *v/i* prick; AUTO get a flat tire, *Br* get a puncture **3** *v/r* **~se** *con aguja etc* prick o.s.; F (*inyectarse*) shoot up P; **se nos pinchó una rueda** we got a flat (tire) *o Br* a puncture; **pinchazo** *m herida* prick; *dolor* sharp pain; AUTO flat (tire), *Br* puncture; F flop F

pinche[1] *m* cook's assistant

pinche[2] *adj Méx* F rotten F; *C.Am.*, *Méx* (*tacaño*) tight-fisted

pincho *m* GASTR bar snack

pingajo *m* F rag

ping-pong *m* ping-pong

pingüino *m* ZO penguin

pino *m* BOT pine; **hacer el ~** do a handstand

pinol(e) *m C.Am.*, *Méx* cornstarch, *Br* cornflour; *L.Am.* roasted corn

pinta *f* pint; *aspecto* looks *pl*; **tener buena ~** *fig* look inviting

pintalabios *m* lipstick

pintar <1a> **1** *v/t* paint; **no ~ nada** *fig* F not count **2** *v/r* **~se** put on one's makeup

pintor *m*, **~a** *f* painter; **~ (de brocha gorda)** (house) painter; **pintoresco** *adj* picturesque; **pintura** *f sustancia* paint; *obra* painting

pinza *f clothes pin*, *Br* clothes peg; ZO claw; **~s** tweezers; *L.Am.* (*alicates*) pliers

piña *f del pino* pine cone; *fruta* pineapple; **piñón** *m* BOT pine nut; TÉC pinion

piojo *m* ZO louse; **~s** *pl* lice *pl*

piola *f L.Am.* cord, twine; **piolín** *m Arg* cord, twine

pionero 1 *adj* pioneering **2** *m*, **-a** *f tb fig* pioneer

pipa *f* pipe; **~s semillas** sunflower seeds; **pasarlo ~** F have a great time

pipí *m* F pee F; **_hacer ~_** F pee F

pipiolo *m C.Am., Méx* F kid F; **~s** *pl C.Am.* F (*dinero*) cash *sg*

pique *m* resentment; (*rivalidad*) rivalry; **_irse a ~_** *fig* go under, go to the wall

piqueta *f herramienta* pickax(e); *en cámping* tentpeg

piquete *m* POL picket

pirado *adj* F crazy F

piragua *f* canoe; **piragüista** *m/f* DEP canoeist

pirámide *f* pyramid

piraña *f* ZO piranha

pirarse <1a> *v/r* F (*marcharse*) clear off F; **_~ por alguien_** F lose one's head over s.o. F

pirata *m/f* pirate; **_~ informático_** hacker; **piratear** <1a> *v/t* INFOR pirate

pirenaico *adj* Pyrenean; **Pirineos** *mpl* Pyrenees

pirómano *m*, **-a** *f* pyromaniac; JUR arsonist

piropo *m* compliment

pirotécnico *adj* fireworks *atr*

piruleta *f*, **pirulí** *m* lollipop

pis *m* F pee F; **_hacer ~_** F have a pee F

pisada *f* footstep; *huella* footprint; **pisapapeles** *m* paperweight; **pisar** <1a> *v/t* step on; *uvas* tread; *fig* (*maltratar*) walk all over; *idea* steal; **_~ a alguien_** step on s.o.'s foot

piscifactoría *f* fish farm

piscina *f* swimming pool

Piscis *m/f inv* ASTR Pisces

piso *m* apartment, *Br* flat; (*planta*) floor

pisotear <1a> *v/t* trample

pista *f* track, trail; (*indicio*) clue; *de atletismo* track; **_~ de aterrizaje_** AVIA runway; **_~ de baile_** dance floor; **_~ de tenis / squash_** tennis / squash court; **_seguir la ~ a alguien_** be on the trail of s.o.

pistacho *m* BOT pistachio

pisto *m* GASTR *mixture of tomatoes, peppers etc cooked in oil*; *C.Am., Méx* F (*dinero*) cash, dough F

pistola *f* pistol

pistón *m* piston

pitada *f* (*abucheo*) whistle; *S.Am. de cigarrillo* puff; **pitar** <1a> **1** *v/i* whistle; *con bocina* beep, hoot; *L.Am.* (*fumar*) smoke; **_salir pitando_** F dash off F **2** *v/t* (*abuchear*) whistle at; *penalti, falta etc* call, *Br* blow for; *silbato* blow; **pitazo** *m L.Am.* whistle; **pitear** <1a> *v/i L.Am.* blow a whistle; **pitido** *m* whistle; *con bocina* beep, hoot

pitillo *m* cigarette; *hecho a mano* roll-up

pito *m* whistle; (*bocina*) horn; **_me importa un ~_** F I don't give a hoot F

pitón *m* ZO python; **pitonisa** *f* fortune-teller

pitorrearse <1a> *v/r*: **_~ de alguien_** F make fun of s.o.

pívot *m en baloncesto* center, *Br* centre

piyama *m L.Am.* pajamas *pl*, *Br* pyjamas *pl*

pizarra *f* blackboard; *piedra* slate

pizca *f* pinch; *Méx* AGR harvest; **_ni ~ de_** not a bit of

pizza *f* pizza

placa *f* (*lámina*) sheet; (*plancha*) plate; (*letrero*) plaque; *Méx* AUTO license plate, *Br* number plate; **_~ madre_** INFOR motherboard; **_~_** (*dental*) plaque; **_~ de matrícula_** AUTO license plate, *Br* number plate

placer <2x> **1** *v/i* please; **_siempre hace lo que le place_** he always does as he pleases **2** *m* pleasure

plácido *adj* placid

plaga *f* AGR pest; MED plague; *fig* scourge; (*abundancia*) glut; **plagado** *adj* infested; (*lleno*) full; **_~ de gente_** swarming with people

plagiar <1b> *v/t* plagiarize; *L.Am.* (*secuestrar*) kidnap; **plagio** *m* plagiarism

plan *m* plan

plana *f*: **_primera ~_** front page

plancha *f para planchar* iron; *en cocina* broiler, *Br* grill; *de metal* sheet; F (*metedura de pata*) goof F; **_a la ~_** GASTR broiled, *Br* grilled; **planchar** <1a> *v/t* iron; *Méx* F (*dar* *plantón*) stand up F; *L.Am.* (*lison-jear*) flatter

planeador *m* glider; **planear** <1a> **1** *v/t* plan **2** *v/i* AVIA glide

planeta *m* planet; **planetario** *m* planetarium

planificación *f* planning; **~ familiar** family planning; **planificar** <1g> *v/t* plan

plano 1 *adj* flat **2** *m* ARQUI plan; *de ciudad* map; *en cine* shot; MAT plane; *fig* level

planta *f* BOT plant; (*piso*) floor; **~ del pie** sole of the foot; **plantación** *f* plantation

plantado *adj*: **dejar a alguien ~** F stand s.o. up F; **plantar** <1a> **1** *v/t* *árbol etc* plant; *tienda de campaña* put up; **~ a alguien** F stand s.o. up F **2** *v/r* **~se** put one's foot down

planteamiento *m de problema* posing; (*perspectiva*) approach; **plantear** <1a> *v/t* *dificultad, problema* pose, create; *cuestión* raise

plantel *m* (*equipo*) team; *L.Am.* staff

plantilla *f para zapato* insole; (*personal*) staff; DEP squad; *para cortar*, INFOR template

plantón *m*: **dar un ~ a alguien** F stand s.o. up F

plasma *m* plasma

plasmar <1a> *v/t* (*modelar*) shape; *fig* (*representar*) express

plasta 1 *m/f* F pain F, drag F **2** *adj*: **ser ~** F be a pain *o* drag F

plástica *f* EDU handicrafts; **plástico** *m* plastic

plastificado *adj* laminated; **plastificar** <1g> *v/t* *documento* laminate

plastilina *f* Plasticine®

plata *f* silver; *L.Am.* F (*dinero*) cash, dough F

plataforma *f tb* POL platform; **~ petrolífera** oil rig

platal *m L.Am.* fortune

plátano *m* banana

plateado *adj Méx* wealthy

plática *f Méx* chat, talk; **platicar** <1g> **1** *v/t L.Am.* tell **2** *v/i Méx* chat, talk

platillo *m*: **~ volante** flying saucer; **~s** MÚS cymbals

platino *m* platinum

plato *m* plate; GASTR dish; **~ principal** main course; **~ preparado / precocinado** ready meal; **~ sopero / hondo** soup dish; **pagar los ~s rotos** F carry the can F

plató *m de película* set; TV studio

platónico *adj* platonic

platudo *adj Chi* rich

plausible *adj* plausible

playa *f* beach; **~ de estacionamiento** *L.Am.* parking lot, *Br* car park; **playeras** *fpl* canvas shoes

playo *adj Rpl* shallow

plaza *f* square; (*vacante*) job opening, *Br* vacancy; *en vehículo* seat; *de trabajo* position; **~ de toros** bull ring

plazo *f* period; (*pago*) instal(l)ment; **a corto / largo ~** in the short / long term; **a ~s** in instal(l)ments

plebiscito *m* plebiscite

plegable *adj* collapsible, folding; **plegar** <1h & 1k> **1** *v/t* fold (up) **2** *v/r* **~se** *fig* submit (**a** to)

plegaria *f* prayer

pleito *m* JUR lawsuit; *fig* dispute; **poner un ~ a alguien** sue s.o.

pleno 1 *adj* full; **en ~ día** in broad daylight **2** *m* plenary session

pliego 1 *vb* → **plegar 2** *m* (*hoja de papel*) sheet (of paper); (*carta*) sealed letter *o* document; **pliegue** *m* fold, crease

plomería *f Méx* plumbing; **plomero** *m Méx* plumber; **plomo** *m* lead; EL fuse; *fig* F drag F; **sin ~** AUTO unleaded

pluma *f* feather; *para escribir* fountain pen; **plumaje** *m* plumage; **plumero** *m para limpiar* feather duster; *CSur para maquillaje* powder puff; **vérsele el ~ a alguien** *fig* F see what s.o. is up to F; **plumífero** *m* F down jacket

plural 1 *adj* plural **2** *m* GRAM plural; **pluralismo** *m* POL pluralism; **pluriempleo** *m* having more than one job

plus *m* bonus

plusmarquista *m/f* record holder

plusvalía *f* COM capital gain

plutonio *m* QUÍM plutonium

pluviosidad *f* rainfall

PNB *abr* (= ***producto nacional bruto***) GNP (= gross national product)

P.º *abr* (= ***Paseo***) Ave (= Avenue)

p.o. *abr* (= ***por orden***) p.p. (per procurationem, by proxy)

población *f gente* population; (*ciudad*) city, town; (*pueblo*) village; *Chi* shanty town; **poblado 1** *adj* populated; *barba* bushy; **~ de** *fig* full of 2 *m* (*pueblo*) settlement; **poblador** *m*, **-a** *f Chi* shanty town dweller; **poblar** <1m> *v/t* populate

pobre 1 *adj económicamente, en calidad* poor 2 *m/f* poor person; *los* **~s** the poor; **pobreza** *f* poverty

pocilga *f* pigpen

pócima *f* concoction

poción *f* potion

poco 1 *adj sg* little, not much; *pl* few, not many; *un ~ de* a little; *unos ~s* a few 2 *adv* little; *trabaja ~* he doesn't work much; *ahora se ve muy ~* it's seldom seen now; *estuvo ~ por aquí* he wasn't around much; *~ conocido* little known; *~ a ~* little by little; *dentro de ~* soon, shortly; *hace ~* a short time ago, not long ago; *por ~* nearly, almost; *¡a ~ no lo hacemos!* *Méx* don't tell me we're not doing it; *de a ~ me fui tranquilizando* *Rpl* little by little I calmed down 3 *m*: *un ~* a little, a bit

podar <1a> *v/t* AGR prune

poder <2t> **1** *v/aux capacidad* can, be able to; *permiso* can, be allowed to; *posibilidad* may, might; *no pude hablar con ella* I wasn't able to talk to her; *¿puedo ir contigo?* can *o* may I come with you?; *¡podías habérselo dicho!* you could have *o* you might have told him **2** *v/i*: *~ con* (*sobreponerse a*) manage, cope with; *me puede* he can beat me; *es franco a más no ~* F he's as frank as they come F; *comimos a más no ~* F we ate to bursting point F; *no puedo más* I can't take any more,

I've had enough; *puede ser* perhaps, maybe; *puede que* perhaps, maybe; *¿se puede?* can I come in?, do you mind if I come in? **3** *m tb* POL power; *en ~ de alguien* in s.o.'s hands; **poderoso** *adj* powerful

podio *m* podium

podólogo *m*, **-a** *f* MED podiatrist, *Br* chiropodist

podrido *adj tb fig* rotten

poema *m* poem; **poesía** *f género* poetry; (*poema*) poem; **poeta** *m/f* poet; **poético** *adj* poetic; **poetisa** *f* poet

polaco 1 *adj* Polish **2** *m*, **-a** *f* Pole

polar *adj* polar

polea *f* TÉC pulley

polémica *f* controversy; **polémico** *adj* controversial

polen *m* BOT pollen

poleo *m* BOT pennyroyal

polera *f Chi* turtle neck (sweater)

poli *m/f* F cop F; *la ~* F the cops *pl* F

policía 1 *f* police **2** *m/f* police officer, policeman; *mujer* police officer, policewoman; **policíaco**, **policiaco** *adj* detective *atr*; **policial** *adj* police *atr*

polideportivo *m* sports center, *Br* sports centre

poliéster *m* polyester

polifacético *adj* versatile, multifaceted

poligamia *f* polygamy

polígloto *m/f* polyglot

polígono *m* MAT polygon; *~ industrial* industrial zone, *Br* industrial estate

polilla *f* ZO moth

polio *f* MED polio; **poliomielitis** *f* MED poliomyelitis

política *f* politics; **políticamente** *adv*: *~ correcto* politically correct; **político 1** *adj* political **2** *m*, **-a** *f* politician

póliza *f* policy; *~ de seguros* insurance policy

polizón *m/f* stowaway

polla *f* V prick V, cock V

pollera *f L.Am.* skirt

pollería *f* poulterer's; **pollito** *m*

P

chick; **pollo** *m* ZO, GASTR chicken; **polluelo** *m* ZO chick

polo *m* GEOG, EL pole; *prenda* polo shirt; DEP polo; ***Polo Norte*** North Pole; ***Polo Sur*** South Pole

polola *f Chi* girlfriend; **pololear** <1a> *v/i Chi* be going steady; **pololo** *m Chi* boyfriend

Polonia Poland

poltrona *f* easy chair

polución *f* pollution; **~ atmosférica** air pollution, atmospheric pollution; **polucionar** <1a> *v/t* pollute

polvo *m* dust; *en química, medicina etc* powder; **~s** *pl* **de talco** talcum powder *sg*; *echar un* **~** V have a screw V; *estar hecho* **~** F be all in F; **pólvora** *f* gunpowder; **polvorín** *m* almacén magazine; *fig* powder keg; **polvorón** *m* GASTR *type of small cake*

pomada *f* cream

pomelo *m* BOT grapefruit

pómez *f*: *~ piedra* **~** pumice stone

pomo *m* doorknob

pompa *f* pomp; *~ de jabón* bubble; *~s* *pl* *fúnebres* ceremonia funeral ceremony *sg*; *establecimiento* funeral parlo(u)r *sg*; **pomposo** *adj* pompous

pómulo *m* ANAT cheekbone

pon *vb* → **poner**

ponchadura *f Méx* flat, *Br* puncture; **ponchar** <1a> **1** *v/t L.Am.* puncture **2** *v/r* **~se** *Méx* get a flat *o Br* puncture

ponche *m* punch

poncho *m* poncho; *pisarse el* **~** *S.Am.* be mistaken

ponderación *f* mesura deliberation; *en estadísticas* weighting

ponencia *f* presentation; EDU paper

poner <2r; *part* **puesto**> **1** *v/t* put; (*añadir*) put in; RAD, TV turn on, switch on; *la mesa* set; *ropa* put on; *telegrama* send; (*escribir*) put down; *en periódico, libro etc* say; *negocio* set up; *huevos* lay; **~ a alguien furioso** make s.o. angry; **~le a alguien con alguien** TELEC put s.o. through to s.o.; **~le una multa a alguien** fine

s.o.; *pongamos que* let's suppose *o* assume that **2** *v/r* **~se** *ropa* put on; *ponte en el banco* go and sit on the bench; *se puso ahí* she stood over there; *dile que se ponga* TELEC tell her to come to the phone; **~se palido** turn pale; **~se furioso** get angry; **~se enfermo** become *o* fall ill; **~se a** start to

pongo¹ *vb* → **poner**

pongo² *m Pe* indentured Indian laborer

poni *m* ZO pony

poniente *m* west

pontífice *m* pontiff; *sumo* **~** Pope

ponzoñoso *adj* poisonous

pop 1 *adj* pop; *música* **~** pop music **2** *m* pop

popa *f* MAR stern

popular *adj* popular; (*del pueblo*) folk *atr*; *barrio* lower-class; **popularidad** *f* popularity; **popularizar** <1f> *v/t* popularize

póquer *m* poker

por *prp* ◊ *motivo* for, because of; *lo hizo* **~** *amor* she did it out of love; *luchó* **~** *sus ideales* he fought for his ideals ◊ *medio* by; **~ avión** by air; **~ correo** by mail, *Br tb* by post ◊ *tiempo*: **~ un segundo** *L.Am.* for a second; **~ la mañana** in the morning ◊ *movimiento*: **~ la calle** down the street; **~ un tunel** through a tunnel; **~ aquí** this way ◊ *posición aproximada* around, about; *está* **~** *aquí* it's around here (somewhere) ◊ *cambio*: **~ cincuenta pesos** for fifty pesos ◊ *otros usos*: **~ hora** an *o* per hour; *dos* **~** *dos* two times two; *¿* **~** *qué?* why?; *el motivo* **~** *el cual or* **~** *el que …* the reason why …

porcelana *f* porcelain, china; *de* **~** porcelain *atr*, china *atr*

porcentaje *m* percentage

porche *f* porch

porción *f* portion

pordiosero *m*, *-a* *f* beggar

porfiar <1c> *v/i* insist (*en* on)

pormenor *m* detail

porno 1 *adj* porn *atr* **2** *m* porn; **pornografía** *f* pornography; **porno-**

gráfico *adj* pornographic

poro *m* pore; **poroso** *adj* porous

poroto *m Rpl, Chi* bean; **~s verdes** *L.Am.* green beans

porque *conj* because; **~ sí** just because

porqué *m* reason

porquería *f* (*suciedad*) filth; F *cosa de poca calidad* piece of trash F

porra *f* baton; (*palo*) club; **¡vete a la ~!** F go to hell! F; **porrazo** *m*: **darle un ~ a alguien** F hit s.o.; **darse** or **pegarse un ~** crash (*contra* into)

porro *m* F joint F

porrón *m container from which wine is poured straight into the mouth*

portaaviones *m inv* aircraft carrier

portada *f* TIP front page; *de revista* cover; ARQUI front

portafolios *m inv* briefcase

portal *m* foyer; (*entrada*) doorway

portaligas *m inv Arg, Chi* garter belt, *Br* suspender belt

portarse <1a> *v/r* behave

portátil *adj* portable

portavoz *m/f* spokesman; *mujer* spokeswoman

portazo *m*: **dar un ~** F slam the door

porte *m* (*aspecto*) appearance, air; (*gasto de correo*) postage

portento *m* wonder; *persona* genius

porteño *Arg* **1** *adj* of Buenos Aires, Buenos Aires *atr* **2** *m*, **-a** *f* native of Buenos Aires

portería *f* reception; *casa* superintendent's apartment, *Br* caretaker's flat; DEP goal; **portero** *m* doorman; *de edificio* superintendent, *Br* caretaker; DEP goalkeeper; **~ automático** intercom, *Br* entryphone

portón *m* large door

Portugal Portugal; **portugués 1** *m/adj* Portuguese **2** *m*, **-esa** *f persona* Portuguese

porvenir *m* future

posada *f C.Am., Méx* Christmas party; (*fonda*) inn

posar <1a> **1** *v/t mano* lay, place (**sobre** on); **~ la mirada en** gaze at **2** *v/r* **~se** *de ave, insecto,* AVIA land

posavasos *m inv* coaster

posdata *f* postscript

poseer <2e> *v/t* possess; (*ser dueño de*) own, possess; **posesión** *f* possession; **tomar ~** (*de un cargo*) POL take up office

posguerra *f* postwar period

posibilidad *f* possibility; **posibilitar** <1a> *v/t* make possible; **posible** *adj* possible; **en lo ~** as far as possible; **hacer todo lo ~** do everything possible; **es ~ que ...** perhaps ...

posición *f tb* MIL, *fig* position; *social* standing, status

positivo *adj* positive

posmoderno *adj* postmodern

poso *m* dregs *pl*

posología *f* dosage

posponer <2r; *part* **pospuesto**> *v/t* postpone; **pospuesto** *part* → **posponer**

posta *f*: **a ~** on purpose

postal 1 *adj* mail *atr*, postal **2** *f* postcard

poste *m* post

póster *m* poster

postergar <1a> *v/t* postpone

posteridad *f* posterity; **posterior** *adj* later, subsequent; (*trasero*) rear *atr*, back *atr*

postizo 1 *adj* false **2** *m* hairpiece

postor *m* bidder; **al mejor ~** to the highest bidder

postrar <1a> **1** *v/t*: **la gripe lo postró** he was laid up with flu **2** *v/r* **~se** prostrate o.s.

postre *m* dessert; **a la ~** in the end

postular <1a> *v/t hipótesis* put forward, advance

póstumo *adj* posthumous

postura *f tb fig* position

pos(t)venta *adj inv* after-sales *atr*

potable *adj* drinkable; *fig* F passable; **agua ~** drinking water

potaje *m* GASTR stew

potasio *m* potassium

potencia *f* power; **en ~** potential; **potencial** *m/adj* potential; **potenciar** <1b> *v/t fig* foster, promote

potentado *m*, **-a** *f* tycoon

potente *adj* powerful

P

potestad *f* authority; **patria ~** parental authority

potingue *m* F *desp* lotion, cream

potro *m* ZO colt

pozo *m* well; MIN shaft; *Rpl* pothole; **un ~ sin fondo** *fig* a bottomless pit

pozol *m* C.Am. corn liquor

pozole *m* Méx corn stew

práctica *f* practice; **practicar** <1g> *v/t* practice, *Br* practise; **deporte** play; **~ la equitación / la esgrima** ride / fence; **práctico** *adj* practical

pradera *f* prairie, grassland; **prado** *m* meadow

pragmático *adj* pragmatic; **pragmatismo** *m* pragmatism

pral. *abr* (= **principal**) first

preámbulo *m* preamble

prebenda *f* sinecure

precalentamiento *m* DEP warm-up

precario *adj* precarious

precaución *f* precaution; **tomar precauciones** take precautions

precavido *adj* cautious

precedente 1 *adj* previous **2** *m* precedent; **preceder** <2a> *v/t* precede

preceptivo *adj* compulsory, mandatory

preciado *adj* precious; **preciarse** <1b> *v/r:* **cualquier fontanero que se precie ...** any self-respecting plumber ...

precinto *m* seal

precio *m* price; **~ de venta al público** recommended retail price; **preciosidad** *f:* **esa casa / chica es una ~** that house / girl is gorgeous *o* beautiful; **precioso** *adj* (*de valor*) precious; (*hermoso*) beautiful; **preciosura** *f* L.Am. F → **preciosidad**

precipicio *m* precipice

precipitación *f* (*prisa*) hurry, haste; **precipitaciones** rain *sg;* **precipitado** *adj* hasty, sudden; **precipitarse** <1a> *v/r* rush; *fig* be hasty

precisamente *adv* precisely; **precisión** *f* precision; **preciso** *adj* precise, accurate; **ser ~** be necessary

preconcebido *adj* preconceived

precoz *adj* early; *niño* precocious

precursor *m,* **~a** *f* precursor, forerunner

predecesor *m,* **~a** *f* predecessor

predecir <3p; *part* **predicho**> *v/t* predict

predestinar <1a> *v/t* predestine

predicado *m* predicate; **predicador** *m,* **~a** *f* preacher; **predicar** <1g> *v/t* preach; **~ con el ejemplo** F practice (*Br* practise) what one preaches

predicción *f* prediction, forecast

predicho *part* → **predecir**

predilecto *adj* favo(u)rite

predisponer <2r> *v/t* prejudice; **predisposición** *f tb* MED predisposition; (*tendencia*) tendency; **una ~ en contra de** a prejudice against; **predispuesto** *adj* predisposed (*a* to)

predominante *adj* predominant; **predominar** <1a> *v/t* predominate

preeminente *adj* preeminent

preescolar *adj* preschool

preestreno *m* preview

preexistente *adj* pre-existing

prefabricado *adj* prefabricated

prefacio *m* preface, foreword

preferencia *f* preference; **preferente** *adj* preferential; **preferible** *adj* preferable (*a* to); **es ~ que ...** it's better if ...; **preferido 1** *part* → **preferir 2** *adj* favo(u)rite; **preferir** <3i> *v/t* prefer

prefijo *m* prefix; TELEC area code, *Br* dialling code

pregonar <1a> *v/t* proclaim, make public

pregunta *f* question; **preguntar** <1a> **1** *v/t* ask **2** *v/i* ask; **~ por algo** ask about sth; **~ por alguien** *paradero* ask for s.o.; *salud etc* ask about s.o. **3** *v/r* **~se** wonder

prehistoria *f* prehistory; **prehistórico** *adj* prehistoric

prejuicio *m* prejudice

prelado *m* prelate

prelavado *m* prewash

preliminar 1 *adj* preliminary; DEP qualifying **2** *m* L.Am. qualifier

preludio *m* prelude

premamá *adj* maternity *atr*

P

prematrimonial *adj* premarital

prematuro 1 *adj* premature **2** *m*, **-a** *f* premature baby

premeditado *adj* premeditated; **premeditación** *f* premeditation; *con* ~ deliberately

premiado 1 *adj* prizewinning **2** *m*, **-a** *f* prizewinner; **premiar** <1b> *v/t* award a prize to; **premio** *m* prize

premisa *f* premise

premonición *f* premonition

premura *f* haste

prenatal *adj* prenatal

prenda *f* item of clothing, garment; *garantía* security; *en juegos* forfeit; *no soltar* ~ not say a word (*sobre* about)

prender <2a; *part* **preso**> **1** *v/t* a *fugitivo* capture; *sujetar* pin up; *L.Am. fuego* light; *L.Am. luz* switch on, turn on; ~ *fuego a* set fire to **2** *v/i de planta* take; (*empezar a arder*) catch; *de moda* catch on

prendería *f Esp* pawnbroker's, pawn shop

prensa *f* press; ~ *amarilla* gutter press; **prensar** <1a> *v/t* press

preñado *adj* pregnant

preñado *adj* pregnant

preocupación *f* worry, concern; **preocupado** *adj* worried (*por* about), concerned (*por* about); **preocupante** *adj* worrying; **preocupar** <1a> **1** *v/t* worry, concern **2** *v/r* ~**se** worry (*por* about); ~**se de** (*encargarse*) look after, take care of

preparación *f* preparation; (*educación*) education; *para trabajo* training; **preparado** *adj* ready, prepared; **preparador** *m*, ~**a** *f*: ~ *físico* trainer; **preparar** <1a> **1** *v/t* prepare, get ready **2** *v/r* ~**se** get ready (*para* for), prepare o.s. (*para* for); *de tormenta, crisis* be brewing; **preparativos** *mpl* preparations

preponderante *adj* predominant

preposición *f* preposition

prepotente *adj* arrogant

prerrogativa *f* prerogative

presa *f* (*dique*) dam; (*embalse*) reservoir; (*víctima*) prey; *L.Am. para comer* bite to eat

presagio *m* omen; sign; (*premonición*) premonition

prescindir <3a> *v/i*: ~ *de* (*privarse de*) do without; (*omitir*) leave out, dispense with; (*no tener en cuenta*) disregard

prescribir <3a; *part* **prescrito**> *v/i* JUR prescribe; **prescrito** *part* → **prescribir**

presencia *f* presence; *buena* ~ smart appearance; **presenciar** <1b> *v/t* witness; (*estar presente a*) attend, be present at

presentación *f* presentation; COM launch; *entre personas* introduction; **presentador** *m*, ~**a** *f* TV presenter; **presentar** <1a> **1** *v/t* present; *a alguien* introduce; *producto* launch; *solicitud* submit **2** *v/r* ~**se** *en sitio* show up; (*darse a conocer*) introduce o.s.; *a examen* take; *de problema, dificultad* arise; *a elecciones* run

presente 1 *adj* present; *tener algo* ~ bear sth in mind; *¡~!* here! **2** *m tiempo* present **3** *m/fpl*: *los* ~**s** those present

presentimiento *m* premonition; **presentir** <3i> *v/t* foresee; *presiento que vendrá* I have a feeling he'll come

preservar <1a> *v/t* protect; **preservativo** *m* condom

presidencia *f* presidency; *de compañía* presidency, *Br* chairmanship; *de comité* chairmanship; **presidencial** *adj* presidential; **presidente** *m*, **-a** *f* president; *de gobierno* premier, prime minister; *de compañía* president, *Br* chairman, *Br mujer* chairwoman; *de comité* chair

presidiario *m*, **-a** *f* prisoner

presidir <3a> *v/t* be president of; *reunión* chair, preside over

presión *f* pressure; ~ *sanguínea* blood pressure; **presionar** <1a> *v/t botón* press; *fig* put pressure on, pressure

preso 1 *part* → **prender 2** *m*, **-a** *f* prisoner

prestación *f* provision; ~ *social sustitutoria* MIL community

service in lieu of military service;
prestado *adj*: **dejar ~** *algo* lend sth;
pedir ~ *algo* borrow sth; **prestamista** *m/f* moneylender; **préstamo**
m loan; **~** *bancario* bank loan;
prestar <1a> *v/t dinero* lend; *ayuda*
give; *L.Am.* borrow; **~** *atención* pay
attention
prestidigitador *m*, **~a** *f* conjurer
prestigio *m* prestige; **prestigioso**
adj prestigious
presumido *adj* conceited; (*coqueto*)
vain; **presumir** <3a> **1** *v/t* presume
2 *v/i* show off; **~** *de algo* boast o
brag about sth; *presume de listo* he
thinks   he's   very   clever;
presuntamente *adv* allegedly;
presunto *adj* alleged, suspected;
presuntuoso *adj* conceited
presuponer <2r; *part* **presupuesto**> *v/t* assume; **presupuesto
1** *part* → **presuponer 2** *m* POL budget
presuroso *adj* hurried
pretencioso *adj* pretentious
pretender <2a> *v/t*: *pretendía
convencerlos* he was trying to
persuade them; **pretendiente** *m de
mujer* suitor
pretensión *f L.Am.* (*arrogancia*)
vanity; *sin pretensiones* unpreten-
tious
pretérito *m* GRAM preterite
pretextar <1a> *v/t* claim; **pretexto** *m*
pretext
prevalecer <2d> *v/i* prevail (*sobre*
over)
prevaricación *f* corruption
prevención *f* prevention
prevenido 1 *part* → **prevenir 2** *adj*
well-prepared; **prevenir** <3s> *v/t*
prevent; (*avisar*) warn (*contra*
against); **preventivo** *adj* preventive, preventative
prever <2v; *part* **previsto**> *v/t* foresee
previo *adj* previous; *sin ~ aviso* without (prior) warning
previsible *adj* foreseeable; **previsión** *f* (*predicción*) forecast; (*preparación*) foresight; **previsor** *adj*

farsighted; **previsto 1** *part* → **prever 2** *adj* foreseen, expected; **tener
~** have planned
prieto *adj L.Am.* dark-skinned
prima *f de seguro* premium; (*pago extra*) bonus
primacía *f* supremacy, primacy;
(*prioridad*) priority; **primario** *adj*
primary
primavera *f* spring; BOT primrose
primer *adj* first
primera *f* first class; AUTO first gear; *a
la ~* first-time; *de ~* F first-class,
first-rate; **primerizo** *adj* inexperienced, green F; *madre* new, first-
time; **primero 1** *adj* first; **~s
auxilios** *pl* first aid *sg* **2** *m*, **-a** *f* first
(one) **3** *adv* first
primitivo *adj* primitive; (*original*)
original
primo *m*, **-a** *f* cousin
primogénito 1 *adj* first **2** *m*, **-a** *f* first
child
primordial *adj* fundamental
primoroso *adj* exquisite
princesa *f* princess
principal *adj* main, principal; *lo ~* the
main o most important thing
príncipe *m* prince
principiante 1 *adj* inexperienced
2 *m/f* beginner; **principio** *m* principle; *en tiempo* beginning; *a ~s de
abril* at the beginning of April; *en ~*
in principle
pringar <1h> **1** *v/t ensuciar* get
greasy; *fig* F get involved (*en* in)
2 *v/r* **~se** get greasy; *fig* F get mixed
up (*en* in); **pringoso** *adj* greasy
prioridad *f* priority; **prioritario** *adj*
priority *atr*
prisa *f* hurry, rush; *darse ~* hurry
(up); *tener ~* be in a hurry o rush
prisión *f* prison, jail; **prisionero 1** *adj*
captive **2** *m*, **-a** *f* prisoner
prismáticos *mpl* binoculars
priva *f Esp* F booze F
privacidad *f* privacy
privación *f acción* deprivation; *sufrir
privaciones* sufffer privation(s) o
hardship
privado 1 *part* → **privar 2** *adj*

private; **privar** <1a> **1** v/t: ~ *a alguien de algo* deprive s.o. of sth **2** v/r ~**se** deprive o.s.: ~*se de algo* deprive o.s. of sth, go without sth; **privatización** f privatization; **privatizar** <1f> v/t privatize

privilegiado adj privileged; (*excelente*) exceptional; **privilegio** m privilege

pro 1 prp for, in aid of; *en ~ de* for **2** m pro; *los ~s y los contras* the pros and cons

proa f MAR bow

probabilidad f probability; **probable** adj probable, likely; *es ~ que venga* she'll probably come

probador m fitting room; **probar** <1m> **1** v/t *teoría* test, try out; (*comer un poco de*) taste, try; (*comer por primera vez*) try **2** v/i try; ~ *a hacer* try doing **3** v/r ~**se** try on; **probeta** f test tube

problema m problem; **problemático** adj problematic

procedencia f origin, provenance; **proceder** <2a> **1** v/i come (*de* from); (*actuar*) proceed; (*ser conveniente*) be fitting; ~ *a* proceed to; ~ *contra alguien* initiate proceedings against s.o. **2** m conduct; **procedimiento** m procedure, method; JUR proceedings pl

procesado m, **-a** f accused, defendant

procesador m INFOR processor; ~ *de textos* word processor

procesamiento m: ~ *de textos* word processing

procesar <1a> v/t INFOR process; JUR prosecute

procesión f procession

proceso m process; JUR trial; ~ *de datos / textos* INFOR data / word processing

proclamar <1a> v/t proclaim

proclive adj given (*a* to)

procrear <1a> v/i breed, procreate fml

procurar <1a> v/t try; *procura no llegar tarde* try not to be late

prodigar <1h> **1** v/t be generous

with **2** v/r ~**se** (*aparecer*) be seen in public

prodigio m wonder, miracle; *persona* prodigy; **prodigioso** adj prodigious

pródigo adj (*generoso*) generous; (*derrochador*) extravagant

producción f production; **producir** <3o> **1** v/t produce; (*causar*) cause **2** v/r ~**se** happen, occur; *se produjo un ruido tremendo* there was a tremendous noise

productividad f productivity; **productivo** adj productive; *empresa* profitable; **producto** m product; ~ *interior bruto* gross domestic product; ~ *nacional bruto* gross national product; **productor** m, **-a** f producer

produjo vb → *producir*

produzco vb → *producir*

proeza f feat, exploit

profana f laywoman; **profanar** <1a> v/t defile, desecrate; **profano 1** adj fig lay atr **2** m layman

profecía f prophecy

profesar <1a> v/t REL profess; fig feel, have; **profesión** f profession; **profesional** m/f & adj professional; **profesor** m, **-a** f teacher; *de universidad* professor, Br lecturer; **profesorado** m faculty, Br staff pl

profeta m prophet; **profetizar** <1f> v/t prophesy

profiláctico 1 adj preventive, prophylactic fml **2** m condom

prófugo m, **-a** f JUR fugitive

profundidad f depth; **profundizar** <1f> v/i: ~ *en algo* go into sth in depth; **profundo** adj deep; *pensamiento, persona* profound

profuso adj abundant, plentiful

programa m program, Br programme; INFOR program; EDU syllabus; ~ *de estudios* curriculum; **programación** f RAD, TV programs pl, Br programmes; INFOR programming; **programador** m, **-a** f programmer; **programar** <1a> v/t *aparato* program, Br programme; INFOR program; (*planear*) schedule

P

progresar <1a> v/i progress, make progress; **progresista** m/f & adj progressive; **progresivo** adj progressive; **progreso** m progress

prohibición f ban (**de** on); **prohibido** adj forbidden; **prohibir** <3a> v/t forbid; oficialmente ban; **prohibitivo** adj precio prohibitive

prójimo m fellow human being

prole f offspring

proletario 1 adj proletarian **2** m, **-a** f proletarian

proliferación f proliferation; **proliferar** <1a> v/t proliferate; **prolífico** adj prolific

prolijo adj long-winded; (minucioso) detailed

prólogo m preface

prolongado adj prolonged, lengthy; **prolongar** <1h> **1** v/t extend, prolong **2** v/r **~se** go o carry on; en espacio extend

promedio m average

promesa f promise; **prometedor** adj bright, promising; **prometer** <2a> **1** v/t promise **2** v/r **~se** get engaged; **prometida** f fiancée; **prometido 1** part → **prometer 2** adj engaged **3** m fiancé

prominente adj prominent

promiscuidad f promiscuity; **promiscuo** adj promiscuous

promoción f promotion; EDU year; **promocionar** <1a> v/t promote; **promotor** m, **~a** f promoter; **~ inmobiliario** developer; **promover** <2h> v/t promote; (causar) provoke, cause

promulgar <1h> v/t ley promulgate

pronombre m GRAM pronoun

pronosticar <1g> v/t forecast; **pronóstico** m MED prognosis; **~ del tiempo** weather forecast

pronto 1 adj prompt **2** adv (dentro de poco) soon; (temprano) early; **de ~** suddenly; **tan ~ como** as soon as

pronunciación f pronunciation; **pronunciar** <1b> v/t pronounce; (decir) say; **~ un discurso** give a speech

propaganda f advertising; POL propaganda; **propagar** <1h> **1** v/t spread **2** v/r **~se** spread

propano m propane

propasarse <1a> v/r go too far

propenso adj prone (**a** to); **ser ~ a hacer** be prone to do, have a tendency to do

propiciar <1b> v/t (favorecer) promote; (causar) bring about; **propicio** adj favo(u)rable

propiedad f property; **propietario** m, **-a** f owner

propina f tip; **propinar** <1a> v/t golpe, paliza give

propio adj own; (característico) characteristic (**de** of), typical (**de** of); (adecuado) suitable (**para** for); **la -a directora** the director herself

proponer <2r; part **propuesto**> v/t propose, suggest

proporción f proportion; **proporcional** adj proportional; **proporcionar** <1a> v/t provide, supply; satisfacción give

proposición f proposal, suggestion

propósito m (intención) intention; (objetivo) purpose; **a ~** on purpose; (por cierto) by the way

propuesta f proposal

propuesto part → **proponer**

propugnar <1a> v/t advocate

propulsar <1a> v/t TÉC propel; fig promote; **propulsor** m (motor) engine

prórroga f DEP overtime, Br extra time; **prorrogar** <1h> v/t plazo extend

prorrumpir <3a> v/i burst (**en** into)

prosa f prose; **prosaico** adj mundane, prosaic

proseguir <3d & 3l> **1** v/t carry on, continue **2** v/i continue (**con** with)

proselitismo m proselytism

prospecto m directions for use pl; de propaganda leaflet

prosperar <1a> v/i prosper, thrive; **prosperidad** f prosperity; **próspero** adj prosperous, thriving

próstata f prostate

prostíbulo m brothel

prostitución f prostitution; **prostituirse** <3g> v/r prostitute o.s.; **prostituta** f prostitute; **prostituto** m male prostitute

protagonista m/f personaje main character; actor, actriz star; de una hazaña hero; mujer heroine; **protagonizar** <1f> v/t star in, play the lead in; incidente play a leading role in

protección f protection; **proteger** <2c> v/t protect (de from)

proteína f protein

protésico m, -a f: ~ **dental** dental technician; **prótesis** f prosthesis

protesta f protest; **protestante** m/f Protestant; **protestar** <1a> **1** v/t protest **2** v/i (quejarse) complain (por, de about); (expresar oposición) protest (contra, por about, against)

protocolo m protocol

prototipo m TÉC prototype

protuberancia f protuberance

prov. abr (= provincia) province

provecho m benefit; ¡buen ~! enjoy (your meal); sacar ~ de benefit from

proveedor m, -a f supplier; ~ de (acceso a) Internet Internet Service Provider, ISP; **proveer** <2e; part provisto> v/t supply; ~ a alguien de algo supply s.o. with sth

provenir <3s> v/i come (de from)

proverbio m proverb

providencia f providence

provincia f province; **provincial** adj provincial; **provinciano 1** adj provincial **2** m, -a f provincial

provisional adj provisional; **provisiones** fpl provisions

provisto 1 part → **proveer 2** adj: ~ de equipped with

provocación f provocation; **provocador** adj provocative; **provocar** <1g> v/t cause; al enfado provoke; sexualmente lead on; ¿te provoca un café? S.Am. how about a coffee?; **provocativo** adj provocative

proxeneta m pimp; **proxenetismo** m procuring

proximidad f proximity; **próximo** adj (siguiente) next; (cercano) near, close

proyección f MAT, PSI projection; de película showing; **proyectar** <1a> v/t project; (planear) plan; película show; sombra cast; **proyectil** m missile; **proyecto** m plan; trabajo project; ~ **de ley** bill; **tener en ~ ha-cer algo** plan to do sth; **proyector** m projector

prudencia f caution, prudence; **prudente** adj careful, cautious

prueba f tb TIP proof; JUR piece of evidence; DEP event; EDU test; a ~ de bala bulletproof; poner algo a ~ put sth to the test

P.S. abr (= postscriptum (posdata)) PS (= postscript)

pseudo... pref pseudo-

pseudónimo m pseudonym

psicoanálisis f (psycho)analysis; **psicoanalista** m/f (psycho)analyst

psicodélico adj psychedelic

psicología f psychology; **psicológi-co** adj psychological; **psicólogo** m, -a f psychologist

psicópata m/f psychopath

psicosis f inv psychosis

psicoterapia f psychotherapy

psiquiatra m/f psychiatrist; **psiquia-tría** f psychiatry; **psiquiátrico** adj psychiatric

psíquico adj psychic

pta abr (= peseta) peseta

ptas abr (= pesetas) pesetas

púa f ZO spine, quill; MÚS plectrum, pick

pub m bar

pubertad f puberty

publicación f publication; **publicar** <1g> **1** v/t publish **2** v/r ~**se** come out, be published; **publicidad** f (divulgación) publicity; COM advertising; (anuncios) advertisements pl; **publicista** m/f advertising executive; **publicitario 1** adj advertising atr **2** m, -a f advertising executive; **público 1** adj public; escuela public, Br state **2** m public; TEA audience; DEP spectators pl,

P

crowd

pucho *m S.Am.* P cigarette butt, *Br* fag end F; **no valer un ~** be completely worthless

pude *vb* → **poder**

púdico *adj* modest

pudín *m* pudding

pudo *vb* → **poder**

pudor *m* modesty

pudrir <3a> 1 *v/t* rot 2 *v/r* -**se** rot; ~**se de envidia** be green with envy

pueblerino *m*, -**a** *f* hick *desp*; **pueblero** *m*, -**a** *f L.Am.* villager; *de pueblo más grande* townsman; *mujer* townswoman; **pueblo** *m* village; *más grande* town

puedo *vb* → **poder**

puente *m* bridge; **hacer ~** have a day off between a weekend and a public holiday

puenting *m* bungee jumping

puerco 1 *adj* dirty; *fig* filthy F 2 *m* ZO pig; ~ **espín** porcupine

puericultura *f* childcare

puerro *m* BOT leek

puerta *f* door; *en valla* gate; DEP goal; ~ **de embarque** gate

puerto *m* MAR port; GEOG pass

Puerto Rico Puerto Rico; **puertorriqueño** 1 *adj* Puerto Rican 2 *m*, -**a** *f* Puerto Rican

pues *conj* well; *fml (porque)* as, since; ~ **bien** well; *¡~ sí!* of course!

puesta *f*: ~ **a punto** tune-up; ~ **de sol** sunset

puestero *m*, -**a** *f L.Am.* stall holder

puesto 1 *part* → **poner** 2 *m lugar* place; *en mercado* stand, stall; MIL post; ~ **(de trabajo)** job 3 *conj*: ~ **que** since, given that

pugnar <1a> *v/i* fight (**por** for; **por hacer** to do)

puja *f (lucha)* struggle; *en subasta* bid; **pujar** <1a> *v/i (luchar)* struggle; *en subasta* bid

pulcro *adj* immaculate

pulga *f* ZO flea; **tener malas ~s** *fig* F be bad-tempered

pulgada *f* inch

pulgar *m* thumb

pulimentar <1a> *v/t* polish; **pulir** <3a> *v/t* polish

pulla *f* gibe

pulmón *m* lung; **pulmonía** *f* MED pneumonia

pulpa *f* pulp

pulpería *f L.Am.* mom-and-pop store, *Br* corner shop; **pulpero** *m*, -**a** *f S.Am.* storekeeper, shopkeeper

púlpito *m* pulpit

pulpo *m* ZO octopus

pulque *m Méx* pulque *(alcoholic drink made from cactus)*; **pulquería** *f Méx* pulque bar

pulsación *f* beat; *al escribir a máquina* key stroke; **pulsar** <1a> *v/t botón, tecla* press

pulsera *f* bracelet

pulso *m* pulse; *fig* steady hand; **tomar el ~ a alguien** take s.o.'s pulse; **tomar el ~ a algo** *fig* take the pulse of sth

pulular <1a> *v/i* mill around

pulverizador *m* spray; **pulverizar** <1f> *v/t* spray; *(convertir en polvo)* pulverize, crush

puma *m* ZO puma, mountain lion

puna *f L.Am.* GEOG high Andean plateau; MED altitude sickness

pundonor *m* pride

punitivo *adj* punitive

punta *f* tip; *(extremo)* end; *de lápiz*, GEOG point; *L.Am. (grupo)* group; **sacar ~ a** sharpen

puntada *f* stitch

puntapié *m* kick

puntera *f* toe

puntería *f* aim

puntero 1 *adj* leading 2 *m* pointer

puntiagudo *adj* pointed, sharp

puntilla *f*: **de ~s** on tippy-toe, *Br* on tiptoe

puntilloso *adj* particular, punctilious *fml*

punto *m* point; *señal* dot; *signo de puntuación* period, *Br* full stop; *en costura, sutura* stitch; **dos ~s** colon; ~ **y coma** semicolon; ~ **muerto** AUTO neutral; ~ **de vista** point of view; **a ~** *(listo)* ready; *(a tiempo)* in time; **de ~** knitted; **en ~** on the dot; **estar a ~ de** be about to; **hacer ~** knit;

hasta cierto ~ up to a point; *empresa f* ~**.com** dot.com (company)
puntuación *f* punctuation; DEP score; EDU grade, mark; **puntual** *adj* punctual; **puntualidad** *f* punctuality; **puntualizar** <1f> *v/t* (*señalar*) point out; (*aclarar*) clarify
punzada *f* sharp *o* stabbing pain; **punzante** *adj* stinging
puñado *m* handful
puñal *m* dagger; **puñalada** *f* stab wound
puñeta *f*: **¡~(s)!** F for heaven's sake! F; *hacer la* ~ *a alguien* F give s.o. a hard time F
puñetazo *m* punch; *dar un* ~ punch
puño *m* fist; *de camisa* cuff; *de bastón*, *paraguas* handle
pupa *f en labio* cold sore; *hacerse* ~ *lenguaje infantil* hurt o.s.
pupila *f* pupil
pupitre *m* desk
pupusa *f L.Am.* filled dumpling
purasangre *m* thoroughbred
puré *m* purée; *sopa* cream; ~ *de patatas* or *papas L.Am.* mashed potatoes
pureza *f* purity
purga *f* POL purge; **purgante** *m/adj* laxative, purgative; **purgatorio** *m*

REL purgatory
purificación *f* purification; **purificar** <1g> *v/t* purify
purista *m/f* purist
puritano 1 *adj* puritanical **2** *m*, **-a** *f* puritan
puro 1 *adj* pure; *casualidad, coincidencia* sheer; *Méx* (*único*) sole, only; *la* **-a** *verdad* the honest truth; *te sirven la* **-a** *comida Méx* they just serve food **2** *m* cigar
púrpura *f* purple
pus *m* pus
puse *vb* → *poder*
pusilánime *adj* fainthearted
puso *vb* → *poder*
puta *f* P whore P; **putada** *f* P dirty trick; **¡qué ~!** shit! P; **putear** <1a> *v/t L.Am.* P swear at; ~ *alguien Esp* give s.o. a hard time, make life difficult for s.o.
puto *adj* P goddamn F, *Br* bloody F; *de puta madre* P great F, fantastic F
putrefacción *f* putrefaction
puzzle *m* jigsaw (puzzle)
PVC *abr* (= *cloruro de polivinilo*) PVC (= polyvinyl chloride)
P.V.P. *abr* (= *precio de venta al público*) RRP (= recommended retail price)
pza. *abr* (= *plaza*) sq (= square)

Q

q.e.p.d. *abr* (= *que en paz descanse*) RIP (= requiescat in pace)
que 1 *pron rel sujeto*: *persona* who, that; *cosa* which, that; *complemento*: *persona* that, whom *fml*; *cosa* that, which; *el coche* ~ *ves* the car you can see, the car that *o* which you can see; *el* ~ the one that **2** *conj* that; *lo mismo* ~ *tú* the same as you; **¡~ entre!** tell him to come in; **¡~ descanses!** sleep well; **¡~ sí!** I said

yes; **¡~ no!** I said no; *es* ~ ... the thing is ...; *yo* ~ *tú* if I were you
qué 1 *adj & pron interr* what; **¿~ pasó?** what happened?; **¿~ día es?** what day is it?; **¿~ vestido prefieres?** which dress do you prefer? **2** *adj & pron int*: **¡~ moto!** what a motorbike!; **¡~ de flores!** what a lot of flowers! **3** *adv*: **¡~ alto es!** he's so tall!; **¡~ bien!** great!
quebrada *f L.Am.* stream

quebradero *m*: **~s de cabeza** F headaches; **quebradizo** *adj* brittle; **quebrado 1** *adj* broken **2** *m* MAT fraction; **quebrantahuesos** *m inv* ZO lammergeier; **quebrantar** <1a> *v/t ley, contrato* break; **quebrar** <1k> **1** *v/t* break **2** *v/i* COM go bankrupt **3** *v/r* **~se** break

quedar <1a> **1** *v/i* (*permanecer*) stay; *en un estado* be; (*sobrar*) be left; **quedó sin resolver** it remained unresolved, it wasn't sorted out; **te queda bien/mal** *de estilo* it suits you/doesn't suit you; *de talla* it fits you/doesn't fit you; **~ cerca** be nearby; **~ con alguien** F arrange to meet (with) s.o.; **~ en algo** agree to sth; **¿queda mucho tiempo?** is there much time left? **2** *v/r* **~se** stay; **~se ciego** go blind; **~se con algo** keep sth; **me quedé sin comer** I ended up not eating

quehaceres *mpl* tasks

queja *f* complaint; **quejarse** <1a> *v/r* complain (**a** to; **de** about); **quejica** *adj* F whining F; **quejido** *m* moan, groan; **quejumbroso** *adj* moaning

quemado *adj* burnt; *Méx* (*desvirtuado*) discredited; **~ por el sol** sunburnt; **oler a ~** smell of burning; **quemadura** *f* burn; **quemar** <1a> **1** *v/t* burn; *con agua* scald; F *recursos* use up; F *dinero* blow F **2** *v/i* be very hot **3** *v/r* **~se** burn o.s.; *de tostada, papeles* burn; *fig* burn o.s. out; *Méx* (*desvirtuarse*) become discredited

quena *f S.Am.* Indian flute

quepo *vb* → **caber**

queque *m L.Am.* cake

querella *f* JUR lawsuit; **querellarse** <1a> *v/r* JUR bring a lawsuit (**contra** against)

querer <2u> *v/t* (*desear*) want; (*amar*) love; **~ decir** mean; **sin ~** unintentionally; **quisiera …** I would like …; **querido 1** *part* → **querer** **2** *adj* dear **3** *m, -a f* darling

queroseno *m* kerosene

querrá *vb* → **querer**

querría *vb* → **querer**

quesadilla *f* quesadilla (*folded tortilla*)

queso *m* cheese; **~ para untar** cheese spread; **~ rallado** grated cheese

quicio *m*: **sacar de ~ a alguien** F drive s.o. crazy F

quid *m*: **el ~ de la cuestión** the nub of the question

quiebra *f* COM bankruptcy

quien *pron rel sujeto* who, that; *objeto* who, whom *fml*, that; **no soy ~ para hacerlo** I'm not the right person to do it

quién *pron* who; **¿~ es?** who is it?; **¿de ~ es este libro?** whose is this book?, who does this book belong to?

quienquiera *pron* whoever

quiero *vb* → **querer**

quieto *adj* still; **¡estáte ~!** keep still!

quijotesco *adj* quixotic

quilate *m* carat

quilla *f* keel

quimera *f* pipe dream

química *f* chemistry; **químico 1** *adj* chemical **2** *m*, **-a f** chemist

quimioterapia *f* MED chemotherapy

quimono *m* kimono

quincalla *f* junk

quince *adj* fifteen; **quincena** *f* two weeks, *Br* fortnight

quiniela *f* lottery where the winners are decided by soccer results

quinientos *adj* five hundred

quinina *f* quinine

quinquenio *m* five-year period

quinta *f* MIL draft, *Br* call-up; **es de mi ~** he's my age

quinteto *m* MÚS quintet

quinto 1 *adj* fifth **2** *m* MIL conscript

quiosco *m* kiosk; **~ de prensa** newsstand, *Br* newsagent's; **quiosquero** *m*, **-a f** newspaper vendor

quirófano *m* operating room, *Br* operating theatre

quiromancia, quiromancía *f* palmistry

quirúrgico *adj* surgical

quise *vb* → **querer**

quisiera *vb* → **querer**

quiso *vb* → **querer**

quisque F: *todo ~* everyone and his brother F, *Br* the world and his wife F

quisquilla *f* ZO shrimp

quisquilloso *adj* touchy

quiste *m* MED cyst

quitaesmalte *m* nail varnish remover

quitamanchas *m inv* stain remover

quitar <1a> **1** *v/t ropa* take off, remove; *obstáculos* remove; *~ algo a alguien* take sth (away) from s.o.; *~ la mesa* clear the table **2** *v/i: ¡quita!* get out of the way! **3** *v/r ~se ropa, gafas* take off; (*apartarse*) get out of the way; *~se algo/a alguien de encima* get rid of s.o./sth; *¡quítate de en medio!* F get out of the way!

quizá(s) *adv* perhaps, maybe

quórum *m* quorum

R

rabadilla *f* ANAT coccyx

rábano *m* BOT radish; *me importa un ~* F I don't give a damn F

rabia *f* MED rabies *sg*; *dar ~ a alguien* make s.o. mad; *tener ~ a alguien* have it in for s.o.; **rabiar** <1b> *v/i: ~ de dolor* be in agony; *hacer ~ a alguien* *fig* F jerk s.o.'s chain F, pull s.o.'s leg F; *~ por* be dying for

rabieta *f* tantrum

rabino *m* rabbi

rabo *m* tail

rabón *adj* L.Am. *animal* short-tailed

rácano *adj* F stingy F, mean

racha *f* spell

racial *adj* racial

racimo *m* bunch

ración *f* share; (*porción*) serving, portion; **racional** *adj* rational; **racionalizar** <1f> *v/t* rationalize; **racionamiento** *m* rationing; **racionar** <1a> *v/t* ration

racismo *m* racism; **racista** *m/f & adj* racist

radar *m* radar

radiación *f* radiation; **radiactividad** *f* radioactivity; **radiactivo** *adj* radioactive; **radiador** *m* radiator; **radiante** *adj* radiant; **radiar** <1b> *v/t* radiate

radical *m/f & adj* radical; **radicalismo** *m* radicalism; **radicar** <1g> *v/i* stem (*en* from), lie (*en* in)

radio 1 *m* MAT radius; QUÍM radium; *L.Am.* radio; *en un ~ de* within a radius of; *~ de acción* range **2** *f* radio; *~ despertador* clock radio

radioaficionado *m* radio ham

radiocasete *m* radio cassette player

radiodifusión *f* broadcasting

radiofónico *adj* radio *atr*

radiografía *f* X-ray; **radiografiar** <1c> *v/t* X-ray

radiología *f* radiology; **radiólogo** *m*, **-a** *f* radiologist

radiotaxi *m* radio taxi

radiotelegrafista *m/f* radio operator

radioyente *m/f* listener

ráfaga *f* gust; *de balas* burst

rafia *f* raffia

rafting *m* rafting

ragú *m* GASTR ragout

raído *adj* threadbare

rail, raíl *m* rail

raíz *f* root; *~ cuadrada/cúbica* MAT square/cube root; *a ~ de* as a result of; *echar raíces de persona* put down roots

raja *f* (*rodaja*) slice; (*corte*) cut; (*grieta*) crack; **rajar** <1a> **1** *v/t fruta* cut, slice; *cerámica* crack; *neumático* slash **2** v/i F gossip **3** v/r **~se** fig F back out F

rajatabla: **a ~** strictly, to the letter

ralentí m: **al ~** AUTO idling; FOT in slow motion; **ralentizar** <1f> v/t slow down

rallador m grater; **rallar** <1a> v/t GASTR grate

rally(e) m rally

rama f branch; POL wing; **andarse por las ~s** beat about the bush; **ramificación** f ramification

ramo m COM sector; **~ de flores** bunch of flowers

rampa f ramp; **~ de lanzamiento** launch pad

ramplón adj vulgar

rana f ZO frog

ranchera f typical Mexican song

ranchero 1 adj: **canción -a** romantic ballad; **música -a** music of northern Mexico **2** m L.Am. rancher; **rancho** m Méx small farm; L.Am. (barrio de chabolas) shanty town

rancio adj rancid; fig ancient

rango m rank; **de alto ~** high-ranking

ranking m ranking

ranura f slot

rapapolvo m F telling-off F

rapar <1a> v/t pelo crop

rapaz 1 adj predatory; **ave ~** bird of prey **2** m, **-a** f F kid F

rape m pescado anglerfish; **al ~** pelo cropped

rapidez f speed, rapidity; **rápido 1** adj quick, fast **2** m rapids pl

rapiña f pillage

raptar <1a> v/t kidnap; **rapto** m kidnap; **raptor** m, **~a** f kidnapper

raqueta f racket

raquítico adj fig rickety

rareza f scarcity, rarity; **raro** adj rare

ras m: **a ~ de tierra** at ground level; **rasante** adj vuelo low

rasca f L.Am.: **pegarse una ~** F get plastered F; **rascacielos** m inv sky-scraper; **rascado** adj L.Am. F plastered F; **rascar** <1g> v/t scratch;

superficie scrape, scratch

rasero m: **medir por el mismo ~** treat equally

rasgado adj boca wide; **ojos ~s** almond-shaped eyes; **rasgar** <1h> v/t tear (up); **rasgo** m feature; **a grandes ~s** broadly speaking; **rasguño** m MED scratch

raso 1 adj flat, level; **soldado ~** private **2** m material satin; **al ~** in the open air

raspa f fishbone; L.Am. F (reprimanda) telling-off; **raspado** m Méx water ice; **raspadura** f scrape; **raspar** <1a> **1** v/t scrape; con lija sand **2** v/i be rough

rastra f: **entrar a ~s** drag o.s. in, crawl in; **rastreador** adj: **perro ~** tracker dog; **rastrear** <1a> **1** v/t persona track; bosque, zona comb **2** v/i rake; **rastrero** adj mean, low; **rastrillo** m rake; **rastro** m flea market; (huella) trace; **desaparecer sin dejar ~** vanish without trace; **rastrojo** m stubble

rasurar <1a> v/t shave

rata f ZO rat

ratero m, **-a** f petty thief

raticida m rat poison

ratificar <1g> v/t POL ratify

rato m time, while; **~s libres** spare time sg; **al poco ~** after a short time o while; **todo el ~** all the time; **un buen ~** a good while, a pretty long time; **pasar el ~** pass the time; **he pasado un buen / mal ~** I've had a great / an awful time

ratón m ZO, INFOR mouse; **ratonera** f mouse trap

raudal m: **tienen dinero a ~es** they've got loads of money F; **raudo** adj swift

raya f GRAM dash; ZO ray; de pelo part, Br parting; **a** or **de ~s** striped; **pasarse de la ~** overstep the mark, go too far; **rayado** adj disco, superficie scratched

rayano adj bordering (**en** on)

rayar <1a> **1** v/t scratch; (tachar) cross out **2** v/i border (**en** on), verge (**en** on)

rayo *m* FÍS ray; METEO (bolt of) lightning; **~ láser** laser beam; **~ X** X-ray; **~s ultravioleta** ultraviolet rays

raza *f* race; *de animal* breed

razón *f* reason; **a ~ de** *precio* at; **dar la ~ a alguien** admit that s.o. is right; **entrar en ~** see sense; **perder la ~** lose one's mind; **tener ~** be right; **razonable** *adj* reasonable; **razonamiento** *m* reasoning; **razonar** <1a> *v/i* reason

RDSI *abr* (= **Red Digital de Servicios Integrados**) ISDN (= Integrated Services Digital Network)

reacción *f* reaction (**a** to); **avión a ~** jet (aircraft); **reaccionar** <1a> *v/i* react (**a** to); **reaccionario 1** *adj* reactionary **2** *m*, **-a** *f* reactionary

reacio *adj* reluctant (**a** to)

reactivación *f* COM revival, upturn; **reactivar** <1a> *v/t* COM revive

reactor *m* reactor; (*motor*) jet engine

reafirmar <1a> **1** *v/t* reaffirm **2** *v/r* **~se: se en** *idea* reassert

reajuste *m* adjustment; **~ ministerial** POL cabinet reshuffle

real *adj* (*regio*) royal; (*verdadero*) real

realeza *f* royalty

realidad *f* reality; **en ~** in fact, in reality; **realismo** *m* realism; **realista 1** *adj* realistic **2** *m/f* realist

realización *f* fulfil(l)ment; RAD, TV production; **realizador** *m*, **~a** *f* *de película* director; RAD, TV producer; **realizar** <1f> **1** *v/t* *tarea* carry out; RAD, TV produce; COM realize **2** *v/r* **~se** *de persona* fulfil(l) o.s.

realquilar <1a> *v/t* sublet

realzar <1f> *v/t* highlight

reanimación *f* revival; **reanimar** <1a> *v/t* revive

reanudación *f* resumption; **reanudar** <1a> *v/t* resume

reaparecer <2d> *v/i* reappear; **reaparición** *f* reappearance

reaseguro *m* reinsurance

rebaja *f* reduction; **~s de verano/**

invierno summer / winter sale; **rebajar** <1a> **1** *v/t* *precio* lower, reduce; *mercancías* reduce **2** *v/r* **~se** lower o.s., humble o.s.

rebanada *f* slice; **rebanar** <1a> *v/t* slice

rebañar <1a> *v/t*: **~ algo** wipe sth clean

rebaño *m* flock

rebasar <1a> *v/t* Méx AUTO pass, Br overtake

rebatir <3a> *v/t* *razones* rebut, refute

rebeca *f* cardigan

rebeco *m* ZO chamois

rebelarse <1a> *v/r* rebel; **rebelde 1** *adj* rebel *atr* **2** *m/f* rebel; **rebeldía** *f* rebelliousness; **rebelión** *f* rebellion

reblandecer <2d> *v/t* soften

rebobinar <1a> *v/t* rewind

rebosar <1a> *v/i* overflow

rebotar <1a> **1** *v/t* bounce; (*disgustar*) annoy **2** *v/i* bounce, rebound; **rebote** *m* bounce; **de ~** on the rebound

rebozar <1f> *v/t* GASTR coat

rebuscado *adj* over-elaborate

rebuznar <1a> *v/i* bray

recado *m* errand; *Rpl* (*arnés*) harness; **dejar un ~** leave a message

recaída *f* MED relapse

recalar <1a> *v/i* MAR put in (**en** at), call (**en** at)

recalcar <1g> *v/t* stress, emphasize

recalcitrante *adj* recalcitrant

recalentar <1k> *v/t* *comida* warm o heat up

recámara *f* *de arma de fuego* chamber; *L.Am.* (*dormitorio*) bedroom

recambio *m* COM spare part

recapacitar <1a> *v/t* think over, reflect on

recapitular <1a> *v/t* recap

recargar <1h> *v/t* *batería* recharge; *recipiente* refill; **~ un 5%** charge 5% extra; **recargo** *m* surcharge

recatado *adj* modest; (*cauto*) cautious; **recato** *m* modesty; (*prudencia*) caution

recauchutar <1a> *v/t* *neumáticos* retread

R

recaudación *f acción* collection; *cantidad* takings *pl*; **recaudar** <1a> *v/t impuestos, dinero* collect; **recaudo** *m*: **poner a buen ~** put in a safe place

recelo *m* mistrust

recepción *f en hotel* reception; **recepcionista** *m/f* receptionist; **receptivo** *adj* receptive; **receptor** *m* receiver

recesión *f* recession

receta *f* GASTR recipe; **~ médica** prescription; **recetar** <1a> *v/t* MED prescribe; **recetario** *m* recipe book

rechazar <1f> *v/t* reject; MIL repel; **rechazo** *m* rejection

rechinar <1a> *v/i* creak, squeak

rechistar <1a> *v/i* protest; **sin ~** F without a murmur, without complaining

rechoncho *adj* F dumpy F

rechupete: **de ~** F delicious

recibidor *m* entrance hall; **recibimiento** *m* reception; **recibir** <3a> *v/t* receive; **recibo** *m* (sales) receipt

reciclable *adj* recyclable; **reciclado**, **reciclaje** *m* recycling; **reciclar** <1a> *v/t* recycle

recién *adv* newly; *L.Am.* (*hace poco*) just; **~ casados** newly-weds; **~ nacido** newborn; **~ pintado** wet paint; **~ llegamos** we've only just arrived; **reciente** *adj* recent

recinto *m* premises *pl*; *área* grounds *pl*

recio *adj* sturdy, tough

recipiente *m* container

recíproco *adj* reciprocal

recital *m* recital; **recitar** <1a> *v/t* recite

reclamación *f* complaint; POL claim, demand; **reclamar** <1a> **1** *v/t* claim, demand **2** *v/i* complain; **reclame** *m L.Am.* advertisement

reclamo *m* lure

reclinable *adj*: **asiento ~** reclining seat; **reclinar** <1a> **1** *v/t* rest **2** *v/r* **~se** lean, recline (**contra** against)

recluir <3g> *v/t* imprison, confine;

reclusión *f* JUR imprisonment, confinement; **recluso** *m*, **-a** *f* prisoner

recluta *m/f* recruit; **reclutar** <1a> *v/t tb* COM recruit

recobrar <1a> **1** *v/t* recover **2** *v/r* **~se** recover (**de** from)

recogedor *m* dustpan

recogepelotas *m/f inv* ball boy; *niña* ball girl

recoger <2c> **1** *v/t* pick up, collect; *habitación* tidy up; AGR harvest; (*mostrar*) show **2** *v/r* **~se** go home; **recogida** *f* collection; **~ de basuras** garbage collection, *Br* refuse collection; **~ de equipajes** baggage reclaim

recolectar <1a> *v/t* AGR harvest, bring in

recomendación *f* recommendation; **recomendar** <1k> *v/t* recommend

recompensa *f* reward; **recompensar** <1a> *v/t* reward

recomponer <2r; *part* **recompuesto**> *v/t* mend

reconciliación *f* reconciliation; **reconciliar** <1b> **1** *v/t* reconcile **2** *v/r* **~se** make up (**con** with), be reconciled (**con** with)

recóndito *adj* remote

reconfortar <1a> *v/t* comfort

reconocer <2d> *v/t* recognize; *errores* admit, acknowledge; *area* reconnoiter, *Br* reconnoitre; MED examine; **reconocimiento** *m* recognition; *de error* acknowledg(e)ment; MED examination, check-up; MIL reconnaissance

reconquista *f* reconquest; **reconquistar** <1a> *v/t* reconquer

reconsiderar <1a> *v/t* reconsider

reconstrucción *f* reconstruction; **reconstruir** <3g> *v/t fig* reconstruct

reconvenir <3s> *v/i* JUR counterclaim

reconversión *f* COM restructuring

recopilación *f* compilation; **recopilar** <1a> *v/t* compile

récord 1 *adj* record(-breaking) **2** *m* record

recordar <1m> *v/t* remember, recall; **~ algo a alguien** remind s.o. of sth;

recordatorio *m* reminder

recorrer <2a> *v/t distancia* cover, do; *a pie* walk; *territorio, país* go around, travel around; *camino* go along, travel along; **recorrido** *m* route; DEP round

recortar <1a> *v/t* cut out; *fig* cut; **recorte** *m fig* cutback; **~ de periódico** cutting, clipping; **~ salarial** salary cut

recostarse <1m> *v/r* lie down

recoveco *m* nook, cranny; *en camino* bend

recrearse <1a> *v/r* amuse o.s.; **recreativo** *adj* recreational; *juegos* **~s** amusements; **recreo** *m* recreation; EDU recess, *Br* break

recriminar <1a> *v/t* reproach

recrudecerse <2d> *v/r* intensify

recta *f* DEP straight; **~ final** *tb fig* home straight

rectángulo *m* rectangle

rectificar <1g> *v/t* correct, rectify; *camino* straighten

rectitud *f* rectitude, probity; **recto** *adj* straight; *(honesto)* honest

rector *m* rector, *Br* vice-chancellor; **rectorado** *m* rector's office, *Br* vice-chancellor's office

recuadro *m* TIP inset, box

recubierto *part* → **recubrir**; **recubrir** <3a; *part* **recubierto**> *v/t* cover (**de** with)

recuento *m* count; **~ de votos** recount

recuerdo *m* memory; **da ~s a Luís** give my regards to Luís

recuperación *f tb fig* recovery; **recuperar** <1a> **1** *v/t tiempo* make up; *algo perdido* recover **2** *v/r* **~se** recover (**de** from)

recurrir <3a> **1** *v/t* JUR appeal against **2** *v/i*: **~ a** resort to, turn to; **recurso** *m* JUR appeal; *material* resource; **~s humanos** human resources; **~s naturales** natural resources

red *f* net; INFOR, *fig* network; **caer en las ~es de** *fig* fall into the clutches of; **Red Digital de Servicios Integrados** Integrated Services Digital Network

redacción *f* writing; *de editorial* editorial department; EDU essay; **redactar** <1a> *v/t* write, compose; **redactor** *m*, **~a** *f* editor

redada *f* raid

redentor *m*, **~a** *f* COM redeemer; **el Redentor** REL the Savio(u)r

redoble *m* MÚS (drum)roll

redomado *adj* F total, out-and-out

redonda *f*: **a la ~** around, round about; **redondear** <1a> *v/t para más* round up; *para menos* round down; *(rematar)* round off; **redondo** *adj* round; *negocio* excellent; **caer ~** flop down

reducción *f* reduction; MED setting; **reducido** *adj precio* reduced; *espacio* small, confined; **reducir** <3o> **1** *v/t* reduce (**a** to); MIL overcome **2** *v/r* **~se** come down (**a** to)

reducto *m* redoubt

redujo *vb* → **reducir**

redundancia *f* tautology

redundar <1a> *v/i* have an impact (**en** on)

reeditar <1a> *v/t* republish, reissue

reelegir <3c & 3l> *v/t* re-elect

reembolsar <1a> *v/t* refund; **reembolso** *m* refund; **contra ~** collect on delivery, *Br* cash on delivery, COD

reemplazar <1f> *v/t* replace

reencarnación *f* REL reincarnation

reestructurar <1a> *v/t* restructure

refacción *f L.Am. de edificio* refurbishment; AUTO spare part

referencia *f* reference; **hacer ~ a** refer to, make reference to; **~s** COM references; **referéndum** *m* referendum; **referente** *adj*: **~ a** referring to, relating to; **referirse** <3i> *v/r* refer (**a** to)

refilón *m*: **mirar de ~** glance at

refinado *adj tb fig* refined; **refinar** <1a> *v/t* TÉC refine; **refinería** *f* TÉC refinery

reflector *m* reflector; EL spotlight; **reflejar** <1a> **1** *v/t tb fig* reflect **2** *v/r* **~se** be reflected; **reflejo** *m* reflex; *imagen* reflection; **reflexión** *f fig* reflection, thought; **reflexionar** <1a>

R

v/t reflect on, ponder; **reflexivo** *adj* GRAM reflexive

reflotar <1a> *v/t* COM refloat

reforestar <1a> *v/t* reforest

reforma *f* reform; **~s** *pl* (*obras*) refurbishment *sg*; (*reparaciones*) repairs; **reformador** *m*, **~a** *f* reformer; **reformar** <1a> **1** *v/t* reform; *edificio* refurbish; (*reparar*) repair **2** *v/r* **~se** mend one's ways, reform; **reformatorio** *m* reform school, reformatory; **reformista 1** *adj* reformist, reform *atr* **2** *m/f* reformer

reforzar <1f & 1m> *v/t* reinforce; *vigilancia* increase, step up

refrán *m* saying

refrenar <1a> *v/t* restrain, contain

refrescante *adj* refreshing; **refrescar** <1g> **1** *v/t tb fig* refresh; *conocimientos* brush up **2** *v/i* cool down **3** *v/r* **~se** cool down; **refresco** *m* soda, *Br* soft drink

refriega *f* MIL clash, skirmish

refrigerador *m* refrigerator; **refrigerar** <1a> *v/t* refrigerate; **refrigerio** *m* snack

refuerzo *m* reinforcement; **~s** MIL reinforcements

refugiado *m*, **-a** *f* refugee; **refugiarse** <1b> *v/r* take refuge; **refugio** *m* refuge

refulgente *adj* dazzling

refunfuñar <1a> *v/i* grumble

refutar <1a> *v/t* refute

regadera *f* watering can; *Méx* (*ducha*) shower; *estar como una ~* F be nuts F; **regadío** *m*: *tierra de ~* irrigated land

regalar <1a> *v/t*: *~ algo a alguien* give sth to s.o., give s.o. sth

regaliz *m* BOT licorice, *Br* liquorice

regalo *m* gift, present

regañadientes: *a ~* reluctantly

regañar <1a> **1** *v/t* tell off **2** *v/i* quarrel; **regañina** *f* F telling off

regar <1h & 1k> *v/t* water; AGR irrigate

regata *f* regatta

regatear <1a> *v/t* DEP get past, dodge; *no ~ esfuerzos* spare no effort

regazo *m* lap

regenerar <1a> *v/t* regenerate

regente *m/f* regent

regidor 1 *adj* governing, ruling **2** *m*, **~a** *f* TEA stage manager

régimen *m* POL regime; MED diet; *estar a ~* be on a diet; **regimiento** *m* MIL regiment

regio *adj* regal, majestic; *S.Am.* F (*estupendo*) great F, fantastic F

región *f* region; **regional** *adj* regional; **regionalismo** *m* regionalism

regir <3l & 3c> **1** *v/t* rule, govern **2** *v/i* apply, be in force **3** *v/r* **~se** be guided (*por* by)

registrar <1a> **1** *v/t* register; *casa* search **2** *v/r* **~se** be recorded; *se registró un máximo de 45°C* a high of 45°C was recorded; **registro** *m* register; *de casa* search; *~ civil* register of births, marriages and deaths

regla *f* (*norma*) rule; *para medir* ruler; MED period; *por ~ general* as a rule

reglamentar <1a> *v/t* regulate; **reglamentario** *adj* regulation *atr*; **reglamento** *m* regulation

regocijarse <1a> *v/r* rejoice (*de* at), take delight (*en* in); **regocijo** *m* delight

regodearse <1a> *v/r* gloat (*con* over), delight (*en* in)

regresar <1a> **1** *v/i* return **2** *v/t Méx* return, give back **3** *v/r* **~se** *L.Am.* return; **regreso** *m* return

regüeldo *m* F belch

reguero *m* trail; *como un ~ de pólvora fig* like wildfire

regulación *f* regulation; *de temperatura* control; **regular 1** *adj sin variar* regular; (*común*) ordinary; (*habitual*) regular, normal; (*no muy bien*) so-so **2** <1a> *v/t* TÉC regulate; *temperatura* control; **regularidad** *f* regularity; **regularizar** <1f> *v/t* regularize

regusto *m* aftertaste

rehabilitación *f* MED, *fig* rehabilitation; ARQUI restoration; **rehabilitar**

<1a> v/t ARQUI restore
rehacer <2s; *part* **rehecho**> v/t *película, ropa, cama* remake; *trabajo, ejercicio* redo; *casa, vida* rebuild
rehén *m* hostage
rehice *vb* → **rehacer**
rehizo *vb* → **rehacer**
rehogar <1h> v/t GASTR fry
rehuir <3g> v/t shy away from
rehusar <1a> v/t refuse, decline
reimprimir <3a> v/t reprint
reina *f* queen; **reinado** *m* reign; **reinante** *adj tb fig* reigning; **reinar** <1a> v/i *tb fig* reign
reincidente 1 *adj* repeat **2** *m/f* repeat offender; **reincidir** <3a> v/i reoffend
reincorporarse <1a> v/r return (*a* to)
reino *m tb fig* kingdom; **el Reino Unido** the United Kingdom
reinserción *f*: **~ social** social rehabilitation; **reinsertar** <1a> v/t rehabilitate
reinstaurar <1a> v/t bring back
reintegrarse <1a> v/r return (*a* to); **reintegro** *m* (*en lotería*) prize in the form of a refund of the stake money
reír <3m> **1** v/i laugh **2** v/r **~se** laugh (*de* at)
reiterar <1a> v/t repeat, reiterate
reivindicación *f* claim; **reivindicar** <1g> v/t claim; **~ un atentado** claim responsibility for an attack
reja *f* AGR plowshare, *Br* ploughshare; (*barrote*) bar, railing; **meter entre ~s** *fig* F put behind bars; **rejilla** *f* FERR luggage rack
rejuvenecer <2d> v/t rejuvenate
relación *f* relationship; **relaciones públicas** *pl* public relations, PR *sg*; **relacionado** *adj* related (*con* to); **relacionarse** <1a> v/r be connected (*con* to), be related (*con* to)
relajación *f* relaxation; **relajante** *adj* relaxing; **relajar** <1a> **1** v/t relax **2** v/r **~se** relax; **relajo** *m C.Am., Méx* uproar
relamerse <2a> v/r lick one's lips
relámpago *m* flash of lightning; **viaje ~** flying visit

relatar <1a> v/t tell, relate
relatividad *f* relativity
relativo *adj* relative; **~ a** regarding, about
relato *m* short story
relax *m* relaxation
releer <2e> v/t reread
relegar <1h> v/t relegate
relevante *adj* relevant
relevar <1a> v/t MIL relieve; **~ a alguien de algo** relieve s.o. of sth; **relevo** *m* MIL change; (*sustituto*) relief, replacement; **carrera de ~s** relay (race); **tomar el ~ de alguien** take over from s.o., relieve s.o.
relicario *m* shrine
relieve *m* relief; **poner de ~** highlight
religión *f* religion; **religiosa** *f* nun; **religioso 1** *adj* religious **2** *m* monk
relinchar <1a> v/i neigh
reliquia *f* relic
rellano *m* landing
rellenar <1a> v/t fill; GASTR *pollo, pimientos* stuff; *formulario* fill out, fill in; **relleno 1** *adj* GASTR *pollo, pimientos* stuffed; *pastel* filled **2** *m tb* **en cojín** stuffing; *en pastel* filling
reloj *m* clock; *de pulsera* watch, wristwatch; **~ de pared** wall clock; **~ de sol** sundial; **relojería** *f* watchmaker's; **relojero** *m*, **-a** *f* watchmaker
reluciente *adj* sparkling, glittering
remanso *m* backwater; **~ de paz** *fig* haven of peace
remar <1a> v/i row
remarcar <1g> v/t stress, emphasize
rematar <1a> **1** v/t finish off; *L.Am.* COM auction **2** v/i en *fútbol* shoot; **remate** *m L.Am.* COM auction, sale; *en fútbol* shot; **ser tonto de ~** be a complete idiot
remediar <1b> v/t remedy; **no puedo ~lo** I can't do anything about it; **remedio** *m* remedy; **sin ~** hopeless; **no hay más ~ que ...** there's no alternative but to ...
rememorar <1a> v/t remember
remendar <1k> v/t *con parche* patch;

(*zurcir*) darn

remesa *f* (*envío*) shipment, consignment; *L.Am. dinero* remittance

remezón *m L.Am.* earth tremor

remiendo *m* (*parche*) patch; (*zurcido*) darn

remilgado *adj* fussy, finicky

reminiscencia *f* reminiscence

remiso *adj* reluctant (**a** to)

remite *m en carta* return address; **remitente** *m/f* sender; **remitir** <3a> **1** *v/t* send, ship; *en texto* refer (**a** to) **2** *v/i* MED go into remission; *de crisis* ease (off)

remo *m pala* oar; *deporte* rowing

remodelar <1a> *v/t* redesign, remodel

remojar <1a> *v/t* soak; *L.Am.* F *acontecimiento* celebrate

remojo *m*: **poner a** or **en ~** leave to soak; **remojón** *m* drenching, soaking; **darse un ~** go for a dip

remolacha *f* beet, *Br* beetroot; **~ azucarera** sugar beet

remolcador *m* tug; **remolcar** <1g> *v/t* AUTO, MAR tow

remolino *m de aire* eddy; *de agua* whirlpool

remolón *m*, **-ona** *f* F slacker; **hacerse el ~** slack (off)

remolque *m* AUTO trailer

remontarse <1a> *v/r en el tiempo* go back (**a** to)

remonte *m* ski lift

remorder <2h> *v/t*: **me remuerde la conciencia** I have a guilty conscience; **remordimiento** *m* remorse

remoto *adj* remote; **no tengo ni la más -a idea** I haven't the faintest idea

remover <2h> *v/t* (*agitar*) stir; *L.Am.* (*destituir*) dismiss; *C.Am., Méx* (*quitar*) remove

remplazar *v/t* → **reemplazar**

remuneración *f* remuneration; **remunerar** <1a> *v/t* pay

renacentista *adj* Renaissance *atr*; **renacer** <2d> *v/i fig* be reborn; **Renacimiento** *m* Renaissance

renacuajo *m* ZO tadpole; F *persona* shrimp F

renal *adj* ANAT renal, kidney *atr*

rencilla *f* fight, argument

rencor *m* resentment; **guardar ~ a alguien** bear s.o. a grudge; **rencoroso** *adj* resentful

rendición *f* surrender

rendija *f* crack; (*hueco*) gap

rendimiento *m* performance; FIN yield; (*producción*) output; **rendir** <3l> **1** *v/t honores* pay, do; *beneficio* produce, yield **2** *v/i* perform **3** *v/r* **~se** surrender

renegado 1 *adj* renegade *atr* **2** *m* renegade; **renegar** <1h & 1k> *v/i*: **~ de alguien** disown s.o.; **~ de algo** renounce sth

renegrido *adj* blackened

RENFE *abr* (= **Red Nacional de Ferrocarriles Españoles**) *Spanish rail operator*

renglón *m* line; **a ~ seguido** immediately after

rengo *adj CSur* lame; **renguear** <1a> *v/i CSur* limp, walk with a limp

reno *m* ZO reindeer

renombre *m*: **de ~** famous, renowned

renovación *f* renewal; **renovador** *adj*: **las fuerzas ~es** the forces of renewal; **renovar** <1m> *v/t* renew

renta *f* income; *de casa* rent; **~ per cápita** income per capita; **rentabilidad** *f* profitability; **rentable** *adj* profitable; **rentar** <1a> *v/t* (*arrendar*) rent out; (*alquiler*) rent; *carro* hire

renuente *adj* reluctant, unwilling

renunciar <1b> *v/i*: **~ a** *tabaco, alcohol etc* give up; *puesto* resign; *demanda* drop

reñir <3h & 3l> **1** *v/t* tell off **2** *v/i* quarrel, fight

reo *m*, **-a** *f* accused

reojo: **de ~** out of the corner of one's eye

repantigarse <1h> *v/r* lounge, sprawl

reparación *f* repair; *fig* reparation; **reparar** <1a> **1** *v/t* repair **2** *v/i*: **~ en algo** notice sth; **reparo** *m*: **poner ~s a** find problems with; **no tener ~s**

en have no reservations about

repartición *f S. Am.* department; **repartidor** *m* delivery man; **repartir** <3a> *v/t* (*dividir*) share out, divide up; *productos* deliver; **reparto** *m* (*división*) share-out, distribution; TEA cast; *~ a domicilio* home delivery

repasar <1a> *v/t trabajo* go over again; EDU revise

repecho *m* steep slope

repelente 1 *adj fig* repellent, repulsive; F horrible **2** *m* repellent

repelús *m*: *dar ~ a alguien* F give s.o. the creeps F

repente: *de ~* suddenly; **repentino** *adj* sudden

repercusión *f fig* repercussion; **repercutir** <3a> *v/i* have repercussions (*en* on)

repertorio *m* TEA, MÚS repertoire

repetición *f* repetition; **repetido** *adj* repeated; **repetir** <3l> **1** *v/t* repeat **2** *v/i de comida* repeat **3** *v/r ~se* happen again; **repetitivo** *adj* repetitive

repipi *adj* F (*afectado*) affected; *es tan ~ niño* he's such a know-it-all F

repisa *f* shelf

replantear <1a> *v/t pregunta, problema* bring up again

replegarse <1h & 1k> *v/r* MIL withdraw

repleto *adj* full (*de* of)

réplica *f* replica

replicar <1g> *v/t* reply

repoblar <1m> *v/t* repopulate

repollo *m* BOT cabbage

reponerse <2r; *part repuesto*> *v/r* recover (*de* from)

reportaje *m* story, report; **reportero** *m*, **-a** *f* reporter; *~ gráfico* press photographer

reposacabezas *m inv* AUTO headrest

reposar <1a> *v/i* rest; *de vino* settle

reposera *f L.Am.* lounger

reposición *f* TEA revival; TV repeat

reposo *m* rest

repostar <1a> *v/i* refuel

repostería *f* pastries *pl*

reprender <2a> *v/t* scold, tell off

represa *f* dam; (*embalse*) reservoir

represalia *f* reprisal

representación *f* representation; TEA performance; *en ~ de* on behalf of; **representante** *m/f tb* COM representative; **representar** <1a> *v/t* represent; *obra* put on, perform; *papel* play; *~ menos años* look younger

represión *f* repression

reprimenda *f* reprimand

reprimir <3a> *v/t tb* PSI repress

reprobar <1m> *v/t* condemn; *L.Am.* EDU fail

reprochar <1a> *v/t* reproach; **reproche** *m* reproach

reproducción *f* BIO reproduction; **reproducir** <3o> **1** *v/t* reproduce **2** *v/r ~se* BIO reproduce, breed

reptil *m* ZO reptile

república *f* republic; **republicano 1** *adj* republican **2** *m*, **-a** *f* republican

repudiar <1b> *v/t fml* repudiate; *herencia* renounce

repuesto 1 *part* → **reponer 2** *m* spare part, replacement; *de ~* spare

repugnancia *f* disgust, repugnance; **repugnante** *adj* disgusting, repugnant; **repugnar** <1a> *v/t* disgust, repel

repulsión *f* repulsion; **repulsivo** *adj* repulsive

repuse *vb* → **reponerse**

reputación *f* reputation

requerir <3i> *v/t* require; JUR summons

requesón *m* cottage cheese

requetebién *adv* F really well, brilliantly F

réquiem *m* requiem

requisar <1a> *v/t Arg, Chi* MIL requisition; **requisito** *m* requirement

res *f L.Am.* bull; *carne f de ~* beef; *~es pl* cattle *pl*

resaca *f* MAR undertow, undercurrent; *de beber* hangover

resaltar <1a> **1** *v/t* highlight, stress **2** *v/i* ARQUI jut out; *fig* stand out

resarcirse <3b> *v/r* make up (*de*

for)

resbaladizo *adj* slippery; *fig* tricky; **resbalar** <1a> *v/i* slide; *fig* slip (up); **resbalón** *m* slip; *fig* F slip-up; **resbaloso** *adj* L.Am. slippery

rescatar <1a> *v/t persona, animal* rescue, save; *bienes* save; **rescate** *m de peligro* rescue; *en secuestro* ransom

rescindir <3a> *v/t* cancel; *contrato* terminate; **rescisión** *f* cancellation; *de contrato* termination

reseco *adj* (*seco*) parched; (*flaco*) skinny

resentimiento *m* resentment; **resentirse** <3i> *v/r* get upset; *de rendimiento, calidad* suffer; **~ de algo** suffer from the effects of sth

reseña *f de libro etc* review; **reseñar** <1a> *v/t* review

reserva 1 *f* reservation; **~ natural** nature reserve; **sin ~s** without reservation **2** *m/f* DEP reserve; **reservar** <1a> **1** *v/t* (*guardar*) set aside, put by; *billete* reserve **2** *v/r* **~se** save o.s. (*para* for)

resfriado 1 *adj*: **estar ~** have a cold **2** *m* cold; **resfriarse** <1c> *v/r* catch cold; **resfrío** *m* L.Am. cold

resguardar <1a> **1** *v/t* protect (*de* from) **2** *v/r* **~se** protect o.s. (*de* from); **resguardo** *m* COM counterfoil

residencia *f* residence; **~ de ancianos** *or* **para la tercera edad** retirement home; **residencial 1** *adj* residential **2** *f Arg, Chi* boarding house; **residente 1** *adj* resident **2** *m/f* resident; **residir** <3a> *v/i* reside; **~ en** *fig* lie in; **residual** *adj* residual; (*de desecho*) waste *atr*; **residuo** *m* residue; **~s** waste *sg*

resignación *f actitud* resignation; **resignarse** <1a> *v/r* resign o.s. (*a* to)

resina *f* resin

resistencia *f* resistance; EL, TÉC resistor; **resistir** <3a> **1** *v/i* resist; (*aguantar*) hold out **2** *v/t tentación* resist; *frío, dolor etc* stand, bear **3** *v/r* **~se** be reluctant (*a* to)

resolución *f actitud* determination, decisiveness; *de problema* solution (*de* to); JUR ruling; **resolver** <2h; *part* **resuelto**> **1** *v/t problema* solve **2** *v/r* **~se** decide (*a* to; *por* on)

resonar <1m> *v/i* echo

resoplar <1a> *v/i* snort

resorte *m* spring

respaldar <1a> *v/t* back, support; **respaldo** *m de silla* back; *fig* backing, support

respectar <1a> *v/i*: **por lo que respecta a ...** as regards ..., as far as ... is concerned; **respectivo** *adj* respective; **respecto** *m*: **al ~** on the matter; **con ~ a** regarding, as regards

respetable *adj* respectable; **respetar** <1a> *v/t* respect; **respeto** *m* respect; **respetuoso** *adj* respectful

respiración *f* breathing; **estar con ~ asistida** MED be on a respirator; **respirar** <1a> *v/t & v/i* breathe; **respiratorio** *adj* respiratory; **respiro** *m fig* breather, break

resplandeciente *adj* shining; **resplandor** *m* shine, gleam

responder <2a> **1** *v/t* answer **2** *v/i*: **~ a** answer, reply to; MED respond to; *descripción* fit, match; (*ser debido a*) be due to

responsabilidad *f* responsibility; **responsabilizarse** <1f> *v/r* take responsibility (*de* for); **responsable 1** *adj* responsible (*de* for) **2** *m/f* person responsible (*de* for); **los ~s del crimen** those responsible for the crime

respuesta *f* (*contestación*) reply, answer; *fig* response

resquebrajar <1a> **1** *v/t* crack **2** *v/r* **~se** crack

resquicio *m* gap

resta *f* MAT subtraction

restablecer <2d> **1** *v/t* re-establish **2** *v/r* **~se** recover; **restablecimiento** *m* re-establishment; *de enfermo* recovery

restante 1 *adj* remaining **2** *m/fpl*: **los/las ~s** *pl* the rest *pl*, the remainder *pl*; **restar** <1a> **1** *v/t* subtract; **~ importancia a** play down the importance of **2** v/i remain, be left

restauración f restoration

restaurante m restaurant

restaurar <1a> v/t restore

restituir <3g> v/t restore; *en cargo* reinstate

resto m rest, remainder; **los ~s mortales** the (mortal) remains

restregar <1h & 1k> v/t scrub

restricción f restriction; **restringir** <3c> v/t restrict, limit

resucitar <1a> **1** v/t resuscitate; *fig* revive **2** v/i *de persona* rise from o come back from the dead

resuello m puffing, heavy breathing

resuelto 1 part → **resolver 2** adj decisive, resolute

resultado m result; **sin ~** without success; **resultar** <1a> v/i turn out; **~ caro** prove expensive, turn out to be expensive; **resulta que ...** it turns out that ...

resumen m summary; **en ~** in short; **resumir** <3a> v/t summarize

resurgir <3c> v/i reappear, come back; **resurrección** f REL resurrection

retaguardia f MIL rearguard

retahíla f string

retar <1a> v/t challenge; *Rpl (regañar)* scold, tell off

retardar <1a> v/t delay

retazo m fig snippet, fragment

retención f MED retention; *de persona* detention; **~ fiscal** tax deduction; **retener** <2l> v/t *dinero etc* withhold, deduct; *persona* detain, hold

reticencia f reticence; **reticente** adj reticent

retintín m: **con ~** F sarcastically

retirada f MIL retreat, withdrawal; **retirado** adj *(jubilado)* retired; *(alejado)* remote, out-of-the-way; **retirar** <1a> **1** v/t take away, remove; *acusación, dinero* withdraw **2** v/r **~se** MIL withdraw; **retiro** m *lugar* retreat

reto m challenge; *Rpl (regañina)*

scolding, telling-off

retobado adj L.Am. unruly

retocar <1g> v/t FOT retouch, touch up; *(acabar)* put the finishing touches to

retomar <1a> v/t: **~ algo** fig take sth up again

retoque m FOT touching-up; *(acabado)* finishing touch

retorcer <2b & 2h> v/t twist; **retorcido** adj fig twisted; **retorcijón** m stomach cramp

retórica f rhetoric

retornar <1a> v/i return; **retorno** m return

retortijón m cramps pl, Br stomach cramp

retozar <1f> v/i frolic, romp

retractar <1a> v/t retract, withdraw

retraer <2p; part **retraído**> **1** v/t retract **2** v/r **~se** withdraw; **retraído 1** part → **retraer 2** adj withdrawn

retransmisión f RAD, TV transmission, broadcast; **retransmitir** <3a> v/t transmit, broadcast

retrasado 1 part → **retrasar 2** adj *tren, entrega* late; *con trabajo, pagos* behind; **está ~ en clase** he's lagging behind in class; **~ mental** mentally handicapped; **retrasar 1** v/t hold up; *reloj* put back; *reunión* postpone, put back **2** v/i *de reloj* lose time; *en los estudios* be behind **3** v/r **~se** *(atrasarse)* be late; *de reloj* lose time; *con trabajo, pagos* get behind; **retraso** m delay; **ir con ~** be late

retratar <1a> v/t FOT take a picture of; *fig* depict; **retrato** m picture; **~-robot** composite photo, E-Fit®

retrete m bathroom

retribución f salary

retroactivo adj retroactive; **retroceder** <2a> v/i go back, move back; *fig* back down; **retroceso** m fig backward step; **retrógrado** adj retrograde; **retroproyector** m overhead projector; **retrospectiva** f retrospective; **retrovisor** m AUTO rearview mirror; **~ exterior** wing mirror

retumbar <1a> v/i boom

retuve vb → **retener**

reuma, reúma m MED rheumatism

reunificación f POL reunification

reunión f meeting; de amigos get-together; **reunir** <3a> **1** v/t personas bring together; requisitos meet, fulfil(l); datos gather (together) **2** v/r **~se** meet up, get together; COM meet

reutilizar <1f> v/t re-use

revalorizar <1f> **1** v/t revalue **2** v/r **~se** appreciate (**en** by), increase in value (**en** by)

revaluar <1e> v/t idea re-evaluate

revancha f revenge

revelación f revelation; **revelado** m development; **revelar** <1a> v/t FOT develop

reventa f resale

reventar <1k> **1** v/i burst; **lleno a ~** full to bursting **2** v/t puerta etc break down **3** v/r **~se** burst; **se reventó a trabajar** fig he worked his butt off F; **reventón** m AUTO blowout

reverberar <1a> v/i de sonido reverberate

reverencia f reverence; saludo: de hombre bow; de mujer curtsy; **reverendo** m REL reverend

reversible adj ropa reversible; **reverso** m reverse, back

revés m setback; tenis backhand; **al or del ~** back to front; **con el interior fuera** inside out

revestir <3l> v/t cover (**de** with); **~ gravedad** be serious

revisación f L.Am. check-up.

revisada f L.Am. → **revisión**; **revisar** <1a> v/t check, inspect; **revisión** f check, inspection; AUTO service; **~ técnica** roadworthiness test, Br MOT (test); **~ médica** check-up; **revisor** m, **~a** f FERR (ticket) inspector

revista f magazine; **pasar ~ a** MIL inspect, review; fig review

revivir <3a> **1** v/i revive **2** v/t relive

revocar <1g & 1m> v/t pared render; JUR revoke

revolcarse <1g & 1m> v/r roll around; **revolcón** m tumble; F de amantes roll in the hay F

revolotear <1a> v/t flutter

revoltijo, revoltillo m mess, jumble

revoltoso adj niño naughty

revolución f revolution; **revolucionario 1** adj revolutionary **2** m, **-a** f revolutionary

revólver m revolver

revolver <2h; part **revuelto**> **1** v/t GASTR stir; estómago turn; (desordenar) mess up **2** v/i rummage (**en** in) **3** v/r **~se** del tiempo worsen

revuelo m stir

revuelto 1 part → **revolver 2** adj mar rough; gente restless

rey m king

reyerta f fight

rezagarse <1h> v/r drop back, fall behind

rezar <1f> **1** v/t oración say **2** v/i pray; de texto say; **rezo** m prayer

rezongar <1h> v/i grumble

rezumar <1a> v/t & v/i ooze

ría 1 vb → **reír 2** f estuary

riachuelo m stream

riada f flood

ribera f shore, bank; **riberano** L.Am. **1** adj L.Am. coastal; de río riverside atr **2** m, **-a** f person who lives by the sea/river; **ribereño: ~ de** bordering (on)

rica f rich woman; **rico 1** adj rich; comida delicious; F niño cute, sweet; **~ en vitaminas** rich in vitamins **2** m rich man; **nuevo ~** nouveau riche

ridiculizar <1f> v/t ridicule; **ridículo 1** adj ridiculous **2** m ridicule; **hacer el ~, quedar en ~** make a fool of o.s.

ríe vb → **reír**

riego 1 vb → **regar 2** m AGR irrigation; **~ sanguíneo** blood flow

ríen vb → **reír**

rienda f rein; **dar ~ suelta a** give free rein to

riesgo m risk; **a ~ de** at the risk of; **correr el ~** run the risk (**de** of); **riesgoso** adj L.Am. risky

rifa f raffle; **rifar** <1a> **1** v/t raffle **2** v/r **~se** fig fight over

rifle *m* rifle
rige *vb* → **regir**
rigidez *f* rigidity; *de carácter* inflexibility; *fig* strictness; **rígido** *adj* rigid; *carácter* inflexible; *fig* strict; **rigor** *m* rigo(u)r; **riguroso** *adj* rigorous, harsh
rima *f* rhyme; **rimar** <1a> *v/i* rhyme (**con** with)
rimbombante *adj* ostentatious
rímel *m* mascara
rincón *m* corner
rinde *vb* → **rendir**
rinoceronte *m* ZO rhino, rhinoceros
riña *f* quarrel, fight
riñe *vb* → **reñir**
riñón *m* ANAT kidney; *costar un* ~ F cost an arm and a leg F
riñonera *f* fanny pack, *Br* bum bag
río **1** *m* river; ~ *abajo*/*arriba* up/down river; *el Río de la Plata* the River Plate **2** *vb* → **reír**
rioplatense *adj* of/from the River Plate area, River Plate *atr*
riqueza *f* wealth
risa *f* laugh; ~*s pl* laughter *sg*; *dar* ~ be funny; *morirse de* ~ kill o.s. laughing; *tomar algo a* ~ treat sth as a joke
ristra *f* string
risueño *adj* cheerful
rítmico *adj* rhythmic(al); **ritmo** *m* rhythm; *de desarrollo* rate, pace
rito *m* rite; **ritual** *m*/*adj* ritual
rival *m*/*f* rival; **rivalidad** *f* rivalry; **rivalizar** <1f> *v/i*: ~ *con* rival
rizado *adj* curly; **rizar** <1f> **1** *v/t* curl **2** ~*se* *v/r* curl; **rizo** *m* curl
robar <1a> *v/t persona, banco* rob; *objeto* steal; *naipe* take, pick up
roble *m* BOT oak
robo *m* robbery; *en casa* burglary
robot *m* robot; ~ *de cocina* food processor; **robótica** *f* robotics
robustecer <2d> **1** *v/t* strengthen **2** *v/r* ~*se* become stronger; **robusto** *adj* robust, sturdy
roca *f* rock
roce *m fig* friction; *tener* ~*s con* come into conflict with
rociar <1c> *v/t* spray

rocín *m* F nag
rocío *m* dew
rock *m* MÚS rock
rococó *adj* rococo
rocódromo *m* climbing wall
rocoto *m S.Am.* hot red pepper
rodaballo *m* ZO turbot
rodaja *f* slice
rodaje *m de película* shooting, filming; AUTO breaking in, *Br* running in
rodapié *m* baseboard, *Br* skirting board
rodar <1m> **1** *v/i* roll; *de coche* go, travel (*a* at); *sin rumbo fijo* wander **2** *v/t película* shoot; AUTO break in, *Br* run in
rodear <1a> **1** *v/t* surround **2** *v/r* ~*se* surround o.s. (*de* with); **rodeo** *m* detour; *con caballos y vaqueros etc* rodeo; *andarse con* ~*s* beat about the bush; *hablar sin* ~*s* speak plainly, not beat about the bush
rodilla *f* knee; *de* ~*s* kneeling, on one's knees; *hincarse or ponerse de* ~*s* kneel (down)
rodillo *m* rolling pin; TÉC roller
rododendro *m* BOT rhododendron
roedor *m* rodent; **roer** <2za> *v/t* gnaw; *fig* eat into
rogar <1h & 1m> *v/t* ask for; (*implorar*) beg for, plead for; *hacerse de* ~ play hard to get
rojizo *adj* reddish; **rojo 1** *adj* red; *al* ~ *vivo* red hot **2** *m color* red **3** *m, -a f* POL red, commie F
rol *m* role
rollizo *adj* F chubby
rollo *m* FOT roll; *fig* F drag F; *buen*/*mal* ~ F good/bad atmosphere; *¡qué* ~*!* F what a drag! F
Roma Rome
romance *m* romance; **románico** *m*/*adj* Romanesque; **romano 1** *adj* Roman **2** *m, -a f* Roman; **romántico 1** *m, -a f* romantic **2** *m, -a f* romantic
rombo *m* rhombus
romero *m* BOT rosemary
rompecabezas *m* puzzle; **rompehielos** *m inv* icebreaker

R

romper <2a; *part* **roto**> **1** *v/t* break; (*hacer añicos*) smash; *tela, papel* tear **2** *v/i* break; **~ a** start to; **~ con alguien** break up with s.o. **3** *v/r* **~se** break

rompopo *m* C.Am., Méx bebida eggnog

ron *m* rum

roncar <1g> *v/i* snore

roncha *f* MED bump, swelling

ronco *adj* hoarse; **quedarse ~** go hoarse

ronda *f* round; **rondar** <1a> **1** *v/t* patrol; **me ronda una idea** I have an idea going around in my head **2** *v/i* F hang around

ronquido *m* snore; **~s** *pl* snoring *sg*

ronronear <1a> *v/i de gato* purr

roña *f* grime; **roñoso** *adj* grimy, grubby

ropa *f* clothes *pl*; **~ de cama** bedclothes *pl*; **~ interior** underwear; **~ íntima** L.Am. underwear; **ropero** *m* closet, Br wardrobe

rosa 1 *adj* pink **2** *f* BOT rose; **fresco como una ~** fresh as a daisy; **ver algo de color de ~** see sth through rose-colo(u)red glasses; **rosado 1** *adj* pink; *vino* rosé **2** *m* rosé; **rosal** *m* rosebush

rosario *m* REL rosary; *fig* string

rosbif *m* GASTR roast beef

rosca *f* TÉC thread; GASTR F *pastry similar to a donut*

rosco *m* GASTR *pastry similar to a donut*; **no comerse un ~** P not get anywhere

roscón *m* GASTR *large ring-shaped cake*

rosquilla *f pastry similar to a donut*

rosticería *f* L.Am. *type of deli that sells roast chicken*

rostro *m* face

rotación *f* rotation

rotisería *f* L.Am. deli, delicatessen

roto 1 *part* → **romper 2** *adj pierna etc* broken; (*hecho añicos*) smashed; *tela, papel* torn **3** *m*, **-a** *f* Chi one of the urban poor

rotonda *f* traffic circle, Br roundabout

rotoso *adj* Rpl F scruffy

rotulador *m* fiber-tip, Br fibre-tip, felt-tip; **rótulo** *m* sign

rotundo *adj fig* categorical

rotura *f* breakage; **una ~ de cadera** MED a broken hip

rozadura *f* chafing, rubbing; **rozagante** *adj* healthy; **rozar** <1f> **1** *v/t* rub; (*tocar ligeramente*) brush; *fig* touch on **2** *v/i* rub **3** *v/r* **~se** rub; (*desgastarse*) wear

rte. *abr* (= **remitente**) sender

ruana *f* Ecuad poncho

rubeola, **rubéola** *f* MED German measles *sg*

rubí *m* ruby

rubicundo *adj* ruddy; **rubio** *adj* blond; **tabaco ~** Virginia tobacco

ruborizarse <1f> *v/r* go red, blush

rúbrica *f* heading; *de firma* flourish

rubro *m* L.Am. category, heading

rudeza *f* roughness

rudimentario *adj* rudimentary

rudo *adj* rough

rueda *f* wheel; **~ dentada** cogwheel; **~ de prensa** press conference; **~ de recambio** spare wheel

ruedo *m* TAUR bullring

ruego 1 *vb* → **rogar 2** *m* request

rufián *m* rogue

rugby *m* rugby

rugido *m* roar; **rugir** <3c> *v/i* roar

rugoso *adj superficie* rough

ruido *m* noise; **hacer ~** make a noise; **mucho ~ y pocas nueces** all talk and no action; **ruidoso** *adj* noisy

ruin *adj* despicable, mean; (*tacaño*) mean, miserly

ruina *f* ruin; **llevar a alguien a la ~** *fig* bankrupt s.o.

ruiseñor *m* ZO nightingale

ruleta *f* roulette

ruletero *m* Méx cab *o* taxi driver

rulo *m* roller

rumbeador *m* Rpl tracker; **rumbear** <1a> *v/i* L.Am. head (**para** for)

rumbo *m* course; **tomar ~ a** head for; **perder el ~** *fig* lose one's way

rumboso *adj* lavish

rumiar <1b> *v/t fig* ponder

rumor *m* rumo(u)r; **rumorearse** <1a> *v/r* be rumo(u)red
rupestre *adj*: *pintura* ~ cave painting
ruptura *f de relaciones* breaking off; *de pareja* break-up
rural 1 *adj* rural **2** *m Rpl* station wagon, *Br* estate car; *~es Méx* (ru-

ral) police
Rusia Russia; **ruso 1** *adj* Russian **2** *m*, **-a** *f* Russian
rústico *adj* rustic
ruta *f* route
rutina *f* routine; **rutinario** *adj* routine *atr*

S

S *abr* (= *sur*) S (= South(ern))
S.A. *abr* (= *sociedad anónima*) inc (= incorporated), *Br* plc (= public limited company)
sábado *m* Saturday
sábana *f* sheet; ~ *ajustable* fitted sheet
sabana *f* savanna(h)
sabandija *f* bug, creepy-crawly
sabañón *m* chilblain
sabelotodo *m* F know-it-all F, *Br* know-all F
saber <2n> **1** *v/t* know (*de* about); ~ *hacer algo* know how to do sth, be able to do sth; *no lo supe hasta más tarde* I didn't find out till later; *hacer* ~ *algo a alguien* let s.o. know sth; *¡qué sé yo!* who knows?; *que yo sepa* as far as I know; *sabér-selas todas* F know every trick in the book **2** *v/i* taste (*a* of); *me sabe a quemado* it tastes burnt to me; *me sabe mal fig* it upsets me **3** *m* knowledge, learning
sabiduría *f* wisdom; (*conocimientos*) knowledge; **sabiendas** *fpl*: *a* ~ knowingly; *a* ~ *que* knowing full well that; **sabio 1** *adj* wise; (*sensato*) sensible **2** *m*, **-a** *f* wise person; (*experto*) expert; **sabiondo** *m*, **-a** *f* know-it-all F, *Br* know-all F
sablazo *m*: *dar un* ~ *a alguien* F scrounge money off s.o.
sable *m* saber, *Br* sabre
sablear <1a> *v/t & v/i L.Am.* F

scrounge (*a* from)
sabor *m* flavo(u)r, taste; *dejar mal* ~ *de boca fig* leave a bad taste in the mouth; **saborear** <1a> *v/t* savo(u)r; *fig* relish
sabotaje *m* sabotage; **saboteador** *m*, **-a** *f* saboteur; **sabotear** <1a> *v/t* sabotage
sabroso *adj* tasty; *fig* juicy; *L.Am.* (*agradable*) nice, pleasant; **sabro-sura** *f L.Am.* tasty dish
sabueso *m fig* sleuth
sacacorchos *m inv* corkscrew; **sa-camuelas** *m inv desp* F dentist; **sa-capuntas** *m inv* pencil sharpener
sacar <1g> **1** *v/t* take out; *mancha* take out, remove; *información* get; *disco, libro* bring out; *fotocopias* make; ~ *a alguien a bailar* ask s.o. to dance; ~ *algo en claro* (*entender*) make sense of sth; ~ *de paseo* take for a walk **2** *v/r* ~*se L.Am. ropa* take off
sacarina *f* saccharin(e)
sacerdote *m* priest; **sacerdotisa** *f* priestess
saciar <1b> *v/t fig* satisfy, fulfill; **saciedad** *f*: *repetir algo hasta la* ~ *fig* repeat sth time and again, repeat sth ad nauseam
saco *m* sack; *L.Am.* jacket; ~ *de dormir* sleeping bag; *entrar a* ~ *en* F burst into, barge into F
sacramento *m* sacrament
sacrificar <1g> **1** *v/t* sacrifice;

(*matar*) slaughter **2** *v/r* **~se** make sacrifices (*por* for); **sacrificio** *m* sacrifice; **sacrilegio** *m* sacrilege; **sacristán** *m* sexton; **sacristía** *f* vestry

sacudida *f* shake, jolt; EL shock; **sacudir** <3a> **1** *v/t tb fig* shake; F *niño* beat, wallop F **2** *v/r* **~se** shake off, shrug off; **~se alguien** (*de encima*) get rid of s.o.

sádico 1 *adj* sadistic **2** *m*, **-a** *f* sadist; **sadismo** *m* sadism

safari *m* safari; **~ fotográfico** photographic safari

sagaz *adj* shrewd, sharp

Sagitario *m/f inv* ASTR Sagittarius

sagrado *adj* sacred, holy; **sagrario** *m* tabernacle

Sahara Sahara

sainete *m* TEA short farce, one-act play

sal 1 *f* salt; **~ común** cooking salt; **~ marina** sea salt **2** *vb* → *salir*

sala *f* room, hall; *de cine* screen; JUR court room; **~ de embarque** AVIA departure lounge; **~ de espera** waiting room; **~ de estar** living room; **~ de fiestas** night club; **~ de sesiones** *or* **de juntas** boardroom

saladero *m L.Am.* meat / fish salting factory; **salado** *adj* salted; (*con demasiada sal*) salty; (*no dulce*) savo(u)ry; *fig* funny, witty; *C.Am.*, *Chi*, *Rpl* F pric(e)y F

salamandra *f* ZO salamander

salamanquesa *f* ZO gecko

salami *m* salami

salar <1a> **1** *v/t* add salt to, salt; *para conservar* salt **2** *m Arg* salt mine

salarial *adj* salary *atr*; **salario** *m* salary, pay; **~ base** basic wage; **~ mínimo** minimum wage

salazón *f* salted fish / meat; **en ~** salt *atr*

salchicha *f* sausage; **salchichón** *m* type of spiced sausage

saldar <1a> *v/t disputa* settle; *deuda* settle, pay; *géneros* sell off; **saldo** *m* COM balance; (*resultado*) result; **~ acreedor** credit balance; **~ deudor** debit balance; **de ~** reduced, on

sale

saldré *vb* → *salir*

salero *m* salt cellar; *fig* wit; **saleroso** *adj* funny, witty

salga *vb* → *salir*

salgo *vb* → *salir*

salida *f* exit, way out; TRANSP departure; *de carrera* start; **~ de emergencia** emergency exit; **~ de tono** ill-judged remark

saliente *adj* projecting, protruding; *presidente* retiring, outgoing

salir <3r> **1** *v/i* leave, go out; (*aparecer*) appear, come out; **~ de** (*ir fuera de*) leave, go out of; (*venir fuera de*) leave, come out of; **~ a alguien** take after s.o.; **~ a 1000 pesetas** cost 1000 pesetas; **~ bien / mal** turn out well / badly; **el dibujo no me sale** F I can't get this drawing right; **no me salió el trabajo** I didn't get the job; **~ con alguien** date s.o., go out with s.o.; **~ perdiendo** end up losing **2** *v/r* **~se** *de líquido* overflow; (*dejar*) leave; **~se de la carretera** leave the road, go off the road; **~se con la suya** get what one wants

salitre *m* saltpeter, *Br* saltpetre

saliva *f* saliva; **tragar ~** hold one's tongue

salmo *m* psalm

salmón *m* ZO salmon; **color ~** salmon; **salmonete** *m* ZO red mullet

salmuera *f* pickle, brine

salobre *adj* salt; (*con demasiada sal*) salty

salomónico *adj* just, fair

salón *m* living room; **~ de actos** auditorium, hall; **~ de baile** dance hall; **~ de belleza** beauty parlo(u)r, beautician's

salpicadera *f Méx* AUTO fender, *Br* mudguard; **salpicadero** *m* AUTO dash(board); **salpicadura** *f* stain; **salpicar** <1g> *v/t* splash, spatter (*con* with); *fig* sprinkle, pepper; **salpicón** *m* GASTR *vegetable salad with chopped meat or fish*

salpimentar <1k> *v/t* season (with

salt and pepper)

salsa f GASTR sauce; *baile salsa*; *en su ~ fig* in one's element; **salsera** f sauce boat

saltamontes m inv ZO grasshopper

saltar <1a> **1** v/i jump, leap; ~ *a la vista fig* be obvious, be clear; ~ *sobre* pounce on; ~ *a la comba* jump rope, *Br* skip **2** v/t *valla* jump **3** v/r ~*se* (*omitir*) miss, skip

saltear <1a> v/t GASTR sauté

saltimbanqui m acrobat

salto m leap, jump; ~ *de agua* waterfall; ~ *de altura* high jump; ~ *de longitud* long jump; ~ *mortal* somersault, **saltón** adj: *ojos saltones* bulging eyes

salubridad f L.Am. health; **Salubridad** L.Am. Department of Health; **salud** f health; *¡(a tu) ~!* cheers!; **saludable** adj healthy; **saludar** <1a> v/t say hello to, greet; MIL salute; **saludo** m greeting; MIL salute; ~*s en carta* best wishes

salva f: ~ *de aplausos* round of applause

salvación f REL salvation

salvado m bran

salvador m REL savio(u)r

salvadoreño 1 adj Salvador(e)an **2** m, -a f Salvador(e)an

salvaguardar <1a> v/t safeguard, protect

salvajada f atrocity, act of savagery; *decir una ~* say something outrageous; **salvaje 1** adj wild; (*bruto*) brutal **2** m/f savage; **salvajismo** m savagery

salvamanteles m inv table mat

salvamento m rescue; *buque de ~* life boat

salvapantallas m inv INFOR screensaver

salvar <1a> **1** v/t save; *obstáculo* get round, get over **2** v/r ~*se* escape, get out; **salvavidas** m inv life belt; **salvedad** f (*excepción*) exception

salvo 1 adj healthy; *ponerse a ~* reach safety **2** adv & prp except, save; ~ *error u omisión* errors and omissions ex-

cepted

sambenito m: *le han colgado el ~ de vago* F they've got him down as idle F

sambumbia f L.Am. watery drink

San adj Saint

sanar <1a> **1** v/t cure **2** v/i *de persona* get well, recover; *de herida* heal; **sanatorio** m sanitarium, clinic

sanción f JUR penalty, sanction; **sancionar** <1a> v/t penalize; (*multar*) fine

sancocho m W.I. type of stew

sandalia f sandal

sándalo m BOT sandalwood

sandez f nonsense; *decir sandeces* talk nonsense

sandía f watermelon

sandunga f F wit; **sandunguero** adj L.Am. F witty

sandwich m *tostado* toasted sandwich; *L.Am. sin tostar* sandwich

saneamiento m cleaning up; COM restructuring, rationalization; **sanear** <1a> v/t clean up; COM restructure, rationalize

sangrar <1a> **1** v/t ~ *a alguien fig* F sponge off s.o. **2** v/i bleed; **sangre** f blood; ~ *fría fig* calmness, coolness; *a ~ fría fig* in cold blood; *no llegará la ~ al río* it won't come to that, it won't be that bad; **sangría** f GASTR sangria; **sangriento** adj bloody; **sangrigordo** adj Méx tedious, boring; **sanguijuela** f ZO, *fig* leech; **sanguinario** adj bloodthirsty

sanidad f health; **sanitario** adj (public) health atr; **sanitarios** mpl bathroom fittings; **sano** adj healthy; ~ *y salvo* safe and well; *cortar por lo ~* take drastic measures

sanseacabó: y ~ F and that's that F

santa f Saint

santiamén m: *en un ~* F in an instant

santidad f: *Su Santidad* His Holiness

santiguarse <1i> v/r cross o.s., make the sign of the cross

santo 1 adj holy **2** m saint; ~ *y seña* F password; *¿a ~ de qué?* F what on earth for? F; *no es ~ de mi*

devoción F I don't like him very much; **santuario** *m fig* sanctuary; **santurrón** *m*, **-ona** *f* sanctimonious person

saña *f* viciousness

sapo *m* ZO toad; ***echar ~s y culebras*** *fig* curse and swear

saque *m en tenis* serve; **~ de banda** *en fútbol* throw-in; **~ de esquina** corner (kick); ***tener buen ~*** F have a big appetite

saquear <1a> *v/t* sack, ransack

sarampión *m* MED measles

sarao *m* party

sarape *m Méx* poncho, blanket

sarcasmo *m* sarcasm; **sarcástico** *adj* sarcastic

sarcófago *m* sarcophagus

sardina *f* sardine; ***como ~s en lata*** like sardines

sargento *m* sergeant

sarna *f* MED scabies; **sarnoso** *adj* scabby

sarpullido *m* MED rash

sarro *m* tartar

sarta *f* string, series

sartén *f* frying pan; ***tener la ~ por el mango*** *fig* be the boss, be in the driving seat

sastra *f* tailor(ess); **sastre** *m* tailor

satán *m*, **satanás** *m* Satan; **satánico** *adj* satanic

satélite *m* satellite; ***ciudad ~*** satellite town

satén, **satín** *m* satin

sátira *f* satire; **satírico** *adj* satirical; **satirizar** <1f> *v/t* satirize

satisfacción *f* satisfaction; **satisfacer** <2s; *part* **satisfecho**> *v/t* satisfy; *requisito*, *exigencia* meet, fulfil(l); *deuda* settle, pay off; **satisfactorio** *adj* satisfactory; **satisfecho 1** *part* → **satisfacer 2** *adj* satisfied; *(lleno)* full; ***darse por ~*** be satisfied (*con* with)

saturar <1a> *v/t* saturate

sauce *m* BOT willow; **~ llorón** weeping willow

saúco *m* BOT elder

saudí *m/f & adj* Saudi

saudita *m/f* Saudi

sauna *f* sauna

savia *f* sap

saxofón, **saxófono** *m* saxophone, sax F

sazón *f*: ***a la ~*** at that time; **sazonar** <1a> *v/t* GASTR season

scooter *m* motor scooter

se ◊ *pron complemento indirecto*: *a él* (to) him; *a ella* (to) her; *a usted*, *ustedes* (to) you; *a ellos* (to) them; **~ lo daré** I will give it to him/ her/you/them ◊ *reflexivo*: *con él* himself; *con ella* herself; *cosa* itself; *con usted* yourself; *con ustedes* yourselves; *con ellos* themselves; **~ vistió** he got dressed, he dressed himself; ***se lavó las manos*** she washed her hands; **~ abrazaron** they hugged each other ◊ *oración impersonal*: **~ cree** it is thought; **~ habla español** Spanish spoken

sé *vb* → **saber**

sea *vb* → **ser**

sebo *m* grease, fat

secador *m*: **~ (de pelo)** hair dryer; **secadora** *f* dryer; **secar** <1g> **1** *v/t* dry **2** *v/r* **~se** dry

sección *f* section

secesión *f* POL secession

seco *adj* dry; *fig persona* curt, brusque; ***parar en ~*** stop dead

secreción *f* secretion

secretaria *f* secretary; **~ de dirección** executive secretary; **secretaría** *f* secretary's office; *de organización* secretariat; **secretario** *m tb* POL secretary; **secréter** *m mueble* writing desk; **secretismo** *m* secrecy; **secreto 1** *adj* secret **2** *m* secret; ***un ~ a voces*** an open secret; ***en ~*** in secret

secta *f* sect; **sectario** *adj* sectarian; **sectarismo** *m* sectarianism

sector *m* sector

secuaz *m/f* follower

secuela *f* MED after-effect

secuencia *f* sequence; **secuencial** *adj* INFOR sequential

secuestrador *m*, **~a** *f* kidnapper; **secuestrar** <1a> *v/t barco*, *avión* hijack; *persona* abduct, kidnap;

secuestro *m* de barco, avión hijacking; *de persona* abduction, kidnapping; **~ aéreo** hijacking

secundar <1a> *v/t* support, back; **secundario** *adj* secondary

sed *f tb fig* thirst; **tener ~** be thirsty

seda *f* silk; **como una ~** F as smooth as silk

sedal *m* fishing line

sedante *m* sedative

sede *f de organización* headquarters; *de acontecimiento* site; **~ social** head office

sedentario *adj* sedentary

sedición *f* sedition

sediento *adj* thirsty; **estar ~ de** *fig* thirst for

sedimentar <1a> *v/t* deposit; **sedimento** *m* sediment

sedoso *adj* silky

seducción *f* seduction; *(atracción)* attraction; **seducir** <3o> *v/t* seduce; *(atraer)* attract; *(cautivar)* captivate, charm; **seductor 1** *adj* seductive; *(atractivo)* attractive; *oferta* tempting **2** *m* seducer; **seductora** *f* seductress

segadora *f* reaper, harvester; **segar** <1h & 1k> *v/t* reap, harvest

seglar *adj* secular, lay *atr*

segmento *m* segment

segregación *f* segregation; **~ racial** racial segregation; **segregar** <1h> *v/t* segregate

seguida *f*: **en ~** at once, immediately; **seguido 1** *adj* consecutive, successive; **ir todo ~** go straight on **2** *adv* L.Am. often, frequently; **seguidor** *m*, **~a** *f* follower, supporter; **seguimiento** *m* monitoring; **seguir** <3l & 3d> **1** *v/t* follow; **~ a alguien** follow s.o. **2** *v/i* continue, carry on; **sigue enfadado conmigo** he's still angry with me; **~ haciendo algo** go on doing sth, continue to do sth

según 1 *prp* according to; **~ él** according to him **2** *adv* it depends

segunda *f*: **de ~** *fig* second-rate; **segundero** *m* second hand; **segundo** *m/adj* second

seguridad *f* safety; *contra crimen* security; *(certeza)* certainty; **Seguridad Social** *Esp* Social Security; **seguro 1** *adj* safe; *(estable)* steady; *(cierto)* sure; **es ~** *(cierto)* it's a certainty; **~ de sí mismo** self-confident, sure of o.s. **2** *adv* for sure **3** *m* COM insurance; *de puerta, coche* lock; *L.Am. (imperdible)* safety pin; **poner el ~** lock the door; **ir sobre ~** be on the safe side

seis *adj* six; **seiscientos** *adj* six hundred

seísmo *m* earthquake

selección *f* selection; **~ nacional** DEP national team; **seleccionador** *m*, **~a** *f* DEP: **~ nacional** national team manager; **seleccionar** <1a> *v/t* choose, select; **selectividad** *f en España* university entrance exam; **selecto** *adj* select, exclusive

sellar <1a> *v/t* seal; **sello** *m* stamp; *fig* hallmark; **~ discográfico** record label

selva *f (bosque)* forest; *(jungla)* jungle

semáforo *m* traffic light

semana *f* week; **Semana Santa** Holy Week, Easter; **semanal** *adj* weekly; **semanario** *m* weekly

semblante *m* face

sembrado *m* sown field; **sembrar** <1k> *v/t* sow; *fig: pánico, inquietud etc* spread

semejante 1 *adj* similar; **jamás he oído ~ tontería** I've never heard such nonsense **2** *m* fellow human being, fellow creature; **semejanza** *f* similarity; **semejarse** <1a> *v/r* look alike, resemble each other

semen *m* BIO semen; **semental** *m* *toro* stud bull; *caballo* stallion

semestre *m* six-month period; EDU semester

semicírculo *m* semicircle; **semiconductor** *m* EL semiconductor; **semifinal** *f* DEP semifinal

semilla *f* seed

seminario *m* seminary; **seminarista** *m* seminarian

semítico *adj* Semitic

sémola *f* semolina

S

senado *m* senate; **senador** *m*, **~a** *f* senator

sencillez *f* simplicity; **sencillo 1** *adj* simple **2** *m L.Am.* small change

senda *f* path, track; **senderismo** *m* trekking, hiking; **senderista** *m/f* walker, hiker; **sendero** *m* path, track

sendos, -as *adj pl*: *les entregó ~ diplomas* he presented each of them with a diploma

senil *adj* senile

seno *m tb fig* bosom; **~s** breasts

sensación *f* feeling, sensation; *causar ~ fig* cause a sensation; **sensacional** *adj* sensational; **sensacionalista** *adj* sensationalist

sensatez *f* good sense; **sensato** *adj* sensible

sensibilidad *f* feeling; (*emotividad*) sensitivity; **sensibilizar** <1f> *v/t* make aware (*sobre* of); **sensible** *adj* sensitive; (*apreciable*) appreciable, noticeable; **sensiblero** *adj* sentimental, schmaltzy F; **sensor** *m* sensor; **sensorial** *adj* sensory; **sensual** *adj* sensual; **sensualidad** *f* sensuality

sentada *f* sit-down; **sentado** *adj* sitting, seated; *dar por ~ fig* take for granted, assume; **sentar** <1k> **1** *v/t fig* establish, create; *~ las bases* lay the foundations, pave the way **2** *v/i*: *~ bien a alguien de comida* agree with s.o.; *le sienta bien esa chaqueta* that jacket suits her, she looks good in that jacket **3** *v/r* **~se** sit down

sentencia *f* JUR sentence; **sentenciar** <1b> *v/t* JUR sentence

sentido *m* sense; (*significado*) meaning; *~ común* common sense; *~ del humor* sense of humo(u)r; *perder/recobrar el ~* lose/regain consciousness

sentimental *adj* emotional; *ser ~* be sentimental; **sentimentalismo** *m* sentiment; **sentimiento** *m* feeling; *lo acompaño en el ~* my condolences

sentir 1 *m* feeling, opinion **2** <3i> *v/t* feel; (*percibir*) sense; *lo siento* I'm sorry **3** *v/r ~se* feel; *L.Am.* (*ofenderse*) take offense, *Br* take offence

seña *f* gesture, sign; *me hizo una ~ para que entrara* he gestured to me to go in; *~s pl* address *sg*; *hacer ~s* wave

señal *f* signal; *fig* sign, trace; COM deposit, down payment; *en ~ de* as a token of, as a mark of; **señalado** *adj* special; **señalar** <1a> *v/t* indicate, point out; **señalizar** <1f> *v/t* signpost

Señor *m* Lord

señor 1 *m* gentleman, man; *trato* sir; *escrito* Mr; *el ~ López* Mr López; *los ~es López* Mr and Mrs López; **señora** *f* lady, woman; *trato* ma'am, *Br* madam; *escrito* Mrs, Ms; *la ~ López* Mrs López; *mi ~* my wife; *~s y señores* ladies and gentlemen; **señoría** *f*: *su ~* your Hono(u)r; **señorial** *adj* lordly, noble; **señorita** *f* young lady, young woman; *tratamiento* miss; *escrito* Miss; *la ~ López* Ms López, Miss López

señuelo *m* decoy

sepa *vb* → *saber*

separación *f* separation; *~ de bienes* JUR division of property; **separado** *adj* separated; *por ~* separately; **separar** <1a> **1** *v/t* separate **2** *v/r* **~se** separate, split up F; **separatismo** *m* separatism; **separatista** *m/f & adj* separatist

sepia *f* ZO cuttlefish

sept.^e *abr* (= *septiembre*) Sept. (= September)

septentrional *adj* northern

septiembre *m* September

séptimo *adj* seventh

sepulcro *m* tomb; **sepultar** <1a> *v/t* bury; **sepultura** *f* burial; (*tumba*) tomb; *dar ~ a alguien* bury s.o.

sequedad *f fig* curtness

sequía *f* drought

séquito *m* retinue, entourage

ser <2w; *part sido*> **1** *v/i* be; *~ de Sevilla* be from Seville; *~ de madera/plata* be made of wood/

silver; **es de Juan** it's Juan's, it belongs to Juan; **~ para** be for; **a no ~ que** unless; **¡eso es!** exactly!, that's right!; **es que ...** the thing is ...; **es de esperar** it's to be hoped; **¿cuánto es?** how much is it?; **¿qué es de ti?** how's life?, how're things?; **o sea** in other words **2** *m* being

Serbia Serbia

serenarse <1a> *v/r* calm down; *del tiempo* clear up

serenata *f* MÚS serenade

serenidad *f* calmness, serenity; **sereno 1** *m*: **dormir al ~** sleep outdoors **2** *adj* calm, serene

serial *m* TV, RAD series; **serie** *f* series; **fuera de ~** out of this world, extraordinary

seriedad *f* seriousness; **serio** *adj* serious; (*responsable*) reliable; **en ~** seriously

sermón *m* sermon; **sermonear** <1a> *v/i* preach

seropositivo *adj* MED HIV positive

serpentina *f* streamer; **serpiente** *f* ZO snake; **~ de cascabel** rattlesnake

serranía *f* mountainous region

serrar <1k> *v/t* saw; **serrín** *m* sawdust; **serrucho** *m* handsaw

servicial *adj* obliging, helpful; **servicio** *m* service; **~s** *pl* restroom *sg*, *Br* toilets; **~ doméstico** domestic service; **~ militar** military service; **~ pos(t)venta** after-sales service; **~ de atención al cliente** customer service; **estar de ~** be on duty

servidor *m* INFOR server

servil *adj* servile; **servilismo** *m* servility

servilleta *f* napkin, serviette; **servilletero** *m* napkin ring

servir <3l> **1** *v/t* serve **2** *v/i* be of use; **¿para qué sirve esto?** what is this (used) for?; **no ~ de nada** be no use at all **3** *v/r* **~se** help o.s.; *comida* help oneself to

servodirección *f* power steering

sésamo *m* sesame

sesenta *adj* sixty

sesgar <1h> *v/t* slant, skew

sesión *f* session; *en cine, teatro* show, performance; **sesionar** <1a> *v/i* *L.Am.* be in session

seso *m* ANAT brain; *fig* brains *pl*, sense; **~s** GASTR brains

set *m* *tenis* set

seta *f* BOT mushroom; *venenosa* toadstool

setecientos *adj* seven hundred; **setenta** *adj* seventy

seto *m* hedge

s.e.u.o. *abr* (= *salvo error u omisión*) E & OE (= errors and omissions excepted)

seudónimo *m* pseudonym

severo *adj* severe

sevillanas *fpl* folk dance from Seville

sexismo *m* sexism; **sexista** *m/f & adj* sexist; **sexo** *m* sex

sexto *adj* sixth

sexual *adj* sexual; **sexualidad** *f* sexuality

sexy *adj inv* sexy

shock *m* MED shock

si *conj* if; **~ no** if not; **como ~** as if; **por ~** in case; **me pregunto si vendrá** I wonder whether he'll come

sí 1 *adv* yes **2** *pron tercera persona*: *singular masculino* himself; *femenino* herself; *cosa, animal* itself; *plural* themselves; *usted* yourself; *ustedes* yourselves; **por ~ solo** by himself / itself, on his / its own

siamés *adj* Siamese

sibarita *m* bon vivant, epicure

Siberia Siberia

sicario *m* hired assassin

Sicilia Sicily

SIDA *abr* (= *síndrome de inmunidad deficiente adquirida*) Aids (= acquired immune-deficiency syndrome)

sidecar *m* sidecar

sideral *adj viajes* space *atr*; **espacio ~** outer space

siderurgia *f* iron and steel making

sido *part* → **ser**

sidra *f* cider

siembra *f* sowing

siempre *adv* always; ~ *que* providing that, as long as; *lo de* ~ the same old story; *para* ~ for ever

sien *f* ANAT temple

siendo *vb* → *ser*

siento *vb* → *sentir*

sierra *f* saw; GEOG mountain range

siesta *f* siesta, nap; *dormir la* ~ have a siesta *o* nap

siete *adj* seven

sífilis *f* MED syphilis

siga *vb* → *seguir*

sigilo *m* (*secreto*) secrecy; (*disimulo*) stealth; **sigiloso** *adj* stealthy

sigla *f* abbreviation, acronym

siglo *m* century; *hace* ~*s o un* ~ *que no le veo* fig I haven't seen him in a long long time

signatario *m*, **-a** *f* signatory

significado *m* meaning; **significar** <1g> *v/t* mean, signify; **significativo** *adj* meaningful, significant

signo *m* sign; ~ *de admiración* exclamation mark; ~ *de interrogación* question mark; ~ *de puntuación* punctuation mark

sigo *vb* → *seguir*

siguiente 1 *adj* next, following **2** *pron* next (one)

sílaba *f* syllable

silbar <1a> *v/i & v/t* whistle; **silbato** *m* whistle; **silbido** *m* whistle

silenciador *m* AUTO muffler, *Br* silencer; **silencio** *m* silence; *en* ~ in silence, silently; **silencioso** *adj* silent

silicio *m* QUÍM silicon; **silicona** *f* silicone

silla *f* chair; ~ *de montar* saddle; ~ *de ruedas* wheelchair

sillín *m* saddle

sillón *m* armchair, easy chair

silueta *f* silhouette

silvestre *adj* wild; **silvicultura** *f* forestry

simbiosis *f* symbiosis

simbolismo *m* symbolism; **simbolizar** <1f> *v/t* symbolize; **símbolo** *m* symbol

simétrico *adj* symmetrical

similar *adj* similar; **similitud** *f* similarity

simio *m* ZO ape

simpatía *f* warmth, friendliness; **simpático** *adj* nice, lik(e)able; **simpatizante** *m/f* sympathizer, supporter; **simpatizar** <1f> *v/i* sympathize

simple 1 *adj* simple; (*mero*) ordinary **2** *m/f* simpleton; **simplicidad** *f* simplicity; **simplificar** <1g> *v/t* simplify; **simplista** *adj* simplistic

simposio *m* symposium

simulación *f* simulation; **simulacro** *m* (*cosa falsa*) pretense, *Br* pretence, sham; (*simulación*) simulation; ~ *de incendio* fire drill; **simulador** *m* simulator; **simular** <1a> *v/t* simulate

simultanear <1a> *v/t*: ~ *dos cargos* hold two positions at the same time; **simultáneo** *adj* simultaneous

sin *prp* without; ~ *que* without; ~ *preguntar* without asking

sinagoga *f* synagogue

sinceridad *f* sincerity; **sincero** *adj* sincere

síncope *m* MED blackout

sincronizar <1f> *v/t* synchronize

sindical *adj* (labor, *Br* trade) union *atr*; **sindicalismo** *m* (labor, *Br* trade) union movement; **sindicalista** *m/f* (labor, *Br* trade) union member; **sindicato** *m* (labor, *Br* trade) union

síndrome *m* syndrome

sinfín *m*: *un* ~ *de* ... no end of ...

sinfonía *f* MÚS symphony

singular 1 *adj* singular; fig outstanding, extraordinary **2** *m* GRAM singular

siniestro 1 *adj* sinister **2** *m* accident; (*catástrofe*) disaster

sinnúmero *m*: *un* ~ *de* no end of

sino 1 *m* fate **2** *conj* but; (*salvo*) except; *no cena en casa,* ~ *en el bar* he doesn't have dinner at home, he has it in the bar

sinónimo 1 *adj* synonymous **2** *m* synonym

sinopsis *f inv* synopsis

sinsentido *m* nonsense

sintaxis f syntax

síntesis f inv synthesis; (*resumen*) summary; **sintético** adj synthetic; **sintetizador** m MÚS synthesizer

síntoma m symptom

sintonía f *melodía* theme tune, signature tune; RAD tuning, reception; **estar en la ~ de** RAD be tuned to; **sintonizar** <1f> **1** v/t *radio* tune in **2** v/i fig be in tune (**con** with)

sinuoso adj winding

sinusitis f MED sinusitis

sinvergüenza m/f swine; **¡qué ~!** (*descarado*) what a nerve!

siquiera adv: **ni ~** not even; **~ bebe algo** L.Am. at least have a drink

sirena f siren; MYTH mermaid

Siria Syria

sirve vb → **servir**

sirvienta f maid; **sirviente** m servant

sisar <1a> v/t F pilfer

sísmico adj seismic

sistema m system; **~ operativo** operating system; **sistemático** adj systematic

sitiar <1b> v/t surround, lay siege to; **sitio** m place; (*espacio*) room; **hacer ~** make room; **en ningún ~** nowhere; **~ web** web site; **situación** f situation; **situar** <1e> **1** v/t place, put **2** v/r **~se** be

S.L. abr (= **sociedad limitada**) Ltd (= limited)

slip m underpants pl

s/n abr (= **sin número**) not numbered

sobaco m armpit

sobar <1a> v/t handle, finger; F *sexualmente* grope F

soberanía f sovereignty; **soberano** m, **-a** f sovereign

soberbia f pride, arrogance; **soberbio** adj proud, arrogant; fig superb

sobornar <1a> v/t bribe; **soborno** m bribe

sobra f surplus, excess; **hay de ~** there's more than enough; **~s** leftovers; **sobradamente** adv *conocido* well; **sobrar** <1a> v/t: **sobra comida** there's food left over; **me sobró pintura** I had some paint

left over; **sobraba uno** there was one left

sobre 1 m envelope **2** prp on; **~ esto** about this; **~ las tres** about three o'clock; **~ todo** above all, especially

sobrecargar <1h> v/t overload; **sobrecargo** m AVIA chief flight attendant; MAR purser

sobrecoger <2c> v/t (*asustar*) strike fear into; (*impresionar*) have an effect on

sobredosis f inv overdose

sobrehumano adj superhuman

sobremesa f: **de ~** afternoon atr

sobrenatural adj supernatural

sobrenombre m nickname

sobrentenderse <2g> v/r: **se sobrentiende que ...** needless to say, ...

sobrepasar <1a> **1** v/t exceed, surpass; **me sobrepasa en altura** he is taller than me **2** v/r **~se** go too far; **sobrepeso** m excess weight

sobreponerse <2r; part **sobrepuesto**> v/r: **~ a** overcome, get over

sobrepuesto part → **sobreponerse**

sobresaliente adj outstanding, excellent; **sobresalir** <3r> v/t stick out, protrude; fig excel; **~ entre** stand out among

sobresaltar <1a> **1** v/t startle **2** v/r **~se** jump, start; **sobresalto** m jump, start

sobreseer <2e> v/t JUR dismiss

sobrestimar <1a> v/t overestimate

sobresueldo m bonus

sobrevalorar <1a> v/t overrate

sobrevenir <3s> v/i happen; **de guerra** break out

sobrevivir <3a> v/i survive

sobrevolar <1m> v/t fly over

sobriedad f soberness; *de comida, decoración* simplicity; (*moderación*) restraint

sobrina f niece; **sobrino** m nephew

sobrio adj sober; *comida, decoración* simple; (*moderado*) restrained

socarrón adj sarcastic, snide F

socavar <1a> v/t tb fig undermine

socavón m hollow

sociable adj sociable; **social** adj social; **socialismo** m socialism; **socialista** m/f & adj socialist

sociedad f society; **~ anónima** public corporation, Br public limited company; **~ de consumo** consumer society

socio m, **-a** f de club, asociación etc member; COM partner; **sociología** f sociology

socorrer <2a> v/t help, assist; **socorrista** m/f life guard; **socorro** m help, assistance; **¡~!** help!

soda f soda (water)

sodio m sodium

sofá m sofa

sofisticación f sophistication; **sofisticado** adj sophisticated

sofocante adj suffocating; **sofocar** <1g> **1** v/t suffocate; incendio put out **2** v/r **~se** fig get embarrassed; (irritarse) get angry; **sofoco** m fig embarrassment

sofreír <3m> v/t sauté; **sofrito** m GASTR mixture of fried onions, peppers etc

software m INFOR software

soga f rope; **estar con la ~ al cuello** F be in big trouble F

sois vb → **ser**

soja f soy, Br soya

sol m sun; **hace ~** it's sunny; **tomar el ~** sunbathe

solamente adv only

solapa f lapel

solar m vacant lot

solariego adj: **casa -a** family seat

solario, solárium m solarium

soldado m/f soldier

soldador m welder; **soldadura** f welding, soldering; **soldar** <1m> v/t weld, solder

soleado adj sunny

soledad f solitude, loneliness

solemne adj solemn

soler <2h> v/i: **~ hacer algo** usually do sth; **suele venir temprano** he usually comes early; **solía visitarme** he used to visit me

solera f traditional character

solfeo m (tonic) sol-fa

solicitante m/f applicant; **solicitar** <1a> v/t request; empleo, beca apply for; **solícito** adj attentive; **solicitud** f application, request

solidaridad f solidarity; **solidario** adj supportive, understanding; **solidarizarse** <1f> v/r: **~ con alguien** support s.o., back s.o.; **solidez** f solidity; fig strength; **sólido** adj solid; fig sound

solista m/f soloist

solitaria f ZO tapeworm; **solitario 1** adj solitary; lugar lonely **2** m solitaire, Br patience; **actuó en ~** he acted alone

soliviantar <1a> **1** v/t incite, stir up **2** v/r **~se** v/r rise up, rebel

sollozar <1f> v/i sob; **sollozo** m sob

solo adj single; **estar ~** be alone; **sentirse ~** feel lonely; **un ~ día** a single day; **a solas** alone, by o.s.; **por sí ~** by o.s.

sólo adv only, just

solomillo m GASTR sirloin

solsticio m solstice

soltar <1m> **1** v/t let go of; (librar) release, let go; olor give off **2** v/r **~se** free o.s.; **~se a andar/hablar** begin o start to walk/talk

soltera f single o unmarried woman; **soltero 1** adj single, not married **2** m bachelor, unmarried man; **solterona** f desp old maid

soltura f fluency, ease

soluble adj soluble; **solución** f solution; **solucionar** <1a> v/t solve

solventar <1a> v/t resolve, settle; **solvente** adj solvent

somanta f F beating

sombra f shadow; **a la ~ de un árbol** in the shade of a tree; **a la ~ de** fig under the protection of; **~ de ojos** eye shadow

sombrero m hat; **~ de copa** top hat

sombrilla f sunshade, beach umbrella

sombrío adj fig somber, Br sombre

someter <2a> **1** v/t subject; **~ algo a votación** put sth to the vote **2** v/r **~se** yield (**a** to); **al ley** comply (**a**

with); (*rendirse*) give in (*a* to); *~se a tratamiento* undergo treatment

somier *m* bed base

somnífero *m* sleeping pill

somnolencia *f* sleepiness, drowsiness; **somnoliento** *adj* sleepy, drowsy

somos *vb* → **ser**

son[1] *m* sound; *al ~ de* to the sound of; *en ~ de paz* in peace

son[2] *vb* → **ser**

sonado *adj* F famous, well-known

sonajero *m* rattle

sonámbulo *m* sleep-walker

sonar <1m> **1** *v/i* ring out; *~ a* sound like; *me suena esa voz* I know that voice, that voice sounds familiar **2** *v/r ~se*: *~se (la nariz)* blow one's nose

sonata *f* MÚS sonata

sonda *f* MED catheter; *~ espacial* space probe; **sondaje** *m* L.Am. poll, survey; **sondear** <1a> *v/t fig* survey, poll; **sondeo** *m*: *~ (de opinión)* survey, (opinion) poll

soneto *m* sonnet

sonido *m* sound

soniquete *m* droning

sonreír <3m> *v/i* smile; **sonriente** *adj* smiling; **sonrisa** *f* smile

sonrojar <1a> **1** *v/t*: *~ a alguien* make s.o. blush **2** *v/r ~se* blush; **sonrojo** *m* blush

sonsacar <1g> *v/t*: *~ algo* worm sth out (*a* of), wheedle sth out (*a* of)

sonso *adj* L.Am. F silly

soñador 1 *adj* dreamy **2** *m* dreamer; **soñar** <1m> (*con* about) **1** *v/t* dream about **2** *v/i* dream; *¡ni ~lo!* dream on! F

soñolencia *f* → **somnolencia**; **soñoliento** *adj* → **somnolento**

sopa *f* soup; *estar hecho una ~* F be sopping wet; *hasta en la ~* F all over the place F

sopapo *m* F smack, slap

sopera *f* soup tureen

sopesar <1a> *v/t fig* weigh up

sopetón *m*: *de ~* unexpectedly

soplar <1a> **1** *v/i del viento* blow **2** *v/t vela* blow out; *polvo* blow away;

~ algo a la policía tip the police off about sth; **soplete** *m* welding torch; **soplo** *m*: *en un ~* F in an instant, **soplón** *m* F informer, stool pigeon F

soponcio *m*: *le dio un ~* F he passed out

sopor *m* drowsiness, sleepiness; **soporífero** *adj* soporific

soportal *m* porch

soportar <1a> *v/t fig* put up with, bear; *no puedo ~ a José* I can't stand José; **soporte** *m* support, stand; *~ lógico* INFOR software; *~ físico* INFOR hardware

soprano MÚS **1** *m* soprano **2** *m/f* soprano

sorber <2a> *v/t* sip

sorbete *m* sorbet; *C.Am.* ice cream; **sorbetería** *f C.Am.* ice-cream parlo(u)r

sorbo *m* sip

sordera *f* deafness

sórdido *adj* sordid

sordo 1 *adj* deaf **2** *m*, *-a f* deaf person; *hacerse el ~* turn a deaf ear; **sordomudo 1** *adj* deaf and dumb **2** *m*, *-a f* deaf-mute

sorna *f* sarcasm; *con ~* sarcastically, mockingly

sorocharse <1a> *v/r Pe, Bol* get altitude sickness; **soroche** *m Pe, Bol* altitude sickness

sorprendente *adj* surprising; **sorprender** <2a> *v/t* surprise; **sorpresa** *f* surprise; *de or por ~* by surprise

sortear <1a> *v/t* draw lots for; *obstáculo* get round; **sorteo** *m* (*lotería*) lottery, (prize) draw

sortija *f* ring

sortilegio *m* spell, charm

SOS *m* SOS

sosa *f* QUÍM: *~ cáustica* caustic soda

sosegado *adj* calm; **sosegarse** <1h & 1k> *v/r* calm down

sosería *f* insipidness, dullness

sosiego *m* calm, quiet

soslayo *adj*: *de ~* sideways

soso 1 *adj* tasteless, insipid; *fig* dull **2** *m*, *-a f* stick-in-the-mud F

sospecha *f* suspicion; **sospechar** <1a> **1** *v/t* suspect **2** *v/i* be suspicious; **~ de alguien** suspect someone; **sospechoso 1** *adj* suspicious **2** *m*, **-a** *f* suspect

sostén *m* brassiere, bra; *fig* pillar, mainstay; **sostener** <2l> **1** *v/t familia* support; *opinión* hold **2** *v/r* **~se** support o.s.; *de pie* stand up; *en el poder* stay, remain

sota *f naipes* jack

sotana *f* REL cassock

sótano *m* basement, *Br* cellar

soterrar <1k> *v/t* bury

soviético *adj* Soviet

soy *vb* → **ser**

soya *f L.Am.* soy, *Br* soya

spot *m* TV commercial

spray *m* spray

sprint *m* sprint

squash *m* DEP squash

Sr. *abr* (= **señor**) Mr

Sra. *abr* (= **señora**) Mrs

Sres. *abr* (= **Señores**) Messrs (= Messieurs)

Srta. *abr* (= **Señorita**) Miss

stand *m* COM stand

stock *m* stock; **tener en ~** have in stock

su, sus *adj pos*: *de él* his; *de ella* her; *de cosa* its; *de usted, ustedes* your; *de ellos* their; *de uno* one's

suave *adj* soft, smooth; *sabor, licor* mild; **suavidad** *f* softness, smoothness; *de sabor, licor* mildness; **suavizante** *m de pelo, ropa* conditioner; **suavizar** <1f> *v/t tb fig* soften

subacuático *adj* underwater

subalterno 1 *adj* subordinate **2** *m*, **-a** *f* subordinate

subasta *f* auction; **sacar a ~** put up for auction; **subastar** <1a> *v/t* auction (off)

subcampeón *m* DEP runner-up

subconsciente *m/adj* subconscious

subcontrata(ción) *f* subcontracting

subdesarrollado *adj* underdeveloped; **subdesarrollo** *m* underdevelopment

subdirector *m*, **~a** *f* deputy manager

súbdito *m* subject

subestimar <1a> *v/t* underestimate

subida *f* rise, ascent; **~ de los precios** rise in prices; **subido 1** *part* → **subir** **2** *adj*: **~ de tono** *fig* risqué, racy; **subir** <3a> **1** *v/t cuesta, escalera* go up, climb; *montaña* climb; *objeto* raise, lift; *intereses, precio* raise **2** *v/i para indicar acercamiento* come up; *para indicar alejamiento* go up; *de precio* rise, go up; *a un tren, autobús* get on; *a un coche* get in **3** *v/r* **~se** go up; *a un árbol* climb

súbito *adj*: **de ~** suddenly, all of a sudden

subjetivo *adj* subjective

subjuntivo *m* GRAM subjunctive

sublevar <1a> **1** *v/t* incite to revolt; *fig* infuriate, get angry **2** *v/r* **~se** rise up, revolt

sublimación *f fig* sublimation; **sublime** *adj* sublime, lofty; **subliminal** *adj* subliminal

submarinismo *m* scuba diving; **submarinista** *m/f* scuba diver; **submarino 1** *adj* underwater **2** *m* submarine

subnormal *adj* subnormal

subordinado 1 *adj* subordinate **2** *m*, **-a** *f* subordinate

subproducto *m* by-product

subrayar <1a> *v/t* underline; *fig* underline, emphasize

subrepticio *adj* surreptitious

subsanar <1a> *v/t* put right, rectify

subsidiario *adj* subsidiary

subsidio *m* welfare, *Br* benefit; **~ de paro** *or* **desempleo** unemployment compensation (*Br* benefit)

subsistencia *f* subsistence, survival; *de pobreza, tradición* persistence; **subsistir** <3a> *v/i* live, survive; *de pobreza, tradición* live on, persist

subte *m Rpl* subway, *Br* underground

subterfugio *m* subterfuge

subterráneo 1 *adj* underground **2** *m L.Am.* subway, *Br* underground

subtítulo *m* subtitle

suburbio *m* slum area

subvención *f* subsidy; **subvencio-**

nar <1a> v/t subsidize
subversivo adj subversive
subyacente adj underlying
subyugar <1h> v/t subjugate
succionar <1a> v/t suck
sucedáneo m substitute
suceder <2a> v/i happen, occur; ~ **a** follow; **¿qué sucede?** what's going on?; **sucesión** f succession; ~ **al trono** succession to the throne; **sucesivo** adj successive; **en lo** ~ from now on; **suceso** m event; **sucesor** m, ~**a** f successor
suciedad f dirt; **sucio** adj tb fig dirty
suculento adj succulent
sucumbir <3a> v/i succumb, give in
sucursal f COM branch
sudaca m/f desp South American
sudadera f sweatshirt
Sudáfrica South Africa; **sudafricano** <2a> adj South African 2 m, -**a** f South African
Sudamérica South America; **sudamericano** 1 adj South American 2 m, -**a** f South American
sudar <1a> v/i sweat
sudario m REL shroud
sudeste m southeast; **sudoeste** m southwest
sudor m sweat; **sudoración** f perspiration; **sudoroso** adj sweaty
Suecia Sweden; **sueco** 1 adj Swedish 2 m, -**a** f Swede; **hacerse el** ~ F pretend not to hear, act dumb F
suegra f mother-in-law; **suegro** m father-in-law
suela f de zapato sole
sueldo m salary
suelo m en casa floor; en el exterior earth, ground; AGR soil; **estar por los** ~**s** F be at rock bottom F
suelto 1 adj loose, free; **un pendiente** ~ a single earring; **andar** ~ be at large 2 m loose change
sueño m (estado de dormir) sleep; (fantasía, imagen mental) dream; **tener** ~ be sleepy
suero m MED saline solution; sanguíneo blood serum
suerte f luck; **por** ~ luckily; **echar a** ~**s** toss for, draw lots for; **probar** ~ try one's luck; **suertero** m, -**a** f L.Am. F, **suertudo** m, -**a** f L.Am. F lucky devil F
suéter m sweater
suficiente 1 adj enough, sufficient 2 m EDU pass
sufragar <1h> v/t COM meet, pay; **sufragio** m: ~ **universal** universal suffrage
sufrimiento m suffering; **sufrir** <3a> 1 v/t fig suffer, put up with 2 v/i suffer (de from)
sugerencia f suggestion; **sugerir** <3i> v/t suggest; **sugestionar** <1a> v/t influence; **sugestivo** adj suggestive
suicida 1 adj suicidal 2 m/f suicide victim; **suicidarse** <1a> v/r commit suicide; **suicidio** m suicide
suite f suite
Suiza Switzerland; **suizo** 1 adj Swiss 2 m, -**a** f Swiss 3 m GASTR sugar topped bun
sujetador m brassiere, bra; **sujetapapeles** m inv paperclip; **sujetar** <1a> v/t hold (down), keep in place; (sostener) hold; **sujeto** 1 adj secure 2 m individual; GRAM subject
sulfurarse <1a> v/r fig F blow one's top F
suma f sum; **en** ~ in short; **sumamente** adv extremely, highly; **sumar** <1a> 1 v/t add; **5 y 6 suman 11** 5 and 6 make 11 2 v/i add up 3 v/r ~**se**: ~**se a** join; **sumario** m summary; JUR indictment
sumergir <3c> 1 v/t submerge, immerse 2 v/r ~**se** fig immerse o.s. (en in), throw o.s. (en into)
sumidero m drain
suministrar <1a> v/t supply, provide; **suministro** m supply
sumir <3a> 1 v/t fig plunge, throw (en into) 2 v/r ~**se** fig sink (en into); **sumisión** f submission; **sumiso** adj submissive
sumo adj supreme; **con** ~ **cuidado** with the utmost care; **a lo** ~ at the most

S

suntuoso *adj* sumptuous

supe *vb* → **saber**

supeditar <1a> *v/t* make conditional (*a* upon)

súper *adj* F super F, great F

superable *adj* surmountable; **superación** *f* overcoming, surmounting; **superar** <1a> **1** *v/t persona* beat; *límite* go beyond, exceed; *obstáculo* overcome, surmount **2** *v/r* **~se** surpass o.s., excel o.s.

superávit *m* surplus

superchería *f* trick, swindle

superdotado *adj* gifted

superficial *adj* superficial, shallow; **superficialidad** *f* superficiality, shallowness; **superficie** *f* surface

superfluo *adj* superfluous

superior 1 *adj* upper; *en jerarquía* superior; **ser ~ a** be superior to **2** *m* superior; **superiora** *f* REL Mother Superior; **superioridad** *f* superiority

superlativo *adj* superlative

supermercado *m* supermarket

superpoblación *f* overpopulation

superponer <2r> *v/t* superimpose

superpotencia *f* POL superpower

superpuesto *adj* superimposed

supersónico *adj* supersonic

superstición *f* superstition; **supersticioso** *adj* superstitious

supervisar <1a> *v/t* supervise; **supervisor** *m*, **~a** *f* supervisor

supervivencia *f* survival; **superviviente 1** *adj* surviving **2** *m/f* survivor

suplantar <1a> *v/t* replace, take the place of

suplementario *adj* supplementary; **suplemento** *m* supplement

suplente *m/f* substitute, stand-in

súplica *f* plea; **suplicar** <1g> *v/t cosa* plead for, beg for; *persona* beg

suplicio *m* fig torment, ordeal

suplir <3a> *v/t carencia* make up for; (*sustituir*) substitute

supo *vb* → **saber**

suponer <2r; *part* **supuesto**> *v/t* suppose, assume; **suposición** *f* supposition

supositorio *m* MED suppository

supremacía *f* supremacy; **supremo** *adj* supreme

supresión *f* suppression; *de impuesto, ley* abolition; *de restricción* lifting; *de servicio* withdrawal; **suprimir** <3a> *v/t* suppress; *ley, impuesto* abolish; *restricción* lift; *servicio* withdraw; *puesto de trabajo* cut

supuesto 1 *part* → **suponer 2** *adj* supposed, alleged; **por ~** of course **3** *m* assumption

sur *m* south

surco *m* AGR furrow

sureño *adj* southern

surf(ing) *m* surfing; **surfista** *m/f* surfer

surgir <3c> *v/i fig* emerge; *de problema* come up; *de agua* spout

surrealismo *m* surrealism

surtido 1 *adj* assorted; **bien ~** COM well stocked **2** *m* assortment, range; **surtidor** *m*: **~ de gasolina** or **de nafta** gas pump, *Br* petrol pump; **surtir** <3a> **1** *v/t* supply; **~ efecto** have the desired effect **2** *v/i* spout **3** *v/r* **~se** stock up (*de* with)

susceptible *adj* touchy; **ser ~ de mejora** leave room for improvement

suscitar <1a> *v/t* arouse; *polémica* generate; *escándalo* provoke

suscribir <3a; *part* **suscrito**> **1** *v/t* subscribe to **2** *v/r* **~se** subscribe; **suscripción** *f* subscription; **suscriptor** *m*, **~a** *f* subscriber; **suscrito** *part* → **suscribir**

suspender <2a> **1** *v/t empleado, alumno* suspend; *objeto* hang; *reunión* adjourn; *examen* fail **2** *v/i* EDU fail; **suspense** *m fig* suspense; **suspensión** *f* suspension; **suspenso 1** *adj alumnos* **~s** students who have failed; **en ~** suspended **2** *m* fail; **suspensores** *mpl L.Am.* suspenders, *Br* braces

suspicacia *f* suspicion; **suspicaz** *adj* suspicious

suspirar <1a> *v/i* sigh; **~ por algo** yearn for sth, long for sth; **suspiro**

m sigh

sustancia *f* substance; **sustancial** *adj* substantial; **sustantivo** *m* GRAM noun

sustentar <1a> *v/t* sustain; *familia* support; *opinión* maintain; **sustento** *m* means of support

sustitución *f* substitution; **sustituir** <3g> *v/t:* **~ X por Y** replace X with Y, substitute Y for X; **sustituto** *m* substitute

susto *m* fright, scare; **dar** or **pegar un ~ a alguien** give s.o. a fright

sustraer <2p; *part* **sustraido**> *v/t* subtract, take away; (*robar*) steal; **sustraido** *part* → **sustraer**

susurrar <1a> *v/t* whisper; **susurro** *m* whisper

sutil *adj fig* subtle; **sutileza** *f fig* subtlety

suyo, suya *pron pos: de él* his; *de ella* hers; *de usted, ustedes* yours; *de ellos* theirs; **los ~s** his/her etc folks, his/her etc family; **hacer de las -as** get up to one's old tricks; **salirse con la -a** get one's own way

T

tabaco *m* tobacco

tábano *m* ZO horsefly

tabarra *f:* **dar la ~ a alguien** F bug s.o. F

taberna *f* bar; **tabernero** *m* bar owner; *Br* landlord; (*camarero*) bartender

tabique *m* partition, partition wall

tabla *f de madera* board, plank; PINT panel; (*cuadro*) table; **~ de multiplicar** multiplication table; **~ de planchar** ironing board; **~ de surf** surf board; **acabar** or **quedar en ~s** end in a tie; **tablero** *m* board, plank; *de juego* board; **~ de mandos** or **de instrumentos** AUTO dashboard; **tableta** *f:* **~ de chocolate** chocolate bar; **tablón** *m* plank; **~ de anuncios** bulletin board, *Br* notice board

tabú *m* taboo

tabulador *m tb* INFOR tab key

taburete *m* stool

tacañería *f* F miserliness, stinginess F; **tacaño 1** *adj* F miserly, stingy F **2** *m, -a f* F miser F, tightwad F

tacha *f* flaw, blemish; **sin ~** beyond reproach

tachadura *f* crossing-out

tachar <1a> *v/t* cross out

tacho *m Rpl* (*papelera*) wastepaper basket; *en la calle* garbage can, *Br* litter basket

tachón *m* crossing-out

tachuela *f* thumbtack, *Br* drawing pin

tácito *adj* tacit; **taciturno** *adj* taciturn

taco *m* F (*palabrota*) swear word; *L.Am.* heel; GASTR taco (*filled tortilla*)

tacón *m de zapato* heel; **zapatos de ~** high-heeled shoes

táctica *f* tactics *pl*; **táctico** *adj* tactical

tacto *m* (sense of) touch; *fig* tact, discretion

TAE *abr* (= **tasa anual efectiva**) APR (= annual percentage rate)

tahona *f* bakery

tahúr *m* gambler, card-sharp F

taita *m S.Am.* F dad, pop F; *S.Am.* (*abuelo*) grandfather

tajada *f* GASTR slice; **agarrar una ~** F get drunk; **sacar ~** take a cut F; **tajamar** *m S.Am.* (*dique*) dike; **tajante** *adj* categorical; **tajo** *m* cut

tal 1 *adj* such; **no dije ~ cosa** I said no such thing; **el gerente era un ~**

Lucas the manager was someone called Lucas **2** *adv:* **~ como** such as; **dejó la habitación ~ cual la encontró** she left the room just as she found it; **~ para cual** two of a kind; **~ vez** maybe, perhaps; **¿qué ~?** how's it going?; **¿que ~ la película?** what was the movie like?; **con ~ de que** + *subj* as long as, provided that

tala *f de árboles* felling

taladrar <1a> *v/t* drill; **taladro** *m* drill

talante *m* (*genio, humor*) mood; **un ~ bonachón** a kindly nature; **de mal ~** in a bad mood

talar <1a> *v/t árbol* fell, cut down

talco *m* talc, talcum; **polvos de ~** talcum powder

talego *m* P 1000 pesetas

talento *m* talent

talismán *m* talisman

talla *f* size; (*estatura*) height; *C.Am.* F (*mentira*) lie; **dar la ~** *fig* make the grade; **tallar** <1a> *v/t* carve; *piedra preciosa* cut

tallarín *m* noodle

taller *m* workshop; **~ mecánico** auto repair shop; **~ de reparaciones** repair shop

tallo *m* BOT stalk, stem

talón *m* ANAT heel; COM stub; **~ de Aquiles** *fig* Achilles' heel; **pisar los talones a alguien** be hot on s.o.'s heels; **talonario** *m:* **~ de cheques** check book, *Br* cheque book

tamal *m Méx, C.Am.* tamale (*meat wrapped in a leaf and steamed*)

tamaño 1 *adj:* **~ fallo / problema** such a great mistake / problem **2** *m* size

tambalearse <1a> *v/r* stagger, lurch; *de coche* sway

tambarria *f C.Am., Pe, Bol* F party

también *adv* also, too, as well; **yo ~** me too; **él ~ dice que ...** he also says that ...

tambo *m Rpl* dairy farm; *Méx type of large container*

tambor *m* drum; *persona* drummer; **tamborilear** <1a> *v/i* drum with

one's fingers

tamiz *m* sieve

tampoco *adv* neither; **él ~ va** he's not going either

tampón *m* tampon; *de tinta* ink-pad

tan *adv* so; **~ ... como ...** as ... as ...; **~ sólo** merely

tanatorio *m* funeral parlo(u)r

tanda *f* series, batch; (*turno*) shift; *L.Am.* (commercial) break; **~ de penaltis** DEP penalty shootout

tanga *m* tanga

tangente *f* MAT tangent; **salir** *or* **irse por la ~** F sidestep the issue, duck the question F

tangible *adj fig* tangible

tango *m* tango

tanque *m tb* MIL tank

tantear <1a> *v/t* feel; (*calcular a ojo*) work out roughly; *situación* size up; *persona* sound out; (*probar*) try out; **~ el terreno** *fig* see how the land lies

tantito *adv Méx* a little

tanto 1 *pron* so much; *igual cantidad* as much; **un ~** a little; **~s** *pl* so many *pl*; *igual número* as many; **tienes ~** you have so much; **no hay ~s como ayer** there aren't as many as yesterday; **a las -as de la noche** in the small hours **2** *adv* so much; *igual cantidad* as much; *periodo* so long; **tardó ~ como él** she took as long as him; **~ mejor** so much the better; **no es para ~** it's not such a big deal; **estar al ~** be informed (*de* about); **por lo ~** therefore, so **3** *m* point; **~ por ciento** percentage

tapa *f* lid; **~ dura** hardback

tapacubos *m inv* AUTO hub cap

tapadera *f* lid; *fig* front; **tapadillo** *m:* **de ~** on the sly; **tapado** *m Arg, Chi* coat; **tapar** <1a> **1** *v/t* cover; *recipiente* put the lid on **2** *v/r* **~se** wrap up; **~se los ojos** cover one's eyes

taparrabo *m* loincloth

tapete *m* tablecloth; **poner algo sobre el ~** bring sth up for discussion

tapia *f* wall; **más sordo que una ~** as

deaf as a post

tapicería *f* upholstery; **tapicero** *m*, -**a** *f* upholsterer

tapioca *f* tapioca

tapir *m* tapir

tapiz *m* tapestry; **tapizar** <1f> *v/t* upholster

tapón *m* top, cap; *de baño* plug; *de tráfico* traffic jam; **taponar** <1a> *v/t* block; *herida* swab

tapujo *m*: *sin ~s* openly

taquicardia *f* MED tachycardia

taquigrafía *f* shorthand

taquilla *f* ticket office; TEA box-office; *C.Am.* (*bar*) small bar

taquillero 1 *adj cantante* popular; *una película -a* a hit movie, a box-office hit **2** *m*, -**a** *f* ticket clerk

tara *f* defect

tarado *adj* F stupid, dumb F

tarántula *f* ZO tarantula

tararear <1a> *v/t* hum

tardar <1a> *v/i* take a long time; *tardamos dos horas* we were two hours overdue *o* late; *¡no tardes!* don't be late; *a más ~* at the latest; *¿cuánto se tarda ...?* how long does it take to ...?; **tarde 1** *adv* late; *~ o temprano* sooner or later **2** *f hasta las 5 ó 6* afternoon; *desde las 5 ó 6* evening; *¡buenas ~s!* good afternoon / evening; *por la ~* in the afternoon / evening; *de ~ en ~* from time to time; **tardón** *adj* F slow; (*impuntual*) late

tarea *f* task, job; *~s pl domésticas* housework *sg*

tarifa *f* rate; *de tren* fare; *~ plana* flat rate

tarima *f* platform; *suelo de ~* wooden floor

tarjeta *f* card; *~ amarilla* DEP yellow card; *~ de crédito* credit card; *~ de embarque* AVIA boarding card; *~ de sonido* INFOR sound card; *~ de visita* (business) card; *~ gráfica* INFOR graphics card; *~ inteligente* smart card; *~ monedero* electronic purse; *~ postal* postcard; *~ roja* DEP red card; *~ telefónica* phone card

tarro *m* jar; P (*cabeza*) head

tarta *f* cake; *plana* tart; *~ helada* ice-cream cake

tartamudear <1a> *v/i* stutter, stammer; **tartamudez** *f* stuttering, stammering; **tartamudo 1** *adj* stuttering, stammering; *ser ~* stutter, stammer **2** *m*, -**a** *f* stutterer, stammerer

tartera *f* lunch box

tarugo *m* F blockhead

tarumba F crazy F; *volverse ~* go crazy

tasa *f* rate; (*impuesto*) tax; *~ de desempleo or paro* unemployment rate; **tasar** <1a> *v/t* fix a price for; (*valorar*) assess

tasca *f* F bar

tata *m L.Am.* F (*abuelo*) grandpa F

tatarabuela *f* great-great-grandmother; **tatarabuelo** *m* great-great-grandfather; **tataranieta** *f* great-great-granddaughter; **tataranieto** *m* great-great-grandson

tate *int* F (*ahora caigo*) oh I see; (*cuidado*) look out!

tatuaje *m* tattoo

taurino *adj* bullfighting *atr*

Tauro *m/f inv* ASTR Taurus

tauromaquia *f* bullfighting

taxi *m* cab, taxi; **taxista** *m/f* cab *o* taxi driver

taza *f* cup; *del wáter* bowl; **tazón** *m* bowl

te *pron directo* you; *indirecto* (to) you; *reflexivo* yourself

té *m* tea

teatral *adj fig* theatrical; **teatro** *m tb fig* theater, *Br* theatre

tebeo *m* children's comic

techar <1a> *v/t* roof; **techo** *m* ceiling; (*tejado*) roof; *~ solar* AUTO sunroof; *los sin ~* the homeless; *tocar ~ fig* peak

tecla *f* key; **teclado** *m* MÚS, INFOR keyboard; **teclear** <1a> *v/t* key

técnica *f* technique; **técnico 1** *adj* technical **2** *m/f* technician; *de televisor, lavadora etc* repairman; **tecnología** *f* technology; *alta ~* hi-tech; *~ punta* state-of-the-art technology, leading-edge technology

tecolote *m Méx, C.Am.* (*búho*) owl

tedio *m* tedium; **tedioso** *adj* tedious

teja *f* roof tile; **a toca ~** in hard cash; **tejado** *m* roof

tejanos *mpl* jeans

tejemanejes *mpl* F scheming *sg,* plotting *sg;* **tejer** <2a> **1** *v/t* weave; (*hacer punto*) knit; F *intriga* devise **2** *v/i L.Am.* F plot, scheme; **tejido** *m* fabric; ANAT tissue

tejo *m* BOT yew; **tirar a alguien los ~s** F hit on s.o. F, come on to s.o. F

tejón *m* ZO badger

Tel. *abr* (= **teléfono**) Tel. (= telephone)

tela *f* fabric, material; **~ de araña** spiderweb; **poner en ~ de juicio** call into question; **hay ~ para rato** F there's a lot to be done

telar *m* loom

telaraña *f* spiderweb

tele *f* F TV, *Br* telly F

telebanca *f* telephone banking

telecabina *f* cable car

telecomedia *f* sitcom

telecompra *f* home shopping

telecomunicaciones *fpl* telecommunications

teleconferencia *f* conference call

telediario *m* TV (television) news *sg*

teledirigido *adj* remote-controlled

teléf. *abr* (= **teléfono**) tel. (= telephone)

teleférico *m* cable car

telefilm(e) *m* TV movie

telefonear <1a> *v/t & v/i* call, phone; **telefonema** *m L.Am.* (phone) message; **telefónico** *adj* (tele)phone *atr;* **teléfono** *m* (tele)phone; **~ inalámbrico** cordless (phone); **~ móvil** cellphone, *Br* mobile (phone)

telégrafo *m* telegraph

telegrama *m* telegram

telemando *m* remote control

telemática *f* data comms

telenovela *f* soap (opera)

teleobjetivo *m* FOT telephoto lens

telepatía *f* telepathy

telescópico *adj* telescopic; **telescopio** *m* telescope

teleserie *f* (television) series

telesilla *f* chair lift

telespectador *m,* **~a** *f* (television) viewer

telesquí *m* drag lift

teletexto *m* teletext

teletienda *f* home shopping

teletrabajo *m* teleworking; **teletrabajador** *m,* **~a** *f* teleworker

televidente *m/f* (television) viewer; **televisar** <1a> *v/t* televise; **televisión** *f* television; **~ por cable** cable (television); **~ digital** digital television; **~ de pago** pay-per-view television; **~ vía satélite** satellite television; **televisivo** *adj* television *atr;* **televisor** *m* TV, television (set); **~ en color** color TV

télex *m* telex

telón *m* TEA curtain; **el ~ de acero** POL the Iron Curtain; **~ de fondo** *fig* backdrop, background

telonero *m,* **-a** *f* supporting artist

tema *m* subject, topic; MÚS, *de novela* theme; **temario** *m* syllabus; **temático** *adj* thematic

temblar <1k> *v/i* tremble, shake; *de frío* shiver; **temblor** *m* trembling, shaking; *de frío* shivering; *L.Am.* (*terremoto*) earthquake; **~ de tierra** earth tremor; **tembloroso** *adj* trembling, shaking; *de frío* shivering

temer <2a> **1** *v/t* be afraid of **2** *v/r* **~se** be afraid; **me temo que no podrá venir** I'm afraid he won't be able to come; **~se lo peor** fear the worst

temerario *adj* rash, reckless; **temeridad** *f* rashness, recklessness

temible *adj* terrifying

temor *m* fear

témpano *m* ice floe

temperamento *m* temperament; **temperante** *adj Méx* teetotal

temperatura *f* temperature

tempestad *f* storm; **tempestuoso** *adj tb fig* stormy

templado *adj* warm; *clima* temperate; *fig* moderate, restrained; **templanza** *f* restraint; **templar**

<1a> v/t *ira, nervios etc* calm
templo *m* temple
temporada *f* season; *una ~* a time, some time; **temporal 1** *adj* temporary **2** *m* storm; **temporizador** *m* timer; **tempranear** <1a> v/i L.Am. get up early; **temprano** *adj & adv* early
ten *vb* → **tener**
tenacidad *f* tenacity; **tenaz** *adj* determined, tenacious; **tenaza** *f* pincer, claw; *~s* pincers; *para las uñas* pliers
tendedero *m* clotheshorse, airer
tendencia *f* tendency; *(corriente)* trend
tendencioso *adj* tendentious
tender <2g> **1** v/t *ropa* hang out; *cable* lay; *le tendió la mano* he held out his hand to her **2** v/i: *~ a* tend to **3** v/r *~se* lie down
tenderete *m* stall
tendero *m*, *-a f* storekeeper, shopkeeper
tendido *m* EL: *~ eléctrico* power lines *pl*
tendón *m* ANAT tendon; *~ de Aquiles* Achilles' tendon
tenebroso *adj* dark, gloomy
tenedor *m* fork
tener <2l> **1** v/t have; *~ 10 años* be 10 (years old); *~ un metro de ancho/largo* be one metre (*Br meter*) wide/long; *~ por* consider to be; *tengo que madrugar* I must get up early, I have to *o* I've got to get up early; *conque ¿esas tenemos?* so that's how it is, eh? **2** v/r *~se* stand up; *fig* stand firm; *se tiene por atractivo* he thinks he's attractive
tenga *vb* → **tener**
tengo *vb* → **tener**
tenia *f* ZO tapeworm
teniente *m/f* MIL lieutenant
tenis *m* tennis; *~ de mesa* table tennis; **tenista** *m/f* tennis player
tenor *m* MÚS tenor; *a ~ de* along the lines of
tenorio *m* lady-killer
tensar <1a> v/t tighten; *músculo* tense, tighten; **tensión** *f* te... voltage; MED blood p...
tenso *adj* tense; *cuerda, cab...*
tentación *f* temptation
tentáculo *m* ZO, *fig* tentacle
tentador *adj* tempting; **tentar** <... v/t tempt, entice; **tentativa** *f*... tempt
tentempié *m* F snack
tenue *adj* faint
teñir <3h & 3l> v/t dye; *fig* tinge
teología *f* theology
teorema *m* theorem; **teoría** *f* theory; *en ~* in theory
tequila *m* tequila
terapeuta *m/f* therapist; **terapéutico** *adj* therapeutic; **terapia** *f* therapy
tercer *adj* third; *Tercer Mundo* Third World; **tercermundista** *adj* Third-World *atr*; **tercero** *m/adj* third; **terciarse** <1b> v/r *de oportunidad* come up; **tercio** *m* third
terciopelo *m* velvet
terco *adj* stubborn
tergiversar <1a> v/t distort, twist
termas *fpl* hot springs; **térmico** *adj* heat *atr*
terminación *f* GRAM ending; **terminal 1** *m* INFOR terminal **2** *f* AVIA terminal; *~ de autobuses* bus station; **terminante** *adj* categorical; **terminar** <1a> **1** v/t end, finish **2** v/i end, finish; *(parar)* stop **3** v/r *~se* run out; *(finalizar)* come to an end; *se ha terminado la leche* we've run out of milk, the milk's all gone; **término** *m* end, conclusion; *(palabra)* term; *~ municipal* municipal area; *por ~ medio* on average; *poner ~ a algo* put an end to sth
terminología *f* terminology
termita *f* ZO termite
termo *m* thermos® (flask)
termómetro *m* thermometer; **termostato** *m* thermostat
ternera *f* calf; GASTR veal; **ternero** *m* calf
terno *m* CSur suit
ternura *f* tenderness

T

erracota *f* terracotta

errplén *m* embankment

terrateniente *m/f* landowner

tcrraza *f* terrace; (*balcón*) balcony; (*café*) sidewalk café

terremoto *m* earthquake

terrenal *adj* earthly, worldly

terreno *m* land; *fig* field; **un ~** a plot *o* piece of land; **~ de juego** DEP field

terrestre *adj* animal land *atr*; *transporte* surface *atr*; **la atmósfera ~** the earth's atmosphere

terrible *adj* terrible, awful

territorial *adj* territorial; **territorio** *m* territory

terrón *m* lump, clod; **~ de azúcar** sugar lump

terror *m* terror; **terrorífico** *adj* terrifying; **terrorismo** *m* terrorism; **terrorista 1** *adj* terrorist *atr* **2** *m/f* terrorist

terso *adj* smooth

tertulia *f* TV debate, round table discussion; **tertuliar** <1b> *v/i L.Am.* get together for a discussion

tesina *f* dissertation

tesis *f inv* thesis

tesitura *f* situation

tesón *m* tenacity, determination

tesorero *m*, **-a** *f* treasurer; **tesoro** *m* treasure; **~ público** treasury

test *m* test

testa *f* head

testaferro *m* front man

testamento *m* JUR will

testarudez *f* stubbornness; **testarudo** *adj* stubborn

testículo *m* ANAT testicle

testificar <1g> **1** *v/t* (*probar, mostrar*) be proof of; **~ que** JUR testify that, give evidence that **2** *v/i* testify, give evidence; **testigo 1** *m/f* JUR witness; **~ de cargo** witness for the prosecution; **~ ocular** *or* **presencial** eye witness **2** *m* DEP baton; **testimonio** *m* testimony, evidence

teta *f* F boob F; ZO teat, nipple

tétanos *m* MED tetanus

tetera *f* teapot

tetilla *f de hombre* nipple

tetina *f de biberón* teat

tetrabrik® *m* carton

tétrico *adj* gloomy

textil 1 *adj* textile *atr* **2** *mpl*: **~es** textiles

texto *m* text; **textual** *adj* textual

textura *f* texture

tez *f* complexion

ti *pron* you; *reflexivo* yourself; **¿y a ~ qué te importa?** so what?, what's it to you?

tía *f* aunt; F (*chica*) girl, chick F; **¡~ buena!** F hey gorgeous! F

tianguis *m Méx., C.Am.* market

tibio *adj tb fig* lukewarm

tiburón *m* ZO, *fig* F shark

tic *m* MED tic

ticket *m* (sales) receipt

tictac *m* tick-tock

tiempo *m* time; (*clima*) weather; GRAM tense; **~ libre** spare time, free time; **~ real** INFOR real time; **a ~** in time; **a un ~, al mismo ~** at the same time; **antes de ~ llegar** ahead of time, early; **celebrar victoria** too soon; **con ~** in good time, early; **desde hace mucho ~** for a long time; **hace buen / mal ~** the weather's fine / bad; **hace mucho ~** a long time ago

tienda *f* store, shop; **~ de campaña** tent; **ir de ~s** go shopping

tiene *vb* → **tener**

tientas *fpl*: **andar a ~** *fig* feel one's way; **tiento** *m*: **con ~** *fig* carefully

tierno *adj* soft; *carne* tender; *pan* fresh; *persona* tender-hearted

tierra *f* land; *materia* soil, earth; (*patria*) native land, homeland; **la Tierra** the earth; **~ firme** dry land, terra firma; **echar por ~** ruin, wreck

tieso *adj* stiff, rigid

tiesto *m* flower pot

tifón *m* typhoon

tifus *m* MED typhus

tigre *m* ZO tiger; *L.Am.* puma; *L.Am.* (*leopardo*) jaguar; **tigresa** *f* tigress

tijeras *fpl* scissors

tila *f* lime blossom tea

tildar <1a> *v/t*: **~ a alguien de** *fig* brand s.o. as

tilde f accent; *en ñ* tilde

tilín m: *me hizo ~* F I took an immediate liking to her

timador m, **~a** f cheat; **timar** <1a> v/t cheat

timba f F gambling den

timbal m MÚS kettle drum

timbre m *de puerta* bell; *Méx* (postage) stamp

timidez f shyness, timidity; **tímido** adj shy, timid

timo m confidence trick, swindle

timón m MAR, AVIA rudder

tímpano m ANAT eardrum

tina f large jar; *L.Am.* (*bañera*) (bath)tub

tinglado m fig F mess

tinieblas fpl darkness sg

tino m aim, marksmanship; (*sensatez*) judg(e)ment; *con mucho ~* wisely, sensibly

tinta f ink; *de buena ~* fig on good authority; *medias ~s* fig half measures; **tinte** m dye; fig veneer, gloss

tinterillo m *L.Am.* F shyster F

tintero m inkwell; *dejarse algo en el ~* leave sth unsaid

tintin(e)ar <1a> v/t jingle

tinto adj: *vino ~* red wine

tintorería f dry cleaner's

tío m uncle; F (*tipo*) guy F; F *apelativo* pal F

tiovivo m carousel, merry-go-round

típico adj typical (*de* of); **tipo** m type, kind; F *persona* guy F; COM rate; *~ de cambio* exchange rate; *~ de interés* interest rate; *tener buen ~* be well built; *de mujer* have a good figure

tipográfico adj typographic(al)

tíquet, tiquete m *L.Am.* receipt

tiquismiquis m/f F fuss-budget F, Br fusspot F

tira f strip; *la ~ de* F loads of F, masses of F; *~ y afloja* fig give and take

tirabuzón m curl; (*sacacorchos*) corkscrew

tirachinas m inv slingshot, Br catapult

tirada f TIP print run; *de una ~* in one

go; **tiradero** m *Méx* dump; **tirado** adj P (*barato*) dirt-cheap F; *estar ~* F (*fácil*) be a walkover F o a piece of cake F; **tiradores** mpl *Arg* suspenders, Br braces

tiranía f tyranny; **tirano 1** adj tyrannical **2** m, **-a** f tyrant

tirante 1 adj taut; fig tense **2** m strap; *~s* suspenders, Br braces; **tirantez** f fig tension

tirar <1a> **1** v/t throw; *edificio, persona* knock down; (*volcar*) knock over; *basura* throw away; *dinero* waste, throw away F; TIP print; F *en examen* fail **2** v/i pull, attract; (*disparar*) shoot; *~ a* tend toward; *~ a conservador* have conservative tendencies; *~ de algo* pull sth; *ir tirando* F get by, manage **3** v/r *~se* throw o.s.; F *tiempo* spend; *~se a alguien* P screw s.o. P

tirita f MED Bandaid®, Br plaster

tiritar <1a> v/i shiver

tiro m shot; *~ al blanco* target practice; *al ~ CSur* F at once, right away; *de ~s largos* F dressed up; *ni a ~s* F for love nor money; *le salió el ~ por la culata* F it backfired on him; *le sentó como un ~* F he needed it like a hole in the head F

tirón m tug, jerk; *de un ~* at a stretch, without a break

tiroteo m shooting

tirria f: *tener ~ a alguien* F have it in for s.o. P

tisana f herbal tea

títere m tb fig puppet; *no dejar ~ con cabeza* F spare no-one; **titiritero** m, **-a** f acrobat

titubear <1a> v/i waver, hesitate; **titubeo** m wavering, hesitation

titular m *de periódico* headline; **titularse** <1a> v/r be entitled; **título** m title; *universitario* degree; JUR title; COM bond; *tener muchos ~s* be highly qualified; *a ~ de* as; *~s de crédito* credits

tiza f chalk

tiznar <1a> v/t blacken; **tizón** m ember

tlapalería f *Méx* hardware store

TLC *abr* (= *Tratado de Libre Comercio*) NAFTA (= North American Free Trade Agreement)

toalla *f* towel; **tirar** *or* **arrojar la ~** *fig* throw in the towel; **toallero** *m* towel rail

tobillo *m* ankle

tobogán *m* slide

tocadiscos *m inv* record player

tocado *adj*: **estar ~** *fig* F be crazy

tocador *m* dressing-table

tocante: **en lo ~ a …** with regard to …

tocar <1g> **1** *v/t* touch; MÚS play **2** *v/i* *L.Am.* **a la clase** knock (on the door); *L.Am.* (*sonar la campanita*) ring the doorbell; **te toca jugar** it's your turn **3** *v/r* **~se** touch

tocateja: **a ~** in hard cash

tocayo *m*, **-a** *f* namesake

tocino *m* bacon

tocólogo *m*, **-a** *f* obstetrician

todavía *adv* still, yet; **~ no ha llegado** he still hasn't come, he hasn't come yet; **~ no** not yet

todo 1 *adj* all; **~s los domingos** every Sunday; **~a la clase** the whole *o* the entire class **2** *adv* all; **estaba ~ sucio** it was all dirty; **con ~** all the same; **del ~** entirely, absolutely **3** *pron* all, everything; *pl* everybody, everyone; **ir a por -as** go all out

todoterreno *m* AUTO off-road *o* all-terrain vehicle

toldo *m* awning; *L.Am.* Indian hut

tolerancia *f* tolerance; **tolerar** <1a> *v/t* tolerate

toma *f* FOT shot, take; **~ de conciencia** realization; **~ de corriente** outlet, socket; **~ de posesión** POL taking office; **tomado** *adj Méx* F (*borracho*) drunk; **tomadura** *f*: **~ de pelo** F joke

tomar <1a> **1** *v/t* take; *decisión* make, take; *bebida*, *comida* have; **~la con alguien** F have it in for s.o. F; **~ el sol** sunbathe; **¡toma!** here (you are); **toma y daca** give and take **2** *v/i L.Am.* drink; **~ por la derecha** turn right **3** *v/r* **~se** take; *comida*, *bebida* have; **se lo tomó a pecho**

he took it to heart

tomate *m* tomato

tomavistas *m inv* movie camera, cine camera

tomillo *m* BOT thyme

tomo *m* volume, tome; **un timador de ~ y lomo** F an out-and-out conman

ton *m*: **sin ~ ni son** for no particular reason

tonada *f* song

tonalidad *f* tonality

tonel *m* barrel, cask; **tonelada** *f peso* ton

tónica *f* tonic; **tónico** *m* MED tonic; **tonificar** <1g> *v/t* tone up; **tono** *m* MÚS, MED, PINT tone

tontería *f fig* stupid *o* dumb F thing; **~s** *pl* nonsense *sg*

tonto 1 *adj* silly, foolish **2** *m*, **-a** *f* fool, idiot; **hacer el ~** play the fool; **hacerse el ~** act dumb F

top *m prenda* top

topacio *m* MIN topaz

toparse <1a> *v/r*: **~ con alguien** bump into s.o., run into s.o.

tope *m* limit; *pieza* stop; *Méx en la calle* speed bump; **pasarlo a ~** have a great time; **estar hasta los ~s** F be bursting at the seams F

tópico *m* cliché, platitude

topo *m* ZO mole

toque *m*: **~ de queda** MIL, *fig* curfew; **dar los últimos ~s** put the finishing touches (**a** to)

toquilla *f* shawl

tórax *m* ANAT thorax

torbellino *m* whirlwind

torcer <2b & 2h> **1** *v/t* twist; (*doblar*) bend; (*girar*) turn **2** *v/i* turn; **~ a la derecha** turn right **3** *v/r* **~se** twist, bend; *fig* go wrong; **~se un pie** sprain one's ankle; **torcido** *adj* twisted, bent

toreador *m esp L.Am.* bullfighter; **torear** <1a> **1** *v/i* fight bulls **2** *v/t* fight; *fig* dodge, sidestep; **toreo** *m* bullfighting

torera *f*: **saltarse algo a la ~** F flout sth, disregard sth

torero *m* bullfighter

tormenta f storm; **tormento** m torture

tornado m tornado, twister ⊦

tornarse <1a> v/r *triste, difícil etc* become

torneo m competition, tournament

tornillo m screw; *con tuerca* bolt; *le falta un ~* F he's got a screw loose F

torniquete m turnstile; MED tourniquet

torno m *de alfarería* wheel; *en ~ a* around, about

toro m bull; *ir a los ~s* go to a bullfight; *coger al ~ por los cuernos* take the bull by the horns

toronja f L.Am. grapefruit

torpe adj clumsy; (*tonto*) dense, dim

torpedo m MIL torpedo

torpeza f clumsiness; (*necedad*) stupidity

torre f tower; *~ de control* AVIA control tower

torrencial adj torrential; **torrente** m fig avalanche, flood

torrezno m GASTR fried rasher of bacon

tórrido adj torrid

torrija f GASTR French toast

torta f cake; *plana* tart; F slap; **tortazo** m F crash; (*bofetada*) punch

tortícolis m MED crick in the neck

tortilla f omelette; L.Am. tortilla

tortillera f V dyke F, lesbian

tortuga f ZO tortoise; *marina* turtle; *a paso de ~* fig at a snail's pace

tortuoso adj fig tortuous

tortura f tb fig torture; **torturar** <1a> v/t torture

tos f cough

tosco adj fig rough, coarse

toser <2a> v/i cough

tostada f piece of toast; **tostado** adj (*moreno*) brown, tanned; **tostador** m toaster; **tostar** <1m> 1 v/t toast; *café* roast; *al sol* tan 2 v/r ~se tan, get brown; **tostón** m F bore

total 1 adj total, complete; *en ~* altogether, in total 2 m total; *un ~ de 50 personas* a total of 50 people; **totalidad** f totality; **totalitario** adj totalitarian

tóxico adj toxic; **toxicómano** m, -a f drug addict; **toxina** f toxin

tozudo adj obstinate

trabajador 1 adj hard-working **2** m, ~a f worker; *~ eventual* casual worker; **trabajar** <1a> **1** v/i work **2** v/t work; *tema, músculos* work on; **trabajo** m work; *~ en equipo* team work; *~ temporal* temporary work; *~ a tiempo parcial* part-time work; **trabajoso** adj hard, laborious

trabalenguas m inv tongue twister

trabar <1a> **1** v/t *conversación, amistad* strike up **2** v/r ~se get tangled up

trabucarse <1g> v/r get all mixed up

tracción f TÉC traction; *~ delantera/trasera* front / rear-wheel drive

tractor m tractor

tradición f tradition; **tradicional** adj traditional

traducción f translation; **traducir** <3o> v/t translate; **traductor** m, ~a f translator

traer <2p; part traido> **1** v/t bring; *~ consigo* involve, entail; *este periódico la trae en portada* this newspaper carries it on the front page **2** v/r ~se: *este asunto se las trae* F it's a very tricky matter

traficante m dealer; **traficar** <1g> v/i deal (*en* in); **tráfico** m traffic; *~ de drogas* drug trafficking, drug dealing

tragaperras f inv slot machine

tragar <1h> **1** v/t swallow; *no lo trago* I can't stand him *o* bear him **2** v/r ~se tb fig F swallow

tragedia f tragedy; **trágico** adj tragic

tragicomedia f tragicomedy

trago m mouthful; F *bebida* drink; *de un ~* in one gulp; *pasar un mal ~* fig have a hard time; **tragón** adj greedy

traición f treachery, betrayal; **traicionar** <1a> v/t betray; **traidor 1** adj treacherous **2** m, ~a f traitor

traido part → **traer**

traigo vb → **traer**

tráiler m trailer

traje 1 *m* suit; **~ de baño** swimsuit **2** *vb* → **traer**

trajín *m* hustle and bustle

trajo *vb* → **traer**

trama *f* (*tema*) plot; **tramar** <1a> *v/t complot* hatch

tramitar <1a> *v/t documento: de persona* apply for; *de banco etc* process; **trámite** *m* formality

tramo *m* section, stretch; *de escaleras* flight

trampa *f* trap; (*truco*) scam F, trick; **hacer ~s** cheat

trampilla *f* trapdoor

trampolín *m* diving board

tramposo *m*, **-a** *f* cheat, crook

tranca *f*: **llevaba una ~ increíble** F he was wasted F *o* smashed F; **a ~s y barrancas** with great difficulty

trancazo *m* F dose of flu

trance *m* (*momento difícil*) tough time; **en ~** in a trance

tranquilidad *f* calm, quietness; **tranquilizante** *m* tranquil(l)izer; **tranquilizar** <1f> *v/t*: **~ a alguien** calm s.o. down

tranquillo *m*: **coger el ~ de algo** F get the hang of sth F

tranquilo *adj* calm, quiet; **¡~!** don't worry; **déjame ~** leave me alone

transacción *f* COM deal, transaction;

transar <1a> *v/i L.Am.* (*ser vendido*) sell out

transatlántico 1 *adj* transatlantic **2** *m* liner

transbordador *m* ferry; **~ espacial** space shuttle; **transbordo** *m*: **hacer ~** TRANSP transfer, change

transcendental *adj fig* momentous

transcurrir <3a> *v/i de tiempo* pass, go by; **transcurso** *m* course; *de tiempo* passing

transeúnte *m/f* passer-by

transexual *m/f* transsexual

transferencia *f* COM transfer

transformación *f* transformation; **transformador** *m* EL transformer; **transformar** <1a> *v/t* transform

transfronterizo *adj* cross-border

tránsfuga *m/f* POL defector

transfusión *f*: **~ de sangre** blood transfusion; **transgénico** *adj* genetically modified; **transgredir** <3a> *v/t* infringe

transición *f* transition

transigir <3c> *v/i* compromise, make concessions

transistor *m* transistor

transitivo *adj* GRAM transitive; **tránsito** *m* COM transit; *L.Am.* (*circulación*) traffic

translúcido *adj* translucent

transmisión *f* transmission; **~ de datos** data transmission; **enfermedad de ~ sexual** sexually transmitted disease; **transmitir** <3a> *v/t* spread; RAD, TV broadcast, transmit

transparencia *f para proyectar* transparency, slide; **transparente** *adj* transparent

transpiración *f* perspiration; **transpirar** <1a> *v/i* perspire

transplantar <1a> *v/t* transplant

transportar <1a> *v/t* transport; **transporte** *m* transport

tranvía *m* streetcar, *Br* tram

trapecio *m* trapeze; **trapecista** *m/f* trapeze artist(e)

trapiche *m CSur* sugar mill *o* press

trapicheo *m* F shady deal F

trapo *m viejo* rag; *para limpiar* cloth; **~s** F clothes

trapujear <1a> *v/t & v/i C.Am.* smuggle

tráquea *f* ANAT windpipe, trachea

traqueteo *m* rattle, clatter

tras *prp en el espacio* behind; *en el tiempo* after

trasero 1 *adj* rear *atr*, back *atr* **2** *m* F butt F, *Br* rear end F

trasiego *m fig* bustle

trasladar <1a> **1** *v/t* move; *trabajador* transfer; **2** *v/r* **~se** move (**a** to); **se traslada** *Méx: en negocio* under new management; **traslado** *m* move; *de trabajador* transfer; **~ al aeropuerto** airport transfer

trasluz *m*: **al ~** against the light; **trasnochar** <1a> *v/i* (*acostarse tarde*) go to bed late, stay up late; (*no dormir*) stay up all night; *L.Am.* stay overnight, spend the night;

traspapelar <1a> v/t mislay; **traspasar** <1a> v/t (atravesar) go through; COM transfer

traspié m trip, stumble; **dar un ~** fig slip up, blunder

trasplantar <1a> v/t AGR, MED transplant; **trasplante** m AGR, MED transplant

trastada f F prank, trick; **hacer ~s** get up to mischief; **traste** m: **irse al ~** F fall through, go down the tubes F; **trastero** m lumber room; **trasto** m desp piece of junk; persona good-for-nothing

trastornar <1a> v/t upset; (molestar) inconvenience; **trastorno** m inconvenience; MED disorder

tratado m esp POL treaty; **Tratado de Libre Comercio** North American Free Trade Agreement

tratamiento m treatment; **~ de datos/textos** INFOR data/word processing; **tratar** <1a> **1** v/t treat; (manejar) handle; (dirigirse a) address (de as); gente come into contact with; tema deal with **2** v/i: **~ con alguien** deal with s.o.; **~ de** (intentar) try to **3** v/r **~se**: **¿de qué se trata?** what's it about?; **trato** m de prisionero, animal treatment; COM deal; **malos ~s** pl ill treatment sg, abuse sg,; **tener ~ con alguien** have dealings with s.o.; **¡~ hecho!** it's a deal

trauma m trauma; **traumatizar** <1f> v/t traumatize; **traumatólogo** m, **-a** f trauma specialist, traumatologist

través m: **a ~ de** through; **travesaño** m en fútbol crossbar; **travesía** f crossing

travesti m transvestite, drag artist

travesura f bit of mischief, prank; **travieso** adj niño mischievous

trayecto m journey; **10 dólares por ~** 10 dollars each way; **trayectoria** f fig course, path

trazar <1f> v/t (dibujar) draw; ruta plot, trace; (describir) outline, describe; **trazo** m line

trébol m BOT clover

trece adj thirteen; **mantenerse** or **seguir en sus ~** stand firm, not budge

trecho m stretch, distance

tregua f truce, cease-fire; **sin ~** relentlessly

treinta adj thirty

tremebundo adj horrendous, frightening

tremendo adj awful, dreadful; éxito, alegría tremendous

tren m FERR train; **~ de alta velocidad** high speed train; **~ de lavado** car wash; **vivir a todo ~** F live in style; **estar como un ~** F be absolutely gorgeous

trenca f duffel coat

trenza f plait

trepa m F socialmente social climber; en el trabajo careerist; **trepar** <1a> v/i climb (a up), scale (a sth)

trepidante adj fig frenetic

tres adj three; **trescientos** adj three hundred

tresillo m living-room suite, Br three-piece suite

treta f trick, ploy

triángulo m triangle

tribu f tribe

tribuna f grandstand

tribunal m court; **Tribunal Supremo** Supreme Court

tributo m tribute; (impuesto) tax

triciclo m tricycle

tricotar <1a> v/i knit

trifulca f F brawl, punch-up F

trigo m wheat

trillado adj fig hackneyed, clichéd; **trillar** <1a> v/t AGR thresh

trillizos mpl triplets

trillón m quintillion, Br trillion

trimestral adj quarterly; **trimestre** m quarter; escolar semester, Br term

trinar <1a> v/i trill, warble; **está que trina** fig F he's fuming F, he's hopping mad F

trincar <1g> v/t F criminal catch

trinchera f MIL trench

trineo m sled, sleigh

trino m trill, warble

trío *m* trio

tripa *f* F belly F, gut F; **hacer de ~s corazón** *fig* pluck up courage

triple *m*: **el ~ que el año pasado** three times as much as last year; **triplicar** <1g> *v/t* triple, treble

trípode *m* tripod

tripulación *f* AVIA, MAR crew; **tripular** <1a> *v/t* man

triquiñuela *f* F dodge F, trick

tris *m*: **estuvo en un ~ de caerse** she came within an inch of falling

triste *adj* sad; **tristeza** *f* sadness

triturar <1a> *v/t* grind

triunfador 1 *adj* winning **2** *m*, **~a** *f* winner, victor; **triunfar** <1a> *v/i* triumph, win; **triunfo** *m* triumph, victory; **en naipes** trump

trivial *adj* trivial

triza *f*: **hacer ~s** F *jarrón* smash to bits; *papel*, *vestido* tear to shreds

trocear <1a> *v/t* cut into pieces, cut up

troche: **había errores a ~ y moche** F there were mistakes galore F

trofeo *m* trophy

troglodita *m/f* cave-dweller

troj(e) *f Arg* granary

trola *f* F fib

trolebús *m* trolley bus

tromba *f*: **~ de agua** downpour

trombón *m* MÚS trombone

trombosis *f* MED thrombosis

trompa 1 *adj* F wasted F **2** *f* MÚS horn; ZO trunk

trompazo *m L.Am.* F whack F; **darse un ~ con algo** F bang into sth; **trompearse** <1a> *L.Am.* F fight, lay into each other F

trompeta *f* MÚS trumpet; **trompetista** *m/f* MÚS trumpeter

trompicón *m*: **a trompicones** in fits and starts

trompo *m* spinning top

trona *f* high chair

tronar <1m> *v/i* thunder

troncha *f S.Am.* slice, piece; **tronchante** *adj* F sidesplitting; **troncharse** <1a> *v/r*: **~ de risa** F split one's sides laughing

tronco *m* trunk; *cortado* log; **dormir como un ~** sleep like a log

trono *m* throne

tropa *f* MIL (*soldado raso*) ordinary soldier; **~s** troops

tropel *m*: **en ~** in a mad rush; **salir en ~** pour out

tropezar <1f & 1k> *v/i* trip, stumble

tropical *adj* tropical; **trópico** *m* tropic

tropiezo *m fig* setback

tropilla *f L.Am.* herd

trotar <1a> *v/i fig* gad around; **trote** *m* trot; **ya no estoy para esos ~s** I'm not up to it any more

trozo *m* piece

trucha *f* ZO trout

truco *m* trick; **coger el ~ a algo** F get the hang of sth F

truculento *adj* horrifying

trueno *m* thunder

trueque *m* barter

trufa *f* BOT truffle

truhán *m* rogue

Tte. *abr* (= **Teniente**) Lieut. (= Lieutenant)

tú *pron sg* you; **tratar de ~** address as 'tú'

tu, tus *adj pos* your

tuberculosis *f* MED TB, tuberculosis

tubería *f* pipe; **tubo** *m* tube; **~ de escape** AUTO exhaust (pipe); **por un ~** F an enormous amount

tucán *m* ZO toucan

tuerca *f* TÉC nut

tulipán *m* BOT tulip

tullido *m* cripple

tumba *f* tomb, grave

tumbar <1a> **1** *v/t* knock down **2** *v/r* **~se** lie down; **tumbo** *m* tumble; **ir dando ~s** stagger along; **tumbona** *f* (sun) lounger

tumor *m* MED tumo(u)r

tumulto *m* uproar

tuna *f Méx fruta* prickly pear

tunda *f* F beating

tundra *f* GEOG tundra

túnel *m* tunnel; **~ de lavado** car wash

Túnez Tunisia

túnica *f* tunic

tuntún: **decir algo al buen ~** say sth off the top of one's head

tupé *m* F quiff

tupido *adj pelo* thick; *vegetación* dense, thick

turbante *m* turban

turbar <1a> **1** *v/t* (*emocionar*) upset; *paz, tranquilidad* disturb; (*avergonzar*) embarrass **2** *v/r* **~se** (*emocionarse*) get upset; *de paz, tranquilidad* be disturbed; (*avergonzarse*) get embarrassed

turbina *f* turbine

turbio *adj* cloudy, murky; *fig* shady, murky

turbo *m* turbo

turbulencia *f* turbulence; **turbulento** *adj* turbulent

turco 1 *adj* Turkish **2** *m*, **-a** *f* Turk

turismo *m* tourism; *automóvil* sedan, *Br* saloon (car); **~ rural** tourism in rural areas; **turista** *m/f* tourist; **turístico** *adj* tourist *atr*

turnarse <1a> *v/r* take it in turns; **turno** *m* turn; **~ de noche** night shift; **por ~s** in turns

turquesa *f piedra preciosa* turquoise; **azul ~** turquoise

Turquía Turkey

turrón *m* nougat

turulato *adj* F stunned, dazed

tute *m*: **darse un ~** F work like a dog F, slave F

tutear <1a> *v/t* address as 'tu'

tutiplén: **había comida a ~** F there was loads *o* masses to eat F

tutor *m*, **~a** *f* EDU tutor

tuve *vb* → **tener**

tuvo *vb* → **tener**

tuyo, tuya *pron pos* yours; **los tuyos** your folks, your family

TV *abr* (= **televisión**) TV (= television)

U

u *conj* (*instead of* **o** *before words starting with* o) or

ubicación *f* *L.Am.* location; (*localización*) finding; **ubicado** *adj* located, situated; **ubicar** <1g> **1** *v/t* *L.Am.* place, put; (*localizar*) locate **2** *v/r* **~se** be located, be situated; *en un empleo* get a job; **ubicuo** *adj* ubiquitous

ubre *f* udder

UCI *abr* (= **Unidad de Cuidados Intensivos**) ICU (= Intensive Care Unit)

Ud. *pron* → **usted**

Uds. *pron* → **ustedes**

UE *abr* (= **Unión Europea**) EU (= European Union)

ufano *adj* conceited; (*contento*) proud

ujier *m* usher

úlcera *f* MED ulcer; **ulcerarse** <1a> *v/r* MED become ulcerous, ulcerate

ulterior *adj* subsequent

últimamente *adv* lately; **ultimar** <1a> *v/t* finalize; *L.Am.* (*rematar*) finish off; **ultimátum** *m* ultimatum; **último** *adj* last; (*más reciente*) latest; *piso* top *atr*; **-as noticias** latest news *sg*; **por ~** finally; **está en las -as** he doesn't have long (to live)

ultra *m* POL right-wing extremist; **ultraderecha** *f* POL extreme right

ultrajante *adj* outrageous; *palabras* insulting; **ultrajar** <1a> *v/t* outrage; (*insultar*) insult; **ultraje** *m* outrage; (*insulto*) insult

ultraligero *m* AVIA microlight

ultramarinos *mpl* groceries; **tienda de ~** grocery store, *Br* grocer's (shop)

ultramoderno *adj* ultramodern

ultranza: **a ~** for all one is worth; **un defensor a ~ de algo** an ardent defender of sth

U

ultrasónico *adj* ultrasonic; **ultrasonido** *m* ultrasound

ultratumba *f*: **la vida de ~** life beyond the grave

ultravioleta *adj* ultraviolet

ulular <1a> *v/i de viento* howl; *de búho* hoot

umbilical *adj* ANAT umbilical

umbral *m fig* threshold; **en el ~ de** *fig* on the threshold of

umbrío *adj* shady

un, una *art a*; *antes de vocal y h muda* an; **~os coches/pájaros** some cars / birds

unánime *adj* unanimous; **unanimidad** *f* unanimity; **por ~** unanimously

unción *f fig* unction

undécimo *adj* eleventh

ungir <3c> *v/t* REL anoint; **ungüento** *m* ointment

únicamente *adv* only; **único** *adj* only; *(sin par)* unique; **es ~** it's unique; **hijo ~** only child; **lo ~ que ...** the only thing that ...

unicornio *m* MYTH unicorn

unidad *f* MIL, MAT unit; *(cohesión)* unity; **~ de cuidados intensivos, ~ de vigilancia intensiva** MED intensive care unit; **~ de disco** INFOR disk drive; **~ monetaria** monetary unity; **unido** *adj* united; **una familia ~a** a close-knit family; **unificación** *f* unification; **unificar** <1g> *v/t* unify

uniformar <1a> *v/t fig* standardize; **uniforme 1** *adj* uniform; *superficie* even **2** *m* uniform

unilateral *adj* unilateral

unión *f* union; **Unión Europea** European Union

unir <3a> **1** *v/t* join; *personas* unite; *características* combine (**con** with); *ciudades* link **2** *v/r* **~se** join together; **~se a** join

unisex *adj* unisex

unísono *adj*: **al ~** in unison

unitario *adj* unitary; **precio ~** unit price

universal *adj* universal

universidad *f* university; **~ a distancia** university correspondence school, *Br* Open University; **universitario 1** *adj* university *atr* **2** *m*, **-a** *f* *(estudiante)* university student

universo *m* universe

uno 1 *pron* one; **es la -a** it's one o'clock; **me lo dijo ~** someone *o* somebody told me; **~ a ~, ~ por ~, de ~ en ~** one by one; **no dar ni -a** F not get anything right; **~s cuantos** a few, some; **~s niños** some children; **-as mil pesetas** about a thousand pesetas **2** *m* one; **el ~ de enero** January first, the first of January

untar <1a> *v/t* spread; **~ a alguien** F *(sobornar)* grease s.o.'s palm; **untuoso** *adj fig* oily

uña *f* ANAT nail; ZO claw; **defenderse con ~s y dientes** *fig* F fight tooth and nail; **ser ~ y carne** *personas* be extremely close

uperisado *adj*: **leche -a** UHT milk

uranio *m* uranium

urbanidad *f* civility; **urbanismo** *m* city planning, *Br* town planning; **urbanización** *f* (urban) development; *(colonia)* housing development, *Br* housing estate; **urbanizar** <1f> *v/t terreno* develop; **urbano** *adj* urban; *(cortés)* courteous; **guardia ~** local police officer; **urbe** *f* city

urdir <3a> *v/t complot* hatch

urea *f* urea

uretra *f* ANAT urethra

urgencia *f* urgency; *(prisa)* haste; MED emergency; **~s** *pl* emergency room *sg*, *Br* casualty *sg*; **urgente** *adj* urgent; **urgir** <3c> *v/i* be urgent

urinario *m* urinal

urna *f* urn; **~ electoral** ballot box

urólogo *m* MED urologist

urraca *f* ZO magpie

URSS *abr* (= **Unión de las Repúblicas Socialistas Soviéticas**) HIST USSR (= Union of Soviet Socialist Republics)

urticaria *f* MED hives

Uruguay Uruguay; **uruguayo 1** *adj* Uruguayan **2** *m*, **-a** *f* Uruguayan

usado *adj* (*gastado*) worn; (*de segunda mano*) second hand; **usar** <1a> 1 *v/t* use; *ropa, gafas* wear 2 *v/i*: **listo para ~** ready to use 3 *v/r* **~se** be used; **uso** *m* use; (*costumbre*) custom; *obligatorio el ~ de casco* helmets must be worn; *en buen ~* still in use

usted *pron* you; *tratar de ~* address as 'usted'; **~es** *pl* you; *de ~/~es* your; *es de ~/~es* it's yours

usual *adj* common, usual

usuario *m*, **-a** *f* INFOR user

usufructo *m* JUR usufruct

usura *f* usury; **usurero** *m*, **-a** *f* usurer

usurpar <1a> *v/t* usurp

utensilio *m* tool; *de cocina* utensil; **~s** *pl* equipment *sg*; **~s** *pl* **de pesca** fishing tackle *sg*

útero *m* ANAT uterus

útil 1 *adj* useful 2 *m* tool; **~es** *pl* **de pesca** fishing tackle *sg*; **utilidad** *f* usefulness; **utilitario** 1 *adj* functional, utilitarian 2 *m* AUTO compact; **utilitarismo** *m* utilitarianism; **utilización** *f* use; **utilizar** <1f> *v/t* use

utopía *f* utopia; **utópico** *adj* utopian

uva *f* BOT grape; *estar de mala ~* F be in a foul mood; *tener mala ~* F be a nasty piece of work F

UVI *abr* (= *Unidad de Vigilancia Intensiva*) ICU (= Intensive Care Unit)

úvula *f* ANAT uvula

V

va *vb* → *ir*

vaca *f* cow; GASTR beef; *~ lechera* dairy cow; *~ marina* manatee, sea cow; *mal or enfermedad de las ~s locas* F mad cow disease F

vacaciones *fpl* vacation *sg*, *Br* holiday *sg*; *de ~* on vacation, *Br* on holiday

vacante 1 *adj* vacant, empty 2 *f* job opening, position, *Br* vacancy; *cubrir una ~* fill a position; **vaciar** <1b> 1 *v/t* empty 2 *v/r* **~se** empty

vacilación *f* hesitation; **vacilante** *adj* unsteady; (*dubitativo*) hesitant; **vacilar** <1a> 1 *v/i* hesitate; *de fe, resolución* waver; *de objeto* wobble, rock; *de persona* stagger; *Méx* F (*divertirse*) have fun 2 *v/t* F make fun of

vacío 1 *adj* empty 2 *m* FÍS vacuum; *fig espacio* void; *~ de poder* power vacuum; *~ legal* loophole; *dejar un ~ fig* leave a gap; *envasado al ~* vacuum packed; *hacer el ~ a*

alguien fig ostracize s.o.

vacuna *f* vaccine; **vacunación** *f* vaccination; **vacunar** <1a> *v/t* vaccinate

vacuno *adj* bovine; *ganado ~* cattle *pl*

vacuo *adj fig* vacuous

vadear <1a> *v/t río* ford; *dificultad* get around; **vado** *m* ford; *en la calle* entrance ramp; *~ permanente letrero* keep clear

vagabundear <1a> *v/i* drift around; **vagabundo** 1 *adj perro* stray 2 *m*, **-a** *f* hobo, *Br* tramp; **vagancia** *f* laziness, idleness; **vagar** <1h> *v/i* wander

vagido *m de bebe* cry

vagina *f* ANAT vagina

vago *adj* (*holgazán*) lazy; (*indefinido*) vague; *hacer el ~* laze around

vagón *m de carga* wagon; *de pasajeros* car, *Br* coach; *~ restaurante* dining car, *Br tb* restaurant car

vaguear <1a> *v/i* laze around

V

vaguedad f vagueness

vahído m MED dizzy spell; **vaho** m (*aliento*) breath; (*vapor*) steam

vaina f BOT pod; *S.Am.* F drag F

vainilla f vanilla

vais vb → **ir**

vaivén m to-and-fro, swinging; **vaivenes** fig ups and downs

vajilla f dishes pl; *juego* dinner service, set of dishes

vale m voucher, coupon

valedero adj valid

valentía f bravery

valer <2q> **1** v/t be worth; (*costar*) cost **2** v/i *de billete, carné* be valid; (*estar permitido*) be allowed; (*tener valor*) be worth; (*servir*) be of use; **no ~ para algo** be no good at sth; **vale más caro** it's more expensive; **sus consejos me valieron de mucho** his advice was very useful to me; **más vale …** it's better to …; **más te vale …** you'd better …; **¡vale!** okay, sure **3** v/r **-se** manage (by o.s.); **-se de** make use of

valeriana f BOT valerian

valeroso adj valiant

valga vb → **valer**

valgo vb → **valer**

valía f worth

validar <1a> v/t validate; **validez** f validity; **válido** adj valid

valiente adj brave; *irón* fine

valija f (*maleta*) bag, suitcase, *Br tb* case; **~ diplomática** diplomatic bag

valioso adj valuable

valla f fence; DEP, fig hurdle; **~ publicitaria** billboard, *Br* hoarding; **carrera de ~s** DEP hurdles; **vallado** m fence; **vallar** <1a> v/t fence in

valle m valley

valor m value; (*valentía*) courage; **~ añadido**, *L.Am.* **~ agregado** value added; **~ nominal** de acción nominal value; *de título* par value; **objetos de ~** valuables; **~es** COM securities

valoración f (*tasación*) valuation; **valorar** <1a> v/t value (**en** at); (*estimar*) appreciate, value

vals m waltz

valuar <1e> v/t value

válvula f ANAT, EL valve; **~ de escape** fig safety valve

vampiro m fig vampire

van vb → **ir**

vanagloriarse <1b> v/r boast (**de** about), brag (**de** about)

vandálico adj destructive; **vandalismo** m vandalism; **vándalo** m, **-a** f vandal

vanguardia f MIL vanguard; **de ~** fig avant-garde

vanidad f vanity; **vanidoso** adj conceited, vain; **vano** adj futile, vain; **en ~** in vain

vapor m vapo(u)r; *de agua* steam; **cocinar al ~** steam; **vaporizar** <1f> **1** v/t vaporize **2** v/r **-se** vaporize; **vaporoso** adj vaporous; *fig: vestido* gauzy, filmy

vapulear <1a> v/t beat up; **vapuleo** m beating

vaquería f dairy; **vaquero 1** adj *tela* denim; **pantalones ~s** jeans **2** m cowboy, cowhand; **vaquilla** f heifer

vara f stick; TÉC rod; (*bastón de mando*) staff

varapalo m F (*contratiempo*) hitch F, setback

variable adj variable; *tiempo* changeable; **variación** f variation; **variado** adj varied; **variar** <1c> **1** v/t vary; (*cambiar*) change **2** v/i vary; (*cambiar*) change; **para ~** for a change

varice f MED varicose vein

varicela f MED chickenpox

variedad f variety; **~es** pl vaudeville sg, *Br* variety sg

variopinto adj varied, diverse

varios adj several

varita f: **~ mágica** magic wand

variz f varicose vein

varón m man, male; **varonil** adj manly, virile

vas vb → **ir**

vasallo m vassal

vasco 1 adj Basque; **País Vasco** Basque country **2** m *idioma* Basque **3** m, **-a** f Basque; **Vascongadas** fpl

Basque country *sg*; **vascuence** *m* Basque

vascular *adj* ANAT vascular

vasectomía *f* MED vasectomy

vaselina *f* Vaseline®

vasija *f* container, vessel; **vaso** *m* glass; ANAT vessel

vasto *adj* vast

Vaticano *m* Vatican

vaticinar <1a> *v/t* predict, forecast; **vaticinio** *m* prediction, forecast

vatio *m* EL watt

vaya 1 *vb* → *ir* **2** *int* well!

V.° B.° *abr* (= *visto bueno*) approved, OK

Vd. *pron* → *usted*

Vds. *pron* → *usted*

ve *vb* → *ir*, *ver*

vea *vb* → *ver*

vecindad *f* *Méx* poor area; **vecindario** *m* neighbo(u)rhood; **vecino 1** *adj* neighbo(u)ring **2** *m*, **-a** *f* neighbo(u)r

vedado *m*: **~ de caza** game reserve

vedar <1a> *v/t* ban, prohibit

vedette *f* star

vegetación *f* vegetation; **vegetal 1** *adj* vegetable, plant *atr* **2** *m* vegetable; **vegetar** <1a> *v/i* *fig* vegetate; **vegetariano 1** *adj* vegetarian **2** *m*, **-a** *f* vegetarian

vehemente *adj* vehement

vehículo *m tb fig* vehicle; MED carrier

veinte *m/adj* twenty; **veintena** *f* twenty; *aproximadamente* about twenty

vejación *f* humiliation; **vejar** <1a> *v/t* humiliate

vejestorio *m* F old fossil F, old relic F

vejez *f* old age

vejiga *f* ANAT bladder

vela *f para alumbrar* candle; DEP sailing; *de barco* sail; *a toda ~* F flat out F, all out F; *estar a dos ~s* F be broke F; *pasar la noche en ~* stay up all night; **velada** *f* evening; **velador** *m L.Am. lámpara* bedlamp, *Br* bedside light; *Chi mueble* nightstand, *Br* bedside table; **velar** <1a> *v/i*: *~ por algo* look after sth;

velatorio *m* wake

velcro® *m* Velcro

veleidad *f* fickleness

velero *m* MAR sailing ship

veleta 1 *f* weathervane **2** *m/f fig* weathercock

vello *m* (body) hair

velo *m* veil

velocidad *f* speed; *(marcha)* gear

velódromo *m* velodrome

veloz *adj* fast, speedy

ven *vb* → *venir*

vena *f* ANAT vein; *le dio la ~ y lo hizo* F she just upped and did it F; *estar en ~* F be on form

venado *m* ZO deer

vencedor 1 *adj* winning **2** *m*, **~a** *f* winner

vencejo *m* ZO swift

vencer <2b> **1** *v/t* defeat; *fig (superar)* overcome **2** *v/i* win; COM *de plazo etc* expire; **vencido** *adj*: *darse por ~* admit defeat, give in; *a la tercera va la -a* third time lucky; **vencimiento** *m* expiration, *Br* expiry; *de bono* maturity

venda *f* bandage; **vendaje** *m* MED dressing; **vendar** <1a> *v/t* MED bandage, dress; *~ los ojos a alguien* blindfold s.o.

vendaval *m* gale

vendedor *m*, **~a** *f* seller; **vender** <2a> **1** *v/t* sell; *fig (traicionar)* betray **2** *v/r* *-se* sell o.s.; *~se al enemigo* sell out to the enemy

vendimia *f* grape harvest; **vendimiar** <1b> *v/t uvas* harvest, pick

vendré *vb* → *venir*

veneno *m* poison; **venenoso** *adj* poisonous

venerable *adj* venerable; **venerar** <1a> *v/t* venerate, worship

venéreo *adj* MED venereal

venezolano 1 *adj* Venezuelan **2** *m*, **-a** *f* Venezuelan; **Venezuela** Venezuela

venga *vb* → *venir*

venganza *f* vengeance, revenge; **vengar** <1h> *v/t* avenge **2** *v/r* *~se* take revenge (*de* on; *por* for);

vengativo *adj* vengeful

vengo *vb* → **venir**

venir <3s> **1** *v/i* come; **~ de España** come from Spain; **~ bien** be convenient; **~ mal** be inconvenient; **le vino una idea** an idea occurred to him; **viene a ser lo mismo** it comes down to the same thing; **el año que viene** next year; **¡venga!** come on; **¿a qué viene eso?** why do you say that? **2** *v/r* **~se**: **~se abajo** collapse; *fig: de persona* fall apart, go to pieces

venta *f* sale; **~ por correo** or **por catálogo** mail order; **al detalle** or **al por menor** retail; **en ~** for sale

ventaja *f* advantage; DEP *en carrera, partido* lead; **~ fiscal** tax advantage; **ventajoso** *adj* advantageous

ventana *f* window; **~ de la nariz** nostril; **ventanilla** *f* AVIA, AUTO, FERR window; MAR porthole

ventilación *f* ventilation; **ventilador** *m* fan; **ventilar** <1a> *v/t* air; *fig: problema* talk over; *opiniones* air

ventisca *f* blizzard

ventosa *f* ZO sucker

ventosidad *f* wind, flatulence

ventrílocuo *m* ventriloquist

veo *vb* → **ver**

ver <2v; *part* **visto**> **1** *v/t* see; *televisión* watch; JUR *pleito* hear; *L.Am.* (*mirar*) look at; **está por ~** it remains to be seen; **no puede verla** *fig* he can't stand the sight of her; **no tiene nada que ~ con** it doesn't have anything to do with; **¡a ~!** let's see; **¡hay que ~!** would you believe it!; **ya veremos** we'll see **2** *v/i L.Am.* (*mirar*) look; **ve aquí dentro** *L.Am.* look in here **3** *v/r* **~se** see o.s.; (*encontrarse*) see one another; **¡habráse visto!** would you believe it!; **¡se las verá conmigo!** F he'll have me to deal with!

veranear <1a> *v/i* spend the summer vacation o *Br* holidays; **veraniego** *adj* summer *atr*; **verano** *m* summer

veras *f: de ~* really, truly

verbal *adj* GRAM verbal

verbena *f* (*fiesta*) party

verbo *m* GRAM verb; **verborrea** *f* *desp* verbosity

verdad *f* truth; **a decir ~** to tell the truth; **de ~** real, proper; **no te gusta, ¿~?** you don't like it, do you?; **vas a venir, ¿~?** you're coming, aren't you?; **es ~** it's true, it's the truth; **verdadero** *adj* true; (*cierto*) real

verde 1 *adj* green; *fruta* unripe; F *chiste* blue, dirty; **viejo ~** dirty old man; **poner ~ a alguien** F criticize s.o. **2** *m* green; **los ~s** POL the Greens; **verdoso** *adj* greenish

verdugo *m* executioner

verdulería *f* fruit and vegetable store, *Br* greengrocer's; **verdura** *f*: **~(s)** (*hortalizas*) greens *pl*, (green) vegetables *pl*

vereda *f S.Am.* sidewalk, *Br* pavement; **meter alguien en ~** *fig* put s.o. back on the straight and narrow, bring s.o. into line

veredicto *m* JUR, *fig* verdict

verga *f* rod

vergel *m* orchard

vergonzoso *adj* disgraceful, shameful; (*tímido*) shy; **vergüenza** *f* shame; (*escándalo*) disgrace; **me da ~** I'm embarrassed; **es una ~** it's a disgrace; **no sé cómo no se te cae la cara de ~** you should be ashamed (of yourself)

vericuetos *mpl fig* twists and turns

verídico *adj* true

verificar <1g> *v/t* verify

verja *f* railing; (*puerta*) iron gate

vermú, vermut *m* vermouth

verosímil *adj* realistic; (*creíble*) plausible

verruga *f* wart

versado *adj* well-versed (*en* in)

versar <1a> *v/i*: **~ sobre** deal with, be about

versátil *adj* fickle; *artista* versatile

versículo *m* verse

versión *f* version; **en ~ original** *película* original language version

verso *m* verse

vértebra *f* ANAT vertebra

vertedero *m* dump, tip; **verter** <2g> *v/t* dump; (*derramar*) spill; *fig:*

opinión voice

vertical *adj* vertical

vertido *m* dumping; **~s** *pl* waste *sg*

vertiente *f L.Am.* (*cuesta*) slope; (*lado*) side

vertiginoso *adj* dizzy; (*rápido*) frantic; **vértigo** *m* MED vertigo; **darle a alguien** make s.o. dizzy

vesícula *f* blister; **~ biliar** ANAT gallbladder

vespa® *f* motorscooter

vestíbulo *m de casa* hall; *de edifico público* lobby

vestido *m* dress; *L.Am. de hombre* suit

vestigio *m* vestige, trace

vestir <3l> **1** *v/t* dress; (*llevar puesto*) wear **2** *v/i* dress; **~ de negro** wear black, dress in black; **~ de uniforme** wear a uniform **3** *v/r* **~se** get dressed; (*disfrazarse*) dress up; **~se de algo** wear sth

vestuario *m* DEP locker room; TEA wardrobe

veta *f* MIN vein

vetar <1a> *v/t* POL veto

veterano 1 *adj* veteran; (*experimentado*) experienced **2** *m*, **-a** *f* veteran

veterinario 1 *adj* veterinary **2** *m*, **-a** *f* veterinarian, vet

veto *m* veto

vetusto *adj* ancient

vez *f* time; **a la ~** at the same time; **a su ~** for his/her part; **cada ~ que** every time that; **de ~ en cuando** from time to time; **en ~ de** instead of; **érase una ~** once upon a time, there was; **otra ~** again; **tal ~** perhaps, maybe; **una ~** once; **a veces** sometimes; **muchas veces** (*con frecuencia*) often; **hacer las veces de** *de objeto* serve as; *de persona* act as

vi *vb* → **ver**

vía 1 *f* FERR track; **~ estrecha** FERR narrow gauge; **darle ~ libre a alguien** give s.o. a free hand; **por ~ aérea** by air; **en ~s de** *fig* in the process of **2** *prp* via

viable *adj plan, solución* viable, fea-

sible

viaducto *m* viaduct

viajante *m/f* sales rep; **viajar** <1a> *v/i* travel; **viaje** *m* trip, journey; **~ organizado** package tour; **~ de ida** outward journey; **~ de ida y vuelta** round trip; **~ de novios** honeymoon; **~ de vuelta** return journey; **viajero** *m*, **-a** *f* travel(l)er

viario *adj* road *atr*; **educación -a** instruction in road safety

víbora *f tb fig* viper

vibración *f* vibration; **vibrante** *adj fig* exciting; **vibrar** <1a> *v/i* vibrate

vicaría *f* pastor's house, vicarage; **pasar por la ~** F get married in church

vicecónsul *m* vice-consul

vicepresidente *m*, **-a** *f* POL vice-president; COM vice-president, *Br* deputy chairman

vicerrector *m* vice-rector

viceversa *adv*: **y ~** and vice versa

viciado *adj aire* stuffy; **viciarse** <1b> *v/r* fall into bad habits; **vicio** *m* vice; **pasarlo de ~** F have a great time F; **vicioso** *adj* vicious; (*corrompido*) depraved

vicisitudes *fpl* ups and downs

víctima *f* victim; **victimar** <1a> *v/t L.Am.* kill

victoria *f* victory; **cantar ~** claim victory; **victorioso** *adj* victorious

vicuña *f* ZO vicuna

vid *f* vine

vida *f* life; *esp* TÉC life span; **de por ~** for life; **en mi ~** never (in my life); **ganarse la ~** earn a living; **hacer la ~ imposible a alguien** make s.o.'s life impossible; **~ mía** my love

vidente *m/f* seer, clairvoyant

vídeo *m* video

videocámara *f* video camera

videocas(s)et(t)e *m* video cassette

videoclip *m* pop video

videoconferencia *f* video conference

videojuego *m* video game

videotex(to) *m* videotext

vidriera *f L.Am.* shop window; **vidrio** *m L.Am.* glass; (*ventana*) window

vieira *f* ZO scallop

vieja *f* old woman; **viejo 1** *adj* old **2** *m* old man; **mis ~s** my folks F

viendo *vb* → **ver**

viene *vb* → **venir**

viento *m* wind; **~ en popa** *fig* F splendidly; **contra ~ y marea** *fig* come what may; **hacer ~** be windy; **proclamar a los cuatro ~s** *fig* shout from the rooftops

vientre *m* belly

viernes *m inv* Friday; **Viernes Santo** Good Friday

Vietnam Vietnam; **vietnamita** *adj & m/f* Vietnamese

viga *f* beam, girder

vigente *adj legislación* in force

vigésimo *adj* twentieth

vigilante 1 *adj* watchful, vigilant **2** *m L.Am.* policeman; **~ nocturno** night watchman; **~ jurado** security guard; **vigilar** <1a> **1** *v/i* keep watch **2** *v/t* watch; *a un preso* guard

vigor *m* vigo(u)r; **en ~** in force; **vigoroso** *adj* vigorous

vil *adj* vile, despicable

vilipendiar <1b> *v/t* insult, vilify *fml*; *(despreciar)* revile

villa *f* town

villancico *m* Christmas carol

villano 1 *adj* villainous **2** *m*, **-a** *f* villain

vilo: en ~ in the air; *fig* in suspense, on tenterhooks; **levantar en ~** lift off the ground; **tener a alguien en ~** *fig* keep s.o. in suspense *o* on tenterhooks

vinagre *m* vinegar; **vinagrera** *f* vinegar bottle; *S.Am. (indigestión)* indigestion; **~s** *pl* cruet *sg*; **vinagreta** *f* vinaigrette

vincha *f S.Am.* hairband

vinculante *adj* binding; **vincular** <1a> *v/t* link (**a** to); *(comprometer)* bind; **vínculo** *m* link; *fig (relación)* tie, bond

vindicar <1g> *v/t* vindicate

vine *vb* → **venir**

vinícola *adj región, país* wine-growing *atr; industria* wine-making *atr*

viniendo *vb* → **venir**

vinicultura *f* wine-growing

vino 1 *m* wine; **~ blanco** white wine; **~ de mesa** table wine; **~ tinto** red wine **2** *vb* → **venir**

viña *f* vineyard; **viñatero** *m*, **-a** *f S.Am.* wine grower; **viñedo** *m* vineyard

viñeta *f* TIP vignette

vio *vb* → **ver**

viola *f* MÚS viola

violación *f* rape; *de derechos* violation; **violador** *m*, **-a** *f* rapist; **violar** <1a> *v/t* rape

violencia *f* violence; **violentar** <1a> *v/t puerta* force; *(incomodar)* embarrass; **violento** *adj* violent; *(embarazoso)* embarrassing; *persona* embarrassed

violeta 1 *f* BOT violet **2** *m/adj* violet

violín *m* violin; **violinista** *m/f* violinist; **violonc(h)elo** *m* cello

VIP *m* VIP

viperino *adj* malicious; **lengua -a** sharp tongue

viral *adj* viral

virar <1a> *v/t* MAR, AVIA turn

virgen 1 *adj* virgin; *cinta* blank; **lana ~** pure new wool **2** *f* virgin; **virginidad** *f* virginity

Virgo *m/f inv* ASTR Virgo

virguería *f*: **hace ~s** P he's a whizz F

vírico *adj* viral

viril *adj* virile, manly

virtual *adj* virtual

virtud *f* virtue; **en ~ de** by virtue of; **virtuoso 1** *adj* virtuous **2** *m*, **-a** *f* virtuoso

viruela *f* MED smallpox

virulento *adj* MED, *fig* virulent

virus *m inv* MED virus; **~ informático** computer virus

viruta *f* shaving

visa *f L.Am.* visa

visado *m* visa

vísceras *fpl* guts, entrails; **visceral** *adj fig* gut *atr*, visceral

viscoso *adj* viscous

visera *f de gorra* peak; *de casco* visor

visibilidad *f* visibility; **visible** *adj* visible; *fig* evident, obvious

visillo *m* sheer, *Br* net curtain

visión f vision, sight; fig vision; (opinión) view; **tener ~ de futuro** be forward looking

visita f visit; **~ a domicilio** house call; **~ guiada** guided tour; **hacer una ~ a alguien** visit s.o.; **visitante 1** adj visiting; DEP away **2** m/f visitor; **visitar** <1a> v/t visit

vislumbrar <1a> v/t glimpse

visos mpl: **tener ~ de** show signs of

visón m ZO mink

víspera f eve; **en ~s de** on the eve of

vista f (eye)sight; JUR hearing; **~ cansada** MED tired eyes; **a la ~** COM at sight, on demand; **a primera ~** at first sight; **con ~s a** with a view to; **en ~ de** in view of; **hasta la ~** bye!, see you!; **hacer la ~ gorda** fig F turn a blind eye; **tener ~ para algo** fig have a good eye for sth; **volver la ~ atrás** tb fig look back; **vistazo** m look; **echar un ~ a** take a (quick) look at

viste vb → **ver**, **vestir**

visto 1 part → **ver 2** adj: **está bien ~** it's the done thing; **está mal ~** it's not done, it's not the done thing; **está ~ que** it's obvious that; **estar muy ~** be old hat, not be original; **por lo ~** apparently **3** m check(mark), Br tick; **dar el ~ bueno** give one's approval; **vistoso** adj eye-catching

visual adj visual; **visualizar** <1f> v/t visualize; en pantalla display

vital adj vital; persona lively; **vitalicio** adj life atr, for life; **renta ~a** life annuity; **vitalidad** f vitality, liveliness

vitamina f vitamin

viticultor m, **~a** f wine grower

vítores mpl cheers, acclaim sg; **vitorear** <1a> v/t cheer

vítreo adj vitreous; **vitrificar** <1g> v/t vitrify

vitrina f display cabinet; L.Am. shop window

vitrocerámica f ceramic hob

vituperar <1a> v/t condemn

viuda f widow; **viudedad** f widowhood; **pensión de ~** widow's pen-

sion; **viudo 1** adj widowed **2** m widower; **quedarse ~** be widowed

viva int hurrah!; **¡~ el rey!** long live the king!

vivaz adj bright, sharp

vivencia f experience

víveres mpl provisions

vívido adj vivid

vivienda f housing; (casa) house

vivir <3a> **1** v/t live through, experience **2** v/i live; **~ de algo** live on sth; **vivo** adj alive; color bright; ritmo lively; fig F sharp, smart

vocabulario m vocabulary

vocación f vocation

vocal 1 m/f member **2** f vowel; **vocalista** m/f vocalist; **vocalizar** <1f> v/i vocalize

voceador m, **~a** f Méx newspaper vendor

vocerío m uproar; **vocero** m, **-a** f esp L.Am. spokesperson; **vociferar** <1a> v/i shout

vodka m vodka

volador adj flying

volandas: en ~ fig in the air

volante 1 adj flying **2** m AUTO steering wheel; de vestido flounce; MED referral (slip)

volar <1m> **1** v/i fly; fig vanish **2** v/t fly; edificio blow up

volátil adj tb fig volatile; **volatilizarse** <1f> v/r fig vanish into thin air

volcán m volcano; **volcánico** adj volcanic

volcar <1g & 1m> **1** v/t knock over; (vaciar) empty; barco, coche overturn **2** v/i de coche, barco overturn **3** v/r **~se** tip over; **~se por alguien** F bend over backwards for s.o., go out of one's way for s.o.; **~se en algo** throw o.s. into sth

volea f tenis volley

voleibol m volleyball

voleo m: **a ~** at random

voley-playa m beach volleyball

voltaje m EL voltage

voltear <1a> **1** v/t L.Am. (invertir) turn over; Rpl (tumbar) knock over; **~ el jersey** turn the sweater inside out; **~ la cabeza** turn one's head

V

2 *v/i* roll over; *de campanas* ring out;
voltereta *f* somersault

voltio *m* EL volt

voluble *adj* erratic, unpredictable

volumen *m* TIP, MÚS, RAD volume; **~ de negocios** COM turnover

voluntad *f* will; *buena/mala* ~ good/ill will; **voluntario 1** *adj* volunteer **2** *m*, **-a** *f* volunteer; **voluntarioso** *adj* willing, enthusiastic

voluptuoso *adj* voluptuous

volver <2h; *part* *vuelto*> **1** *v/t página, mirada etc* turn (*a* to; *hacia* toward); **~ a hacer algo** do sth again **3** *v/r* **~se** turn round; **~se loco** go crazy

vomitar <1a> **1** *v/t* throw up; *lava* hurl, throw out **2** *v/i* throw up, be sick; **tengo ganas de** ~ I feel nauseous, *Br* I feel sick; **vómito** *m* MED vomit

vorágine *f* (*remolino*) whirlpool; *fig* whirl

voraz *adj* voracious; *incendio* fierce

vos *pron pers sg Rpl, C.Am., Ven* you

vosotros, vosotras *pron pers pl* you

votación *f* vote, ballot; **votar** <1a> **1** *v/t* (*aprobar*) vote **2** *v/i* vote; **voto** *m* POL vote; **~ en blanco** spoiled ballot paper

voy *vb* → *ir*

voz *f* voice; *fig* rumo(u)r; **~ activa/ pasiva** GRAM active/passive voice;

a media ~ in a hushed voice, in a low voice; **a ~ en grito** at the top of one's voice; **en ~ alta** aloud; **en ~ baja** in a low voice; **correr la ~** spread the word; **llevar la ~ cantante** *fig* call the tune, call the shots; **no tener ~ ni voto** *fig* not have a say; **~ en off** voice-over

vuelco 1 *vb* → *volcar* **2** *m*: **dar un** ~ *fig* F take a dramatic turn; **me dio un ~ el corazón** my heart missed a beat

vuelo 1 *vb* → *volar* **2** *m* flight; **~ chárter** charter flight; **~ nacional** domestic flight; **al ~ coger, cazar** in mid-air; **una falda con ~** a full skirt

vuelta *f* return; *en carrera* lap; **~ de carnero** *L.Am.* half-somersault; **~ al mundo** round-the-world trip; **a la ~** on the way back; **a la ~ de la esquina** *fig* just around the corner; **dar la ~ llave etc** turn; **dar media ~** turn round; **dar una ~** go for a walk; **dar cien ~s a alguien** F be a hundred times better than s.o. F

vuelto 1 *part* → *volver* **2** *m L.Am.* change

vuelvo *vb* → *volver*

vuestro 1 *adj pos* your **2** *pron* yours

vulgar *adj* vulgar, common; *abundante* common; **vulgaridad** *f* vulgarity; **vulgo** *m* lower classes *pl*

vulnerable *adj* vulnerable

W

w. *abr* (= *watio*) w (= watt)

walkman *m* personal stereo

wáter *m* bathroom, toilet

waterpolo *m* DEP water polo

WC *abr* WC

whisky *m* whiskey, *Br* whisky

windsurf(ing) *m* wind-surfing; **windsurfista** *m/f* windsurfer

X

xenofobia *f* xenophobia

xilófono *m* MÚS xylophone

Y

y *conj* and

ya *adv* already; (*ahora mismo*) now; **¡~!** *incredulidad* oh, yeah!, sure!; *comprensión* I know, I understand; *asenso* OK, sure; *al terminar* finished!, done!; **~ no vive aquí** he doesn't live here any more, he no longer lives here; **~ que** since, as; **~ lo sé** I know; **~ viene** she's coming now; **¿lo puede hacer? – ¡~ lo creo!** can she do it? – you bet!; **~ ... ~ ...** either ... or ...

yacaré *m L.Am.* ZO cayman

yacer <2y> *v/i* lie; **yacimiento** *m* MIN deposit

yanqui *m/f* Yankee

yapa *f L.Am.* bit extra (for free); *Pe, Bol* (*propina*) tip

yate *m* yacht

yaya *f* grandma

yayo *m* grandpa

yedra *f* BOT ivy

yegua *f* ZO mare

yema *f* yolk; **~ del dedo** fingertip

yendo *vb* → **ir**

yerba *f L.Am.* grass; **~ mate** maté; **yerbatero** *m*, **-a** *f Rpl* herbalist

yerno *m* son-in-law

yeso *m* plaster

yo *pron* I; **soy ~** it's me; **~ que tú** if I were you

yodo *m* iodine

yoga *m* yoga

yogur *m* yog(h)urt

yonqui *m/f* F junkie

yuca *f* BOT yucca

yugo *m* yoke

Yugoslavia Yugoslavia; **yugoslavo 1** *adj* Yugoslav(ian) **2** *m*, **-a** *f* Yugoslav(ian)

yugular *adj* ANAT jugular

yute *m* jute

yuxtaposición *f* juxtaposition

yuyo *m L.Am.* weed

Z

zacatal *m C.Am.*, *Méx* pasture; **zacate** *m C.Am.*, *Méx* fodder

zafarse <1a> *v/r* get away (*de* from); (*soltarse*) come undone; **~ de algo** (*evitar*) get out of sth

zafio *adj* coarse

zafiro *m* sapphire

zaga *f*: **ir a la ~** bring up the rear

zalamero 1 *adj* flattering; *empalagoso* syrupy, sugary **2** *m*, **-a** *f* flatterer, sweet talker

zamba *f Arg* (*baile*) Argentinian folkdance

zambomba *f* MÚS *type of drum*

zambullirse <3h> *v/r* dive (*en* into); *fig* throw o.s. (*en* into), immerse o.s. (*en* in)

zamparse <1a> *v/r* F wolf down F

zanahoria *f* carrot

zancada *f* stride

zancadilla *f fig* obstacle; ***poner*** or ***echar la ~ a alguien*** trip s.o. up

zancudo *m L.Am.* mosquito

zángano *m* ZO drone; *fig* F lazybones *sg*

zanja *f* ditch; **zanjar** <1a> *v/t fig problemas* settle; *dificultades* overcome

zapatería *f* shoe store, shoe shop; **zapatero** *m*, **-a** *f* shoemaker; **~ remendón** shoe mender; **zapatilla** *f* slipper; *de deporte* sneaker, *Br* trainer

Zapatista *m/f Méx* member or supporter of the Zapatista National Liberation Army

zapato *m* shoe

zapear <1a> *v/i* TV F channel hop; **zapeo**, **zapping** *m* TV F channel hopping

zarandear <1a> *v/t* shake violently, buffet; **~ a alguien** *fig* give s.o. a hard time

zarpa *f* paw

zarpar <1a> *v/i* MAR set sail (*para* for)

zarza *f* BOT bramble; **zarzamora** *f* BOT blackberry

zarzuela *f* MÚS *type of operetta*

zascandilear <1a> *v/i* mess around

zigzaguear <1a> *v/i* zigzag

zinc *m* zinc

zócalo *m* baseboard, *Br* skirting board

zodíaco, **zodiaco** *m* AST zodiac

zona *f* area, zone

zoncería *f L.Am.* F stupid thing; **zonzo** *adj L.Am.* F stupid

zoo *m* zoo; **zoológico 1** *adj* zoological **2** *m* zoo

zoom *m* FOT zoom

zopilote *m L.Am.* ZO turkey buzzard

zorra *f* ZO vixen; P whore P; **zorro 1** *adj* sly, crafty **2** *m* ZO fox; *fig* old fox

zozobrar <1a> *v/i* MAR overturn; *fig* go under

zueco *m* clog

zulo *m* hiding place

zumba *f L.Am.*, *Méx* (*paliza*) beating; **zumbar** <1a> **1** *v/i* buzz; ***me zumban los oídos*** my ears are ringing *o* buzzing **2** *v/t golpe, bofetada* give; **zumbido** *m* buzzing

zumo *m* juice

zurcir <3b> *v/t calcetines* darn; *chaqueta, pantalones* patch

zurdo 1 *adj* left-handed **2** *m*, **-a** *f* left-hander

zurrar <1a> *v/t* TÉC tan; **~ a alguien** F tan s.o.'s hide F

A

a [ə] *stressed* [eɪ] *art* un(a); ***an island*** una isla; ***$5 a ride*** 5 dólares por vuelta

a·back [ə'bæk] *adv:* **taken ~** desconcertado (**by** por)

a·ban·don [ə'bændən] *v/t* abandonar

a·bashed [ə'bæʃt] *adj* avergonzado

a·bate [ə'beɪt] *v/i of storm, flood* amainar

ab·at·toir ['æbətwɑːr] matadero *m*

ab·bey ['æbɪ] abadía *f*

ab·bre·vi·ate [ə'briːvɪeɪt] *v/t* abreviar

ab·bre·vi·a·tion [əbriːvɪ'eɪʃn] abreviatura *f*

ab·di·cate ['æbdɪkeɪt] *v/i* abdicar

ab·di·ca·tion [æbdɪ'keɪʃn] abdicación *f*

ab·do·men ['æbdəmən] abdomen *m*

ab·dom·i·nal [æb'dɑːmɪnl] *adj* abdominal

ab·duct [əb'dʌkt] *v/t* raptar, secuestrar

ab·duc·tion [əb'dʌkʃn] rapto *m*, secuestro *m*

♦ **a·bide by** [ə'baɪd] *v/t* atenerse a

a·bil·i·ty [ə'bɪlətɪ] capacidad *f*, habilidad *f*

a·blaze [ə'bleɪz] *adj* en llamas

a·ble ['eɪbl] *adj (skillful)* capaz, hábil; ***be ~ to*** poder; ***I wasn't ~ to see/hear*** no conseguí *or* pude ver/escuchar

a·ble-bod·ied [eɪbl'bɑːdɪːd] *adj* sano

ab·nor·mal [æb'nɔːrml] *adj* anormal

ab·nor·mal·ly [æb'nɔːrməlɪ] *adv* anormalmente; *behave* de manera anormal

a·board [ə'bɔːrd] **1** *prep* a bordo de **2** *adv* a bordo; ***be ~*** estar a bordo; ***go ~*** subir a bordo

a·bol·ish [ə'bɑːlɪʃ] *v/t* abolir

ab·o·li·tion [æbə'lɪʃn] abolición *f*

a·bort [ə'bɔːrt] *v/t mission, launch* suspender, cancelar; COMPUT cancelar

a·bor·tion [ə'bɔːrʃn] aborto *m (provocado)*; ***have an ~*** abortar

a·bor·tive [ə'bɔːrtɪv] *adj* fallido

a·bout [ə'baʊt] **1** *prep (concerning)* acerca de, sobre; ***what's it ~?*** *of book, movie* ¿de qué trata? **2** *adv (roughly)* más o menos; ***be ~ to ...*** *(be going to)* estar a punto de ...

a·bove [ə'bʌv] **1** *prep* por encima de; ***500 m ~ sea level*** 500 m sobre el nivel del mar; ***~ all*** por encima de todo, sobre todo **2** *adv:* ***on the floor ~*** en el piso de arriba

a·bove-men·tioned [əbʌv'menʃnd] *adj* arriba mencionado

ab·ra·sion [ə'breɪʒn] abrasión *f*

ab·ra·sive [ə'breɪsɪv] *adj personality* abrasivo

a·breast [ə'brest] *adv* de frente, en fondo; ***keep ~ of*** mantenerse al tanto de

a·bridge [ə'brɪdʒ] *v/t* abreviar, condensar

a·broad [ə'brɔːd] *adv live* en el extranjero; *go* al extranjero

a·brupt [ə'brʌpt] *adj departure* brusco, repentino; *manner* brusco, rudo

a·brupt·ly [ə'brʌptlɪ] *adv (suddenly)* repentinamente; *(curtly)* bruscamente

ab·scess ['æbsɪs] absceso *m*

ab·sence ['æbsəns] *of person* ausencia *f*; *(lack)* falta *f*

ab·sent ['æbsənt] *adj* ausente

ab·sen·tee [æbsən'tiː] *n* ausente *m/f*

ab·sen·tee·ism [æbsən'tiːɪzm] absentismo *m*

ab·sent-mind·ed [æbsənt'maɪndɪd] *adj* despistado, distraído

ab·sent-mind·ed·ly [æbsənt'maɪndɪdlɪ] *adv* distraídamente

ab·so·lute ['æbsəluːt] *adj power* absoluto; *idiot* completo; *mess* total

ab·so·lute·ly ['æbsəluːtlɪ] *adv* (*completely*) absolutamente, completamente; **~ not!** ¡en absoluto!; *do you agree? – –* ¿estás de acuerdo? – ¡completamente!

ab·so·lu·tion [æbsə'luːʃn] REL absolución *f*

ab·solve [əb'zɑːlv] *v/t* absolver

ab·sorb [əb'sɔːrb] *v/t* absorber; **~ed in** absorto en

ab·sorb·en·cy [əb'sɔːrbənsɪ] absorbencia *f*

ab·sorb·ent [əb'sɔːrbənt] *adj* absorbente

ab·sorb·ent [əb'sɔːrbənt] 'cot·ton algodón *m* hidrófilo

ab·sorb·ing [əb'sɔːrbɪŋ] *adj* absorbente

ab·stain [əb'steɪn] *v/i from voting* abstenerse

ab·sten·tion [əb'stenʃn] *in voting* abstención *f*

ab·stract ['æbstrækt] *adj* abstracto

ab·struse [əb'struːs] *adj* abstruso

ab·surd [əb'sɜːrd] *adj* absurdo

ab·surd·i·ty [əb'sɜːrdətɪ] lo absurdo

a·bun·dance [ə'bʌndəns] abundancia *f*

a·bun·dant [ə'bʌndənt] *adj* abundante

a·buse¹ [ə'bjuːs] *n* (*insults*) insultos *mpl*; *of thing* maltrato *m*; (*child*) ~ *physical* malos tratos *mpl* a menores; *sexual* agresión *f* sexual a menores

a·buse² [ə'bjuːz] *v/t physically* abusar de; *verbally* insultar

a·bu·sive [ə'bjuːsɪv] *adj language* insultante, injurioso; *become* ~ ponerse a insultar

a·bys·mal [ə'bɪzml] *adj* F (*very bad*) desastroso F

a·byss [ə'bɪs] abismo *m*

AC ['eɪsiː] *abbr* (= *alternating current*) CA (= corriente *f* alterna)

ac·a·dem·ic [ækə'demɪk] **1** *n* académico(-a) *m(f)*, profesor(a) *m(f)* **2** *adj* académico

a·cad·e·my [ə'kædəmɪ] academia *f*

ac·cel·e·rate [ək'seləreɪt] *v/t & v/i* acelerar

ac·cel·e·ra·tion [əksselə'reɪʃn] aceleración *f*

ac·cel·e·ra·tor [ək'seləreɪtər] *of car* acelerador *m*

ac·cent ['æksənt] *when speaking* acento *m*; (*emphasis*) énfasis *m*

ac·cen·tu·ate [ək'sentʊeɪt] *v/t* acentuar

ac·cept [ək'sept] *v/t & v/i* aceptar

ac·cep·ta·ble [ək'septəbl] *adj* aceptable

ac·cept·ance [ək'septəns] aceptación *f*

ac·cess ['ækses] **1** *n* acceso *m*; *have* ~ *to computer* tener acceso a; *child* tener derecho a visitar **2** *v/t also* COMPUT acceder a

'ac·cess code COMPUT código *m* de acceso

ac·ces·si·ble [ək'sesəbl] *adj* accesible

ac·ces·sion [ək'seʃn] acceso *m*

ac·ces·so·ry [ək'sesərɪ] *for wearing* accesorio *m*, complemento *m*; LAW cómplice *m/f*

'ac·cess road carretera *f* de acceso

'ac·cess time COMPUT tiempo *m* de acceso

ac·ci·dent ['æksɪdənt] accidente *m*; *by* ~ por casualidad

ac·ci·den·tal [æksɪ'dentl] *adj* accidental

ac·ci·den·tal·ly [æksɪ'dentlɪ] *adv* sin querer

ac·claim [ə'kleɪm] **1** *n* alabanza *f*, aclamación *f*; *meet with* ~ ser alabado *or* aclamado **2** *v/t* alabar, aclamar

ac·cla·ma·tion [əklə'meɪʃn] aclamación *f*

ac·cli·mate, ac·cli·ma·tize [ə'klaɪmət, ə'klaɪmətaɪz] *v/t* aclimatarse

ac·com·mo·date [ə'kɑːmədeɪt] *v/t* alojar; *requirements* satisfacer, hacer frente a

ac·com·mo·da·tions [əkɑːmə'deɪʃnz] *npl* alojamiento *m*

ac·com·pa·ni·ment [ə'kʌmpənɪmənt] MUS acompañamiento *m*

ac·com·pa·nist [ə'kʌmpənɪst] MUS acompañante *m/f*

ac·com·pa·ny [ə'kʌmpənɪ] *v/t* (*pret & pp* **-ied**) *also* MUS acompañar

ac·com·plice [ə'kʌmplɪs] cómplice *m/f*

ac·com·plish [ə'kʌmplɪʃ] *v/t task* realizar; *goal* conseguir, lograr

ac·com·plished [ə'kʌmplɪʃt] *adj* consumado

ac·com·plish·ment [ə'kʌmplɪʃ-mənt] *of a task* realización *f*; (*talent*) habilidad *f*; (*achievement*) logro *m*

ac·cord [ə'kɔːrd] acuerdo *m*; *of one's own* ~ de motu propio

ac·cord·ance [ə'kɔːrdəns]: *in* ~ *with* de acuerdo con

ac·cord·ing [ə'kɔːrdɪŋ] *adv*: ~ *to* según

ac·cord·ing·ly [ə'kɔːrdɪŋlɪ] *adv* (*consequently*) por consiguiente; (*appropriately*) como corresponde

ac·cor·di·on [ə'kɔːrdɪən] acordeón *m*

ac·cor·di·on·ist [ə'kɔːrdɪənɪst] acordeonista *m/f*

ac·count [ə'kaʊnt] *financial* cuenta *f*; (*report, description*) relato *m*, descripción *f*; *give an* ~ *of* relatar, describir; *on no* ~ de ninguna manera, bajo ningún concepto; *on* ~ *of a* causa de; *take sth into* ~, *take* ~ *of sth* tener algo en cuenta, tener en cuenta algo

♦ **account for** *v/t* (*explain*) explicar; (*make up, constitute*) suponer, constituir

ac·count·a·bil·i·ty [əkaʊntə'bɪlətɪ] responsabilidad *f*

ac·coun·ta·ble [ə'kaʊntəbl] *adj* responsable (*to* ante); *be held* ~ ser considerado responsable

ac·coun·tant [ə'kaʊntənt] contable *m/f*, L.Am. contador(a) *m(f)*

ac'count hold·er titular *m/f* de una cuenta

ac'count num·ber número *m* de cuenta

ac·counts [ə'kaʊnts] *npl* contabilidad *f*

ac·cu·mu·late [ə'kjuːmjʊleɪt] **1** *v/t*

acumular **2** *v/i* acumularse

ac·cu·mu·la·tion [əkjuːmjʊ'leɪʃn] acumulación *f*

ac·cu·ra·cy ['ækjʊrəsɪ] precisión *f*

ac·cu·rate ['ækjʊrət] *adj* preciso

ac·cu·rate·ly ['ækjʊrətlɪ] *adv* con precisión

ac·cu·sa·tion [ækjuː'zeɪʃn] acusación *f*

ac·cuse [ə'kjuːz] *v/t*: ~ *s.o. of sth* acusar a alguien de algo; *be* ~*d of* LAW ser acusado de

ac·cused [ə'kjuːzd] *n* LAW acusado(-a) *m(f)*

ac·cus·ing [ə'kjuːzɪŋ] *adj* acusador

ac·cus·ing·ly [ə'kjuːzɪŋlɪ] *adv say* en tono acusador; *he looked at me* ~ me lanzó una mirada acusadora

ac·cus·tom [ə'kʌstəm] *v/t* acostumbrar; *get* ~*ed to* acostumbrarse a; *be* ~*ed to* estar acostumbrado a

ace [eɪs] *in cards* as *m*; (*in tennis: shot*) ace *m*

ache [eɪk] **1** *n* dolor *m* **2** *v/i* doler

a·chieve [ə'tʃiːv] *v/t* conseguir, lograr

a·chieve·ment [ə'tʃiːvmənt] *of ambition* consecución *f*, logro *m*; (*thing achieved*) logro *m*

ac·id ['æsɪd] *n* ácido *m*

a·cid·i·ty [ə'sɪdətɪ] acidez *f*; *fig* sarcasmo *m*

ac·id 'rain lluvia *f* ácida

'ac·id test *fig* prueba *f* de fuego

ac·knowl·edge [ək'nɑːlɪdʒ] *v/t* reconocer; ~ *receipt of a letter* acusar recibo de una carta

ac·knowl·edg(e)·ment [ək'nɑːlɪdʒ-mənt] reconocimiento *m*; *of a letter* acuse *m* de recibo

ac·ne ['æknɪ] MED acné *m*, acne *m*

a·corn ['eɪkɔːrn] BOT bellota *f*

a·cous·tics [ə'kuːstɪks] acústica *f*

ac·quaint [ə'kweɪnt] *v/t fml*: *be* ~*ed with* conocer

ac·quaint·ance [ə'kweɪntəns] *person* conocido(-a) *m(f)*

ac·qui·esce [ækwɪ'es] *v/i fml* acceder

ac·qui·es·cence [ækwɪ'esns] *fml* aquiescencia *f*

ac·quire [ə'kwaɪr] *v/t* adquirir

ac·qui·si·tion [ækwɪ'zɪʃn] adquisición f

ac·quis·i·tive [æ'kwɪzətɪv] adj consumista

ac·quit [ə'kwɪt] v/t LAW absolver

ac·quit·tal [ə'kwɪtl] LAW absolución f

a·cre ['eɪkər] acre m (4.047m2)

ac·ri·mo·ni·ous [ækrɪ'moʊnɪəs] adj áspero, agrio

ac·ro·bat ['ækrəbæt] acróbata m/f

ac·ro·bat·ic [ækrə'bætɪk] adj acrobático

ac·ro·bat·ics [ækrə'bætɪks] npl acrobacias fpl

ac·ro·nym ['ækrənɪm] acrónimo m

a·cross [ə'krɑːs] **1** prep al otro lado de; **she lives ~ the street** vive al otro lado de la calle; **sail ~ the Atlantic** cruzar el Atlántico navegando **2** adv de un lado a otro; **it's too far to swim ~** está demasiado lejos como para cruzar a nado; **once you're ~** cuando hayas llegado al otro lado; **10 m ~** 10 m de ancho

a·cryl·ic [ə'krɪlɪk] adj acrílico

act [ækt] **1** v/i THEA actuar; (pretend) hacer teatro; **~ as** actuar or hacer de **2** n (deed), of play acto m; in vaudeville número m; (law) ley f; **it's just an ~** (pretense) es puro teatro; **~ of God** caso m fortuito

act·ing ['æktɪŋ] **1** n in a play interpretación f; as profession teatro m **2** adj (temporary) en funciones

ac·tion ['ækʃn] acción f; **out of ~** machine sin funcionar; person fuera de combate; **take ~** actuar; **bring an ~ against** LAW demandar a

ac·tion 're·play TV repetición f (de la jugada)

ac·tive ['æktɪv] adj also GRAM activo; party member en activo

ac·tiv·ist ['æktɪvɪst] POL activista m/f

ac·tiv·i·ty [æk'tɪvətɪ] actividad f

ac·tor ['æktər] actor m

ac·tress ['æktrɪs] actriz f

ac·tu·al ['æktʃʊəl] adj verdadero, real

ac·tu·al·ly ['æktʃʊəlɪ] adv (in fact, to tell the truth) en realidad; **did you ~ see her?** ¿de verdad llegaste a verla?; **he ~ did it!** ¡aunque parezca mentira lo hizo!; **~, I do know him** (stressing converse) pues sí, de hecho lo conozco; **~, it's not finished yet** el caso es que todavía no está terminado

ac·u·punc·ture ['ækjəpʌŋktʃər] acupuntura f

a·cute [ə'kjuːt] adj pain agudo; sense muy fino

a·cute·ly [ə'kjuːtlɪ] adv (extremely) extremadamente; **~ aware** plenamente consciente

AD [eɪ'diː] abbr (= anno Domini) D.C. (= después de Cristo)

ad [æd] → **advertisement**

ad·a·mant ['ædəmənt] adj firme

Ad·am's ap·ple [ædəmz'æpəl] nuez f

a·dapt [ə'dæpt] **1** v/t adaptar **2** v/i of person adaptarse

a·dapt·a·bil·i·ty [ədæptə'bɪlətɪ] adaptabilidad f

a·dapt·a·ble [ə'dæptəbl] adj adaptable

a·dap·ta·tion [ædæp'teɪʃn] of play etc adaptación f

a·dapt·er [ə'dæptər] electrical adaptador m

add [æd] **1** v/t añadir; MATH sumar **2** v/i of person sumar

♦ **add on** v/t 15% etc sumar

♦ **add up 1** v/t sumar **2** v/i fig cuadrar

ad·der ['ædər] víbora f

ad·dict ['ædɪkt] adicto(-a) m(f); **drug ~** drogadicto(-a) m(f)

ad·dict·ed [ə'dɪktɪd] adj adicto; **be ~ to** ser adicto a

ad·dic·tion [ə'dɪkʃn] adicción f

ad·dic·tive [ə'dɪktɪv] adj adictivo

ad·di·tion [ə'dɪʃn] MATH suma f; to list, company etc incorporación f; of new drive etc instalación f; **in ~** además; **in ~ to** además de

ad·di·tion·al [ə'dɪʃnl] adj adicional

ad·di·tive ['ædɪtɪv] aditivo m

add-on ['ædɑːn] extra m, accesorio m

ad·dress [ə'dres] **1** n dirección f; **form of ~** tratamiento m **2** v/t letter dirigir; audience dirigirse a; **how do you ~ the judge?** ¿qué tratamiento se le da al juez?

ad'dress book agenda f de direcciones

ad·dress·ee [ædre'siː] destinatario(-a) m(f)

ad·ept ['ædept] adj experto; **be ~ at** ser un experto en

ad·e·quate ['ædɪkwət] adj suficiente; (satisfactory) aceptable

ad·e·quate·ly ['ædɪkwətlɪ] adv suficientemente; (satisfactorily) aceptablemente

ad·here [əd'hɪr] v/i adherirse
◆ adhere to v/t surface adherirse a; rules cumplir

ad·he·sive [əd'hiːsɪv] n adhesivo m

ad·he·sive 'plas·ter esparadrapo m

ad·he·sive 'tape cinta f adhesiva

ad·ja·cent [ə'dʒeɪsnt] adj adyacente

ad·jec·tive ['ædʒɪktɪv] adjetivo m

ad·join [ə'dʒɔɪn] v/t lindar con

ad·join·ing [ə'dʒɔɪnɪŋ] adj contiguo

ad·journ [ə'dʒɜːrn] v/i of court, meeting aplazar

ad·journ·ment [ə'dʒɜːrnmənt] aplazamiento m

ad·just [ə'dʒʌst] v/t ajustar, regular

ad·just·a·ble [ə'dʒʌstəbl] adj ajustable, regulable

ad·just·ment [ə'dʒʌstmənt] ajuste m; psychological adaptación f

ad lib [æd'lɪb] **1** adj improvisado **2** adv improvisadamente **3** v/i (pret & pp -bed) improvisar

ad·min·is·ter [əd'mɪnɪstər] v/t administrar

ad·min·is·tra·tion [ədmɪnɪ'streɪʃn] administración f

ad·min·is·tra·tive [ədmɪnɪ'strətɪv] adj administrativo

ad·min·is·tra·tor [əd'mɪnɪstreɪtər] administrador(a) m(f)

ad·mi·ra·ble ['ædmərəbl] adj admirable

ad·mi·ra·bly ['ædmərəblɪ] adv admirablemente

ad·mi·ral ['ædmərəl] almirante m

ad·mi·ra·tion [ædmə'reɪʃn] admiración f

ad·mire [əd'maɪr] v/t admirar

ad·mir·er [əd'maɪrər] admirador(a) m(f)

ad·mir·ing [əd'maɪrɪŋ] adj de admiración

ad·mir·ing·ly [əd'maɪrɪŋlɪ] adv con admiración

ad·mis·si·ble [əd'mɪsəbl] adj admisible

ad·mis·sion [əd'mɪʃn] (confession) confesión f; **~ free** entrada gratis

ad·mit [əd'mɪt] v/t (pret & pp -ted) to a place dejar entrar; to school, organization admitir; to hospital ingresar; (confess) confesar; (accept) admitir

ad·mit·tance [əd'mɪtəns] admisión f; **no ~** prohibido el paso

ad·mit·ted·ly [əd'mɪtɪdlɪ] adv: **he didn't use those exact words, ~** es verdad que no utilizó exactamente esas palabras

ad·mon·ish [əd'mɑːnɪʃ] v/t fml reprender

a·do [ə'duː]: **without further ~** sin más dilación

ad·o·les·cence [ædə'lesns] adolescencia f

ad·o·les·cent [ædə'lesnt] **1** n adolescente m/f **2** adj de adolescente

a·dopt [ə'dɑːpt] v/t child, plan adoptar

a·dop·tion [ə'dɑːpʃn] of child adopción f

a·dop·tive 'par·ents [ədɑːptɪv] npl padres mpl adoptivos

a·dor·a·ble [ə'dɔːrəbl] adj encantador

ad·o·ra·tion [ædə'reɪʃn] adoración f

a·dore [ə'dɔːr] v/t adorar; **I ~ chocolate** me encanta el chocolate

a·dor·ing [ə'dɔːrɪŋ] adj expression lleno de adoración; **his ~ fans** sus entregados fans

ad·ren·al·in [ə'drenəlɪn] adrenalina f

a·drift [ə'drɪft] adj a la deriva; fig perdido

ad·u·la·tion [ædʊ'leɪʃn] adulación f

a·dult ['ædʌlt] **1** *n* adulto(-a) *m(f)*
2 *adj* adulto

a·dult ed·u·ca·tion educación *f* para adultos

a·dul·ter·ous [ə'dʌltərəs] *adj relationship* adúltero

a·dul·ter·y [ə'dʌltərɪ] adulterio *m*

'a·dult film *euph* película *f* para adultos

ad·vance [əd'væns] **1** *n money* adelanto *m*; *in science,* MIL avance *m*; **in ~** con antelación; *get money* por adelantado; **48 hours in ~** con 48 horas de antelación; **make ~s** (*make progress*) avanzar, progresar; *sexually* insinuarse **2** *v/i* MIL avanzar; (*make progress*) avanzar, progresar **3** *v/t theory* presentar; *sum of money* adelantar; *human knowledge, a cause* hacer avanzar

ad·vance 'book·ing reserva *f* (anticipada)

ad·vanced [əd'vænst] *adj country, level, learner* avanzado

ad·vance 'no·tice aviso *m* previo

ad·vance 'pay·ment pago *m* por adelantado

ad·van·tage [əd'væntɪdʒ] ventaja *f*; *there's no ~ to be gained* no se gana nada; *it's to your ~* te conviene; *take ~ of* aprovecharse de

ad·van·ta·geous [ædvən'teɪdʒəs] *adj* ventajoso

ad·vent ['ædvent] *fig* llegada *f*

'ad·vent cal·en·dar calendario *m* de Adviento

ad·ven·ture [əd'ventʃər] aventura *f*

ad·ven·tur·ous [əd'ventʃərəs] *adj person* aventurero; *investment* arriesgado

ad·verb ['ædvɜːrb] adverbio *m*

ad·ver·sa·ry ['ædvərserɪ] adversario(-a) *m(f)*

ad·verse ['ædvɜːrs] *adj* adverso

ad·vert ['ædvɜːrt] → *advertisement*

ad·ver·tise ['ædvərtaɪz] **1** *v/t* anunciar **2** *v/i* anunciarse, poner un anuncio

ad·ver·tise·ment [ədvɜːr'taɪsmənt] anuncio *m*

ad·ver·tis·er ['ædvərtaɪzər] anun-

ciante *m/f*

ad·ver·tis·ing ['ædvərtaɪzɪŋ] publicidad *f*

'ad·ver·tis·ing a·gen·cy agencia *f* de publicidad; **'ad·ver·tis·ing budg·et** presupuesto *m* para publicidad; **'ad·ver·tis·ing cam·paign** campaña *f* publicitaria; **'ad·ver·tis·ing rev·e·nue** ingresos *mpl* por publicidad

ad·vice [əd'vaɪs] consejo *m*; *he gave me some ~* me dio un consejo; *take s.o.'s ~* seguir el consejo de alguien

ad·vis·a·ble [əd'vaɪzəbl] *adj* aconsejable

ad·vise [əd'vaɪz] *v/t person, caution* aconsejar; *government* asesorar; *I ~ you to leave* te aconsejo que te vayas

ad·vis·er [əd'vaɪzər] asesor(a) *m(f)*

ad·vo·cate ['ædvəkeɪt] *v/t* abogar por

aer·i·al ['erɪəl] *n* antena *f*

aer·i·al 'pho·to·graph fotografía *f* aérea

aer·o·bics [e'roʊbɪks] *nsg* aerobic *m*

aer·o·dy·nam·ic [eroʊdaɪ'næmɪk] *adj* aerodinámico

aer·o·nau·ti·cal [eroʊ'nɒtɪkl] *adj* aeronáutico

aer·o·plane ['eroʊpleɪn] *Br* avión *m*

aer·o·sol ['erəsɑːl] aerosol *m*

aer·o·space in·dus·try ['erəspeɪs] industria *f* aeroespacial

aes·thet·ic *etc Br* → *esthetic etc*

af·fa·ble ['æfəbl] *adj* afable

af·fair [ə'fer] (*matter, business*) asunto *m*; (*love ~*) aventura *f*, lío *m*; *foreign ~s* asuntos *mpl* exteriores; *have an ~ with* tener una aventura *or* lío con

af·fect [ə'fekt] *v/t also* MED afectar

af·fec·tion [ə'fekʃn] afecto *m*, cariño *m*

af·fec·tion·ate [ə'fekʃnət] *adj* afectuoso, cariñoso

af·fec·tion·ate·ly [ə'fekʃnətlɪ] *adv* con afecto, cariñosamente

af·fin·i·ty [ə'fɪnətɪ] afinidad *f*

af·fir·ma·tive [ə'fɜːrmətɪv] *adj* afirmativo; *answer in the ~* responder

af·flu·ence ['æfluəns] prosperidad *f*, riqueza *f*

af·flu·ent ['æfluənt] *adj* próspero, acomodado; **~ *society*** sociedad *f* opulenta

af·ford [ə'fɔːrd] *v/t* permitirse; **be able to ~ sth** *financially* poder permitirse algo; **I can't ~ the time** no tengo tiempo

af·ford·a·ble [ə'fɔːrdəbl] *adj* asequible

a·float [ə'flout] *adj boat* a flote; **keep the company ~** mantener la compañía a flote

a·fraid [ə'freid] *adj*: **be ~** tener miedo; **be ~ of** tener miedo de; **I'm ~ of cats** tengo miedo a los gatos; **he's of the dark** le da miedo la oscuridad; **I'm ~ of annoying him** me da miedo enfadarle; **I'm ~** *expressing regret* me temo; **he's very ill, I'm ~** me temo que está muy enfermo; **I'm ~ so** (me) temo que sí; **I'm ~ not** (me) temo que no

a·fresh [ə'freʃ] *adv* de nuevo

Af·ri·ca ['æfrikə] África

Af·ri·can ['æfrikən] **1** *adj* africano **2** *n* africano(-a) *m(f)*

af·ter ['æftər] **1** *prep* después de; **~ all** después de todo; **~ that** después de eso; **it's ten ~ two** son las dos y diez **2** *adv* (*afterward*) después; **the day ~** el día siguiente

af·ter·math ['æftərmæθ] *time* periodo *m* posterior (**of** a); *state of affairs* repercusiones *fpl*

af·ter·noon [æftər'nuːn] tarde *f*; **in the ~** por la tarde; **this ~** esta tarde; **good ~** buenas tardes

'af·ter sales serv·ice servicio *m* posventa; **'af·ter·shave** loción *f* para después del afeitado, after shave *m*; **'af·ter·taste** regusto *m*

af·ter·ward ['æftərwərd] *adv* después

a·gain [ə'gein] *adv* otra vez; **I never saw him ~** no lo volví a ver

a·gainst [ə'genst] *prep lean* contra; **the USA ~ Brazil** SP Estados Unidos contra Brasil; **I'm ~ the idea** es-

toy en contra de la idea; **what do you have ~ her?** ¿que tienes en contra de ella?; **~ the law** ilegal

age [eidʒ] **1** *n of person, object* edad *f*; (*era*) era *f*; **at the ~ of ten** a los diez años; **under ~** menor de edad; **she's five years of ~** tiene cinco años **2** *v/i* envejecer

aged¹ [eidʒd] *adj*: **~ 16** con 16 años de edad

a·ged² ['eidʒid] **1** *adj*: **her ~ parents** sus ancianos padres **2** *n*: **the ~** los ancianos

'age group grupo *m* de edades

'age lim·it límite *m* de edad

a·gen·cy ['eidʒənsi] agencia *f*

a·gen·da [ə'dʒendə] orden *m* del día; **on the ~** en el orden del día

a·gent ['eidʒənt] agente *m/f*, representante *m/f*

ag·gra·vate ['ægrəveit] *v/t* agravar; (*annoy*) molestar

ag·gre·gate ['ægrigət] *n* SP: **win on ~** ganar en el total de la eliminatoria

ag·gres·sion [ə'greʃn] agresividad *f*

ag·gres·sive [ə'gresiv] *adj* agresivo; (*dynamic*) agresivo, enérgico

ag·gres·sive·ly [ə'gresivli] *adv* agresivamente

a·ghast [ə'gæst] *adj* horrorizado

ag·ile ['ædʒəl] *adj* ágil

a·gil·i·ty [ə'dʒiləti] agilidad *f*

ag·i·tate ['ædʒiteit] *v/i*: **~ for** hacer campaña a favor de

ag·i·tat·ed ['ædʒiteitid] *adj* agitado

ag·i·ta·tion [ædʒi'teiʃn] agitación *f*

ag·i·ta·tor [ædʒi'teitər] agitador(a) *m(f)*

ag·nos·tic [æg'nɑːstik] *n* agnóstico(-a) *m(f)*

a·go [ə'gou] *adv*: **2 days ~** hace dos días; **long ~** hace mucho tiempo; **how long ~?** ¿hace cuánto tiempo?; **how long ~ did he leave?** ¿hace cuánto se marchó?

a·gog [ə'gɑːg] *adj*: **be ~ at sth** estar emocionado con algo

ag·o·nize ['ægənaiz] *v/i* atormentarse (**over** por), angustiarse (**over** por)

ag·o·niz·ing ['ægənaiziŋ] *adj* pain

atroz; **wait** angustioso

ag·o·ny ['ægənɪ] agonía *f*

a·gree [ə'griː] **1** *v/i* estar de acuerdo; *of figures* coincidir; (*reach agreement*) ponerse de acuerdo; *I* ~ estoy de acuerdo; *it doesn't* ~ *with me of food* no me sienta bien **2** *v/t price* acordar; ~ *that sth should be done* acordar que hay que hacer algo

a·gree·a·ble [ə'griːəbl] *adj* (*pleasant*) agradable; *be* ~ *fml* (*in agreement*) estar de acuerdo

a·gree·ment [ə'griːmənt] (*consent, contract*) acuerdo *m*; *reach* ~ *on* llegar a un acuerdo sobre

ag·ri·cul·tur·al [ægrɪ'kʌltʃərəl] *adj* agrícola

ag·ri·cul·ture ['ægrɪkʌltʃər] agricultura *f*

a·head [ə'hed] *adv position* delante; *movement* adelante; *in race* por delante, en cabeza; *be* ~ *of* estar por delante de; *plan/think* ~ planear con antelación/pensar con anticipación

aid [eɪd] **1** *n* ayuda *f*; *come to s.o.'s* ~ acudir a ayudar a alguien **2** *v/t* ayudar

aide [eɪd] asistente *m/f*

Aids [eɪdz] *nsg* sida *m*

ail·ing ['eɪlɪŋ] *adj economy* débil, frágil

ail·ment ['eɪlmənt] achaque *m*

aim [eɪm] **1** *n in shooting* puntería *f*; (*objective*) objetivo *m* **2** *v/i in shooting* apuntar; ~ *at doing sth,* ~ *to do sth* tener como intención hacer algo **3** *v/t remark* dirigir; *he* ~*ed the gun at me* me apuntó con la pistola; *be* ~*ed at of remark etc* estar dirigido a; *of gun* estar apuntando a

aim·less ['eɪmlɪs] *adj* sin objetivos

air [er] **1** *n* aire *m*; *by* ~ *travel* en avión; *send mail* por correo aéreo; *in the open* ~ al aire libre; *on the* ~ RAD, TV en el aire **2** *v/t room* airear; *fig: views* airear, ventilar

'**air·bag** airbag *m*, bolsa *f* de aire; '**air·base** base *f* aérea; '**air·con·di-**

tioned *adj* con aire acondicionado, climatizado; '**air·con·di·tion·ing** aire *m* acondicionado; '**air·craft** avión *m*, aeronave *f*; '**air·craft car·ri·er** portaaviones *m inv*; '**air cy·lin·der** (*for diver*) escafandra *f* autónoma; '**air fare** (precio *m* del) *Span* billete *m or L.Am.* boleto *m* de avión; '**air·field** aeródromo *m*, campo *m* de aviación; '**air force** fuerza *f* aérea; '**air host·ess** azafata *f*, *L.Am.* aeromoza *f*; '**air let·ter** aerograma *m*; '**air·lift 1** *n* puente *m* aéreo **2** *v/t* transportar mediante puente aéreo; '**air·line** línea *f* aérea; '**air·lin·er** avión *m* de pasajeros; '**air·mail**: *by* ~ por correo aéreo; '**air·plane** avión *m*; '**air·pock·et** bolsa *f* de aire; '**air pol·lu·tion** contaminación *f* del aire; '**air·port** aeropuerto *m*; '**air·sick**: *get* ~ marearse (*en avión*); '**air·space** espacio *m* aéreo; '**air ter·mi·nal** terminal *f* aérea; '**air·tight** *adj container* hermético; '**air traf·fic** tráfico *m* aéreo; '**air-traf·fic con·trol** control *m* del tráfico aéreo; **air-traf·fic con·trol·ler** controlador(a) *m(f)* del tráfico aéreo

air·y ['erɪ] *adj room* aireado

aisle [aɪl] pasillo *m*

'**aisle seat** asiento *m* de pasillo

a·jar [ə'dʒɑːr] *adj*: *be* ~ estar entreabierto

a·lac·ri·ty [ə'lækrətɪ] presteza *f*

a·larm [ə'lɑːrm] **1** *n* alarma *f*; *raise the* ~ dar la alarma **2** *v/t* alarmar

a'larm clock reloj *m* despertador

a·larm·ing [ə'lɑːrmɪŋ] *adj* alarmante

a·larm·ing·ly [ə'lɑːrmɪŋlɪ] *adv* de forma alarmante

al·bum ['ælbəm] *for photographs,* (*record*) álbum *m*

al·co·hol ['ælkəhɒːl] alcohol *m*

al·co·hol·ic [ælkə'hɒːlɪk] **1** *n* alcohólico(-a) *m(f)* **2** *adj* alcohólico

a·lert [ə'lɜːrt] **1** *n signal* alerta *f*; *be on the* ~ estar alerta **2** *v/t* alertar **3** *adj* alerta

al·ge·bra ['ældʒɪbrə] álgebra *f*

al·i·bi ['ælɪbaɪ] coartada *f*

a·li·en ['eɪlɪən] **1** *n* (*foreigner*) extranjero(-a) *m(f)*; *from space* extraterrestre *m/f* **2** *adj* extraño; *be* ~ *to s.o.* ser ajeno a alguien

a·li·en·ate ['eɪlɪəneɪt] *v/t* alienar, provocar el distanciamiento de

a·light [ə'laɪt] *adj* en llamas

a·lign [ə'laɪn] *v/t* alinear

a·like [ə'laɪk] **1** *adj:* *be* ~ parecerse **2** *adv* igual; *old and young* ~ viejos y jóvenes sin distinción

al·i·mo·ny ['ælɪmənɪ] pensión *f* alimenticia

a·live [ə'laɪv] *adj:* *be* ~ estar vivo

all [ɔːl] **1** *adj* todo(s) **2** *pron* todo; ~ *of us / them* todos nosotros / ellos; *he ate* ~ *of it* se lo comió todo; *that's* ~, *thanks* eso es todo, gracias; *for* ~ *I care* para lo que me importa; *for* ~ *I know* por lo que sé **3** *adv:* ~ *at once* (*suddenly*) de repente; (*at the same time*) a la vez; ~ *but* (*except*) todos menos; (*nearly*) casi; ~ *the better* mucho mejor; ~ *the time* desde el principio; *they're not at* ~ *alike* no se parecen en nada; *not at* ~! ¡en absoluto!; *two* – SP empate a dos; ~ *right* → *alright*

al·lay [ə'leɪ] *v/t* apaciguar

al·le·ga·tion [ælɪ'geɪʃn] acusación *f*

al·lege [ə'ledʒ] *v/t* alegar

al·leged [ə'ledʒd] *adj* presunto

al·leg·ed·ly [ə'ledʒɪdlɪ] *adv* presuntamente, supuestamente

al·le·giance [ə'liːdʒəns] lealtad *f*

al·ler·gic [ə'lɜːrdʒɪk] *adj* alérgico; *be* ~ *to* ser alérgico a

al·ler·gy ['ælərdʒɪ] alergia *f*

al·le·vi·ate [ə'liːvɪeɪt] *v/t* aliviar

al·ley ['ælɪ] callejón *m*

al·li·ance [ə'laɪəns] alianza *f*

al·lo·cate ['æləkeɪt] *v/t* asignar

al·lo·ca·tion [æləˈkeɪʃn] asignación *f*

al·lot [ə'lɑːt] *v/t* (*pret & pp* -**ted**) asignar

al·low [ə'laʊ] *v/t* (*permit*) permitir; (*calculate for*) calcular; *it's not* ~*ed* no está permitido; *he* ~*ed us to leave* nos permitió salir

♦ **allow for** *v/t* tener en cuenta

al·low·ance [ə'laʊəns] (*money*) asig-

nación *f*; (*pocket money*) paga *f*; *make* ~*s for weather etc* tener en cuenta; *for person* disculpar

al·loy ['ælɔɪ] aleación *f*

'all-pur·pose *adj* multiuso; **'all-round** *adj* completo; **'all-time**: *be at an* ~ *low* haber alcanzado un mínimo histórico

♦ **al·lude to** [ə'luːd] *v/t* aludir a

al·lur·ing [ə'lʊrɪŋ] *adj* atractivo, seductor

all-wheel 'drive *adj* con tracción a las cuatro ruedas

al·ly ['ælaɪ] *n* aliado(-a) *m(f)*

al·mond ['ɑːmənd] almendra *f*

al·most ['ɔːlmoʊst] *adv* casi

a·lone [ə'loʊn] *adj* solo

a·long [ə'lɒːŋ] **1** *prep* (*situated beside*) a lo largo de; *walk* ~ *this path* sigue por esta calle **2** *adv*: *would you like to come* ~? ¿te gustaría venir con nosotros?; *he always brings the dog* ~ siempre trae al perro; ~ *with* junto con; *all* ~ (*all the time*) todo el tiempo, desde el principio

a·long·side [ələːŋˈsaɪd] *prep* (*in cooperation with*) junto a; (*parallel to*) al lado de

a·loof [ə'luːf] *adj* distante, reservado

a·loud [ə'laʊd] *adv* en voz alta

al·pha·bet ['ælfəbet] alfabeto *m*

al·pha·bet·i·cal [ælfə'betɪkl] *adj* alfabético

al·read·y [ɒl'redɪ] *adv* ya

al·right [ɒl'raɪt] *adj* (*not hurt, in working order*) bien; *is it* ~ *to leave now?* (*permitted*) ¿puedo irme ahora?; *is it* ~ *to take these out of the country?* ¿se pueden sacar éstos del país?; *is it* ~ *with you if I ...?* ¿te importa si ...?; ~, *you can have one!* de acuerdo, ¡puedes tomar uno!; ~, *I heard you!* vale, ¡te he oído!; *everything is* ~ *now between them* vuelven a estar bien; *that's* ~ (*don't mention it*) de nada; (*I don't mind*) no importa

al·so ['ɒːlsoʊ] *adv* también

al·tar ['ɒːltər] altar *m*

al·ter ['ɒːltər] *v/t* alterar

al·ter·a·tion [ɒːltə'reɪʃn] alteración f

al·ter·nate 1 v/i ['ɒːltərneɪt] alternar **2** adj ['ɒːltərnət] alterno

al·ter·nat·ing cur·rent ['ɒːltərneɪtɪŋ] corriente f alterna

al·ter·na·tive [ɒːlt'ɜːrnətɪv] **1** n alternativa f **2** adj alternativo

al·ter·na·tive·ly [ɒːlt'ɜːrnətɪvlɪ] adv si no

al·though [ɒːl'ðoʊ] conj aunque, si bien

al·ti·tude ['æltɪtuːd] of plane, city altitud f; of mountain altura f

al·to·geth·er [ɒːltə'geðər] adv (completely) completamente; (in all) en total

al·tru·ism ['æltruːɪzm] altruismo m

al·tru·is·tic [æltruː'ɪstɪk] adj altruista

a·lu·min·i·um [æljʊ'mɪnɪəm] Br, **a·lu·mi·num** [ə'luːmənəm] aluminio m

al·ways ['ɒːlweɪz] adv siempre

a.m. ['eɪem] abbr (= **ante meridiem**) a.m.; **at 11** ~ a las 11 de la mañana

am·a·teur ['æmətʃʊr] n unskilled aficionado(-a) m(f); SP amateur m/f

am·a·teur·ish ['æmətʃʊrɪʃ] adj pej chapucero

a·maze [ə'meɪz] v/t asombrar

a·mazed [ə'meɪzd] adj asombrado; **we were ~ to hear …** nos asombró oír …

a·maze·ment [ə'meɪzmənt] asombro m

a·maz·ing [ə'meɪzɪŋ] adj (surprising) asombroso; F (very good) alucinante F

a·maz·ing·ly [ə'meɪzɪŋlɪ] adv increíblemente

Am·a·zon ['æməzən] n: **the** ~ el Amazonas

Am·a·zo·ni·an [æmə'zoʊnɪən] adj amazónico

am·bas·sa·dor [æm'bæsədər] embajador(a) m(f)

am·ber ['æmbər] adj ámbar; **at** ~ en

ámbar

am·bi·dex·trous [æmbɪ'dekstrəs] adj ambidiestro

am·bi·ence ['æmbɪəns] ambiente m

am·bi·gu·i·ty [æmbɪ'gjuːətɪ] ambigüedad f

am·big·u·ous [æm'bɪgjʊəs] adj ambiguo

am·bi·tion [æm'bɪʃn] also pej ambición f

am·bi·tious [æm'bɪʃəs] adj ambicioso

am·biv·a·lent [æm'bɪvələnt] adj ambivalente

am·ble ['æmbl] v/i deambular

am·bu·lance ['æmbjʊləns] ambulancia f

am·bush ['æmbʊʃ] **1** n emboscada f **2** v/t tender una emboscada a

a·mend [ə'mend] v/t enmendar

a·mend·ment [ə'mendmənt] enmienda f

a·mends [ə'mendz] npl: **make ~ for** compensar

a·men·i·ties [ə'miːnətɪz] npl servicios mpl

A·mer·i·ca [ə'merɪkə] continent América; USA Estados mpl Unidos

A·mer·i·can [ə'merɪkən] **1** adj North American estadounidense **2** n North American estadounidense m/f

A'mer·i·can plan pensión f completa

a·mi·a·ble ['eɪmɪəbl] adj afable, amable

a·mi·ca·ble ['æmɪkəbl] adj amistoso

a·mi·ca·bly ['æmɪkəblɪ] adv amistosamente

am·mu·ni·tion [æmjʊ'nɪʃn] munición f, fig argumentos mpl

am·ne·sia [æm'niːzɪə] amnesia f

am·nes·ty ['æmnəstɪ] amnistía f

a·mong(st) [ə'mʌŋ(st)] prep entre

a·mor·al [eɪ'mɒːrəl] adj amoral

a·mount [ə'maʊnt] cantidad f; (sum of money) cantidad f, suma f

♦**amount to** v/t ascender a; **his contribution didn't amount to much** su contribución no fue gran cosa

am·phib·i·an [æm'fɪbɪən] anfibio m

am·phib·i·ous [æm'fɪbɪəs] *adj animal, vehicle* anfibio

am·phi·the·a·tre ['æmfɪθɪətər] *Br* **am·phi·the·a·tre** ['æmfɪθɪətər] anfiteatro *m*

am·ple ['æmpl] *adj* abundante; **$4 will be ~** 4 dólares serán más que suficientes

am·pli·fi·er ['æmplɪfaɪr] amplificador *m*

am·pli·fy ['æmplɪfaɪ] *v/t* (*pret & pp* **-ied**) *sound* amplificar

am·pu·tate ['æmpjuteɪt] *v/t* amputar

am·pu·ta·tion [æmpju'teɪʃn] amputación *f*

a·muse [ə'mjuːz] *v/t* (*make laugh etc*) divertir; (*entertain*) entretener

a·muse·ment [ə'mjuːzmənt] (*merriment*) diversión *f*; (*entertainment*) entretenimiento *m*; **~s** (*games*) juegos *mpl*; **what do you do for ~?** ¿qué haces para entretenerte?; **to our great ~** para nuestro regocijo

a'muse·ment ar·cade [ɑːr'keɪd] salón *m* de juegos recreativos

a'muse·ment park parque *m* de atracciones

a·mus·ing [ə'mjuːzɪŋ] *adj* divertido

an [æn] *unstressed* [ən] → **a**

an·a·bol·ic ster·oid [ænə'bɑːlɪk] esteroide *m* anabolizante

a·nae·mi·a *etc Br* → **anemia** *etc*

an·aes·thet·ic *etc Br* → **anesthetic** *etc*

an·a·log ['ænəlɔːg] *adj* analógico

a·nal·o·gy [ə'nælədʒɪ] analogía *f*

a·nal·y·sis [ə'næləsɪs] (*pl* **analyses** [ə'næləsiːz]) análisis *m inv*; (*psychoanalysis*) psicoanálisis *m inv*

an·a·lyst ['ænəlɪst] analista *m/f*; PSYCH psicoanalista *m/f*

an·a·lyt·i·cal [ænə'lɪtɪkl] *adj* analítico

an·a·lyze ['ænəlaɪz] *v/t* analizar; (*psychoanalyse*) psicoanalizar

an·arch·y ['ænərkɪ] anarquía *f*

a·nat·o·my [ə'nætəmɪ] anatomía *f*

an·ces·tor ['ænsestər] antepasado(-a) *m(f)*

an·chor ['æŋkər] **1** *n* NAUT ancla *f*; TV presentador(a) *m(f)* **2** *v/i* NAUT anclar

an·cient ['eɪnʃənt] *adj* antiguo

an·cil·lar·y [æn'sɪlərɪ] *adj staff* auxiliar

and [ənd] *stressed* [ænd] *conj* y

An·de·an ['ændɪən] *adj* andino

An·des ['ændiːz] *npl*: **the ~** los Andes

an·ec·dote ['ænɪkdoʊt] anécdota *f*

a·ne·mia [ə'niːmɪə] anemia *f*

a·ne·mic [ə'niːmɪk] *adj* anémico

an·es·thet·ic [ænəs'θetɪk] *n* anestesia *f*

an·es·the·tist [ə'niːsθətɪst] anestesista *m/f*

an·gel ['eɪndʒl] REL ángel *m*; *fig* ángel *m*, cielo *m*

an·ger ['æŋgər] **1** *n* enfado *m*, enojo *m* **2** *v/t* enfadar, enojar

an·gi·na [æn'dʒaɪnə] angina *f* (de pecho)

an·gle ['æŋgl] *n* ángulo *m*

an·gry ['æŋgrɪ] *adj* enfadado, enojado; **be ~ with s.o.** estar enfadado *or* enojado con alguien

an·guish ['æŋgwɪʃ] angustia *f*

an·gu·lar ['æŋgjʊlər] *adj* anguloso

an·i·mal ['ænɪml] animal *m*

an·i·ma·ted ['ænɪmeɪtɪd] *adj* animado

an·i·ma·ted car'toon dibujos *mpl* animados

an·i·ma·tion [ænɪ'meɪʃn] (*liveliness*), *of cartoon* animación *f*

an·i·mos·i·ty [ænɪ'mɑːsətɪ] animosidad *f*

an·kle ['æŋkl] tobillo *m*

an·nex ['æneks] **1** *n building* edificio *m* anexo **2** *v/t state* anexionar

an·nexe ['æneks] *n Br* edificio *m* anexo

an·ni·hi·late [ə'naɪəleɪt] *v/t* aniquilar

an·ni·hi·la·tion [ənaɪə'leɪʃn] aniquilación *f*

an·ni·ver·sa·ry [ænɪ'vɜːrsərɪ] (*wedding ~*) aniversario *m*

an·no·tate ['ænəteɪt] *v/t report* anotar

an·nounce [ə'naʊns] *v/t* anunciar

an·nounce·ment [ə'naʊnsmənt] anuncio *m*

an·nounc·er [ə'naʊnsər] TV, RAD

presentador(a) *m(f)*

an·noy [ə'nɔɪ] *v/t* molestar, irritar; **be ~ed** estar molesto *or* irritado

an·noy·ance [ə'nɔɪəns] *(anger)* irritación *f*, *(nuisance)* molestia *f*

an·noy·ing [ə'nɔɪɪŋ] *adj* molesto, irritante

an·nu·al ['ænʊəl] *adj* anual

an·nu·i·ty [ə'nuːətɪ] anualidad *f*

an·nul [ə'nʌl] *v/t (pret & pp -led) marriage* anular

an·nul·ment [ə'nʌlmənt] anulación *f*

a·non·y·mous [ə'nɑːnɪməs] *adj* anónimo

an·o·rak ['ænəræk] *Br* anorak *m*

an·o·rex·i·a [ænə'reksɪə] anorexia *f*

an·o·rex·ic [ænə'reksɪk] *adj* anoréxico

an·oth·er [ə'nʌðər] **1** *adj* otro **2** *pron* otro(-a) *m(f)*; **they helped one ~** se ayudaron (el uno al otro); **do they know one ~?** ¿se conocen?

ans·wer ['ænsər] **1** *n to letter, person, question* respuesta *f*, contestación *f*; *to problem* solución *f* **2** *v/t letter, person, question* responder, contestar; **~ the door** abrir la puerta; **~ the telephone** responder *or Span* coger al teléfono
- **answer back** *v/t & v/i* contestar, replicar
- **answer for** *v/t* responder de

ans·wer·phone ['ænsərfoʊn] TELEC contestador *m* (automático)

ant [ænt] hormiga *f*

an·tag·o·nism [æn'tægənɪzm] antagonismo *m*

an·tag·o·nis·tic [æntægə'nɪstɪk] *adj* hostil

an·tag·o·nize [æn'tægənaɪz] *v/t* antagonizar, enfadar

Ant·arc·tic [ænt'ɑːrktɪk] *n*: **the ~** el Antártico

an·te·na·tal [æntɪ'neɪtl] *adj* prenatal

an·ten·na [æn'tenə] *of insect, for TV* antena *f*

an·thol·o·gy [æn'θɑːlədʒɪ] antología *f*

an·thro·pol·o·gy [ænθrə'pɑːlədʒɪ] antropología *f*

an·ti·bi·ot·ic [æntɪbaɪ'ɑːtɪk] *n* anti-

biótico *m*

an·ti·bod·y ['æntɪbɑːdɪ] anticuerpo *m*

an·tic·i·pate [æn'tɪsɪpeɪt] *v/t* esperar, prever

an·tic·i·pa·tion [æntɪsɪ'peɪʃn] expectativa *f*, previsión *f*

an·ti·clock·wise ['æntɪklɑː kwaɪz] *adv Br* en dirección contraria a las agujas del reloj

an·tics ['æntɪks] *npl* payasadas *fpl*

an·ti·dote ['æntɪdoʊt] antídoto *m*

an·ti·freeze ['æntɪfriːz] anticongelante *m*

an·tip·a·thy [æn'tɪpəθɪ] antipatía *f*

an·ti·quat·ed ['æntɪkweɪtɪd] *adj* anticuado

an·tique [æn'tiːk] *n* antigüedad *f*

an'tique deal·er anticuario(-a) *m(f)*

an·tiq·ui·ty [æn'tɪkwətɪ] antigüedad *f*

an·ti·sep·tic [æntɪ'septɪk] **1** *adj* antiséptico **2** *n* antiséptico *m*

an·ti·so·cial [æntɪ'soʊʃl] *adj* antisocial, poco sociable

an·ti·vi·rus pro·gram [æntɪ'vaɪrəs] COMPUT (programa *m*) antivirus *m inv*

anx·i·e·ty [æŋ'zaɪətɪ] ansiedad *f*

anx·ious ['æŋkʃəs] *adj* preocupado; *(eager)* ansioso; **be ~ for** *for news etc* esperar ansiosamente

an·y ['enɪ] **1** *adj*: **are there ~ diskettes / glasses?** ¿hay disquetes / vasos?; **is there ~ bread / improvement?** ¿hay algo de pan / alguna mejora?; **there aren't ~ diskettes / glasses** no hay disquetes / vasos; **there isn't ~ bread / improvement** no hay pan / ninguna mejora; **have you ~ idea at all?** ¿tienes alguna idea?; **~ one of them could win** cualquiera de ellos podría ganar **2** *pron* alguno(-a); **do you have ~?** ¿tienes alguno(s)?; **there aren't ~ left** no queda ninguno; **there isn't ~ left** no queda; **~ of them could be guilty** cualquiera de ellos podría ser culpable **3** *adv*: **is that ~ better / easier?** ¿es mejor / más fácil así?; **I**

don't like it ~ more ya no me gusta
an·y·bod·y ['enɪbɒːdɪ] *pron* alguien;
there wasn't ~ there no había nadie allí
an·y·how ['enɪhaʊ] *adv* en todo caso, de todos modos; *if I can help you ~, please let me know* si puedo ayudarte de alguna manera, por favor dímelo
an·y·one ['enɪwʌn] → *anybody*
an·y·thing ['enɪθɪŋ] *pron* algo; *with negatives* nada; *I didn't hear ~* no oí nada; *~ but* todo menos; *~ else?* ¿algo más?
an·y·way ['enɪweɪ] → *anyhow*
an·y·where ['enɪweɪr] *adv* en alguna parte; *is Peter ~ around?* ¿está Peter por ahí?; *he never goes ~* nunca va a ninguna parte; *I can't find it ~* no lo encuentro por ninguna parte
a·part [ə'pɑːrt] *adv* aparte; *the two cities are 250 miles ~* las dos ciudades están a 250 millas la una de la otra; *live ~ of people* vivir separado; *~ from* aparte de
a·part·ment [ə'pɑːrtmənt] apartamento *m*, Span piso *m*
a·part·ment block bloque *m* de apartamentos *or* Span pisos
ap·a·thet·ic [æpə'θetɪk] *adj* apático
ap·a·thy ['æpəθɪ] apatía *f*
ape [eɪp] simio *m*
a·pe·ri·tif [ə'perɪtiːf] aperitivo *m*
ap·er·ture ['æpərtʃər] PHOT apertura *f*
a·piece [ə'piːs] *adv* cada uno
a·pol·o·get·ic [əpɑːlə'dʒetɪk] *adj letter* de disculpa; *he was very ~ about ...* pedía constantes disculpas por ...
a·pol·o·gize [ə'pɑːlədʒaɪz] *v/i* disculparse, pedir perdón
a·pol·o·gy [ə'pɑːlədʒɪ] disculpa *f*; *owe s.o. an ~* deber disculpas a alguien
a·pos·tle [ə'pɑːsl] REL apóstol *m*
a·pos·tro·phe [ə'pɑːstrəfɪ] GRAM apóstrofo *m*
ap·pall [ə'pɒːl] *v/t* horrorizar, espantar

ap·pal·ling [ə'pɒːlɪŋ] *adj* horroroso
ap·pa·ra·tus [æpə'reɪtəs] aparatos *mpl*
ap·par·ent [ə'pærənt] *adj* aparente, evidente; *become ~ that* hacerse evidente que
ap·par·ent·ly [ə'pærəntlɪ] *adv* al parecer, por lo visto
ap·pa·ri·tion [æpə'rɪʃn] *(ghost)* aparición *f*
ap·peal [ə'piːl] **1** *n (charm)* atractivo *m*; *for funds etc* llamamiento *m*; LAW apelación *f* **2** *v/i* LAW apelar
♦ **appeal for** *v/t* solicitar
♦ **appeal to** *v/t (be attractive to)* atraer a
ap·peal·ing [ə'piːlɪŋ] *adj idea, offer* atractivo; *glance* suplicante
ap·pear [ə'pɪr] *v/i* aparecer; *in court* comparecer; *(look, seem)* parecer; *it ~s that ...* parece que ...
ap·pear·ance [ə'pɪrəns] aparición *f*; *in court* comparecencia *f*; *(look)* apariencia *f*, aspecto *m*; *put in an ~* hacer acto de presencia
ap·pease [ə'piːz] *v/t* apaciguar
ap·pen·di·ci·tis [əpendɪ'saɪtɪs] apendicitis *m*
ap·pen·dix [ə'pendɪks] MED, *of book* apéndice *m*
ap·pe·tite ['æpɪtaɪt] *also fig* apetito *m*
ap·pe·tiz·er ['æpɪtaɪzər] aperitivo *m*
ap·pe·tiz·ing ['æpɪtaɪzɪŋ] *adj* apetitoso
ap·plaud [ə'plɒːd] **1** *v/i* aplaudir **2** *v/t also fig* aplaudir
ap·plause [ə'plɒːz] aplauso *m*
ap·ple ['æpl] manzana *f*
ap·ple 'pie tarta *f* de manzana
ap·ple 'sauce compota *f* de manzana
ap·pli·ance [ə'plaɪəns] aparato *m*; *household* electrodoméstico *m*
ap·plic·a·ble [ə'plɪkəbl] *adj* aplicable; *it's not ~ to foreigners* no se aplica a extranjeros
ap·pli·cant ['æplɪkənt] solicitante *m/f*
ap·pli·ca·tion [æplɪ'keɪʃn] *for job, passport etc* solicitud *f*; *for university*

solicitud *f* (de admisión)

ap·pli'ca·tion form *for passport etc* impreso *m* de solicitud; *for university* impreso *m* de solicitud de admisión

ap·ply [əˈplaɪ] **1** *v/t* (*pret & pp* **-ied**) *rules, solution, ointment* aplicar **2** *v/i* (*pret & pp* **-ied**) *of rule, law* aplicarse

♦ **apply for** *v/t* *job, passport* solicitar; *university* solicitar el ingreso en

♦ **apply to** *v/t* (*contact*) dirigirse a; (*affect*) aplicarse a

ap·point [əˈpɔɪnt] *v/t to position* nombrar, designar

ap·point·ment [əˈpɔɪntmənt] *to position* nombramiento *m*, designación *f*; *meeting* cita *f*; **make an ~ with the doctor** pedir hora con el doctor

ap'point·ments di·a·ry agenda *f* de citas

ap·prais·al [əˈpreɪz(ə)l] evaluación *f*

ap·pre·cia·ble [əˈpriːʃəbl] *adj* apreciable

ap·pre·ci·ate [əˈpriːʃɪeɪt] **1** *v/t* (*value*) apreciar; (*be grateful for*) agradecer; (*acknowledge*) ser consciente de; **thanks, I ~ it** te lo agradezco **2** *v/i* FIN revalorizarse

ap·pre·ci·a·tion [əˌpriːʃɪˈeɪʃn] *of kindness etc* agradecimiento *m*; *of music etc* aprecio *m*

ap·pre·ci·a·tive [əˈpriːʃətɪv] *adj* agradecido

ap·pre·hen·sive [æprɪˈhensɪv] *adj* aprensivo, temeroso

ap·pren·tice [əˈprentɪs] aprendiz(a) *m(f)*

ap·proach [əˈprəʊtʃ] **1** *n* aproximación *f*; (*proposal*) propuesta *f*; *to problem* enfoque *m* **2** *v/t* (*get near to*) aproximarse a; (*contact*) ponerse en contacto con; *problem* enfocar

ap·proach·a·ble [əˈprəʊtʃəbl] *person* accesible

ap·pro·pri·ate¹ [əˈprəʊprɪət] *adj* apropiado, adecuado

ap·pro·pri·ate² [əˈprəʊprɪeɪt] *v/t also euph* apropiarse de

ap·prov·al [əˈpruːvl] aprobación *f*

ap·prove [əˈpruːv] **1** *v/i*: **my parents don't ~** a mis padres no les parece bien **2** *v/t* aprobar

♦ **approve of** *v/t* aprobar; **her parents don't approve of me** no les gusto a sus padres

ap·prox·i·mate [əˈprɑːksɪmət] *adj* aproximado

ap·prox·i·mate·ly [əˈprɑːksɪmətlɪ] *adv* aproximadamente

ap·prox·i·ma·tion [əprɑːksɪˈmeɪʃn] aproximación *f*

APR [eɪpiːˈɑː] *abbr* (= **annual percentage rate**) TAE *f* (= tasa *f* anual equivalente)

a·pri·cot [ˈæprɪkɑːt] albaricoque *m*, *L.Am.* damasco *m*

A·pril [ˈeɪprəl] abril *m*

apt [æpt] *adj remark* oportuno; **be ~ to ...** ser propenso a ...

ap·ti·tude [ˈæptɪtuːd] aptitud *f*; **he has a natural ~ for ...** tiene aptitudes naturales para ...

'ap·ti·tude test prueba *f* de aptitud

a·quar·i·um [əˈkweriəm] acuario *m*

A·quar·i·us [əˈkweriəs] ASTR Acuario *m/f inv*

a·quat·ic [əˈkwætɪk] *adj* acuático

Ar·ab [ˈærəb] **1** *adj* árabe **2** *n* árabe *m/f*

Ar·a·bic [ˈærəbɪk] **1** *adj* árabe **2** *n* árabe *m*

ar·a·ble [ˈærəbl] *adj* arable, cultivable

ar·bi·tra·ry [ˈɑːrbɪtrerɪ] *adj* arbitrario

ar·bi·trate [ˈɑːrbɪtreɪt] *v/i* arbitrar

ar·bi·tra·tion [ɑːrbɪˈtreɪʃn] arbitraje *m*

ar·bi·tra·tor [ˈɑːrbɪˈtreɪtər] árbitro(-a) *m(f)*

arch [ɑːrtʃ] *n* arco *m*

ar·chae·ol·o·gy *etc Br* → **archeology** *etc*

ar·cha·ic [ɑːrˈkeɪɪk] *adj* arcaico

ar·che·o·log·i·cal [ɑːrkɪəˈlɑːdʒɪkl] *adj* arqueológico

ar·che·ol·o·gist [ɑːrkɪˈɑːlədʒɪst] arqueólogo(-a) *m(f)*

ar·che·ol·o·gy [ɑːrkɪˈɑːlədʒɪ] arqueología *f*

ar·cher ['ɑːrtʃər] arquero(-a) m(f)

ar·chi·tect ['ɑːrkɪtekt] arquitecto(-a) m(f)

ar·chi·tec·tur·al [ɑːrkɪ'tektʃərəl] adj arquitectónico

ar·chi·tec·ture ['ɑːrkɪtektʃər] arquitectura f

ar·chives ['ɑːrkaɪvz] npl archivos mpl

arch·way ['ɑːrtʃweɪ] arco m

Arc·tic ['ɑːrktɪk] n: **the** ~ el Ártico

ar·dent ['ɑːrdənt] adj ardiente, ferviente

ar·du·ous ['ɑːrdjuəs] adj arduo

ar·e·a ['eɪrɪə] área f, zona f; of activity, study etc área f, ámbito m

'ar·e·a code TELEC prefijo m

a·re·na [ə'riːnə] SP estadio m

Ar·gen·ti·na [ɑːrdʒən'tiːnə] Argentina

Ar·gen·tin·i·an [ɑːrdʒən'tɪnɪən] **1** adj argentino **2** n argentino(-a) m(f)

ar·gu·a·bly ['ɑːrgjuəblɪ] adv posiblemente

ar·gue ['ɑːrgjuː] **1** v/i (quarrel) discutir; (reason) argumentar **2** v/t: ~ **that** argumentar que ...

ar·gu·ment ['ɑːrgjumənt] (quarrel) discusión f; (reasoning) argumento m

ar·gu·men·ta·tive [ɑːrgjuˈmentətɪv] adj discutidor

a·ri·a ['ɑːrɪə] MUS aria f

ar·id ['ærɪd] adj land árido

Ar·i·es ['eriːz] ASTR Aries m/f inv

a·rise [ə'raɪz] v/i (pret **arose**, pp **arisen**) of situation, problem surgir

a·ris·en [ə'rɪzn] pp → **arise**

ar·is·toc·ra·cy [ærɪ'stɑːkrəsɪ] aristocracia f

ar·is·to·crat [ə'rɪstəkræt] aristócrata m/f

a·ris·to·crat·ic [ærɪstə'krætɪk] adj aristocrático

a·rith·me·tic [ə'rɪθmətɪk] aritmética f

arm[1] [ɑːrm] n of person, chair brazo m

arm[2] [ɑːrm] v/t armar

ar·ma·ments ['ɑːrməmənts] npl armamento m

arm·chair ['ɑːrmtʃer] sillón m

armed [ɑːrmd] adj armado

armed 'forc·es npl fuerzas fpl armadas

armed 'rob·ber·y atraco m a mano armada

ar·mor, Br **ar·mour** ['ɑːrmər] armadura f

ar·mored 've·hi·cle, Br **ar·moured 've·hi·cle** ['ɑːrmərd] vehículo m blindado

arm·pit ['ɑːrmpɪt] sobaco m

arms [ɑːrmz] npl (weapons) armas fpl

ar·my ['ɑːrmɪ] ejército m

a·ro·ma [ə'roumə] aroma m

a·rose [ə'rouz] pret → **arise**

a·round [ə'raund] **1** prep (enclosing) alrededor de; **it's ~ the corner** está a la vuelta de la esquina; **he lives ~ here** vive por aquí **2** adv (in the area) por ahí; (encircling) alrededor; (roughly) alrededor de, aproximadamente; (with expressions of time) en torno a; **walk ~** pasear; **she has been ~** (has traveled, is experienced) tiene mucho mundo; **he's still ~** F (alive) todavía está rondando por ahí F

a·rouse [ə'rauz] v/t despertar; sexually excitar

ar·range [ə'reɪndʒ] v/t (put in order) ordenar; furniture ordenar, disponer; flowers, music arreglar; meeting, party etc organizar; time and place acordar; **I've ~d to meet her** he quedado con ella

♦ **arrange for** v/t: **I arranged for Jack to collect it** quedé para que Jack lo recogiera

ar·range·ment [ə'reɪndʒmənt] (plan) plan m, preparativo m; (agreement) acuerdo m; (layout: of furniture etc) orden m, disposición f; of flowers, music arreglo m; **I've made ~s for the neighbors to water my plants** he quedado con los vecinos para que rieguen mis plantas

ar·rears [ə'rɪərz] npl atrasos mpl; **be in ~** of person ir atrasado

ar·rest [ə'rest] **1** *n* detención *f*, arresto *m*; **be under ~** estar detenido *or* arrestado **2** *v/t* detener, arrestar

ar·riv·al [ə'raɪvl] llegada *f*; **on your ~** al llegar; **~s** *at airport* llegadas *fsg*

ar·rive [ə'raɪv] *v/i* llegar

♦ **arrive at** *v/t place, decision etc* llegar a

ar·ro·gance ['ærəgəns] arrogancia *f*

ar·ro·gant ['ærəgənt] *adj* arrogante

ar·ro·gant·ly ['ærəgəntlɪ] *adv* con arrogancia

ar·row ['ærou] flecha *f*

arse [ɑːrs] *Br* P culo *m* P

ar·se·nic ['ɑːrsənɪk] arsénico *m*

ar·son ['ɑːrsn] incendio *m* provocado

ar·son·ist ['ɑːrsənɪst] pirómano(-a) *m(f)*

art [ɑːrt] arte *m*; **the ~s** las artes

ar·te·ry ['ɑːrtərɪ] MED arteria *f*

'art gal·ler·y *public* museo *m*; *private* galería *f* de arte

ar·thri·tis [ɑːr'θraɪtɪs] artritis *f*

ar·ti·choke ['ɑːrtɪʧouk] alcachofa *f*, *L.Am.* alcaucil *m*

ar·ti·cle ['ɑːrtɪkl] artículo *m*

ar·tic·u·late [ɑːr'tɪkjulət] *adj person* elocuente

ar·ti·fi·cial [ɑːrtɪ'fɪʃl] *adj* artificial

ar·ti·fi·cial in·tel·li·gence inteligencia *f* artificial

ar·til·le·ry [ɑːr'tɪlərɪ] artillería *f*

ar·ti·san ['ɑːrtɪzæn] artesano(-a) *m(f)*

ar·tist ['ɑːrtɪst] (*painter, artistic person*) artista *m/f*

ar·tis·tic [ɑːr'tɪstɪk] *adj* artístico

'arts de·gree licenciatura *f* en letras

as [æz] **1** *conj* (*while, when*) cuando; (*because, like*) como; ~ **if** como si; ~ **usual** como de costumbre; ~ **necessary** como sea necesario **2** *adv* como; ~ **high** / **pretty** ~ ... tan alto / guapa como ...; ~ **much** ~ **that?** ¿tanto? **3** *prep* como; **work** ~ **a team** trabajar en equipo; ~ **a child** / **schoolgirl** cuando era un niño / una colegiala; **work** ~ **a teacher** / **translator** trabajar como profesor / traductor; ~ **for** por lo

que respecta a; ~ **Hamlet** en el papel del Hamlet

asap ['eɪzæp] *abbr* (= **as soon as possible**) cuanto antes

as·bes·tos [æz'bestɑːs] amianto *m*, asbesto *m*

As·cen·sion [ə'senʃn] REL Ascensión *f*

ash [æʃ] ceniza *f*; **~es** *of person* cenizas *fpl*

a·shamed [ə'ʃeɪmd] *adj* avergonzado, *L.Am.* apenado; **be ~ of** estar avergonzado *or L.Am.* apenado de; **you should be ~ of yourself** debería darte vergüenza *or L.Am.* pena; **it's nothing to be ~ of** no tienes por qué avergonzarte *or L.Am.* apenarte

'ash can cubo *m* de la basura

a·shore [ə'ʃɔːr] *adv* en tierra; **go ~** desembarcar

ash·tray ['æʃtreɪ] cenicero *m*

A·sia ['eɪʃə] Asia

A·sian ['eɪʃən] **1** *adj* asiático **2** *n* asiático(-a) *m(f)*

a·side [ə'saɪd] *adv* a un lado; **move ~ please** apártense, por favor; **he took me ~** me llevó aparte; ~ **from** aparte de

ask [æsk] **1** *v/t person* preguntar; *question* hacer; (*invite*) invitar; *favor* pedir; **can I ~ you something?** ¿puedo hacerte una pregunta?; ~ *s.o.* **for sth** pedir algo a alguien; **he ~ed me to leave** me pidió que me fuera; ~ *s.o.* **about sth** preguntar por algo a alguien **2** *v/i*: **all you need to do is ~** no tienes más que pedirlo

♦ **ask after** *v/t person* preguntar por

♦ **ask for** *v/t* pedir; *person* preguntar por

♦ **ask out** *v/t* invitar a salir

ask·ing price ['æskɪŋ] precio *m* de salida

a·sleep [ə'sliːp] *adj* dormido; **be (fast) ~** estar (profundamente) dormido; **fall ~** dormirse, quedarse dormido

as·par·a·gus [ə'spærəgəs] espárragos *mpl*

as·pect ['æspɛkt] aspecto *m*

as·phalt ['æsfælt] *n* asfalto *m*

as·phyx·i·ate [æ'sfiksieit] *v/t* asfixiar

as·phyx·i·a·tion [əsfiksi'eiʃn] asfixia *f*

as·pi·ra·tion [æspə'reiʃn] aspiración *f*

as·pi·rin ['æsprin] aspirina *f*

ass¹ [æs] (*idiot*) burro(-a) *m(f)*

ass² [æs] P (*backside*) culo P; (*sex*) sexo *m*

as·sai·lant [ə'seilənt] asaltante *m/f*

as·sas·sin [ə'sæsin] asesino(-a) *m(f)*

as·sas·sin·ate [ə'sæsineit] *v/t* asesinar

as·sas·sin·a·tion [əsæsi'neiʃn] asesinato *m*

as·sault [ə'sɒːlt] **1** *n* agresión *f*; (*attack*) ataque *m* **2** *v/t* atacar, agredir

as·sem·ble [ə'sembl] **1** *v/t parts* montar **2** *v/i of people* reunirse

as·sem·bly [ə'sembli] *of parts* montaje *m*; POL asamblea *f*

as'sem·bly line cadena *f* de montaje

as'sem·bly plant planta *f* de montaje

as·sent [ə'sent] *v/i* asentir, dar el consentimiento

as·sert [ə'sɜːrt] *v/t* afirmar, hacer valer; ~ *o.s.* mostrarse firme

as·ser·tive [ə'sɜːrtiv] *adj person* seguro y firme

as·sess [ə'ses] *v/t situation* evaluar; *value* valorar

as·sess·ment [ə'sesmənt] evaluación *f*

as·set ['æset] FIN activo *m*; *fig* ventaja *f*; *she's an ~ to the company* es un gran valor para la compañía

ass·hole ['æshoʊl] V ojete *m* V; (*idiot*) *Span* gilipollas *m/f inv* V, *L.Am.* pendejo(-a) *m(f)* V

as·sign [ə'sain] *v/t* asignar

as·sign·ment [ə'sainmənt] (*task, study*) trabajo *m*

as·sim·i·late [ə'simileit] *v/t information* asimilar; *person into group* integrar

as·sist [ə'sist] *v/t* ayudar

as·sist·ance [ə'sistəns] ayuda *f*, asistencia *f*

as·sis·tant [ə'sistənt] ayudante *m/f*; *Br in store* dependiente(-a) *m(f)*

as·sis·tant di'rec·tor director(a) *m(f)* adjunto

as·sis·tant 'man·ag·er *of business* subdirector(a) *m(f)*; *of hotel, restaurant, store* subdirector(a) *m(f)*, subgerente *m/f*

as·so·ci·ate 1 *v/t* [ə'souʃieit] asociar; *he has long been ~d with the Ballet* ha estado vinculado al Ballet durante mucho tiempo **2** *v/i* [ə'souʃieit]: ~ *with* relacionarse con **3** *n* [ə'souʃiət] colega *m/f*

as·so·ci·ate pro'fes·sor profesor(a) *m(f)* adjunto(a)

as·so·ci·a·tion [əsousi'eiʃn] asociación *f*; *in ~ with* conjuntamente con

as·sort·ed [ə'sɒːrtid] *adj* surtido, diverso

as·sort·ment [ə'sɒːrtmənt] *of food* surtido *m*; *of people* diversidad *f*

as·sume [ə'suːm] *v/t* (*suppose*) suponer

as·sump·tion [ə'sʌmpʃn] suposición *f*

as·sur·ance [ə'ʃurəns] garantía *f*; (*confidence*) seguridad *f*

as·sure [ə'ʃur] *v/t* (*reassure*) asegurar

as·sured [ə'ʃurd] *adj* (*confident*) seguro

as·ter·isk ['æstərisk] asterisco *m*

asth·ma ['æsmə] asma *f*

asth·mat·ic [æs'mætik] *adj* asmático

as·ton·ish [ə'stɑːniʃ] *v/t* asombrar, sorprender; *be ~ed* estar asombrado *or* sorprendido

as·ton·ish·ing [ə'stɑːniʃiŋ] *adj* asombroso, sorprendente

as·ton·ish·ing·ly [ə'stɑːniʃiŋli] *adv* asombrosamente

as·ton·ish·ment [ə'stɑːniʃmənt] asombro *m*, sorpresa *f*

as·tound [ə'staund] *v/t* pasmar

as·tound·ing [ə'staundiŋ] *adj* pasmoso

a·stray [ə'strei] *adv*: *go* ~ extraviarse; *morally* descarriarse

a·stride [ə'straɪd] **1** *adv* a horcajadas **2** *prep* a horcajadas sobre

as·trol·o·ger [ə'strɑːlədʒər] astrólogo(-a) *m(f)*

as·trol·o·gy [ə'strɑːlədʒɪ] astrología *f*

as·tro·naut ['æstrənɔːt] astronauta *m/f*

as·tron·o·mer [ə'strɑːnəmər] astrónomo(-a) *m(f)*

as·tro·nom·i·cal [æstrə'nɑːmɪkl] *adj price etc* astronómico

as·tron·o·my [ə'strɑːnəmɪ] astronomía *f*

as·tute [ə'stuːt] *adj* astuto, sagaz

a·sy·lum [ə'saɪləm] (*mental ~*) manicomio *m*; *political* asilo *m*

at [ət] *stressed* [æt] *prep with places* en; ~ *Joe's house* en casa de Joe; *bar* en el bar de Joe; ~ *the door* a la puerta; ~ *10 dollars* a 10 dólares; ~ *the age of 18* a los 18 años; ~ *5 o'clock* a las 5; ~ *150 km/h* a 150 km./h.; *be good/bad* ~ *sth* ser bueno/malo haciendo algo

ate [eɪt] *pret* → *eat*

a·the·ism ['eɪθɪɪzm] ateísmo *m*

a·the·ist ['eɪθɪɪst] ateo(-a) *m(f)*

ath·lete ['æθliːt] atleta *m/f*

ath·let·ic [æθ'letɪk] *adj* atlético

ath·let·ics [æθ'letɪks] atletismo *m*

At·lan·tic [ət'læntɪk] *n*: *the* ~ el Atlántico

at·las ['ætləs] atlas *m inv*

ATM [eɪtiː'em] *abbr* (= *automatic teller machine*) cajero *m* automático

at·mos·phere ['ætməsfɪr] *of earth* atmósfera *f*; (*ambience*) ambiente *m*

at·mos·pher·ic pol·lu·tion [ætməs'ferɪk] contaminación *f* atmosférica

at·om ['ætəm] átomo *m*

'at·om bomb bomba *f* atómica

a·tom·ic [ə'tɑːmɪk] *adj* atómico

a·tom·ic 'en·er·gy energía *f* atómica *or* nuclear

a·tom·ic 'waste desechos *mpl* radiactivos

a·tom·iz·er ['ætəmaɪzər] atomiza-

dor *m*

a·tone [ə'toun] *v/i*: ~ *for* expiar

a·tro·cious [ə'troufəs] *adj* atroz, terrible

a·troc·i·ty [ə'trɑːsətɪ] atrocidad *f*

at·tach [ə'tætʃ] *v/t* sujetar, fijar; *importance* atribuir; *be ~ed to* (*fond of*) tener cariño a

at·tach·ment [ə'tætʃmənt] (*fondness*) cariño *m* (*to* por); *to e-mail* archivo *m* adjunto

at·tack [ə'tæk] **1** *n* ataque *m* **2** *v/t* atacar

at·tempt [ə'tempt] **1** *n* intento *m*; *an* ~ *on the world record* un intento de batir el récord del mundo **2** *v/t* intentar

at·tend [ə'tend] *v/t* acudir a

♦ *attend to* *v/t* ocuparse de; *customer* atender

at·tend·ance [ə'tendəns] asistencia *f*

at·tend·ant [ə'tendənt] *in museum etc* vigilante *m/f*

at·ten·tion [ə'tenʃn] atención *f*; *bring sth to s.o.'s* ~ informar a alguien de algo; *your* ~ *please* atención, por favor; *pay* ~ prestar atención

at·ten·tive [ə'tentɪv] *adj listener* atento

at·tic ['ætɪk] ático *m*

at·ti·tude ['ætɪtuːd] actitud *f*

attn *abbr* (= *for the attention of*) atn (= a la atención de)

at·tor·ney [ə'tɜːrnɪ] abogado(-a) *m(f)*; *power of* ~ poder *m* (notarial)

at·tract [ə'trækt] *v/t* atraer; ~ *attention* llamar la atención; ~ *s.o.'s attention* atraer la atención de alguien; *be ~ed to s.o.* sentirse atraído por alguien

at·trac·tion [ə'trækʃn] atracción *f*, atractivo *m*; *romantic* atracción *f*

at·trac·tive [ə'træktɪv] *adj* atractivo

at·trib·ute¹ [ə'trɪbjuːt] *v/t* atribuir; ~ *sth to ...* atribuir algo a ...

at·trib·ute² ['ætrɪbjuːt] *n* atributo *m*

au·ber·gine ['oubərʒiːn] *Br* berenjena *f*

auc·tion ['ɒːkʃn] **1** *n* subasta *f*, *L.Am.* remate *m* **2** *v/t* subastar, *L.Am.* rematar

♦ **auction off** *v/t* subastar, *L.Am.* rematar

auc·tio·neer [ɒːkʃə'nɪr] subastador(a) *m(f)*, *L.Am.* rematador(a) *m(f)*

au·da·cious [ɒː'deɪʃəs] *adj plan* audaz

au·dac·i·ty [ɒː'dæsətɪ] audacia *f*

au·di·ble ['ɒːdəbl] *adj* audible

au·di·ence ['ɒːdɪəns] *in theater, at show* público *m*, espectadores *mpl*; *TV* audiencia *f*

au·di·o ['ɒːdɪoʊ] *adj* de audio

au·di·o·vi·su·al [ɒːdɪoʊ'vɪʒʊəl] *adj* audiovisual

au·dit ['ɒːdɪt] **1** *n* auditoría *f* **2** *v/t* auditar; *course* asistir de oyente a

au·di·tion [ɒː'dɪʃn] **1** *n* audición *f* **2** *v/i* hacer una prueba

au·di·tor ['ɒːdɪtər] auditor(a) *m(f)*

au·di·to·ri·um [ɒːdɪ'tɔːrɪəm] *of theater etc* auditorio *m*

Au·gust ['ɒːgəst] agosto *m*

aunt [ænt] tía *f*

au pair [oʊ'per] au pair *m/f*

au·ra ['ɒːrə] aura *f*

aus·pic·es ['ɒːspɪsɪz] *npl* auspicios *mpl*; *under the ~ of* bajo los auspicios de

aus·pi·cious [ɒː'spɪʃəs] *adj* propicio

aus·tere [ɒː'stiːr] *adj interior* austero

aus·ter·i·ty [ɒːs'terətɪ] *economic* austeridad *f*

Aus·tra·li·a [ɒː'streɪlɪə] Australia

Aus·tra·li·an [ɒː'streɪlɪən] **1** *adj* australiano **2** *n* australiano(-a) *m(f)*

Aus·tri·a ['ɒːstrɪə] Austria

Aus·tri·an ['ɒːstrɪən] **1** *adj* austriaco **2** *n* austriaco(-a) *m(f)*

au·then·tic [ɒː'θentɪk] *adj* auténtico

au·then·tic·i·ty [ɒːθen'tɪsətɪ] autenticidad *f*

au·thor ['ɒːθər] *of story, novel* escritor(a) *m(f)*; *of text* autor(a) *m(f)*

au·thor·i·tar·i·an [əθɑːrɪ'terɪən] *adj* autoritario

au·thor·i·ta·tive [ə'θɑːrɪtətɪv] *adj* autorizado

au·thor·i·ty [ə'θɑːrətɪ] autoridad *f*; *(permission)* autorización *f*; *be an ~ on* ser una autoridad en; *the authorities* las autoridades

au·thor·i·za·tion [ɒːθəraɪ'zeɪʃn] autorización *f*

au·thor·ize ['ɒːθəraɪz] *v/t* autorizar; *be ~d to* ... estar autorizado para ...

au·tis·tic [ɒː'tɪstɪk] *adj* autista

au·to·bi·og·ra·phy [ɒːtəbaɪ'ɑːgrəfɪ] autobiografía *f*

au·to·crat·ic [ɒːtə'krætɪk] *adj* autocrático

au·to·graph ['ɒːtəgræf] autógrafo *m*

au·to·mate ['ɒːtəmeɪt] *v/t* automatizar

au·to·mat·ic [ɒːtə'mætɪk] **1** *adj* automático **2** *n car* (coche *m*) automático *m*; *gun* pistola *f* automática; *washing machine* lavadora *f* automática

au·to·mat·i·cal·ly [ɒːtə'mætɪklɪ] *adv* automáticamente

au·to·ma·tion [ɒːtə'meɪʃn] automatización *f*

au·to·mo·bile ['ɒːtəmoubiːl] automóvil *m*, coche *m*, *L.Am.* carro *m*, *Rpl* auto *m*

'au·to·mo·bile in·dus·try industria *f* automovilística

au·ton·o·mous [ɒː'tɑːnəməs] *adj* autónomo

au·ton·o·my [ɒː'tɑːnəmɪ] autonomía *f*

au·to·pi·lot ['ɒːtoupaɪlət] piloto *m* automático

au·top·sy ['ɒːtɑːpsɪ] autopsia *f*

au·tumn ['ɒːtəm] *Br* otoño *m*

aux·il·ia·ry [ɒːg'zɪljərɪ] *adj* auxiliar

a·vail [ə'veɪl] **1** *n*: *to no ~* en vano **2** *v/t*: *~ o.s. of* aprovechar

a·vai·la·ble [ə'veɪləbl] *adj* disponible

av·a·lanche ['ævəlænʃ] avalancha *f*, alud *m*

av·a·rice ['ævərɪs] avaricia *f*

av·e·nue ['ævənuː] avenida *f*; *fig* camino *m*

av·e·rage ['ævərɪdʒ] **1** *adj* medio; *(of mediocre quality)* regular **2** *n* promedio *m*, media *f*; *above/below ~*

por encima/por debajo del promedio; **on** ~ como promedio, de media **3** *v/t: I ~ six hours of sleep a night* duermo seis horas cada noche como promedio *or* de media
◆ **average out** *v/t* calcular el promedio *or* la media de
◆ **average out at** *v/t* salir a
a·verse [ə'vɜːrs] *adj: not be ~ to* no ser reacio a
a·ver·sion [ə'vɜːrʃn] aversión *f*; **have an ~ to** tener aversión a
a·vert [ə'vɜːrt] *v/t one's eyes* apartar; *crisis* evitar
a·vi·a·tion [eɪvɪ'eɪʃn] aviación *f*
av·id ['ævɪd] *adj* ávido
av·o·ca·do [ɑːvə'kɑːdoʊ] aguacate *m, S.Am.* palta *f*
a·void [ə'vɔɪd] *v/t* evitar; *you've been ~ing me* has estado huyendo de mí
a·wait [ə'weɪt] *v/t* aguardar, esperar
a·wake [ə'weɪk] *adj* despierto; *it kept me ~* no me dejó dormir
a·ward [ə'wɔːrd] **1** *n* (*prize*) premio *m* **2** *v/t prize, damages* conceder
a·ware [ə'wer] *adj: be ~ of sth* ser consciente de algo; *become ~ of*
sth darse cuenta de algo
a·ware·ness [ə'wernɪs] conciencia *f*
a·way [ə'weɪ] *adv: look* ~ mirar hacia otra parte; *I'll be ~ until ...* traveling voy a estar fuera hasta ...; *sick* no voy a ir hasta ...; *it's 2 miles* ~ está a 2 millas; *Christmas is still six weeks* ~ todavía quedan seis semanas para Navidad; *take sth ~ from s.o.* quitar algo a alguien; *put sth* ~ guardar algo
a'way game SP partido *m* fuera de casa
awe·some ['ɒːsəm] *adj* F (*terrific*) alucinante F
aw·ful ['ɒːfəl] *adj* horrible, espantoso; *I feel* ~ me siento fatal
aw·ful·ly ['ɒːfəlɪ] *adv* F (*very*) tremendamente; *~ bad* malísimo
awk·ward ['ɒːkwərd] *adj* (*clumsy*) torpe; (*difficult*) difícil; (*embarrassing*) embarazoso; *feel ~* sentirse incómodo
awn·ing ['ɒːnɪŋ] toldo *m*
ax, *Br* **axe** [æks] **1** *n* hacha *f* **2** *v/t project etc* suprimir; *budget, job* recortar
ax·le ['æksl] eje *m*

B

BA [biː'eɪ] *abbr* (= **Bachelor of Arts**) Licenciatura *f* en Filosofía y Letras
ba·by ['beɪbɪ] *n* bebé *m*
'ba·by boom explosión *f* demográfica
'ba·by car·riage ['kærɪdʒ] cochecito *m* de bebé
ba·by·ish ['beɪbɪɪʃ] *adj* infantil
'ba·by-sit *v/i* (*pret & pp* **-sat**) hacer de *Span* canguro *or* *L.Am.* babysitter
'ba·by-sit·ter ['sɪtər] *Span* canguro *m/f, L.Am.* babysitter *m/f*
bach·e·lor ['bætʃələr] soltero *m*

back [bæk] **1** *n of person, clothes* espalda *f*; *of car, bus, house* parte *f* trasera *or* de atrás; *of paper, book* dorso *m*; *of drawer* fondo *m*; *of chair* respaldo *m*; SP defensa *m/f*; *in ~ in store* en la trastienda; *in the ~ (of the car)* atrás (del coche); *at the ~ of the bus* en la parte trasera *or* de atrás del autobús; *~ to front* del revés; *at the ~ of beyond* en el quinto pino **2** *adj* trasero; *~ road* carretera *f* secundaria **3** *adv* atrás; *please stand ~* pongase más para atrás; *2 meters ~ from the edge* a 2 metros del borde; **~ in 1935** allá por el año 1935; **give sth ~ to s.o.** devolver algo a alguien; **she'll be ~ tomorrow** volverá mañana; **when are you coming ~?** ¿cuándo volverás?; **take sth ~ to the store** *because unsatisfactory* devolver algo a la tienda; **they wrote/phoned ~** contestaron a la carta/a la llamada; **he hit me ~** me devolvió el golpe **4** *v/t* (*support*) apoyar, respaldar; *horse* apostar por **5** *v/i* **he ~ed into the garage** entró en el garaje marcha atrás

◆ **back away** *v/i* alejarse (hacia atrás)

◆ **back down** *v/i* echarse atrás

◆ **back off** *v/i* echarse atrás

◆ **back onto** *v/t* dar por la parte de atrás a

◆ **back out** *v/i of commitment* echarse atrás

◆ **back up 1** *v/t* (*support*) respaldar; *file* hacer una copia de seguridad de; **traffic was backed up all the way to …** el atasco llegaba hasta … **2** *v/i in car* dar marcha atrás; *of drains* atascarse

'**back·ache** dolor *m* de espalda; '**back·bit·ing** cotilleo *m*, chismorreo *m*; '**back·bone** ANAT columna *f* vertebral, espina *f* dorsal; *fig* (*courage*) agallas *fpl*; *fig* (*mainstay*) columna *f* vertebral; '**back·break·ing** *adj* extenuante, deslomador; **back 'burn·er: put sth on the ~** aparcar algo; '**back·date** *v/t:* **a salary increase ~d to 1st January** una subida salarial con efecto retroactivo a partir del 1 de enero; '**back·door** puerta *f* trasera
back·er ['bækər]: **the ~s of the movie** *financially* las personas que financiaron la película
back'fire *v/i fig:* **it ~d on us** nos salió el tiro por la culata; '**back·ground** *n* fondo *m*; *of person* origen *m*, historia *f* personal; *of situation* contexto *m*; **she prefers to stay in the ~** prefiere permanecer en un segundo plano; '**back·hand** *n in tennis*

revés *m*
back·ing ['bækɪŋ] *n* (*support*) apoyo *m*, respaldo *m*; MUS acompañamiento *m*
'**back·ing group** MUS grupo *m* de acompañamiento
'**back·lash** reacción *f* violenta; '**back·log** acumulación *f*; '**back·pack 1** *n* mochila *f* **2** *v/i* viajar con la mochila a cuestas; '**back·pack·er** mochilero(-a) *m(f)*; '**back·pack·ing** viajes *mpl* con la mochila a cuestas; '**back·ped·al** *v/i fig* echarse atrás, dar marcha atrás; '**back seat** *of car* asiento *m* trasero *or* de atrás; **back-seat 'driv·er: he's a terrible ~** va siempre incordiando al conductor con sus comentarios; '**back·space (key)** (tecla *f* de) retroceso *m*; '**back·stairs** *npl* escalera *f* de servicio; '**back street** callejuela *f*; '**back streets** *npl* callejuelas *fpl*; *poorer, dirtier part of a city* zonas *fpl* deprimidas; '**back·stroke** SP espalda *f*; '**back·track** *v/i* volver atrás, retroceder; '**back·up** (*support*) apoyo *m*, respaldo *m*; *for police* refuerzos *mpl*; COMPUT copia *f* de seguridad; **take a ~** COMPUT hacer una copia de seguridad; '**back·up disk** COMPUT disquete *m* con la copia de seguridad
back·ward ['bækwərd] **1** *adj child* retrasado; *society* atrasado; *glance* hacia atrás **2** *adv* hacia atrás
back'yard jardín *m* trasero; **in s.o.'s ~** *fig* en la misma puerta de alguien
ba·con ['beɪkn] tocino *m*, *Span* bacon *m*
bac·te·ri·a [bæk'tɪrɪə] *npl* bacterias *fpl*
bad [bæd] *adj* malo; *before singular masculine noun* mal; *cold, headache etc* fuerte; *mistake, accident* grave; **I've had a ~ day** he tenido un mal día; **smoking is ~ for you** fumar es malo; **it's not ~** no está mal; **that's really too ~** (*shame*) es una verdadera pena; **feel ~ about** (*guilty*) sentirse mal por; **I'm ~ at math** se me dan mal las matemáticas;

B

Friday's ~, how about Thursday? el viernes me viene mal, ¿qué tal el jueves?

bad 'debt deuda *f* incobrable

badge [bædʒ] insignia *f*, chapa *f*; *of policeman* placa *f*

bad·ger ['bædʒər] *v/t* acosar, importunar

bad 'lan·guage palabrotas *fpl*

bad·ly ['bædlɪ] *adv injured* gravemente; *damaged* seriamente; *work* mal; *I did really ~ in the exam* el examen me salió fatal; *he hasn't done ~ in life, business etc* no le ha ido mal; *you're ~ in need of a haircut* necesitas urgentemente un corte de pelo; *he is ~ off poor* anda mal de dinero

bad-man·nered [bæd'mænərd] *adj*: *be ~* tener malos modales

bad·min·ton ['bædmɪntən] bádminton *m*

bad-tem·pered [bæd'tempərd] *adj* malhumorado

baf·fle ['bæfl] *v/t* confundir, desconcertar; *be ~d* estar confundido *or* desconcertado; *I'm ~d why she left* no consigo entender por qué se fue

baf·fling ['bæflɪŋ] *adj mystery, software* desconcertante, incomprensible

bag [bæg] bolsa *f*; *for school* cartera *f*; (*purse*) bolso *m*, *S.Am.* cartera *f*, *Mex* bolsa *f*

bag·gage ['bægɪdʒ] equipaje *m*

'bag·gage car RAIL vagón *m* de equipajes; **'bag·gage check** consigna *f*; **'bag·gage re·claim** ['ri:kleɪm] recogida *f* de equipajes

bag·gy ['bægɪ] *adj* ancho, holgado

'bag·pipes *npl* gaita *f*

bail [beɪl] *n* LAW libertad *f* bajo fianza; (*money*) fianza *f*; *on ~* bajo fianza

♦ **bail out 1** *v/t* LAW pagar la fianza de **2** *v/i of airplane* tirarse en paracaídas

bait [beɪt] *n* cebo *m*

bake [beɪk] *v/t* hornear, cocer al horno

baked po'ta·to *Span* patata *f* or

L.Am. papa *f* asada (*con piel*)

bak·er ['beɪkər] panadero(-a) *m(f)*

bak·er·y ['beɪkərɪ] panadería *f*

bak·ing pow·der ['beɪkɪŋ] levadura *f*

bal·ance ['bæləns] **1** *n* equilibrio *m*; (*remainder*) resto *m*; *of bank account* saldo *m* **2** *v/t* poner en equilibrio; *~ the books* cuadrar las cuentas **3** *v/i* mantenerse en equilibrio; *of accounts* cuadrar

bal·anced ['bælənst] *adj* (*fair*) objetivo; *diet, personality* equilibrado

bal·ance of 'pay·ments balanza *f* de pagos; **bal·ance of 'trade** balanza *f* comercial; **'bal·ance sheet** balance *m*

bal·co·ny ['bælkənɪ] *of house* balcón *m*; *in theater* anfiteatro *m*

bald [bɔːld] *adj* calvo; *he's going ~* se está quedando calvo; *~ spot* calva *f*

bald·ing ['bɔːldɪŋ] *adj* medio calvo

Bal·kan ['bɔːlkən] *adj* balcánico

Bal·kans ['bɔːlkənz] *npl*: *the ~* los Balcanes

ball [bɔːl] *tennis-ball size* pelota *f*; *football size* balón *m*, pelota *f*; *billiard-ball size* bola *f*; *on the ~* fig despierto; *play ~* fig cooperar; *the ~'s in his court* le toca actuar a él, la pelota está en su tejado

bal·lad ['bæləd] balada *f*

ball 'bear·ing rodamiento *m* de bolas

bal·le·ri·na [bælə'riːnə] bailarina *f*

bal·let [bæˈleɪ] ballet *m*

'bal·let danc·er bailarín (-ina) *m(f)*

ball game (*baseball game*) partido *m* de béisbol; *that's a different ~* F esa es otra cuestión F

bal·lis·tic mis·sile [bəˈlɪstɪk] misil *m* balístico

bal·loon [bəˈluːn] globo *m*

bal·loon·ist [bəˈluːnɪst] piloto *m* de globo aerostático

bal·lot ['bælət] **1** *n* voto *m* **2** *v/t members* consultar por votación

'bal·lot box urna *f*

'bal·lot pa·per papeleta *f*

'ball·park (*baseball*) campo *m* de

béisbol; *you're in the right* ~ F no vas descaminado; '**ball·park fig·ure** F cifra *f* aproximada; '**ball·point (pen)** bolígrafo *m*, *Mex* pluma *f*, *Rpl* birome *m*

balls [bɔ:lz] *npl* ∨ huevos *mpl* ∨; (*courage*) huevos *mpl* ∨

bam·boo [bæm'bu:] *n* bambú *m*

ban [bæn] **1** *n* prohibición *f* **2** *v/t* (*pret & pp* -*ned*) prohibir; ~ *s.o. from doing sth* prohibir a alguien que haga algo

ba·nal [bə'næl] *adj* banal

ba·na·na [bə'nænə] plátano *m*, *Rpl* banana *f*

band [bænd] banda *f*; *pop* grupo *m*

ban·dage ['bændɪdʒ] **1** *n* vendaje *m* **2** *v/t* vendar

'**Band-Aid®** *Span* tirita *f*, *L.Am.* curita *f*

B&B [bi:n'bi:] *abbr* (= *bed and breakfast*) hostal *m* familiar

ban·dit ['bændɪt] bandido *m*

'**band·wagon**: *jump on the* ~ subirse al carro

ban·dy ['bændɪ] *adj legs* arqueado

bang [bæŋ] **1** *n noise* estruendo *m*, estrépito *m*; (*blow*) golpe *m*; *the door closed with a* ~ la puerta se cerró de un portazo **2** *v/t door* cerrar de un portazo; (*hit*) golpear; ~ *o.s. on the head* golpearse la cabeza **3** *v/i* dar golpes; *the door ~ed shut* la puerta se cerró de un portazo

ban·gle ['bæŋgl] brazalete *m*, pulsera *f*

bangs [bæŋz] *npl* flequillo *m*

ban·is·ters ['bænɪstərz] *npl* barandilla *f*

ban·jo ['bændʒoʊ] banjo *m*

bank[1] [bæŋk] *of river* orilla *f*

bank[2] [bæŋk] **1** *n* FIN banco *m* **2** *v/i*: *I* ~ *with* ... mi banco es el ... **3** *v/t money* ingresar, depositar

♦ **bank on** *v/t* contar con; *don't bank on it* no cuentes con ello

'**bank ac·count** cuenta *f* (bancaria); '**bank bal·ance** saldo *m* bancario; '**bank bill** billete *m*

bank·er ['bæŋkər] banquero *m*

'**bank·er's card** tarjeta *f* bancaria

bank·ing ['bæŋkɪŋ] banca *f*

'**bank loan** préstamo *m* bancario; '**bank man·ag·er** director(a) *m(f)* de banco; '**bank rate** tipo *m* de interés bancario; '**bank·roll** *v/t* financiar

bank·rupt ['bæŋkrʌpt] **1** *adj* en bancarrota *or* quiebra; *go* ~ quebrar, ir a la quiebra; *of person* arruinarse **2** *v/t* llevar a la quiebra

bank·rupt·cy ['bæŋkrʌpsɪ] *of person, company* quiebra *f*, bancarrota *f*

'**bank state·ment** extracto *m* bancario

ban·ner ['bænər] pancarta *f*

banns [bænz] *npl* amonestaciones *fpl*

ban·quet ['bæŋkwɪt] *n* banquete *m*

ban·ter ['bæntər] *n* bromas *fpl*

bap·tism ['bæptɪzm] bautismo *m*

bap·tize [bæp'taɪz] *v/t* bautizar

bar[1] [bɑr] *n of iron* barra *f*; *of chocolate* tableta *f*; *for drinks* bar *m*; (*counter*) barra *f*; *a* ~ *of soap* una pastilla de jabón; *be behind* ~*s* (*in prison*) estar entre barrotes

bar[2] [bɑr] *v/t* (*pret & pp* -*red*) *from premises* prohibir la entrada a; ~ *s.o. from doing sth* prohibir a alguien que haga algo

bar[3] [bɑr] *prep* (*except*) excepto

bar·bar·i·an [bɑr'beriən] bárbaro(-a) *m(f)*

bar·bar·ic [bɑr'bærɪk] *adj* brutal, inhumano

bar·be·cue ['bɑrbɪkju:] **1** *n* barbacoa *f* **2** *v/t* cocinar en la barbacoa

barbed 'wire [bɑrbd] alambre *f* de espino

bar·ber ['bɑrbər] barbero *m*

bar·bi·tu·rate [bɑr'bɪtjərət] barbitúrico *m*

'**bar code** código *m* de barras

bare [ber] *adj* (*naked*) desnudo; (*empty: room*) vacío; *mountainside* pelado, raso; *floor* descubierto; *in one's* ~ *feet* descalzo

'**bare·foot** *adj* descalzo

bare·head·ed [ber'hedɪd] *adj* sin sombrero

B

'**bare·ly** ['berlɪ] *adv* apenas; *he's ~ five* acaba de cumplir cinco años

bar·gain ['bɑːrgɪn] **1** *n* (*deal*) trato *m*; (*good buy*) ganga *f*; *into the ~* además **2** *v/i* regatear, negociar

♦ **bargain for** *v/t* (*expect*) imaginarse, esperar

barge [bɑːrdʒ] *n* NAUT barcaza *f*

♦ **barge into** *v/t person* tropezarse con; *room* irrumpir en

bar·i·tone ['bærɪtoʊn] *n* barítono *m*

bark[1] [bɑːrk] **1** *n of dog* ladrido *m* **2** *v/i* ladrar

bark[2] [bɑːrk] *of tree* corteza *f*

bar·ley ['bɑːrlɪ] cebada *f*

barn [bɑːrn] granero *m*

ba·rom·e·ter [bə'rɑːmɪtər] *also fig* barómetro *m*

Ba·roque [bə'rɑːk] *adj* barroco

bar·racks ['bærəks] *npl* MIL cuartel *m*

bar·rage [bə'rɑːʒ] MIL barrera *f* (de fuego); *fig* aluvión *m*

bar·rel ['bærəl] (*container*) tonel *m*, barril *m*

bar·ren ['bærən] *adj land* yermo, árido

bar·rette [bə'ret] pasador *m*

bar·ri·cade [bærɪ'keɪd] *n* barricada *f*

bar·ri·er ['bærɪər] *also fig* barrera *f*; *language ~* barrera *f* lingüística

bar·ring ['bɑːrɪŋ] *prep* salvo, excepto; *~ accidents* salvo imprevistos

bar·ris·ter ['bærɪstər] *Br* abogado(-a) *m(f)* (*que aparece en tribunales*)

bar·row ['bæroʊ] carretilla *f*

'**bar ten·der** camarero(-a) *m(f)*, *L.Am.* mesero(-a) *m(f)*, *Rpl* mozo(-a) *m(f)*

bar·ter ['bɑːrtər] **1** *n* trueque *m* **2** *v/t* cambiar, trocar (*for* por)

base [beɪs] **1** *n bottom, center* base *f*; *~ camp* campamento *m* base **2** *v/t* basar (*on* en); *be ~d in of soldier* estar destinado en; *of company* tener su sede en

'**base·ball** *ball* pelota *f* de béisbol; *game* béisbol *m*; '**base·ball bat** bate *m* de béisbol; '**base·ball cap** gorra *f* de béisbol; '**base·ball**

'**play·er** jugador(a) *m(f)* de béisbol, *L.Am.* pelotero(-a) *m(f)*

'**base·board** rodapié *m*

base·less ['beɪslɪs] *adj* infundado

base·ment ['beɪsmənt] *of house, store* sótano *m*

'**base rate** FIN tipo *m* de interés básico

bash [bæʃ] **1** *n* F porrazo *m* F **2** *v/t* F dar un porrazo a F

ba·sic ['beɪsɪk] *adj* (*rudimentary*) básico; *room* modesto, sencillo; *language skills* elemental; (*fundamental*) fundamental; *~ salary* sueldo *m* base

ba·sic·al·ly ['beɪsɪklɪ] *adv* básicamente

ba·sics ['beɪsɪks] *npl*: *the ~* lo básico, los fundamentos; *get down to ~* centrarse en lo esencial

bas·il ['bæzɪl] albahaca *f*

ba·sin ['beɪsn] *for washing* barreño *m*; *in bathroom* lavabo *m*

ba·sis ['beɪsɪs] (*pl bases* ['beɪsiːz]) base *f*; *on the ~ of what you've told me* de acuerdo con lo que me has dicho

bask [bæsk] *v/i* tomar el sol

bas·ket ['bæskɪt] cesta *f*; *in basketball* canasta *f*

'**bas·ket·ball** *game* baloncesto *m*, *L.Am.* básquetbol *m*; *ball* balón *m or* pelota *f* de baloncesto; *~ player* baloncestista *m/f*, *L.Am.* basquebolista *m/f*

Basque [bæsk] **1** *adj* vasco **2** *n person* vasco(-a) *m(f)*; *language* vasco *m*

bass [beɪs] **1** *n part, singer* bajo *m*; *instrument* contrabajo *m* **2** *adj* bajo

bas·tard ['bæstərd] ilegítimo(-a) *m(f)*, bastardo(-a) *m(f)*; P cabrón(-ona) *m(f)* P; *poor ~* pobre desgraciado; *stupid ~* desgraciado

bat[1] [bæt] **1** *n for baseball* bate *m*; *for table tennis* pala *f* **2** *v/i* (*pret & pp -ted*) *in baseball* batear

bat[2] [bæt] *v/t* (*pret & pp -ted*): *he didn't ~ an eyelid* no se inmutó

bat[3] [bæt] (*animal*) murciélago *m*

batch [bætʃ] *n of students* tanda *f*; *of*

data conjunto *m*; *of bread* hornada *f*; *of products* lote *m*

ba·ted ['beɪtɪd] *adj:* **with ~ breath** con la respiración contenida

bath [bæθ] baño *m*; **have a ~, take a ~** darse *or* tomar un baño

bathe [beɪð] *v/i* (*swim, have a bath*) bañarse

'**bath mat** alfombra *f* de baño; '**bath·robe** albornoz *m*; '**bath-room** *for bath, washing hands,* cuarto *m* de baño; (*toilet*) servicio *m*, *L.Am.* baño *m*; '**bath tow·el** toalla *f* de baño; '**bath·tub** bañera *f*

bat·on [bə'tɑːn] *of conductor* batuta *f*

bat·tal·i·on [bə'tæliən] MIL batallón *m*

bat·ter ['bætər] *n* masa *f*; *in baseball* bateador(a) *m(f)*

bat·tered ['bætərd] *adj* maltratado

bat·ter·y ['bætərɪ] *in watch, flashlight* pila *f*; *in computer, car* batería *f*

'**bat·ter·y charg·er** ['tʃɑːrdʒər] cargador *m* de pilas/baterías

bat·ter·y-op·er·at·ed ['ɑːpəreɪtɪd] *adj* que funciona con pilas

bat·tle ['bætl] **1** *n also fig* batalla *f* **2** *v/i against illness etc* luchar

'**bat·tle·field**, '**bat·tle·ground** campo *m* de batalla

'**bat·tle·ship** acorazado *m*

bawd·y ['bɒdɪ] *adj* picante, subido de tono

bawl [bɒːl] *v/i* (*shout*) gritar, vociferar; (*weep*) berrear

♦**bawl out** *v/t* F echar la bronca a F

bay [beɪ] (*inlet*) bahía *f*

bay·o·net ['beɪənet] *n* bayoneta *f*

bay 'win·dow ventana *f* en saliente

BC [biːˈsiː] *abbr* (= **before Christ**) A.C. (= antes de Cristo)

be [biː] ◊ *v/i* (*pret* **was**/**were**, *pp* **been**) *permanent characteristics, profession, nationality* ser; *position, temporary condition* estar; **was she there?** ¿estaba allí?; **it's me** soy yo; **how much is**/**are ...?** ¿cuánto es/son ...?; **there is, there are** hay; **~ careful** ten cuidado; **don't ~ sad** no estés triste ◊ **has the mailman been?** ¿ha venido el cartero?; **I've**

never been to Japan no he estado en Japón; **I've been here for hours** he estado aquí horas ◊ *tags:* **that's right, isn't it?** eso es, ¿no?; **she's Chinese, isn't she?** es china, ¿verdad? ◊ *v/aux:* **I am thinking** estoy pensando; **he was running** corría; **you're ~ing stupid** estás siendo un estúpido ◊ *obligation:* **you are to do what I tell you** harás lo que yo te diga; **I was to help him escape** se suponía que le iba a ayudar a escaparse; **you are not to tell anyone** no debes decírselo a nadie ◊ *passive:* **he was arrested** fue detenido, lo detuvieron; **they have been sold** se han vendido

♦**be in for** *v/t:* **he's in for a big disappointment** se va a llevar una gran desilusión

beach [biːtʃ] *n* playa *f*

'**beach ball** pelota *f* de playa

'**beach·wear** ropa *f* playera

beads [biːdz] *npl* cuentas *fpl*

beak [biːk] pico *m*

'**be-all: the ~ and end-all** lo más importante del mundo

beam [biːm] **1** *n in ceiling etc* viga *f* **2** *v/i* (*smile*) sonreír de oreja a oreja **3** *v/t* (*transmit*) emitir

bean [biːn] judía *f*, alubia *f*, *L.Am.* frijol *m*, *S.Am.* poroto *m*; **green ~s** judías *fpl* verdes, *Mex* ejotes *mpl*, *S.Am.* porotos *mpl* verdes; **coffee ~s** granos *mpl* de café; **be full of ~s** F estar lleno de vitalidad

'**bean·bag** *cojín relleno de bolitas*

bear¹ [ber] *animal* oso(-a) *m(f)*

bear² [ber] **1** *v/t* (*pret* **bore**, *pp* **borne**) *weight* resistir; *costs* correr con; (*tolerate*) aguantar, soportar; *child* dar a luz; **she bore him six children** le dio seis hijos **2** *v/i* (*pret* **bore**, *pp* **borne**): **bring pressure to ~ on** ejercer presión sobre

♦**bear out** *v/t* (*confirm*) confirmar

bear·a·ble ['berəbl] *adj* soportable

beard [bɪrd] barba *f*

beard·ed ['bɪrdɪd] *adj* con barba

bear·ing ['berɪŋ] *in machine* rodamiento *m*, cojinete *m*; **that has no ~**

B

on the case eso no tiene nada que ver con el caso

'**bear mar·ket** FIN mercado *m* a la baja

beast [biːst] *animal* bestia *f*; *person* bestia *m/f*

beat [biːt] **1** *n of heart* latido *m*; *of music* ritmo *m* **2** *v/i* (*pret* **beat**, *pp* **beaten**) *of heart* latir; *of rain* golpear; ~ *about the bush* andarse por las ramas **3** *v/t* (*pret* **beat**, *pp* **beaten**) *in competition* derrotar, ganar a; (*hit*) pegar a; (*pound*) golpear; ~ *it!* F ¡lárgate! F; *it ~s me* no logro entender

♦ **beat up** *v/t* dar una paliza a

beat·en ['biːtən] **1** *adj*: *off the ~ track* retirado **2** *pp* → **beat**

beat·ing ['biːtɪŋ] (*physical*) paliza *f*

beat-up *adj* F destartalado F

beau·ti·cian [bjuːˈtɪʃn] esteticista *m/f*

beau·ti·ful ['bjuːtəfəl] *adj woman, house, day, story, movie* bonito, precioso, *L.Am.* lindo; *smell, taste, meal* delicioso, *L.Am.* rico; *vacation* estupendo; *thanks, that's just ~!* ¡muchísimas gracias, está maravilloso!

beau·ti·ful·ly ['bjuːtɪfəlɪ] *adv cooked, done* perfectamente, maravillosamente

beaut·y ['bjuːtɪ] belleza *f*

'**beaut·y par·lor**, *Br* '**beaut·y par·lour** ['pɑːrlər] salón *m* de belleza

bea·ver ['biːvər] castor *m*

♦ **beaver away** *v/i* F trabajar como un burro F

be·came [bɪˈkeɪm] *pret* → **become**

be·cause [bɪˈkɑːz] *conj* porque; ~ *it was too expensive* porque era demasiado caro; ~ *of* debido a, a causa de; ~ *of you, we can't go* gracias a ti, no podemos ir

beck·on ['bekn] *v/i* hacer señas

be·come [bɪˈkʌm] (*pret* **became**, *pp* **become**) hacerse, volverse; *it became clear that ...* quedó claro que ...; *he became a priest* se hizo sacerdote; *she's becoming very forgetful* cada vez es más olvidadiza; *what's ~ of her?* ¿qué fue de

ella?

be·com·ing [bɪˈkʌmɪŋ] *adj* favorecedor, apropiado

bed [bed] *n* cama *f*; *of flowers* macizo *m*; *of sea* fondo *m*; *of river* cauce *m*, lecho *m*; *go to ~* ir a la cama; *he's still in ~* aún está en la cama; *go to ~ with s.o.* irse a la cama *or* acostarse con alguien

'**bed-clothes** *npl* ropa *f* de cama

bed·ding ['bedɪŋ] ropa *f* de cama

bed·lam ['bedləm] F locura *f*, jaleo *m*

bed·rid·den ['bedrɪdən] *adj*: *be ~* estar postrado en cama; '**bed·room** dormitorio *m*, *L.Am.* cuarto *m*; '**bed·side**: *be at the ~ of* estar junto a la cama de; '**bed·spread** colcha *f*; '**bed·time** hora *f* de irse a la cama

bee [biː] abeja *f*

beech [biːtʃ] haya *f*

beef [biːf] **1** *n* carne *f* de vaca *or* vacuna; F (*complaint*) queja *f* **2** *v/i* F (*complain*) quejarse

♦ **beef up** *v/t* reforzar, fortalecer

'**beef·bur·ger** hamburguesa *f*

'**bee·hive** colmena *f*

'**bee·line**: *make a ~ for* ir directamente a

been [bɪn] *pp* → **be**

beep [biːp] **1** *n* pitido *m* **2** *v/i* pitar **3** *v/t* (*call on pager*) llamar con el buscapersonas

beep·er ['biːpər] buscapersonas *m inv*, *Span* busca *m*

beer [bɪr] cerveza *f*

beet [biːt] remolacha *f*

bee·tle ['biːtl] escarabajo *m*

be·fore [bɪˈfɔːr] **1** *prep* (*time*) antes de; (*space, order*) antes de, delante de **2** *adv* antes; *I've seen this movie ~* ya he visto esta película; *have you been to Japan ~?* ¿habías estado antes *or* ya en Japón?; *the week/ day ~* la semana / el día anterior **3** *conj* antes de que

be·fore·hand *adv* de antemano

be·friend [bɪˈfrend] *v/t* hacerse amigo de

beg [beg] **1** *v/i* (*pret & pp* **-ged**) mendigar, pedir **2** *v/t* (*pret & pp*

-ged): ~ *s.o. to do sth* rogar *or* suplicar a alguien que haga algo

began [bɪ'gæn] *pret* → **begin**

beg·gar ['begər] *n* mendigo(-a) *m(f)*

be·gin [bɪ'gɪn] **1** *v/i* (*pret began, pp begun*) empezar, comenzar; *to ~ with* (*at first*) en un primer momento, al principio; (*in the first place*) para empezar **2** *v/t* (*pret began, pp begun*) empezar, comenzar; *~ to do sth, ~ doing sth* empezar *or* comenzar a hacer algo

be·gin·ner [bɪ'gɪnər] principiante *m/f*

be·gin·ning [bɪ'gɪnɪŋ] principio *m*, comienzo *m*; (*origin*) origen *m*

be·grudge [bɪ'grʌdʒ] *v/t* (*envy*) envidiar; (*give reluctantly*) dar a regañadientes

be·gun [bɪ'gʌn] *pp* → **begin**

be·half [bɪ'hɑːf]: *on ~ of, in ~ of* en nombre de; *on my/ his ~* en nombre mío/ suyo

be·have [bɪ'heɪv] *v/i* comportarse, portarse; *~ (o.s.)* comportarse *or* portarse bien; *~ (yourself)!* ¡pórtate bien!

be·hav·ior, *Br* **be·hav·iour** [bɪ'heɪvɪər] comportamiento *m*, conducta *f*

be·hind [bɪ'haɪnd] **1** *prep in position, order* detrás de; *in progress* por detrás de; *be ~ ...* (*responsible for*) estar detrás de ...; (*support*) respaldar ... **2** *adv* (*at the back*) detrás; *be ~ with sth* estar atrasado con algo; *leave ~* dejarse algo

beige [beɪʒ] *adj* beige, *Span* beis

be·ing ['biːɪŋ] *existence, creature* ser *m*

be·lat·ed [bɪ'leɪtɪd] *adj* tardío

belch [beltʃ] **1** *n* eructo *m* **2** *v/i* eructar

Bel·gian ['beldʒən] **1** *adj* belga **2** *n* belga *m/f*

Bel·gium ['beldʒəm] Bélgica

be·lief [bɪ'liːf] creencia *f*; *it's my ~ that* creo que

be·lieve [bɪ'liːv] *v/t* creer
♦ **believe in** *v/t* creer en

be·liev·er [bɪ'liːvər] REL creyente

m/f; fig partidario(a) *m(f)* (*in* de)

be·lit·tle [bɪ'lɪtl] *v/t* menospreciar

Be·lize [be'liːz] *n* Belice

bell [bel] *of bike, door, school* timbre *m; of church* campana *f*

'bell·hop botones *m inv*

bel·lig·er·ent [bɪ'lɪdʒərənt] *adj* beligerante

bel·low ['beloʊ] **1** *n* bramido *m* **2** *v/i* bramar

bel·ly ['belɪ] *of person* estómago *m*, barriga *f*; (*fat stomach*) barriga *f*, tripa *f; of animal* panza *f*

'bel·ly·ache *v/i* F refunfuñar

be·long [bɪ'lɒːŋ] *v/i*: *where does this ~?* ¿dónde va esto?; *I don't ~ here* no encajo aquí
♦ **belong to** *v/t of object, money* pertenecer a; *club* pertenecer a, ser socio de

be·long·ings [bɪ'lɒːŋɪŋz] *npl* pertenencias *fpl*

be·loved [bɪ'lʌvɪd] *adj* querido

be·low [bɪ'loʊ] **1** *prep in amount, rate, level* por debajo de **2** *adv* abajo; *in text* más abajo; *see* ~ véase más abajo; *10 degrees ~* 10 grados bajo cero

belt [belt] *n* cinturón *m; tighten one's ~ fig* apretarse el cinturón

bench [bentʃ] *seat* banco *m*; (*work~*) mesa *f* de trabajo

'bench·mark punto *m* de referencia

bend [bend] **1** *n* curva *f* **2** *v/t* (*pret & pp bent*) doblar **3** *v/i* (*pret & pp bent*) torcer, girar; *of person* flexionarse
♦ **bend down** *v/i* agacharse

bend·er ['bendər] F parranda *f*

be·neath [bɪ'niːθ] **1** *prep* debajo de; *she thinks a job like that is ~ her* cree que un trabajo como ése le supondría rebajarse **2** *adv* abajo

ben·e·fac·tor ['benɪfæktər] benefactor(a) *m(f)*

ben·e·fi·cial [benɪ'fɪʃl] *adj* beneficioso

ben·e·fi·ci·a·ry [benɪ'fɪʃərɪ] beneficiario(-a) *m(f)*

ben·e·fit ['benɪfɪt] **1** *n* beneficio *m*, ventaja *f* **2** *v/t* beneficiar **3** *v/i* bene-

B

ficiarse

be·nev·o·lence [bɪ'nevələns] benevolencia *f*

be·nev·o·lent [bɪ'nevələnt] *adj* benevolente

be·nign [bɪ'naɪn] *adj* agradable; MED benigno

bent [bent] *pret & pp* → **bend**

be·queath [bɪ'kwiːð] *v/t also fig* legar

be·quest [bɪ'kwest] legado *m*

be·reaved [bɪ'riːvd] *npl:* **the ~** los familiares del difunto

be·ret [bə'reɪ] boina *f*

ber·ry ['berɪ] baya *f*

ber·serk [bər'zɜːrk] *adv:* **go ~** F volverse loco

berth [bɜːrθ] *on ship* litera *f*; *on train* camarote *m*; *for ship* amarradero *m*; **give s.o. a wide ~** evitar a alguien

be·seech [bɪ'siːtʃ] *v/t:* **~ s.o. to do sth** suplicar a alguien que haga algo

be·side [bɪ'saɪd] *prep* al lado de, junto a; **be ~ o.s.** estar fuera de sí; **that's ~ the point** eso no tiene nada que ver

be·sides [bɪ'saɪdz] **1** *adv* además **2** *prep* (*apart from*) aparte de, además de

be·siege [bɪ'siːdʒ] *v/t also fig* asediar

best [best] **1** *adj* mejor **2** *adv* mejor; **which did you like ~?** ¿cuál te gustó más?; **it would be ~ if ...** sería mejor si ...; **I like her ~** ella es la que más me gusta **3** *n:* **do one's ~** hacer todo lo posible; **the ~** *person, thing* el /la mejor; **we insist on the ~** insistimos en lo mejor; **we'll just have to make the ~ of it** tendremos que arreglárnoslas; **all the ~!** ¡buena suerte!, ¡que te vaya bien!

best be'fore date fecha *f* de caducidad; **best 'man** *at wedding* padrino *m*; **'best-sell·er** éxito *m* de ventas, best-seller *m*

bet [bet] **1** *n* apuesta *f*; **place a ~** hacer una apuesta **2** *v/t & v/i also fig* apostar; **I ~ he doesn't come** apuesto a que no viene; **you ~!** ¡ya lo creo!

be·tray [bɪ'treɪ] *v/t* traicionar; *husband, wife* engañar

be·tray·al [bɪ'treɪəl] traición *f*; *of husband, wife* engaño *m*

bet·ter ['betər] **1** *adj* mejor; **get ~ in** *skills, health* mejorar; **he's ~ in health** está mejor **2** *adv* mejor; **you'd ~ ask permission** sería mejor que pidieras permiso; **I'd really ~ not** mejor no; **all the ~ for us** tanto mejor para nosotros; **I like her ~** me gusta más ella

bet·ter·'off *adj* (*wealthier*) más rico

be·tween [bɪ'twiːn] *prep* entre; **~ you and me** entre tú y yo

bev·er·age ['bevərɪdʒ] *fml* bebida *f*

be·ware [bɪ'wer] *v/t:* **~ of** tener cuidado con

be·wil·der [bɪ'wɪldər] *v/t* desconcertar

be·wil·der·ment [bɪ'wɪldərmənt] desconcierto *m*

be·yond [bɪ'jɑːnd] **1** *prep in space* más allá de; **she has changed ~ recognition** ha cambiado tanto que es difícil reconocerla; **it's ~ me** (*don't understand*) no logro entender; (*can't do it*) no me es imposible **2** *adv* más allá

bi·as ['baɪəs] *n against* prejuicio *m*; *in favor of* favoritismo *m*

bi·as(s)ed ['baɪəst] *adj* parcial

bib [bɪb] *for baby* babero *m*

Bi·ble ['baɪbl] Biblia *f*

bib·li·cal ['bɪblɪkl] *adj* bíblico

bib·li·og·ra·phy [bɪblɪ'ɑːɡrəfɪ] bibliografía *f*

bi·car·bon·ate of so·da [baɪ'kɑːr-bəneɪt] bicarbonato *m* sódico

bi·cen·ten·ni·al [baɪsen'tenɪəl] bicentenario *m*

bi·ceps ['baɪseps] *npl* bíceps *mpl*

bick·er ['bɪkər] *v/i* reñir, discutir

bi·cy·cle ['baɪsɪkl] bicicleta *f*

bid [bɪd] **1** *n at auction* puja *f*; (*attempt*) intento *m* **2** *v/i* (*pret & pp* **bid**) *at auction* pujar

bid·der ['bɪdər] postor(a) *m(f)*; **the highest ~** el mejor postor

bi·en·ni·al [baɪ'enɪəl] *adj* bienal

bi·fo·cals [baɪ'foʊkəlz] *npl* gafas *fpl*

B

or L.Am. lentes *mpl* bifocales

big [bɪg] **1** *adj* grande; *before singular nouns* gran; **my ~ brother/ sister** mi hermano/hermana mayor; **~ name** nombre *m* importante **2** *adv*: **talk** ~ alardear, fanfarronear

big·a·mist ['bɪgəmɪst] bígamo(-a) *m(f)*

big·a·mous ['bɪgəməs] *adj* bígamo

big·a·my ['bɪgəmɪ] bigamia *f*

'big·head F creído(-a) *m(f)* F

big·head·ed [bɪg'hedɪd] *adj* F creído F

big·ot ['bɪgət] fanático(-a) *m(f)*, intolerante *m/f*

bike [baɪk] **1** *n* F bici *f* F; *motorbike* moto *f* F **2** *v/i* ir en bici

bik·er ['baɪkər] motero(-a) *m(f)*

bi·ki·ni [bɪ'ki:nɪ] biquini *m*

bi·lat·er·al [baɪ'lætərəl] *adj* bilateral

bi·lin·gual [baɪ'lɪŋgwəl] *adj* bilingüe

bill [bɪl] **1** *n for gas, electricity* factura *f*, recibo *m*; *Br in hotel, restaurant* cuenta *f*; *(money)* billete *m*; POL proyecto *m* de ley; *(poster)* cartel *m* **2** *v/t (invoice)* enviar la factura a

'bill·board valla *f* publicitaria

'bill·fold cartera *f*, billetera *f*

bil·liards ['bɪljərdz] *nsg* billar *m*

bil·lion ['bɪljən] mil millones *mpl*, millardo *m*

bill of ex'change FIN letra *f* de cambio

bill of 'sale escritura *f* de compraventa

bin [bɪn] *n* cubo *m*

bi·na·ry ['baɪnərɪ] *adj* binario

bind [baɪnd] *v/t (pret & pp bound) (connect)* unir; *(tie)* atar; *(LAW: oblige)* obligar

bind·ing ['baɪndɪŋ] **1** *adj agreement, promise* vinculante **2** *n of book* tapa *f*

bi·noc·u·lars [bɪ'nɑːkjʊlərz] *npl* prismáticos *mpl*

bi·o·chem·ist [baɪoʊ'kemɪst] bioquímico(-a) *m(f)*

bi·o·chem·is·try [baɪoʊ'kemɪstrɪ] bioquímica *f*

bi·o·de·gra·da·ble [baɪoʊdɪ'greɪdəbl] *adj* biodegradable

bi·og·ra·pher [baɪ'ɑːgrəfər] biógrafo(-a) *m(f)*

bi·og·ra·phy [baɪ'ɑːgrəfɪ] biografía *f*

bi·o·log·i·cal [baɪoʊ'lɑːdʒɪkl] *adj* biológico; **~ parents** padres *mpl* biológicos; **~ detergent** detergente *m* biológico

bi·ol·o·gist [baɪ'ɑːlədʒɪst] biólogo(-a) *m(f)*

bi·ol·o·gy [baɪ'ɑːlədʒɪ] biología *f*

bi·o·tech·nol·o·gy [baɪoʊtek'nɑːlədʒɪ] biotecnología *f*

bird [bɜːrd] ave *f*, pájaro *m*

'bird·cage jaula *f* para pájaros; **bird of 'prey** ave *f* rapaz; **'bird sanc·tu·a·ry** reserva *f* de aves; **bird's eye 'view** vista *f* panorámica; **get a ~'s eye view of sth** ver algo a vista de pájaro

bi·ro® ['baɪroʊ] *Br* bolígrafo *m*, *Mex* pluma *f*, *Rpl* birome *m*

birth [bɜːrθ] *also fig* nacimiento *m*; *(labor)* parto *m*; **give ~ to** *child* dar a luz; *of animal* parir; **date of ~** fecha *f* de nacimiento; **the land of my ~** mi tierra natal

'birth cer·tif·i·cate partida *f* de nacimiento; **'birth con·trol** control *m* de natalidad; **'birth·day** cumpleaños *m inv*; **happy ~!** ¡feliz cumpleaños!; **'birth·day cake** tarta *f* de cumpleaños; **'birth·mark** marca *f* de nacimiento, antojo *m*; **'birth·place** lugar *m* de nacimiento; **'birth·rate** tasa *f* de natalidad

bis·cuit ['bɪskɪt] bollo *m*, panecillo *m*; *Br* galleta *f*

bi·sex·u·al ['baɪsekʃʊəl] **1** *adj* bisexual **2** *n* bisexual *m/f*

bish·op ['bɪʃəp] obispo *m*

bit¹ [bɪt] *n (piece)* trozo *m*; *(part)* parte *f*; *of puzzle* pieza *f*; COMPUT bit *m*; **a ~** *(a little)* un poco; **let's sit down for a ~** sentémonos un rato; **you haven't changed a ~** no has cambiado nada; **a ~ of** *(a little)* un poco de; **a ~ of news** una noticia; **a ~ of advice** un consejo; **~ by ~** poco a poco; **I'll be there in a ~** estaré allí dentro de un rato

bit² [bɪt] *pret* → **bite**

B

bitch [bɪtʃ] **1** *n dog* perra *f*; F *woman* zorra *f* F **2** *v/i* F (*complain*) quejarse

bitch·y ['bɪtʃɪ] *adj* F *person* malicioso; *remark* a mala leche F

bite [baɪt] **1** *n of dog* mordisco *m*; *of spider, mosquito* picadura *f*; *of snake* mordedura *f*, picadura *f*; *of food* bocado *m*; *let's have a ~ (to eat)* vamos a comer algo **2** *v/t* (*pret bit*, *pp bitten*) *of dog* morder; *of mosquito, flea* picar; *of snake* picar, morder; *~ one's nails* morderse las uñas **3** *v/i* (*pret bit*, *pp bitten*) *of dog* morder; *of mosquito, flea* picar; *of snake* morder, picar; *of fish* picar

bit·ten ['bɪtn] *pp* → *bite*

bit·ter ['bɪtər] *adj taste* amargo; *person* resentido; *weather* helador; *argument* agrio

bit·ter·ly ['bɪtərlɪ] *adv resent* amargamente; *it's ~ cold* hace un frío helador

bi·zarre [bɪ'zɑːr] *adj* extraño, peculiar

blab [blæb] *v/i* (*pret & pp -bed*) F irse de la lengua F

blab·ber·mouth ['blæbərmaʊθ] F bocazas *m/f inv* F

black [blæk] **1** *adj* negro; *coffee* solo; *tea* sin leche; *fig* negro, aciago **2** *n* (*color*) negro *m*; (*person*) negro(-a) *m(f)*; *be in the ~* FIN no estar en números rojos; *in ~ and white* en blanco y negro; *in writing* por escrito

♦ **black out** *v/i* perder el conocimiento

'black·ber·ry mora *f*; **'black·bird** mirlo *m*; **'black·board** pizarra *f*, encerado *m*; **black 'box** caja *f* negra; **black 'cof·fee** café *m* solo; **black e'con·o·my** economía *f* sumergida

black·en ['blækn] *v/t fig: person's name* manchar

black 'eye ojo *m* morado; **'black·head** espinilla *f*, punto *m* negro; **'black·list 1** *n* lista *f* negra **2** *v/t* poner en la lista negra; **'black·mail 1** *n* chantaje *m*; *emotional ~* chantaje *m* emocional **2** *v/t* chantajear; **'black·mail·er**

chantajista *m/f*; **black 'mar·ket** mercado *m* negro

black·ness ['blæknɪs] oscuridad *f*

'black·out ELEC apagón *m*; MED desmayo *m*; *have a ~* desmayarse

'black·smith herrero *m*

blad·der ['blædər] vejiga *f*

blade [bleɪd] *n of knife, sword* hoja *f*; *of propeller* pala *f*; *of grass* brizna *f*

blame [bleɪm] **1** *n* culpa *f*; *I got the ~ for it* me echaron la culpa **2** *v/t* culpar; *~ s.o. for sth* culpar a alguien de algo

bland [blænd] *adj smile* insulso; *food* insípido, soso

blank [blæŋk] **1** *adj* (*not written on*) en blanco; *tape* virgen; *look* inexpresivo **2** *n* (*empty space*) espacio *m* en blanco; *my mind's a ~* tengo la mente en blanco

blank 'check, *Br* **blank 'cheque** cheque *m* en blanco

blan·ket ['blæŋkɪt] *n* manta *f*, *L.Am.* frazada *f*; *a ~ of snow* un manto de nieve

blare [bler] *v/i* retumbar

♦ **blare out 1** *v/i* retumbar **2** *v/t* emitir a todo volumen

blas·pheme [blæs'fiːm] *v/i* blasfemar

blas·phe·my ['blæsfəmɪ] blasfemia *f*

blast [blæst] **1** *n* (*explosion*) explosión *f*; (*gust*) ráfaga *f* **2** *v/t tunnel* abrir (con explosivos); *rock* volar; *~!* F ¡mecachis! F

♦ **blast off** *v/i of rocket* despegar

'blast fur·nace alto horno *m*

'blast-off despegue *m*

bla·tant ['bleɪtənt] *adj* descarado

blaze [bleɪz] **1** *n* (*fire*) incendio *m*; *a ~ of color* una explosión de color **2** *v/i of fire* arder

♦ **blaze away** *v/i with gun* disparar sin parar

blaz·er ['bleɪzər] americana *f*

bleach [bliːtʃ] **1** *n for clothes* lejía *f*; *for hair* decolorante *m* **2** *v/t hair* aclarar, decolorar

bleak [bliːk] *adj countryside* inhóspito; *weather* desapacible; *future* desolador

blear·y-eyed ['blɪrɪaɪd] *adj* con ojos de sueño

bleat [bliːt] *v/i of sheep* balar

bled [bled] *pret & pp →* **bleed**

bleed [bliːd] **1** *v/i* (*pret & pp* **bled**) sangrar; *he's ~ing internally* tiene una hemorragia interna; *~ to death* desangrarse **2** *v/t* (*pret & pp* **bled**) *fig* sangrar

bleed·ing ['bliːdɪŋ] *n* hemorragia *f*

bleep [bliːp] **1** *n* pitido *m* **2** *v/i* pitar **3** *v/t* (*call on pager*) llamar con el buscapersonas

bleep·er ['bliːpər] buscapersonas *m inv, Span* busca *m*

blem·ish ['blemɪʃ] **1** *n* imperfección *f* **2** *v/t reputation* manchar

blend [blend] **1** *n of coffee etc* mezcla *f; fig* combinación *f* **2** *v/t* mezclar

♦ **blend in 1** *v/i of person in environment* pasar desapercibido; *of animal with surroundings etc* confundirse; *of furniture etc* combinar **2** *v/t in cooking* añadir

blend·er ['blendər] *machine* licuadora *f*

bless [bles] *v/t* bendecir; (*God*) *~ you!* ¡que Dios te bendiga!; *in response to sneeze* ¡Jesús!; *be ~ed with* tener la suerte de tener

bless·ing ['blesɪŋ] *also fig* bendición *f*

blew [bluː] *pret →* **blow**

blind [blaɪnd] **1** *adj* ciego; *corner* sin visibilidad; *be ~ to sth fig* no ver algo **2** *npl: the ~* los ciegos, los invidentes **3** *v/t of sun* cegar; *she was ~ed in an accident* se quedó ciega a raíz de un accidente

blind 'al·ley callejón *m* sin salida; **blind 'date** cita *f* a ciegas; **'blind·fold 1** *n* venda *f* **2** *v/t* vendar los ojos a **3** *adv* con los ojos cerrados

blind·ing ['blaɪndɪŋ] *adj light* cegador; *headache* terrible

blind·ly ['blaɪndlɪ] *adv* a ciegas; *fig* ciegamente

'blind spot *in road* punto *m* sin visibilidad; *in driving mirror* ángulo *m* muerto; (*ability that is lacking*) pun-

to *m* flaco

blink [blɪŋk] *v/i* parpadear

blink·ered ['blɪŋkərd] *adj fig* cerrado

blip [blɪp] *on radar screen* señal *f*, luz *f*; *it's just a ~ fig* es algo momentáneo

bliss [blɪs] felicidad *f*; *it was ~* fue fantástico

blis·ter ['blɪstər] **1** *n* ampolla *f* **2** *v/i* ampollarse; *of paint* hacer burbujas

bliz·zard ['blɪzərd] ventisca *f*

bloat·ed ['bloʊtɪd] *adj* hinchado

blob [blɑːb] *of liquid* goterón *m*

bloc [blɑːk] POL bloque *m*

block [blɑːk] **1** *n* bloque *m; buildings* manzana *f, L.Am.* cuadra *f; of shares* paquete *m;* (*blockage*) bloqueo *m* **2** *v/t* bloquear; *sink* atascar

♦ **block in** *v/t with vehicle* bloquear el paso a

♦ **block out** *v/t light* impedir el paso de

♦ **block up** *v/t sink etc* atascar

block·ade [blɑːˈkeɪd] **1** *n* bloqueo *m* **2** *v/t* bloquear

block·age ['blɑːkɪdʒ] obstrucción *f*

block·bust·er ['blɑːkbʌstər] gran éxito *m*

block 'let·ters *npl* letras *fpl* mayúsculas

blond [blɑːnd] *adj* rubio

blonde [blɑːnd] *n woman* rubia *f*

blood [blʌd] sangre *f; in cold ~* a sangre fría

'blood al·co·hol lev·el nivel *m* de alcohol en sangre; **'blood bank** banco *m* de sangre; **'blood bath** baño *m* de sangre; **'blood do·nor** donante *m/f* de sangre; **'blood group** grupo *m* sanguíneo

blood·less ['blʌdlɪs] *adj coup* incruento, pacífico

'blood poi·son·ing septicemia *f*; **'blood pres·sure** tensión *f* (arterial), presión *f* sanguínea; **'blood re·la·tion**: *she's not a ~ of mine* no nos unen lazos de sangre; **'blood sam·ple** muestra *f* de sangre; **'blood·shed** derramamiento *m* de sangre; **'blood·shot** *adj* enrojecido; **'blood·stain** mancha *f* de sangre; **'blood·stained** *adj* ensangrentado, manchado de sangre; '**blood-stream** flujo *m* sanguíneo; '**blood test** análisis *m inv* de sangre; '**blood·thirst·y** *adj* sanguinario; *movie* macabro; '**blood trans-fu·sion** transfusión *f* sanguínea; '**blood ves·sel** vaso *m* sanguíneo

blood·y ['blʌdɪ] *adj hands etc* ensangrentado; *battle* sangriento

bloom [bluːm] **1** *n* flor *f*; **in ~** en flor **2** *v/i also fig* florecer

blos·som ['blɑːsəm] **1** *n* flores *fpl* **2** *v/i also fig* florecer

blot [blɑːt] **1** *n* mancha *f*, borrón *m*; **be a ~ on the landscape** estropear el paisaje **2** *v/t* (*pret & pp* **-ted**) (*dry*) secar

♦ **blot out** *v/t* borrar; *sun, view* ocultar

blotch [blɑːtʃ] *on skin* erupción *f*, mancha *f*

blotch·y ['blɑːtʃɪ] *adj*: **~ skin** piel con erupciones

blouse [blauz] blusa *f*

blow¹ [bloʊ] *n* golpe *m*

blow² [bloʊ] **1** *v/t* (*pret* **blew**, *pp* **blown**) *smoke* exhalar; *whistle* tocar; F (*spend*) fundir F; F *opportunity* perder, desaprovechar; **~ one's nose** sonarse (la nariz) **2** *v/i* (*pret* **blew**, *pp* **blown**) *of wind, person* soplar; *of whistle* sonar; *of fuse* fundirse; *of tire* reventarse

♦ **blow off 1** *v/t* llevarse **2** *v/i* salir volando

♦ **blow out 1** *v/t candle* apagar **2** *v/i of candle* apagarse

♦ **blow over 1** *v/t* derribar, hacer caer **2** *v/i* caerse, derrumbarse; *of storm* amainar; *of argument* calmarse

♦ **blow up 1** *v/t with explosives* volar; *balloon* hinchar; *photograph* ampliar **2** *v/i* explotar; F (*become angry*) ponerse furioso

'**blow-dry** *v/t* (*pret & pp* **-ied**) secar (*con secador*)

'**blow-job** V mamada *f* V

blown [bloʊn] *pp* → **blow**

'**blow·out** *of tire* reventón *m*; F (*big meal*) comilona *f* F

'**blow-up** *of photo* ampliación *f*

blue [bluː] **1** *adj* azul; F *movie* porno *inv* F **2** *n* azul *m*

'**blue·ber·ry** arándano *m*; **blue 'chip** *adj* puntero, de primera fila; **blue-'col·lar work·er** trabajador(a) *m(f)* manual; '**blue·print** plano *m*; *fig* proyecto *m*, plan *m*

blues [bluːz] *npl* MUS blues *m inv*; **have the ~** estar deprimido

'**blues sing·er** cantante *m/f* de blues

bluff [blʌf] **1** *n* (*deception*) farol *m* **2** *v/i* ir de farol

blunder ['blʌndər] **1** *n* error *m* de bulto, metedura *f* de pata **2** *v/i* cometer un error de bulto, meter la pata

blunt [blʌnt] *adj pencil* sin punta; *knife* desafilado; *person* franco

blunt·ly ['blʌntlɪ] *adv speak* francamente

blur [blɜːr] **1** *n* imagen *f* desenfocada; *everything is a ~* todo está desenfocado **2** *v/t* (*pret & pp* **-red**) desdibujar

blurb [blɜːrb] *on book* nota *f* promocional

♦ **blurt out** [blɜːrt] *v/t* soltar

blush [blʌʃ] **1** *n* rubor *m*, sonrojo *m* **2** *v/i* ruborizarse, sonrojarse

blush·er ['blʌʃər] *cosmetic* colorete *m*

blus·ter ['blʌstər] *v/i* protestar encolerizadamente

blus·ter·y ['blʌstərɪ] *adj* tempestuoso

BO [biː'oʊ] *abbr* (= **body odor**) olor *m* corporal

board [bɔːrd] **1** *n* tablón *m*, tabla *f*; *for game* tablero *m*; *for notices* tablón *m*; **~ (of directors)** consejo *m* de administración; **on ~** *on plane, boat, train* a bordo; **take on ~** *comments etc* aceptar, tener en cuenta; (*fully realize truth of*) asumir; **across the ~** de forma general **2** *v/t airplane etc* embarcar; *train* subir a **3** *v/i of passengers* embarcar; **~ with** *as lodger* hospedarse con

♦ **board up** *v/t* cubrir con tablas

board·er ['bɔːrdər] huésped *m/f*

'**board game** juego *m* de mesa

'**board·ing card** tarjeta *f* de embarque; '**board·ing house** hostal *m*, pensión *f*; '**board·ing pass** tarjeta *f* de embarque; '**board·ing school** internado *m*

'**board meet·ing** reunión *f* del consejo de administración; '**board room** sala *f* de reuniones *or* juntas; '**board·walk** paseo marítimo con tablas

boast [boust] **1** *n* presunción *f*, jactancia *f* **2** *v/i* presumir, alardear (*about* de)

boat [bout] barco *m*; *small, for leisure* barca *f*; **go by ~** ir en barco

bob[1] [ba:b] *haircut* corte *m* a lo chico

bob[2] [ba:b] *v/i* (*pret & pp* **-bed**) *of boat etc* mecerse

♦ **bob up** *v/i* aparecer

'**bob·sled**, '**bob·sleigh** bobsleigh *m*

bod·ice ['ba:dɪs] cuerpo *m*

bod·i·ly ['ba:dɪlɪ] **1** *adj* corporal; *needs* físico; *function* fisiológico **2** *adv eject* en volandas

bod·y ['ba:dɪ] cuerpo *m*; *dead* cadáver *m*; ~ *of water* masa *f* de agua

'**bod·y·guard** guardaespaldas *m/f inv*; '**bod·y lan·guage** lenguaje *m* corporal; '**bod·y o·dor**, *Br* '**bod·y o·dour** olor *m* corporal; '**bod·y pierc·ing** piercing *m*, perforaciones *fpl* corporales; '**bod·y·shop** MOT taller *m* de carrocería; '**bod·y stock·ing** malla *f*; '**bod·y suit** body *m*; '**bod·y·work** MOT carrocería *f*

bog·gle ['ba:gl] *v/i*: *it ~s the mind!* ¡no quiero ni pensarlo!

bo·gus ['bougəs] *adj* falso

boil[1] [bɔɪl] *n* (*swelling*) forúnculo

boil[2] [bɔɪl] **1** *v/t liquid* hervir; *egg, vegetables* cocer **2** *v/i* hervir

♦ **boil down to** *v/t* reducirse a

♦ **boil over** *v/i of milk etc* salirse

boil·er ['bɔɪlər] caldera *f*

'**boil·ing point** ['bɔɪlɪŋ] *of liquid* punto *m* de ebullición; *reach* ~ *fig* perder la paciencia

bois·ter·ous ['bɔɪstərəs] *adj* escandaloso

bold [bould] **1** *adj* valiente, audaz;

text en negrita **2** *n print* negrita *f*; *in* ~ en negrita

Bo·liv·i·a [bə'lɪvɪə] *n* Bolivia

Bo·liv·i·an [bə'lɪvɪən] **1** *adj* boliviano **2** *n* boliviano(-a) *m(f)*

bol·ster ['boulstər] *v/t confidence* reforzar

bolt [boult] **1** *n on door* cerrojo *m*, pestillo *m*; *with nut* perno *m*; *of lightning* rayo *m*; *like a ~ from the blue* de forma inesperada **2** *adv*: ~ *upright* erguido **3** *v/t* (*fix with bolts*) atornillar; *close* cerrar con cerrojo *or* pestillo **4** *v/i* (*run off*) fugarse, escaparse

bomb [ba:m] **1** *n* bomba *f* **2** *v/t* MIL bombardear; *of terrorist* poner una bomba en

bom·bard [ba:m'ba:rd] *v/t also fig* bombardear

'**bomb at·tack** atentado *m* con bomba

bomb·er ['ba:mər] *airplane* bombardero *m*; *terrorist* terrorista *m/f* (*que pone bombas*)

'**bomb·er jack·et** cazadora *f* de aviador

'**bomb·proof** *adj* a prueba de bombas; '**bomb scare** amenaza *f* de bomba; '**bomb·shell** *fig*: *news* bomba *f*

bond [ba:nd] **1** *n* (*tie*) unión *f*; FIN bono *m* **2** *v/i of glue* adherirse

bone [boun] **1** *n* hueso *m*; *of fish* espina *f* **2** *v/t meat* deshuesar; *fish* quitar las espinas a

bon·fire ['ba:nfaɪr] hoguera *f*

bon·net *Br of car* capó *m*

bo·nus ['bounəs] *money plus m*, bonificación *f*; (*something extra*) ventaja *f* adicional; *a Christmas ~* un plus por Navidad

boo [bu:] **1** *n* abucheo *m* **2** *v/t & v/i* abuchear

boob [bu:b] *n* P (*breast*) teta *f* P

boo·boo ['bu:bu:] *n* F metedura *f* de pata

book [buk] **1** *n* libro *m*; *of matches* caja *f* (*de solapa*) **2** *v/t* (*reserve*) reservar; *of policeman* multar **3** *v/i* (*serve*) reservar, hacer una reserva

'book·case estantería f, librería f
booked up [bʊkt'ʌp] adj lleno, completo; *person* ocupado
book·ie ['bʊkɪ] F corredor(a) m(f) de apuestas
book·ing ['bʊkɪŋ] (*reservation*) reserva f
'book·ing clerk taquillero(-a) m(f)
'book·keep·er tenedor(a) m(f) de libros
'book·keep·ing contabilidad f
book·let ['bʊklɪt] folleto m
'book·mak·er corredor(a) m(f) de apuestas
books [bʊks] npl (*accounts*) contabilidad f; *do the* ~ llevar la contabilidad
'book·sell·er librero(-a) m(f);
'book·shelf (*pl* -shelves) estante m; 'book·stall puesto m de venta de libros; 'book·store librería f;
'book to·ken vale m para comprar libros
boom¹ [buːm] 1 n boom m 2 v/i of *business* desarrollarse, experimentar un boom
boom² [buːm] n *noise* estruendo m
boon·ies ['buːnɪz] npl F: *they live out in the* ~ viven en el quinto pino F
boor [bʊr] basto m, grosero m
boor·ish ['bʊrɪʃ] adj basto, grosero
boost [buːst] 1 n *to sales, economy* impulso m; *your confidence needs a* ~ necesitas algo que te dé más confianza 2 v/t *production, prices* estimular; *morale* levantar
boot [buːt] n bota f; *Br of car* maletero m, *C.Am.*, *Mex* cajuela f, *Rpl* baúl m
♦ boot out v/t F echar
♦ boot up v/t & v/i COMPUT arrancar
booth [buːð] *at market, fair* cabina f, *at exhibition* puesto m, stand m; (*in restaurant*) mesa rodeada por bancos fijos
booze [buːz] n F bebida f, *Span* priva f F
bor·der ['bɔːrdər] 1 n *between countries* frontera f; (*edge*) borde m; *on clothing* ribete m 2 v/t *country* limitar con; *river* bordear

♦ border on limitar con; (*be almost*) rayar en
'bor·der·line adj: *a ~ case* un caso dudoso
bore¹ [bɔːr] 1 v/t *hole* taladrar; *~ a hole in sth* taladrar algo
bore² [bɔːr] 1 n (*person*) pesado(-a) m(f), pelma m/f inv F 2 v/t aburrir
bore³ [bɔːr] pret → *bear²*
bored [bɔːrd] adj aburrido; *I'm* ~ me aburro, estoy aburrido
bore·dom ['bɔːrdəm] aburrimiento m
bor·ing ['bɔːrɪŋ] adj aburrido; *be* ~ ser aburrido
born [bɔːrn] adj: *be* ~ nacer; *where were you ~?* ¿dónde naciste?; *be a ~ teacher* haber nacido para ser profesor
borne [bɔːrn] pp → *bear²*
bor·row ['baːroʊ] v/t tomar prestado
bos·om ['bʊzm] *of woman* pecho m
boss [baːs] jefe(-a) m(f)
♦ boss around v/t dar órdenes a
boss·y ['baːsɪ] adj mandón
bo·tan·i·cal [bə'tænɪkl] adj botánico
bo·tan·ic(·al) 'gar·dens npl jardín m botánico
bot·a·nist ['baːtənɪst] botánico(-a) m(f)
bot·a·ny ['baːtənɪ] botánica f
botch [baːtʃ] v/t arruinar, estropear
both [boʊθ] 1 adj & pron ambos, los dos; *I know* ~ (*of the*) *brothers* conozco a ambos hermanos, conozco a los dos hermanos; *~ of them* ambos, los dos 2 adv: *~ my mother and I* tanto mi madre como yo; *he's ~ handsome and intelligent*; *is it business or pleasure?* – ~ ¿es de negocios o de placer? – las dos cosas
both·er ['baːðər] 1 n molestias fpl; *it's no* ~ no es ninguna molestia 2 v/t (*disturb*) molestar; (*worry*) preocupar 3 v/i preocuparse; *don't ~!* (*you needn't do it*) ¡no te preocupes!; *you needn't have ~ed* no deberías haberte molestado
bot·tle ['baːtl] 1 n botella f; *for baby*

biberón *m* **2** *v/t* embotellar

♦ **bottle up** *v/t* feelings reprimir, contener

'**bot·tle bank** contenedor *m* de vidrio

bot·tled wa·ter ['bɑːtld] agua *f* embotellada

'**bot·tle·neck** *n* in road embotellamiento *m*, atasco *m*; in production cuello *m* de botella

'**bot·tle-o·pen·er** abrebotellas *m inv*

bot·tom ['bɑːtəm] **1** adj inferior, de abajo **2** *n* of drawer, case, pan, garden fondo *m*; of hill, page pie *m*; of pile parte *f* inferior, (underside) parte *f* de abajo; of street final *m*; (buttocks) trasero *m*; **at the ~ of the screen** en la parte inferior de la pantalla

♦ **bottom out** *v/i* tocar fondo

bot·tom 'line (financial outcome) saldo *m* final; (real issue) realidad *f*

bought [bɔːt] pret & pp → **buy**

boul·der ['boʊldər] roca *f* redondeada

bounce [baʊns] **1** *v/t* ball botar **2** *v/i* of ball botar, rebotar; on sofa etc saltar; of rain rebotar; of check ser rechazado

bounc·er ['baʊnsər] portero *m*, gorila *m*

bounc·y ['baʊnsɪ] adj ball que bota bien; cushion, chair mullido

bound¹ [baʊnd] adj: **be ~ to do sth** (obliged to) estar obligado a hacer algo; **she's ~ to call an election soon** (sure to) seguro que convoca elecciones pronto

bound² [baʊnd] adj: **be ~ for** of ship llevar destino a

bound³ [baʊnd] **1** *n* (jump) salto *m* **2** *v/i* saltar

bound⁴ [baʊnd] pret & pp → **bind**

bound·a·ry ['baʊndərɪ] límite *m*; between countries frontera *f*

bound·less ['baʊndlɪs] adj ilimitado, infinito

bou·quet [buˈkeɪ] flowers ramo *m*

bour·bon ['bɜːrbən] bourbon *m*

bout [baʊt] MED ataque *m*; in boxing combate *m*

bou·tique [buːˈtiːk] boutique *f*

bow¹ [baʊ] **1** *n* as greeting reverencia *f* **2** *v/i* saludar con la cabeza **3** *v/t* head inclinar

bow² [boʊ] (knot) lazo *m*; MUS, for archery arco *m*

bow³ [baʊ] of ship proa *f*

bow·els ['baʊəlz] npl entrañas fpl

bowl¹ [boʊl] for rice, cereals etc cuenco *m*; for soup plato *m* sopero; for salad ensaladera *f*; for washing barreño *m*, palangana *f*

bowl² [boʊl] **1** *n* (ball) bola *f* **2** *v/i* in bowling lanzar la bola

♦ **bowl over** *v/t* fig (astonish) impresionar, maravillar

bowl·ing ['boʊlɪŋ] bolos mpl

'**bowl·ing al·ley** bolera *f*

bow 'tie [boʊ] pajarita *f*

box¹ [bɑːks] *n* container caja *f*; on form casilla *f*

box² [bɑːks] *v/i* boxear

box·er ['bɑːksər] boxeador(a) *m(f)*

'**box·er shorts** npl calzoncillos mpl, boxers mpl

box·ing ['bɑːksɪŋ] boxeo *m*

'**box·ing glove** guante *m* de boxeo; '**box·ing match** combate *m* de boxeo; '**box·ing ring** cuadrilátero *m*, ring *m*

'**box num·ber** at post office apartado *m* de correos

'**box of·fice** taquilla *f*, L.Am. boletería *f*

boy [bɔɪ] niño *m*, chico *m*; (son) hijo *m*

boy·cott ['bɔɪkɑːt] **1** *n* boicot *m* **2** *v/t* boicotear

'**boy·friend** novio *m*

boy·ish ['bɔɪɪʃ] adj varonil

boy'scout boy scout *m*

bra [brɑː] sujetador *m*, sostén *m*

brace [breɪs] on teeth aparato *m*

brace·let ['breɪslɪt] pulsera *f*

brack·et ['brækɪt] for shelf escuadra *f*; (square) ~ in text corchete *m*

brag [bræg] *v/i* (pret & pp **-ged**) presumir, fanfarronear

braid [breɪd] *n* in hair trenza *f*; trimming trenzado *m*

braille [breɪl] braille *m*

brain [breɪn] cerebro *m*; **use your ~**

utiliza la cabeza

'**brain dead** *adj* MED clínicamente muerto

brain·less ['breɪnlɪs] *adj* F estúpido

brains [breɪnz] *npl* (*intelligence*) inteligencia *f*; **the ~ of the operation** el cerebro de la operación

'**brain·storm** idea *f* genial; **brain·storm·ing** ['breɪnstɔːrmɪŋ] tormenta *f* de ideas; '**brain sur·geon** neurocirujano(-a) *m(f)*; '**brain sur·ger·y** neurocirugía *f*; '**brain tu·mor**, *Br* '**brain tu·mour** tumor *m* cerebral; '**brain·wash** *v/t* lavar el cerebro a; '**brain·wave** (*brilliant idea*) idea *f* genial

brain·y ['breɪnɪ] *adj* F: **be ~** tener mucho coco F, ser una lumbrera

brake [breɪk] **1** *n* freno *m* **2** *v/i* frenar

'**brake flu·id** MOT líquido *m* de frenos; '**brake light** MOT luz *f* de frenado; '**brake ped·al** MOT pedal *m* del freno

branch [bræntʃ] *n of tree* rama *f*, *of bank, company* sucursal *f*

♦ **branch off** *v/i of road* bifurcarse

♦ **branch out** *v/i* diversificarse; **they've branched out into furniture** han empezado a trabajar también con muebles

brand [brænd] **1** *n* marca *f* **2** *v/t*: **be ~ed a liar** ser tildado de mentiroso

brand 'im·age imagen *f* de marca

bran·dish ['brændɪʃ] *v/t* blandir

brand 'lead·er marca *f* líder del mercado; **brand 'loy·al·ty** lealtad *f* a una marca; '**brand name** nombre *m* comercial; **brand-'new** *adj* nuevo, flamante

bran·dy ['brændɪ] brandy *m*, coñac *m*

brass [bræs] *alloy* latón *m*; **the ~** MUS los metales

brass 'band banda *f* de música

bras·sière [brə'zɪr] sujetador *m*, sostén *m*

brat [bræt] *pej* niñato(-a) *m(f)*

bra·va·do [brə'vɑːdoʊ] bravuconería *f*

brave [breɪv] *adj* valiente, valeroso

brave·ly ['breɪvlɪ] *adv* valientemente, valerosamente

brav·er·y ['breɪvərɪ] valentía *f*, valor *m*

brawl [brɔːl] **1** *n* pelea *f* **2** *v/i* pelearse

brawn·y ['brɔːnɪ] *adj* fuerte, musculoso

Bra·zil [brə'zɪl] Brasil

Bra·zil·ian [brə'zɪlɪən] **1** *adj* brasileño **2** *n* brasileño(-a) *m(f)*

breach [briːtʃ] *n* (*violation*) infracción *f*, incumplimiento *m*; *in party* ruptura *f*

breach of 'con·tract LAW incumplimiento *m* de contrato

bread [bred] *n* pan *m*

'**bread·crumbs** *npl for cooking* pan *m* rallado; *for birds* migas *fpl*

'**bread knife** cuchillo *m* del pan

breadth [bredθ] *of road* ancho *m*; *of knowledge* amplitud *f*

'**bread·win·ner**: **be the ~** ser el que gana el pan

break [breɪk] **1** *n in bone etc* fractura *f*, rotura *f*, (*rest*) descanso *m*; *in relationship* separación *f* temporal; **give s.o. a ~** F (*opportunity*) ofrecer una oportunidad a alguien; **take a ~** descansar; **without a ~** *work, travel* sin descanso **2** *v/t* (*pret* **broke**, *pp* **broken**) *device* romper, estropear; *stick* romper, partir; *arm, leg* fracturar, romper; *glass, egg* romper; *rules, law* violar, incumplir; *promise* romper; *news* dar; *record* batir **3** *v/i* (*pret* **broke**, *pp* **broken**) *of device* romperse, estropearse; *of glass, egg* romperse; *of stick* partirse, romperse; *of news* saltar; *of storm* estallar, comenzar; *of boy's voice* cambiar

♦ **break away** *v/i* (*escape*) escaparse; *from family* separarse; *from organization* escindirse; *from tradition* romper (*from* con)

♦ **break down 1** *v/i of vehicle* averiarse, estropearse; *of machine* estropearse; *of talks* romperse; *in tears* romper a llorar; *mentally* venirse abajo **2** *v/t door* derribar; *figures* detallar, desglosar

♦ **break even** *v/i* COM cubrir gastos

♦ **break in** *v/i* (*interrupt*) interrumpir;

of burglar entrar

♦ **break off 1** *v/t* partir; *relationship* romper; ***they've broken it off*** han roto **2** *v/i* (*stop talking*) interrumpirse

♦ **break out** *v/i* (*start up*) comenzar; *of fighting* estallar; *of disease* desatarse; *of prisoners* escaparse, darse a la fuga; ***he broke out in a rash*** le salió un sarpullido

♦ **break up 1** *v/t into component parts* descomponer; *fight* poner fin a **2** *v/i of ice* romperse; *of couple* terminar, separarse; *of band* separarse; *of meeting* terminar

break·a·ble ['breɪkəbl] *adj* rompible, frágil

break·age ['breɪkɪdʒ] rotura *f*

'**break·down** *of vehicle, machine* avería *f*; *of talks* ruptura *f*; (*nervous* ~) crisis *f inv* nerviosa; *of figures* desglose *m*

break-'e·ven point punto *m* de equilibrio

break·fast ['brekfəst] *n* desayuno *m*; ***have*** ~ desayunar

'**break·fast tel·e·vi·sion** televisión *f* matinal

'**break-in** entrada *f* (*mediante la fuerza*); *robbery* robo *m*; ***we've had a*** ~ han entrado a robar; '**break-through** *in plan, negotiations* paso *m* adelante; *of science, technology* avance *m*; '**break-up** *of marriage, partnership* ruptura *f*, separación *f*

breast [brest] *of woman* pecho *m*

'**breast·feed** *v/t* (*pret & pp* ***breastfed***) amamantar

'**breast·stroke** braza *f*

breath [breθ] respiración *f*; ***get your*** ~ ***back*** recobrar el aliento; ***be out of*** ~ estar sin respiración; ***take a deep*** ~ respira hondo

Breath·a·lyz·er® ['breθəlaɪzər] alcoholímetro *m*

breathe [briːð] **1** *v/i* respirar **2** *v/t* (*inhale*) aspirar, respirar; (*exhale*) exhalar, espirar

♦ **breathe in** *v/t & v/i* aspirar, inspirar

♦ **breathe out** *v/i* espirar

breath·ing ['briːðɪŋ] *n* respiración *f*

breath·less ['breθlɪs] *adj*: ***arrive*** ~ llegar sin respiración, llegar jadeando

breath·less·ness ['breθlɪsnɪs] dificultad *f* para respirar

breath·tak·ing ['breθteɪkɪŋ] *adj* impresionante, sorprendente

bred [bred] *pret & pp* → ***breed***

breed [briːd] **1** *n* raza *f* **2** *v/t* (*pret & pp* ***bred***) criar; *plants* cultivar; *fig* causar, generar **3** *v/i* (*pret & pp* ***bred***) *of animals* reproducirse

breed·er ['briːdər] *of animals* criador(a) *m(f)*; *of plants* cultivador(a) *m(f)*

breed·ing ['briːdɪŋ] *of animals* cría *f*; *of plants* cultivo *m*; *of person* educación *f*

breed·ing ground *fig* caldo *m* de cultivo

breeze [briːz] brisa *f*

breez·i·ly ['briːzɪlɪ] *adv fig* jovialmente, tranquilamente

breez·y ['briːzɪ] *adj* ventoso; *fig* jovial, tranquilo

brew [bruː] **1** *v/t beer* elaborar; *tea* preparar, hacer **2** *v/i of storm* avecinarse; *of trouble* fraguarse

brew·er ['bruːər] fabricante *m/f* de cerveza

brew·er·y ['bruːərɪ] fábrica *f* de cerveza

bribe [braɪb] **1** *n* soborno *m*, *Mex* mordida *f*, *S.Am.* coima *f* **2** *v/t* sobornar

brib·er·y ['braɪbərɪ] soborno *m*, *Mex* mordida *f*, *S.Am.* coima *f*

brick [brɪk] ladrillo *m*

'**brick·lay·er** albañil *m/f*

brid·al suite ['braɪdl] suite *f* nupcial

bride [braɪd] novia *f* (*en boda*)

'**bride·groom** novio *m* (*en boda*)

'**brides·maid** dama *f* de honor

bridge[1] [brɪdʒ] **1** *n also* NAUT puente *m*; *of nose* caballete *m* **2** *v/t gap* superar, salvar

bridge[2] [brɪdʒ] *card game* bridge *m*

bri·dle ['braɪdl] *n* brida *f*

brief[1] ['briːf] *adj* breve, corto

brief[2] [briːf] **1** *n* (*mission*) misión *f* **2** *v/t*: ~ ***s.o. on sth*** informar a alguien de algo

brief·case maletín *m*

brief·ing ['bri:fɪŋ] reunión *f* informativa

brief·ly ['bri:flɪ] *adv* (*for a short period of time*) brevemente; (*in a few words*) en pocas palabras; (*to sum up*) en resumen

briefs [bri:fs] *npl for women* bragas *fpl*; *for men* calzoncillos *mpl*

bright [braɪt] *adj color* vivo; *smile* radiante; *future* brillante, prometedor; (*sunny*) soleado, luminoso; (*intelligent*) inteligente

♦**bright·en up** ['braɪtn] **1** *v/t* alegrar **2** *v/i of weather* aclararse; *of face, person* animarse

bright·ly ['braɪtlɪ] *adv shine* intensamente, fuerte; *smile* alegremente

bright·ness ['braɪtnɪs] *of light* brillo *m*; *of weather* luminosidad *f*; *of smile* alegría *f*; (*intelligence*) inteligencia *f*

bril·liance ['brɪljəns] *of person* genialidad *f*; *of color* resplandor *m*

bril·liant ['brɪljənt] *adj sunshine etc* resplandeciente, radiante; (*very good*) genial; (*very intelligent*) brillante

brim [brɪm] *of container* borde *m*; *of hat* ala *f*

brim·ful ['brɪmfəl] *adj* rebosante

bring [brɪŋ] *v/t* (*pret & pp* **brought**) traer; ~ *it here, will you* tráelo aquí, por favor; *can I* ~ *a friend?* ¿puedo traer a un amigo?, ¿puedo venir con un amigo?

♦**bring about** *v/t* ocasionar; *bring about peace* traer la paz

♦**bring around** *v/t from a faint* hacer volver en sí; (*persuade*) convencer, persuadir

♦**bring back** *v/t* (*return*) devolver; (*re-introduce*) reinstaurar; *memories* traer

♦**bring down** *v/t fence, tree* tirar, echar abajo; *government* derrocar; *bird, airplane* derribar; *rates, inflation, price* reducir

♦**bring in** *v/t interest, income* generar; *legislation* introducir; *verdict* pronunciar

♦**bring on** *v/t illness* provocar

♦**bring out** *v/t book, video, new product* sacar

♦**bring to** *v/t from a faint* hacer volver en sí

♦**bring up** *v/t child* criar, educar; *subject* mencionar, sacar a colación; (*vomit*) vomitar

brink [brɪŋk] borde *m*; *be on the* ~ *of* (*doing*) *sth fig* estar a punto de (hacer) algo

brisk [brɪsk] *adj person, voice* enérgico; *walk* rápido; *trade* animado

bris·tle ['brɪsl] *v/i: the streets are bristling with policemen* las calles están atestadas de policías

bris·tles ['brɪslz] *npl on chin* pelos *mpl*; *of brush* cerdas *fpl*

Brit [brɪt] F británico(-a) *m(f)*

Brit·ain ['brɪtn] Gran Bretaña

Brit·ish ['brɪtɪʃ] **1** *adj* británico **2** *npl*: *the* ~ los británicos

Brit·on ['brɪtn] británico(-a) *m(f)*

brit·tle ['brɪtl] *adj* frágil, quebradizo

broach [brəʊtʃ] *v/t subject* sacar a colación

broad [brɔːd] **1** *adj* ancho; *smile* amplio; (*general*) general; *in* ~ *daylight* a plena luz del día **2** *n* F (*woman*) tía *f* F

broad·cast **1** *n* emisión *f*; *a live* ~ una retransmisión en directo **2** *v/t* emitir, retransmitir

broad·cast·er presentador(a) *m(f)*

broad·cast·ing televisión *f*

broad·en ['brɔːdn] **1** *v/i* ensancharse, ampliarse **2** *v/t* ensanchar; ~ *one's horizons* ampliar los horizontes

broad·jump salto *m* de longitud

broad·ly ['brɔːdlɪ] *adv* en general; ~ *speaking* en términos generales

broad·mind·ed [brɔːd'maɪndɪd] *adj* tolerante, abierto

broad·mind·ed·ness [brɔːd'maɪndɪdnɪs] mentalidad *f* abierta

broc·co·li ['brɑːkəlɪ] brécol *m*, brócoli *m*

bro·chure ['brəʊʃər] folleto *m*

broil [brɔɪl] *v/t* asar a la parrilla

broil·er ['brɔɪlər] *on stove* parrilla *f*;

chicken pollo *m* (para asar)

broko [broʊk] **1** *adj* F: **be ~** *temporarily* estar sin blanca F; *long term* estar arruinado; **go ~** (*go bankrupt*) arruinarse **2** *pret* → **break**

bro·ken ['broʊkn] **1** *adj* roto; *home* deshecho; **they talk in ~ English** chapurrean el inglés **2** *pp* → **break**

bro·ken-heart·ed [broʊkn'hɑːrtɪd] *adj* desconsolado, destrozado

bro·ker ['broʊkər] corredor(a) *m(f)*, agente *m/f*

bron·chi·tis [brɑːŋ'kaɪtɪs] bronquitis *f*

bronze [brɑːnz] *n* bronce *m*

'bronze med·al medalla *f* de bronce

brooch [broʊtʃ] broche *m*

brood [bruːd] *v/i of person* darle vueltas a las cosas; **~ about sth** darle vueltas a algo

broom [bruːm] escoba *f*

broth [brɑːθ] *soup* sopa *f*; *stock* caldo *m*

broth·el ['brɑːθl] burdel *m*

broth·er ['brʌðər] hermano *m*

'broth·er-in-law (*pl* **brothers-in-law**) cuñado *m*

broth·er·ly ['brʌðərlɪ] *adj* fraternal

brought [brɔːt] *pret & pp* → **bring**

brow [braʊ] (*forehead*) frente *f*; *of hill* cima *f*

brown [braʊn] **1** *n* marrón *m*, *L.Am.* color *m* café **2** *adj* marrón; *eyes, hair* castaño; (*tanned*) moreno **3** *v/t in cooking* dorar **4** *v/i in cooking* dorarse

'brown·bag *v/t* (*pret & pp* **-ged**) F: **~ it** llevar la comida al trabajo

Brown·ie ['braʊnɪ] escultista *f*

'Brown·ie points *npl* tantos *mpl*; **earn ~** anotarse tantos

brown·ie ['braʊnɪ] (*cake*) pastel *m* de chocolate y nueces

'brown-nose *v/t* P lamer el culo a P; **brown 'pa·per** papel *m* de estraza; **brown 'pa·per bag** bolsa *f* de cartón; **brown 'sug·ar** azúcar *m or f* moreno(-a)

browse [braʊz] **1** *v/i in store* echar una ojeada; **~ through a book** hojear un libro **2** *v/t the Web* navegar por

brows·er ['braʊzər] COMPUT navegador *m*

bruise [bruːz] **1** *n* magulladura *f*, cardenal *f*; *on fruit* maca *f* **2** *v/t arm, fruit* magullar; (*emotionally*) herir **3** *v/i of person* hacerse cardenales; *of fruit* macarse

bruis·ing ['bruːzɪŋ] *adj fig* doloroso

brunch [brʌntʃ] combinación de desayuno y almuerzo

bru·nette [bruː'net] *n* morena *f*

brunt [brʌnt]: **this area bore the ~ of the flooding** esta zona fue la más castigada por la inundación; **we bore the ~ of the layoffs** fuimos los más perjudicados por los despidos

brush [brʌʃ] **1** *n* cepillo *m*; *conflict* roce *m* **2** *v/t* cepillar; (*touch lightly*) rozar; (*move away*) quitar

♦ **brush against** *v/t* rozar

♦ **brush aside** *v/t* hacer caso omiso a, no hacer caso a

♦ **brush off** *v/t* sacudir; *criticism* no hacer caso a

♦ **brush up** *v/t* repasar

'brush·work PAINT pincelada *f*

brusque [brʊsk] *adj* brusco

Brus·sels ['brʌslz] Bruselas

Brus·sels 'sprouts *npl* coles *fpl* de Bruselas

bru·tal ['bruːtl] *adj* brutal

bru·tal·i·ty [bruː'tælətɪ] brutalidad *f*

bru·tal·ly ['bruːtəlɪ] *adv* brutalmente; **be ~ frank** ser de una sinceridad aplastante

brute [bruːt] *n* bruto *m/f*

brute 'force fuerza *f* bruta

bub·ble ['bʌbl] *n* burbuja *f*

'bub·ble bath baño *m* de espuma; **'bub·ble gum** chicle *m*; **'bub·ble wrap** *n* plástico *m* para embalar (*con burbujas*)

bub·bly ['bʌblɪ] *n* F (*champagne*) champán *m*

buck[1] [bʌk] *n* F (*dollar*) dólar *m*

buck[2] [bʌk] *v/i of horse* corcovear

buck[3] [bʌk] *n*: **pass the ~** escurrir el bulto

buck·et ['bʌkɪt] *n* cubo *m*

buck·le[1] ['bʌkl] **1** *n* hebilla *f* **2** *v/t belt* abrochar

buck·le² ['bʌkl] *v/i of metal* combarse
♦ **buckle down** *v/i* ponerse a trabajar
bud [bʌd] *n* BOT capullo *m*, brote *m*
bud·dy ['bʌdɪ] F *amigo(-a) m(f)*, *Span* colega *m/f* F; *form of address* *Span* colega *m/f* F, *L.Am.* compadre *m/f* F
budge [bʌdʒ] **1** *v/t* mover; *(make reconsider)* hacer cambiar de opinión **2** *v/i* moverse; *(change one's mind)* cambiar de opinión
bud·ger·i·gar ['bʌdʒərɪgɑːr] periquito *m*
bud·get ['bʌdʒɪt] **1** *n* presupuesto *m*; **be on a ~** tener un presupuesto limitado **2** *v/i* administrarse
♦ **budget for** *v/t* contemplar en el presupuesto
bud·gie ['bʌdʒɪ] F periquito *m*
buff¹ [bʌf] *adj color* marrón claro
buff² [bʌf] *n* aficionado(-a) *m(f)*; *a movie ~* un cinéfilo
buf·fa·lo ['bʌfələu] búfalo *m*
buff·er ['bʌfər] RAIL tope *m*; COMPUT búfer *m*; *fig* barrera *f*
buf·fet¹ ['bufeɪ] *n (meal)* bufé *m*
buf·fet² ['bʌfɪt] *v/t of wind* sacudir
bug [bʌg] **1** *n insect* bicho *m*; *virus* virus *m inv*; *(spying device)* micrófono *m* oculto; COMPUT error *m* **2** *v/t* (*pret & pp -ged*) *room* colocar un micrófono en; F *(annoy)* fastidiar F, jorobar F
bug·gy ['bʌgɪ] *for baby* silla *f* de paseo
bu·gle [bjuːgl] corneta *f*, clarín *m*
build [bɪld] **1** *n of person* constitución *f*, complexión *f* **2** *v/t* (*pret & pp* **built**) construir, edificar
♦ **build up 1** *v/t strength* aumentar; *relationship* fortalecer; *collection* acumular **2** *v/i of dirt* acumularse; *of pressure, excitement* aumentar
'build·er ['bɪldər] albañil *m/f*; *company* constructora *f*
'build·ing ['bɪldɪŋ] edificio *m*; *activity* construcción *f*
'build·ing blocks *npl for child* piezas *fpl* de construcción; **'build·ing site**

obra *f*; **'build·ing so·ci·e·ty** *Br* caja *f* de ahorros; **'build·ing trade** industria *f* de la construcción
'build-up *(accumulation)* accumulación *f*; *after all the ~ publicity* después de tantas expectativas
built [bɪlt] *pret & pp* → **build**
built-in ['bɪltɪn] *adj cupboard* empotrado; *flash* incorporado
built-up 'ar·e·a zona *f* urbanizada
bulb [bʌlb] BOT bulbo *m*; *(light ~)* bombilla *f*, *L.Am.* foco *m*
bulge [bʌldʒ] **1** *n* bulto *m*, abultamiento *m* **2** *v/i of eyes* salirse de las órbitas; *of wall* abombarse
bu·lim·i·a [buˈlɪmɪə] bulimia *f*
bulk [bʌlk] *the ~ of* el grueso *or* la mayor parte de; *in ~* a granel
'bulk·y ['bʌlkɪ] *adj* voluminoso
bull [bul] *animal* toro *m*
bull·doze ['buldəuz] *v/t (demolish)* demoler, derribar; *~ s.o. into sth fig* obligar a alguien a hacer algo
bull·doz·er ['buldəuzər] bulldozer *m*
bul·let ['bulɪt] bala *f*
bul·le·tin ['bulɪtɪn] boletín *m*
'bul·le·tin board *on wall* tablón de anuncios; COMPUT tablón *m* de anuncios, BBS *f*
'bul·let-proof *adj* antibalas *inv*
'bull fight corrida *f* de toros; **'bull fight·er** torero(-a) *m(f)*; **'bull fight·ing** tauromaquia *f*, los toros; **'bull mar·ket** FIN mercado *m* al alza; **'bull ring** plaza *f* de toros; **'bull's-eye** diana *f*, blanco *m*; *hit the ~* dar en el blanco; **'bull·shit** F V *Span* gilipollez *f* V, *L.Am.* pendejada *f* V **2** *v/i* (*pret & pp -ted*) V decir *Span* gilipolleces V *or L.Am.* pendejadas V
bul·ly ['bulɪ] **1** *n* matón(-ona) *m(f)*; *child* abusón(-ona) *m(f)* **2** *v/t* (*pret & pp -ied*) intimidar
bul·ly·ing ['bulɪɪŋ] *n* intimidación *f*
bum [bʌm] F **1** *n (tramp)* vagabundo(-a) *m(f)*; *(worthless person)* inútil *m/f* **2** *adj (useless)* inútil **3** *v/t* (*pret & pp -med*) *cigarette etc* gorronear
♦ **bum around** *v/i* F *travel* vaga-

bundear (**in** por); (*be lazy*) vaguear

bum·ble·bee ['bʌmblbi:] abejorro *m*

bump [bʌmp] **1** *n* (*swelling*) chichón *m*; *on road* bache *m*; **get a ~ on the head** darse un golpe en la cabeza **2** *v/t* golpear

♦ **bump into** *v/t table* chocar con; (*meet*) encontrarse con

♦ **bump off** *v/t* F (*murder*) cargarse a F

♦ **bump up** *v/t* F *prices* aumentar

bump·er ['bʌmpər] **1** *n* MOT parachoques *m inv*; **the traffic was ~ to ~** el tráfico estaba colapsado **2** *adj* (*extremely good*) excepcional, extraordinario

'**bump-start** *v/t car* arrancar un coche empujándolo; *fig: economy* reanimar

bump·y ['bʌmpɪ] *adj* con baches; *flight* movido

bun [bʌn] *hairstyle* moño *m*; *for eating* bollo *m*

bunch [bʌntʃ] *of people* grupo *m*; *of keys* manojo *m*; *of flowers* ramo *m*; *of grapes* racimo *m*; **thanks a ~** *iron* no sabes lo que te lo agradezco

bun·dle ['bʌndl] *of clothes* fardo *m*; *of wood* haz *m*

♦ **bundle up** *v/t* liar; (*dress warmly*) abrigar

bun·gee jump·ing ['bʌndʒɪdʒʌmpɪŋ] puenting *m*

bun·gle ['bʌŋgl] *v/t* echar a perder

bunk [bʌŋk] litera *f*

bunk beds *npl* literas *fpl*

buoy [bɔɪ] *n* NAUT boya *f*

buoy·ant ['bɔɪənt] *adj* animado, optimista; *economy* boyante

bur·den ['bɜːrdn] **1** *n also fig* carga *f* **2** *v/t*: **~ s.o. with sth** *fig* cargar a alguien con algo

bu·reau ['bjʊroʊ] (*chest of drawers*) cómoda *f*; (*office*) departamento *m*, oficina *f*; **a translation ~** una agencia de traducción

bu·reauc·ra·cy [bjʊ'rɑːkrəsɪ] burocracia *f*

bu·reau·crat ['bjʊrəkræt] burócrata *m/f*

bu·reau·crat·ic [bjʊrə'krætɪk] *adj* burocrático

burg·er ['bɜːrgər] hamburguesa *f*

bur·glar ['bɜːrglər] ladrón(-ona) *m(f)*

'**bur·glar a·larm** alarma *f* antirrobo

bur·glar·ize ['bɜːrglərɑɪz] *v/t* robar

bur·glar·y ['bɜːrglərɪ] robo *m*

bur·i·al ['berɪəl] entierro *m*

bur·ly ['bɜːrlɪ] *adj* corpulento, fornido

burn [bɜːrn] **1** *n* quemadura *f* **2** *v/t* (*pret & pp **burnt***) quemar; **be ~t to death** morir abrasado **3** *v/i* (*pret & pp **burnt***) *of wood, meat, in sun* quemarse

♦ **burn down 1** *v/t* incendiar **2** *v/i* incendiarse

♦ **burn out** *v/t*: **burn o.s. out** quemarse; **a burned-out car** un coche carbonizado

burn·er ['bɜːrnər] *on cooker* placa *f*

'**burn·out** F (*exhaustion*) agotamiento *m*

burnt [bɜːrnt] *pret & pp →* **burn**

burp [bɜːrp] **1** *n* eructo *m* **2** *v/i* eructar **3** *v/t baby* hacer eructar a

burst [bɜːrst] **1** *n in water pipe* rotura *f*; *of gunfire* ráfaga *f*; **in a ~ of energy** en un arrebato de energía **2** *adj tire* reventado **3** *v/t* (*pret & pp **burst***) *balloon* reventar **4** *v/i* (*pret & pp **burst***) *of balloon, tire* reventar; **~ into a room** irrumpir en una habitación; **~ into tears** echarse a llorar; **~ out laughing** echarse a reír

bur·y ['berɪ] *v/t* (*pret & pp **-ied***) enterrar; **be buried under** (*covered by*) estar sepultado por; **~ o.s. in work** meterse de lleno en el trabajo

bus [bʌs] **1** *n local* autobús *m*, *Mex* camión *m*, *Arg* colectivo *m*, *C.Am.* guagua *f*; *long distance* autobús *m*, *Span* autocar *m*; **school ~** autobús *m* escolar **2** *v/t* (*pret & pp **-sed***) llevar en autobús

'**bus·boy** ayudante *m* de camarero

'**bus driv·er** conductor(a) *m(f)* de autobús

bush [bʊʃ] *plant* arbusto *m*; *type of countryside* monte *m*

B

bushed [buʃt] *adj* F (*tired*) molido F

bush·y ['buʃɪ] *adj* beard espeso

busi·ness ['bɪznɪs] negocios *mpl*; (*company*) empresa *f*; (*sector*) sector *m*; (*affair, matter*) asunto *m*; *as subject of study* empresariales *fpl*; **on ~** de negocios; *that's none of your ~!* ¡no es asunto tuyo!; *mind your own ~!* ¡no te metas en lo que no te importa!

'**busi·ness card** tarjeta *f* de visita; '**busi·ness class** clase *f* ejecutiva; '**busi·ness hours** *npl* horario *m* de oficina; **busi·ness·like** ['bɪznɪslaɪk] *adj* eficiente; '**busi·ness lunch** almuerzo *m* de negocios; '**busi·ness·man** hombre *m* de negocios, ejecutivo *m*; '**busi·ness meet·ing** reunión *f* de negocios; '**busi·ness school** escuela *f* de negocios; '**busi·ness stud·ies** *nsg course* empresariales *mpl*; '**busi·ness trip** viaje *m* de negocios; '**busi·ness·wom·an** mujer *f* de negocios, ejecutiva *f*

'**bus lane** carril *m* bus; '**bus shel·ter** marquesina *f*; '**bus sta·tion** estación *f* de autobuses; '**bus stop** parada *f* de autobús

bust¹ [bʌst] *n of woman* busto *m*

bust² [bʌst] **1** *adj* F (*broken*) escacharrado F; **go ~** quebrar **2** *v/t* F escacharrar F

'**bus tick·et** billete *m or L.Am.* boleto *m* de autobús

♦ **bus·tle around** ['bʌsl] *v/i* trajinar

'**bust-up** F corte *m* F

bust·y ['bʌstɪ] *adj* pechugona

bus·y ['bɪzɪ] **1** *adj also* TELEC ocupado; *full of people* abarrotado; *of restaurant etc: making money* ajetreado; *the line was ~* estaba ocupado, *Span* comunicaba; *she leads a very ~ life* lleva una vida muy ajetreada; *be ~ doing sth* estar ocupado *or* atareado haciendo algo **2** *v/t* (*pret & pp -ied*): **~ o.s. with sth** entretenerse con algo

'**bus·y·bod·y** metomentodo *m/f*, entrometido(-a) *m(f)*

'**bus·y sig·nal** señal *f* de ocupado *or Span* comunicando

but [bʌt] *unstressed* [bət] **1** *conj* pero; *it's not me ~ my father you want* no me quieres a mí sino a mi padre; **~ then** (*again*) pero **2** *prep*: *all ~ him* todos excepto él; *the last ~ one* el penúltimo; *the next ~ one* el próximo no, el otro; *the next page ~ one* la página siguiente a la próxima; *~ for you* si no hubiera sido por ti; *nothing ~ the best* sólo lo mejor

butch·er ['butʃər] carnicero(-a) *m(f)*; *murderer* asesino(-a) *m(f)*

butt [bʌt] **1** *n of cigarette* colilla *f*; *of joke* blanco *m*; F (*buttocks*) trasero *m* F **2** *v/t* dar un cabezazo a; *of goat, bull* embestir

♦ **butt in** *v/i* inmiscuirse, entrometerse

but·ter ['bʌtər] **1** *n* mantequilla *f* **2** *v/t* untar de mantequilla

♦ **butter up** *v/t* F hacer la pelota a F

'**but·ter·fly** *insect* mariposa *f*

but·tocks ['bʌtəks] *npl* nalgas *fpl*

but·ton ['bʌtn] **1** *n on shirt, machine* botón *m*; (*badge*) chapa *f* **2** *v/t* abotonar

♦ **button up** *v/t* abotonar

'**but·ton·hole 1** *n in suit* ojal *m* **2** *v/t* acorralar

bux·om ['bʌksəm] *adj* de amplios senos

buy [baɪ] **1** *n* compra *f*, adquisición *f* **2** *v/t* (*pret & pp bought*) comprar; *can I ~ you a drink?* ¿quieres tomar algo?; *$5 doesn't ~ much* con 5 dólares no se puede hacer gran cosa

♦ **buy off** *v/t* (*bribe*) sobornar

♦ **buy out** *v/t* COM comprar la parte de

♦ **buy up** *v/t* acaparar

buy·er [baɪr] comprador(a) *m(f)*

buzz [bʌz] **1** *n* zumbido *m*; *she gets a real ~ out of it* F (*thrill*) le vuelve loca, le entusiasma **2** *v/i of insect* zumbar; *with buzzer* llamar por el interfono **3** *v/t with buzzer* llamar por el interfono a

♦ **buzz off** *v/i* F largarse F, *Span* pirarse F

buz·zard ['bʌzərd] ratonero *m*
buzz·er ['bʌzər] timbre *m*
'buzz·word palabra *f* de moda
by [baɪ] **1** *prep to show agent* por;
(near, next to) al lado de, junto a; *(no later than)* no más tarde de; *mode of transport* en; **she rushed ~ me** pasó rápidamente por mi lado; **as we drove ~ the church** cuando pasábamos por la iglesia; **side ~ side** uno junto al otro; **~ day/night** de día/noche; **~ bus/train** en autobús/tren; **~ the dozen** por docenas; **~ the hour/ton** por hora/por tonelada; **~ my watch** en mi reloj; **~ nature** por naturaleza; **a play ~ ...** una obra de ...; **~ o.s.** *without company* solo; **I did it ~ myself** lo

hice yo solito; **~ a couple of minutes** por un par de minutos; **2 ~ 1** *measurement* 2 por 4; **~ this time tomorrow** mañana a esta hora; **~ this time next year** el año que viene por estas fechas; **go ~**, **pass ~** pasar **2** *adv*: **~ and ~** *(soon)* dentro de poco
bye(-bye) [baɪ] adiós
by·gones ['baɪgɑːnz]: **let ~ be ~** lo pasado, pasado está; **'by·pass 1** *n road* circunvalación *f*; MED bypass *m* **2** *v/t* sortear; **'by-prod·uct** subproducto *m*; **by·stand·er** ['baɪstændər] transeúnte *m/f*
byte [baɪt] byte *m*
'by·word: **be a ~ for sth** ser sinónimo de algo

C

cab [kæb] *(taxi)* taxi *m*; *of truck* cabina *f*
cab·a·ret ['kæbəreɪ] cabaret *m*
cab·bage ['kæbɪdʒ] col *f*, repollo *m*
'cab driv·er taxista *m/f*
cab·in ['kæbɪn] *of plane* cabina *f*; *of ship* camarote *m*
'cab·in at·tend·ant auxiliar *m/f* de vuelo
'cab·in crew personal *m* de a bordo
cab·i·net ['kæbɪnɪt] armario *m*; POL gabinete *m*; **drinks ~** mueble *m* bar; **medicine ~** botiquín *m*; **display ~** vitrina *f*
'cab·i·net mak·er ebanista *m/f*
ca·ble ['keɪbl] cable *m*; **~ (TV)** televisión *f* por cable
'ca·ble car teleférico *m*
'ca·ble tel·e·vi·sion televisión *f* por cable
'cab stand parada *f* de taxis
cac·tus ['kæktəs] cactus *m inv*
CAD [kæd] *abbr* (= **computer assisted design**) CAD *m* (= dise-

ño asistido por *Span* ordenador *or L.Am.* computadora)
ca·dav·er [kə'dævər] cadáver *m*
cad·die ['kædɪ] **1** *n in golf* caddie *m/f* **2** *v/i* hacer de caddie
ca·det [kə'det] cadete *m*
cadge [kædʒ] *v/t* F: **~ sth from s.o.** gorronear algo a alguien
Cae·sar·e·an *Br* → **Cesarean**
caf·é ['kæfeɪ] café *m*, cafetería *f*
caf·e·te·ri·a [kæfɪ'tɪrɪə] cafetería *f*, cantina *f*
caf·feine ['kæfiːn] cafeína *f*
cage [keɪdʒ] jaula *f*
ca·gey ['keɪdʒɪ] *adj* cauteloso, reservado; **he's ~ about how old he is** es muy reservado con respecto a su edad
ca·hoots [kə'huːts] *npl* F: **be in ~ with s.o.** estar conchabado con alguien
ca·jole [kə'dʒoul] *v/t* engatusar, persuadir
cake [keɪk] **1** *n big* tarta *f*; *small pas-*

tel *m*; **be a piece of ~** F estar chupado F **2** *v/i* endurecerse

ca·lam·i·ty [kə'læmətɪ] calamidad *f*

cal·ci·um ['kælsɪəm] calcio *m*

cal·cu·late ['kælkjʊleɪt] *v/t* calcular

cal·cu·lat·ing ['kælkjʊleɪtɪŋ] *adj* calculador

cal·cu·la·tion [kælkjʊ'leɪʃn] cálculo
m

cal·cu·la·tor ['kælkjʊleɪtər] calculadora *f*

cal·en·dar ['kælɪndər] calendario *m*

calf¹ [kæf] (*pl* **calves** [kævz])
(*young cow*) ternero(-a) *m(f)*,
becerro(-a) *m(f)*

calf² [kæf] (*pl* **calves** [kævz]) *of leg*
pantorrilla *f*

'calf·skin *n* piel *f* de becerro

cal·i·ber, *Br* cal·i·bre ['kælɪbər] *of
gun* calibre *m*; **a man of his ~** un
hombre de su calibre

Cal·i·for·ni·an [kælɪ'fɔːnɪən] **1** *adj*
californiano **2** *n* californiano(-a)
m(f)

call [kɔːl] **1** *n* llamada *f*; (*demand*)
llamamiento *m*; **there's a ~ for you**
tienes una llamada, te llaman; **I'll
give you a ~ tomorrow** te llamaré
mañana; **make a ~** hacer una llamada; **a ~ for help** una llamada de
socorro; **be on ~** estar de guardia
2 *v/t also* TELEC llamar; *meeting* convocar; **he ~ed him a liar** le llamó
mentiroso; **what have they ~ed
the baby?** ¿qué nombre le han
puesto al bebé?; **but we ~ him Tom**
pero le llamamos Tom; **s.o.
names** insultar a alguien; **I ~ed his
name** lo llamé **3** *v/i also* TELEC llamar; (*visit*) pasarse; **can I tell him
who's ~ing?** ¿quién le llama?; **~ for
help** pedir ayuda a gritos

♦ **call at** *v/t* (*stop at*) pasarse por; *of
train* hacer parada en

♦ **call back 1** *v/t* (*phone again*) volver a llamar; (*return call*) devolver
la llamada; (*summon*) hacer volver
2 *v/i on phone* volver a llamar;
(*make another visit*) volver a pasar

♦ **call for** *v/t* (*collect*) pasar a recoger;
(*demand*) pedir, exigir; (*require*) re-

querir

♦ **call in 1** *v/t* (*summon*) llamar **2** *v/i*
(*phone*) llamar; **he called in sick**
llamó para decir que estaba enfermo

♦ **call off** *v/t* (*cancel*) cancelar; *strike*
desconvocar

♦ **call on** *v/t* (*urge*) instar; (*visit*) visitar

♦ **call out** *v/t* (*shout*) gritar; (*summon*) llamar

♦ **call up** *v/t* (*on phone*) llamar;
COMPUT abrir, visualizar

'call cen·ter, *Br* 'call cen·tre centro
m de atención telefónica

call·er ['kɔːlər] *on phone* persona *f*
que llama; (*visitor*) visitante *m/f*

'call girl prostituta *f* (*que concierta
sus citas por teléfono*)

cal·lous ['kæləs] *adj* cruel, desalma-
do

cal·lous·ly ['kæləslɪ] *adv* cruelmente

cal·lous·ness ['kæləsnɪs] crueldad *f*

calm [kɑːm] **1** *adj sea* tranquilo;
weather apacible; *person* tranquilo,
sosegado; **please keep ~** por favor
mantengan la calma **2** *n* calma *f*

♦ **calm down 1** *v/t* calmar, tranquilizar **2** *v/i of sea, weather* calmarse; *of
person* calmarse, tranquilizarse

calm·ly ['kɑːmlɪ] *adv* con calma,
tranquilamente

cal·o·rie ['kælərɪ] caloría *f*

cam·cor·der ['kæmkɔːrdər] videocámara *f*

came [keɪm] *pret* → **come**

cam·e·ra ['kæmərə] cámara *f*

'cam·e·ra·man cámara *m*, camarógrafo *m*

cam·i·sole ['kæmɪsoʊl] camisola *f*

cam·ou·flage ['kæməflɑːʒ] **1** *n*
camuflaje *m* **2** *v/t* camuflar

camp [kæmp] **1** *n* campamento *m*;
make ~ acampar; **refugee ~** campo
m de refugiados **2** *v/i* acampar

cam·paign [kæm'peɪn] **1** *n* campaña
f **2** *v/i* hacer campaña (**for** a favor
de)

cam·paign·er [kæm'peɪnər] defen-
sor(a) *m(f)* (**for** de); **a ~ against
racism** una persona que hace cam-

paña contra el racismo

camp·er ['kæmpər] *person* campista *m/f*; *vehicle* autocaravana *f*

camp·ing ['kæmpɪŋ] acampada *f*; *on campsite* camping *m*; **go ~** ir de acampada *or* camping

'camp·site camping *m*

cam·pus ['kæmpəs] campus *m*

can¹ [kæn] *unstressed* [kən] *v/aux* (*pret* **could**) ◊ (*ability*) poder; *~ you swim?* ¿sabes nadar?; *~ you hear me?* ¿me oyes?; *I can't see* no veo; *~ you speak French?* ¿hablas francés?; *~ he call me back?* ¿me podría devolver la llamada?; *as fast/ well as you ~* tan rápido/bien como puedas ◊ (*permission*) poder; *~ I help you?* ¿te puedo ayudar?; *~ I have a beer/ coffee?* ¿me pones una cerveza/un café?; *that can't be right* debe haber un error

can² [kæn] **1** *n for drinks etc* lata *f* **2** *v/t* (*pret & pp* **-ned**) enlatar

Can·a·da ['kænədə] Canadá

Ca·na·di·an [kə'neɪdɪən] **1** *adj* canadiense **2** *n* canadiense *m/f*

ca·nal [kə'næl] *waterway* canal *m*

ca·nar·y [kə'nerɪ] canario *m*

can·cel ['kænsl] *v/t* (*pret & pp* **-ed**, *Br* **-led**) cancelar

can·cel·la·tion [kænsə'leɪʃn] cancelación *f*

can·cel·la·tion fee tarifa *f* de cancelación de reserva

can·cer ['kænsər] cáncer *m*

Can·cer ['kænsər] *ASTR* Cáncer *m/f inv*

can·cer·ous ['kænsərəs] *adj* canceroso

c & f *abbr* (= *cost and freight*) C&F (= costo y flete)

can·did ['kændɪd] *adj* sincero, franco

can·di·da·cy ['kændɪdəsɪ] candidatura *f*

can·di·date ['kændɪdət] *for position* candidato(-a) *m(f)*; *in exam* candidato(-a) *m(f)*, examinando(-a) *m(f)*

can·did·ly ['kændɪdlɪ] *adv* sinceramente, francamente

can·died ['kændiːd] *adj* confitado

can·dle ['kændl] vela *f*

'can·dle·stick candelero *m*; *short* palmatoria *f*

can·dor, *Br* **can·dour** ['kændər] sinceridad *f*, franqueza *f*

can·dy ['kændɪ] (*sweet*) caramelo *m*; (*sweets*) dulces *mpl*; *a box of ~* una caja de caramelos *or* dulces

cane [keɪn] caña *f*; *for walking* bastón *m*

can·is·ter ['kænɪstər] bote *m*

can·na·bis ['kænəbɪs] cannabis *m*, hachís *m*

canned [kænd] *adj fruit, tomatoes* enlatado, en lata; (*recorded*) grabado

can·ni·bal·ize ['kænɪbəlaɪz] *v/t* canibalizar

can·not ['kænɑːt] → **can¹**

can·ny ['kænɪ] *adj* (*astute*) astuto

ca·noe [kə'nuː] canoa *f*, piragua *f*

'can o·pen·er abrelatas *m inv*

can't [kænt] → **can**

can·tan·ker·ous [kæn'tæŋkərəs] *adj* arisco, cascarrabias

can·teen [kæn'tiːn] *in plant* cantina *f*, cafetería *f*

can·vas ['kænvəs] *for painting* lienzo *m*; *material* lona *f*

can·vass ['kænvəs] **1** *v/t* (*seek opinion of*) preguntar **2** *v/i* POL hacer campaña (*for* en favor de)

can·yon ['kænjən] cañón *m*

cap [kæp] *n hat* gorro *m*; *with peak* gorra *f*; *of bottle, jar* tapón *m*; *of pen, lens* tapa *f*

ca·pa·bil·i·ty [keɪpə'bɪlətɪ] capacidad *f*; *it's beyond my capabilities* no entra dentro de mis posibilidades

ca·pa·ble ['keɪpəbl] *adj* (*efficient*) capaz, competente; *be ~ of* ser capaz de

ca·pac·i·ty [kə'pæsətɪ] capacidad *f*; *of car engine* cilindrada *f*; *a ~ crowd* un lleno absoluto; *in my ~ as ...* en mi calidad de ...

cap·i·tal ['kæpɪtl] *n city* capital *f*; *letter* mayúscula *f*; *money* capital *m*

cap·i·tal ex'pend·i·ture inversión *f* en activo fijo; **cap·i·tal 'gains tax**

impuesto *m* sobre las plusvalías; **cap·i·tal 'growth** crecimiento *m* del capital

cap·i·tal·ism ['kæpɪtəlɪzm] capitalismo *m*

'cap·i·tal·ist ['kæpɪtəlɪst] **1** *adj* capitalista **2** *n* capitalista *m/f*

♦ **cap·i·tal·ize on** ['kæpɪtəlaɪz] *v/t* aprovecharse de

cap·i·tal 'let·ter letra *f* mayúscula

cap·i·tal 'pun·ish·ment pena *f* capital, pena *f* de muerte

ca·pit·u·late [kə'pɪtʊleɪt] *v/i* capitular

ca·pit·u·la·tion [kæpɪtʊ'leɪʃn] capitulación *f*

Cap·ri·corn ['kæprɪkɔːrn] ASTR Capricornio *m/f inv*

cap·size [kæp'saɪz] **1** *v/i* volcar **2** *v/t* hacer volcar

cap·sule ['kæpsʊl] *of medicine* cápsula *f*; (*space ~*) cápsula *f* espacial

cap·tain ['kæptɪn] *n of ship, team*, MIL capitán(-ana) *m(f)*; *of aircraft* comandante *m/f*

cap·tion ['kæpʃn] *n* pie *m* de foto

cap·ti·vate ['kæptɪveɪt] *v/t* cautivar, fascinar

cap·tive ['kæptɪv] **1** *adj* prisionero **2** *n* prisionero(-a) *m(f)*

cap·tive 'mar·ket mercado *m* cautivo

cap·tiv·i·ty [kæp'tɪvətɪ] cautividad *f*

cap·ture ['kæptʃər] **1** *n of city* toma *f*; *of criminal, animal* captura *f* **2** *v/t person, animal* capturar; *city, building* tomar; *market share* ganar; (*portray*) captar

car [kɑːr] coche *m*, *L.Am.* carro *m*, *Rpl* auto *m*; *of train* vagón *m*; **by ~** en coche

ca·rafe [kə'ræf] garrafa *f*, jarra *f*

car·at ['kærət] quilate *m*

car·bo·hy·drate [kɑːrboʊ'haɪdreɪt] carbohidrato *m*

'car bomb coche *m* bomba

car·bon·at·ed ['kɑːrbəneɪtɪd] *adj drink* con gas

car·bon mon·ox·ide [kɑːrbənmən-'ɑːksaɪd] monóxido *m* de carbono

car·bu·ret·er, **car·bu·ret·or** [kɑːr-

bʊ'retər] carburador *m*

car·cass ['kɑːrkəs] cadáver *m*

car·cin·o·gen [kɑːr'sɪnədʒen] agente *m* cancerígeno *or* carcinogéno

car·cin·o·gen·ic [kɑːrsɪnə'dʒenɪk] *adj* cancerígeno, carcinogéno

card [kɑːrd] *to mark occasion*, COMPUT, *business* tarjeta *f*; (*post~*) (*tarjeta f*) postal *f*; (*playing ~*) carta *f*, naipe *m*; **game of ~s** partida *f* de cartas

'card·board cartón *m*

card·board 'box caja *f* de cartón

car·di·ac ['kɑːrdɪæk] *adj* cardíaco

car·di·ac ar'rest paro *m* cardíaco

car·di·gan ['kɑːrdɪgən] cárdigan *m*

car·di·nal ['kɑːrdɪnl] *n* REL cardenal *m*

'card in·dex fichero *m*; **'card key** llave *f* tarjeta; **'card phone** teléfono *m* de tarjeta

care [ker] **1** *n* cuidado *m*; (*medical ~*) asistencia *f* médica; (*worry*) preocupación *f*; **care of →** c/o; **take ~** (*be cautious*) tener cuidado; **take ~** (**of yourself**)! (*goodbye*) ¡cuídate!; **take ~ of** *dog, tool, house, garden* cuidar; *baby* cuidar (de); (*deal with*) ocuparse de; *I'll take ~ of the bill* yo pago la cuenta; (*handle*) **with ~!** *on label* frágil **2** *v/i* preocuparse; *I don't ~!* ¡me da igual!; *I couldn't ~ less* ¡me importa un pimiento!; *if you really ~d ...* si de verdad te importara ...

♦ **care about** *v/t* preocuparse por

♦ **care for** *v/t* (*look after: person*) cuidar; (*look after: plant*) cuidar; *he doesn't care for me the way he used to* ya no le gusto como antes; *would you care for a drink?* ¿le apetece tomar algo?

ca·reer [kə'rɪr] carrera *f*; **~ prospects** perspectivas *fpl* profesionales

ca'reers of·fi·cer asesor(a) *m(f)* de orientación profesional

'care·free *adj* despreocupado

care·ful ['kerfəl] *adj* (*cautious, thorough*) cuidadoso; **be ~** tener cuidado; (**be**) **~!** ¡(ten) cuidado!

care·ful·ly ['kerfəlɪ] *adv* (*with caution*) con cuidado; *worded etc* cuidadosamente

care·less ['kerlɪs] *adj* descuidado; *you are so ~!* ¡qué descuidado eres!

care·less·ly ['kerlɪslɪ] *adv* descuidadamente

car·er ['kerər] *persona que cuida de un familiar o enfermo*

ca·ress [kə'res] **1** *n* caricia *f* **2** *v/t* acariciar

care·tak·er ['kerteɪkər] conserje *m*

'**care-worn** *adj* agobiado

'**car fer·ry** ferry *m*, transbordador *m*

car·go ['kɑːrgoʊ] cargamento *m*

car·i·ca·ture ['kærɪkətʃər] *n* caricatura *f*

car·ing ['kerɪŋ] *adj person* afectuoso, bondadoso; *society* solidario

'**car me·chan·ic** mecánico(-a) *m(f)* de coches *or* automóviles

car·nage ['kɑːrnɪdʒ] matanza *f*, carnicería *f*

car·na·tion [kɑːr'neɪʃn] clavel *m*

car·ni·val ['kɑːrnɪvl] feria *f*

car·ol ['kærəl] *n* villancico *m*

car·ou·sel [kærə'sel] *at airport* cinta *f* transportadora de equipajes; *for slide projector* carro *m*; (*merry-go-round*) tiovivo *m*

'**car park** *Br* estacionamiento *m*, *Span* aparcamiento *m*

car·pen·ter ['kɑːrpɪntər] carpintero(-a) *m(f)*

car·pet ['kɑːrpɪt] alfombra *f*

'**car phone** teléfono *m* de coche; '**car·pool** *n* acuerdo para compartir el vehículo entre varias personas que trabajan en el mismo sitio; '**car port** estacionamiento *m* con techo; '**car ra·di·o** autorradio *m*; '**car ren·tal** alquiler *m* de coches *or* automóviles

car·ri·er ['kærɪər] *company* transportista *m*; *airline* línea *f* aérea; *of disease* portador(a) *m(f)*

car·rot ['kærət] zanahoria *f*

car·ry ['kærɪ] **1** *v/t* (*pret & pp* -*ied*) *of person* llevar; *disease* ser portador de; *of ship, plane, bus etc* transportar; *proposal* aprobar; *be ~ing a child of pregnant woman* estar embarazada; *get carried away* dejarse llevar por la emoción, emocionarse **2** *v/i* (*pret & pp* -*ied*) *of sound* oírse

♦ **carry on 1** *v/i* (*continue*) seguir, continuar; (*make a fuss*) organizar un escándalo; (*have an affair*) tener un lío **2** *v/t* (*conduct*) mantener; *business* efectuar

♦ **carry out** *survey etc* llevar a cabo

'**car seat** *for child* asiento *m* para niño

cart [kɑːrt] carro *m*; *for shopping* carrito *m*

car·tel [kɑːr'tel] cartel *m*

car·ton ['kɑːrtn] *for storage, transport* caja *f* de cartón; *for milk etc* cartón *m*, tetrabrik *m* ®; *for eggs, of cigarettes* cartón *m*

car·toon [kɑːr'tuːn] *in newspaper, magazine* tira *f* cómica; *on TV, movie* dibujos *mpl* animados

car·toon·ist [kɑːr'tuːnɪst] dibujante *m/f* de chistes

car·tridge ['kɑːrtrɪdʒ] *for gun* cartucho *m*

carve [kɑːrv] *v/t meat* trinchar; *wood* tallar

carv·ing ['kɑːrvɪŋ] *figure* talla *f*

'**car wash** lavado *m* de automóviles

case¹ [keɪs] *container* funda *f*; *of scotch, wine etc* caja *f*; *Br* (*suitcase*) maleta *f*

case² [keɪs] *n instance, criminal*, MED caso *m*; LAW causa *f*; *I think there's a ~ for dismissing him* creo que hay razones fundadas para despedirlo; *the ~ for the prosecution* (los argumentos jurídicos de) la acusación; *in ~ ...* por si ...; *in ~ of emergency* en caso de emergencia; *in any ~* en cualquier caso; *in that ~* en ese caso

'**case his·to·ry** MED historial *m* médico

'**case·load** número *m* de casos

cash [kæʃ] **1** *n* (*dinero m en*) efectivo *m*; *I'm a bit short of ~* no tengo mucho dinero; *~ down* al contado;

C

pay (in) ~ pagar en efectivo **2** *v/t check* hacer efectivo

♦ **cash in on** *v/t* sacar provecho de

'**cash cow** fuente *f* de ingresos; '**cash desk** caja *f*; **cash 'dis·count** descuento *m* por pago al contado; '**cash flow** flujo *m* de caja, cash-flow *m*; ~ *problems* problemas *mpl* de liquidez

cash·ier [kæ'ʃɪr] *n in store etc* cajero(-a) *m(f)*

cash·mere ['kæʃmɪr] *adj* cachemir *m*

'**cash·point** cajero *m* automático

'**cash re·gis·ter** caja *f* registradora

ca·si·no [kə'si:nou] casino *m*

cas·ket ['kæskɪt] *(coffin)* ataúd *m*

cas·se·role ['kæsərool] *n meal* guiso *m*; *container* cacerola *f*, cazuela *f*

cas·sette [kə'set] cinta *f*, casete *m*

cas'sette play·er, **cas'sette re·cord·er** casete *m*

cast [kæst] **1** *n of play* reparto *m*; *(mold)* molde *m* **2** *v/t (pret & pp cast)* *doubt, suspicion* proyectar; *metal* fundir; *play* seleccionar el reparto de; *they* ~ *Alan as ...* le dieron a Alan el papel de ...

♦ **cast off** *v/i of ship* soltar amarras

caste [kæst] casta *f*

cast·er ['kæstər] *on chair etc* ruedecita *f*

Cas·til·ian [kæs'tɪliən] **1** *adj* castellano **2** *n person* castellano(-a) *m(f)*; *language* castellano *m*

cast 'i·ron *n* hierro *m* fundido

cast-'i·ron *adj* de hierro fundido

cas·tle ['kæsl] castillo *m*

'**cast·or** ['kæstər] → **caster**

cas·trate [kæ'streɪt] *v/t* castrar

cas·tra·tion [kæ'streɪʃn] castración *f*

cas·u·al ['kæʒuəl] *adj (chance)* casual; *(offhand)* despreocupado; *(not formal)* informal; *(not permanent)* eventual; *it was just a* ~ *remark* no era más que un comentario hecho de pasada; *he was very* ~ *about the whole thing* parecía no darle mucha importancia al asunto; ~ *sex* relaciones *fpl* sexuales (con parejas) ocasionales

cas·u·al·ly ['kæʒuəli] *adv dressed* de manera informal; *say* a la ligera

cas·u·al·ty ['kæʒuəltɪ] víctima *f*

'**cas·u·al wear** ropa *f* informal

cat [kæt] gato *m*

Cat·a·lan ['kætələn] **1** *adj* catalán **2** *n person* catalán(-ana) *m(f)*; *language* catalán *m*

cat·a·log, *Br* **cat·a·logue** ['kætəlɑ:g] *n* catálogo *m*

cat·a·lyst ['kætəlɪst] catalizador *m*

cat·a·lyt·ic con'vert·er [kætə'lɪtɪk] catalizador *m*

cat·a·pult ['kætəpʌlt] **1** *v/t fig to fame, stardom* catapultar, lanzar **2** *n* catapulta *f*; *toy* tirachinas *m inv*

cat·a·ract ['kætərækt] MED catarata *f*

ca·tas·tro·phe [kə'tæstrəfɪ] catástrofe *f*

cat·a·stroph·ic [kætə'strɑ:fɪk] *adj* catastrófico

catch [kætʃ] **1** *n parada f (sin que la pelota toque el suelo)*; *of fish* captura *f*, pesca *f*; *(locking device)* cierre *m*; *(problem)* pega *f*; *there has to be a* ~ tiene que haber una trampa **2** *v/t (pret & pp caught)* *ball* agarrar, *Span* coger; *animal* atrapar; *escaped prisoner* capturar; *(get on: bus, train)* tomar, *Span* coger; *(not miss: bus, train)* alcanzar, *Span* coger; *fish* pescar; *in order to speak to* alcanzar, pillar; *(hear)* oír; *illness* agarrar, *Span* coger; ~ *(a) cold* agarrar *or Span* coger un resfriado, resfriarse; ~ *s.o.'s eye of person, object* llamar la atención de alguien; ~ *sight of*, ~ *a glimpse of* ver; ~ *s.o. doing sth* atrapar *or Span* coger a alguien haciendo algo

♦ **catch on** *v/i (become popular)* cuajar, ponerse de moda; *(understand)* darse cuenta

♦ **catch up** *v/i:* **catch up with s.o.** alcanzar a alguien; *he's having to work hard to catch up* tiene que trabajar muy duro para ponerse al día

♦ **catch up on** *v/t:* **catch up on one's sleep** recuperar sueño;

there's a lot of work to catch up on hay mucho trabajo atrasado

catch-22 [kætʃˈtwentɪˈtuː]: ***it's a ~ situation*** es como la pescadilla que se muerde la cola

catch·er [ˈkætʃər] *in baseball* cácher *m*, cátcher *m*

catch·ing [ˈkætʃɪŋ] *adj also fig* contagioso

catch·y [ˈkætʃɪ] *adj tune* pegadizo

cat·e·gor·ic [kætəˈgɑːrɪk] *adj* categórico

cat·e·gor·i·cal·ly [kætəˈgɑːrɪklɪ] *adv* categóricamente

cat·e·go·ry [ˈkætəgɔːrɪ] categoría *f*

♦ **ca·ter for** [ˈkeɪtər] *v/t (meet the needs of)* cubrir las necesidades de; *(provide food for)* organizar la comida para

ca·ter·er [ˈkeɪtərər] hostelero(-a) *m(f)*

ca·ter·pil·lar [ˈkætərpɪlər] oruga *f*

ca·the·dral [kəˈθiːdrl] catedral *f*

Cath·o·lic [ˈkæθəlɪk] **1** *adj* católico **2** *n* católico(-a) *m(f)*

Ca·thol·i·cism [kəˈθɑːlɪsɪzm] catolicismo *m*

'cat's eyes *on road* captafaros *mpl (en el centro de la calzada)*

cat·sup [ˈkætsʌp] ketchup *m*, catchup *m*

cat·tle [ˈkætl] *npl* ganado *m*

cat·ty [ˈkætɪ] *adj* malintencionado

'cat·walk pasarela *f*

caught [kɔːt] *pret & pp* → **catch**

cau·li·flow·er [ˈkɔːlɪflaʊər] coliflor *f*

cause [kɔːz] **1** *n* causa *f*; *(grounds)* motivo *m*, razón *f* **2** *v/t* causar, provocar

caus·tic [ˈkɔːstɪk] *adj fig* cáustico

cau·tion [ˈkɔːʃn] **1** *n (carefulness)* precaución *f*, prudencia *f* **2** *v/t (warn)* prevenir (***against*** contra)

cau·tious [ˈkɔːʃəs] *adj* cauto, prudente

cau·tious·ly [ˈkɔːʃəslɪ] *adv* cautelosamente, con prudencia

cav·al·ry [ˈkævəlrɪ] caballería *f*

cave [keɪv] cueva *f*

♦ **cave in** *v/i of roof* hundirse

cav·i·ar [ˈkævɪɑːr] caviar *m*

cav·i·ty [ˈkævətɪ] caries *f inv*

cc¹ [siːˈsiː] **1** *abbr* (= ***carbon copy***) copia *f* **2** *v/t memo* enviar una copia de; *person* enviar una copia a

cc² [siːˈsiː] *abbr* (= ***cubic centimeters***) cc (centímetros *mpl* cúbicos); MOT cilindrada *f*

CD [siːˈdiː] *abbr* (= ***compact disc***) CD *m* (= disco *m* compacto)

CD play·er (reproductor *m* de) CD *m*; **CD-ROM** [siːdiːˈrɑːm] CD-ROM *m*; **CD-ROM drive** lector *m* de CD-ROM

cease [siːs] **1** *v/i* cesar **2** *v/t* suspender; ***~ doing sth*** dejar de hacer algo

'cease-fire alto *m* el fuego

cei·ling [ˈsiːlɪŋ] *of room* techo *m*; *(limit)* tope *m*, límite *m*

cel·e·brate [ˈselɪbreɪt] **1** *v/i*: ***let's ~ with a bottle of champagne*** celebrémoslo con una botella de champán **2** *v/t* celebrar, festejar; *(observe)* celebrar

cel·e·brat·ed [ˈselɪbreɪtɪd] *adj* célebre; ***be ~ for*** ser célebre por

cel·e·bra·tion [selɪˈbreɪʃn] celebración *f*

ce·leb·ri·ty [sɪˈlebrətɪ] celebridad *f*

cel·e·ry [ˈselərɪ] apio *m*

cel·i·ba·cy [ˈselɪbəsɪ] celibato *m*

cel·i·bate [ˈselɪbət] *adj* célibe

cell [sel] *for prisoner, in spreadsheet* celda *f*; BIO célula *f*

cel·lar [ˈselər] sótano *m*; *for wine* bodega *f*

cel·list [ˈtʃelɪst] violonchelista *m/f*

cel·lo [ˈtʃeloʊ] violonchelo *m*

cel·lo·phane [ˈseləfeɪn] celofán *m*

'cell phone, cel·lu·lar phone [ˈseljələr] (teléfono *m*) móvil *m*, *L.Am.* (teléfono *m*) celular *m*

ce·ment [sɪˈment] **1** *n* cemento *m* **2** *v/t* colocar con cemento; *friendship* consolidar

cem·e·ter·y [ˈsemətərɪ] cementerio *m*

cen·sor [ˈsensər] *v/t* censor(a) *m(f)*

cen·sus [ˈsensəs] censo *m*

cent [sent] céntimo *m*

C

cen·te·na·ry [sen'ti:nərı] centenario *m*

cen·ter ['sentər] **1** *n* centro *m*; **in the ~ of** en el centro de **2** *v/t* centrar
♦ **center on** *v/t* centrarse en

cen·ter of 'grav·i·ty centro *m* de gravedad

cen·ti·grade ['sentıgreıd] *adj* centígrado; **10 degrees ~** 10 grados centígrados

cen·ti·me·ter, *Br* **cen·ti·me·tre** ['sentımi:tər] centímetro *m*

cen·tral ['sentrəl] *adj* central; *location*, *apartment* céntrico; **~ Chicago** el centro de Chicago; **be ~ to sth** ser el eje de algo

Cen·tral A'mer·i·ca *n* Centroamérica, América Central; **Cen·tral A'mer·i·can 1** *adj* centroamericano, de (la) América *f* Central **2** *n* centroamericano(-a) *m(f)*; **central 'heat·ing** calefacción *f* central

cen·tral·ize ['sentrəlaız] *v/t* centralizar

cen·tral 'lock·ing MOT cierre *m* centralizado

cen·tral 'pro·ces·sing u·nit unidad *f* central de proceso

cen·tre *Br* → **center**

cen·tu·ry ['sentʃərı] siglo *m*

CEO [si:i:'ou] *abbr* (= *Chief Executive Officer*) consejero(-a) *m(f)* delegado

ce·ram·ic [sı'ræmık] *adj* de cerámica

ce·ram·ics [sı'ræmıks] (*pl: objects*) objetos *mpl* de cerámica; (*sing: art*) cerámica *f*

ce·re·al ['sırıəl] (*grain*) cereal *m*; (*breakfast ~*) cereales *mpl*

cer·e·mo·ni·al [serı'mounıəl] **1** *adj* ceremonial **2** *n* ceremonial *m*

cer·e·mo·ny ['serımənı] (*event, ritual*) ceremonia *f*

cer·tain ['sɜ:rtn] *adj* (*sure*) seguro; (*particular*) cierto; **I'm ~** estoy seguro; **a ~ Mr S.** un cierto Sr. S.; **make ~** asegurarse; **know/say for ~** saber / decir con certeza

cer·tain·ly ['sɜ:rtnlı] *adv* (*definitely*) claramente; (*of course*) por supues-

to; **~ not!** ¡por supuesto que no!

cer·tain·ty ['sɜ:rtntı] (*confidence*) certeza *f*, certidumbre *f*; (*inevitability*) seguridad *f*; **it's a ~** es seguro; **he's a ~ for the gold medal** va a ganar seguro la medalla de oro

cer·tif·i·cate [sər'tıfıkət] (*qualification*) título *m*; (*official paper*) certificado *m*

cer·ti·fied pub·lic ac·count·ant ['sɜ:rtıfaıd] censor(a) *m(f)* jurado de cuentas

cer·ti·fy ['sɜ:rtıfaı] *v/t* (*pret & pp -ied*) certificar

Ce·sar·e·an [sı'zerıən] *n* cesárea *f*

ces·sa·tion [se'seıʃn] cese *m*

c/f *abbr* (= *cost and freight*) CF (= costo y flete)

CFC [si:ef'si:] *abbr* (= *chlorofluorocarbon*) CFC *m* (= clorofluorocarbono *m*)

chain [tʃeın] **1** *n also of hotels etc* cadena *f* **2** *v/t* encadenar; **~ sth / s.o. to sth** encadenar algo / a alguien a algo

chain re'ac·tion reacción *f* en cadena; **'chain-smoke** *v/i* fumar un cigarrillo tras otro, fumar como un carretero; **'chain-smok·er** persona que fuma un cigarrillo tras otro; **'chain store** *store* tienda *f* (de una cadena); *company* cadena *f* de tiendas

chair [tʃer] **1** *n* silla *f*; (*arm~*) sillón *m*; *at university* cátedra *f*; **the ~** (*electric ~*) la silla eléctrica; *at meeting* la presidencia; **take the ~** ocupar la presidencia **2** *v/t meeting* presidir

'chair lift telesilla *f*;

'chair·man presidente *m*

chair·man·ship ['tʃermənʃıp] presidencia *f*

'chair·per·son presidente(-a) *m(f)*

'chair·wom·an presidenta *f*

cha·let ['ʃæleı] chalet *m*, chalé *m*

chal·ice ['tʃælıs] REL cáliz *m*

chalk [tʃɔ:k] *for writing* tiza *f*; *in soil* creta *f*

chal·lenge ['tʃælındʒ] **1** *n* (*difficulty*) desafío *m*, reto *m*; *in race, competition* ataque *m* **2** *v/t* desafiar, retar; (*call into question*) cuestionar

chal·len·ger ['tʃælɪndʒər] aspirante *m/f*

chal·len·ging ['tʃælɪndʒɪŋ] *adj job, undertaking* estimulante

cham·ber·maid ['tʃeɪmbərmeɪd] camarera *f* (de hotel); **'cham·ber mu·sic** música *f* de cámara; **Cham·ber of 'Com·merce** Cámara *f* de Comercio

cham·ois (leath·er) ['ʃæmɪ] ante *m*

cham·pagne [ʃæm'peɪn] champán *m*

cham·pi·on ['tʃæmpɪən] **1** *n* SP campeón(-ona) *m(f)*; *of cause* abanderado (-a) *m(f)* **2** *v/t* (*cause*) abanderar

cham·pi·on·ship ['tʃæmpɪənʃɪp] campeonato *m*

chance [tʃæns] (*possibility*) posibilidad *f*; (*opportunity*) oportunidad *f*; (*risk*) riesgo *m*; (*luck*) casualidad *f*, suerte *f*; *there's not much ~ of that happening* no es probable que ocurra; *leave nothing to* ~ no dejar nada a la improvisación; *by* ~ por casualidad; *take a* ~ correr el riesgo; *I'm not taking any* ~*s* no voy a correr ningún riesgo

chan·de·lier [ʃændə'lɪr] araña *f* (de luces)

change [tʃeɪndʒ] **1** *n* cambio *m*; (*small coins*) suelto *m*; *from purchase* cambio *m*, *Span* vuelta *f*, *L.Am.* vuelto *m*; *a* ~ *is as good as a rest* a veces cambiar es lo mejor; *that makes a nice* ~ eso es una novedad bienvenida; *for a* ~ para variar; *a* ~ *of clothes* una muda **2** *v/t* cambiar; ~ *trains* hacer transbordo; ~ *one's clothes* cambiarse de ropa **3** *v/i* cambiar; (*put on different clothes*) cambiarse; (*take different train/bus*) hacer transbordo; *the lights* ~*d to green* el semáforo se puso verde

change·a·ble ['tʃeɪndʒəbl] *adj* variable, cambiante

'change·o·ver transición *f* (*to* a); *in relay race* relevo *m*

chang·ing room ['tʃeɪndʒɪŋ] SP vestuario *m*; *in shop* probador *m*

chan·nel ['tʃænl] *on TV, at sea* canal *m*

chant [tʃænt] **1** REL canto *m*; *of fans* cántico *m*; *of demonstrators* consigna *f* **2** *v/i* gritar **3** *v/t* corear

cha·os ['keɪɑs] caos *m*; *it was* ~ *at the airport* la situación en el aeropuerto era caótica

cha·ot·ic [keɪ'ɑːtɪk] *adj* caótico

chap [tʃæp] *n Br* F tipo *m* F, *Span* tío *m* F

chap·el ['tʃæpl] capilla *f*

chapped [tʃæpt] *adj lips* cortado; *hands* agrietado

chap·ter ['tʃæptər] capítulo *m*; *of organization* sección *f*

char·ac·ter ['kærɪktər] *nature, personality, in printing* carácter *m*; *person, in book, play* personaje *m*; *he's a real* ~ es todo un personaje

char·ac·ter·is·tic [kærɪktə'rɪstɪk] **1** *n* característica *f* **2** *adj* característico

char·ac·ter·is·ti·cal·ly [kærɪktə'rɪstɪklɪ] *adv* de modo característico; *he was* ~ *rude* fue grosero como de costumbre

char·ac·ter·ize ['kærɪktəraɪz] *v/t* (*be typical of*) caracterizar; (*describe*) describir, clasificar

cha·rade [ʃə'rɑːd] *fig* farsa *f*

char·broiled ['tʃɑːrbrɔɪld] *adj* a la brasa

char·coal ['tʃɑːrkoʊl] *for barbecue* carbón *m* vegetal; *for drawing* carboncillo *m*

charge [tʃɑːrdʒ] **1** *n* (*fee*) tarifa *f*; LAW cargo *m*, acusación *f*; *free of* ~ gratis; *bank* ~*s* comisiones *fpl* bancarias; *will that be cash or* ~*?* ¿pagará en efectivo o con tarjeta?; *be in* ~ estar a cargo; *take* ~ hacerse cargo **2** *v/t sum of money* cobrar; (*put on account*) pagar con tarjeta; LAW acusar (*with* de); *battery* cargar; *please* ~ *it to my account* cárguelo a mi cuenta **3** *v/i* (*attack*) cargar

'charge ac·count cuenta *f* de crédito

'**charge card** tarjeta *f* de compra

cha·ris·ma [kə'rɪzmə] carisma *m*

char·is·ma·tic [kærɪz'mætɪk] *adj* carismático

char·i·ta·ble ['tʃærɪtəbl] *adj* *institution, donation* de caridad; *person* caritativo

char·i·ty ['tʃærətɪ] *assistance* caridad *f*; *organization* entidad *f* benéfica

char·la·tan ['ʃɑːrlətən] charlatán (-ana) *m(f)*

charm [tʃɑːrm] **1** *n* (*appealing quality*) encanto *m*; *on bracelet etc* colgante *m* **2** *v/t* (*delight*) encantar

charm·ing ['tʃɑːrmɪŋ] *adj* encantador

charred [tʃɑːrd] *adj* carbonizado

chart [tʃɑːrt] (*diagram*) gráfico *m*; (*map*) carta *f* de navegación; **the ~s** MUS las listas de éxitos

'**char·ter flight** vuelo *m* chárter

chase [tʃeɪs] **1** *n* persecución *f* **2** *v/t* perseguir

♦ **chase away** *v/t* ahuyentar

chas·sis ['ʃæsɪ] *of car* chasis *m inv*

chat [tʃæt] **1** *n* charla *f*, *Mex* plática *f* **2** *v/i* (*pret* & *pp* **-ted**) charlar, *Mex* platicar

chat·ter ['tʃætər] **1** *n* cháchara *f* **2** *v/i* *talk* parlotear; *of teeth* castañetear

'**chat·ter·box** charlatán(-ana) *m(f)*

chat·ty ['tʃætɪ] *adj* *person* hablador

chauf·feur ['ʃoʊfər] *n* chófer *m*, *L.Am.* chofer *m*

'**chauf·feur-driv·en** *adj* con chófer *or L.Am.* chofer

chau·vin·ist ['ʃoʊvɪnɪst] *n* (*male ~*) machista *m*

chau·vin·ist·ic [ʃoʊvɪ'nɪstɪk] *adj* chovinista; (*sexist*) machista

cheap [tʃiːp] *adj* (*inexpensive*) barato; (*nasty*) chabacano; (*mean*) tacaño

cheat [tʃiːt] **1** *n* (*person*) tramposo(-a) *m(f)* **2** *v/t* engañar; **~ s.o. out of sth** estafar algo a alguien **3** *v/i* in *exam* copiar; *in cards etc* hacer trampa; **~ on one's wife** engañar a la esposa

check¹ [tʃek] **1** *adj* *shirt* a cuadros **2** *n* cuadro *m*

check² [tʃek] FIN cheque *m*; *in restaurant etc* cuenta *f*; **~ please** la cuenta, por favor

check³ [tʃek] **1** *n* *to verify sth* comprobación *f*; **keep in ~**, **hold in ~** mantener bajo control; **keep a ~ on** llevar el control de **2** *v/t* (*verify*) comprobar; *machinery* inspeccionar; (*restrain, stop*) contener, controlar; *with a ~mark* poner un tic en; *coat* dejar en el guardarropa; *package* dejar en consigna **3** *v/i* comprobar; **~ for** comprobar

♦ **check in** *v/i* *at airport* facturar; *at hotel* registrarse

♦ **check off** *v/t* marcar (*como comprobada*)

♦ **check on** *v/t* vigilar

♦ **check out 1** *v/i of hotel* dejar el hotel **2** *v/t* (*look into*) investigar; *club, restaurant etc* probar

♦ **check up on** *v/t* hacer averiguaciones sobre, investigar

♦ **check with** *v/t of person* hablar con; (*tally: of information*) concordar con

'**check·book** talonario *m* de cheques, *L.Am.* chequera *f*

checked [tʃekt] *adj* *material* a cuadros

check·er·board ['tʃekərbɔːrd] tablero *m* de ajedrez

check·ered ['tʃekərd] *adj* *pattern* a cuadros; *career* accidentado

check·ers ['tʃekərz] *nsg* damas *fpl*

'**check-in** (**coun·ter**) mostrador *m* de facturación

check·ing ac·count ['tʃekɪŋ] cuenta *f* corriente

'**check-in time** hora *f* de facturación; '**check·list** lista *f* de verificación; '**check mark** tic *m*; '**check·mate** *n* jaque *m* mate; '**check-out** caja *f*; '**check-out time** *from hotel* hora *f* de salida; '**check·point** control *m*; '**check·room** *for coats* guardarropa *m*; *for baggage* consigna *f*; '**check·up** *medical* chequeo *m* (médico), revisión *f* (médica); *dental* revisión *f* (en el dentista)

cheek [tʃi:k] ANAT mejilla *f*
'cheek·bone pómulo *m*
cheer [tʃɪr] **1** *n* ovación *f*; *~s!* toast
¡salud!; *the ~s of the fans* los vítores de los aficionados **2** *v/t* ovacionar, vitorear **3** *v/i* lanzar vítores
♦ cheer on *v/t* animar
♦ cheer up **1** *v/i* animarse **2** *v/t* animar
cheer·ful ['tʃɪrfəl] *adj* alegre, contento
cheer·ing ['tʃɪrɪŋ] *n* vítores *mpl*
cheer·i·o [tʃɪri'ou] *Br* F ¡chao! F
'cheer·lead·er animadora *f*
cheese [tʃi:z] queso *m*
'cheese·burg·er hamburguesa *f* de
queso
'cheese·cake tarta *f* de queso
chef [ʃef] chef *m*, jefe *m* de cocina
chem·i·cal ['kemɪkl] **1** *adj* químico
2 *n* producto *m* químico
chem·i·cal 'war·fare guerra *f* química
chem·ist ['kemɪst] *in laboratory*
químico(-a) *m(f)*; *Br dispensing*
farmacéutico(-a) *m(f)*
chem·is·try ['kemɪstrɪ] química *f*, *fig*
sintonía *f*, química *f*
chem·o·ther·a·py [ki:mou'θerəpɪ]
quimioterapia *f*
cheque [tʃek] *Br* → *check²*
cher·ish ['tʃerɪʃ] *v/t photo etc* apreciar mucho, tener mucho cariño a;
person querer mucho; *hope* albergar
cher·ry ['tʃerɪ] *fruit* cereza *f*; *tree* cerezo *m*
cher·ub ['tʃerəb] *in painting, sculpture*
querubín *m*
chess [tʃes] ajedrez *m*
'chess·board tablero *m* de ajedrez
'chess·man, 'chess·piece pieza *f*
de ajedrez
chest [tʃest] *of person* pecho *m*; *box*
cofre *m*; *get sth off one's ~* desahogarse
chest·nut ['tʃesnʌt] castaña *f*; *tree*
castaño *m*
chest of 'draw·ers cómoda *f*
chew [tʃu:] *v/t* mascar, masticar; *of*
dog, rats mordisquear

♦ chew out *v/t* F echar una bronca a
F
chew·ing gum ['tʃu:ɪŋ] chicle *m*
chic [ʃi:k] *adj* chic, elegante
chick [tʃɪk] *young chicken* pollito *m*;
young bird polluelo *m*; F *girl* nena *f* F
chick·en ['tʃɪkɪn] **1** *n* gallina *f*; *food*
pollo *m*; F *(coward)* gallina *f* F **2** *adj*
F *(cowardly)* cobarde; *be ~* ser
un(a) gallina F
♦ chicken out *v/i* F acobardarse
'chick·en·feed F calderilla *f*
chief [tʃi:f] **1** *n* jefe(-a) *m(f)* **2** *adj*
principal
chief ex·ec·u·tive 'of·fi·cer conse-
jero(-a) *m(f)* delegado
chief·ly ['tʃi:flɪ] *adv* principalmente
chil·blain ['tʃɪlbleɪn] sabañón *m*
child [tʃaɪld] *(pl children* ['tʃɪldrən])
niño(-a) *m(f)*; *son* hijo *m*; *daughter*
hija *f*; *pej* niño(-a) *m(f)*, crío(-a)
m(f)
'child a·buse malos tratos *mpl* a menores; 'child·birth parto *m*;
child·hood ['tʃaɪldhʊd] infancia *f*
child·ish ['tʃaɪldɪʃ] *adj pej* infantil
child·ish·ly ['tʃaɪldɪʃlɪ] *adv pej* de
manera infantil
child·ish·ness ['tʃaɪldɪʃnɪs] *pej* in-
fantilismo *m*
child·less ['tʃaɪldlɪs] *adj* sin hijos
child·like ['tʃaɪldlaɪk] *adj* infantil
'child·mind·er niñero(-a) *m(f)*
'child·ren ['tʃɪldrən] *pl* → *child*
Chil·e ['tʃɪlɪ] *n* Chile
Chil·e·an ['tʃɪlɪən] **1** *adj* chileno **2** *n*
chileno(-a) *m(f)*
chill [tʃɪl] **1** *n illness* resfriado *m*;
there's a ~ in the air hace bastante
fresco **2** *v/t wine* poner a enfriar
♦ chill out *v/i* P tranquilizarse
chil·(l)i (pep·per) ['tʃɪlɪ] chile *m*,
Span guindilla *f*
chill·y ['tʃɪlɪ] *adj weather, welcome*
fresco; *I'm feeling a bit ~* tengo
fresco
chime [tʃaɪm] *v/i* campanada *f*
chim·ney ['tʃɪmnɪ] chimenea *f*
chim·pan·zee [tʃɪm'pænzi:] chimpancé *m*
chin [tʃɪn] barbilla *f*

Chi·na ['tʃaɪnə] China
chi·na ['tʃaɪnə] porcelana f
Chi·nese [tʃaɪ'niːz] **1** adj chino **2** n (language) chino m; (person) chino(-a) m(f)
chink [tʃɪŋk] gap resquicio m; sound tintineo m
chip [tʃɪp] **1** n of wood viruta f; of stone lasca f; damage mella f; in gambling ficha f; **~s** patatas fpl fritas **2** v/t (pret & pp **-ped**) (damage) mellar
♦ **chip in** v/i (interrupt) interrumpir; with money poner dinero
chip·munk ['tʃɪpmʌŋk] ardilla f listada
chi·ro·prac·tor ['kaɪroʊpræktər] quiropráctico(-a) m(f)
chirp [tʃɜːrp] v/i piar
chis·el ['tʃɪzl] n for stone cincel m; for wood formón m
chit·chat ['tʃɪtʃæt] charla f
chiv·al·rous ['ʃɪvlrəs] adj caballeroso
chive [tʃaɪv] cebollino m
chlo·rine ['klɔːriːn] cloro m
chlor·o·form ['klɔːrəfɔːrm] n cloroformo m
choc·a·hol·ic [tʃɑːkə'hɑːlɪk] n F adicto(-a) al chocolate
chock-full [tʃɑːk'fʊl] adj F de bote en bote F
choc·o·late ['tʃɑːkələt] chocolate m; a box of **~s** una caja de bombones; hot **~** chocolate m caliente
'choc·o·late cake pastel m de chocolate
choice [tʃɔɪs] **1** n elección f; (selection) selección f; you have a **~** of rice or potatoes puedes elegir entre arroz y patatas; the **~** is yours tú eliges; I had no **~** no tuve alternativa **2** adj (top quality) selecto
choir [kwaɪr] coro m
'choir·boy niño m de coro
choke [tʃoʊk] **1** n MOT estárter m **2** v/i ahogarse; **~** on sth atragantarse con algo **3** v/t estrangular; screams ahogar
cho·les·te·rol [kə'lestəroʊl] colesterol m

choose [tʃuːz] v/t & v/i (pret **chose**, pp **chosen**) elegir, escoger
choos·ey ['tʃuːzɪ] adj F exigente
chop [tʃɑːp] **1** n meat chuleta f; with one **~** of the ax con un hachazo **2** v/t (pret & pp **-ped**) wood cortar; meat trocear; vegetables picar
♦ **chop down** v/t tree talar
chop·per ['tʃɑːpər] F (helicopter) helicóptero m
'chop·sticks npl palillos mpl (chinos)
cho·ral ['kɔːrəl] adj coral
chord [kɔːrd] MUS acorde m
chore [tʃɔːr] tarea f
chor·e·o·graph ['kɔːrɪəgræf] v/t coreografiar
chor·e·og·ra·pher [kɔːrɪ'ɑːgrəfər] coreógrafo(-a) m(f)
chor·e·og·ra·phy [kɔːrɪ'ɑːgrəfɪ] coreografía f
cho·rus ['kɔːrəs] singers coro m; of song estribillo m
chose [tʃoʊz] pret → **choose**
cho·sen ['tʃoʊzn] pp → **choose**
Christ [kraɪst] Cristo; **~!** ¡Dios mío!
chris·ten ['krɪsn] v/t bautizar
chris·ten·ing ['krɪsnɪŋ] bautizo m
Chris·tian ['krɪstʃən] **1** n cristiano(-a) m(f) **2** adj cristiano
Chris·ti·an·i·ty [krɪstɪ'ænətɪ] cristianismo m
'Chris·tian name nombre m de pila
Christ·mas ['krɪsməs] Navidad(es) f(pl); **at ~** en Navidad(es); Merry **~!** ¡Feliz Navidad!
'Christ·mas card crismas m inv, tarjeta f de Navidad; **Christ·mas 'Day** día f de Navidad; **'Christ·mas 'Eve** Nochebuena f; **'Christ·mas pres·ent** regalo m de Navidad; **'Christ·mas tree** árbol m de Navidad
chrome, chro·mi·um [kroʊm, 'kroʊmɪəm] cromo m
chro·mo·some ['kroʊməsoʊm] cromosoma m
chron·ic ['krɑːnɪk] adj crónico
chron·o·log·i·cal [krɑːnə'lɑːdʒɪkl] adj cronológico; **in ~** order en orden cronológico

chrys·an·the·mum [krɪˈsænθəməm] crisantemo *m*

chub·by [ˈtʃʌbɪ] *adj* rechoncho

chuck [tʃʌk] *v/t* F tirar

♦ **chuck out** *v/t* F *object* tirar; *person* echar

chuck·le [ˈtʃʌkl] **1** *n* risita *f* **2** *v/i* reírse por lo bajo

chum [tʃʌm] amigo(-a) *m(f)*

chum·my [ˈtʃʌmɪ] *adj* F: **be ~ with** ser amiguete de F

chunk [tʃʌŋk] trozo *m*

chunk·y [ˈtʃʌŋkɪ] *adj sweater* grueso; *person*, *build* cuadrado, fornido

church [tʃɜːrtʃ] iglesia *f*

church 'hall *sala parroquial empleada para diferentes actividades*; **church 'serv·ice** oficio *m* religioso; **'church·yard** cementerio *m* (al lado de iglesia)

churl·ish [ˈtʃɜːrlɪʃ] *adj* maleducado, grosero

chute [ʃuːt] rampa *f*; *for garbage* colector *m* de basura

CIA [siːaɪˈeɪ] *abbr* (= *Central Intelligence Agency*) CIA *f* (= Agencia *f* Central de Inteligencia)

ci·der [ˈsaɪdər] sidra *f*

CIF [siːaɪˈef] *abbr* (= *cost, insurance, freight*) CIF (= costo, seguro y flete)

ci·gar [sɪˈɡɑːr] (cigarro *m*) puro *m*

cig·a·rette [sɪɡəˈret] cigarrillo *m*

cig·a·rette end colilla *f*; **cig·a·rette light·er** encendedor *m*, mechero *m*; **cig·a·rette pa·per** papel *m* de fumar

cin·e·ma [ˈsɪnɪmə] cine *m*

cin·na·mon [ˈsɪnəmən] canela *f*

cir·cle [ˈsɜːrkl] **1** *n* círculo *m* **2** *v/t* (*draw ~ around*) poner un círculo alrededor de; *his name was ~d in red* su nombre tenía un círculo rojo alrededor **3** *v/i of plane, bird* volar en círculo

cir·cuit [ˈsɜːrkɪt] circuito *m*; (*lap*) vuelta *f*

'cir·cuit board COMPUT placa *f or* tarjeta *f* de circuitos; **'cir·cuit break·er** ELEC cortacircuitos *m inv*; **'cir·cuit train·ing** SP: *do ~* hacer

circuitos de entrenamiento

cir·cu·lar [ˈsɜːrkjələr] **1** *n giving information* circular *f* **2** *adj* circular

cir·cu·late [ˈsɜːrkjuleɪt] **1** *v/i* circular **2** *v/t memo* hacer circular

cir·cu·la·tion [sɜːrkjuˈleɪʃn] circulación *f*; *of newspaper, magazine* tirada *f*

cir·cum·fer·ence [sərˈkʌmfərəns] circunferencia *f*

cir·cum·stan·ces [ˈsɜːrkəmstənsɪs] *npl* circunstancias *fpl*; *financial* situación *f* económica; *under no ~* en ningún caso, de ninguna manera; *under the ~* dadas las circunstancias

cir·cus [ˈsɜːrkəs] circo *m*

cir·rho·sis (of the liv·er) [sɪˈrousɪs] cirrosis *f* (hepática)

cis·tern [ˈsɪstɜːrn] cisterna *f*

cite [saɪt] *v/t* citar

cit·i·zen [ˈsɪtɪzn] ciudadano(-a) *m(f)*

cit·i·zen·ship [ˈsɪtɪznʃɪp] ciudadanía *f*

cit·rus [ˈsɪtrəs] *adj* cítrico; *~ fruit* cítrico *m*

cit·y [ˈsɪtɪ] ciudad *f*

cit·y 'cen·ter, *Br* **cit·y 'cen·tre** centro *m* de la ciudad

cit·y 'hall ayuntamiento *m*

civ·ic [ˈsɪvɪk] *adj* cívico

civ·il [ˈsɪvl] *adj* civil; (*polite*) cortés

civ·il en·gi·neer ingeniero(-a) *m(f)* civil

ci·vil·ian [sɪˈvɪljən] **1** *n* civil *m/f* **2** *adj clothes* de civil

ci·vil·i·ty [sɪˈvɪlɪtɪ] cortesía *f*

civ·i·li·za·tion [sɪvəlaɪˈzeɪʃn] civilización *f*

civ·i·lize [ˈsɪvəlaɪz] *v/t* civilizar

civ·il 'rights *npl* derechos *mpl* civiles; **civ·il 'ser·vant** funcionario(-a) *m(f)*; **civ·il 'ser·vice** administración *f* pública; **civ·il 'war** guerra *f* civil

claim [kleɪm] **1** *n* (*request*) reclamación *f* (*for* de); (*right*) derecho *m*; (*assertion*) afirmación *f* **2** *v/t* (*ask for as a right*) reclamar; (*assert*) afirmar; *lost property* reclamar; *they have*

~ed responsibility for the attack se han atribuido la responsabilidad del ataque

claim·ant ['kleɪmənt] reclamante *m/f*

clair·voy·ant [kler'vɔɪənt] *n* clarividente *m/f*, vidente *m/f*

clam [klæm] almeja *f*
♦ **clam up** *v/i* (*pret & pp* **-med**) F cerrarse, callarse

clam·ber ['klæmbər] *v/i* trepar (*over* por)

clam·my ['klæmɪ] *adj* húmedo

clam·or, *Br* **clam·our** ['klæmər] *noise* griterío *m*; *outcry* clamor *m*
♦ **clamor for** *v/t justice* clamar por; *ice cream* pedir a gritos

clamp [klæmp] **1** *n fastener* abrazadera *f*, mordaza *f* **2** *v/t fasten* sujetar con abrazadera; *car* poner un cepo a
♦ **clamp down** *v/i* actuar contundentemente
♦ **clamp down on** *v/t* actuar contundentemente contra

clan [klæn] clan *m*

clan·des·tine [klæn'destɪn] *adj* clandestino

clang [klæŋ] **1** *n* sonido *m* metálico **2** *v/i* resonar; *the metal door ~ed shut* la puerta metálica se cerró con gran estrépito

clap [klæp] *v/t & v/i* (*pret & pp* **-ped**) (*applaud*) aplaudir

clar·et ['klærɪt] *wine* burdeos *m inv*

clar·i·fi·ca·tion [klærɪfɪ'keɪʃn] aclaración *f*

clar·i·fy ['klærɪfaɪ] *v/t* (*pret & pp* **-ied**) aclarar

clar·i·net [klærɪ'net] clarinete *m*

clar·i·ty ['klærətɪ] claridad *f*

clash [klæʃ] **1** *n* choque *m*, enfrentamiento *m*; *of personalities* choque *m* **2** *v/i* chocar, enfrentarse; *of colors* desentonar; *of events* coincidir

clasp [klæsp] **1** *n* broche *m*, cierre *m* **2** *v/t in hand* estrechar

class [klæs] **1** *n lesson*, *students* clase *f*; *social ~* clase *f* social **2** *v/t* clasificar (*as* como)

clas·sic ['klæsɪk] **1** *adj* clásico **2** *n*

clásico *m*

clas·si·cal ['klæsɪkl] *adj music* clásico

clas·si·fi·ca·tion [klæsɪfɪ'keɪʃn] clasificación *f*

clas·si·fied ['klæsɪfaɪd] *adj information* reservado

'clas·si·fied ad(ver·tise·ment) anuncio *m* por palabras

clas·si·fy ['klæsɪfaɪ] *v/t* (*pret & pp* **-ied**) clasificar

'class·mate compañero(-a) *m(f)* de clase; **'class·room** clase *f*, aula *f*; **''class war·fare** lucha *f* de clases

class·y ['klæsɪ] *adj* F con clase

clat·ter ['klætər] **1** *n* estrépito *m* **2** *v/i* hacer ruido

clause [klɔːz] *in agreement* cláusula *f*; GRAM cláusula *f*, oración *f*

claus·tro·pho·bi·a [klɔːstrə'fəʊbɪə] claustrofobia *f*

claw [klɔː] **1** *n also fig* garra *f*; *of lobster* pinza *f* **2** *v/t* (*scratch*) arañar

clay [kleɪ] arcilla *f*

clean [kliːn] **1** *adj* limpio **2** *adv* F (*completely*) completamente **3** *v/t* limpiar; *~ one's teeth* limpiarse los dientes; *I must have my coat ~ed* tengo que llevar el abrigo a la tintorería
♦ **clean out** *v/t room*, *closet* limpiar por completo; *fig* desplumar
♦ **clean up 1** *v/t also fig* limpiar; *papers* recoger **2** *v/i* limpiar; (*wash*) lavarse; *on stock market etc* ganar mucho dinero

clean·er ['kliːnər] *person* limpiador(a) *m(f)*; (*dry*) ~ tintorería *f*

clean·ing wom·an ['kliːnɪŋ] señora *f* de la limpieza

cleanse [klenz] *v/t skin* limpiar

cleans·er ['klenzər] *for skin* loción *f* limpiadora

cleans·ing cream ['klenzɪŋ] crema *f* limpiadora

clear [klɪr] **1** *adj* claro; *weather*, *sky* despejado; *water* transparente; *conscience* limpio; *I'm not ~ about it* no lo tengo claro; *I didn't make myself ~* no me expliqué claramente **2** *adv* **stand ~ of the doors** apartarse de las puertas; **_steer ~ of_** evitar 3 _v/t roads etc_ despejar; _(acquit)_ absolver; _(authorize)_ autorizar; _(earn)_ ganar, sacar; **_the guards ~ed everybody out of the room_** los guardias sacaron a todo el mundo de la habitación; **_you're ~ed for takeoff_** tiene autorización _or_ permiso para despegar; **_~ one's throat_** carraspear 4 _v/i of sky, mist_ despejarse; _of face_ alegrarse

♦ **clear away** _v/t_ quitar

♦ **clear off** _v/i_ F largarse F

♦ **clear out 1** _v/t closet_ ordenar, limpiar **2** _v/i_ marcharse

♦ **clear up 1** _v/i_ ordenar; _of weather_ despejarse; _of illness, rash_ desaparecer **2** _v/t (tidy)_ ordenar; _mystery, problem_ aclarar

clear·ance ['klɪrəns] _space_ espacio _m_; _(authorization)_ autorización _f_

clear·ance sale liquidación _f_

clear·ing ['klɪrɪŋ] claro _m_

clear·ly ['klɪrlɪ] _adv_ claramente; **_she is ~ upset_** está claro que está disgustada

cleav·age ['kliːvɪdʒ] escote _m_

cleav·er ['kliːvər] cuchillo _m_ de carnicero

clem·en·cy ['klemənsɪ] clemencia _f_

clench [klentʃ] _v/t teeth, fist_ apretar

cler·gy ['klɜːrdʒɪ] clero _m_

cler·gy·man ['klɜːrdʒɪmæn] clérigo _m_

clerk [klɜːrk] _administrative_ oficinista _m/f_; _in store_ dependiente(-a) _m/f_

clev·er ['klevər] _adj person, animal_ listo; _idea, gadget_ ingenioso

clev·er·ly ['klevərlɪ] _adv designed_ ingeniosamente

cli·ché ['kliːʃeɪ] tópico _m_, cliché _m_

cli·chéd ['kliːʃeɪd] _adj_ estereotipado

click [klɪk] **1** _n_ COMPUT clic _m_ **2** _v/i_ hacer clic

♦ **click on** _v/t_ COMPUT hacer clic en

cli·ent ['klaɪənt] cliente _m/f_

cli·en·tele [kliːən'tel] clientela _f_

cli·mate ['klaɪmət] _also fig_ clima _m_

'cli·mate change cambio _m_ climático

cli·mat·ic [klaɪ'mætɪk] _adj_ climático

cli·max ['klaɪmæks] _n_ clímax _m_, punto _m_ culminante

climb [klaɪm] **1** _n up mountain_ ascensión _f_, escalada _f_ **2** _v/t hill, ladder_ subir; _mountain_ subir, escalar; _tree_ trepar a **3** _v/i_ subir (**_into_** a); _up mountain_ subir, escalar; _of inflation etc_ subir

♦ **climb down** _v/i from ladder etc_ bajar

climb·er ['klaɪmər] _person_ escalador(a) _m(f)_, alpinista _m/f_, _L.Am._ andinista _m/f_

climb·ing ['klaɪmɪŋ] escalada _f_, alpinismo _m_, _L.Am._ andinismo _m_

climb·ing wall rocódromo _m_

clinch [klɪntʃ] _v/t deal_ cerrar; **_that ~es it!_** ¡ahora sí que está claro!

cling [klɪŋ] _v/i (pret & pp **clung**) of clothes_ pegarse al cuerpo

♦ **cling to** _v/t person, idea_ aferrarse a

'cling·film plástico _m_ transparente (para alimentos)

cling·y ['klɪŋɪ] _adj child, boyfriend_ pegajoso

clin·ic ['klɪnɪk] clínica _f_

clin·i·cal ['klɪnɪkl] _adj_ clínico

clink [klɪŋk] **1** _n noise_ tintineo _m_ **2** _v/i_ tintinear

clip¹ [klɪp] **1** _n fastener_ clip _m_ **2** _v/t (pret & pp -ped)_: **_~ sth to sth_** sujetar algo a algo

clip² [klɪp] **1** _n extract_ fragmento _m_ **2** _v/t (pret & pp -ped) hair, grass_ cortar; _hedge_ podar

clip·pers ['klɪpərz] _npl for hair_ maquinilla _f_; _for nails_ cortaúñas _m inv_; _for gardening_ tijeras _fpl_ de podar

clip·ping ['klɪpɪŋ] _from newspaper_ recorte _m_

clique [kliːk] camarilla _f_

cloak _n_ capa _f_

'cloak·room _Br_ guardarropa _m_

clock [klɑːk] reloj _m_

'clock ra·di·o radio _m_ despertador; **'clock·wise** _adv_ en el sentido de las agujas del reloj; **'clock·work**: **_it went like ~_** salió a la perfección

♦ **clog up** [klɑːg] **1** _v/i (pret & pp -ged)_ bloquearse **2** _v/t (pret & pp -ged)_ bloquear

clone [kloʊn] **1** *n* clon *m* **2** *v/t* clonar

close¹ [kloʊs] **1** *adj family* cercano; *friend* íntimo; **bear a ~ resemblance to** parecerse mucho a; **the ~st town** la ciudad más cercana; **be ~ to s.o.** *emotionally* estar muy unido a alguien **2** *adv* cerca; **~ to the school** cerca del colegio; **~ at hand** a mano; **~ by** cerca

close² [kloʊz] **1** *v/t* cerrar **2** *v/i of door, shop* cerrar; *of eyes* cerrarse

♦ **close down** *v/t & v/i* cerrar

♦ **close in** *v/i of fog* echarse encima; *of troops* aproximarse, acercarse

♦ **close up 1** *v/t building* cerrar **2** *v/i* (*move closer*) juntarse

closed [kloʊzd] *adj store, eyes* cerrado

closed-cir·cuit 'tel·e·vi·sion circuito *m* cerrado de televisión

'close-knit *adj* muy unido

close·ly ['kloʊslɪ] *adv listen, watch* atentamente; *cooperate* de cerca

clos·et ['klɑːzɪt] armario *m*

close-up ['kloʊsʌp] primer plano *m*

clos·ing date ['kloʊzɪŋ] fecha *f* límite

'clos·ing time hora *f* de cierre

clo·sure ['kloʊʒər] cierre *m*

clot [klɑːt] **1** *n of blood* coágulo *m* **2** *v/i* (*pret & pp* **-ted**) *of blood* coagular

cloth [klɑːθ] (*fabric*) tela *f*, tejido *m*; *for cleaning* trapo *m*

clothes [kloʊðz] *npl* ropa *f*

'clothes brush cepillo *m* para la ropa; **'clothes hang·er** percha *f*; **'clothes·horse** tendedero *m* plegable; **'clothes·line** cuerda *f* de tender la ropa; **'clothes peg**, **'clothes·pin** pinza *f* (de la ropa)

cloth·ing ['kloʊðɪŋ] ropa *f*

cloud [klaʊd] *n* nube *f*; **a ~ of dust** una nube de polvo

♦ **cloud over** *v/i of sky* nublarse

'cloud·burst chaparrón *m*

cloud·less ['klaʊdlɪs] *adj sky* despejado

cloud·y ['klaʊdɪ] *adj* nublado

clout [klaʊt] *fig* (*influence*) influencia *f*

clove of 'gar·lic [kloʊv] diente *m* de ajo

clown [klaʊn] *also fig* payaso *m*

club [klʌb] *n weapon* palo *m*, garrote *m*; *in golf* palo *m*; *organization* club *m*; **~s** *in cards* tréboles

clue [kluː] pista *f*; **I haven't a ~** F (*don't know*) no tengo idea F; **he hasn't a ~** F (*is useless*) no tiene ni idea F

clued-up [kluːd'ʌp] *adj* F puesto F; **be ~ on sth** F estar puesto sobre algo F

clump [klʌmp] *n of earth* terrón *m*; *of flowers etc* grupo *m*

clum·si·ness ['klʌmzɪnɪs] torpeza *f*

clum·sy ['klʌmzɪ] *adj person* torpe

clung [klʌŋ] *pret & pp* → **cling**

clus·ter ['klʌstər] **1** *n* grupo *m* **2** *v/i of people* apiñarse; *of houses* agruparse

clutch [klʌtʃ] **1** *n* MOT embrague *m* **2** *v/t* agarrar

♦ **clutch at** *v/t* agarrarse a

clut·ter ['klʌtər] **1** *n* desorden *m*; **all the ~ on my desk** la cantidad de cosas que hay encima de mi mesa **2** *v/t* (*also:* **~ up**) abarrotar

Co. *abbr* (= **Company**) Cía. (= Compañía *f*)

c/o *abbr* (= **care of**) en el domicilio de

coach [koʊtʃ] **1** *n* (*trainer*) entrenador(a) *m(f)*; *of singer, actor* profesor(a) *m(f)*; *Br* (*bus*) autobús *m* **2** *v/t footballer* entrenar; *singer* preparar

coach·ing ['koʊtʃɪŋ] entrenamiento *m*

co·ag·u·late [koʊ'ægjʊleɪt] *v/i of blood* coagularse

coal [koʊl] carbón *m*

co·a·li·tion [koʊə'lɪʃn] coalición *f*

'coal·mine mina *f* de carbón

coarse [kɔːrs] *adj* áspero; *hair* basto; (*vulgar*) basto, grosero

coarse·ly ['kɔːrslɪ] *adv* (*vulgarly*) de manera grosera; **~ ground coffee** café molido grueso

coast [koʊst] *n* costa *f*; **at the ~** en la costa

coast·al ['koustl] *adj* costero

coast·er ['koustər] *posavasos m inv*

'coast·guard *organization* servicio *m* de guardacostas; *person* guardacostas *m/f inv*

'coast·line litoral *m*, costa *f*

coat [kout] **1** *n* chaqueta *f*, *L.Am.* saco *m*; (*over~*) abrigo *m*; *of animal* pelaje *m*; *of paint etc* capa *f*, mano *f* **2** *v/t* (*cover*) cubrir (**with** de)

'coat·hang·er percha *f*

coat·ing ['koutɪŋ] capa *f*

co·au·thor ['kouɒ:θər] **1** *n* coautor(a) *m(f)* **2** *v/t*: ~ *a book* escribir un libro conjuntamente

coax [kouks] *v/t* persuadir; ~ *sth out of s.o.* sonsacar algo a alguien

cob·bled ['kɑ:bld] *adj* adoquinado

cob·ble·stone ['kɑ:blstoun] adoquín *m*

cob·web ['kɑ:bweb] telaraña *f*

co·caine [kə'keɪn] cocaína *f*

cock [kɑ:k] *n* (*chicken*) gallo *m*; (*any male bird*) macho *m*

cock·eyed [kɑ:k'aɪd] *adj* F *idea etc* ridículo

'cock·pit *of plane* cabina *f*

cock·roach ['kɑ:kroutʃ] cucaracha *f*

'cock·tail cóctel *m* (*bebida*)

'cock·tail par·ty cóctel *m* (*fiesta*)

'cock·tail shak·er coctelera *f*

cock·y ['kɑ:kɪ] *adj* F creído, chulo

co·coa ['koukou] *drink* cacao *m*

co·co·nut ['koukənʌt] coco *m*

'co·co·nut palm cocotero *m*

COD [si:ou'di:] *abbr* (= *collect on delivery*) entrega *f* contra reembolso

cod·dle ['kɑ:dl] *v/t sick person* cuidar; *pej: child* mimar

code [koud] *n* código *m*; **in ~** cifrado

co·ed·u·ca·tion·al [kouedu'keɪʃnl] *adj* mixto

co·erce [kou'ɜ:rs] *v/t* coaccionar

co·ex·ist [kouɪg'zɪst] *v/i* coexistir

co·ex·ist·ence [kouɪg'zɪstəns] coexistencia *f*

cof·fee ['kɑ:fɪ] café *m*; *a cup of ~* un café

'cof·fee bean grano *m* de café;

'cof·fee break pausa *f* para el café;

'cof·fee cup taza *f* de café;

'cof·fee grind·er ['graɪndər] molinillo *m* de café; **'cof·fee mak·er** cafetera *f* (para preparar); **'cof·fee pot** cafetera *f* (para servir); **'cof·fee shop** café *m*, cafetería *f*; **'cof·fee ta·ble** mesa *f* de centro

cof·fin ['kɑ:fɪn] féretro *m*, ataúd *m*

cog [kɑ:g] diente *m*

co·gnac ['kɑ:njæk] coñac *m*

'cog·wheel rueda *f* dentada

co·hab·it [kou'hæbɪt] *v/i* cohabitar

co·her·ent [kou'hɪrənt] *adj* coherente

coil [kɔɪl] **1** *n of rope* rollo *m*; *of smoke* espiral *f*; *of snake* anillo *m* **2** *v/t*: ~ (**up**) enrollar

coin [kɔɪn] *n* moneda *f*

co·in·cide [kouɪn'saɪd] *v/i* coincidir

co·in·ci·dence [kou'ɪnsɪdəns] coincidencia *f*

coke [kouk] P (*cocaine*) coca *f*

Coke® [kouk] Coca-Cola® *f*

cold [kould] **1** *adj also fig* frío; *I'm* (*feeling*) ~ tengo frío; *it's* ~ *of weather* hace frío; *in* ~ *blood* a sangre fría; *get* ~ *feet* F ponerse nervioso **2** *n* frío *m*; MED resfriado *m*; *I have a* ~ estoy resfriado, tengo un resfriado

cold-blood·ed [kould'blʌdɪd] *adj* de sangre fría; *fig: murder* a sangre fría

cold call·ing ['kɒ:lɪŋ] COM *visitas o llamadas comerciales hechas sin cita previa*

'cold cuts *npl* fiambres *mpl*

cold·ly ['kouldlɪ] *adv* fríamente, con frialdad

cold·ness ['kouldnɪs] frialdad *f*

'cold sore calentura *f*

cole·slaw ['koulslɒ:] *ensalada de col, cebolla, zanahoria y mayonesa*

col·ic ['kɑ:lɪk] cólico *m*

col·lab·o·rate [kə'læbəreɪt] *v/i* colaborar (**on** en)

col·lab·o·ra·tion [kəlæbə'reɪʃn] colaboración *f*

col·lab·o·ra·tor [kə'læbəreɪtər] colaborador(a) *m(f)*; *with enemy* colaboracionista *m/f*

col·lapse [kə'læps] *v/i of roof, buil-*

ding hundirse, desplomarse; *of person* desplomarse

col·lap·si·ble [kəˈlæpsəbl] *adj* plegable

col·lar [ˈkɑːlər] cuello *m*; *for dog* collar *m*

'col·lar·bone clavícula *f*

col·league [ˈkɑːliːg] colega *m/f*

col·lect [kəˈlekt] **1** *v/t* recoger; *as hobby* coleccionar **2** *v/i* (*gather together*) reunirse **3** *adv*: *call* ~ llamar a cobro revertido

col·lect call llamada *f* a cobro revertido

col·lect·ed [kəˈlektɪd] *adj works, poems etc* completo; *person* sereno

col·lec·tion [kəˈlekʃn] colección *f*; *in church* colecta *f*

col·lec·tive [kəˈlektɪv] *adj* colectivo

col·lec·tive 'bar·gain·ing negociación *f* colectiva

col·lec·tor [kəˈlektər] coleccionista *m/f*

col·lege [ˈkɑːlɪdʒ] universidad *f*

col·lide [kəˈlaɪd] *v/i* chocar, colisionar (*with* con *or* contra)

col·li·sion [kəˈlɪʒn] choque *m*, colisión *f*

col·lo·qui·al [kəˈloʊkwɪəl] *adj* coloquial

Co·lom·bi·a [kəˈlʌmbɪə] Colombia *f*

Co·lom·bi·an [kəˈlʌmbɪən] **1** *adj* colombiano **2** *n* colombiano(-a) *m(f)*

co·lon [ˈkoʊlən] *punctuation* dos puntos *mpl*; ANAT colon *m*

colo·nel [ˈkɜːrnl] coronel *m*

co·lo·ni·al [kəˈloʊnɪəl] *adj* colonial

co·lo·nize [ˈkɑːlənaɪz] *v/t country* colonizar

co·lo·ny [ˈkɑːlənɪ] colonia *f*

col·or [ˈkʌlər] **1** *n* color *m*; *in* ~ *movie etc* en color; ~*s* MIL bandera *f* **2** *v/t one's hair* teñir **3** *v/i* (*blush*) ruborizarse

'col·or-blind *adj* daltónico

col·ored [ˈkʌlərd] *adj person* de color

'col·or fast *adj* que no destiñe

col·or·ful [ˈkʌlərfəl] *adj* lleno de colores; *account* colorido

col·or·ing [ˈkʌlərɪŋ] color *m*

'col·or pho·to·graph fotografía *f* en color; **'col·or scheme** combinación *f* de colores; **'col·or TV** televisión *f* en color

co·los·sal [kəˈlɑːsl] *adj* colosal

col·our *etc Br* → **color** *etc*

colt [koʊlt] potro *m*

Co·lum·bus [kəˈlʌmbəs] Colón *m*

col·umn [ˈkɑːləm] *architectural, of text* columna *f*

col·umn·ist [ˈkɑːləmɪst] columnista *m/f*

co·ma [ˈkoʊmə] coma *m*; *be in a* ~ estar en coma

comb [koʊm] **1** *n* peine *m* **2** *v/t hair, area* peinar; ~ *one's hair* peinarse

com·bat [ˈkɑːmbæt] **1** *n* combate *m* **2** *v/t* combatir

com·bi·na·tion [kɑːmbɪˈneɪʃn] combinación *f*

com·bine [kəmˈbaɪn] **1** *v/t* combinar; *ingredients* mezclar **2** *v/i* combinarse

com·bine har·vest·er [kɑːmbaɪnˈhɑːrvɪstər] cosechadora *f*

com·bus·ti·ble [kəmˈbʌstɪbl] *adj* combustible

com·bus·tion [kəmˈbʌstʃn] combustión *f*

come [kʌm] *v/i* (*pret* **came**, *pp* **come**) *toward speaker* venir; *toward listener* ir; *of train, bus* llegar, venir; *don't* ~ *too close* no te acerques demasiado; *you'll* ~ *to like it* llegará a gustarte; *how* ~*?* F ¿y eso?; *how* ~ *you've stopped going to the club?* ¿cómo es que has dejado de ir al club?

♦ **come about** *v/i* (*happen*) pasar, suceder

♦ **come across 1** *v/t* (*find*) encontrar **2** *v/i*: *his humor comes across as ...* su humor da la impresión de ser ...; *she comes across as ...* da la impresión de ser ...

♦ **come along** *v/i* (*come too*) venir; (*turn up*) aparecer; (*progress*) marchar; *why don't you come along?* ¿por qué no te vienes con nosotros?

♦ **come apart** *v/i* desmontarse;

C

(break) romperse

♦ **come around** *v/i to s.o.'s home* venir, pasarse; *(regain consciousness)* volver en sí

♦ **come away** *v/i (leave)* salir; *of button etc* caerse

♦ **come back** *v/i* volver; *it came back to me* lo recordé

♦ **come by 1** *v/i* pasarse **2** *v/t (acquire)* conseguir; *how did you come by that bruise?* ¿cómo te has dado ese golpe?

♦ **come down 1** *v/i* bajar; *of rain, snow* caer **2** *v/t: he came down the stairs* bajó las escaleras

♦ **come for** *v/t (attack)* atacar; *(collect: thing)* venir a por; *(collect: person)* venir a buscar a

♦ **come forward** *v/i (present o.s.)* presentarse

♦ **come from** *v/t (travel from)* venir de; *(originate from)* ser de

♦ **come in** *v/i* entrar; *of train* llegar; *of tide* subir; *come in!* ¡entre!, ¡adelante!

♦ **come in for** *v/t* recibir; *come in for criticism* recibir críticas

♦ **come in on** *v/t: come in on a deal* participar en un negocio

♦ **come off** *v/i of handle etc* soltarse, caerse; *of paint etc* quitarse

♦ **come on** *v/i (progress)* marchar, progresar; *come on!* ¡vamos!; *oh come on, you're exaggerating* ¡vamos, hombre!, estás exagerando

♦ **come out** *v/i* salir; *of book* publicarse; *of stain* irse, quitarse; *of gay* declararse homosexual públicamente

♦ **come to 1** *v/t place* llegar a; *of hair, dress, water* llegar hasta; *that comes to $70* eso suma 70 dólares **2** *v/i (regain consciousness)* volver en sí

♦ **come up** *v/i* subir; *of sun* salir; *something has come up* ha surgido algo

♦ **come up with** *v/t solution* encontrar; *John came up with a great idea* a John se le ocurrió una idea estupenda

'**come·back** regreso *m*; *make a ~* regresar

co·me·di·an [kə'mi:dɪən] humorista *m/f; pej* payaso(-a) *m(f)*

'**come·down** gran decepción *f*

com·e·dy ['kɑ:mədɪ] comedia *f*

com·et ['kɑ:mɪt] cometa *m*

come·up·pance [kʌm'ʌpəns] *n* F: *he'll get his ~* tendrá su merecido

com·fort ['kʌmfərt] **1** *n* comodidad *f*, confort *m; (consolation)* consuelo *m* **2** *v/t* consolar

com·for·ta·ble ['kʌmfərtəbl] *adj chair* cómodo; *house, room* cómodo, confortable; *be ~ of person* estar cómodo; *financially* estar en una situación holgada

com·ic ['kɑ:mɪk] **1** *n to read* cómic *m; (comedian)* cómico(-a) *m(f)* **2** *adj* cómico

com·i·cal ['kɑ:mɪkl] *adj* cómico

'**com·ic book** cómic *m*

'**com·ics** ['kɑ:mɪks] *npl* tiras *fpl* cómicas

'**com·ic strip** tira *f* cómica

com·ma ['kɑ:mə] coma *f*

com·mand [kə'mænd] **1** *n* orden *f* **2** *v/t* ordenar, mandar

com·man·deer [kɑ:mən'dɪr] *v/t* requisar

com·mand·er [kə'mændər] comandante *m/f*

com·mand·er-in-'chief comandante *m/f* en jefe

com·mand·ing of·fi·cer [kə'mændɪŋ] oficial *m/f* al mando

com·mand·ment [kə'mændmənt] mandamiento *m: the Ten Commandments* REL los Diez Mandamientos

com·mem·o·rate [kə'meməreɪt] *v/t* conmemorar

com·mem·o·ra·tion [kəmemə'reɪʃn]: *in ~ of* en conmemoración de

com·mence [kə'mens] *v/t & v/i* comenzar

com·mend [kə'mend] *v/t* encomiar, elogiar

com·mend·a·ble [kə'mendəbl] *adj* encomiable

com·men·da·tion [kəmen'deɪʃn] *for bravery* mención *f*

com·men·su·rate [kə'menʃərət] *adj*: ~ **with** acorde con

com·ment ['kɑːment] **1** *n* comentario *m*; *no ~!* ¡sin comentarios! **2** *v/i* hacer comentarios (**on** sobre)

com·men·ta·ry ['kɑːməntərɪ] comentarios *mpl*

com·men·tate ['kɑːmənteɪt] *v/i* hacer de comentarista

com·men·ta·tor ['kɑːmənteɪtər] comentarista *m/f*

com·merce ['kɑːmɜːrs] comercio *m*

com·mer·cial [kə'mɜːrʃl] **1** *adj* comercial **2** *n* (*advert*) anuncio *m* (publicitario)

com·mer·cial 'break pausa *f* publicitaria

com·mer·cial·ize [kə'mɜːrʃlaɪz] *v/t Christmas* comercializar

com·mer·cial 'trav·el·er, *Br* **com·mer·cial 'trav·el·ler** viajante *m/f* de comercio

com·mis·e·rate [kə'mɪzəreɪt] *v/i*: *he ~d with me on my failure to get the job* me dijo cuánto sentía que no hubiera conseguido el trabajo

com·mis·sion [kə'mɪʃn] **1** *n* (*payment, committee*) comisión *f*; (*job*) encargo *m* **2** *v/t*: *she has been commissioned ...* se le ha encargado ...

com·mit [kə'mɪt] *v/t* (*pret & pp* **-ted**) *crime* cometer; *money* comprometer; *~ o.s.* comprometerse

com·mit·ment [kə'mɪtmənt] compromiso *m* (**to** con); *he's afraid of ~* tiene miedo de comprometerse

com·mit·tee [kə'mɪtɪ] comité *m*

com·mod·i·ty [kə'mɑːdətɪ] *raw material* producto *m* básico; *product* bien *m* de consumo

com·mon ['kɑːmən] *adj* común; *in ~* al igual (**with** que); *have sth in ~ with s.o.* tener algo en común con alguien

com·mon·er ['kɑːmənər] plebeyo(-a) *m(f)*

com·mon 'law wife esposa *f* de hecho

com·mon·ly ['kɑːmənlɪ] *adv* comúnmente

'com·mon·place *adj* común

com·mon 'sense sentido *m* común

com·mo·tion [kə'mouʃn] alboroto *m*

com·mu·nal [kə'mjuːnl] *adj* comunal

com·mu·nal·ly [kə'mjuːnəlɪ] *adv* en comunidad

com·mu·ni·cate [kə'mjuːnɪkeɪt] **1** *v/i* comunicarse **2** *v/t* comunicar

com·mu·ni·ca·tion [kəmjuːnɪ'keɪʃn] comunicación *f*

com·mu·ni·ca·tions *npl* comunicaciones *fpl*

com·mu·ni'ca·tions sat·el·lite satélite *m* de telecomunicaciones

com·mu·ni·ca·tive [kə'mjuːnɪkətɪv] *adj person* comunicativo

Com·mu·nion [kə'mjuːnjən] REL comunión *f*

com·mu·ni·qué [kə'mjuːnɪkeɪ] comunicado *m*

Com·mu·nism ['kɑːmjʊnɪzəm] comunismo *m*

Com·mu·nist ['kɑːmjʊnɪst] **1** *adj* comunista **2** *n* comunista *m/f*

com·mu·ni·ty [kə'mjuːnətɪ] comunidad *f*

com'mu·ni·ty cen·ter, *Br* **com'mu·ni·ty cen·tre** centro *m* comunitario

com'mu·ni·ty serv·ice servicios *mpl* a la comunidad (como pena)

com·mute [kə'mjuːt] **1** *v/i* viajar al trabajo; *~ to work* viajar al trabajo **2** *v/t* LAW conmutar

com·mut·er [kə'mjuːtər] *persona que viaja al trabajo*

com'mut·er traf·fic *tráfico generado por los que se desplazan al trabajo*

com'mut·er train *tren de cercanías que utilizan los que se desplazan al trabajo*

com·pact 1 *adj* [kəm'pækt] compacto **2** *n* ['kɑːmpækt] MOT utilitario *m*

com·pact 'disc (disco *m*) compacto *m*

com·pan·ion [kəm'pænjən] compañero(-a) *m(f)*

com·pan·ion·ship [kəm'pænjənʃɪp] compañía *f*

com·pa·ny ['kʌmpənɪ] COM empresa *f*, compañía *f*; (*companionship, guests*) compañía *f*; **keep s.o. ~** hacer compañía a alguien

com·pa·ny 'car coche *m* de empresa

com·pa·ny 'law derecho *m* de sociedades

com·pa·ra·ble ['kɑːmpərəbl] *adj* comparable

com·par·a·tive [kəm'pærətɪv] **1** *adj* (*relative*) relativo; *study* comparado; GRAM comparativo; **~ form** GRAM comparativo *m* **2** *n* GRAM comparativo *m*

com·par·a·tive·ly [kəm'pærətɪvlɪ] *adv* relativamente

com·pare [kəm'per] **1** *v/t* comparar; **~d with ...** comparado con ...; **you can't ~ them** no se pueden comparar **2** *v/i* compararse

com·par·i·son [kəm'pærɪsn] comparación *f*; **there's no ~** no hay punto de comparación

com·part·ment [kəm'pɑːrtmənt] compartimento *m*

com·pass ['kʌmpəs] brújula *f*; (**a pair of**) **~es** GEOM un compás

com·pas·sion [kəm'pæʃn] compasión *f*

com·pas·sion·ate [kəm'pæʃənət] *adj* compasivo

com·pas·sion·ate 'leave *permiso laboral por muerte o enfermedad grave de un familiar*

com·pat·i·bil·i·ty [kəmpætə'bɪlɪtɪ] compatibilidad *f*

com·pat·i·ble [kəm'pætəbl] *adj* compatible; **we're not ~** no somos compatibles

com·pel [kəm'pel] *v/t* (*pret & pp* **-led**) obligar

com·pel·ling [kəm'pelɪŋ] *adj* *argument* poderoso; *movie, book* fascinante

com·pen·sate ['kɑːmpənseɪt] **1** *v/t* **with** *money* compensar **2** *v/i* **~ for** compensar

com·pen·sa·tion [kɑːmpən'seɪʃn] (*money*) indemnización *f*; (*reward, comfort*) compensación *f*

com·pete [kəm'piːt] *v/i* competir

(**for** por)

com·pe·tence ['kɑːmpɪtəns] competencia *f*

com·pe·tent ['kɑːmpɪtənt] *adj* competente; **I'm not ~ to judge** no estoy capacitado para juzgar

com·pe·tent·ly ['kɑːmpɪtəntlɪ] *adv* competentemente

com·pe·ti·tion [kɑːmpə'tɪʃn] (*contest*) concurso *m*; SP competición *f*; (*competitors*) competencia *f*; **the government wants to encourage ~** el gobierno quiere fomentar la competencia

com·pet·i·tive [kəm'petətɪv] *adj* competitivo

com·pet·i·tive·ly [kəm'petətɪvlɪ] *adv* competitivamente: **~ priced** con un precio muy competitivo

com·pet·i·tive·ness [kəm'petɪtɪvnɪs] COM competitividad *f*; *of person* espíritu *m* competitivo

com·pet·i·tor [kəm'petɪtər] *in contest* concursante *m/f*; SP competidor(a) *m(f)*, contrincante *m/f*; COM competidor(a) *m(f)*

com·pile [kəm'paɪl] *v/t* compilar

com·pla·cen·cy [kəm'pleɪsənsɪ] complacencia *f*

com·pla·cent [kəm'pleɪsənt] *adj* complaciente

com·plain [kəm'pleɪn] *v/i* quejarse, protestar; *to shop, manager* quejarse; **~ of** MED estar aquejado de

com·plaint [kəm'pleɪnt] queja *f*, protesta *f*; MED dolencia *f*

com·ple·ment ['kɑːmplɪmənt] *v/t* complementar; **they ~ each other** se complementan

com·ple·men·ta·ry [kɑːmplɪ'men-tərɪ] *adj* complementario; **the two are ~** los dos se complementan

com·plete [kəm'pliːt] **1** *adj* (*total*) absoluto, total; (*full*) completo; (*finished*) finalizado, terminado **2** *v/t* task, building etc finalizar, terminar; *course* completar; *form* rellenar

com·plete·ly [kəm'pliːtlɪ] *adv* completamente

com·ple·tion [kəm'pliːʃn] finalización f, terminación f

com·plex ['kɑ:mpleks] **1** adj complejo **2** n also PSYCH complejo m

com·plex·ion [kəm'plekʃn] facial tez f

com·plex·i·ty [kəm'pleksɪtɪ] complejidad f

com·pli·ance [kəm'plaɪəns] cumplimiento (**with** de)

com·pli·cate ['kɑ:mplɪkeɪt] v/t complicar

com·pli·cat·ed ['kɑ:mplɪkeɪtɪd] adj complicado

com·pli·ca·tion [kɑ:mplɪ'keɪʃn] complicación f; **~s** MED complicaciones fpl

com·pli·ment ['kɑ:mplɪmənt] **1** n cumplido m **2** v/t hacer un cumplido a (**on** por)

com·pli·men·ta·ry [kɑ:mplɪ'mentərɪ] adj elogioso; (free) de regalo, gratis

'**com·pli·ments slip** nota f de cortesía

com·ply [kəm'plaɪ] v/i (pret & pp -ied) cumplir; **~ with** cumplir

com·po·nent [kəm'poʊnənt] pieza f, componente m

com·pose [kəm'poʊz] v/t also MUS componer; **be ~d of** estar compuesto de; **~ o.s.** serenarse

com·posed [kəm'poʊzd] adj (calm) sereno

com·pos·er [kəm'poʊzər] MUS compositor(a) m(f)

com·po·si·tion [kɑ:mpə'zɪʃn] also MUS composición f; (essay) redacción f

com·po·sure [kəm'poʊʒər] compostura f

com·pound ['kɑ:mpaʊnd] n CHEM compuesto m

com·pound 'in·ter·est interés m compuesto or combinado

com·pre·hend [kɑ:mprɪ'hend] v/t (understand) comprender

com·pre·hen·sion [kɑ:mprɪ'henʃn] comprensión f

com·pre·hen·sive [kɑ:mprɪ'hensɪv] adj detallado

com·pre·hen·sive in'sur·ance seguro m a todo riesgo

com·pre·hen·sive·ly [kɑ:mprɪ'hensɪvlɪ] adv detalladamente

com·press 1 n ['kɑ:mpres] MED compresa f **2** v/t [kəm'pres] air, gas comprimir; information condensar

com·prise [kəm'praɪz] v/t comprender; **be ~d of** constar de

com·pro·mise ['kɑ:mprəmaɪz] **1** n solución f negociada; **I've had to make ~s all my life** toda mi vida he tenido que hacer concesiones **2** v/i transigir, efectuar concesiones **3** v/t principles traicionar; (jeopardize) poner en peligro; **~ o.s.** ponerse en un compromiso

com·pul·sion [kəm'pʌlʃn] PSYCH compulsión f

com·pul·sive [kəm'pʌlsɪv] adj behavior compulsivo; reading absorbente

com·pul·so·ry [kəm'pʌlsərɪ] adj obligatorio

com·put·er [kəm'pju:tər] Span ordenador m, L.Am. computadora f; **have sth on ~** tener algo en el Span ordenador or L.Am. computadora

com·put·er-aid·ed de'sign [kəmp-ju:tər'eɪdɪd] diseño m asistido por Span ordenador or L.Am. computadora; **com·put·er-aid·ed man·u-'fac·ture** fabricación f asistida por Span ordenador or L.Am. computadora; **com·put·er-con'trolled** adj controlado por Span ordenador or L.Am. computadora; **com'puter game** juego m de Span ordenador or L.Am. computadora

com·put·er·ize [kəm'pju:təraɪz] v/t informatizar, L.Am. computarizar

com·put·er 'lit·er·ate adj con conocimientos de informática or L.Am. computación; **com·put·er 'sci·ence** informática f, L.Am. computación f; **com·put·er 'sci·en·tist** informático(-a) m(f)

com·put·ing [kəm'pju:tɪŋ] n informática f, L.Am. computación f

com·rade ['kɑ:mreɪd] (friend) compañero(-a) m(f); POL camarada m/f

com·rade·ship [ˈkɑːmreɪdʃɪp] ca·maradería f

con [kɑːn] **1** n F timo m **2** v/t (pret & pp **-ned**) F timar F

con·ceal [kənˈsiːl] v/t ocultar

con·ceal·ment [kənˈsiːlmənt] ocultación f

con·cede [kənˈsiːd] v/t (admit) admitir, reconocer

con·ceit [kənˈsiːt] engreimiento m, presunción f

con·ceit·ed [kənˈsiːtɪd] adj engreido, presuntuoso

con·ceiv·a·ble [kənˈsiːvəbl] adj concebible

con·ceive [kənˈsiːv] v/i of woman concebir; ~ of (imagine) imaginar

con·cen·trate [ˈkɑːnsəntreɪt] **1** v/i concentrarse **2** v/t one's attention, energies concentrar

con·cen·trat·ed [ˈkɑːnsəntreɪtɪd] adj juice etc concentrado

con·cen·tra·tion [kɑːnsənˈtreɪʃn] concentración f

con·cept [ˈkɑːnsept] concepto m

con·cep·tion [kənˈsepʃn] of child concepción f

con·cern [kənˈsɜːrn] **1** n (anxiety, care) preocupación f; (business) asunto m; (company) empresa f; **it's none of your** ~ no es asunto tuyo; **cause** ~ preocupar, inquietar **2** v/t (involve) concernir, incumbir; (worry) preocupar, inquietar; ~ **o.s. with** preocuparse de

con·cerned [kənˈsɜːrnd] adj (anxious) preocupado, inquieto (about por); (caring) preocupado (about por); (involved) en cuestión; **as far as I'm** ~ por lo que a mí respecta

con·cern·ing [kənˈsɜːrnɪŋ] prep en relación con, sobre

con·cert [ˈkɑːnsərt] concierto m

con·cert·ed [kənˈsɜːrtɪd] adj (joint) concertado, conjunto

'con·cert·mas·ter primer violín m/f

con·cer·to [kənˈʃertoʊ] concierto m

con·ces·sion [kənˈseʃn] (compromise) concesión f

con·cil·i·a·to·ry [kənsɪliˈeɪtərɪ] adj conciliador

con·cise [kənˈsaɪs] adj conciso

con·clude [kənˈkluːd] v/t & v/i (deduce, end) concluir (from de)

con·clu·sion [kənˈkluːʒn] (deduction, end) conclusión f; **in** ~ en conclusión

con·clu·sive [kənˈkluːsɪv] adj concluyente

con·coct [kənˈkɑːkt] v/t meal, drink preparar; excuse, story urdir

con·coc·tion [kənˈkɑːkʃn] food menjunje m; drink brebaje m, pócima f

con·crete [ˈkɑːŋkriːt] **1** adj concreto; ~ **jungle** jungla f de asfalto **2** n hormigón m, L.Am. concreto m

con·cur [kənˈkɜːr] v/i (pret & pp -red) coincidir

con·cus·sion [kənˈkʌʃn] conmoción f cerebral

con·demn [kənˈdem] v/t condenar; building declarar en ruina

con·dem·na·tion [kɑːndəmˈneɪʃn] of action condena f

con·den·sa·tion [kɑːndenˈseɪʃn] on walls, windows condensación f

con·dense [kənˈdens] **1** v/t (make shorter) condensar **2** v/i of steam condensarse

con·densed 'milk [kənˈdensd] leche f condensada

con·de·scend [kɑːndɪˈsend] v/i: **he ~ed to speak to me** se dignó a hablarme

con·de·scend·ing [kɑːndɪˈsendɪŋ] adj (patronizing) condescendiente

con·di·tion [kənˈdɪʃn] **1** n (state) condiciones fpl; of health estado m; illness enfermedad f; (requirement, term) condición f; ~**s** (circumstances) condiciones fpl; **on** ~ **that ...** a condición de que ...; **you're in no** ~ **to drive** no estás en condiciones de conducir **2** v/t PSYCH condicionar

con·di·tion·al [kənˈdɪʃnl] **1** adj acceptance condicional **2** n GRAM condicional m

con·di·tion·er [kənˈdɪʃnər] for hair suavizante m, acondicionador m; for fabric suavizante m

con·di·tion·ing [kən'dɪʃnɪŋ] PSYCH condicionamiento *m*

con·do ['kɑ:ndoʊ] F *apartment* apartamento *m*, Span piso *m*; *building* bloque de apartamentos

con·do·len·ces [kən'doʊlənsɪz] *npl* condolencias *fpl*

con·dom ['kɑ:ndəm] condón *m*, preservativo *m*

con·do·min·i·um [kɑ:ndə'mɪniəm] → **condo**

con·done [kən'doʊn] *v/t actions* justificar

con·du·cive [kən'du:sɪv] *adj:* **~ to** propicio para

con·duct 1 *n* ['kɑ:ndʌkt] (*behavior*) conducta *f* **2** *v/t* [kən'dʌkt] (*carry out*) realizar, hacer; ELEC conducir; MUS dirigir; **~ o.s.** comportarse

con·duct·ed 'tour [kən'dʌktɪd] visita *f* guiada

con·duc·tor [kən'dʌktər] MUS director(a) *m(f)* de orquesta; *on train* revisor(-a) *m(f)*; PHYS conductor *m*

cone [koʊn] GEOM, *on highway* cono *m*; *for ice cream* cucurucho *m*; *of pine tree* piña *f*

con·fec·tion·er [kən'fekʃənər] pastelero(-a) *m(f)*

con·fec·tion·ers' sug·ar azúcar *m or f* glas

con·fec·tion·e·ry [kən'fekʃənərɪ] (*candy*) dulces *mpl*

con·fed·e·ra·tion [kənfedə'reɪʃn] confederación *f*

con·fer [kən'fɜ:r] **1** *v/t* (*pret & pp* **-red**): **~ sth on s.o.** (*bestow*) conferir *or* otorgar algo a alguien **2** *v/i* (*pret & pp* **-red**) (*discuss*) deliberar

con·fe·rence ['kɑ:nfərəns] congreso *m*; *discussion* conferencia *f*

'con·fe·rence room sala *f* de conferencias

con·fess [kən'fes] **1** *v/t* confesar **2** *v/i* confesar; REL confesarse; **~ to a weakness for sth** confesar una debilidad por algo

con·fes·sion [kən'feʃn] confesión *f*; **I've a ~ to make** tengo algo que confesar

con·fes·sion·al [kən'feʃnl] REL confesionario *m*

con·fes·sor [kən'fesər] REL confesor *m*

con·fide [kən'faɪd] **1** *v/t* confiar **2** *v/i*: **~ in s.o.** confiarse a alguien

con·fi·dence ['kɑ:nfɪdəns] confianza *f*; (*secret*) confidencia *f*; **in ~** en confianza, confidencialmente

con·fi·dent ['kɑ:nfɪdənt] *adj* (*self-assured*) seguro de sí mismo; (*convinced*) seguro

con·fi·den·tial [kɑ:nfɪ'denʃl] *adj* confidencial, secreto

con·fi·den·tial·ly [kɑ:nfɪ'denʃlɪ] *adv* confidencialmente

con·fi·dent·ly ['kɑ:nfɪdəntlɪ] *adv* con seguridad

con·fine [kən'faɪn] *v/t* (*imprison*) confinar, recluir; (*restrict*) limitar; **be ~d to one's bed** tener que guardar cama

con·fined [kən'faɪnd] *adj space* limitado

con·fine·ment [kən'faɪnmənt] (*imprisonment*) reclusión *f*; MED parto *m*

con·firm [kən'fɜ:rm] *v/t* confirmar

con·fir·ma·tion [kɑ:nfər'meɪʃn] confirmación *f*

con·firmed [kən'fɜ:rmd] *adj* (*inveterate*) empedernido; **I'm a ~ believer in ...** creo firmemente en ...

con·fis·cate ['kɑ:nfɪskeɪt] *v/t* confiscar

con·flict 1 *n* ['kɑ:nflɪkt] conflicto *m* **2** *v/i* [kən'flɪkt] (*clash*) chocar; **~ing loyalties** lealtades *fpl* encontradas

con·form [kən'fɔ:rm] *v/i* ser conformista; **~ to** *to standards etc* ajustarse a

con·form·ist [kən'fɔ:rmɪst] *n* conformista *m/f*

con·front [kən'frʌnt] *v/t* (*face*) hacer frente a, enfrentarse; (*tackle*) hacer frente a

con·fron·ta·tion [kɑ:nfrən'teɪʃn] confrontación *f*, enfrentamiento *m*

con·fuse [kən'fju:z] *v/t* confundir; **~ s.o. with s.o.** confundir a alguien con alguien

con·fused [kən'fju:zd] *adj person*

con·fun·dido; *situation*, *piece of writing* confuso

con·fus·ing [kən'fjuːzɪŋ] *adj* confuso

con·fu·sion [kən'fjuːʒn] (*muddle*, *chaos*) confusión *f*

con·geal [kən'dʒiːl] *v/i of blood* coagularse; *of fat* solidificarse

con·gen·ial [kən'dʒiːnɪəl] *adj person* simpático, agradable; *occasion*, *place* agradable

con·gen·i·tal [kən'dʒenɪtl] *adj* MED congénito

con·gest·ed [kən'dʒestɪd] *adj roads* congestionado

con·ges·tion [kən'dʒestʃn] *also* MED congestión *f*; **traffic ~** congestión *f* circulatoria

con·grat·u·late [kən'grætʃʊleɪt] *v/t* felicitar

con·grat·u·la·tions [kəngrætʃʊ'leɪʃnz] *npl* felicitaciones *fpl*; **~ on ...** felicidades por ...; **let me offer my ~** permita que le dé la enhorabuena

con·grat·u·la·to·ry [kəngrætʃʊ'leɪtəri] *adj* de felicitación

con·gre·gate ['kɑːŋgrɪgeɪt] *v/i* (*gather*) congregarse

con·gre·ga·tion [kɑːŋgrɪ'geɪʃn] REL congregación *f*

con·gress ['kɑːŋgres] (*conference*) congreso *m*; **Congress** *in US* Congreso *m*

Con·gres·sion·al [kən'greʃnl] *adj* del Congreso

Con·gress·man ['kɑːŋgresmən] congresista *m*

Con·gress·wo·man ['kɑːŋgreswʊmən] congresista *f*

co·ni·fer ['kɑːnɪfər] conífera *f*

con·jec·ture [kən'dʒektʃər] *n* (*speculation*) conjetura *f*

con·ju·gate ['kɑːndʒʊgeɪt] *v/t* GRAM conjugar

con·junc·tion [kən'dʒʌŋkʃn] GRAM conjunción *f*; **in ~ with** junto con

con·junc·ti·vi·tis [kəndʒʌŋktɪ'vaɪtɪs] conjuntivitis *f*

♦ **con·jure up** ['kʌndʒər] *v/t* (*produce*) hacer aparecer; (*evoke*) evocar

con·jur·er, con·jur·or ['kʌndʒərər]

(*magician*) prestidigitador(a) *m(f)*

con·jur·ing tricks ['kʌndʒərɪŋ] *npl* juegos *mpl* de manos

con man ['kɑːnmæn] ⌐ timador *m* F

con·nect [kə'nekt] *v/t* conectar; (*link*) relacionar, vincular; *to power supply* enchufar

con·nect·ed [kə'nektɪd] *adj*: **be well-~** estar bien relacionado; **be ~ with** estar relacionado con

con·nect·ing flight [kə'nektɪŋ] vuelo *m* de conexión

con·nec·tion [kə'nekʃn] conexión *f*; *when traveling* conexión *f*, enlace; (*personal contact*) contacto *m*; **in ~ with** en relación con

con·nois·seur [kɑːnə'sɜːr] entendido(-a) *m(f)*

con·quer ['kɑːŋkər] *v/t* conquistar; *fig*: *fear etc* vencer

con·quer·or ['kɑːŋkərər] conquistador(a) *m(f)*

con·quest ['kɑːŋkwest] *of territory* conquista *f*

con·science ['kɑːnʃəns] conciencia *f*; **a guilty ~** un sentimiento de culpa; **it was on my ~** me remordía la conciencia

con·sci·en·tious [kɑːnʃɪ'enʃəs] *adj* concienzudo

con·sci·en·tious·ness [kɑːnʃɪ'enʃəsnəs] aplicación *f*

con·sci·en·tious ob·ject·or objetor(a) *m(f)* de conciencia

con·scious ['kɑːnʃəs] *adj* consciente; **be ~ of** ser consciente de

con·scious·ly ['kɑːnʃəslɪ] *adv* conscientemente

con·scious·ness ['kɑːnʃəsnɪs] (*awareness*) conciencia *f*; MED con(s)ciencia *f*; **lose/regain ~** quedar inconsciente / volver en sí

con·sec·u·tive [kən'sekjʊtɪv] *adj* consecutivo

con·sen·sus [kən'sensəs] consenso *m*

con·sent [kən'sent] **1** *n* consentimiento *m* **2** *v/i* consentir (**to** en)

con·se·quence ['kɑːnsɪkwəns] (*result*) consecuencia *f*; **as a ~ of** como consecuencia de

con·se·quent·ly ['kɑːnsɪkwəntlɪ] *adv* (*therefore*) por consiguiente

con·ser·va·tion [kɑːnsər'veɪʃn] (*preservation*) conservación *f*, protección *f*

con·ser·va·tion·ist [kɑːnsər'veɪʃnɪst] ecologista *m/f*

con·ser·va·tive [kən'sɜːrvətɪv] *adj* (*conventional*) conservador; *estimate* prudente

con·ser·va·to·ry [kən'sɜːrvətɔːrɪ] MUS conservatorio *m*

con·serve 1 *n* ['kɑːnsɜːrv] (*jam*) compota *f* **2** *v/t* [kən'sɜːrv] conservar

con·sid·er [kən'sɪdər] *v/t* (*regard*) considerar; (*show regard for*) mostrar consideración por; (*think about*) considerar; *it is ~ed to be ...* se considera que es ...

con·sid·er·a·ble [kən'sɪdrəbl] *adj* considerable

con·sid·er·a·bly [kən'sɪdrəblɪ] *adv* considerablemente

con·sid·er·ate [kən'sɪdərət] *adj* considerado

con·sid·er·ate·ly [kən'sɪdərətlɪ] *adv* con consideración

con·sid·er·a·tion [kənsɪdə'reɪʃn] (*thoughtfulness, concern*) consideración *f*; (*factor*) factor *m*; *take sth into ~* tomar algo en consideración; *after much ~* tras muchas deliberaciones; *your proposal is under ~* su propuesta está siendo estudiada

con·sign·ment [kən'saɪnmənt] COM envío *m*

♦ **con·sist of** [kən'sɪst] *v/t* consistir en

con·sis·ten·cy [kən'sɪstənsɪ] (*texture*) consistencia *f*; (*unchangingness*) coherencia *f*, consecuencia *f*; *of player* regularidad *f*, constancia *f*

con·sis·tent [kən'sɪstənt] *adj person* coherente, consecuente; *improvement, change* constante

con·sis·tent·ly [kən'sɪstəntlɪ] *adv perform* con regularidad *or* constancia; *improve* continuamente; *he's ~ late* llega tarde sistemáticamente

con·so·la·tion [kɑːnsə'leɪʃn] consuelo *m*; *if it's any ~* si te sirve de consuelo

con·sole [kən'soʊl] *v/t* consolar

con·sol·i·date [kən'sɑːlɪdeɪt] *v/t* consolidar

con·so·nant ['kɑːnsənənt] *n* GRAM consonante *f*

con·sor·ti·um [kən'sɔːrtɪəm] consorcio *m*

con·spic·u·ous [kən'spɪkjʊəs] *adj* llamativo; *he felt very ~* sentía que estaba llamando la atención

con·spir·a·cy [kən'spɪrəsɪ] conspiración *f*

con·spir·a·tor [kən'spɪrətər] conspirador(a) *m(f)*

con·spire [kən'spaɪr] *v/i* conspirar

con·stant ['kɑːnstənt] *adj* (*continuous*) constante

con·stant·ly ['kɑːnstəntlɪ] *adv* constantemente

con·ster·na·tion [kɑːnstər'neɪʃn] consternación *f*

con·sti·pat·ed ['kɑːnstɪpeɪtɪd] *adj* estreñido

con·sti·pa·tion [kɑːnstɪ'peɪʃn] estreñimiento *m*

con·sti·tu·ent [kən'stɪtjʊənt] *n* (*component*) elemento *m* constitutivo, componente *m*

con·sti·tute ['kɑːnstɪtuːt] *v/t* constituir

con·sti·tu·tion [kɑːnstɪ'tuːʃn] constitución *f*

con·sti·tu·tion·al [kɑːnstɪ'tuːʃənl] *adj* POL constitucional

con·straint [kən'streɪnt] (*restriction*) restricción *f*, límite *m*

con·struct [kən'strʌkt] *v/t building etc* construir

con·struc·tion [kən'strʌkʃn] construcción *f*; *under ~* en construcción

con·struc·tion in·dus·try sector *m* de la construcción; **con'struc·tion site** obra *f*; **con'struc·tion work·er** obrero(-a) *m(f)* de la construcción

con·struc·tive [kən'strʌktɪv] *adj* constructivo

con·sul ['kɑːnsl] cónsul *m/f*

con·su·late ['kɑːnsʊlət] consulado *m*

con·sult [kən'sʌlt] *v/t* (*seek the advice of*) consultar

con·sul·tan·cy [kən'sʌltənsɪ] *company* consultoría *f*, asesoría *f*; (*advice*) asesoramiento *m*

con·sul·tant [kən'sʌltənt] *n* (*adviser*) asesor(a) *m*(*f*), consultor(a) *m*(*f*)

con·sul·ta·tion [kɑːnsl'teɪʃn] consulta *f*; **have a ~ with** consultar con

con·sume [kən'suːm] *v/t* consumir

con·sum·er [kən'suːmər] (*purchaser*) consumidor(a) *m*(*f*)

con·sum·er con·fi·dence confianza *f* de los consumidores; **con'sum·er goods** *npl* bienes *mpl* de consumo; **con'sum·er so·ci·e·ty** sociedad *f* de consumo

con·sump·tion [kən'sʌmpʃn] consumo *m*

con·tact ['kɑːntækt] **1** *n* contacto; **keep in ~ with s.o.** mantenerse en contacto con alguien; **come into ~ with s.o.** entrar en contacto con alguien **2** *v/t* contactar con, ponerse en contacto con

'con·tact lens lentes *fpl* de contacto, *Span* lentillas *fpl*

'con·tact num·ber número *m* de contacto

con·ta·gious [kən'teɪdʒəs] *adj also fig* contagioso

con·tain [kən'teɪn] *v/t* (*hold, hold back*) contener; **~ o.s.** contenerse

con·tain·er [kən'teɪnər] (*recipient*) recipiente *m*; COM contenedor *m*

con·tain·er ship buque *m* de transporte de contenedores

con·tam·i·nate [kən'tæmɪneɪt] *v/t* contaminar

con·tam·i·na·tion [kəntæmɪ'neɪʃn] contaminación *f*

con·tem·plate ['kɑːntəmpleɪt] *v/t* contemplar

con·tem·po·ra·ry [kən'tempərerɪ] **1** *adj* contemporáneo **2** *n* contemporáneo(-a) *m*(*f*)

con·tempt [kən'tempt] desprecio *m*, desdén *m*; **be beneath ~** ser despreciable

con·temp·ti·ble [kən'temptəbl] *adj* despreciable

con·temp·tu·ous [kən'temptʃʊəs] *adj* despectivo

con·tend [kən'tend] *v/i:* **~ for ...** competir por ...; **~ with** enfrentarse a

con·tend·er [kən'tendər] SP, POL contendiente *m*/*f*; *against champion* aspirante *m*/*f*

con·tent¹ ['kɑːntent] *n* contenido *m*

con·tent² [kən'tent] **1** *adj* satisfecho; **I'm quite ~ to sit here** me contento con sentarme aquí **2** *v/t:* **~ o.s. with** contentarse con

con·tent·ed [kən'tentɪd] *adj* satisfecho

con·ten·tion [kən'tenʃn] (*assertion*) argumento *m*; **be in ~ for** tener posibilidades de ganar

con·ten·tious [kən'tenʃəs] *adj* polémico

con·tent·ment [kən'tentmənt] satisfacción *f*

con·tents ['kɑːntents] *npl of house, letter, bag etc* contenido *m*; *list: in book* tabla *f* de contenidos

con·test¹ ['kɑːntest] *n* (*competition*) concurso *m*; (*struggle, for power*) lucha *f*

con·test² [kən'test] *v/t leadership etc* presentarse como candidato a; *decision, will* impugnar

con·tes·tant [kən'testənt] concursante *m*/*f*; *in competition* competidor(a) *m*(*f*)

con·text ['kɑːntekst] contexto *m*; **look at sth in ~ / out of ~** examinar algo en contexto / fuera de contexto

con·ti·nent ['kɑːntɪnənt] *n* continente *m*

con·ti·nen·tal [kɑːntɪ'nentl] *adj* continental

con·tin·gen·cy [kən'tɪndʒənsɪ] contingencia *f*, eventualidad *f*

con·tin·u·al [kən'tɪnjʊəl] *adj* continuo

con·tin·u·al·ly [kən'tɪnjʊəlɪ] *adv* continuamente

con·tin·u·a·tion [kəntɪnjʊ'eɪʃn]

continuación f

con·tin·ue [kən'tɪnjuː] **1** v/t continuar; **to be ~d** continuará; **he ~d to drink** continuó bebiendo **2** v/i continuar

con·ti·nu·i·ty [kɑːntɪ'njuːətɪ] continuidad f

con·tin·u·ous [kən'tɪnjuəs] adj continuo

con·tin·u·ous·ly [kən'tɪnjuəslɪ] adv continuamente, ininterrumpidamente

con·tort [kən'tɔːrt] v/t face contraer; body contorsionar

con·tour ['kɑːntʊr] contorno m

con·tra·cep·tion [kɑːntrə'sepʃn] anticoncepción f

con·tra·cep·tive [kɑːntrə'septɪv] n (device, pill) anticonceptivo m

con·tract¹ ['kɑːntrækt] n contrato m

con·tract² [kən'trækt] **1** v/i (shrink) contraerse **2** v/t illness contraer

con·trac·tor [kən'træktər] contratista m/f; **building ~** constructora f

con·trac·tu·al [kən'træktuəl] adj contractual

con·tra·dict [kɑːntrə'dɪkt] v/t statement desmentir; person contradecir

con·tra·dic·tion [kɑːntrə'dɪkʃn] contradicción f

con·tra·dic·to·ry [kɑːntrə'dɪktərɪ] adj account contradictorio

con·trap·tion [kən'træpʃn] F artilugio m F

con·trar·y¹ ['kɑːntrərɪ] **1** adj contrario; **~ to** al contrario de **2** n: **on the ~** al contrario

con·tra·ry² [kən'trerɪ] adj (perverse) difícil

con·trast 1 n ['kɑːntræst] contraste m; **by ~** por contraste **2** v/t & v/i [kən'træst] contrastar

con·trast·ing [kən'træstɪŋ] adj opuesto

con·tra·vene [kɑːntrə'viːn] v/t contravenir

con·trib·ute [kən'trɪbjuːt] **1** v/i contribuir (**to** a) **2** v/t money, time, suggestion contribuir con, aportar

con·tri·bu·tion [kɑːntrɪ'bjuːʃn] money contribución f; to political

party, church donación f; of time, effort, to debate contribución f, aportación f; to magazine colaboración f

con·trib·u·tor [kən'trɪbjutər] of money donante m/f; to magazine colaborador(a) m(f)

con·trol [kən'troʊl] **1** n control m; **take / lose ~ of** tomar / perder el control de; **lose ~ of o.s.** perder el control; **circumstances beyond our ~** circunstancias ajenas a nuestra voluntad; **be in ~ of** controlar; **we're in ~ of the situation** tenemos la situación controlada or bajo control; **get out of ~** descontrolarse; **under ~** bajo control; **~s** of aircraft, vehicle controles mpl; (restrictions) controles mpl **2** v/t (pret & pp **-led**) (govern) controlar, dominar; (restrict, regulate) controlar; **~ o.s.** controlarse

con'trol cen·ter, Br **con'trol cen·tre** centro m de control

con'trol freak F persona obsesionada con controlar todo

con·trolled 'sub·stance [kən'troʊld] estupefaciente m

con·trol·ling 'in·ter·est [kən'troʊlɪŋ] FIN participación f mayoritaria, interés m mayoritario

con'trol pan·el panel m de control

con'trol tow·er torre f de control

con·tro·ver·sial [kɑːntrə'vɜːrʃl] adj polémico, controvertido

con·tro·ver·sy ['kɑːntrəvɜːrsɪ] polémica f, controversia f

con·va·lesce [kɑːnvə'les] v/i convalecer

con·va·les·cence [kɑːnvə'lesns] convalecencia f

con·vene [kən'viːn] v/t convocar

con·ve·ni·ence [kən'viːnɪəns] conveniencia f; **at your / my ~** a su / mi conveniencia; **all (modern) ~s** todas las comodidades

con·ve·ni·ence food comida f preparada

con·ve·ni·ence store tienda f de barrio

con·ve·ni·ent [kən'viːnɪənt] adj location, device conveniente; time, *arrangement* oportuno; *it's very ~ living so near the office* vivir cerca de la oficina es muy cómodo; *the apartment is ~ for the station* el apartamento está muy cerca de la estación; *I'm afraid Monday isn't ~* me temo que el lunes no me va bien

con·ve·ni·ent·ly [kən'viːnɪəntlɪ] *adv* convenientemente; *~ located for theaters* situado cerca de los teatros

con·vent ['kaːnvənt] convento *m*

con·ven·tion [kən'venʃn] *(tradition)* convención *f*; *(meeting)* congreso *m*

con·ven·tion·al [kən'venʃnl] *adj* convencional

con'ven·tion cen·ter, *Br* con'ven·tion cen·tre palacio *m* de congresos

con·ven·tion·eer [kən'venʃnɪr] congresista *m/f*

♦ con·verge on [kən'vɜːrdʒ] *v/t* converger en

con·ver·sant [kən'vɜːrsənt] *adj*: *be ~ with* estar familiarizado con

con·ver·sa·tion [kaːnvər'seɪʃn] conversación *f*; *make ~* conversar; *have a ~* mantener una conversación

con·ver·sa·tion·al [kaːnvər'seɪʃnl] *adj* coloquial

con·verse ['kaːnvɜːrs] *n (opposite)*: *the ~* lo opuesto

con·verse·ly [kən'vɜːrslɪ] *adv* por lo contrario

con·ver·sion [kən'vɜːrʃn] conversión *f*

con·ver·sion ta·ble tabla *f* de conversión

con·vert **1** *n* ['kaːnvɜːrt] converso(-a) *m(f)* (*to* a) **2** *v/t* [kən'vɜːrt] convertir

con·ver·ti·ble [kən'vɜːrtəbl] *n car* descapotable *m*

con·vey [kən'veɪ] *v/t (transmit)* transmitir; *(carry)* transportar

con·vey·or belt [kən'veɪər] cinta *f* transportadora

con·vict **1** *n* ['kaːnvɪkt] convicto(-a) *m(f)* **2** *v/t* [kən'vɪkt] LAW: *~ s.o. of sth* declarar a alguien culpable de

algo

con·vic·tion [kən'vɪkʃn] LAW condena *f*; *(belief)* convicción *f*

con·vince [kən'vɪns] *v/t* convencer: *I'm ~d he's lying* estoy convencido de que miente

con·vinc·ing [kən'vɪnsɪŋ] *adj* convincente

con·viv·i·al [kən'vɪvɪəl] *adj (friendly)* agradable

con·vul·sion [kən'vʌlʃn] MED convulsión *f*

cook [kʊk] **1** *n* cocinero(-a) *m(f)*: *I'm a good ~* soy un buen cocinero, cocino bien **2** *v/t* cocinar; *a ~ed meal* una comida caliente **3** *v/i* cocinar

'cook·book libro *m* de cocina

cook·e·ry ['kʊkərɪ] cocina *f*

cook·ie ['kʊkɪ] galleta *f*

cook·ing ['kʊkɪŋ] food cocina *f*

cool [kuːl] **1** *n*: *keep one's ~* F mantener la calma; *lose one's ~* F perder la calma **2** *adj weather, breeze* fresco; *drink* frío; *(calm)* tranquilo, sereno; *(unfriendly)* frío; P *(great)* Span guay P, *L.Am.* chévere P, *Mex* padre P, *Rpl* copante P **3** *v/i of food, interest* enfriarse; *of tempers* calmarse **4** *v/t*: *~ it* F cálmate

♦ cool down **1** *v/i* enfriarse; *of weather* refrescar; *fig: of tempers* calmarse, tranquilizarse **2** *v/t food* enfriar; *fig* calmar, tranquilizar

cool·ing-'off pe·ri·od fase *f* de reflexión

co·op·e·rate [koʊ'aːpəreɪt] *v/i* cooperar

co·op·e·ra·tion [koʊaːpə'reɪʃn] cooperación *f*

co·op·e·ra·tive [koʊ'aːpərətɪv] **1** *n* COM cooperativa *f* **2** *adj* COM conjunto; *(helpful)* cooperativo

co·or·di·nate [koʊ'ɔːrdɪneɪt] *v/t activities* coordinar

co·or·di·na·tion [koʊɔːrdɪ'neɪʃn] coordinación *f*

cop [kaːp] *n* F poli *m/f* F

cope [koʊp] *v/i* arreglárselas; *~ with*

poder con

cop·i·er ['kɑːpɪər] *machine* foto-copiadora *f*

co·pi·lot ['koʊpaɪlət] copiloto *m/f*

co·pi·ous ['koʊpɪəs] *adj* copioso

cop·per ['kɑːpər] *n metal* cobre *m*

cop·y ['kɑːpɪ] **1** *n* copia *f*; *of book* ejemplar *m*; *of record, CD* copia *f*; *(written material)* texto *m*; **make a ~ of a file** COMPUT hacer una copia de un archivo **2** *v/t* (*pret & pp -ied*) copiar

'**cop·y cat** F copión (-ona) *m(f)* F, copiota *m/f* F; '**cop·y·cat crime** *delito inspirado en otro*; '**cop·y·right** *n* copyright *m*, derechos *mpl* de reproducción; '**cop·y·writ·er** *in advertising* creativo(-a) *m(f)* (*de publicidad*)

cor·al ['kɑːrəl] coral *m*

cord [kɔːrd] *(string)* cuerda *f*, cordel *m*; *(cable)* cable *m*

cor·di·al ['kɔːrdʒəl] *adj* cordial

cord·less 'phone ['kɔːrdlɪs] teléfono *m* inalámbrico

cor·don ['kɔːrdn] cordón *m*
♦ **cordon off** *v/t* acordonar

cords [kɔːrdz] *npl pants* pantalones *mpl* de pana

cor·du·roy ['kɔːrdərɔɪ] pana *f*

core [kɔːr] **1** *n of fruit* corazón *m*; *of problem* meollo *m*; *of organization, party* núcleo *m* **2** *v/t fruit* sacar el corazón a **3** *adj issue, meaning* central

co·ri·an·der ['kɑːrɪændər] cilantro *m*

cork [kɔːrk] *in bottle* (tapón *m* de) corcho *m*; *material* corcho *m*

'**cork·screw** *n* sacacorchos *m inv*

corn [kɔːrn] *grain* maíz *m*

cor·ner ['kɔːrnər] **1** *n of page, street* esquina *f*; *of room* rincón *m*; *(bend: on road)* curva *f*; *in soccer* córner *m*, saque *m* de esquina; **in the ~** en el rincón; **I'll meet you on the ~** te veré en la esquina **2** *v/t person* arrinconar; **~ a market** monopolizar un mercado **3** *v/i of driver, car* girar

'**cor·ner kick** *in soccer* saque *m* de esquina, córner *m*

'**corn·flakes** *npl* copos *mpl* de maíz

'**corn·starch** harina *f* de maíz

corn·y ['kɔːrnɪ] *adj* F *(sentimental)* cursi F; *joke* manido

cor·o·na·ry ['kɑːrənerɪ] **1** *adj* coronario **2** *n* infarto *m* de miocardio

cor·o·ner ['kɑːrənər] *oficial encargado de investigar muertes sospechosas*

cor·po·ral ['kɔːrpərəl] *n* cabo *m/f*

cor·po·ral 'pun·ish·ment castigo *m* corporal

cor·po·rate ['kɔːrpərət] *adj* COM corporativo, de empresa; **~ image** imagen *f* corporativa; **~ loyalty** lealtad *f* a la empresa

cor·po·ra·tion [kɔːrpəˈreɪʃn] *(business)* sociedad *f* anónima

corps [kɔːr] *nsg* cuerpo *m*

corpse [kɔːrps] cadáver *m*

cor·pu·lent ['kɔːrpjʊlənt] *adj* corpulento

cor·pus·cle ['kɔːrpʌsl] corpúsculo *m*

cor·ral [kəˈræl] *n* corral *m*

cor·rect [kəˈrekt] **1** *adj* correcto; *time* exacto; **you are ~** tiene razón **2** *v/t* corregir

cor·rec·tion [kəˈrekʃn] corrección *f*

cor·rect·ly [kəˈrektlɪ] *adv* correctamente

cor·re·spond [kɑːrɪˈspɑːnd] *v/i (match)* corresponderse; **~ to** corresponder a; **~ with** corresponderse con; *(write letters)* mantener correspondencia con

cor·re·spon·dence [kɑːrɪˈspɑːndəns] *(matching)* correspondencia *f*, relación *f*; *(letters)* correspondencia *f*

cor·re·spon·dent [kɑːrɪˈspɑːndənt] *(letter writer)* correspondiente *m/f*; *(reporter)* corresponsal *m/f*

cor·re·spon·ding [kɑːrɪˈspɑːndɪŋ] *adj (equivalent)* correspondiente

cor·ri·dor ['kɔːrɪdər] *in building* pasillo *m*

cor·rob·o·rate [kəˈrɑːbəreɪt] *v/t* corroborar

cor·rode [kəˈroʊd] **1** *v/t* corroer **2** *v/i* corroerse

cor·ro·sion [kəˈroʊʒn] corrosión *f*

cor·ru·gat·ed 'card·board ['kɑːrə-geɪtɪd] cartón m ondulado
cor·ru·gat·ed 'i·ron chapa f ondula-da
cor·rupt [kə'rʌpt] **1** adj corrupto; COMPUT corrompido **2** v/t corromper; (bribe) sobornar
cor·rup·tion [kə'rʌpʃn] corrupción f
cos·met·ic [kɑːz'metɪk] adj cosmé-tico; fig superficial
cos·met·ics [kɑːz'metɪks] npl cosméticos mpl
cos·met·ic 'sur·geon especialista m/f en cirugía estética
cos·met·ic 'sur·ger·y cirugía f esté-tica
cos·mo·naut ['kɑːzmənɔːt] cosmo-nauta m/f
cos·mo·pol·i·tan [kɑːzmə'pɑːlɪtən] adj city cosmopolitano
cost¹ [kɑːst] **1** n also fig costo m, Span coste m; **at all ~s** cueste lo que cueste; **I've learnt to my ~** por desgracia he aprendido **2** v/t (pret & pp cost) money, time costar; **how much does it ~?** ¿cuánto cuesta?
cost² [kɑːst] v/t (pret & pp -ed) FIN proposal, project estimar el costo de
cost and 'freight COM costo or Span coste y flete
Cos·ta Ri·ca ['kɑːstə'riːkə] n Costa Rica
Cos·ta Ri·can ['kɑːstə'riːkən] **1** adj costarricense **2** n costarricense m/f
'**cost-con·scious** adj consciente del costo or Span coste; '**cost-ef·fec·tive** adj rentable; '**cost, in·sur·ance, freight** COM costo or Span coste, seguro y flete
cost·ly ['kɑːstlɪ] adj mistake caro
cost of 'liv·ing costo m or Span coste m de la vida
cost 'price precio m de costo or Span coste
cos·tume ['kɑːstuːm] for actor traje m
cos·tume 'jew·el·lery Br, **cos·tume** 'jew·el·ry bisutería f
'**cos·y** Br → **cozy**
cot [kɑːt] (camp-bed) catre m
cot·tage ['kɑːtɪdʒ] casa f de campo,

casita f
cot·tage 'cheese queso m fresco
cot·ton ['kɑːtn] **1** n algodón m **2** adj de algodón
♦ **cotton on** v/i F darse cuenta
♦ **cotton on to** v/t F darse cuenta de
♦ **cotton to** v/t F: **I never cottoned to her** nunca me cayó bien
cot·ton 'can·dy algodón m dulce
cot·ton 'wool Br algodón m (hidrófilo)
couch [kaʊtʃ] n sofá m
'**couch po·ta·to** F teleadicto(-a) m(f)
cou·chette [kuː'ʃet] litera f
cough [kɑːf] **1** n tos f; to get attention carraspeo m **2** v/i toser; to get attention carraspear
♦ **cough up 1** v/t blood etc toser; F money soltar, Span apoquinar F **2** v/i F (pay) soltar dinero, Span apoquinar F
'**cough med·i·cine**, '**cough syr·up** jarabe m para la tos
could [kʊd] **1** v/aux: ~ **I have my key?** ¿me podría dar la llave?; ~ **you help me?** ¿me podrías ayudar?; **this ~ be our bus** puede que éste sea nuestro autobús; **you ~ be right** puede que tengas razón; **I ~n't say for sure** no sabría decirlo con seguridad; **he ~ have got lost** a lo mejor se ha perdido; **you ~ have warned me!** ¡me podías haber avisado! **2** pret → **can**
coun·cil ['kaʊnsl] n (assembly) conse-jo m
'**coun·cil·man** concejal m
coun·cil·or ['kaʊnsələr] concejal(a) m(f)
coun·sel ['kaʊnsl] **1** n (advice) conse-jo m; (lawyer) abogado(-a) m(f) **2** v/t course of action aconsejar; person ofrecer apoyo psicológico a
coun·sel·ing, Br **coun·sel·ling** ['kaʊnslɪŋ] apoyo m psicológico
coun·sel·lor, **coun·sel·or** ['kaʊnslər] (adviser) consejero(-a) m(f); of student orientador(a) m(f); LAW abogado(-a) m(f)
count¹ [kaʊnt] **1** n (number arrived

at) cuenta f; (*action of ~ing*) recuento m; in baseball, boxing cuenta f; **what is your ~?** ¿cuántos has contado?; **keep ~ of** llevar la cuenta de; **lose ~ of** perder la cuenta de; **at the last ~** en el último recuento **2** *v/i* to ten etc contar; (*be important*) contar; (*qualify*) contar, valer **3** *v/t* contar
♦ **count on** *v/t* contar con

count² [kaʊnt] *nobleman* conde m

'count·down cuenta f atrás

coun·te·nance ['kaʊntənəns] *v/t* tolerar

coun·ter¹ ['kaʊntər] *n in shop* mostrador m; *in café* barra f; *in game* ficha f

coun·ter² ['kaʊntər] **1** *v/t* contrarrestar **2** *v/i* (*retaliate*) responder

coun·ter³ ['kaʊntər] *adv*: **run ~ to** estar en contra de

'coun·ter·act *v/t* contrarrestar

coun·ter·at·tack 1 *n* contraataque m **2** *v/i* contraatacar

'coun·ter·bal·ance 1 *n* contrapeso m **2** *v/t* contrarrestar, contrapesar

coun·ter'clock·wise *adv* en sentido contrario al de las agujas del reloj

coun·ter·es·pi·o·nage contraespionaje m

coun·ter·feit ['kaʊntərfɪt] **1** *v/t* falsificar **2** *adj* falso

'coun·ter·part (*person*) homólogo(-a) m(f)

coun·ter·pro'duc·tive *adj* contraproducente

'coun·ter·sign *v/t* refrendar

coun·tess ['kaʊntes] condesa f

count·less ['kaʊntlɪs] *adj* incontables

coun·try ['kʌntrɪ] *n* (*nation*) país m; *as opposed to town* campo m; **in the ~** en el campo

coun·try and 'west·ern MUS música f *country*; **'coun·try·man** (*fellow ~*) compatriota m; **'coun·try·side** campo m

coun·ty ['kaʊntɪ] condado m

coup [kuː] POL golpe m (de Estado); *fig* golpe m de efecto

cou·ple ['kʌpl] *n* pareja f; **just a ~** un par; **a ~ of** un par de

cou·pon ['kuːpɑːn] cupón m

cour·age ['kʌrɪdʒ] valor m, coraje m

cou·ra·geous [kə'reɪdʒəs] *adj* valiente

cou·ra·geous·ly [kə'reɪdʒəslɪ] *adv* valientemente

cou·ri·er ['kʊrɪr] (*messenger*) mensajero(-a) m(f); *with tourist party* guía m/f

course [kɔːrs] *n* (*series of lessons*) curso m; (*part of meal*) plato m; *of ship, plane* rumbo m; *for horse race* circuito m; *for golf* campo m; *for skiing, marathon* recorrido m; **change ~** *of ship, plane* cambiar de rumbo; **of ~** (*certainly*) claro, por supuesto; (*naturally*) por supuesto; **~ not** claro que no; **~ of action** táctica f; **~ of treatment** tratamiento m; **in the ~ of ...** durante ...

court [kɔːrt] *n* LAW tribunal m; (*courthouse*) palacio m de justicia; SP pista f, cancha f; **take s.o. to ~** llevar a alguien a juicio

'court case proceso m, causa f

cour·te·ous ['kɜːrtɪəs] *adj* cortés

cour·te·sy ['kɜːrtəsɪ] cortesía f

'court·house palacio m de justicia; **court 'mar·tial 1** *n* consejo m de guerra **2** *v/t* formar un consejo de guerra a; **'court or·der** orden f judicial; **'court·room** sala f de juicios; **'court·yard** patio m

cous·in ['kʌzn] primo(-a) m(f)

cove [koʊv] (*small bay*) cala f

cov·er ['kʌvər] **1** *n protective* funda f; *of book, magazine* portada f; (*shelter*) protección f; (*insurance*) cobertura f; **~s for bed** manta y sábanas fpl; **we took ~ from the rain** nos pusimos a cubierto de la lluvia **2** *v/t* cubrir
♦ **cover up 1** *v/t* cubrir; *scandal* encubrir **2** *v/i* disimular; **cover up for s.o.** encubrir a alguien

cov·er·age ['kʌvərɪdʒ] *by media* cobertura f informativa

cov·er·ing let·ter ['kʌvrɪŋ] carta f

cov·ert [koʊ'vɜːrt] *adj* encubierto

'cov·er-up encubrimiento m

cow [kaʊ] vaca f

cow·ard ['kauərd] cobarde *m/f*

cow·ard·ice ['kauərdɪs] cobardía *f*

cow·ard·ly ['kauərdlɪ] *adj* cobarde

'**cow·boy** vaquero *m*

cow·er ['kauər] *v/i* agacharse, amilanarse

co-work·er ['kouwɜrkər] compañero(a) *m(f)* de trabajo

coy [kɔɪ] *adj* (*evasive*) evasivo; (*flirtatious*) coqueto

co·zy ['kouzɪ] *adj room* acogedor; *job* cómodo

CPU [si:pi:'ju:] *abbr* (= *central processing unit*) CPU *f* (= unidad *f* central de proceso)

crab [kræb] *n* cangrejo *m*

crack [kræk] **1** *n* grieta *f*, *in cup, glass* raja *f*; (*joke*) chiste *m* (malo) **2** *v/t cup, glass* rajar; *nut* cascar; *code* descifrar; F (*solve*) resolver; **~ a joke** contar un chiste **3** *v/i* rajarse; *get* **~ing** F poner manos a la obra F

♦ **crack down on** *v/t* castigar severamente

♦ **crack up** *v/i* sufrir una crisis nerviosa; F (*laugh*) desternillarse F

'**crack·brained** *adj* chiflado F

'**crack·down** medidas *fpl* severas

cracked [krækt] *adj cup, glass* rajado; F (*crazy*) chiflado F

crack·er ['krækər] *to eat* galleta *f* salada

crack·le ['krækl] *v/i of fire* crepitar

cra·dle ['kreɪdl] *n for baby* cuna *f*

craft[1] [kræft] NAUT embarcación *f*

craft[2] [kræft] (*skill*) arte *m*; (*trade*) oficio *m*

crafts·man ['kræftsmən] artesano *m*

craft·y ['kræftɪ] *adj* astuto

crag [kræg] *rock* peñasco *m*, risco *m*

cram [kræm] *v/t* (*pret & pp* **-med**) embutir

cramp [kræmp] *n* calambre *m*; *stomach* ~ retorcijón *m*

cramped [kræmpt] *adj room* pequeño

cramps [kræmps] *npl* calambre *m*; *stomach* ~ retorcijón *m*

cran·ber·ry ['krænberɪ] arándano *m* agrio

crane [kreɪn] **1** *n machine* grúa *f* **2** *v/t*:

~ *one's neck* estirar el cuello

crank [kræŋk] *n person* maniático(-a) *m(f)*, persona *f* rara

'**crank·shaft** cigüeñal *m*

crank·y ['kræŋkɪ] *adj* (*bad-tempered*) gruñón

crap [kræp] P **1** *n* (*excrement*) mierda *f* P; (*nonsense*) Span gilipolleces *fpl* P, *L.Am.* pendejadas *fpl* P, *Rpl* boludeces *fpl* P; (*poor quality item*) mierda *f* P **2** *v/i* (*defecate*) cagar V

crash [kræʃ] **1** *n noise* estruendo *m*, estrépito *m*; *accident* accidente *m*; COM quiebra *f*, crac *m*; COMPUT bloqueo *m*; *a* ~ *of thunder* un trueno **2** *v/i of car, airplane* estrellarse (*into* con *or* contra); *of thunder* sonar; COM *of market* hundirse, desplomarse; COMPUT bloquearse, colgarse; F (*sleep*) dormir, *Span* sobar F; *the waves* ~*ed onto the shore* las olas chocaban contra la orilla; *the vase* ~*ed to the ground* el jarrón se cayó con estruendo **3** *v/t car* estrellar

♦ **crash out** *v/i* F (*fall asleep*) dormirse, *Span* quedarse sobado

'**crash bar·ri·er** quitamiedos *m inv*; '**crash course** curso *m* intensivo; '**crash di·et** dieta *f* drástica; '**crash hel·met** casco *m* protector; '**crash-land** *v/i* realizar un aterrizaje forzoso; '**crash land·ing** aterrizaje *m* forzoso

crate [kreɪt] (*packing case*) caja *f*

cra·ter ['kreɪtər] *of volcano* cráter *m*

crave [kreɪv] *v/t* ansiar

crav·ing ['kreɪvɪŋ] ansia *f*, deseo *m*; *of pregnant woman* antojo *m*; *I have a* ~ *for ...* me apetece muchísimo ...

crawl [krɔːl] **1** *n in swimming* crol *m*; *at a* ~ (*very slowly*) muy lentamente **2** *v/i on floor* arrastrarse; *of baby* andar a gatas; (*move slowly*) avanzar lentamente

♦ **crawl with** *v/t* estar abarrotado de

cray·fish ['kreɪfɪʃ] *freshwater* cangrejo *m* de río; *saltwater* langosta *f*

cray·on ['kreɪɑːn] *n* lápiz *m* de color

craze [kreɪz] locura *f* (*for* de); *the latest* ~ la última locura *or* moda

cra·zy ['kreɪzɪ] *adj* loco; *be ~ about* estar loco por

creak [kri:k] **1** *n of hinge, door* chirrido *m*; *of floor* crujido *m* **2** *v/i of hinge, door* chirriar; *of floor, shoes* crujir

creak·y ['kri:kɪ] *adj hinge, door* que chirría; *floor, shoes* que cruje

cream [kri:m] **1** *n for skin* crema *f*; *for coffee, cake* nata *f*; *(color)* crema *m* **2** *adj* crema

cream 'cheese queso *m* blanco para untar

cream·er ['kri:mər] *(pitcher)* jarra *f* para la nata; *for coffee* leche *f* en polvo

cream·y ['kri:mɪ] *adj (with lots of cream)* cremoso

crease [kri:s] **1** *n accidental* arruga *f*; *deliberate* raya *f* **2** *v/t accidentally* arrugar

cre·ate [kri:'eɪt] *v/t & v/i* crear

cre·a·tion [kri:'eɪʃn] *creación f*

cre·a·tive [kri:'eɪtɪv] *adj* creativo

cre·a·tor [kri:'eɪtər] creador(a) *m(f)*; *(founder)* fundador(a) *m(f)*; *the Creator* REL el Creador

crea·ture ['kri:tʃər] *animal, person* criatura *f*

crèche [kreʃ] *for children* guardería *f* (infantil); REL nacimiento *m*, belén *m*

cred·i·bil·i·ty [kredə'bɪlətɪ] credibilidad *f*

cred·i·ble ['kredəbl] *adj* creíble

cred·it ['kredɪt] **1** *n* FIN, *(honor)* crédito *m*; *be in ~* tener un saldo positivo; *get the ~ for sth* recibir reconocimiento por algo **2** *v/t (believe)* creer; *~ an amount to an account* abonar una cantidad en una cuenta

cred·i·ta·ble ['kredɪtəbl] *adj* estimable, honorable

'cred·it card tarjeta *f* de crédito

'cred·it lim·it límite *m* de crédito

cred·i·tor ['kredɪtər] acreedor(a) *m(f)*

'cred·it·wor·thy *adj* solvente

cred·u·lous ['kredʊləs] *adj* crédulo

creed [kri:d] *(beliefs)* credo *m*

creek [kri:k] *(stream)* arroyo *m*

creep [kri:p] **1** *n pej* asqueroso(-a) *m(f)* **2** *v/i (pret & pp crept)* moverse sigilosamente

creep·er ['kri:pər] BOT enredadera *f*

creeps [kri:ps] *npl* F: *the house/ he gives me the ~* la casa/él me pone la piel de gallina F

creep·y ['kri:pɪ] *adj* F espeluznante F

cre·mate [krɪ'meɪt] *v/t* incinerar

cre·ma·tion [krɪ'meɪʃn] incineración *f*

cre·ma·to·ri·um [kremə'tɔ:rɪəm] crematorio *m*

crept [krept] *pret & pp → creep*

cres·cent ['kresənt] *n shape* medialuna *f*; *~ moon* cuarto *m* creciente

crest [krest] *of hill* cima *f*; *of bird* cresta *f*

crest·fal·len *adj* abatido

crev·ice ['krevɪs] grieta *f*

crew [kru:] *n of ship, airplane* tripulación *f*; *of repairmen etc* equipo *m*; *(crowd, group)* grupo *m*, pandilla *f*

'crew cut rapado *m*

'crew neck cuello *m* redondo

crib [krɪb] *n for baby* cuna *f*

crick [krɪk]: *have a ~ in the neck* tener tortícolis

crick·et ['krɪkɪt] *insect* grillo *m*

crime [kraɪm] *(offense)* delito *m*; *serious, also fig* crimen *m*

crim·i·nal ['krɪmɪnl] **1** *n* delincuente *m/f*, criminal *m/f* **2** *adj (relating to crime)* criminal; (LAW: *not civil)* penal; *(shameful)* vergonzoso; *act* delictivo; *it's ~ (shameful)* es un crimen

crim·son ['krɪmzn] *adj* carmesí

cringe [krɪndʒ] *v/i with embarrassment* sentir vergüenza

crip·ple ['krɪpl] **1** *n (disabled person)* inválido(-a) *m(f)* **2** *v/t person* dejar inválido; *fig: country, industry* paralizar

cri·sis ['kraɪsɪs] *(pl crises* ['kraɪsi:z]*)* crisis *f inv*

crisp [krɪsp] *adj weather, air* fresco; *lettuce, apple, bacon* crujiente; *new shirt, bills* flamante

cri·te·ri·on [kraɪ'tɪrɪən] *(standard)* criterio *m*

crit·ic ['krɪtɪk] crítico(-a) m(f)

crit·i·cal ['krɪtɪkl] adj (making criticisms, serious) crítico; moment etc decisivo

crit·i·cal·ly ['krɪtɪklɪ] adv speak etc en tono de crítica; ~ **ill** en estado crítico

crit·i·cism ['krɪtɪsɪzm] crítica f

crit·i·cize ['krɪtɪsaɪz] v/t criticar

croak [krəʊk] **1** n of frog croar m **2** v/i of frog croar

cro·chet ['krəʊʃeɪ] **1** n ganchillo m **2** v/t hacer a ganchillo

crock·e·ry ['krɑːkərɪ] vajilla f

croc·o·dile ['krɑːkədaɪl] cocodrilo m

cro·cus ['krəʊkəs] azafrán m

cro·ny ['krəʊnɪ] ⊢ amiguete m/f ⊢

crook [krʊk] n ladrón (-ona) m(f); dishonest trader granuja m/f

crook·ed ['krʊkɪd] adj (not straight) torcido; (dishonest) deshonesto

crop [krɑːp] **1** n also fig cosecha f; plant grown cultivo m **2** v/t (pret & pp **-ped**) hair cortar; photo recortar
♦ **crop up** v/i salir

cross [krɑːs] **1** adj (angry) enfadado, enojado **2** n cruz f **3** v/t (go across) cruzar; ~ **o.s.** REL santiguarse; ~ **one's legs** cruzar las piernas; **keep one's fingers ~ed** cruzar los dedos; **it never ~ed my mind** no se me ocurrió **4** v/i (go across) cruzar; of lines cruzarse, cortarse
♦ **cross off, cross out** v/t tachar

'cross·bar of goal larguero m; of bicycle barra f; in high jump listón m; **'cross-check 1** n comprobación f **2** v/t comprobar; **cross-coun·try** ('ski·ing) esquí m de fondo

crossed 'check, Br **crossed 'cheque** [krɑːst] cheque m cruzado

cross-ex·am·i·na·tion LAW interrogatorio m; **cross-ex'am·ine** v/t LAW interrogar; **cross-'eyed** adj bizco

cross·ing ['krɑːsɪŋ] NAUT travesía f

'cross·roads nsg also fig encrucijada f; **'cross-sec·tion** of people muestra f representativa; **'cross·walk** paso m de peatones; **'cross·word** (**puz·zle**) crucigrama m

crotch [krɑːtʃ] of person, pants entrepierna f

crouch [kraʊtʃ] v/i agacharse

crow [krəʊ] n bird corneja f; **as the ~ flies** en línea recta

'crow·bar palanca f

crowd [kraʊd] n multitud f, muchedumbre f; at sports event público m

crowd·ed ['kraʊdɪd] adj abarrotado (**with** de)

crown [kraʊn] **1** n on head, tooth corona f **2** v/t tooth poner una corona a

cru·cial ['kruːʃl] adj crucial

cru·ci·fix ['kruːsɪfɪks] crucifijo m

cru·ci·fix·ion [kruːsɪ'fɪkʃn] crucifixión f

cru·ci·fy ['kruːsɪfaɪ] v/t (pret & pp **-ied**) also fig crucificar

crude [kruːd] **1** adj (vulgar) grosero; (unsophisticated) primitivo **2** n: ~ (**oil**) crudo m

crude·ly ['kruːdlɪ] adv speak groseramente; made de manera primitiva

cru·el ['kruːəl] adj cruel (**to** con)

cru·el·ty ['kruːəltɪ] crueldad f (**to** con)

cruise [kruːz] **1** n crucero m; **go on a ~** ir de crucero **2** v/i of people hacer un crucero; of car a velocidad de crucero; of plane volar

cruis·ing speed ['kruːzɪŋ] of vehicle velocidad f de crucero; fig: of project etc ritmo m normal

crumb [krʌm] miga f

crum·ble ['krʌmbl] **1** v/t desmigajar **2** v/i of bread desmigajarse; of stonework desmenuzarse; fig: of opposition etc desmoronarse

crum·bly ['krʌmblɪ] adj cookie que se desmigaja; stonework que se desmenuza

crum·ple ['krʌmpl] **1** v/t (crease) arrugar **2** v/i (collapse) desplomarse

crunch [krʌntʃ] **1** n: **when it comes to the ~** a la hora de la verdad **2** v/i of snow, gravel crujir

cru·sade [kruː'seɪd] n also fig cruzada f

crush [krʌʃ] **1** n (crowd) muchedumbre *f*; **have a ~ on** estar loco por **2** *v/t* aplastar; (*crease*) arrugar; **they were ~ed to death** murieron aplastados **3** *v/i* (*crease*) arrugarse

crust [krʌst] *on bread* corteza *f*

crust·y ['krʌstɪ] *adj bread* crujiente

crutch [krʌtʃ] *walking aid* muleta *f*

cry [kraɪ] **1** *n* (*call*) grito *m*; **have a ~** llorar **2** *v/t* (*pret & pp -ied*) (*call*) gritar **3** *v/i* (*pret & pp -ied*) (*weep*) llorar

♦ **cry out** *v/t & v/i* gritar

♦ **cry out for** *v/t* (*need*) pedir a gritos

cryp·tic ['krɪptɪk] *adj* críptico

crys·tal ['krɪstl] cristal *m*

crys·tal·lize ['krɪstəlaɪz] **1** *v/t* cristalizar **2** *v/i* cristalizarse

cub [kʌb] cachorro *m*; *of bear* osezno *m*

Cu·ba ['kjuːbə] Cuba

Cu·ban ['kjuːbən] **1** *adj* cubano **2** *n* cubano(-a) *m(f)*

cube [kjuːb] *shape* cubo *m*

cu·bic ['kjuːbɪk] *adj* cúbico

cu·bic ca'pac·i·ty TECH cilindrada *f*

cu·bi·cle ['kjuːbɪkl] (*changing room*) cubículo *m*

cu·cum·ber ['kjuːkʌmbər] pepino *m*

cud·dle ['kʌdl] **1** *n* abrazo **2** *v/t* abrazar

cud·dly ['kʌdlɪ] *adj kitten etc* tierno

cue [kjuː] *n for actor etc* pie *m*, entrada *f; for pool* taco *m*

cuff [kʌf] **1** *n of shirt* puño *m; of pants* vuelta *f*; (*blow*) cachete *m*; **off the ~** improvisado **2** *v/t* (*hit*) dar un cachete a

'**cuff link** gemelo *m*

cul-de-sac ['kʌldəsæk] callejón *m* sin salida

cu·li·nar·y ['kʌlɪnərɪ] *adj* culinario

cul·mi·nate ['kʌlmɪneɪt] *v/i* culminar (**in** en)

cul·mi·na·tion [kʌlmɪ'neɪʃn] culminación *f*

cul·prit ['kʌlprɪt] culpable *m/f*

cult [kʌlt] (*sect*) secta *f*

cul·ti·vate ['kʌltɪveɪt] *v/t also fig* cultivar

cul·ti·vat·ed ['kʌltɪveɪtɪd] *adj person* culto

cul·ti·va·tion [kʌltɪ'veɪʃn] *of land* cultivo *m*

cul·tur·al ['kʌltʃərəl] *adj* cultural

cul·ture ['kʌltʃər] *artistic* cultura *f*

cul·tured ['kʌltʃərd] *adj* (*cultivated*) culto

'**cul·ture shock** choque *m* cultural

cum·ber·some ['kʌmbərsəm] *adj* engorroso

cu·mu·la·tive ['kjuːmjʊlətɪv] *adj* acumulativo

cun·ning ['kʌnɪŋ] **1** *n* astucia *f* **2** *adj* astuto

cup [kʌp] *n* taza *f*; *trophy* copa *f*

cup·board ['kʌbərd] armario *m*

'**cup fi·nal** final *f* de (la) copa

cu·po·la ['kjuːpələ] cúpula *f*

cu·ra·ble ['kjʊrəbl] *adj* curable

cu·ra·tor [kjʊ'reɪtər] conservador(a) *m(f)*

curb [kɜːrb] **1** *n of street* bordillo *m; on powers etc* freno *m* **2** *v/t* frenar

cur·dle ['kɜːrdl] *v/i of milk* cortarse

cure [kjʊr] **1** *n* MED cura *f* **2** *v/t* MED, *meat* curar

cur·few ['kɜːrfjuː] toque *m* de queda

cu·ri·os·i·ty [kjʊrɪ'ɑːsətɪ] (*inquisitiveness*) curiosidad *f*

cu·ri·ous ['kjʊrɪəs] *adj* (*inquisitive, strange*) curioso

cu·ri·ous·ly ['kjʊrɪəslɪ] *adv* (*inquisitively*) con curiosidad; (*strangely*) curiosamente; **~ enough** curiosamente

curl [kɜːrl] **1** *n in hair* rizo *m; of smoke* voluta *f* **2** *v/t hair* rizar; (*wind*) enroscar **3** *v/i of hair* rizarse; *of leaf, paper etc* ondularse

♦ **curl up** *v/i* acurrucarse

curl·y ['kɜːrlɪ] *adj hair* rizado; *tail* enroscado

cur·rant ['kʌrənt] (*dried fruit*) pasa *f* de Corinto

cur·ren·cy ['kʌrənsɪ] *money* moneda *f*; **foreign ~** divisas *fpl*

cur·rent ['kʌrənt] **1** *n in sea*, ELEC corriente *f* **2** *adj* (*present*) actual

'**cur·rent ac·count** *Br* cuenta *f* corriente; **cur·rent af'fairs** *npl* la actualidad; **cur·rent af'fairs pro·gram**, *Br* **cur·rent af'fairs pro·**

gramme programa *m* de actualidad; **cur·rent e'vents** *npl* la actualidad

cur·rent·ly ['kʌrəntlɪ] *adv* actualmente

cur·ric·u·lum [kə'rɪkjʊləm] plan *m* de estudios

cur·ric·u·lum vi·tae ['viːtaɪ] *Br* currículum *m* vitae

cur·ry ['kʌrɪ] curry *m*

curse [kɜːrs] **1** *n* (*spell*) maldición *f*; (*swearword*) palabrota *f* **2** *v/t* maldecir; (*swear at*) insultar **3** *v/i* (*swear*) decir palabrotas

cur·sor ['kɜːrsər] COMPUT cursor *m*

cur·so·ry ['kɜːrsərɪ] *adj* rápido, superficial

curt [kɜːrt] *adj* brusco, seco

cur·tail [kɜːr'teɪl] *v/t* acortar

cur·tain ['kɜːrtn] cortina *f*; THEA telón *m*

curve [kɜːrv] **1** *n* curva *f* **2** *v/i* (*bend*) curvarse

cush·ion ['kʊʃn] **1** *n for couch etc* cojín *m* **2** *v/t blow, fall* amortiguar

cus·tard ['kʌstərd] natillas *fpl*

cus·to·dy ['kʌstədɪ] *of children* custodia *f*; **in ~** LAW detenido

cus·tom ['kʌstəm] (*tradition*) costumbre *f*; COM clientela *f*; **it's the ~ in France** es costumbre en Francia; **as was his ~** como era costumbre en él

cus·tom·a·ry ['kʌstəmərɪ] *adj* acostumbrado, de costumbre; **it is ~ to ...** es costumbre ...

cus·tom-'built *adj* hecho de encargo

cus·tom·er ['kʌstəmər] cliente(-a) *m(f)*

cus·tom·er re'la·tions *npl* relaciones *fpl* con los clientes

cus·tom·er 'serv·ice atención *f* al cliente

cus·tom-'made *adj* hecho de encargo

cus·toms ['kʌstəmz] *npl* aduana *f*

'cus·toms clear·ance despacho *m* de aduanas; **'cus·toms in·spec·tion** inspección *f* aduanera; **'cus·toms of·fi·cer** funciona-

rio(-a) *m(f)* de aduanas

cut [kʌt] **1** *n with knife etc, of garment* corte *m*; (*reduction*) recorte (**in** de) **2** *v/t* (*pret* & *pp* **cut**) cortar; (*reduce*) recortar; *hours* acortar; **get one's hair ~** cortarse el pelo; **I've ~ my finger** me he cortado el dedo

♦ **cut back 1** *v/i in costs* recortar gastos **2** *v/t staff numbers* recortar

♦ **cut down 1** *v/t tree* talar, cortar **2** *v/i in expenses* gastar menos; *in smoking / drinking* fumar / beber menos

♦ **cut down on** *v/t*: **cut down on the cigarettes** fumar menos; **cut down on chocolate** comer menos chocolate

♦ **cut off** *v/t with knife, scissors etc* cortar; (*isolate*) aislar; **I was cut off** se me ha cortado la comunicación

♦ **cut out** *v/t with scissors* recortar; (*eliminate*) eliminar; **cut that out!** F ¡ya está bien! F; **be cut out for sth** estar hecho para algo

♦ **cut up** *v/t meat etc* trocear

'cut·back recorte *m*

cute [kjuːt] *adj* (*pretty*) guapo, lindo; (*sexually attractive*) atractivo; (*smart, clever*) listo; **it looks really ~ on you** eso te queda muy mono

cu·ti·cle ['kjuːtɪkl] cutícula *f*

'cut-off date fecha *f* límite; **cut-'price** *adj goods* rebajado; *store* de productos rebajados; **'cut-throat** *adj competition* despiadado

cut·ting ['kʌtɪŋ] **1** *n from newspaper etc* recorte *m* **2** *adj remark* hiriente

cy·ber·space ['saɪbərspeɪs] ciberespacio *m*

cy·cle ['saɪkl] **1** *n* (*bicycle*) bicicleta *f*; (*series of events*) ciclo *m* **2** *v/i* ir en bicicleta

'cy·cle path vía *f* para bicicletas; *part of roadway* carril *m* bici

cy·cling ['saɪklɪŋ] ciclismo *m*

cy·clist ['saɪklɪst] ciclista *m/f*

cyl·in·der ['sɪlɪndər] cilindro *m*

cy·lin·dri·cal [sɪ'lɪndrɪkl] *adj* cilíndrico

cyn·ic ['sɪnɪk] escéptico(-a) *m(f)*, suspicaz *m/f*

cyn·i·cal ['sınıkl] *adj* escéptico, suspicaz

cyn·i·cal·ly ['sınıklı] *adv smile, say* con escepticismo *or* suspicacia

cyn·i·cism ['sınısızm] escepticismo *m*, suspicacia *f*

cy·press ['saıprəs] ciprés *m*

cyst [sıst] quiste *m*

Czech [tʃek] **1** *adj* checo; **the ~ Republic** la República Checa **2** *n person* checo(-a) *m(f)*; *language* checo *m*

D

DA *abbr* (= **district attorney**) fiscal *m/f* (del distrito)

dab [dæb] **1** *n small amount* pizca *f* **2** *v/t* (*pret & pp* **-bed**) (*remove*) quitar; (*apply*) poner

♦ **dab·ble in** ['dæbl] *v/t* ser aficionado a

dad [dæd] *talking to him* papá *m*; *talking about him* padre *m*

dad·dy ['dædı] *talking to him* papi *m*; *talking about him* padre *m*

daf·fo·dil ['dæfədıl] narciso *m*

dag·ger ['dægər] daga *f*

dai·ly ['deılı] **1** *n* (*paper*) diario *m* **2** *adj* diario

dain·ty ['deıntı] *adj* grácil, delicado

dair·y ['derı] *on farm* vaquería *f*

'dair·y prod·ucts *npl* productos *mpl* lácteos

dais ['deıls] tarima *f*

dai·sy ['deızı] margarita *f*

dam [dæm] **1** *n for water* presa *f* **2** *v/t* (*pret & pp* **-med**) *river* embalsar

dam·age ['dæmıdʒ] **1** *n* daños *mpl*; *fig: to reputation etc* daño *m* **2** *v/t also fig* dañar; **you're damaging your health** estás perjudicando tu salud

dam·a·ges ['dæmıdʒız] *npl* LAW daños *mpl* y perjuicios

dam·ag·ing ['dæmıdʒıŋ] *adj* perjudicial

dame [deım] F (*woman*) mujer *f*, *Span* tía *f* F

damn [dæm] **1** *int* F ¡mecachis! F **2** *n* F: *I don't give a ~!* ¡me importa

un pimiento! F **3** *adj* F maldito F **4** *adv* F muy; *a ~ stupid thing* una tontería monumental **5** *v/t* (*condemn*) condenar; *~ it!* F ¡maldita sea! F; *I'm ~ed if ...* F ya lo creo que ... F

damned [dæmd] → **damn** *adj, adv*

damn·ing ['dæmıŋ] *adj evidence* condenatorio; *report* crítico

damp [dæmp] *adj* húmedo

damp·en ['dæmpən] *v/t* humedecer

dance [dæns] **1** *n* baile *m* **2** *v/i* bailar; **would you like to ~?** ¿le gustaría bailar?

danc·er ['dænsər] bailarín (-ina) *m(f)*

danc·ing ['dænsıŋ] baile *m*

dan·de·li·on ['dændılaıən] diente *m* de león

dan·druff ['dændrʌf] caspa *f*

dan·druff sham'poo champú *m* anticaspa

Dane [deın] danés(-esa) *m(f)*

dan·ger ['deındʒər] peligro *m*; *be in ~* estar en peligro; *be out of ~ of patient* estar fuera de peligro; *be in no ~* no estar en peligro

dan·ger·ous ['deındʒərəs] *adj* peligroso

dan·ger·ous 'driv·ing conducción *f* peligrosa

dan·ger·ous·ly ['deındʒərəslı] *adv drive* peligrosamente; *~ ill* gravemente enfermo

dan·gle ['dæŋgl] **1** *v/t* balancear **2** *v/i*

colgar
Da·nish ['deɪnɪʃ] **1** *adj* danés **2** *n*
language danés *m*
'Da·nish (pas·try) pastel *m* de hojaldre (*dulce*)
dare [der] **1** *v/i* atreverse; *how ~*
you! ¡cómo te atreves! **2** *v/t*: - *to do*
sth atreverse a hacer algo; *~ s.o. to*
do sth desafiar a alguien para que
haga algo
dare·dev·il ['derdevɪl] temerario(-a)
m(f)
dar·ing ['derɪŋ] *adj* atrevido
dark [dɑːrk] **1** *n* oscuridad *f*; *in the ~*
en la oscuridad; *after ~* después de
anochecer; *keep s.o. in the ~*
about sth *fig* no revelar algo a alguien **2** *adj* oscuro; *hair* oscuro, moreno; *~ green / blue* verde / azul oscuro
dark·en ['dɑːrkn] *v/i of sky* oscure-
cerse
dark 'glass·es *npl* gafas *fpl* oscuras,
L.Am. lentes *fpl* oscuras
dark·ness ['dɑːrknɪs] oscuridad *f*; *in*
~ a oscuras
'dark·room PHOT cuarto *m* oscuro
dar·ling ['dɑːrlɪŋ] **1** *n* cielo *m*; *yes*
my ~ sí cariño **2** *adj* encantador; *~*
Ann, how are you? querida Ann,
¿cómo estás?
darn¹ [dɑːrn] **1** *n* (*mend*) zurcido *m*
2 *v/t* (*mend*) zurcir
darn², darned [dɑːrn, dɑːrnd] →
damn adj, adv
dart [dɑːrt] **1** *n for throwing* dardo *m*
2 *v/i* lanzarse, precipitarse
darts [dɑːrts] *nsg* dardos *mpl*
'dart(s)·board diana *f*
dash [dæʃ] **1** *n punctuation* raya *f*;
(*small amount*) chorrito *m*; (MOT:
~board) salpicadero *m*; *make a ~*
for correr hacia **2** *v/i* correr; *he ~ed*
downstairs bajó las escaleras corriendo **3** *v/t hopes* frustrar, truncar
♦ **dash off 1** *v/i* irse **2** *v/t* (*write*
quickly) escribir rápidamente
'dash·board salpicadero *m*
da·ta ['deɪtə] datos *mpl*
'da·ta·base base *f* de datos; **da·ta**
'cap·ture captura *f* de datos; **da·ta**

'pro·cess·ing proceso *m or* tratamiento *m* de datos; **da·ta**
pro'tec·tion protección *f* de datos;
da·ta 'stor·age almacenamiento
m de datos
date¹ [deɪt] *fruit* dátil *m*
date² [deɪt] **1** *n* fecha *f*; (*meeting*) cita
f; (*person*) pareja *f*; *what's the ~*
today? ¿qué fecha es hoy?, ¿a qué
fecha estamos?; *out of ~ clothes* pasado de moda; *passport* caducado;
up to ~ al día **2** *v/t letter, check* fe-
char; (*go out with*) salir con; *that ~s*
you (*shows your age*) eso demues-
tra lo viejo que eres
dat·ed ['deɪtɪd] *adj* anticuado
daub [dɒːb] *v/t* embadurnar
daugh·ter ['dɒːtər] hija *f*
'daugh·ter-in-law (*pl daughters-*
in-law) nuera *f*
daunt [dɒːnt] *v/t* acobardar, desalentar
daw·dle ['dɒːdl] *v/i* perder el tiempo
dawn [dɒːn] **1** *n* amanecer *m*, alba *f*;
fig: of new age albores *mpl* **2** *v/i*
amanecer; *it ~ed on me that ...* me
di cuenta de que …
day [deɪ] día *m*; *what ~ is it today?*
¿qué día es hoy?, ¿a qué día estamos?; *~ off* día *m* de vacaciones; *by*
~ durante el día; *~ by ~* día tras día;
the ~ after el día siguiente; *the ~*
after tomorrow pasado mañana;
the ~ before el día anterior; *the ~*
before yesterday anteayer; *~ in*
out un día sí y otro también; *in*
those ~s en aquellos tiempos; *one*
~ un día; *the other ~* (*recently*) el
otro día; *let's call it a ~!* ¡dejémos-
lo!
'day·break amanecer *m*, alba *f*; **'day**
care servicio *m* de guardería;
'day·dream 1 *n* fantasía *f* **2** *v/i* soñar despierto; **'day dream·er**
soñador(a) *m(f)*; **'day·light** luz *f*
del día; **'day·light 'sav·ing time**
horario *m* de verano; **'day·time:** *in*
the ~ durante el día; **'day trip** excursión *f* en el día
daze [deɪz] *n*: *in a ~* aturdido
dazed [deɪzd] *adj* aturdido

daz·zle ['dæzl] *v/t also fig* deslumbrar

DC [di:'si:] *abbr* (= *direct current*) cc (= corriente *f* continua); (= *District of Columbia*) Distrito *m* de Columbia

dead [ded] **1** *adj person, plant* muerto; *battery* agotado; *light bulb* fundido; F *place* muerto F; *the phone is ~* no hay línea **2** *adv* F (*very*) tela de F, la mar de F; *~ beat*, *~ tired* hecho polvo; *that's ~ right* tienes toda la razón del mundo **3** *npl*: *the ~* (*~ people*) los muertos; *in the ~ of night* a altas horas de la madrugada

dead·en ['dedn] *v/t pain, sound* amortiguar

dead 'end *street* callejón *m* sin salida; **dead-'end job** trabajo *m* sin salidas; **dead 'heat** empate *m*; **'dead·line** fecha *f* tope; *for newspaper, magazine* hora *f* de cierre; *meet a ~* cumplir un plazo; **'dead·lock** *n in talks* punto *m* muerto

dead·ly ['dedli] *adj* (*fatal*), F (*boring*) mortal F

deaf [def] *adj* sordo

deaf-and-'dumb *adj* sordomudo

deaf·en ['defn] *v/t* ensordecer

deaf·en·ing ['defnɪŋ] *adj* ensordecedor

deaf·ness ['defnɪs] sordera *f*

deal [di:l] **1** *n* acuerdo *m*; *I thought we had a ~* creía que habíamos hecho un trato; *it's a ~!* ¡trato hecho!; *a good ~* (*bargain*) una ocasión; (*a lot*) mucho; *a great ~ of* (*lots*) mucho(s) **2** *v/t* (*pret & pp* **dealt**) *cards* repartir; *~ a blow to* asestar un golpe a

♦ **deal in** *v/t* (*trade in*) comerciar con; *deal in drugs* traficar con drogas

♦ **deal out** *v/t cards* repartir

♦ **deal with** *v/t* (*handle*) tratar; *situation* hacer frente a; *customer, applications* encargarse de; (*do business with*) hacer negocios con

deal·er ['di:lər] (*merchant*) comerciante *m/f*; (*drug ~*) traficante *m/f*

deal·ing ['di:lɪŋ] (*drug ~*) tráfico *m*

deal·ings ['di:lɪŋz] *npl* (*business*) tratos *mpl*

dealt [delt] *pret & pp* → **deal**

dean [di:n] *of college* decano(-a) *m(f)*

dear [dɪr] *adj* querido; (*expensive*) caro; *Dear Sir* Muy Sr. Mío; *Dear Richard/Margaret* Querido Richard/Querida Margaret; (*oh*) *~!*, *~ me!* ¡oh, cielos!

dear·ly ['dɪrlɪ] *adv love* muchísimo

death [deθ] muerte *f*

'death cer·tif·i·cate certificado *m* de defunción; **'death pen·al·ty** pena *f* de muerte; **'death toll** saldo *m* de víctimas mortales

de·ba·ta·ble [dɪ'beɪtəbl] *adj* discutible

de·bate [dɪ'beɪt] **1** *n also* POL debate *m* **2** *v/i* debatir; *I ~d with myself whether to go* me debatía entre ir o no ir **3** *v/t* debatir

de·bauch·er·y [dɪ'bɔ:tʃərɪ] libertinaje *m*

deb·it ['debɪt] **1** *n* cargo *m* **2** *v/t account* cargar en; *amount* cargar

'deb·it card tarjeta *f* de débito

deb·ris [də'bri:] *nsg of building* escombros *mpl; of airplane* restos *mpl*

debt [det] deuda *f*; *be in ~ financially* estar endeudado

debt·or ['detər] deudor(-a) *m(f)*

de·bug [di:'bʌg] *v/t* (*pret & pp* **-ged**) *room* limpiar de micrófonos; COMPUT depurar

dé·but ['deɪbju:] *n* debut *m*

dec·ade ['dekeɪd] década *f*

dec·a·dence ['dekədəns] decadencia *f*

dec·a·dent ['dekədənt] *adj* decadente

de·caf·fein·at·ed [dɪ'kæfɪneɪtɪd] *adj* descafeinado

de·cant·er [dɪ'kæntər] licorera *f*

de·cap·i·tate [dɪ'kæpɪteɪt] *v/t* decapitar

de·cay [dɪ'keɪ] **1** *n of wood, plant* putrefacción *f; of civilization* declive *m; in teeth* caries *f inv* **2** *v/i of wood, plant* pudrirse; *of civilization* decaer; *of teeth* cariarse

de·ceased [dɪ'siːst]: **the ~** el difunto/la difunta

de·ceit [dɪ'siːt] engaño *m*, mentira *f*

de·ceit·ful [dɪ'siːtfəl] *adj* mentiroso

de·ceive [dɪ'siːv] *v/t* engañar

De·cem·ber [dɪ'sembər] diciembre *m*

de·cen·cy ['diːsənsɪ] decencia *f*; **he had the ~ to ...** tuvo la delicadeza de ...

de·cent ['diːsənt] *adj* decente; (*adequately dressed*) presentable

de·cen·tral·ize [diː'sentrəlaɪz] *v/t* descentralizar

de·cep·tion [dɪ'sepʃn] engaño *m*

de·cep·tive [dɪ'septɪv] *adj* engañoso

de·cep·tive·ly [dɪ'septɪvlɪ] *adv*: **it looks ~ simple** parece muy fácil

dec·i·bel ['desɪbel] decibelio *m*

de·cide [dɪ'saɪd] **1** *v/t* decidir **2** *v/i* decidir; **you ~** decide tú

de·cid·ed [dɪ'saɪdɪd] *adj* (*definite*) tajante

de·cid·er [dɪ'saɪdər]: **this match will be the ~** este partido será el que decida

dec·i·du·ous [dɪ'sɪduəs] *adj* de hoja caduca

dec·i·mal ['desɪml] *n* decimal *m*

dec·i·mal 'point coma *f* (decimal)

dec·i·mate ['desɪmeɪt] *v/t* diezmar

de·ci·pher [dɪ'saɪfər] *v/t* descifrar

de·ci·sion [dɪ'sɪʒn] decisión *f*; **come to a ~** llegar a una decisión

de'ci·sion-mak·er: **who's the ~ here?** ¿quién toma aquí las decisiones?

de·ci·sive [dɪ'saɪsɪv] *adj* decidido; (*crucial*) decisivo

deck [dek] *of ship* cubierta *f*; *of cards* baraja *f*

'deck·chair tumbona *f*

dec·la·ra·tion [deklə'reɪʃn] (*statement*) declaración *f*

de·clare [dɪ'kler] *v/t* (*state*) declarar

de·cline [dɪ'klaɪn] **1** *n* (*fall*) descenso *m*; *in standards* caída *f*; *in health* empeoramiento *m* **2** *v/t invitation* declinar; **~ to comment** declinar hacer declaraciones **3** *v/i* (*refuse*) rehusar; (*decrease*) declinar; *of health* empeorar

de·clutch [diː'klʌtʃ] *v/i* desembragar

de·code [diː'koʊd] *v/t* descodificar

de·com·pose [diːkəm'poʊz] *v/i* descomponerse

déc·or ['deɪkɔːr] decoración *f*

dec·o·rate ['dekəreɪt] *v/t with paint* pintar; *with paper* empapelar; (*adorn*) decorar; *soldier* condecorar

dec·o·ra·tion [dekə'reɪʃn] *paint* pintado *m*; *paper* empapelado *m*; (*ornament*) decoración *f*

dec·o·ra·tive ['dekərətɪv] *adj* decorativo

dec·o·ra·tor ['dekəreɪtər] (*interior ~*) decorador(a) *m(f)*; *with paint* pintor(a) *m(f)*; *with wallpaper* empapelador(a) *m(f)*

de·co·rum [dɪ'kɔːrəm] decoro *m*

de·coy ['diːkɔɪ] *n* señuelo *m*

de·crease 1 *n* ['diːkriːs] disminución *f*, reducción *f* (*in* de) **2** *v/t* [dɪ'kriːs] disminuir, reducir **3** *v/i* [dɪ'kriːs] disminuir, reducirse

de·crep·it [dɪ'krepɪt] *adj car, coat, shoes* destartalado; *person* decrépito

ded·i·cate ['dedɪkeɪt] *v/t book etc* dedicar; **~ o.s. to.** dedicarse a

ded·i·ca·ted [dedɪkeɪtɪd] *adj* dedicado

ded·i·ca·tion [dedɪ'keɪʃn] *in book* dedicatoria *f*; *to cause, work* dedicación *f*

de·duce [dɪ'duːs] *v/t* deducir

de·duct [dɪ'dʌkt] *v/t* descontar

de·duc·tion [dɪ'dʌkʃn] *from salary*, (*conclusion*) deduccción *f*

deed [diːd] *n* (*act*) acción *f*, obra *f*; LAW escritura *f*

dee·jay ['diːdʒeɪ] F disk jockey *m/f*, *Span* pincha *m/f* F

deem [diːm] *v/t* estimar

deep [diːp] *adj* profundo; *color* intenso; **be in ~ trouble** estar metido en serios apuros

deep·en ['diːpn] **1** *v/t* profundizar **2** *v/i* hacerse más profundo; *of crisis, mystery* agudizarse

'deep freeze *n* congelador *m*; **'deep-froz·en food** comida *f* con-

gelada; **'deep-fry** v/t (pret & pp
-ied) freír (en mucho aceite); **deep
'fry·er** freidora f

deer [dɪr] (pl **deer**) ciervo m

de·face [dɪ'feɪs] v/t desfigurar, dañar

def·a·ma·tion [defə'meɪʃn] difamación f

de·fam·a·to·ry [dɪ'fæmətərɪ] adj difamatorio

de·fault ['diːfɔːlt] adj COMPUT por
defecto

de·feat [dɪ'fiːt] **1** n derrota f **2** v/t derrotar; of task, problem derrotar,
vencer

de·feat·ist [dɪ'fiːtɪst] adj attitude derrotista

de·fect ['diːfekt] n defecto m

de·fec·tive [dɪ'fektɪv] adj defectuoso

de·fence etc Br → **defense** etc

de·fend [dɪ'fend] v/t defender

de·fend·ant [dɪ'fendənt] acusado(-a) m(f); in civil case demandado(-a) m(f)

de·fense [dɪ'fens] defensa f; **come
to s.o.'s ~** salir en defensa de alguien

de·fense budg·et POL presupuesto
m de defensa

de·fense law·yer abogado(-a) m(f)
defensor(a)

de·fense·less [dɪ'fenslɪs] adj indefenso

de·fense play·er SP defensa m/f;
De'fense Se·cre·ta·ry POL ministro(-a) m(f) de Defensa; in USA
secretario m de Defensa; **de'fense
wit·ness** LAW testigo m/f de la defensa

de·fen·sive [dɪ'fensɪv] **1** n: **on the ~**
a la defensiva; **go on the ~** ponerse
a la defensiva **2** adj weaponry defensivo; **stop being so ~!** ¡no hace
falta que te pongas tan a la defensiva!

de·fen·sive·ly [dɪ'fensɪvlɪ] adv a la
defensiva

de·fer [dɪ'fɜːr] v/t (pret & pp **-red**)
(postpone) aplazar, diferir

de·fer·ence ['defərəns] deferencia f

def·er·en·tial [defə'renʃl] adj deferente

de·fi·ance [dɪ'faɪəns] desafío m; **in ~
of** desafiando

de·fi·ant [dɪ'faɪənt] adj desafiante

de·fi·cien·cy [dɪ'fɪʃənsɪ] (lack) deficiencia f, carencia f

de·fi·cient [dɪ'fɪʃənt] adj deficiente,
carente; **be ~ in ...** carecer de ...

def·i·cit ['defɪsɪt] déficit m

de·fine [dɪ'faɪn] v/t word, objective
definir

def·i·nite ['defɪnɪt] adj date, time,
answer definitivo; improvement claro; (certain) seguro; **nothing ~ has
been arranged** no se ha acordado
nada de forma definitiva

def·i·nite 'ar·ti·cle GRAM artículo m
determinado or definido

def·i·nite·ly ['defɪnɪtlɪ] adv con certeza, sin lugar a dudas

def·i·ni·tion [defɪ'nɪʃn] definición f

def·i·ni·tive [dɪ'fɪnətɪv] adj definitivo

de·flect [dɪ'flekt] v/t desviar; criticism distraer; **be ~ed from** desviarse
de

de·for·est·a·tion [difɑːrɪs'teɪʃn]
deforestación f

de·form [dɪ'fɔːrm] v/t deformar

de·for·mi·ty [dɪ'fɔːrmɪtɪ] deformidad f

de·fraud [dɪ'frɔːd] v/t defraudar

de·frost [diː'frɔːst] v/t food, fridge
descongelar

deft [deft] adj hábil, diestro

de·fuse [diː'fjuːz] v/t bomb desactivar; situation calmar

de·fy [dɪ'faɪ] v/t (pret & pp **-ied**) desafiar

de·gen·e·rate [dɪ'dʒenəreɪt] v/i degenerar; **~ into** degenerar en

de·grade [dɪ'greɪd] v/t degradar

de·grad·ing [dɪ'greɪdɪŋ] adj position,
work degradante

de·gree [dɪ'griː] from university título m; of temperature, angle, latitude
grado m; **there is a ~ of truth in
that** hay algo de verdad en eso; **a ~
of compassion** algo de compasión;
by ~s gradualmente; **get one's ~**
graduarse, L.Am. egresar

de·hy·drat·ed [diːhaɪˈdreɪtɪd] *adj* deshidratado

de·ice [diːˈaɪs] *v/t* deshelar

de·ic·er [diːˈaɪsər] *spray* descongelador *m*, descongelante *m*

deign [deɪn] *v/i*: ~ *to* dignarse a

de·i·ty [ˈdiːɪtɪ] deidad *f*

de·ject·ed [dɪˈdʒektɪd] *adj* abatido, desanimado

de·lay [dɪˈleɪ] **1** *n* retraso *m* **2** *v/t* retrasar; *be ~ed* llevar retraso **3** *v/i* retrasarse

del·e·gate [ˈdelɪɡət] **1** *n* delegado(-a) *m(f)* **2** [ˈdelɪɡeɪt] *v/t task* delegar; *person* delegar en

del·e·ga·tion [delɪˈɡeɪʃn] delegación *f*

de·lete [dɪˈliːt] *v/t* borrar; (*cross out*) tachar; ~ *where not applicable* táchese donde no corresponda

de·le·tion [dɪˈliːʃn] *act* borrado *m*; *that deleted* supresión *f*

del·i [ˈdelɪ] → *delicatessen*

de·lib·e·rate 1 *adj* [dɪˈlɪbərət] deliberado, intencionado **2** *v/i* [dɪˈlɪbəreɪt] deliberar

de·lib·e·rate·ly [dɪˈlɪbərətlɪ] *adv* deliberadamente, a propósito

del·i·ca·cy [ˈdelɪkəsɪ] delicadeza *f*; *of health* fragilidad *f*; *food* exquisitez *f*, manjar *m*

del·i·cate [ˈdelɪkət] *adj fabric, problem* delicado; *health* frágil

del·i·ca·tes·sen [delɪkəˈtesn] *tienda de productos alimenticios de calidad*

del·i·cious [dɪˈlɪʃəs] *adj* delicioso

de·light [dɪˈlaɪt] *n* placer *m*

de·light·ed [dɪˈlaɪtɪd] *adj* encantado; *I'd be ~ to come* me encantaría venir

de·light·ful [dɪˈlaɪtfəl] *adj* encantador

de·lim·it [diːˈlɪmɪt] *v/t* delimitar

de·lir·i·ous [dɪˈlɪrɪəs] *adj* MED delirante; (*ecstatic*) entusiasmado; *she's ~ about the new job* está como loca con el nuevo trabajo

de·liv·er [dɪˈlɪvər] *v/t* entregar, repartir; *message* dar; *baby* dar a luz; *speech* pronunciar

de·liv·er·y [dɪˈlɪvərɪ] *of goods, mail* entrega *f*, reparto *m*; *of baby* parto *m*

de·liv·er·y charge gastos *mpl* de envío; **de·liv·er·y date** fecha *f* de entrega; **de·liv·er·y man** repartidor *m*; **de·liv·er·y note** nota *f* de entrega; **de·liv·er·y serv·ice** servicio *m* de reparto; **de·liv·er·y van** furgoneta *f* de reparto

de·lude [dɪˈluːd] *v/t* engañar; *you're deluding yourself* te estás engañando a ti mismo

de·luge [ˈdeljuːdʒ] **1** *n* diluvio *m*; *fig* avalancha *f* **2** *v/t fig* inundar (*with* de)

de·lu·sion [dɪˈluːʒn] engaño *m*; *you're under a ~ if you think …* te engañas si piensas que …

de luxe [dəˈluːks] *adj* de lujo

♦**delve into** [delv] *v/t* rebuscar en

de·mand [dɪˈmænd] **1** *n* exigencia *f*; *by union* reivindicación *f*; COM demanda *f*; *in ~* solicitado **2** *v/t* exigir; (*require*) requerir

de·mand·ing [dɪˈmændɪŋ] *adj job* que exige mucho; *person* exigente

de·mean·ing [dɪˈmiːnɪŋ] *adj* degradante

de·ment·ed [dɪˈmentɪd] *adj* demente

de·mise [dɪˈmaɪz] *fallecimiento m*; *fig* desaparición *f*

dem·i·tasse [ˈdemɪtæs] taza *f* de café

dem·o [ˈdemoʊ] *protest* manifestación *f*; *of video etc* maqueta *f*

de·moc·ra·cy [dɪˈmɑːkrəsɪ] democracia *f*

dem·o·crat [ˈdeməkræt] demócrata *m/f*; *Democrat* POL Demócrata *m/f*

dem·o·crat·ic [deməˈkrætɪk] *adj* democrático

dem·o·crat·ic·al·ly [deməˈkrætɪklɪ] *adv* democráticamente

'dem·o disk disco *m* de demostración

de·mo·graph·ic [demoʊˈɡræfɪk] *adj* demográfico

de·mol·ish [dɪˈmɑːlɪʃ] *v/t building* demoler; *argument* destruir, echar por tierra

dem·o·li·tion [deməˈlɪʃn] *of building* demolición *f*; *of argument* destrucción *f*

de·mon [ˈdiːmən] demonio *m*

dem·on·strate [ˈdemənstreɪt] **1** *v/t* demostrar **2** *v/i politically* manifestarse

dem·on·stra·tion [demənˈstreɪʃn] demostración *f*; *protest* manifestación *f*

de·mon·stra·tive [dɪˈmɑːnstrətɪv] *adj person* extrovertido, efusivo; GRAM demostrativo

de·mon·stra·tor [ˈdemənstreɪtər] *protester* manifestante *m/f*

de·mor·al·ized [dɪˈmɔːrəlaɪzd] *adj* desmoralizado

de·mor·al·iz·ing [dɪˈmɔːrəlaɪzɪŋ] *adj* desmoralizador

de·mote [diːˈmoʊt] *v/t* degradar

de·mure [dɪˈmjʊər] *adj* solemne, recatado

den [den] *(study)* estudio *m*

de·ni·al [dɪˈnaɪəl] *of rumor, accusation* negación *f*; *of request* denegación *f*

den·im [ˈdenɪm] tela *f* vaquera

den·ims [ˈdenɪmz] *npl (jeans)* vaqueros *mpl*

Den·mark [ˈdenmɑːrk] Dinamarca

de·nom·i·na·tion [dɪnɑːmɪˈneɪʃn] *of money* valor *m*; *religious* confesión *f*

de·nounce [dɪˈnaʊns] *v/t* denunciar

dense [dens] *adj smoke, fog* denso; *foliage* espeso; *crowd* compacto; F *(stupid)* corto

dense·ly [ˈdenslɪ] *adv*: **~ populated** densamente poblado

den·si·ty [ˈdensɪtɪ] *of population* densidad *f*

dent [dent] **1** *n* abolladura *f* **2** *v/t* abollar

den·tal [ˈdentl] *adj* dental; **~ surgeon** odontólogo(-a) *m(f)*

den·ted [ˈdentɪd] *adj* abollado

den·tist [ˈdentɪst] dentista *m/f*

den·tist·ry [ˈdentɪstrɪ] odontología *f*

den·tures [ˈdentʃərz] *npl* dentadura *f* postiza

Den·ver boot [ˈdenvər] cepo *m*

de·ny [dɪˈnaɪ] *v/t (pret & pp -ied)*

charge, rumor negar; *right, request* denegar

de·o·do·rant [diːˈoʊdərənt] desodorante *m*

de·part [dɪˈpɑːrt] *v/i* salir; **~ from** *(deviate from)* desviarse de

de·part·ment [dɪˈpɑːrtmənt] departamento *m*; *of government* ministerio *m*

De·part·ment of 'De·fense Ministerio *m* de Defensa; **De·part·ment of 'State** Ministerio *m* de Asuntos Exteriores; **De·part·ment of the In·te·ri·or** Ministerio *m* del Interior; **de'part·ment store** grandes almacenes *mpl*

de·par·ture [dɪˈpɑːrtʃər] salida *f*; *of person from job* marcha *f*; *(deviation)* desviación *f*; **a new ~ for** *government, organization* una innovación; *for company* un cambio; *for actor, artist, writer* una nueva experiencia

de'par·ture lounge sala *f* de embarque

de'par·ture time hora *f* de salida

de·pend [dɪˈpend] *v/i* depender; **that ~s** depende; **it ~s on the weather** depende del tiempo; **I ~ on you** dependo de ti

de·pen·da·ble [dɪˈpendəbl] *adj* fiable

de·pen·dant [dɪˈpendənt] → **dependent**

de·pen·dence, de·pen·den·cy [dɪˈpendəns, dɪˈpendənsɪ] dependencia *f*

de·pen·dent [dɪˈpendənt] **1** *n* persona a cargo de otra; **how many ~s do you have?** ¿cuántas personas tiene a su cargo? **2** *adj* dependiente (**on** de)

de·pict [dɪˈpɪkt] *v/t* describir

de·plete [dɪˈpliːt] *v/t* agotar, mermar

de·plor·a·ble [dɪˈplɔːrəbl] *adj* deplorable

de·plore [dɪˈplɔːr] *v/t* deplorar

de·ploy [dɪˈplɔɪ] *v/t (use)* utilizar; *(position)* desplegar

de·pop·u·la·tion [diːpɑːpjəˈleɪʃn] despoblación *f*

de·port [dɪ'pɔːrt] v/t deportar
de·por·ta·tion [diːpɔːr'teɪʃn] deportación f
de·por·ta·tion or·der orden f de deportación
de·pose [dɪ'pəʊz] v/t deponer
de·pos·it [dɪ'pɑːzɪt] **1** n in bank, of oil depósito m; of coal yacimiento m; on purchase señal f, depósito m **2** v/t money depositar, Span ingresar; (put down) depositar
de·pos·it ac·count Br cuenta f de ahorro or de depósito
dep·o·si·tion [diːpoʊ'zɪʃn] LAW declaración f
dep·ot ['diːpəʊ] (train station) estación f de tren; (bus station) estación f de autobuses; for storage depósito m
de·praved [dɪ'preɪvd] adj depravado
de·pre·ci·ate [dɪ'priːʃieɪt] v/i FIN depreciarse
de·pre·ci·a·tion [dɪpriːʃi'eɪʃn] FIN depreciación f
de·press [dɪ'pres] v/t person deprimir
de·pressed [dɪ'prest] adj person deprimido
de·press·ing [dɪ'presɪŋ] adj deprimente
de·pres·sion [dɪ'preʃn] MED, economic depresión f; meteorological borrasca f
dep·ri·va·tion [deprɪ'veɪʃn] privación f
de·prive [dɪ'praɪv] v/t privar; **~ s.o. of sth** privar a alguien de algo
de·prived [dɪ'praɪvd] adj desfavorecido
depth [depθ] profundidad f; of color intensidad f; **in ~** (thoroughly) en profundidad; **in the ~s of winter** en pleno invierno; **be out of one's ~** in water no tocar el fondo; fig: in discussion etc saber muy poco
dep·u·ta·tion [depjʊ'teɪʃn] delegación f
♦ dep·u·tize for ['depjʊtaɪz] v/t sustituir
dep·u·ty ['depjʊtɪ] segundo(-a)

m(f)
'dep·u·ty lead·er vicelíder m/f
de·rail [dɪ'reɪl] v/t hacer descarrilar; **be ~ed** of train descarrilar
de·ranged [dɪ'reɪndʒd] adj perturbado, trastornado
de·reg·u·late [dɪ'regjʊleɪt] v/t liberalizar, desregular
de·reg·u·la·tion [dɪregjʊ'leɪʃn] liberalización f, desregulación f
der·e·lict ['derəlɪkt] adj en ruinas
de·ride [dɪ'raɪd] v/t ridiculizar, mofarse de
de·ri·sion [dɪ'rɪʒn] burla f, mofa f
de·ri·sive [dɪ'raɪsɪv] adj burlón
de·ri·sive·ly [dɪ'raɪsɪvlɪ] adv burlonamente
de·ri·so·ry [dɪ'raɪsərɪ] adj amount, salary irrisorio
de·riv·a·tive [dɪ'rɪvətɪv] adj (not original) poco original
de·rive [dɪ'raɪv] v/t obtener, encontrar; **be ~d from** of word derivar(se) de
der·ma·tol·o·gist [dɜːrmə'tɑːlədʒɪst] dermatólogo(-a) m(f)
de·rog·a·to·ry [dɪ'rɑːgətɔːrɪ] adj despectivo
de·scend [dɪ'send] **1** v/t descender por; **be ~d from** descender de **2** v/i descender; of mood, darkness caer
de·scen·dant [dɪ'sendənt] descendiente m/f
de·scent [dɪ'sent] descenso m; (ancestry) ascendencia f
de·scribe [dɪ'skraɪb] v/t describir; **~ sth as sth** definir a algo como algo
de·scrip·tion [dɪ'skrɪpʃn] descripción f
des·e·crate ['desɪkreɪt] v/t profanar
des·e·cra·tion [desɪ'kreɪʃn] profanación f
de·seg·re·gate [diː'segrəgeɪt] v/t acabar con la segregación racial en
des·ert¹ ['dezərt] n also fig desierto m
de·sert² [dɪ'zɜːrt] **1** v/t (abandon) abandonar **2** v/i of soldier desertar
de·sert·ed [dɪ'zɜːrtɪd] adj desierto
de·sert·er [dɪ'zɜːrtər] MIL desertor(a) m(f)

D

de·ser·ti·fi·ca·tion [dɪzɜːrtɪfɪ'keɪʃn] desertización *f*

de·ser·tion [dɪ'zɜːrʃn] (*abandonment*) abandono *m*; MIL deserción *f*

des·ert 'is·land isla *f* desierta

de·serve [dɪ'zɜːrv] *v/t* merecer

de·sign [dɪ'zaɪn] **1** *n* diseño *m*; (*pattern*) motivo *m* **2** *v/t* diseñar

des·ig·nate ['dezɪgneɪt] *v/t person* designar; *area* declarar

de·sign·er [dɪ'zaɪnər] diseñador(a) *m(f)*

de'sign·er clothes *npl* ropa *f* de diseño

de'sign fault defecto *m* de diseño

de'sign school escuela *f* de diseño

de·sir·a·ble [dɪ'zaɪrəbl] *adj* deseable; *house* apetecible, atractivo

de·sire [dɪ'zaɪr] *n* deseo *m*; *I have no ~ to see him* no me apetece verle

desk [desk] *in classroom* pupitre *m*; *in home, office* mesa *f*; *in hotel* recepción *f*

'desk clerk recepcionista *m/f*; **'desk di·a·ry** agenda *f*; **'desk·top** *also on screen* escritorio *m*; *computer* Span ordenador *m* de escritorio, *L.Am.* computadora *f* de escritorio; **desk·top 'pub·lish·ing** autoedición *f*

des·o·late ['desələt] *adj place* desolado

de·spair [dɪ'sper] **1** *n* desesperación *f*; *in ~* desesperado **2** *v/i* desesperarse; *I ~ of finding something to wear* he perdido la esperanza de encontrar algo para ponerme

des·per·ate ['despərət] *adj* desesperado; *be ~* estar desesperado; *be ~ for a drink / cigarette* necesitar una bebida / un cigarrillo desesperadamente

des·per·a·tion [despə'reɪʃn] desesperación *f*; *an act of ~* un acto desesperado

des·pic·a·ble [dɪs'pɪkəbl] *adj* despreciable

de·spise [dɪ'spaɪz] *v/t* despreciar

de·spite [dɪ'spaɪt] *prep* a pesar de

de·spon·dent [dɪ'spɑːndənt] *adj* abatido, desanimado

des·pot ['despɑːt] déspota *m/f*

des·sert [dɪ'zɜːrt] postre *m*

des·ti·na·tion [destɪ'neɪʃn] destino *m*

des·tined ['destɪnd] *adj*: *be ~ for fig* estar destinado a

des·ti·ny ['destɪnɪ] destino *m*

des·ti·tute ['destɪtuːt] *adj* indigente; *be ~* estar en la miseria

de·stroy [dɪ'strɔɪ] *v/t* destruir

de·stroy·er [dɪ'strɔɪr] NAUT destructor *m*

de·struc·tion [dɪ'strʌkʃn] destrucción *f*

de·struc·tive [dɪ'strʌktɪv] *adj* destructivo; *child* revoltoso

de·tach [dɪ'tætʃ] *v/t* separar, soltar

de·tach·a·ble [dɪ'tætʃəbl] *adj* desmontable, separable

de·tached [dɪ'tætʃt] *adj (objective)* distanciado

de·tach·ment [dɪ'tætʃmənt] (*objectivity*) distancia *f*

de·tail ['diːteɪl] *n* detalle *m*; *in ~* en detalle

de·tailed ['diːteɪld] *adj* detallado

de·tain [dɪ'teɪn] *v/t (hold back)* entretener; *as prisoner* detener

de·tain·ee [diːteɪn'iː] detenido(-a) *m(f)*

de·tect [dɪ'tekt] *v/t* percibir; *of device* detectar

de·tec·tion [dɪ'tekʃn] *of criminal, crime* descubrimiento *m*; *of smoke etc* detección *f*

de·tec·tive [dɪ'tektɪv] detective *m/f*

de·tec·tive nov·el novela *f* policiaca *or* de detectives

de·tec·tor [dɪ'tektər] detector *m*

dé·tente ['deɪtɑːnt] POL distensión *f*

de·ten·tion [dɪ'tenʃn] (*imprisonment*) detención *f*

de·ter [dɪ'tɜːr] *v/t (pret & pp -red)* disuadir; *~ s.o. from doing sth* disuadir a alguien de hacer algo

de·ter·gent [dɪ'tɜːrdʒənt] detergente *m*

de·te·ri·o·rate [dɪ'tɪriəreɪt] *v/i* deteriorarse; *of weather* empeorar

de·te·ri·o·ra·tion [dɪtɪriə'reɪʃn] deterioro *m*; *of weather* empeoramiento *m*

de·ter·mi·na·tion [dɪtɜːrmɪˈneɪʃn] (*resolution*) determinación *f*

de·ter·mine [dɪˈtɜːrmɪn] *v/t* (*establish*) determinar

de·ter·mined [dɪˈtɜːrmɪnd] *adj* resuelto, decidido; *I'm ~ to succeed* estoy decidido a triunfar

de·ter·rent [dɪˈterənt] *n* elemento *m* disuasorio; *act as a ~* actuar como elemento disuasorio; *nuclear ~* disuasión *f* nuclear

de·test [dɪˈtest] *v/t* detestar

de·test·a·ble [dɪˈtestəbl] *adj* detestable

de·to·nate [ˈdetəneɪt] **1** *v/t* hacer detonar *or* explotar **2** *v/i* detonar, explotar

de·to·na·tion [detəˈneɪʃn] detonación *f*, explosión *f*

de·tour [ˈdiːtur] *n* rodeo *m*; (*diversion*) desvío *m*; *make a ~* dar un rodeo

♦ **de·tract from** [dɪˈtrækt] *v/t achievement* quitar méritos a; *beauty* quitar atractivo a

de·tri·ment [ˈdetrɪmənt]: *to the ~ of* en detrimento de

de·tri·men·tal [detrɪˈmentl] *adj* perjudicial (*to* para)

deuce [duːs] *in tennis* deuce *m*

de·val·u·a·tion [diːvæljuˈeɪʃn] *of currency* devaluación *f*

de·val·ue [diːˈvæljuː] *v/t currency* devaluar

dev·a·state [ˈdevəsteɪt] *v/t crops, countryside, city* devastar; *fig: person* asolar

dev·a·stat·ing [ˈdevəsteɪtɪŋ] *adj* devastador

de·vel·op [dɪˈveləp] **1** *v/t film* revelar; *land, site* urbanizar; *activity, business* desarrollar; (*originate*) desarrollar; (*improve on*) perfeccionar; *illness, cold* contraer **2** *v/i* (*grow*) desarrollarse; *~ into* convertirse en

de·vel·op·er [dɪˈveləpər] *of property* promotor(a) *m(f)* inmobiliario(-a)

de·vel·op·ing 'coun·try [dɪˈveləpɪŋ] país *m* en vías de desarrollo

de·vel·op·ment [dɪˈveləpmənt] *of*

film revelado *m*; *of land, site* urbanización *f*; *of business, country* desarrollo *m*; (*event*) acontecimiento *m*; (*origination*) desarrollo *m*; (*improving*) perfeccionamiento *m*

de·vice [dɪˈvaɪs] *tool* aparato *m*, dispositivo *m*

dev·il [ˈdevl] *also fig* diablo *m*, demonio *m*

de·vi·ous [ˈdiːvɪəs] *adj* (*sly*) retorcido

de·vise [dɪˈvaɪz] *v/t* idear

de·void [dɪˈvɔɪd] *adj*: *be ~ of* estar desprovisto de

dev·o·lu·tion [diːvəˈluːʃn] POL traspaso *m* de competencias

de·vote [dɪˈvoʊt] *v/t* dedicar (*to* a)

de·vot·ed [dɪˈvoʊtɪd] *adj* son *etc* afectuoso; *be ~ to s.o.* tener mucho cariño a alguien

de·vo·tee [dɪvoʊˈtiː] entusiasta *m/f*

de·vo·tion [dɪˈvoʊʃn] devoción *f*

de·vour [dɪˈvaʊər] *v/t food, book* devorar

de·vout [dɪˈvaʊt] *adj* devoto

dew [duː] rocío *m*

dex·ter·i·ty [dekˈsterətɪ] destreza *f*

di·a·be·tes [daɪəˈbiːtiːz] *nsg* diabetes *f*

di·a·bet·ic [daɪəˈbetɪk] **1** *n* diabético(-a) *m(f)* **2** *adj* diabético; *foods* para diabéticos

di·ag·nose [ˈdaɪəgnoʊz] *v/t* diagnosticar; *she has been ~d as having cancer* se le ha diagnosticado un cáncer

di·ag·no·sis [daɪəgˈnoʊsɪs] (*pl di·agnoses* [daɪəgˈnoʊsiːz]) diagnóstico *m*

di·ag·o·nal [daɪˈægənl] *adj* diagonal

di·ag·o·nal·ly [daɪˈægənlɪ] *adv* diagonalmente, en diagonal

di·a·gram [ˈdaɪəgræm] diagrama *m*

di·al [ˈdaɪl] **1** *n of clock* esfera *f*; *of instrument* cuadrante *m*; TELEC disco *m* **2** *v/t & v/i* (*pret & pp* ***-ed***, Br ***-led***) TELEC marcar

di·a·lect [ˈdaɪəlekt] dialecto *m*

di·al·ling tone *Br* → **dial tone**

di·a·log, *Br* **di·a·logue** [ˈdaɪəlɑːg] diálogo *m*

di·a·log box COMPUT ventana *f* de diálogo

'di·al tone tono *m* de marcar

di·am·e·ter [daɪˈæmɪtər] diámetro *m*; *a circle 6 cms in ~* un círculo de 6 cms. de diámetro

di·a·met·ri·cal·ly [daɪəˈmetrɪkəlɪ] *adv*: *~ opposed* diametralmente opuesto

di·a·mond [ˈdaɪmənd] *also in cards* diamante *m*; *shape* rombo *m*

di·a·per [ˈdaɪpər] pañal *m*

di·a·phragm [ˈdaɪəfræm] ANAT, *contraceptive* diafragma *m*

di·ar·rhe·a, *Br* **di·ar·rhoe·a** [daɪəˈriːə] diarrea *f*

di·a·ry [ˈdaɪrɪ] *for thoughts* diario *m*; *for appointments* agenda *f*

dice [daɪs] **1** *n* dado *m*; *pl* dados *mpl* **2** *v/t food* cortar en dados

di·chot·o·my [daɪˈkɑːtəmɪ] dicotomía *f*

dic·tate [dɪkˈteɪt] *v/t* dictar

dic·ta·tion [dɪkˈteɪʃn] dictado *m*

dic·ta·tor [dɪkˈteɪtər] POL dictador(a) *m(f)*

dic·ta·to·ri·al [dɪktəˈtɔːrɪəl] *adj* dictatorial

dic·ta·tor·ship [dɪkˈteɪtərʃɪp] dictadura *f*

dic·tion·a·ry [ˈdɪkʃənerɪ] diccionario *m*

did [dɪd] *pret* → **do**

die [daɪ] *v/i* morir; *~ of cancer* / *Aids* morir de cáncer / sida; *I'm dying to know* / *leave* me muero de ganas de saber / marchar

♦ **die away** *v/i of noise* desaparecer

♦ **die down** *v/i of noise* irse apagando; *of storm* amainar; *of fire* irse extinguiendo; *of excitement* calmarse

♦ **die out** *v/i of custom, species* desaparecer

die·sel [ˈdiːzl] *fuel* gasoil *m*, gasóleo *m*

di·et [ˈdaɪət] **1** *n* (*regular food*) dieta *f*; *for losing weight, for health reasons* dieta *f*, régimen *m* **2** *v/i to lose weight* hacer dieta *or* régimen

di·e·ti·tian [daɪəˈtɪʃn] experto(-a) *m(f)* en dietética

dif·fer [ˈdɪfər] *v/i* (*be different*) ser distinto; (*disagree*) discrepar; *the male ~s from the female in ...* el macho se diferencia de la hembra por ...

dif·fe·rence [ˈdɪfrəns] diferencia *f*; *it doesn't make any ~* (*doesn't change anything*) no cambia nada; (*doesn't matter*) da lo mismo

dif·fe·rent [ˈdɪfrənt] *adj* diferente, distinto (*from*, *than* de)

dif·fe·ren·ti·ate [dɪfəˈrenʃɪeɪt] *v/i* diferenciar, distinguir (*between* entre); *~ between* treat differently establecer diferencias entre

dif·fe·rent·ly [ˈdɪfrəntlɪ] *adv* de manera diferente

dif·fi·cult [ˈdɪfɪkəlt] *adj* difícil

dif·fi·cul·ty [ˈdɪfɪkəltɪ] dificultad *f*; *with* ~ con dificultades

dif·fi·dence [ˈdɪfɪdəns] retraimiento *m*

dif·fi·dent [ˈdɪfɪdənt] *adj* retraído

dig [dɪg] *v/t & v/i* (*pret & pp* **dug**) cavar

♦ **dig out** *v/t* (*find*) encontrar

♦ **dig up** *v/t* levantar, cavar; *information* desenterrar

di·gest [daɪˈdʒest] *v/t also fig* digerir

di·gest·i·ble [daɪˈdʒestəbl] *adj food* digerible

di·ges·tion [daɪˈdʒestʃn] digestión *f*

di·ges·tive [daɪˈdʒestɪv] *adj* digestivo

dig·ger [ˈdɪgər] *machine* excavadora *f*

di·git [ˈdɪdʒɪt] (*number*) dígito *m*; *a 4 ~ number* un número de 4 dígitos

di·gi·tal [ˈdɪdʒɪtl] *adj* digital

dig·ni·fied [ˈdɪgnɪfaɪd] *adj* digno

dig·ni·ta·ry [ˈdɪgnɪterɪ] dignatario(-a) *m(f)*

dig·ni·ty [ˈdɪgnɪtɪ] dignidad *f*

di·gress [daɪˈgres] *v/i* divagar, apartarse del tema

di·gres·sion [daɪˈgreʃn] digresión *f*

dike [daɪk] *wall* dique *m*

di·lap·i·dat·ed [dɪˈlæpɪdeɪtɪd] *adj* destartalado

di·late [daɪˈleɪt] *v/i of pupils* dilatarse

di·lem·ma [dɪˈlemə] dilema *m*; *be in*

a ~ estar en un dilema

dil·et·tante [dɪlə'tæntɪ] diletante *m/f*

dil·i·gent ['dɪlɪdʒənt] *adj* diligente

di·lute [daɪ'luːt] *v/t* diluir

dim [dɪm] **1** *adj room* oscuro; *light* tenue; *outline* borroso, confuso; *(stupid)* tonto; *prospects* remoto **2** *v/t* (*pret & pp* **-med**): atenuar; ~ *the headlights* poner las luces cortas **3** *v/i* (*pret & pp* **-med**) *of lights* atenuarse

dime [daɪm] *moneda de diez centavos*

di·men·sion [daɪ'menʃn] dimensión *f*

di·min·ish [dɪ'mɪnɪʃ] *v/t & v/i* disminuir

di·min·u·tive [dɪ'mɪnjutɪv] **1** *n* diminutivo *m* **2** *adj* diminuto

dim·ple ['dɪmpl] hoyuelo *m*

din [dɪn] *n* estruendo *m*

dine [daɪn] *v/i fml* cenar

din·er ['daɪnər] *person* comensal *m/f*; *restaurant* restaurante *m* barato

din·ghy ['dɪŋgɪ] *(small yacht)* bote *m* de vela; *(rubber boat)* lancha *f* neumática

din·gy ['dɪndʒɪ] *adj* sórdido; *(dirty)* sucio

din·ing car ['daɪnɪŋ] RAIL vagón *m* restaurante, coche *m* comedor; **'din·ing room** comedor *m*; **'din·ing ta·ble** mesa *f* de comedor

din·ner ['dɪnər] *in the evening* cena *f*; *at midday* comida *f*; *(formal gathering)* cena *f* de gala

'din·ner guest invitado(-a) *m(f)* a cenar; **'din·ner jack·et** esmoquin *m*; **'din·ner par·ty** cena *f*; **'din·ner serv·ice** vajilla *f*

di·no·saur ['daɪnəsɔːr] dinosaurio *m*

dip [dɪp] **1** *n* (*swim*) baño *m*, zambullida *f*; *for food* salsa *f*; *(slope)* inclinación *f*, pendiente *f*; *(depression)* hondonada *f* **2** *v/t* (*pret & pp* **-ped**) meter; ~ *the headlights* poner las luces cortas **3** *v/i* (*pret & pp* **-ped**) *of road* bajar

di·plo·ma [dɪ'ploumə] diploma *m*

di·plo·ma·cy [dɪ'plouməsɪ] *also fig* diplomacia *f*

di·plo·mat ['dɪpləmæt] diplomáti-

co(-a) *m(f)*

di·plo·mat·ic [dɪplə'mætɪk] *adj also fig* diplomático

dip·lo·mat·i·cal·ly [dɪplə'mætɪklɪ] *adv* de forma diplomática

dip·lo·mat·ic im·mu·ni·ty inmunidad *f* diplomática

dire [daɪr] *adj* terrible; *be in* ~ *need of* necesitar acuciantemente

di·rect [daɪ'rekt] **1** *adj* directo **2** *v/t play, movie, attention* dirigir; *can you* ~ *me to the museum?* ¿me podría indicar cómo se va al museo?

di·rect 'cur·rent ELEC corriente *f* continua

di·rec·tion [dɪ'rekʃn] dirección *f*; ~*s to get to a place* indicaciones *fpl*; *(instructions)* instrucciones *fpl*; *for medicine* posología *f*; *let's ask for* ~*s* preguntemos cómo se va; ~*s for use* modo *m* de empleo

di·rec·tion 'in·di·ca·tor MOT intermitente *m*

di·rec·tive [dɪ'rektɪv] directiva *f*

di·rect·ly [dɪ'rektlɪ] **1** *adv* (*straight*) directamente; *(soon)* pronto; *(immediately)* ahora mismo **2** *conj* en cuanto

di·rec·tor [dɪ'rektər] director(a) *m(f)*

di·rec·to·ry [dɪ'rektərɪ] directorio *m*; TELEC guía *f* telefónica

dirt [dɜːrt] suciedad *f*

'dirt cheap *adj* F tirado F

dirt·y ['dɜːrtɪ] **1** *adj* sucio; *(pornographic)* pornográfico, obsceno **2** *v/t* (*pret & pp* **-ied**) ensuciar

dirt·y 'trick jugarreta *f*; *play a* ~ *on s.o.* hacer una jugarreta a alguien

dis·a·bil·i·ty [dɪsə'bɪlətɪ] discapacidad *f*, minusvalía *f*

dis·a·bled [dɪs'eɪbld] **1** *n*: *the* ~ los discapacitados *mpl* **2** *adj* discapacitado

dis·ad·van·tage [dɪsəd'væntɪdʒ] *(drawback)* desventaja *f*; *be at a* ~ estar en desventaja

dis·ad·van·taged [dɪsəd'væntɪdʒd] *adj* desfavorecido

dis·ad·van·ta·geous [dɪsædvæn-

'teɪdʒəs] *adj* desventajoso, desfavorable

dis·a·gree [dɪsə'griː] *v/i of person* no estar de acuerdo, discrepar; *let's agree to* ~ aceptemos que no nos vamos a poner de acuerdo

♦ **disagree with** *v/t of person* no estar de acuerdo con, discrepar con; *of food* sentar mal; *lobster disagrees with me* la langosta me sienta mal

dis·a·gree·a·ble [dɪsə'griːəbl] *adj* desagradable

dis·a·gree·ment [dɪsə'griːmənt] desacuerdo *m*; (*argument*) discusión *f*

dis·ap·pear [dɪsə'pɪr] *v/i* desaparecer

dis·ap·pear·ance [dɪsə'pɪrəns] desaparición *f*

dis·ap·point [dɪsə'pɔɪnt] *v/t* desilusionar, decepcionar

dis·ap·point·ed [dɪsə'pɔɪntɪd] *adj* desilusionado, decepcionado

dis·ap·point·ing [dɪsə'pɔɪntɪŋ] *adj* decepcionante

dis·ap·point·ment [dɪsə'pɔɪntmənt] desilusión *f*, decepción *f*

dis·ap·prov·al [dɪsə'pruːvl] desaprobación *f*

dis·ap·prove [dɪsə'pruːv] *v/i* desaprobar, estar en contra; ~ *of* desaprobar, estar en contra de

dis·ap·prov·ing [dɪsə'pruːvɪŋ] *adj* desaprobatorio, de desaprobación

dis·ap·prov·ing·ly [dɪsə'pruːvɪŋlɪ] *adv* con desaprobación

dis·arm [dɪs'ɑːrm] **1** *v/t* desarmar **2** *v/i* desarmarse

dis·ar·ma·ment [dɪs'ɑːrməmənt] desarme *m*

dis·arm·ing [dɪs'ɑːrmɪŋ] *adj* cautivador

dis·as·ter [dɪ'zæstər] desastre *m*

di'sas·ter ar·e·a zona *f* catastrófica; *fig* (*person*) desastre *m*

di·sas·trous [dɪ'zæstrəs] *adj* desastroso

dis·band [dɪs'bænd] **1** *v/t* disolver **2** *v/i* disolverse

dis·be·lief [dɪsbə'liːf] incredulidad *f*;

in ~ con incredulidad

disc [dɪsk] (*CD*) compact *m* (disc)

dis·card [dɪ'skɑːrd] *v/t* desechar; *boyfriend* deshacerse de

di·scern [dɪ'sɜːrn] *v/t* distinguir, percibir

di·scern·i·ble [dɪ'sɜːrnəbl] *adj* perceptible

di·scern·ing [dɪ'sɜːrnɪŋ] *adj* entendido, exigente

dis·charge 1 *n* ['dɪstʃɑːrdʒ] *from hospital* alta *f*; *from army* licencia *f* **2** *v/t* [dɪs'tʃɑːrdʒ] *from hospital* dar el alta a; *from army* licenciar; *from job* despedir

di·sci·ple [dɪ'saɪpl] *religious* discípulo *m*

dis·ci·pli·nar·y [dɪsɪ'plɪnərɪ] *adj* disciplinario

dis·ci·pline ['dɪsɪplɪn] **1** *n* disciplina *f* **2** *v/t child, dog* castigar; *employee* sancionar

'disc jock·ey disc jockey *m/f*, *Span* pinchadiscos *m/f inv*

dis·claim [dɪs'kleɪm] *v/t* negar

dis·close [dɪs'klous] *v/t* revelar

dis·clo·sure [dɪs'klouʒər] revelación *f*

dis·co ['dɪskou] discoteca *f*

dis·col·or, *Br* **dis·col·our** [dɪs'kʌlər] *v/i* decolorar

dis·com·fort [dɪs'kʌmfərt] (*pain*) molestia *f*; (*embarrassment*) incomodidad *f*

dis·con·cert [dɪskən'sɜːrt] *v/t* desconcertar

dis·con·cert·ed [dɪskən'sɜːrtɪd] *adj* desconcertado

dis·con·nect [dɪskə'nekt] *v/t* desconectar

dis·con·so·late [dɪs'kɑːnsələt] *adj* desconsolado

dis·con·tent [dɪskən'tent] descontento *m*

dis·con·tent·ed [dɪskən'tentɪd] *adj* descontento

dis·con·tin·ue [dɪskən'tɪnjuː] *v/t product* dejar de producir; *bus, train service* suspender; *magazine* dejar de publicar

dis·cord ['dɪskɔːrd] MUS discordancia *f*; *in relations* discordia *f*

dis·co·theque ['dɪskətek] discoteca *f*

dis·count 1 *n* ['dɪskaʊnt] descuento *m* **2** *v/t* [dɪs'kaʊnt] *goods* descontar; *theory* descartar

dis·cour·age [dɪs'kʌrɪdʒ] *v/t* (*dissuade*) disuadir (**from** de); (*dishearten*) desanimar, desalentar

dis·cour·age·ment [dɪs'kʌrɪdʒmənt] disuasión *f*; (*being disheartened*) desánimo *m*, desaliento *m*

dis·cov·er [dɪ'skʌvər] *v/t* descubrir

dis·cov·er·er [dɪ'skʌvərər] descubridor(a) *m(f)*

dis·cov·e·ry [dɪ'skʌvəri] descubrimiento *m*

dis·cred·it [dɪs'kredɪt] *v/t* desacreditar

di·screet [dɪ'skriːt] *adj* discreto

di·screet·ly [dɪ'skriːtlɪ] *adv* discretamente

di·screp·an·cy [dɪ'skrepənsɪ] discrepancia *f*

di·scre·tion [dɪ'skreʃn] discreción *f*; **at your** ~ a discreción; **use your** ~ usa tu criterio

di·scrim·i·nate [dɪ'skrɪmɪneɪt] *v/i* discriminar (**against** contra); ~ **between** (*distinguish*) distinguir entre

di·scrim·i·nat·ing [dɪ'skrɪmɪneɪtɪŋ] *adj* entendido, exigente

di·scrim·i·na·tion [dɪskrɪmɪ'neɪʃn] *sexual, racial etc* discriminación *f*

dis·cus ['dɪskəs] SP *object* disco *m*; *event* lanzamiento *m* de disco

di·scuss [dɪ'skʌs] *v/t* discutir; *of article* analizar

di·scus·sion [dɪ'skʌʃn] discusión *f*

'dis·cus throw·er lanzador(a) *m(f)* de disco

dis·dain [dɪs'deɪn] *n* desdén *m*

dis·ease [dɪ'ziːz] enfermedad *f*

dis·em·bark [dɪsəm'baːrk] *v/i* desembarcar

dis·en·chant·ed [dɪsən'tʃæntɪd] *adj*: ~ **with** desencantado con

dis·en·gage [dɪsən'geɪdʒ] *v/t* soltar

dis·en·tan·gle [dɪsən'tæŋgl] *v/t* desenredar

dis·fig·ure [dɪs'fɪgər] *v/t* desfigurar

dis·grace [dɪs'greɪs] **1** *n* vergüenza *f*; **it's a** ~! ¡qué vergüenza!; **in** ~ desacreditado **2** *v/t* deshonrar

dis·grace·ful [dɪs'greɪsfəl] *adj behavior, situation* vergonzoso, lamentable

dis·grunt·led [dɪs'grʌntld] *adj* descontento

dis·guise [dɪs'gaɪz] **1** *n* disfraz *m*; **in** ~ disfrazado **2** *v/t voice, handwriting* cambiar; *fear, anxiety* disfrazar; ~ **o.s. as** disfrazarse de; **he was ~d as** iba disfrazado de

dis·gust [dɪs'gʌst] **1** *n* asco *m*, repugnancia *f*; **in** ~ asqueado **2** *v/t* dar asco a, repugnar; **I'm ~ed by ...** me da asco *or* me repugna ...

dis·gust·ing [dɪs'gʌstɪŋ] *adj habit, smell, food* asqueroso, repugnante; **it is** ~ **that ...** da asco que ..., es repugnante que ...

dish [dɪʃ] (*part of meal, container*) plato *m*

'dish·cloth paño *m* de cocina

dis·heart·ened [dɪs'haːrtnd] *adj* desalentado, descorazonado

dis·heart·en·ing [dɪs'haːrtnɪŋ] *adj* descorazonador

di·shev·eled [dɪ'ʃevld] *adj hair, clothes* desaliñado; *person* despeinado

dis·hon·est [dɪs'aːnɪst] *adj* deshonesto

dis·hon·est·y [dɪs'aːnɪstɪ] deshonestidad *f*

dis·hon·or [dɪs'aːnər] *n* deshonra *f*; **bring** ~ **on** deshonrar a

dis·hon·o·ra·ble [dɪs'aːnərəbl] *adj* deshonroso

dis·hon·our *etc Br* → **dishonor** *etc*

'dish·wash·er *person* lavaplatos *m/f inv*; *machine* lavavajillas *m inv*, lavaplatos *m inv*; **'dish·wash·ing liq·uid** lavavajillas *m inv*; **'dish·wa·ter** agua *f* de lavar los platos

dis·il·lu·sion [dɪsɪ'luːʒn] *v/t* desilusionar

dis·il·lu·sion·ment [dɪsɪ'luːʒnmənt]

desilusión f

dis·in·clined [dɪsɪn'klaɪnd] *adj*: **she was ~ to believe him** no estaba inclinada a creerle

dis·in·fect [dɪsɪn'fekt] *v/t* desinfectar

dis·in·fec·tant [dɪsɪn'fektənt] desinfectante *m*

dis·in·her·it [dɪsɪn'herɪt] *v/t* desheredar

dis·in·te·grate [dɪs'ɪntəgreɪt] *v/i* desintegrarse; *of marriage* deshacerse

dis·in·terest·ed [dɪs'ɪntərestɪd] *adj* (*unbiased*) desinteresado

dis·joint·ed [dɪs'dʒɔɪntɪd] *adj* deshilvanado

disk [dɪsk] *also* COMPUT disco *m*; **on ~** en disco

'disk drive COMPUT unidad *f* de disco

disk·ette [dɪs'ket] disquete *m*

dis·like [dɪs'laɪk] **1** *n* antipatía *f* **2** *v/t*: **she ~s being kept waiting** no le gusta que la hagan esperar; **I ~ him** no me gusta

dis·lo·cate ['dɪsləkeɪt] *v/t shoulder* dislocar

dis·lodge [dɪs'lɑːdʒ] *v/t* desplazar, mover de su sitio

dis·loy·al [dɪs'lɔɪəl] *adj* desleal

dis·loy·al·ty [dɪs'lɔɪəltɪ] deslealtad *f*

dis·mal ['dɪzməl] *adj weather* horroroso, espantoso; *news, prospect* negro; *person (sad)* triste; *person (negative)* negativo; *failure* estrepitoso

dis·man·tle [dɪs'mæntl] *v/t* desmantelar

dis·may [dɪs'meɪ] **1** *n* (*alarm*) consternación *f*, (*disappointment*) desánimo *m* **2** *v/t* consternar

dis·miss [dɪs'mɪs] *v/t employee* despedir; *suggestion* rechazar; *idea, possibility* descartar

dis·miss·al [dɪs'mɪsl] *of employee* despido *m*

dis·mount [dɪs'maunt] *v/i* desmontar

dis·o·be·di·ence [dɪsə'biːdɪəns] desobediencia *f*

dis·o·be·di·ent [dɪsə'biːdɪənt] *adj* desobediente

dis·o·bey [dɪsə'beɪ] *v/t* desobedecer

dis·or·der [dɪs'ɔːrdər] (*untidiness*) desorden *m*; (*unrest*) desórdenes *mpl*; MED dolencia *f*

dis·or·der·ly [dɪs'ɔːrdərlɪ] *adj room, desk* desordenado; *mob* alborotado

dis·or·gan·ized [dɪs'ɔːrgənaɪzd] *adj* desorganizado

dis·o·ri·ent·ed [dɪs'ɔːrɪəntɪd] *adj* desorientado

dis·own [dɪs'oun] *v/t* repudiar, renegar de

dis·par·ag·ing [dɪ'spærɪdʒɪŋ] *adj* despreciativo

dis·par·i·ty [dɪ'spærətɪ] disparidad *f*

dis·pas·sion·ate [dɪ'spæʃənət] *adj* (*objective*) desapasionado

dis·patch [dɪ'spætʃ] *v/t* (*send*) enviar

dis·pen·sa·ry [dɪ'spensərɪ] *in pharmacy* dispensario *m*

♦ **dis·pense with** [dɪ'spens] *v/t* prescindir de

dis·perse [dɪ'spɜːrs] **1** *v/t* dispersar **2** *v/i of crowd* dispersarse; *of mist* disiparse

dis·pir·it·ed [dɪ'spɪrɪtɪd] *adj* desalentado, abatido

dis·place [dɪs'pleɪs] *v/t* (*supplant*) sustituir

di·splay [dɪ'spleɪ] **1** *n* muestra *f*; *in store window* objetos *mpl* expuestos; COMPUT pantalla *f*; **be on ~** estar expuesto **2** *v/t emotion* mostrar; *at exhibition, for sale* exponer; COMPUT visualizar

di·splay cab·i·net *in museum, shop* vitrina *f*

dis·please [dɪs'pliːz] *v/t* desagradar, disgustar

dis·plea·sure [dɪs'pleʒər] desagrado *m*, disgusto *m*

dis·po·sa·ble [dɪ'spouzəbl] *adj* desechable; **~ income** ingreso(s) *m(pl)* disponible(s)

dis·pos·al [dɪ'spouzl] eliminación *f*; **I am at your ~** estoy a su disposición; **put sth at s.o.'s ~** poner algo a disposición de alguien

♦ **dis·pose of** [dɪ'spouz] *v/t* (*get rid*

of) deshacerse de

dis·posed [dɪsˈpəʊzd] *adj*: **be ~ to do sth** (*willing*) estar dispuesto a hacer algo; **be well ~ toward** estar bien dispuesto hacia

dis·po·si·tion [dɪspəˈzɪʃn] (*nature*) carácter *m*

dis·pro·por·tion·ate [dɪsprəˈpɔːrʃənət] *adj* desproporcionado

dis·prove [dɪsˈpruːv] *v/t* refutar

di·spute [dɪˈspjuːt] **1** *n* disputa *f*; *industrial* conflicto *m* laboral **2** *v/t* discutir; (*fight over*) disputarse; **I don't ~ that** eso no lo discuto

dis·qual·i·fi·ca·tion [dɪskwɑːlɪfɪˈkeɪʃn] descalificación *f*

dis·qual·i·fy [dɪsˈkwɑːlɪfaɪ] *v/t* (*pret & pp* **-ied**) descalificar

dis·re·gard [dɪsrəˈgɑːrd] **1** *n* indiferencia *f* **2** *v/t* no tener en cuenta

dis·re·pair [dɪsrəˈper]: *in a state of ~* deteriorado

dis·rep·u·ta·ble [dɪsˈrepjʊtəbl] *adj* poco respetable; *area* de mala reputación

dis·re·spect [dɪsrəˈspekt] falta *f* de respeto

dis·re·spect·ful [dɪsrəˈspektfəl] *adj* irrespetuoso

dis·rupt [dɪsˈrʌpt] *v/t train service* trastornar, alterar; *meeting, class* interrumpir

dis·rup·tion [dɪsˈrʌpʃn] *of train service* alteración *f*; *of meeting, class* interrupción *f*

dis·rup·tive [dɪsˈrʌptɪv] *adj* perjudicial; *he's very ~ in class* causa muchos problemas en clase

dis·sat·is·fac·tion [dɪssætɪsˈfækʃn] insatisfacción *f*

dis·sat·is·fied [dɪsˈsætɪsfaɪd] *adj* insatisfecho

dis·sen·sion [dɪsˈsenʃn] disensión *f*

dis·sent [dɪˈsent] **1** *n* discrepancia *f* **2** *v/i*: *~ from* disentir de

dis·si·dent [ˈdɪsɪdənt] *n* disidente *m/f*

dis·sim·i·lar [dɪsˈsɪmɪlər] *adj* distinto

dis·so·ci·ate [dɪˈsəʊʃɪeɪt] *v/t* disociar; *~ o.s. from* disociarse de

dis·so·lute [ˈdɪsəluːt] *adj* disoluto

dis·so·lu·tion [dɪsəluːʃn] POL disolución *f*

dis·solve [dɪˈzɑːlv] **1** *v/t substance* disolver **2** *v/i of substance* disolverse

dis·suade [dɪˈsweɪd] *v/t* disuadir; *~ s.o. from doing sth* disuadir a alguien de hacer algo

dis·tance [ˈdɪstəns] **1** *n* distancia *f*; *in the ~* en la lejanía **2** *v/t* distanciar; *~ o.s. from* distanciarse de

dis·tant [ˈdɪstənt] *adj place, time, relative* distante, lejano; *fig* (*aloof*) distante

dis·taste [dɪsˈteɪst] desagrado *m*

dis·taste·ful [dɪsˈteɪstfəl] *adj* desagradable

dis·till·er·y [dɪsˈtɪlərɪ] destilería *f*

dis·tinct [dɪˈstɪŋkt] *adj* (*clear*) claro; (*different*) distinto; *as ~ from* a diferencia de

dis·tinc·tion [dɪˈstɪŋkʃn] (*differentiation*) distinción *f*; *hotel/product of ~* un hotel/producto destacado

dis·tinc·tive [dɪˈstɪŋktɪv] *adj* característico

dis·tinct·ly [dɪˈstɪŋktlɪ] *adv* claramente, con claridad; (*decidedly*) verdaderamente

dis·tin·guish [dɪˈstɪŋgwɪʃ] *v/t* distinguir (*between* entre)

dis·tin·guished [dɪˈstɪŋgwɪʃt] *adj* distinguido

dis·tort [dɪˈstɔːrt] *v/t* distorsionar

dis·tract [dɪˈstrækt] *v/t* distraer

dis·trac·tion [dɪˈstrækʃn] distracción *f*; *drive s.o. to ~* sacar a alguien de quicio

dis·traught [dɪˈstrɔːt] *adj* angustiado, consternado

dis·tress [dɪˈstres] **1** *n* sufrimiento *m*; *in ~ of ship, aircraft* en peligro **2** *v/t* (*upset*) angustiar

dis·tress·ing [dɪˈstresɪŋ] *adj* angustiante

dis'tress sig·nal señal *m* de socorro

dis·trib·ute [dɪˈstrɪbjuːt] *v/t* distribuir, repartir; COM distribuir

dis·tri·bu·tion [dɪstrɪˈbjuːʃn] distribución *f*

dis·tri·bu·tion ar·range·ment COM

acuerdo *m* de distribución

dis·trib·u·tor [dɪsˈtrɪbjuːtər] COM distribuidor(a) *m(f)*

dis·trict [ˈdɪstrɪkt] *(area)* zona *f*; *(neighborhood)* barrio *m*

dis·trict at·tor·ney fiscal *m/f* del distrito

dis·trust [dɪsˈtrʌst] **1** *n* desconfianza *f* **2** *v/t* desconfiar de

dis·turb [dɪsˈtɜːrb] *v/t (interrupt)* molestar; *(upset)* preocupar; **do not ~** no molestar

dis·turb·ance [dɪsˈtɜːrbəns] *(interruption)* molestia *f*; **~s** *(civil unrest)* disturbios *mpl*

dis·turbed [dɪsˈtɜːrbd] *adj (concerned, worried)* preocupado, inquieto; *mentally* perturbado

dis·turb·ing [dɪsˈtɜːrbɪŋ] *adj (worrying)* inquietante; **you may find some scenes ~** algunas de las escenas pueden herir la sensibilidad del espectador

dis·used [dɪsˈjuːzd] *adj* abandonado

ditch [dɪtʃ] **1** *n* zanja *f* **2** *v/t* F *(get rid of)* deshacerse de; *boyfriend* plantar F; *plan* abandonar

dith·er [ˈdɪðər] *v/i* vacilar

dive [daɪv] **1** *n* salto *m* de cabeza; *underwater* inmersión *f*; *of plane* descenso *m* en picado; F *bar etc* antro *m* F; **take a ~** F *of dollar etc* desplomarse **2** *v/i (pret also dove)* tirarse de cabeza; *underwater* bucear; *of plane* descender en picado

div·er [ˈdaɪvər] *off board* saltador(a) *m(f)* de trampolín; *underwater* buceador(a) *m(f)*

di·verge [daɪˈvɜːrdʒ] *v/i* bifurcarse

di·verse [daɪˈvɜːrs] *adj* diverso

di·ver·si·fi·ca·tion [daɪvɜːrsɪfɪˈkeɪʃn] COM diversificación *f*

di·ver·si·fy [daɪˈvɜːrsɪfaɪ] *v/i (pret & pp -ied)* COM diversificarse

di·ver·sion [daɪˈvɜːrʃn] *for traffic* desvío *m*; *to distract attention* distracción *f*

di·ver·si·ty [daɪˈvɜːrsətɪ] diversidad *f*

di·vert [daɪˈvɜːrt] *v/t traffic, attention* desviar

di·vest [daɪˈvest] *v/t*: **~ s.o. of sth** despojar a alguien de algo

di·vide [dɪˈvaɪd] *v/t also fig* dividir; **~ 16 by 4** dividir 16 entre 4

div·i·dend [ˈdɪvɪdend] FIN dividendo *m*; **pay ~s** *fig* resultar beneficioso

di·vine [dɪˈvaɪn] *adj also* F divino

div·ing [ˈdaɪvɪŋ] *from board* salto *m* de trampolín; *(scuba ~)* buceo *m*, submarinismo *m*

'div·ing board trampolín *m*

di·vis·i·ble [dɪˈvɪzəbl] *adj* divisible

di·vi·sion [dɪˈvɪʒn] división *f*

di·vorce [dɪˈvɔːrs] **1** *n* divorcio *m*; **get a ~** divorciarse **2** *v/t* divorciarse de; **get ~d** divorciarse **3** *v/i* divorciarse

di·vorced [dɪˈvɔːrst] *adj* divorciado

di·vor·cee [dɪvɔːrˈsiː] divorciado(-a) *m(f)*

di·vulge [daɪˈvʌldʒ] *v/t* divulgar, dar a conocer

DIY [diːaɪˈwaɪ] *abbr (= do it yourself)* bricolaje *m*

DI'Y store tienda *f* de bricolaje

diz·zi·ness [ˈdɪzɪnɪs] mareo *m*

diz·zy [ˈdɪzɪ] *adj* mareado; **feel ~** estar mareado

DJ [ˈdiːdʒeɪ] *abbr (= disc jockey)* disc jockey *m/f*, *Span* pinchadiscos *m/f inv*; *(= dinner jacket)* esmoquin *m*

DNA [diːenˈeɪ] *abbr (= deoxyribonucleic acid)* AND *m (=* ácido *m* desoxirribonucleico)

do [duː] **1** *v/t (pret did, pp done)* hacer; *100 mph etc* ir a; **~ one's hair** arreglarse el pelo; **what are you ~ing tonight?** ¿qué vas a hacer esta noche?; **I don't know what to ~** no sé qué hacer; **~ it right now!** hazlo ahora mismo; **have one's hair done** ir al peluquero **2** *v/i (pret did, pp done) (be suitable, enough)*: **that'll ~ nicely** eso bastará; **that will ~!** ¡ya vale!; **~ well** *of business* ir bien; **he's ~ing well** le van bien las cosas; **well done!** *(congratulations!)* ¡bien hecho!; **how ~ you ~?** encantado de conocerle **3** v/aux: **~ you know him?** ¿lo conoces?; **I don't know** no sé; **~ you like Des Moines? – yes I ~** ¿te gusta Des Moines? – sí; **he works hard, doesn't he?** trabaja mucho, ¿verdad?; **don't you believe me?** ¿no me crees?; **you ~ believe me, don't you?** me crees, ¿verdad?; **you don't know the answer, ~ you? – no I don't** no sabes la respuesta, ¿no es así? – no, no la sé

♦ **do away with** v/t (*abolish*) abolir

♦ **do in** v/t F (*exhaust*) machacar F; **I'm done in** estoy hecho polvo F

♦ **do out of** v/t: **do s.o. out of sth** timar alguien a algo F

♦ **do up** v/t (*renovate*) renovar; *buttons, coat* abrocharse; *laces* atarse

♦ **do with** v/t: **I could do with ...** no me vendría mal ...; **he won't have anything to do with it** (*won't get involved*) no quiere saber nada de ello

♦ **do without 1** v/i: **you'll have to do without** te las tendrás que arreglar **2** v/t pasar sin

do·cile ['dousəl] *adj* dócil

dock¹ [dɑːk] **1** *n* NAUT muelle *m* **2** v/i *of ship* atracar; *of spaceship* acoplarse

dock² [dɑːk] *n* LAW banquillo *m* (de los acusados)

'**dock·yard** Br astillero *m*

doc·tor ['dɑːktər] *n* MED médico *m*; *form of address* doctor *m*

doc·tor·ate ['dɑːktərət] doctorado *m*

doc·trine ['dɑːktrɪn] doctrina *f*

doc·u·dra·ma ['dɑːkjudrɑːmə] docudrama *f*

doc·u·ment ['dɑːkjumənt] *n* documento *m*

doc·u·men·ta·ry [dɑːkjuˈmentərɪ] *n program* documental *m*

doc·u·men·ta·tion [dɑːkjumenˈteɪʃn] documentación *f*

dodge [dɑːdʒ] v/t *blow, person* esquivar; *issue, question* eludir

doe [dou] *deer* cierva *f*

dog [dɑːg] **1** *n* perro(-a) *m(f)* **2** v/t

(*pret & pp* **-ged**) *of bad luck* perseguir

'**dog catch·er** perrero(-a) *m(f)*

dog-eared ['dɑːgɪrd] *adj book* sobado, con las esquinas dobladas

dog·ged ['dɑːgɪd] *adj* tenaz

dog·gie ['dɑːgɪ] *in children's language* perrito *m*

dog·gy bag ['dɑːgɪbæg] *bolsa para las sobras de la comida*

'**dog·house: be in the ~** F haber caído en desgracia

dog·ma ['dɑːgmə] dogma *m*

dog·mat·ic [dɑːgˈmætɪk] *adj* dogmático

do-good·er ['duːgudər] *pej* buen(a) samaritano(-a) *m(f)*

'**dog tag** MIL chapa *f* de identificación

'**dog-tired** *adj* F hecho polvo F

do-it-your·self [duːɪtjərˈself] bricolaje *m*

dol·drums ['douldrəmz]: **be in the ~** *of economy* estar en un bache; *of person* estar deprimido

♦ **dole out** v/t repartir

doll [dɑːl] *toy* muñeca *f*; F *woman* muñeca *f* F

♦ **doll up** v/t: **get dolled up** emperifollarse

dol·lar ['dɑːlər] dólar *m*

dol·lop ['dɑːləp] *n* F cucharada *f*

dol·phin ['dɑːlfɪn] delfín *m*

dome [doum] *of building* cúpula *f*

do·mes·tic [dəˈmestɪk] **1** *adj chores* doméstico, del hogar; *news, policy* nacional **2** *n* empleado(-a) *m(f)* del hogar

do·mes·tic 'an·i·mal animal *m* doméstico

do·mes·ti·cate [dəˈmestɪkeɪt] v/t *animal* domesticar; **be ~d** *of person* estar domesticado

do'mes·tic flight vuelo *m* nacional

dom·i·nant ['dɑːmɪnənt] *adj* dominante

dom·i·nate ['dɑːmɪneɪt] v/t dominar

dom·i·na·tion [dɑːmɪˈneɪʃn] dominación *f*

dom·i·neer·ing [dɑːmɪˈnɪrɪŋ] *adj* dominante

dom·i·no ['dɑːmɪnoʊ] ficha f de dominó; *play ~es* jugar al dominó

do·nate [doʊ'neɪt] v/t donar

do·na·tion [doʊ'neɪʃn] donación f, donativo m; MED donación f

done [dʌn] pp → **do**

don·key ['dɑːŋkɪ] burro m

do·nor ['doʊnər] *of money*, MED donante m/f

do·nut ['doʊnʌt] dónut m

doo·dle ['duːdl] v/i garabatear

doom [duːm] n (*fate*) destino m; (*ruin*) fatalidad f

doomed [duːmd] adj project condenado al fracaso; *we are ~* (*bound to fail*) estamos condenados al fracaso; (*going to die*) vamos a morir

door [dɔːr] puerta f; *there's someone at the ~* hay alguien en la puerta

'**door·bell** timbre m; '**door·knob** pomo m; '**door·man** portero m; '**door·mat** felpudo m; '**door·step** umbral m; '**door·way** puerta f

dope [doʊp] **1** n (*drugs*) droga f; F (*idiot*) lelo(-a) m(f); F (*information*) información f **2** v/t drogar

dor·mant ['dɔːrmənt] adj plant aletargado; *volcano* inactivo

dor·mi·to·ry ['dɔːrmɪtɔːrɪ] dormitorio m (colectivo); (*hall of residence*) residencia f de estudiantes

dos·age ['doʊsɪdʒ] dosis f inv

dose [doʊs] n dosis f inv

dot [dɑːt] n punto m; *on the ~* (*exactly*) en punto

◆ **dote** on [doʊt] v/t adorar a

dot.com (**com·pa·ny**) [dɑːt'kɑːm] empresa f punto.com

dot·ing ['doʊtɪŋ] adj: *my ~ aunt* mi tía, que tanto me adora

dot·ted line ['dɑːtɪd] línea f de puntos

dou·ble ['dʌbl] **1** n person doble m/f; room habitación f doble **2** adj doble; *inflation is now in ~ figures* la inflación ha superado ya el 10% **3** adv: *they offered me ~ what the others did* me ofrecieron el doble que la otra gente **4** v/t doblar, duplicar **5** v/i doblarse, duplicarse; *it ~s*

as ... hace también de ...

◆ **double back** v/i (*go back*) volver sobre sus pasos

◆ **double up** v/i in pain doblarse; (*share*) compartir habitación

doub·le-'bass contrabajo m; **doub·le 'bed** cama f de matrimonio; **doub·le-breast·ed** [dʌbl-'brestɪd] adj cruzado; **doub·le-'check** v/t & v/i volver a comprobar; **doub·le 'chin** papada f; **doub·le'cross** v/t engañar, traicionar; **doub·le 'glaz·ing** doble acristalamiento m; **doub·le'park** v/i aparcar en doble fila; '**doub·le-quick** adj: *in ~ time* muy rápidamente; '**doub·le room** habitación f doble

doub·les ['dʌblz] in tennis dobles mpl

doubt [daʊt] **1** n duda f; (*uncertainty*) dudas fpl; *be in ~* ser incierto; *not be in ~* estar claro; *no ~* (*probably*) sin duda **2** v/t dudar; *we never ~ed you* nunca dudamos de ti

doubt·ful ['daʊtfəl] adj remark, look dubitativo; *be ~ of person* tener dudas; *it is ~ whether ...* es dudoso que ...

doubt·ful·ly ['daʊtfəlɪ] adv lleno de dudas

doubt·less ['daʊtlɪs] adv sin duda, indudablemente

dough [doʊ] masa f; F (*money*) Span pasta f F, *L.Am.* plata f F

dove[1] [dʌv] also fig paloma f

dove[2] [doʊv] pret → **dive**

dow·dy ['daʊdɪ] adj poco elegante

Dow Jones Av·er·age [daʊdʒoʊnz-'ævərɪdʒ] índice m Dow Jones

down[1] [daʊn] n (*feathers*) plumón m

down[2] [daʊn] **1** adv (*downward*) (hacia) abajo; *pull the shade ~* baja la persiana; *put it ~ on the table* ponlo en la mesa; *when the leaves come ~* cuando se caen las hojas; *cut ~ a tree* cortar un árbol; *she was ~ on her knees* estaba arrodillada; *the plane was shot ~* el avión fue abatido; *~ there* allá abajo; *fall ~* caerse; *die ~* amainar; *$200*

~ (*as deposit*) una entrada de 200 dólares; ~ **south** hacia el sur; **be ~** *of price, rate* haber bajado; *of numbers, amount* haber descendido; (*not working*) no funcionar; F (*depressed*) estar deprimido *or* con la depre **2** *prep*: **run ~ the stairs** bajar las escaleras corriendo; **the lava rolled ~ the hill** la lava descendía por la colina; **walk ~ the street** andar por la calle; **the store is halfway ~ Baker Street** la tienda está a mitad de Baker Street; **~ the corridor** por el pasillo **3** *v/t* (*swallow*) tragar; (*destroy*) derribar

'**down-and-out** *n* vagabundo(-a) *m(f)*; '**down-cast** *adj* deprimido; '**down-fall** caída *f*; **be s.o.'s ~** *of alcohol etc* ser la perdición de alguien; '**downgrade** *v/t* degradar; **the hurricane has been ~d to a storm** el huracán ha sido reducido a la categoría de tormenta; **down-heart-ed** [daʊnˈhɑːrtɪd] *adj* abatido; **down'hill** *adv* cuesta abajo; **go ~** *fig* ir cuesta abajo; '**down-hill ski-ing** descenso *m*; '**down-load** *v/t* COMPUT descargar, bajar; '**down-mark-et** *adj* barato; '**down pay-ment** entrada *f*; **make a ~ on sth** pagar la entrada de algo; '**down-play** *v/t* quitar importancia a; '**down-pour** chaparrón *m*, aguacero *m*; '**down-right 1** *adj* lie evidente; *idiot* completo **2** *adv* *dangerous* extremadamente; *stupid* completamente; '**down-side** (*disadvantage*) desventaja *f*, inconveniente *m*; '**down-size 1** *v/t* car reducir el tamaño de; *company* reajustar la plantilla de **2** *v/i* of *company* reajustar la plantilla; '**down-stairs 1** *adj* del piso de abajo; **my ~ neighbors** los vecinos de abajo **2** *adv*: **the kitchen is ~** la cocina está en el piso de abajo; **I ran ~** bajé corriendo; **down-to-'earth** *adj* *approach, person* práctico, realista; '**down-town 1** *n* centro *m* **2** *adj* del centro **2** *adv*: **I'm going ~** voy al centro; **he lives ~** vive en el

centro; '**down-turn** *in economy* bajón *m*

'**down-ward** [ˈdaʊnwərd] **1** *adj* descendente **2** *adv* a la baja

doze [doʊz] **1** *n* cabezada *f*, sueño *m* **2** *v/i* echar una cabezada
♦ **doze off** *v/i* quedarse dormido
doz-en [ˈdʌzn] docena *f*; **~s of** F montonadas de F

drab [dræb] *adj* gris

draft [dræft] **1** *n of air* corriente *f*; *of document* borrador *m*; MIL reclutamiento *m*; **~** (*beer*), **beer on ~** cerveza *f* de barril **2** *v/t document* redactar un borrador de; MIL reclutar
'**draft dodg-er** prófugo(-a) *m(f)*
draft-ee [dræftˈiː] recluta *m/f*
drafts-man [ˈdræftsmən] delineante *m/f*
draft-y [ˈdræftɪ] *adj*: **it's ~ here** hace mucha corriente aquí

drag [dræg] **1** *n*: **it's a ~ having to ...** F es un latazo tener que ...F; **he's a ~ F** es un peñazo F; **the main ~ F** la calle principal; **in ~** vestido de mujer **2** *v/t* (*pret & pp -ged*) (*pull*) arrastrar; (*search*) dragar; **~ s.o. into sth** (*involve*) meter a alguien en algo; **~ sth out of s.o.** (*get information from*) arrancar algo de alguien **3** *v/i* (*pret & pp -ged*) of time pasar despacio; *of show, movie* ser pesado
♦ **drag away** *v/t*: **drag o.s. away from the TV** despegarse de la TV
♦ **drag in** *v/t into conversation* introducir
♦ **drag on** *v/i* (*last long time*) alargarse
♦ **drag out** *v/t* (*prolong*) alargar
♦ **drag up** *v/t* F (*mention*) sacar a relucir
drag-on [ˈdrægn] dragón *m*; *fig* bruja *f*

drain [dreɪn] **1** *n pipe* sumidero *m*, desagüe *m*; *under street* alcantarilla *f*; **a ~ on resources** una sangría en los recursos **2** *v/t water, vegetables* escurrir; *land* drenar; *glass, tank, oil* vaciar; *person* agotar **3** *v/i of dishes* escurrir

D

◆**drain away** *v/i of liquid* irse

◆**drain off** *v/t water* escurrir

drain·age ['dreɪnɪdʒ] *(drains)* desagües *mpl*; *of water from soil* drenaje *m*

'**drain·pipe** tubo *m* de desagüe

dra·ma ['drɑːmə] *(art form)* drama *m*, teatro *m*; *(excitement)* dramatismo *m*; *(play: on TV)* drama *m*, obra *f* de teatro

dra·mat·ic [drə'mætɪk] *adj* dramático; *scenery* espectacular

dra·mat·i·cal·ly [drə'mætɪklɪ] *adv say* con dramatismo, de manera dramática; *decline, rise, change etc* espectacularmente

dram·a·tist ['dræmətɪst] dramaturgo(-a) *m(f)*

dram·a·ti·za·tion [dræmətaɪ'zeɪʃn] *(play)* dramatización *f*

dram·a·tize ['dræmətaɪz] *v/t also fig* dramatizar

drank [dræŋk] *pret* → **drink**

drape [dreɪp] *v/t cloth* cubrir; **~d in** *(covered with)* cubierto con

drap·er·y ['dreɪpərɪ] ropajes *mpl*

drapes [dreɪps] *npl* cortinas *fpl*

dras·tic ['dræstɪk] *adj* drástico

draught *Br* → **draft**

draw [drɔː] **1** *n in match, competition* empate *m*; *in lottery* sorteo *m*; *(attraction)* atracción *f* **2** *v/t (pret drew, pp drawn) picture, map* dibujar; *cart* tirar de; *curtain* correr; *in lottery* sortear; *gun, knife* sacar; *(attract)* atraer; *(lead)* llevar; *from bank account* sacar, retirar **3** *v/i (pret drew, pp drawn)* dibujar; *in match, competition* empatar; **~ near** acercarse

◆**draw back 1** *v/i (recoil)* echarse atrás **2** *v/t (pull back)* retirar

◆**draw on 1** *v/i (approach)* aproximarse **2** *v/t (make use of)* utilizar

◆**draw out** *v/t wallet, money from bank* sacar

◆**draw up** *v/t document* redactar; *chair* acercar **2** *v/i of vehicle* parar

'**draw·back** desventaja *f*, inconveniente *m*

draw·er[1] [drɔːr] *of desk etc* cajón *m*

draw·er[2] [drɔːr]: *she's a good* ~ dibuja muy bien

draw·ing ['drɔːɪŋ] dibujo *m*

'**draw·ing board** tablero *m* de dibujo; *go back to the* ~ *fig* volver a empezar otra vez

'**draw·ing pin** *Br* chincheta *f*

drawl [drɔːl] *n* acento *m* arrastrado

drawn [drɔːn] *pp* → **draw**

dread [dred] *v/t* tener pavor a; *I* ~ *him ever finding out* me da pavor pensar que lo pueda llegar a descubrir; *I* ~ *going to the dentist* me da pánico ir al dentista

dread·ful ['dredfəl] *adj* horrible, espantoso; *it's a* ~ *pity you won't be there* es una auténtica pena que no vayas a estar ahí

dread·ful·ly ['dredfəlɪ] *adv* F *(extremely)* terriblemente, espantosamente F; *behave* fatal

dream [driːm] **1** *n* sueño *m* **2** *adj*: *win your* ~ *house!* ¡gane la casa de sus sueños! **3** *v/t* soñar; *(day~)* soñar (despierto) **4** *v/i* soñar; *(day~)* soñar (despierto); *I* ~*t about you last night* anoche soñé contigo

◆**dream up** *v/t* inventar

dream·er ['driːmər] *(day~)* soñador(a) *m(f)*

dream·y ['driːmɪ] *adj voice, look* soñador

drear·y ['drɪrɪ] *adj* triste, deprimente

dredge [dredʒ] *v/t harbor, canal* dragar

◆**dredge up** *v/t fig* sacar a relucir

dregs [dregz] *npl of coffee* posos *mpl*; *the* ~ *of society* la escoria de la sociedad

drench [drentʃ] *v/t* empapar; *get* ~*ed* empaparse

dress [dres] **1** *n for woman* vestido *m*; *(clothing)* traje *m*; *he has no* ~ *sense* no sabe vestir(se); *the company has a* ~ *code* la compañía tiene unas normas sobre la ropa que deben llevar los empleados **2** *v/t person* vestir; *wound* vendar; *get* ~*ed* vestirse **3** *v/i (get* ~*ed)* vestirse; *well, in black etc* vestir(se) (*in* de)

♦**dress up** *v/i* arreglarse, vestirse elegante; (*wear a disguise*) disfrazarse (*as* de)

'**dress cir·cle** piso *m* principal

dress·er ['dresər] (*dressing table*) tocador *f*; *in kitchen* aparador *m*

dress·ing ['dresɪŋ] *for salad* aliño *m*, *Span* arreglo *m*; *for wound* vendaje *m*

dress·ing 'down regaño *m*; *give s.o. a ~* regañar a alguien; '**dress·ing room** *in theater* camerino *m*; '**dress·ing ta·ble** tocador *f*

'**dress·mak·er** modisto(-a) *m(f)*

'**dress re·hears·al** ensayo *m* general

dress·y ['dresɪ] *adj* F elegante

drew [dru:] *pret* → *draw*

drib·ble ['drɪbl] *v/i of person, baby* babear; *of water* gotear; SP driblar

dried [draɪd] *adj fruit etc* seco

dri·er [draɪr] → *dryer*

drift [drɪft] **1** *n of snow* ventisquero *m* **2** *v/i of snow* amontonarse; *of ship* ir a la deriva; (*go off course*) desviarse del rumbo; (*of person*) vagar

♦**drift apart** *v/i of couple* distanciarse

drift·er ['drɪftər] vagabundo(-a) *m(f)*

drill [drɪl] **1** *n tool* taladro *m*; *exercise* simulacro *m*; MIL instrucción *f* **2** *v/t hole* taladrar, perforar **3** *v/i for oil* hacer perforaciones; MIL entrenarse

dril·ling rig ['drɪlɪŋrɪg] (*platform*) plataforma *f* petrolífera

dri·ly ['draɪlɪ] *adv remark* secamente, lacónicamente

drink [drɪŋk] **1** *n* bebida *f*; *a ~ of ...* un vaso de ...; *go for a ~* ir a tomar algo **2** *v/t* (*pret drank, pp drunk*) beber **3** *v/i* (*pret drank, pp drunk*) beber, *L.Am.* tomar; *I don't ~* no bebo

♦**drink up 1** *v/i* (*finish drink*) acabarse la bebida **2** *v/t* (*drink completely*) beberse todo

drink·a·ble ['drɪŋkəbl] *adj* potable

drink 'driv·ing conducción *f* bajo los efectos del alcohol

drink·er ['drɪŋkər] bebedor(a) *m(f)*

drink·ing ['drɪŋkɪŋ]: *I'm worried about his ~* me preocupa que beba tanto; *a ~ problem* un problema con la bebida

'**drink·ing wa·ter** agua *f* potable

'**drinks ma·chine** máquina *f* expendedora de bebidas

drip [drɪp] **1** *n* gota *f*; MED gotero *m*, suero *m* **2** *v/i* (*pret & pp -ped*) gotear

'**drip-dry** *adj* que no necesita planchado

drip·ping ['drɪpɪŋ] *adv*: *~ wet* empapado

drive [draɪv] **1** *n outing* vuelta *f*, paseo *m* (en coche); (*energy*) energía *f*; COMPUT unidad *f*; (*campaign*) campaña *f*; *it's a short ~ from the station* está a poca distancia en coche de la estación; *with left- / right-hand ~* MOT con el volante a la izquierda / a la derecha **2** *v/t* (*pret drove, pp driven*) *vehicle* conducir, *L.Am.* manejar; (*own*) tener; (*take in car*) llevar (en coche); TECH impulsar; *that noise / he is driving me mad* ese ruido / él me está volviendo loco **3** *v/i* (*pret drove, pp driven*) conducir, *L.Am.* manejar; *don't drink and ~* si bebes, no conduzcas; *I ~ to work* voy al trabajo en coche

♦**drive at** *v/t*: *what are you driving at?* ¿qué insinuas?

♦**drive away 1** *v/t* llevarse en un coche; (*chase off*) ahuyentar **2** *v/i* marcharse

♦**drive in** *v/t nail* remachar

♦**drive off** → *drive away*

'**drive-in** *n* (*movie theater*) autocine *m*

driv·el ['drɪvl] *n* tonterías *fpl*

driv·en ['drɪvn] *pp* → *drive*

driv·er ['draɪvər] conductor(a) *m(f)*; COMPUT controlador *m*

'**driv·er's li·cense** carné *m* de conducir

drive-thru ['draɪvθru:] *restaurante /*

banco etc en el que se atiende al cliente sin que salga del coche

'**drive·way** camino *m* de entrada

driv·ing ['draɪvɪŋ] **1** *n* conducción *f*; *his ~ is appalling* conduce *or L.Am.* maneja fatal **2** *adj* rain torrencial

driv·ing 'force fuerza *f* motriz; '**driv·ing in·struc·tor** profesor(a) *m(f)* de autoescuela; '**driv·ing les·son** clase *f* de conducir; '**driv·ing li·cence** *Br* carné *m* de conducir; '**driv·ing school** autoescuela *f*; '**driv·ing test** examen *m* de conducir *or L.Am.* manejar

driz·zle ['drɪzl] **1** *n* llovizna *f* **2** *v/i* lloviznar

drone [droʊn] *n noise* zumbido *m*

droop [druːp] *v/i of plant* marchitarse; *her shoulders ~ed* se encorvó

drop [drɑːp] **1** *n* gota *f*; *in price, temperature* caída *f* **2** *v/t* (*pret & pp -ped*) *object* dejar caer; *person from car* dejar; *person from team* excluir; (*stop seeing*) abandonar; *charges, demand etc* retirar; (*give up*) dejar; *~ a line to* mandar unas líneas a **3** *v/i* (*pret & pp -ped*) caer, caerse; (*decline*) caer; *of wind* amainar

♦ **drop in** *v/i* (*visit*) pasar a visitar

♦ **drop off 1** *v/t person* dejar; (*deliver*) llevar **2** *v/i* (*fall asleep*) dormirse; (*decline*) disminuir

♦ **drop out** *v/i* (*withdraw*) retirarse; *drop out of school* abandonar el colegio

'**drop·out** (*from school*) alumno que ha abandonado los estudios; *from society* marginado(-a) *m(f)*

drops [drɑːps] *npl for eyes* gotas *fpl*

drought [draʊt] sequía *f*

drove [droʊv] *pret* → **drive**

drown [draʊn] **1** *v/i* ahogarse **2** *v/t person, sound* ahogar; *be ~ed* ahogarse

drow·sy ['draʊzi] *adj* soñoliento(-a)

drudg·e·ry ['drʌdʒərɪ] *the job is sheer ~* el trabajo es terriblemente pesado

drug [drʌg] **1** *n* MED, *illegal* droga *f*; *be on ~s* drogarse **2** *v/t* (*pret & pp -ged*) drogar

'**drug ad·dict** drogadicto(-a) *m(f)*

'**drug deal·er** traficante *m/f* (de drogas)

drug·gist ['drʌgɪst] farmacéutico(-a) *m(f)*

'**drug·store** *tienda en la que se venden medicinas, cosméticos, periódicos y que a veces tiene un bar*

'**drug traf·fick·ing** tráfico *m* de drogas

drum [drʌm] *n* MUS tambor *m*; *container* barril *m*

♦ **drum into** *v/t* (*pret & pp -med*) *drum sth into s.o.* meter algo en la cabeza de alguien

♦ **drum up** *v/t*: *drum up support* buscar apoyos

drum·mer ['drʌmər] tambor *m*, tamborilero(-a) *m(f)*

'**drum·stick** MUS baqueta *f*; *of poultry* muslo *m*

drunk [drʌŋk] **1** *n* borracho(-a) *m(f)* **2** *adj* borracho; *get ~* emborracharse **3** *pp* → **drink**

drunk·en ['drʌŋkn] *voices, laughter* borracho; *party* con mucho alcohol

dry [draɪ] **1** *adj* seco; *where alcohol is banned* donde está prohibido el consumo de alcohol **2** *v/t & v/i* (*pret & pp -ied*) secar

♦ **dry out** *v/i* secarse; *of alcoholic* desintoxicarse

♦ **dry up** *v/i of river* secarse; F (*be quiet*) cerrar el pico F

'**dry-clean** *v/t* limpiar en seco; '**dry clean·er** tintorería *f*; '**dry-clean·ing** (*clothes*): *would you pick up my ~ for me?* ¿te importaría recogerme la ropa de la tintorería?

dry·er ['draɪr] *machine* secadora *f*

DTP [diːtiːˈpiː] *abbr* (= *desk-top publishing*) autoedición *f*

du·al ['duːəl] *adj* doble

dub [dʌb] *v/t* (*pret & pp -bed*) *movie* doblar

du·bi·ous ['duːbɪəs] *adj* dudoso; (*having doubts*) inseguro; *I'm still ~ about the idea* todavía tengo mis dudas sobre la idea

duch·ess ['dʌtʃɪs] duquesa *f*

duck [dʌk] **1** n pato m, pata f **2** v/i agacharse **3** v/t one's head agachar; *question* eludir

dud [dʌd] n ⌐ (*false bill*) billete m falso

due [du:] adj (*proper*) debido; *the money ~ me* el dinero que se me debe; *payment is now ~* el pago se debe hacer efectivo ahora; *is there a train ~ soon?* ¿va a pasar un tren pronto?; *when is the baby ~?* ¿cuando está previsto que nazca el bebé?; *he's ~ to meet him next month* tiene previsto reunirse con él el próximo mes; *~ to* (*because of*) debido a; *be ~ to* (*be caused by*) ser debido a; *in ~ course* en su debido momento

dues [du:z] npl cuota f

du·et [du:'et] MUS dúo m

dug [dʌg] pret & pp → **dig**

duke [du:k] duque m

dull [dʌl] adj *weather* gris; *sound, pain* sordo; (*boring*) aburrido, soso

du·ly ['du:lɪ] adv (*as expected*) tal y como se esperaba; (*properly*) debidamente

dumb [dʌm] adj (*mute*) mudo; F (*stupid*) estúpido; *a pretty ~ thing to do* una tontería

dumb·found·ed [dʌm'faʊndɪd] adj boquiabierto

dump [dʌmp] **1** n for garbage vertedero m, basurero m; (*unpleasant place*) lugar m de mala muerte **2** v/t (*deposit*) dejar; (*dispose of*) deshacerse de; *toxic waste, nuclear waste* verter

dump·ling ['dʌmplɪŋ] bola de masa dulce o salada

dune [du:n] duna f

dung [dʌŋ] estiércol m

dun·ga·rees [dʌŋɡə'ri:z] npl pantalones mpl de trabajo

dunk [dʌŋk] v/t *in coffee etc* mojar

du·o ['du:oʊ] MUS dúo m

du·plex (a·part·ment) ['du:pleks] dúplex m

du·pli·cate 1 n ['du:plɪkət] duplicado m; *in ~* por duplicado **2** v/t ['du:plɪkeɪt] (*copy*) duplicar, hacer

un duplicado de; (*repeat*) repetir

du·pli·cate 'key llave f duplicada

du·ra·ble ['dʊrəbl] adj *material* duradero, durable; *relationship* duradero

du·ra·tion [dʊ'reɪʃn] duración f; *for the ~ of her visit* mientras dure su visita

du·ress [dʊ'res]: *under ~* bajo coacción

dur·ing ['dʊrɪŋ] prep durante

dusk [dʌsk] crepúsculo m, anochecer m

dust [dʌst] **1** n polvo m **2** v/t quitar el polvo a; *~ sth with sth* (*sprinkle*) espolvorear algo con algo

dust·er ['dʌstər] (*cloth*) trapo m del polvo

'**dust jack·et** sobrecubierta f

'**dust·pan** recogedor m

dust·y ['dʌstɪ] adj polvoriento

Dutch [dʌtʃ] **1** adj holandés; *go ~* F pagar a escote F **2** n (*language*) neerlandés m; *the ~* los holandeses

du·ty ['du:tɪ] deber m; (*task*) obligación f, tarea f; *on goods* impuesto m; *be on ~* estar de servicio; *be off ~* estar fuera de servicio

du·ty-'free 1 adj libre de impuestos **2** n productos mpl libres de impuestos

du·ty-'free shop tienda f libre de impuestos

DVD [di:vi:'di:] abbr (= *digital versatile disk*) DVD m

dwarf [dwɔ:rf] **1** n enano m **2** v/t empequeñecer

♦**dwell on** [dwel] v/t: *dwell on the past* pensar en el pasado; *don't dwell on what he said* no des demasiada importancia a lo que ha dicho

dwin·dle ['dwɪndl] v/i disminuir, menguar

dye [daɪ] **1** n tinte m **2** v/t teñir

dy·ing ['daɪɪŋ] adj *person* moribundo; *industry, tradition* en vías de desaparición

dy·nam·ic [daɪ'næmɪk] adj dinámico

dy·na·mism ['daɪnəmɪzm] dinamismo m

dy·na·mite ['daɪnəmaɪt] n dinamita f

dy·na·mo ['daɪnəmoʊ] TECH dinamo *f*, dínamo *f*

dy·nas·ty ['daɪnəstɪ] dinastía *f*

dys·lex·i·a [dɪs'leksɪə] dislexia *f*

dys·lex·ic [dɪs'leksɪk] **1** *adj* disléxico **2** *n* disléxico(-a) *m(f)*

D

E

each [iːtʃ] **1** *adj* cada **2** *adv*: **he gave us one ~** nos dio uno a cada uno; **they're $1.50 ~** valen 1.50 dólares cada uno **3** *pron* cada uno; **~ other** el uno al otro; **we love ~ other** nos queremos

ea·ger ['iːgər] *adj* ansioso; **she's always ~ to help** siempre está deseando ayudar

ea·ger 'bea·ver F entusiasta *m/f*

ea·ger·ly ['iːgərlɪ] *adv* ansiosamente

ea·ger·ness ['iːgərnɪs] entusiasmo *m*

ea·gle ['iːgl] águila *f*

ea·gle-eyed [iːgl'aɪd] *adj* con vista de lince

ear¹ [ɪr] *of person, animal* oreja *f*; *for music* oído *m*

ear² [ɪr] *of corn* espiga *f*

'ear·ache dolor *m* de oídos; **'ear·drum** tímpano *m*; **'ear·lobe** lóbulo *m*

ear·ly ['ɜːrlɪ] **1** *adj* (*not late*) temprano; (*ahead of time*) anticipado; (*farther back in time*) primero; (*in the near future*) pronto; *music* antiguo; **let's have an ~ supper** cenemos temprano; **in ~ October** a principios de octubre; **in the ~ hours of the morning** a primeras horas de la madrugada; **an ~ Picasso** un Picasso de su primera época; **I'm an ~ riser** soy madrugador **2** *adv* (*not late*) pronto, temprano; (*ahead of time*) antes de tiempo; **it's too ~ to say** es demasiado pronto como para poder decir nada; **earlier than** antes que

'ear·ly bird madrugador(a) *m(f)*

ear·mark ['ɪrmɑːrk] *v/t* destinar; **~ sth for sth** destinar algo a algo

earn [ɜːrn] *v/t salary* ganar; *interest* devengar; *holiday, drink etc* ganarse; **~ one's living** ganarse la vida

ear·nest ['ɜːrnɪst] *adj* serio; **in ~** en serio

earn·ings ['ɜːrnɪŋz] *npl* ganancias *fpl*

'ear·phones *npl* auriculares *mpl*; **'ear-pierc·ing** *adj* estrepitoso; **'ear·plug** tapón *m* para el oído; **'ear·ring** pendiente *m*; **'ear·shot**: **within ~** al alcance del oído; **out of ~** fuera del alcance del oído

earth [ɜːrθ] (*soil*) tierra *f*; (*world, planet*) Tierra *f*; **where on ~ ...?** F ¿dónde diablos ...? F

earth·en·ware ['ɜːrθnwer] *n* loza *f*

earth·ly ['ɜːrθlɪ] *adj* terrenal; **it's no ~ use** F no sirve para nada

earth·quake ['ɜːrθkweɪk] terremoto *m*

earth-shat·ter·ing ['ɜːrθʃætərɪŋ] *adj* extraordinario

ease [iːz] **1** *n* facilidad *f*; **be at (one's) ~, feel at ~** sentirse cómodo; **feel ill at ~** sentirse incómodo **2** *v/t (relieve)* aliviar **3** *v/i of pain* disminuir

♦ ease off 1 *v/t (remove)* quitar con cuidado **2** *v/i of pain* disminuir; *of rain* amainar

ea·sel ['iːzl] caballete *m*

eas·i·ly ['iːzəlɪ] *adv* (*with ease*) fácilmente; (*by far*) con diferencia

east [iːst] **1** *n* este *m* **2** *adj* oriental, este; *wind* del este **3** *adv travel* hacia el este

Eas·ter ['iːstər] Pascua *f*; *period* Semana f Santa

Eas·ter 'Day Domingo *m* de Resurrección

'Eas·ter egg huevo *m* de pascua

eas·ter·ly ['i:stərlɪ] *adj* del este

Eas·ter 'Mon·day Lunes *m* Santo

east·ern ['i:stərn] *adj* del este; (*oriental*) oriental

east·er·ner ['i:stərnər] *habitante de la costa este estadounidense*

Eas·ter 'Sun·day Domingo *m* de Resurrección

east·ward ['i:stwərd] *adv* hacia el este

eas·y ['i:zɪ] *adj* fácil; (*relaxed*) tranquilo; *take things ~ (slow down)* tomarse las cosas con tranquilidad; *take it ~! (calm down)* ¡tranquilízate!

'eas·y chair sillón *m*

eas·y-go·ing ['i:zɪgoʊɪŋ] *adj* tratable

eat [i:t] *v/t & v/i* (*pret ate*, *pp eaten*) comer

♦ **eat out** *v/i* comer fuera

♦ **eat up** *v/t* comerse; *fig: use up* acabar con

eat·a·ble ['i:təbl] *adj* comestible

eat·en ['i:tn] *pp* → *eat*

eau de Co·logne [oʊdəkə'loʊn] agua *f* de colonia

eaves [i:vz] *npl* alero *m*

eaves·drop ['i:vzdrɑ:p] *v/i* (*pret & pp -ped*) escuchar a escondidas (*on s.o.* alguien)

ebb [eb] *v/i of tide* bajar

♦ **ebb away** *v/i fig of courage, strength* desvanecerse

e-busi·ness ['i:bɪznɪs] comercio *m* electrónico

ec·cen·tric [ɪk'sentrɪk] **1** *adj* excéntrico **2** *n* excéntrico(-a) *m(f)*

ec·cen·tric·i·ty [ɪksen'trɪsɪtɪ] excentricidad *f*

ech·o ['ekoʊ] **1** *n* eco *m* **2** *v/i* resonar **3** *v/t words* repetir; *views* mostrar acuerdo con

e-clipse [ɪ'klɪps] **1** *n* eclipse *m* **2** *v/t fig* eclipsar

e·co·lo·gi·cal [i:kə'lɑ:dʒɪkl] *adj* ecológico

e·co·lo·gi·cal·ly [i:kə'lɑ:dʒɪklɪ] *adv* ecológicamente

e·co·lo·gi·cal·ly 'friend·ly *adj* ecológico

e·col·o·gist [ɪ'kɑ:lədʒɪst] ecologista *m/f*

e·col·o·gy [i:'kɑ:lədʒɪ] ecología *f*

ec·o·nom·ic [i:kə'nɑ:mɪk] *adj* económico

ec·o·nom·i·cal [i:kə'nɑ:mɪkl] *adj* (*cheap*) económico; (*thrifty*) cuidadoso

ec·o·nom·i·cal·ly [i:kə'nɑ:mɪklɪ] *adv* (*in terms of economics*) económicamente; (*thriftily*) de manera económica

ec·o·nom·ics [i:kə'nɑ:mɪks] *nsg* (*science*) economía *f*; (*npl: financial aspects*) aspecto *m* económico

e·con·o·mist [ɪ'kɑ:nəmɪst] economista *m/f*

e·con·o·mize [ɪ'kɑ:nəmaɪz] *v/i* economizar, ahorrar

♦ **economize on** *v/t* economizar, ahorrar

e·con·o·my [ɪ'kɑ:nəmɪ] *of a country* economía *f*; (*saving*) ahorro *m*

e'con·o·my class clase *f* turista; **e'con·o·my drive** intento *m* de ahorrar; **e'con·o·my size** tamaño *m* económico

e·co·sys·tem ['i:koʊsɪstm] ecosistema *m*

e·co·tour·ism ['i:koʊtʊrɪzm] ecoturismo *m*

ec·sta·sy ['ekstəsɪ] éxtasis *m*

ec·sta·tic [ɪk'stætɪk] *adj* muy emocionado, extasiado

Ec·ua·dor ['ekwədɔ:r] *n* Ecuador

Ec·ua·dore·an [ekwə'dɔ:rən] **1** *adj* ecuatoriano **2** *n* ecuatoriano(-a) *m(f)*

ec·ze·ma ['eksmə] eczema *f*

edge [edʒ] **1** *n of knife* filo *m*; *of table, seat, road, cliff* borde *m*; *in voice* irritación *f*; *on ~* tenso **2** *v/t* ribetear **3** *v/i* (*move slowly*) acercarse despacio

edge·wise ['edʒwaɪz] *adv* de lado; *I couldn't get a word in ~* no me dejó decir una palabra

edg·y ['edʒɪ] *adj* tenso

ed·i·ble ['edɪbl] *adj* comestible

ed·it ['edɪt] *v/t text* corregir; *book* editar; *newspaper* dirigir; *TV program, movie* montar

e·di·tion [ɪ'dɪʃn] edición *f*

ed·i·tor ['edɪtər] *of text, book* editor(a) *m(f)*; *of newspaper* director(a) *m(f)*; *of TV program, movie* montador(a) *m(f)*; *sports/political ~* redactor(a) *m(f)* de deportes/política

ed·i·to·ri·al [edɪ'tɔːrɪəl] **1** *adj* editorial **2** *n in newspaper* editorial *m*

EDP [iːdiː'piː] *abbr* (= *electronic data processing*) procesamiento *m* electrónico de datos

ed·u·cate ['edʒəkeɪt] *v/t child* educar; *consumers* concienciar

ed·u·cat·ed ['edʒəkeɪtɪd] *adj person* culto

ed·u·ca·tion [edʒə'keɪʃn] educación *f*; *the ~ system* el sistema educativo

ed·u·ca·tion·al [edʒə'keɪʃnl] *adj* educativo; (*informative*) instructivo

eel [iːl] anguila *f*

ee·rie ['ɪrɪ] *adj* escalofriante

ef·fect [ɪ'fekt] efecto *m*; *take ~ of medicine, drug* hacer efecto; *come into ~ of law* entrar en vigor

ef·fec·tive [ɪ'fektɪv] *adj* (*efficient*) efectivo; (*striking*) impresionante; *~ May 1* a partir del 1 de mayo

ef·fem·i·nate [ɪ'femɪnət] *adj* afeminado

ef·fer·ves·cent [efər'vesnt] *adj* efervescente; *personality* chispeante

ef·fi·cien·cy [ɪ'fɪʃənsɪ] *of person* eficiencia *f*; *of machine* rendimiento *m*; *of system* eficacia *f*

ef·fi·cient [ɪ'fɪʃənt] *adj person* eficiente; *machine* de buen rendimiento; *method* eficaz

ef·fi·cient·ly [ɪ'fɪʃəntlɪ] *adv* eficientemente

ef·flu·ent ['eflʊənt] aguas *fpl* residuales

ef·fort ['efərt] (*struggle, attempt*) esfuerzo *m*

ef·fort·less ['efərtlɪs] *adj* fácil

ef·fron·te·ry [ɪ'frʌntərɪ] desvergüenza *f*

ef·fu·sive [ɪ'fjuːsɪv] *adj* efusivo

e.g. [iː'dʒiː] p. ej.

e·gal·i·tar·i·an [ɪgælɪ'terɪən] *adj* igualitario

egg [eg] huevo *m*; *of woman* óvulo *m*

♦**egg on** *v/t* incitar

'egg·cup huevera *f*; **'egg·head** F cerebrito(-a) *m(f)* F; **'egg·plant** berenjena *f*; **'egg·shell** cáscara *f* de huevo; **'egg tim·er** reloj *m* de arena

e·go ['iːgou] PSYCH ego *m*; (*self-esteem*) amor *m* propio

e·go·cen·tric [iːgou'sentrɪk] *adj* egocéntrico

e·go·ism ['iːgouɪzm] egoismo *m*

e·go·ist ['iːgouɪst] egoísta *m/f*

E·gypt ['iːdʒɪpt] Egipto

E·gyp·tian [ɪ'dʒɪpʃn] **1** *adj* egipcio **2** *n* egipcio(-a) *m(f)*

ei·der·down ['aɪdərdaun] *quilt* edredón *m*

eight [eɪt] ocho

eigh·teen [eɪ'tiːn] dieciocho

eigh·teenth [eɪ'tiːnθ] *n & adj* decimoctavo

eighth [eɪtθ] *n & adj* octavo

eigh·ti·eth ['eɪtɪɪθ] *n & adj* octogésimo

eigh·ty ['eɪtɪ] ochenta

ei·ther ['aɪðər] **1** *adj* cualquiera de los dos; *with negative constructions* ninguno de los dos; (*both*) cada, ambos; *he wouldn't accept ~ of the proposals* no quería aceptar ninguna de las dos propuestas **2** *pron* cualquiera de los dos; *with negative constructions* ninguno de los dos **3** *adv* tampoco; *I won't go ~* yo tampoco iré **4** *conj*: *~ ... or choice* o ... o; *with negative constructions* ni ... ni

e·ject [ɪ'dʒekt] **1** *v/t* expulsar **2** *v/i from plane* eyectarse

♦**eke out** [iːk] *v/t* (*make last*) hacer durar

el [el] → *elevated railroad*

e·lab·o·rate 1 *adj* [ɪ'læbərət] elaborado 2 v/t [ɪ'læbəreɪt] elaborar 3 v/i [ɪ'læbəreɪt] dar detalles

e·lab·o·rate·ly [ɪ'læbəreɪtlɪ] adv elaboradamente

e·lapse [ɪ'læps] v/i pasar

e·las·tic [ɪ'læstɪk] 1 adj elástico 2 n elástico m

e·las·ti·ca·ted [ɪ'læstɪkeɪtɪd] adj elástico

e·las·ti·ci·ty [ɪlæs'tɪsətɪ] elasticidad f

e·las·ti·cized [ɪ'læstɪsaɪzd] adj elástico

e·lat·ed [ɪ'leɪtɪd] adj eufórico

el·a·tion [ɪ'leɪʃn] euforia f

el·bow ['elbou] 1 n codo m 2 v/t dar un codazo a; ~ out of the way apartar a codazos

el·der ['eldər] 1 adj mayor 2 n mayor m/f; she's two years my ~ es dos años mayor que yo

el·der·ly ['eldərlɪ] 1 adj mayor 2 n: the ~ las personas mayores

el·dest ['eldəst] 1 adj mayor 2 n mayor m/f; the ~ el mayor

e·lect [ɪ'lekt] v/t elegir; ~ to do sth decidir hacer algo

e·lect·ed [ɪ'lektɪd] adj elegido

e·lec·tion [ɪ'lekʃn] elección f; call an ~ convocar elecciones

e'lec·tion cam·paign campaña f electoral

e'lec·tion day día m de las elecciones

e·lec·tive [ɪ'lektɪv] adj opcional; subject optativo

e·lec·tor [ɪ'lektər] elector(a) m(f), votante m/f

e·lec·to·ral sys·tem [ɪ'lektərəl] sistema m electoral

e·lec·to·rate [ɪ'lektərət] electorado m

e·lec·tric [ɪ'lektrɪk] adj eléctrico; fig atmosphere electrizado

e·lec·tri·cal [ɪ'lektrɪkl] adj eléctrico

e·lec·tri·cal en·gi'neer ingeniero(-a) m(f) electrónico

e·lec·tri·cal en·gi'neer·ing ingeniería f electrónica

e·lec·tric 'blan·ket manta f or L.Am. cobija f eléctrica

e·lec·tric 'chair silla f eléctrica

e·lec·tri·cian [ɪlek'trɪʃn] electricista m/f

e·lec·tri·ci·ty [ɪlek'trɪsətɪ] electricidad f

e·lec·tric 'ra·zor maquinilla f eléctrica

e·lec·tric 'shock descarga f eléctrica

e·lec·tri·fy [ɪ'lektrɪfaɪ] v/t (pret & pp -ied) electrificar; fig electrizar

e·lec·tro·cute [ɪ'lektrəkjuːt] v/t electrocutar

e·lec·trode [ɪ'lektroud] electrodo m

e·lec·tron [ɪ'lektrɑːn] electrón m

e·lec·tron·ic [ɪlek'trɑːnɪk] adj electrónico

e·lec·tron·ic da·ta 'pro·ces·sing procesamiento m electrónico de datos

e·lec·tron·ic 'mail correo m electrónico

e·lec·tron·ics [ɪlek'trɑːnɪks] electrónica f

el·e·gance ['elɪɡəns] elegancia f

el·e·gant ['elɪɡənt] adj elegante

el·e·gant·ly ['elɪɡəntlɪ] adv elegantemente

el·e·ment ['elɪmənt] also CHEM elemento m

el·e·men·ta·ry [elɪ'mentərɪ] adj (rudimentary) elemental

el·e'men·ta·ry school escuela f primaria

el·e'men·ta·ry teacher maestro(-a) m(f)

el·e·phant ['elɪfənt] elefante m

el·e·vate ['elɪveɪt] v/t elevar

el·e·vat·ed 'rail·road ['elɪveɪtɪd] ferrocarril m elevado

el·e·va·tion [elɪ'veɪʃn] (altitude) altura f

el·e·va·tor ['elɪveɪtər] ascensor m

el·e·ven [ɪ'levn] once

el·e·venth [ɪ'levnθ] n & adj undécimo; at the ~ hour justo en el último minuto

el·i·gi·ble ['elɪdʒəbl] adj que reúne los requisitos; ~ to vote con derecho al voto; be ~ to do sth tener derecho a hacer algo

el·i·gi·ble ˈbach·e·lor buen partido *m*

e·lim·i·nate [ɪˈlɪmɪneɪt] *v/t* eliminar; *poverty* acabar con; *(rule out)* descartar

e·lim·i·na·tion [ɪˈlɪmɪneɪʃn] eliminación *f*

e·lite [eɪˈliːt] **1** *n* élite *f* **2** *adj* de élite

elk [elk] ciervo *m* canadiense

e·lipse [ɪˈlɪps] elipse *f*

elm [elm] olmo *m*

e·lope [ɪˈloʊp] *v/i* fugarse con un amante

el·o·quence [ˈeləkwəns] elocuencia *f*

el·o·quent [ˈeləkwənt] *adj* elocuente

el·o·quent·ly [ˈeləkwəntlɪ] *adv* elocuentemente

El Sal·va·dor [elˈsælvədɔːr] *n* El Salvador

else [els] *adv*: *anything ~?* ¿algo más?; *if you have nothing ~ to do* si no tienes nada más que hacer; *no one ~* nadie más; *everyone ~ is going* todos (los demás) van, va todo el mundo; *who ~ was there?* ¿quién más estaba allí?; *someone ~* otra persona; *something ~* algo más; *let's go somewhere ~* vamos a otro sitio; *or ~* si no

else·where [ˈelsweər] *adv* en otro sitio

e·lude [ɪˈluːd] *v/t (escape from)* escapar de; *(avoid)* evitar; *the name ~s me* no recuerdo el nombre

e·lu·sive [ɪˈluːsɪv] *adj* evasivo

e·ma·ci·at·ed [ɪˈmeɪsɪeɪtɪd] *adj* demacrado

e-mail [ˈiːmeɪl] **1** *n* correo *m* electrónico **2** *v/t person* mandar un correo electrónico a

'e-mail ad·dress dirección *f* de correo electrónico, dirección *f* electrónica

e·man·ci·pat·ed [ɪˈmænsɪpeɪtɪd] *adj* emancipado

e·man·ci·pa·tion [ɪmænsɪˈpeɪʃn] emancipación *f*

em·balm [ɪmˈbɑːm] *v/t* embalsamar

em·bank·ment [ɪmˈbæŋkmənt] *of river* dique *m*; RAIL terraplén *m*

em·bar·go [emˈbɑːrɡoʊ] embargo *m*

em·bark [ɪmˈbɑːrk] *v/i* embarcar

♦ **embark on** *v/t* embarcarse en

em·bar·rass [ɪmˈbærəs] *v/t* avergonzar; *he ~ed me in front of everyone* me hizo pasar vergüenza delante de todos

em·bar·rassed [ɪmˈbærəst] *adj* avergonzado; *I was ~ to ask* me daba vergüenza preguntar

em·bar·rass·ing [ɪmˈbærəsɪŋ] *adj* embarazoso

em·bar·rass·ment [ɪmˈbærəsmənt] embarazo *m*, apuro *m*

em·bas·sy [ˈembəsɪ] embajada *f*

em·bel·lish [ɪmˈbelɪʃ] *v/t* adornar; *story* exagerar

em·bers [ˈembərz] *npl* ascuas *fpl*

em·bez·zle [ɪmˈbezl] *v/t* malversar

em·bez·zle·ment [ɪmˈbezlmənt] malversación *f*

em·bez·zler [ɪmˈbezlər] malversador(a) *m(f)*

em·bit·ter [ɪmˈbɪtər] *v/t* amargar

em·blem [ˈembləm] emblema *m*

em·bod·i·ment [ɪmˈbɑːdɪmənt] personificación *f*

em·bod·y [ɪmˈbɑːdɪ] *v/t (pret & pp -ied)* personificar

em·bo·lism [ˈembəlɪzm] embolia *f*

em·boss [ɪmˈbɑːs] *v/t metal* repujar; *paper* grabar en relieve

em·brace [ɪmˈbreɪs] **1** *n* abrazo *m* **2** *v/t (hug)* abrazar; *(take in)* abarcar **3** *v/i of two people* abrazarse

em·broi·der [ɪmˈbrɔɪdər] *v/t* bordar; *fig* adornar

em·broi·der·y [ɪmˈbrɔɪdərɪ] bordado *m*

em·bry·o [ˈembrɪoʊ] embrión *m*

em·bry·on·ic [embrɪˈɑːnɪk] *adj fig* embrionario

em·e·rald [ˈemərəld] esmeralda *f*

e·merge [ɪˈmɜːrdʒ] *v/i (appear)* emerger, salir; *of truth* aflorar; *it has ~d that* se ha descubierto que

e·mer·gen·cy [ɪˈmɜːrdʒənsɪ] emergencia *f*; *in an ~* en caso de emergencia

emer·gen·cy 'ex·it salida *f* de emergencia; **e'mer·gen·cy land·ing**

aterrizaje *m* forzoso; **e'mer·gen·cy ser·vi·ces** *npl* servicios *mpl* de urgencia

em·er·y board |'eməri| lima *f* de uñas

em·i·grant ['emɪɡrənt] emigrante *m/f*

em·i·grate ['emɪɡreɪt] *v/i* emigrar

em·i·gra·tion [emɪ'ɡreɪʃn] emigración *f*

Em·i·nence ['emɪnəns] REL: *His ~* Su Eminencia

em·i·nent ['emɪnənt] *adj* eminente

em·i·nent·ly ['emɪnəntlɪ] *adv* sumamente

e·mis·sion [ɪ'mɪʃn] *of gases* emisión *f*

e·mit [ɪ'mɪt] *v/t* (*pret & pp* **-ted**) emitir; *heat, odor* desprender

e·mo·tion [ɪ'moʊʃn] emoción *f*

e·mo·tion·al [ɪ'moʊʃənl] *adj problems, development* sentimental; (*full of emotion*) emotivo

em·pa·thize ['empəθaɪz] *v/i:* ~ *with* identificarse con

em·per·or ['empərər] emperador *m*

em·pha·sis ['emfəsɪs] *in word* acento *m*; *fig* énfasis *m*

em·pha·size ['emfəsaɪz] *v/t syllable* acentuar; *fig* hacer hincapié en

em·phat·ic [ɪm'fætɪk] *adj* enfático

em·pire ['empaɪr] imperio *m*

em·ploy [ɪm'plɔɪ] *v/t* emplear; *he's ~ed as a ...* trabaja de ...

em·ploy·ee [emplɔɪ'iː] empleado(-a) *m(f)*

em·ploy·er [em'plɔɪər] empresario(-a) *m(f)*

em·ploy·ment [em'plɔɪmənt] empleo *m*; (*work*) trabajo *m*; *be looking for ~* buscar trabajo

em'ploy·ment a·gen·cy agencia *f* de colocaciones

em·press ['empris] emperatriz *f*

emp·ti·ness ['emptɪnɪs] vacío *m*

emp·ty ['emptɪ] **1** *adj* vacío; *promise* vana **2** *v/t* (*pret & pp* **-ied**) *drawer, pockets* vaciar; *glass, bottle* acabar **3** *v/i* (*pret & pp* **-ied**) *of room, street* vaciarse

em·u·late ['emjʊleɪt] *v/t* emular

e·mul·sion [ɪ'mʌlʃn] *paint* emulsión *f*

en·a·ble [ɪ'neɪbl] *v/t* permitir; ~ *s.o. to do sth* permitir a alguien hacer algo

en·act [ɪ'nækt] *v/t law* promulgar; THEA representar

e·nam·el [ɪ'næml] *n* esmalte *m*

enc *abbr* (= *enclosure(s)*) documento(s) *m(pl)* adjunto(s)

en·chant·ing [ɪn'tʃæntɪŋ] *adj* encantador

en·cir·cle [ɪn'sɜːrkl] *v/t* rodear

encl *abbr* (= *enclosure(s)*) documento(s) *m(pl)* adjunto(s)

en·close [ɪn'kloʊz] *v/t in letter* adjuntar; *area* rodear; *please find ~d ...* remito adjunto ...

en·clo·sure [ɪn'kloʊʒər] *with letter* documento *m* adjunto

en·core ['ɑːŋkɔːr] bis *m*

en·coun·ter [ɪn'kaʊntər] **1** *n* encuentro *m* **2** *v/t person* encontrarse con; *problem, resistance* tropezar con

en·cour·age [ɪn'kʌrɪdʒ] *v/t* animar; *violence* fomentar

en·cour·age·ment [ɪn'kʌrɪdʒmənt] ánimo *m*

en·cour·ag·ing [ɪn'kʌrɪdʒɪŋ] *adj* alentador

♦**en·croach on** [ɪn'kroʊtʃ] *v/t land* invadir; *rights* usurpar; *time* quitar

en·cy·clo·pe·di·a [ɪnsaɪklə'piːdɪə] enciclopedia *f*

end [end] **1** *n of journey, month* final *m*; (*extremity*) extremo *m*; (*bottom*) fondo *m*; (*conclusion, purpose*) fin *m*; *at the other ~ of town* al otro lado de la ciudad; *in the ~* al final; *for hours on ~* durante horas y horas; *stand sth on ~* poner de pie algo; *at the ~ of July* a finales de julio; *in the ~* al final; *put an ~ to* poner fin a **2** *v/t* terminar, finalizar **3** *v/i* terminar

♦**end up** *v/i* acabar

en·dan·ger [ɪn'deɪndʒər] *v/t* poner en peligro

en'dan·gered spe·cies *nsg* especie *f* en peligro de extinción

en·dear·ing [ɪnˈdɪrɪŋ] adj simpático
en·deav·or [ɪnˈdevər] 1 n esfuerzo m 2 v/t procurar
en·dem·ic [ɪnˈdemɪk] adj endémico
end·ing [ˈendɪŋ] final m; GRAM terminación f
end·less [ˈendlɪs] adj interminable
en·dorse [ɪnˈdɔːrs] v/t check endosar; candidacy apoyar; product representar
en·dorse·ment [ɪnˈdɔːrsmənt] of check endoso m; of candidacy apoyo m; of product representación f
end ˈprod·uct producto m final
end reˈsult resultado m final
en·dur·ance [ɪnˈdʊrəns] resistencia f
en·dure [ɪnˈdʊər] 1 v/t resistir 2 v/i (last) durar
en·dur·ing [ɪnˈdʊrɪŋ] adj duradero
end-ˈus·er usuario(-a) m(f) final
en·e·my [ˈenəmɪ] enemigo(-a) m(f)
en·er·get·ic [enərˈdʒetɪk] adj enérgico
en·er·get·ic·al·ly [enərˈdʒetɪklɪ] adv enérgicamente
en·er·gy [ˈenərdʒɪ] energía f
ˈen·er·gy-sav·ing adj device que ahorra energía
ˈen·er·gy sup·ply suministro m de energía
en·force [ɪnˈfɔːrs] v/t hacer cumplir
en·gage [ɪnˈgeɪdʒ] 1 v/t (hire) contratar 2 v/i TECH engranar
♦ engage in v/t dedicarse a
en·gaged [ɪnˈgeɪdʒd] adj to be married prometido; get ~ prometerse
en·gage·ment [ɪnˈgeɪdʒmənt] (appointment, to be married) compromiso m; MIL combate m
enˈgage·ment ring anillo m de compromiso
en·gag·ing [ɪnˈgeɪdʒɪŋ] adj smile, person atractivo
en·gine [ˈendʒɪn] motor m
en·gi·neer [endʒɪˈnɪr] 1 n ingeniero(-a) m(f); NAUT, RAIL maquinista m/f 2 v/t fig: meeting etc tramar
en·gi·neer·ing [endʒɪˈnɪrɪŋ] ingeniería f
En·gland [ˈɪŋglənd] Inglaterra f

En·glish [ˈɪŋglɪʃ] 1 adj inglés(-esa) 2 n language inglés m; the ~ los ingleses
Eng·lish ˈChan·nel Canal m de la Mancha; ˈEn·glish·man inglés m; ˈEn·glish·wom·an inglesa f
en·grave [ɪnˈgreɪv] v/t grabar
en·grav·ing [ɪnˈgreɪvɪŋ] grabado m
en·grossed [ɪnˈgroʊst] adj absorto (in en)
en·gulf [ɪnˈgʌlf] v/t devorar
en·hance [ɪnˈhæns] v/t realzar
e·nig·ma [ɪˈnɪgmə] enigma m
e·nig·mat·ic [enɪgˈmætɪk] adj enigmático
en·joy [ɪnˈdʒɔɪ] v/t disfrutar; ~ o.s. divertirse; ~ (your meal)! ¡que aproveche!
en·joy·a·ble [ɪnˈdʒɔɪəbl] adj agradable
en·joy·ment [ɪnˈdʒɔɪmənt] diversión f
en·large [ɪnˈlɑːrdʒ] v/t ampliar
en·large·ment [ɪnˈlɑːrdʒmənt] ampliación f
en·light·en [ɪnˈlaɪtn] v/t educar
en·list [ɪnˈlɪst] 1 v/i MIL alistarse 2 v/t: I ~ed his help conseguí que me ayudara
en·liv·en [ɪnˈlaɪvn] v/t animar
en·mi·ty [ˈenmətɪ] enemistad f
e·nor·mi·ty [ɪˈnɔːrmətɪ] magnitud f
e·nor·mous [ɪˈnɔːrməs] adj enorme; satisfaction, patience inmenso
e·nor·mous·ly [ɪˈnɔːrməslɪ] adv enormemente
e·nough [ɪˈnʌf] 1 adj pron suficiente, bastante; will $50 be ~? ¿llegará con 50 dólares?; I've had ~! ¡estoy harto!; that's ~, calm down! ¡ya basta, tranquilízate! 2 adv suficientemente, bastante; the bag isn't big ~ la bolsa no es lo suficientemente or bastante grande; strangely ~ curiosamente
en·quire [ɪnˈkwaɪr] → inquire
en·raged [ɪnˈreɪdʒd] adj enfurecido
en·rich [ɪnˈrɪtʃ] v/t enriquecer
en·roll [ɪnˈroʊl] v/i matricularse
en·roll·ment [ɪnˈroʊlmənt] matrícula f

en·sue [ɪn'suː] *v/i* sucederse

en suite [ˈɑːnswiːt] *adj*: **~ bathroom** baño *m* privado

en·sure [ɪn'ʃʊər] *v/t* asegurar

en·tail [ɪn'teɪl] *v/t* conllevar

en·tan·gle [ɪn'tæŋgl] *v/t in rope* enredar; **become ~d in** enredarse *in*; **become ~d with** *in love affair* liarse con

en·ter ['entər] **1** *v/t room, house* entrar en; *competition* participar en; *person, horse in race* inscribir; (*write down*) COMPUT introducir **2** *v/i* entrar; THEA entrar en escena; *in competition* inscribirse **3** *n* COMPUT intro *m*

en·ter·prise ['entərpraɪz] (*initiative*) iniciativa *f*; (*venture*) empresa *f*

en·ter·pris·ing ['entərpraɪzɪŋ] *adj* con iniciativa

en·ter·tain [entər'teɪn] **1** *v/t* (*amuse*) entretener; (*consider: idea*) considerar **2** *v/i* (*have guests*): **we ~ a lot** recibimos a mucha gente

en·ter·tain·er [entər'teɪnər] artista *m/f*

en·ter·tain·ing [entər'teɪnɪŋ] *adj* entretenido

en·ter·tain·ment [entər'teɪnmənt] entretenimiento *m*

en·thrall [ɪn'θrɔːl] *v/t* cautivar

en·thu·si·as·m [ɪn'θuːzɪæzm] entusiasmo *m*

en·thu·si·ast [ɪn'θuːzɪæst] entusiasta *m/f*

en·thu·si·as·tic [ɪnθuːzɪ'æstɪk] *adj* entusiasta; **be ~ about sth** estar entusiasmado con algo

en·thu·si·as·tic·al·ly [ɪnθuːzɪ'æstɪklɪ] *adv* con entusiasmo

en·tice [ɪn'taɪs] *v/t* atraer

en·tire [ɪn'taɪr] *adj* entero; **the ~ school is going** va a ir todo el colegio

en·tire·ly [ɪn'taɪrlɪ] *adv* completamente

en·ti·tle [ɪn'taɪtld] *v/t*: **~ s.o. to sth** dar derecho a alguien a algo; **be ~d to** tener derecho a

en·ti·tled [ɪn'taɪtld] *adj book* titulado

en·trance ['entrəns] entrada *f*; THEA entrada *f* en escena

en·tranced [ɪn'trænst] *adj* encantado

'en·trance ex·am(·i·na·tion) examen *m* de acceso

'en·trance fee (cuota *f* de) entrada *f*

en·trant ['entrənt] participante *m/f*

en·treat [ɪn'triːt] *v/t* suplicar; **~ s.o. to do sth** suplicar a alguien que haga algo

en·trenched [ɪn'trentʃt] *adj attitudes* arraigado

en·tre·pre·neur [ɑːntrəprə'nɜːr] empresario(-a) *m(f)*

en·tre·pre·neur·i·al [ɑːntrəprə'nɜːrɪəl] *adj* empresarial

en·trust [ɪn'trʌst] *v/t* confiar; **~ s.o. with sth, ~ sth to s.o.** confiar algo a alguien

en·try ['entrɪ] entrada *f*; *for competition* inscripción *f*; *in diary etc* entrada *f*; *no* ~ prohibida la entrada; **the winning ~ was painted by ...** el cuadro ganador fue pintado por ...

'en·try form impreso *m* de inscripción; **'en·try·phone** portero *m* automático; **'en·try vi·sa** visado *m*

e·nu·me·rate [ɪ'nuːməreɪt] *v/t* enumerar

en·vel·op [ɪn'veləp] *v/t* cubrir

en·ve·lope ['envələʊp] sobre *m*

en·vi·a·ble ['envɪəbl] *adj* envidiable

en·vi·ous ['envɪəs] *adj* envidioso; **be ~ of s.o.** tener envidia de alguien

en·vi·ron·ment [ɪn'vaɪrənmənt] (*nature*) medio *m* ambiente; (*surroundings*) entorno *m*, ambiente *m*

en·vi·ron·men·tal [ɪnvaɪrən'məntl] *adj* medioambiental

en·vi·ron·men·tal·ist [ɪnvaɪrən'məntlɪst] ecologista *m/f*

en·vi·ron·men·tal·ly 'friend·ly [ɪnvaɪrən'məntəlɪ] *adj* ecológico, que no daña el medio ambiente

en·vi·ron·men·tal pol·lu·tion contaminación *f* medioambiental

en·vi·ron·men·tal pro'tec·tion protección *f* medioambiental

en·vi·rons [ɪn'vaɪrənz] *npl* alrededores *mpl*

en·vis·age [ɪn'vɪzɪdʒ] *v/t* imaginar

en·voy ['envɔɪ] enviado(-a) *m(f)*

en·vy ['envɪ] **1** *n* envidia *f*; **be the ~ of** ser la envidia de **2** *v/t* (*pret & pp -ied*) envidiar; **~ s.o. sth** envidiar a alguien por algo

e·phem·er·al [ɪ'femərəl] *adj* efímero

ep·ic ['epɪk] **1** *n* epopeya *f* **2** *adj journey* épico; **a task of ~ proportions** una tarea monumental

ep·i·cen·ter, *Br* **ep·i·cen·tre** ['epɪsentər] epicentro *m*

ep·i·dem·ic [epɪ'demɪk] epidemia *f*

ep·i·lep·sy ['epɪlepsɪ] epilepsia *f*

ep·i·lep·tic [epɪ'leptɪk] epiléptico(-a) *m(f)*

ep·i·lep·tic 'fit ataque *m* epiléptico

ep·i·log, *Br* **ep·i·logue** ['epɪlɑːg] epílogo *m*

ep·i·sode ['epɪsoʊd] *of story, soap opera* episodio *m*, capítulo *m*; (*happening*) episodio *m*; **let's forget the whole ~** olvidemos lo sucedido

ep·i·taph ['epɪtæf] epitafio *m*

e·poch ['iːpɑːk] época *f*

e·poch-mak·ing ['iːpɑːkmeɪkɪŋ] *adj* que hace época

e·qual ['iːkwl] **1** *adj* igual; **~ amounts of milk and water** la misma cantidad de leche y de agua; **~ opportunities** igualdad *f* de oportunidades; **be ~ to** *a task* estar capacitado para **2** *n* igual *m/f* **3** *v/t* (*pret & pp -ed*, *Br -led*) *with numbers* equivaler; (*be as good as*) igualar; **four times twelve ~s 48** cuatro por doce, (igual a) cuarenta y ocho

e·qual·i·ty [ɪ'kwɑːlətɪ] igualdad *f*

e·qual·ize ['iːkwəlaɪz] **1** *v/t* igualar **2** *v/i* SP empatar

e·qual·iz·er ['iːkwəlaɪzər] SP gol *m* del empate

e·qual·ly ['iːkwəlɪ] *adv* igualmente; *share, divide* en partes iguales

e·qual 'rights *npl* igualdad *f* de derechos

e·quate [ɪ'kweɪt] *v/t* equiparar

e·qua·tion [ɪ'kweɪʒn] MATH ecuación *f*

e·qua·tor [ɪ'kweɪtər] ecuador *m*

e·qui·lib·ri·um [iːkwɪ'lɪbrɪəm] equilibrio *m*

e·qui·nox ['iːkwɪnɑːks] equinoccio *m*

e·quip [ɪ'kwɪp] *v/t* (*pret & pp -ped*) equipar; **he's not ~ped to handle it** *fig* no está preparado para llevarlo

e·quip·ment [ɪ'kwɪpmənt] equipo *m*

eq·ui·ty ['ekwətɪ] FIN acciones *fpl* ordinarias

e·quiv·a·lent [ɪ'kwɪvələnt] **1** *adj* equivalente; **be ~ to** equivaler a **2** *n* equivalente *m*

e·ra ['ɪrə] era *f*

e·rad·i·cate [ɪ'rædɪkeɪt] *v/t* erradicar

e·rase [ɪ'reɪz] *v/t* borrar

e·ras·er [ɪ'reɪzər] *for pencil* goma *f* (de borrar); *for chalk* borrador *m*

e·rect [ɪ'rekt] **1** *adj* erguido **2** *v/t* levantar, erigir

e·rec·tion [ɪ'rekʃn] *of building etc* construcción *f*; *of penis* erección *f*

er·go·nom·ic [ɜːrgoʊ'nɑːmɪk] *adj furniture* ergonómico

e·rode [ɪ'roʊd] *v/t also fig* erosionar

e·ro·sion [ɪ'roʊʒn] *also fig* erosión *f*

e·rot·ic [ɪ'rɑːtɪk] *adj* erótico

e·rot·i·cism [ɪ'rɑːtɪsɪzm] erotismo *m*

er·rand ['erənd] recado *m*; **run ~s** hacer recados

er·rat·ic [ɪ'rætɪk] *adj* irregular; *course* errático

er·ror ['erər] error *m*

'er·ror mes·sage COMPUT mensaje *m* de error

e·rupt [ɪ'rʌpt] *v/i of volcano* entrar en erupción; *of violence* brotar; *of person* explotar

e·rup·tion [ɪ'rʌpʃn] *of volcano* erupción *f*; *of violence* brote *m*

es·ca·late ['eskəleɪt] *v/i* intensificarse

es·ca·la·tion [eskə'leɪʃn] intensificación *f*

es·ca·la·tor ['eskəleɪtər] escalera *f* mecánica

es·cape [ɪ'skeɪp] **1** *n of prisoner, animal* fuga *f*; *of gas* escape *m*, fuga *f*; **have a narrow ~** escaparse por los pelos **2** *v/i of prisoner, animal, gas* escaparse **3** *v/t*: *the word ~s me* no consigo recordar la palabra

es'cape chute AVIA tobogán *m* de emcrgencia

es·cort 1 *n* ['eskɔːrt] acompañante *m/f*; (*guard*) escolta *m/f*; *under ~* escoltado **2** *v/t* [ɪ'skɔːrt] escoltar; *socially* acompañar

es·pe·cial [ɪ'speʃl] → *special*

es·pe·cial·ly [ɪ'speʃlɪ] *adv* especialmente

es·pi·o·nage ['espɪənɑːʒ] espionaje *m*

es·pres·so (cof·fee) [es'presoʊ] café *m* exprés

es·say ['eseɪ] *n creative* redacción *f*; *factual* trabajo *m*

es·sen·tial [ɪ'senʃl] *adj* esencial; *the ~ thing is …* lo esencial es …

es·sen·tial·ly [ɪ'senʃlɪ] *adv* esencialmente

es·tab·lish [ɪ'stæblɪʃ] *v/t company* fundar; (*create, determine*) establecer; *~ o.s. as* establecerse como

es·tab·lish·ment [ɪ'stæblɪʃmənt] *firm, shop etc* establecimiento *m*; *the Establishment* el orden establecido

es·tate [ɪ'steɪt] (*area of land*) finca *f*; (*possessions of dead person*) patrimonio *m*

es'tate a·gen·cy *Br* agencia *f* inmobiliaria

es·thet·ic [ɪs'θetɪk] *adj* estético

es·ti·mate ['estɪmət] **1** *n* estimación *f*; *for job* presupuesto *m* **2** *v/t* estimar; *~d time of arrival* hora *f* estimada de llegada

es·ti·ma·tion [estɪ'meɪʃn] estima *f*; *he has gone up/down in my ~* le tengo en más/menos estima; *in my ~ (opinion)* a mi parecer

es·tranged [ɪs'treɪndʒd] *adj wife, husband* separado

es·tu·a·ry ['estʃəwerɪ] estuario *m*

ETA [iːtiː'eɪ] *abbr* (= *estimated time of arrival*) hora *f* estimada de llegada

etc [et'setrə] *abbr* (= *et cetera*) etc (= etcétera)

etch·ing ['etʃɪŋ] aguafuerte *m*

e·ter·nal [ɪ'tɜːrnl] *adj* eterno

e·ter·ni·ty [ɪ'tɜːrnətɪ] eternidad *f*

eth·i·cal ['eθɪkl] *adj* ético

eth·ics ['eθɪks] ética *f*; *code of ~* código *m* ético

eth·nic ['eθnɪk] *adj* étnico

eth·nic 'group grupo *m* étnico

eth·nic mi'nor·i·ty minoría *f* étnica

EU [iː'juː] *abbr* (= *European Union*) UE *f* (=Unión *f* Europea)

eu·phe·mism ['juːfəmɪzm] eufemismo *m*

eu·pho·ri·a [juː'fɔːrɪə] euforia *f*

eu·ro ['jʊroʊ] euro *m*

Eu·rope ['jʊrəp] Europa *f*

Eu·ro·pe·an [jʊrə'pɪən] **1** *adj* europeo **2** *n* europeo(-a) *m(f)*

Eu·ro·pe·an Com'mis·sion Comisión *f* Europea; **Eu·ro·pe·an 'Par·lia·ment** Parlamento *m* Europeo; **Eu·ro'pe·an plan** media pensión *f*; **Eu·ro·pe·an 'Un·ion** Unión *f* Europea

eu·tha·na·si·a [juːθə'neɪzɪə] eutanasia *f*

e·vac·u·ate [ɪ'vækjʊeɪt] *v/t* evacuar

e·vade [ɪ'veɪd] *v/t* evadir

e·val·u·ate [ɪ'væljʊeɪt] *v/t* evaluar

e·val·u·a·tion [ɪvæljʊ'eɪʃn] evaluación *f*

e·van·gel·ist [ɪ'vændʒəlɪst] evangelista *m/f*

e·vap·o·rate [ɪ'væpəreɪt] *v/i of water* evaporarse; *of confidence* desvanecerse

e·vap·o·ra·tion [ɪvæpə'reɪʃn] *of water* evaporación *f*

e·va·sion [ɪ'veɪʒn] evasión *f*

e·va·sive [ɪ'veɪsɪv] *adj* evasivo

eve [iːv] víspera *f*

e·ven ['iːvn] **1** *adj* (*regular*) regular; (*level*) llano; *number* par; *distribution* igualado; *I'll get ~ with him* me las pagará **2** *adv* incluso; *~ bigger/better* incluso *or* aún mayor/mejor; *not ~* ni siquiera; *~ so* aun así; *~ if* aunque; *~ if he begged me* aunque me lo suplicara **3** *v/t*: *~ the score* empatar, igualar el marcador

eve·ning ['iːvnɪŋ] tarde *f*; *after dark*

noche *f*; *in the* ~ por la tarde / noche; *this* ~ esta tarde / noche; *yesterday* ~ anoche *f*; *good* ~ buenas noches

'eve·ning class clase *f* nocturna; 'eve·ning dress *for woman* traje *f* de noche; *for man* traje *f* de etiqueta; eve·ning 'pa·per periódico *m* de la tarde *or* vespertino

e·ven·ly ['iːvnlɪ] *adv* (*regularly*) regularmente

e·vent [ɪ'vent] acontecimiento *m*; SP prueba *f*; *at all* ~*s* en cualquier caso

e·vent·ful [ɪ'ventfəl] *adj* agitado, lleno de incidentes

e·ven·tu·al [ɪ'ventʃuəl] *adj* final

e·ven·tu·al·ly [ɪ'ventʃuəlɪ] *adv* finalmente

ev·er ['evər] *adv*: *if I* ~ *hear you ...* como te oiga ...; *have you* ~ *been to Colombia?* ¿has estado alguna vez en Colombia?; *for* ~ siempre; ~ *since* desde entonces; ~ *since she found out about it* desde que se enteró de ello; ~ *since I've known him* desde que lo conozco

ev·er·green ['evərgriːn] *n* árbol *m* de hoja perenne

ev·er·last·ing [evər'læstɪŋ] *adj love* eterno

ev·ery ['evrɪ] *adj* cada; *I see him* ~ *day* le veo todos los días; *you have* ~ *reason to ...* tienes toda la razón para ...; *one in* ~ *ten* uno de cada diez; ~ *other day* cada dos días; ~ *now and then* de vez en cuando

ev·ery·bod·y ['evrɪbaːdɪ] → *everyone*

ev·ery·day ['evrɪdeɪ] *adj* cotidiano

ev·ery·one ['evrɪwʌn] *pron* todo el mundo

ev·ery·thing ['evrɪθɪŋ] *pron* todo

ev·ery·where ['evrɪwer] *adv* en *or* por todos sitios; (*wherever*) dondequiera que

e·vict [ɪ'vɪkt] *v/t* desahuciar

ev·i·dence ['evɪdəns] *also* LAW prueba(s) *f*(*pl*); *give* ~ prestar declaración

ev·i·dent ['evɪdənt] *adj* evidente

ev·i·dent·ly ['evɪdəntlɪ] *adv* (*clearly*)

evidentemente; (*apparently*) aparentemente, al parecer

e·vil ['iːvl] 1 *adj* malo 2 *n* mal *m*

e·voke [ɪ'vouk] *v/t image* evocar

ev·o·lu·tion [iːvə'luːʃn] evolución *f*

e·volve [ɪ'vaːlv] *v/i* evolucionar

ewe [juː] oveja *f*

ex- [eks] *pref* ex-

ex [eks] F (*former wife, husband*) ex *m*/f F

ex·act [ɪg'zækt] *adj* exacto

ex·act·ing [ɪg'zæktɪŋ] *adj* exigente; *task* duro

ex·act·ly [ɪg'zæktlɪ] *adv* exactamente

ex·ag·ge·rate [ɪg'zædʒəreɪt] *v/t* & *v/i* exagerar

ex·ag·ge·ra·tion [ɪgzædʒə'reɪʃn] exageración *f*

ex·am [ɪg'zæm] examen *m*; *take an* ~ hacer un examen; *pass / fail an* ~ aprobar / suspender un examen

ex·am·i·na·tion [ɪgzæmɪ'neɪʃn] examen *m*; *of patient* reconocimiento *m*

ex·am·ine [ɪg'zæmɪn] *v/t* examinar; *patient* reconocer

ex·am·in·er [ɪg'zæmɪnər] EDU examinador(a) *m*(*f*)

ex·am·ple [ɪg'zæmpl] ejemplo *m*; *for* ~ por ejemplo; *set a good / bad* ~ dar buen / mal ejemplo

ex·as·pe·rat·ed [ɪg'zæspəreɪtɪd] *adj* exasperado

ex·as·pe·rat·ing [ɪg'zæspəreɪtɪŋ] *adj* exasperante

ex·ca·vate ['ekskəveɪt] *v/t* excavar

ex·ca·va·tion [ekskə'veɪʃn] excavación *f*

ex·ca·va·tor ['ekskəveɪtər] excavadora *f*

ex·ceed [ɪk'siːd] *v/t* (*be more than*) exceder; (*go beyond*) sobrepasar

ex·ceed·ing·ly [ɪk'siːdɪŋlɪ] *adj* sumamente

ex·cel [ɪk'sel] 1 *v/i* (*pret & pp* -led) sobresalir (*at* en) 2 *v/t* (*pret & pp* -led): ~ *o.s.* superarse a sí mismo

ex·cel·lence ['eksələns] excelencia *f*

ex·cel·lent ['eksələnt] *adj* excelente

ex·cept [ɪk'sept] *prep* excepto; ~ *for* a excepción de; ~ *that* sólo que

ex·cep·tion [ɪk'sepʃn] excepción *f*;
with the ~ of a excepción de; **take
~ to** molestarse por

ex·cep·tion·al [ɪk'sepʃnl] *adj* excepcional

ex·cep·tion·al·ly [ɪk'sepʃnlɪ] *adv*
(*extremely*) excepcionalmente

ex·cerpt ['eksɜːrpt] extracto *m*

ex·cess [ɪk'ses] **1** *n* exceso *m*;
eat / drink to ~ comer / beber en exceso; **in ~ of** superior a **2** *adj* excedente

ex·cess 'bag·gage exceso *m* de
equipaje

ex·cess 'fare suplemento *m*

ex·ces·sive [ɪk'sesɪv] *adj* excesivo

ex·change [ɪks'tʃeɪndʒ] **1** *n* intercambio *m*; **in ~** a cambio (**for** de)
2 *v/t* cambiar

ex'change rate FIN tipo *m* de cambio

ex·ci·ta·ble [ɪk'saɪtəbl] *adj* excitable

ex·cite [ɪk'saɪt] *v/t* (*make enthusiastic*) entusiasmar

ex·cit·ed [ɪk'saɪtɪd] *adj* emocionado,
excitado; *sexually* excitado; **get ~**
emocionarse; **get ~ about** emocionarse *or* excitarse con

ex·cite·ment [ɪk'saɪtmənt] emoción
f, excitación *f*

ex·cit·ing [ɪk'saɪtɪŋ] *adj* emocionante, excitante

ex·claim [ɪk'skleɪm] *v/t* exclamar

ex·cla·ma·tion [eksklə'meɪʃn] exclamación *f*

ex·cla'ma·tion point signo *m* de admiración

ex·clude [ɪk'sklu:d] *v/t* excluir;
possibility descartar

ex·clud·ing [ɪk'sklu:dɪŋ] *prep* excluyendo

ex·clu·sive [ɪk'sklu:sɪv] *adj* exclusivo

ex·com·mu·ni·cate [ekskə'mju:nɪkeɪt] *v/t* REL excomulgar

ex·cru·ci·a·ting [ɪk'skru:ʃɪeɪtɪŋ] *adj*
pain terrible

ex·cur·sion [ɪk'skɜːrʃn] excursión *f*

ex·cuse **1** *n* [ɪk'skju:s] excusa *f* **2** *v/t*
[ɪk'skju:z] (*forgive*) excusar, perdonar; (*allow to leave*) disculpar; **~ s.o.**

from sth dispensar a alguien de
algo; **~ me** to get past, interrupting
perdone, disculpe; *to get attention*
perdone, oiga

e·x·e·cute ['eksɪkju:t] *v/t criminal,
plan* ejecutar

ex·e·cu·tion [eksɪ'kju:ʃn] *of criminal, plan* ejecución *f*

ex·e·cu·tion·er [eksɪ'kju:ʃnər] verdugo *m*

ex·ec·u·tive [ɪg'zekjʊtɪv] ejecutivo(-a) *m(f)*

ex·ec·u·tive 'brief·case maletín *m*
de ejecutivo

ex·ec·u·tive 'wash·room baño *m*
para ejecutivos

ex·em·pla·ry [ɪg'zemplərɪ] *adj* ejemplar

ex·empt [ɪg'zempt] *adj* exento; **be ~
from** estar exento de

ex·er·cise ['eksərsaɪz] **1** *n* ejercicio
m; **take ~** hacer ejercicio **2** *v/t
muscle* ejercitar; *dog* pasear; *caution*
proceder con; **~ restraint** controlarse **3** *v/i* hacer ejercicio

'ex·er·cise bike bicicleta *f* estática

'ex·er·cise book EDU cuaderno *m* de
ejercicios

ex·ert [ɪg'zɜːrt] *v/t authority* ejercer;
~ o.s. esforzarse

ex·er·tion [ɪg'zɜːrʃn] esfuerzo *m*

ex·hale [eks'heɪl] *v/t* exhalar

ex·haust [ɪg'zɒːst] **1** *n fumes* gases
mpl de la combustión; *pipe* tubo *m*
de escape **2** *v/t* (*tire*) cansar; (*use up*)
agotar

ex·haust·ed [ɪg'zɒːstɪd] *adj* (*tired*)
agotado

ex'haust fumes *npl* gases *mpl* de la
combustión

ex·haust·ing [ɪg'zɒːstɪŋ] *adj* agotador

ex·haus·tion [ɪg'zɒːstʃn] agotamiento *m*

ex·haus·tive [ɪg'zɒːstɪv] *adj* exhaustivo

ex'haust pipe tubo *m* de escape

ex·hib·it [ɪg'zɪbɪt] **1** *n in exhibition*
objeto *m* expuesto **2** *v/t of gallery*
exhibir; *of artist* exponer; (*give
evidence of*) mostrar

E

ex·hi·bi·tion [eksɪ'bɪʃn] exposición *f*; *of bad behavior, skill* exhibición *f*

ex·hi·bi·tion·ist [eksɪ'bɪʃnɪst] exhibicionista *m/f*

ex·hil·a·rat·ing [ɪɡ'zɪləreɪtɪŋ] *adj* estimulante

ex·ile ['eksaɪl] **1** *n* exilio *m*; *person* exiliado(-a) *m(f)* **2** *v/t* exiliar

ex·ist [ɪɡ'zɪst] *v/i* existir; **~ on** subsistir a base de

ex·ist·ence [ɪɡ'zɪstəns] existencia *f*; **be in ~** existir; **come into ~** crearse, nacer

ex·ist·ing [ɪɡ'zɪstɪŋ] *adj* existente

ex·it ['eksɪt] **1** *n* salida *f*; THEA salida *f*, mutis *m* **2** *v/i* COMPUT salir

ex·on·e·rate [ɪɡ'zɑːnəreɪt] *v/t* exonerar

ex·or·bi·tant [ɪɡ'zɔːrbɪtənt] *adj* exorbitante

ex·ot·ic [ɪɡ'zɑːtɪk] *adj* exótico

ex·pand [ɪk'spænd] **1** *v/t* expandir **2** *v/i* expandirse; *of metal* dilatarse

♦ **expand on** *v/t* desarrollar

ex·panse [ɪk'spæns] extensión *f*

ex·pan·sion [ɪk'spænʃn] expansión *f*; *of metal* dilatación *f*

ex·pat·ri·ate [eks'pætrɪət] **1** *adj* expatriado **2** *n* expatriado(-a) *m(f)*

ex·pect [ɪk'spekt] **1** *v/t* esperar; *(suppose)* imaginar(se); *(demand)* exigir **2** *v/i*: **be ~ing** *(be pregnant)* estar en estado; **I ~ so** eso espero, creo que sí

ex·pec·tant [ɪk'spektənt] *adj crowd* expectante

ex·pec·tant 'moth·er futura madre *f*

ex·pec·ta·tion [ekspek'teɪʃn] expectativa *f*

ex·pe·di·ent [ɪk'spiːdɪənt] *adj* oportuno, conveniente

ex·pe·di·tion [ekspɪ'dɪʃn] expedición *f*

ex·pel [ɪk'spel] *v/t (pret & pp -led) person* expulsar

ex·pend [ɪk'spend] *v/t energy* gastar

ex·pend·a·ble [ɪk'spendəbl] *adj person* prescindible

ex·pen·di·ture [ɪk'spendɪtʃər] gasto *m*

ex·pense [ɪk'spens] gasto *m*; **at great ~** gastando mucho dinero; **at the company's ~** a cargo de la empresa; **a joke at my ~** una broma a costa mía; **at the ~ of his health** a costa de su salud

ex'pense ac·count cuenta *f* de gastos

ex·pen·ses [ɪk'spensɪz] *npl* gastos *mpl*

ex·pen·sive [ɪk'spensɪv] *adj* caro

ex·pe·ri·ence [ɪk'spɪrɪəns] **1** *n* experiencia *f* **2** *v/t* experimentar

ex·pe·ri·enced [ɪk'spɪrɪənst] *adj* experimentado

ex·per·i·ment [ɪk'sperɪmənt] **1** *n* experimento *m* **2** *v/i* experimentar; **~ on** *animals* experimentar con; **~ with** *(try out)* probar

ex·per·i·men·tal [ɪksperɪ'mentl] *adj* experimental

ex·pert ['ekspɜːrt] **1** *adj* experto **2** *n* experto(-a) *m(f)*

ex·pert ad'vice la opinión de un experto

ex·per·tise [ekspɜːr'tiːz] destreza *f*, pericia *f*

ex·pire [ɪk'spaɪr] *v/i* caducar

ex·pi·ry [ɪk'spaɪrɪ] *of lease, contract* vencimiento *m*; *of passport* caducidad *f*

ex'pi·ry date *of food, passport* fecha *f* de caducidad; **be past its ~** haber caducado

ex·plain [ɪk'spleɪn] **1** *v/t* explicar **2** *v/i* explicarse

ex·pla·na·tion [eksplə'neɪʃn] explicación *f*

ex·plan·a·tor·y [ɪk'splænətɔːrɪ] *adj* explicativo

ex·plic·it [ɪk'splɪsɪt] *adj instructions* explícito

ex·plic·it·ly [ɪk'splɪsɪtlɪ] *adv state* explícitamente; *forbid* terminantemente

ex·plode [ɪk'sploʊd] **1** *v/i of bomb* explotar **2** *v/t bomb* hacer explotar

ex·ploit¹ ['eksplɔɪt] *n* hazaña *f*

ex·ploit² [ɪk'splɔɪt] *v/t person, resources* explotar

ex·ploi·ta·tion [eksplɔɪ'teɪʃn] *of person* explotación *f*

ex·plo·ra·tion [eksplə'reɪʃn] exploración *f*

ex·plor·a·to·ry [ɪk'splɔːrətɔrɪ] *adj surgery* exploratorio

ex·plore [ɪk'splɔːr] *v/t country etc* explorar; *possibility* estudiar

ex·plor·er [ɪk'splɔːrər] explorador(a) *m(f)*

ex·plo·sion [ɪk'sploʊʒn] *of bomb, in population* explosión *f*

ex·plo·sive [ɪk'sploʊsɪv] *n* explosivo *m*

ex·port ['ekspɔːrt] **1** *n action* exportación *f*; *item* producto *m* de exportación; **ex·ports** exportaciones *fpl* **2** *v/t also* COMPUT exportar

'ex·port cam·paign campaña *f* de exportación

ex·port·er ['ekspɔːrtər] exportador(a) *m(f)*

ex·pose [ɪk'spoʊz] *v/t (uncover)* exponer; *scandal* sacar a la luz; **he's been ~d as a liar** ha quedado como un mentiroso

ex·po·sure [ɪk'spoʊʒər] exposición *f*; PHOT foto(grafía) *f*

ex·press [ɪk'spres] **1** *adj (fast)* rápido; *(explicit)* expreso **2** *n train* expreso *m*; *bus* autobús *m* directo **3** *v/t* expresar; **~ o.s. well / clearly** expresarse bien / con claridad

ex·press el·e·va·tor *ascensor rápido que sólo para en algunos pisos*

ex·pres·sion [ɪk'spreʃn] *voiced* muestra *f*; *phrase, on face* expresión *f*; **read with ~** leer con sentimiento

ex·pres·sive [ɪk'spresɪv] *adj* expresivo

ex·press·ly [ɪk'spreslɪ] *adv state* expresamente; *forbid* terminantemente

ex·press·way [ɪk'spresweɪ] autopista *f*

ex·pul·sion [ɪk'spʌlʃn] *from school, of diplomat* expulsión *f*

ex·qui·site [ek'skwɪzɪt] *adj (beautiful)* exquisito

ex·tend [ɪk'stend] **1** *v/t house, investigation* ampliar; *(make wider)* ensan-

char; *(make bigger)* agrandar; *runway, path* alargar; *contract, visa* prorrogar; *thanks, congratulations* extender **2** *v/i of garden etc* llegar

ex·ten·sion [ɪk'stenʃn] *to house* ampliación *f*; *of contract, visa* prórroga *f*; TELEC extensión *f*

ex·ten·sion ca·ble cable *m* de extensión

ex·ten·sive [ɪk'stensɪv] *adj damage* cuantioso; *knowledge* considerable; *search* extenso, amplio

ex·tent [ɪk'stent] alcance *m*; **to such an ~ that** hasta el punto de que; **to a certain ~** hasta cierto punto

ex·ten·u·at·ing cir·cum·stanc·es [ɪk'stenuːeɪtɪŋ] *npl* circunstancias *fpl* atenuantes

ex·te·ri·or [ɪk'stɪrɪər] **1** *adj* exterior **2** *n* exterior *m*

ex·ter·mi·nate [ɪk'stɜːrmɪneɪt] *v/t* exterminar

ex·ter·nal [ɪk'stɜːrnl] *adj (outside)* exterior, externo

ex·tinct [ɪk'stɪŋkt] *adj species* extinguido

ex·tinc·tion [ɪk'stɪŋkʃn] *of species* extinción *f*

ex·tin·guish [ɪk'stɪŋgwɪʃ] *v/t fire* extinguir, apagar; *cigarette* apagar

ex·tin·guish·er [ɪk'stɪŋgwɪʃər] extintor *m*

ex·tort [ɪk'stɔːrt] *v/t* obtener mediante extorsión; **~ money from** extorsionar a

ex·tor·tion [ɪk'stɔːrʃn] extorsión *f*

ex·tor·tion·ate [ɪk'stɔːrʃənət] *adj prices* desorbitado

ex·tra ['ekstrə] **1** *n* extra *m*; *in movie* extra *m/f* **2** *adj* extra; **meals are ~** las comidas se pagan aparte; **that's $1 ~** cuesta 1 dólar más **3** *adv* super; **~ strong** extrafuerte; **~ special** muy especial

ex·tra 'charge recargo *m*

ex·tract[1] ['ekstrækt] *n* extracto *m*

ex·tract[2] [ɪk'strækt] *v/t* sacar; *coal, oil, tooth* extraer; *information* sonsacar

ex·trac·tion [ɪk'strækʃn] *of oil, coal, tooth* extracción *f*

ex·tra·dite ['ekstrədaɪt] v/t extraditar

ex·tra·di·tion [ekstrə'dɪʃn] extradición f

ex·tra·di·tion trea·ty tratado m de extradición

ex·tra·mar·i·tal [ekstrə'mærɪtl] adj extramarital

ex·tra·or·di·nar·i·ly [ekstrɔːrdɪn'erɪlɪ] adv extraordinariamente

ex·tra·or·di·na·ry [ɪk'strɔːrdɪnerɪ] adj extraordinario

ex·trav·a·gance [ɪk'strævəgəns] with money despilfarro m; of claim etc extravagancia f

ex·trav·a·gant [ɪk'strævəgənt] adj with money despilfarrador; claim extravagante

ex·treme [ɪk'striːm] **1** n extremo m **2** adj extremo; views extremista

ex·treme·ly [ɪk'striːmlɪ] adv extremadamente, sumamente

ex·trem·ist [ɪk'striːmɪst] extremista

m/f

ex·tri·cate ['ekstrɪkeɪt] v/t liberar

ex·tro·vert ['ekstrəvɜːrt] **1** adj extrovertido **2** n extrovertido(-a) m(f)

ex·u·be·rant [ɪg'zuːbərənt] adj exuberante

ex·ult [ɪg'zʌlt] v/i exultar

eye [aɪ] **1** n of person, needle ojo m; **keep an ~ on** (look after) estar pendiente de; (monitor) estar pendiente de, vigilar **2** v/t mirar

'eye·ball globo m ocular; **'eye·brow** ceja f; **'eye·catch·ing** adj llamativo; **'eye·glass·es** npl gafas fpl, L.Am. anteojos mpl, L.Am. lentes mpl; **'eye·lash** pestaña f; **'eye·lid** párpado m; **'eye·lin·er** lápiz m de ojos; **'eye·sha·dow** sombra f de ojos; **'eye·sight** vista f; **'eye·sore** engendro m, monstruosidad f; **'eye strain** vista f cansada; **'eye·wit·ness** testigo m/f ocular

F

F abbr (= **Fahrenheit**) F

fab·ric ['fæbrɪk] (material) tejido m

fab·u·lous ['fæbjʊləs] adj fabuloso, estupendo

fab·u·lous·ly ['fæbjʊləslɪ] adv rich tremendamente; beautiful increíblemente

fa·çade [fə'sɑːd] of building, person fachada f

face [feɪs] **1** n cara f; **~ to ~** cara a cara; **lose ~** padecer una humillación **2** v/t (be opposite) estar enfrente de; (confront) enfrentarse a

♦ **face up to** v/t hacer frente a

'face·cloth toallita f; **'face·lift** lifting m, estiramiento m de piel; **'face pack** mascarilla f (facial); **face 'val·ue: take sth at ~** tomarse algo literalmente

fa·cial ['feɪʃl] n limpieza f de cutis

fa·cil·i·tate [fə'sɪlɪteɪt] v/t facilitar

fa·cil·i·ties [fə'sɪlɪtɪz] npl instalaciones fpl

fact [fækt] hecho m; **in ~**, **as a matter of ~** de hecho

fac·tion ['fækʃn] facción f

fac·tor ['fæktər] factor m

fac·to·ry ['fæktərɪ] fábrica f

fac·ul·ty ['fækəltɪ] (hearing etc), at university facultad f

fad [fæd] moda f

fade [feɪd] v/i of colors desteñirse, perder color; of memories desvanecerse

fad·ed ['feɪdɪd] adj color, jeans desteñido, descolorido

fag¹ [fæg] F (homosexual) maricón m F

fag² [fæg] *Br F (cigarette)* pitillo *m* F

Fahr·en·heit [ˈfærənhaɪt] *adj* Fahrenheit

fail [feɪl] **1** *v/i* fracasar; *of plan* fracasar, fallar **2** *v/t exam* suspender **3** *n:* **without ~** sin falta

fail·ing [ˈfeɪlɪŋ] *n* fallo *m*

fail·ure [ˈfeɪljər] fracaso *m*; *in exam* suspenso *m*; **I feel such a ~** me siento un fracasado

faint [feɪnt] **1** *adj line, smile* tenue; *smell, noise* casi imperceptible **2** *v/i* desmayarse

faint·ly [ˈfeɪntlɪ] *adv smile, smell* levemente

fair¹ [fer] *n* COM feria *f*

fair² [fer] *adj hair* rubio; *complexion* claro; *(just)* justo

fair·ly [ˈferlɪ] *adv treat* justamente, con justicia; *(quite)* bastante

fair·ness [ˈfernɪs] *of treatment* imparcialidad *f*

fai·ry [ˈferɪ] hada *f*

'fai·ry tale cuento *m* de hadas

faith [feɪθ] fe *f*, confianza *f*; REL fe *f*

faith·ful [ˈfeɪθfəl] *adj* fiel; **be ~ to one's partner** ser fiel a la pareja

faith·ful·ly [ˈfeɪθfəlɪ] *adv* religiosamente

fake [feɪk] **1** *n* falsificación *f* **2** *adj* falso **3** *v/t (forge)* falsificar; *(feign)* fingir

Falk·land Is·lands [ˈfɔːlklənd] *npl:* **the ~** las Islas Malvinas

fall¹ [fɔːl] *n season* otoño *m*

fall² [fɔːl] **1** *v/i (pret fell, pp fallen) of person* caerse; *of government, prices, temperature, night* caer; **it ~s on a Tuesday** cae en martes; **~ ill** enfermar, caer enfermo; **I fell off the wall** me caí del muro **2** *n* caída *f*

♦ **fall back on** *v/t* recurrir a

♦ **fall behind** *v/i with work, studies* retrasarse

♦ **fall down** *v/i* caerse

♦ **fall for** *v/t person* enamorarse de; *(be deceived by)* dejarse engañar por; **I'm amazed you fell for it** me sorprende mucho que picaras

♦ **fall out** *v/i of hair* caerse; *(argue)* pelearse

♦ **fall over** *v/i* caerse

♦ **fall through** *v/i of plans* venirse abajo

fal·len [ˈfɔːlən] *pp →* **fall**

fal·li·ble [ˈfæləbl] *adj* falible

'fall·out lluvia *f* radiactiva

false [fɑːls] *adj* falso

false a'larm falsa alarma *f*

false·ly [ˈfɑːlslɪ] *adv:* **be ~ accused of sth** ser acusado falsamente de algo

false 'start *in race* salida *f* nula

false 'teeth *npl* dentadura *f* postiza

fal·si·fy [ˈfɑːlsɪfaɪ] *v/t (pret & pp -ied)* falsificar

fame [feɪm] fama *f*

fa·mil·i·ar [fəˈmɪljər] *adj* familiar; **get ~** *(intimate)* tomarse demasiadas confianzas; **be ~ with sth** estar familiarizado con algo; **that looks ~** eso me resulta familiar; **that sounds ~** me suena

fa·mil·i·ar·i·ty [fəmɪlɪˈærɪtɪ] *with subject etc* familiaridad *f*

fa·mil·i·ar·ize [fəˈmɪljəraɪz] *v/t:* **~ o.s. with ...** familiarizarse con ...

fam·i·ly [ˈfæməlɪ] familia *f*

fam·i·ly 'doc·tor médico *m/f* de familia; **'fam·i·ly name** apellido *m*; **fam·i·ly 'plan·ning** planificación *f* familiar; **fam·i·ly 'plan·ning clin·ic** clínica *f* de planificación familiar; **fam·i·ly 'tree** árbol *m* genealógico

fam·ine [ˈfæmɪn] hambruna *f*

fam·ished [ˈfæmɪʃt] *adj* F: **I'm ~** estoy muerto de hambre F

fa·mous [ˈfeɪməs] *adj* famoso; **be ~ for ...** ser famoso por ...

fan¹ [fæn] *n (supporter)* seguidor(a) *m(f)*; *of singer, band* admirador(a) *m(f)*, fan *m/f*

fan² [fæn] **1** *n electric* ventilador *m*; *handheld* abanico *m* **2** *v/t (pret & pp -ned)* abanicar; **~ o.s.** abanicarse

fa·nat·ic [fəˈnætɪk] *n* fanático(-a) *m(f)*

fa·nat·i·cal [fəˈnætɪkl] *adj* fanático

fa·nat·i·cism [fəˈnætɪsɪzm] fanatismo *m*

'fan belt MOT correa *f* del ventilador

'**fan club** club *m* de fans

fan·cy '**dress** disfraz *m*

fan·cy· '**dress par·ty** fiesta *f* de disfraces

fang [fæŋ] colmillo *m*

'**fan mail** cartas *fpl* de los fans

fan·ny pack ['fænɪ] riñonera *f*

fan·ta·size ['fæntəsaɪz] *v/i* fantasear (*about* sobre)

fan·tas·tic [fæn'tæstɪk] *adj* (*very good*) fantástico, excelente; (*very big*) inmenso

fan·tas·tic·al·ly [fæn'tæstɪklɪ] *adv* (*extremely*) sumamente, increíblemente

fan·ta·sy ['fæntəsɪ] fantasía *f*

far [fɑːr] *adv* lejos; (*much*) mucho; ~ *bigger/ faster* mucho más grande / rápido; ~ *away* lejos; *how ~ is it to ...?* ¿a cuánto está ...?; *as ~ as the corner/ hotel* hasta la esquina/ el hotel; *as ~ as I can see* tal y como lo veo yo; *as ~ as I know* que yo sepa; *you've gone too ~ in behavior* te has pasado; *so ~ so good* por ahora muy bien

farce [fɑːrs] farsa *f*

fare [fer] *n price* tarifa *f*; *actual money* dinero *m*

Far '**East** Lejano Oriente *m*

fare·well [fer'wel] *n* despedida *f*

fare·well par·ty fiesta *f* de despedida

far·fetched [fɑːr'fetʃt] *adj* inverosímil, exagerado

farm [fɑːrm] *n* granja *f*

farm·er ['fɑːrmər] granjero(-a) *m(f)*

'**farm·house** granja *f*, alquería *f*

farm·ing ['fɑːrmɪŋ] *n* agricultura *f*

'**farm·work·er** trabajador(a) *m(f)* del campo

'**farm·yard** corral *m*

far- '**off** *adj* lejano

far·sight·ed [fɑːr'saɪtɪd] *adj* previsor; *optically* hipermétrope

fart [fɑːrt] **1** *n* F pedo *m* F **2** *v/i* F tirarse un pedo F

far·ther ['fɑːrðər] *adv* más lejos; ~ *away* más allá, más lejos

far·thest ['fɑːrðəst] *adv travel etc* más lejos

fas·ci·nate ['fæsɪneɪt] *v/t* fascinar; *be ~d by ...* estar fascinado por ...

fas·ci·nat·ing ['fæsɪneɪtɪŋ] *adj* fascinante

fas·ci·na·tion [fæsɪ'neɪʃn] fascinación *f*

fas·cism ['fæʃɪzm] fascismo *m*

fas·cist ['fæʃɪst] **1** *n* fascista *m/f* **2** *adj* fascista

fash·ion ['fæʃn] *n* moda *f*; (*manner*) modo *m*, manera *f*; *in ~* de moda; *out of ~* pasado de moda

fash·ion·a·ble ['fæʃnəbl] *adj* de moda

fash·ion·a·bly ['fæʃnəblɪ] *adv dressed* a la moda

'**fash·ion-con·scious** *adj* que sigue la moda; '**fash·ion de·sign·er** modisto(-a) *m(f)*; '**fash·ion mag·a·zine** revista *f* de modas; '**fash·ion show** desfile *f* de moda, pase *m* de modelos

fast¹ [fæst] **1** *adj* rápido; *be ~ of clock* ir adelantado **2** *adv* rápido; *stuck ~* atascado; ~ *asleep* profundamente dormido

fast² [fæst] *n not eating* ayuno *m*

fas·ten ['fæsn] **1** *v/t window, lid* cerrar (*poniendo el cierre*); *dress* abrochar; ~ *sth onto sth* asegurar algo a algo **2** *v/i of dress etc* abrocharse

fas·ten·er ['fæsnər] *for dress, lid* cierre *f*

fast '**food** comida *f* rápida; **fast·food** '**res·tau·rant** restaurante *f* de comida rápida; **fast** '**for·ward 1** *n on video etc* avance *m* rápido **2** *v/i* avanzar; '**fast lane** *on road* carril *m* rápido; *in the ~ fig:* of life con un tren de vida acelerado; '**fast train** (tren *m*) rápido *m*

fat [fæt] **1** *adj* gordo **2** *n on meat, for baking* grasa *f*

fa·tal ['feɪtl] *adj illness* mortal; *error* fatal

fa·tal·i·ty [fə'tælətɪ] víctima *f* mortal

fa·tal·ly ['feɪtəlɪ] *adv* mortalmente; ~ *injured* herido mortalmente

fate [feɪt] destino *m*

fat·ed ['feɪtɪd] *adj:* *be ~ to do sth* estar predestinado a hacer algo

'fat-free *adj* sin grasas

fa·ther ['fɑːðər] *n* padre *m*; **Father Martin** REL el Padre Martin

fa·ther·hood ['fɑːðərhʊd] paternidad *f*

'fa·ther-in-law (*pl* **fathers-in-law**) suegro *m*

fa·ther·ly ['fɑːðəlɪ] *adj* paternal

fath·om ['fæðəm] *n* NAUT braza *f*

♦**fathom out** *v/t fig* entender

fa·tigue [fə'tiːg] *n* cansancio *m*, fatiga *f*

fat·so ['fætsoʊ] F gordinflón (-ona) *m(f)* F

fat·ten ['fætn] *v/t animal* engordar

fat·ty ['fætɪ] **1** *adj* graso **2** *n* F (*person*) gordinflón (-ona) *m(f)* F

fau·cet ['fɔːsɪt] *Span* grifo *m*, *L.Am.* llave *f*

fault [fɔːlt] *n* (*defect*) fallo *m*; **it's your/my ~** es culpa tuya/mía; **find ~ with ...** encontrar defectos a ...

fault·less ['fɔːltlɪs] *adj* impecable

fault·y ['fɔːltɪ] *adj goods* defectuoso

fa·vor ['feɪvər] **1** *n* favor *m*; **do s.o. a ~** hacer un favor a alguien; **do me a ~!** (*don't be stupid*) ¡haz el favor!; **in ~ of ...** a favor de ...; **be in ~ of ...** estar a favor de ... **2** *v/t* (*prefer*) preferir

fa·vo·ra·ble ['feɪvərəbl] *adj reply etc* favorable

fa·vo·rite ['feɪvərɪt] **1** *n* favorito(-a) *m(f)*; *food* comida *f* favorita **2** *adj* favorito

fa·vor·it·ism ['feɪvrɪtɪzm] favoritismo *m*

fa·vour *etc Br* → **favor** *etc*

fax [fæks] **1** *n* fax *m*; **send sth by ~** enviar algo por fax **2** *v/t* enviar por fax; **~ sth to s.o.** enviar algo por fax a alguien

FBI [efbiː'aɪ] *abbr* (= **Federal Bureau of Investigation**) FBI *m*

fear [fɪr] **1** *n* miedo *m*, temor *m* **2** *v/t* temer, tener miedo a

fear·less ['fɪrlɪs] *adj* valiente, audaz

fear·less·ly ['fɪrlɪslɪ] *adv* sin miedo

fea·si·bil·i·ty stud·y [fiːzə'bɪlətɪ] estudio *m* de viabilidad

fea·si·ble ['fiːzəbl] *adj* factible, viable

feast [fiːst] *n* banquete *m*, festín *m*

feat [fiːt] *n* hazaña *f*, proeza *f*

fea·ther ['feðər] pluma *f*

fea·ture ['fiːtʃər] **1** *n on face* rasgo *m*, facción *f*; *of city, building, plan, style* característica *f*; *article in paper* reportaje *m*; *movie* largometraje *f*; **make a ~ of ...** destacar ... **2** *v/t*: *a movie featuring ...* una película en la que aparece ...

'fea·ture film largometraje *m*

Feb·ru·a·ry ['februeri] febrero *m*

fed [fed] *pret & pp* → **feed**

fed·e·ral ['fedərəl] *adj* federal

fed·e·ra·tion [fedə'reɪʃn] federación *f*

fed 'up *adj* F harto, hasta las narices F; **be ~ with ...** estar harto *or* hasta las narices de ...

fee [fiː] *of lawyer, doctor, consultant* honorarios *mpl*; *for entrance* entrada *f*; *for membership* cuota *f*

fee·ble ['fiːbl] *adj person, laugh* débil; *attempt* flojo; *excuse* pobre

feed [fiːd] *v/t* (*pret & pp* **fed**) alimentar, dar de comer a

'feed·back *n* reacción *f*; **we'll give you some ~ as soon as possible** le daremos nuestra opinión *or* nuestras reacciones lo antes posible

feel [fiːl] **1** *v/t* (*pret & pp* **felt**) (*touch*) tocar; (*sense*) sentir; (*think*) creer, pensar; **you can ~ the difference** se nota la diferencia **2** *v/i* (*pret & pp* **felt**): **it ~s silk/cotton** tiene la textura de la seda/algodón; **your hand ~s hot** tienes la mano caliente; **I ~ hungry** tengo hambre; **I ~ tired** estoy cansado; **how are you ~ing today?** ¿cómo te encuentras hoy?; **how does it ~ to be rich?** ¿qué se siente siendo rico?; **do you ~ like a drink/meal?** ¿te apetece una bebida/comida?; **I ~ like going/staying** me apetece ir/quedarme; **I don't ~ like it** no me apetece

♦**feel up** *v/t sexually* manosear

♦**feel up to** *v/t* sentirse con fuerzas

para

feel·er ['fi:lər] *of insect* antena *f*

'feel-good fac·tor sensación *f* positiva

feel·ing ['fi:lɪŋ] sentimiento *m*; (*sensation*) sensación *f*; *what are your ~s about it?* ¿qué piensas sobre ello?; *I have this ~ that ...* tengo el presentimiento de que ...

feet [fi:t] *pl →* **foot**

fe·line ['fi:laɪn] *adj* felino

fell [fel] *pret →* **fall**

fel·low ['feloʊ] *n* (*man*) tipo *m*

fel·low 'cit·i·zen conciudadano(-a) *m(f)*; **fel·low 'coun·try·man** compatriota *m/f*; **fel·low 'man** prójimo *m*

fel·o·ny ['felənɪ] delito *m* grave

felt [felt] **1** *n* fieltro *m* **2** *pret & pp →* **feel**

felt 'tip, felt-tip 'pen rotulador *m*

fe·male ['fi:meɪl] **1** *adj animal, plant* hembra; *relating to people* femenino **2** *n of animals, plants* hembra *f*; *person* mujer *f*

fem·i·nine ['femɪnɪn] **1** *adj also* GRAM femenino **2** *n* GRAM femenino *m*

fem·i·nism ['femɪnɪzm] feminismo *m*

fem·i·nist ['femɪnɪst] **1** *n* feminista *m/f* **2** *adj* feminista

fence [fens] *n around garden etc* cerca *f*, valla *f*; F *criminal* perista *m/f*; *sit on the ~* nadar entre dos aguas

♦ **fence in** *v/t land* cercar, vallar

fenc·ing ['fensɪŋ] SP esgrima *f*

fend [fend] *v/i*: *~ for o.s.* valerse por sí mismo

fend·er ['fendər] MOT aleta *f*

fer·ment¹ [fə'ment] *v/i of liquid* fermentar

fer·ment² ['fɜ:rment] *n* (*unrest*) agitación *f*

fer·men·ta·tion [fɜ:rmen'teɪʃn] fermentación *f*

fern [fɜ:rn] helecho *m*

fe·ro·cious [fə'roʊʃəs] *adj* feroz

fer·ry ['ferɪ] *n* ferry *m*, transbordador *m*

fer·tile ['fɜ:rtəl] *adj* fértil

fer·til·i·ty [fɜ:r'tɪlətɪ] fertilidad *f*

fer·til·i·ty drug medicamento *m* para el tratamiento de la infertilidad

fer·ti·lize ['fɜ:rtəlaɪz] *v/t* fertilizar

fer·ti·liz·er ['fɜ:rtəlaɪzər] *for soil* fertilizante *m*

fer·vent ['fɜ:rvənt] *adj admirer* ferviente

fer·vent·ly ['fɜ:rvəntlɪ] *adv* fervientemente

fes·ter ['festər] *v/i of wound* enconarse

fes·ti·val ['festɪvl] festival *m*

fes·tive ['festɪv] *adj* festivo; *the ~ season* la época navideña, las Navidades

fes·tiv·i·ties [fe'stɪvətɪz] *npl* celebraciones *fpl*

fe·tal ['fi:tl] *adj* fetal

fetch [fetʃ] *v/t person* recoger; *thing* traer, ir a buscar; *price* alcanzar

fe·tus ['fi:təs] feto *m*

feud [fju:d] **1** *n* enemistad *f* **2** *v/i* estar enemistado

fe·ver ['fi:vər] fiebre *f*

fe·ver·ish ['fi:vərɪʃ] *adj* con fiebre; *fig: excitement* febril

few [fju:] **1** *adj* (*not many*) pocos; *a ~* unos pocos; *quite a ~, a good ~* (*a lot*) bastantes **2** *pron* (*not many*) pocos(-as); *a ~* (*some*) unos pocos; *quite a ~, a good ~* (*a lot*) bastantes; *~ of them could speak English* de ellos muy pocos hablaban inglés

fewer ['fju:ər] *adj* menos; *~ than* menos que; *with numbers* menos de

fi·an·cé [fɪ'ɑ:nseɪ] prometido *m*, novio *m*

fi·an·cée [fɪ'ɑ:nseɪ] prometida *f*, novia *f*

fi·as·co [fɪ'æskoʊ] fiasco *m*

fib [fɪb] *n* F bola *f* F

fi·ber ['faɪbər] *n* fibra *f*

'fi·ber·glass *n* fibra *f* de vidrio; **fi·ber 'op·tic** *adj* de fibra óptica; **fi·ber 'op·tics** tecnología *f* de la fibra óptica

fi·bre *Br →* **fiber**

fick·le ['fɪkl] *adj* inconstante,

mudable

fic·tion ['fɪkʃn] n (novels) literatura f
de ficción; (made-up story) ficción f

fic·tion·al ['fɪkʃnl] adj de ficción

fic·ti·tious [fɪkˈtɪʃəs] adj ficticio

fid·dle ['fɪdl] **1** n (violin) violín m
2 v/i: ~ **around with** enredar con
3 v/t accounts, result amañar

fi·del·i·ty [fɪˈdelətɪ] fidelidad f

fidg·et ['fɪdʒɪt] v/i moverse; **stop**
~ing! ¡estáte quieto!

fidg·et·y ['fɪdʒɪtɪ] adj inquieto

field [fiːld] n (football, crops etc) campo
m; for sport campo m, L.Am. cancha
f; (competitors in race) participantes
mpl

field·er ['fiːldər] in baseball
fildeador(-a) m(f)

'**field e·vents** npl pruebas fpl de salto y lanzamiento

fierce [fɪrs] adj animal feroz; wind,
storm violento

fierce·ly ['fɪrslɪ] adv ferozmente

fi·er·y ['faɪrɪ] adj fogoso, ardiente

fif·teen [fɪfˈtiːn] quince

fif·teenth [fɪfˈtiːnθ] n & adj decimo-
quinto

fifth [fɪfθ] n & adj quinto

fif·ti·eth ['fɪftɪθ] n & adj quincuagé-
simo

fif·ty ['fɪftɪ] cincuenta

fif·ty-'fif·ty adv a medias

fig [fɪg] higo m

fight [faɪt] **1** n lucha f, pelea f;
(argument) pelea f; fig: for survival,
championship etc lucha f; in boxing
combate m; **have a ~** (argue) pelearse **2** v/t (pret & pp **fought**)
enemy, person luchar contra, pelear
contra; in boxing pelear contra;
disease, injustice luchar contra, combatir **3** v/i (pret & pp **fought**) luchar, pelear; (argue) pelearse

♦**fight for** v/t one's rights, a cause luchar por

fight·er ['faɪtər] combatiente m/f;
airplane caza m; (boxer) púgil m;
she's a ~ tiene espíritu combativo

fight·ing ['faɪtɪŋ] n physical, verbal
peleas fpl; MIL luchas fpl, combates
mpl

fig·u·ra·tive ['fɪgjərətɪv] adj figurado

fig·ure ['fɪgər] **1** n figura f; (digit) cifra f **2** v/t F (think) imaginarse, pensar

♦**figure on** v/t F (plan) pensar

♦**figure out** v/t (understand) entender; calculation resolver

'**fig·ure skat·er** patinador(a) m(f)
artístico(-a)

'**fig·ure skat·ing** patinaje m artístico

file[1] [faɪl] **1** n of documents expediente m; COMPUT archivo m, fichero m
2 v/t documents archivar

♦**file away** v/t documents archivar

file[2] [faɪl] n for wood, fingernails lima
f

'**file cab·i·net** archivador m

'**file man·ag·er** COMPUT administrador m de archivos

fi·li·al ['fɪlɪəl] adj filial

fill [fɪl] **1** v/t llenar; tooth empastar,
L.Am. emplomar **2** n: **eat one's ~**
hincharse

♦**fill in** v/t form, hole rellenar; **fill s.o.**
in poner a alguien al tanto

♦**fill in for** v/t sustituir a

♦**fill out 1** v/t form rellenar **2** v/i (get
fatter) engordar

♦**fill up 1** v/t llenar (hasta arriba)
2 v/i of stadium, theater llenarse

fil·let ['fɪlɪt] n filete m

fill·ing ['fɪlɪŋ] **1** n in sandwich relleno
m; in tooth empaste m, L.Am.
emplomadura f **2** adj: **be ~ of food**
llenar mucho

'**fill·ing sta·tion** estación f de servicio, gasolinera f

film [fɪlm] **1** n for camera carrete m;
(movie) película f **2** v/t person, event
filmar

'**film-mak·er** cineasta m/f

'**film star** estrella f de cine

fil·ter ['fɪltər] **1** n filtro m **2** v/t coffee,
liquid filtrar

♦**filter through** v/i of news reports filtrarse

'**fil·ter pa·per** papel m de filtro

'**fil·ter tip** (cigarette) cigarrillo m con
filtro

filth [fɪlθ] suciedad f, mugre f

F

filth·y ['fɪlθɪ] *adj* sucio, mugriento; *language etc* obsceno

fin [fɪn] *of fish* aleta *f*

fi·nal ['faɪnl] **1** *adj* (*last*) último; *decision* final, definitivo **2** *n* SP final *f*

fi·na·le [fɪ'nælɪ] final *m*

fi·nal·ist ['faɪnəlɪst] finalista *m/f*

fi·nal·ize ['faɪnəlaɪz] *v/t plans, design* ultimar

fi·nal·ly ['faɪnəlɪ] *adv* finalmente, por último; (*at last*) finalmente, por fin

fi·nance ['faɪnæns] **1** *n* finanzas *fpl* **2** *v/t* financiar

fi·nan·ces ['faɪnænsɪz] *npl* finanzas *fpl*

fi·nan·cial [faɪ'nænʃl] *adj* financiero

fi·nan·cial·ly [faɪ'nænʃəlɪ] *adv* económicamente

fi·nan·cial 'year *Br* ejercicio *m* económico

fi·nan·cier [faɪ'nænsɪr] financiero(-a) *m(f)*

find [faɪnd] *v/t* (*pret & pp* **found**) encontrar, hallar; *if you ~ it too hot/cold* si te parece demasiado frío/caliente; *~ s.o. innocent/guilty* LAW declarar a alguien inocente/culpable; *I ~ it strange that ...* me sorprende que ...; *how did you ~ the hotel?* ¿qué te pareció el hotel?

♦ **find out 1** *v/t* descubrir, averiguar **2** *v/i* (*discover*) descubrir; *can you try to find out?* ¿podrías enterarte?

find·ings ['faɪndɪŋz] *npl of report* conclusiones *fpl*

fine¹ [faɪn] *adj day, weather* bueno; *wine, performance, city* excelente; *distinction, line* fino; *how's that? – that's ~* ¿qué tal está? – bien; *that's ~ by me* por mí no hay ningún problema; *how are you? – ~* ¿cómo estás? – bien

fine² [faɪn] **1** *n* multa *f* **2** *v/t* multar, poner una multa a

fine-'tooth comb: *go through sth with a ~* revisar algo minuciosamente

fine-'tune *v/t engine, fig* afinar, hacer los últimos ajustes a

fin·ger ['fɪŋgər] **1** *n* dedo *m* **2** *v/t* tocar

'fin·ger·nail *n* uña *f*; **'fin·ger·print 1** *n* huella *f* digital *or* dactilar **2** *v/t* tomar las huellas digitales *or* dactilares a; **'fin·ger·tip** punta *f* del dedo; *have sth at one's ~s* saberse algo al dedillo

fin·i·cky ['fɪnɪkɪ] *adj person* quisquilloso; *design* enrevesado

fin·ish ['fɪnɪʃ] **1** *v/t* acabar, terminar; *~ doing sth* acabar *or* terminar de hacer algo **2** *v/i* acabar, terminar **3** *n of product* acabado *m*; *of race* final *f*

♦ **finish off** *v/t* acabar, terminar

♦ **finish up** *v/t food* acabar, terminar; *he finished up liking it* acabó gustándole

♦ **finish with** *v/t boyfriend etc* cortar con

fin·ish·ing line ['fɪnɪʃɪŋ] línea *f* de meta

Fin·land ['fɪnlənd] Finlandia

Finn [fɪn] finlandés (-esa) *m(f)*

Finn·ish ['fɪnɪʃ] **1** *adj* finlandés **2** *n language* finés *m*

fir [fɜːr] abeto *m*

fire [faɪr] **1** *n* fuego *m*; *electric, gas* estufa *f*; (*blaze*) incendio *m*; (*bonfire, campfire etc*) hoguera *f*; *be on ~* estar ardiendo; *catch ~* prender; *set sth on ~, set ~ to sth* prender fuego a algo **2** *v/i* (*shoot*) disparar (*on/at* sobre/a) **3** *v/t* F (*dismiss*) despedir

'fire a·larm alarma *f* contra incendios; **'fire·arm** arma *f* de fuego; **'fire·crack·er** petardo *m*; **'fire de·part·ment** (cuerpo *m* de) bomberos *mpl*; **'fire door** puerta *f* contra incendios; **'fire drill** simulacro *m* de incendio; **'fire en·gine** coche *m* de bomberos; **'fire es·cape** salida *f* de incendios; **'fire ex·tin·guish·er** extintor *m*; **'fire fight·er** bombero (-a) *m(f)*; **'fire·guard** pantalla *f*, parachispas *m inv*; **'fire·man** bombero *m*; **'fire·place** chimenea *f*, hogar *m*; **'fire sta·tion** parque *m* de bomberos; **'fire truck** coche *m* de bomberos; **'fire·wood** leña *f*; **'fire·works** *npl* fuegos *mpl* artificiales

firm¹ [fɜːrm] *adj* firme; *a ~ deal* un acuerdo en firme

firm² [fɜːrm] *n* COM empresa *f*

first [fɜːrst] **1** *adj* primero; *who's ~ please?* ¿quién es el primero, por favor? **2** *n* primero(-a) *m(f)* **3** *adv* primero; *~ of all* (*for one reason*) en primer lugar; *at ~* al principio

first 'aid primeros *mpl* auxilios; **first-'aid box, first-'aid kit** botiquín *m* de primeros auxilios; **'first·born** *adj* primogénito; **'first class 1** *adj* ticket, seat de primera (clase); (*very good*) excelente **2** *adv* travel en primera (clase); **first 'floor** planta *f* baja, Br primer piso *m*; **first'hand** *adj* de primera mano; **First 'La·dy** of US primera dama *f*

first·ly ['fɜːrstlɪ] *adv* en primer lugar

first 'name nombre *m* (de pila); **first 'night** estreno *m*; **first of'fend·er** delincuente *m/f* sin antecedentes; **first of'fense** primer delito *m*; **first-'rate** *adj* excelente

fis·cal ['fɪskl] *adj* fiscal

fis·cal 'year año *m* fiscal

fish [fɪʃ] **1** *n* (*pl* **fish**) pez *m*; *to eat* pescado *m*; *drink like a ~* F beber como un cosaco F; *feel like a ~ out of water* sentirse fuera de lugar **2** *v/i* pescar

'fish·bone espina *f* (de pescado)

fish·er·man ['fɪʃərmən] pescador *m*

fish·ing ['fɪʃɪŋ] pesca *f*

'fish·ing boat (barco *m*) pesquero *m*; **'fish·ing line** sedal *m*; **'fish·ing rod** caña *f* de pescar

'fish stick palito *m* de pescado

fish·y ['fɪʃɪ] *adj* F (*suspicious*) sospechoso

fist [fɪst] puño *m*

fit¹ [fɪt] *n* MED ataque *m*; *a ~ of rage/jealousy* un arrebato de cólera/un ataque de celos

fit² [fɪt] *adj* physically en forma; morally adecuado; *he's not ~ to be President* no está en condiciones

ser Presidente; *keep ~* mantenerse en forma

fit³ [fɪt] **1** *v/t* (*attach*) colocar; *these pants don't ~ me any more* estos pantalones ya no me entran; *it ~s you perfectly* te queda perfectamente **2** *v/i* (*pret & pp* **-ted**) of clothes quedar bien; of piece of furniture etc caber **3** *n*: *it's a good ~* of jacket etc queda bien; of piece of furniture cabe bien; *it's a tight ~* no hay mucho espacio

♦ **fit in 1** *v/i* of person in group encajar; *it fits in with our plans* encaja con nuestros planes **2** *v/t*: *fit s.o. in* into schedule etc hacer un hueco a alguien

fit·ful ['fɪtfəl] *adj* sleep intermitente

fit·ness ['fɪtnɪs] physical buena forma *f*

'fit·ness cen·ter, Br **'fit·ness cen·tre** gimnasio *m*

fit·ted 'kitch·en ['fɪtɪd] cocina *f* a medida

fit·ted 'sheet sábana *f* ajustable

fit·ter ['fɪtər] *n* técnico(-a) *m(f)*

fit·ting ['fɪtɪŋ] *adj* apropiado

fit·tings ['fɪtɪŋz] *npl* equipamiento *m*

five [faɪv] cinco

fix [fɪks] **1** *n* (*solution*) solución *f*; *be in a ~* F estar en un lío F **2** *v/t* (*attach*) fijar; (*repair*) arreglar, reparar; (*arrange: meeting etc*) organizar; lunch preparar; *dishonestly: match etc* amañar; *~ sth onto sth* fijar algo a algo; *I'll ~ you a drink* te prepararé una bebida

♦ **fix up** *v/t* meeting organizar

fixed [fɪkst] *adj* fijo

fix·ings ['fɪkɪŋz] *npl* guarnición *f*

fix·ture ['fɪkstʃər] (*in room*) parte fija del mobiliario o la decoración de una habitación

♦ **fiz·zle out** ['fɪzl] *v/i* F quedarse en nada

flab [flæb] on body grasa *f*

flab·ber·gast ['flæbərgæst] *v/t* F: *be ~ed* quedarse estupefacto or Span alucinado F

flab·by ['flæbɪ] *adj* muscles etc fofo

F

flag¹ [flæg] *n* bandera *f*

flag² [flæg] *v/i* (*pret & pp* **-ged**) (*tire*) desfallecer

'flag·pole asta *f* (de bandera)

fla·grant ['fleɪgrənt] *adj* flagrante

'flag·ship *fig* estandarte *m*; **'flag·staff** asta *f* (de bandera); **'flag·stone** losa *f*

flair [fler] (*talent*) don *m*; ***have a natural ~ for*** tener dotes para

flake [fleɪk] *n of snow* copo *m*; *of skin* escama *f*; *of plaster* desconchón *m*

♦ **flake off** *v/i of skin* descamarse; *of plaster, paint* desconcharse

flak·y ['fleɪkɪ] *adj skin* con escamas; *paint* desconchado

flak·y 'pas·try hojaldre *m*

flam·boy·ant [flæm'bɔɪənt] *adj personality* extravagante

flam·boy·ant·ly [flæm'bɔɪəntlɪ] *adv dressed* extravagantemente

flame [fleɪm] llama *f*; ***go up in ~s*** ser pasto de las llamas

fla·men·co [flə'meŋkou] flamenco *m*

fla'men·co danc·er bailaor(a) *m(f)*

flam·ma·ble ['flæməbl] *adj* inflamable

flan [flæn] tarta *f*

flank [flæŋk] **1** *n of horse etc* costado *m*; MIL flanco *m* **2** *v/t* flanquear

flap [flæp] **1** *n of envelope, pocket* solapa *f*; *of table* hoja *f*; ***be in a ~*** F estar histérico F **2** *v/t* (*pret & pp* **-ped**) *wings* batir **3** *v/i* (*pret & pp* **-ped**) *of flag etc* ondear

flare [fler] **1** *n* (*distress signal*) bengala *f*; *in dress* vuelo *m* **2** *v/t*: **~** ***one's nostrils*** hinchar las narices resoplando

♦ **flare up** *v/i of violence* estallar; *of illness, rash* exacerbarse, empeorar; *of fire* llamear; (*get very angry*) estallar

flash [flæʃ] **1** *n of light* destello *m*; PHOT flash *m*; ***in a ~*** F en un abrir y cerrar de ojos; ***have a ~ of inspiration*** tener una inspiración repentina; ***a ~ of lightning*** un relámpago **2** *v/i of light* destellar **3** *v/t* **~** ***one's headlights*** echar las luces

'flash·back *in movie* flash-back *m*, escena *f* retrospectiva

flash·er ['flæʃər] MOT intermitente *m*

'flash·light linterna *f*; PHOT flash *m*

flash·y ['flæʃɪ] *adj pej* ostentoso, chillón

flask [flæsk] (*hip ~*) petaca *f*

flat¹ [flæt] **1** *adj surface, land* llano, plano; *beer* sin gas; *battery* descargado; *tire* desinflado; *shoes* bajo; MUS bemol; ***and that's ~*** F y sanseacabó F **2** *adv* MUS demasiado bajo; **~** ***out*** *work, run, drive* a tope **3** *n* (*~ tire*) pinchazo *m*

flat² [flæt] *n Br* apartamento *m*, *Span* piso *m*

flat-chest·ed [flæt'tʃestɪd] *adj* plana de pecho

flat·ly ['flætlɪ] *adv refuse, deny* rotundamente

'flat rate tarifa *f* única

flat·ten ['flætn] *v/t land, road* allanar, aplanar; *by bombing, demolition* arrasar

flat·ter ['flætər] *v/t* halagar, adular

flat·ter·er ['flætərər] adulador(a) *m(f)*

flat·ter·ing ['flætərɪŋ] *adj comments* halagador; *color, clothes* favorecedor

flat·ter·y ['flætərɪ] halagos *mpl*, adulación *f*

flat·u·lence ['flætjʊləns] flatulencia *f*

'flat·ware (*cutlery*) cubertería *f*

flaunt [flɔːnt] *v/t* hacer ostentación de, alardear de

flau·tist ['flɔːtɪst] flautista *m/f*

fla·vor ['fleɪvər] **1** *n* sabor *m* **2** *v/t food* condimentar

fla·vor·ing ['fleɪvərɪŋ] *n* aromatizante *m*

fla·vour *etc Br* → **flavor** *etc*

flaw [flɔː] *n* defecto *m*, fallo *m*

flaw·less ['flɔːlɪs] *adj* impecable

flea [fliː] pulga *f*

fleck [flek] mota *f*

fled [fled] *pret & pp* → **flee**

flee [fliː] *v/i* (*pret & pp* **fled**) escapar, huir

fleece [fliːs] *v/t* F desplumar F

fleet [fliːt] *n* NAUT, *of vehicles* flota *f*

fleet·ing ['fliːtɪŋ] *adj visit etc* fugaz; **catch a ~ glimpse of** vislumbrar fugazmente a

flesh [fleʃ] *n* carne *f*; *of fruit* pulpa *f*; **meet/see s.o. in the ~** conocer/ver a alguien en persona

flew [fluː] *pret →* **fly**

flex [fleks] *v/t muscles* flexionar

flex·i·bil·i·ty [fleksə'bɪlətɪ] flexibilidad *f*

flex·i·ble ['fleksəbl] *adj* flexible

'flex·time ['flekstaɪm] *n* horario *m* flexible

flick [flɪk] *v/t tail* sacudir; **he ~ed a fly off his hand** espantó una mosca que tenía en la mano; **she ~ed her hair out of her eyes** se apartó el pelo de los ojos

♦ **flick through** *v/t book, magazine* hojear

flick·er ['flɪkər] *v/i of light, screen* parpadear

fli·er [flaɪr] *(circular)* folleto *m*

flies [flaɪz] *npl Br on pants* bragueta *f*

flight [flaɪt] *n in airplane* vuelo *m*; *(fleeing)* huida *f*; **not capable of ~** incapaz de volar; **~ (of stairs)** tramo *m* (de escaleras)

'flight at·tend·ant auxiliar *m/f* de vuelo; **'flight crew** tripulación *f*; **'flight deck** AVIA cabina *f* del piloto; **'flight num·ber** número *m* de vuelo; **'flight path** ruta *f* de vuelo; **'flight re·cord·er** caja *f* negra; **'flight time** *departure* hora *f* del vuelo; *duration* duración *f* del vuelo

flight·y ['flaɪtɪ] *adj* inconstante

flim·sy ['flɪmzɪ] *adj structure, furniture* endeble; *dress, material* débil; *excuse* pobre

flinch [flɪntʃ] *v/i* encogerse

fling [flɪŋ] **1** *v/t (pret & pp* **flung**) arrojar, lanzar; **~ o.s. into a chair** dejarse caer en una silla **2** *n* F *(affair)* aventura *f*

♦ **flip over** [flɪp] *v/i* volcar

♦ **flip through** *v/t (pret & pp* **-ped**) *magazine* hojear

flip·per ['flɪpər] *for swimming* aleta *f*

flirt [flɜːrt] **1** *v/i* flirtear, coquetear **2** *n* ligón (-ona) *m(f)*

flir·ta·tious [flɜːr'teɪʃəs] *adj* coqueto

float [fləʊt] *v/t also* FIN flotar

float·ing vot·er ['fləʊtɪŋ] votante *m/f* indeciso(-a)

flock [flɑːk] **1** *n of sheep* rebaño *m* **2** *v/i* acudir en masa

flog [flɑːg] *v/t (pret & pp* **-ged**) *(whip)* azotar

flood [flʌd] **1** *n* inundación *f* **2** *v/t of river* inundar

♦ **flood in** *v/i* llegar en grandes cantidades

flood·ing ['flʌdɪŋ] inundaciones *fpl*

'flood·light *n* foco *m*

flood-lit ['flʌdlɪt] *adj match* con luz artificial

'flood wa·ters *npl* crecida *f*

floor [flɔːr] *n* suelo *m*; *(story)* piso *m*

'floor·board *n* tabla *f* del suelo; **'floor cloth** trapo *m* del suelo; **'floor lamp** lámpara *f* de pie

flop [flɑːp] **1** *v/i (pret & pp* **-ped**) dejarse caer; F *(fail)* pinchar F **2** *n* F *(failure)* pinchazo *m* F

flop·py ['flɑːpɪ] *adj ears* caído; *hat* blando; *(weak)* flojo

flop·py ('**disk**) disquete *m*

flor·ist ['flɔːrɪst] florista *m/f*

floss [flɑːs] **1** *n for teeth* hilo *m* dental **2** *v/t*: **~ one's teeth** limpiarse los dientes con hilo dental

flour [flaʊr] harina *f*

flour·ish ['flʌrɪʃ] *v/i of plant* crecer rápidamente; *of business, civilization* florecer, prosperar

flour·ish·ing ['flʌrɪʃɪŋ] *adj business, trade* floreciente, próspero

flow [fləʊ] **1** *v/i* fluir **2** *n* flujo *m*

'flow·chart diagrama *m* de flujo

flow·er [flaʊr] **1** *n* flor *f* **2** *v/i* florecer

'flow·er·bed parterre *m*; **'flow·er·pot** tiesto *m*, maceta *f*; **'flow·er show** exposición *f* floral

flow·er·y ['flaʊrɪ] *adj pattern* floreado; *style of writing* florido

flown [fləʊn] *pp →* **fly**

flu [fluː] gripe *f*

fluc·tu·ate ['flʌktjʊeɪt] *v/i* fluctuar

fluc·tu·a·tion [flʌktjʊ'eɪʃn] fluctua-

F

F

ción f

flu·en·cy ['fluːənsɪ] *in a language* fluidez *f*

flu·ent ['fluːənt] *adj:* **he speaks ~ Spanish** habla español con soltura

flu·ent·ly ['fluːəntlɪ] *adv speak, write* con soltura

fluff [flʌf] *material* pelusa *f*

fluff·y ['flʌfɪ] *adj* esponjoso; **~ toy** juguete *m* de peluche

fluid ['fluːɪd] *n* fluido *m*

flung [flʌŋ] *pret & pp* → **fling**

flunk [flʌŋk] *v/t* F *subject* suspender, *Span* catear *F*

flu·o·res·cent [fluˈresnt] *adj light* fluorescente

flur·ry ['flʌrɪ] *of snow* torbellino *m*

flush [flʌʃ] **1** *v/t:* ~ **the toilet** tirar de la cadena; **~ sth down the toilet** tirar algo por el retrete **2** *v/i* (*go red in the face*) ruborizarse; **the toilet won't ~** la cisterna no funciona **3** *adj* (*level*): **be ~ with ...** estar a la misma altura que ...

♦**flush away** *v/t:* **flush sth away** *down toilet* tirar algo por el retrete

♦**flush out** *v/t rebels etc* hacer salir

flus·ter ['flʌstər] *v/t:* **get ~ed** ponerse nervioso

flute [fluːt] MUS flauta *f;* *glass* copa *f* de champán

flut·ist ['fluːtɪst] flautista *m/f*

flut·ter ['flʌtər] *v/i of bird, wings* aletear; *of flag* ondear; *of heart* latir con fuerza

fly¹ [flaɪ] *n insect* mosca *f*

fly² [flaɪ] *n on pants* bragueta *f*

fly³ [flaɪ] *v/i* (*pret* **flew**, *pp* **flown**) *of bird, airplane* volar; *in airplane* volar, ir en avión; *of flag* ondear; ~ **into a rage** enfurecerse; **she flew out of the room** salió a toda prisa de la habitación **2** *v/t* (*pret* **flew**, *pp* **flown**) *airplane* pilotar; *airline* volar con; (*transport by air*) enviar por avión

♦**fly away** *v/i of bird* salir volando; *of airplane* alejarse

♦**fly back** *v/i* (*travel back*) volver en avión

♦**fly in 1** *v/i of airplane, passengers*

llegar en avión **2** *v/t supplies etc* transportar en avión

♦**fly off** *v/i of hat etc* salir volando

♦**fly out** *v/i* irse (*en avión*); **when do you fly out?** ¿cuándo os vais?

♦**fly past** *v/i in formation* pasar volando en formación; *of time* volar

fly·ing ['flaɪɪŋ] *n* volar *m*

fly·ing 'sau·cer platillo *m* volante

foam [foʊm] *n on liquid* espuma *f*

foam 'rub·ber gomaespuma *f*

FOB [efoʊˈbiː] *abbr* (= **free on board**) fab (= franco a bordo)

fo·cus ['foʊkəs] **1** *n of attention,* PHOT foco *m;* **be in ~ / out of ~** PHOT estar enfocado / desenfocado **2** *v/t:* **~ one's attention on** concentrar la atención en **3** *v/i* enfocar

♦**focus on** *v/t problem, issue* concentrarse en; PHOT enfocar

fod·der ['fɑːdər] *n* forraje *m*

fog [fɑːg] *n* niebla *f*

♦**fog up** *v/i* (*pret & pp* **-ged**) empañarse

'fog·bound *adj* paralizado por la niebla

fog·gy ['fɑːgɪ] *adj* neblinoso, con niebla; **it's ~** hay niebla; **I haven't the foggiest idea** no tengo la más remota idea

foi·ble ['fɔɪbl] manía *f*

foil¹ [fɔɪl] *n* papel *m* de aluminio

foil² [fɔɪl] *v/t* (*thwart*) frustrar

fold¹ [foʊld] **1** *v/t paper etc* doblar; ~ **one's arms** cruzarse de brazos **2** *v/i of business* quebrar **3** *n in cloth etc* pliegue *m*

♦**fold up 1** *v/t* plegar **2** *v/i of chair, table* plegarse

fold² [foʊld] *n for sheep etc* redil *m*

fold·er ['foʊldər] *for documents,* COMPUT carpeta *f*

fold·ing ['foʊldɪŋ] *adj* plegable; ~ **chair** silla *f* plegable

fo·li·age ['foʊlɪɪdʒ] follaje *m*

folk [foʊk] *npl* (*people*) gente *f;* **my ~s** (*family*) mi familia; **evening ~s** F buenas noches, gente F

'folk dance baile *m* popular; **'folk mu·sic** música *f* folk *or* popular; **'folk sing·er** cantante *m/f* de folk;

'folk song canción m/f folk or popular

fol·low ['fɑːlou] **1** v/t seguir; (understand) entender; **~ me** sígueme **2** v/i logically deducirse; **it ~s from this that ...** de esto se deduce que ...; **you go first and I'll ~** tú ve primero que yo te sigo; **the requirements are as ~s** los requisitos son los siguientes

♦follow up v/t letter, inquiry hacer el seguimiento de

fol·low·er ['fɑːlouər] seguidor(a) m(f)

fol·low·ing ['fɑːlouɪŋ] **1** adj siguiente **2** n people seguidores(-as) mpl (fpl); **the ~** lo siguiente

'fol·low-up meet·ing reunión f de seguimiento

'fol·low-up vis·it to doctor etc visita f de seguimiento

fol·ly ['fɑːlɪ] (madness) locura f

fond [fɑːnd] adj (loving) cariñoso; memory entrañable; **he's ~ of travel/music** le gusta viajar/la música; **I'm very ~ of him** le tengo mucho cariño

fon·dle ['fɑːndl] v/t acariciar

fond·ness ['fɑːndnɪs] for s.o. cariño m (for por); for wine, food afición f (for por)

font [fɑːnt] for printing tipo m; in church pila f bautismal

food [fuːd] comida f

'food chain cadena f alimentaria

food·ie ['fuːdɪ] F gourmet m/f

'food mix·er robot m de cocina

food poi·son·ing ['fuːdpɔɪznɪŋ] intoxicación f alimentaria

fool [fuːl] **1** n tonto(-a) m(f), idiota m/f; **you stupid ~!** ¡estúpido!; **make a ~ of o.s.** ponerse en ridículo **2** v/t engañar

♦fool around v/i hacer el tonto; sexually tener un lío

♦fool around with v/t knife, drill etc enredar con algo; sexually tener un lío con

'fool·har·dy adj temerario

fool·ish ['fuːlɪʃ] adj tonto

fool·ish·ly ['fuːlɪʃlɪ] adv: **I ~ ...** come-

tí la tontería de ...

'fool·proof adj infalible

foot [fut] (pl feet [fiːt]) also measurement pie m; of animal pata f; **on ~** a pie, caminando, andando; **I've been on my feet all day** llevo todo el día de pie; **be back on one's feet** estar recuperado; **at the ~ of the page/hill** al pie de la página/de la colina; **put one's ~ in it** F meter la pata F

foot·age ['futɪdʒ] secuencias fpl, imágenes fpl

'foot·ball Br (soccer) fútbol m; American style fútbol m americano; ball balón m or pelota f (de fútbol)

'foot·ball play·er American style jugador(a) m(f) de fútbol americano; Br in soccer jugador(a) m(f) de fútbol, futbolista m/f

'foot·bridge puente m peatonal

foot·er ['futər] in document pie m de página

foot·hills ['futhɪlz] npl estribaciones fpl

'foot·hold n in climbing punto m de apoyo; **gain a ~** fig introducirse

foot·ing ['futɪŋ] (basis): **put the business back on a secure ~** volver a afianzar la empresa; **lose one's ~** perder el equilibrio; **be on the same/a different ~** estar/no estar en igualdad de condiciones; **be on a friendly ~ with ...** tener relaciones de amistad con ...

foot·lights ['futlaɪts] npl candilejas fpl; 'foot·mark pisada f; 'foot·note nota f a pie de página; 'foot·path sendero m; 'foot·print pisada f; 'foot·step paso m; **follow in s.o.'s ~s** seguir los pasos de alguien; 'foot·stool escabel m; 'foot·wear calzado m

for [fər, fɔːr] prep ◊ purpose, destination etc para; **a train ~ ...** un tren para or hacia ...; **clothes ~ children** ropa para niños; **it's too big/small ~ you** te queda demasiado grande/pequeño; **this is ~ you** esto es para ti; **what's ~ lunch?** ¿qué hay para comer?; **the steak is ~ me** el filete es para mí; **what is this ~?**

¿para qué sirve esto?; **what ~?** ¿para qué? ◊ *time* durante; **~ three days/two hours** durante tres días/dos horas; **it lasts ~ two hours** dura dos horas; **please get it done ~ Monday** por favor tenlo listo (para) el lunes ◊ *distance*: **I walked ~ a mile** caminé una milla; **it stretches for 100 miles** se extiende 100 millas ◊ *(in favor of)*: **I am ~ the idea** estoy a favor de la idea ◊ *(instead of, in behalf of)*: **let me do that ~ you** déjame que te lo haga; **we are agents ~ ...** somos representantes de ... ◊ *(in exchange for)*: **I bought it ~ $25** lo compré por 25 dólares: **how much did you sell it ~?** ¿por cuánto lo vendiste?

for·bade [fərˈbæd] *pret* → **forbid**

for·bid [fərˈbɪd] *v/t* (*pret* **forbade**, *pp* **forbidden**) prohibir; **~ s.o. to do sth** prohibir a alguien hacer algo

for·bid·den [fərˈbɪdn] **1** *adj* prohibido; **smoking/parking ~** prohibido fumar/aparcar **2** *pp* → **forbid**

for·bid·ding [fərˈbɪdɪŋ] *adj person, tone, look* amenazador; *rockface* imponente; *prospect* intimidador

force [fɔːrs] **1** *n* fuerza *f*; **come into ~ of law etc** entrar en vigor; **the ~s** MIL las fuerzas **2** *v/t door, lock* forzar; **~ s.o. to do sth** forzar a alguien a hacer algo; **~ sth open** forzar algo
♦ **force back** *v/t tears* contener

forced [fɔːrst] *adj* forzado

forced 'land·ing aterrizaje *m* forzoso

force·ful [ˈfɔːrsfəl] *adj argument* poderoso; *speaker* vigoroso; *character* enérgico

force·ful·ly [ˈfɔːrsfəlɪ] *adv* de manera convincente

for·ceps [ˈfɔːrseps] *npl* MED fórceps *m inv*

for·ci·ble [ˈfɔːrsəbl] *adj entry* por la fuerza

for·ci·bly [ˈfɔːrsəblɪ] *adv* por la fuerza

ford [fɔːrd] *n* vado *m*

fore [fɔːr] *n*: **come to the ~** salir a la palestra

'fore·arm antebrazo *m*; **fore·bears** [ˈfɔːrberz] *npl* antepasados *mpl*; 'fore·bod·ing [fərˈboʊdɪŋ] premonición *f*; 'fore·cast **1** *n* pronóstico *m*; *of weather* pronóstico *m* (del tiempo) **2** *v/t* (*pret & pp* **forecast**) pronosticar; 'fore·court *(of garage)* explanada en la parte de delante; fore·fa·thers [ˈfɔːrfɑːðərz] *npl* ancestros *mpl*; 'fore·fin·ger (dedo *m*) índice *m*; 'fore·front: **be in the ~ of** estar a la vanguardia de; 'fore·gone *adj*: **that's a ~ conclusion** eso ya se sabe de antemano; 'fore·ground primer plano *m*; 'fore·hand *in tennis* derecha *f*; 'fore·head frente *f*

for·eign [ˈfɑːrən] *adj* extranjero; **a ~ holiday** unas vacaciones en el extranjero

for·eign af'fairs *npl* asuntos *mpl* exteriores; for·eign 'aid ayuda *f* al exterior; for·eign 'bod·y cuerpo *m* extraño; for·eign 'cur·ren·cy divisa *f* extranjera

for·eign·er [ˈfɑːrənər] extranjero(-a) *m(f)*

for·eign ex'change divisas *fpl*; for·eign 'lan·guage idioma *m* extranjero; 'For·eign Of·fice *in UK* Ministerio *m* de Asuntos Exteriores; for·eign 'pol·i·cy política *f* exterior; For·eign 'Sec·re·ta·ry *in UK* Ministro(-a) *m(f)* de Asuntos Exteriores

'fore·man capataz *m*

'fore·most *adj* principal

fo·ren·sic 'med·i·cine [fəˈrensɪk] medicina *f* forense

fo·ren·sic 'sci·en·tist forense *m/f*

'fore·run·ner predecesor(a) *m(f)*; fore·see *v/t* (*pret* **foresaw**, *pp* **foreseen**) prever; fore·see·a·ble [fɔːrˈsiːəbl] *adj* previsible; **in the ~ future** en un futuro próximo; fore·'seen *pp* → **foresee**; 'fore·sight previsión *f*

for·est [ˈfɑːrɪst] bosque *m*

for·est·ry [ˈfɑːrɪstrɪ] silvicultura *f*

'fore·taste anticipo *m*

fore·tell v/t (pret & pp **foretold**) predecir

for·ev·er [fə'revər] adv siempre; **I will remember this day ~** no me olvidaré nunca de ese día

fore·word ['fɔːrwɜːrd] prólogo m

for·feit ['fɔːrfət] v/t (lose) perder; (give up) renunciar a

for·gave [fər'geɪv] pret → **forgive**

forge [fɔːrdʒ] v/t falsificar

♦ **forge ahead** v/i progresar rápidamente

forg·er ['fɔːrdʒər] falsificador(a) m(f)

forg·er·y ['fɔːrdʒərɪ] falsificación f

for·get [fər'get] v/t (pret **forgot**, pp **forgotten**) olvidar; **I forgot his name** se me olvidó su nombre; **~ to do sth** olvidarse de hacer algo

for·get·ful [fər'getfəl] adj olvidadizo

for·get-me-not flower nomeolvides m inv

for·give [fər'gɪv] v/t & v/i (pret **forgave**, pp **forgiven**) perdonar

for·giv·en [fər'gɪvn] pp → **forgive**

for·give·ness [fər'gɪvnɪs] perdón m

for·got [fər'gɑːt] pret → **forget**

for·got·ten [fər'gɑːtn] pp → **forget**

fork [fɔːrk] n for eating tenedor m; for garden horca f; in road bifurcación f

♦ **fork out** v/t & v/i F (pay) apoquinar F

forked adj tongue bífido; stick bifurcado

fork·lift 'truck carretilla f elevadora

form [fɔːrm] **1** n shape forma f; (document) formulario m, impreso m; **be on/off ~** estar/no estar en forma **2** v/t in clay etc moldear; friendship establecer; opinion formarse; past tense etc formar; (constitute) formar, constituir **3** v/i (take shape, develop) formarse

form·al ['fɔːrml] adj formal; recognition etc oficial; dress de etiqueta

for·mal·i·ty [fər'mælətɪ] formalidad f

for·mal·ly ['fɔːrməlɪ] adv speak, behave formalmente; accepted, recognized oficialmente

for·mat ['fɔːrmæt] **1** v/t (pret & pp

-ted) diskette, document formatear **2** n of paper, program etc formato m

for·ma·tion [fɔːr'meɪʃn] formación f; **~ flying** vuelo m en formación

for·ma·tive ['fɔːrmətɪv] adj formativo; **in his ~ years** en sus años de formación

for·mer ['fɔːrmər] adj antiguo; **the ~** el primero; **the ~ arrangement** la situación de antes

for·mer·ly ['fɔːrmərlɪ] adv antiguamente

for·mi·da·ble ['fɔːrmɪdəbl] adj personality formidable; opponent, task terrible

for·mu·la ['fɔːrmjulə] MATH, CHEM, fig fórmula f

for·mu·late ['fɔːrmjuleɪt] v/t (express) formular

for·ni·cate ['fɔːrnɪkeɪt] v/i fml fornicar

for·ni·ca·tion [fɔːrnɪ'keɪʃn] fml fornicación f

fort [fɔːrt] MIL fuerte m

forth [fɔːrθ] adv: **back and ~** de un lado para otro; **and so ~** y así sucesivamente; **from that day ~** desde ese día en adelante

forth·com·ing ['fɔːrθkʌmɪŋ] adj (future) próximo; personality comunicativo

'forth·right adj directo

for·ti·eth ['fɔːrtɪɪθ] n & adj cuadragésimo

fort·night ['fɔːrtnaɪt] Br quincena f

for·tress ['fɔːrtrɪs] MIL fortaleza f

for·tu·nate ['fɔːrtʃnət] adj afortunado

for·tu·nate·ly ['fɔːrtʃnətlɪ] adv afortunadamente

for·tune ['fɔːrtʃən] (fate, money) fortuna f; (luck) fortuna f, suerte f; **tell s.o.'s ~** decir a alguien la buenaventura

'for·tune-tell·er adivino(-a) m(f)

for·ty ['fɔːrtɪ] cuarenta; **have ~ winks** F echarse una siestecilla F

fo·rum ['fɔːrəm] fig foro m

for·ward ['fɔːrwərd] **1** adv hacia delante **2** adj pej: person atrevido **3** n SP delantero(-a) m(f) **4** v/t letter reexpedir

'for·ward·ing ad·dress ['fɔːrwərd-ɪŋ] *dirección a la que reexpedir correspondencia*

'for·ward·ing a·gent COM transitario(-a) *m(f)*

'for·ward-look·ing *adj* con visión de futuro, moderno

fos·sil ['fɑːsəl] fósil *m*

fos·sil·ized ['fɑːsəlaɪzd] *adj* fosilizado

fos·ter ['fɑːstər] *v/t child* acoger, adoptar (temporalmente); *attitude, belief* fomentar

'fos·ter child niño(-a) *m(f)* en régimen de acogida; **'fos·ter home** hogar *m* de acogida; **'fos·ter par·ents** *npl* familia *f* de acogida

fought [fɔːt] *pret & pp →* **fight**

foul [faul] **1** *n* SP falta *f* **2** *adj smell, taste* asqueroso; *weather* terrible **3** *v/t* SP hacer (una) falta a

found¹ [faund] *v/t school etc* fundar

found² [faund] *pret & pp →* **find**

foun·da·tion [faun'deɪʃn] *of theory etc* fundamento *m*; (*organization*) fundación *f*

foun·da·tions [faun'deɪʃnz] *npl of building* cimientos *mpl*

found·er ['faundər] *n* fundador(a) *m(f)*

found·ing ['faundɪŋ] *n* fundación *f*

foun·dry ['faundrɪ] fundición *f*

foun·tain ['fauntɪn] fuente *f*

'foun·tain pen pluma *f* (estilográfica)

four [fɔːr] cuatro; *on all ~s* a gatas, a cuatro patas

four-let·ter 'word palabrota *f*; **four-post·er** (**'bed**) cama *f* de dosel; **'four-star** *adj hotel etc* de cuatro estrellas

four·teen [fɔːr'tiːn] catorce

four·teenth [fɔːr'tiːnθ] *n & adj* decimocuarto

fourth [fɔːrθ] *n & adj* cuarto

four-wheel 'drive MOT vehículo *m* con tracción a las cuatro ruedas; *type of drive* tracción *f* a las cuatro ruedas

fowl [faul] ave *f* de corral

fox [fɑːks] **1** *n* zorro *m* **2** *v/t* (*puzzle*) dejar perplejo

foy·er ['fɔɪər] vestíbulo *m*

frac·tion ['frækʃn] fracción *f*; MATH fracción *f*, quebrado *m*

frac·tion·al·ly ['frækʃnəlɪ] *adv* ligeramente

frac·ture ['fræktʃər] **1** *n* fractura *f* **2** *v/t* fracturar; *he ~d his arm* se fracturó el brazo

fra·gile ['frædʒəl] *adj* frágil

frag·ment ['frægmənt] *n* fragmento *m*

frag·men·ta·ry [fræg'məntərɪ] *adj* fragmentario

fra·grance ['freɪgrəns] fragancia *f*

fra·grant ['freɪgrənt] *adj* fragante

frail [freɪl] *adj* frágil, delicado

frame [freɪm] **1** *n of picture, window* marco *m*; *of eyeglasses* montura *f*; *of bicycle* cuadro *m*; *~ of mind* estado *m* de ánimo **2** *v/t picture* enmarcar; F *person* tender una trampa a

'frame-up F trampa *f*

'frame·work estructura *f*; *for agreement* marco *m*

France [fræns] Francia

fran·chise ['fræntʃaɪz] *n for business* franquicia *f*

frank [fræŋk] *adj* franco

frank·furt·er ['fræŋkfɜːrtər] salchicha *f* de Fráncfort

frank·ly ['fræŋklɪ] *adv* francamente

frank·ness ['fræŋknɪs] franqueza *f*

fran·tic ['fræntɪk] *adj* frenético

fran·ti·cal·ly ['fræntɪklɪ] *adv* frenéticamente

fra·ter·nal [frə'tɜːrnl] *adj* fraternal

fraud [frɔːd] fraude *m*; *person* impostor(a) *m(f)*

fraud·u·lent ['frɔːdjʊlənt] *adj* fraudulento

fraud·u·lent·ly ['frɔːdjʊləntlɪ] *adv* fraudulentamente

frayed [freɪd] *adj cuffs* deshilachado

freak [friːk] **1** *n unusual event* fenómeno *m* anormal; *two-headed person, animal etc* monstruo *m*, monstruosidad *f*; F *strange person* bicho *m* raro F; *a movie / jazz ~* un fanático del cine / jazz F **2** *adj wind,* *storm etc* anormal

freck·le ['frekl] peca *f*

free [fri:] **1** *adj* libre; *no cost* gratis, gratuito; *are you ~ this afternoon?* ¿estás libre esta tarde?; *~ and easy* relajado; *for ~ travel, get sth* gratis **2** *v/t prisoners* liberar

free·bie ['fri:bɪ] F regalo *m*; *as a ~* de regalo

free·dom ['fri:dəm] libertad *f*

free·dom of 'speech libertad *f* de expresión

free·dom of the 'press libertad *f* de prensa

free 'en·ter·prise empresa *f* libre; **free 'kick** *in soccer* falta *f*, golpe *m* franco; **free·lance** ['fri:læns] **1** *adj* autónomo, free-lance **2** *adv*: *work ~* trabajar como autónomo *or* free-lance; **free·lanc·er** ['fri:lænsər] autónomo(-a) *m(f)*, free-lance *m/f*; **free·load·er** ['fri:loʊdər] F gorrón (-ona) *m(f)*

free·ly ['fri:lɪ] *adv admit* libremente

free mar·ket e'con·o·my economía *f* de libre mercado; **free-range 'chick·en** pollo *m* de corral; **free-range 'eggs** *npl* huevos *mpl* de corral; **free 'sam·ple** muestra *f* gratuita; **free 'speech** libertad *f* de expresión; **'free·way** autopista *f*; **free'wheel** *v/i on bicycle* ir sin pedalear; **free 'will** libre albedrío *m*; *he did it of his own ~* lo hizo por propia iniciativa

freeze [fri:z] **1** *v/t* (*pret* **froze**, *pp* **frozen**) *food, wages, video* congelar; *river* congelar, helar **2** *v/i* (*pret* **froze**, *pp* **frozen**) *of water* congelarse, helarse

♦ **freeze over** *v/i of river* helarse

'freeze-dried *adj* liofilizado

freez·er ['fri:zər] congelador *m*

freez·ing ['fri:zɪŋ] **1** *adj* muy frío; *it's ~* (*cold*) *of weather* hace mucho frío; *of water* está muy frío; *I'm ~* (*cold*) tengo mucho frío **2** *n*: *10 degrees below ~* diez grados bajo cero

'freez·ing com·part·ment congelador *m*

'freez·ing point punto *m* de conge-

lación

freight [freɪt] *n* transporte; *costs* flete *m*

'freight car *on train* vagón *m* de mercancías

freight·er ['freɪtər] *ship* carguero *m*; *airplane* avión *m* de carga

'freight train tren *m* de mercancías

French [frentʃ] **1** *adj* francés **2** *n language* francés *m*; *the ~* los franceses

French 'bread pan *m* de barra; **French 'doors** *npl* puerta *f* cristalera; **'French fries** *npl* Span patatas *fpl* or *L.Am.* papas *fpl* fritas; **'French·man** francés *m*; **'French·wom·an** francesa *f*

fren·zied ['frenzɪd] *adj attack, activity* frenético; *mob* desenfrenado

fren·zy ['frenzɪ] frenesí *m*; *whip s.o. into a ~* poner a alguien frenético

fre·quen·cy ['fri:kwənsɪ] *also* RAD frecuencia *f*

fre·quent¹ ['fri:kwənt] *adj* frecuente; *how ~ are the trains?* ¿con qué frecuencia pasan trenes?

fre·quent² [frɪ'kwent] *v/t bar* frecuentar

fre·quent·ly ['fri:kwəntlɪ] *adv* con frecuencia

fres·co ['freskoʊ] fresco *m*

fresh [freʃ] *adj* fresco; *start* nuevo; *don't you get ~ with your mother!* ¡no seas descarado con tu madre!

fresh 'air aire *m* fresco

fresh·en ['freʃn] *v/i of wind* refrescar

♦ **freshen up** *v/i* refrescarse **2** *v/t room, paintwork* renovar, revivir

fresh·ly ['freʃlɪ] *adv* recién

'fresh·man estudiante *m/f* de primer año

fresh·ness ['freʃnɪs] frescura *f*

'fresh·wa·ter *adj* de agua dulce

fret [fret] *v/i* (*pret & pp* **-ted**) ponerse nervioso, inquietarse

Freud·i·an ['frɔɪdɪən] *adj* freudiano

fric·tion ['frɪkʃn] PHYS rozamiento *m*; *between people* fricción *f*

'fric·tion tape cinta *f* aislante

Fri·day ['fraɪdeɪ] viernes *m inv*

fridge [frɪdʒ] nevera *f*, frigorífico *m*

fried 'egg [fraɪd] huevo *m* frito

fried po'ta·toes *npl* Span patatas *fpl* or *L.Am.* papas *fpl* fritas

friend [frend] amigo(-a) *m(f)*; **make ~s** *of one person* hacer amigos; *of two people* hacerse amigos; **make ~s with s.o.** hacerse amigo de alguien

friend·li·ness ['frendlɪnɪs] simpatía *f*

friend·ly ['frendlɪ] *adj atmosphere* agradable; *person* agradable, simpático; *(easy to use)* fácil de usar; *argument, match, relations* amistoso; **be ~ with s.o.** *(be friends)* ser amigo de alguien

'friend·ship ['frendʃɪp] amistad *f*

fries [fraɪz] *npl* Span patatas *fpl* or *L.Am.* papas *fpl* fritas

fright [fraɪt] susto *m*; **give s.o. a ~** dar un susto a alguien, asustar a alguien; **scream with ~** gritar asustado

fright·en ['fraɪtn] *v/t* asustar; **be ~ed** estar asustado, tener miedo; **don't be ~ed** no te asustes, no tengas miedo; **be ~ed of** tener miedo de

♦ **frighten away** *v/t* ahuyentar, espantar

fright·en·ing ['fraɪtnɪŋ] *adj noise, person, prospect* aterrador, espantoso

fri·gid ['frɪdʒɪd] *adj sexually* frígido

frill [frɪl] *on dress etc* volante *m*; *(fancy extra)* extra *m*

frill·y ['frɪlɪ] *adj* de volantes

fringe [frɪndʒ] *on dress, curtains etc* flecos *mpl*; *Br in hair* flequillo *m*; *(edge)* margen *m*

'fringe ben·e·fits *npl* ventajas *fpl* adicionales

frisk [frɪsk] *v/t* cachear

frisk·y ['frɪskɪ] *adj puppy etc* juguetón

♦ **frit·ter away** ['frɪtər] *v/t time* desperdiciar; *fortune* despilfarrar

fri·vol·i·ty [frɪ'vɑːlətɪ] frivolidad *f*

friv·o·lous ['frɪvələs] *adj* frívolo

frizz·y ['frɪzɪ] *adj hair* crespo

frog [frɑːg] rana *f*

'frog·man hombre *m* rana

from [frɑːm] *prep* ◊ *in time* desde; **~ 9 to 5 (o'clock)** de 9 a 5; **~ the 18th century** desde el siglo XVIII; **~ today on** a partir de hoy; **~ next Tuesday** a partir del próximo martes ◊ *in space* de, desde; **~ here to there** de *or* desde aquí hasta allí; **we drove here ~ Las Vegas** vinimos en coche desde Las Vegas ◊ *origin* de; **a letter ~ Jo** una carta de Jo; **it doesn't say who it's ~** no dice de quién es; **I am ~ New Jersey** soy de Nueva Jersey; **made ~ bananas** hecho con plátanos ◊ *(because of)*: **tired ~ the journey** cansado del viaje; **it's ~ overeating** es por comer demasiado

front [frʌnt] **1** *n of building, book* portada *f*; *(cover organization)* tapadera *f*; MIL, *of weather* frente *m*; **in ~** delante; *in a race* en cabeza; **the car in ~** el coche de delante; **in ~ of** delante de; **at the ~ of** en la parte de delante de **2** *adj wheel, seat* delantero **3** *v/t TV program* presentar

front 'cov·er portada *f*; **front 'door** puerta *f* principal; **front 'en·trance** entrada *f* principal

fron·tier ['frʌntɪr] frontera *f*; *fig: of knowledge, science* límite *m*

front 'line MIL línea *f* del frente; **front 'page** *of newspaper* portada *f*, primera *f* plana; **front page 'news** *nsg* noticia *f* de portada *or* de primera plana; **front 'row** primera fila *f*; **front seat 'pas·sen·ger** *in car* pasajero(-a) *m(f)* de delante; **front-wheel 'drive** tracción *f* delantera

frost [frɑːst] *n* escarcha *f*; **there was a ~ last night** anoche cayó una helada

'frost·bite congelación *f*

'frost·bit·ten *adj* congelado

frost·ed glass ['frɑːstɪd] vidrio *m* esmerilado

frost·ing ['frɑːstɪŋ] *on cake* glaseado *m*

frost·y ['frɑːstɪ] *adj weather* gélido; *fig: welcome* glacial

froth [frɑːθ] *n* espuma *f*

froth·y ['frɑːθɪ] *adj cream etc* espumoso

frown [fraʊn] **1** *n*: **what's that ~ for?** ¿por qué frunces el ceño? **2** *v/i* fruncir el ceño

froze [frəʊz] *pret* → **freeze**

fro·zen ['frəʊzn] **1** *adj ground, food* congelado; *wastes* helado; **I'm ~** F estoy helado *or* congelado F **2** *pp* → **freeze**

fro·zen 'food comida *f* congelada

fruit [fruːt] fruta *f*

'fruit cake bizcocho *m* de frutas

fruit·ful ['fruːtfəl] *adj discussions etc* fructífero

'fruit juice *Span* zumo *m* or *L.Am* jugo *m* de fruta

fruit 'sal·ad macedonia *f*

frus·trate [frʌ'streɪt] *v/t person, plans* frustrar

frus·trat·ed [frʌ'streɪtɪd] *adj* frustrado

frus·trat·ing [frʌ'streɪtɪŋ] *adj* frustrante

frus·tra·tion [frʌ'streɪʃn] frustración *f*

fry [fraɪ] *v/t* (*pret & pp* **-ied**) freír

'fry·pan sartén *f*

fuck [fʌk] *v/t* V *Span* follar con V, *L.Am.* coger V; **~!** ¡joder! V; **~ him!** ¡que se joda! V

♦ **fuck off** *v/i* V: **fuck off!** ¡vete a la mierda! V

fuck·ing ['fʌkɪŋ] **1** *adj* V puto V **2** *adv* V: **it's ~ crazy** es un estupidez ¡coño!; **it was ~ brilliant!** ¡estuvo de puta madre! V

fu·el ['fjʊəl] **1** *n* combustible *m* **2** *v/t fig* avivar

fu·gi·tive ['fjuːdʒətɪv] *n* fugitivo(-a) *m(f)*

ful·fil *Br*, **ful·fill** [fʊl'fɪl] *v/t dream* cumplir, realizar; *task* realizar; *contract* cumplir; **feel ~ed** *in job, life* sentirse realizado

ful·fill·ing [fʊl'fɪlɪŋ] *adj*: **I have a ~ job** mi trabajo me llena

ful·fil·ment *Br*, **ful·fill·ment** [fʊl'fɪlmənt] *of contract etc* cumplimiento *m*; *moral, spiritual* satisfacción *f*

full [fʊl] *adj* lleno; *account, schedule* completo; *life* pleno; **~ of** *of water etc* lleno de; **~ up** *hotel etc, with food* lleno; **pay in ~** pagar al contado

full-'cov·er·age (*insurance*) seguro *m* a todo riesgo; **'full-grown** *adj* completamente desarrollado; **'full-length** *adj dress* de cuerpo entero; **~ movie** largometraje *m*; **full 'moon** luna *f* llena; **full 'stop** *Br* punto *m*; **full 'time 1** *adj worker, job* a tiempo completo **2** *adv work* a tiempo completo

ful·ly ['fʊlɪ] *adv* completamente; *describe* en detalle

fum·ble ['fʌmbl] *v/t ball* dejar caer

♦ **fumble around** *v/i* rebuscar

fume [fjuːm] *v/i*: **be fuming** F *with anger* echar humo F

fumes [fjuːmz] *npl* humos *mpl*

fun [fʌn] diversión *f*; **it was great ~** fue muy divertido; **bye, have ~!** ¡adiós, que lo paséis bien!; **for ~** para divertirse; **make ~ of** burlarse de

func·tion ['fʌŋkʃn] **1** *n* (*purpose*) función *f*; (*reception etc*) acto *m* **2** *v/i* funcionar; **~ as** hacer de

func·tion·al ['fʌŋkʃnl] *adj* funcional

fund [fʌnd] **1** *n* fondo *m* **2** *v/t project etc* financiar

fun·da·men·tal [fʌndə'mentl] *adj* fundamental; (*crucial*) esencial

fun·da·men·tal·ist [fʌndə'mentlɪst] *n* fundamentalista *m/f*

fun·da·men·tal·ly [fʌndə'mentlɪ] *adv* fundamentalmente

fund·ing ['fʌndɪŋ] (*money*) fondos *mpl*, financiación *f*

fu·ne·ral ['fjuːnərəl] funeral *m*

'fu·ne·ral di·rec·tor encargado(-a) *m(f)* de una funeraria

'fu·ne·ral home funeraria *f*

fun·gus ['fʌŋgəs] hongos *mpl*

fu·nic·u·lar ('rail·way') [fjuː'nɪkjʊlər] funicular *m*

fun·nel ['fʌnl] *n of ship* chimenea *f*

fun·nies ['fʌnɪz] *npl* F sección de humor

fun·ni·ly ['fʌnɪlɪ] *adv* (*oddly*) de modo extraño; (*comically*) de for-

ma divertida; **~ enough** curiosamente

fun·ny ['fʌnɪ] *adj* (*comical*) divertido, gracioso; (*odd*) curioso, raro;
that's not ~ eso no tiene gracia

'fun·ny bone hueso *m* de la risa

fur [fɜ:r] piel *f*

fu·ri·ous ['fjʊrɪəs] *adj* (*angry*) furioso; (*intense*) furioso, feroz; *effort* febril; **at a ~ pace** a un ritmo vertiginoso

fur·nace ['fɜ:rnɪs] horno *m*

fur·nish ['fɜ:rnɪʃ] *v/t room* amueblar;
(*supply*) suministrar

fur·ni·ture ['fɜ:rnɪʧər] mobiliario *m*,
muebles *mpl*; **a piece of ~** un mueble

fur·ry ['fɜ:rɪ] *adj animal* peludo

fur·ther ['fɜ:rðər] **1** *adj* (*additional*)
adicional; (*more distant*) más lejano;
there's been a ~ development ha
pasado algo nuevo; **until ~ notice**
hasta nuevo aviso; **have you
anything ~ to say?** ¿tiene algo más
que añadir? **2** *adv walk, drive* más
lejos; **~, I want to say ...** además,
quiero decir ...; **two miles ~** (**on**)
dos millas más adelante **3** *v/t cause
etc* promover

fur·ther·more *adv* es más

fur·thest ['fɜ:ðɪst] **1** *adj:* **the ~ point
north** el punto más al norte; **the ~
stars** las estrellas más lejanas **2** *adv*
más lejos; **this is the ~ north I've
ever been** nunca había estado tan

al norte

fur·tive ['fɜ:rtɪv] *adj glance* furtivo

fur·tive·ly ['fɜ:rtɪvlɪ] *adv* furtivamente

fu·ry ['fjʊrɪ] (*anger*) furia *f*, ira *f*

fuse [fju:z] **1** *n* ELEC fusible *m* **2** *v/i*
ELEC fundirse; **the lights have ~d**
se han fundido los plomos **3** *v/t*
ELEC fundir

'fuse·box caja *f* de fusibles

fu·se·lage ['fju:zəlɑ:ʒ] fuselaje *m*

'fuse wire fusible *m* (*hilo*)

fu·sion ['fju:ʒn] fusión *f*

fuss [fʌs] *n* escándalo *m*; **make a ~**
armar un escándalo; **make a ~ of**
(*be very attentive to*) deshacerse en
atenciones con

fuss·y ['fʌsɪ] *adj person* quisquilloso;
design etc recargado; **be a ~ eater**
ser un quisquilloso a la hora de comer

fu·tile ['fju:tl] *adj* inútil, vano

fu·til·i·ty [fju:'tɪlətɪ] inutilidad *f*

fu·ture ['fju:ʧər] **1** *n also* GRAM
futuro *m*; **in ~** en el futuro **2** *adj* futuro

fu·tures ['fju:ʧərz] *npl* FIN futuros
mpl

'fu·tures mar·ket FIN mercado *m* de
futuros

fu·tur·is·tic [fju:ʧə'rɪstɪk] *adj design*
futurista

fuze [fju:z] → **fuse**

fuzz·y ['fʌzɪ] *adj hair* crespo; (*out of
focus*) borroso

G

gab [gæb] *n:* **have the gift of the ~** F
tener labia F

gab·ble ['gæbl] *v/i* farfullar

♦ **gab around** [gæd] *v/i* (*pret & pp
-ded*) pendonear

gad·get ['gæʤɪt] artilugio *m*, chisme *m*

gaffe [gæf] metedura *f* de pata

gag [gæg] **1** *n over mouth* mordaza *f*;
(*joke*) chiste *m* **2** *v/t* (*pret & pp
-ged*) *also fig* amordazar

gain [geɪn] *v/t* (*acquire*) ganar; *victory*
obtener; **~ speed** cobrar velocidad;
~ 10 pounds engordar 10 libras

ga·la ['gælə] gala *f*

gal·ax·y ['gæləksı] AST galaxia *f*

gale [geɪl] vendaval *m*

gal·lant ['gælənt] *adj* galantc

gall blad·der ['gɔ:lblædər] vesícula *f* biliar

gal·le·ry ['gælərı] *for art* museo *m*; *in theater* galería *f*

gal·ley ['gælı] *on ship* cocina *f*

♦ gal·li·vant around ['gælɪvænt] *v/i* pendonear

gal·lon ['gælən] galón *m* (en EE.UU. 3,785 litros, en GB 4,546); ~s of tea F toneladas de té F

gal·lop ['gæləp] *v/i* galopar

gal·lows ['gæloʊz] *npl* horca *f*

gall·stone ['gɔ:lstoʊn] cálculo *m* biliar

ga·lore [gə'lɔ:r] *adj*: apples/novels ~ manzanas/novelas a montones

gal·va·nize ['gælvənaɪz] *v/t* TECH galvanizar; ~ s.o. into activity hacer que alguien se vuelva más activo

gam·ble ['gæmbl] *v/i* jugar

gam·bler ['gæmblər] jugador(a) *m(f)*

gam·bling ['gæmblıŋ] *n* juego *m*

game [geɪm] *n* (sport) partido *m*; children's, in tennis juego *m*

'game re·serve coto *m* de caza

gang [gæŋ] *of friends* cuadrilla *f*, pandilla *f*; *of criminals* banda *f*

♦ gang up on *v/t* compincharse contra

'gang rape 1 *n* violación *f* colectiva 2 *v/t* violar colectivamente

gan·grene ['gæŋgri:n] MED gangrena *f*

gang·ster ['gæŋstər] gángster *m*

'gang war·fare lucha *f* entre bandas

'gang·way pasarela *f*

gap [gæp] *in wall* hueco *m*; *for parking, in figures* espacio *m*; *in time* intervalo *m*; *in conversation* interrupción *f*; *between two people's characters* diferencia *f*

gape [geɪp] *v/i of person* mirar boquiabierto

♦ gape at *v/t* mirar boquiabierto a

gap·ing ['geɪpıŋ] *adj hole* enorme

gar·age [gə'rɑ:ʒ] *n for parking* garaje *m*; *for repairs* taller *m*; Br *for gas* gasolinera *f*

gar·bage ['gɑ:rbɪdʒ] basura *f*; fig (nonsense) tonterías *fpl*; (poor quality goods) basura *f*, porquería *f*

'gar·bage bag bolsa *f* de la basura; 'gar·bage can cubo *m* de la basura; *in street* papelera *f*; 'gar·bage truck camión *m* de la basura

gar·bled ['gɑ:rbld] *adj message* confuso

gar·den ['gɑ:rdn] jardín *m*

'gar·den cen·ter, Br 'gar·den cen·tre vivero *m*, centro *m* de jardinería

gar·den·er ['gɑ:rdnər] aficionado(-a) *m(f)* a la jardinería; *professional* jardinero(-a) *m(f)*

gar·den·ing ['gɑ:rdnıŋ] jardinería *f*

gar·gle ['gɑ:rgl] *v/i* hacer gárgaras

gar·goyle ['gɑ:rgɔɪl] ARCHI gárgola *f*

gar·ish ['gerıʃ] *adj color* chillón; design estridente

gar·land ['gɑ:rlənd] *n* guirnalda *f*

gar·lic ['gɑ:rlık] ajo *m*

gar·lic 'bread pan *m* con ajo

gar·ment ['gɑ:rmənt] prenda *f* (de vestir)

gar·nish ['gɑ:rnıʃ] *v/t* guarnecer (with con)

gar·ri·son ['gærısn] *n place* plaza *f*; troops guarnición *f*

gar·ter ['gɑ:rtər] liga *f*

gas [gæs] *n* gas *m*; (gasoline) gasolina *f*, Rpl nafta *f*

gash [gæʃ] *n* corte *m* profundo

gas·ket ['gæskıt] junta *f*

gas·o·line ['gæsəli:n] gasolina *f*, Rpl nafta *f*

gasp [gæsp] 1 *n* grito *m* apagado 2 *v/i* lanzar un grito apagado; ~ for breath luchar por respirar

'gas ped·al acelerador *m*; 'gas pipe·line gasoducto *m*; 'gas pump surtidor *m* (de gasolina); 'gas sta·tion gasolinera *f*, S.Am. bomba *f*; gas stove cocina *f* de gas

gas·tric ['gæstrık] *adj* MED gástrico

gas·tric 'flu MED gripe *f* gastrointestinal; gas·tric 'juic·es *npl* jugos *mpl* gástricos; **gas·tric 'ul·cer** MED úlcera *f* gástrica

gate [geɪt] *of house, at airport* puerta *f*; *made of iron* verja *f*

'**gate·crash** *v/t*: ~ *a party* colarse en una fiesta

'**gate·way** *also fig* entrada *f*

gath·er ['gæðər] **1** *v/t facts, information:* reunir; **am I to ~ that ...?** ¿debo entender que ...?; ~ *speed* ganar velocidad **2** *v/i of crowd* reunirse

♦ **gather up** *v/t possessions* recoger

gath·er·ing ['gæðərɪŋ] *n* (*group of people*) grupo *m* de personas

gau·dy ['gɔːdɪ] *adj* chillón, llamativo

gauge [geɪdʒ] **1** *n* indicador *m* **2** *v/t pressure* medir, calcular; *opinion* estimar, evaluar

gaunt [gɔːnt] *adj* demacrado

gauze [gɔːz] gasa *f*

gave [geɪv] *pret* → **give**

gaw·ky ['gɔːkɪ] *adj* desgarbado

gawp [gɔːp] *v/i* F mirar boquiabierto; *don't just stand there ~ing!* ¡no te quedes ahí boquiabierto!

gay [geɪ] **1** *n* (*homosexual*) homosexual *m*, gay *m* **2** *adj* homosexual, gay

gaze [geɪz] **1** *n* mirada *f* **2** *v/i* mirar fijamente

♦ **gaze at** *v/t* mirar fijamente

GB [dʒiː'biː] *abbr* (= *Great Britain*) GB (= Gran Bretaña)

GDP [dʒiːdiː'piː] *abbr* (= *gross domestic product*) PIB *m* (= producto *m* interior bruto)

gear [gɪr] *n* (*equipment*) equipo *m*; *in vehicles* marcha *f*

'**gear·box** MOT caja *f* de cambios

'**gear le·ver**, '**gear shift** MOT palanca *f* de cambios

geese [giːs] *pl* → **goose**

gel [dʒel] *for hair* gomina *f*; *for shower* gel *m*

gel·a·tine ['dʒelətiːn] gelatina *f*

gel·ig·nite ['dʒelɪgnaɪt] gelignita *f*

gem [dʒem] gema *f*; *fig* (*book etc*) joya *f*; (*person*) cielo *m*

Gem·i·ni ['dʒemɪnaɪ] ASTR Géminis *m/f inv*

gen·der ['dʒendər] género *m*

gene [dʒiːn] gen *m*; *it's in his ~s* lo lleva en los genes

gen·e·ral ['dʒenrəl] **1** *n* MIL general *m*; *in ~* en general, por lo general **2** *adj* general

gen·e·ral e'lec·tion elecciones *fpl* generales

gen·er·al·i·za·tion [dʒenrəlaɪ'zeɪʃn] generalización *f*; *that's a ~* eso es generalizar

gen·er·al·ize ['dʒenrəlaɪz] *v/i* generalizar

gen·er·al·ly ['dʒenrəlɪ] *adv* generalmente, por lo general; ~ *speaking* en términos generales

gen·e·rate ['dʒenəreɪt] *v/t* generar; *a feeling* provocar

gen·e·ra·tion [dʒenə'reɪʃn] generación *f*

gen·e'ra·tion gap conflicto *m* generacional

gen·e·ra·tor ['dʒenəreɪtər] generador *m*

ge·ner·ic drug [dʒə'nerɪk] MED medicamento *m* genérico

gen·e·ros·i·ty [dʒenə'rɑːsətɪ] generosidad *f*

gen·e·rous ['dʒenərəs] *adj* generoso

ge·net·ic [dʒɪ'netɪk] *adj* genético

ge·net·i·cal·ly [dʒɪ'netɪklɪ] *adv* genéticamente; ~ *modified crops* transgénico; *be ~ modified* estar modificado genéticamente

ge·net·ic 'code código *m* genético; **ge·net·ic en·gi'neer·ing** ingeniería *f* genética; **ge·net·ic 'fin·ger·print** identificación *f* genética

ge·net·i·cist [dʒɪ'netɪsɪst] genetista *m/f*, especialista *m/f* en genética

ge·net·ics [dʒɪ'netɪks] genética *f*

ge·ni·al ['dʒiːnjəl] *adj* afable, cordial

gen·i·tals ['dʒenɪtlz] *npl* genitales *mpl*

ge·ni·us ['dʒiːnjəs] genio *m*

gen·o·cide ['dʒenəsaɪd] genocidio *m*

gen·tle ['dʒentl] *adj person* tierno, delicado; *touch, detergent* suave; *breeze* suave, ligero; *slope* poco inclinado; *be ~ with it, it's fragile* ten

mucho cuidado con él, es frágil
gen·tle·man ['dʒentlmən] caballero
m; *he's a real ~* es todo un caballero
gen·tle·ness ['dʒentlnɪs] *of person*
ternura *f*, delicadeza; *of touch,
detergent, breeze* suavidad *f*; *of slope*
poca inclinación *f*
gen·tly ['dʒentlɪ] *adv* con delicadeza,
poco a poco; *a breeze blew ~* sopla
una ligera *or* suave brisa
gents [dʒents] *nsg toilet* servicio *m*
de caballeros
gen·u·ine ['dʒenʊɪn] *adj antique* genuino, auténtico; *(sincere)* sincero
gen·u·ine·ly ['dʒenʊɪnlɪ] *adv* realmente, de verdad
ge·o·graph·i·cal [dʒɪə'græfɪkl] *adj
features* geográfico
ge·og·ra·phy [dʒɪ'ɑːgrəfɪ] geografía
f
ge·o·log·i·cal [dʒɪə'lɑːdʒɪkl] *adj*
geológico
ge·ol·o·gist [dʒɪ'ɑːlədʒɪst] geólogo(-a) *m(f)*
ge·ol·o·gy [dʒɪ'ɑːlədʒɪ] geología *f*
ge·o·met·ric, ge·o·met·ri·cal
[dʒɪə'metrɪk(l)] *adj* geométrico
ge·om·e·try [dʒɪ'ɑːmətrɪ] geometría
f
ge·ra·ni·um [dʒə'reɪnɪəm] geranio
m
ger·i·at·ric [dʒerɪ'ætrɪk] **1** *adj* geriátrico **2** *n* anciano(-a) *m(f)*
germ [dʒɜːrm] *also fig* germen *m*
Ger·man ['dʒɜːrmən] **1** *adj* alemán **2** *n person* alemán (-ana) *m(f)*;
language alemán *m*
Ger·man 'mea·sles *nsg* rubeola *f*
Ger·man 'shep·herd pastor *m* alemán
Ger·ma·ny ['dʒɜːrmənɪ] Alemania
ger·mi·nate ['dʒɜːrmɪneɪt] *v/i of seed*
germinar
germ 'war·fare guerra *f* bacteriológica
ges·tic·u·late [dʒe'stɪkjʊleɪt] *v/i*
gesticular
ges·ture ['dʒestʃər] *n also fig* gesto *m*
get [get] **1** *v/t (pret got, pp got, gotten) (obtain)* conseguir; *(fetch)*

traer; *(receive: letter, knowledge, respect)* recibir; *(catch: bus, train etc)*
tomar, *Span* coger; *(understand)* entender; *you can ~ them at the
corner shop* los puedes comprar
en la tienda de la esquina; *can I ~
you something to drink?* ¿quieres
tomar algo?; *~ tired* cansarse; *~
drunk* emborracharse; *I'm ~ting
old* me estoy haciendo mayor; *~
the TV fixed* hacer que arreglen la
televisión; *~ s.o. to do sth* hacer
que alguien haga algo; *~ to do sth
(have opportunity)* llegar a hacer
algo; *~ one's hair cut* cortarse el
pelo; *~ sth ready* preparar algo; *~
going (leave)* marcharse, irse; *have
got* tener; *he's got a lot of money*
tiene mucho dinero; *I have got to
study / verlo; I don't want to, but
I've got to* no quiero, pero tengo
que hacerlo; *~ to know* llegar a
conocer **2** *v/i (arrive)* llegar
♦ **get along** *v/i (come to party etc)* ir;
with s.o. llevarse bien; *how are you
getting along at school?* ¿cómo te
van las cosas en el colegio?; *the
patient is getting along nicely* el
paciente está progresando satisfactoriamente
♦ **get around** *v/i (travel)* viajar; *(be
mobile)* desplazarse
♦ **get at** *v/t (criticize)* meterse con;
(imply, mean) querer decir
♦ **get away 1** *v/i (leave)* marcharse,
irse **2** *v/t: get sth away from s.o.*
quitar algo a alguien
♦ **get away with** *v/t* salir impune de;
get away with it salirse con la suya;
she lets him get away with anything le permite todo; *I'll let you
get away with it this time* por esta
vez te perdonaré
♦ **get back 1** *v/i (return)* volver; *I'll
get back to you on that tomorrow*
le responderé a eso mañana **2** *v/t
(obtain again)* recuperar
♦ **get by** *v/i (pass)* pasar; *financially*
arreglárselas
♦ **get down 1** *v/i from ladder etc*

bajarse (*from* de); (*duck etc*) agacharse **2** *v/t* (*depress*) desanimar, deprimir

♦ **get down to** *v/t* (*start: work*) ponerse a; **get down to the facts** ir a los hechos

♦ **get in 1** *v/i* (*arrive*) llegar; *to car* subir(se), meterse; **how did they get in?** *of thieves, mice etc* ¿cómo entraron? **2** *v/t to suitcase etc* meter

♦ **get into** *v/t house* entrar en, meterse en; *car* subir(se) a, meterse en; *computer system* introducirse en

♦ **get off 1** *v/i from bus etc* bajarse; (*finish work*) salir; (*not be punished*) librarse **2** *v/t* (*remove*) quitar; *clothes, hat, footgear* quitarse; **get off my bike!** ¡bájate de mi bici!; **get off the grass!** ¡no pises la hierba!

♦ **get off with** *v/t:* **get off with a small fine** tener que pagar sólo una pequeña multa

♦ **get on 1** *v/i to bike, bus, train* montarse, subirse; (*be friendly*) llevarse bien; (*advance: of time*) hacerse tarde; (*become old*) hacerse mayor; (*make progress*) progresar; **it's getting on** *getting late* se está haciendo tarde; **he's getting on** se está haciendo mayor; **he's getting on for 50** está a punto de cumplir 50 **2** *v/t:* **get on the bus/one's bike** montarse en el autobús/la bici; **get one's shoes on** ponerse los zapatos; **I can't get these pants on** estos pantalones no me entran

♦ **get out 1** *v/i of car, prison etc* salir; **get out!** ¡vete!, ¡fuera de aquí!; **let's get out of here** ¡salgamos de aquí!; **I don't get out much these days** últimamente no salgo mucho **2** *v/t nail, sth jammed* sacar, extraer; *stain* quitar; *gun, pen* sacar

♦ **get over** *v/t fence etc* franquear; *disappointment* superar; *lover etc* olvidar

♦ **get over with** *v/t* terminar con; **let's get it over with** quitémonoslo de encima

♦ **get through** *v/i on telephone* conectarse; **obviously I'm just not**

getting through está claro que no me estoy haciendo entender; **get through to s.o.** (*make self understood*) comunicarse con alguien

♦ **get up 1** *v/i* levantarse **2** *v/t* (*climb*) subir

'**get·a·way** *from robbery* fuga *f*, huida *f*

'**get·a·way car** coche *m* utilizado en la fuga

'**get-to·geth·er** reunión *f*

ghast·ly ['gæstlɪ] *adj* terrible

gher·kin ['gɜːrkɪn] pepinillo *m*

ghet·to ['getou] gueto *m*

ghost [goust] fantasma *m*

ghost·ly ['goustlɪ] *adj* fantasmal

'**ghost town** ciudad *f* fantasma

ghoul [guːl] macabro(-a) *m(f)*, morboso(-a) *m(f)*

ghoul·ish ['guːlɪʃ] *adj* macabro, morboso

gi·ant ['dʒaɪənt] **1** *n* gigante *m* **2** *adj* gigantesco, gigante

gib·ber·ish ['dʒɪbərɪʃ] F memeces *fpl* F, majaderías *fpl* F

gibe [dʒaɪb] *n* pulla *f*

gib·lets ['dʒɪblɪts] *npl* menudillos *mpl*

gid·di·ness ['gɪdɪnɪs] mareo *m*

gid·dy ['gɪdɪ] *adj* mareado; **feel ~** estar mareado

gift [gɪft] regalo *m*

gift cer·ti·fi·cate vale *m* de regalo

gift·ed ['gɪftɪd] *adj* con talento

'**gift-wrap 1** *n* papel *m* de regalo **2** *v/t* (*pret & pp* **-ped**) envolver para regalo

gig [gɪg] F concierto *m*, actuación *f*

gi·ga·byte ['gɪgəbaɪt] COMPUT gigabyte *m*

gi·gan·tic [dʒaɪ'gæntɪk] *adj* gigantesco

gig·gle ['gɪgl] **1** *v/i* soltar risitas **2** *n* risita *f*

gig·gly ['gɪglɪ] *adj* que suelta risitas

gill [gɪl] *of fish* branquia *f*

gilt [gɪlt] *n* dorado *m*; **~s** FIN valores *mpl* del Estado

gim·mick ['gɪmɪk] truco *m*, reclamo *m*

gim·mick·y ['gɪmɪkɪ] *adj* superficial,

artificioso

gin [dʒɪn] ginebra f; **~ and tonic** gintonic m

gin·ger ['dʒɪndʒər] n spice jengibre m

'**gin·ger·bread** pan m de jengibre

gin·ger·ly ['dʒɪndʒərlɪ] adv cuidadosamente, delicadamente

gip·sy ['dʒɪpsɪ] gitano(-a) m(f)

gi·raffe [dʒɪ'ræf] jirafa f

gir·der ['gɜːrdər] viga f

girl [gɜːrl] chica f; (**young**) ~ niña f, chica f

'**girl·friend** of boy novia f; of girl amiga f

girl·ie mag·a·zine ['gɜːrlɪ] revista f porno

girl·ish ['gɜːrlɪʃ] adj de niñas

girl 'scout escultista f, scout f

gist [dʒɪst] esencia f

give [gɪv] v/t (pret **gave**, pp **given**) dar; as present regalar; (supply: electricity etc) proporcionar; talk, lecture dar, pronunciar; cry, groan soltar; **~ her my love** dale recuerdos (de mi parte); **~ s.o. a present** hacer un regalo a alguien

♦ **give away** v/t as present regalar; (betray) traicionar; **give o.s. away** descubrirse, traicionarse

♦ **give back** v/t devolver

♦ **give in 1** v/i (surrender) rendirse **2** v/t (hand in) entregar

♦ **give off** v/t smell, fumes emitir, despedir

♦ **give onto** v/t (open onto) dar a

♦ **give out 1** v/t leaflets etc repartir **2** v/i of supplies, strength agotarse

♦ **give up 1** v/t smoking etc dejar de; **give o.s. up to the police** entregarse a la policía **2** v/i (stop making effort) rendirse; **I find it hard to give up** me cuesta mucho dejarlo

♦ **give way** v/i of bridge etc hundirse

give-and-'take toma m y daca

giv·en ['gɪvn] pp → **give**

'**giv·en name** nombre m de pila

gla·ci·er ['gleɪʃər] glaciar m

glad [glæd] adj contento, alegre; **I was ~ to see you** me alegré de verte

glad·ly ['glædlɪ] adv con mucho gusto

glam·or ['glæmər] atractivo m, glamour m

glam·or·ize ['glæməraɪz] v/t hacer atractivo, ensalzar

glam·or·ous ['glæmərəs] adj atractivo, glamoroso

glam·our Br → **glamor**

glance [glæns] **1** n ojeada f, vistazo **2** v/i echar una ojeada or vistazo

♦ **glance at** v/t echar una ojeada or vistazo a

gland [glænd] glándula f

glan·du·lar 'fe·ver ['glændʒələr] mononucleosis f inv infecciosa

glare [gler] **1** n of sun, headlights resplandor m **2** v/i of headlights resplandecer

♦ **glare at** v/t mirar con furia a

glar·ing ['glerɪŋ] adj mistake garrafal

glar·ing·ly ['glerɪŋlɪ] adv: **it's ~ obvious** está clarísimo

glass [glæs] material vidrio m; for drink vaso m

glass 'case vitrina f

glass·es npl gafas fpl, L.Am. lentes mpl, L.Am. anteojos mpl

glaze [gleɪz] n vidriado m

♦ **glaze over** v/i of eyes vidriarse

glazed [gleɪzd] adj expression vidrioso

gla·zi·er ['gleɪzɪr] cristalero(-a) m(f), vidriero(-a) m(f)

glaz·ing ['gleɪzɪŋ] cristales mpl, vidrios mpl

gleam [gliːm] **1** n resplandor m, brillo m **2** v/i resplandecer, brillar

glee [gliː] júbilo m, regocijo m

glee·ful ['gliːfəl] adj jubiloso

glib [glɪb] adj fácil

glib·ly ['glɪblɪ] adv con labia

glide [glaɪd] v/i of bird, plane planear; of piece of furniture deslizarse

glid·er ['glaɪdər] planeador m

glid·ing ['glaɪdɪŋ] n sport vuelo m sin motor

glim·mer ['glɪmər] **1** n of light brillo m tenue; **~ of hope** rayo m de esperanza **2** v/i brillar tenuemente

glimpse [glɪmps] **1** n vistazo m;

catch a ~ of vislumbrar **2** *v/t* vislumbrar

glint [glɪnt] **1** *n* destello *m*; *in eyes* centelleo *m* **2** *v/i of light* destellar; *of eyes* centellear

glis·ten ['glɪsn] *v/i* relucir, centellear

glit·ter ['glɪtər] *v/i* resplandecer, destellar

glit·ter·ati [glɪtə'rɑːtɪ] *npl* famosos *mpl*

gloat [gloʊt] *v/i* regodearse

♦**gloat over** *v/t* regodearse de

glo·bal ['gloʊbl] *adj* global

glo·bal e'con·o·my economía *f* global; **glo·bal 'mar·ket** mercado *m* global; **glo·bal 'warm·ing** calentamiento *m* global

globe [gloʊb] *(the earth)* globo *m*; *(model of earth)* globo *m* terráqueo

gloom [gluːm] *(darkness)* tinieblas *fpl*, oscuridad *f*; *mood* abatimiento *m*, melancolía *f*

gloom·i·ly ['gluːmɪlɪ] *adv* con abatimiento, melancólicamente

gloom·y ['gluːmɪ] *adj room* tenebroso, oscuro; *mood, person* abatido, melancólico

glo·ri·ous ['glɔːrɪəs] *adj weather, day* espléndido, maravilloso; *victory* glorioso

glo·ry ['glɔːrɪ] *n* gloria *f*

gloss [glɑːs] *n (shine)* lustre *m*, brillo *m*; *(general explanation)* glosa *f*

♦**gloss over** *v/t* pasar por alto

glos·sa·ry ['glɑːsərɪ] *n* glosario *m*

'**gloss paint** pintura *f* brillante

gloss·y ['glɑːsɪ] **1** *adj paper* cuché, satinado **2** *n magazine* revista *f* en color (en papel cuché *or* satinado)

glove [glʌv] guante *m*

'**glove com·part·ment** guantera *f*

'**glove pup·pet** marioneta *f* de guiñol (de guante)

glow [gloʊ] **1** *n of light, fire* resplandor *m*, brillo *m*; *in cheeks* rubor *m* **2** *v/i of light, fire* resplandecer, brillar; *of cheeks* ruborizarse

glow·er [glaʊr] *v/i* fruncir el ceño

glow·ing ['gloʊɪŋ] *adj description* entusiasta

glu·cose ['gluːkoʊs] glucosa *f*

glue [gluː] **1** *n* pegamento *m*, cola *f* **2** *v/t* pegar, encolar; **~ sth to sth** pegar *or* encolar algo a algo; **be ~d to the radio / TV** F estar pegado a la radio / televisión F

glum [glʌm] *adj* sombrío, triste

glum·ly ['glʌmlɪ] *adv* con tristeza

glut [glʌt] *n* exceso *m*, superabundancia *f*

glut·ton ['glʌtən] glotón(-ona) *m(f)*

glut·ton·y ['glʌtənɪ] gula *f*, glotonería *f*

GMT [dʒiːem'tiː] *abbr* (= **Greenwich Mean Time**) hora *f* del meridiano de Greenwich

gnarled [nɑːrld] *adj* nudoso

gnat [næt] *tipo de mosquito*

gnaw [nɔː] *v/t bone* roer

GNP [dʒiːen piː] *abbr* (= **gross national product**) PNB *m* (= producto *m* nacional bruto)

go [goʊ] **1** *n:* **on the ~** en marcha **2** *v/i (pret went, pp gone)* ir (**to** a); *(leave)* irse, marcharse; *(work, function)* funcionar; *(come out: of stain etc)* irse; *(cease: of pain etc)* pasarse; *(match: of colors etc)* ir bien, pegar; **~ shopping / jogging** ir de compras / a hacer footing; **I must be ~ing** me tengo que ir; **let's ~!** ¡vamos!; **~ for a walk** ir a pasear *or* a dar un paseo; **~ to bed** ir(se) a la cama; **~ to school** ir al colegio; **how's the work ~ing?** ¿cómo va el trabajo?; **they're ~ing for $50** *(being sold at)* se venden por 50 dólares; **hamburger to ~** hamburguesa para llevar; **be all gone** *(finished)* haberse acabado; **~ green** ponerse verde; **be ~ing to do sth** ir a hacer algo

♦**go ahead** *v/i and do sth* seguir adelante; **can I? – sure, go ahead** ¿puedo? – por supuesto, adelante

♦**go ahead with** *v/t plans etc* seguir adelante con

♦**go along with** *v/t suggestion* aceptar

♦**go at** *v/t (attack)* atacar

♦**go away** *v/i of person* irse, marcharse; *of rain, pain, clouds* desaparecer

♦ **go back** *v/i* (*return*) volver; (*date back*) remontarse; *we go back a long way* nos conocemos desde hace tiempo; *go back to sleep* volver a dormirse

♦ **go by** *v/i* of car, time pasar

♦ **go down** *v/i* bajar; *of sun* ponerse; *of ship* hundirse; *go down well/ badly of suggestion etc* sentar bien / mal

♦ **go for** *v/t* (*attack*) atacar; *I don't much go for gin* no me va mucho la ginebra

♦ **go in** *v/i to room, house* entrar; *of sun* ocultarse; (*fit: of part etc*) ir, encajar

♦ **go in for** *v/t competition, race* tomar parte en; *I used to go in for badminton quite a lot* antes jugaba mucho al bádminton

♦ **go off 1** *v/i* (*leave*) marcharse; *of bomb* explotar, estallar; *of gun* dispararse; *of alarm* saltar; *of milk etc* echarse a perder **2** *v/t: I've gone off whiskey* ya no me gusta el whisky

♦ **go on** *v/i* (*continue*) continuar; (*happen*) ocurrir, pasar; *go on, do it!* (*encouraging*) ¡venga, hazlo!; *what's going on?* ¿qué pasa?

♦ **go on at** *v/t* (*nag*) meterse con

♦ **go out** *v/i of person* salir; *of light, fire* apagarse

♦ **go out with** *v/t romantically* salir con

♦ **go over** *v/t* (*check*) examinar; (*do again*) repasar

♦ **go through** *v/t illness, hard times* atravesar; (*check*) revisar, examinar; (*read through*) estudiar

♦ **go under** *v/i* (*sink*) hundirse; *of company* ir a la quiebra

♦ **go up** *v/i* subir

♦ **go without 1** *v/t food etc* pasar sin **2** *v/i* pasar privaciones

goad [goud] *v/t* pinchar; *~ s.o. into doing sth* pinchar a alguien para que haga algo

'**go-a-head 1** *n* luz *f* verde; *when we get the ~* cuando nos den la luz verde **2** *adj* (*enterprising, dynamic*) di-

námico

goal [goul] SP *target* portería *f, L.Am.* arco *m*; SP *point* gol *m*; (*objective*) objetivo *m*, meta *f*

goal·ie ['gouli] F portero(-a) *m(f)*, *L.Am.* arquero(-a) *m(f)*

'**goal·keep·er** portero(-a) *m(f)*, guardameta *m/f, L.Am.* arquero(-a) *m(f)*; '**goal kick** saque *m* de puerta; '**goal·mouth** portería *f*; '**goal·post** poste *m*

goat [gout] cabra *f*

gob·ble ['gabl] *v/t* engullir

♦ **gobble up** *v/t* engullir

gob·ble·dy·gook ['gabldɪguːk] F jerigonza *f* F

'**go-be·tween** intermediario(-a) *m(f)*

god [gad] dios *m*; *thank God!* ¡gracias a Dios!; *oh God!* ¡Dios mío!

'**god·child** ahijado(-a) *m(f)*

'**god·daugh·ter** ahijada *f*

'**god·dess** ['gadɪs] diosa *f*

'**god·fa·ther** *also in mafia* padrino *m*; **god·for·sak·en** ['gadfərseɪkən] *adj place* dejado de la mano de Dios; '**god·moth·er** madrina *f*; '**god·pa·rent** *man* padrino *m*; *woman* madrina *f*; '**god·send** regalo *m* del cielo; '**god·son** ahijado *m*

go·fer ['goufər] F recadero(-a) *m(f)*

gog·gles ['gaglz] *npl* gafas *fpl*

go·ing ['gouɪŋ] *adj price etc* vigente; *~ concern* empresa *f* en marcha

go·ings-on [gouɪŋz'ɑːn] *npl* actividades *fpl*

gold [gould] **1** *n* oro *m* **2** *adj* de oro

gold·en ['gouldn] *adj sky, hair* dorado

gold·en 'hand·shake *gratificación entregada tras la marcha de un directivo*

gold·en 'wed·ding (**an·ni·ver·sa·ry**) *bodas fpl* de oro

'**gold·fish** pez *m* de colores; '**gold med·al** medalla *f* de oro; '**gold mine** *fig* mina *f*; '**gold·smith** orfebre *m/f*

golf [galf] golf *m*

'**golf ball** pelota *f* de golf; '**golf club** *organization* club *m* de golf; *stick*

G

palo *m* de golf; **'golf course** campo *m* de golf

golf·er ['gɑːlfər] golfista *m/f*

gone [gɑːn] *pp* → **go**

gong [gɑːŋ] gong *m*

good [gʊd] *adj* bueno; *food* bueno, rico; *a* ~ *many* muchos; *he's* ~ *at chess* se le da muy bien el ajedrez; *be* ~ *for s.o.* ser bueno para alguien

good·bye [gʊd'baɪ] adiós *m*, despedida *f*; *say* ~ *to s.o., wish s.o.* ~ decir adiós a alguien, despedirse de alguien

'good-for-noth·ing *n* inútil *m/f*; **Good 'Fri·day** Viernes *m inv* Santo; **good-hu·mored**, *Br* **good-hu·moured** [gʊd'hjuːmərd] *adj* jovial, afable; **good-look·ing** [gʊd'lʊkɪŋ] *adj woman, man* guapo; **good-na·tured** [gʊd'neɪtʃərd] bondadoso

good·ness ['gʊdnɪs] *moral* bondad *f*; *of fruit etc* propiedades *fpl*, valor *m* nutritivo; *thank* ~! ¡gracias a Dios!

goods [gʊdz] *npl* COM mercancías *fpl*, productos *mpl*

good·will buena voluntad *f*

good·y-good·y ['gʊdɪgʊdɪ] *n* F: *she's a real* ~ es demasiado buena-za F

goo·ey ['guːɪ] *adj* pegajoso

goof [guːf] *v/i* F meter la pata F

goose [guːs] (*pl* **geese** [giːs]) ganso *m*, oca *f*

goose·ber·ry ['gʊzberɪ] grosella *f*; **'goose bumps** *npl* carne *f* de gallina; **'goose pim·ples** *npl* carne *f* de gallina

gorge [gɔːrdʒ] **1** *n* garganta *f*, desfiladero *m* **2** *v/t*: ~ *o.s. on sth* comer algo hasta hartarse

gor·geous ['gɔːrdʒəs] *adj weather* maravilloso; *dress, hair* precioso; *woman, man* buenísimo; *smell* estupendo

go·ril·la [gə'rɪlə] gorila *m*

gosh [gɑːʃ] *int* ¡caramba!, ¡vaya!

go-'slow huelga *f* de celo

gos·pel ['gɑːspl] *in Bible* evangelio *m*; *it's the* ~ *truth* es la pura verdad

gos·sip ['gɑːsɪp] **1** *n* cotilleo *m*; *person* cotilla *m/f* **2** *v/i* cotillear

'gos·sip col·umn ecos *mpl* de sociedad

'gos·sip col·um·nist escritor(a) *m(f)* de los ecos de sociedad

gos·sipy ['gɑːsɪpɪ] *adj letter* lleno de cotilleos

got [gɑːt] *pret & pp* → **get**

got·ten ['gɑːtn] *pp* → **get**

gour·met ['gʊrmeɪ] *n* gastrónomo(-a) *m(f)*, gourmet *m/f*

gov·ern ['gʌvərn] *v/t country* gobernar

gov·ern·ment ['gʌvərnmənt] gobierno *m*

gov·er·nor ['gʌvərnər] gobernador(a) *m(f)*

gown [gaʊn] *long dress* vestido *m*; *wedding dress* traje *m*; *of academic, judge* toga *f*; *of surgeon* bata *f*

grab [græb] *v/t* (*pret & pp* **-bed**) agarrar; *food* tomar; ~ *some sleep* dormir

grace [greɪs] *of dancer etc* gracia *f*, elegancia *f*; *say* ~ *at meal* bendecir la mesa

grace·ful ['greɪsfəl] *adj* elegante

grace·ful·ly ['greɪsfəlɪ] *adv move* con gracia *or* elegancia

gra·cious ['greɪʃəs] *adj person* amable; *style, living* elegante; **good** ~! ¡Dios mío!

grade [greɪd] **1** *n quality* grado *m*; EDU curso *m*; (*mark*) nota *f* **2** *v/t* clasificar

'grade cross·ing paso *m* a nivel

'grade school escuela *f* primaria

gra·di·ent ['greɪdɪənt] pendiente *f*

grad·u·al ['grædʒʊəl] *adj* gradual

grad·u·al·ly ['grædʒʊəlɪ] *adv* gradualmente, poco a poco

grad·u·ate ['grædʒʊət] **1** *n* licenciado (-a) *m(f)*; *from high school* bachiller *m/f* **2** *v/i from university* licenciarse, *L.Am.* egresarse; *from high school* sacar el bachillerato

grad·u·a·tion [grædʒʊ'eɪʃn] graduación *f*

graf·fi·ti [grə'fiːtiː] graffiti *m*

graft [græft] **1** *n* BOT, MED injerto *m*; *corruption* corrupción *f* **2** *v/t* BOT, MED injertar

grain [greɪn] grano *m*; *in wood* veta *f*;
  go against the ~ ir contra la naturaleza de alguien

gram [græm] gramo *m*

gram·mar ['græmər] gramática *f*

gram·mat·i·cal [grə'mætɪkl] *adj* gramatical

gram·mat·i·cal·ly [grə'mætɪklɪ] *adv* gramaticalmente

grand [grænd] **1** *adj* grandioso; F (*very good*) estupendo, genial **2** *n* F (*$1000*) mil dólares

gran·dad ['grændæd] F abuelito *m*

'grand·child nieto(-a) *m(f)*

'grand·daugh·ter nieta *f*

gran·deur ['grændʒər] grandiosidad *f*

'grand·fa·ther abuelo *m*

'grand·fa·ther clock reloj *m* de pie

gran·di·ose ['grændɪoʊs] *adj* grandioso

grand 'jur·y jurado *m* de acusación, gran jurado; **'grand·ma** F abuelita *f*, yaya *f* F; **'grand·moth·er** abuela *f*; **'grand·pa** F abuelito *m*, yayo *m* F; **'grand·par·ents** *npl* abuelos *mpl*; **grand pi'an·o** piano *m* de cola; **grand 'slam** gran slam *m*; **'grand·son** nieto *m*; **'grand·stand** tribuna *f*

gran·ite ['grænɪt] granito *m*

gran·ny ['grænɪ] F abuelita *f*, yaya *f* F

grant [grænt] **1** *n money* subvención *f* **2** *v/t* conceder; **take sth for ~ed** dar algo por sentado; **take s.o. for ~ed** no apreciar a alguien lo suficiente

gran·u·lat·ed sug·ar ['grænʊleɪtɪd] azúcar *m or f* granulado(-a)

gran·ule ['grænjuːl] gránulo *m*

grape [greɪp] uva *f*

'grape·fruit pomelo *m*, *L.Am.* toronja *f*; **'grape·fruit juice** *Span* zumo *m* de pomelo, *L.Am.* jugo *m* de toronja; **'grape·vine**: **I've heard through the ~ that ...** me ha contado un pajarito que ...

graph [græf] gráfico *m*, gráfica *f*

graph·ic ['græfɪk] **1** *adj* (*vivid*) gráfico **2** *n* COMPUT gráfico *m*

graph·ic·al·ly ['græfɪklɪ] *adv* descri-

be gráficamente

graph·ic de'sign·er diseñador(a) *m(f)* gráfico(-a)

♦ **grap·ple with** ['græpl] *v/t attacker* forcejear con; *problem etc* enfrentarse a

grasp [græsp] **1** *n physical* asimiento *m*; *mental* comprensión *f* **2** *v/t physically* agarrar; (*understand*) comprender

grass [græs] *n* hierba *f*

'grass·hop·per saltamontes *m inv*; **grass 'roots** *npl people* bases *fpl*; **grass 'wid·ow** mujer cuyo marido está a menudo ausente durante largos periodos de tiempo; **grass 'wid·ow·er** hombre cuya mujer está a menudo ausente durante largos periodos de tiempo

gras·sy ['græsɪ] *adj* lleno de hierba

grate¹ [greɪt] *n metal* parrilla *f*, reja *f*

grate² [greɪt] **1** *v/t in cooking* rallar **2** *v/i of sound* rechinar

grate·ful ['greɪtfʊl] *adj* agradecido; **we are ~ for your help** (le) agradecemos su ayuda; **I'm ~ to him** le estoy agradecido

grate·ful·ly ['greɪtfəlɪ] *adv* con agradecimiento

grat·er ['greɪtər] rallador *m*

grat·i·fy ['grætɪfaɪ] *v/t* (*pret & pp -ied*) satisfacer, complacer

grat·ing ['greɪtɪŋ] **1** *n* reja *f* **2** *adj sound, voice* chirriante

grat·i·tude ['grætɪtuːd] gratitud *f*

gra·tu·i·tous [grə'tuːɪtəs] *adj* gratuito

gra·tu·i·ty [grə'tuːətɪ] propina *f*, gratificación *f*

grave¹ [greɪv] *n* tumba *f*, sepultura *f*

grave² [greɪv] *adj* grave

grav·el ['grævl] *n* gravilla *f*

'grave·stone lápida *f*

'grave·yard cementerio *m*

♦ **grav·i·tate toward** ['grævɪteɪt] *v/t* verse atraído por

grav·i·ty ['grævətɪ] PHYS gravedad *f*

gra·vy ['greɪvɪ] jugo *m* (de la carne)

gray [greɪ] *adj* gris; **be going ~** encanecer

G

gray-haired [greɪ'herd] *adj* canoso

'gray·hound galgo *m*

graze¹ [greɪz] *v/i of cow etc* pastar, pacer

graze² [greɪz] **1** *v/t arm etc* rozar, arañar **2** *n* rozadura *f*, arañazo *m*

grease [gri:s] *n* grasa *f*

grease·proof 'pa·per papel *m* de cera *or* parafinado

greas·y ['gri:sɪ] *adj food, hands, plate* grasiento; *hair, skin* graso

great [greɪt] *adj* grande, *before singular noun* gran; F (*very good*) estupendo, genial F; *how was it? – ~!* ¿cómo fue? – ¡estupendo *or* genial!; *~ to see you again!* ¡me alegro de volver a verte!

Great 'Brit·ain Gran Bretaña; **great-'grand·child** bisnieto(-a) *m(f)*; **great-'grand·daugh·ter** bisnieta *f*; **great-'grand·fa·ther** bisabuelo *m*; **great-'grand·moth·er** bisabuela *f*; **great-'grand·par·ents** *npl* bisabuelos *mpl*; **great-'grand·son** bisnieto *m*

great·ly ['greɪtlɪ] *adv* muy

great·ness ['greɪtnɪs] grandeza *f*

Greece [gri:s] Grecia

greed [gri:d] *for money* codicia *f*; *for food* gula *f*, glotonería *f*

greed·i·ly ['gri:dɪlɪ] *adv* con codicia; *eat* con gula *or* glotonería

greed·y ['gri:dɪ] *adj food* glotón; *for money* codicioso

Greek [gri:k] **1** *adj* griego **2** *n person* griego(-a) *m(f)*; *language* griego *m*

green [gri:n] *adj* verde; *environmentally* ecologista, verde

green 'beans *npl* judías *fpl* verdes, *L.Am.* porotos *mpl* verdes, *Mex* ejotes *mpl*; **'green belt** cinturón *m* verde; **'green card** (*work permit*) permiso *m* de trabajo; **'green·field site** terreno *m* edificable en el campo; **'green·horn** F novato(-a) *m(f)* F; **'green·house** invernadero *m*; **'green·house ef·fect** efecto *m* invernadero; **'green·house gas** gas *m* invernadero

greens [gri:nz] *npl* verduras *f*

green 'thumb: *have a ~* tener buena mano con la jardinería

greet [gri:t] *v/t* saludar

greet·ing ['gri:tɪŋ] saludo *m*

'greet·ing card tarjeta *f* de felicitación

gre·gar·i·ous [grɪ'gerɪəs] *adj person* sociable

gre·nade [grɪ'neɪd] granada *f*

grew [gru:] *pret* → **grow**

grey *Br* → **gray**

grid [grɪd] reja *f*, rejilla *f*

'grid·iron SP *campo de fútbol americano*

'grid·lock *in traffic* paralización *f* del tráfico

grief [gri:f] dolor *m*, aflicción *f*

grief-strick·en ['gri:fstrɪkn] *adj* afligido

griev·ance ['gri:vəns] queja *f*

grieve [gri:v] *v/i* sufrir; *~ for s.o.* llorar por alguien

grill [grɪl] **1** *n on window* reja *f* **2** *v/t* (*interrogate*) interrogar

grille [grɪl] reja *f*

grim [grɪm] *adj face* severo; *prospects* desolador; *surroundings* lúgubre

gri·mace ['grɪməs] *n* gesto *m*, mueca *f*

grime [graɪm] mugre *f*

grim·ly ['grɪmlɪ] *adv speak* en tono grave

grim·y ['graɪmɪ] *adj* mugriento

grin [grɪn] **1** *n* sonrisa *f* (amplia) **2** *v/i* (*pret & pp -ned*) sonreír abiertamente

grind [graɪnd] *v/t* (*pret & pp ground*) *coffee* moler; *meat* picar; *~ one's teeth* hacer rechinar los dientes

grip [grɪp] **1** *n*: *he lost his ~ on the rope* se le escapó la cuerda; *be losing one's ~* (*losing one's skills*) estar perdiendo el control **2** *v/t* (*pret & pp -ped*) agarrar

gripe [graɪp] **1** *n* F queja *f* **2** *v/i* F quejarse

grip·ping ['grɪpɪŋ] *adj* apasionante

gris·tle ['grɪsl] cartílago *m*

grit [grɪt] **1** *n* (*dirt*) arenilla *f*; *for roads* gravilla *f* **2** *v/t* (*pret & pp -ted*): *~ one's teeth* apretar los dientes

grit·ty ['grɪtɪ] *adj* F *book, movie etc* duro F, descarnado

groan [groʊn] **1** *n* gemido *m* **2** *v/i* gemir

gro·cer ['groʊsər] tendero(-a) *m(f)*

gro·cer·ies ['groʊsərɪz] *npl* comestibles *mpl*

gro·cer·y store ['groʊsərɪ] tienda *f* de comestibles *or Mex* abarrotes

grog·gy ['grɑːgɪ] *adj* F grogui F

groin [grɔɪn] ANAT ingle *f*

groom [gruːm] **1** *n for bride* novio *m*; *for horse* mozo *m* de cuadra **2** *v/t horse* almohazar; *(train, prepare)* preparar; *well ~ed in appearance* bien arreglado

groove [gruːv] ranura *f*

grope [groʊp] **1** *v/i in the dark* caminar a tientas **2** *v/t sexually* manosear

♦ **grope for** *v/t door handle, the right word* intentar encontrar

gross [groʊs] *adj (coarse, vulgar)* grosero; *(exaggeration)* tremendo; *error* craso; FIN bruto

gross do·mes·tic 'prod·uct producto *m* interior bruto

gross na·tion·al 'prod·uct producto *m* nacional bruto

ground¹ [graʊnd] **1** *n* suelo *m*, tierra *f*; *(reason)* motivo *m*; ELEC tierra *f*; *on the ~* en el suelo **2** *v/t* ELEC conectar a tierra

ground² [graʊnd] *pret & pp* → **grind**

'ground con·trol control *m* de tierra

'ground crew personal *m* de tierra

ground·ing ['graʊndɪŋ] *in subject* fundamento *m*; *he's had a good ~ in electronics* tiene buenos fundamentos de electrónica

ground·less ['graʊndlɪs] *adj* infundado

ground 'meat carne *f* picada; **'ground·nut** cacahuete *m*, *L.Am.* maní *m*, *Mex* cacahuate *m*; **'ground plan** plano *m*; **'ground staff** SP personal *m* de mantenimiento; *at airport* personal *m* de tierra; **'ground·work** trabajos *mpl* preliminares

group [gruːp] **1** *n* grupo *m* **2** *v/t* agrupar

group·ie ['gruːpɪ] F grupi *f* F

group 'ther·a·py terapia *f* de grupo

grouse [graʊs] **1** *n* F queja *f* **2** *v/i* quejarse, refunfuñar

grov·el ['grɑːvl] *v/i fig* arrastrarse

grow [groʊ] **1** *v/i* (*pret* **grew**, *pp* **grown**) crecer; *of number, amount* crecer, incrementarse; *~ old/ tired* envejecer/cansarse **2** *v/t* (*pret* **grew**, *pp* **grown**) *flowers* cultivar

♦ **grow up** *v/i of person, city* crecer; **grow up!** ¡no seas crío!

growl [graʊl] **1** *n* gruñido *m* **2** *v/i* gruñir

grown [groʊn] *pp* → **grow**

grown-up ['groʊnʌp] **1** *n* adulto(-a) *m(f)* **2** *adj* maduro

growth [groʊθ] *of person, economy* crecimiento *m*; *(increase)* incremento *m*; MED bulto *m*

grub [grʌb] *of insect* larva *f*, gusano *m*

grub·by ['grʌbɪ] *adj* mugriento *m*

grudge [grʌdʒ] **1** *n* rencor *m*; *bear s.o. a ~* guardar rencor a alguien **2** *v/t*: *~ s.o. sth feel envy* envidiar algo a alguien

grudg·ing ['grʌdʒɪŋ] *adj* rencoroso

grudg·ing·ly ['grʌdʒɪŋlɪ] *adv* de mala gana

gru·el·ing, *Br* **gru·el·ling** ['gruːəlɪŋ] *adj* agotador

gruff [grʌf] *adj* seco, brusco

grum·ble ['grʌmbl] *v/i* murmurar, refunfuñar

grum·bler ['grʌmblər] quejica *m/f*

grump·y ['grʌmpɪ] *adj* cascarrabias

grunt [grʌnt] **1** *n* gruñido *m* **2** *v/i* gruñir

guar·an·tee [gærən'tiː] **1** *n* garantía *f*; *~ period* periodo *m* de garantía **2** *v/t* garantizar

guar·an·tor [gærən'tɔːr] garante *m/f*

guard [gɑːrd] **1** *n (security ~)* guardia *m/f*, guarda *m/f*; MIL guardia *f*; *in prison* guardián (-ana) *m(f)*; *be on one's ~ against* estar en guardia contra **2** *v/t* guardar, proteger

♦ **guard against** *v/t* evitar

'guard dog perro *m* guardián

guard·ed ['gɑːrdɪd] *adj reply* cauteloso

G

guard·i·an ['gɑːrdɪən] LAW tutor(a) *m(f)*

guard·i·an 'an·gel ángel *m* de la guardia

Gua·te·ma·la [gwætə'mɑːlə] *n* Guatemala

Gua·te·ma·lan [gwætə'mɑːlən] **1** *adj* guatemalteco **2** *n* guatemalteco(-a) *m(f)*

guer·ril·la [gə'rɪlə] guerrillero(-a) *m(f)*

guer·ril·la 'war·fare guerra *f* de guerrillas

guess [ges] **1** *n* conjetura *f*, suposición *f* **2** *v/t the answer* adivinar; *I ~ so* me imagino *or* supongo que sí; *I ~ not* me imagino *or* supongo que no **3** *v/i* adivinar

'guess·work conjeturas *fpl*

guest [gest] invitado(-a) *m(f)*

'guest·house casa *f* de huéspedes

'guest·room habitación *f* para invitados

guf·faw [gʌ'fɔː] **1** *n* carcajada *f*, risotada *f* **2** *v/i* carcajearse

guid·ance ['gaɪdəns] orientación *f*, consejo *m*

guide [gaɪd] **1** *n person* guía *m/f*; *book* guía *f* **2** *v/t* guiar

'guide·book guía *f*

guid·ed mis·sile ['gaɪdɪd] misil *m* teledirigido

'guide dog *Br* perro *m* lazarillo

guid·ed 'tour visita *f* guiada

'guide·lines ['gaɪdlaɪnz] *npl* directrices *fpl*, normas *fpl* generales

guilt [gɪlt] culpa *f*, culpabilidad *f*; LAW culpabilidad *f*

guilt·y ['gɪltɪ] *adj also* LAW culpable; *be ~ of sth* ser culpable de algo; *have a ~ conscience* tener remordimientos de conciencia

guin·ea pig ['gɪnɪpɪg] conejillo *m* de Indias, cobaya *f*; *fig* conejillo *m* de Indias

guise [gaɪz] apariencia *f*; *under the ~ of* bajo la apariencia de

gui·tar [gɪ'tɑːr] guitarra *f*

gui'tar case estuche *m* de guitarra

gui·tar·ist [gɪ'tɑːrɪst] guitarrista *m/f*

gui'tar play·er guitarrista *m/f*

gulf [gʌlf] golfo *m*; *fig* abismo *m*; *the Gulf* el Golfo

Gulf of 'Mex·i·co Golfo *m* de México

gull [gʌl] *bird* gaviota *f*

gul·let ['gʌlɪt] ANAT esófago *m*

gul·li·ble ['gʌlɪbl] *adj* crédulo, ingenuo

gulp [gʌlp] **1** *n of water etc* trago *m* **2** *v/i in surprise* tragar saliva

♦ **gulp down** *v/t drink* tragar; *food* engullir

gum¹ [gʌm] *in mouth* encía *f*

gum² [gʌm] *n* (*glue*) pegamento *m*, cola *f*; (*chewing ~*) chicle *m*

gump·tion ['gʌmpʃn] sentido *m* común

gun [gʌn] *pistol, revolver* pistola *f*; *rifle* rifle *m*; *cannon* cañón *m*

♦ **gun down** *v/t* (*pret & pp* **-ned**) matar a tiros

'gun·fire disparos *mpl*; **'gun·man** hombre *m* armado; **'gun·point**: *at ~* a punta de pistola; **'gun·shot** disparo *m*, tiro *m*; **'gun·shot wound** herida *f* de bala

gur·gle ['gɜːrgl] *v/i of baby* gorjear; *of drain* gorgotear

gu·ru ['guːruː] *fig* gurú *m*

gush [gʌʃ] *v/i of liquid* manar, salir a chorros

gush·y ['gʌʃɪ] *adj* F (*enthusiastic*) efusivo, exagerado

gust [gʌst] ráfaga *f*

gus·to ['gʌstoʊ] entusiasmo *m*

gust·y ['gʌstɪ] *adj weather* ventoso, con viento racheado; *~ wind* viento *m* racheado

gut [gʌt] **1** *n* intestino *m*; F (*stomach*) tripa *f* F **2** *v/t* (*pret & pp* **-ted**) (*destroy*) destruir

guts [gʌts] *npl* F (*courage*) agallas *fpl* F

guts·y ['gʌtsɪ] *adj* F (*brave*) valiente, con muchas agallas F

gut·ter ['gʌtər] *on sidewalk* cuneta *f*; *on roof* canal *m*, canalón *m*

guy [gaɪ] F tipo *m* F, *Span* tío *m* F; *hey, you ~s* eh, gente

guz·zle ['gʌzl] *v/t* tragar, engullir

gym [dʒɪm] gimnasio *m*

gym·na·si·um [dʒɪm'neɪzɪəm] gimnasio *m*

gym·nast ['dʒɪmnæst] gimnasta *m/f*

gym·nas·tics [dʒɪm'næstɪks] gimnasia *f*

'gym shoes *npl Br* zapatillas *fpl* de gimnasia

gy·nae·col·o·gy *etc Br* → **gynecology** *etc*

gy·ne·col·o·gist [gaɪnɪ'kɑːlədʒɪst] ginecólogo(-a) *m(f)*

gy·ne·col·o·gy [gaɪnɪ'kɑːlədʒɪ] ginecología *f*

gyp·sy ['dʒɪpsɪ] gitano(-a) *m(f)*

H

hab·it ['hæbɪt] hábito *m*, costumbre *m*; **get into the ~ of doing sth** adquirir el hábito de hacer algo

hab·it·a·ble ['hæbɪtəbl] *adj* habitable

hab·i·tat ['hæbɪtæt] hábitat *m*

ha·bit·u·al [hə'bɪtʊəl] *adj* habitual

hack [hæk] *n poor writer* gacetillero(-a) *m(f)*

hack·er ['hækər] COMPUT pirata *m/f* informático(-a)

hack·neyed ['hæknɪd] *adj* manido

had [hæd] *pret & pp* → **have**

had·dock ['hædək] eglefino *m*

haem·or·rhage *Br* → **hemorrhage**

hag·gard ['hægərd] *adj* demacrado

hag·gle ['hægl] *v/i* regatear; **~ over sth** regatear algo

hail [heɪl] *n* granizo *m*

'hail·stone piedra *f* de granizo

'hail·storm granizada *f*

hair [her] pelo *m*, cabello *m*; *single* pelo *m*; *(body ~)* vello *m*; **have short/ long ~** tener el pelo corto/largo

'hair·brush cepillo *m*; **'hair·cut** corte *m* de pelo; **have a ~** cortarse el pelo; **'hair·do** peinado *m*; **'hair·dress·er** peluquero(-a) *m(f)*; **at the ~** en la peluquería; **'hair·dry·er** secador *m* (de pelo)

hair·less ['herlɪs] *adj* sin pelo

'hair·pin horquilla *f*; **hair·pin 'curve** curva *f* muy cerrada; **hair-rais·ing** ['heɪrɪzɪŋ] *adj* espeluznante; **hair remov·er** [her'muːvər] depilatorio *m*; **'hair's breadth** *fig*: **by a ~** por un pelo; **hair-split·ting** ['hersplɪtɪŋ] *n* sutilezas *fpl*; **'hair spray** laca *f*; **'hair·style** peinado *m*; **'hair·styl·ist** estilista *m/f*, peluquero(-a) *m(f)*

hair·y ['herɪ] *adj arm, animal* peludo; F *(frightening)* espeluznante

half [hæf] **1** *n* (*pl* **halves** [hævz]) mitad *f*; **~ past ten, ~ after ten** las diez y media; **~ an hour** media hora; **~ a pound** media libra; **go halves with s.o. on sth** ir a medias con alguien en algo **2** *adj* medio; **at ~ price** a mitad de precio **3** *adv* a medias; **~ finished** a medio acabar

half-heart·ed [hæf'hɑːrtɪd] *adj* desganado; **'half note** MUS nota *f* blanca; **half 'pay** media paga *f*; **half 'time 1** *n* SP descanso *m* **2** *adj* SP: **~ score** marcador *m* en el descanso; **half'way 1** *adj stage, point* intermedio **2** *adv* a mitad de camino

hall [hɔːl] *large room* sala *f*; *(hallway in house)* vestíbulo *m*

Hal·low·e'en [hæloʊ'wiːn] *víspera de Todos los Santos*

halo ['heɪloʊ] halo *m*

halt [hɔːlt] **1** *v/i* detenerse **2** *v/t* detener **3** *n* alto *m*; **come to a ~** detenerse

halve [hæv] *v/t input, costs, effort* reducir a la mitad; *apple* partir por la mitad

ham [hæm] jamón *m*

ham·burg·er ['hæmbɜːrgər] hamburguesa *f*

ham·mer ['hæmər] **1** *n* martillo *m* **2** *v/i*: **~ at the door** golpear la puerta

ham·mock ['hæmək] hamaca *f*

ham·per¹ ['hæmpər] *n for food* cesta *f*

ham·per² *v/t (obstruct)* estorbar, obstaculizar

ham·ster ['hæmstər] hámster *m*

hand [hænd] *n* mano *f*; *of clock* manecilla *f*; *(worker)* brazo *m*; **at ~, to ~** a mano; **at first ~** de primera mano, directamente; **by ~** a mano; **on the one ~ ..., on the other ~** por una parte ..., por otra parte; **the work is in ~** el trabajo se está llevando a cabo; **on your right ~** a mano derecha; **~s off!** ¡fuera las manos!; **~s up!** ¡arriba las manos!; **change ~s** cambiar de manos; **give s.o. a ~** echar una mano a alguien

♦ **hand down** *v/t* transmitir

♦ **hand in** *v/t* entregar

♦ **hand on** *v/t* pasar

♦ **hand out** *v/t* repartir

♦ **hand over** *v/t* entregar

'**hand·bag** bolso *m*, *L.Am.* cartera *f*; '**hand·bag·gage** equipaje *m* de mano; '**hand·book** manual *m*; '**hand·cuff** *v/t* esposar; **hand·cuffs** ['hæn(d)kʌfs] *npl* esposas *fpl*

hand·i·cap ['hændɪkæp] *n* desventaja *f*

hand·i·capped ['hændɪkæpt] *adj physically* minusválido, disminuido; **~ by lack of funds** en desventaja por carecer de fondos

hand·i·craft ['hændɪkræft] artesanía *f*

hand·i·work ['hændɪwɜːrk] manualidades *fpl*

hand·ker·chief ['hæŋkərtʃɪf] pañuelo *m*

han·dle ['hændl] **1** *n of door* manilla *f*; *of suitcase* asa *f*; *of pan, knife* mango *m* **2** *v/t goods, difficult person* manejar; *case, deal* llevar, encargarse de; **let me ~ this** deja que me ocupe yo de esto

han·dle·bars ['hændlbɑːrz] *npl* manillar *m*, *L.Am.* manubrio *m*

'**hand lug·gage** equipaje *m* de mano; **hand·made** [hæn(d)'meɪd] *adj* hecho a mano; '**hand·rail** barandilla *f*; '**hand·shake** apretón *m* de manos

hands-off [hændz'ɑːf] *adj* no intervencionista

hand·some ['hænsəm] *adj* guapo, atractivo

hands-on [hændz'ɑːn] *adj* práctico; **he has a ~ style of management** le gusta implicarse en todos los aspectos de la gestión

'**hand·writ·ing** caligrafía *f*

hand·writ·ten ['hændrɪtn] *adj* escrito a mano

hand·y ['hændɪ] *adj tool, device* práctico; **it might come in ~** nos puede venir muy bien

hang [hæŋ] **1** *v/t (pret & pp hung) picture* colgar; *person* colgar, ahorcar (*pret & pp -ed*) **2** *v/i (pret & pp hung)* colgar; *of dress, hair* caer, colgar **3** *n*: **get the ~ of sth** F agarrarle el tranquillo a algo F

♦ **hang around** *v/i*: **he's always hanging around on the street corner** siempre está rondando por la esquina

♦ **hang on** *v/i (wait)* esperar

♦ **hang on to** *v/t (keep)* conservar; **do you mind if I hang on to it for a while?** ¿te importa si me lo quedo durante un tiempo?

♦ **hang up** *v/i* TELEC colgar

han·gar ['hæŋər] hangar *m*

hang·er ['hæŋər] *for clothes* percha *f*

hang glid·er ['hæŋɡlaɪdər] *person* piloto *m* de ala delta; *device* ala *f* delta

hang glid·ing ['hæŋɡlaɪdɪŋ] ala *f* delta

'**hang·o·ver** resaca *f*

♦ **han·ker after** ['hæŋkər] *v/t* anhelar

han·kie, han·ky ['hæŋkɪ] F pañuelo *m*

hap·haz·ard [hæp'hæzərd] *adj* descuidado

hap·pen ['hæpn] *v/i* ocurrir, pasar, suceder; **if you ~ to see him** si por casualidad lo vieras; **what has ~ed to you?** ¿qué te ha pasado?

♦ **happen across** *v/t* encontrar por

casualidad

hap·pen·ing ['hæpnɪŋ] suceso *m*

hap·pi·ly ['hæpɪlɪ] *adv* alegremente; *(luckily)* afortunadamente

hap·pi·ness ['hæpɪnɪs] felicidad *f*

hap·py ['hæpɪ] *adj* feliz, contento; *coincidence* afortunado

hap·py-go-'luck·y *adj* despreocupado

'hap·py hour *franja horaria en la que las bebidas se venden más baratas*

har·ass [hə'ræs] *v/t* acosar; *enemy* asediar, hostigar

har·assed [hər'æst] *adj* agobiado

har·ass·ment [hə'ræsmənt] acoso *m*

har·bor, *Br* **har·bour** ['hɑːrbər] **1** *n* puerto *m* **2** *v/t criminal* proteger; *grudge* albergar

hard [hɑːrd] **1** *adj* duro; *(difficult)* difícil; *facts, evidence* real; *~ of hearing* duro de oído **2** *adv hit, rain* fuerte; *work* duro; *try ~ to do sth* esforzarse por hacer algo

'hard·back *n* libro *m* de tapas duras; **hard-boiled** [hɑːrd'bɔɪld] *adj egg* duro; **'hard cop·y** copia *f* impresa; **'hard core** *n (pornography)* porno *m* duro; **hard 'cur·ren·cy** divisa *f* fuerte; **hard 'disk** disco *m* duro

hard·en ['hɑːrdn] **1** *v/t* endurecer **2** *v/i of glue, attitude* endurecerse

'hard hat casco *m*; *(construction worker)* obrero(-a) *m(f)* (de la construcción); **hard·head·ed** [hɑːrd-'hedɪd] *adj* pragmático; **hard·heart·ed** [hɑːrd'hɑːrtɪd] *adj* insensible; **hard 'line** línea *f* dura; *take a ~ line on* adoptar una línea dura en cuanto a; **hard'lin·er** partidario(-a) *m(f)* de la línea dura

hard·ly ['hɑːrdlɪ] *adv* apenas; *did you agree? – ~!* ¿estuviste de acuerdo? – ¡en absoluto!

hard·ness ['hɑːrdnɪs] dureza *f*; *(difficulty)* dificultad *f*

hard'sell venta *f* agresiva

hard·ship ['hɑːrdʃɪp] penuria *f*, privación *f*

hard 'up *adj: be ~* andar mal de dinero; **'hard·ware** ferretería *f*; COMPUT hardware *m*; **'hard·ware store** fe-

rretería *f*; **hard-work·ing** [hɑːrd-'wɜːrkɪŋ] *adj* trabajador

har·dy ['hɑːrdɪ] *adj* resistente

hare [her] liebre *f*

hare-brained ['herbreɪnd] *adj* alocado

harm [hɑːrm] **1** *n* daño *m*; *it wouldn't do any ~ to buy two* por comprar dos no pasa nada **2** *v/t* hacer daño a, dañar

harm·ful ['hɑːrmfəl] *adj* dañino, perjudicial

harm·less ['hɑːrmlɪs] *adj* inofensivo; *fun* inocente

har·mo·ni·ous [hɑːr'moʊnɪəs] *adj* armonioso

har·mo·nize ['hɑːrmənaɪz] *v/i* armonizar

har·mo·ny ['hɑːrmənɪ] MUS, *fig* armonía *f*

harp [hɑːrp] *n* arpa *f*

♦**harp on about** *v/t* F dar la lata con F

har·poon [hɑːr'puːn] *n* arpón *m*

harsh [hɑːʃ] *adj words* duro, severo; *color* chillón; *light* potente

harsh·ly ['hɑːrʃlɪ] *adv* con dureza *or* severidad

har·vest ['hɑːrvɪst] *n* cosecha *f*

hash [hæʃ] F: *make a ~ of* fastidiar

hash browns *npl Span* patatas *fpl or L.Am.* papas *fpl* fritas

hash·ish ['hæʃiːʃ] hachís *m*

'hash mark almohadilla *f*, *el signo* '#'

haste [heɪst] *n* prisa *f*

has·ten ['heɪsn] *v/i: ~ to do sth* apresurarse en hacer algo

hast·i·ly ['heɪstɪlɪ] *adv* precipitadamente

hast·y ['heɪstɪ] *adj* precipitado

hat [hæt] sombrero *m*

hatch [hætʃ] *n for serving food* trampilla *f*; *on ship* escotilla *f*

♦**hatch out** *v/i of eggs* romperse; *of chicks* salir del cascarón

hatch·et ['hætʃɪt] hacha *f*; *bury the ~* enterrar el hacha de guerra

hate [heɪt] **1** *n* odio *m* **2** *v/t* odiar

ha·tred ['heɪtrɪd] odio *m*

haugh·ty ['hɔːtɪ] *adj* altanero

haul [hɔːl] **1** *n of fish* captura *f*; *from*

robbery botín m **2** v/t (*pull*) arrastrar

haul·age ['hɔːlɪdʒ] transporte m

haul·i·er ['hɔːlɪr] transportista m

haunch [hɔːntʃ] *of person* trasero m;
of animal pierna f

haunt [hɔːnt] **1** v/t: *this place is ~ed*
en este lugar hay fantasmas **2** n lugar m favorito

haunt·ing ['hɔːntɪŋ] *adj tune* fascinante

Ha·van·a [hə'vænə] n La Habana

have [hæv] **1** v/t (*pret & pp had*)
(*own*) tener; *I don't ~ a TV* no tengo
televisión ◊ *breakfast, lunch* tomar
◊: *can I ~ a coffee?* ¿me da un
café?; *can I ~ more time?* ¿me puede dar más tiempo? ◊ *must: ~ (got)
to* tener que ◊ *causative: I'll ~ it
faxed to you* te lo mandaré por fax;
I'll ~ it repaired haré que lo arreglen; *I had my hair cut* me corté el
pelo **2** v/aux: *I ~ eaten* he comido; *~
you seen her?* ¿la has visto?
♦ **have back** v/t: *when can I have it
back?* ¿cuándo me lo devolverá?
♦ **have on** v/t (*wear*) llevar puesto; *do
you have anything on for tonight?*
have planned ¿tenéis algo planeado
para esta noche?

ha·ven ['heɪvn] *fig* refugio m

hav·oc ['hævək] estragos mpl; *play ~
with* hacer estragos en

hawk [hɔːk] n *also fig* halcón m

hay [heɪ] heno m

'hay fe·ver fiebre f del heno

haz·ard ['hæzərd] n riesgo m, peligro
m

'haz·ard lights npl MOT luces fpl de
emergencia

haz·ard·ous ['hæzərdəs] adj peligroso, arriesgado; *~ waste* residuos mpl
peligrosos

haze [heɪz] neblina f

ha·zel ['heɪzl] n tree avellano m

'ha·zel·nut avellana f

haz·y ['heɪzɪ] adj image, memories
confuso, vago; *I'm a bit ~ about it* no
lo tengo muy claro

he [hiː] pron él; *~ is French / a doctor*
es francés / médico; *you're funny,*

~'s not tú tienes gracia, él no

head [hed] **1** n cabeza f; (boss, leader)
jefe(-a) m(f); Br: *of school* direc-
tor(a) m(f); *on beer* espuma f; *of nail,
line* cabeza f; *$15 a ~* 15 dólares por
cabeza; *~s or tails?* ¿cara o cruz?; *at
the ~ of the list* encabezando la lista; *~ over heels* fall rodando; *fall in
love* locamente **2** v/t (lead) estar a la
cabeza de; *ball* cabecear
♦ **head for** v/t dirigirse a or hacia

'head·ache dolor m de cabeza

'head·band cinta f para la cabeza

head·er ['hedər] in soccer cabezazo
m; *in document* encabezamiento m

'head·hunt v/t COM buscar, captar

'head·hunt·er COM cazatalentos m/f
inv

head·ing ['hedɪŋ] *in list* encabezamiento m

'head·lamp faro m; **'head·light** faro
m; **'head·line** n *in newspaper* titular
m; *make the ~s* saltar a los titulares;
'head·long *adv fall* de cabeza;
'head·mas·ter director m; **'head-
mis·tress** directora f; **head 'of·fice**
of company central f; **head·'on
1** adv *crash* de frente **2** adj *crash*
frontal; **'head·phones** npl auriculares mpl; **'head·quar·ters** npl *of
party, organization* sede f; *of army*
cuartel m general; **'head·rest** reposacabezas f inv; **'head·room** under
bridge gálibo m; *in car* espacio m vertical; **'head·scarf** pañuelo m (para
la cabeza); **'head·strong** adj cabe-
zudo, testarudo; **head 'teach·er** Br
director(a) m(f); **head 'wait·er**
maître m; **'head·wind** viento m contrario

head·y ['hedɪ] adj *drink, wine etc* que
se sube a la cabeza

heal [hiːl] v/t curar
♦ **heal up** v/i curarse

health [helθ] salud f; *your ~!* ¡a tu salud!

'health club gimnasio m (*con piscina,
pista de tenis, sauna etc*); **'health
food** comida f integral; **'health
food store** tienda f de comida integral; **'health in·su·rance** seguro m

de enfermedad; '**health re·sort** centro *m* de reposo

health·y ['helθɪ] *adj person* sano; *food, lifestyle* saludable; *economy* saneado

heap [hiːp] *n* montón *m*
♦ **heap up** *v/t* amontonar

hear [hɪr] *v/t & v/i* (*pret & pp heard*) oír
♦ **hear about** *v/t*: **have you heard about Mike?** ¿te has enterado de lo de Mike?; **they're bound to hear about it sooner or later** se van a enterar tarde o temprano
♦ **hear from** *v/t* (*have news from*) tener noticias de

hear·ing ['hɪrɪŋ] oído *m*; LAW vista *f*; **his ~ is not so good now** ahora ya no oye tan bien; **she was within ~ / out of ~** estaba / no estaba lo suficientemente cerca como para oírlo

'**hear·ing aid** audífono *m*

'**hear·say** rumores *mpl*; **by ~** de oídas

hearse [hɜːrs] coche *m* fúnebre

heart [hɑːrt] *also fig* corazón *m*; *of problem* meollo *m*; **know sth by ~** saber algo de memoria; **~s** *in cards* corazones *mpl*

'**heart at·tack** infarto *m*; '**heart·beat** latido *m*; '**heart·break·ing** ['hɑːrtbreɪkɪŋ] *adj* desgarrador; '**heart·brok·en** *adj* descorazonado; '**heart·burn** acidez *f* (de estómago); '**heart fail·ure** paro *m* cardíaco; '**heart·felt** ['hɑːrtfelt] *adj sympathy* sincero

hearth [hɑːrθ] chimenea *f*

heart·less ['hɑːrtlɪs] *adj* despiadado

heart-rend·ing ['hɑːrtrendɪŋ] *adj plea, sight* desgarrador; '**heart throb** F ídolo *m*; '**heart trans·plant** transplante *m* de corazón

heart·y ['hɑːrtɪ] *adj appetite* voraz; *meal* copioso; *person* cordial, campechano

heat [hiːt] *n* calor *m*
♦ **heat up** *v/t* calentar

heat·ed ['hiːtɪd] *adj swimming pool* climatizado; *discussion* acalorado

heat·er ['hiːtər] *in room* estufa *f*; **turn on the ~** *in car* enciende la calefac-

ción

hea·then ['hiːðn] *n* pagano(-a) *m(f)*

heat·ing ['hiːtɪŋ] calefacción *f*

'**heat·proof**, '**heat-re·sis·tant** *adj* resistente al calor; '**heat·stroke** insolación *f*; '**heat·wave** ola *f* de calor

heave [hiːv] *v/t* (*lift*) subir

heav·en ['hevn] cielo *m*; **good ~s!** ¡Dios mío!

heav·en·ly ['hevnlɪ] *adj* F divino F

heav·y ['hevɪ] *adj* pesado; *cold, rain, accent, loss* fuerte; *smoker, drinker* empedernido; *loss of life* grande; *bleeding* abundante; **there's ~ traffic** hay mucho tráfico

heav·y·du·ty *adj* resistente

'**heav·y·weight** *adj* SP de los pesos pesados

heck·le ['hekl] *v/t* interrumpir (*molestando*)

hec·tic ['hektɪk] *adj* vertiginoso, frenético

hedge [hedʒ] *n* seto *m*

hedge·hog ['hedʒhɑːg] erizo *m*

heed [hiːd] *n*: **pay ~ to ...** hacer caso de ...

heel [hiːl] *of foot* talón *m*; *of shoe* tacón *m*

'**heel bar** zapatería *f*

hef·ty ['heftɪ] *adj weight, suitcase* pesado; *person* robusto

height [haɪt] altura *f*; **at the ~ of the season** en plena temporada

height·en ['haɪtn] *v/t effect, tension* intensificar

heir [er] heredero *m*

heir·ess ['erɪs] heredera *f*

held [held] *pret & pp* → **hold**

hel·i·cop·ter ['helɪkɒptər] helicóptero *m*

hell [hel] infierno *m*; **what the ~ are you doing / do you want?** F ¿qué demonios estás haciendo / quieres?; F: **go to ~!** F ¡vete a paseo! F; **a ~ of a lot** F un montonazo F; **a ~ of a nice guy** F un tipo muy simpático *or* Span legal F

hel·lo [hə'lou] hola; TELEC ¿sí?, *Span* ¿diga?, *S. Am.* ¿alo?, *Rpl* ¿oigo?, *Mex* ¿bueno?; **say ~ to s.o.** saludar a alguien

helm [helm] NAUT timón *m*

hel·met ['helmɪt] casco *m*

help [help] **1** *n* ayuda *f*; **~!** ¡socorro! **2** *v/t* ayudar; *just ~ yourself to food* toma lo que quieras; *I can't ~ it* no puedo evitarlo; *I couldn't ~ laughing* no pude evitar reírme

help·er ['helpər] ayudante *m/f*

help·ful ['helpfəl] *adj advice* útil; *person* servicial

help·ing ['helpɪŋ] *of food* ración *f*

help·less ['helplɪs] *adj* (*unable to cope*) indefenso; (*powerless*) impotente

help·less·ly ['helplɪslɪ] *adv* impotentemente

help·less·ness ['helplɪsnɪs] impotencia *f*

'**help screen** COMPUT pantalla *f* de ayuda

hem [hem] *n of dress etc* dobladillo *m*

hem·i·sphere ['hemɪsfɪr] hemisferio *m*

'**hem·line** bajo *m*

hem·or·rhage ['hemərɪdʒ] **1** *n* hemorragia *f* **2** *v/i* sangrar

hen [hen] gallina *f*

hench·man ['hentʃmən] *pej* sicario *m*

'**hen par·ty** despedida *f* de soltera

hen·pecked ['henpekt] *adj*: **~ husband** calzonazos *mpl*

hep·a·ti·tis [hepə'taɪtɪs] hepatitis *f*

her [hɜːr] **1** *adj* su; **~ ticket**su entrada; **~ books** sus libros **2** *pron direct object* la; *indirect object* le; *after prep* ella; *I know ~* la conozco; *I gave ~ the keys* le di las llaves; *I sold it to ~* se lo vendí; *this is for ~* esto es para ella; *who do you mean? – ~* ¿a quién te refieres? – a ella

herb [ɜːrb] hierba *f*

herb(·al) '**tea** ['ɜːrb(əl)] infusión *f*

herd [hɜːrd] *n* rebaño *m*; *of elephants* manada *f*

here [hɪr] *adv* aquí; *over ~* aquí; *~'s to you!* as toast ¡a tu salud!; *~ you are giving sth* ¡aquí tienes!; *~ we are! finding sth* ¡aquí está!

he·red·i·ta·ry [hə'redɪterɪ] *adj disease* hereditario

he·red·i·ty [hə'redɪtɪ] herencia *f*

her·i·tage ['herɪtɪdʒ] patrimonio *m*

her·mit ['hɜːrmɪt] ermitaño(-a) *m(f)*

her·ni·a ['hɜːrnɪə] MED hernia *f*

he·ro ['hɪrou] héroe *m*

he·ro·ic [hɪ'rouɪk] *adj* heroico

he·ro·i·cal·ly [hɪ'rouɪklɪ] *adv* heroicamente

her·o·in ['herouɪn] heroína *f*

'**her·o·in ad·dict** heroinómano(-a) *m(f)*

her·o·ine ['herouɪn] heroína *f*

her·o·ism ['herouɪzm] heroísmo *m*

her·on ['herən] garza *f*

her·pes ['hɜːrpiːz] MED herpes *m*

her·ring ['herɪŋ] arenque *m*

hers [hɜːrz] *pron* el suyo, la suya; *~ are red* los suyos son rojos; *that book is ~* ese libro es suyo; *a cousin of ~* un primo suyo

her·self [hɜːr'self] *pron reflexive* se; *emphatic* ella misma; *she hurt ~* se hizo daño; *when she saw ~ in the mirror* cuando se vio en el espejo; *she saw it ~* lo vio ella misma; *by ~* (*alone*) sola; (*without help*) ella sola, ella misma

hes·i·tant ['hezɪtənt] *adj* indeciso

hes·i·tant·ly ['hezɪtəntlɪ] *adv* con indecisión

hes·i·tate ['hezɪteɪt] *v/i* dudar, vacilar

hes·i·ta·tion [hezɪ'teɪʃn] vacilación *f*

het·er·o·sex·u·al [hetərou'sekʃuəl] *adj* heterosexual

hey·day ['heɪdeɪ] apogeo *m*

hi [haɪ] *int* ¡hola!

hi·ber·nate ['haɪbərneɪt] *v/i* hibernar

hic·cup ['hɪkʌp] *n* hipo *m*; (*minor problem*) tropiezo *m*, traspié *m*; *have the ~s* tener hipo

hick [hɪk] *pej* F palurdo(-a) *m(f)* F, pueblerino(-a) *m(f)* F

'**hick town** *pej* F ciudad *f* provinciana

hid [hɪd] *pret* → **hide**

hid·den ['hɪdn] **1** *adj meaning, treasure* oculto **2** *pp* → **hide**

hid·den a'gen·da *fig* objetivo *m* secreto

hide[1] [haɪd] **1** *v/t* (*pret* **hid**, *pp* **hidden**) esconder **2** *v/i* (*pret* **hid**, *pp* **hidden**) esconderse

hide² *n of animal* piel *f*
hide-and-'seek escondite *m*
'hide·a·way escondite *m*
hid·e·ous ['hɪdɪəs] *adj* espantoso, horrendo; *person* repugnante
hid·ing¹ ['haɪdɪŋ] *(beating)* paliza *f*
hid·ing² ['haɪdɪŋ]: *be in* ~ estar escondido; *go into* ~ esconderse
'hid·ing place escondite *m*
hi·er·ar·chy ['haɪrərɪkɪ] jerarquía *f*
hi-fi ['haɪfaɪ] equipo *m* de alta fidelidad
high [haɪ] **1** *adj* alto; *wind* fuerte; *(on drugs)* colocado P; *have a very ~ opinion of* tener muy buena opinión de; *it is ~ time you understood* ya va siendo hora de que entiendas **2** *n* MOT directa *f*; *in statistics* máximo *m*; EDU escuela *f* secundaria, *Span* instituto *m* **3** *adv*: ~ *in the sky* en lo alto; *that's as ~ as we can go* eso es lo máximo que podemos ofrecer
'high·brow *adj* intelectual; **'high·chair** trona *f*; **high-'class** *adj* de categoría; **high 'div·ing** salto *m* de trampolín; **high-'fre·quen·cy** *adj* de alta frecuencia; **high-'grade** *adj* de calidad superior; **high-hand·ed** [haɪ'hændɪd] *adj* despótico; **high-heeled** [haɪ'hiːld] *adj* de tacón alto; **'high jump** salto *m* de altura; **high-'lev·el** *adj* de alto nivel; **'high life** buena vida *f*; **'high·light 1** *n (main event)* momento *m* cumbre; *in hair* reflejo *m* **2** *v/t with pen* resaltar; COMPUT seleccionar, *Span* **'high·light·er** *pen* fluorescente *m*
high·ly ['haɪlɪ] *adv desirable, likely* muy; *be ~ paid* estar muy bien pagado; *think ~ of s.o.* tener una buena opinión de alguien
high per'form·ance *adj drill, battery* de alto rendimiento; **high-pitched** [haɪ'pɪtʃt] *adj* agudo; **'high point** *of life, career* punto *m* culminante; **high-pow·ered** [haɪ'paʊərd] *adj engine* potente; *intellectual* de alto(s) vuelo(s); *salesman* enérgico; **high 'pres·sure 1** *n weather* altas presiones *fpl* **2** *adj* TECH a gran presión;

salesman agresivo; *job, lifestyle* muy estresante; **high 'priest** sumo sacerdote *m*; **'high school** escuela *f* secundaria, *Span* instituto *m*; **high so'ci·e·ty** alta sociedad *f*; **high-speed 'train** tren *m* de alta velocidad; **high-'strung** *adj* muy nervioso; **high 'tide** marea *f* alta; **high 'wa·ter**: *at* ~ con la marea alta; **'high·way** autopista *f*; **'high wire** *in circus* cuerda *f* floja
hi·jack ['haɪdʒæk] **1** *v/t plane, bus* secuestrar **2** *n of plane, bus* secuestro *m*
hi·jack·er ['haɪdʒækər] *of plane, bus* secuestrador(a) *m(f)*
hike¹ [haɪk] **1** *n* caminata *f* **2** *v/i* caminar
hike² [haɪk] *n in prices* subida *f*
hik·er ['haɪkər] senderista *m/f*
hik·ing ['haɪkɪŋ] senderismo *m*
'hik·ing boots *npl* botas *fpl* de senderismo
hi·lar·i·ous [hɪ'lerɪəs] *adj* divertidísimo, graciosísimo
hill [hɪl] colina *f*; *(slope)* cuesta *f*
hill·bil·ly ['hɪlbɪlɪ] F *rústico* montañés; **'hill·side** ladera *f*; **'hill·top** cumbre *f*
hill·y ['hɪlɪ] *adj* con colinas
hilt [hɪlt] puño *m*
him [hɪm] *pron direct object* lo; *indirect object* le; *after prep* él; *I know* ~ lo conozco; *I gave* ~ *the keys* le di las llaves; *I sold it to* ~ se lo vendí; *this is for* ~ esto es para él; *who do you mean?* – ~ ¿a quién te refieres? – a él
him·self [hɪm'self] *pron reflexive* se; *emphatic* él mismo; *he hurt* ~ se hizo daño; *when he saw* ~ *in the mirror* cuando se vio en el espejo; *he saw it* ~ lo vio él mismo; *by* ~ *(alone)* solo; *(without help)* él solo, él mismo
hind [haɪnd] *adj* trasero
hin·der ['hɪndər] *v/t* obstaculizar, entorpecer
hin·drance ['hɪndrəns] estorbo *m*, obstáculo *m*
hind·sight ['haɪndsaɪt]: *with* ~ a posteriori

hinge [hɪndʒ] *n* bisagra *f*
♦ **hinge on** *v/t* depender de
hint [hɪnt] *n* (*clue*) pista *f*; (*piece of advice*) consejo *m*; (*implied suggestion*) indirecta *f*; *of red, sadness etc* rastro *m*
hip [hɪp] *n* cadera *f*
hip 'pock·et bolsillo *m* trasero
hip·po·pot·a·mus [hɪpə'pɑːtəməs] hipopótamo *m*
hire [haɪr] *v/t* alquilar
his [hɪz] **1** *adj* su; ~ *ticket* su entrada; ~ *books* sus libros **2** *pron* el suyo, la suya; ~ *are red* los suyos son rojos; *that ticket is* ~ esa entrada es suya; *a cousin of* ~ un primo suyo
His·pan·ic [hɪ'spænɪk] **1** *n* hispano(-a) *m(f)* **2** *adj* hispano, hispánico
hiss [hɪs] *v/i of snake, audience* silbar
his·to·ri·an [hɪ'stɔːrɪən] historiador(a) *m(f)*
his·tor·ic [hɪ'stɑːrɪk] *adj* histórico
his·tor·i·cal [hɪ'stɑːrɪkl] *adj* histórico
his·to·ry ['hɪstərɪ] historia *f*
hit [hɪt] **1** *v/t* (*pret & pp hit*) golpear; (*collide with*) chocar contra; *he was* ~ *by a bullet* le alcanzó una bala; *it suddenly* ~ *me* (*I realized*) de repente me di cuenta; ~ *town* (*arrive*) llegar a la ciudad **2** *n* (*blow*) golpe *m*; MUS, (*success*) éxito *m*
♦ **hit back** *v/i physically* devolver el golpe; *verbally, with actions* responder
♦ **hit on** *v/t idea* dar con; (*flirt with*) intentar ligar con
♦ **hit out at** *v/t* (*criticize*) atacar
hit-and-run *adj:* ~ *accident* accidente en el que el vehículo causante se da a la fuga
hitch [hɪtʃ] **1** *n* (*problem*) contratiempo *m*; *without a* ~ sin ningún contratiempo **2** *v/t* (*fix*) enganchar; ~ *a ride* hacer autoestop **3** *v/i* (*hitchhike*) hacer autoestop
♦ **hitch up** *v/t wagon, trailer* enganchar
'hitch·hike *v/i* hacer autoestop;
'hitch·hik·er autoestopista *m/f*;
'hitch·hik·ing autoestop *m*

hi-'tech 1 *n* alta tecnología *f* **2** *adj* de alta tecnología
'hit·list lista *f* de blancos; **'hit·man** asesino *m* a sueldo; **hit-or-'miss** *adj* a la buena ventura; **'hit squad** grupo *m* de intervención especial
HIV [eɪtʃaɪ'viː] *abbr* (= *human immunodeficiency virus*) VIH *m* (= virus *m inv* de la inmunodeficiencia humana)
hive [haɪv] *for bees* colmena *f*
♦ **hive off** *v/t* COM (*separate off*) desprenderse de
HIV-'pos·i·tive *adj* seropositivo
hoard [hɔːrd] **1** *n* reserva *f* **2** *v/t* hacer acopio de; *money* acumular
hoard·er ['hɔːrdər] acaparador(a) *m(f)*
hoarse [hɔːrs] *adj* ronco
hoax [hoʊks] *n* bulo *m*, engaño *m*; *bomb* ~ amenaza *f* falsa de bomba
hob·ble ['hɑːbl] *v/i* cojear
hob·by ['hɑːbɪ] hobby *m*, afición *f*
ho·bo ['hoʊboʊ] F vagabundo(-a) *m(f)*
hock·ey ['hɑːkɪ] (*ice* ~) hockey *m* sobre hielo
hog [hɑːg] *n* (*pig*) cerdo *m*, *L.Am.* chancho *m*
hoist [hɔɪst] **1** *n* montacargas *m inv*; *manual* elevador *m* **2** *v/t* (*lift*) levantar, subir; *flag* izar
ho·kum ['hoʊkəm] F (*nonsense*) tonterías *fpl*; (*sentimental stuff*) cursilería *f*
hold [hoʊld] **1** *v/t* (*pret & pp held*) *in hand* llevar; (*support, keep in place*) sostener; (*contain*) contener; *job, post* ocupar; *course* mantener; ~ *my hand* dame la mano; ~ *one's breath* aguantar la respiración; *he can* ~ *his drink* sabe beber; ~ *s.o. responsible* hacer a alguien responsable; ~ *that ...* (*believe, maintain*) mantener que ...; ~ *the line, please* TELEC espere, por favor **2** *n in ship, plane* bodega *f*; *take* ~ *of sth* agarrar algo; *lose one's* ~ *on sth on rope* soltar algo; *on reality* perder el contacto con

algo

♦ **hold against** v/t: **hold sth against s.o.** tener algo contra alguien

♦ **hold back 1** v/t *crowds* contener; *facts, information* guardar **2** v/i (*not tell all*): *I'm sure he's holding back* estoy seguro de que no dice todo lo que sabe

♦ **hold on** v/i (*wait*) esperar; *now hold on a minute!* ¡un momento!

♦ **hold on to** v/t (*keep*) guardar; *belief* aferrarse a

♦ **hold out 1** v/t *hand* tender; *prospect* ofrecer **2** v/i *of supplies* durar; (*survive*) resistir, aguantar

♦ **hold up** v/t *hand* levantar; *bank etc* atracar; (*make late*) retrasar; *I was held up by the traffic* he llegado tarde por culpa del tráfico; *hold s.o. up as an example* poner a alguien como ejemplo

♦ **hold with** v/t (*approve of*): *I don't hold with that sort of behavior* no me parece bien ese tipo de comportamiento

hold·er ['houldər] (*container*) receptáculo m; *of passport, ticket etc* titular m/f; *of record* poseedor(a) m(f)

'hold·ing com·pa·ny holding m

'hold·up (*robbery*) atraco m; (*delay*) retraso m

hole [houl] *in sleeve, wood, bag* agujero m; *in ground* hoyo m

hol·i·day ['hɑːlədei] *single day* día m de fiesta; *Br: period* vacaciones fpl; *take a ~* tomarse vacaciones

Hol·land ['hɑːlənd] Holanda

hol·low ['hɑːlou] *adj object* hueco; *cheeks* hundido; *promise* vacío

hol·ly ['hɑːlɪ] acebo m

hol·o·caust ['hɑːləkɒst] holocausto m

hol·o·gram ['hɑːləgræm] holograma m

hol·ster ['houlstər] pistolera f

ho·ly ['houlɪ] *adj* santo

Ho·ly 'Spir·it Espíritu m Santo

'Ho·ly Week Semana f Santa

home [houm] **1** n *casa* f; (*native country*) tierra f; *for old people* residencia f; *New York is my ~* Nueva

York es mi hogar; *at ~* also SP en casa; (*in country*) en mi/su/nuestra tierra; *make yourself at ~* ponte cómodo; *at ~ and abroad* en el país y en el extranjero; *work from ~* trabajar desde casa **2** *adv* a casa; *go ~* ir a casa; *to country* ir a mi/tu/su tierra; *to town, part of country* ir a mi/tu/su ciudad

'home ad·dress domicilio m; **home 'bank·ing** telebanca f, banca f electrónica; **'home·com·ing** vuelta f a casa; **home com'put·er** Span ordenador m, L.Am. computadora f doméstica; **'home game** partido m en casa

home·less ['houmlɪs] **1** *adj* sin casa **2** *npl*: *the ~* los sin casa

'home·lov·ing *adj* hogareño

home·ly ['houmlɪ] *adj* (*homeloving*) hogareño; (*not good-looking*) feúcho

home'made *adj* casero

home 'mov·ie película f casera

ho·me·op·a·thy [houmi'ɑːpəθɪ] homeopatía f

'home page *web site* página f personal; *on web site* página f inicial; **'home·sick** *adj* nostálgico; *be ~* tener morriña; **'home town** ciudad f natal

home·ward ['houmwərd] *adv to own house* a casa; *to own country* a mi/tu/su país

'home·work EDU deberes mpl

'home·work·ing COM teletrabajo m

hom·i·cide ['hɑːmɪsaid] *crime* homicidio m; *police department* brigada f de homicidios

hom·o·graph ['hɑːməgræf] homógrafo m

ho·mo·pho·bi·a [hɑːmə'foubɪə] homofobia f

ho·mo·sex·u·al [hɑːmə'sekʃuəl] **1** *adj* homosexual **2** n homosexual m/f

Hon·du·ran [hɑːn'durən] **1** *adj* hondureño **2** n hondureño(-a) m(f)

Hon·du·ras [hɑːn'durəs] n Honduras

hon·est ['ɑːnɪst] *adj* honrado

hon·est·ly ['ɑːnɪstlɪ] *adv* honradamente; **~!** ¡desde luego!

hon·es·ty [ˈɑːnɪstɪ] honradez *f*

hon·ey [ˈhʌnɪ] miel *f*; F (*darling*) cariño *m*, vida *f* mía

'hon·ey·comb panal *m*

'hon·ey·moon *n* luna *f* de miel

honk [hɑːŋk] *v/t horn* tocar

hon·or [ˈɑːnər] **1** *n* honor *m* **2** *v/t* honrar

hon·or·a·ble [ˈɑːnrəbl] *adj* honorable

hon·our *etc Br* → **honor** *etc*

hood [hʊd] *over head* capucha *f*; *over cooker* campana *f* extractora; MOT capó *m*; F (*gangster*) matón(-ona) *m(f)*

hood·lum [ˈhuːdləm] matón(-ona) *m(f)*

hoof [huːf] casco *m*

hook [hʊk] gancho *m*; *to hang clothes on* colgador *m*; *for fishing* anzuelo *m*; **off the ~** TELEC descolgado

hooked [hʊkt] *adj* enganchado (**on** a)

hook·er [ˈhʊkər] F fulana *f* F

hook·y [ˈhʊkɪ] F: **play ~** hacer novillos, *Mex* irse de pinta, *S.Am.* hacerse la rabona

hoo·li·gan [ˈhuːlɪgən] gamberro(-a) *m(f)*

hoo·li·gan·ism [ˈhuːlɪgənɪzm] gamberrismo *m*

hoop [huːp] aro *m*

hoot [huːt] *v/t horn* tocar **2** *v/i of car* dar bocinazos; *of owl* ulular

hop[1] [hɑːp] *n plant* lúpulo *m*

hop[2] [hɑːp] *v/i* (*pret & pp* **-ped**) saltar

hope [hoʊp] **1** *n* esperanza *f* **2** *v/i* esperar; **~ for sth** esperar algo; **we all ~ for peace** todos ansiamos la paz; **I ~ so** eso espero; **I ~ not** espero que no **3** *v/t*: **I ~ you like it** espero que te guste

hope·ful [ˈhoʊpfəl] *adj* prometedor; **I'm ~ that ...** espero que ...

hope·ful·ly [ˈhoʊpfəlɪ] *adv say, wait* esperanzadamente; **~ he hasn't forgotten** esperemos que no se haya olvidado

hope·less [ˈhoʊplɪs] *adj position, prospect* desesperado; (*useless: person*) inútil

ho·ri·zon [həˈraɪzn] horizonte *m*

hor·i·zon·tal [hɑːrɪˈzɑːntl] *adj* horizontal

hor·mone [ˈhɔːrmoʊn] hormona *f*

horn [hɔːrn] *of animal* cuerno *m*; MOT bocina *f*, claxon *m*

hor·net [ˈhɔːrnɪt] avispón *m*

horn-rimmed 'spec·ta·cles [ˈhɔːrnrɪmd] *npl* gafas *fpl* de concha

horn·y [ˈhɔːrnɪ] *adj* F *sexually* cachondo F

hor·o·scope [ˈhɑːrəskoʊp] horóscopo *m*

hor·ri·ble [ˈhɑːrɪbl] *adj* horrible; *person* muy antipático

hor·ri·fy [ˈhɑːrɪfaɪ] *v/t* (*pret & pp* **-ied**) horrorizar; **I was horrified** me quedé horrorizado

hor·ri·fy·ing [ˈhɑːrɪfaɪɪŋ] *adj* horroroso

hor·ror [ˈhɑːrər] horror *m*

'hor·ror mov·ie película *f* de terror

hors d'œu·vre [ɔːrˈdɜːrv] entremés *m*

horse [hɔːrs] caballo *m*

'horse·back: on ~ a caballo; **horse 'chest·nut** castaño *m* de Indias; **'horse·pow·er** caballo *m* (de vapor); **'horse race** carrera *f* de caballos; **'horse·shoe** herradura *f*

hor·ti·cul·ture [ˈhɔːrtɪkʌltʃər] horticultura *f*

hose [hoʊz] *n* manguera *f*

hos·pice [ˈhɑːspɪs] hospital *m* para enfermos terminales

hos·pi·ta·ble [hɑːˈspɪtəbl] *adj* hospitalario

hos·pi·tal [ˈhɑːspɪtl] hospital *m*; **go into the ~** ir al hospital

hos·pi·tal·i·ty [hɑːspɪˈtælətɪ] hospitalidad *f*

host [hoʊst] *n at party, reception* anfitrión *m*; *of TV program* presentador(a) *m(f)*

hos·tage [ˈhɑːstɪdʒ] rehén *m*; **take s.o. ~** tomar a alguien como rehén

'hos·tage tak·er *persona que toma rehenes*

hos·tel [ˈhɑːstl] *for students* residencia *f*; (*youth ~*) albergue *m*

hos·tess ['houstɪs] *at party, reception* anfitriona *f*; *on airplane* azafata *f*; *in bar* cabaretera *f*

hos·tile ['hɑːstl] *adj* hostil

hos·til·i·ty [hɑːˈstɪlətɪ] *of attitude etc* hostilidad *f*; **hostilities** hostilidades *fpl*

hot [hɑːt] *adj weather* caluroso; *object, water, food* caliente; *(spicy)* picante; **it's** ~ *of weather* hace calor; **I'm** ~ tengo calor; **she's pretty** ~ **at math** F *(good)* es una fenómena con las matemáticas F

'hot dog perrito *m* caliente

ho·tel [hou'tel] hotel *m*

'hot·plate placa *f*

'hot spot *military, political* punto *m* caliente

hour [aʊr] hora *f*

hour·ly ['aʊrlɪ] *adj*: **at** ~ **intervals** a intervalos de una hora; **an** ~ **bus** un autobús que pasa cada hora

house [haʊs] *n* casa *f*; **at your** ~ en tu casa

'house·boat barco-vivienda *f*; **'house·break·ing** allanamiento *m* de morada; **'house·hold** hogar *m*; **house·hold 'name** nombre *m* conocido; **'house hus·band** amo *m* de casa; **'house·keep·er** ama *f* de llaves; **'house·keep·ing** *activity* tareas *fpl* domésticas; *money* dinero *m* para gastos domésticos; **House of Rep·re·sent·a·tives** *npl* Cámara *f* de Representantes; **house·warm·ing (par·ty)** ['haʊswɔːrmɪŋ] fiesta *f* de estreno de una casa; **'house·wife** ama *f* de casa; **'house·work** tareas *fpl* domésticas

hous·ing ['haʊzɪŋ] vivienda *f*; TECH cubierta *f*

'hous·ing con·di·tions *npl* condiciones *fpl* de la vivienda

hov·el ['hɑːvl] chabola *f*

hov·er ['hɑːvər] *v/i of bird* cernerse; *of helicopter* permanecer inmóvil en el aire

'hov·er·craft aerodeslizador *m*, hovercraft *m*

how [haʊ] *adv* cómo; ~ **are you?** ¿cómo estás?; ~ **about ...?** ¿qué te

parece ...?; ~ **about a drink?** ¿te apetece tomar algo?; ~ **much?** ¿cuánto?; ~ **much is it?** *cost* ¿cuánto vale *or* cuesta?; ~ **many?** ¿cuántos?; ~ **often?** ¿con qué frecuencia?; ~ **funny/sad!** ¡qué divertido/triste!

how·ev·er *adv* sin embargo; ~ **big/ rich/small they are** independientemente de lo grandes/ricos/pequeños que sean

howl [haʊl] *v/i of dog* aullido *m*; *of person in pain* alarido *m*; *with laughter* risotada *f*

hub [hʌb] *of wheel* cubo *m*

'hub·cap tapacubos *m inv*

♦**hud·dle together** ['hʌdl] *v/i* apiñarse, acurrucarse

hue [hjuː] tonalidad *f*

huff [hʌf]: **be in a** ~ estar enfurruñado

hug [hʌg] *v/t* (*pret & pp* **-ged**) abrazar

huge [hjuːdʒ] *adj* enorme

hull [hʌl] *of ship* casco *m*

hul·la·ba·loo [hʌləbəˈluː] alboroto *m*

hum [hʌm] **1** *v/t song, tune* tararear **2** *v/i of person* tararear; *of machine* zumbar

hu·man ['hjuːmən] **1** *n* humano *m* **2** *adj* humano; ~ **error** error *m or* fallo *m* humano

human 'be·ing ser *m* humano

hu·mane [hjuːˈmeɪn] *adj* humano

hu·man·i·tar·i·an [hjuːmænɪˈterɪən] *adj* humanitario

hu·man·i·ty [hjuːˈmænətɪ] humanidad *f*

human 'race raza *f* humana

human re'sources *npl* recursos *mpl* humanos

hum·ble ['hʌmbl] *adj* humilde

hum·drum ['hʌmdrʌm] *adj* monótono, anodino

hu·mid ['hjuːmɪd] *adj* húmedo

hu·mid·i·fi·er [hjuːˈmɪdɪfaɪr] humidificador *m*

hu·mid·i·ty [hjuːˈmɪdətɪ] humedad *f*

hu·mil·i·ate [hjuːˈmɪlɪeɪt] *v/t* humillar

hu·mil·i·at·ing [hjuːˈmɪlɪeɪtɪŋ] *adj*

humillante

hu·mil·i·a·tion [hju:mɪlɪ'eɪʃn] humillación f

hu·mil·i·ty [hju:'mɪlətɪ] humildad f

hu·mor ['hju:mər] humor m; **sense of ~** sentido m del humor

hu·mor·ous ['hju:mərəs] adj gracioso

hu·mour Br → **humor**

hump [hʌmp] **1** n of camel, person joroba f; on road bache m **2** v/t F (carry) acarrear

hunch [hʌntʃ] n (idea) presentimiento m, corazonada f

hun·dred ['hʌndrəd] cien m; **a ~ dollars** cien dólares; **~s of birds** cientos or centenares de aves; **a ~ and one** ciento uno; **two ~** doscientos

hun·dredth ['hʌndrədθ] n & adj centésimo

'**hun·dred·weight** 43 kilogramos

hung [hʌŋ] pret & pp → **hang**

Hun·gar·i·an [hʌŋ'gerɪən] **1** adj húngaro **2** n person húngaro(-a) m(f); language húngaro m

Hun·ga·ry ['hʌŋgərɪ] Hungría

hun·ger ['hʌŋgər] n hambre f

hung-'o·ver adj: **be ~** tener resaca

hun·gry ['hʌŋgrɪ] adj hambriento; **I'm ~** tengo hambre

hunk [hʌŋk] cacho m, pedazo m; F **man** cachas m inv F

hun·ky-dor·y [hʌŋkɪ'dɔːrɪ] adj F: **everything's ~** todo va de perlas

hunt [hʌnt] **1** n caza f, búsqueda f **2** v/t animal cazar

♦ **hunt for** v/t buscar

hunt·er ['hʌntər] cazador(a) m(f)

hunt·ing ['hʌntɪŋ] caza f

hur·dle ['hɜːrdl] SP valla f; fig obstáculo m

hur·dler ['hɜːrdlər] SP vallista m/f

hur·dles npl SP vallas fpl

hurl [hɜːrl] v/t lanzar

hur·ray [hʊ'reɪ] int ¡hurra!

hur·ri·cane ['hʌrɪkən] huracán m

hur·ried ['hʌrɪd] adj apresurado

hur·ry ['hʌrɪ] **1** n prisa f; **be in a ~** tener prisa **2** v/i (pret & pp **-ied**) darse prisa

♦ **hurry up** v/i darse prisa; **hurry up!**

¡date prisa! **2** v/t meter prisa a

hurt [hɜːrt] **1** v/i (pret & pp **hurt**) doler; **does it ~?** ¿te duele? **2** v/t (pret & pp **hurt**) physically hacer daño a; emotionally herir; **I've ~ my hand** me he hecho daño en la mano; **did he ~ you?** ¿te hizo daño?

hus·band ['hʌzbənd] marido m

hush [hʌʃ] n silencio m; **~!** ¡silencio!

♦ **hush up** v/t scandal etc acallar

husk [hʌsk] of peanuts etc cáscara f

hus·ky ['hʌskɪ] adj voice áspero

hus·tle ['hʌsl] **1** n agitación f; **~ and bustle** ajetreo m **2** v/t person empujar

hut [hʌt] cabaña f, refugio m; workman's cobertizo m

hy·a·cinth ['haɪəsɪnθ] jacinto m

hy·brid ['haɪbrɪd] n híbrido m

hy·drant ['haɪdrənt] boca f de riego or de incendios

hy·draul·ic [haɪ'drɔːlɪk] adj hidráulico

hy·dro·e·lec·tric [haɪdroʊɪ'lektrɪk] adj hidroeléctrico

'**hy·dro·foil** ['haɪdrəfɔɪl] boat hidroplaneador m

hy·dro·gen ['haɪdrədʒən] hidrógeno m

'**hy·dro·gen bomb** bomba f de hidrógeno

hy·giene ['haɪdʒiːn] higiene f

hy·gien·ic [haɪ'dʒiːnɪk] adj higiénico

hymn [hɪm] himno m

hype [haɪp] n bombo m

hy·per·ac·tive [haɪpər'æktɪv] adj hiperactivo

hy·per·sen·si·tive [haɪpər'sensɪtɪv] adj hipersensible

hy·per·ten·sion [haɪpər'tenʃn] hipertensión f

hy·per·text ['haɪpərtekst] COMPUT hipertexto m

hy·phen ['haɪfn] guión m

hyp·no·sis [hɪp'noʊsɪs] hipnosis f

hyp·no·ther·a·py [hɪpnoʊ'θerəpɪ] hipnoterapia f

hyp·no·tize ['hɪpnətaɪz] v/t hipnotizar

hy·po·chon·dri·ac [haɪpə'kɑːndriæk] n hipocondríaco(-a) m(f)

hy·poc·ri·sy [hɪ'pɑːkrəsɪ] hipocresía f

hyp·o·crite ['hɪpəkrɪt] hipócrita m/f

hyp·o·crit·i·cal [hɪpə'krɪtɪkl] *adj* hipócrita

hy·po·ther·mi·a [haɪpou'θɜːrmɪə] hipotermia f

hy·poth·e·sis [haɪ'pɑːθəsɪs] (*pl* **hypotheses** [haɪ'pɑːθəsiːz]) hipótesis f inv

hy·po·thet·i·cal [haɪpə'θetɪkl] *adj* hipotético

hys·ter·ec·to·my [hɪstə'rektəmɪ] histerectomía f

hys·te·ri·a [hɪ'stɪrɪə] histeria f

hys·ter·i·cal [hɪ'sterɪkl] *adj person, laugh* histérico; F (*very funny*) tronchante F; **become ~** ponerse histérico

hys·ter·ics [hɪ'sterɪks] *npl* ataque f de histeria; (*laughter*) ataque f de risa

I

I [aɪ] *pron* yo; **~ am English / a student** soy inglés / estudiante; **you're crazy, ~'m not** tú estás loco, yo no

ice [aɪs] *in drink, on road* hielo m; **break the ~** *fig* romper el hielo
♦ **ice up** *v/i of engine, wings* helarse

ice·berg ['aɪsbɜːrg] iceberg m; **'ice·box** nevera f, *Rpl* heladera f; **'ice·break·er** *ship* rompehielos m inv; **'ice cream** helado m; **'ice cream par·lor**, *Br* **'ice cream par·lour** heladería f; **'ice cube** cubito m de hielo

iced [aɪst] *adj drink* helado

iced 'cof·fee café m helado

'ice hock·ey hockey m sobre hielo; **'ice skate** pista f de hielo; **'ice skate** patín m de cuchilla; **'ice skat·ing** patinaje m sobre hielo

i·ci·cle ['aɪsɪkl] carámbano m

i·con ['aɪkɑːn] *also* COMPUT icono m

i·cy ['aɪsɪ] *adj road* con hielo; *surface* helado; *welcome* frío

ID [aɪ'diː] *abbr* (= *identity*) documentación f; **you got any ~ on you?** ¿lleva algún tipo de documentación?

i·dea [aɪ'diːə] idea f; **good ~!** ¡buena idea!; **I have no ~** no tengo ni idea; **it's not a good ~ to ...** no es buena idea ...

i·deal [aɪ'diːəl] *adj* (*perfect*) ideal

i·deal·is·tic [aɪdiːə'lɪstɪk] *adj* idealista

i·deal·ly [aɪ'diːəlɪ] *adv*: **~ situated** en una posición ideal; **~, we would do it like this** lo ideal sería que lo hiciéramos así

i·den·ti·cal [aɪ'dentɪkl] *adj* idéntico

i·den·ti·fi·ca·tion [aɪdentɪfɪ'keɪʃn] identificación f; *papers etc* documentación f

i·den·ti·fy [aɪ'dentɪfaɪ] *v/t* (*pret & pp -ied*) identificar

i·den·ti·ty [aɪ'dentətɪ] identidad f; **~ card** carné m de identidad

i·de·o·log·i·cal [aɪdɪə'lɑːdʒɪkl] *adj* ideológico

i·de·ol·o·gy [aɪdɪ'ɑːlədʒɪ] ideología f

id·i·om ['ɪdɪəm] (*saying*) modismo m

id·i·o·mat·ic [ɪdɪə'mætɪk] *adj natural* natural

id·i·o·syn·cra·sy [ɪdɪə'sɪŋkrəsɪ] peculiaridad f, rareza f

id·i·ot ['ɪdɪət] idiota m/f, estúpido(-a) m/f

id·i·ot·ic [ɪdɪ'ɑːtɪk] *adj* idiota, estúpido

i·dle ['aɪdl] **1** *adj not working* desocupado; (*lazy*) vago; *threat* vano; *machinery* inactivo **2** *v/i of engine* funcionar al ralentí

◆ idle away *v/t the time etc* pasar ociosamente

i·dol ['aɪdl] ídolo *m*

i·dol·ize ['aɪdəlaɪz] *v/t* idolatrar

i·dyl·lic [ɪ'dɪlɪk] *adj* idílico

if [ɪf] *conj* si; **~ only I hadn't shouted at her** ojalá no le hubiera gritado

ig·nite [ɪg'naɪt] *v/t* inflamar

ig·ni·tion [ɪg'nɪʃn] *in car* encendido *m*; **~ key** llave *m* de contacto

ig·no·rance ['ɪgnərəns] ignorancia *f*

ig·no·rant ['ɪgnərənt] *adj* ignorante; (*rude*) maleducado; **be ~ of sth** desconocer *or* ignorar algo

ig·nore [ɪg'nɔːr] *v/t* ignorar; COMPUT omitir

ill [ɪl] *adj* enfermo; **fall ~, be taken ~** caer enfermo; **feel ~ at ease** no sentirse a gusto, sentirse incómodo

il·le·gal [ɪ'liːgl] *adj* ilegal

il·le·gi·ble [ɪ'ledʒəbl] *adj* ilegible

il·le·git·i·mate [ɪlɪ'dʒɪtɪmət] *adj child* ilegítimo

ill-fat·ed [ɪl'feɪtɪd] *adj* infortunado

il·li·cit [ɪ'lɪsɪt] *adj* ilícito

il·lit·e·rate [ɪ'lɪtərət] *adj* analfabeto

ill-man·nered [ɪl'mænərd] *adj* maleducado

ill-na·tured [ɪl'neɪtʃərd] *adj* malhumorado

ill·ness ['ɪlnɪs] enfermedad *f*

il·log·i·cal [ɪ'lɑːdʒɪkl] *adj* ilógico

ill-tem·pered [ɪl'tempərd] *adj* malhumorado

ill'treat *v/t* maltratar

il·lu·mi·nate [ɪ'luːmɪneɪt] *v/t building etc* iluminar

il·lu·mi·nat·ing [ɪ'luːmɪneɪtɪŋ] *adj remarks etc* iluminador, esclarecedor

il·lu·sion [ɪ'luːʒn] ilusión *f*

il·lus·trate ['ɪləstreɪt] *v/t* ilustrar

il·lus·tra·tion [ɪlə'streɪʃn] ilustración *f*

il·lus·tra·tor [ɪlə'streɪtər] ilustrador(a) *m(f)*

ill 'will rencor *m*

im·age ['ɪmɪdʒ] imagen *f*; **he's the ~ of his father** es la viva imagen de su padre

'im·age-con·scious *adj* preocupado por la imagen

i·ma·gi·na·ble [ɪ'mædʒɪnəbl] *adj* imaginable; **the smallest size ~** la talla más pequeña que se pueda imaginar

i·ma·gi·na·ry [ɪ'mædʒɪnəri] *adj* imaginario

i·ma·gi·na·tion [ɪmædʒɪ'neɪʃn] imaginación *f*; **it's all in your ~** son imaginaciones tuyas

i·ma·gi·na·tive [ɪ'mædʒɪnətɪv] *adj* imaginativo

i·ma·gine [ɪ'mædʒɪn] *v/t* imaginar, imaginarse; **I can just ~ it** me lo imagino; **you're imagining things** son imaginaciones tuyas

im·be·cile ['ɪmbəsiːl] imbécil *m/f*

IMF [aɪem'ef] *abbr* (= **International Monetary Fund**) FMI *m* (= Fondo *m* Monetario Internacional)

im·i·tate ['ɪmɪteɪt] *v/t* imitar

im·i·ta·tion [ɪmɪ'teɪʃn] imitación *f*; **learn by ~** aprender imitando

im·mac·u·late [ɪ'mækjʊlət] *adj* inmaculado

im·ma·te·ri·al [ɪmə'tɪrɪəl] *adj* (*not relevant*) irrelevante

im·ma·ture [ɪmə'tʃʊər] *adj* inmaduro

im·me·di·ate [ɪ'miːdɪət] *adj* inmediato; **the ~ family** los familiares más cercanos; **in the ~ neighborhood** en las inmediaciones

im·me·di·ate·ly [ɪ'miːdɪətlɪ] *adv* inmediatamente; **~ after the bank/church** justo después del banco/la iglesia

im·mense [ɪ'mens] *adj* inmenso

im·merse [ɪ'mɜːrs] *v/t* sumergir; **~ o.s. in** sumergirse en

im·mer·sion heat·er [ɪ'mɜːrʃn] calentador *m* de agua eléctrico

im·mi·grant ['ɪmɪgrənt] *n* inmigrante *m/f*

im·mi·grate ['ɪmɪgreɪt] *v/i* inmigrar

im·mi·gra·tion [ɪmɪ'greɪʃn] inmigración *f*; **Immigration** *government department* (Departamento *m* de) Inmigración *f*

im·mi·nent ['ɪmɪnənt] *adj* inminente

im·mo·bi·lize [ɪ'moʊbɪlaɪz] *v/t factory* paralizar; *person, car* inmovilizar

im·mo·bi·liz·er [ɪˈmoʊbɪlaɪzər] *on car* inmovilizador *m*

im·mod·e·rate [ɪˈmɑːdərət] *adj* desmedido, exagerado

im·mor·al [ɪˈmɔːrəl] *adj* inmoral

im·mor·al·i·ty [ɪmɔːˈrælɪtɪ] inmoralidad *f*

im·mor·tal [ɪˈmɔːrtl] *adj* inmortal

im·mor·tal·i·ty [ɪmɔːrˈtælɪtɪ] inmortalidad *f*

im·mune [ɪˈmjuːn] *adj to illness, infection* inmune; *from ruling, requirement* con inmunidad

im'mune sys·tem MED sistema *m* inmunológico

im·mu·ni·ty [ɪˈmjuːnətɪ] inmunidad *f*

im·pact [ˈɪmpækt] *n* impacto *m*; *the warning had no ~ on him* el aviso no le hizo cambiar lo más mínimo

im·pair [ɪmˈper] *v/t* dañar

im·paired [ɪmˈperd] *adj*: *with ~ hearing/sight* con problemas auditivos/visuales

im·par·tial [ɪmˈpɑːrʃl] *adj* imparcial

im·pass·a·ble [ɪmˈpæsəbl] *adj road* intransitable

im·passe [ˈɪmpæs] *in negotations etc* punto *m* muerto

im·pas·sioned [ɪmˈpæʃnd] *adj speech, plea* apasionado

im·pas·sive [ɪmˈpæsɪv] *adj* impasible

im·pa·tience [ɪmˈpeɪʃəns] impaciencia *f*

im·pa·tient [ɪmˈpeɪʃənt] *adj* impaciente

im·pa·tient·ly [ɪmˈpeɪʃəntlɪ] *adv* impacientemente

im·peach [ɪmˈpiːtʃ] *v/t President* iniciar un proceso de destitución contra

im·pec·ca·ble [ɪmˈpekəbl] *adj* impecable

im·pec·ca·bly [ɪmˈpekəblɪ] *adv* impecablemente

im·pede [ɪmˈpiːd] *v/t* dificultar

im·ped·i·ment [ɪmˈpedɪmənt] *in speech* defecto *m* del habla

im·pend·ing [ɪmˈpendɪŋ] *adj* inminente

im·pen·e·tra·ble [ɪmˈpenɪtrəbl] *adj* impenetrable

im·per·a·tive [ɪmˈperətɪv] **1** *adj* imprescindible **2** *n* GRAM imperativo *m*

im·per·cep·ti·ble [ɪmpɜːrˈseptɪbl] *adj* imperceptible

im·per·fect [ɪmˈpɜːrfekt] **1** *adj* imperfecto **2** *n* GRAM imperfecto *m*

im·pe·ri·al [ɪmˈpɪrɪəl] *adj* imperial

im·per·son·al [ɪmˈpɜːrsənl] *adj* impersonal

im·per·so·nate [ɪmˈpɜːrsəneɪt] *v/t as a joke* imitar; *illegally* hacerse pasar por

im·per·ti·nence [ɪmˈpɜːrtɪnəns] impertinencia *f*

im·per·ti·nent [ɪmˈpɜːrtɪnənt] *adj* impertinente

im·per·tur·ba·ble [ɪmpərˈtɜːrbəbl] *adj* imperturbable

im·per·vi·ous [ɪmˈpɜːrvɪəs] *adj*: *~ to* inmune a

im·pe·tu·ous [ɪmˈpetʃʊəs] *adj* impetuoso

im·pe·tus [ˈɪmpɪtəs] *of campaign etc* ímpetu *m*

im·ple·ment **1** *n* [ˈɪmplɪmənt] utensilio *m* **2** *v/t* [ˈɪmplɪment] *measures etc* poner en práctica

im·pli·cate [ˈɪmplɪkeɪt] *v/t* implicar; *~ s.o. in sth* implicar a alguien en algo

im·pli·ca·tion [ɪmplɪˈkeɪʃn] consecuencia *f*; *the ~ is that ...* implica que ...

im·pli·cit [ɪmˈplɪsɪt] *adj* implícito; *trust* inquebrantable

im·plore [ɪmˈplɔːr] *v/t* implorar

im·ply [ɪmˈplaɪ] *v/t* (*pret & pp -ied*) implicar; *are you ~ing I lied?* ¿insinúas que mentí?

im·po·lite [ɪmpəˈlaɪt] *adj* maleducado

im·port [ˈɪmpɔːrt] **1** *n* importación *f* **2** *v/t* importar

im·por·tance [ɪmˈpɔːrtəns] importancia *f*

im·por·tant [ɪmˈpɔːrtənt] *adj* importante

im·por·ter [ɪmˈpɔːrtər] importador(a) *m(f)*

im·pose [ɪmˈpoʊz] *v/t tax* imponer; ~ *o.s. on s.o.* molestar a alguien

im·pos·ing [ɪmˈpoʊzɪŋ] *adj* imponente

im·pos·si·bil·i·ty [ɪmpɑːsɪˈbɪlɪtɪ] imposibilidad *f*

im·pos·si·ble [ɪmˈpɑːsɪbəl] *adj* imposible

im·pos·tor [ɪmˈpɑːstər] impostor(a) *m(f)*

im·po·tence [ˈɪmpətəns] impotencia *f*

im·po·tent [ˈɪmpətənt] *adj* impotente

im·pov·er·ished [ɪmˈpɑːvərɪʃt] *adj* empobrecido

im·prac·ti·cal [ɪmˈpræktɪkəl] *adj* poco práctico

im·press [ɪmˈpres] *v/t* impresionar; *be ~ed by s.o./ sth* quedar impresionado por alguien/algo; *I'm not ~ed* no me parece nada extraordinario

im·pres·sion [ɪmˈpreʃn] impresión *f*; (*impersonation*) imitación *f*; *make a good/ bad ~ on s.o.* causar a alguien buena/mala impresión; *I get the ~ that …* me da la impresión de que …

im·pres·sion·a·ble [ɪmˈpreʃənəbl] *adj* influenciable

im·pres·sive [ɪmˈpresɪv] *adj* impresionante

im·print [ˈɪmprɪnt] *n of credit card* impresión *f*

im·pris·on [ɪmˈprɪzn] *v/t* encarcelar

im·pris·on·ment [ɪmˈprɪznmənt] encarcelamiento *m*

im·prob·a·ble [ɪmˈprɑːbəbəl] *adj* improbable

im·prop·er [ɪmˈprɑːpər] *adj behavior* incorrecto

im·prove [ɪmˈpruːv] *v/t & v/i* mejorar

im·prove·ment [ɪmˈpruːvmənt] mejora *f*, mejoría *f*

im·pro·vise [ˈɪmprəvaɪz] *v/i* improvisar

im·pu·dent [ˈɪmpjʊdənt] *adj* insolente, desvergonzado

im·pulse [ˈɪmpʌls] impulso *m*; *do sth on an ~* hacer algo impulsivamente

'im·pulse buy compra *f* impulsiva

im·pul·sive [ɪmˈpʌlsɪv] *adj* impulsivo

im·pu·ni·ty [ɪmˈpjuːnətɪ] impunidad *f*; *with ~* impunemente

im·pure [ɪmˈpjʊr] *adj* impuro

in [ɪn] **1** *prep* ◇ en; ~ *Washington* en Washington; ~ *the street* en la calle; *put it ~ your pocket* métetelo en el bolsillo; *wounded ~ the leg/ arm* herido en la pierna/el brazo ◇ ~ *1999* en 1999; ~ *two hours from now* dentro de dos horas; (*over period of*) en dos horas; ~ *the morning* por la mañana; ~ *the summer* en verano; ~ *August* en agosto ◇ ~ *English/ Spanish* en inglés/español; ~ *a loud voice* en voz alta; ~ *his style* en su estilo; ~ *yellow* de amarillo ◇ ~ *crossing the road* (*while*) al cruzar la calle; ~ *agreeing to this* (*by virtue of*) al expresar acuerdo con esto ◇ ~ *his novel* en su novela; ~ *Faulkner* en Faulkner ◇ *three ~ all* tres en total; *one ~ ten* uno de cada diez **2** *adv*: *is he ~?* *at home* ¿está en casa?; *is the express ~ yet?* ¿ha llegado ya el expreso?; *when the diskette is ~* cuando el disquete está dentro; ~ *here* aquí dentro **3** *adj* (*fashionable, popular*) de moda

in·a·bil·i·ty [ɪnəˈbɪlɪtɪ] incapacidad *f*

in·ac·ces·si·ble [ɪnəkˈsesɪbl] *adj* inaccesible

in·ac·cu·rate [ɪnˈækjʊrət] *adj* inexacto

in·ac·tive [ɪnˈæktɪv] *adj* inactivo

in·ad·e·quate [ɪnˈædɪkwət] *adj* insuficiente

in·ad·vis·a·ble [ɪnədˈvaɪzəbl] *adj* poco aconsejable

in·an·i·mate [ɪnˈænɪmət] *adj* inanimado

in·ap·pro·pri·ate [ɪnəˈproʊprɪət] *adj remark*, *thing to do* inadecuado, improcedente; *choice* inapropiado

in·ar·tic·u·late [ɪnɑːrˈtɪkjʊlət] *adj*: *be ~* expresarse mal

in·au·di·ble [ɪnˈɔːdəbl] *adj* inaudible

in·au·gu·ral [ɪˈnɔːgjʊrəl] *adj speech* inaugural

in·au·gu·rate [ɪ'nɔ:gjʊreɪt] *v/t* inaugurar

in·born ['ɪnbɔ:rn] *adj* innato

in·breed·ing ['ɪnbri:dɪŋ] endogamia *f*

Inc. *abbr* (= *Incorporated*) S.A. (= sociedad *f* anónima)

in·cal·cu·la·ble [ɪn'kælkjʊləbl] *adj damage* incalculable

in·ca·pa·ble [ɪn'keɪpəbl] *adj* incapaz; *be ~ of doing sth* ser incapaz de hacer algo

in·cen·di·a·ry de'vice [ɪn'sendɪrɪ] artefacto *m* incendiario

in·cense[1] ['ɪnsens] *n* incienso *m*

in·cense[2] [ɪn'sens] *v/t* encolerizar

in·cen·tive [ɪn'sentɪv] incentivo *m*

in·ces·sant [ɪn'sesnt] *adj* incesante

in·ces·sant·ly [ɪn'sesntlɪ] *adv* incesantemente

in·cest ['ɪnsest] incesto *m*

inch [ɪntʃ] *n* pulgada *f*

in·ci·dent ['ɪnsɪdənt] incidente *m*

in·ci·den·tal [ɪnsɪ'dentl] *adj* sin importancia; *~ expenses* gastos *mpl* varios

in·ci·den·tal·ly [ɪnsɪ'dentlɪ] *adv* a propósito

in·cin·e·ra·tor [ɪn'sɪnəreɪtər] incinerador *m*

in·ci·sion [ɪn'sɪʒn] incisión *f*

in·ci·sive [ɪn'saɪsɪv] *adj* incisivo

in·cite [ɪn'saɪt] *v/t* incitar; *~ s.o. to do sth* incitar a alguien a que haga algo

in·clem·ent [ɪn'klemənt] *adj* inclemente

in·cli·na·tion [ɪnklɪ'neɪʃn] (*tendency, liking*) inclinación *f*

in·cline [ɪn'klaɪn] *v/t: be ~d to do sth* tender a hacer algo

in·close, in·clos·ure → *enclose, enclosure*

in·clude [ɪn'klu:d] *v/t* incluir

in·clud·ing [ɪn'klu:dɪŋ] *prep* incluyendo

in·clu·sive [ɪn'klu:sɪv] **1** *adj price* total, global **2** *prep: ~ of* incluyendo, incluido **3** *adv: from Monday to Thursday ~* de lunes al jueves, ambos inclusive; *it costs $1000 ~* cuesta 1.000 dólares todo incluido

in·co·her·ent *adj* incoherente

in·come ['ɪnkəm] ingresos *mpl*

'in·come tax impuesto *m* sobre la renta

in·com·ing ['ɪnkʌmɪŋ] *adj tide* que sube; *~ flight* vuelo *m* que llega; *~ mail* correo *m* recibido; *~ calls* llamadas *fpl* recibidas

in·com·pa·ra·ble [ɪn'kɑ:mpərəbl] *adj* incomparable

in·com·pat·i·bil·i·ty [ɪnkəmpætɪ'bɪlɪtɪ] incompatibilidad *f*

in·com·pat·i·ble [ɪnkəm'pætɪbl] *adj* incompatible

in·com·pe·tence [ɪn'kɑ:mpɪtəns] incompetencia *f*

in·com·pe·tent [ɪn'kɑ:mpɪtənt] *adj* incompetente

in·com·plete [ɪnkəm'pli:t] *adj* incompleto

in·com·pre·hen·si·ble [ɪnkɑ:mprɪ'hensɪbl] *adj* incomprensible

in·con·ceiv·a·ble [ɪnkən'si:vəbl] *adj* inconcebible

in·con·clu·sive [ɪnkən'klu:sɪv] *adj* no concluyente

in·con·gru·ous [ɪn'kɑ:ŋgrʊəs] *adj* incongruente

in·con·sid·er·ate [ɪnkən'sɪdərət] *adj* desconsiderado

in·con·sis·tent [ɪnkən'sɪstənt] *adj argument, behavior* incoherente, inconsecuente; *player* irregular; *be ~ with sth* no ser consecuente con algo

in·con·so·la·ble [ɪnkən'soʊləbl] *adj* inconsolable, desconsolado

in·con·spic·u·ous [ɪnkən'spɪkjʊəs] *adj* discreto

in·con·ve·ni·ence [ɪnkən'vi:nɪəns] *n* inconveniencia *f*

in·con·ve·ni·ent [ɪnkən'vi:nɪənt] *adj* inconveniente, inoportuno

in·cor·po·rate [ɪn'kɔ:rpəreɪt] *v/t* incorporar

in·cor·po·rat·ed [ɪn'kɔ:rpəreɪtɪd] *adj* COM: *ABC Incorporated* ABC, sociedad *f* anónima

in·cor·rect [ɪnkə'rekt] *adj* incorrecto

in·cor·rect·ly [ɪnkə'rektlɪ] *adv* incorrectamente

in·cor·ri·gi·ble [ɪnˈkɑːrɪdʒəbl] *adj* incorregible

in·crease [ɪnˈkriːs] *v/t & v/i* aumentar **2** *n* [ˈɪnkriːs] aumento *m*

in·creas·ing [ɪnˈkriːsɪŋ] *adj* creciente

in·creas·ing·ly [ɪnˈkriːsɪŋlɪ] *adv* cada vez más; *we're getting ~ concerned* cada vez estamos más preocupados

in·cred·i·ble [ɪnˈkredɪbl] *adj* (*amazing, very good*) increíble

in·crim·i·nate [ɪnˈkrɪmɪneɪt] *v/t* incriminar; *~ o.s.* incriminarse

in·cu·ba·tor [ˈɪŋkjʊbeɪtər] incubadora *f*

in·cur [ɪnˈkɜːr] *v/t* (*pret & pp* **-red**) *costs* incurrir en; *debts* contraer; *s.o's anger* provocar

in·cu·ra·ble [ɪnˈkjʊrəbl] *adj* incurable

in·debt·ed [ɪnˈdetɪd] *adj*: *be ~ to s.o.* estar en deuda con alguien

in·de·cent [ɪnˈdiːsnt] *adj* indecente

in·de·ci·sive [ɪndɪˈsaɪsɪv] *adj* indeciso

in·de·ci·sive·ness [ɪndɪˈsaɪsɪvnɪs] indecisión *f*

in·deed [ɪnˈdiːd] *adv* (*in fact*) ciertamente, efectivamente; *yes, agreeing* ciertamente, en efecto; *very much ~* muchísimo; *thank you very much ~* muchísimas gracias

in·de·fi·na·ble [ɪndɪˈfaɪnəbl] *adj* indefinible

in·def·i·nite [ɪnˈdefɪnɪt] *adj* indefinido; *~ article* GRAM artículo *m* indefinido

in·def·i·nite·ly [ɪnˈdefɪnɪtlɪ] *adv* indefinidamente

in·del·i·cate [ɪnˈdelɪkət] *adj* poco delicado

in·dent 1 *n* [ˈɪndent] *in text* sangrado *m* **2** *v/t* [ɪnˈdent] *line* sangrar

in·de·pen·dence [ɪndɪˈpendəns] independencia *f*

In·de·pen·dence Day Día *m* de la Independencia

in·de·pen·dent [ɪndɪˈpendənt] *adj* independiente

in·de·pen·dent·ly [ɪndɪˈpendəntlɪ] *adv deal with* por separado; *~ of* al margen de

in·de·scri·ba·ble [ɪndɪˈskraɪbəbl] *adj* indescriptible

in·de·scrib·a·bly [ɪndɪˈskraɪbəblɪ] *adv* indescriptiblemente

in·de·struc·ti·ble [ɪndɪˈstrʌktəbl] *adj* indestructible

in·de·ter·mi·nate [ɪndɪˈtɜːrmɪnət] *adj* indeterminado

in·dex [ˈɪndeks] *n for book* índice *m*

'in·dex card ficha *f*; **'in·dex fin·ger** (dedo *m*) índice *m*; **in·dex-'linked** *adj Br* indexado

In·di·a [ˈɪndɪə] (la) India

In·di·an [ˈɪndɪən] **1** *adj* indio **2** *n from India* indio(-a) *m(f)*, hindú *m/f*; *American* indio(-a) *m(f)*

In·di·an 'sum·mer *in northern hemisphere* veranillo *m* de San Martín; *in southern hemisphere* veranillo *m* de San Juan

in·di·cate [ˈɪndɪkeɪt] **1** *v/t* indicar **2** *v/i when driving* poner el intermitente

in·di·ca·tion [ɪndɪˈkeɪʃn] indicio *m*

in·di·ca·tor [ˈɪndɪkeɪtər] *Br on car* intermitente *m*

in·dict [ɪnˈdaɪt] *v/t* acusar

in·dif·fer·ence [ɪnˈdɪfrəns] indiferencia *f*

in·dif·fer·ent [ɪnˈdɪfrənt] *adj* indiferente; (*mediocre*) mediocre; *are you totally ~ to the way I feel?* ¿no te importa lo más mínimo lo que sienta yo?

in·di·ges·ti·ble [ɪndɪˈdʒestɪbl] *adj* indigesto

in·di·ges·tion [ɪndɪˈdʒesʧn] indigestión *f*

in·dig·nant [ɪnˈdɪgnənt] *adj* indignado

in·dig·na·tion [ɪndɪgˈneɪʃn] indignación *f*

in·di·rect [ɪndɪˈrekt] *adj* indirecto

in·di·rect·ly [ɪndɪˈrektlɪ] *adv* indirectamente

in·dis·creet [ɪndɪˈskriːt] *adj* indiscreto

in·dis·cre·tion [ɪndɪˈskreʃn] indiscreción *f*

in·dis·crim·i·nate [ɪndɪˈskrɪmɪnət]

adj indiscriminado

in·dis·pen·sa·ble [ɪndɪ'spensəbl] *adj* indispensable, imprescindible

in·dis·posed [ɪndɪ'spoʊzd] *adj* (*not well*) indispuesto; **be ~** hallarse indispuesto

in·dis·pu·ta·ble [ɪndɪ'spju:təbl] *adj* indiscutible

in·dis·pu·ta·bly [ɪndɪ'spju:təblɪ] *adv* indiscutiblemente

in·dis·tinct [ɪndɪ'stɪŋkt] *adj* indistinto, impreciso

in·dis·tin·guish·a·ble [ɪndɪ'stɪŋgwɪʃəbl] *adj* indistinguible

in·di·vid·u·al [ɪndɪ'vɪdʒʊəl] **1** *n* individuo *m* **2** *adj* individual

in·di·vid·u·a·list [ɪndɪ'vɪdʒʊəlɪst] *adj* individualista

in·di·vid·u·al·ly [ɪndɪ'vɪdʒʊəlɪ] *adv* individualmente

in·di·vis·i·ble [ɪndɪ'vɪzɪbl] *adj* indivisible

in·doc·tri·nate [ɪn'dɑ:ktrɪneɪt] *v/t* adoctrinar

in·do·lence ['ɪndələns] indolencia *f*

in·do·lent ['ɪndələnt] *adj* indolente

In·do·ne·sia [ɪndə'ni:ʒə] Indonesia

In·do·ne·sian [ɪndə'ni:ʒən] **1** *adj* indonesio **2** *n person* indonesio(-a) *m(f)*

in·door ['ɪndɔːr] *adj activities* de interior; *sport* de pista cubierta; *arena* cubierto; *athletics* en pista cubierta

in·doors [ɪn'dɔːrz] *adv* dentro

in·dorse → **endorse**

in·dulge [ɪn'dʌldʒ] **1** *v/t o.s., one's tastes* satisfacer **2** *v/i*: **~ in a pleasure** entregarse a un placer; **if I might ~ in a little joke** si se me permite contar un chiste

in·dul·gent [ɪn'dʌldʒənt] *adj* indulgente

in·dus·tri·al [ɪn'dʌstrɪəl] *adj* industrial; **~ action** acciones *fpl* reivindicativas

in·dus·tri·al dis·pute conflicto *m* laboral

in·dus·tri·al·ist [ɪn'dʌstrɪəlɪst] industrial *m/f*

in·dus·tri·al·ize [ɪn'dʌstrɪəlaɪz] **1** *v/t* industrializar **2** *v/i* industrializarse

in·dus·tri·al 'waste residuos *mpl* industriales

in·dus·tri·ous [ɪn'dʌstrɪəs] *adj* trabajador, aplicado

in·dus·try ['ɪndəstrɪ] industria *f*

in·ef·fec·tive [ɪnɪ'fektɪv] *adj* ineficaz

in·ef·fec·tu·al [ɪnɪ'fektʃʊəl] *adj person* inepto, incapaz

in·ef·fi·cient [ɪnɪ'fɪʃənt] *adj* ineficiente

in·el·i·gi·ble [ɪn'elɪdʒɪbl] *adj*: **be ~** no reunir las condiciones

in·ept [ɪ'nept] *adj* inepto

in·e·qual·i·ty [ɪnɪ'kwɑ:lɪtɪ] desigualdad *f*

in·es·ca·pa·ble [ɪnɪ'skeɪpəbl] *adj* inevitable

in·es·ti·ma·ble [ɪn'estɪməbl] *adj* inestimable

in·ev·i·ta·ble [ɪn'evɪtəbl] *adj* inevitable

in·ev·i·ta·bly [ɪn'evɪtəblɪ] *adv* inevitablemente

in·ex·cu·sa·ble [ɪnɪk'skju:zəbl] *adj* inexcusable, injustificable

in·ex·haus·ti·ble [ɪnɪg'zɒ:stəbl] *adj supply* inagotable

in·ex·pen·sive [ɪnɪk'spensɪv] *adj* barato, económico

in·ex·pe·ri·enced [ɪnɪk'spɪrɪənst] *adj* inexperto

in·ex·plic·a·ble [ɪnɪk'splɪkəbl] *adj* inexplicable

in·ex·pres·si·ble [ɪnɪk'spresɪbl] *adj joy* indescriptible

in·fal·li·ble [ɪn'fælɪbl] *adj* infalible

in·fa·mous ['ɪnfəməs] *adj* infame

in·fan·cy ['ɪnfənsɪ] infancia *f*

in·fant ['ɪnfənt] bebé *m*

in·fan·tile ['ɪnfəntaɪl] *adj pej* infantil, pueril

in·fan·try ['ɪnfəntrɪ] infantería *f*

in·fan·try 'sol·dier soldado *m/f* de infantería, infante *m/f*

in·fat·u·at·ed [ɪn'fætʃʊeɪtɪd] *adj*: **be ~ with s.o.** estar encaprichado de alguien

in·fect [ɪn'fekt] *v/t* infectar; **he ~ed everyone with his cold** contagió el resfriado a todo el mundo; **become ~ed** *of wound* infectarse; *of person*

contagiarse
in·fec·tion [ɪnˈfekʃn] infección f
in·fec·tious [ɪnˈfekʃəs] adj disease infeccioso; laughter contagioso
in·fer [ɪnˈfɜːr] v/t (pret & pp -red) inferir, deducir (from de)
in·fe·ri·or [ɪnˈfɪrɪər] adj inferior (to a)
in·fe·ri·or·i·ty [ɪnfɪrɪˈɑːrətɪ] in quality inferioridad f
in·fe·ri·or·i·ty com·plex complejo m de inferioridad
in·fer·tile [ɪnˈfɜːrtl] adj woman, plant estéril; soil estéril, yermo
in·fer·til·i·ty [ɪnfərˈtɪlɪtɪ] esterilidad f
in·fi·del·i·ty [ɪnfɪˈdelɪtɪ] infidelidad f
in·fil·trate [ˈɪnfɪltreɪt] v/t infiltrarse en
in·fi·nite [ˈɪnfɪnət] adj infinito
in·fin·i·tive [ɪnˈfɪnətɪv] infinitivo m
in·fin·i·ty [ɪnˈfɪnətɪ] infinidad f
in·firm [ɪnˈfɜːrm] adj enfermo, achacoso
in·fir·ma·ry [ɪnˈfɜːrmərɪ] enfermería f
in·fir·mi·ty [ɪnˈfɜːrmətɪ] debilidad f
in·flame [ɪnˈfleɪm] v/t despertar
in·flam·ma·ble [ɪnˈflæməbl] adj inflamable
in·flam·ma·tion [ɪnfləˈmeɪʃn] MED inflamación f
in·flat·a·ble [ɪnˈfleɪtəbl] adj dinghy hinchable, inflable
in·flate [ɪnˈfleɪt] v/t tire, dinghy hinchar, inflar; economy inflar
in·fla·tion [ɪnˈfleɪʃən] inflación f
in·fla·tion·a·ry [ɪnˈfleɪʃənərɪ] adj inflacionario, inflacionista
in·flec·tion [ɪnˈflekʃn] inflexión f
in·flex·i·ble [ɪnˈfleksɪbl] adj inflexible
in·flict [ɪnˈflɪkt] v/t infligir (on a)
'in-flight adj: ~ entertainment entretenimiento m durante el vuelo
in·flu·ence [ˈɪnfluəns] 1 n influencia f; be a good/bad ~ on s.o. tener una buena/mala influencia en alguien 2 v/t influir en, influenciar
in·flu·en·tial [ɪnfluˈenʃl] adj influyente
in·flu·en·za [ɪnfluˈenzə] gripe f
in·form [ɪnˈfɔːrm] 1 v/t informar; ~

s.o. about sth informar a alguien de algo; please keep me ~ed por favor manténme informado 2 v/i: ~ on s.o. delatar a alguien
in·for·mal [ɪnˈfɔːrml] adj informal
in·for·mal·i·ty [ɪnfɔːrˈmælɪtɪ] informalidad f
in·form·ant [ɪnˈfɔːrmənt] confidente m/f
in·for·ma·tion [ɪnfərˈmeɪʃn] información f; a piece of ~ una información
in·for·ma·tion 'sci·ence informática f; in·for·ma·tion 'sci·en·tist informático(-a) m(f); in·for·ma·tion tech·nol·o·gy tecnologías fpl de la información
in·for·ma·tive [ɪnˈfɔːrmətɪv] adj informativo; you're not being very ~ no estás dando mucha información
in·form·er [ɪnˈfɔːrmər] confidente m/f
in·fra·red [ɪnfrəˈred] adj infrarrojo
in·fra·struc·ture [ˈɪnfrəstrʌkʃər] infraestructura f
in·fre·quent [ɪnˈfriːkwənt] adj poco frecuente
in·fu·ri·ate [ɪnˈfjʊrɪeɪt] v/t enfurecer, exasperar
in·fu·ri·at·ing [ɪnˈfjʊrɪeɪtɪŋ] adj exasperante
in·fuse [ɪnˈfjuːz] v/i of tea infundir
in·fu·sion [ɪnˈfjuːʒn] (herb tea) infusión f
in·ge·ni·ous [ɪnˈdʒiːnɪəs] adj ingenioso
in·ge·nu·i·ty [ɪndʒɪˈnuːətɪ] lo ingenioso
in·got [ˈɪŋgət] lingote m
in·gra·ti·ate [ɪnˈgreɪʃɪeɪt] v/t: ~ o.s. with s.o. congraciarse con alguien
in·grat·i·tude [ɪnˈgrætɪtuːd] ingratitud f
in·gre·di·ent [ɪnˈgriːdɪənt] also fig ingrediente m
in·hab·it [ɪnˈhæbɪt] v/t habitar
in·hab·it·a·ble [ɪnˈhæbɪtəbl] adj habitable
in·hab·it·ant [ɪnˈhæbɪtənt] habitante m/f
in·hale [ɪnˈheɪl] 1 v/t inhalar 2 v/i

when smoking tragarse el humo

in·ha·ler [ɪnˈheɪlər] inhalador *m*

in·her·it [ɪnˈherɪt] *v/t* heredar

in·her·i·tance [ɪnˈherɪtəns] herencia *f*

in·hib·it [ɪnˈhɪbɪt] *v/t growth* impedir; *conversation* inhibir, cohibir

in·hib·it·ed [ɪnˈhɪbɪtɪd] *adj* inhibido, cohibido

in·hi·bi·tion [ɪnhɪˈbɪʃn] inhibición *f*

in·hos·pi·ta·ble [ɪnhɑːˈspɪtəbl] *adj person* inhospitalario; *city, climate* inhóspito

'in-house 1 *adj facilities* en el lugar de trabajo; **~ team** equipo *m* en plantilla **2** *adv work* en la empresa

in·hu·man [ɪnˈhjuːmən] *adj* inhumano

i·ni·tial [ɪˈnɪʃl] **1** *adj* inicial **2** *n* inicial *f* **3** *v/t (write ~s on)* poner las iniciales en

i·ni·tial·ly [ɪˈnɪʃlɪ] *adv* inicialmente, al principio

i·ni·ti·ate [ɪˈnɪʃɪeɪt] *v/t* iniciar

i·ni·ti·a·tion [ɪnɪʃɪˈeɪʃn] iniciación *f*, inicio *m*

i·ni·ti·a·tive [ɪˈnɪʃətɪv] iniciativa *f*; **do sth on one's own ~** hacer algo por iniciativa propia

in·ject [ɪnˈdʒekt] *v/t drug, fuel, capital* inyectar

in·jec·tion [ɪnˈdʒekʃn] *of drug, fuel, capital* inyección *f*

'in-joke *it's an* **~** es un chiste que entendemos nosotros

in·jure [ˈɪndʒər] *v/t* lesionar; **he ~d his leg** se lesionó la pierna

in·jured [ˈɪndʒərd] **1** *adj leg* lesionado; *feelings* herido **2** *npl:* **the ~** los heridos

in·ju·ry [ˈɪndʒərɪ] lesión *f*; *wound* herida *f*

'in·ju·ry time SP tiempo *m* de descuento

in·jus·tice [ɪnˈdʒʌstɪs] injusticia *f*

ink [ɪŋk] tinta *f*

ink·jet (**'prin·ter**) impresora *f* de chorro de tinta

in·land [ˈɪnlənd] *adj* interior; *mail* nacional

in-laws [ˈɪnlɔːz] *npl* familia *f* política

in·lay [ˈɪnleɪ] *n* incrustación *f*

in·let [ˈɪnlet] *of sea* ensenada *f*; *in machine* entrada *f*

in·mate [ˈɪnmeɪt] *of prison* recluso(-a) *m(f)*; *of mental hospital* paciente *m/f*

inn [ɪn] posada *f*, mesón *m*

in·nate [ɪˈneɪt] *adj* innato

in·ner [ˈɪnər] *adj* interior; **the ~ ear** el oído interno

in·ner 'cit·y barrios degradados del centro de la ciudad; **~ decay** degradación *f* del centro de la ciudad

'in·ner·most *adj feelings* más íntimo; *recess* más recóndito

in·ner 'tube cámara *f* (de aire)

in·no·cence [ˈɪnəsəns] inocencia *f*

in·no·cent [ˈɪnəsənt] *adj* inocente

in·noc·u·ous [ɪˈnɑːkjʊəs] *adj* inocuo

in·no·va·tion [ɪnəˈveɪʃn] innovación *f*

in·no·va·tive [ɪnəˈveɪtɪv] *adj* innovador

in·no·va·tor [ˈɪnəveɪtər] innovador(a) *m(f)*

in·nu·me·ra·ble [ɪˈnuːmərəbl] *adj* innumerable

i·noc·u·late [ɪˈnɑːkjʊleɪt] *v/t* inocular

i·noc·u·la·tion [ɪnɑːkjʊˈleɪʃn] inoculación *f*

in·of·fen·sive [ɪnəˈfensɪv] *adj* inofensivo

in·or·gan·ic [ɪnɔːrˈgænɪk] *adj* inorgánico

'in-pa·tient paciente *m/f* interno(-a)

in·put [ˈɪnpʊt] **1** *n into project etc* contribución *f*, aportación *f*; COMPUT entrada *f* **2** *v/t (pret & pp* **-ted** *or* **input***) into project* contribuir, aportar; COMPUT introducir

in·quest [ˈɪnkwest] investigación *f* (**into** sobre)

in·quire [ɪnˈkwaɪr] *v/i* preguntar; **~ into sth** investigar algo

in·quir·y [ɪnˈkwaɪrɪ] consulta *f*, pregunta *f*; *into rail crash etc* investigación *f*

in·quis·i·tive [ɪnˈkwɪzətɪv] *adj* curioso, inquisitivo

in·sane [ɪnˈseɪn] *adj person* loco, demente; *idea* descabellado

in·san·i·ta·ry [ɪnˈsænɪterɪ] *adj* antihigiénico

in·san·i·ty [ɪnˈsænɪtɪ] locura *f*, demencia *f*

in·sa·ti·a·ble [ɪnˈseɪʃəbl] *adj* insaciable

in·scrip·tion [ɪnˈskrɪpʃn] inscripción *f*

in·scru·ta·ble [ɪnˈskruːtəbl] *adj* inescrutable

in·sect [ˈɪnsekt] insecto *m*

in·sec·ti·cide [ɪnˈsektɪsaɪd] insecticida *f*

'in·sect re·pel·lent repelente *m* contra insectos

in·se·cure [ɪnsɪˈkjʊr] *adj* inseguro

in·se·cu·ri·ty [ɪnsɪˈkjʊrɪtɪ] inseguridad *f*

in·sen·si·tive [ɪnˈsensɪtɪv] *adj* insensible

in·sen·si·tiv·i·ty [ɪnsensɪˈtɪvɪtɪ] insensibilidad *f*

in·sep·a·ra·ble [ɪnˈseprəbl] *adj* inseparable

in·sert 1 *n* [ˈɪnsɜːrt] *in magazine etc* encarte *m* **2** *v/t* [ɪnˈsɜːrt] *coin, finger, diskette* introducir, meter; *extra text* insertar

in·ser·tion [ɪnˈsɜːrʃn] *act* introducción, inserción *f; of text* inserción *f*

in·side [ɪnˈsaɪd] **1** *n of house, box* interior *m*; **somebody on the ~** algún de dentro; **~ out** del revés; **turn sth ~ out** dar la vuelta a algo *(de dentro a fuera)*; **know sth ~ out** saberse algo al dedillo **2** *prep* dentro de; **~ the house** dentro de la casa; **~ of 2 hours** dentro de 2 horas **3** *adv* stay, remain dentro; *go, carry* adentro; **we went ~** entramos **4** *adj:* **~ information** información *f* confidencial; **~ lane** SP calle *f* de dentro; *on road* carril *m* de la derecha; **~ pocket** bolsillo *m* interior

in·sid·er [ɪnˈsaɪdər] *persona con acceso a información confidencial*

in·sid·er 'trad·ing FIN uso *m* de información privilegiada

in·sides [ɪnˈsaɪdz] *npl* tripas *fpl*

in·sid·i·ous [ɪnˈsɪdɪəs] *adj* insidioso

in·sight [ˈɪnsaɪt]: **this film offers an ~ into local customs** esta película permite hacerse una idea de las costumbres locales; **full of ~** muy perspicaz

in·sig·nif·i·cant [ɪnsɪgˈnɪfɪkənt] *adj* insignificante

in·sin·cere [ɪnsɪnˈsɪr] *adj* poco sincero, falso

in·sin·cer·i·ty [ɪnsɪnˈserɪtɪ] falta *f* de sinceridad

in·sin·u·ate [ɪnˈsɪnueɪt] *v/t (imply)* insinuar

in·sist [ɪnˈsɪst] *v/i* insistir; **please keep it, I ~** por favor, insisto en que te lo quedes

♦ insist on *v/t* insistir en

in·sis·tent [ɪnˈsɪstənt] *adj* insistente

in·so·lent [ˈɪnsələnt] *adj* insolente

in·sol·u·ble [ɪnˈsɑːljubl] *adj problem* irresoluble; *substance* insoluble

in·sol·vent [ɪnˈsɑːlvənt] *adj* insolvente

in·som·ni·a [ɪnˈsɑːmnɪə] insomnio *m*

in·spect [ɪnˈspekt] *v/t* inspeccionar

in·spec·tion [ɪnˈspekʃn] inspección *f*

in·spec·tor [ɪnˈspektər] *in factory, of police* inspector(a) *m(f); on buses* revisor(a) *m(f)*

in·spi·ra·tion [ɪnspəˈreɪʃn] inspiración *f*

in·spire [ɪnˈspaɪr] *v/t respect etc* inspirar; **be ~d by s.o. / sth** estar inspirado por alguien / algo

in·sta·bil·i·ty [ɪnstəˈbɪlɪtɪ] *of character, economy* inestabilidad *f*

in·stall [ɪnˈstɔːl] *v/t* instalar

in·stal·la·tion [ɪnstəˈleɪʃn] instalación *f; military ~* instalación *f* militar

in·stal·ment *Br*, **in·stall·ment** [ɪnˈstɔːlmənt] *of story, TV drama etc* episodio *m; payment* plazo *m*

in·stall·ment plan compra *f* a plazos

in·stance [ˈɪnstəns] *(example)* ejemplo *m;* **for ~** por ejemplo

in·stant [ˈɪnstənt] **1** *adj* instantáneo **2** *n* instante *m;* **in an ~** en un instante

in·stan·ta·ne·ous [ɪnstənˈteɪnɪəs] *adj* instantáneo

in·stant 'cof·fee café *m* instantáneo

in·stant·ly [ˈɪnstəntlɪ] *adv* al instante

in·stead [ɪn'sted] adv: **I'll take that one ~** me llevaré mejor ese otro; **would you like coffee ~?** ¿preferiría mejor café?; **I'll have coffee ~ of tea** tomaré café en vez de té; **he went ~ of me** fue en mi lugar

in·step [ɪnstep] empeine *m*

in·stinct ['ɪnstɪŋkt] instinto *m*

in·stinc·tive [ɪn'stɪŋktɪv] adj instintivo

in·sti·tute ['ɪnstɪtuːt] **1** *n* instituto *m*; *for elderly* residencia *f* de ancianos; *for mentally ill* psiquiátrico *m* **2** *v/t new law* establecer; *inquiry* iniciar

in·sti·tu·tion [ɪnstɪ'tuːʃn] institución *f*; (*setting up*) iniciación *f*

in·struct [ɪn'strʌkt] *v/t* (*order*) dar instrucciones a; (*teach*) instruir; **~ s.o. to do sth** (*order*) ordenar a alguien que haga algo

in·struc·tion [ɪn'strʌkʃn] instrucción *f*; **~s for use** instrucciones *fpl* de uso

in·struc·tion man·u·al manual *m* de instrucciones

in·struc·tive [ɪn'strʌktɪv] adj instructivo

in·struc·tor [ɪn'strʌktər] instructor(a) *m(f)*

in·stru·ment ['ɪnstrʊmənt] MUS, *tool* instrumento *m*

in·sub·or·di·nate [ɪnsə'bɔːrdɪnət] adj insubordinado

in·suf·fi·cient [ɪnsə'fɪʃt] adj insuficiente

in·su·late ['ɪnsəleɪt] *v/t also* ELEC aislar

in·su·la·tion [ɪnsə'leɪʃn] ELEC aislamiento *m*; *against cold* aislamiento *m* (térmico)

in·su·lin ['ɪnsəlɪn] insulina *f*

in·sult **1** *n* ['ɪnsʌlt] insulto *m* **2** *v/t* [ɪn'sʌlt] insultar

in·sur·ance [ɪn'ʃʊrəns] seguro *m*

in·sur·ance com·pa·ny compañía *f* de seguros, aseguradora *f*; **in'sur·ance pol·i·cy** póliza *f* de seguros; **in'sur·ance pre·mi·um** prima *f* (del seguro)

in·sure [ɪn'ʃʊr] *v/t* asegurar

in·sured [ɪn'ʃʊrd] **1** adj asegurado

2 *n*: **the ~** el asegurado, la asegurada

in·sur·moun·ta·ble [ɪnsər'maʊntəbl] adj insuperable

in·tact [ɪn'tækt] adj (*not damaged*) intacto

in·take ['ɪnteɪk] *of college etc* remesa *f*; **we have an annual ~ of 300 students** cada año admitimos a 300 alumnos

in·te·grate ['ɪntɪgreɪt] *v/t* integrar (*into* en)

in·te·grat·ed 'cir·cuit ['ɪntɪgreɪtɪd] circuito *m* integrado

in·teg·ri·ty [ɪn'tegrətɪ] (*honesty*) integridad *f*; **a man of ~** un hombre íntegro

in·tel·lect ['ɪntəlekt] intelecto *m*

in·tel·lec·tu·al [ɪntə'lektʃʊəl] **1** adj intelectual **2** *n* intelectual *m/f*

in·tel·li·gence [ɪn'telɪdʒəns] inteligencia *f*; (*information*) información *f* secreta

in'tel·li·gence of·fi·cer agente *m/f* del servicio de inteligencia

in'tel·li·gence ser·vice servicio *m* de inteligencia

in·tel·li·gent [ɪn'telɪdʒənt] adj inteligente

in·tel·li·gi·ble [ɪn'telɪdʒəbl] adj inteligible

in·tend [ɪn'tend] *v/t*: **~ to do sth** tener la intención de hacer algo; **that's not what I ~ed** esa no era mi intención

in·tense [ɪn'tens] adj sensation, pleasure, heat, pressure intenso; personality serio

in·ten·si·fy [ɪn'tensɪfaɪ] (pret & pp **-ied**) **1** *v/t* effect, pressure intensificar **2** *v/i* intensificarse

in·ten·si·ty [ɪn'tensətɪ] intensidad *f*

in·ten·sive [ɪn'tensɪv] adj study, training, treatment intensivo

in·ten·sive 'care (u·nit) MED (unidad *f* de) cuidados *mpl* intensivos

in·ten·sive 'course of language study curso *m* intensivo

in·tent [ɪn'tent] adj: **be ~ on doing sth** (*determined to do*) estar decidido a hacer algo; **be ~ on sth** (*concentrating on*) estar concentrado haciendo algo

in·ten·tion [ɪn'tenʃn] intención *f*; *I have no ~ of ...* (*refuse to*) no tengo intención de ...

in·ten·tion·al [ɪn'tenʃənl] *adj* intencionado

in·ten·tion·al·ly [ɪn'tenʃnlɪ] *adv* a propósito, adrede

in·ter·ac·tion [ɪntər'ækʃn] interacción *f*

in·ter·ac·tive [ɪntər'æktɪv] *adj* interactivo

in·ter·cede [ɪntər'siːd] *v/i* interceder

in·ter·cept [ɪntər'sept] *v/t* interceptar

in·ter·change ['ɪntərtʃeɪndʒ] *n of highways* nudo *m* vial

in·ter·change·a·ble [ɪntər'tʃeɪndʒəbl] *adj* intercambiable

in·ter·com ['ɪntərkɑːm] *in office, ship* interfono *m*; *for front door* portero *m* automático

in·ter·course ['ɪntərkɔːrs] *sexual* coito *m*

in·ter·de·pend·ent [ɪntərdɪ'pendənt] *adj* interdependiente

in·ter·est ['ɪntrəst] **1** *n also FIN* interés *m*; *take an ~ in sth* interesarse por algo **2** *v/t* interesar

in·ter·est·ed ['ɪntrəstɪd] *adj* interesado; *be ~ in sth* estar interesado en algo; *thanks, but I'm not ~* gracias, pero no me interesa

in·ter·est-free 'loan préstamo *m* sin intereses

in·ter·est·ing ['ɪntrəstɪŋ] *adj* interesante

'in·ter·est rate tipo *m* de interés

in·ter·face ['ɪntərfeɪs] **1** *n* interface *m*, interfaz *f* **2** *v/i* relacionarse

in·ter·fere [ɪntər'fɪr] *v/i* interferir, entrometerse

♦ interfere with *v/t* afectar a; *the lock had been interfered with* alguien había manipulado la cerradura

in·ter·fer·ence [ɪntər'fɪrəns] intromisión *f*; *on radio* interferencia *f*

in·te·ri·or [ɪn'tɪrɪər] **1** *adj* interior **2** *n* interior *m*; *Department of the Interior* Ministerio *m* del Interior

in·te·ri·or 'dec·o·ra·tor interiorista *m/f*, decorador(a) *m(f)* de interiores; **in·te·ri·or de'sign** interiorismo *m*; **in·te·ri·or de'sign·er** interiorista *m/f*

in·ter·lude ['ɪntərluːd] *at theater* entreacto *m*, intermedio *m*; *at concert* intermedio *m*; (*period*) intervalo *m*

in·ter·mar·ry [ɪntər'mærɪ] *v/i* (*pret & pp* -ied) casarse (*con miembros de otra raza, religión o grupo*); *the two tribes intermarried* los dos tribus se casaron entre sí

in·ter·me·di·ar·y [ɪntər'miːdɪərɪ] *n* intermediario

in·ter·me·di·ate [ɪntər'miːdɪət] *adj* intermedio *m*

in·ter·mis·sion [ɪntər'mɪʃn] *in theater* entreacto *m*, intermedio *m*; *in movie theater* intermedio *m*, descanso *m*

in·tern [ɪn'tɜːrn] *v/t* recluir

in·ter·nal [ɪn'tɜːrnl] *adj* interno

in·ter·nal com'bus·tion en·gine motor *m* de combustión interna

in·ter·nal·ly [ɪn'tɜːrnəlɪ] *adv* internamente

In·ter·nal 'Rev·e·nue (Ser·vice) Hacienda *f*, *Span* Agencia *f* Tributaria

in·ter·na·tion·al [ɪntər'næʃnl] *adj* internacional

In·ter·na·tion·al Court of 'Jus·tice Tribunal *m* Internacional de Justicia

in·ter·na·tion·al·ly [ɪntər'næʃnəlɪ] *adv* internacionalmente

In·ter·na·tion·al 'Mon·e·tar·y Fund Fondo *m* Monetario Internacional

In·ter·net ['ɪntərnet] Internet *f*; *on the ~* en Internet

in·ter·nist [ɪn'tɜːrnɪst] internista *m/f*

in·ter·pret [ɪn'tɜːrprɪt] *v/t & v/i* interpretar

in·ter·pre·ta·tion [ɪntɜːrprɪ'teɪʃn] interpretación *f*

in·ter·pret·er [ɪn'tɜːrprɪtər] intérprete *m/f*

in·ter·re·lat·ed [ɪntərrɪ'leɪtɪd] *adj facts* interrelacionado

in·ter·ro·gate [ɪn'terəgeɪt] *v/t* interrogar

in·ter·ro·ga·tion [ɪntərə'geɪʃn] interrogatorio *m*

in·ter·rog·a·tive [ɪntər'rɑːgətɪv] *n* GRAM (forma *f*) interrogativa *f*

in·ter·ro·ga·tor [ɪntərə'geɪtər] interrogador(a) *m(f)*

in·ter·rupt [ɪntər'rʌpt] *v/t* & *v/i* interrumpir

in·ter·rup·tion [ɪntər'rʌpʃn] interrupción *f*

in·ter·sect [ɪntər'sekt] **1** *v/t* cruzar **2** *v/i* cruzarse

in·ter·sec·tion ['ɪntərsekʃn] (*crossroads*) intersección *f*

in·ter·state ['ɪntərsteɪt] *n* autopista *f* interestatal

in·ter·val ['ɪntərvl] intervalo *m*; *in theater* entreacto *m*, intermedio *m*; *at concert* intermedio *m*

in·ter·vene [ɪntər'viːn] *v/i of person, police etc* intervenir

in·ter·ven·tion [ɪntər'venʃn] intervención *f*

in·ter·view ['ɪntərvjuː] **1** *n* entrevista *f* **2** *v/t* entrevistar

in·ter·view·ee [ɪntərvjuː'iː] *on TV* entrevistado(-a) *m(f)*; *for job* candidato(-a) *m(f)*

in·ter·view·er ['ɪntərvjuːər] entrevistador(a) *m(f)*

in·tes·tine [ɪn'testɪn] intestino *m*

in·ti·ma·cy ['ɪntɪməsɪ] *of friendship* intimidad *f*; *sexual* relaciones *fpl* íntimas

in·ti·mate ['ɪntɪmət] *adj* íntimo

in·tim·i·date [ɪn'tɪmɪdeɪt] *v/t* intimidar

in·tim·i·da·tion [ɪntɪmɪ'deɪʃn] intimidación *f*

in·to ['ɪntʊ] *prep* en; *he put it ~ his suitcase* lo puso en su maleta; *translate ~ English* traducir al inglés; *he's ~ classical music* F (*likes*) le gusta *or Span* le va mucho la música clásica; *he's ~ local politics* F (*is involved with*) está muy metido en el mundillo de la política local; *when you're ~ the job* cuando te hayas metido en el trabajo

in·tol·e·ra·ble [ɪn'tɑːlərəbl] *adj* intolerable

in·tol·e·rant [ɪn'tɑːlərənt] *adj* intolerante

in·tox·i·cat·ed [ɪn'tɑːksɪkeɪtɪd] *adj* ebrio, embriagado

in·tran·si·tive [ɪn'trænsɪtɪv] *adj* intransitivo

in·tra·ve·nous [ɪntrə'viːnəs] *adj* intravenoso

in·trep·id [ɪn'trepɪd] *adj* intrépido

in·tri·cate ['ɪntrɪkət] *adj* intrincado, complicado

in·trigue 1 *n* ['ɪntriːg] intriga *f* **2** *v/t* [ɪn'triːg] intrigar; *I would be ~d to know ...* tendría curiosidad por saber ...

in·trigu·ing [ɪn'triːgɪŋ] *adj* intrigante

in·tro·duce [ɪntrə'duːs] *v/t* presentar; *new technique etc* introducir; *may I ~ ...?* permítame presentarle a ...; *~ s.o. to a new sport* iniciar a alguien en un deporte nuevo

in·tro·duc·tion [ɪntrə'dʌkʃn] *to person* presentación *f*; *to a new food, sport etc* iniciación *f*; *in book, of new techniques* e introducción *f*

in·tro·vert ['ɪntrəvɜːrt] *n* introvertido(-a) *m(f)*

in·trude [ɪn'truːd] *v/i* molestar

in·trud·er [ɪn'truːdər] intruso(-a) *m(f)*

in·tru·sion [ɪn'truːʒn] intromisión *f*

in·tu·i·tion [ɪntuː'ɪʃn] intuición *f*

in·vade [ɪn'veɪd] *v/t* invadir

in·val·id¹ [ɪn'vælɪd] *adj* nulo

in·va·lid² ['ɪnvəlɪd] *n* MED minusválido(-a) *m(f)*

in·val·i·date [ɪn'vælɪdeɪt] *v/t claim, theory* invalidar

in·val·u·a·ble [ɪn'væljʊbl] *adj help, contributor* inestimable

in·var·i·a·bly [ɪn'veɪrɪəblɪ] *adv* (*always*) invariablemente, siempre

in·va·sion [ɪn'veɪʒn] invasión *f*

in·vent [ɪn'vent] *v/t* inventar

in·ven·tion [ɪn'venʃn] *action* invención *f*; *thing invented* invento *m*

in·ven·tive [ɪn'ventɪv] *adj* inventivo, imaginativo

in·ven·tor [ɪn'ventər] inventor(-a) *m(f)*

in·ven·to·ry ['ɪnvəntɔːrɪ] inventario *m*

in·verse [ɪn'vɜːrs] *adj order* inverso

in·vert [ɪn'vɜːrt] *v/t* invertir

in·ver·te·brate [ɪn'vɜːrtɪbrət] *n* invertebrado *m*

in·vert·ed 'com·mas [ɪn'vɜːrtɪd] *npl* comillas *fpl*

in·vest [ɪn'vest] *v/t & v/i* invertir (*in* en)

in·ves·ti·gate [ɪn'vestɪgeɪt] *v/t* investigar

in·ves·ti·ga·tion [ɪnvestɪ'geɪʃn] investigación *f*

in·ves·ti·ga·tive 'jour·nal·ism [ɪn'vestɪgətɪv] periodismo *m* de investigación

in·vest·ment [ɪn'vestmənt] inversión *f*

in'vest·ment bank banco *m* de inversiones

in·ves·tor [ɪn'vestər] inversor(a) *m(f)*

in·vig·or·at·ing [ɪn'vɪgəreɪtɪŋ] *adj climate* vigorizante

in·vin·ci·ble [ɪn'vɪnsəbl] *adj* invencible

in·vis·i·ble [ɪn'vɪzɪbl] *adj* invisible

in·vi·ta·tion [ɪnvɪ'teɪʃn] invitación *f*

in·vite [ɪn'vaɪt] *v/t* invitar

♦ **invite in** *v/t*: *invite s.o. in* invitar a alguien a que entre

in·voice ['ɪnvɔɪs] **1** *n* factura *f* **2** *v/t customer* enviar la factura a

in·vol·un·ta·ry [ɪn'vɑːləntərɪ] *adj* involuntario

in·volve [ɪn'vɑːlv] *v/t hard work, expense* involucrar, entrañar; *it would ~ emigrating* supondría emigrar; *this doesn't ~ you* esto no tiene nada que ver contigo; *what does it ~?* ¿en qué consiste?; *get ~d with sth* involucrarse *or* meterse en algo; *the police didn't want to get ~d* la policía no quería intervenir; *get ~d with s.o. emotionally, romantically* tener una relación sentimental con alguien

in·volved [ɪn'vɑːlvd] *adj* (*complex*) complicado

in·volve·ment [ɪn'vɑːlvmənt] *in a*

project, crime etc participación *f*, intervención *f*

in·vul·ne·ra·ble [ɪn'vʌlnərəbl] *adj* invulnerable

in·ward ['ɪnwərd] **1** *adj feeling, smile* interior **2** *adv* hacia dentro

in·ward·ly ['ɪnwərdlɪ] *adv* por dentro

i·o·dine ['aɪoʊdiːn] yodo *m*

IOU [aɪoʊ'juː] *abbr* (= *I owe you*) pagaré *m*

IQ [aɪ'kjuː] *abbr* (= *intelligence quotient*) cociente *m* intelectual

I·ran [ɪ'rɑːn] Irán

I·ra·ni·an [ɪ'reɪnɪən] **1** *adj* iraní **2** *n* iraní *m/f*

I·raq [ɪ'ræk] Iraq, Irak

I·ra·qi [ɪ'rækɪ] **1** *adj* iraquí **2** *n* iraquí *m/f*

Ire·land ['aɪrlənd] Irlanda

i·ris ['aɪrɪs] *of eye* iris *m inv*; *flower* lirio *m*

I·rish ['aɪrɪʃ] *adj* irlandés

'I·rish·man irlandés *m*

'I·rish·wom·an irlandesa *f*

i·ron ['aɪərn] **1** *n substance* hierro *m*; *for clothes* plancha *f* **2** *v/t shirts etc* planchar

i·ron·ic(·al) [aɪ'rɑːnɪk(l)] *adj* irónico

i·ron·ing ['aɪərnɪŋ] planchado *m*; *do the ~* planchar

'i·ron·ing board tabla *f* de planchar

'i·ron·works fundición *f*

i·ron·y ['aɪrənɪ] ironía *f*; *the ~ of it all is that ...* lo irónico del tema es que ...

ir·ra·tion·al [ɪ'ræʃənl] *adj* irracional

ir·rec·on·ci·la·ble [ɪrekən'saɪləbl] *adj* irreconciliable

ir·re·cov·e·ra·ble [ɪrɪ'kʌvərəbl] *adj* irrecuperable

ir·re·gu·lar [ɪ'regjʊlər] *adj* irregular

ir·rel·e·vant [ɪ'reləvənt] *adj* irrelevante

ir·rep·a·ra·ble [ɪ'repərəbl] *adj* irreparable

ir·re·place·a·ble [ɪrɪ'pleɪsəbl] *adj object, person* irreemplazable

ir·re·pres·si·ble [ɪrɪ'presəbl] *adj sense of humor* incontenible; *person* irreprimible

ir·re·proach·a·ble [ɪrɪ'proʊtʃəbl] *adj*

irreprochable

ir·re·sis·ti·ble [ɪrɪ'zɪstəbl] *adj* irresistible

ir·re·spec·tive [ɪrɪ'spektɪv] *adv*: ~ *of* independientemente de

ir·re·spon·si·ble [ɪrɪ'spɑːnsəbl] *adj* irresponsable

ir·re·trie·va·ble [ɪrɪ'triːvəbl] *adj* irrecuperable

ir·rev·e·rent [ɪ'revərənt] *adj* irreverente

ir·rev·o·ca·ble [ɪ'revəkəbl] *adj* irrevocable

ir·ri·gate ['ɪrɪgeɪt] *v/t* regar

ir·ri·ga·tion [ɪrɪ'geɪʃn] riego *m*

ir·ri·ga·tion ca'nal acequia *f*

ir·ri·ta·ble ['ɪrɪtəbl] *adj* irritable

ir·ri·tate ['ɪrɪteɪt] *v/t* irritar

ir·ri·tat·ing ['ɪrɪteɪtɪŋ] *adj* irritante

ir·ri·ta·tion [ɪrɪ'teɪʃn] irritación *f*

Is·lam ['ɪzlɑːm] (el) Islam

Is·lam·ic [ɪz'læmɪk] *adj* islámico

is·land ['aɪlənd] isla *f*

is·land·er ['aɪləndər] isleño(-a) *m(f)*

i·so·late ['aɪsəleɪt] *v/t* aislar

i·so·lat·ed ['aɪsəleɪtɪd] *adj* aislado

i·so·la·tion [aɪsə'leɪʃn] *of a region* aislamiento *m*; *in* ~ aisladamente

i·so'la·tion ward pabellón *m* de enfermedades infecciosas

ISP [aɪes'piː] *abbr* (= *Internet service provider*) proveedor *m* de (acceso a) Internet

Is·rael ['ɪzreɪl] Israel

Is·rae·li [ɪz'reɪli] **1** *adj* israelí **2** *n person* israelí *m/f*

is·sue ['ɪʃuː] **1** *n* (*matter*) tema *m*, asunto *m*; *of magazine* número *m*; *the point at* ~ el tema que se debate; *take* ~ *with s.o./sth* discrepar de

algo/alguien **2** *v/t coins* emitir; *passport, visa etc* expedir; *warning* dar; ~ *s.o. with sth* entregar algo a alguien

IT [aɪ'tiː] *abbr* (= *information technology*) tecnologías *fpl* de la información; ~ *department* departamento *m* de informática

it [ɪt] *pron as object* lo *m*, la *f*; *what color is* ~? – ~ *is red* ¿de qué color es? – es rojo; ~*'s raining* llueve; ~*'s me/him* soy yo/es él; ~*'s Charlie here* TELEC soy Charlie; ~*'s your turn* te toca; *that's* ~! (*that's right*) ¡eso es!; (*finished*) ¡ya está!

I·tal·ian [ɪ'tæljən] **1** *adj* italiano **2** *n person* italiano(-a) *m(f)*; *language* italiano *m*

i·tal·ic [ɪ'tælɪk] *adj* cursiva

i·tal·ics [ɪ'tælɪks] *npl* cursiva *f*

I·ta·ly ['ɪtəli] Italia

itch [ɪtʃ] **1** *n* picor *m* **2** *v/i* picar

i·tem ['aɪtəm] *in list, accounts,* (*article*) artículo *m*; *on agenda* punto *m*; *of news* noticia *f*

i·tem·ize ['aɪtəmaɪz] *v/t invoice* detallar

i·tin·e·ra·ry [aɪ'tɪnəreri] itinerario *m*

its [ɪts] *poss adj* su; *where is* ~ *box?* ¿dónde está su caja?; *the dog has hurt* ~ *leg* el perro se ha hecho daño en la pata

it's [ɪts] → *it is, it has*

it·self [ɪt'self] *pron reflexive* se; *the dog hurt* ~ el perro se hizo daño; *the hotel* ~ *is fine* el hotel en sí (mismo) está bien; *by* ~ (*alone*) aislado, solo; (*automatically*) solo

i·vo·ry ['aɪvəri] marfil *m*

i·vy ['aɪvi] hiedra *f*

I

J

jab [dʒæb] v/t (*pret & pp* **-bed**) clavar

jab·ber ['dʒæbər] v/i parlotear

jack [dʒæk] MOT gato m; *in cards* jota f

♦ **jack up** v/t MOT levantar con el gato

jack·et ['dʒækɪt] (*coat*) chaqueta f; *of book* sobrecubierta f

jack·et po·ta·to *Span* patata f or *L.Am.* papa f asada (*con piel*)

jack·knife v/i derrapar (*por la parte del remolque*)

'**jack·pot** gordo m; **he hit the ~** le tocó el gordo

ja·cuz·zi® [dʒə'ku:zɪ] jacuzzi m

jade [dʒeɪd] n jade m

jad·ed ['dʒeɪdɪd] adj harto; *appetite* hastiado

jag·ged ['dʒægɪd] adj accidentado

jag·u·ar ['dʒægʊər] jaguar m

jail [dʒeɪl] n cárcel f; **he's in ~** está en la cárcel

jam¹ [dʒæm] n *for bread* mermelada f

jam² [dʒæm] **1** n MOT atasco m; F (*difficulty*) aprieto m; **be in a ~** estar en un aprieto **2** v/t (*pret & pp* **-med**) (*ram*) meter, embutir; (*cause to stick*) atascar; *broadcast* provocar interferencias en; **be ~med** *of roads* estar colapsado; *of door, window* estar atascado; **~ on the brakes** dar un frenazo **3** v/i (*pret & pp* **-med**) (*stick*) atascarse; **all ten of us managed to ~ into the car** nos las arreglamos para meternos los diez en el coche

jam-'packed adj F abarrotado (**with** de)

jan·i·tor ['dʒænɪtər] portero(-a) m(f)

Jan·u·a·ry ['dʒænʊerɪ] enero m

Ja·pan [dʒə'pæn] Japón

Jap·a·nese [dʒæpə'ni:z] **1** adj japonés **2** n *person* japonés(-esa) m(f); *language* japonés m; **the ~** los japo-neses

jar¹ [dʒɑ:r] n *container* tarro m

jar² [dʒɑ:r] v/i (*pret & pp* **-red**) *of noise* rechinar; **~ on** rechinar en

jar·gon ['dʒɑ:rgən] jerga f

jaun·dice ['dʒɔ:ndɪs] n ictericia f

jaun·diced ['dʒɔ:ndɪst] adj fig resentido

jaunt [dʒɔ:nt] n excursión f; **go on a ~** ir de excursión

jaunt·y ['dʒɔ:ntɪ] adj desenfadado

jav·e·lin ['dʒævlɪn] (*spear*) jabalina f; *event* (lanzamiento m de) jabalina f

jaw [dʒɔ:] n mandíbula f

jay·walk·er ['dʒeɪwɔ:kər] peatón(-ona) m(f) imprudente

'**jay·walk·ing** cruzar la calle de manera imprudente

jazz [dʒæz] n jazz m

♦ **jazz up** v/t F animar

jeal·ous ['dʒeləs] adj celoso; **be ~ in love** tener celos de; *of riches etc* tener envidia de

jeal·ous·ly ['dʒeləslɪ] adv celosamente; *relating to possessions* con envidia

jeal·ous·y ['dʒeləsɪ] celos mpl; *of possessions* envidia f

jeans [dʒi:nz] npl vaqueros mpl, jeans mpl

jeep [dʒi:p] jeep m

jeer [dʒɪr] **1** n abucheo m **2** v/i abuchear; **~ at** burlarse de

Jel·lo® ['dʒelou] gelatina f

jel·ly ['dʒelɪ] mermelada f

'**jel·ly bean** gominola f

'**jel·ly·fish** medusa f

jeop·ar·dize ['dʒepərdaɪz] v/t poner en peligro

jeop·ar·dy ['dʒepərdɪ]: **be in ~** estar en peligro

jerk¹ [dʒɜ:rk] **1** n sacudida f **2** v/t dar un tirón a

jerk² [dʒɜ:rk] n F imbécil m/f, *Span*

gilipollas *m/f inv* F

jerk·y ['dʒɜːrkɪ] *adj movement* brusco

jer·sey ['dʒɜːrzɪ] *(sweater)* suéter *m*, *Span* jersey *m*

jest[dʒest] **1** *n* broma *f*; **in ~** en broma **2** *v/i* bromear

Je·sus ['dʒiːzəs] Jesús

jet [dʒet] **1** *n of water* chorro *m*; *(nozzle)* boquilla *f*; *(airplane)* reactor *m*, avión *m* a reacción **2** *v/i* (*pret & pp* -ted) *travel* viajar en avión

jet-'black *adj* azabache; **'jet en·gine** reactor *m*; **'jet·lag** desfase *m* horario, jet lag *m*

jet·ti·son ['dʒetɪsn] *v/t also fig* tirar por la borda

jet·ty ['dʒetɪ] malecón *m*

Jew [dʒuː] judío(-a) *m(f)*

jew·el ['dʒuːəl] joya *f*, alhaja *f*; *fig: person* joya *f*

jew·el·er, *Br* **jew·el·ler** ['dʒuːlər] joyero(-a) *m(f)*

jew·el·ry *Br* **jew·el·ry** ['dʒuːlrɪ] joyas *fpl*, alhajas *fpl*

Jew·ish ['dʒuːɪʃ] *adj* judío

jif·fy ['dʒɪfɪ] F: **in a ~** en un periquete F

jig·saw (puz·zle) ['dʒɪgsɔː] rompecabezas *m inv*, puzzle *m*

jilt [dʒɪlt] *v/t* dejar plantado

jin·gle ['dʒɪŋgl] **1** *n (song)* melodía *f* publicitaria **2** *v/i of keys, coins* tintinear

jinx [dʒɪŋks] *n* gafe *m*; **there's a ~ on this project** este proyecto está gafado

jit·ters ['dʒɪtərz] *npl* F: **I got the ~** me entró el pánico *or Span* canguelo F

jit·ter·y ['dʒɪtərɪ] *adj* F nervioso

job [dʒaːb] *(employment)* trabajo *m*, empleo *m*; *(task)* tarea *f*, trabajo *m*; **it's not my ~ to answer the phone** no me corresponde a mí contestar el teléfono; **I have a few ~s to do around the house** tengo que hacer unas cuantas cosas en la casa; **out of a ~** sin trabajo *or* empleo; **it's a good ~ you warned me** menos mal que me avisaste; **you'll have a ~** (*it'll be difficult*) te va a costar Dios y ayuda

'job de·scrip·tion (descripción *f* de las) responsabilidades *fpl* del puesto

'job hunt *v/i*: **be ~ing** buscar trabajo

job·less ['dʒaːblɪs] *adj* desempleado, *Span* parado

job sat·is·fac·tion satisfacción *f* con el trabajo

jock·ey ['dʒaːkɪ] *n* jockey *m/f*

jog [dʒaːg] **1** *n*: **go for a ~** ir a hacer jogging *or* footing **2** *v/i* (*pret & pp* -ged) *as exercise* hacer jogging *or* footing **3** *v/t* (*pret & pp* -ged) ~ **s.o.'s memory** refrescar la memoria de alguien; **somebody ~ged my elbow** alguien me dio en el codo

♦ **jog along** *v/i* F ir tirando P

jog·ger ['dʒaːgər] *person* persona *f* que hace jogging *or* footing; *shoe* zapatilla *f* de jogging *or* footing

jog·ging ['dʒaːgɪŋ] jogging *m*, footing *m*; **go ~** ir a hacer jogging *or* footing

'jog·ging suit chándal *m*

john [dʒaːn] P *(toilet)* baño *m*, váter *m*

join [dʒɔɪn] **1** *n* juntura *f* **2** *v/i of roads, rivers* juntarse; *(become a member)* hacerse socio **3** *v/t (connect)* unir; *person* unirse a; *club* hacerse socio de; *(go to work for)* entrar en; *of road* desembocar en; **I'll ~ you at the theater** me reuniré contigo en el teatro

♦ **join in** *v/i* participar

♦ **join up** *v/i Br* MIL alistarse

join·er ['dʒɔɪnər] carpintero(-a) *m(f)*

joint [dʒɔɪnt] **1** *n* ANAT articulación *f*; *in woodwork* junta *f*; *of meat* pieza *f*, F *(place)* garito *m* F; *of cannabis* porro *m* F, canuto *m* F **2** *adj (shared)* conjunto

joint ac'count cuenta *f* conjunta

joint 'ven·ture empresa *f* conjunta

joke [dʒoʊk] **1** *n story* chiste *m*; *(practical ~)* broma *f*; **play a ~ on** gastar una broma a; **it's no ~** no tiene ninguna gracia **2** *v/i* bromear

jok·er ['dʒoʊkər] *person* bromista *m/f*, F *pej* payaso(-a) *m(f)*; *in cards* comodín *m*

jok·ing ['dʒoʊkɪŋ]: **~ apart** bromas aparte

jok·ing·ly ['dʒoʊkɪŋlɪ] *adv* en broma

jol·ly ['dʒɑːlɪ] *adj* alegre

jolt [dʒoʊlt] **1** *n* (*jerk*) sacudida *f* **2** *v/t* (*push*) **somebody ~ed my elbow** alguien me dio en el codo

jos·tle ['dʒɑːsl] *v/t* empujar

♦**jot down** [dʒɑːt] *v/t* (*pret & pp* **-ted**) apuntar, anotar

jour·nal ['dʒɜːrnl] (*magazine*) revista *f*; (*diary*) diario *m*

jour·nal·ism ['dʒɜːrnəlɪzm] periodismo *m*

jour·nal·ist ['dʒɜːrnəlɪst] periodista *m/f*

jour·ney ['dʒɜːrnɪ] *n* viaje *m*

jo·vi·al ['dʒoʊvɪəl] *adj* jovial

joy [dʒɔɪ] alegría *f*, gozo *m*

'joy·stick COMPUT joystick *m*

ju·bi·lant ['dʒuːbɪlənt] *adj* jubiloso

ju·bi·la·tion [dʒuːbɪ'leɪʃn] júbilo *m*

judge [dʒʌdʒ] **1** *n* LAW juez *m/f*, jueza *f*; *in competition* juez *m/f*, miembro *m* del jurado **2** *v/t* juzgar; (*estimate*) calcular **3** *v/i* juzgar; **~ for yourself** júzgalo por ti mismo

judg(e)·ment ['dʒʌdʒmənt] LAW fallo *m*; (*opinion*) juicio *m*; **an error of ~** una equivocación; **he showed good ~** mostró tener criterio; **against my better ~** a pesar de no estar convencido; **the Last Judgment** REL el Juicio Final

'Judg(e)·ment Day Día *m* del Juicio Final

ju·di·cial [dʒuː'dɪʃl] *adj* judicial

ju·di·cious [dʒuː'dɪʃəs] *adj* juicioso

ju·do ['dʒuːdoʊ] judo *m*

jug·gle ['dʒʌgl] *v/t also fig* hacer malabarismos con

jug·gler ['dʒʌglər] malabarista *m/f*

juice [dʒuːs] *n* Span zumo *m*, L.Am. jugo *m*

juic·y ['dʒuːsɪ] *adj* jugoso; *news, gossip* jugoso, sabroso

juke·box ['dʒuːkbɑːks] máquina *f* de discos

Ju·ly [dʒʊ'laɪ] julio *m*

jum·ble ['dʒʌmbl] *n* revoltijo *m*

♦**jumble up** *v/t* revolver

jum·bo (jet) ['dʒʌmboʊ] jumbo *m*

'jum·bo(-sized) *adj* gigante

jump [dʒʌmp] **1** *n* salto *m*; (*increase*) incremento *m*, subida *f*; **give a ~ of surprise** dar un salto **2** *v/i* saltar; (*increase*) dispararse; **you made me ~!** ¡me diste un susto!; **~ to one's feet** ponerse de pie de un salto; **~ to conclusions** sacar conclusiones precipitadas **3** *v/t fence etc* saltar; F (*attack*) asaltar; **~ the lights** saltarse el semáforo, pasarse un semáforo en rojo

♦**jump at** *v/t opportunity* no dejar escapar

jump·er¹ ['dʒʌmpər] *dress* pichi *m*

jump·er² ['dʒʌmpər] SP saltador(a) *m(f)*; *horse* caballo *m* de saltos

jump·y ['dʒʌmpɪ] *adj* nervioso; **get ~** ponerse nervioso

junc·tion ['dʒʌŋkʃn] *of roads* cruce *m*

junc·ture ['dʒʌŋktʃər] *fml*: **at this ~** en esta coyuntura

June [dʒuːn] junio *m*

jun·gle ['dʒʌŋgl] selva *f*, jungla *f*

ju·ni·or ['dʒuːnjər] **1** *adj* (*subordinate*) de rango inferior; (*younger*) más joven **2** *n in rank* subalterno(-a) *m(f)*; **she is ten years my ~** es diez años más joven que yo

ju·ni·or 'high escuela *f* secundaria (*para alumnos de entre 12 y 14 años*)

junk [dʒʌŋk] *n* trastos *mpl*

'junk food comida *f* basura

junk·ie ['dʒʌŋkɪ] F drogota *m/f*

'junk mail propaganda *f* postal; **'junk shop** cacharrería *f*; **'junk·yard** depósito *m* de chatarra

ju·ris·dic·tion [dʒʊrɪs'dɪkʃn] LAW jurisdicción *f*

ju·ror ['dʒʊrər] miembro *m* del jurado

ju·ry ['dʒʊrɪ] jurado *m*

just [dʒʌst] **1** *adj law, cause* justo **2** *adv* (*barely*) justo; (*exactly*) justo, justamente; (*only*) sólo, solamente; **have ~ done sth** acabar de hacer algo; **I've ~ seen her** la acabo de ver; **~ about** (*almost*) casi; **I was ~ about to leave when ...** estaba a punto de salir cuando ...; **~ like that**

(*abruptly*) de repente; **~ now** (*at the moment*) ahora mismo; **I saw her ~ now** (*a few moments ago*) la acabo de ver; **~ you wait!** ¡ya verás!; **~ be quiet!** ¡cállate de una vez!

jus·tice ['dʒʌstɪs] justicia *f*

jus·ti·fi·a·ble [dʒʌstɪ'faɪəbl] *adj* justificable

jus·ti·fi·a·bly [dʒʌstɪ'faɪəblɪ] *adv* justificadamente

jus·ti·fi·ca·tion [dʒʌstɪfɪ'keɪʃn] justificación *f*; **there's no ~ for behavior like that** ese comportamiento es injustificable *or* no tiene justificación

jus·ti·fy ['dʒʌstɪfaɪ] *v/t* (*pret & pp -ied*) *also text* justificar

just·ly ['dʒʌstlɪ] *adv* (*fairly*) con justicia; (*rightly*) con razón

jut out [dʒʌt] *v/i* (*pret & pp -ted*) sobresalir

ju·ve·nile ['dʒuːvənl] **1** *adj crime* juvenil; *court* de menores; *pej* infantil **2** *n fml* menor *m/f*

ju·ve·nile de·lin·quen·cy delincuencia *f* juvenil

ju·ve·nile de·lin·quent delincuente *m/f* juvenil

K

k [keɪ] *abbr* (= *kilobyte*) k (= kilobyte *m*); (= *thousand*) mil

kan·ga·roo [kæŋgə'ruː] canguro *m*

ka·ra·te [kə'rɑːtɪ] kárate *m*

ka·ra·te chop golpe *m* de kárate

ke·bab [kɪ'bæb] pincho *m*, brocheta *f*

♦ **keel over** *v/i* of structure desplomarse; *of person* desmayarse

keen [kiːn] *adj interest* gran; *competition* reñido

keep [kiːp] **1** *n* (*maintenance*) manutención *f*; **for ~s** F para siempre **2** *v/t* (*pret & pp* **kept**) guardar; (*not lose*) conservar; (*detain*) entretener; *family* mantener; *animals* tener, criar; **you can ~ it** (*it's for you*) te lo puedes quedar; **~ trying!** ¡sigue intentándolo!; **don't ~ interrupting!** ¡deja de interrumpirme!; **~ a promise** cumplir una promesa; **~ s.o. company** hacer compañía a alguien; **~ s.o. waiting** hacer esperar a alguien; **he can't ~ anything to himself** no sabe guardar un secreto; **I kept the news of the accident to myself** no dije nada sobre el accidente; **~ sth from s.o.** ocultar algo a

alguien; **we kept the news from him** no le contamos la noticia **3** *v/i* (*pret & pp* **kept**) *of food, milk* aguantar, conservarse; **~ calm!** ¡tranquilízate!; **~ quiet!** ¡cállate!

♦ **keep away 1** *v/i*: **keep away from that building** no te acerques a ese edificio **2** *v/t*: **keep the children away from the stove** no dejes que los niños se acerquen a la cocina

♦ **keep back** *v/t* (*hold in check*) contener; *information* ocultar

♦ **keep down** *v/t voice* bajar; *costs, inflation etc* reducir; *food* retener; **tell the kids to keep the noise down** diles a los niños que no hagan tanto ruido; **I can't keep anything down** devuelvo todo lo que como

♦ **keep in** *v/t in school* castigar (*a quedarse en clase*); **the hospital's keeping her in** la tienen en observación

♦ **keep off 1** *v/t* (*avoid*) evitar; **keep off the grass!** ¡prohibido pisar el césped! **2** *v/i*: **if the rain keeps off** si no llueve

♦ **keep on 1** *v/i* continuar; **if you keep on interrupting me** si no de-

jas de interrumpirme; ***keep on
trying*** sigue intentándolo **2** *v/t*: ***the
company kept them on*** la empresa
los mantuvo en el puesto; ***keep
your coat on!*** ¡no te quites el abrigo!

♦ **keep on at** *v/t* (*nag*): ***my parents
keep on at me to get a job*** mis padres no dejan de decirme que bus-
que un trabajo

♦ **keep out 1** *v/t*: ***it keeps the cold
out*** protege del frío; ***they must be
kept out*** no pueden entrar **2** *v/i*: ***I
told you to keep out!*** *of a place* ¡te
dije que no entraras!; ***I would keep
out of it if I were you*** *of discussion
etc* yo en tu lugar no me metería;
keep out *as sign* prohibida la entrada, prohibido el paso

♦ **keep to** *v/t path* seguir; *rules* cumplir, respetar

♦ **keep up 1** *v/i when walking, running
etc* seguir *or* mantener el ritmo
(***with*** de); ***keep up with s.o.*** (*stay in
touch with*) mantener contacto con
alguien **2** *v/t pace* seguir, mantener;
payments estar al corriente de; *bridge, pants* sujetar

keep·ing ['kiːpɪŋ] *n*: ***be in ~ with***
decor combinar con; ***in ~ with***
promises de acuerdo con

'**keep·sake** recuerdo *m*

keg [keg] barril *m*

ken·nel ['kenl] *n* caseta *f* del perro

ken·nels ['kenlz] *npl* residencia *f* canina

kept [kept] *pret & pp* → **keep**

ker·nel ['kɜːrnl] almendra *f*

ker·o·sene ['kerəsiːn] queroseno *m*

ketch·up ['ketʃʌp] ketchup *m*

ket·tle ['ketl] hervidor *m*

key [kiː] **1** *n to door, drawer* llave *f*; *on
keyboard, piano* tecla *f*; *of piece of
music* clave *f*; *on map* leyenda *f* **2** *adj*
(*vital*) clave, crucial **3** *v/t & v/i*
COMPUT teclear

♦ **key in** *v/t data* introducir, teclear

'**key·board** COMPUT, MUS teclado *m*;
key·board·er COMPUT opera-
dor(a) *m(f)*, *persona que introduce
datos en el ordenador*; '**key·card** tar-

jeta *f* (de hotel)

keyed-up [kiːd'ʌp] *adj* nervioso

'**key·hole** ojo *m* de la cerradura;
'**key·note 'speech** discurso *m* central; '**key·ring** llavero *m*

kha·ki ['kækɪ] *adj* caqui

kick [kɪk] **1** *n* patada *f*; ***he got a ~ out
of watching them suffer*** disfrutó
viéndoles sufrir; (*just*) ***for ~s*** F por
diversión **2** *v/t* dar una patada a; F
habit dejar **3** *v/i of person* patalear;
of horse, mule cocear

♦ **kick around** *v/t ball* dar patadas a; F
(*discuss*) comentar

♦ **kick in** *v/t* P *money* apoquinar F

♦ **kick off** *v/i* comenzar, sacar de centro; F (*start*) empezar

♦ **kick out** *v/t of bar, company* echar;
of country, organization expulsar

♦ **kick up** *v/t*: ***kick up a fuss*** montar
un numerito

'**kick·back** F (*bribe*) soborno *m*

'**kick·off** SP saque *m*

kid [kɪd] **1** *n* F (*child*) crío *m* F, niño *m*;
when I was a ~ cuando era peque-
ño; ***~ brother*** hermano *m* pequeño;
~ sister hermana *f* pequeña **2** *v/t*
(*pret & pp* **-ded**) F tomar el pelo a **3** *v/i* (*pret & pp* **-ded**) F bromear; ***I
was only ~ding*** estaba bromeando

kid·der ['kɪdər] F vacilón *m* F

kid 'gloves: ***handle s.o. with ~*** tratar
a alguien con guante de seda

kid·nap ['kɪdnæp] *v/t* (*pret & pp*
-ped) secuestrar

kid·nap·(p)er ['kɪdnæpər] secuestrador *m*

'**kid·nap·(p)ing** ['kɪdnæpɪŋ] secuestro *m*

kid·ney ['kɪdnɪ] ANAT riñón *m*; *in
cooking* riñones *mpl*

'**kid·ney bean** alubia *f* roja de riñón

'**kid·ney ma·chine** MED riñón *m* artificial, máquina *f* de diálisis

kill [kɪl] *v/t* matar; ***the drought ~ed
all the plants*** las plantas murieron
como resultado de la sequía; ***I had
six hours to ~*** tenía seis horas sin
nada que hacer; ***be ~ed in an
accident*** matarse en un accidente,
morirse en un accidente; ***~ o.s.*** suici-

darse; ~ **o.s. laughing** F morirse de
risa F

kil·ler ['kılər] (*murderer*) asesino *m*;
be a ~ *of disease* ser mortal

kil·ling ['kılıŋ] *n* asesinato *m*; **make a
~** F (*lots of money*) forrarse F

kil·ling·ly ['kılıŋlı] *adv* F: ~ **funny**
para morirse de risa

kiln [kıln] horno *m*

ki·lo ['ki:lou] kilo *m*

ki·lo·byte ['kıloubaıt] COMPUT kilobyte *m*

ki·lo·gram ['kılougræm] kilogramo
m

ki·lo·me·ter, *Br* **ki·lo·me·tre**
[kı'lɑːmıtər] kilómetro *m*

kind¹ [kaınd] *adj* agradable, amable

kind² [kaınd] *n* (*sort*) tipo *m*; (*make,
brand*) marca *f*; **all ~s of people**
toda clase de personas; **I did
nothing of the ~!** ¡no hice nada parecido!; **~ of ...** *sad, lonely, etc* un
poco ...; **that's very ~ of you** gracias
por tu amabilidad

kin·der·gar·ten ['kındərgɑːrtn]
guardería *f*, jardín *m* de infancia

kind-heart·ed [kaınd'hɑːrtıd] *adj*
agradable, amable

kind·ly ['kaındlı] **1** *adj* amable, agradable **2** *adv* con amabilidad; **~ don't
interrupt** por favor, no me inte-
rrumpa; **~ lower your voice** ¿le importaría hablar más bajo?

kind·ness ['kaındnıs] amabilidad *f*

king [kıŋ] rey *m*

king·dom ['kıŋdəm] reino *m*

king-size(d) *adj* F *cigarettes* extra-
largo; **~ bed** cama *f* de matrimonio
grande

kink [kıŋk] *n in hose etc* doblez *f*

kink·y ['kıŋkı] *adj* F vicioso

ki·osk ['kiːɑːsk] quiosco *m*

kiss [kıs] **1** *n* beso *m* **2** *v/t* besar **3** *v/i*
besarse

kiss of 'life boca *f* a boca, respiración
f artificial; **give s.o. the ~** hacer a alguien el boca a boca

kit [kıt] (*equipment*) equipo *m*; **tool ~**
caja *f* de herramientas

kitch·en ['kıtʃın] cocina *f*

kitch·en·ette [kıtʃı'net] *cocina pe-*

queña

**kitch·en 'sink: you've got every-
thing but the ~** F llevas la casa a
cuestas F

kite [kaıt] *for flying* cometa *f*

kit·ten ['kıtn] gatito *m*

kit·ty ['kıtı] *money* fondo *m*

klutz [klʌts] F (*clumsy person*) mana-
zas *m* F

knack [næk] habilidad *f*; **he has a ~
of upsetting people** tiene la habilidad de disgustar a la gente; **I soon
got the ~ of the new machine** le
pillé el truco a la nueva máquina rápidamente

knead [niːd] *v/t dough* amasar

knee [niː] *n* rodilla *f*

'knee·cap *n* rótula *f*

kneel [niːl] *v/i* (*pret & pp* **knelt**) arrodillarse

'knee-length *adj* hasta la rodilla

knelt [nelt] *pret & pp →* **kneel**

knew [nuː] *pret →* **know**

knick-knacks ['nıknæks] *npl* F bara-
tijas *fpl*

knife [naıf] **1** *n* (*pl* **knives** [naıvz]) *for
food* cuchillo *m*; *carried outside* na-
vaja *f* **2** *v/t* acuchillar, apuñalar

knight [naıt] *n* caballero *m*

knit [nıt] **1** *v/t* (*pret & pp* **-ted**) tejer
2 *v/i* (*pret & pp* **-ted**) tricotar

♦ **knit together** *v/i of broken bone*
soldarse

knit·ting ['nıtıŋ] punto *m*

'knit·ting nee·dle aguja *f* para hacer
punto

'knit·wear prendas *fpl* de punto

knob [nɑːb] *on door* pomo *m*; *on
drawer* tirador *m*; *of butter* nuez *f*,
trocito *m*

knock [nɑːk] **1** *n on door*, (*blow*) golpe *m*; **there was a ~ on the door** llamaron a la puerta **2** *v/t* (*hit*) golpear;
F (*criticize*) criticar, meterse con
F; **he was ~ed to the ground** le
tiraron al suelo **3** *v/i on the door* lla-

♦ **knock around 1** *v/t* F (*beat*) pegar a
2 *v/i* F (*travel*) viajar

♦ **knock down** *v/t of car* atropellar;
building tirar; *object* tirar al suelo; F

K

(*reduce the price of*) rebajar
♦ **knock off 1** *v/t* P (*steal*) mangar P
2 *v/i* F (*stop work for the day*) acabar,
Span plegar F
♦ **knock out** *v/t* (*make unconscious*)
dejar K.O.; *of medicine* dejar para el
arrastre F; *power lines etc* destruir;
(*eliminate*) eliminar
♦ **knock over** *v/t* tirar; *of car* atropellar
'**knock·down** *adj*: *at a ~ price* tirado;
knock-kneed [nɑːkˈniːd] *adj* pati-
zambo; '**knock·out** *n in boxing* K.O.
m
knot [nɑːt] **1** *n* nudo *m* **2** *v/t* (*pret &*
pp **-ted**) anudar
knot·ty [ˈnɑːtɪ] *adj problem* complicado
know [noʊ] **1** *v/t* (*pret* **knew**, *pp*
known) *fact, language, how to do sth*
saber; *person, place* conocer;
(*recognize*) reconocer; *will you let*
him ~ that ...? ¿puedes decirle que
...? **2** *v/i* (*pret* **knew**, *pp* **known**) saber; *I don't ~* no (lo) sé; *yes, I ~* sí,
lo sé **3** *n*: *people in the ~* los entera-
dos
'**know·how** pericia *f*

know·ing [ˈnoʊɪŋ] *adj* cómplice
know·ing·ly [ˈnoʊɪŋlɪ] *adv* (*wittingly*)
deliberadamente; *smile etc* con com-
plicidad
'**know-it-all** F sabiondo F
knowl·edge [ˈnɑːlɪdʒ] conocimiento
m; *to the best of my ~* por lo que sé;
have a good ~ of ... tener buenos
conocimientos de ...
knowl·edge·a·ble [ˈnɑːlɪdʒəbl] *adj*:
she's very ~ about music sabe mucho de música
known [noʊn] *pp* → **know**
knuck·le [ˈnʌkl] nudillo *m*
♦ **knuckle down** *v/i* F aplicarse F
♦ **knuckle under** *v/i* F pasar por el
aro F
KO [keɪˈoʊ] (*knockout*) K.O.
Ko·ran [kəˈræn] Corán *m*
Ko·re·a [kəˈriːə] Corea
Ko·re·an [kəˈriːən] **1** *adj* coreano **2** *n*
coreano(a) *m(f)*; *language* coreano
m
ko·sher [ˈkoʊʃər] *adj* REL kosher; F
legal F
kow·tow [ˈkaʊtaʊ] *v/i* F reverenciar
ku·dos [ˈkjuːdɑːs] reconocimiento
m, prestigio *m*

L

lab [læb] laboratorio *m*
la·bel [ˈleɪbl] **1** *n* etiqueta *f* **2** *v/t* (*pret*
& pp **-ed**, *Br* **-led**) *bags* etiquetar
la·bor [ˈleɪbər] *n* (*work*) trabajo *m*; *in*
pregnancy parto *m*; *be in ~* estar de
parto
la·bor·a·to·ry [ˈlæbrətɔːrɪ] laboratorio *m*
la·bor·a·to·ry tech·ni·cian técni-
co(-a) *m(f)* de laboratorio
la·bored [ˈleɪbərd] *adj style, speech*
elaborado
la·bor·er [ˈleɪbərər] obrero(-a) *m(f)*
la·bo·ri·ous [ləˈbɔːrɪəs] *adj* laborioso

'**la·bor u·nion** sindicato *m*
'**la·bor ward** MED sala *f* de partos
la·bour *etc Br* → **labor** *etc*
lace [leɪs] *n material* encaje *m*; *for*
shoe cordón *m*
♦ **lace up** *v/t shoes* atar
lack [læk] **1** *n* falta *f*, carencia *f* **2** *v/t*
carecer de; *he ~s confidence* le fal-
ta confianza **3** *v/i*: *be ~ing* faltar
lac·quer [ˈlækər] *n for hair* laca *f*
lad [læd] muchacho *m*, chico *m*
lad·der [ˈlædər] *n* escalera *f* (de
mano)
la·den [ˈleɪdn] *adj* cargado (*with* de)

la·dies room ['leɪdi:z] servicio *m* de señoras

la·dle ['leɪdl] *n* cucharón *m*, cazo *m*

la·dy ['leɪdɪ] señora *f*

la·dy·bug mariquita *f*

la·dy·like *adj* femenino

lag [læg] *v/t* (*pret & pp -ged*) *pipes* revestir con aislante

♦ **lag behind** *v/i* quedarse atrás

la·ger ['lɑ:gər] cerveza *f* rubia

la·goon [lə'gu:n] laguna *f*

laid [leɪd] *pret & pp* → **lay**

laid-back [leɪd'bæk] *adj* tranquilo, despreocupado

lain [leɪn] *pp* → **lie**

lake [leɪk] lago *m*

lamb [læm] *animal, meat* cordero *m*

lame [leɪm] *adj person* cojo; *excuse* pobre

la·ment [lə'ment] **1** *n* lamento *m* **2** *v/t* lamentar

lam·en·ta·ble ['læməntəbl] *adj* lamentable

lam·i·nat·ed ['læmɪneɪtɪd] *adj surface* laminado; *paper* plastificado

lam·i·nat·ed 'glass cristal *m* laminado

lamp [læmp] lámpara *f*

'lamp·post farola *f*

'lamp·shade pantalla *f* (*de lámpara*)

land [lænd] **1** *n* tierra *f*; *by ~* por tierra; *on ~* en tierra; *work on the ~ as farmer* trabajar la tierra **2** *v/t airplane* aterrizar; *job* conseguir **3** *v/i of airplane* aterrizar; *of capsule on the moon* alunizar; *of ball, sth thrown* caer; *it ~ed right on top of his head* le cayó justo en la cabeza

land·ing ['lændɪŋ] *n of airplane* aterrizaje *m*; *on moon* alunizaje *m*; *of staircase* rellano *m*

'land·ing field pista *f* de aterrizaje; **'land·ing gear** tren *m* de aterrizaje; **'land·ing strip** pista *f* de aterrizaje

'land·la·dy *of hostel etc* dueña *f*; *of rented room* casera *f*; *Br: of bar* patrona *f*; **'land·lord** *of hostel etc* dueño *m*; *of rented room* casero *m*; *Br: of bar* patrón *m*; **'land·mark** punto *m* de referencia; *fig* hito *m*; **'land own·er** terrateniente *m/f*; **land·scape**

['lændskeɪp] **1** *n* (*also painting*) paisaje *m* **2** *adv print* en formato apaisado; **'land·slide** corrimiento *m* de tierras, **'land·slide 'vic·to·ry** victoria *f* arrolladora

lane [leɪn] *in country* camino *m*, vereda *f*; (*alley*) callejón *m*; MOT carril *m*

lan·guage ['læŋgwɪdʒ] lenguaje *m*; *of nation* idioma *f*, lengua *f*

'lan·guage lab laboratorio *m* de idiomas

lank [læŋk] *adj hair* lacio

lank·y ['læŋkɪ] *adj person* larguirucho

lan·tern ['læntərn] farol *f*

lap¹ [læp] *n of track* vuelta *f*

lap² [læp] *n of water* chapoteo *m*

♦ **lap up** *v/t* (*pret & pp -ped*) *drink, milk* beber a lengüetadas; *flattery* deleitarse con

lap³ [læp] *n of person* regazo *m*

la·pel [lə'pel] solapa *f*

lapse [læps] **1** *n* (*mistake, slip*) desliz *m*; *of time* lapso *m*; *a ~ of attention* un momento de distracción; *a ~ of memory* un olvido **2** *v/i of membership* vencer; *~ into silence / despair* sumirse en el silencio / la desesperación; *she ~d into English* empezó a hablar en inglés

lap·top ['læptɔ:p] COMPUT ordenador *m* portátil, *L.Am.* computadora *f* portátil

lar·ce·ny ['lɑ:rsənɪ] latrocinio *m*

lard [lɑ:rd] manteca *f* de cerdo

lar·der ['lɑ:rdər] despensa *f*

large [lɑ:rdʒ] *adj* grande; *be at ~ of criminal, wild animal* andar suelto

large·ly ['lɑ:rdʒlɪ] *adv* (*mainly*) en gran parte, principalmente

lark [lɑ:rk] *bird* alondra *f*

lar·va ['lɑ:rvə] larva *f*

lar·yn·gi·tis [lærɪn'dʒaɪtɪs] laringitis *f*

lar·ynx ['lærɪŋks] laringe *f*

la·ser ['leɪzər] láser *m*

'la·ser beam rayo *m* láser

'la·ser print·er impresora *f* láser

lash¹ [læʃ] *v/t with whip* azotar

♦ **lash down** *v/t with rope* amarrar

♦ **lash out** *v/i with fists, words* atacar (*at* a), arremeter (*at* contra)

lash² [læʃ] *n* (*eyelash*) pestaña *f*

last¹ [læst] **1** *adj in series* último; (*preceding*) anterior; **~ Friday** el viernes pasado; **~ but one** penúltimo; **~ night** anoche; **~ but not least** por último, pero no por ello menos importante **2** *adv* **at ~** por fin, al fin

last² [læst] *v/i* durar

last·ing ['læstɪŋ] *adj* duradero

last·ly ['læstlɪ] *adv* por último, finalmente

latch [lætʃ] *n* pestillo *m*

late [leɪt] **1** *adj:* **the bus is ~ again** el autobús vuelve a llegar tarde; **it's ~** es tarde; **it's getting ~** se está haciendo tarde; **of ~** últimamente, recientemente; **the ~ 19th century** la última parte del siglo XIX; **in the ~ 19th century** a finales del siglo XIX **2** *adv arrive, leave* tarde

late·ly ['leɪtlɪ] *adv* últimamente, recientemente

lat·er ['leɪtər] *adv* más tarde; **see you ~!** ¡hasta luego!; **~ on** más tarde

lat·est ['leɪtɪst] *adj news, girlfriend* último

lathe [leɪð] *n* torno *m*

la·ther ['lɑːðər] *n from soap* espuma *f*; **in a ~** (*sweaty*) empapado de sudor

Lat·in ['lætɪn] **1** *adj* latino **2** *n* latín *m*

Lat·in A'mer·i·ca Latinoamérica, América Latina

Lat·in A'mer·i·can 1 *n* latinoamericano(-a) *m(f)* **2** *adj* latinoamericano

La·ti·no [læ'tiːnoʊ] **1** *adj* latino **2** *n* latino(-a)

lat·i·tude ['lætɪtuːd] *geographical* latitud *f*; (*freedom to act*) libertad *f*

lat·ter ['lætər] **1** *adj* último **2** *n:* **Mr Brown and Mr White, of whom the ~ was ...** el Señor Brown y el Señor White, de quien el segundo *or* este último era ...

laugh [læf] **1** *n* risa *f*; **it was a ~** F fue genial **2** *v/i* reírse

◆ **laugh at** *v/t* reírse de

'laugh·ing stock: make o.s. a ~ ponerse en ridículo; **become a ~** ser el hazmerreír

laugh·ter ['læftər] risas *fpl*

launch [lɒːntʃ] *n small boat* lancha *f*; *of ship* botadura *f*; *of rocket, new product* lanzamiento *m* **2** *v/t rocket, new product* lanzar; *ship* botar

'launch cer·e·mo·ny ceremonia *f* de lanzamiento

'launch(·ing) pad plataforma *f* de lanzamiento

laun·der ['lɒːndər] *v/t clothes* lavar (y planchar); *money* blanquear

laun·dro·mat ['lɒːndrəmæt] lavandería *f*

laun·dry ['lɒːndrɪ] *place* lavadero *m*; *dirty clothes* ropa *f* sucia; *clean clothes* ropa *f* lavada; **do the ~** lavar la ropa, *Span* hacer la colada

lau·rel ['lɑːrəl] laurel *m*

lav·a·to·ry ['lævətɔːrɪ] *place* cuarto *m* de baño, lavabo *m*; *equipment* retrete *m*

lav·en·der ['lævəndər] espliego *m*, lavanda *f*

lav·ish ['lævɪʃ] *adj* espléndido

law [lɒː] ley *f*; *subject* derecho *m*; **be against the ~** estar prohibido, ser ilegal

law-a·bid·ing ['lɒːəbaɪdɪŋ] *adj* respetuoso con la ley

'law court juzgado *m*

law·ful ['lɒːfəl] *adj* legal; *wife* legítimo

law·less ['lɒːlɪs] *adj* sin ley

lawn [lɒːn] césped *m*

'lawn mow·er cortacésped *m*

'law·suit pleito *m*

law·yer ['lɒːjər] abogado(-a) *m(f)*

lax [læks] *adj* poco estricto

lax·a·tive ['læksətɪv] *n* laxante *m*

lay¹ [leɪ] *v/t* (*pret & pp* **laid**) (*put down*) dejar, poner; *eggs* poner; V *sexually* tirarse a V

lay² [leɪ] *pret* → **lie**

◆ **lay into** *v/t* (*attack*) arremeter contra

◆ **lay off** *v/t workers* despedir

◆ **lay on** *v/t* (*provide*) organizar

◆ **lay out** *v/t objects* colocar, disponer; *page* diseñar, maquetar

'lay-by *Br: on road* área *f* de descanso

lay·er ['leɪər] estrato *m*; *of soil, paint* capa *f*

'lay·man laico *m*

'**lay-off** despido *m*
'**lay-out** diseño *m*
♦ **laze around** [leɪz] *v/i* holgazanear
la·zy ['leɪzɪ] *adj person* holgazán, perezoso; *day* ocioso
lb *abbr* (= *pound*) libra *f* (*de peso*)
LCD [elsiː'diː] *abbr* (= *liquid crystal display*) LCD, pantalla *f* de cristal líquido
lead¹ [liːd] **1** *v/t* (*pret & pp* **led**) *procession, race* ir al frente de; *company, team* dirigir; (*guide, take*) conducir **2** *v/i* (*pret & pp* **led**) *in race, competition* ir en cabeza; (*provide leadership*) tener el mando; *a street ~ing off the square* una calle que sale de la plaza; *where is this ~ing?* ¿adónde nos lleva esto? **3** *n in race* ventaja *f*; *be in the ~* estar en cabeza; *take the ~* ponerse en cabeza; *lose the ~* perder la cabeza
♦ **lead on** *v/i* (*go in front*) ir delante
♦ **lead up to** *v/t* preceder a; *I wonder what she's leading up to* me pregunto a dónde quiere ir a parar
lead² [liːd] *for dog* correa *f*
lead³ [led] *substance* plomo *m*
lead·ed ['ledɪd] *adj gas* con plomo
lead·er ['liːdər] líder *m*
lead·er·ship ['liːdərʃɪp] *of party etc* liderazgo *m*
'**lead·er·ship con·test** pugna *f* por el liderazgo
lead-free ['ledfriː] *adj gas* sin plomo
lead·ing ['liːdɪŋ] *adj runner* en cabeza; *company, product* puntero
'**lead·ing-edge** *adj company* en la vanguardia; *technology* de vanguardia
leaf [liːf] (*pl* **leaves** [liːvz]) hoja *f*
♦ **leaf through** *v/t* hojear
leaf·let ['liːflət] folleto *m*
league [liːg] liga *f*
leak [liːk] **1** *n in roof* gotera *f*; *in pipe* agujero *m*; *of air, gas* fuga *f*, escape *m*; *of information* filtración *f* **2** *v/i of boat* hacer agua; *of pipe* tener un agujero; *of liquid, gas* fugarse, escaparse
♦ **leak out** *v/i of air, gas* fugarse, escaparse; *of news* filtrarse

leak·y ['liːkɪ] *adj pipe* con agujeros; *boat* que hace agua
lean¹ [liːn] **1** *v/i* (*be at an angle*) estar inclinado; *~ against sth* apoyarse en algo **2** *v/t* apoyar
lean² [liːn] *adj meat* magro; *style, prose* pobre, escueto
leap [liːp] **1** *n* salto *m*; *a great ~ forward* un gran salto adelante **2** *v/i* (*pret & pp* **-ed** *or* **leapt**) saltar; *he ~t over the fence* saltó la valla; *they ~t into the river* se tiraron al río
leapt [lept] *pret & pp* → **leap**
'**leap year** año *m* bisiesto
learn [lɜrn] **1** *v/t* aprender; (*hear*) enterarse de; *~ how to do sth* aprender a hacer algo **2** *v/i* aprender
learn·er ['lɜrnər] estudiante *m/f*
learn·ing ['lɜrnɪŋ] *n* (*knowledge*) conocimientos *mpl*; *act* aprendizaje *m*
'**learn·ing curve** curva *f* de aprendizaje; *be on the ~* tener que aprender cosas nuevas
lease [liːs] **1** *n* (contrato *m* de) arrendamiento *m* **2** *v/t apartment, equipment* arrendar
♦ **lease out** *v/t apartment, equipment* arrendar
lease 'pur·chase arrendamiento *m* con opción de compra
leash [liːʃ] *for dog* correa *f*
least [liːst] **1** *adj* (*slightest*) menor; *the ~ amount, money, baggage* menos; *there's not the ~ reason to ...* no hay la más mínima razón para que ... **2** *adv* menos **3** *n* lo menos; *he drank the ~* fue el que menos bebió; *not in the ~ surprised* en absoluto sorprendido; *at ~* por lo menos
leath·er ['leðər] **1** *n* piel *f*, cuero *m* **2** *adj* de piel, de cuero
leave [liːv] **1** *n* (*vacation*) permiso *m*; *on ~* de permiso **2** *v/t* (*pret & pp* **left**) *city, place* marcharse de, irse de; *person, food, memory,* (*forget*) dejar; *let's ~ things as they are* dejemos las cosas tal y como están; *how did you ~ things with him?* ¿cómo quedaron las cosas con él?; *~ s.o. / sth alone* (*not touch, not interfere with*) dejar a alguien / algo en paz; *be left*

L

quedar; *there is nothing left* no queda nada; *I only have one left* sólo me queda uno 3 *v/i* (*pret & pp* *left*) *of person* marcharse, irse; *of plane*, *train*, *bus* salir

♦ **leave behind** *v/t intentionally* dejar; (*forget*) dejarse

♦ **leave on** *v/t hat*, *coat* dejar puesto; *TV*, *computer* dejar encendido

♦ **leave out** *v/t word*, *figure* omitir; (*not put away*) no guardar; *leave me out of this* a mí no me metas en esto

'**leav·ing par·ty** fiesta *f* de despedida

lec·ture ['lektʃər] 1 *n* clase *f*; *to general public* conferencia *f* 2 *v/i at university* dar clases (*in* de); *to general public* dar una conferencia

'**lec·ture hall** sala *f* de conferencias

lec·tur·er ['lektʃərər] profesor(a) *m*(*f*)

LED [eli:'di:] *abbr* (= *light-emitting diode*) LED *m* (= diodo *m* emisor de luz)

led [led] *pret & pp* → **lead¹**

ledge [ledʒ] *of window* alféizar *f*; *on rock face* saliente *m*

ledg·er ['ledʒər] COM libro *m* mayor

leek [li:k] puerro *m*

leer [lɪr] *n sexual* mirada *f* impúdica; *evil* mirada *f* maligna

left¹ [left] 1 *adj* izquierdo 2 *n also* POL izquierda *f*; *on the* ~ a la izquierda; *to the* ~ *turn*, *look* a la izquierda 3 *adv turn*, *look* a la izquierda

left² [left] *pret & pp* → **leave**

'**left-hand** *adj* de la izquierda; *on your* ~ *side* a tu izquierda; **left-hand 'drive**: *this car is* ~ este coche tiene el volante a la izquierda; **left-'hand·ed** *adj* zurdo; **left 'lug·gage (of·fice)** *Br* consigna *f*; **left-o·vers** *npl food* sobras *fpl*; '**left-wing** *adj* POL izquierdista, de izquierdas

leg [leg] *of person* pierna *f*; *of animal* pata *f*; *pull s.o.'s* ~ tomar el pelo a alguien

leg·a·cy ['legəsɪ] legado *m*

le·gal ['li:gl] *adj* legal

le·gal ad'vis·er asesor(a) *m*(*f*) jurídico(-a)

le·gal·i·ty [lɪ'gælətɪ] legalidad *f*

le·gal·ize ['li:gəlaɪz] *v/t* legalizar

le·gend ['ledʒənd] leyenda *f*

le·gen·da·ry ['ledʒəndrɪ] *adj* legendario

le·gi·ble ['ledʒəbl] *adj* legible

le·gis·late ['ledʒɪsleɪt] *v/i* legislar

le·gis·la·tion [ledʒɪs'leɪʃn] legislación *f*

le·gis·la·tive ['ledʒɪslətɪv] *adj* legislativo

le·gis·la·ture ['ledʒɪslətʃər] POL legislativo *m*

le·git·i·mate [lɪ'dʒɪtɪmət] *adj* legítimo

'**leg room** espacio *m* para las piernas

lei·sure ['li:ʒər] ocio *m*; *I look forward to having more* ~ deseando tener más tiempo libre; *do it at your* ~ tómate tu tiempo para hacerlo

lei·sure·ly ['li:ʒəlɪ] *adj pace*, *lifestyle* tranquilo, relajado

'**lei·sure time** tiempo *m* libre

le·mon ['lemən] limón *m*

le·mon·ade [lemə'neɪd] limonada *f*

'**le·mon juice** zumo *m* de limón, *L.Am.* jugo *m* de limón

le·mon 'tea té *m* con limón

lend [lend] *v/t* (*pret & pp* **lent**) prestar

length [leŋθ] longitud *f*; (*piece*: *of material etc*) pedazo *m*; *at* ~ *describe*, *explain* detalladamente; (*finally*) finalmente

length·en ['leŋθən] *v/t* alargar

length·y ['leŋθɪ] *adj speech*, *stay* largo

le·ni·ent ['li:nɪənt] *adj* indulgente, poco severo

lens [lenz] *of camera* objetivo *m*, lente *f*; *of eyeglasses* cristal *m*; *of eye* cristalino *m*; (*contact* ~) lente *m* de contacto, *Span* lentilla *f*

'**lens cov·er** *of camera* tapa *f* del objetivo

Lent [lent] REL Cuaresma *f*

lent [lent] *pret & pp* → **lend**

len·til ['lentl] lenteja *f*

len·til 'soup sopa *f* de lentejas

Le·o ['li:ou] ASTR Leo *m*/*f inv*

leop·ard ['lepərd] leopardo *m*

le·o·tard ['li:outɑːrd] malla *f*

les·bi·an ['lezbɪən] 1 *n* lesbiana *f*

2 *adj* lésbico, lesbiano

less [les] *adv* menos; **it costs ~** cuesta menos; **~ than $200** menos de 200 dólares

les·sen ['lesn] **1** *v/t* disminuir **2** *v/i* reducirse, disminuir

les·son ['lesn] lección *f*

let [let] *v/t* (*pret & pp* **let**) (*allow*) dejar, permitir; **~ s.o. do sth** dejar a alguien hacer algo; **~ me go!** ¡déjame!; **~ him come in!** ¡déjale entrar!; **~'s go/ stay** vamos / quedémonos; **~'s not argue** no discutamos; **~ alone** mucho menos; **~ go of sth of rope, handle** soltar algo; **~ go of me!** ¡suéltame!

♦ **let down** *v/t hair* soltarse; *blinds* bajar; (*disappoint*) decepcionar, defraudar; *dress, pants* alargar

♦ **let in** *v/t to house* dejar pasar

♦ **let off** *v/t* (*not punish*) perdonar; *from car* dejar; **the court let him off with a small fine** el tribunal sólo le impuso una pequeña multa

♦ **let out** *v/t of room, building* alquilar, *Mex* rentar; *jacket etc* agrandar; *groan, yell* soltar

♦ **let up** *v/i* (*stop*) amainar

le·thal ['li:θl] *adj* letal

le·thar·gic [lɪ'θɑːrdʒɪk] *adj* aletargado, apático

leth·ar·gy ['leθərdʒɪ] sopor *m*, apatía *f*

let·ter ['letər] *of alphabet* letra *f*; *in mail* carta *f*

'**let·ter·box** *Br* buzón *m*; '**let·ter·head** (*heading*) membrete *m*; (*headed paper*) papel *m* con membrete; **let·ter of 'cred·it** COM carta *f* de crédito

let·tuce ['letɪs] lechuga *f*

'**let·up**: **without a ~** sin interrupción

leu·ke·mia [luːˈkiːmɪə] leucemia *f*

lev·el ['levl] **1** *adj field, surface* nivelado, llano; *in competition, scores* igualado; **draw ~ with s.o.** *in race* ponerse a la altura de alguien **2** *n on scale, in hierarchy, (amount)* nivel *m*; **on the ~** F (*honest*) honrado

lev·el-head·ed [levl'hedɪd] *adj* ecuánime, sensato

le·ver ['levər] **1** *n* palanca *f* **2** *v/t*: **~ sth open** abrir algo haciendo palanca

lev·er·age ['levrɪdʒ] apalancamiento *m*, (*influence*) influencia *f*

lev·y ['levɪ] *v/t* (*pret & pp* **-ied**) *taxes* imponer

lewd [luːd] *adj* obsceno

li·a·bil·i·ty [laɪəˈbɪlətɪ] (*responsibility*) responsabilidad *f*; (*likeliness*) propensión *f* (**to** a)

li·a·bil·i·ty in·sur·ance seguro *m* a terceros

li·a·ble ['laɪəbl] *adj* (*responsible*) responsable (**for** de); **be ~ to** (*likely*) ser propenso a

♦ **li·aise with** [lɪ'eɪz] *v/t* actuar de enlace con

li·ai·son [lɪ'eɪzɑːn] (*contacts*) contacto *m*, enlace *m*

li·ar [laɪr] mentiroso(-a) *m(f)*

li·bel ['laɪbl] **1** *n* calumnia *f*, difamación *f* **2** *v/t* calumniar, difamar

lib·e·ral ['lɪbərəl] *adj* (*broad-minded*), POL liberal; (*generous*: *portion etc*) abundante

lib·e·rate ['lɪbəreɪt] *v/t* liberar

lib·e·rat·ed ['lɪbəreɪtɪd] *adj* liberado

lib·e·ra·tion [lɪbə'reɪʃn] liberación *f*

lib·er·ty ['lɪbərtɪ] libertad *f*; **at ~ of prisoner etc** en libertad; **be at ~ to do sth** tener libertad para hacer algo

Li·bra ['liːbrə] ASTR Libra *m/f inv*

li·brar·i·an [laɪ'brerɪən] bibliotecario(-a) *m(f)*

li·bra·ry ['laɪbrerɪ] biblioteca *f*

Lib·y·a ['lɪbɪə] Libia

Lib·y·an ['lɪbɪən] **1** *adj* libio **2** *n* libio(-a) *m(f)*

lice [laɪs] *pl* → **louse**

li·cence *Br* → **license 1** *n*

li·cense ['laɪsns] **1** *n* permiso *m*, licencia *f* **2** *v/t* autorizar; **be ~d** tener permiso *or* licencia

'**li·cense num·ber** (*número m de*) matrícula *f*

'**li·cense plate** *of car* (placa *f* de) matrícula *f*

lick [lɪk] **1** *n* lamedura *f* **2** *v/t* lamer; **~ one's lips** relamerse

lick·ing ['lɪkɪŋ] F (*defeat*): **we got a ~** nos dieron una paliza F

L

li·co·rice ['lıkərıs] regaliz *m*

lid [lıd] (*top*) tapa *f*

lie¹ [laı] **1** *n* (*untruth*) mentira *f* **2** *v/i* mentir

lie² [laı] *v/i* (*pret* **lay,** *pp* **lain**) *of person* estar tumbado; *of object* estar; (*be situated*) estar, encontrarse; **~ on your stomach** túmbate boca abajo
♦ **lie down** *v/i* tumbarse

'lie-in: *Br* **have a ~** quedarse un rato más en la cama

lieu [luː]: **in ~ of** en lugar de

lieu·ten·ant [luˈtenənt] teniente *m/f*

life [laıf] (*pl* **lives** [laıvz]) vida *f*; *of machine* vida *f*, duración *f*; **that's ~!** ¡así es la vida!

'life belt salvavidas *m inv*; **'life·boat** *from ship* bote *m* salvavidas; *from land* lancha *f* de salvamento; **'life ex·pect·an·cy** esperanza *f* de vida; **'life·guard** socorrista *m/f*; **'life his·to·ry** historia *f* de la vida; **life im·pris·on·ment** cadena *f* perpetua; **'life in·sur·ance** seguro *m* de vida; **'life jack·et** chaleco *m* salvavidas

life·less ['laıflıs] *adj* sin vida

life·like ['laıflaık] *adj* realista

'life·long *adj* de toda la vida; **'life pre·serv·er** salvavidas *m inv*; **'life·sav·ing** *adj medical equipment, drug* que salva vidas; **'life·sized** *adj* de tamaño natural; **'life-threat·en·ing** *adj* que puede ser mortal; **'life·time** vida *f*; **in my ~** durante mi vida

lift [lıft] **1** *v/t* levantar **2** *v/i of fog* disiparse **3** *n Br* (*elevator*) ascensor *m*; **give s.o. a ~** llevar a alguien (en coche)
♦ **lift off** *v/i of rocket* despegar

'lift-off *of rocket* despegue *m*

lig·a·ment ['lıgəmənt] ligamento *m*

light¹ [laıt] **1** *n* luz *f*; **in the ~ of** a la luz de; **have you got a ~?** ¿tienes fuego? **2** *v/t* (*pret & pp* **-ed** *or* **lit**) *fire, cigarette* encender; (*illuminate*) iluminar **3** *adj color, sky* claro; *room* luminoso

light² [laıt] **1** *adj* (*not heavy*) ligero **2** *adv:* **travel ~** viajar ligero de equipaje

♦ **light up 1** *v/t* (*illuminate*) iluminar **2** *v/i* (*start to smoke*) encender un cigarrillo

'light bulb bombilla *f*

light·en¹ ['laıtn] *v/t color* aclarar

light·en² ['laıtn] *v/t load* aligerar

♦ **lighten up** *v/i of person* alegrarse; **come on, lighten up** venga, no te tomes las cosas tan en serio

light·er ['laıtər] *for cigarettes* encendedor *m*, *Span* mechero *m*

light-head·ed [laıt'hedıd] *adj* (*dizzy*) mareado; **light-'heart·ed** [laıt'hɑːrtıd] *adj* alegre; **'light·house** faro *m*

light·ing ['laıtıŋ] iluminación *f*

light·ly ['laıtlı] *adv touch* ligeramente; **get off ~** salir bien parado

light·ness¹ ['laıtnıs] *of room, color* claridad *f*

light·ness² ['laıtnıs] *in weight* ligereza *f*

light·ning ['laıtnıŋ]: **a flash of ~** un relámpago; **they were struck by ~** les cayó un rayo

'light·ning con·duc·tor pararrayos *m inv*

'light pen lápiz *m* óptico; **'light·weight** *n in boxing* peso *m* ligero; **'light year** año *m* luz

like¹ [laık] **1** *prep* como; **be ~ s.o.** ser como alguien; **what is she ~?** ¿cómo es?; **it's not ~ him** (*not his character*) no es su estilo **2** *conj* F (*as*) como; **~ I said** como dije

like² [laık] *v/t:* **I ~ it / her** me gusta; **I would ~ ...** querría ...; **I would ~ to ...** me gustaría ...; **would you ~ ...?** ¿querrías ...?; **would you ~ to ...?** ¿querrías ...?; **she ~s to swim** le gusta nadar; **if you** ~ si quieres

like·a·ble ['laıkəbl] *adj* simpático

like·li·hood ['laıklıhʊd] probabilidad *f*; **in all ~** con toda probabilidad

like·ly ['laıklı] *adj* (*probable*) probable; **not ~!** ¡ni hablar!

like·ness ['laıknıs] (*resemblance*) parecido *m*

'like·wise ['laıkwaız] *adv* igualmente; **pleased to meet you – ~!** encantado de conocerle – ¡lo mismo digo!

lik·ing ['laɪkɪŋ] afición *f* (*for* a); *to your* ~ a su gusto; *take a* ~ *to s.o.* tomar cariño a alguien

li·lac ['laɪlək] *flower* lila *f*; *color* lila *m*

li·ly ['lɪlɪ] lirio *m*

li·ly of the 'val·ley lirio *m* de los valles

limb [lɪm] miembro *m*

lime¹ [laɪm] *fruit, tree* lima *f*

lime² [laɪm] *substance* cal *f*

lime'green *adj* verde lima

'lime·light: be in the ~ estar en el candelero

lim·it ['lɪmɪt] **1** *n* límite *m*; *within* ~*s* dentro de un límite; *be off* ~*s of place* ser zona prohibida; *that's the* ~! ¡es el colmo! F **2** *v/t* limitar

lim·i·ta·tion [lɪmɪ'teɪʃn] limitación *f*

lim·it·ed 'com·pa·ny *Br* sociedad *f* limitada

li·mo ['lɪmoʊ] F limusina *f*

lim·ou·sine ['lɪməziːn] limusina *f*

limp¹ [lɪmp] *adj* flojo

limp² [lɪmp] *n*: *he has a* ~ cojea

line¹ [laɪn] *n of text, on road*, TELEC línea *f*; *of trees* fila *f*, hilera *f*; *of people* fila *f*, cola *f*; *of business* especialidad *f*; *what* ~ *are you in?* ¿a qué te dedicas?; *the* ~ *is busy* está ocupado, *Span* está comunicando; *hold the* ~ no cuelgue; *draw the* ~ *at sth* no estar dispuesto a hacer algo; ~ *of inquiry* línea *f* de investigación; ~ *of reasoning* argumentación *f*; *stand in* ~ hacer cola; *in* ~ *with ...* (*conforming with*) en las mismas líneas que

line² [laɪn] *v/t with lining* forrar

♦ **line up** *v/i* hacer cola

lin·e·ar ['lɪnɪər] *adj* lineal

lin·en ['lɪnɪn] *material* lino *m*; (*sheets etc*) ropa *f* blanca

lin·er ['laɪnər] *ship* transatlántico *m*

lines·man ['laɪnzmən] SP juez *m* de línea, linier *m*

lin·ger ['lɪŋgər] *v/i of person* entretenerse; *of pain* persistir

lin·ge·rie ['lænʒəriː] lencería *f*

lin·guist ['lɪŋgwɪst] lingüista *m/f*; *she's a good* ~ se le dan bien los idiomas

lin·guis·tic [lɪŋ'gwɪstɪk] *adj* lingüístico

lin·ing ['laɪnɪŋ] *of clothes* forro *m*; *of brakes, pipe* revestimiento *m*

link [lɪŋk] **1** *n* (*connection*) conexión *f*; *between countries* vínculo *m*; *in chain* eslabón *m* **2** *v/t* conectar

♦ **link up** *v/i* encontrarse; TV conectar

li·on ['laɪən] león *m*

lip [lɪp] labio *m*

'lip·read *v/i* (*pret & pp* **-read** [red]) leer los labios

'lip·stick barra *f* de labios

li·queur [lɪ'kjʊr] licor *m*

liq·uid ['lɪkwɪd] **1** *n* líquido *m* **2** *adj* líquido

liq·ui·date ['lɪkwɪdeɪt] *v/t assets* liquidar; F (*kill*) cepillarse a F

liq·ui·da·tion [lɪkwɪ'deɪʃn] liquidación *f*; *go into* ~ ir a la quiebra

liq·ui·di·ty [lɪ'kwɪdɪtɪ] FIN liquidez *f*

liq·uid·ize ['lɪkwɪdaɪz] *v/t* licuar

liq·uid·iz·er ['lɪkwɪdaɪzər] licuadora *f*

liq·uor ['lɪkər] bebida *f* alcohólica

'liq·uor store tienda *f* de bebidas alcohólicas

lisp [lɪsp] **1** *n* ceceo *m* **2** *v/i* cecear

list [lɪst] **1** *n* lista *f* **2** *v/t* enumerar; COMPUT listar

lis·ten ['lɪsn] *v/i* escuchar; *I tried to persuade him, but he wouldn't* ~ intenté convencerle, pero no me hizo ningún caso

♦ **listen in** *v/i* escuchar

♦ **listen to** *v/t radio, person* escuchar

lis·ten·er ['lɪsnər] *to radio* oyente *m/f*; *he's a good* ~ sabe escuchar

list·ings mag·a·zine ['lɪstɪŋz] guía *f* de espectáculos

list·less ['lɪstlɪs] *adj* apático, lánguido

lit [lɪt] *pret & pp* → **light**

li·ter ['liːtər] litro *m*

lit·e·ral ['lɪtərəl] *adj* literal

lit·e·ral·ly ['lɪtərəlɪ] *adv* literalmente

lit·e·ra·ry ['lɪtərerɪ] *adj* literario

lit·e·rate ['lɪtərət] *adj* culto; *be* ~ saber leer y escribir

lit·e·ra·ture ['lɪtrətʃər] literatura *f*; *about a product* folletos *mpl*, prospectos *mpl*

li·tre *Br* → **liter**

lit·ter ['lɪtər] basura *f*; *of animal* camada *f*

'**lit·ter bas·ket** *Br* papelera *f*

lit·tle ['lɪtl] **1** *adj* pequeño; *the ~ ones* los pequeños **2** *n* poco *m*; *the ~ I know* lo poco que sé; *a ~* un poco; *a ~ bread/wine* un poco de pan/vino; *a ~ is better than nothing* más vale poco que nada **3** *adv* poco; *~ by ~* poco a poco; *a ~ better/bigger* un poco mejor/más grande; *a ~ before 6* un poco antes de las 6

live¹ [lɪv] *v/i* vivir

♦ **live on 1** *v/t* rice, bread sobrevivir a base de **2** *v/i (continue living)* sobrevivir, vivir

♦ **live up**: *live it up* pasarlo bien

♦ **live up to** *v/t* responder a

♦ **live with** *v/t person* vivir con

live² [laɪv] *adj broadcast* en directo; *ammunition* real; *wire* con corriente

live·li·hood ['laɪvlɪhʊd] vida *f*, sustento *m*; *earn one's ~* ganarse la vida

live·li·ness ['laɪvlɪnɪs] *of person, music* vivacidad *f*; *of debate* lo animado

live·ly ['laɪvlɪ] *adj* animado

liv·er ['lɪvər] MED, *food* hígado *m*

live·stock ['laɪvstɑːk] ganado *m*

liv·id ['lɪvɪd] *adj (angry)* enfurecido, furioso

liv·ing ['lɪvɪŋ] **1** *adj* vivo **2** *n* vida *f*; *what do you do for a ~?* ¿en qué trabajas?; *earn one's ~* ganarse la vida; *standard of ~* estándar *m* de vida

'**liv·ing room** sala *f* de estar, salón *m*

liz·ard ['lɪzərd] lagarto *m*

load [loʊd] **1** *n also* ELEC carga *f*; *~s of* F montones de F **2** *v/t car, truck, gun* cargar; *camera* poner el carrete a; COMPUT: *software* cargar (en memoria)

load·ed ['loʊdɪd] F *adj (very rich)* forrado F; *(drunk)* como una cuba

loaf [loʊf] *n (pl loaves* [loʊvz]*)* pan *m*; *a ~ of bread* una barra de pan, un pan

♦ **loaf around** *v/i* F gandulear F

loaf·er ['loʊfər] *shoe* mocasín *m*

loan [loʊn] **1** *n* préstamo *m*; *on ~* prestado **2** *v/t* prestar; *~ s.o. sth* prestar algo a alguien

loathe [loʊð] *v/t* detestar, aborrecer

loath·ing ['loʊðɪŋ] odio *m*, aborrecimiento *m*

lob·by ['lɑːbɪ] *n in hotel, theater* vestíbulo *m*; POL lobby *m*, grupo *m* de presión

lobe [loʊb] *of ear* lóbulo *m*

lob·ster ['lɑːbstər] langosta *f*

lo·cal ['loʊkl] **1** *adj* local; *the ~ people* la gente del lugar; *I'm not ~* no soy de aquí **2** *n*: *the ~s* los del lugar; *are you a ~?* ¿eres de aquí?

'**lo·cal call** TELEC llamada *f* local; **lo·cal e'lec·tions** *npl* elecciones *fpl* municipales; **lo·cal 'gov·ern·ment** administración *f* municipal

lo·cal·i·ty [loʊ'kælətɪ] localidad *f*

lo·cal·ly ['loʊkəlɪ] *adv live, work* cerca, en la zona; *it's well known ~* es muy conocido en la zona; *they are grown ~* son cultivados en la región

lo·cal 'pro·duce productos *mpl* del lugar

'**lo·cal time** hora *f* local

lo·cate [loʊ'keɪt] *v/t new factory etc* emplazar, ubicar; *(identify position of)* situar; *be ~d* encontrarse

lo·ca·tion [loʊ'keɪʃn] *(siting)* emplazamiento *m*; *(identifying position of)* localización *f*; *on ~ movie* en exteriores

lock¹ [lɑːk] *of hair* mechón *m*

lock² [lɑːk] **1** *n on door* cerradura *f* **2** *v/t door* cerrar (con llave)

♦ **lock away** *v/t* guardar bajo llave

♦ **lock in** *v/t person* encerrar

♦ **lock out** *v/t of house* dejar fuera; *I locked myself out* me dejé las llaves dentro

♦ **lock up** *v/t in prison* encerrar

lock·er ['lɑːkər] taquilla *f*

'**lock·er room** vestuario *m*

'**lock·et** ['lɑːkɪt] guardapelo *m*

lock·smith ['lɑːksmɪθ] cerrajero(-a) *m(f)*

lo·cust ['loʊkəst] langosta *f*

lodge [lɑːdʒ] **1** *v/t complaint* presentar **2** *v/i of bullet* alojarse

lodg·er [ˈlɑːdʒər] húesped *m/f*

loft [lɑːft] buhardilla *f*, desván *m*

loft·y [ˈlɑːftɪ] *adj heights*, *ideals* elevado

log [lɑːg] *n wood* tronco *m*; *written record* registro *m*

◆ **log off** *v/i* (*pret & pp* **-ged**) salir

◆ **log on** *v/i* entrar

◆ **log on to** *v/t* entrar a

'**log·book** *captain's* cuaderno *m* de bitácora; *driver's* documentación *f* del vehículo

log 'cab·in cabaña *f*

log·ger·heads [ˈlɑːgərhedz]: **be at ~** estar enfrentado

lo·gic [ˈlɑːdʒɪk] lógica *f*

lo·gic·al [ˈlɑːdʒɪkl] *adj* lógico

lo·gic·al·ly [ˈlɑːdʒɪklɪ] *adv* lógicamente

lo·gis·tics [ləˈdʒɪstɪks] logística *f*

lo·go [ˈlougou] logotipo *m*

loi·ter [ˈlɔɪtər] *v/i* holgazanear

lol·li·pop [ˈlɑːlɪpɑːp] piruleta *f*

Lon·don [ˈlʌndən] Londres

lone·li·ness [ˈlounlɪnɪs] *of person*, *place* soledad *f*

lone·ly [ˈlounlɪ] *adj person* solo; *place* solitario

lon·er [ˈlounər] solitario(-a) *m(f)*

long[1] [lɔːŋ] **1** *adj* largo; *it's a ~ way* hay un largo camino; *it's two feet ~* mide dos pies de largo; *the movie is three hours ~* la película dura tres horas **2** *adv* mucho tiempo; *don't be ~* no tardes mucho; *5 weeks is too ~* 5 semanas son mucho tiempo; *will it take ~?* ¿llevará mucho tiempo?; *that was ~ ago* eso fue hace mucho tiempo; *before ~* al poco tiempo; *we can't wait any ~er* no podemos esperar más tiempo; *she no ~er works here* ya no trabaja aquí; *so ~ as* (*provided*) siempre que; *so ~!* ¡hasta la vista!

long[2] [lɔːŋ] *v/i*: *~ for sth home* echar en falta algo; *change* anhelar *or* desear algo; *be ~ing to do sth* anhelar *or* desear hacer algo

long-'dis·tance *adj race* de fondo; *flight* de larga distancia; *a ~ phone-call* una llamada de larga distancia, una conferencia interurbana

lon·gev·i·ty [lɑːnˈdʒevɪtɪ] longevidad *f*

long·ing [ˈlɔːŋɪŋ] *n* anhelo *m*, deseo *m*

lon·gi·tude [ˈlɑːŋgɪtuːd] longitud *f*

'**long jump** salto *m* de longitud; '**long-range** *adj missile* de largo alcance; *forecast* a largo plazo; **long-sight·ed** [lɔːŋˈsaɪtɪd] *adj* hipermétrope; **long-sleeved** [lɔːŋˈsliːvd] *adj* de manga larga; **long-'stand·ing** *adj* antiguo; '**long-term** *adj* a largo plazo; ' **long wave** RAD onda *f* larga; '**long-wind·ed** [lɔːŋˈwɪndɪd] *adj* prolijo

look [luk] **1** *n* (*appearance*) aspecto *m*; (*glance*) mirada *f*; *give s.o.* / *sth a ~* mirar a alguien / mirar algo; *have a ~ at sth* (*examine*) echar un vistazo a algo; *can I have a ~?* ¿puedo echarle un vistazo?; *can I have a ~ around?* *in store etc* ¿puedo echar un vistazo?; *~s* (*beauty*) atractivo *m*, guapura *f* **2** *v/i* mirar; (*search*) buscar; (*seem*) parecer; *you ~ tired* / *different* pareces cansado / diferente; *he ~s about 25* aparenta 25 años; *how do things ~ to you?* ¿qué te parece cómo están las cosas?; *that ~s good* se ve muy buena pinta

◆ **look after** *v/t children* cuidar (de); *property*, *interests* proteger

◆ **look ahead** *v/i fig* mirar hacia el futuro

◆ **look around 1** *v/i* mirar **2** *v/t museum*, *city* dar una vuelta por

◆ **look at** *v/t* mirar; (*examine*) estudiar; (*consider*) considerar; *it depends how you look at it* depende de cómo lo mires

◆ **look back** *v/i* mirar atrás

◆ **look down on** *v/t* mirar por encima del hombro a

◆ **look for** *v/t* buscar

◆ **look forward to** *v/t* estar deseando; *I'm looking forward to the vacation* tengo muchas ganas de empezar las vacaciones

♦ **look in on** v/t (*visit*) hacer una visita a

♦ **look into** v/t (*investigate*) investigar

♦ **look on 1** v/i (*watch*) quedarse mirando **2** v/t: **look on s.o./ sth as** (*consider*) considerar a alguien/ algo como

♦ **look out** v/t *garden, street* dar a

♦ **look out** v/i *through, from window etc* mirar; (*pay attention*) tener cuidado; **look out!** ¡cuidado!

♦ **look out for** v/t *buscar*; (*be on guard against*) tener cuidado con

♦ **look out of** v/t *window* mirar por

♦ **look over** v/t *translation* revisar, repasar; *house* inspeccionar

♦ **look through** v/t *magazine, notes* echar un vistazo a, hojear

♦ **look to** v/t (*rely on*): **we look to you for help** acudimos a usted en busca de ayuda

♦ **look up 1** v/i *from paper etc* levantar la mirada; (*improve*) mejorar **2** v/t *word, phone number* buscar; (*visit*) visitar

♦ **look up to** v/t (*respect*) admirar

'**look•out** *person* centinela *m*, vigía *m*; **be on the ~ for** estar buscando

♦ **loom up** [luːm] v/i aparecer (*out of* de entre)

loon•y ['luːnɪ] **1** n F chalado(-a) m(f) F **2** adj F chalado F

loop [luːp] n bucle m

'**loop•hole** *in law etc* resquicio m or vacío m legal

loose [luːs] *adj connection, button* suelto; *clothes* suelto, holgado; *morals* disoluto, relajado; *wording* impreciso; **~ change** suelto m, L.Am. sencillo m; **~ ends** of problem, discussion cabos mpl sueltos

loose•ly ['luːslɪ] *adv worded* vagamente

loos•en ['luːsn] v/t *collar, knot* aflojar

loot [luːt] **1** n botín m **2** v/i saquear

loot•er ['luːtər] saqueador(a) m(f)

♦ **lop off** [lɑːp] v/t (*pret & pp* **-ped**) *branch* cortar; podar

lop-sid•ed [lɑːp'saɪdɪd] *adj* torcido; *balance of committee etc* desigual

Lord [lɔːrd] (*God*) Señor m

Lord's 'Prayer padrenuestro m

lor•ry ['lɒrɪ] Br camión m

lose [luːz] **1** v/t (*pret & pp* **lost**) *object, match* perder **2** v/i (*pret & pp* **lost**) SP perder; *of clock* retrasarse; **I'm lost** me he perdido; **get lost!** F ¡vete a paseo!

♦ **lose out** v/i salir perdiendo

los•er ['luːzər] perdedor(-a) m(f); F *in life* fracasado(-a) m(f)

loss [lɑːs] pérdida f; **make a ~** tener pérdidas; **I'm at a ~ what to say** no sé qué decir

lost [lɑːst] **1** adj perdido **2** pret & pp → **lose**

lost-and-'found, Br **lost 'prop•er•ty** (**of•fice**) oficina f de objetos perdidos

lot [lɑːt]: **a ~** (*of*), **~s** (*of*) mucho, muchos; **a ~ of books**, **~s of books** muchos libros; **a ~ of butter**, **~s of butter** mucha mantequilla; **a ~ better/ easier** mucho mejor/más fácil

lo•tion ['loʊʃn] loción f

lot•te•ry ['lɑːtərɪ] lotería f

loud [laʊd] *adj voice, noise* fuerte; *music* fuerte, alto; *color* chillón

loud'speak•er altavoz m, L.Am. altoparlante m

lounge [laʊndʒ] *in house* salón m

♦ **lounge around** v/i holgazanear

'**lounge suit** Br traje m de calle

louse [laʊs] (*pl lice* [laɪs]) piojo m

lous•y ['laʊzɪ] *adj* F asqueroso F; **I feel ~** me siento de pena F

lout [laʊt] gamberro m

lov•a•ble ['lʌvəbl] *adj* adorable, encantador

love [lʌv] **1** n amor m; *in tennis* nada f; **be in ~** estar enamorado (**with** de); **fall in ~** enamorarse (**with** de); **make ~** hacer el amor; **make ~ to ...** hacer el amor con; **yes, my ~** sí, amor **2** v/t *person, country, wine* amar; **she ~s to watch tennis** le encanta ver tenis

'**love af•fair** aventura f amorosa; '**love let•ter** carta f de amor; '**love-life** vida f amorosa

love·ly ['lʌvlɪ] *adj face, hair, color, tune* precioso, lindo; *person, character* encantador; *holiday, weather, meal* estupendo; **we had a ~ time** nos lo pasamos de maravilla

lov·er ['lʌvər] amante *m/f*

lov·ing ['lʌvɪŋ] *adj* cariñoso

lov·ing·ly ['lʌvɪŋlɪ] *adv* con cariño

low [loʊ] **1** *adj bridge, salary, price, voice, quality* bajo; **be feeling ~** estar deprimido; **we're ~ on gas / tea** nos queda poca gasolina / té **2** *n in weather* zona *f* de bajas presiones, borrasca *f*; *in sales, statistics* mínimo *m*

low·brow ['loʊbraʊ] *adj* poco intelectual, popular; **low-'cal·o·rie** *adj* bajo en calorías; **'low-cut** *adj dress* escotado

low·er ['loʊər] *v/t to the ground, hemline, price* bajar; *flag* arriar; *pressure* reducir

'low-fat *adj* de bajo contenido graso; **'low·key** *adj* discreto, mesurado; **'low·lands** *npl* tierras *fpl* bajas; **low-'pres·sure ar·e·a** zona *f* de bajas presiones, borrasca *f*; **low 'sea·son** temporada *f* baja; **'low tide** marea *f* baja

loy·al ['lɔɪəl] *adj* leal, fiel (**to** a)

loy·al·ly ['lɔɪəlɪ] *adv* lealmente, fielmente

loy·al·ty ['lɔɪəltɪ] lealtad *f* (**to** a)

loz·enge ['lɑːzɪndʒ] *shape* rombo *m*; *tablet* pastilla *f*

Ltd *abbr* (= **limited**) S.L. (= sociedad *f* limitada)

lu·bri·cant ['luːbrɪkənt] lubricante *m*

lu·bri·cate ['luːbrɪkeɪt] *v/t* lubricar

lu·bri·ca·tion [luːbrɪ'keɪʃn] lubricación *f*

lu·cid ['luːsɪd] *adj* (*clear, sane*) lúcido

luck [lʌk] suerte *f*; **bad** ~ mala suerte; **good ~!** ¡buena suerte!

♦ **luck out** *v/i* F tener mucha suerte

luck·i·ly ['lʌkɪlɪ] *adv* afortunadamente, por suerte

luck·y ['lʌkɪ] *adj person, coincidence* afortunado; *day, number* de la suerte; **you were ~** tuviste suerte; **she's**

~ to be alive tiene suerte de estar con vida; **that's ~!** ¡qué suerte!

lu·cra·tive ['luːkrətɪv] *adj* lucrativo

lu·di·crous ['luːdɪkrəs] *adj* ridículo

lug [lʌg] *v/t* (*pret & pp* **-ged**) arrastrar

lug·gage ['lʌgɪdʒ] equipaje *m*

luke·warm ['luːkwɔːrm] *adj water* tibio, templado; *reception* indiferente

lull [lʌl] **1** *n in storm, fighting* tregua *f*; *in conversation* pausa *f* **2** *v/t*: **~ s.o. into a false sense of security** dar a alguien una falsa sensación de seguridad

lul·la·by ['lʌləbaɪ] canción *f* de cuna, nana *f*

lum·ba·go [lʌm'beɪgoʊ] lumbago *m*

lum·ber ['lʌmbər] *n* (*timber*) madera *f*

lu·mi·nous ['luːmɪnəs] *adj* luminoso

lump [lʌmp] *n of sugar, earth* terrón *m*; (*swelling*) bulto *m*

♦ **lump together** *v/t* agrupar

lump 'sum pago *m* único

lump·y ['lʌmpɪ] *adj liquid, sauce* grumoso; *mattress* lleno de bultos

lu·na·cy ['luːnəsɪ] locura *f*

lu·nar ['luːnər] *adj* lunar

lu·na·tic ['luːnətɪk] *n* lunático(-a) *m(f)*, loco(-a) *m(f)*

lunch [lʌntʃ] *n* almuerzo *m*, comida *f*; **have ~** almorzar, comer

'lunch box fiambrera *f*; **'lunch break** pausa *f* para el almuerzo; **'lunch hour** hora *f* del almuerzo; **'lunchtime** hora *f* del almuerzo

lung [lʌŋ] pulmón *m*

'lung can·cer cáncer *m* de pulmón

♦ **lunge at** [lʌndʒ] *v/t* arremeter contra

lurch [lɜːrtʃ] *v/i of drunk* tambalearse; *of ship* dar sacudidas

lure [lʊr] **1** *n* atractivo *m* **2** *v/t* atraer

lu·rid ['lʊrɪd] *adj color* chillón; *details* espeluznante

lurk [lɜːrk] *v/i of person* estar oculto, estar al acecho

lus·cious ['lʌʃəs] *adj fruit, dessert* jugoso, exquisito; F *woman, man* cautivador

lush [lʌʃ] *adj vegetation* exuberante

lust [lʌst] *n* lujuria *f*

L

lux·u·ri·ous [lʌgˈʒʊrɪəs] *adj* lujoso

lux·u·ri·ous·ly [lʌgˈʒʊrɪəslɪ] *adv* lujosamente

lux·u·ry [ˈlʌkʃərɪ] **1** *n* lujo *m* **2** *adj* de lujo

lymph gland [ˈlɪmfglænd] ganglio *m* linfático

lynch [lɪntʃ] *v/t* linchar

lyr·i·cist [ˈlɪrɪsɪst] letrista *m/f*

lyr·ics [ˈlɪrɪks] *npl* letra *f*

M

MA [emˈeɪ] *abbr* (= **Master of Arts**) Máster *m* en Humanidades

ma'am [mæm] señora *f*

ma·chine [məˈʃiːn] **1** *n* máquina *f* **2** *v/t with sewing machine* coser a máquina; TECH trabajar a máquina

ma·chine gun *n* ametralladora *f*

ma·chine-'read·a·ble *adj* legible por *Span* el ordenador *or L.Am.* la computadora

ma·chin·e·ry [məˈʃiːnərɪ] (*machines*) maquinaria *f*

ma·chine trans·la·tion traducción *f* automática

ma·chis·mo [məˈkɪzmoʊ] machismo *m*

mach·o [ˈmætʃoʊ] *adj* macho

mack·in·tosh [ˈmækɪntɑːʃ] impermeable *m*

mac·ro [ˈmækroʊ] COMPUT macro *m*

mad [mæd] *adj* (*insane*) loco; F (*angry*) enfadado; *a ~ idea* una idea disparatada; *be ~ about* F estar loco por; *drive s.o. ~* volver loco a alguien; *go ~* (*become insane, with enthusiasm*) volverse loco; *like ~* F *run, work* como un loco F; *Pa got real ~ when I told him* papá se puso hecho una furia cuando se lo conté

mad·den [ˈmædən] *v/t* (*infuriate*) sacar de quicio

mad·den·ing [ˈmædnɪŋ] *adj* exasperante

made [meɪd] *pret & pp* → **make**

'mad·house *fig* casa *f* de locos

mad·ly [ˈmædlɪ] *adv* como loco; *~ in love* locamente enamorado

'mad·man loco *m*

mad·ness [ˈmædnɪs] locura *f*

Ma·don·na [məˈdɑːnə] madona *f*

Ma·fi·a [ˈmɑːfɪə]: *the ~* la mafia

mag·a·zine [mægəˈziːn] *printed* revista *f*

mag·got [ˈmægət] gusano *m*

Ma·gi [ˈmeɪdʒaɪ] REL: *the ~* los Reyes Magos

mag·ic [ˈmædʒɪk] **1** *n* magia *f*; *as if by ~*, *like ~* como por arte de magia **2** *adj* mágico; *there's nothing ~ about it* no tiene nada de mágico

mag·i·cal [ˈmædʒɪkl] *adj* mágico

ma·gi·cian [məˈdʒɪʃn] *performer* mago(-a) *m(f)*

ma·gic 'spell hechizo *m*; **ma·gic 'trick** truco *m* de magia; **mag·ic 'wand** varita *f* mágica

mag·nan·i·mous [mægˈnænɪməs] *adj* magnánimo

mag·net [ˈmægnɪt] imán *m*

mag·net·ic [mægˈnetɪk] *adj* magnético; *fig: personality* cautivador

mag·net·ic 'stripe banda *f* magnética

mag·net·ism [ˈmægnetɪzm] *of person* magnetismo *m*

mag·nif·i·cence [mægˈnɪfɪsəns] magnificencia *f*

mag·nif·i·cent [mægˈnɪfɪsənt] *adj* magnífico

mag·ni·fy [ˈmægnɪfaɪ] *v/t* (*pret & pp -ied*) aumentar; *difficulties* magnificar

'mag·ni·fy·ing glass lupa *f*

mag·ni·tude ['mægnɪtuːd] magnitud f

ma·hog·a·ny [mə'hɑːgənɪ] caoba f

maid [meɪd] (*servant*) criada f; *in hotel* camarera f

'**maid·en name** ['meɪdn] apellido m de soltera

maid·en 'voy·age viaje m inaugural

mail [meɪl] **1** n correo m; **put sth in the ~** echar algo al correo **2** v/t *letter* enviar (por correo)

'**mail·box** *also* COMPUT buzón m

'**mail·ing list** lista f de direcciones

'**mail·man** cartero m; **mail-'or·der cat·a·log**, *Br* **mail-'or·der cat·a·logue** catálogo m de venta por correo; **mail-'or·der firm** empresa f de venta por correo; '**mail·shot** mailing m

maim [meɪm] v/t mutilar

main [meɪn] *adj* principal; **she's alive, that's the ~ thing** está viva, que es lo principal

'**main course** plato m principal; **main 'en·trance** entrada f principal; '**main·frame** *Span* ordenador m central, *L.Am.* computadora f central; '**main·land** tierra f firme; **on the ~** en el continente

main·ly ['meɪnlɪ] *adv* principalmente

main 'road carretera f general

'**main street** calle f principal

main·tain [meɪn'teɪn] v/t mantener

main·te·nance ['meɪntənəns] mantenimiento m; **pay** pagar una pensión alimenticia

'**main·te·nance costs** *npl* gastos *mpl* de mantenimiento

'**main·te·nance staff** personal m de mantenimiento

ma·jes·tic [mə'dʒestɪk] *adj* majestuoso

ma·jes·ty ['mædʒestɪ] majestuosidad f; **Her Majesty** Su Majestad

ma·jor ['meɪdʒər] **1** *adj* (*significant*) importante, principal; **in C ~** MUS en C mayor **2** n MIL comandante m

♦ **major in** v/i especializarse en

ma·jor·i·ty [mə'dʒɑːrətɪ] *also* POL mayoría f; **be in the ~** ser mayoría

make [meɪk] **1** n (*brand*) marca f **2** v/t

(*pret & pp* **made**) hacer; *cars* fabricar, producir; *movie* rodar; *speech* pronunciar; (*earn*) ganar; MATH hacer; **two and two ~ four** dos y dos son cuatro; **~ s.o. do sth** (*force to*) obligar a alguien a hacer algo; (*cause to*) hacer que alguien haga algo; **you can't ~ me do it!** ¡no puedes obligarme a hacerlo!; **~ s.o. happy/ angry** hacer feliz/enfadar a alguien; **~ a decision** tomar una decisión; **made in Japan** hecho en Japón; **~ it** (*catch bus, train*) llegar a tiempo; (*come*) ir; (*succeed*) tener éxito; (*survive*) sobrevivir; **what time do you ~ it?** ¿qué hora llevas?; **~ believe** imaginarse; **~ do with** conformarse con; **what do you ~ of it?** ¿qué piensas?

♦ **make for** v/t (*go toward*) dirigirse hacia

♦ **make off** v/i escaparse

♦ **make off with** v/t (*steal*) llevarse

♦ **make out** v/t *list* hacer, elaborar; *check* extender; (*see*) distinguir; (*imply*) pretender

♦ **make over** v/t (*transfer*) ceder

♦ **make up 1** v/i *of woman, actor* maquillarse; *after quarrel* reconciliarse **2** v/t *story, excuse* inventar; *face* maquillar; (*constitute*) suponer, formar; **be made up of** estar compuesto de; **make up one's mind** decidirse; **make it up** *after quarrel* reconciliarse

♦ **make up for** v/t compensar por

'**make-be·lieve** n ficción f, fantasía f

mak·er ['meɪkər] (*manufacturer*) fabricante m

make·shift ['meɪkʃɪft] *adj* improvisado

make-up ['meɪkʌp] (*cosmetics*) maquillaje m

'**make-up bag** bolsa f del maquillaje

mal·ad·just·ed [mælə'dʒʌstɪd] *adj* inadaptado

male [meɪl] **1** *adj* (*masculine*) masculino; *animal, bird, fish* macho; **~ bosses** los jefes varones; **a ~ teacher** un profesor **2** n *man* hombre m, varón m; *animal, bird, fish*

M

macho *m*

male 'chau·vin·ism machismo *m*;
male chau·vin·ist 'pig machista *m*;
male 'nurse enfermero *m*

ma·lev·o·lent [mə'levələnt] *adj* malévolo

mal·func·tion [mæl'fʌŋkʃn] **1** *n* fallo *m* (**in** de) **2** *v/i* fallar

mal·ice ['mælɪs] malicia *f*

ma·li·cious [mə'lɪʃəs] *adj* malicioso

ma·lig·nant [mə'lɪgnənt] *adj tumor* maligno

mall [mɔːl] (*shopping ~*) centro *m* comercial

mal·nu·tri·tion [mælnuː'trɪʃn] desnutrición *f*

mal·treat [mæl'triːt] *v/t* maltratar

mal·treat·ment [mæl'triːtmənt] maltrato *m*

mam·mal ['mæml] mamífero *m*

man [mæn] **1** *n* (*pl* **men** [men]) hombre *m*; (*humanity*) el hombre; *in checkers* ficha *f* **2** *v/t* (*pret & pp* **-ned**) *telephones, front desk* atender; *spacecraft* tripular

man·age ['mænɪdʒ] **1** *v/t business* dirigir; *money* gestionar; *suitcase* poder con; **~ to ...** conseguir ... **2** *v/i* (*cope*) arreglárselas

man·age·a·ble ['mænɪdʒəbl] *adj* (*easy to handle*) manejable; (*feasible*) factible

man·age·ment ['mænɪdʒmənt] (*managing*) gestión *f*, administración *f*; (*managers*) dirección *f*

man·age·ment 'buy·out *compra de una empresa por sus directivos*; man·age·ment con'sult·ant *consultor(a)* m(f) *en administración de empresas*; 'man·age·ment stud·ies *estudios* mpl *de administración de empresas*; 'man·age·ment team *equipo* m *directivo*

man·ag·er ['mænɪdʒər] *of hotel, company director(a)* m(f); *of shop, restaurant* encargado(a) m(f)

man·a·ge·ri·al [mænɪ'dʒɪrɪəl] *adj* de gestión; *a ~ post* un puesto directivo

man·ag·ing di'rec·tor director(a) m(f) gerente

man·da·rin (or·ange) ['mændərɪn-('ɔːrɪndʒ)] mandarina *f*

man·date ['mændeɪt] (*authority*) mandato *m*; (*task*) tarea *f*

man·da·to·ry ['mændətɔːrɪ] *adj* obligatorio

mane [meɪn] *of horse* crines *fpl*

ma·neu·ver [mə'nuːvər] **1** *n* maniobra *f* **2** *v/t* maniobrar; *she ~ed him into giving her the assignment* consiguió convencerle para que le diera el trabajo

man·gle ['mæŋgl] *v/t* (*crush*) destrozar

man·han·dle ['mænhændl] *v/t* mover a la fuerza

man·hood ['mænhʊd] (*maturity*) madurez *f*; (*virility*) virilidad *f*

'man-hour hora-hombre *f*

'man·hunt persecución *f*

ma·ni·a ['meɪnɪə] (*craze*) pasión *f*

ma·ni·ac ['meɪnɪæk] F chiflado(-a) m(f) F

man·i·cure ['mænɪkjʊr] manicura *f*

man·i·fest ['mænɪfest] **1** *adj* manifiesto **2** *v/t* manifestar; *~ itself* manifestarse

ma·nip·u·late [mə'nɪpjəleɪt] *v/t person, bones* manipular

ma·nip·u·la·tion [mənɪpjə'leɪʃn] *of person, bones* manipulación *f*

ma·nip·u·la·tive [mə'nɪpjələtɪv] *adj* manipulador

man'kind la humanidad

man·ly ['mænlɪ] *adj* (*brave*) de hombres; (*strong*) varonil

'man-made *adj fibers, materials* sintético; *crater, structure* artificial

man·ner ['mænər] *of doing sth* manera *f*, modo *m*; (*attitude*) actitud *f*

man·ners ['mænərz] *npl* modales *mpl*; *good / bad ~* buena / mala educación; *have no ~* ser un maleducado

ma·noeu·vre *Br* → **maneuver**

'man·pow·er (*workers*) mano *f* de obra; *for other tasks* recursos *mpl* humanos

man·sion ['mænʃn] mansión *f*

'man·slaugh·ter *Br* homicidio *m* sin premeditación

man·tel·piece ['mæntlpiːs] repisa *f* de chimenea

man·u·al ['mænjʊəl] **1** *adj* manual **2** *n* manual *m*

man·u·al·ly ['mænjʊəlɪ] *adv* a mano

man·u·fac·ture [mænjʊ'fæktʃər] **1** *n* fabricación *f* **2** *v/t equipment* fabricar

man·u·fac·tur·er [mænjʊ'fæktʃərər] fabricante *m*

man·u·fac·tur·ing [mænjʊ'fæktʃərɪŋ] *adj industry* manufacturero

ma·nure [mə'nʊr] estiércol *m*

man·u·script ['mænjʊskrɪpt] manuscrito *m*

man·y ['menɪ] **1** *adj* muchos; *take as ~ apples as you like* toma todas las manzanas que quieras; *not ~ people / taxis* no mucha gente / muchos taxis; *too ~ problems / beers* demasiados problemas / demasiadas cervezas **2** *pron* muchos; *a great ~, a good ~* muchos; *how ~ do you need?* ¿cuántos necesitas?; *as ~ as 200 are still missing* hay hasta 200 desaparecidos

'**man-year** año-hombre *m*

map [mæp] mapa *m*

♦ **map out** *v/t* (*pret & pp -ped*) proyectar

ma·ple ['meɪpl] arce *m*

mar [mɑːr] *v/t* (*pret & pp -red*) empañar

mar·a·thon ['mærəθɑːn] *race* maratón *m* or *f*

mar·ble ['mɑːrbl] *material* mármol *m*

March [mɑːrtʃ] marzo *m*

march [mɑːrtʃ] **1** *n* marcha *f* **2** *v/i* marchar

march·er ['mɑːrtʃər] manifestante *m / f*

Mardi Gras ['mɑːrdɪɡrɑː] martes *m inv* de Carnaval

mare [mer] yegua *f*

mar·ga·rine [mɑːrdʒə'riːn] margarina *f*

mar·gin ['mɑːrdʒɪn] *also* COM margen *m*

mar·gin·al ['mɑːrdʒɪnl] *adj (slight)* marginal

mar·gin·al·ly ['mɑːrdʒɪnlɪ] *adv*

(slightly) ligeramente

mar·i·hua·na, mar·i·jua·na [mærɪ'hwɑːnə] marihuana *f*

ma·ri·na [mə'riːnə] puerto *m* deportivo

mar·i·nade [mærɪ'neɪd] *n* adobo *m*

mar·i·nate ['mærɪneɪt] *v/t* adobar, marinar

ma·rine [mə'riːn] **1** *adj* marino **2** *n* MIL marine *m / f*, infante *m / f* de marina

mar·i·tal ['mærɪtl] *adj* marital

mar·i·tal 'sta·tus estado *m* civil

mar·i·time ['mærɪtaɪm] *adj* marítimo

mar·jo·ram ['mɑːrdʒərəm] mejorana *f*

mark [mɑːrk] **1** *n* señal *f*, marca *f*; *(stain)* marca *f*, mancha *f*; *(sign, token)* signo *m*, señal *f*; *(trace)* señal *f*; EDU nota *f*; *leave one's ~* dejar huella **2** *v/t (stain)* manchar; EDU calificar; *(indicate, commemorate)* marcar **3** *v/i of fabric* mancharse

♦ **mark down** *v/t goods* rebajar

♦ **mark out** *v/t with a line etc* marcar; *fig (set apart)* distinguir

♦ **mark up** *v/t price* subir; *goods* subir de precio

marked [mɑːrkt] *adj (definite)* marcado, notable

mark·er ['mɑːrkər] *(highlighter)* rotulador *m*

mar·ket ['mɑːrkɪt] **1** *n* mercado *m*; *(stock ~)* bolsa *f*; *on the ~* en el mercado **2** *v/t* comercializar

mar·ket·a·ble ['mɑːrkɪtəbl] *adj* comercializable

mar·ket e'con·o·my economía *f* de mercado

'**mar·ket for·ces** *npl* fuerzas *fpl* del mercado

mar·ket·ing ['mɑːrkɪtɪŋ] marketing *m*

'**mar·ket·ing cam·paign** campaña *f* de marketing; '**mar·ket·ing de·part·ment** departamento *m* de marketing; '**mar·ket·ing mix** marketing mix *m*, *el producto, el precio, la distribución y la promoción*; '**mar·ket·ing strat·e·gy** estrategia *f* de marketing

M

mar·ket 'lead·er líder *m* del mercado; **'mar·ket·place** *in town* plaza *f* del mercado; *for commodities* mercado *m*; **mar·ket re'search** investigación *f* de mercado; **mar·ket 'share** cuota *f* de mercado

mark-up ['maːrkʌp] margen *m*

mar·ma·lade ['maːrməleɪd] mermelada *f* de naranja

mar·quee [maːr'kiː] carpa *f*

mar·riage ['mærɪdʒ] matrimonio *m*; *event* boda *f*

'mar·riage cer·tif·i·cate certificado *m* de matrimonio

mar·riage 'guid·ance coun·se·lor consejero(-a) *m(f)* matrimonial

mar·ried ['mærɪd] *adj* casado; *be ~ to ...* estar casado con ...

mar·ried 'life vida *f* matrimonial

mar·ry ['mærɪ] *v/t (pret & pp -ied)* casarse con; *of priest* casar; *get married* casarse

marsh [maːrʃ] pantano *m*, ciénaga *f*

mar·shal ['maːrʃl] *n in police* jefe(-a) *m(f)* de policía; *in security service* miembro *m* del servicio de seguridad

marsh·mal·low [maːrʃ'mæloʊ] dulce de consistencia blanda

marsh·y ['maːrʃɪ] *adj* pantanoso

mar·tial arts [maːrʃl'aːrts] *npl* artes *fpl* marciales

mar·tial 'law ley *f* marcial

mar·tyr ['maːrtər] mártir *m/f*

mar·tyred ['maːrtərd] *adj fig* de mártir

mar·vel ['maːrvl] maravilla *f*

♦ **marvel at** *v/t* maravillarse de

mar·ve·lous, *Br* **mar·vel·lous** ['maːrvələs] *adj* maravilloso

Marx·ism ['maːrksɪzm] marxismo *m*

Marx·ist ['maːrksɪst] **1** *adj* marxista **2** *n* marxista *m/f*

mar·zi·pan ['maːrzɪpæn] mazapán *m*

mas·ca·ra [mæ'skærə] rímel *m*

mas·cot ['mæskət] mascota *f*

mas·cu·line ['mæskjʊlɪn] *adj* masculino

mas·cu·lin·i·ty [mæskjʊ'lɪnətɪ] *(virility)* masculinidad *f*

mash [mæʃ] *v/t* hacer puré de, majar

mashed po·ta·toes [mæʃt] *npl* puré *m* de patatas *or L.Am.* papas

mask [mæsk] **1** *n* máscara *f*; *to cover mouth, nose* mascarilla *f* **2** *v/t feelings* enmascarar

'mask·ing tape cinta *f* adhesiva de pintor

mas·o·chism ['mæsəkɪzm] masoquismo *m*

mas·o·chist ['mæsəkɪst] masoquista *m/f*

ma·son ['meɪsn] cantero *m*

ma·son·ry ['meɪsnrɪ] albañilería *f*

mas·que·rade [mæskə'reɪd] **1** *n fig* mascarada *f* **2** *v/i: ~ as* hacerse pasar por

mass¹ [mæs] **1** *n (great amount)* gran cantidad *f*; *(body)* masa *f*; *the ~es* las masas; *~es of* F un montón de F **2** *v/i* concentrarse

mass² [mæs] REL misa *f*

mas·sa·cre ['mæsəkər] **1** *n* masacre *f*, matanza *f*; F *in sport* paliza *f* **2** *v/t* masacrar; F *in sport* dar una paliza a

mas·sage ['mæsaːʒ] **1** *n* masaje *m* **2** *v/t* dar un masaje en; *figures* maquillar

'mas·sage par·lor, *Br* **'mas·sage par·lour** salón *m* de masajes

mas·seur [mæ'sɜːr] masajista *m*

mas·seuse [mæ'sɜːrz] masajista *f*

mas·sive ['mæsɪv] *adj* enorme; *heart attack* muy grave

mass 'me·di·a *npl* medios *mpl* de comunicación; **mass-pro'duce** *v/t* fabricar en serie; **mass pro'duc·tion** fabricación *f* en serie

mast [mæst] *of ship* mástil *m*; *for radio signal* torre *f*

mas·ter ['mæstər] **1** *n of dog* dueño *m*, amo *m*; *of ship* patrón *m*; *be a ~ of* ser un maestro de **2** *v/t skill, language, situation* dominar

'mas·ter bed·room dormitorio *m* principal

'mas·ter key llave *f* maestra

mas·ter·ly ['mæstəlɪ] *adj* magistral

'mas·ter·mind 1 *n* cerebro *m* **2** *v/t* dirigir, organizar; **Mas·ter of 'Arts** Máster *m* en Humanidades; **mas·ter of 'cer·e·mo·nies** maes-

tro *m* de ceremonias; '**mas·ter·piece** obra *f* maestra
'**mas·ter's** (**de·gree**) máster *m*
mas·ter·y ['mæstərɪ] dominio *m*
mas·tur·bate ['mæstərbeɪt] *v/i* masturbarse
mat [mæt] *for floor* estera *f*; *for table* salvamanteles *m inv*
match[1] [mætʃ] *for cigarette* cerilla *f*, fósforo *m*
match[2] [mætʃ] **1** *n* SP partido *m*; *in chess* partida *f*; **be no ~ for s.o.** no estar a la altura de alguien; **meet one's ~** encontrar la horma de su zapato **2** *v/t* (*be the same as*) coincidir con; (*be in harmony with*) hacer juego con; (*equal*) igualar **3** *v/i of colors, patterns* hacer juego
'**match·box** caja *f* de cerillas
'**match·ing** ['mætʃɪŋ] *adj* a juego
'**match stick** cerilla *f*, fósforo *m*
mate [meɪt] **1** *n of animal* pareja *f*; NAUT oficial *m/f* **2** *v/i* aparearse; **these birds ~ for life** estas aves viven con la misma pareja toda la vida
ma·te·ri·al [mə'tɪrɪəl] **1** *n* (*fabric*) tejido *m*; (*substance*) material *m*; **~s** materiales *mpl* **2** *adj* material
ma·te·ri·al·ism [mə'tɪrɪəlɪzm] materialismo *m*
ma·te·ri·al·ist [mətɪrɪə'lɪst] materialista *m/f*
ma·te·ri·al·is·tic [mətɪrɪə'lɪstɪk] *adj* materialista
ma·te·ri·al·ize [mə'tɪrɪəlaɪz] *v/i* (*appear*) aparecer; (*come into existence*) hacerse realidad
ma·ter·nal [mə'tɜːrnl] *adj* maternal
ma·ter·ni·ty [mə'tɜːrnətɪ] maternidad *f*
ma·ter·ni·ty dress vestido *m* premamá; **ma·ter·ni·ty leave** baja *f* por maternidad; **ma·ter·ni·ty ward** pabellón *m* de maternidad
math [mæθ] matemáticas *fpl*
math·e·mat·i·cal [mæθə'mætɪkl] *adj* matemático
math·e·ma·ti·cian [mæθmə'tɪʃn] matemático(-a) *m(f)*
math·e·mat·ics [mæθ'mætɪks] matemáticas *fpl*

maths *Br* → **math**
mat·i·née ['mætɪneɪ] sesión *f* de tarde
ma·tri·arch ['meɪtrɪɑːrk] matriarca *f*
mat·ri·mo·ny ['mætrəmoʊnɪ] matrimonio *m*
matt [mæt] *adj* mate
mat·ter ['mætər] **1** *n* (*affair*) asunto *m*; PHYS materia *f*; **you're only making ~s worse** sólo estás empeorando las cosas; **as a ~ of course** automáticamente; **as a ~ of fact** de hecho; **what's the ~?** ¿qué pasa?; **no ~ what she says** diga lo que diga **2** *v/i* importar; **it doesn't ~** no importa
mat·ter-of-'fact *adj* tranquilo
mat·tress ['mætrɪs] colchón *m*
ma·ture [mə'tʃʊr] **1** *adj* maduro **2** *v/i of person* madurar; *of insurance policy etc* vencer
ma·tu·ri·ty [mə'tʃʊrətɪ] madurez *f*
maul [mɔːl] *v/t of lion, tiger* atacar; *of critics* destrozar
max·i·mize ['mæksɪmaɪz] *v/t* maximizar
max·i·mum ['mæksɪməm] **1** *adj* máximo; **it will cost \$500 ~** costará 500 dólares como máximo **2** *n* máximo *m*
May [meɪ] mayo *m*
may [meɪ] *v/aux* ◊ *possibility*: **it ~ rain** puede que llueva; **you ~ be right** puede que tengas razón; **it ~ not happen** puede que no ocurra ◊ *permission* poder; **~ I help / smoke?** ¿puedo ayudar / fumar?
may·be ['meɪbɪ] *adv* quizás, tal vez
'**May Day** el Primero de Mayo
may·o, may·on·naise ['meɪoʊ, meɪə-'neɪz] mayonesa *f*
may·or [mer] alcalde *m*
maze [meɪz] laberinto *m*
MB *abbr* (= **megabyte**) MB (= megabyte *m*)
MBA [embɪ'eɪ] *abbr* (= **Master of Business Administration**) MBA *m* (= Máster *m* en Administración de Empresas)
MBO [embɪ'oʊ] *abbr* (= **management buyout**) compra de una em-

M

presa por sus directivos

MC [em'si:] *abbr* (= *master of cere-monies*) maestro *m* de ceremonias

MD [em'di:] *abbr* (= *Doctor of Medi-cine*) Doctor(a) *m(f)* en Medicina; (= *managing director*) director(a) *m(f)* gerente

me [mi:] *pron direct & indirect object* me; *after prep* mí; *he knows* ~ me conoce; *he gave* ~ *the keys* me dio las llaves; *he sold it to* ~ me lo vendió; *this is for* ~ esto es para mí; *who do you mean,* ~? ¿a quién te refieres?, ¿a mí?; *with* ~ conmigo; *it's* ~ soy yo; *taller than* ~ más alto que yo

mead·ow ['medou] prado *m*

mea·ger, *Br* **mea·gre** ['mi:gər] *adj* escaso, exiguo

meal [mi:l] comida *f*; *enjoy your* ~ ¡que aproveche!

'**meal·time** hora *f* de comer

mean¹ [mi:n] *adj with money* tacaño; (*nasty*) malo, cruel; *that was a* ~ *thing to say* ha estado fatal que dijeras eso

mean² [mi:n] **1** *v/t* (*pret & pp* **meant**) (*intend to say*) querer decir; (*signify*) querer decir, significar; *you weren't* ~*t to hear that* no era mi intención que oyeras eso; ~ *to do sth* tener la intención de hacer algo; *be* ~*t for* ser para; *of remark* ir dirigido a; *doesn't it* ~ *anything to you?* (*doesn't it matter?*) ¿no te importa para nada? **2** *v/i* (*pret & pp* **meant**): ~ *well* tener buena intención

mean·ing ['mi:nɪŋ] *of word* significado *m*

mean·ing·ful ['mi:nɪŋfəl] *adj* (*comprehensible*) con sentido; (*constructive*), *glance* significativo

mean·ing·less ['mi:nɪŋlɪs] *adj* sin sentido

means [mi:nz] *npl financial* medios *mpl*; (*nsg: way*) medio *m*; *a* ~ *of transport* un medio de transporte; *by all* ~ (*certainly*) por supuesto; *by all* ~ *check my figures* comprueba mis cifras, faltaría más; *by no* ~ *rich/poor* ni mucho menos rico/pobre; *by* ~ *of* mediante

meant [ment] *pret & pp* → **mean²**

mean·time ['mi:ntaɪm] **1** *adv* mientras tanto **2** *n*: *in the* ~ mientras tanto

mea·sles ['mi:zlz] *nsg* sarampión *m*

mea·sure ['meʒər] **1** *n* (*step*) medida *f*; *we've had a* ~ *of success* (*certain amount*) hemos tenido cierto éxito **2** *v/t & v/i* medir

♦ **measure out** *v/t area, drink, medici-ne* medir; *sugar, flour, ingredients* pesar

♦ **measure up** *v/i* estar a la altura (*to* de)

mea·sure·ment ['meʒərmənt] medida *f*; *system of* ~ sistema *m* de medidas

'**mea·sur·ing tape** cinta *f* métrica

meat [mi:t] carne *f*

'**meat·ball** albóndiga *f*

'**meat·loaf** masa de carne cocinada en forma de barra de pan

me·chan·ic [mɪ'kænɪk] mecánico(-a) *m(f)*

me·chan·i·cal [mɪ'kænɪkl] *adj also fig* mecánico

me·chan·i·cal en·gi·neer ingeniero(-a) *m(f)* industrial

me·chan·i·cal en·gi·neer·ing ingeniería *f* industrial

me·chan·i·cal·ly [mɪ'kænɪklɪ] *adv also fig* mecánicamente

mech·a·nism ['mekənɪzm] mecanismo *m*

mech·a·nize ['mekənaɪz] *v/t* mecanizar

med·al ['medl] medalla *f*

med·a·list, *Br* **med·al·list** ['medəlɪst] medallista *m/f*

med·dle ['medl] *v/i* entrometerse; *don't* ~ *with the TV* no enredes con la televisión

me·di·a ['mi:dɪə] *npl*: *the* ~ los medios de comunicación

'**me·di·a cov·er·age** cobertura *f* informativa; '**me·di·a e·vent** acontecimiento *m* informativo; **me·di·a** '**hype** revuelo *m* informativo

me·di·an strip [mi:dɪən'strɪp] mediana *f*

'**me·di·a stud·ies** ciencias *fpl* de la

información

me·di·ate ['miːdɪeɪt] *v/i* mediar

me·di·a·tion [miːdɪ'eɪʃn] mediación *f*

me·di·a·tor ['miːdɪeɪtər] mediador(a) *m(f)*

med·i·cal ['medɪkl] **1** *adj* médico **2** *n* reconocimiento *m* médico

'**med·i·cal cer·tif·i·cate** certificado *m* médico; '**med·i·cal ex·am·i·na·tion** reconocimiento *m* médico; '**med·i·cal his·to·ry** historial *m* médico; '**med·i·cal pro·fes·sion** profesión *f* médica; (*doctors*) médicos *mpl*; '**med·i·cal rec·ord** ficha *f* médica

Med·i·care ['medɪker] seguro de enfermedad para los ancianos en Estados Unidos

med·i·cat·ed ['medɪkeɪtɪd] *adj* medicinal

med·i·ca·tion [medɪ'keɪʃn] medicamento *m*, medicina *f*

me·di·ci·nal [mɪ'dɪsɪnl] *adj* medicinal

med·i·cine ['medsən] *science* medicina *f*; (*medication*) medicina *f*, medicamento *m*

'**med·i·cine cab·i·net** botiquín *m*

med·i·e·val [medɪ'iːvl] *adj* medieval

me·di·o·cre [miːdɪ'oʊkər] *adj* mediocre

me·di·oc·ri·ty [miːdɪ'ɑːkrətɪ] *of work etc, person* mediocridad *f*

med·i·tate ['medɪteɪt] *v/i* meditar

med·i·ta·tion [medɪ'teɪʃn] meditación *f*

Med·i·ter·ra·ne·an [medɪtə'reɪnɪən] **1** *adj* mediterráneo **2** *n*: **the ~** el Mediterráneo

me·di·um ['miːdɪəm] **1** *adj* (*average*) medio; *steak* a punto **2** *n* size talla *f* media; (*means*) medio *m*; (*spiritualist*) médium *m/f*

me·di·um-sized ['miːdɪəmsaɪzd] *adj* de tamaño medio; **me·di·um 'term**: *in the ~* a medio plazo; '**me·di·um wave** RAD onda *f* media

med·ley ['medlɪ] (*assortment*) mezcla *f*

meek [miːk] *adj* manso, dócil

meet [miːt] **1** *v/t* (*pret & pp **met***) *by appointment* encontrarse con, reunirse con; *by chance, of eyes* encontrarse con; (*get to know*) conocer; (*collect*) ir a buscar; *in competition* enfrentarse con; (*satisfy*) satisfacer; **~ a deadline** cumplir un plazo **2** *v/i* (*pret & pp **met***) encontrarse; *in competition* enfrentarse; *of committee etc* reunirse; **have you two met?** ¿os conocíais? **3** *n* SP reunión *f*

♦ **meet with** *v/t* person, opposition, approval encontrar con; **my attempts met with failure** mis intentos fracasaron

meet·ing ['miːtɪŋ] *by chance* encuentro *m*; *of committee, in business* reunión *f*; **he's in a ~** está reunido

'**meet·ing place** lugar *m* de encuentro

meg·a·byte ['megəbaɪt] COMPUT megabyte *m*

mel·an·chol·y ['melənkəlɪ] *adj* melancólico

mel·low ['meloʊ] **1** *adj* suave **2** *v/i of person* suavizarse, sosegarse

me·lo·di·ous [mɪ'loʊdɪəs] *adj* melodioso

mel·o·dra·mat·ic [melədrə'mætɪk] *adj* melodramático

mel·o·dy ['melədɪ] melodía *f*

mel·on ['melən] melón *m*

melt [melt] **1** *v/i* fundirse, derretirse **2** *v/t* fundir, derretir

♦ **melt away** *v/i* fig desvanecerse

♦ **melt down** *v/t* metal fundir

melt·ing pot ['meltɪŋpɑːt] fig crisol *m*

mem·ber ['membər] miembro *m*

Mem·ber of 'Con·gress diputado(-a) *m(f)*

Mem·ber of 'Par·lia·ment Br diputado(-a) *m(f)*

mem·ber·ship ['membərʃɪp] afiliación *f*; (*number of members*) número *m* de miembros; **he applied for ~ of the club** solicitó ser admitido en el club

'**mem·ber·ship card** tarjeta *f* de socio

mem·brane ['membreɪn] membrana *f*

M

me·men·to [me'mentoʊ] recuerdo *m*

mem·o ['memoʊ] nota *f*

mem·oirs ['memwɑːrz] *npl* memorias *fpl*

'**mem·o pad** bloc *m* de notas

mem·o·ra·ble ['memərəbl] *adj* memorable

me·mo·ri·al [mɪ'mɔːrɪəl] **1** *adj* conmemorativo **2** *n* monumento *m* conmemorativo

Me'mo·ri·al Day Día *f* de los Caídos

mem·o·rize ['meməraɪz] *v/t* memorizar

mem·o·ry ['memərɪ] (*recollection*) recuerdo *m*; (*power of recollection*), COMPUT memoria *f*; **I have no ~ of the accident** no recuerdo el accidente; **have a good/bad ~** tener buena/mala memoria; **in ~ of** en memoria de

men [men] *pl* → **man**

men·ace ['menɪs] **1** *n* amenaza *f*; *person* peligro *m* **2** *v/t* amenazar

men·ac·ing ['menɪsɪŋ] *adj* amenazador

mend [mend] **1** *v/t* reparar; *clothes* coser, remendar; *shoes* remendar **2** *n*: **be on the ~** *after illness* estar recuperándose

me·ni·al ['miːnɪəl] *adj* ingrato, penoso

men·in·gi·tis [menɪn'dʒaɪtɪs] meningitis *f*

men·o·pause ['menəpɔːz] menopausia *f*

'**men's room** servicio *m* de caballeros

men·stru·ate ['menstrʊeɪt] *v/i* menstruar

men·stru·a·tion [menstrʊ'eɪʃn] menstruación *f*

men·tal ['mentl] *adj* mental; F (*crazy*) chiflado F, pirado F

men·tal a'rith·me·tic cálculo *m* mental; **men·tal 'cru·el·ty** crueldad *f* mental; '**men·tal hos·pi·tal** hospital *m* psiquiátrico; **men·tal 'ill·ness** enfermedad *f* mental

men·tal·i·ty [men'tælətɪ] mentalidad *f*

men·tal·ly ['mentəlɪ] *adv* (*inwardly*) mentalmente

men·tal·ly 'hand·i·capped *adj* con minusvalía psíquica

men·tal·ly 'ill *adj*: **be ~** sufrir una enfermedad mental

men·tion ['menʃn] **1** *n* mención *f*; **she made no ~ of it** no lo mencionó **2** *v/t* mencionar; **don't ~ it** (*you're welcome*) no hay de qué

men·tor ['mentɔːr] mentor(a) *m(f)*

men·u ['menuː] *for food*, COMPUT menú *m*

mer·ce·na·ry ['mɜːrsɪnərɪ] **1** *adj* mercenario **2** *n* MIL mercenario(-a) *m(f)*

mer·chan·dise ['mɜːrtʃəndaɪz] mercancías *fpl*, *L.Am.* mercadería *f*

mer·chant ['mɜːrtʃənt] comerciante *m/f*

mer·chant 'bank *Br* banco *m* mercantil

mer·ci·ful ['mɜːrsɪfəl] *adj* compasivo, piadoso

mer·ci·ful·ly ['mɜːrsɪfəlɪ] *adv* (*thankfully*) afortunadamente

mer·ci·less ['mɜːrsɪlɪs] *adj* despiadado

mer·cu·ry ['mɜːrkjʊrɪ] mercurio *m*

mer·cy ['mɜːrsɪ] clemencia *f*, compasión *f*; **be at s.o.'s ~** estar a merced de alguien

mere [mɪr] *adj* mero, simple

mere·ly ['mɪrlɪ] *adv* meramente, simplemente

merge [mɜːrdʒ] *v/i of two lines etc* juntarse, unirse; *of companies* fusionarse

merg·er ['mɜːrdʒər] COM fusión *f*

mer·it ['merɪt] **1** *n* (*worth*) mérito *m*; (*advantage*) ventaja *f*; **she got the job on ~** consiguió el trabajo por méritos propios **2** *v/t* merecer

mer·ry ['merɪ] *adj* alegre; **Merry Christmas!** ¡Feliz Navidad!

'**mer·ry-go-round** tiovivo *m*

mesh [meʃ] malla *f*

mess [mes] (*untidiness*) desorden *m*; (*trouble*) lío *m*; **I'm in a bit of a ~** estoy metido en un lío; **be a ~** *of room, desk* estar desordenado; *of hair* estar revuelto; *of situation, s.o.'s life* ser un desastre

♦ **mess around 1** *v/i* enredar **2** *v/t person* jugar con

♦ **mess around with** *v/t* enredar con; *s.o.'s wife* tener un lío con

♦ **mess up** *v/t room, papers* desordenar; *task* convertir en una chapuza; *plans, marriage* estropear, arruinar

mes·sage ['mesɪdʒ] *also of movie etc* mensaje *m*

mes·sen·ger ['mesɪndʒər] *(courier)* mensajero(-a) *m(f)*

mess·y ['mesɪ] *adj room, person* desordenado; *job* sucio; *divorce, situation* desagradable

met [met] *pret & pp* → **meet**

me·tab·o·lism [mə'tæbəlɪzm] metabolismo *m*

met·al ['metl] **1** *n* metal *m* **2** *adj* metálico

me·tal·lic [mɪ'tælɪk] *adj* metálico

met·a·phor ['metəfər] metáfora *f*

me·te·or ['miːtɪər] meteoro *m*

me·te·or·ic [miːtɪ'ɑːrɪk] *adj fig* meteórico

me·te·or·ite ['miːtɪəraɪt] meteorito *m*

me·te·or·o·log·i·cal [miːtɪrə'lɑːdʒɪkl] *adj* meteorológico

me·te·or·ol·o·gist [miːtɪə'rɑːlədʒɪst] meteorólogo(-a) *m(f)*

me·te·o·rol·o·gy [miːtɪə'rɑːlədʒɪ] meteorología *f*

me·ter[1] ['miːtər] *for gas, electricity* contador *m*; *(parking ~)* parquímetro *m*

me·ter[2] ['miːtər] *unit of length* metro *m*

'**me·ter read·ing** lectura *f* del contador

meth·od ['meθəd] método *m*

me·thod·i·cal [mɪ'θɑːdɪkl] *adj* metódico

me·thod·i·cal·ly [mɪ'θɑːdɪklɪ] *adv* metódicamente

me·tic·u·lous [mə'tɪkjʊləs] *adj* meticuloso, minucioso

me·tre *Br* → **meter**[2]

met·ric ['metrɪk] *adj* métrico

me·trop·o·lis [mɪ'trɑːpəlɪs] metrópolis *f inv*

met·ro·pol·i·tan [metrə'pɑːlɪtən] *adj* metropolitano

mew [mjuː] → **miaow**

Mex·i·can ['meksɪkən] **1** *adj* mexicano, mejicano **2** *n* mexicano(-a) *m(f)*, mejicano(-a) *m(f)*

Mex·i·co ['meksɪkoʊ] México, Méjico

Mex·i·co 'Cit·y *n* Ciudad *f* de México, *Mex* México, *Mex* el Distrito Federal, *Mex* el D.F.

mez·za·nine (floor) ['mezəniːn] entresuelo *m*

mi·aow [mɪaʊ] **1** *n* maullido *m* **2** *v/i* maullar

mice [maɪs] *pl* → **mouse**

mick·ey mouse [mɪkɪ'maʊs] *adj pej* P *course, qualification* de tres al cuarto P

mi·cro·bi·ol·o·gy [maɪkroʊbaɪ'ɑːlədʒɪ] microbiología *f*; '**mi·cro·chip** microchip *m*; '**mi·cro·cli·mate** microclima *m*; **mi·cro·cosm** ['maɪkroʊkɑːzm] microcosmos *m inv*; '**mi·cro·e·lec·tron·ics** microelectrónica *f*; '**mi·cro·film** microfilm *m*; '**mi·cro·or·gan·ism** microorganismo *m*; '**mi·cro·phone** micrófono *m*; '**mi·cro'pro·ces·sor** microprocesador *m*; '**mi·cro·scope** microscopio *m*; **mi·cro·scop·ic** [maɪkrə'skɑːpɪk] *adj* microscópico; '**mi·cro·wave** oven microondas *m inv*

mid·air [mɪd'er]: **in ~** en pleno vuelo

mid·day [mɪd'deɪ] mediodía *m*

mid·dle ['mɪdl] **1** *adj* del medio; *the ~ child of five* el tercero de cinco hermanos **2** *n* medio *m*; *it's the ~ of the night!* ¡estamos en plena noche!; *in the ~ of floor, room* en medio de; *of period of time* a mitad *or* mediados de; *in the ~ of winter* en pleno invierno; *be in the ~ of doing sth* estar ocupado haciendo algo

'**mid·dle-aged** *adj* de mediana edad; '**Mid·dle Ag·es** *npl* Edad *f* Media; **mid·dle-'class** *adj* de clase media; '**mid·dle class(es)** clases *fpl* medias; **Mid·dle 'East** Oriente *m* Medio; '**mid·dle·man** intermediario *m*;

mid·dle 'man·age·ment mandos
mpl intermedios; **mid·dle 'name**
segundo nombre *m*; **'mid·dle·
weight** *boxer* peso *m* medio
mid·dling ['mɪdlɪŋ] *adj* regular
mid·field·er [mɪd'fiːldər] centro-
campista *m/f*
midg·et ['mɪdʒɪt] *adj* en miniatura
'mid·night ['mɪdnaɪt] medianoche *f*;
at ~ a medianoche; **'mid·sum·mer**
pleno verano *m*; **'mid·way** *adv*:
we'll stop for lunch ~ pararemos
para comer a mitad de camino; ~
through the meeting a mitad de la
reunión; **'mid·week** *adv* a mitad de
semana; **'Mid·west** Medio Oeste *m*
(de Estados Unidos); **'mid·wife** comadrona *f*; **'mid·win·ter** pleno invierno *m*
might[1] [maɪt] *v/aux* poder, ser posible
que; *I ~ be late* puede *or* es posible
que llegue tarde; *it ~ never happen*
puede *or* es posible que no ocurra
nunca; *he ~ have left* a lo mejor se
ha ido; *you ~ have told me!* ¡me lo
podías haber dicho!
might[2] [maɪt] (*power*) poder *m*, fuerza *f*
might·y ['maɪtɪ] **1** *adj* poderoso **2** *adv*
F (*extremely*) muy, cantidad de F
mi·graine ['miːgreɪn] migraña *f*
mi·grant work·er ['maɪgrənt]
trabajador(a) *m(f)* itinerante
mi·grate [maɪ'greɪt] *v/i* emigrar
mi·gra·tion [maɪ'greɪʃn] emigración
f
mike [maɪk] F micro *m* F
mild [maɪld] *adj weather*, *climate* apacible; *cheese*, *voice* suave; *curry etc* no
muy picante; *person* afable, apacible
mil·dew ['mɪlduː] moho *m*
mild·ly ['maɪldlɪ] *adv say sth* con suavidad; *spicy* ligeramente; *to put it* ~
por no decir algo peor
mild·ness ['maɪldnɪs] *of weather*,
voice suavidad *f*; *of person* afabili-
dad *f*
mile [maɪl] milla *f*; *be ~s better /
easier* F ser mil veces mejor / más
fácil F
mile·age ['maɪlɪdʒ] millas *fpl* recorri-

das; *unlimited* ~ kilometraje *m* ilimitado
'mile·stone *fig* hito *m*
mil·i·tant ['mɪlɪtənt] **1** *adj* militante
2 *n* militante *m/f*
mil·i·ta·ry ['mɪlɪterɪ] **1** *adj* militar **2** *n*:
the ~ el ejército, las fuerzas armadas
mil·i·ta·ry a'cad·e·my academia *f*
militar; **mil·i·ta·ry po'lice** policía *f*
militar; **mil·i·ta·ry 'serv·ice** servicio *m* militar
mi·li·tia [mɪ'lɪʃə] milicia *f*
milk [mɪlk] **1** *n* leche *f* **2** *v/t* ordeñar
milk 'choc·o·late chocolate *m* con
leche; **milk of mag'ne·sia** leche *f*
de magnesia; **'milk·shake** batido *m*
'milk·y ['mɪlkɪ] *adj with lots of milk*
con mucha leche; *made with milk*
con leche
Milk·y 'Way Vía *f* Láctea
mill [mɪl] *for grain* molino *m*; *for textiles* fábrica *f* de tejidos
♦ **mill around** *v/i* pulular
mil·len·ni·um [mɪ'lenɪəm] milenio *m*
mil·li·gram, *Br* **mil·li·gramme**
['mɪlɪgræm] miligramo *m*
mil·li·me·ter, *Br* **mil·li·me·tre**
['mɪlimiːtər] milímetro *m*
mil·lion ['mɪljən] millón *m*
mil·lion·aire [mɪljə'ner] millona-
rio(-a) *m(f)*
mime [maɪm] *v/t* representar con ges-
tos
mim·ic ['mɪmɪk] **1** *n* imitador(a)
m(f) **2** *v/t* (*pret & pp -ked*) imitar
mince [mɪns] *v/t* picar
'mince·meat carne *f* picada
mince 'pie *empanada de carne picada*
mind [maɪnd] **1** *n* mente *f*; *it's
uppermost in my* ~ es lo que más
me preocupa; *it's all in your* ~ son
imaginaciones tuyas; *be out of
one's* ~ haber perdido el juicio;
bear o keep sth in ~ recordar; *I've a
good ~ to ...* estoy considerando seriamente ...; *change one's* ~ cambiar de opinión; *it didn't enter my* ~
no se me ocurrió; *give s.o. a piece
of one's* ~ cantarle a alguien las
cuarenta; *make up one's* ~ decidirse; *have something on one's* ~ te-

ner algo en la cabeza; **keep one's ~ on sth** concentrarse en algo **2** v/t (*look after*) cuidar (de); (*heed*) prestar atención a; **I don't ~ what we do** no me importa lo que hagamos; **do you ~ if I smoke?, do you ~ my smoking?** ¿le importa que fume?; **would you ~ opening the window?** ¿le importaría abrir la ventana?; **~ the step!** ¡cuidado con el escalón!; **~ your own business!** ¡métete en tus asuntos! **3** v/i: **~!** ¡ten cuidado!; **never ~!** ¡no importa!; **I don't ~** no me importa, me da igual

mind-bog-gling ['maindbɑ:glɪŋ] *adj* increíble

mind-less ['maindlɪs] *adj violence* gratuito

mine¹ [main] *pron* el mío, la mía; **~ are red** los míos son rojos; **that book is ~** eso libro es mío; **a cousin of ~** un primo mío

mine² [main] **1** *n for coal etc* mina *f* **2** v/i: **~ for** extraer

mine³ [main] **1** *n* (*explosive*) mina *f* **2** v/t minar

'mine-field MIL campo *m* de minas; *fig* campo *m* minado

min-er ['mainər] minero(-a) *m(f)*

min-e-ral ['minərəl] *n* mineral *m*

'min-e-ral wa-ter agua *f* mineral

'mine-sweep-er NAUT dragaminas *m inv*

min-gle ['miŋgl] *v/i of sounds, smells* mezclarse; *at party* alternar

min-i ['mini] *skirt* minifalda *f*

min-i-a-ture ['minitʃər] *adj* en miniatura

'min-i-bus microbús *m*

min-i-mal ['minɪməl] *adj* mínimo

min-i-mal-ism ['minɪməlɪzm] minimalismo *m*

min-i-mize ['minɪmaiz] *v/t risk, delay* minimizar, reducir al mínimo; (*downplay*) minimizar, quitar importancia a

min-i-mum ['minɪməm] **1** *adj* mínimo **2** *n* mínimo *m*

min-i-mum 'wage salario *m* mínimo

min-ing ['mainiŋ] minería *f*

'min-i-se-ries *nsg* TV miniserie *f*

'min-i-skirt minifalda *f*

min-is-ter ['minɪstər] POL ministro(-a) *m(f)*; REL ministro(-a) *m(f)*, pastor(a) *m(f)*

min-is-te-ri-al [minɪ'stiriəl] *adj* ministerial

min-is-try ['minɪstri] POL ministerio *m*

mink [miŋk] *animal, fur* visón *m*; *coat* abrigo *m* de visón

mi-nor ['mainər] **1** *adj problem, setback* menor, pequeño; *operation, argument* de poca importancia; *aches and pains* leve; *in D* ~ MUS en D menor **2** *n* LAW menor *m/f* de edad

mi-nor-i-ty [mai'nɑ:rəti] minoría *f*; **be in the ~** ser minoría

mint [mint] *n herb* menta *f*; *chocolate* pastilla *f* de chocolate con sabor a menta; *hard candy* caramelo *m* de menta

mi-nus ['mainəs] **1** *n* (*~ sign*) (signo *m* de) menos *m* **2** *prep* menos; *temperatures of ~ 18* temperaturas de 18 grados bajo cero

mi-nus-cule ['minəskju:l] *adj* minúsculo

min-ute¹ ['minit] *of time* minuto *m*; *in a ~* (*soon*) en un momento; *just a ~* un momento

mi-nute² [mai'nu:t] *adj* (*tiny*) diminuto, minúsculo; (*detailed*) minucioso; *in ~ detail* minuciosamente

'min-ute hand ['minit] minutero *m*

mi-nute-ly [mai'nu:tli] *adv in detail* minuciosamente; (*very slightly*) mínimamente

min-utes ['minits] *npl of meeting* acta(s) *f(pl)*

mir-a-cle ['mirəkl] *n* milagro *m*

mi-rac-u-lous [mi'rækjuləs] *adj* milagroso

mi-rac-u-lous-ly [mi'rækjuləsli] *adv* milagrosamente

mi-rage ['mirɑ:ʒ] espejismo *m*

mir-ror ['mirər] **1** *n* espejo *m*; MOT (*espejo m*) retrovisor *m* **2** v/t reflejar

mis-an-thro-pist [mi'zænθrəpist] misántropo(-a) *m(f)*

mis-ap-pre-hen-sion [misæpri'henʃn]: **be under a ~** estar equivocado

mis·be·have [mɪsbə'heɪv] *v/i* portarse mal

mis·be·hav·ior, *Br* **mis·be·hav·iour** [mɪsbə'heɪvɪər] mal comportamiento *m*

mis·cal·cu·late [mɪs'kælkjʊleɪt] *v/t & v/i* calcular mal

mis·cal·cu·la·tion [mɪs'kælkjʊleɪʃn] error *m* de cálculo

mis·car·riage ['mɪskærɪdʒ] MED aborto *m* (espontáneo); **~ of justice** error *m* judicial

mis·car·ry ['mɪskærɪ] *v/i* (*pret & pp -ied*) *of plan* fracasar

mis·cel·la·ne·ous [mɪsə'leɪnɪəs] *adj* diverso; **put it in the file marked "~"** ponlo en la carpeta de "varios"

mis·chief ['mɪstʃɪf] (*naughtiness*) travesura *f*, trastada *f*

mis·chie·vous ['mɪstʃɪvəs] *adj* (*naughty*) travieso; (*malicious*) malicioso

mis·con·cep·tion [mɪskən'sepʃn] idea *f* equivocada

mis·con·duct [mɪs'kɑːndʌkt] mala conducta *f*

mis·con·strue [mɪskən'struː] *v/t* malinterpretar

mis·de·mea·nor, *Br* **mis·de·mea·nour** [mɪsdə'miːnər] falta *f*, delito *m* menor

mi·ser ['maɪzər] avaro(-a) *m(f)*

mis·e·ra·ble ['mɪzrəbl] *adj* (*unhappy*) triste, infeliz; *weather, performance* horroroso

mi·ser·ly ['maɪzərlɪ] *adj person* avaro; **a ~ $150** 150 míseros dólares

mis·e·ry ['mɪzərɪ] (*unhappiness*) tristeza *f*, infelicidad *f*; (*wretchedness*) miseria *f*

mis·fire [mɪs'faɪr] *v/i of joke, scheme* salir mal

mis·fit ['mɪsfɪt] *in society* inadaptado(-a) *m(f)*

mis·for·tune [mɪs'fɔːrtʃən] desgracia *f*

mis·giv·ings [mɪs'ɡɪvɪŋz] *npl* recelo *m*, duda *f*

mis·guid·ed [mɪs'ɡaɪdɪd] *adj person* equivocado; *attempt, plan* desacer-

tado

mis·han·dle [mɪs'hændl] *v/t situation* llevar mal

mis·hap ['mɪshæp] contratiempo *m*

mis·in·form [mɪsɪn'fɔːrm] *v/t* informar mal

mis·in·ter·pret [mɪsɪn'tɜːrprɪt] *v/t* malinterpretar

mis·in·ter·pre·ta·tion [mɪsɪntɜːrprɪ'teɪʃn] mala interpretación *f*

mis·judge [mɪs'dʒʌdʒ] *v/t person, situation* juzgar mal

mis·lay [mɪs'leɪ] *v/t* (*pret & pp -laid*) perder

mis·lead [mɪs'liːd] *v/t* (*pret & pp -led*) engañar

mis·lead·ing [mɪs'liːdɪŋ] *adj* engañoso

mis·man·age [mɪs'mænɪdʒ] *v/t* gestionar mal

mis·man·age·ment [mɪs'mænɪdʒmənt] mala gestión *f*

mis·match ['mɪsmætʃ]: **there's a ~ between the two sets of figures** los dos grupos de cifras no se corresponden

mis·placed ['mɪspleɪst] *adj loyalty* inmerecido; *enthusiasm* inoportuno

mis·print ['mɪsprɪnt] errata *f*

mis·pro·nounce [mɪsprə'naʊns] *v/t* pronunciar mal

mis·pro·nun·ci·a·tion [mɪsprənʌnsɪ'eɪʃn] pronunciación *f* incorrecta

mis·read [mɪs'riːd] *v/t* (*pret & pp -read* [red]) *word, figures* leer mal; *situation* malinterpretar

mis·rep·re·sent [mɪsreprɪ'zent] *v/t* deformar, tergiversar

miss[1] [mɪs]: **Miss Smith** la señorita Smith; **~!** ¡señorita!

miss[2] [mɪs] **1** *n SP* fallo *m*; **give sth a ~** *meeting, party etc* no ir a algo **2** *v/t target* no dar en; *emotionally* echar de menos; *bus, train, airplane* perder; (*not notice*) pasar por alto; (*not be present at*) perderse; **I ducked and he ~ed me** me agaché y no me dio; **you just ~ed her** (*she's just left*) se acaba de marchar; **we must have ~ed the turnoff** nos hemos debido pasar el desvío; **you don't ~ much!**

¡no se te escapa una!; **~ *a class*** faltar a una clase **3** v/i fallar

mis·shap·en [mɪsˈʃeɪpən] adj deforme

mis·sile [ˈmɪsəl] misil m; (sth thrown) arma f arrojadiza

miss·ing [ˈmɪsɪŋ] adj desaparecido; **be ~** of person, plane haber desaparecido; **the ~ money** el dinero que falta

mis·sion [ˈmɪʃn] task misión f; people delegación f

mis·sion·a·ry [ˈmɪʃənrɪ] REL misionero(-a) m(f)

mis·spell [mɪsˈspel] v/t escribir incorrectamente

mist [mɪst] neblina f

♦ **mist over** v/i of eyes empañarse

♦ **mist up** v/i of mirror, window empañarse

mis·take [mɪˈsteɪk] **1** n error m, equivocación f; **make a ~** cometer un error or una equivocación, equivocarse; **by ~** por error or equivocación **2** v/t (pret **mistook**, pp **mistaken**) confundir; **~ X for Y** confundir X con Y

mis·tak·en [mɪˈsteɪkən] **1** adj erróneo, equivocado; **be ~** estar equivocado **2** pp → **mistake**

mis·ter [ˈmɪstər] → **Mr**

mis·took [mɪˈstʊk] pret → **mistake**

mis·tress [ˈmɪstrɪs] lover amante f, querida f; of servant ama f; of dog dueña f, ama f

mis·trust [mɪsˈtrʌst] **1** n desconfianza f (of en) **2** v/t desconfiar de

mist·y [ˈmɪstɪ] adj weather neblinoso; eyes empañado; color borroso

mis·un·der·stand [mɪsʌndərˈstænd] v/t (pret & pp **-stood**) entender mal

mis·un·der·stand·ing [mɪsʌndərˈstændɪŋ] (mistake) malentendido m; (argument) desacuerdo m

mis·use 1 n [mɪsˈjuːs] uso m indebido **2** v/t [mɪsˈjuːz] usar indebidamente

miti·ga·ting cir·cum·stanc·es [ˈmɪtɪɡeɪtɪŋ] npl circunstancias fpl atenuantes

mitt [mɪt] in baseball guante m de béisbol

mit·ten [ˈmɪtn] mitón m

mix [mɪks] **1** n (mixture) mezcla f; cooking: ready to use preparado m **2** v/t mezclar; cement preparar; **~ the flour in well** mezclar la harina bien **3** v/i socially relacionarse

♦ **mix up** v/t (confuse) confundir (**with** con); (put in wrong order) revolver, desordenar; **be mixed up** emotionally tener problemas emocionales; of figures estar confundido; of papers estar revuelto or desordenado; **be mixed up in** estar metido en; **get mixed up with** verse liado con

♦ **mix with** v/t (associate with) relacionarse con

mixed [mɪkst] adj feelings contradictorio; reactions, reviews variado

mixed 'mar·riage matrimonio m mixto

mix·er [ˈmɪksər] for food batidora f; drink refresco m (para mezclar con bebida alcohólica); **she's a good ~** es muy sociable

mix·ture [ˈmɪkstʃər] mezcla f; medicine preparado m

mix-up [ˈmɪksʌp] confusión f

moan [moʊn] **1** n of pain gemido m **2** v/i in pain gemir

mob [maːb] **1** n muchedumbre f **2** v/t (pret & pp **-bed**) asediar, acosar

mo·bile [ˈmoʊbəl] **1** adj person con movilidad; (that can be moved) móvil; **she's a lot less ~ now** ahora tiene mucha menos movilidad **2** n móvil m

mo·bile 'home casa f caravana

mo·bile 'phone Br teléfono m móvil

mo·bil·i·ty [məˈbɪlətɪ] movilidad f

mob·ster [ˈmaːbstər] gángster m

mock [maːk] **1** adj fingido, simulado; **~ exams/elections** exámenes mpl / elecciones fpl de prueba **2** v/t burlarse de

mock·er·y [ˈmaːkərɪ] (derision) burlas fpl; (travesty) farsa f

mock-up [ˈmaːkʌp] (model) maqueta f, modelo m

mode [moʊd] (form), COMPUT modo

M

m; **~ of transportation** medio *m* de transporte

mod·el ['mɑːdl] **1** *adj employee, husband* modélico, modelo; **~ boat/ plane** maqueta *f* de un barco / avión **2** *n miniature* maqueta *f*, modelo *m*; (*pattern*) modelo *m*; (*fashion ~*) modelo *m/f*; **male ~** modelo *m* **3** *v/t* (*pret & pp* **-ed**, *Br* **-led**): **~ clothes** trabajar de modelo; **she ~s swimsuits** trabaja de modelo de bañadores **4** *v/i* (*pret & pp* **-ed**, *Br* **-led**) *for designer* trabajar de modelo; *for artist, photographer* posar

mo·dem ['moʊdem] módem *m*

mod·e·rate 1 *adj* ['mɑːdərət] moderado **2** *n* ['mɑːdərət] POL moderado(-a) *m(f)* **3** *v/t* ['mɑːdəreɪt] moderar

mod·e·rate·ly ['mɑːdərətlɪ] *adv* medianamente, razonablemente

mod·e·ra·tion [mɑːdə'reɪʃn] moderación *f*; **in ~** con moderación

mod·ern ['mɑːdn] *adj* moderno; **in the ~ world** en el mundo contemporáneo

mod·ern·i·za·tion [mɑːdənaɪ'zeɪʃn] modernización *f*

mod·ern·ize ['mɑːdənaɪz] **1** *v/t* modernizar **2** *v/i of business, country* modernizarse

mod·ern ˈlan·gua·ges *npl* lenguas *fpl* modernas

mod·est ['mɑːdɪst] *adj* modesto

mod·es·ty ['mɑːdɪstɪ] modestia *f*

mod·i·fi·ca·tion [mɑːdɪfɪ'keɪʃn] modificación *f*

mod·i·fy ['mɑːdɪfaɪ] *v/t* (*pret & pp* **-ied**) modificar

mod·u·lar ['mɑːdʊlər] *adj furniture* por módulos

mod·ule ['mɑːduːl] módulo *m*

moist [mɔɪst] *adj* húmedo

moist·en ['mɔɪsn] *v/t* humedecer

mois·ture ['mɔɪstʃər] humedad *f*

mois·tur·iz·er ['mɔɪstʃəraɪzər] *for skin* crema *f* hidratante

mo·lar ['moʊlər] muela *f*, molar *m*

mo·las·ses [mə'læsɪz] *nsg* melaza *f*

mold¹ [moʊld] *on food* moho *m*

mold² [moʊld] **1** *n* molde *m* **2** *v/t clay,*

character moldear

mold·y ['moʊldɪ] *adj food* mohoso

mole [moʊl] *on skin* lunar *m*

mo·lec·u·lar [mə'lekjʊlər] *adj* molecular

mol·e·cule ['mɑːlɪkjuːl] molécula *f*

mo·lest [mə'lest] *v/t child, woman* abusar sexualmente de

mol·ly·cod·dle ['mɑːlɪkɑːdl] *v/t* F mimar, consentir

mol·ten ['moʊltən] *adj* fundido

mom [mɑːm] F mamá *f*

mo·ment ['moʊmənt] momento *m*; **at the ~** en estos momentos, ahora mismo; **for the ~** por el momento, por ahora

mo·men·tar·i·ly [moʊmən'terɪlɪ] *adv* (*for a moment*) momentáneamente; (*in a moment*) de un momento a otro

mo·men·ta·ry ['moʊmənterɪ] *adj* momentáneo

mo·men·tous [mə'mentəs] *adj* trascendental, muy importante

mo·men·tum [mə'mentəm] impulso *m*

mon·arch ['mɑːnərk] monarca *m/f*

mon·ar·chy ['mɑːnərkɪ] monarquía *f*

mon·as·tery ['mɑːnəsterɪ] monasterio *m*

mo·nas·tic [mə'næstɪk] *adj* monástico

Mon·day ['mʌndeɪ] lunes *m inv*

mon·e·ta·ry ['mʌnɪterɪ] *adj* monetario

mon·ey ['mʌnɪ] dinero *m*

ˈmon·ey belt faltriquera *f*; **ˈmon·ey-lend·er** prestamista *m/f*; **ˈmon·ey mar·ket** mercado *m* monetario; **ˈmon·ey or·der** giro *m* postal

mon·grel ['mʌŋgrəl] perro *m* cruzado

mon·i·tor ['mɑːnɪtər] **1** *n* COMPUT monitor *m* **2** *v/t* controlar

monk [mʌŋk] monje *m*

mon·key ['mʌŋkɪ] mono *m*; F *child* diablillo *m* F

♦ monkey around with *v/t* F enredar con

ˈmon·key wrench llave *f* inglesa

mon·o·gram ['mɑːnəgræm] monograma *m*

mon·o·grammed ['mɑːnəgræmd] *adj* con monograma

mon·o·log, *Br* **mon·o·logue** ['mɑːnəlɑːg] monólogo *m*

mo·nop·o·lize [məˈnɑːpəlaɪz] *v/t* monopolizar

mo·nop·o·ly [məˈnɑːpəli] monopolio *m*

mo·not·o·nous [məˈnɑːtənəs] *adj* monótono

mo·not·o·ny [məˈnɑːtəni] monotonía *f*

mon·soon [mɑːnˈsuːn] monzón *m*

mon·ster ['mɑːnstər] *n* monstruo *m*

mon·stros·i·ty [mɑːnˈstrɑːsətɪ] monstruosidad *f*

mon·strous ['mɑːnstrəs] *adj* (*frightening, huge*) monstruoso; (*shocking*) escandaloso

month [mʌnθ] mes *m*; **how much do you pay a ~?** ¿cuánto pagas al mes?

month·ly ['mʌnθlɪ] **1** *adj* mensual **2** *adv* mensualmente **3** *n magazine* revista *f* mensual

mon·u·ment ['mɑːnʊmənt] monumento *m*

mon·u·ment·al [mɑːnʊ'mentl] *adj fig* monumental

mood [muːd] (*frame of mind*) humor *m*; (*bad* ~) mal humor *m*; *of meeting, country* atmósfera *f*; *be in a good/ bad* ~ estar de buen / mal humor; *I'm in the ~ for a pizza* me apetece una pizza

mood·y ['muːdɪ] *adj* temperamental; (*bad-tempered*) malhumorado

moon [muːn] *n* luna *f*

'**moon·light 1** *n* luz *f* de luna **2** *v/i* F estar pluriempleado irregularmente; *he's ~ing as a barman* tiene un segundo empleo de camarero

'**moon·lit** *adj* iluminado por la luna

moor [mʊr] *v/t boat* atracar

moor·ing ['mʊrɪŋ] atracadero *m*

moose [muːs] alce *m* americano

mop [mɑːp] **1** *n for floor* fregona *f*; *for dishes* estropajo *m* (*con mango*) **2** *v/t* (*pret & pp* **-ped**) *floor* fregar; *eyes, face* limpiar

♦ **mop up** *v/t* limpiar; MIL acabar con

mope [moʊp] *v/i* estar abatido

mor·al ['mɔːrəl] **1** *adj* moral; *person, behavior* moralista **2** *n of story* moraleja *f*; **~s** moral *f*, moralidad *f*

mo·rale [məˈræl] moral *f*

mo·ral·i·ty [məˈrælətɪ] moralidad *f*

mor·bid ['mɔːrbɪd] *adj* morboso

more [mɔːr] **1** *adj* más; *there are no ~ eggs* no quedan huevos; *some ~ tea?* ¿más té?; *~ and ~ students / time* cada vez más estudiantes / tiempo **2** *adv* más; *~ important* más importante; *~ often* más a menudo; *~ and ~* cada vez más; *~ or less* más o menos; *once ~* una vez más; *he paid ~ than $100 for it* pagó más de 100 dólares por él; *he earns ~ than I do* gana más que yo; *I don't live there any ~* ya no vivo allí **3** *pron* más; *do you want some ~?* ¿quieres más?; *a little ~* un poco más

more·o·ver [mɔːrˈoʊvər] *adv* además, lo que es más

morgue [mɔːrg] depósito *m* de cadáveres

morn·ing ['mɔːrnɪŋ] mañana *f*; *in the ~* por la mañana; *this ~* esta mañana; *tomorrow ~* mañana por la mañana; *good ~* buenos días

morn·ing 'sick·ness náuseas *fpl* matutinas (*típicas del embarazo*)

mo·ron ['mɔːrɑːn] F imbécil *m/f* F, subnormal *m/f* F

mo·rose [məˈroʊs] *adj* hosco, malhumorado

mor·phine ['mɔːrfiːn] morfina *f*

mor·sel ['mɔːrsl] pedacito *m*

mor·tal ['mɔːrtl] **1** *adj* mortal **2** *n* mortal *m/f*

mor·tal·i·ty [mɔːrˈtælətɪ] mortalidad *f*

mor·tar¹ ['mɔːrtər] MIL mortero *m*

mor·tar² ['mɔːrtər] (*cement*) mortero *m*, argamasa *f*

mort·gage ['mɔːrgɪdʒ] **1** *n* hipoteca *f*, préstamo *m* hipotecario **2** *v/t* hipotecar

mor·ti·cian [mɔːrˈtɪʃn] encargado(-a) *m(f)* de una funeraria

mor·tu·a·ry ['mɔːrtʊerɪ] depósito *m* de cadáveres

mo·sa·ic [moʊˈzeɪɪk] mosaico *m*

M

Mos·cow ['mɑːskəʊ] Moscú

Mos·lem ['mʊzlɪm] **1** adj musulmán **2** n musulmán(-ana) m(f)

mosque [mɑːsk] mezquita f

mos·qui·to [mɑːˈskiːtəʊ] mosquito m

moss [mɑːs] musgo m

moss·y ['mɑːsɪ] adj cubierto de musgo

most [məʊst] **1** adj la mayoría de **2** adv (very) muy, sumamente; *the ~ beautiful / interesting* el más hermoso/interesante; *that's the one I like ~* ése es el que más me gusta; *~ of all* sobre todo **3** pron la mayoría de; *I've read ~ of her novels* he leído la mayoría de sus novelas; *at (the) ~* como mucho; *make the ~ of* aprovechar al máximo

most·ly ['məʊstlɪ] adv principalmente, sobre todo

mo·tel [məʊˈtel] motel m

moth [mɑːθ] mariposa f nocturna; (clothes ~) polilla f

'moth·ball bola f de naftalina

moth·er ['mʌðər] **1** n madre f **2** v/t mimar

'moth·er·board COMPUT placa f madre

'moth·er·hood maternidad f

Moth·er·ing 'Sun·day → **Mother's Day**

'moth·er-in-law (pl **mothers-in-law**) suegra f

moth·er·ly ['mʌðərlɪ] adj maternal

moth·er-of-'pearl nácar m; **'Mother's Day** Día f de la Madre; **'moth·er tongue** lengua f materna

mo·tif [məʊˈtiːf] motivo m

mo·tion ['məʊʃn] **1** n (movement) movimiento m; (proposal) moción f; *put o set things in ~* poner las cosas en marcha **2** v/t: *he ~ed me forward* me indicó con un gesto que avanzara

mo·tion·less ['məʊʃnlɪs] adj inmóvil

mo·ti·vate ['məʊtɪveɪt] v/t person motivar

mo·ti·va·tion [məʊtɪˈveɪʃn] motivación f

mo·tive ['məʊtɪv] motivo m

mo·tor ['məʊtər] motor m

'mo·tor·bike moto f; **'mo·tor·boat** lancha f motora; **mo·tor·cade** ['məʊtəkeɪd] caravana f, desfile m de coches; **'mo·tor·cy·cle** motocicleta f; **'mo·tor·cy·clist** motociclista m/f; **'mo·tor home** autocaravana f

mo·tor·ist ['məʊtərɪst] conductor(a) m(f), automovilista m/f

'mo·tor me·chan·ic mecánico(-a) m(f) (de automóviles); **'mo·tor rac·ing** carreras fpl de coches; **'mo·tor·scoot·er** vespa® f; **'mo·tor ve·hi·cle** vehículo m de motor; **'mo·tor·way** Br autopista f

mot·to ['mɑːtəʊ] lema m

mould etc Br → **mold** etc

mound [maʊnd] montículo m

mount [maʊnt] **1** n (mountain) monte m; (horse) montura f; **Mount McKinley** el Monte McKinley **2** v/t steps subir; horse, bicycle montar en; campaign, photo montar **3** v/i aumentar, crecer

♦ **mount up** v/i acumularse

moun·tain ['maʊntɪn] montaña f

'moun·tain bike bicicleta f de montaña

moun·tain·eer [maʊntɪˈnɪr] montañero(-a) m(f), alpinista m/f, L.Am. andinista m/f

moun·tain·eer·ing [maʊntɪˈnɪrɪŋ] montañismo m, alpinismo m, L.Am. andinismo m

moun·tain·ous ['maʊntɪnəs] adj montañoso

mount·ed po'lice ['maʊntɪd] policía f montada

mourn [mɔːrn] **1** v/t llorar **2** v/i: *~ for s.o.* llorar la muerte de alguien

mourn·er ['mɔːrnər] doliente m/f

mourn·ful ['mɔːrnfəl] adj voice, face triste

mourn·ing ['mɔːrnɪŋ] luto m, duelo m; *be in ~* estar de luto; *wear ~* vestir de luto

mouse [maʊs] (pl **mice** [maɪs]) also COMPUT ratón m

'mouse mat COMPUT alfombrilla f

mous·tache → **mustache**

M

mouth [mauθ] *of person* boca *f*; *of river* desembocadura *f*

mouth·ful ['mauθfəl] *of food* bocado *m*; *of drink* trago *m*

'**mouth·or·gan** armónica *f*; '**mouth·piece** *of instrument* boquilla *f*; *(spokesperson)* portavoz *m/f*; '**mouth·wash** enjuague *m* bucal, elixir *m* bucal; '**mouth·wa·ter·ing** *adj* apetitoso

move [muːv] **1** *n in chess, checkers* movimiento *m*; *(step, action)* paso *m*; *(change of house)* mudanza *f*; **make the first ~** dar el primer paso; **get a ~ on!** F ¡espabílate! F; **don't make a ~!** ¡ni te muevas! **2** *v/t object* mover; *(transfer)* trasladar; *emotionally* conmover; **~ those papers out of your way** aparta esos papeles; **~ house** mudarse de casa **3** *v/i* moverse; *(transfer)* trasladarse

♦ **move around** *v/i in room* andar; *from place to place* trasladarse, mudarse

♦ **move away** *v/i* alejarse, apartarse; *(move house)* mudarse

♦ **move in** *v/i to house, neighborhood* mudarse; *to office* trasladarse

♦ **move on** *v/i to another town* mudarse; *to another job* cambiarse; *to another subject* pasar a hablar de

♦ **move out** *v/i of house* mudarse; *of area* marcharse

♦ **move up** *v/i in league* ascender, subir; *(make room)* correrse

move·ment ['muːvmənt] *also organization*, MUS movimiento *m*

mov·ers ['muːvərz] *npl firm* empresa *f* de mudanzas; *(men)* empleados *mpl* de una empresa de mudanzas

mov·ie ['muːvɪ] película *f*; **go to a ~ o the ~s** ir al cine

mov·ie·go·er ['muːvɪɡouər] aficionado(a) *m/f* al cine

'**mov·ie the·a·ter** cine *m*, sala *f* de cine

mov·ing ['muːvɪŋ] *adj that can move* movible; *emotionally* conmovedor

mow [mou] *v/t grass* cortar

♦ **mow down** *v/t* segar la vida de

mow·er ['mouər] cortacésped *m*

MP [em'piː] *abbr* (= **Member of Parliament**) *Br* diputado(-a) *m(f)*; *abbr* (= **Military Policeman**) policía *m* militar

mph [empiː'eɪtʃ] *abbr* (= **miles per hour**) millas *fpl* por hora

Mr ['mɪstər] Sr.

Mrs ['mɪsɪz] Sra.

Ms [mɪz] Sra. *(casada o no casada)*

much [mʌtʃ] **1** *adj* mucho; **so money** tanto dinero; **as ~ ... as ...** tanto ... como **2** *adv* mucho; **I don't like him ~** no me gusta mucho; **he's ~ more intelligent than ...** es mucho más inteligente que ...; **the house is ~ too large for one person** la casa es demasiado grande para una sola persona; **very ~** mucho; **thank you very ~** muchas gracias; **I love you very ~** te quiero muchísimo; **too ~** demasiado **3** *pron* mucho; **what did she say? – nothing ~** ¿qué dijo? – no demasiado; **as ~ as ...** tanto ... como; **it may cost as ~ as half a million dollars** puede que haya malversado hasta medio millón de dólares; **I thought as ~** eso es lo que pensaba

muck [mʌk] *(dirt)* suciedad *f*

mu·cus ['mjuːkəs] mocos *mpl*, mucosidad *f*

mud [mʌd] barro *m*

mud·dle ['mʌdl] **1** *n* lío *m* **2** *v/t person* liar; **you've gotten the story all ~d** te has hecho un lío con la historia

♦ **muddle up** *v/t* desordenar; *(confuse)* liar

mud·dy ['mʌdɪ] *adj* embarrado

mues·li ['mjuːzlɪ] muesli *m*

muf·fin ['mʌfɪn] magdalena *f*

muf·fle ['mʌfl] *v/t* ahogar, amortiguar

♦ **muffle up** *v/i* abrigarse

muf·fler ['mʌflər] MOT silenciador *m*

mug[1] [mʌɡ] *for tea, coffee* taza *f*; F *(face)* jeta *f* F, *Span* careto *m* F

mug[2] [mʌɡ] *v/t (pret & pp* **-ged***) (attack)* atracar

mug·ger ['mʌɡər] atracador(a) *m(f)*

mug·ging ['mʌɡɪŋ] atraco *m*

mug·gy ['mʌɡɪ] *adj* bochornoso

M

mule [mjuːl] *animal* mulo(-a) *m(f)*; (*slipper*) pantufla *f*

♦ **mull over** [mʌl] *v/t* reflexionar sobre

mul·ti·lat·e·ral [mʌltɪ'lætərəl] *adj* POL multilateral

mul·ti·lin·gual [mʌltɪ'lɪŋgwəl] *adj* multilingüe

mul·ti·me·di·a [mʌltɪ'miːdɪə] **1** *n* multimedia *f* **2** *adj* multimedia

mul·ti·na·tion·al [mʌltɪ'næʃnl] **1** *adj* multinacional **2** *n* COM multinacional *f*

mul·ti·ple ['mʌltɪpl] *adj* múltiple

mul·ti·ple 'choice ques·tion pregunta *f* tipo test

mul·ti·ple scle·ro·sis [skle'rousɪs] esclerosis *f* múltiple

mul·ti·pli·ca·tion [mʌltɪplɪ'keɪʃn] multiplicación *f*

mul·ti·ply ['mʌltɪplaɪ] **1** *v/t* (*pret & pp -ied*) multiplicar **2** *v/i* (*pret & pp -ied*) multiplicarse

mum·my ['mʌmɪ] *Br* mamá *f*

mum·ble ['mʌmbl] **1** *n* murmullo *m* **2** *v/t* farfullar **3** *v/i* hablar entre dientes

mumps [mʌmps] *nsg* paperas *fpl*

munch [mʌntʃ] *v/t & v/i* mascar

mu·ni·ci·pal [mjuː'nɪsɪpl] *adj* municipal

mu·ral ['mjuərəl] mural *m*

mur·der ['mɜːrdər] **1** *n* asesinato *m* **2** *v/t person* asesinar, matar; *song* destrozar

mur·der·er ['mɜːrdərər] asesino(-a) *m(f)*

mur·der·ous ['mɜːrdrəs] *adj rage, look* asesino

murk·y ['mɜːrkɪ] *adj water* turbio, oscuro; *fig* turbio

mur·mur ['mɜːrmər] **1** *n* murmullo *m* **2** *v/t* murmurar

mus·cle ['mʌsl] músculo *m*

mus·cu·lar ['mʌskjʊlər] *adj pain, strain* muscular; *person* musculoso

muse [mjuːz] *v/i* meditar, reflexionar (*on* sobre)

mu·se·um [mjuː'zɪəm] museo *m*

mush·room ['mʌʃrʊm] **1** *n* seta *f*, hongo *m*; (*button ~*) champiñón *m*

2 *v/i* crecer rápidamente

mu·sic ['mjuːzɪk] música *f*; *in written form* partitura *f*

mu·sic·al ['mjuːzɪkl] **1** *adj* musical; *person* con talento para la música **2** *n* musical *m*

'mu·sic(·al) box caja *f* de música

mu·sic·al 'in·stru·ment instrumento *m* musical

mu·si·cian [mjuː'zɪʃn] músico(-a) *m(f)*

mus·sel ['mʌsl] mejillón *m*

must [mʌst] *v/aux* ◊ *necessity* tener que, deber; *I ~ be on time* tengo que *or* debo llegar a la hora; *do you have to leave now? yes, I ~* ¿tienes que marcharte ahora? – sí, debo marcharme; *I ~n't be late* no tengo que llegar tarde, no debo llegar tarde ◊ *probability* deber de; *it ~ be about 6 o'clock* deben de ser las seis; *they ~ have arrived by now* ya deben de haber llegado

mus·tache [mə'stæʃ] bigote *m*

mus·tard ['mʌstərd] mostaza *f*

must·y ['mʌstɪ] *adj room* que huele a humedad; *smell* a humedad

mute [mjuːt] *adj animal* mudo

mut·ed ['mjuːtɪd] *adj color* apagado; *criticism* débil

mu·ti·late ['mjuːtɪleɪt] *v/t* mutilar

mu·ti·ny ['mjuːtɪnɪ] **1** *n* motín *m* **2** *v/i* (*pret & pp -ied*) amotinarse

mut·ter ['mʌtər] *v/t & v/i* murmurar

mut·ton ['mʌtn] carnero *m*

mu·tu·al ['mjuːtʃʊəl] *adj* mutuo

muz·zle ['mʌzl] **1** *n of animal* hocico *m*; *for dog* bozal *m* **2** *v/t* poner un bozal a; *~ the press* amordazar a la prensa

my [maɪ] *adj* mi; *~ house* mi casa; *~ parents* mis padres

my·op·ic [maɪ'ɑːpɪk] *adj* miope

my·self [maɪ'self] *pron reflexive* me; *emphatic* yo mismo(-a); *when I saw ~ in the mirror* cuando me vi en el espejo; *I saw it ~* lo vi yo mismo; *by ~* (*alone*) solo; (*without help*) yo solo, yo mismo

mys·te·ri·ous [mɪ'stɪrɪəs] *adj* misterioso

mys·te·ri·ous·ly [mɪˈstɪrɪəslɪ] *adv* misteriosamente

mys·te·ry [ˈmɪstərɪ] misterio *m*; **~ (story)** relato *m* de misterio

mys·ti·fy [ˈmɪstɪfaɪ] *v/t* (*pret & pp -ied*) dejar perplejo

myth [mɪθ] *also fig* mito *m*

myth·i·cal [ˈmɪθɪkl] *adj* mítico

my·thol·o·gy [mɪˈθɑːlədʒɪ] mitología *f*

N

nab [næb] *v/t* (*pret & pp -bed*) F (*take for o.s.*) pescar F, agarrar

nag [næg] **1** *v/i* (*pret & pp -ged*) *of person* dar la lata **2** *v/t* (*pret & pp -ged*): **~ s.o. to do sth** dar la lata a alguien para que haga algo

nag·ging [ˈnægɪŋ] *adj person* quejica; *doubt* persistente; *pain* continuo

nail [neɪl] *for wood* clavo *m*; *on finger, toe* uña *f*

'**nail clip·pers** *npl* cortaúñas *m inv*; '**nail file** lima *f* de uñas; '**nail pol·ish** esmalte *m* de uñas; '**nail pol·ish re·mov·er** quitaesmaltes *m inv*; '**nail scis·sors** *npl* tijeras *fpl* de manicura; '**nail var·nish** esmalte *m* de uñas

na·ive [naɪˈiːv] *adj* ingenuo

na·ked [ˈneɪkɪd] *adj* desnudo; **to the ~ eye** a simple vista

name [neɪm] **1** *n* nombre *m*; **what's your ~?** ¿cómo te llamas?; **call s.o. ~s** insultar a alguien; **make a ~ for o.s.** hacerse un nombre **2** *v/t*: **they ~d him Ben** le llamaron Ben

♦ **name for** *v/t*: **name s.o. for s.o.** poner a alguien el nombre de alguien

name·ly [ˈneɪmlɪ] *adv* a saber

'**name·sake** tocayo(-a) *m(f)*, homónimo(-a) *m(f)*

'**name·tag** *on clothing etc* etiqueta *f*

nan·ny [ˈnænɪ] niñera *f*

nap [næp] *n* cabezada *f*; **have a ~** echar una cabezada

nape [neɪp]: **~ of the neck** nuca *f*

nap·kin [ˈnæpkɪn] (*table ~*) servilleta *f*; (*sanitary ~*) compresa *f*

nar·cot·ic [nɑrˈkɑːtɪk] *n* narcótico *m*, estupefaciente *m*

nar'cot·ics a·gent agente *m/f* de la brigada de estupefacientes

nar·rate [nəˈreɪt] *v/t* narrar

nar·ra·tion [nəˈreɪʃn] (*telling*) narración *f*

nar·ra·tive [ˈnærətɪv] **1** *n* (*story*) narración *f* **2** *adj poem, style* narrativo

nar·ra·tor [nəˈreɪtər] narrador(a) *m(f)*

nar·row [ˈnæroʊ] *adj street, bed, victory* estrecho; *views, mind* cerrado

nar·row·ly [ˈnæroʊlɪ] *adv win* por poco; **~ escape sth** escapar por poco de algo

nar·row-mind·ed [næroʊˈmaɪndɪd] *adj* cerrado

na·sal [ˈneɪzl] *adj voice* nasal

nas·ty [ˈnæstɪ] *adj person, smell* desagradable, asqueroso; *thing to say* malintencionado; *weather* horrible; *cut, wound* feo; *disease* serio

na·tion [ˈneɪʃn] nación *f*

na·tion·al [ˈnæʃənl] **1** *adj* nacional **2** *n* ciudadano(-a) *m(f)*

na·tion·al 'an·them himno *m* nacional

na·tion·al 'debt deuda *f* pública

na·tion·al·ism [ˈnæʃənəlɪzm] nacionalismo *m*

na·tion·al·i·ty [næʃəˈnælətɪ] nacionalidad *f*

na·tion·al·ize [ˈnæʃənəlaɪz] *v/t industry etc* nacionalizar

na·tion·al 'park parque *m* nacional

na·tive [ˈneɪtɪv] **1** *adj* nativo; **~**

tongue lengua *f* materna **2** *n* nativo(-a) *m*(*f*), natural *m*/*f*; *tribesman* nativo(-a) *m*(*f*), indígena *m*/*f*; ***he's a ~ of New York*** es natural de Nueva York

na·tive 'coun·try país *m* natal

na·tive 'speak·er hablante *m*/*f* nativo(-a)

NATO ['neɪtou] *abbr* (= ***North Atlantic Treaty Organization***) OTAN *f* (= Organización *f* del Tratado del Atlántico Norte)

nat·u·ral ['nætʃrəl] *adj* natural

nat·u·ral 'gas gas *m* natural

nat·u·ral·ist ['nætʃrəlɪst] naturalista *m*/*f*

nat·u·ral·ize ['nætʃrəlaɪz] *v*/*t*: ***become ~d*** naturalizarse, nacionalizarse

nat·u·ral·ly ['nætʃrəlɪ] *adv* (*of course*) naturalmente; *behave, speak* con naturalidad; (*by nature*) por naturaleza

nat·u·ral 'sci·ence ciencias *fpl* naturales

nat·u·ral 'sci·en·tist experto(-a) *m*(*f*) en ciencias naturales

na·ture ['neɪtʃər] naturaleza *f*

na·ture re'serve reserva *f* natural

naugh·ty ['nɒːtɪ] *adj* travieso, malo; *photograph, word etc* picante

nau·se·a ['nɒːzɪə] náusea *f*

nau·se·ate ['nɒːzɪeɪt] *v*/*t* (*disgust*) dar náuseas a

nau·se·at·ing ['nɒːzɪeɪtɪŋ] *adj smell, taste* nauseabundo; *person* repugnante

nau·seous ['nɒːʃəs] *adj* nauseabundo; ***feel ~*** tener náuseas

nau·ti·cal ['nɒːtɪkl] *adj* náutico

'nau·ti·cal mile milla *f* náutica

na·val ['neɪvl] *adj* naval

'na·val base base *f* naval

na·vel ['neɪvl] ombligo *m*

nav·i·ga·ble ['nævɪɡəbl] *adj river* navegable

nav·i·gate ['nævɪɡeɪt] *v*/*i in ship, airplane*, COMPUT navegar; *in car* hacer de copiloto

nav·i·ga·tion [nævɪ'ɡeɪʃn] navegación *f*; *in car* direcciónes *fpl*

nav·i·ga·tor ['nævɪɡeɪtər] *on ship* oficial *m* de derrota; *in airplane* navegante *m*/*f*; *in car* copiloto *m*/*f*

na·vy ['neɪvɪ] armada *f*, marina *f* (de guerra)

na·vy 'blue 1 *n* azul *m* marino **2** *adj* azul marino

near [nɪr] **1** *adv* cerca; ***come a bit ~er*** acércate un poco más **2** *prep* cerca de; ***~ the bank*** cerca del banco; ***do you go ~ the bank?*** ¿pasa cerca del banco? **3** *adj* cercano, próximo; ***the ~est bus stop*** la parada de autobús más cercana *or* próxima; ***in the ~ future*** en un futuro próximo

near·by [nɪr'baɪ] *adv live* cerca

near·ly ['nɪrlɪ] *adv* casi

near-sight·ed [nɪr'saɪtɪd] *adj* miope

neat [niːt] *adj* ordenado; *whiskey* solo, seco; *solution* ingenioso; F (*terrific*) genial F, estupendo F

ne·ces·sar·i·ly ['nesəserəlɪ] *adv* necesariamente

ne·ces·sa·ry ['nesəserɪ] *adj* necesario, preciso; ***it is ~ to ...*** es necesario ..., hay que ...

ne·ces·si·tate [nɪ'sesɪteɪt] *v*/*t* exigir, hacer necesario

ne·ces·si·ty [nɪ'sesɪtɪ] (*being necessary*) necesidad *f*; (*something necessary*) necesidad *f*, requisito *m* imprescindible

neck [nek] *n* cuello *m*

neck·lace ['neklɪs] collar *m*; **'neck·line** *of dress* escote *m*; **'neck·tie** corbata *f*

née [neɪ] *adj* de soltera

need [niːd] **1** *n* necesidad *f*; ***if ~ be*** si fuera necesario; ***in ~*** necesitado; ***be in ~ of sth*** necesitar algo; ***there's no ~ to be rude/upset*** no hace falta ser grosero / que te enfades **2** *v*/*t* necesitar; ***you'll ~ to buy one*** tendrás que comprar uno; ***you don't ~ to wait*** no hace falta que esperes; ***I ~ to talk to you*** tengo que *or* necesito hablar contigo; ***~ I say more?*** ¿hace falta que añada algo?

nee·dle ['niːdl] *for sewing, injection, on dial* aguja *f*

'nee·dle·work costura *f*

need·y ['niːdɪ] *adj* necesitado

neg·a·tive ['negətɪv] *adj* negativo; ***answer in the ~*** dar una respuesta negativa

ne·glect [nɪ'glekt] **1** *n* abandono *m*, descuido *m* **2** *v/t garden, one's health* descuidar, desatender; ***~ to do sth*** no hacer algo

ne·glect·ed [nɪ'glektɪd] *adj garden* abandonado, descuidado; *author* olvidado; ***feel ~*** sentirse abandonado

neg·li·gence ['neglɪdʒəns] negligencia *f*

neg·li·gent ['neglɪdʒənt] *adj* negligente

neg·li·gi·ble ['neglɪdʒəbl] *adj quantity, amount* insignificante

ne·go·ti·a·ble [nɪ'goʊʃəbl] *adj salary, contract* negociable

ne·go·ti·ate [nɪ'goʊʃɪeɪt] **1** *v/i* negociar **2** *v/t deal, settlement* negociar; *obstacles* franquear, salvar; *bend in road* tomar

ne·go·ti·a·tion [nɪgoʊʃɪ'eɪʃn] negociación *f*; ***be under ~*** estar siendo negociado

ne·go·ti·a·tor [nɪ'goʊʃɪeɪtər] negociador(a) *m(f)*

Ne·gro ['niːgroʊ] negro(-a) *m(f)*

neigh [neɪ] *v/i* relinchar

neigh·bor ['neɪbər] vecino(-a) *m(f)*

neigh·bor·hood ['neɪbərhʊd] *in town* vecindario *m*, barrio *m*; ***in the ~ of ...*** *fig* alrededor de ...

neigh·bor·ing ['neɪbərɪŋ] *adj house, state* vecino, colindante

neigh·bor·ly ['neɪbərlɪ] *adj* amable

neigh·bour *etc* Br → **neighbor** *etc*

nei·ther ['niːðər] **1** *adj* ninguno; ***~ applicant was any good*** ninguno de los candidatos era bueno **2** *pron* ninguno(-a) *m(f)* **3** *adv*: ***~ ... nor ...*** ni ... ni ... **4** *conj*: ***~ do I*** yo tampoco; ***~ can I*** yo tampoco

ne·on light ['niːɑːn] luz *f* de neón

neph·ew ['nefjuː] sobrino *m*

nerd [nɜːrd] F petardo(-a) *m(f)* F

nerve [nɜːrv] nervio *m*; *(courage)* valor *m*; *(impudence)* descaro *m*; ***it's bad for my ~s*** me pone de los nervios; ***get on s.o.'s ~s*** sacar de quicio

a alguien

nerve-rack·ing ['nɜːrvrækɪŋ] *adj* angustioso, exasperante

ner·vous ['nɜːrvəs] *adj person* nervioso, inquieto; *twitch* nervioso; ***I'm ~ about meeting them*** la reunión con ellos me pone muy nervioso

ner·vous 'break·down crisis *f inv* nerviosa

ner·vous 'en·er·gy energía *f*

ner·vous·ness ['nɜːrvəsnɪs] nerviosismo *m*

ner·vous 'wreck manojo *m* de nervios

nerv·y ['nɜːrvɪ] *adj (fresh)* descarado

nest [nest] *n* nido *m*

nes·tle ['nesl] *v/i* acomodarse

net[1] [net] *for fishing, tennis* red *f*

net[2] [net] *adj price, weight* neto

net 'cur·tain visillo *m*

net 'pro·fit beneficio *m* neto

'net·work *of contacts, cells,* COMPUT red *f*

neu·rol·o·gist [nuː'rɑːlədʒɪst] neurólogo(-a) *m(f)*

neu·ro·sis [nuː'roʊsɪs] neurosis *f inv*

neu·rot·ic [nuː'rɑːtɪk] *adj* neurótico

neu·ter ['nuːtər] *v/t animal* castrar

neu·tral ['nuːtrl] **1** *adj country* neutral; *color* neutro **2** *n gear* punto *m* muerto; ***in ~*** en punto muerto

neu·tral·i·ty [nuː'trælətɪ] neutralidad *f*

neu·tral·ize ['nuːtrəlaɪz] *v/t* neutralizar

nev·er ['nevər] *adv* nunca; ***you're ~ going to believe this*** no te vas a creer esto; ***you ~ promised, did you?*** no lo llegaste a prometer, ¿verdad?

nev·er-'end·ing *adj* interminable

nev·er·the·less [nevərðə'les] *adv* sin embargo, no obstante

new [nuː] *adj* nuevo; ***this system is still ~ to me*** todavía no me he hecho con este sistema; ***I'm ~ to the job*** soy nuevo en el trabajo; ***that's nothing ~*** no es nada nuevo

'new·born *adj* recién nacido

new·com·er ['nuːkʌmər] recién

llegado(-a) m(f)

new·ly ['nu:lɪ] adv (recently) recientemente, recién

new·ly·weds [wedz] npl recién casados mpl

new 'moon luna f nueva

news [nu:z] nsg also RAD noticias fpl; on TV noticias fpl, telediario m; **that's ~ to me** no sabía eso

'news a·gen·cy agencia f de noticias; **'news·cast** TV noticias fpl, telediario m; on radio noticias fpl; **'news·cast·er** TV presentador(a) m(f) de informativos; **'news·deal·er** quiosquero(-a) m(f); **'news flash** flash m informativo, noticia f de última hora; **'news·pa·per** periódico m; **'news·read·er** TV etc presentador(a) m(f) de informativos; **'news re·port** reportaje m; **'news·stand** quiosco m; **'news·ven·dor** vendedor(a) m(f) de periódicos

'New Year año m nuevo; **Happy ~!** ¡Feliz Año Nuevo!; **New Year's 'Day** Día m de Año Nuevo; **New Year's 'Eve** Nochevieja f; **New York** [jɔ:rk] 1 adj neoyorquino 2 n: ~ (City) Nueva York; **New York·er** ['jɔ:rkər] n neoyorquino(-a) m(f); **New Zea·land** ['zi:lənd] Nueva Zelanda; **New Zea·land·er** ['zi:ləndər] neozelandés(-esa) m(f), neocelandés(-esa) m(f)

next [nekst] 1 adj in time próximo, siguiente; in space siguiente, de al lado; **~ week** la próxima semana, la semana que viene; **the ~ week he came back again** volvió a la semana siguiente; **who's ~?** ¿quién es el siguiente? 2 adv luego, después; **~, we're going to study …** a continuación, vamos a estudiar …; **~ to** (beside) al lado de; (in comparison with) en comparación con

next-'door 1 adj neighbor de al lado 2 adv live al lado

next of 'kin pariente m más cercano

nib·ble ['nɪbl] v/t mordisquear

Nic·a·ra·gua [nɪkə'rɑ:gwə] Nicaragua

Nic·a·ra·guan [nɪkə'rɑ:gwən] 1 adj nicaragüense 2 n nicaragüense m/f

nice [naɪs] adj trip, house, hair bonito, L.Am. lindo; person agradable, simpático; weather bueno, agradable; meal, food bueno, rico; **be ~ to your sister!** ¡trata bien a tu hermana!; **that's very ~ of you** es muy amable de tu parte

nice·ly ['naɪslɪ] adv written, presented bien; (pleasantly) amablemente

ni·ce·ties ['naɪsətɪz] npl sutilezas fpl, refinamientos mpl; **social ~** cumplidos mpl

niche [ni:ʃ] in market hueco m, nicho m; (special position) hueco m

nick [nɪk] n (cut) muesca f, mella f; **in the ~ of time** justo a tiempo

nick·el ['nɪkl] níquel m; (coin) moneda de cinco centavos

'nick·name n apodo m, mote m

niece [ni:s] sobrina f

nig·gard·ly ['nɪgərdlɪ] adj amount, person mísero

night [naɪt] noche f; **tomorrow ~** mañana por la noche; **11 o'clock at ~** las 11 de la noche; **travel by ~** viajar de noche; **during the ~** por la noche; **stay the ~** quedarse a dormir; **a room for 2 ~s** una habitación para 2 noches; **work ~s** trabajar de noche; **good ~** buenas noches; **in the middle of the ~** en mitad de la noche

'night·cap drink copa f (tomada antes de ir a dormir); **'night·club** club m nocturno, discoteca f; **'night·dress** camisón m; **'night·fall**: **at ~** al anochecer; **'night flight** vuelo m nocturno; **'night·gown** camisón m

nigh·tin·gale ['naɪtɪŋgeɪl] ruiseñor m

'night·life vida f nocturna

night·ly ['naɪtlɪ] 1 adj: **a ~ event** algo que sucede todas las noches 2 adv todas las noches

'night·mare also fig pesadilla f; **'night por·ter** portero m de noche; **'night school** escuela f nocturna; **'night shift** turno m de noche; **'night·shirt** camisa f de dormir;

'night·spot local *m* nocturno; **'night·time**: *at ~*, *in the ~* por la noche

nil [nɪl] *Br* cero

nim·ble ['nɪmbl] *adj* ágil

nine [naɪn] nueve

nine·teen [naɪn'tiːn] diecinueve

nine·teenth [naɪn'tiːnθ] *n & adj* decimonoveno

nine·ti·eth ['naɪntɪɪθ] *n & adj* nonagésimo

nine·ty ['naɪntɪ] noventa

ninth [naɪnθ] *n & adj* noveno

nip [nɪp] *n* (*pinch*) pellizco *m*; (*bite*) mordisco *m*

nip·ple ['nɪpl] pezón *m*

ni·tro·gen ['naɪtrədʒn] nitrógeno *m*

no [noʊ] **1** *adv* no **2** *adj*: *there's ~ coffee/ tea left* no queda café / té; *I have ~ family/ money* no tengo familia/ dinero; *I'm ~ linguist/ expert* no soy un lingüista / experto; *~ smoking/ parking* prohibido fumar/ aparcar

no·bil·i·ty [noʊ'bɪlətɪ] nobleza *f*

no·ble ['noʊbl] *adj* noble

no·bod·y ['noʊbədɪ] *pron* nadie; *~ knows* nadie lo sabe; *there was ~ at home* no había nadie en casa

nod [nɑːd] **1** *n* movimiento *m* de la cabeza **2** *v/i* (*pret & pp* **-ded**) asentir con la cabeza

◆ **nod off** *v/i* (*fall asleep*) quedarse dormido

no-hop·er [noʊ'hoʊpər] F inútil *m/f* F

noise [nɔɪz] ruido *m*

nois·y ['nɔɪzɪ] *adj* ruidoso

nom·i·nal ['nɑːmɪnl] *adj amount* simbólico

nom·i·nate ['nɑːmɪneɪt] *v/t* (*appoint*) nombrar; *~ s.o. for a post* (*propose*) proponer a alguien para un puesto

nom·i·na·tion [nɑːmɪ'neɪʃn] (*appointment*) nombramiento *m*; (*proposal*) nominación *f*; *who was your ~?* ¿a quién propusiste?

nom·i·nee [nɑːmɪ'niː] candidato(-a) *m(f)*

non ... [nɑːn] no ...

non·al·co·hol·ic *adj* sin alcohol

non·a·ligned *adj* no alineado

non·cha·lant ['nɑːnʃələnt] *adj* despreocupado

non·com·mis·sioned 'of·fi·cer suboficial *m/f*

non·com·mit·tal *adj person, response* evasivo

non·de·script ['nɑːndɪskrɪpt] *adj* anodino

none [nʌn] *pron*: *~ of the students* ninguno de los estudiantes; *~ of the water* nada del agua; *there are ~ left* no queda ninguno; *there is ~ left* no queda nada

non·en·ti·ty nulidad *f*

none·the·less [nʌnðə'les] *adv* sin embargo, no obstante

non·ex·ist·ent *adj* inexistente

non·fic·tion no ficción *f*

non(·in)'flam·ma·ble *adj* incombustible, no inflamable

non·in·ter·fer·ence, **non·in·ter·'ven·tion** no intervención *f*

non-'i·ron *adj shirt* que no necesita plancha

'no-no: *that's a ~* F de eso nada

no-'non·sense *adj approach* directo

non·'pay·ment impago *m*

non·pol'lut·ing *adj* que no contamina

non·'res·i·dent *n* no residente *m/f*

non·re·turn·a·ble [nɑːnrɪ'tɜːrnəbl] *adj* no retornable

non·sense ['nɑːnsəns] disparate *m*, tontería *f*; *don't talk ~* no digas disparates *or* tonterías; *~, it's easy!* tonterías, ¡es fácil!

non·'skid *adj tires* antideslizante

non·'slip *adj surface* antideslizante

non·'smok·er *person* no fumador(a) *m(f)*

non·'stand·ard *adj* no estándar

non·'stick *adj pans* antiadherente

non·'stop **1** *adj flight, train* directo, sin escalas; *chatter* ininterrumpido **2** *adv fly, travel* directamente; *chatter, argue* sin parar

non·'swim·mer: *be a ~* no saber nadar

non·'u·nion *adj* no sindicado

non·'vi·o·lence no violencia *f*

non·'vi·o·lent *adj* no violento

N

noo·dles ['nu:dlz] *npl* tallarines *mpl* (chinos)

nook [nʊk] rincón *m*

noon [nu:n] mediodía *m*; *at* ~ al mediodía

'no-one → *nobody*

noose [nu:s] lazo *m* corredizo

nor [nɔ:r] *conj* ni; ~ *do I* yo tampoco, ni yo

norm [nɔ:rm] norma *f*

nor·mal ['nɔ:rml] *adj* normal

nor·mal·i·ty [nɔ:r'mælətɪ] normalidad *f*

nor·mal·ize ['nɔ:rməlaɪz] *v/t relationships* normalizar

nor·mal·ly ['nɔ:rməlɪ] *adv* (*usually*) normalmente; (*in a normal way*) normalmente, con normalidad

north [nɔ:rθ] **1** *n* norte *m*; *to the* ~ *of* al norte de **2** *adj* norte **3** *adv travel* al norte; ~ *of* al norte de

North Am·er·i·ca América del Norte, Norteamérica; **North Am·er·i·can 1** *n* norteamericano(-a) *m(f)* **2** *adj* norteamericano; **north'east** *n* nordeste *m*, noreste *m*

nor·ther·ly ['nɔ:rðəlɪ] *adj* norte, del norte

nor·thern ['nɔ:rðən] norteño, del norte

nor·thern·er ['nɔ:rðənər] norteño(-a) *m(f)*

North Ko·re·a Corea del Norte; **North Ko·re·an 1** *adj* norcoreano **2** *n* norcoreano(-a) *m(f)*; **North 'Pole** Polo *m* Norte

north·ward ['nɔ:rðwərd] *adv travel* hacia el norte

north·west [nɔ:rð'west] *n* noroeste *m*

Nor·way ['nɔ:rweɪ] Noruega

Nor·we·gian [nɔ:r'wi:dʒən] **1** *adj* noruego **2** *n person* noruego(-a) *m(f)*; *language* noruego *m*

nose [noʊz] nariz *m*; *of animal* hocico *m*; *it was right under my* ~*!* ¡lo tenía delante de mis narices!

♦ **nose around** *v/i* F husmear

'nose·bleed: *have a* ~ sangrar por la nariz

nos·tal·gia [nɑ:'stældʒə] nostalgia *f*

nos·tal·gic [nɑ:'stældʒɪk] *adj* nostálgico

nos·tril ['nɑ:strəl] ventana *f* de la nariz

nos·y ['noʊzɪ] *adj* F entrometido

not [nɑ:t] *adv* no; ~ *this one, that one* éste no, ése; ~ *now* ahora no; ~ *like that* así no; ~ *before Tuesday* / *next week* no antes del martes / de la próxima semana; ~ *for me, thanks* para mí no, gracias; ~ *a lot* no mucho; *it's* ~ *ready* / *allowed* no está listo / permitido; *I don't know* no lo sé; *he didn't help* no ayudó

no·ta·ble ['noʊtəbl] *adj* notable

no·ta·ry ['noʊtərɪ] notario(-a) *m(f)*

notch [nɑ:tʃ] *n* muesca *f*, mella *f*

note [noʊt] *n written*, MUS nota *f*; *take* ~*s* tomar notas; *take* ~ *of sth* prestar atención a algo

♦ **note down** *v/t* anotar

'note·book cuaderno *m*, libreta *f*; COMPUT *Span* ordenador *m* portátil, *L.Am.* computadora *f* portátil

not·ed ['noʊtɪd] *adj* destacado

'note·pad bloc *m* de notas

'note·pa·per papel *m* de carta

noth·ing ['nʌθɪŋ] *pron* nada; ~ *but* sólo; ~ *much* no mucho; *for* ~ (*for free*) gratis; (*for no reason*) por nada; *I'd like* ~ *better* me encantaría

no·tice ['noʊtɪs] **1** *n on bulletin board*, *in street* cartel *m*, letrero *m*; (*advance warning*) aviso *m*; *in newspaper* anuncio *m*; *at short* ~ con poca antelación; *until further* ~ hasta nuevo aviso; *give s.o. his* / *her* ~ to quit job despedir a alguien; *to leave house* comunicar a alguien que tiene que abandonar la casa; *hand in one's* ~ *to employer* presentar la dimisión; *four weeks'* ~ cuatro semanas de preaviso; *take* ~ *of sth* observar algo, prestar atención a algo; *take no* ~ *of s.o.* / *sth* no hacer caso de alguien / algo **2** *v/t* notar, fijarse en

no·tice·a·ble ['noʊtɪsəbl] *adj* apreciable, evidente

no·ti·fy ['noʊtɪfaɪ] *v/t* (*pret & pp -ied*) notificar, informar

no·tion ['noʊʃn] noción *f*, idea *f*

no·tions ['noʊʃnz] *npl* artículos *mpl* de costura

no·to·ri·ous [noʊ'tɔːrɪəs] *adj* de mala fama

nou·gat ['nuːgət] *especie de turrón*

noun [naʊn] nombre *m*, sustantivo *m*

nou·rish·ing ['nʌrɪʃɪŋ] *adj* nutritivo

nou·rish·ment ['nʌrɪʃmənt] alimento *m*, alimentación *f*

nov·el ['nɑːvl] *n* novela *f*

nov·el·ist ['nɑːvlɪst] novelista *m/f*

nov·el·ty ['nɑːvəltɪ] (*being new*) lo novedoso; (*sth new*) novedad *f*

No·vem·ber [noʊ'vembər] noviembre *m*

nov·ice ['nɑːvɪs] principiante *m/f*

now [naʊ] *adv* ahora; **~ and again**, **~ and then** de vez en cuando; **by ~** ya; **from ~ on** de ahora en adelante; **right ~** ahora mismo; **just ~** (*at this moment*) en este momento; (*a little while ago*) hace un momento; **~, ~!** ¡vamos!, ¡venga!; **~, where did I put it?** ¿y ahora dónde lo he puesto?

now·a·days ['naʊədeɪz] *adv* hoy en día

no·where ['noʊwer] *adv* en ningún lugar; **it's ~ near finished** no está acabado ni mucho menos; **he was ~ to be seen** no se le veía en ninguna parte

noz·zle ['nɑːzl] boquilla *f*

nu·cle·ar ['nuːklɪər] *adj* nuclear

nu·cle·ar 'en·er·gy energía *f* nuclear; **nu·cle·ar 'fis·sion** ['fɪʃn] fisión *f* nuclear; **'nu·cle·ar-free** *adj* desnuclearizado; **nu·cle·ar 'phys·ics** física *f* nuclear; **nu·cle·ar 'pow·er** energía *f* nuclear; POL potencia *f* nuclear; **nu·cle·ar 'pow·er sta·tion** central *f* nuclear; **nu·cle·ar re'ac·tor** reactor *m* nuclear; **nu·cle·ar 'waste** residuos *mpl* nucleares; **nu·cle·ar 'weap·on** arma *f* nuclear

nude [nuːd] **1** *adj* desnudo **2** *n paint-ing* desnudo *m*; **in the ~** desnudo

nudge [nʌdʒ] *v/t* dar un toque con el codo a

nud·ist ['nuːdɪst] *n* nudista *m/f*

nui·sance ['nuːsns] incordio *m*, molestia *f*; **make a ~ of o.s.** dar la lata; **what a ~!** ¡qué incordio!

nuke [nuːk] *v/t* F atacar con armas nucleares

null and 'void [nʌl] *adj* nulo y sin efecto

numb [nʌm] *adj* entumecido; *emotionally* insensible

num·ber ['nʌmbər] **1** *n* número *m*; **a ~ of people** un cierto número de personas **2** *v/t* (*put a ~ on*) numerar

nu·mer·al ['nuːmərəl] número *m*

nu·me·rate ['nuːmərət] *adj* que sabe sumar y restar

nu·me·rous ['nuːmərəs] *adj* numeroso

nun [nʌn] monja *f*

nurse [nɜːrs] enfermero(-a) *m(f)*

nur·se·ry ['nɜːrsərɪ] guardería *f*; *for plants* vivero *m*

'nur·se·ry rhyme canción *f* infantil; **'nur·se·ry school** parvulario *m*, jardín *m* de infancia; **'nur·se·ry school teach·er** profesor(a) *m(f)* de parvulario

nurs·ing ['nɜːrsɪŋ] enfermería *f*

'nurs·ing home *for old people* residencia *f*

nut [nʌt] nuez *f*; *for bolt* tuerca *f*; **~s** F (*testicles*) pelotas *fpl* F

'nut·crack·ers *npl* cascanueces *m inv*

nu·tri·ent ['nuːtrɪənt] nutriente *m*

nu·tri·tion [nuː'trɪʃn] nutrición *f*

nu·tri·tious [nuː'trɪʃəs] *adj* nutritivo

nuts [nʌts] *adj* F (*crazy*) chalado F, pirado F; **be ~ about s.o.** estar colado por alguien F

'nut·shell *in a ~* en una palabra

nut·ty ['nʌtɪ] *adj taste* a nuez; F (*crazy*) chalado F, pirado F

ny·lon ['naɪlɑːn] **1** *n* nylon *m* **2** *adj* de nylon

N

O

oak [oʊk] *tree, wood* roble *m*

oar [ɔːr] remo *m*

o·a·sis [oʊ'eɪsɪs] (*pl **oases*** [oʊ'eɪsiːz]) *also fig* oasis *m inv*

oath [oʊθ] LAW, (*swearword*) juramento *m*; **on ~** bajo juramento

'oat·meal harina *f* de avena

oats [oʊts] *npl* copos *mpl* de avena

o·be·di·ence [oʊ'biːdɪəns] obediencia *f*

o·be·di·ent [oʊ'biːdɪənt] *adj* obediente

o·be·di·ent·ly [oʊ'biːdɪəntlɪ] *adv* obedientemente

o·bese [oʊ'biːs] *adj* obeso

o·bes·i·ty [oʊ'biːsɪtɪ] obesidad *f*

o·bey [oʊ'beɪ] *v/t* obedecer

o·bit·u·a·ry [ə'bɪtʊerɪ] *n* necrología *f*, obituario *m*

ob·ject¹ [ˈɑːbdʒɪkt] *n also* GRAM objeto *m*; (*aim*) objetivo *m*

ob·ject² [əb'dʒekt] *v/i* oponerse

♦ **object to** *v/t* oponerse a

ob·jec·tion [əb'dʒekʃn] objeción *f*

ob·jec·tio·na·ble [əb'dʒekʃnəbl] *adj* (*unpleasant*) desagradable

ob·jec·tive [əb'dʒektɪv] **1** *adj* objetivo **2** *n* objetivo *m*

ob·jec·tive·ly [əb'dʒektɪvlɪ] *adv* objetivamente

ob·jec·tiv·i·ty [əb'dʒektɪvətɪ] objetividad *f*

ob·li·ga·tion [ɑːblɪ'geɪʃn] obligación *f*; **be under an ~ to s.o.** tener una obligación para con alguien

ob·lig·a·to·ry [ə'blɪgətɔːrɪ] *adj* obligatorio

o·blige [ə'blaɪdʒ] *v/t* obligar; ***much ~d!*** muy agradecido

o·blig·ing [ə'blaɪdʒɪŋ] *adj* atento, servicial

o·blique [ə'bliːk] **1** *adj reference* indirecto **2** *n in punctuation* barra *f* inclinada

o·blit·er·ate [ə'blɪtəreɪt] *v/t city* destruir, arrasar; *memory* borrar

o·bliv·i·on [ə'blɪvɪən] olvido *m*; ***fall into ~*** caer en el olvido

o·bliv·i·ous [ə'blɪvɪəs] *adj*: ***be ~ of sth*** no ser consciente de algo

ob·long [ˈɑːblɒŋ] *adj* rectangular

ob·nox·ious [əb'nɑːkʃəs] *adj person* detestable, odioso; *smell* repugnante

ob·scene [ɑːb'siːn] *adj* obsceno; *salary, poverty* escandaloso

ob·scen·i·ty [əb'senətɪ] obscenidad *f*

ob·scure [əb'skjʊr] *adj* oscuro

ob·scu·ri·ty [əb'skjʊrətɪ] oscuridad *f*

ob·ser·vance [əb'zɜːrvns] *of festival* práctica *f*

ob·ser·vant [əb'zɜːrvnt] *adj* observador

ob·ser·va·tion [ɑːbzə'veɪʃn] *of nature, stars* observación *f*; (*comment*) observación *f*, comentario *m*

ob·ser·va·to·ry [əb'zɜːrvətɔːrɪ] observatorio *m*

ob·serve [əb'zɜːrv] *v/t* observar

ob·serv·er [əb'zɜːrvər] observador(a) *m(f)*

ob·sess [ɑːb'ses] *v/t* obsesionar; ***be ~ed by/with*** estar obsesionado con/por

ob·ses·sion [ɑːb'seʃn] obsesión *f*

ob·ses·sive [ɑːb'sesɪv] *adj* obsesivo

ob·so·lete [ˈɑːbsəliːt] *adj* obsoleto

ob·sta·cle [ˈɑːbstəkl] obstáculo *m*

ob·ste·tri·cian [ɑːbstə'trɪʃn] obstetra *m/f*, tocólogo(-a) *m(f)*

ob·stet·rics [ɑːb'stetrɪks] obstetricia *f*, tocología *f*

ob·sti·na·cy [ˈɑːbstɪnəsɪ] obstinación *f*

ob·sti·nate [ˈɑːbstɪnət] *adj* obstinado

ob·sti·nate·ly [ˈɑːbstɪnətlɪ] *adv* obstinadamente

ob·struct [əbˈstrʌkt] v/t *road* obstruir; *investigation, police* obstaculizar

ob·struc·tion [əbˈstrʌkʃn] *on road etc* obstrucción f

ob·struc·tive [əbˈstrʌktɪv] *adj behavior, tactics* obstruccionista

ob·tain [əbˈteɪn] v/t obtener, lograr

ob·tain·a·ble [əbˈteɪnəbl] *adj products* disponible

ob·tru·sive [əbˈtruːsɪv] *adj* molesto; *the plastic chairs are rather ~* las sillas de plástico desentonan por completo

ob·tuse [əbˈtuːs] *adj fig* duro de mollera

ob·vi·ous [ˈɑːbvɪəs] *adj* obvio, evidente

ob·vi·ous·ly [ˈɑːbvɪəslɪ] *adv* obviamente; *~!* ¡por supuesto!

oc·ca·sion [əˈkeɪʒn] ocasión f

oc·ca·sion·al [əˈkeɪʒnəl] *adj* ocasional, esporádico; *I like the ~ Scotch* me gusta tomarme un whisky de vez en cuando

oc·ca·sion·al·ly [əˈkeɪʒnlɪ] *adv* ocasionalmente, de vez en cuando

oc·cult [əˈkʌlt] **1** *adj* oculto **2** *n: the ~* lo oculto

oc·cu·pant [ˈɑːkjʊpənt] ocupante m/f

oc·cu·pa·tion [ɑːkjʊˈpeɪʃn] ocupación f

oc·cu·pa·tion·al 'ther·a·pist [ɑːkjʊˈpeɪʃnl] terapeuta m/f ocupacional

oc·cu·pa·tion·al 'ther·a·py terapia f ocupacional

oc·cu·py [ˈɑːkjʊpaɪ] v/t (*pret & pp -ied*) ocupar

oc·cur [əˈkɜːr] v/i (*pret & pp -red*) ocurrir, suceder; *it ~red to me that ...* se me ocurrió que ...

oc·cur·rence [əˈkʌrəns] acontecimiento m

o·cean [ˈəʊʃn] océano m

o·ce·a·nog·ra·phy [əʊʃnˈɑːgrəfɪ] oceanografía f

o'clock [əˈklɑːk]: *at five / six ~* a las cinco / seis

Oc·to·ber [ɑːkˈtəʊbər] octubre m

oc·to·pus [ˈɑːktəpəs] pulpo m

OD [əʊˈdiː] v/i F: *~ on drug* tomar una sobredosis de

odd [ɑːd] *adj* (*strange*) raro, extraño; (*not even*) impar; *the ~ one out* el bicho raro; *50 ~* cerca de 50

'odd·ball F bicho m raro F

odds [ɑːdz] *npl*: *be at ~ with sth / s.o.* no concordar con algo / estar peleado con alguien; *the ~ are 10 to one* las apuestas están en 10 a 1; *the ~ are that ...* lo más probable es que ...; *against all the ~* contra lo que se esperaba

odds and 'ends *npl objects* cacharros *mpl*; *things to do* cosillas *fpl*

'odds-on *adj favorite* indiscutible

o·di·ous [ˈəʊdɪəs] *adj* odioso

o·dom·e·ter [əʊˈdɑːmətər] cuentakilómetros m inv

o·dor, *Br* **o·dour** [ˈəʊdər] olor m

of [ɑːv], [əv] *prep possession* de; *the name ~ the street / hotel* el nombre de la calle / del hotel; *the color ~ the car* el color del coche; *five minutes ~ twelve* las doce menos cinco, *L.Am* cinco para los doce; *die ~ cancer* morir de cáncer; *love ~ money / adventure* amor por el dinero / la aventura; *~ the three this is ...* de los tres éste es ...

off [ɑːf] **1** *prep*: *~ the main road* (*away from*) apartado de la carretera principal; (*leading off*) saliendo de la carretera principal; *$20 ~ the price* una rebaja en el precio de 20 dólares; *he's ~ his food* no come nada, está desganado **2** *adv*: *be ~ of light, TV, machine* estar apagado; *of brake, lid, top* no estar puesto; *not at work* faltar; *on vacation* estar de vacaciones; (*canceled*) estar cancelado; *we're ~ tomorrow* (*leaving*) nos vamos mañana; *I'm ~ to New York* me voy a Nueva York; *with his pants / hat ~* sin los pantalones / el sombrero; *take a day ~* tomarse un día de fiesta *or* un día libre; *it's 3 miles ~* está a tres millas de distancia; *it's a long way ~ in distance* está muy lejos; *in future* todavía queda mucho tiempo; **he got into his car and drove ~** se subió al coche y se marchó; **~ and on** de vez en cuando **3** *adj*: **the ~ switch** el interruptor de apagado

of·fence *Br* → **offense**

of·fend [ə'fend] *v/t* (*insult*) ofender

of·fend·er [ə'fendər] LAW delincuente *m/f*

of·fense [ə'fens] LAW delito *m*; **take ~ at sth** ofenderse por algo

of·fen·sive [ə'fensɪv] **1** *adj behavior, remark* ofensivo; *smell* repugnante **2** *n* (MIL: *attack*) ofensiva *f*; **go on(to) the ~** pasar a la ofensiva

of·fer ['ɑːfər] **1** *n* oferta *f* **2** *v/t* ofrecer; **~ s.o. sth** ofrecer algo a alguien

off'hand *adj attitude* brusco

of·fice ['ɑːfɪs] *building* oficina *f*; *room* oficina *f*, despacho *m*; *position* cargo *m*

'of·fice block bloque *m* de oficinas

'of·fice hours *npl* horas *fpl* de oficina

of·fi·cer ['ɑːfɪsər] MIL oficial *m/f*; in *police* agente *m/f*

of·fi·cial [ə'fɪʃl] **1** *adj* oficial **2** *n* funcionario(-a) *m(f)*

of·fi·cial·ly [ə'fɪʃlɪ] *adv* oficialmente

of·fi·ci·ate [ə'fɪʃieɪt] *v/i*: **with X officiating** con X celebrando la ceremonia

of·fi·cious [ə'fɪʃəs] *adj* entrometido

'off-line *adv work* fuera de línea; **be ~** *of printer etc* estar desconectado; **go ~** desconectarse

'off-peak *adj rates* en horas valle, fuera de las horas punta

'off-sea·son **1** *adj rates, vacation* temporada baja **2** *n* temporada *f* baja

'off·set *v/t* (*pret & pp* **-set**) *losses, disadvantage* compensar

'off·shore *adj drilling rig* cercano a la costa; *investment* en el exterior

'off·side **1** *adj wheel etc* del lado del conductor **2** *adv* SP fuera de juego

'off·spring *of person* vástagos *mpl*, hijos *mpl*; *of animal* crías *fpl*

off-the-'rec·ord *adj* confidencial

'off-white *adj* blancuzco

of·ten ['ɑːfn] *adv* a menudo, frecuentemente *m*

oil [ɔɪl] **1** *n for machine, food, skin* aceite *m*; *petroleum* petróleo *m* **2** *v/t hinges, bearings* engrasar

'oil change cambio *m* del aceite; 'oil com·pa·ny compañía *f* petrolera; 'oil·field yacimiento *m* petrolífero; 'oil-fired *adj central heating* de gasóleo *or* fuel; 'oil paint·ing óleo *m*; 'oil-pro·duc·ing coun·try país *m* productor de petróleo; 'oil re·fin·e·ry refinería *f* de petróleo; 'oil rig plataforma *f* petrolífera; 'oil·skins *npl* ropa *f* impermeable; 'oil slick marea *f* negra; 'oil tank·er petrolero *m*; 'oil well pozo *m* petrolífero

oil·y ['ɔɪlɪ] *adj* grasiento

oint·ment ['ɔɪntmənt] ungüento *m*, pomada *f*

ok [oʊ'keɪ] *adj, adv* F: **can I? - ~** ¿puedo? – de acuerdo *or* Span vale; **is it ~ with you if …?** ¿te parecería bien si …?; **does that look ~?** ¿queda bien?; **that's ~ by me** por mí, ningún problema; **are you ~?** (*well, not hurt*) ¿estás bien?; **are you ~ for Friday?** ¿te va bien el viernes?; **he's ~** (*is a good guy*) es buena persona; **is this bus ~ for …?** ¿este autobús va a …?

old [oʊld] *adj* viejo; (*previous*) anterior, antiguo; **an ~ man/ woman** un anciano / una anciana, un viejo / una vieja; **how ~ are you/ is he?** ¿cuántos años tienes / tiene?; **he's getting ~** está haciéndose mayor

old 'age vejez *f*

old-'fash·ioned *adj clothes, style, ideas* anticuado, pasado de moda; *word* anticuado

ol·ive ['ɑːlɪv] aceituna *f*, oliva *f*

'ol·ive oil aceite *m* de oliva

O·lym·pic 'Games [ə'lɪmpɪk] *npl* Juegos *mpl* Olímpicos

om·e·let, *Br* om·e·lette ['ɑːmlɪt] tortilla *f* (francesa)

om·i·nous ['ɑːmɪnəs] *adj* siniestro

o·mis·sion [oʊ'mɪʃn] omisión *f*

o·mit [ə'mɪt] *v/t* (*pret & pp* **-ted**) omitir; **~ to do sth** no hacer algo

om·nip·o·tent [ɑːm'nɪpətənt] *adj*

omnipotente

om·nis·ci·ent [ɑːmˈnɪsɪənt] adj omnisciente

on [ɑːn] **1** prep en; **~ the table/wall** en la mesa/la pared; **~ the bus/ train** en el autobús/el tren; **~ TV/ the radio** en la televisión/la radio; **~ Sunday** el domingo; **~ the 1st of ...** el uno de ...; **this is ~ me** (*I'm paying*) invito yo; **have you any money ~ you?** ¿llevas dinero encima?; **~ his arrival/departure** cuando llegue/se marche; **~ hearing this** al escuchar esto **2** adv: **be ~** of light, TV, computer etc estar encendido or L.Am. prendido; of brake, lid, top estar puesto; of meeting etc: be scheduled to happen haber sido acordado; **it's ~ at 5 am** of TV program lo dan or Span a las cinco; **what's ~ tonight?** on TV etc ¿qué dan or Span ponen esta noche?; (*what's planned?*) ¿qué planes hay para esta noche?; **with his hat ~** con el sombrero puesto; **you're ~** (*I accept your offer etc*) trato hecho; **~ you go** (*go ahead*) adelante; **walk/talk ~** seguir caminando/hablando; **and so ~** etcétera; **~ and ~** sin parar **3** adj: **the ~ switch** el interruptor de encendido

once [wʌns] **1** adv (*one time, formerly*) una vez; **~ again, ~ more** una vez más; **at ~** (*immediately*) de inmediato, inmediatamente; **all at ~** (*suddenly*) de repente; (**all**) **at ~** (*together*) al mismo tiempo; **~ upon a time there was ...** érase una vez ...; **~ in a while** de vez en cuando; **~ and for all** de una vez por todas; **for ~** por una vez **2** conj una vez que; **~ you have finished** una vez que hayas acabado

one [wʌn] **1** number uno m **2** adj un(a); **~ day** un día **3** pron uno(-a); **which ~?** ¿cuál?; **~ by ~** enter, deal with uno por uno; **we help ~ another** nos ayudamos mutuamente; **what can ~ say/do?** ¿qué puede uno decir/hacer?; **the little ~s** los pequeños; **I for ~** yo personalmente

one-'off n (*unique event, person*) hecho m aislado; (*exception*) excepción f

one-par·ent 'fam·i·ly familia f monoparental

one'self pron uno(-a) mismo(-a) m(f); **do sth by ~** hacer algo sin ayuda; **look after ~** cuidarse; **be by ~** estar solo

one-sid·ed [wʌnˈsaɪdɪd] adj discussion, fight desigual; **one-track 'mind** hum: **have a ~** ser un obseso; **'one-way street** calle f de sentido único; **'one-way tick·et** billete m de ida

on·ion [ˈʌnjən] cebolla f

'on-line adv en línea; **go ~ to** conectarse a

'on-line serv·ice COMPUT servicio m en línea

on·look·er [ˈɑːnlʊkər] espectador(a) m(f), curioso(-a) m(f)

on·ly [ˈoʊnlɪ] **1** adv sólo, solamente; **he was here ~ yesterday** estuvo aquí ayer mismo; **not ~ ... but ... also ...; ~ just** por poco **2** adj único; **~ son** hijo único

'on·set comienzo m

'on·side adv SP en posición reglamentaria

on-the-job 'train·ing formación f continua

on·to [ˈɑːntuː] prep: **put sth ~ sth** (*on top of*) poner algo encima de algo

on·ward [ˈɑːnwərd] adv hacia adelante; **from ... ~** de ... en adelante

ooze [uːz] **1** v/i of liquid, mud rezumar **2** v/t rezumar; **he ~s charm** rezuma or rebosa encanto

o·paque [oʊˈpeɪk] adj glass opaco

OPEC [ˈoʊpek] abbr (= **Organization of Petroleum Exporting Countries**) OPEP f (= Organización f de Países Exportadores de Petróleo)

o·pen [ˈoʊpən] **1** adj also honest abierto; **in the ~ air** al aire libre **2** v/t abrir **3** v/i of door, shop abrir; of flower abrirse

♦ **open up** v/i of person abrirse

O

o·pen-'air *adj meeting, concert* al aire libre; *pool* descubierto; **'o·pen day** jornada *f* de puertas abiertas; **o·pen-'end·ed** *adj contract etc* abierto

o·pen·ing ['oupənɪŋ] *in wall etc* abertura *f*; *(beginning: of film, novel etc)* comienzo *m*; *(job)* puesto *m* vacante

'o·pen·ing hours *npl* horario *m* de apertura

o·pen·ly ['oupənlɪ] *adv (honestly, frankly)* abiertamente

o·pen-mind·ed [oupən'maɪndɪd] *adj* de mentalidad abierta; **o·pen 'plan of·fice** oficina *f* de planta abierta; **'o·pen tick·et** billete *m* abierto

op·e·ra ['ɑ:pərə] ópera *f*

'op·e·ra glass·es *npl* gemelos *mpl*, prismáticos *mpl*; **'op·e·ra house** (teatro *m* de la) ópera *f*; **'op·e·ra sing·er** cantante *m/f* de ópera

op·e·rate ['ɑ:pəreɪt] **1** *v/i of company* operar, actuar; *of airline, bus service,* MED operar; *of machine* funcionar (**on** con) **2** *v/t machine* manejar

♦ **operate on** *v/t* MED operar; **they operated on his leg** le operaron de la pierna

'op·e·rat·ing in·struc·tions *npl* instrucciones *fpl* de funcionamiento; **'op·e·rat·ing room** MED quirófano *m*; **'op·e·rat·ing sys·tem** COMPUT sistema *m* operativo

op·e·ra·tion [ɑ:pə'reɪʃn] MED operación *f*; *of machine* manejo *m*; **~s of** *company* operaciones *fpl*, actividades *fpl*; **have an ~** MED ser operado

op·e·ra·tor ['ɑ:pəreɪtər] TELEC operador(a) *m(f)*; *of machine* operario(-a) *m(f)*; *(tour ~)* operador *m* turístico

oph·thal·mol·o·gist [ɑ:fθæl'mɑ:lədʒɪst] oftalmólogo(-a) *m(f)*

o·pin·ion [ə'pɪnjən] opinión *f*; **in my ~** en mi opinión

o'pin·ion poll encuesta *f* de opinión

op·po·nent [ə'pounənt] oponente *m/f*, adversario(-a) *m(f)*

op·por·tune ['ɑ:pərtu:n] *adj fml* oportuno

op·por·tun·ist [ɑ:pər'tu:nɪst] oportunista *m/f*

op·por·tu·ni·ty [ɑ:pər'tu:nətɪ] oportunidad *f*

op·pose [ə'pouz] *v/t* oponerse a; **be ~d to ...** estar en contra de ...; **John, as ~d to George ...** John, al contrario que George ...

op·po·site ['ɑ:pəzɪt] **1** *adj* contrario; *views, characters, meaning* opuesto; **the ~ side of town / end of the road** el otro lado de la ciudad / el otro extremo de la calle; **the ~ sex** el sexo opuesto **2** *n:* **the ~ of** lo contrario de

op·po·site 'num·ber homólogo(-a) *m(f)*

op·po·si·tion [ɑ:pə'zɪʃn] *to plan,* POL oposición *f*

op·press [ə'pres] *v/t the people* oprimir

op·pres·sive [ə'presɪv] *adj rule, dictator* opresor; *weather* agobiante

opt [ɑ:pt] *v/t:* **~ to do sth** optar por hacer algo

op·ti·cal il·lu·sion ['ɑ:ptɪkl] ilusión *f* óptica

op·ti·cian [ɑ:p'tɪʃn] óptico(-a) *m(f)*

op·ti·mism ['ɑ:ptɪmɪzm] optimismo *m*

op·ti·mist ['ɑ:ptɪmɪst] optimista *m/f*

op·ti·mis·tic [ɑ:ptɪ'mɪstɪk] *adj* optimista

op·ti·mis·tic·al·ly [ɑ:ptɪ'mɪstɪklɪ] *adv* con optimismo

op·ti·mum ['ɑ:ptɪməm] **1** *adj* óptimo **2** *n:* **the ~** lo ideal

op·tion ['ɑ:pʃn] opción *f*

op·tion·al ['ɑ:pʃnl] *adj* optativo

op·tion·al 'ex·tras *npl* accesorios *mpl* opcionales

or [ɔ:r] *conj* o; *before a word beginning with the letter o* u

o·ral ['ɔ:rəl] *adj exam, sex* oral; *hygiene* bucal

or·ange ['ɔ:rɪndʒ] **1** *adj* naranja **2** *n fruit* naranja *f; color* naranja *m*

or·ange·ade ['ɔ:rɪndʒeɪd] naranjada *f*

'or·ange juice *Span* zumo *m or* L.Am. jugo *m* de naranja

or·a·tor ['ɔ:rətər] orador(a) *m(f)*

or·bit ['ɔːrbɪt] **1** *n of earth* órbita *f* **2** *v/t the earth* girar alrededor de

or·chard ['ɔːrtʃərd] huerta *f* (de frutales)

or·ches·tra ['ɔːrkɪstrə] orquesta *f*

or·chid ['ɔːrkɪd] orquídea *f*

or·dain [ɔːr'deɪn] *v/t* ordenar

or·deal [ɔːr'diːl] calvario *m*, experiencia *f* penosa

or·der ['ɔːrdər] **1** *n* (*command*) orden *f*; (*sequence, being well arranged*) orden *m*; *for goods* pedido *m*; **take s.o.'s ~** *in restaurant* preguntar a alguien lo que va a tomar; *in ~ to* para; *out of ~* (*not functioning*) estropeado; (*not in sequence*) desordenado **2** *v/t* (*put in sequence, proper layout*) ordenar; *goods* pedir, encargar; *meal* pedir; **~ s.o. to do sth** ordenar a alguien hacer algo *or* que haga algo **3** *v/i in restaurant* pedir

or·der·ly ['ɔːrdəlɪ] **1** *adj lifestyle* ordenado, metódico **2** *n in hospital* celador(a) *m(f)*

or·di·nal (num·ber) ['ɔːrdɪnl] (número *m*) ordinal *m*

or·di·nar·i·ly [ɔːrdɪ'nerɪlɪ] *adv* (*as a rule*) normalmente

or·di·nary ['ɔːrdɪnerɪ] *adj* común, normal

ore [ɔːr] mineral, mena *f*

or·gan ['ɔːrgən] ANAT, MUS órgano *m*

or·gan·ic [ɔːr'gænɪk] *adj food* ecológico, biológico; *fertilizer* orgánico

or·gan·i·cal·ly [ɔːr'gænɪklɪ] *adv grown* ecológicamente, biológicamente

or·gan·ism ['ɔːrgənɪzm] organismo *m*

or·gan·i·za·tion [ɔːrgənaɪ'zeɪʃn] organización *f*

or·gan·ize ['ɔːrgənaɪz] *v/t* organizar

or·gan·ized 'crime crimen *m* organizado

or·gan·iz·er ['ɔːrgənaɪzər] *person* organizador(a) *m(f)*

or·gasm ['ɔːrgæzm] orgasmo *m*

O·ri·ent ['ɔːrɪənt] Oriente

o·ri·ent ['ɔːrɪənt] *v/t* (*direct*) orientar; **~ o.s.** (*get bearings*) orientarse

O·ri·en·tal [ɔːrɪ'entl] **1** *adj* oriental **2** *n* oriental *m/f*

or·i·gin ['ɑːrɪdʒɪn] origen *m*

o·rig·i·nal [ə'rɪdʒənl] **1** *adj* (*not copied, first*) original **2** *n painting etc* original *m*

o·rig·i·nal·i·ty [ərɪdʒən'ælətɪ] originalidad *f*

o·rig·i·nal·ly [ə'rɪdʒənəlɪ] *adv* originalmente; (*at first*) originalmente, en un principio

o·rig·i·nate [ə'rɪdʒɪneɪt] **1** *v/t scheme, idea* crear **2** *v/i of idea, belief* originarse; *of family* proceder

o·rig·i·na·tor [ə'rɪdʒɪneɪtər] *of scheme etc* creador(a) *m(f)*; **he's not an ~** no es un creador nato

or·na·ment ['ɔːrnəmənt] *n* adorno *m*

or·na·men·tal [ɔːrnə'mentl] *adj* ornamental

or·nate [ɔːr'neɪt] *adj style, architecture* recargado

or·phan ['ɔːrfn] *n* huérfano(-a) *m(f)*

or·phan·age ['ɔːrfənɪdʒ] orfanato *m*

or·tho·dox ['ɔːrθədɑːks] *adj* REL, *fig* ortodoxo

or·tho·pe·dic [ɔːrθə'piːdɪk] *adj* ortopédico

os·ten·si·bly [ɑː'stensəblɪ] *adv* aparentemente

os·ten·ta·tion [ɑːsten'teɪʃn] ostentación *f*

os·ten·ta·tious [ɑːsten'teɪʃəs] *adj* ostentoso

os·ten·ta·tious·ly [ɑːsten'teɪʃəslɪ] *adv* de forma ostentosa

os·tra·cize ['ɑːstrəsaɪz] *v/t* condenar al ostracismo

oth·er ['ʌðər] **1** *adj* otro; **~ people might not agree** puede que otros no estén de acuerdo; **the ~ day** (*recently*) el otro día; **every ~ day/person** cada dos días/personas **2** *n*: **the ~** el otro; **the ~s** los otros

oth·er·wise ['ʌðərwaɪz] **1** *conj* de lo contrario, si no **2** *adv* (*differently*) de manera diferente

ot·ter ['ɑːtər] nutria *f*

ought [ɔːt] *v/aux*: *I/you ~ to know* debo/debes saberlo; *you ~ to have done it* deberías haberlo hecho

ounce [aʊns] onza f

our [aʊr] adj nuestro m, nuestra f; **~ brother** nuestro hermano; **~ books** nuestros libros

ours [aʊrz] pron el nuestro, la nuestra; **~ are red** los nuestros son rojos; **that book is ~** ese libro es nuestro; **a friend of ~** un amigo nuestro

our·selves [aʊrˈselvz] pron reflexive nos; emphatic nosotros mismos mpl, nosotras mismas fpl; **we hurt ~** nos hicimos daño; **when we saw ~ in the mirror** cuando nos vimos en el espejo; **we saw it ~** lo vimos nosotros mismos; **by ~** (alone) solos; (without help) nosotros solos, nosotras mismos

oust [aʊst] v/t from office derrocar

out [aʊt] adv: **be ~** of light, fire estar apagado; of flower estar en flor; (not at home, not in building), of sun haber salido; of calculations estar equivocado; (be published) haber sido publicado; (no longer in competition) estar eliminado; (no longer in fashion) estar pasado de moda; **the secret is ~** el secreto ha sido revelado; **~ here in Dallas** aquí en Dallas; **he's ~ in the garden** está en el jardín; (get) **~!** ¡vete!; (get) **~ of my room!** ¡fuera de mi habitación!; **that's ~!** (out of the question) ¡eso es imposible!; **he's ~ to win** (fully intends to) va a por la victoria

out·board ˈmo·tor motor m de fueraborda

ˈout·break of violence, war estallido m

ˈout·build·ing edificio m anexo

ˈout·burst emotional arrebato m, arranque m

ˈout·cast paria m/f

ˈout·come resultado m

ˈout·cry protesta f

outˈdat·ed adj anticuado

outˈdo v/t (pret -did, pp -done) superar

outˈdoor adj toilet, activities, life al aire libre

outˈdoors adv fuera

out·er [ˈaʊtər] adj wall etc exterior

out·er ˈspace espacio m exterior

ˈout·fit (clothes) traje m, conjunto m; (company, organization) grupo m

ˈout·go·ing adj flight saliente; personality extrovertido

outˈgrow v/t (pret -grew, pp -grown) old ideas dejar atrás

out·ing [ˈaʊtɪŋ] (trip) excursión f

outˈlast v/t durar más que

ˈout·let of pipe desagüe m; for sales punto m de venta; ELEC enchufe m

ˈout·line 1 n of person, building etc perfil m, contorno m; of plan, novel resumen m **2** v/t plans etc resumir

outˈlive v/t sobrevivir a

ˈout·look (prospects) perspectivas fpl

ˈout·ly·ing adj areas periférico

outˈnum·ber v/t superar en número

out of prep ◊ motion fuera de; **run ~ the house** salir corriendo de la casa; **it fell ~ the window** se cayó por la ventana ◊ position: **20 miles ~ Detroit** a 20 millas de Detroit ◊ cause por; **~ jealousy / curiosity** por celos / curiosidad ◊ without: **we're ~ gas / beer** no nos queda gasolina / cerveza ◊ from a group de cada; **5 ~ 10** 5 de cada 10

out-of-ˈdate adj anticuado, desfasado

out-of-the-ˈway adj apartado

ˈout·pa·tient paciente m/f externo(-a)

ˈout·pa·tients' (clin·ic) clínica f ambulatoria

outˈper·form v/t superar a

ˈout·put 1 n of factory producción f; COMPUT salida f **2** v/t (pret & pp -ted or **output**) (produce) producir

outˈrage 1 n feeling indignación f; act ultraje m, atrocidad f **2** v/t indignar, ultrajar; **I was ~d to hear ...** me indignó escuchar que ...

out·ra·geous [aʊtˈreɪdʒəs] adj acts atroz; prices escandaloso

ˈout·right 1 adj winner absoluto **2** adv win completamente; kill en el acto

outˈrun v/t (pret -ran, pp -run) correr más que

'out·set principio *m*, comienzo *m*; *from the* ~ desde el principio *or* comienzo

out'shine *v/t* (*pret & pp* **-shone**) eclipsar

'out·side **1** *adj surface, wall* exterior; *lane* de fuera **2** *adv* sit, go fuera **3** *prep* fuera de; (*apart from*) aparte de **4** *n of building, case etc* exterior *m*; *at the* ~ a lo sumo

out·side 'broad·cast emisión *f* desde exteriores

out·sid·er [aut'saɪdər] *in life* forastero(-a) *m(f)*; ~ *be an* ~ *in election, race* no ser uno de los favoritos

'out·size *adj clothing* de talla especial

'out·skirts *npl* afueras *fpl*

out'smart → **outwit**

out'stand·ing*adj success, quality* destacado, sobresaliente; *writer*, *athlete* excepcional; FIN: *invoice*, *sums* pendiente

out·stretched ['autstretʃt] *adj hands* extendido

out'vote*v/t: be* ~*d* perder la votación

out·ward ['autwərd] *adj appearance* externo; ~ *journey* viaje *m* de ida

out·ward·ly ['autwərdlɪ] *adv* aparentemente

out'weigh *v/t* pesar más que

out'wit*v/t* (*pret & pp* **-ted**) mostrarse más listo que

o·val ['ouvl] *adj* oval, ovalado

o·va·ry ['ouvərɪ] ovario *m*

o·va·tion [ou'veɪʃn] ovación *f*; *give s.o. a standing* ~ aplaudir a alguien de pie

ov·en ['ʌvn] horno *m*

'ov·en glove, 'ov·en mitt manopla *f* para el horno; 'ov·en·proof *adj* refractario; 'ov·en·read·y *adj* listo para el horno

o·ver ['ouvər] **1** *prep* (*above*) sobre, encima de; (*across*) al otro lado de; (*more than*) más de; (*during*) durante; *she walked* ~ *the street* cruzó la calle; *travel all* ~ *Brazil* viajar por todo Brasil; *let's talk* ~ *a drink/meal* hablemos mientras tomamos una bebida/comemos; *we're* ~ *the worst* lo peor ya ha

pasado; ~ *and above* además de **2** *adv*: *be* ~ (*finished*) haber acabado; *there were just 6* ~ sólo quedaban seis; ~ *to you* (*your turn*) te toca a ti; ~ *in Japan* allá en Japón; ~ *here/there* por aquí/allá; *it hurts all* ~ me duele por todas partes; *painted white all* ~ pintado todo de blanco; *it's all* ~ se ha acabado; ~ *and* ~ *again* una y otra vez; *do sth* ~ (*again*) volver a hacer algo

o·ver·all ['ouvərɔ:l] **1** *adj length* total **2** *adv* (*in general*) en general; *it measures six feet* ~ mide en total seis pies

o·ver·alls ['ouvərɔ:lz] *npl Span* mono *m*, *L.Am.* overol *m*

o·ver'awe *v/t* intimidar; *be* ~*d by s.o./sth* sentirse intimidado por alguien/algo

o·ver'bal·ance *v/i* perder el equilibrio

o·ver'bear·ing *adj* dominante, despótico

'o·ver·board *adv* por la borda; *man* ~*!* ¡hombre al agua!; *go* ~ *for s.o./sth* entusiasmarse muchísimo con alguien/algo

'o·ver·cast *adj day* nublado; *sky* cubierto

o·ver'charge *v/t customer* cobrar de más a

'o·ver·coat abrigo *m*

o·ver'come *v/t* (*pret* **-came**, *pp* **-come**) *difficulties*, *shyness* superar, vencer; *be* ~ *by emotion* estar embargado por la emoción

o·ver'crowd·ed *adj train* atestado; *city* superpoblado

o·ver'do *v/t* (*pret* **-did**, *pp* **-done**) (*exaggerate*) exagerar; *in cooking* recocer, cocinar demasiado; *you're* ~*ing things* te estás excediendo

o·ver'done *adj meat* demasiado hecho

'o·ver·dose *n* sobredosis *f inv*

'o·ver·draft descubierto *m*; *have an* ~ tener un descubierto

o·ver'draw *v/t* (*pret* **-drew**, *pp* **-drawn**) *account* dejar al descubierto; *be $800* ~*n* tener un descubierto de 800 dólares

o·ver·dressed *adj* demasiado trajeado

'o·ver·drive MOT superdirecta *f*

o·ver·due *adj*: **his apology was long** ~ se debía haber disculpado hace tiempo

o·ver·es·ti·mate *v/t abilities, value* sobreestimar

o·ver·ex·pose *v/t photograph* sobreexponer

'o·ver·flow[1] *n pipe* desagüe *m*, rebosadero *m*

o·ver·flow[2] *v/i of water* desbordarse

o·ver·grown *adj garden* abandonado, cubierto de vegetación; **he's an** ~ **baby** es como un niño

o·ver·haul *v/t engine, plans* revisar

'o·ver·head 1 *adj lights, railway* elevado **2** *n* FIN gastos *mpl* generales

o·ver·hear *v/t (pret & pp* **-heard***)* oír por casualidad

o·ver·heat·ed *adj* recalentado

o·ver·joyed [ouvər'dʒɔɪd] *adj* contentísimo, encantado

'o·ver·kill: **that's** ~ eso es exagerar

'o·ver·land 1 *adj route* terrestre **2** *adv travel* por tierra

o·ver·lap *v/i (pret & pp* **-ped***) of tiles etc* solaparse; *of periods of time* coincidir; *of theories* tener puntos en común

o·ver·leaf *adv*: **see** ~ véase al dorso

o·ver·load *v/t vehicle,* ELEC sobrecargar

o·ver·look *v/t of tall building etc* dominar; *(not see)* pasar por alto

o·ver·ly ['ouvərlɪ] *adv* excesivamente, demasiado

'o·ver·night *adv travel* por la noche; **stay** ~ quedarse a pasar la noche

o·ver·night 'bag bolso *m* de viaje

o·ver·paid *adj*: **be** ~ cobrar demasiado

'o·ver·pass paso *m* elevado

o·ver·pop·u·lat·ed [ouvər'pɑːpjuleɪtɪd] *adj* superpoblado

o·ver·pow·er *v/t physically* dominar

o·ver·pow·er·ing [ouvər'pauɪrŋ] *adj smell* fortísimo; *sense of guilt* insoportable

o·ver·priced [ouvər'praɪst] *adj* demasiado caro

o·ver·rat·ed [ouvə'reɪtɪd] *adj* sobrevalorado

o·ver·re·act *v/i* reaccionar exageradamente

o·ver·ride *v/t (pret* **-rode***, pp* **-ridden***)* anular

o·ver·rid·ing *adj concern* primordial

o·ver·rule *v/t decision* anular

o·ver·run *v/t (pret* **-ran***, pp* **-run***) country* invadir; *time* superar; **be** ~ **with** estar plagado de

o·ver·seas 1 *adv live, work* en el extranjero; *go* al extranjero **2** *adj* extranjero

o·ver·see *v/t (pret* **-saw***, pp* **-seen***)* supervisar

o·ver·shad·ow *v/t fig* eclipsar

'o·ver·sight descuido *m*

o·ver·sim·pli·fi·ca·tion simplificación *f* excesiva

o·ver·sim·pli·fy *v/t (pret & pp* **-ied***)* simplificar en exceso

o·ver·sleep *v/i (pret & pp* **-slept***)* quedarse dormido

o·ver·state *v/t* exagerar

o·ver·state·ment exageración *f*

o·ver·step *v/t (pret & pp* **-ped***) fig* traspasar; ~ **the mark** propasarse, pasarse de la raya

o·ver·take *v/t (pret* **-took***, pp* **-taken***) in work, development* adelantarse a; *Br* MOT adelantar

o·ver·throw[1] *v/t (pret* **-threw***, pp* **-thrown***)* derrocar

'o·ver·throw[2] *n* derrocamiento *m*

'o·ver·time 1 *n* SP: **in** ~ en la prórroga **2** *adv*: **work** ~ hacer horas extras

'o·ver·ture ['ouvərtʃur] MUS obertura *f*; **make** ~**s to** establecer contactos con

o·ver·turn 1 *v/t vehicle* volcar; *object* dar la vuelta a; *government* derribar **2** *v/i of vehicle* volcar

'o·ver·view visión *f* general

o·ver·weight *adj* con sobrepeso; **be** ~ estar demasiado gordo

o·ver·whelm [ouvər'welm] *v/t with work* abrumar, inundar; *with emotion* abrumar; **be** ~**ed by** by *response* estar abrumado por

o·ver·whelm·ing [oʊvər'welmɪŋ] *adj feeling* abrumador; *majority* aplastante

o·ver·work 1 *n* exceso *m* de trabajo **2** *v/i* trabajar en exceso **3** *v/t* hacer trabajar en exceso

owe [oʊ] *v/t* deber; **~ s.o. \$500** deber a alguien 500 dólares; **how much do I ~ you?** ¿cuánto te debo?

ow·ing to ['oʊɪŋ] *prep* debido a

owl [aʊl] búho *m*

own¹ [oʊn] *v/t* poseer; **who ~s the restaurant?** ¿de quién es el restaurante?, ¿quién es el propietario del restaurante?

own² [oʊn] **1** *adj* propio **2** *pron*: **a car/an apartment of my ~** mi propio coche/apartamento; **on my/his ~** yo/él solo

♦ **own up** *v/i* confesar

own·er ['oʊnər] dueño(-a) *m(f)*, propietario(-a) *m(f)*

own·er·ship ['oʊnərʃɪp] propiedad *f*

ox [ɑːks] (*pl* **oxen** ['ɑːksn]) buey *m*

ox·ide ['ɑːksaɪd] óxido *m*

ox·y·gen ['ɑːksɪdʒən] oxígeno *m*

oy·ster ['ɔɪstər] ostra *f*

oz *abbr* (= **ounce(s)**) onza(s) *f(pl)*

o·zone ['oʊzoʊn] ozono *m*

'o·zone lay·er capa *f* de ozono

P

PA [piː'eɪ] *abbr* (= **personal assistant**) secretario(-a) *m(f)* personal

pace [peɪs] **1** *n* (*step*) paso *m*; (*speed*) ritmo *m* **2** *v/i*: **~ up and down** pasear de un lado a otro

'pace·mak·er MED marcapasos *m inv*; SP liebre *f*

Pa·cif·ic [pə'sɪfɪk]: **the ~** (*Ocean*) el (Océano) Pacífico

pac·i·fi·er ['pæsɪfaɪər] chupete *m*

pac·i·fism ['pæsɪfɪzm] pacifismo *m*

pac·i·fist ['pæsɪfɪst] *n* pacifista *m/f*

pac·i·fy ['pæsɪfaɪ] *v/t* (*pret & pp* **-ied**) tranquilizar; *country* pacificar

pack [pæk] **1** *n* (*back~*) mochila *f*; *of cereal, food, cigarettes* paquete *m*; *of cards* baraja *f* **2** *v/t item of clothing etc* meter en la maleta; *goods* empaquetar; *groceries* meter en una bolsa; **~ one's bag/suitcase** hacer la bolsa/la maleta **3** *v/i* hacer la maleta

pack·age ['pækɪdʒ] **1** *n* paquete *m* **2** *v/t in packs* embalar; *idea, project* presentar

'pack·age deal *for holiday* paquete *m*

'pack·age tour viaje *m* organizado

pack·ag·ing ['pækɪdʒɪŋ] *of product* embalaje *m*; *of idea, project* presentación *f*; **it's all ~** *fig* es sólo imagen

packed [pækt] *adj* (*crowded*) abarrotado

pack·et ['pækɪt] paquete *m*

pact [pækt] pacto *m*

pad¹ [pæd] **1** *n for protection* almohadilla *f*; *for absorbing liquid* compresa *f*; *for writing* bloc *m* **2** *v/t* (*pret & pp* **-ded**) *with material* acolchar; *speech, report* meter paja en

pad² *v/i* (*pret & pp* **-ded**) (*move quietly*) caminar silenciosamente

pad·ded shoulders ['pædɪd] hombreras *fpl*

pad·ding ['pædɪŋ] *material* relleno *m*; *in speech etc* paja *f*

pad·dle ['pædəl] **1** *n for canoe* canalete *m*, remo *m* **2** *v/i in canoe* remar; *in water* chapotear

pad·dock ['pædək] potrero *m*

pad·lock ['pædlɑːk] **1** *n* candado *m* **2** *v/t gate* cerrar con candado; **I ~ed**

my bike to the railings até mi bicicleta a la verja con candado

page[1] [peɪdʒ] *n of book etc* página *f*; **~ number** número *m* de página

page[2] [peɪdʒ] *v/t (call)* llamar; *by PA* llamar por megafonía; *by beeper* llamar por el buscapersonas *or Span* busca

pag·er ['peɪdʒər] buscapersonas *m inv*, *Span* busca *m*

paid [peɪd] *pret & pp →* **pay**

paid em'ploy·ment empleo *m* remunerado

pail [peɪl] cubo *m*

pain [peɪn] dolor *m*; **be in ~** sentir dolor; **take ~s to ...** tomarse muchas molestias por ...; **a ~ in the neck** F una lata F, un tostón F

pain·ful ['peɪnfəl] *adj* dolorido; *blow, condition, subject* doloroso; *(laborious)* difícil; **my arm is still very ~** me sigue doliendo mucho el brazo

pain·ful·ly ['peɪnfəlɪ] *adv (extremely, acutely)* extremadamente

pain·kill·er ['peɪnkɪlər] analgésico *m*

pain·less ['peɪnlɪs] *adj* indoloro; **be completely ~** doler nada

pains·tak·ing ['peɪnzteɪkɪŋ] *adj* meticuloso

paint [peɪnt] **1** *n* pintura *f* **2** *v/t* pintar

paint·brush ['peɪntbrʌʃ] *large* brocha *f*; *small* pincel *m*

paint·er ['peɪntər] *decorator* pintor(a) *m(f)* (de brocha gorda); *artist* pintor(a) *m(f)*

paint·ing ['peɪntɪŋ] *activity* pintura *f*; *picture* cuadro *m*

paint·work ['peɪntwɜːrk] pintura *f*

pair [per] *of shoes, gloves, objects* par *m*; *of people, animals* pareja *f*

pa·ja·ma 'jack·et camisa *f* de pijama

pa·ja·ma 'pants *npl* pantalón *m* de pijama

pa·ja·mas [pəˈdʒɑːməz] *npl* pijama *m*

Pa·ki·stan [pɑːkɪˈstɑːn] Paquistán, Pakistán

Pa·ki·sta·ni [pɑːkɪˈstɑːnɪ] **1** *n* paquistaní *m/f*, pakistaní *m/f* **2** *adj* paquistaní, pakistaní

pal [pæl] F *(friend)* amigo(-a) *m(f)*,

Span colega *m/f* F; **hey ~, got a light?** oye amigo *or Span* tío, ¿tienes fuego?

pal·ace ['pælɪs] palacio *m*

pal·ate ['pælət] paladar *m*

pa·la·tial [pəˈleɪʃl] *adj* palaciego

pale [peɪl] *adj person* pálido; **she went ~** palideció; **~ pink/blue** rosa/azul claro

Pal·e·stine ['pæləstaɪn] Palestina

Pal·e·stin·i·an [pæləˈstɪnɪən] **1** *n* palestino(-a) *m(f)* **2** *adj* palestino

pal·let ['pælɪt] palé *m*

pal·lor ['pælər] palidez *f*

palm [pɑːm] *of hand* palma *f*; *tree* palmera *f*

pal·pi·ta·tions [pælpɪˈteɪʃnz] *npl* MED palpitaciones *fpl*

pal·try ['pɒːltrɪ] *adj* miserable

pam·per ['pæmpər] *v/t* mimar

pam·phlet ['pæmflɪt] *for information* folleto *m*; *political* panfleto *m*

pan [pæn] **1** *n for cooking* cacerola *f*; *for frying* sartén *f* **2** *v/t (pret & pp -ned)* F *(criticize)* poner por los suelos F

♦ **pan out** *v/i (develop)* salir

Pan·a·ma ['pænəmɑː] Panamá

Pan·a·ma Ca'nal: the ~ el Canal de Panamá

Pan·a·ma 'Cit·y Ciudad *f* de Panamá

Pan·a·ma·ni·an [pænəˈmeɪnɪən] **1** *adj* panameño **2** *n* panameño(-a) *m(f)*

pan·cake ['pænkeɪk] crepe *m*, *L.Am.* panqueque *m*

pan·da ['pændə] (oso *m*) panda *m*

pan·de·mo·ni·um [pændɪˈmoʊnɪəm] pandemónium *m*, pandemonio *m*

♦ **pan·der to** *v/t* complacer

pane [peɪn] *of glass* hoja *f*

pan·el ['pænl] panel *m*; *people* grupo *m*, panel *m*

pan·el·ing, *Br* **pan·el·ling** ['pænəlɪŋ] paneles *mpl*; *of ceiling* artesonado *m*

pang [pæŋ] **~s of hunger** retortijones *mpl*; **~s of remorse** remordimientos *mpl*

'pan·han·dle *v/i* F mendigar

pan·ic ['pænɪk] **1** *n* pánico *m* **2** *v/i*

(*pret & pp* **-ked**) ser preso del pánico; ***don't ~*** ¡que no cunda el pánico!
'**pan·ic buy·ing** FIN compra *f* provocada por el pánico; '**pan·ic sel·ling** FIN venta *f* provocada por el pánico; '**pan·ic-strick·en** preso del pánico
pan·o·ra·ma [pænəˈrɑːmə] panorama *m*
pa·no·ram·ic [pænəˈræmɪk] *adj view* panorámico
pan·sy [ˈpænzɪ] *flower* pensamiento *m*
pant [pænt] *v/i* jadear
pan·ties [ˈpæntɪz] *npl Span* bragas *fpl, L.Am.* calzones *mpl*
pan·ti·hose → **pantyhose**
pants [pænts] *npl* pantalones *mpl*
pan·ty·hose [ˈpæntɪhoʊz] medias *fpl*, pantis *mpl*
pa·pal [ˈpeɪpəl] *adj* papal
pa·per [ˈpeɪpər] **1** *n* papel *m*; (*news~*) periódico *m*; *academic* estudio *m*; *at conference* ponencia *f*; (*examination ~*) examen *m*; **~s** (*documents*) documentos *mpl, of vehicle,* (*identity ~s*) papeles *mpl*, documentación *f*; ***a piece of ~*** un trozo de papel **2** *adj* de papel **3** *v/t room, walls* empapelar
'**pa·per·back** libro *m* en rústica; '**pa·per 'bag** bolsa *f* de papel; '**pa·per boy** repartidor *m* de periódicos; '**pa·per clip** clip *m*; '**pa·per cup** vaso *m* de papel; '**pa·per·work** papeleo *m*
par [pɑːr] *in golf* par *m*; ***be on a ~ with*** ser comparable a; ***feel below ~*** sentirse en baja forma
par·a·chute [ˈpærəʃuːt] **1** *n* paracaídas *m inv* **2** *v/i* saltar en paracaídas **3** *v/t troops, supplies* lanzar en paracaídas
par·a·chut·ist [ˈpærəʃuːtɪst] paracaidista *m/f*
pa·rade [pəˈreɪd] **1** *n procession* desfile *m* **2** *v/i* desfilar; (*walk about*) pasearse **3** *v/t knowledge, new car* hacer ostentación de
par·a·dise [ˈpærədaɪs] paraíso *m*
par·a·dox [ˈpærədɑːks] paradoja *f*
par·a·dox·i·cal [pærəˈdɑːksɪkl] *adj* paradójico
par·a·dox·i·cal·ly [pærəˈdɑːksɪklɪ]

adv paradójicamente
par·a·graph [ˈpærəgræf] párrafo *m*
Par·a·guay [ˈpærəgwaɪ] Paraguay
Par·a·guay·an [pærəˈgwaɪən] **1** *adj* paraguayo **2** *n* paraguayo(-a) *m(f)*
par·al·lel [ˈpærəlel] **1** *n* GEOM paralela *f*; GEOG paralelo *m*; *fig* paralelismo *m*; ***draw a ~*** establecer un paralelismo; ***do two things in ~*** hacer dos cosas al mismo tiempo **2** *adj also fig* paralelo **3** *v/t* (*match*) equipararse a
pa·ral·y·sis [pəˈræləsɪs] parálisis *f*
par·a·lyze [ˈpærəlaɪz] *v/t also fig* paralizar
par·a·med·ic [pærəˈmedɪk] *n* auxiliar *m/f* sanitario(-a)
pa·ram·e·ter [pəˈræmɪtər] parámetro *m*
par·a·mil·i·tar·y [pærəˈmɪlɪterɪ] **1** *adj* paramilitar **2** *n* paramilitar *m/f*
par·a·mount [ˈpærəmaunt] *adj* supremo, extremo; ***be ~*** ser de importancia capital
par·a·noi·a [pærəˈnɔɪə] paranoia *f*
par·a·noid [ˈpærənɔɪd] *adj* paranoico
par·a·pher·na·li·a [pærəfərˈneɪlɪə] parafernalia *f*
par·a·phrase [ˈpærəfreɪz] *v/t* parafrasear
par·a·pleg·ic [pærəˈpliːdʒɪk] *n* parapléjico(-a) *m(f)*
par·a·site [ˈpærəsaɪt] *also fig* parásito *m*
par·a·sol [ˈpærəsɑːl] sombrilla *f*
par·a·troop·er [ˈpærətruːpər] paracaidista *m/f* (*militar*)
par·cel [ˈpɑːrsl] *n* paquete *m*
♦ **parcel up** *v/t* empaquetar
parch [pɑːrtʃ] *v/t* secar; ***be ~ed*** F *of person* estar muerto de sed F
par·don [ˈpɑːrdn] **1** *n* LAW indulto *m*; ***I beg your ~?*** (*what did you say?*) ¿cómo ha dicho?; ***I beg your ~*** (*I'm sorry*) discúlpeme **2** *v/t* perdonar; LAW indultar; ***~ me?*** ¿perdón?, ¿qué?
pare [per] *v/t* (*peel*) pelar
par·ent [ˈperənt] *father* padre *m*; *mother* madre *f*; ***my ~s*** mis padres
pa·ren·tal [pəˈrentl] *adj* de los padres

P

par·ent com·pa·ny empresa *f* matriz

pa·ren·the·sis [pə'renθəsɪs] (*pl* **parentheses** [pə'renθəsi:z]) paréntesis *m inv*

par·ent-'teach·er as·so·ci·a·tion asociación *f* de padres y profesores

par·ish ['pærɪʃ] parroquia *f*

park¹ [pɑːrk] *n* parque *m*

park² [pɑːrk] *v/t & v/i* MOT estacionar, *Span* aparcar

par·ka ['pɑːrkə] parka *f*

par·king ['pɑːrkɪŋ] MOT estacionamiento *m*, *Span* aparcamiento *m*; **no ~** prohibido aparcar

'**par·king brake** freno *m* de mano; '**par·king disc** disco *m* (de aparcamiento); '**par·king ga·rage** párking *m*, *Span* aparcamiento *m*; '**par·king lot** estacionamiento *m*, *Span* aparcamiento *m* (*al aire libre*); '**par·king me·ter** parquímetro *m*; '**par·king place** (plaza *f* de) estacionamiento *or Span* aparcamiento, sitio *m* para estacionar *or Span* aparcar; '**par·king tick·et** multa *f* de estacionamiento

par·lia·ment ['pɑːrləmənt] parlamento *m*

par·lia·men·ta·ry [pɑːrlə'mentərɪ] *adj* parlamentario

pa·role [pə'roʊl] **1** *n* libertad *f* condicional; **be on ~** estar en libertad condicional **2** *v/t* poner en libertad condicional; **be ~d** salir en libertad condicional

par·rot ['pærət] *n* loro *m*

pars·ley ['pɑːrslɪ] perejil *m*

part [pɑːrt] **1** *n* (*portion, area*) parte *f*; (*episode*) parte *f*, episodio *m*; *of machine* pieza *f* (de repuesto); *in play, film* papel *m*; *in hair* raya *f*; **take ~ in** tomar parte en **2** *adv* (*partly*) en parte; **~ American, ~ Spanish** medio americano medio español; **~ fact, ~ fiction** con una parte de realidad y una parte de ficción **3** *v/i* separarse **4** *v/t*: **~ one's hair** hacerse la raya

♦ **part with** *v/t* desprenderse de

'**part ex·change**: **take sth in ~** lle-

varse algo como parte del pago

par·tial ['pɑːrʃl] *adj* (*incomplete*) parcial; **be ~ to** tener debilidad por

par·tial·ly ['pɑːrʃəlɪ] *adv* parcialmente

par·ti·ci·pant [pɑːr'tɪsɪpənt] participante *m/f*

par·ti·ci·pate [pɑːr'tɪsɪpeɪt] *v/i* participar

par·ti·ci·pa·tion [pɑːrtɪsɪ'peɪʃn] participación *f*

par·ti·cle ['pɑːrtɪkl] PHYS partícula *f*; (*small amount*) pizca *f*

par·tic·u·lar [pər'tɪkjələr] *adj* (*specific*) particular, concreto; (*demanding*) exigente; *about friends, employees* selectivo; *pej* especial, quisquilloso; *you know how ~ she is* ya sabes lo especial que es; *this ~ morning* precisamente esta mañana; *in ~* en particular; *it's a ~ favorite of mine* es uno de mis preferidos

par·tic·u·lar·ly [pər'tɪkjələrlɪ] *adv* particularmente, especialmente

par·ti·tion [pɑːr'tɪʃn] **1** *n* (*screen*) tabique *m*; *of country* partición *f*, división *f* **2** *v/t* country dividir

♦ **partition off** *v/t* dividir con tabiques

part·ly ['pɑːrtlɪ] *adv* en parte

part·ner ['pɑːrtnər] COM socio(-a) *m(f)*; *in relationship* compañero(-a) *m(f)*; *in tennis, dancing* pareja *f*

part·ner·ship ['pɑːrtnərʃɪp] COM sociedad *f*; *in particular activity* colaboración *f*

part of 'speech parte *f* de la oración; '**part own·er** copropietario(-a) *m(f)*; '**part-time 1** *adj* a tiempo parcial **2** *adv work* a tiempo parcial; **part-'tim·er**: **be a ~** trabajar a tiempo parcial

par·ty ['pɑːrtɪ] **1** *n* (*celebration*) fiesta *f*; POL partido *m*; (*group of people*) grupo *m*; **be a ~ to** tomar parte en **2** *v/i* (*pret & pp* **-ied**) F salir de marcha F

pass [pæs] **1** *n for entry, SP* pase *m*; *in mountains* desfiladero *m*; **make a ~ at** tirarle los tejos a **2** *v/t* (*hand*) pasar; (*go past*) pasar por delante de;

(*overtake*) adelantar; (*go beyond*) sobrepasar; (*approve*) aprobar; **~ an exam** aprobar un examen; **~ sentence** LAW dictar sentencia; **~ the time** pasar el tiempo **3** *v/i of time* pasar; *in exam* aprobar; (*go away*) pasarse

♦ **pass around** *v/t* repartir

♦ **pass away** *v/i euph* fallecer, pasar a mejor vida

♦ **pass by 1** *v/t* (*go past*) pasar por **2** *v/i* (*go past*) pasarse

♦ **pass on 1** *v/t* information, book pasar; **~ the savings to ...** *of supermarket etc* revertir el ahorro en ... **2** *v/i* (*euph: die*) fallecer, pasar a mejor vida

♦ **pass out** *v/i* (*faint*) desmayarse

♦ **pass through** *v/t* town pasar por

♦ **pass up** *v/t* opportunity dejar pasar

pass·a·ble ['pæsəbl] *adj* road transitable; (*acceptable*) aceptable

pas·sage ['pæsɪdʒ] (*corridor*) pasillo *m*; *from poem, book* pasaje *m*; *of time* paso *m*

pas·sage·way ['pæsɪdʒweɪ] pasillo *m*

pas·sen·ger ['pæsɪndʒər] pasajero(-a) *m(f)*

'pas·sen·ger seat asiento *m* de pasajero

pas·ser·by [pæsər'baɪ] (*pl* **passers-by**) transeúnte *m/f*

pas·sion ['pæʃn] pasión *f*; **a crime of ~** un crimen pasional

pas·sion·ate ['pæʃnət] *adj* lover apasionado; (*fervent*) fervoroso

pas·sive ['pæsɪv] **1** *adj* pasivo **2** *n* GRAM (voz *f*) pasiva *f*; **in the ~** en pasiva

'pass mark EDU nota *f* mínima para aprobar; **Pass·o·ver** ['pæsouvər] REL Pascua *f* de los hebreos; **pass·port** ['pæspɔːrt] pasaporte *m*; **'pass·port con·trol** control *m* de pasaportes; **'pass·word** contraseña *f*

past [pæst] **1** *adj* (*former*) pasado; **his ~ life** su pasado; **the ~ few days** los últimos días; **that's all ~ now** todo eso es agua pasada **2** *n* pasado; **in the ~** antiguamente **3** *prep in*

position después de; **it's half ~ two** son las dos y media; **it's ~ seven o'clock** pasan de las siete; **it's ~ your bedtime** hace rato que tenías que haberte ido a la cama **4** *adv*: **run/walk ~** pasar

pas·ta ['pæstə] pasta *f*

paste [peɪst] **1** *n* (*adhesive*) cola *f* **2** *v/t* (*stick*) pegar

pas·tel ['pæstl] **1** *n* color pastel *m* **2** *adj* pastel

pas·time ['pæstaɪm] pasatiempo *m*

pas·tor ['pæstər] vicario *m*

past par·ti·ci·ple GRAM participio *m* pasado

pas·tra·mi [pæ'strɑːmɪ] pastrami *m*, carne de vaca ahumada con especias

pas·try ['peɪstrɪ] *for pie* masa *f*; *small cake* pastel *m*

'past tense GRAM (tiempo *m*) pasado *m*

pas·ty ['peɪstɪ] *adj complexion* pálido

pat [pæt] **1** *n* palmadita *f*; **give s.o. a ~ on the back** *fig* dar una palmadita a alguien en la espalda **2** *v/t* (*pret & pp* **-ted**) dar palmaditas a

patch [pætʃ] **1** *n on clothing* parche *m*; (*area*) mancha *f*; **a bad ~** (*period of time*) un mal momento, una mala racha; **~es of fog** zonas de niebla; **not be a ~ on** *fig* no tener ni punto de comparación con **2** *v/t clothing* remendar

♦ **patch up** *v/t* (*repair temporarily*) hacer un remiendo a, arreglar a medias; *quarrel* solucionar

patch·work ['pætʃwɜːrk] **1** *n needlework* labor *f* de retazo **2** *adj* hecho de remiendos

patch·y ['pætʃɪ] *quality* desigual; *work, performance* irregular

pâ·té [pɑː'teɪ] paté *m*

pa·tent ['peɪtnt] **1** *adj* patente, evidente **2** *n for invention* patente *f* **3** *v/t invention* patentar

pa·tent 'leath·er charol *m*

pa·tent·ly ['peɪtntlɪ] (*clearly*) evidentemente, claramente

pa·ter·nal [pə'tɜːrnl] *relative* paterno; *pride, love* paternal

pa·ter·nal·ism [pə'tɜːrnlɪzm] paternalismo *m*

pa·ter·nal·is·tic [pətɜːrnl'ɪstɪk] *adj* paternalista

pa·ter·ni·ty [pə'tɜːrnɪtɪ] paternidad *f*

path [pæθ] *also fig* camino *m*

pa·thet·ic [pə'θetɪk] *adj invoking pity* patético; F (*very bad*) lamentable F

path·o·log·i·cal [pæθə'lɑːdʒɪkl] *adj* patológico

pa·thol·o·gist [pə'θɑːlədʒɪst] patólogo(-a) *m(f)*

pa·thol·o·gy [pə'θɑːlədʒɪ] patología *f*

pa·tience ['peɪʃns] paciencia *f*

pa·tient ['peɪʃnt] **1** *n* paciente *m/f* **2** *adj* paciente; *just be ~!* ¡ten paciencia!

pa·tient·ly ['peɪʃntlɪ] *adv* pacientemente

pat·i·o ['pætɪoʊ] patio *m*

pat·ri·ot ['peɪtrɪət] patriota *m/f*

pat·ri·ot·ic [peɪtrɪ'ɑːtɪk] *adj* patriótico

pa·tri·ot·ism ['peɪtrɪətɪzm] patriotismo *m*

pa·trol [pə'troʊl] **1** *n* patrulla *f*; *be on ~* estar de patrulla **2** *v/t* (*pret & pp -led*) *streets, border* patrullar

pa'trol car coche *m* patrulla; pa'trol·man policía *m*, patrullero *m*; pa'trol wag·on furgón *m* policial

pa·tron ['peɪtrən] *of store, movie theater* cliente *m/f*; *of artist, charity etc* patrocinador(a) *m(f)*

pa·tron·ize ['pætrənaɪz] *v/t person* tratar con condescendencia *or* como a un niño

pa·tron·iz·ing ['pætrənaɪzɪŋ] condescendiente

pa·tron 'saint santo(-a) *m(f)* patrón(-ona), patrón(-ona) *m(f)*

pat·ter ['pætər] **1** *n of rain etc* repiqueteo *m*; F *of salesman* parloteo *m* F **2** *v/i* repiquetear

pat·tern ['pætərn] *n on wallpaper, fabric* estampado *m*; *for knitting, sewing* diseño *m*; (*model*) modelo *m*; *in behavior, events* pauta *f*

pat·terned ['pætərnd] *adj* estampado

paunch [pɔːntʃ] barriga *f*

pause [pɔːz] **1** *n* pausa *f* **2** *v/i* parar; *when speaking* hacer una pausa **3** *v/t tape* poner en pausa

pave [peɪv] *with concrete* pavimentar; *with slabs* adoquinar; *~ the way for fig* preparar el terreno para

pave·ment ['peɪvmənt] (*roadway*) calzada *f*; Br (*sidewalk*) acera *f*

pav·ing stone ['peɪvɪŋ] losa *f*

paw [pɔː] **1** *n of animal* pata *f*; F (*hand*) pezuña *f* F **2** *v/t* F sobar F

pawn[1] [pɔːn] *n in chess* peón *m*; *fig* títere *m*

pawn[2] [pɔːn] *v/t* empeñar

'pawn·bro·ker prestamista *m/f*

'pawn·shop casa *f* de empeños

pay [peɪ] **1** *n* paga *f*, sueldo *m*; *in the ~ of* a sueldo de **2** *v/t* (*pret & pp paid*) *employee, sum, bill* pagar; *~ attention* prestar atención; *~ s.o. a compliment* hacer un cumplido a alguien **3** *v/i* (*pret & pp paid*) pagar; (*be profitable*) ser rentable; *it doesn't ~ to …* no conviene …; *~ for purchase* pagar; *you'll ~ for this! fig* ¡me las pagarás!

♦ pay back *v/t person* devolver el dinero a; *loan* devolver

♦ pay in *v/t to bank* ingresar

♦ pay off **1** *v/t debt* liquidar; (*bribe*) sobornar **2** *v/i* (*be profitable*) valer la pena

♦ pay up *v/i* pagar

pay·a·ble ['peɪəbl] *adj* pagadero

'pay·check, Br 'pay cheque cheque *m* del sueldo

'pay·day día *m* de paga

pay·ee [peɪ'iː] beneficiario(-a) *m(f)*

'pay en·ve·lope sobre *m* con la paga

pay·er ['peɪər] pagador(a) *m(f)* *they are good ~s* pagan puntualmente

pay·ment ['peɪmənt] pago *m*

'pay phone teléfono *m* público; 'pay·roll *salarios mpl; employees* nómina *f*; *be on the ~* estar en nómina; 'pay·slip nómina *f* (*papel*)

PC [piː'siː] *abbr* (= *personal computer*) PC *m*, Span ordenador *m or* L.Am. computadora personal; (= *politically correct*) políticamente correcto

pea [piː] *Span* guisante *m*, *L.Am.* arveja *f*, *Mex* chícharo *m*

peace [piːs] paz *f*; *(quietness)* tranquilidad

peace·a·ble ['piːsəbl] *adj person* pacífico

'**Peace Corps** *organización gubernamental estadounidense de ayuda al desarrollo*

peace·ful ['piːsfəl] *adj* tranquilo; *demonstration* pacífico

peace·ful·ly ['piːsfəlɪ] *adv* pacíficamente

peach [piːtʃ] *fruit* melocotón *m*, *L.Am.* durazno *m*; *tree* melocotonero *m*, *L.Am.* duraznero *m*

pea·cock ['piːkɑːk] pavo *m* real

peak [piːk] **1** *n of mountain* cima *f*; *mountain* pico *m*; *fig* clímax *m* **2** *v/i* alcanzar el máximo

'**peak hours** *npl* horas *fpl* punta

pea·nut ['piːnʌt] cacahuete *m*, *L.Am.* maní *m*, *Mex* cacahuate *m*; **get paid ~s** F cobrar una miseria F; **that's ~s to him** F eso es calderilla para él F

pea·nut 'but·ter crema *f* de cacahuete

pear [per] pera *f*

pearl [pɜːrl] perla *f*

peas·ant ['peznt] campesino(-a) *m(f)*

peb·ble ['pebl] guijarro *m*

pe·can ['piːkən] pacana *f*

peck [pek] **1** *n bite* picotazo *m*; *kiss* besito *m* **2** *v/t bite* picotear; *kiss* dar un besito a

pe·cu·li·ar [pɪ'kjuːljər] *adj (strange)* raro; **~ to** *(special)* característico de

pe·cu·li·ar·i·ty [pɪkjuːlɪ'ærətɪ] *(strangeness)* rareza *f*; *(special feature)* peculiaridad *f*, característica *f*

ped·al ['pedl] **1** *n of bike* pedal *m* **2** *v/i (turn ~s)* pedalear; *(cycle)* recorrer en bicicleta

pe·dan·tic [pɪ'dæntɪk] *adj* puntilloso

ped·dle ['pedl] *v/t drugs* traficar *or* trapichear con

ped·es·tal ['pedəstl] *for statue* pedestal *m*

pe·des·tri·an [pɪ'destrɪən] *n* pea-

pe·des·tri·an 'cros·sing paso *m* de peatones

pe·di·at·ric [piːdɪ'ætrɪk] *adj* pediátrico

pe·di·a·tri·cian [piːdɪə'trɪʃn] pediatra *m/f*

pe·di·at·rics [piːdɪ'ætrɪks] pediatría *f*

ped·i·cure ['pedɪkjʊr] pedicura *f*

ped·i·gree ['pedɪgriː] **1** *n of animal* pedigrí; *of person* linaje *m* **2** *adj* con pedigrí

pee [piː] *v/i* F hacer pis F, mear F

peek [piːk] **1** *n* ojeada *f*, vistazo *m* **2** *v/i* echar una ojeada *or* vistazo

peel [piːl] **1** *n* piel *f* **2** *v/t fruit, vegetables* pelar **3** *v/i of nose, shoulders* pelarse; *of paint* levantarse

♦ **peel off 1** *v/t wrapper etc* quitar; *jacket etc* quitarse **2** *v/i of wrapper* quitarse

peep [piːp] → **peek**

peep·hole ['piːphoʊl] mirilla *f*

peer[1] [pɪr] *n (equal)* igual *m*

peer[2] [pɪr] *v/i* mirar; **~ through the mist** buscar con la mirada entre la niebla; **~ at** forzar la mirada para ver

peeved [piːvd] F mosqueado F

peg [peg] *n for hat, coat* percha *f*; *for tent* clavija *f*; **off the ~** de confección

pe·jo·ra·tive [pɪ'dʒɑːrətɪv] *adj* peyorativo

pel·let ['pelɪt] pelotita *f*; *(bullet)* perdigón *m*

pelt [pelt] **1** *v/t*: **~ s.o. with sth** tirar algo a alguien **2** *v/i*: **they ~ed along the road** F fueron a toda mecha por la carretera F; **it's ~ing down** F está diluviando F

pel·vis ['pelvɪs] pelvis *f*

pen[1] [pen] *n (ballpoint ~)* bolígrafo *m*; *(fountain ~)* pluma *f* (estilográfica)

pen[2] [pen] *(enclosure)* corral *m*

pen[3] [pen] → **penitentiary**

pe·nal·ize ['piːnəlaɪz] *v/t* penalizar

pen·al·ty ['penltɪ] sanción *f*; SP penalti *m*; **take the ~** *in soccer* lanzar el penalti

P

'pen·al·ty ar·e·a SP área *f* de castigo; 'pen·al·ty clause LAW cláusula *f* de penalización; 'pen·al·ty kick (lanzamiento *m* de) penalti *m*; pen·al·ty 'shoot-out tanda *f* de penaltis; 'pen·al·ty spot punto *m* de penalti

pen·cil ['pensɪl] lápiz *m*

pen·cil sharp·en·er sacapuntas *m inv*

pen·dant ['pendənt] *necklace* colgante *m*

pend·ing ['pendɪŋ] **1** *prep* en espera de **2** *adj* pendiente; *be ~ awaiting a decision* estar pendiente; *about to happen* ser inminente

pen·e·trate ['penɪtreɪt] *v/t (pierce)* penetrar; *market* penetrar en

pen·e·trat·ing ['penɪtreɪtɪŋ] *adj stare, scream* penetrante; *analysis* exhaustivo

pen·e·tra·tion [penɪ'treɪʃn] penetración *f*; *of defences* incursión *f*; *of market* entrada *f*

'pen friend amigo(-a) *m(f)* por correspondencia

pen·guin ['peŋgwɪn] pingüino *m*

pen·i·cil·lin [penɪ'sɪlɪn] penicilina *f*

pe·nin·su·la [pə'nɪnsʊlə] península *f*

pe·nis ['piːnɪs] pene *m*

pen·i·tence ['penɪtəns] *(remorse)* arrepentimiento *m*

pen·i·tent ['penɪtənt] *adj* arrepentido

pen·i·tent·ia·ry [penɪ'tenʃərɪ] prisión *f*, cárcel *f*

'pen name seudónimo *m*

pen·nant ['penənt] banderín *f*

pen·ni·less ['penɪlɪs] *adj* sin un centavo

pen·ny ['penɪ] penique *m*

'pen pal amigo(-a) *m(f)* por correspondencia

pen·sion ['penʃn] pensión *f*

♦ pension off *v/t* jubilar

'pen·sion fund fondo *m* de pensiones

'pen·sion scheme plan *m* de jubilación

pen·sive ['pensɪv] *adj* pensativo

Pen·ta·gon ['pentəgɑːn]: *the ~* el Pentágono

pen·tath·lon [pen'tæθlən] pentatlón *m*

Pen·te·cost ['pentɪkɑːst] Pentecostés *m*

pent·house ['penthaʊs] ático *m (de lujo)*

pent-up ['pentʌp] *adj* reprimido

pe·nul·ti·mate [pe'nʌltɪmət] *adj* penúltimo

peo·ple ['piːpl] *npl* gente *f*; *(individuals)* personas *fpl*; *(nsg: race, tribe)* pueblo *m*; *the ~ (citizens)* el pueblo, los ciudadanos; *the Spanish ~* los españoles; *a lot of ~ think ...* muchos piensan que ...; *~ say ...* se dice que ..., dicen que ...

pep·per ['pepər] *spice* pimienta *f*; *vegetable* pimiento *m*

pep·per·mint *candy* caramelo *m* de menta

pep talk ['peptɔːk]: *give a ~* decir unas palabras de aliento

per [pɜːr] *prep* por; *~ annum* al año, por año

per·ceive [pər'siːv] *v/t with senses* percibir; *(view, interpret)* interpretar

per·cent [pər'sent] *adv* por ciento

per·cen·tage [pər'sentɪdʒ] porcentaje *m*, tanto *m* por ciento

per·cep·ti·ble [pər'septəbl] *adj* perceptible

per·cep·ti·bly [pər'septəblɪ] *adv* visiblemente

per·cep·tion [pər'sepʃn] *through senses* percepción *f*; *of situation* apreciación *f*; *(insight)* perspicacia *f*

per·cep·tive [pər'septɪv] *adj* perceptivo

perch [pɜːrtʃ] **1** *n for bird* percha *f* **2** *v/i of bird* posarse; *of person* sentarse

per·co·late ['pɜːrkəleɪt] *v/i of coffee* filtrarse

per·co·la·tor ['pɜːrkəleɪtər] cafetera *f* de filtro

per·cus·sion [pər'kʌʃn] percusión *f*

per·cus·sion in·stru·ment instrumento *m* de percusión

pe·ren·ni·al [pə'renɪəl] *n* BOT árbol *m* de hoja perenne

per·fect **1** *n* ['pɜːrfɪkt] GRAM pretéri-

to *m* perfecto **2** *adj* perfecto **3** *v/t*
[pər'fekt] perfeccionar

por·fec·tion [pər'fekʃn] perfección *f*;
do sth to ~ hacer algo a la perfección

per·fec·tion·ist [pər'fekʃnɪst] *n* perfeccionista *m/f*

per·fect·ly ['pɜːrfɪktlɪ] perfectamente; *(totally)* completamente

per·fo·rat·ed ['pɜːrfəreɪtɪd] *adj line* perforado

per·fo·ra·tions [pɜːrfə'reɪʃnz] *npl* perforaciones *fpl*

per·form [pə'fɔːrm] **1** *v/t (carry out)* realizar, llevar a cabo; *of actors, musician etc* interpretar, representar **2** *v/i of actor, musician, dancer* actuar; *of machine* funcionar

per·form·ance [pə'fɔːrməns] *by actor, musician etc* actuación *f*, interpretación *f*; *of play* representación *f*; *of employee* rendimiento *m*; *of official, company, in sport* actuación *f*; *of machine* rendimiento *m*

per'form·ance car coche *m* de gran rendimiento

per·form·er [pə'fɔːrmər] intérprete *m/f*

per·fume ['pɜːrfjuːm] perfume *m*

per·func·to·ry [pər'fʌŋktərɪ] *adj* superficial

per·haps [pər'hæps] *adv* quizá(s), tal vez; *~ it's not too late* puede que no sea demasiado tarde

per·il ['perəl] peligro *m*

per·il·ous ['perələs] *adj* peligroso

pe·rim·e·ter [pə'rɪmɪtər] perímetro *m*

pe·rim·e·ter fence cerca *f*

pe·ri·od ['pɪrɪəd] periodo *m*, período *m*; *(menstruation)* periodo *m*, regla *f*; *punctuation mark* punto *m*; *I don't want to, ~!* F ¡no me da la gana y punto! F

pe·ri·od·ic [pɪrɪ'ɑːdɪk] *adj* periódico

pe·ri·od·i·cal [pɪrɪ'ɑːdɪkl] *n* publicación *f* periódica

pe·ri·od·i·cal·ly [pɪrɪ'ɑːdɪklɪ] *adv* periódicamente, con periodicidad

pe·riph·e·ral [pə'rɪfərəl] **1** *adj (not crucial)* secundario **2** *n* COMPUT pe-

rifércio *m*

pe·riph·e·ry [pə'rɪfərɪ] periferia *f*

per·ish ['perɪʃ] *v/i of rubber* estropearse, picarse; *of person* perecer

per·ish·a·ble ['perɪʃəbl] *adj food* perecedero

per·jure ['pɜːrdʒər] *v/t:* **~ o.s.** perjurar

per·ju·ry ['pɜːrdʒərɪ] perjurio *m*

perk [pɜːrk] *n of job* ventaja *f*

♦ **perk up 1** *v/t* animar **2** *v/i* animarse

perk·y ['pɜːrkɪ] *(cheerful)* animado

perm [pɜːrm] **1** *n* permanente *f* **2** *v/t* hacer la permanente; *she had her hair ~ed* se hizo la permanente

per·ma·nent ['pɜːrmənənt] *adj* permanente

per·ma·nent·ly ['pɜːrmənəntlɪ] *adv* permanentemente

per·me·a·ble ['pɜːrmɪəbl] *adj* permeable

per·me·ate ['pɜːrmɪeɪt] *v/t* impregnar

per·mis·si·ble [pər'mɪsəbl] *adj* permisible

per·mis·sion [pər'mɪʃn] permiso *m*; *ask s.o.'s ~ to ...* pedir permiso a alguien para ...

per·mis·sive [pər'mɪsɪv] *adj* permisivo

per·mit ['pɜːrmɪt] **1** *n* licencia *f* **2** *v/t (pret & pp -ted)* [pər'mɪt] permitir; *~ s.o. to do sth* permitir a alguien que haga algo

per·pen·dic·u·lar [pɜːrpən'dɪkjulər] *adj* perpendicular

per·pet·u·al [pər'petʃuəl] *adj* perpetuo; *interruptions* continuo

per·pet·u·al·ly [pər'petʃuəlɪ] *adv* constantemente

per·pet·u·ate [pər'petʃueɪt] *v/t* perpetuar

per·plex [pər'pleks] *v/t* dejar perplejo

per·plexed [pər'plekst] *adj* perplejo

per·plex·i·ty [pər'pleksɪtɪ] perplejidad *f*

per·se·cute ['pɜːrsɪkjuːt] *v/t* perseguir; *(hound)* acosar

per·se·cu·tion [pɜːrsɪ'kjuːʃn] persecución *f*; *(harassment)* acoso *m*

per·se·cu·tor [pɜːrsɪ'kjuːtər] perseguidor(a) *m(f)*

per·se·ver·ance [pɜːrsɪˈvɪrəns] perseverancia *f*

per·se·vere [pɜːrsɪˈvɪr] *v/i* perseverar

per·sist [pərˈsɪst] *v/i* persistir; **~ in** persistir en

per·sis·tence [pərˈsɪstəns] (*perseverance*) perseverancia *f*; (*continuation*) persistencia *f*

per·sis·tent [pərˈsɪstənt] *adj person, questions* perseverante; *rain, unemployment etc* persistente

per·sis·tent·ly [pərˈsɪstəntlɪ] *adv* (*continually*) constantemente

per·son [ˈpɜːrsn] persona *f*; **in ~** en persona

per·son·al [ˈpɜːrsnl] *adj* (*private*) personal; *life* privado; **don't make ~ remarks** no hagas comentarios personales

per·son·al as·sist·ant secretario(a) *m(f)* personal; **'per·son·al col·umn** sección *f* de anuncios personales; **per·son·al com'put·er** *Span* ordenador *m* personal, *L.Am.* computadora *f* personal; **per·son·al 'hy·giene** higiene *f* personal

per·son·al·i·ty [pɜːrsəˈnælətɪ] personalidad *f*; (*celebrity*) personalidad *f*, personaje *m*

per·son·al·ly [ˈpɜːrsənəlɪ] *adv* (*for my part*) personalmente; (*in person*) en persona; **don't take it ~** no te lo tomes como algo personal

per·son·al 'or·gan·iz·er organizador *m* personal; **per·son·al 'pro·noun** pronombre *m* personal; **per·son·al 'ster·e·o** walkman *m* ®

per·son·i·fy [pɜːrˈsɑːnɪfaɪ] *v/t* (*pret & pp -ied*) *of person* personificar

per·son·nel [pɜːrsəˈnel] *employees, department* personal *m*

per·son'nel man·a·ger director(a) *m(f)* de personal

per·spec·tive [pərˈspektɪv] PAINT perspectiva *f*; **get sth into ~** poner algo en perspectiva

per·spi·ra·tion [pɜːrspɪˈreɪʃn] sudor *m*, transpiración *f*

per·spire [pərˈspaɪr] *v/i* sudar, transpirar

per·suade [pərˈsweɪd] *v/t person* persuadir; **~ s.o. to do sth** persuadir a alguien para que haga algo

per·sua·sion [pərˈsweɪʒn] persuasión *f*

per·sua·sive [pərˈsweɪsɪv] persuasivo

per·ti·nent [ˈpɜːrtɪnənt] *adj fml* pertinente

per·turb [pərˈtɜːrb] *v/t* perturbar

per·turb·ing [pərˈtɜːrbɪŋ] *adj* perturbador

Pe·ru [pəˈruː] *n* Perú

pe·ruse [pəˈruːz] *v/t fml* leer atentamente

Pe·ru·vi·an [pəˈruːvɪən] **1** *adj* peruano **2** *n* peruano(-a) *m(f)*

per·va·sive [pərˈveɪsɪv] *adj influence, ideas* dominante

per·verse [pərˈvɜːrs] *adj* (*awkward*) terco; **just to be ~** sólo para llevar la contraria

per·ver·sion [pərˈvɜːrʃn] *sexual* perversión *f*

per·vert [ˈpɜːrvɜːrt] *n sexual* pervertido(-a) *m(f)*

pes·si·mism [ˈpesɪmɪzm] pesimismo *m*

pes·si·mist [ˈpesɪmɪst] pesimista *m/f*

pes·si·mist·ic [pesɪˈmɪstɪk] *adj* pesimista

pest [pest] plaga *f*; F *person* tostón *m* F

pes·ter [ˈpestər] *v/t* acosar; **~ s.o. to do sth** molestar *or* dar la lata a alguien para que haga algo

pes·ti·cide [ˈpestɪsaɪd] pesticida *f*

pet [pet] **1** *n animal* animal *m* doméstico *or* de compañía; (*favorite*) preferido(-a) *m(f)* **2** *adj* preferido, favorito **3** *v/t* (*pret & pp -ted*) *animal* acariciar **4** *v/i* (*pret & pp -ted*) *of couple* magrearse F

pet·al [ˈpetl] pétalo *m*

♦ **pe·ter out** [ˈpiːtər] *v/i of rain* amainar; *of rebellion* irse extinguiendo; *of path* ir desapareciendo

pe·tite [pəˈtiːt] *adj* chiquito(-a); *size* menudo

pe·ti·tion [pə'tɪʃn] n petición f

'pet name nombre m cariñoso

pet·ri·fled ['petrɪfaɪd] adj person petrificado; scream, voice aterrorizado

pet·ri·fy ['petrɪfaɪ] v/t (pret & pp -ied) dejar petrificado

pet·ro·chem·i·cal [petrou'kemɪkl] adj petroquímico

pet·rol ['petrl] Br gasolina f, Arg nafta f

pe·tro·le·um [pɪ'trouliəm] petróleo m

pet·ting ['petɪŋ] magreo m F

pet·ty ['petɪ] adj person, behavior mezquino; details, problem sin importancia

pet·ty 'cash dinero m para gastos menores

pet·u·lant ['petʃələnt] adj caprichoso

pew [pjuː] banco m (de iglesia)

pew·ter ['pjuːtər] peltre m

phar·ma·ceu·ti·cal [fɑːrmə'suːtɪkl] adj farmacéutico

phar·ma·ceu·ti·cals [fɑːmə'suːtɪklz] npl fármacos mpl

phar·ma·cist ['fɑːrməsɪst] in store farmacéutico(-a) m(f)

phar·ma·cy ['fɑːrməsɪ] store farmacia f

phase [feɪz] fase f; **go through a difficult ~** atravesar una mala etapa

♦ phase in v/t introducir gradualmente

♦ phase out v/t eliminar gradualmente

PhD [piːeɪtʃ'diː] abbr (= **Doctor of Philosophy**) Doctorado m

phe·nom·e·nal [fɪ'nɑːmɪnl] adj fenomenal

phe·nom·e·nal·ly [fɪ'nɑːmɪnlɪ] adv extraordinariamente; stupid increíblemente

phe·nom·e·non [fɪ'nɑːmɪnɑːn] fenómeno m

phil·an·throp·ic [fɪlən'θrɑːpɪk] adj filantrópico

phi·lan·thro·pist [fɪ'lænθrəpɪst] filántropo(-a) m(f)

phi·lan·thro·py [fɪ'lænθrəpɪ] filantropía f

Phil·ip·pines ['fɪlɪpiːnz] npl: **the ~** las Filipinas

phil·is·tine ['fɪlɪstaɪn] n filisteo(-a) m(f)

phi·los·o·pher |lɪ'lɑːsəfər] filósofo(-a) m(f)

phil·o·soph·i·cal [fɪlə'sɑːfɪkl] adj filosófico

phi·los·o·phy [fɪ'lɑːsəfɪ] filosofía f

pho·bi·a ['foubɪə] fobia f

phone [foun] **1** n teléfono m; **be on the ~** (have a ~) tener teléfono; be talking estar hablando por teléfono **2** v/t llamar (por teléfono) a **3** v/i llamar (por teléfono)

'phone book guía f (de teléfonos); 'phone booth cabina f (de teléfonos); 'phone·call llamada f (telefónica); 'phone card tarjeta f telefónica; 'phone num·ber número m de teléfono

pho·net·ics [fə'netɪks] fonética f

pho·n(e)y ['founɪ] adj F falso

pho·to ['foutou] foto f

'pho·to al·bum álbum m de fotos; 'pho·to·cop·i·er fotocopiadora f; 'pho·to·cop·y **1** n fotocopia f **2** v/t (pret & pp -ied) fotocopiar

pho·to·gen·ic [foutou'dʒenɪk] adj fotogénico

pho·to·graph ['foutəgræf] **1** n fotografía f **2** v/t fotografiar

pho·tog·ra·pher [fə'tɑːgrəfər] fotógrafo(-a) m(f)

pho·tog·ra·phy [fə'tɑːgrəfɪ] fotografía f

phrase [freɪz] **1** n frase f **2** v/t expresar

'phrase·book guía f de conversación

phys·i·cal ['fɪzɪkl] **1** adj físico **2** n MED reconocimiento m médico

phys·i·cal 'hand·i·cap minusvalía f física

phys·i·cal·ly ['fɪzɪklɪ] adv físicamente

phys·i·cal·ly 'hand·i·cap·ped disminuído(-a) m(f) físico

phy·si·cian [fɪ'zɪʃn] médico(-a) m(f)

phys·i·cist ['fɪzɪsɪst] físico(-a) m(f)

phys·ics ['fɪzɪks] física f

phys·i·o·ther·a·pist [fɪzɪou'θerəpıst] fisioterapeuta *m/f*

phys·i·o·ther·a·py [fızıoʊ'θerəpı] fisioterapia *f*

phy·sique [fɪ'ziːk] físico *m*

pi·a·nist ['pıənıst] pianista *m/f*

pi·an·o [pı'ænoʊ] piano *m*

pick [pɪk] **1** *n*: **take your ~** elige el que prefieras **2** *v/t* (*choose*) escoger, elegir; *flowers, fruit* recoger; **~ one's nose** meterse el dedo en la nariz **3** *v/i*: **~ and choose** ser muy exigente

♦ **pick at** *v/t*: **pick at one's food** comer como un pajarito

♦ **pick on** *v/t* (*treat unfairly*) meterse con; (*select*) elegir

♦ **pick out** *v/t* (*identify*) identificar

♦ **pick up 1** *v/t object* recoger, *Span* coger; *habit* adquirir, *Span* coger; *illness* contraer, *Span* coger; *in car, from ground, from airport etc* recoger; *telephone* descolgar; *language, skill* aprender; (*buy*) comprar; *criminal* detener; **pick s.o. up** *sexually* ligar con alguien **2** *v/i* (*improve*) mejorar

pick·et ['pɪkɪt] **1** *n of strikers* piquete *m* **2** *v/t* hacer piquete delante de

'**pick·et fence** valla *f* de estacas

'**pick·et line** piquete *m*

pick·le ['pɪkl] *v/t* encurtir; *fish* poner en escabeche; *meat* poner en adobo

pick·les ['pɪklz] *npl* (*dill ~*) encurtidos *mpl*

'**pick·pock·et** carterista *m/f*

pick-up (truck) ['pɪkʌp] camioneta *f*

pick·y ['pɪkı] *adj* F tiquismiquis F

pic·nic ['pɪknɪk] **1** *n* picnic *m* **2** *v/i* (*pret & pp* **-ked**) ir de picnic

pic·ture ['pɪktʃər] **1** *n* (*photo*) fotografía *f*; (*painting*) cuadro *m*; (*illustration*) dibujo *m*; (*movie*) película *f*; *on TV* imagen *f*; **keep s.o. in the ~** mantener a alguien al día **2** *v/t* imaginar

'**pic·ture book** libro *m* ilustrado

pic·ture 'post·card postal *f*

pic·tur·esque [pɪktʃə'resk] *adj* pintoresco

pie [paı] pastel *m*

piece [piːs] (*fragment*) fragmento *m*;

component, in board game pieza *f*; **a ~ of pie / bread** un trozo de pastel / una rebanada de pan; **a ~ of advice** un consejo; **go to ~s** derrumbarse; **take to ~s** desmontar

♦ **piece together** *v/t broken plate* recomponer; *facts, evidence* reconstruir

piece·meal ['piːsmiːl] *adv* poco a poco

piece·work ['piːswɜːrk] trabajo *m* a destajo

pier [pır] *at seaside* malecón *m*

pierce [pırs] *v/t* (*penetrate*) perforar; *ears* agujerear

pierc·ing ['pırsıŋ] *adj scream* desgarrador; *gaze* penetrante; *wind* cortante

pig [pıg] *also fig* cerdo *m*; *greedy* glotón(-a) *m(f)*

pi·geon ['pıdʒın] paloma *f*

'**pi·geon·hole 1** *n* casillero *m* **2** *v/t person* encasillar; *proposal* archivar

pig·gy·bank ['pıgıbæŋk] hucha *f*

pig·head·ed [pıg'hedıd] *adj* F cabezota F; '**pig·pen** *also fig* pocilga *f*; '**pig·skin** piel *f* de cerdo; '**pig·tail** coleta *f*

pile [paıl] montón *m*, pila *f*; **a ~ of work** F un montón de trabajo F

♦ **pile up 1** *v/i of work, bills* acumularse **2** *v/t* amontonar

piles [paılz] *nsg* MED hemorroides *fpl*

pile-up ['paılʌp] MOT choque *m* múltiple

pil·fer·ing ['pılfərıŋ] hurtos *mpl*

pil·grim ['pılgrım] peregrino(-a) *m(f)*

pil·grim·age ['pılgrımıdʒ] peregrinación *f*

pill [pıl] pastilla *f*; **be on the ~** tomar la píldora

pil·lar ['pılər] pilar *m*

pil·lion ['pıljən] *of motor bike* asiento *m* trasero

pil·low ['pıloʊ] *n* almohada *f*

'**pill·ow·case**, '**pil·low·slip** funda *f* de almohada

pi·lot ['paılət] **1** *n of airplane* piloto *m/f*; *for ship* práctico *m* **2** *v/t airplane* pilotar

'**pi·lot scheme** plan *m* piloto

pimp [pɪmp] *n* proxeneta *m*, *Span* chulo *m* F

pim·ple ['pɪmpl] grano *m*

PIN [pɪn] (= *personal identification number*) PIN *m* (= número *m* de identificación personal)

pin [pɪn] **1** *n for sewing* alfiler *m*; *in bowling* bolo *m*; (*badge*) pin *m*; ELEC clavija *f*; *safety ~* imperdible *m* **2** *v/t* (*pret & pp* *-ned*) (*hold down*) mantener; (*attach*) sujetar

◆ **pin down** *v/t*: *pin s.o. down to a date* forzar a alguien a concretar una fecha

◆ **pin up** *v/t notice* sujetar con chinchetas

pin·cers ['pɪnsərz] *npl of crab* pinzas *fpl*; *tool* tenazas *fpl*; *a pair of ~* unas tenazas *fpl*

pinch [pɪntʃ] **1** *n* pellizco *m*; *of salt, sugar etc* pizca *f*; *at ~* si no queda otro remedio; *with numbers* como máximo **2** *v/t* pellizcar **3** *v/i of shoes* apretar

pine[1] [paɪn] *n tree* pino *m*; *wood* (madera *f* de) pino *m*

pine[2] [paɪn] *v/i*: *~ for* echar de menos

pine·ap·ple ['paɪnæpl] piña *f*, *L.Am.* ananá(s) *f*

ping [pɪŋ] **1** *n* sonido *m* metálico **2** *v/i* hacer un sonido metálico

ping-pong ['pɪŋpɑːŋ] pimpón *m*, ping-pong *m*

pink [pɪŋk] *adj* rosa

pin·na·cle ['pɪnəkl] *fig* cima *f*

'**pin·point** *v/t* determinar

pins and 'nee·dles *npl* hormigueo *m*

'**pin·stripe** *adj* a rayas

pint [paɪnt] pinta *f*, *medida equivalente a 0,473 litros en Estados Unidos o a 0,568 litros en Gran Bretaña*

'**pin-up** modelo *m/f* de revista

pi·o·neer [paɪə'nɪr] **1** *n* pionero(-a) *m*(*f*) **2** *v/t* ser pionero en

pi·o·neer·ing [paɪə'nɪrɪŋ] *adj work* pionero

pi·ous ['paɪəs] piadoso

pip [pɪp] *n of fruit* pepita *f*

pipe [paɪp] **1** *n for smoking* pipa *f*; *for water, gas, sewage* tubería *f* **2** *v/t* conducir por tuberías

◆ **pipe down** *v/i* F cerrar el pico F

piped mu·sic [paɪpt'mjuːzɪk] hilo *m* musical

'**pipe·line** *for oil* oleoducto *m*; *for gas* gasoducto *m*; *in the ~ fig* en trámite

pip·ing hot [paɪpɪŋ'hɑːt] *adj* muy caliente

pi·rate ['paɪrət] **1** *n* pirata *m/f* **2** *v/t software* piratear

Pis·ces ['paɪsiːz] ASTR Piscis *m/f inv*

piss [pɪs] **1** *v/i* P (*urinate*) mear P **2** *n* P (*urine*) meada *f* P

pissed [pɪst] *adj* P (*annoyed*) cabreado P; *Br* P (*drunk*) borracho, pedo F

pis·tol ['pɪstl] pistola *f*

pis·ton ['pɪstən] pistón *m*

pit [pɪt] *n* (*hole*) hoyo *m*; (*coal mine*) mina *f*; *in fruit* hueso *m*

pitch[1] [pɪtʃ] *n* MUS tono *m*

pitch[2] [pɪtʃ] **1** *v/i in baseball* lanzar la pelota **2** *v/t tent* montar; *ball* lanzar

'**pitch black** *adj* negro como el carbón

pitch·er[1] ['pɪtʃər] *baseball player* lanzador(a) *m*(*f*), pítcher *m/f*

pitch·er[2] ['pɪtʃər] *container* jarra *f*

pith [pɪθ] *of citrus fruit* piel *f* blanca

pit·e·ous ['pɪtɪəs] *adj* patético

'**pit·fall** ['pɪtfɔːl] dificultad *f*

pit·i·ful ['pɪtɪfəl] *adj sight* lastimoso; *excuse, attempt* lamentable

pit·i·less ['pɪtɪləs] *adj* despiadado

pits [pɪts] *npl in motor racing* boxes *mpl*

'**pit stop** *in motor racing* parada *f* en boxes

pit·tance ['pɪtns] miseria *f*

pit·y ['pɪtɪ] **1** *n* pena *f*, lástima *f*; *it's a ~ that* es una pena *or* lástima que; *what a ~!* ¡qué pena!; *take ~ on* compadecerse de **2** *v/t* (*pret & pp* *-ied*) *person* compadecerse de

piv·ot ['pɪvət] *v/i* pivotar

piz·za ['piːtsə] pizza *f*

plac·ard ['plækɑːrd] pancarta *f*

place [pleɪs] **1** *n* sitio *m*, lugar *m*; *in race, competition* puesto *m*; (*seat*) sitio *m*, asiento *m*; *I've lost my ~ in book* no sé por dónde iba; *at my / his ~* en mi / su casa; *in ~ of* en lugar de;

feel out of ~ sentirse fuera de lugar;
take ~ tener lugar, llevarse a cabo;
in the first ~ (*firstly*) en primer lugar; (*in the beginning*) en principio
2 v/t (*put*) poner, colocar; *I know you but I can't quite* ~ *you* te conozco pero no recuerdo de qué; ~ *an order* hacer un pedido

'place mat mantel *m* individual
plac·id ['plæsɪd] *adj* apacible
pla·gia·rism ['pleɪdʒərɪzm] plagio *m*
pla·gia·rize ['pleɪdʒəraɪz] v/t plagiar
plague [pleɪg] **1** *n* plaga *f* **2** v/t (*bother*) molestar
plain¹ [pleɪn] *n* llanura *f*
plain² [pleɪn] **1** *adj* (*clear, obvious*) claro; (*not fancy*) simple; (*not pretty*) feo/lo; (*not patterned*) liso; (*blunt*) directo; ~ *chocolate* chocolate amargo **2** *adv* verdaderamente; *it's* ~ *crazy* es una verdadera locura
'plain-clothes: *in* ~ de paisano
plain·ly ['pleɪnlɪ] *adv* (*clearly*) evidentemente; (*bluntly*) directamente; (*simply*) con sencillez; *he's* ~ *upset* está claro que está enfadado
plain [pleɪn] *adj* sencillo
plain·tiff ['pleɪntɪf] demandante *m/f*
plain·tive ['pleɪntɪv] *adj* quejumbroso
plan [plæn] **1** *n* (*project, intention*) plan *m*; (*drawing*) plano *m*; *wedding* ~*s* preparaciones *fpl* para la boda **2** v/t (*pret & pp* -*ned*) (*prepare*) planear; (*design*) hacer los planos de; *to do sth, ~ on doing sth* planear hacer algo **3** v/i (*pret & pp* -*ned*) hacer planes
plane¹ [pleɪn] *n* (*airplane*) avión *m*
plane² [pleɪn] *tool* cepillo *m*
plan·et ['plænɪt] planeta *f*
plank [plæŋk] *of wood* tablón *m*; *fig: of policy* punto *m*
plan·ning ['plænɪŋ] planificación *f*; *at the* ~ *stage* en fase de estudio
plant¹ [plænt] **1** *n* planta *f* **2** v/t plantar
plant² [plænt] *n* (*factory*) fábrica *f*, planta *f*; (*equipment*) maquinaria *f*
plan·ta·tion [plæn'teɪʃn] plantación *f*
plaque [plæk] *on wall, teeth* placa *f*

plas·ter ['plæstər] **1** *n on wall, ceiling* yeso *m* **2** v/t *wall, ceiling* enyesar; *be* ~*ed with* estar recubierto de
'plas·ter cast escayola *f*
plas·tic ['plæstɪk] **1** *n* plástico *m* **2** *adj* (*made of* ~) de plástico
plas·tic 'bag bolsa *f* de plástico;
'plas·tic (mon·ey) plástico *m*, tarjetas *fpl* de pago; **plas·tic 'sur·geon** cirujano(-a) *m(f)* plástico(-a); **plas·tic 'sur·ge·ry** cirugía *f* estética
plate [pleɪt] *n for food* plato *m*; (*sheet of metal*) chapa *f*; PHOT placa *f*
pla·teau ['plætoʊ] *n* meseta *f*
plat·form ['plætfɔːrm] (*stage*) plataforma *f*; *of railroad station* andén *m*; *fig: political* programa *m*
plat·i·num ['plætɪnəm] **1** *n* platino *m* **2** *adj* de platino
plat·i·tude ['plætɪtuːd] tópico *m*
pla·ton·ic [plə'tɑːnɪk] *adj relationship* platónico
pla·toon [plə'tuːn] *of soldiers* sección *f*
plat·ter ['plætər] *for meat, fish* fuente *f*
plau·si·ble ['plɔːzəbl] *adj* plausible
play [pleɪ] **1** *n in theater, on TV* obra *f* (de teatro); *of children, in match,* TECH juego *m* **2** v/i jugar; *of musician* tocar **3** v/t *musical instrument* tocar; *piece of music* intepretar, tocar; *game* jugar; *tennis, football* jugar; *opponent* jugar contra; (*perform: Macbeth etc*) representar; *particular role* interpretar, hacer el papel de; ~ *a joke on* gastar una broma a
♦ **play around** v/i F (*be unfaithful*) acostarse con otras personas
♦ **play down** v/t quitar importancia a
♦ **play up** v/i *of machine* dar problemas; *of child* dar guerra
play·act ['pleɪækt] v/i (*pretend*) fingir
play·boy ['pleɪbɔɪ] playboy *m*
play·er ['pleɪr] SP jugador(a) *m(f)*; (*musician*) intérprete *m/f*; (*actor*) actor *m*, actriz *f*
play·ful ['pleɪfəl] *adj punch etc* de broma

play·ground ['pleɪgraʊnd] zona f de juegos

'**play·group** guardería f

play·ing card ['pleɪŋkɑːrd] carta f

play·ing field ['pleɪŋfiːld] campo m de deportes

play·mate ['pleɪmeɪt] compañero(-a) m(f) de juego

play·wright ['pleɪraɪt] autor(a) m(f)

pla·za ['plɑːzə] for shopping centro m comercial

plc [piːel'siː] Br abbr (= **public limited company**) S.A. f (= sociedad f anónima)

plea [pliː] n súplica f

plead [pliːd] v/i: ~ **for mercy** pedir clemencia; ~ **guilty / not guilty** declararse culpable / inocente; **she ~ed with me not to go** me suplicó que no fuera

pleas·ant ['pleznt] adj agradable

please [pliːz] 1 adv por favor; **more tea? – yes, ~** ¿más té? – sí, por favor; ~ **do** claro que sí, por supuesto 2 v/t complacer; ~ **yourself!** ¡haz lo que quieras!

pleased [pliːzd] adj contento, (satisfied) satisfecho; ~ **to meet you** encantado de conocerle; **I'm very ~ to be here** estoy muy contento de estar aquí

pleas·ing ['pliːzɪŋ] adj agradable

pleas·ure ['pleʒər] (happiness, satisfaction, delight) satisfacción f; as opposed to work placer m; **it's a ~** (you're welcome) no hay de qué; **with ~** faltaría más

pleat [pliːt] n in skirt tabla f

pleat·ed skirt ['pliːtɪd] falda f de tablas

pledge [pledʒ] 1 n (promise) promesa f; (guarantee) compromiso m; (money) donación f; **Pledge of Allegiance** juramento de lealtad a la bandera estadounidense 2 v/t (promise) prometer; (guarantee) comprometerse; money donar

plen·ti·ful ['plentɪfəl] adj abundante

plen·ty ['plentɪ] (abundance) abundancia f; ~ **of books / food** muchos libros / mucha comida; **we have ~ of**

room tenemos espacio más que suficiente; **that's ~** es suficiente; **there's ~ for everyone** hay (suficiente) para todos

pli·a·ble ['plaɪəbl] adj flexible

pli·ers ['plaɪərz] npl alicates mpl; **a pair of ~** unos alicates

plight [plaɪt] situación f difícil

plod [plɑːd] v/i (pret & pp -**ded**) (walk) arrastrarse

♦ **plod on** v/i with a job avanzar laboriosamente

plod·der ['plɑːdər] (at work, school) persona no especialmente lista pero muy trabajadora

plot[1] [plɑːt] n (land) terreno m

plot[2] [plɑːt] 1 n (conspiracy) complot m; of novel argumento m 2 v/t (pret & pp -**ted**) tramar 3 v/i (pret & pp -**ted**) conspirar

plot·ter ['plɑːtər] conspirador(a) m(f); COMPUT plóter m

plough Br, **plow** [plaʊ] 1 n arado m 2 v/t & v/i arar

♦ **plow back** v/t profits reinvertir

pluck [plʌk] v/t eyebrows depilar; chicken desplumar

♦ **pluck up** v/t: **pluck up courage to …** reunir el valor para …

plug [plʌg] 1 n for sink, bath tapón m; electrical enchufe m; (spark ~) bujía f; **give a book a ~** dar publicidad a un libro 2 v/t (pret & pp -**ged**) hole tapar; new book etc hacer publicidad de

♦ **plug away at** v/t F trabajar con esfuerzo en

♦ **plug in** v/t enchufar

plum [plʌm] 1 n fruit ciruela f; tree ciruelo m 2 adj F: **a ~ job** un chollo de trabajo

plum·age ['pluːmɪdʒ] plumaje m

plumb [plʌm] adj vertical

♦ **plumb in** v/t washing machine conectar a la red del agua

plumb·er ['plʌmər] Span fontanero(-a) m(f), L.Am. plomero(-a) m(f)

plumb·ing ['plʌmɪŋ] pipes tuberías fpl

plume [pluːm] (feather) pluma f; of

smoke nube *f*

plum·met ['plʌmɪt] *v/i of airplane, prices* caer en picado

plump [plʌmp] *adj* rellenito

◆ **plump for** *v/t* F decidirse por

plunge [plʌndʒ] **1** *n* salto *m*; *in prices* caída *f*; **take the ~** dar el paso **2** *v/i* precipitarse; *of prices* caer en picado **3** *v/t* hundir; *(into water)* sumergir; **the city was ~d into darkness** la ciudad quedó inmersa en la oscuridad; **the news ~d him into despair** la noticia lo hundió en la desesperación

plung·ing ['plʌndʒɪŋ] *adj neckline* escotado

plu·per·fect ['pluː'pɜːrfɪkt] *n* GRAM pluscuamperfecto *m*

plu·ral ['plʊərəl] **1** *n* plural *m* **2** *adj* plural

plus [plʌs] **1** *prep* más; **I want John ~ two other volunteers ...** quiero a John y a otros dos voluntarios **2** *adj* más de; **$500 ~** más de 500 dólares **3** *n symbol* signo *m* más; *(advantage)* ventaja *f* **4** *conj (moreover, in addition)* además

plush [plʌʃ] *adj* lujoso

'plus sign signo *m* más

ply·wood ['plaɪwʊd] madera *f* contrachapada

PM [piː'em] *Br abbr (= Prime Minister)* Primer(a) *m(f)* Ministro(-a)

p.m. [piː'em] *abbr (= post meridiem)* p.m.; **at 3 ~** a las 3 de la tarde; **at 11 ~** a las 11 de la noche

pneu·mat·ic [nuː'mætɪk] *adj* neumático

pneu·mat·ic 'drill martillo *m* neumático

pneu·mo·ni·a [nuː'moʊnɪə] pulmonía *f*, neumonía *f*

poach[1] [poʊtʃ] *v/t cook* hervir

poach[2] [poʊtʃ] *v/t & v/i (hunt)* cazar furtivamente; *fish* pescar furtivamente

poached egg [poʊtʃt'eg] huevo *m* escalfado

poach·er ['poʊtʃər] *of game* cazador(a) *m(f)* furtivo(-a); *of fish* pescador(a) *m(f)* furtivo(-a)

P.O. Box [piː'oʊbɑːks] apartado *m* de correos

pock·et ['pɑːkɪt] **1** *n* bolsillo *m*; **line one's own ~s** llenarse los bolsillos; **be $10 out of ~** salir perdiendo 10 dólares **2** *adj radio, dictionary* de bolsillo **3** *v/t* meter en el bolsillo

'pock·et·book *(purse)* bolso *m*; *(billfold)* cartera *f*; *book* libro *m* de bolsillo; **pock·et 'cal·cu·la·tor** calculadora *f* de bolsillo; **'pock·et·knife** navaja *f*

po·di·um ['poʊdɪəm] podio *m*

po·em ['poʊɪm] poema *m*

po·et ['poʊɪt] poeta *m/f*, poetisa *f*

po·et·ic [poʊ'etɪk] *adj* poético

po·et·ic 'jus·tice justicia *f* divina

po·et·ry ['poʊɪtrɪ] poesía *f*

poign·ant ['pɔɪnjənt] *adj* conmovedor

point [pɔɪnt] **1** *n of pencil, knife* punta *f*; *in competition, argument* punto *m*; *(purpose)* objetivo *m*; *(moment)* momento *m*; *in decimals* coma *f*; **what's the ~ of telling him?** ¿qué se consigue diciéndoselo?; **the ~ I'm trying to make ...** lo que estoy intentando decir ...; **at one ~** en un momento dado; **that's beside the ~** eso no viene a cuento; **be on the ~ of** estar a punto de; **get to the ~** ir al grano; **the ~ is ...** la cuestión es que ...; **there's no ~ in waiting / trying** no vale la pena esperar / intentarlo **2** *v/i* señalar con el dedo **3** *v/t*: **he ~ed the gun at me** me apuntó con la pistola

◆ **point out** *v/t sights* indicar; *advantages etc* destacar

◆ **point to** *v/t with finger* señalar con el dedo; *fig (indicate)* indicar

'point-blank 1 *adj refusal, denial* categórico; **at ~ range** a quemarropa **2** *adv refuse, deny* categóricamente

point·ed ['pɔɪntɪd] *adj remark* mordaz

point·er ['pɔɪntər] *for teacher* puntero *m*; *(hint)* consejo *m*; *(sign, indication)* indicador *m*

point·less ['pɔɪntləs] *adj* inútil; **it's ~ trying** no sirve de nada intentarlo '**point of sale** *place* punto *m* de venta; *promotional material* material *m* promocional

'**point of view** punto *m* de vista

poise [pɔɪz] confianza *f*

poised [pɔɪzd] *adj person* con aplomo

poi·son ['pɔɪzn] **1** *n* veneno *m* **2** *v/t* envenenar

poi·son·ous ['pɔɪznəs] *adj* venenoso

poke [pouk] **1** *n* empujón *m* **2** *v/t* (*prod*) empujar; (*stick*) clavar; **he ~d his head out of the window** asomó la cabeza por la ventana; **~ fun at** reírse de; **~ one's nose into** F meter las narices en F

♦ **poke around** *v/i* F husmear

pok·er ['poukər] *card game* póquer *m*

pok·y ['poukɪ] *adj* F (*cramped*) enano, minúsculo

Po·land ['pouland] Polonia

po·lar ['poulər] *adj* polar

po·lar '**bear** oso *m* polar *or* blanco

po·lar·ize ['poulraɪz] *v/t* polarizar

Pole [poul] polaco(-a) *m*(*f*)

pole[1] [poul] *for support* poste *m*; *for tent, pushing things* palo *m*

pole[2] [poul] *of earth* polo *m*

'**pole star** estrella *f* polar; '**pole-vault** salto *m* con pértiga; '**pole-vault·er** saltador(a) *m*(*f*) de pértiga

po·lice [pə'liːs] *n* policía *f*

po·lice car coche *m* de policía; **po'lice·man** policía *m*; **po'lice state** estado *m* policial; **po'lice sta·tion** comisaría *f* (de policía); **po'lice·wo·man** (mujer *f*) policía *f*

pol·i·cy[1] ['paːlɪsɪ] política *f*

pol·i·cy[2] ['paːlɪsɪ] (*insurance ~*) póliza *f*

po·li·o ['pouliou] polio *f*

Pol·ish ['poulɪʃ] **1** *adj* polaco **2** *n* polaco *m*

pol·ish ['paːlɪʃ] **1** *n* abrillantador *m*; (*nail ~*) esmalte *m* de uñas **2** *v/t* dar brillo a; *speech* pulir

♦ **polish off** *v/t food* acabar, comerse

♦ **polish up** *v/t skill* perfeccionar

pol·ished ['paːlɪʃt] *adj performance* brillante

po·lite [pə'laɪt] *adj* educado

po·lite·ly [pə'laɪtlɪ] *adv* educadamente

po·lite·ness [pə'laɪtnɪs] educación *f*

po·lit·i·cal [pə'lɪtɪkl] *adj* político

po·lit·i·cal·ly cor·rect [pə'lɪtɪklɪ kə'rekt] políticamente correcto

pol·i·ti·cian [paːlɪ'tɪʃn] político(-a) *m*(*f*)

pol·i·tics ['paːlətɪks] política *f*; **I'm not interested in ~** no me interesa la política; **what are his ~?** ¿cuáles son sus ideas políticas?

poll [poul] **1** *n* (*survey*) encuesta *f*, sondeo *m*; **the ~s** (*election*) las elecciones; **go to the ~s** (*vote*) acudir a las urnas **2** *v/t people* sondear; *votes* obtener

pol·len ['paːlən] polen *m*

'**pol·len count** concentración *f* de polen en el aire

poll·ing booth ['poulɪŋ] cabina *f* electoral

'**poll·ing day** día *m* de las elecciones

poll·ster ['poulstər] encuestador(a) *m*(*f*)

pol·lu·tant [pə'luːtənt] contaminante *m*

pol·lute [pə'luːt] *v/t* contaminar

pol·lu·tion [pə'luːʃn] contaminación *f*

po·lo ['poulou] SP polo *m*

'**po·lo neck** *sweater* suéter *m* de cuello alto

'**po·lo shirt** polo *m*

pol·y·es·ter [paːlɪ'estər] poliéster *m*

pol·y·eth·yl·ene [paːlɪ'eθiliːn] polietileno *m*

pol·y·sty·rene [paːlɪ'staɪriːn] poliestireno *m*

pol·y·un·sat·u·rat·ed [paːlɪʌn'sæt-jəreɪtɪd] *adj* poliinsaturado

pom·pous ['paːmpəs] *adj* pomposo

pond [paːnd] estanque *m*

pon·der ['paːndər] *v/i* reflexionar

pon·tiff ['paːntɪf] pontífice *m*

po·ny ['pounɪ] poni *m*

'**po·ny·tail** coleta *f*

poo·dle ['puːdl] caniche *m*

pool[1] [puːl] (*swimming ~*) piscina *f*, *L.Am.* pileta *f*, *Mex* alberca *f*; *of*

P

water, blood charco *m*

pool² [puːl] *game* billar *m* americano

pool³ [puːl] **1** *n (common fund)* bote *m*, fondo *m* común **2** *v/t resources* juntar

'**pool hall** sala *f* de billares

'**pool table** mesa *f* de billar americano

poop [puːp] *n* F caca *f* F

pooped [puːpt] *adj* F hecho polvo F

poor [pur] **1** *adj* pobre; *(not good)* mediocre, malo; *be in ~ health* estar enfermo; **~ old Tony!** ¡pobre(cito) Tony! **2** *npl: the ~* los pobres

poor·ly ['pulɪ] **1** *adv* mal **2** *adj (unwell): feel ~* encontrarse mal

pop¹ [paːp] **1** *n noise* pequeño ruido *m* **2** *v/i (pret & pp -ped) of balloon etc* estallar **3** *v/t (pret & pp -ped) cork* hacer saltar; *balloon* pinchar

pop² [paːp] **1** *n* MUS pop *m* **2** *adj* pop

pop³ [paːp] F *(father)* papá *m* F

pop⁴ [paːp] *v/t (pret & pp -ped)* F *(put)* meter

♦ **pop up** *v/i* F *(appear)* aparecer

'**pop con·cert** concierto *m* (de música) pop

pop·corn ['paːpkɔːrn] palomitas *fpl* de maíz

pope [poup] papa *m*

'**pop group** grupo *m* (de música) pop

pop·py ['paːpɪ] amapola *f*

Pop·sicle® ['paːpsɪkl] polo *m (helado)*

'**pop song** canción *f* pop

pop·u·lar ['paːpjʊlər] *adj* popular; *contrary to ~ belief* contrariamente a lo que se piensa

pop·u·lar·i·ty [paːpjuˈlærətɪ] popularidad *f*

pop·u·late ['paːpjʊleɪt] *v/t* poblar

pop·u·la·tion [paːpjuˈleɪʃn] población *f*

porce·lain ['pɔːrsəlɪn] **1** *n* porcelana *f* **2** *adj* de porcelana

porch [pɔːrtʃ] porche *m*

por·cu·pine ['pɔːrkjʊpaɪn] puercoespín *m*

pore [pɔːr] *of skin* poro *m*

♦ **pore over** *v/t* estudiar detenidamente

pork [pɔːrk] cerdo *m*

porn [pɔːrn] *n* F porno *m* F

porn(o) [pɔːrn, 'pɔːrnou] *adj* F porno F

por·no·graph·ic [pɔːrnəˈgræfɪk] *adj* pornográfico

porn·og·ra·phy [pɔːrˈnɑːgrəfɪ] pornografía *f*

po·rous ['pɔːrəs] *adj* poroso

port¹ [pɔːrt] *n town, area* puerto *m*

port² [pɔːrt] *adj (left-hand)* a babor

por·ta·ble ['pɔːrtəbl] **1** *adj* portátil **2** *n* COMPUT portátil *m*; *TV* televisión *f* portátil

por·ter ['pɔːrtər] *for luggage* mozo(-a) *m(f)*

port·hole ['pɔːrthoul] NAUT portilla *f*

por·tion ['pɔːrʃn] parte *f*; *of food* ración *f*

por·trait ['pɔːrtreɪt] **1** *n* retrato *m* **2** *adv print* en formato vertical

por·tray [pɔːrˈtreɪ] *of artist, photographer* retratar; *of actor* interpretar; *of author* describir

por·tray·al [pɔːrˈtreɪəl] *by actor* interpretación *f*, representación *f*; *by author* descripción *f*

Por·tu·gal ['pɔːrtʃʊgl] Portugal

Por·tu·guese [pɔːrtʃʊˈgiːz] **1** *adj* portugués **2** *n person* portugués(-esa) *m(f)*; *language* portugués *m*

pose [pouz] **1** *n (pretense)* pose *f*; *it's all a ~* no es más que una pose **2** *v/i for artist, photographer* posar; **~ as** hacerse pasar por **3** *v/t:* **~ a problem / a threat** representar un problema / una amenaza

posh [paːʃ] *adj Br* F elegante, *pej* pijo

po·si·tion [pəˈzɪʃn] **1** *n* posición *f*; *(stance, point of view)* postura *f*; *(job)* puesto *m*, empleo *m*; *(status)* posición *f (social)* **2** *v/t* situar, colocar

pos·i·tive ['paːzətɪv] *adj* positivo; *be ~ (sure)* estar seguro

pos·i·tive·ly ['paːzətɪvlɪ] *adv (decidedly)* verdaderamente, sin lugar a dudas; *(definitely)* claramente

pos·sess [pəˈzes] *v/t* poseer

pos·ses·sion [pəˈzeʃn] posesión *f*; **~s** posesiones *fpl*

pos·ses·sive [pəˈzesɪv] *adj person,* GRAM posesivo

pos·si·bil·i·ty [pɑːsəˈbɪlətɪ] posibilidad *f*; **there is a ~ that ...** cabe la posibilidad de que ...

pos·si·ble [ˈpɑːsəbl] *adj* posible; **the shortest/ quickest route ~** la ruta más corto/ rápido posible; **the best ~ ...** el mejor ...

possibly [ˈpɑːsəblɪ] *adv* (*perhaps*) puede ser, quizás; **that can't ~ be right** no puede ser; **they're doing everything they ~ can** están haciendo todo lo que pueden; **could you ~ tell me ...?** ¿tendría la amabilidad de decirme ...?

post[1] [poust] **1** *n of wood, metal* poste *m* **2** *v/t* pegar; *on notice board* poner; *profits* presentar; **keep s.o. ~ed** mantener a alguien al corriente

post[2] [poust] **1** *n* (*place of duty*) puesto *m* **2** *v/t soldier, employee* destinar; *guards* apostar

post[3] [poust] *Br* **1** *n* (*mail*) correo *m* **2** *v/t letter* echar al correo

post·age [ˈpoustɪdʒ] franqueo *m*

post·age stamp *fml* sello *m*, *L.Am.* estampilla *f*, *Mex* timbre *m*

post·al [ˈpoustl] *adj* postal

post·card (tarjeta *f*) postal *f*;

post·code *Br* código *m* postal;

post·date *v/t* posfechar

post·er [ˈpoustər] póster *m*, *L.Am.* afiche *m*

pos·te·ri·or [pɑːˈstɪrɪər] *n* (*hum: buttocks*) trasero *m*

pos·ter·i·ty [pɑːˈsterətɪ] posteridad *f*; **for ~** para la posteridad

post·grad·u·ate [ˈpoustgrædʒuət] **1** *n* posgraduado(-a) *m(f)* **2** *adj* de posgrado

post·hu·mous [ˈpɑːstuməs] *adj* póstumo

post·hu·mous·ly [ˈpɑːstuməslɪ] *adv* póstumamente

post·ing [ˈpoustɪŋ] (*assignment*) destino *m*

post·mark [ˈpoustmɑːrk] *n* matasellos *m inv*

post·mor·tem [poust'mɔːrtəm] *n* autopsia *f*

post of·fice oficina *f* de correos

post·pone [poust'poun] *v/t* posponer, aplazar

post·pone·ment [poust'pounmənt] aplazamiento *m*

pos·ture [ˈpɑːstʃər] postura *f*

post-war *adj* de posguerra

pot[1] [pɑːt] *for cooking* olla *f*, *for coffee* cafetera *f*, *for tea* tetera *f*, *for plant* maceta *f*

pot[2] [pɑːt] F (*marijuana*) maría *f* F

po·ta·to [pəˈteɪtou] *Span* patata *f*, *L.Am.* papa *f*

po·ta·to chips, *Br* **po·ta·to crisps** *npl Span* patatas *fpl* fritas, *L.Am.* papas *fpl* fritas

pot·bel·ly [ˈpɑːtbelɪ] barriga *f*

po·tent [ˈpoutənt] *adj* potente

po·ten·tial [pəˈtenʃl] **1** *adj* potencial **2** *n* potencial *m*

po·ten·tial·ly [pəˈtenʃəlɪ] *adv* potencialmente

pot·hole [ˈpɑːthoul] *in road* bache *m*

pot·ter [ˈpɑːtər] *n* alfarero(-a) *m(f)*

pot·ter·y [ˈpɑːtərɪ] *n* alfarería *f*

pot·ty [ˈpɑːtɪ] *n for baby* orinal *m*

pouch [pautʃ] *bag* bolsa *f*; *for tobacco* petaca *f*; *for amunition* cartuchera *f*; *for mail* saca *f*

poul·try [ˈpoultrɪ] *birds* aves *fpl* de corral; *meat* carne *f* de ave

pounce [pauns] *v/i of animal* saltar; *fig* echarse encima

pound[1] [paund] *n weight* libra *f* (*453,6 gr*)

pound[2] [paund] *n for strays* perrera *f*; *for cars* depósito *m*

pound[3] [paund] *v/i of heart* palpitar con fuerza; **~ on** (*hammer on*) golpear en

pound 'ster·ling libra *f* esterlina

pour [pɔːr] **1** *v/t into a container* verter; (*spill*) derramar; **~ s.o. some coffee** servir café a alguien **2** *v/i: it's ~ing* (*with rain*) está lloviendo a cántaros

♦ **pour out** *v/t liquid* servir; *troubles* contar

pout [paut] *v/i* hacer un mohín

pov·er·ty [ˈpɑːvərtɪ] pobreza *f*

pov·er·ty-strick·en [ˈpɑːvərtɪstrɪkn] depauperado

pow·der [ˈpaudər] **1** *n* polvo *m*; *for*

P

face polvos *mpl*, colorete *m* **2** *v/t face* empolvarse

pow·er ['pauər] **1** *n* (*strength*) fuerza *f*; *of engine* potencia; (*authority*) poder *m*; (*energy*) energía *f*; (*electricity*) electricidad *f*; **in ~** POL en el poder; **fall from ~** POL perder el poder **2** *v/t*: **be ~ed by** estar impulsado por

'**pow·er-as·sist·ed steering** dirección *f* asistida; '**pow·er cut** apagón *m*; '**pow·er fail·ure** apagón *m*

pow·er·ful ['pauərfəl] *adj* poderoso; *car* potente; *drug* fuerte

pow·er·less ['pauərlıs] *adj* impotente; **be ~ to …** ser incapaz de …

'**pow·er line** línea *f* de conducción eléctrica; '**pow·er out·age** apagón *m*; '**pow·er sta·tion** central *f* eléctrica; '**pow·er steer·ing** dirección *f* asistida; '**pow·er u·nit** fuente *f* de alimentación

PR [piː'ɑːr] *abbr* (= **public relations**) relaciones *fpl* públicas

prac·ti·cal ['præktıkl] *adj* práctico; *layout* funcional

prac·ti·cal 'joke broma *f* (*que se gasta*)

prac·tic·al·ly ['præktıklı] *adv behave, think* de manera práctica; (*almost*) prácticamente, casi

prac·tice ['præktıs] **1** *n* práctica *f*; (*rehearsal*) ensayo *m*; (*custom*) costumbre *f*; **in ~** (*in reality*) en la práctica; **be out of ~** estar desentrenado; **~ makes perfect** a base de práctica se aprende **2** *v/i* practicar; *of musician* ensayar; *of footballer* entrenarse **3** *v/t* practicar; *law, medicine* ejercer

prac·tise *Br* → **practice** *v/i* & *v/t*

prag·mat·ic [præg'mætık] *adj* pragmático

prag·ma·tism ['prægmətızm] pragmatismo *m*

prai·rie ['prerı] pradera *f*

praise [preız] **1** *n* elogio *m*, alabanza *f* **2** *v/t* elogiar

'**praise·wor·thy** *adj* elogiable

prank [præŋk] travesura *f*

prat·tle ['prætl] *v/i* F parlotear F

pray [preı] *v/i* rezar

prayer [prer] oración *f*

preach [priːtʃ] **1** *v/i in church* predicar; (*moralize*) sermonear **2** *v/t sermon* predicar

preach·er ['priːtʃər] predicador(a) *m(f)*

pre·am·ble [priː'æmbl] preámbulo *m*

pre·car·i·ous [prı'kerıəs] *adj* precario

pre·car·i·ous·ly [prı'kerıəslı] *adv* precariamente

pre·cau·tion [prı'kɒːʃn] precaución *f*; **as a ~** como precaución

pre·cau·tion·a·ry [prı'kɒːʃnrı] *adj measure* preventivo

pre·cede [prı'siːd] *v/t in time* preceder; (*walk in front of*) ir delante de

pre·ce·dent ['presıdənt] precedente *m*

pre·ce·ding [prı'siːdıŋ] *adj week, chapter* anterior

pre·cinct ['priːsıŋkt] (*district*) distrito *m*

pre·cious ['preʃəs] *adj* preciado; *gem* precioso

pre·cip·i·tate [prı'sıpıteıt] *v/t crisis* precipitar

pré·cis ['preısiː] *n* resumen *m*

pre·cise [prı'saıs] *adj* preciso

pre·cise·ly [prı'saıslı] *adv* exactamente

pre·ci·sion [prı'sıʒn] precisión *f*

pre·co·cious [prı'kouʃəs] *adj child* precoz

pre·con·ceived ['priːkənsiːvd] *adj idea* preconcebido

pre·con·di·tion [priːkən'dıʃn] condición *f* previa

pred·a·tor ['predətər] *animal* depredador(a) *m(f)*

pred·a·to·ry ['predətɔːrı] *adj* depredador

pre·de·ces·sor ['priːdısesər] *in job* predecesor(a) *m(f)*; *machine* modelo *m* anterior

pre·des·ti·na·tion [priːdestı'neıʃn] predestinación *f*

pre·des·tined ['priːdestınd] *adj*: **be ~ to** estar predestinado a

pre·dic·a·ment [prı'dıkəmənt] apuro *m*

pre·dict [prɪ'dɪkt] *v/t* predecir, pronosticar

pre·dict·a·ble [prɪ'dɪktəbl] *adj* predecible

pre·dic·tion [prɪ'dɪkʃn] predicción *f*, pronóstico *m*

pre·dom·i·nant [prɪ'dɑːmɪnənt] *adj* predominante

pre·dom·i·nant·ly [prɪ'dɑːmɪnəntlɪ] *adv* predominantemente

pre·dom·i·nate [prɪ'dɑːmɪneɪt] *v/i* predominar

pre·fab·ri·cat·ed [priː'fæbrɪkeɪtɪd] *adj* prefabricado

pref·ace ['prefɪs] *n* prólogo *m*, prefacio *m*

pre·fer [prɪ'fɜːr] *v/t* (*pret & pp -red*) preferir; *~ X to Y* preferir X a Y; *~ to do* preferir hacer

pref·e·ra·ble ['prefərəbl] *adj* preferible; *anywhere is ~ to this* cualquier sitio es mejor que éste

pref·e·ra·bly ['prefərəblɪ] *adv* preferentemente

pref·e·rence ['prefərəns] preferencia *f*

pref·er·en·tial [prefə'renʃl] *adj* preferente

pre·fix ['priːfɪks] prefijo *m*

preg·nan·cy ['pregnənsɪ] embarazo *m*

preg·nant ['pregnənt] *adj woman* embarazada; *animal* preñada

pre·heat ['priːhiːt] *v/t oven* precalentar

pre·his·tor·ic [priːhɪs'tɑːrɪk] *adj* prehistórico

pre·judge [priː'dʒʌdʒ] *v/t* prejuzgar, juzgar de antemano

prej·u·dice ['predʒʊdɪs] **1** *n* prejuicio *m* **2** *v/t person* predisponer, influir; *chances* perjudicar

prej·u·diced ['predʒʊdɪst] *adj* parcial, predispuesto

pre·lim·i·na·ry [prɪ'lɪmɪnerɪ] *adj* preliminar

pre·mar·i·tal [priː'mærɪtl] *adj* prematrimonial

pre·ma·ture ['priːmətʊr] *adj* prematuro

pre·med·i·tat·ed [priː'medɪteɪtɪd] *adj* premeditado

prem·i·er ['premɪr] *n* (*Prime Minister*) primer(a) ministro(-a) *m(f)*

prem·i·ère ['premɪer] *n* estreno *m*

prem·is·es ['premɪsɪz] *npl* local *m*

pre·mi·um ['priːmɪəm] *n in insurance* prima *f*

pre·mo·ni·tion [premə'nɪʃn] premonición *f*, presentimiento *m*

pre·na·tal [priː'neɪtl] *adj* prenatal

pre·oc·cu·pied [prɪ'ɑːkjʊpaɪd] *adj* preocupado

prep·a·ra·tion [prepə'reɪʃn] preparación *f*; *in ~ for* como preparación a; *~s* preparativos *mpl*

pre·pare [prɪ'per] **1** *v/t* preparar; *be ~d to do sth* be willing estar dispuesto a hacer algo; *be ~d for sth* be expecting, ready estar preparado para algo **2** *v/i* prepararse

prep·o·si·tion [prepə'zɪʃn] preposición *f*

pre·pos·ter·ous [prɪ'pɑːstərəs] *adj* ridículo, absurdo

pre·req·ui·site [priː'rekwɪzɪt] requisito *m* previo

pre·scribe [prɪ'skraɪb] *v/t of doctor* recetar

pre·scrip·tion [prɪ'skrɪpʃn] MED receta *f*

pres·ence ['prezns] presencia *f*; *in the ~ of* en presencia de, delante de

pres·ence of 'mind presencia *f* de ánimo

pres·ent¹ ['preznt] **1** *adj* (*current*) actual; *be ~* estar presente **2** *n: the ~ also* GRAM el presente; *at ~* en este momento

pres·ent² ['preznt] *n* (*gift*) regalo *m*

pres·ent³ [prɪ'zent] *v/t* presentar; *award* entregar; *~ s.o. with sth*, *~ sth to s.o.* entregar algo a alguien

pre·sen·ta·tion [prezn'teɪʃn] *to audience* presentación *f*

pres·ent-day [preznt'deɪ] *adj* actual

pre·sent·er [prɪ'zentər] presentador(a) *m(f)*

pres·ent·ly ['prezntlɪ] *adv* (*at the moment*) actualmente; (*soon*) pronto

'pres·ent tense tiempo *m* presente

pres·er·va·tion [prezər'veɪʃn] conservación f; *of standards, peace* mantenimiento *m*

pre·ser·va·tive [prɪˈzɜːrvətɪv] *n* conservante *m*

pre·serve [prɪˈzɜːrv] **1** *n* (*domain*) dominio *m* **2** *v/t standards, peace etc* mantener; *food, wood* conservar

pre·side [prɪˈzaɪd] *v/i at meeting* presidir; **~ over** *meeting* presidir

pres·i·den·cy [ˈprezɪdənsɪ] presidencia *f*

pres·i·dent [ˈprezɪdnt] POL, *of company* presidente(-a) *m(f)*

pres·i·den·tial [prezɪˈdenʃl] *adj* presidencial

press [pres] **1** *n*: *the* **~** la prensa **2** *v/t button* pulsar, presionar; (*urge*) presionar; (*squeeze*) apretar; *clothes* planchar **3** *v/i*: **~ for** presionar para obtener

'**press a·gen·cy** agencia *f* de prensa

'**press con·fer·ence** rueda *f* or conferencia *f* de prensa

press·ing [ˈpresɪŋ] *adj* urgente

pres·sure [ˈpreʃər] **1** *n* presión *f*; *be* **under ~** estar sometido a presión; *he is under* **~ to resign** lo están presionando para que dimita **2** *v/t* presionar

pres·tige [preˈstiːʒ] prestigio *m*

pres·ti·gious [preˈstɪdʒəs] *adj* prestigioso

pre·su·ma·bly [prɪˈzuːməblɪ] *adv* presumiblemente, probablemente

pre·sume [prɪˈzuːm] *v/t* suponer; *they were ~d dead* los dieron por muertos; **~ to do sth** *fml* tomarse la libertad de hacer algo

pre·sump·tion [prɪˈzʌmpʃn] *of innocence, guilt* presunción *f*

pre·sump·tu·ous [prɪˈzʌmptʊəs] *adj* presuntuoso

pre·sup·pose [priːsəˈpoʊz] *v/t* presuponer

pre·tax [ˈpriːtæks] *adj* antes de impuestos

pre·tence *Br* → **pretense**

pre·tend [prɪˈtend] **1** *v/t* fingir, hacer como si; *claim* pretender; **~ to be s.o.** hacerse pasar por alguien; *the children are ~ing to be spacemen*

los niños están jugando a que son astronautas **2** *v/i* fingir

pre·tense [prɪˈtens] farsa *f*

pre·ten·tious [prɪˈtenʃəs] *adj* pretencioso

pre·text [ˈpriːtekst] pretexto *m*

pret·ty [ˈprɪtɪ] **1** *adj village, house, fabric etc* bonito, lindo; *child, woman* guapo, lindo **2** *adv* (*quite*) bastante

pre·vail [prɪˈveɪl] *v/i* (*triumph*) prevalecer

pre·vail·ing [prɪˈveɪlɪŋ] *adj* predominante

pre·vent [prɪˈvent] *v/t* impedir, evitar; **~ s.o. (from) doing sth** impedir que alguien haga algo

pre·ven·tion [prɪˈvenʃn] prevención *f*

pre·ven·tive [prɪˈventɪv] *adj* preventivo

pre·view [ˈpriːvjuː] **1** *n of movie, exhibition* preestreno *m* **2** *v/t* hacer la presentación previa de

pre·vi·ous [ˈpriːvɪəs] *adj* anterior, previo

pre·vi·ous·ly [ˈpriːvɪəslɪ] *adv* anteriormente, antes

pre·war [ˈpriːwɔːr] *adj* de preguerra, de antes de la guerra

prey [preɪ] *n* presa *f*; **~ to** presa de

◆ **prey on** *v/t* atacar; *fig: of con man etc* aprovecharse de

price [praɪs] **1** *n* precio *m* **2** *v/t* COM poner precio a

price·less [ˈpraɪslɪs] *adj* que no tiene precio

'**price tag** etiqueta *f* del precio

'**price war** guerra *f* de precios

pric·ey [ˈpraɪsɪ] *adj* F carillo F

prick[1] [prɪk] **1** *n in pain* punzada *f* **2** *v/t* (*jab*) pinchar

prick[2] [prɪk] *n* ∨ (*penis*) polla *f* ∨, carajo *m* ∨; ∨ *person Span* gilipollas *m inv* ∨, *L.Am.* pendejo *m* ∨

◆ **prick up** *v/t*: *prick up one's ears of dog* aguzar las orejas; *of person* prestar atención

prick·le [ˈprɪkl] *on plant* espina *f*

prick·ly [ˈprɪklɪ] *adj beard, plant* que pincha; (*irritable*) irritable

pride [praɪd] **1** *n in person, achieve-*

ment orgullo *m*; (*self-respect*) amor *m* propio **2** *v/t*: **~ o.s. on** enorgullecerse de

priest [pri:st] sacerdote *m*; (*parish ~*) cura *m*

pri·ma·ri·ly [praɪˈmerɪlɪ] *adv* principalmente

pri·ma·ry [ˈpraɪmərɪ] **1** *adj* principal **2** *n* POL elecciones *fpl* primarias

prime [praɪm] **1** *n*: **be in one's ~** estar en la flor de la vida **2** *adj example, reason* primordial; **of ~ importance** de suprema importancia

prime 'min·is·ter primer(a) ministro *m(f)*

'prime time *n* TV horario *m* de mayor audiencia

prim·i·tive [ˈprɪmɪtɪv] *adj* primitivo

prince [prɪns] príncipe *m*

prin·cess [prɪnˈses] princesa *f*

prin·ci·pal [ˈprɪnsəpl] **1** *adj* principal **2** *n of school* director(a) *m(f)*; *of university* rector(a) *m(f)*

prin·ci·pal·ly [ˈprɪnsəplɪ] *adv* principalmente

prin·ci·ple [ˈprɪnsəpl] principio *m*; **on ~** por principios; **in ~** en principio

print [prɪnt] **1** *n in book, newspaper etc* letra *f*; (*photograph*) grabado *m*; **out of ~** agotado **2** *v/t* imprimir; (*use block capitals*) escribir en mayúsculas

◆ **print out** *v/t* imprimir

print·ed mat·ter [ˈprɪntɪd] impresos *mpl*

print·er [ˈprɪntər] *person* impresor(a) *m(f)*; *machine* impresora *f*; *company* imprenta *f*

print·ing press [ˈprɪntɪŋpres] imprenta *f*

'print·out copia *f* impresa

pri·or [praɪr] **1** *adj* previo **2** *prep*: **~ to** antes de

pri·or·i·tize [praɪˈɔːrətaɪz] *v/t* (*put in order of priority*) ordenar atendiendo a las prioridades; (*give priority to*) dar prioridad a

pri·or·i·ty [praɪˈɑːrətɪ] prioridad *f*; **have ~** tener prioridad

pris·on [ˈprɪzn] prisión *f*, cárcel *f*

pris·on·er [ˈprɪznər] prisionero(-a)

m(f); **take s.o. ~** hacer prisionero a alguien

pris·on·er of 'war prisionero(-a) *m(f)* de guerra

priv·a·cy [ˈprɪvəsɪ] intimidad *f*

pri·vate [ˈpraɪvət] **1** *adj* privado **2** *n* MIL soldado *m/f* raso; **in ~** en privado

pri·vate·ly [ˈpraɪvətlɪ] *adv* (*in private*) en privado; *with one other* a solas; (*inwardly*) para sí; **~ owned** en manos privadas

'pri·vate sec·tor sector *m* privado

pri·va·tize [ˈpraɪvətaɪz] *v/t Br* privatizar

priv·i·lege [ˈprɪvəlɪdʒ] (*special treatment*) privilegio *m*; (*honor*) honor *m*

priv·i·leged [ˈprɪvəlɪdʒd] *adj* privilegiado

prize [praɪz] **1** *n* premio *m* **2** *v/t* apreciar, valorar

prize·win·ner [ˈpraɪzwɪnər] premiado(-a) *m(f)*

prize·win·ning [ˈpraɪzwɪnɪŋ] *adj* premiado

pro[1] [prou] *n*: **the ~s and cons** los pros y los contras

pro[2] [prou] → **professional**

pro[3] [prou]: **be ~ ...** (*in favor of*) estar a favor de; **the ~ Clinton Democrats** los demócratas partidarios de Clinton

prob·a·bil·i·ty [prɑːbəˈbɪlətɪ] probabilidad *f*

prob·a·ble [ˈprɑːbəbl] *adj* probable

prob·a·bly [ˈprɑːbəblɪ] *adv* probablemente

pro·ba·tion [prəˈbeɪʃn] *in job* período *m* de prueba; LAW libertad *f* condicional; **be given ~** ser puesto en libertad condicional

pro·ba·tion of·fi·cer *oficial encargado de la vigilancia de los que están en libertad condicional*

pro·ba·tion pe·ri·od *in job* período *m* de prueba

probe [proub] **1** *n* (*investigation*) investigación *f*; *scientific* sonda *f* **2** *v/t* examinar; (*investigate*) investigar

prob·lem [ˈprɑːbləm] problema *m*; **no ~!** ¡claro!

P

pro·ce·dure [prəˈsiːdʒər] procedimiento *m*

pro·ceed [prəˈsiːd] *v/i* (*go: of people*) dirigirse; *of work etc* proseguir, avanzar; **~ to do sth** pasar a hacer algo

pro·ceed·ings [prəˈsiːdɪŋz] *npl* (*events*) actos *mpl*

pro·ceeds [ˈproʊsiːdz] *npl* recaudación *f*

pro·cess [ˈprɑːses] **1** *n* proceso *m*; **in the ~** (*while doing it*) al hacerlo **2** *v/t food* tratar; *raw materials, data* procesar; *application* tramitar

pro·ces·sion [prəˈseʃn] *n* desfile *m*; *religious* procesión *f*

pro·ces·sor [ˈprɑːsesər] procesador *m*

pro·claim [prəˈkleɪm] *v/t* declarar, proclamar

prod [prɑːd] **1** *n* empujoncito *m* **2** *v/t* (*pret & pp -ded*) dar un empujoncito a; *with elbow* dar un codazo a

prod·i·gy [ˈprɑːdɪdʒɪ]: (*child*) ~ niño(-a) *m(f)* prodigio

prod·uce[1] [ˈprɑːduːs] *n* productos *mpl* del campo

pro·duce[2] [prəˈduːs] *v/t* producir; (*manufacture*) fabricar; (*bring out*) sacar

pro·duc·er [prəˈduːsər] productor(a) *m(f)*; (*manufacturer*) fabricante *m/f*

prod·uct [ˈprɑːdʌkt] producto *m*

pro·duc·tion [prəˈdʌkʃn] producción *f*

pro'duc·tion ca·pac·i·ty capacidad *f* de producción

pro'duc·tion costs *npl* costos *mpl* de producción

pro·duc·tive [prəˈdʌktɪv] *adj* productivo

pro·duc·tiv·i·ty [prɑːdʌkˈtɪvətɪ] productividad *f*

pro·fane [prəˈfeɪn] *adj language* profano

pro·fess [prəˈfes] *v/t* manifestar

pro·fes·sion [prəˈfeʃn] profesión *f*; **what's your ~?** ¿a qué se dedica?

pro·fes·sion·al [prəˈfeʃnl] **1** *adj* profesional; **turn ~** hacerse profesional

2 *n* profesional *m/f*

pro·fes·sion·al·ly [prəˈfeʃnlɪ] *adv play sport* profesionalmente; (*well, skillfully*) con profesionalidad

pro·fes·sor [prəˈfesər] catedrático(-a) *m(f)*

pro·fi·cien·cy [prəˈfɪʃnsɪ] competencia *f*

pro·fi·cient [prəˈfɪʃnt] competente; (*skillful*) hábil

pro·file [ˈproʊfaɪl] *of face* perfil *m*

prof·it [ˈprɑːfɪt] **1** *n* beneficio *m* **2** *v/i*: **~ by, ~ from** beneficiarse de

prof·it·a·bil·i·ty [prɑːfɪtəˈbɪlətɪ] rentabilidad *f*

prof·it·a·ble [ˈprɑːfɪtəbl] *adj* rentable

'prof·it mar·gin margen *m* de beneficios

pro·found [prəˈfaʊnd] *adj* profundo

pro·found·ly [prəˈfaʊndlɪ] *adv* profundamente, enormemente

prog·no·sis [prɑːgˈnoʊsɪs] pronóstico *m*

pro·gram [ˈproʊɡræm] **1** *n* programa *m* **2** *v/t* (*pret & pp -med*) COMPUT programar

pro·gramme *Br* → **program**

pro·gram·mer [ˈproʊɡræmər] programador(a) *m(f)*

pro·gress 1 *n* [ˈprɑːgres] progreso *m*; **make ~** hacer progresos; **in ~** en curso **2** *v/i* [prəˈgres] (*advance in time*) avanzar; (*move on*) pasar; (*make ~*) progresar; **how is the work ~ing?** ¿cómo avanza el trabajo?

pro·gres·sive [prəˈgresɪv] *adj* (*enlightened*) progresista; (*which progresses*) progresivo

pro·gres·sive·ly [prəˈgresɪvlɪ] *adv* progresivamente

pro·hib·it [prəˈhɪbɪt] *v/t* prohibir

pro·hi·bi·tion [proʊhɪˈbɪʃn] prohibición *f*; **during Prohibition** durante la ley seca

pro·hib·i·tive [prəˈhɪbɪtɪv] *adj prices* prohibitivo

proj·ect[1] [ˈprɑːdʒekt] *n* (*plan, undertaking*) proyecto *m*; EDU trabajo *m*; (*housing area*) barriada *f* de viviendas sociales

pro·ject² [prə'dʒekt] **1** v/t movie proyectar; figures, sales calcular **2** v/i (stick out) sobresalir

pro·jec·tion [prə'dʒekʃn] (forecast) previsión f

pro·jec·tor [prə'dʒektər] for slides proyector m

pro·lif·ic [prə'lɪfɪk] adj writer, artist prolífico

pro·log, Br **pro·logue** ['proʊlɑːg] prólogo m

pro·long [prə'lɒːŋ] v/t prolongar

prom [prɑːm] (school dance) baile de fin de curso

prom·i·nent ['prɑːmɪnənt] adj nose, chin prominente; (significant) destacado

prom·is·cu·i·ty [prɑːmɪ'skjuːətɪ] promiscuidad f

prom·is·cu·ous [prə'mɪskjʊəs] adj promiscuo

prom·ise ['prɑːmɪs] **1** n promesa f **2** v/t prometer; she ~d to help prometió ayudar; ~ sth to s.o. prometer algo a alguien **3** v/i: do you ~? ¿lo prometes?

prom·is·ing ['prɑːmɪsɪŋ] adj prometedor

pro·mote [prə'moʊt] v/t employee ascender; (encourage, foster) promover; COM promocionar

pro·mot·er [prə'moʊtər] of sports event promotor(a) m(f)

pro·mo·tion [prə'moʊʃn] of employee ascenso m; of scheme, idea, COM promoción f

prompt [prɑːmpt] **1** adj (on time) puntual; (speedy) rápido **2** adv: at two o'clock ~ a las dos en punto **3** v/t (cause) provocar; actor apuntar **4** n COMPUT mensaje m; go to the c ~ ir a c:\

prompt·ly ['prɑːmptlɪ] adv (on time) puntualmente; (immediately) inmediatamente

prone [proʊn] adj: be ~ to ser propenso a

pro·noun ['proʊnaʊn] pronombre m

pro·nounce [prə'naʊns] v/t word pronunciar; (declare) declarar

pro·nounced [prə'naʊnst] adj accent marcado; views fuerte

pron·to ['prɑːntoʊ] adv F ya, en seguida

pro·nun·ci·a·tion [prənʌnsɪ'eɪʃn] pronunciación f

proof [pruːf] n prueba(s) f(pl); of book prueba f

prop [prɑːp] **1** v/t (pret & pp **-ped**) apoyar **2** n THEA accesorio m

♦ **prop up** v/t apoyar

prop·a·gan·da [prɑːpə'gændə] propaganda f

pro·pel [prə'pel] v/t (pret & pp **-led**) propulsar

pro·pel·lant [prə'pelənt] in aerosol propelente m

pro·pel·ler [prə'pelər] of boat hélice f

prop·er ['prɑːpər] adj (real) de verdad; (fitting) adecuado; it's not ~ no está bien; put it back in its ~ place vuelve a ponerlo en su sitio

prop·er·ly ['prɑːpərlɪ] adv (correctly) bien; (fittingly) adecuadamente

prop·er·ty ['prɑːpərtɪ] propiedad f; (land) propiedad(es) f(pl)

'**prop·er·ty de·vel·op·er** promotor(-a) m(f) inmobiliario f

proph·e·cy ['prɑːfəsɪ] profecía f

proph·e·sy ['prɑːfəsaɪ] v/t (pret & pp **-ied**) profetizar

pro·por·tion [prə'pɔːrʃn] proporción f; a large ~ of North Americans gran parte de los norteamericanos; ~s (dimensions) proporciones fpl

pro·por·tion·al [prə'pɔːrʃnl] adj proporcional

pro·por·tion·al rep·re·sen·ta·tion POL representación f proporcional

pro·pos·al [prə'poʊzl] (suggestion) propuesta f; of marriage proposición f

pro·pose [prə'poʊz] **1** v/t (suggest) sugerir, proponer; (plan) proponerse **2** v/i (make offer of marriage) pedir la mano (to a)

prop·o·si·tion [prɑːpə'zɪʃn] **1** n propuesta f **2** v/t woman hacer proposiciones a

pro·pri·e·tor [prə'praɪətər] propietario(-a) m(f)

pro·pri·e·tress [prə'praɪətrɪs] pro-

P

pietaria *f*

prose [prouz] prosa *f*

pros·e·cute ['prɑːsɪkjuːt] *v/t* LAW procesar

pros·e·cu·tion [prɑːsɪ'kjuːʃn] LAW procesamiento *m*; *lawyers* acusación *f*; **he's facing ~** lo van a procesar

pros·e·cu·tor → **public prosecutor**

pros·pect ['prɑːspekt] **1** *n* (*chance, likelihood*) probabilidad *f*; (*thought of something in the future*) perspectiva *f*; **~s** perspectivas *fpl* (de futuro) **2** *v/i*: **~ for gold** buscar

pro·spec·tive [prə'spektɪv] *adj* potencial

pros·per ['prɑːspər] *v/i* prosperar

pros·per·i·ty [prɑː'sperətɪ] prosperidad *f*

pros·per·ous ['prɑːspərəs] *adj* próspero

pros·ti·tute ['prɑːstɪtuːt] *n* prostituta *f*; **male ~** prostituto *m*

pros·ti·tu·tion [prɑːstɪ'tuːʃn] prostitución *f*

pros·trate ['prɑːstreɪt] *adj* postrado; **be ~ with grief** estar postrado por el dolor

pro·tect [prə'tekt] *v/t* proteger

pro·tec·tion [prə'tekʃn] protección *f*

pro·tec·tion mon·ey *dinero pagado a delincuentes a cambio de obtener protección*; *paid to terrorists* impuesto *m* revolucionario

pro·tec·tive [prə'tektɪv] *adj* protector

pro·tec·tive 'cloth·ing ropa *f* protectora

pro·tec·tor [prə'tektər] protector(a) *m(f)*

pro·tein ['proutiːn] proteína *f*

pro·test 1 *n* ['proutest] protesta *f* **2** *v/t* [prə'test] protestar, quejarse de; (*object to*) protestar contra **3** *v/i* [prə'test] protestar

Prot·es·tant ['prɑːtɪstənt] **1** *n* protestante *m/f* **2** *adj* protestante

pro·test·er [prə'testər] manifestante *m/f*

pro·to·col ['proutəkɑːl] protocolo *m*

pro·to·type ['proutətaɪp] prototipo *m*

pro·tract·ed [prə'træktɪd] *adj* prolongado, largo

pro·trude [prə'truːd] *v/i* sobresalir

pro·trud·ing [prə'truːdɪŋ] *adj* saliente; *ears, teeth* prominente

proud [praud] *adj* orgulloso; **be ~ of** estar orgulloso de

proud·ly ['praudlɪ] *adv* con orgullo, orgullosamente

prove [pruːv] *v/t* demostrar, probar

prov·erb ['prɑːvɜːrb] proverbio *m*, refrán *m*

pro·vide [prə'vaɪd] *v/t* proporcionar; **~ sth to s.o., ~ s.o. with sth** proporcionar algo a alguien; **~d (that)** (*on condition that*) con la condición de que, siempre que

♦ **provide for** *v/t family* mantener; *of law etc* prever

prov·ince ['prɑːvɪns] provincia *f*

pro·vin·cial [prə'vɪnʃl] *adj city* provincial; *pej: attitude* de pueblo, provinciano

pro·vi·sion [prə'vɪʒn] (*supply*) suministro *m*; *of law, contract* disposición *f*

pro·vi·sion·al [prə'vɪʒnl] *adj* provisional

pro·vi·so [prə'vaɪzou] condición *f*

prov·o·ca·tion [prɑːvə'keɪʃn] provocación *f*

pro·voc·a·tive [prə'vɑːkətɪv] *adj* provocador; *sexually* provocativo

pro·voke [prə'vouk] *v/t* (*cause, annoy*) provocar

prow [prau] NAUT proa *f*

prow·ess ['prauɪs] proezas *fpl*

prowl [praul] *v/i of tiger, burglar* merodear

prowl·er ['praulər] merodeador(a) *m(f)*

prox·im·i·ty [prɑːk'sɪmətɪ] proximidad *f*

prox·y ['prɑːksɪ] (*authority*) poder *m*; *person* apoderado(-a) *m(f)*

prude [pruːd] mojigato(-a) *m(f)*

pru·dence ['pruːdns] prudencia *f*

pru·dent ['pruːdnt] *adj* prudente

prud·ish ['pruːdɪʃ] *adj* mojigato

prune¹ [pruːn] *n* ciruela *f* pasa

prune² [pruːn] *v/t plant* podar; *fig* reducir

pry [praɪ] v/i (pret & pp **-ied**) entrometerse

♦ **pry into** v/t entrometerse en

PS [ˈpiːes] abbr (= **postscript**) PD (= posdata f)

pseu·do·nym [ˈsuːdənɪm] pseudónimo m

psy·chi·at·ric [saɪkɪˈætrɪk] adj psiquiátrico

psy·chi·a·trist [saɪˈkaɪətrɪst] psiquiatra m/f

psy·chi·a·try [saɪˈkaɪətrɪ] psiquiatría f

psy·chic [ˈsaɪkɪk] adj research paranormal; **I'm not ~** no soy vidente

psy·cho·a·nal·y·sis [saɪkouənˈæləsɪs] psicoanálisis m

psy·cho·an·a·lyst [saɪkouˈænəlɪst] psicoanalista m/f

psy·cho·an·a·lyze [saɪkouˈænəlaɪz] v/t psicoanalizar

psy·cho·log·i·cal [saɪkəˈlɑːdʒɪkl] adj psicológico

psy·cho·log·i·cal·ly [saɪkəˈlɑːdʒɪklɪ] adv psicológicamente

psy·chol·o·gist [saɪˈkɑːlədʒɪst] psicólogo(-a) m(f)

psy·chol·o·gy [saɪˈkɑːlədʒɪ] psicología f

psy·cho·path [ˈsaɪkoupæθ] psicópata m/f

psy·cho·so·mat·ic [saɪkousəˈmætɪk] adj psicosomático

PTO [piːtiːˈou] abbr (= **please turn over**) véase al dorso

pub [pʌb] Br bar m

pu·ber·ty [ˈpjuːbərtɪ] pubertad f

pu·bic hair [ˈpjuːbɪk] vello m púbico

pub·lic [ˈpʌblɪk] **1** adj público **2** n: **the ~** el público; **in ~** en público

pub·li·ca·tion [pʌblɪˈkeɪʃn] publicación f

pub·lic 'hol·i·day día m festivo

pub·lic·i·ty [pʌbˈlɪsətɪ] publicidad f

pub·li·cize [ˈpʌblɪsaɪz] v/t (make known) publicar, hacer público; COM dar publicidad a

pub·lic 'li·bra·ry biblioteca f pública

pub·lic·ly [ˈpʌblɪklɪ] adv públicamente

pub·lic 'pros·e·cu·tor fiscal m/f; **pub·lic re'la·tions** npl relaciones públicas fpl; **'pub·lic school** colegio m público; Br colegio m privado; **'pub·lic sec·tor** sector m público

pub·lish [ˈpʌblɪʃ] v/t publicar

pub·lish·er [ˈpʌblɪʃər] person editor(a) m(f); company editorial f

pub·lish·ing [ˈpʌblɪʃɪŋ] industria f editorial

'pub·lish·ing com·pa·ny editorial f

pud·dle [ˈpʌdl] charco m

Puer·to Ri·can [pwertouˈriːkən] **1** adj portorriqueño, puertorriqueño **2** n portorriqueño(-a) m(f), puertorriqueño(-a) m(f)

Puer·to Ri·co [pwertouˈriːkou] Puerto Rico

puff [pʌf] **1** n of wind racha f; from cigarette calada f; of smoke bocanada f **2** v/i (pant) resoplar; **~ on a ciga·rette** dar una calada a un cigarrillo

puff·y [ˈpʌfɪ] adj eyes, face hinchado

puke [pjuːk] **1** n P substance vomitona f P **2** v/i P echar la pota P

pull [pul] **1** n on rope tirón m; F (appeal) gancho m F; F (influence) enchufe m F **2** v/t (drag) arrastrar; (tug) tirar de; tooth sacar; **~ a mus·cle** sufrir un tirón en un músculo **3** v/i tirar

♦ **pull ahead** v/i in race, competition adelantarse

♦ **pull apart** v/t (separate) separar

♦ **pull away** v/t apartar

♦ **pull down** v/t (lower) bajar; (demolish) derribar

♦ **pull in** v/i of bus, train llegar

♦ **pull off** v/t quitar; item of clothing quitarse; F conseguir

♦ **pull out 1** v/t sacar; troops retirar; **2** v/i retirarse; of ship salir

♦ **pull over** v/i parar en el arcén

♦ **pull through** v/i from an illness recuperarse

♦ **pull together 1** v/i (cooperate) cooperar **2** v/t: **pull o.s. together** tranquilizarse

♦ **pull up 1** v/t (raise) subir; item of clothing subirse; plant, weeds arrancar **2** v/i of car etc parar

pul·ley ['pʊlɪ] polea f
pull·o·ver ['pʊlouvər] suéter m, Span jersey m
pulp [pʌlp] of fruit pulpa f; for paper-making pasta f
pul·pit ['pʊlpɪt] púlpito m
pul·sate [pʌl'seɪt] v/i of heart, blood palpitar; of music vibrar
pulse [pʌls] pulso m
pul·ver·ize ['pʌlvəraɪz] v/t pulverizar
pump [pʌmp] **1** n bomba f; (gas ~) surtidor m **2** v/t bombear
♦ **pump up** v/t inflar
pump·kin ['pʌmpkɪn] calabaza f
pun [pʌn] juego m de palabras
punch [pʌntʃ] **1** n blow puñetazo m; implement perforadora f **2** v/t with fist dar un puñetazo a; hole, ticket agujerear
'**punch line** golpe m, punto m culminante
punc·tu·al ['pʌŋktʃʊəl] adj puntual
punc·tu·al·i·ty [pʌŋktʃʊ'ælətɪ] puntualidad f
punc·tu·al·ly ['pʌŋktʃʊəlɪ] adv puntualmente
punc·tu·ate ['pʌŋktʃʊeɪt] v/t puntuar
punc·tu·a·tion ['pʌŋktʃʊ'eɪʃn] puntuación f
punc·tu'a·tion mark signo m de puntuación
punc·ture ['pʌŋktʃər] **1** n perforación f **2** v/t perforar
pun·gent ['pʌndʒənt] adj fuerte
pun·ish ['pʌnɪʃ] v/t person castigar
pun·ish·ing ['pʌnɪʃɪŋ] adj schedule exigente; pace fuerte
pun·ish·ment ['pʌnɪʃmənt] castigo m
punk (**rock**) ['pʌŋk(rɑːk)] MUS (música f) punk m
pu·ny ['pjuːnɪ] adj person enclenque
pup [pʌp] cachorro m
pu·pil¹ ['pjuːpl] of eye pupila f
pu·pil² ['pjuːpl] (student) alumno(-a) m(f)
pup·pet ['pʌpɪt] also fig marioneta f
'**pup·pet gov·ern·ment** gobierno m títere
pup·py ['pʌpɪ] cachorro m
pur·chase¹ ['pɜːrtʃəs] **1** n adquisi-

ción f, compra f **2** v/t adquirir, comprar
pur·chase² ['pɜːrtʃəs] (grip) agarre m
pur·chas·er ['pɜːrtʃəsər] comprador(a) m(f)
pure [pjʊr] adj puro; ~ new wool pura lana f virgen
pure·ly ['pjʊrlɪ] adv puramente
pur·ga·to·ry ['pɜːrgətɔːrɪ] purgatorio m
purge [pɜːrdʒ] **1** n of political party purga f **2** v/t purgar f
pu·ri·fy ['pjʊrɪfaɪ] v/t (pret & pp -ied) water depurar
pu·ri·tan ['pjʊrɪtən] puritano(-a) m(f)
pu·ri·tan·i·cal [pjʊrɪ'tænɪkl] adj puritano
pu·ri·ty ['pjʊrɪtɪ] pureza f
pur·ple ['pɜːrpl] adj morado
Pur·ple 'Heart MIL medalla concedida a los soldados heridos en combate
pur·pose ['pɜːrpəs] (aim, goal) propósito m, objeto m; on ~ a propósito; what is the ~ of your visit? ¿cuál es el objeto de su visita?
pur·pose·ful ['pɜːrpəsfəl] adj decidido
pur·pose·ly ['pɜːrpəslɪ] adv decididamente
purr [pɜːr] v/i of cat ronronear
purse [pɜːrs] n (pocket book) bolso m; Br for money monedero m
pur·sue [pər'suː] v/t person perseguir; career ejercer; course of action proseguir
pur·su·er [pər'suːər] perseguidor(a) m(f)
pur·suit [pər'suːt] (chase) persecución f; of happiness etc búsqueda f; (activity) actividad f; those in ~ los perseguidores
pus [pʌs] pus m
push [pʊʃ] **1** n (shove) empujón m; at the ~ of a button apretando un botón **2** v/t (shove) empujar; button apretar, pulsar; (pressurize) presionar; F drugs pasar, mercadear con; be ~ed for cash F estar pelado F, estar sin un centavo; be ~ed for time F ir mal de tiempo F; be ~ing 40 F ron-

dar los 40 **3** *v/i* empujar

♦ **push ahead** *v/i* seguir adelante

♦ **push along** *v/t cart etc* empujar

♦ **push away** *v/t* apartar

♦ **push off** *v/t lid* destapar

♦ **push on** *v/i* (*continue*) continuar

♦ **push up** *v/t prices* hacer subir

push·er ['pʊʃər] F *of drugs* camello *m* F

push-up ['pʊʃʌp] flexión *f* (de brazos)

push·y ['pʊʃi] *adj* F avasallador, agresivo

puss, pus·sy (**cat**) [pʊs, 'pʊsi (kæt)] F minino *m* F

♦ **pussyfoot around** ['pʊsifʊt] *v/i* F andarse con rodeos

put [pʊt] *v/t* (*pret & pp* **put**) poner; *question* hacer; **~ the cost at …** estimar el costo en …

♦ **put across** *v/t idea etc* hacer llegar

♦ **put aside** *v/t money* apartar, ahorrar; *work* dejar a un lado

♦ **put away** *v/t in closet etc* guardar; *in institution* encerrar; F (*consume*) consumir, cepillarse F; *money* apartar, ahorrar; *animal* sacrificar

♦ **put back** *v/t* (*replace*) volver a poner

♦ **put by** *v/t money* apartar, ahorrar

♦ **put down** *v/t* dejar; *deposit* entregar; *rebellion* reprimir; (*belittle*) dejar en mal lugar; **put down in writing** poner por escrito; **put one's foot down** *in car* apretar el acelerador; (*be firm*) plantarse; **put sth down to sth** (*attribute*) atribuir algo a algo

♦ **put forward** *v/t idea etc* proponer, presentar

♦ **put in** *v/t* meter; *time* dedicar; *request, claim* presentar

♦ **put in for** *v/t* (*apply for*) solicitar

♦ **put off** *v/t light, radio, TV* apagar; (*postpone*) posponer, aplazar; (*deter*) desalentar; (*repel*) desagradar; **I was put off by the smell** el olor me quitó las ganas; **that put me off shellfish for life** me quitó las ganas de volver a comer marisco

♦ **put on** *v/t light, radio, TV* encender, *L.Am.* prender; *tape, music* poner; *jacket, shoes, eye glasses* ponerse; (*perform*) representar; (*assume*) fingir; **put on make-up** maquillarse; **put on the brake** frenar; **put on weight** engordar; **she's just putting it on** está fingiendo

♦ **put out** *v/t hand* extender; *fire, light* apagar

♦ **put through** *v/t*: **put s.o. through to s.o.** *on phone* poner a alguien con alguien

♦ **put together** *v/t* (*assemble, organize*) montar

♦ **put up** *v/t hand, fence, building* levantar; *person* alojar; *prices* subir; *poster, notice* colocar; *money* aportar; **put your hands up!** ¡arriba las manos!; **put up for sale** poner en venta

♦ **put up with** *v/t* (*tolerate*) aguantar

putt [pʌt] *v/i* SP golpear con el putter

put·ty ['pʌti] masilla *f*

puz·zle ['pʌzl] **1** *n* (*mystery*) enigma *m*; *game* pasatiempos *mpl*; (*jigsaw*) puzzle *m*; (*crossword*) crucigrama *m* **2** *v/t* desconcertar; **one thing ~s me** hay algo que no acabo de entender

puz·zling ['pʌzliŋ] *adj* desconcertante

PVC [piːviː'siː] *abbr* (= *polyvinyl chloride*) PVC *m* (= cloruro *m* de polivinilo)

py·ja·mas *Br* → **pajamas**

py·lon ['paɪlən] torre *f* de alta tensión

P

quack¹ [kwæk] **1** n of duck graznido m **2** v/i graznar

quack² [kwæk] n F (bad doctor) matasanos m/f inv F

quad·ran·gle ['kwɑ:dræŋgl] figure cuadrángulo m; courtyard patio m

quad·ru·ped ['kwɑ:drʊped] cuadrúpedo m

quad·ru·ple ['kwɑ:drʊpl] v/i cuadruplicarse

quad·ru·plets ['kwɑ:drʊplɪts] npl cuatrillizos(-as) mpl (fpl)

quads [kwɑ:dz] npl F cuatrillizos(-as) mpl (fpl)

quag·mire ['kwɑ:gmaɪr] fig atolladero m

quail [kweɪl] v/i temblar (**at** ante)

quaint [kweɪnt] adj cottage pintoresco; (eccentric: ideas etc) extraño

quake [kweɪk] **1** n (earthquake) terremoto m **2** v/i of earth, with fear temblar

qual·i·fi·ca·tion [kwɑ:lɪfɪ'keɪʃn] from university etc título m; **have the right ~s for a job** estar bien cualificado para un trabajo

qual·i·fied ['kwɑ:lɪfaɪd] adj doctor, engineer, plumber etc titulado; (restricted) limitado; **I am not ~ to judge** no estoy en condiciones de poder juzgar

qual·i·fy ['kwɑ:lɪfaɪ] **1** v/t (pret & pp **-ied**) of degree, course etc habilitar; remark etc matizar **2** v/i (pret & pp **-ied**) (get degree etc) titularse, L.Am. egresar; in competition calificarse; **that doesn't ~ as ...** eso no cuenta como ...

qual·i·ty ['kwɑ:lətɪ] calidad f; (characteristic) cualidad f

qual·i·ty con'trol control m de calidad

qualm [kwɑ:m]: **have no ~s about ...** no tener reparos en ...

quan·da·ry ['kwɑ:ndərɪ] dilema m

quan·ti·fy ['kwɑ:ntɪfaɪ] v/t (pret & pp **-ied**) cuantificar

quan·ti·ty ['kwɑ:ntətɪ] cantidad f

quan·tum 'phys·ics ['kwɑ:ntəm] física f cuántica

quar·an·tine ['kwɑ:rənti:n] cuarentena f

quar·rel ['kwɑ:rəl] **1** n pelea f **2** v/i (pret & pp **-ed**, Br **-led**) pelearse

quar·rel·some ['kwɑ:rəlsʌm] adj peleón

quar·ry¹ ['kwɑ:rɪ] in hunt presa f

quar·ry² ['kwɑ:rɪ] for mining cantera f

quart [kwɔ:rt] cuarto m de galón

quar·ter ['kwɔ:rtər] cuarto m; 25 cents cuarto m de dólar; part of town barrio m; **a ~ of an hour** un cuarto de hora; **a ~ of 5** las cinco menos cuarto, L.Am. un cuarto para las cinco; **a ~ after 5** las cinco y cuarto

'quar·ter·back SP quarterback m, en fútbol americano, jugador que dirige el juego de ataque; **quar·ter·'fi·nal** cuarto m de final; **quar·ter·'fi·nal·ist** cuartofinalista m/f

quar·ter·ly ['kwɔ:rtərlɪ] **1** adj trimestral **2** adv trimestralmente

'quar·ter·note MUS negra f

quar·ters ['kwɔ:rtərz] npl MIL alojamiento m

quar·tet [kwɔ:r'tet] MUS cuarteto m

quartz [kwɔ:rts] cuarzo m

quash [kwɑ:ʃ] v/t rebellion aplastar, sofocar; court decision revocar

qua·ver ['kweɪvər] **1** n in voice temblor m **2** v/i of voice temblar

quea·sy ['kwi:zɪ] adj mareado; **get ~** marearse

queen [kwi:n] reina f

queen 'bee abeja f reina

queer [kwɪr] adj (peculiar) raro, extraño

queer·ly ['kwɪrlɪ] adv de manera extraña

quell [kwel] *v/t protest* acallar; *riot* aplastar, sofocar

quench [kwentʃ] *v/t thirst* apagar, saciar; *flames* apagar

que·ry ['kwɪrɪ] **1** *n* duda *f*, pregunta *f* **2** *v/t* (*pret & pp -ied*) (*express doubt about*) cuestionar; (*check*) comprobar; **~ sth with s.o.** preguntar algo a alguien

quest [kwest] busca *f*

ques·tion ['kwestʃn] **1** *n* pregunta *f*; (*matter*) cuestión *f*, asunto *m*; **in ~** (*being talked about*) en cuestión; (*in doubt*) en duda; **it's a ~ of money/ time** es una cuestión de dinero/ tiempo; **that's out of the ~** eso es imposible **2** *v/t person* preguntar a; LAW interrogar; (*doubt*) cuestionar, poner en duda

ques·tion·a·ble ['kwestʃnəbl] *adj* cuestionable, dudoso

ques·tion·ing ['kwestʃnɪŋ] **1** *adj look, tone* inquisitivo **2** *n* interrogatorio *m*

'ques·tion mark signo *m* de interrogación

ques·tion·naire [kwestʃə'ner] cuestionario *m*

queue [kjuː] *n Br* cola *f*

quib·ble ['kwɪbl] *v/i* discutir (*por algo insignificante*)

quick [kwɪk] *adj* rápido; **be ~!** ¡date prisa!; **let's have a ~ drink** vamos a tomarnos algo rápidamente; **can I have a ~ look?** ¿me dejas echarle un vistazo?; **that was ~!** ¡qué rápido!

quick·ly ['kwɪklɪ] *adv* rápidamente, rápido, deprisa

'quick·sand arenas *fpl* movedizas; **'quick·sil·ver** azogue *m*; **quick·wit·ted** [kwɪk'wɪtɪd] *adj* agudo

qui·et ['kwaɪət] *adj* tranquilo; *engine* silencioso; **keep ~ about sth** guardar silencio sobre algo; **~!** ¡silencio!

♦ **qui·et·en down** ['kwaɪətn] **1** *v/t children, class* tranquilizar, hacer callar **2** *v/i of children* tranquilizarse, callarse; *of political situation* calmarse

qui·et·ly ['kwaɪətlɪ] *adv* (*not loudly*) silenciosamente; (*without fuss*) discretamente; (*peacefully*) tranquilamente; **speak ~** hablar en voz baja

quiet·ness ['kwaɪətnɪs] *of voice* suavidad *f*; *of night, street* silencio *m*, calma *f*

quilt [kwɪlt] *on bed* edredón *m*

quilt·ed ['kwɪltɪd] *adj* acolchado

quin·ine ['kwɪniːn] quinina *f*

quin·tet [kwɪn'tet] MUS quinteto *m*

quip [kwɪp] **1** *n joke* broma *f*; *remark* salida *f* **2** *v/i* (*pret & pp -ped*) bromear

quirk [kwɜːrk] peculiaridad *f*, rareza *f*

quirk·y ['kwɜːrkɪ] *adj* peculiar, raro

quit [kwɪt] **1** *v/t* (*pret & pp quit*) *job* dejar, abandonar; **~ doing sth** dejar de hacer algo **2** *v/i* (*pret & pp quit*) (*leave job*) dimitir; COMPUT salir

quite [kwaɪt] *adv* (*fairly*) bastante; (*completely*) completamente; **not ~ ready** no listo del todo; **I didn't ~ understand** no entendí bien; **is that right? – not ~** ¿es verdad? – no exactamente; **~!** ¡exactamente!; **~ a lot** bastante; **~ a few** bastantes; **it was ~ a surprise** fue toda una sorpresa

quits [kwɪts] *adj:* **be ~ with s.o.** estar en paz con alguien

quit·ter ['kwɪtər] F *persona que abandona fácilmente*

quiv·er ['kwɪvər] *v/i* estremecerse

quiz [kwɪz] **1** *n* concurso *m* (*de preguntas y respuestas*) **2** *v/t* (*pret & pp -zed*) interrogar (*about* sobre)

'quiz mas·ter presentador de un concurso de preguntas y respuestas

'quiz pro·gram, *Br* **'quiz pro·gramme** programa *m* concurso (*de preguntas y respuestas*)

quo·ta ['kwoʊtə] cuota *f*

quo·ta·tion [kwoʊ'teɪʃn] *from author* cita *f*; (*price*) presupuesto *m*

quo'ta·tion marks *npl* comillas *fpl*

quote [kwoʊt] **1** *n from author* cita *f*; (*price*) presupuesto *m*; (*quotation mark*) comilla *f*; **in ~s** entre comillas **2** *v/t text* citar; *price* dar **3** *v/i:* **~ from an author** citar de un autor

Q

R

rab·bi ['ræbaɪ] rabino *m*
rab·bit ['ræbɪt] conejo *m*
rab·ble ['ræbl] chusma *f*, multitud *f*
rab·ble-rous·er ['ræblraʊzər] agitador(a) *m(f)*
ra·bies ['reɪbiːz] *nsg* rabia *f*
rac·coon [rə'kuːn] mapache *m*
race¹ [reɪs] *n of people* raza *f*
race² [reɪs] **1** *n* SP carrera *f*; *the ~s horse races* las carreras **2** *v/i (run fast)* correr; *he ~d through his meal/work* acabó su comida/trabajo a toda velocidad **3** *v/t* correr contra; *I'll ~ you* te echo una carrera
'race·course hipódromo *m*;
'race·horse caballo *m* de carreras;
'race riot disturbios *mpl* raciales;
'race·track circuito *m*; *for horses* hipódromo *m*
ra·cial ['reɪʃl] *adj* racial; *~ equality* igualdad *f* racial
rac·ing ['reɪsɪŋ] carreras *fpl*
rac·ism ['reɪsɪzm] racismo *m*
rac·ist ['reɪsɪst] **1** *n* racista *m/f* **2** *adj* racista
rack [ræk] **1** *n (for bikes)* barras para aparcar bicicletas; *for bags on train* portaequipajes *m inv*; *for CDs* mueble *m* **2** *v/t*: *~ one's brains* devanarse los sesos
rack·et¹ ['rækɪt] SP raqueta *f*
rack·et² ['rækɪt] *(noise)* jaleo *m*; *(criminal activity)* negocio *m* sucio
ra·dar ['reɪdɑːr] radar *m*
'ra·dar screen pantalla *f* de radar
'ra·dar trap control *m* de velocidad por radar
ra·di·al **'tire**, *Br* **ra·di·al** **'tyre** ['reɪdɪəl] neumático *m* radial
ra·di·ance ['reɪdɪəns] esplendor *m*, brillantez *f*
ra·di·ant ['reɪdɪənt] *adj smile, appearance* resplandeciente, brillante
ra·di·ate ['reɪdɪeɪt] *v/i of heat, light* irradiar
ra·di·a·tion [reɪdɪ'eɪʃn] PHYS radiación *f*
ra·di·a·tor ['reɪdɪeɪtər] *in room, car* radiador *m*
rad·i·cal ['rædɪkl] **1** *adj* radical **2** *n* POL radical *m/f*
rad·i·cal·ism ['rædɪkəlɪzm] POL radicalismo *m*
rad·i·cal·ly ['rædɪklɪ] *adv* radicalmente
ra·di·o ['reɪdɪoʊ] radio *f*; *on the ~* en la radio; *by ~* por radio
ra·di·o·ac·tive [reɪdɪoʊ'æktɪv] *adj* radiactivo; **ra·di·o·ac·tive 'waste** residuos *mpl* radiactivos; **ra·di·o·ac·tiv·i·ty** [reɪdɪoʊæk'tɪvɪtɪ] radiactividad *f*; **ra·di·o a'larm** radio *m* despertador
ra·di·og·ra·pher [reɪdɪ'ɑːgrəfər] técnico(-a) *m(f)* de rayos X
ra·di·og·ra·phy [reɪdɪ'ɑːgrəfɪ] radiografía *f*
'ra·di·o sta·tion emisora *f* de radio;
'ra·di·o tax·i radiotaxi *m*; **ra·di·o·'ther·a·py** radioterapia *f*
rad·ish ['rædɪʃ] rábano *m*
ra·di·us ['reɪdɪəs] radio *m*
raf·fle ['ræfl] *n* rifa *f*
raft [ræft] balsa *f*
raf·ter ['ræftər] viga *f*
rag [ræg] *n for cleaning etc* trapo *m*; *in ~s* con harapos
rage [reɪdʒ] **1** *n* ira *f*, cólera *f*; *be in a ~* estar encolerizado; *be all the ~* F estar arrasando F **2** *v/i of storm* bramar
rag·ged ['rægɪd] *adj* andrajoso
raid [reɪd] **1** *n by troops* incursión *f*; *by police* redada *f*; *by robbers* atraco *m*; FIN ataque *m*, incursión *f* **2** *v/t of troops* realizar una incursión en; *of police* realizar una redada en; *of robbers* atracar; *fridge, orchard* sa-

quear

raid·er ['reɪdər] *on bank etc* atracador(a) *m(f)*

rail [reɪl] *n on track* riel *m*, carril *m*; (*hand~*) pasamanos *m inv*, baranda *f*; *for towel* barra *f*; *by ~* en tren

rail·ings ['reɪlɪŋz] *npl around park etc* verja *f*

'**rail·road** ferrocarril *m*; '**rail·road sta·tion** estación *f* de ferrocarril *or* de tren; '**rail·way** *Br* ferrocarril *m*

rain [reɪn] **1** *n* lluvia *f*; *in the ~* bajo la lluvia **2** *v/i* llover; *it's ~ing* llueve

'**rain·bow** arco *m* iris; '**rain·check**: *can I take a ~ on that?* F ¿lo podríamos aplazar para algún otro momento?; '**rain·coat** impermeable *m*; '**rain·drop** gota *f* de lluvia; '**rain·fall** pluviosidad *f*, precipitaciones *fpl*; '**rain for·est** selva *f*; '**rain·proof** *adj fabric* impermeable; '**rain·storm** tormenta *f*, aguacero *m*

rain·y ['reɪnɪ] *adj* lluvioso; *it's ~* llueve mucho

'**rain·y sea·son** estación *f* de las lluvias

raise [reɪz] **1** *n in salary* aumento *m* de sueldo **2** *v/t shelf etc* levantar; *offer* incrementar; *children* criar; *question* plantear; *money* reunir

rai·sin ['reɪzn] pasa *f*

rake [reɪk] *n for garden* rastrillo *m*
♦ **rake up** *v/t leaves* rastrillar; *fig* sacar a la luz

ral·ly ['rælɪ] *n (meeting, reunion)* concentración *f*; *political* mitin *m*; MOT rally *m*; *in tennis* peloteo *m*
♦ **rally round 1** *v/i (pret & pp -ied)* acudir a ayudar **2** *v/t (pret & pp -ied)*: *rally round s.o.* acudir a ayudar a alguien

RAM [ræm] COMPUT *abbr (= random access memory)* RAM *f (= memoria f de acceso aleatorio)*

ram [ræm] **1** *n* carnero *m* **2** *v/t (pret & pp -med) ship, car* embestir

ram·ble ['ræmbl] **1** *n walk* caminata *f*, excursión *f* **2** *v/i in walk* caminar; *in speaking* divagar; *(talk incoherently)* hablar sin decir nada coherente

ram·bler ['ræmblər] *walker*

senderista *m/f*, excursionista *m/f*

ram·bling ['ræmblɪŋ] **1** *n walking* senderismo *m*; *in speech* divagaciones *fpl* **2** *adj speech* inconexo

ramp [ræmp] rampa *f*; *for raising vehicle* elevador *m*

ram·page ['ræmpeɪdʒ] **1** *v/i* pasar arrasando con todo **2** *n*: *go on the ~* pasar arrasando con todo

ram·pant ['ræmpənt] *adj inflation* galopante

ram·part ['ræmpɔːrt] muralla *f*

ram·shack·le ['ræmʃækl] *adj* destartalado, desvencijado

ran [ræn] *pret* → *run*

ranch [rænʃ] rancho *m*

ranch·er ['rænʃər] ranchero(-a) *m(f)*

ran·cid ['rænsɪd] *adj* rancio

ran·cor ['rænkər] rencor *m*

R & D [ɑːrən'diː] *abbr (= research and development)* I+D *f (= investigación f y desarrollo)*

ran·dom ['rændəm] **1** *adj* al azar; *~ sample* muestra *f* aleatoria **2** *n*: *at ~* al azar

ran·dy ['rændɪ] *adj Br* F cachondo F; *it makes me ~* me pone cachondo

rang [ræŋ] *pret* → *ring*

range [reɪndʒ] *n of products* gama *f*; *of gun, airplane* alcance *m*; *of voice* registro *m*; *of mountains* cordillera *f*; *at close ~* de cerca **2** *v/i*: *~ from X to Y* ir desde X a Y

rang·er ['reɪndʒər] guardabosques *m/f inv*

rank [ræŋk] **1** *n* MIL, *in society* rango *m*; *the ~s* MIL la tropa **2** *v/t* clasificar
♦ **rank among** *v/t* figurar entre

ran·kle ['ræŋkl] *v/i* doler; *it still ~s (with him)* todavía le duele

ran·sack ['rænsæk] *v/t* saquear

ran·som ['rænsəm] *n* rescate *m*; *hold s.o. to ~* pedir un rescate por alguien

'**ran·som mon·ey** (dinero *m* del) rescate *m*

rant [rænt] *v/i*: *~ and rave* despotricar

rap [ræp] **1** *n at door etc* golpe *m*; MUS rap *m* **2** *v/t (pret & pp -ped) table etc* golpear

♦ **rap at** *v/t window etc* golpear
rape¹ [reɪp] **1** *n* violación *f* **2** *v/t* violar
rape² [reɪp] *n* BOT colza *f*
'**rape vic·tim** víctima *m/f* de una violación
rap·id ['ræpɪd] *adj* rápido
ra·pid·i·ty [rə'pɪdətɪ] rapidez *f*
rap·id·ly ['ræpɪdlɪ] *adv* rápidamente
rap·ids ['ræpɪdz] *npl* rápidos *mpl*
rap·ist ['reɪpɪst] violador(a) *m(f)*
rap·port [ræ'pɔːr] relación *f*; *we have a good ~* nos entendemos muy bien
rap·ture ['ræptʃər]: *go into ~s over* extasiarse con
rap·tur·ous ['ræptʃərəs] *adj* clamoroso
rare [rer] *adj* raro; *steak* poco hecho
rare·ly ['rerlɪ] *adv* raramente, raras veces
rar·i·ty ['rerətɪ] rareza *f*
ras·cal ['ræskl] pícaro(-a) *m(f)*
rash¹ [ræʃ] *n* MED sarpullido *m*, erupción *f* cutánea
rash² [ræʃ] *adj action, behavior* precipitado
rash·ly ['ræʃlɪ] *adv* precipitadamente
rasp·ber·ry ['ræzberɪ] frambuesa *f*
rat [ræt] *n* rata *f*
rate [reɪt] **1** *n of exchange* tipo *m*; *of pay* tarifa *f*; *(price)* tarifa *f*, precio *m*; *(speed)* ritmo *m*; *~ of interest* FIN tipo *m* de interés; *at this ~ (at this speed)* a este ritmo; *(if we carry on like this)* si seguimos así; *at any ~ (anyway)* en todo caso; *(at least)* por lo menos **2** *v/t*: *~ s.o. as ...* considerar a alguien (como) ...; *~ s.o. highly* tener buena opinión de alguien
rather ['ræðər] *adv (fairly, quite)* bastante; *I would ~ stay here* preferiría quedarme aquí; *or would you ~ ...?* ¿o preferiría ...?
rat·i·fi·ca·tion [rætɪfɪ'keɪʃn] ratificación *f*
rat·i·fy ['rætɪfaɪ] *v/t (pret & pp -ied)* ratificar
rat·ings ['reɪtɪŋz] *npl* índice *m* de audiencia
ra·ti·o ['reɪʃɪoʊ] proporción *f*
ra·tion ['ræʃn] **1** *n* ración *f* **2** *v/t*

supplies racionar
ra·tion·al ['ræʃnl] *adj* racional
ra·tion·al·i·ty [ræʃə'nælɪtɪ] racionalidad *f*
ra·tion·al·i·za·tion [ræʃənəlaɪ'zeɪʃn] racionalización *f*
ra·tion·al·ize ['ræʃənəlaɪz] **1** *v/t* racionalizar **2** *v/i* buscar una explicación racional
ra·tion·al·ly ['ræʃənlɪ] *adv* racionalmente
'**rat race** vida frenética y competitiva
rat·tle ['rætl] **1** *n noise* traqueteo *m*, golpeteo *m*; *toy* sonajero *m* **2** *v/t chains etc* entrechocar **3** *v/i of chains etc* entrechocarse; *of crates* traquetear
♦ **rattle off** *v/t poem, list of names* decir rápidamente
♦ **rattle through** *v/t* hacer rápidamente
'**rat·tle·snake** serpiente *f* de cascabel
rau·cous ['rɒkəs] *adj laughter, party* estridente
rav·age ['rævɪdʒ] **1** *n*: *the ~s of time* los estragos del tiempo **2** *v/t* arrasar; *~d by war* arrasado por la guerra
rave [reɪv] **1** *v/i (talk deliriously)* delirar; *(talk wildly)* desvariar; *~ about sth (be very enthusiastic)* estar muy entusiasmado con algo **2** *n party* fiesta *f* tecno
ra·ven ['reɪvn] cuervo *m*
rav·e·nous ['rævənəs] *adj (very hungry)* famélico; *have a ~ appetite* tener un hambre canina
rav·e·nous·ly ['rævənəslɪ] *adv* con voracidad
rave re'view crítica *f* muy entusiasta
ra·vine [rə'viːn] barranco *m*
rav·ing ['reɪvɪŋ] *adv*: *~ mad* chalado
rav·ish·ing ['rævɪʃɪŋ] *adj* encantador, cautivador
raw [rɒ] *adj meat, vegetable* crudo; *sugar* sin refinar; *iron* sin tratar
raw ma'te·ri·als *npl* materias *fpl* primas
ray [reɪ] rayo *m*; *a ~ of hope* un rayo de esperanza
raze [reɪz] *v/t*: *~ to the ground* arra-

sar *or* asolar por completo

ra·zor ['reɪzər] maquinilla *f* de afeitar

'ra·zor blade cuchilla *f* de afeitar

re [riː] *prep* COM con referencia a

reach [riːtʃ] **1** *n:* **within ~** al alcance; **out of ~** fuera del alcance **2** *v/t* llegar a; *decision, agreement, conclusion* alcanzar, llegar a; **can you ~ it?** ¿alcanzas?, ¿llegas?

♦**reach out** *v/i* extender el brazo

re·act [rɪ'ækt] *v/i* reaccionar

re·ac·tion [rɪ'ækʃn] reacción *f*

re·ac·tion·ar·y [rɪ'ækʃnrɪ] **1** *n* POL reaccionario(-a) *m(f)* **2** *adj* POL reaccionario

re·ac·tor [rɪ'æktər] *nuclear reactor m*

read [riːd] (*pret & pp* **read**[red]) **1** *v/t also* COMPUT leer **2** *v/i* leer; **~ to s.o.** leer a alguien

♦**read out** *v/t* leer en voz alta

♦**read up on** *v/t* leer mucho sobre, estudiar

rea·da·ble ['riːdəbl] *adj handwriting* legible; *book* ameno

read·er ['riːdər] *person* lector(a) *m(f)*

read·i·ly ['redɪlɪ] *adv admit, agree* de buena gana

read·i·ness ['redɪnɪs]: **in a state of ~** preparado par actuar; **their ~ to help** la facilidad con la que ayudaron

read·ing ['riːdɪŋ] *activity* lectura *f*; **take a ~ from the meter** leer el contador

'read·ing mat·ter lectura *f*

re·ad·just [riːə'dʒʌst] **1** *v/t equipment, controls* reajustar **2** *v/i to conditions* volver a adaptarse

read-'on·ly file COMPUT archivo *m* sólo de lectura

read-'on·ly mem·o·ry COMPUT memoria *f* sólo de lectura

read·y ['redɪ] *adj* (*prepared*) listo, preparado; (*willing*) dispuesto; **get (o.s.) ~** prepararse; **get sth ready** preparar algo

read·y 'cash dinero *m* contante y sonante; **read·y-made** *adj stew etc* precocinado; *solution* ya hecho; **read·y-to-wear** *adj* de confección

re·al [riːl] *adj* real; *surprise, genius* auténtico; **he's a ~ idiot** es un auténtico idiota

're·al es·tate bienes *mpl* inmuebles

're·al es·tate a·gent agente *m/f* inmobiliario(-a)

re·al·ism ['rɪəlɪzəm] realismo *m*

re·al·ist ['rɪəlɪst] realista *m/f*

re·al·is·tic [rɪə'lɪstɪk] *adj* realista

re·al·is·tic·al·ly [rɪə'lɪstɪklɪ] *adv* realísticamente

re·al·i·ty [rɪ'ælətɪ] realidad *f*

re·al·i·za·tion [rɪələr'zeɪʃn]: **the ~ dawned on me that ...** me di cuenta de que ...

re·al·ize ['rɪəlaɪz] *v/t* darse cuenta de; FIN (*yield*) realizar; (*sell*) liquidar; **I ~ now that ...** ahora me doy cuenta de que ...

re·al·ly ['rɪəlɪ] *adv in truth* de verdad; *big, small* muy; **I am ~ ~ sorry** lo siento en el alma; **~?** ¿de verdad?; **not ~ as reply** la verdad es que no

're·al time *n* COMPUT tiempo *m* real

're·al-time *adj* COMPUT en tiempo real

re·al·tor ['riːltər] agente *m/f* inmobiliario(-a)

re·al·ty ['riːltɪ] bienes *mpl* inmuebles

reap [riːp] *v/t* cosechar

re·ap·pear [riːə'pɪr] *v/i* reaparecer

re·ap·pear·ance [riːə'pɪrəns] reaparición *f*

rear [rɪr] **1** *n* parte *f* de atrás **2** *adj legs* de atrás; *seats, wheels, lights* trasero

rear 'end 1 *n* F *of person* trasero *m* **2** *v/t* MOT F dar un golpe por atrás a

rear 'light *of car* luz *f* trasera

re·arm [riː'ɑːrm] **1** *v/t* rearmar **2** *v/i* rearmarse

'rear·most *adj* último

re·ar·range [riːə'reɪndʒ] *v/t flowers* volver a colocar; *furniture* reordenar; *schedule, meetings* cambiar

rear·view 'mir·ror espejo *m* retrovisor

rea·son ['riːzn] **1** *n faculty* razón *f*; (*cause*) razón *f*, motivo *m*; **see/ listen to ~** atender a razones **2** *v/i:* **~ with s.o.** razonar con alguien

rea·so·na·ble ['riːznəbl] *adj person*

R

razonable; *a ~ number of people* un buen número de personas

rea·son·a·bly ['riːznəblɪ] *adv act, behave* razonablemente; *(quite)* bastante

rea·son·ing ['riːznɪŋ] razonamiento *m*

re·as·sure [riːə'ʃʊr] *v/t* tranquilizar; *she ~d us of her continued support* nos aseguró que continuábamos contando con su apoyo

re·as·sur·ing [riːə'ʃʊrɪŋ] *adj* tranquilizador

re·bate ['riːbeɪt] *money back* reembolso *m*

reb·el¹ ['rebl] *n* rebelde *m/f*; *~ troops* tropas *fpl* rebeldes

re·bel² [rɪ'bel] *v/i (pret & pp -led)* rebelarse

reb·el·lion [rɪ'beljən] rebelión *f*

reb·el·lious [rɪ'beljəs] *adj* rebelde

reb·el·lious·ly [rɪ'beljəslɪ] *adv* con rebeldía

reb·el·lious·ness [rɪ'beljəsnɪs] rebeldía *f*

re·bound [rɪ'baʊnd] *v/i* of ball etc rebotar

re·buff [rɪ'bʌf] *n* desaire *m*, rechazo *m*

re·build ['riːbɪld] *v/t (pret & pp -built)* reconstruir

re·buke [rɪ'bjuːk] *v/t* reprender

re·call [rɪ'kɒːl] *v/t goods* retirar del mercado; *(remember)* recordar

re·cap ['riːkæp] *v/i (pret & pp -ped)* recapitular

re·cap·ture [riː'kæptʃər] *v/t* MIL reconquistar; *criminal* volver a detener

re·cede [rɪ'siːd] *v/i* of flood waters retroceder

re·ced·ing [rɪ'siːdɪŋ] *adj forehead, chin* hundido; *have a ~ hairline* tener entradas

re·ceipt [rɪ'siːt] *for purchase* recibo *m*; *acknowledge ~ of sth* acusar recibo de algo; *~s* FIN ingresos *mpl*

re·ceive [rɪ'siːv] *v/t* recibir

re·ceiv·er [rɪ'siːvər] *of letter* destinatario(-a) *m(f)*; TELEC auricular *m*; *for radio* receptor *m*

re·ceiv·er·ship [rɪ'siːvərʃɪp]: *be in ~* estar en suspensión de pagos

re·cent ['riːsnt] *adj* reciente

re·cent·ly ['riːsntlɪ] *adv* recientemente

re·cep·tion [rɪ'sepʃn] recepción *f*; *(welcome)* recibimiento *m*

re'cep·tion desk recepción *f*

re·cep·tion·ist [rɪ'sepʃnɪst] recepcionista *m/f*

re·cep·tive [rɪ'septɪv] *adj*: *be ~ to sth* ser receptivo a algo

re·cess ['riːses] *n in wall etc* hueco *m*; EDU recreo *m*; *of legislature* periodo *m* vacacional

re·ces·sion [rɪ'seʃn] *economic* recesión *f*

re·charge [riː'tʃɑːrdʒ] *v/t battery* recargar

re·ci·pe ['resəpɪ] receta *f*

're·ci·pe book libro *m* de cocina, recetario *m*

re·cip·i·ent [rɪ'sɪpɪənt] *of parcel etc* destinatario(-a) *m(f)*; *of payment* receptor(a) *m(f)*

re·cip·ro·cal [rɪ'sɪprəkl] *adj* recíproco

re·cit·al [rɪ'saɪtl] MUS recital *m*

re·cite [rɪ'saɪt] *v/t poem* recitar; *details, facts* enumerar

reck·less ['reklɪs] *adj* imprudente; *driving* temerario

reck·less·ly ['reklɪslɪ] *adv* con imprudencia; *drive* con temeridad

reck·on ['rekən] *v/t (think, consider)* estimar, considerar; *I ~ it won't happen* creo que no va a pasar
♦ **reckon on** *v/t* contar con
♦ **reckon with** *v/t*: *have s.o. / sth to reckon with* tener que vérselas con alguien / algo

reck·on·ing ['rekənɪŋ] estimaciones *fpl*, cálculos *mpl*; *by my ~* según mis cálculos

re·claim [rɪ'kleɪm] *v/t land from sea* ganar, recuperar; *lost property, rights* reclamar

re·cline [rɪ'klaɪn] *v/i* reclinarse

re·clin·er [rɪ'klaɪnər] *chair* sillón *m* reclinable

re·cluse [rɪ'kluːs] solitario(-a) *m(f)*

rec·og·ni·tion [rekəg'nɪʃn] *of state, s.o.'s achievements* reconocimiento *m*; **in ~ of** en reconocimiento a; **be changed beyond ~** estar irreconocible

rec·og·niz·a·ble [rekəg'naɪzəbl] *adj* reconocible

rec·og·nize ['rekəgnaɪz] *v/t* reconocer

re·coil [rɪ'kɔɪl] *v/i* echarse atrás, retroceder

rec·ol·lect [rekə'lekt] *v/t* recordar

rec·ol·lec·tion [rekə'lekʃn] recuerdo *m*; **I have no ~ of the accident** no me acuerdo del accidente

rec·om·mend [rekə'mend] *v/t* recomendar

rec·om·men·da·tion [rekəmen'deɪʃn] recomendación *f*

rec·om·pense ['rekəmpens] *n* recompensa *f*

rec·on·cile ['rekənsaɪl] *v/t people* reconciliar; *differences, facts* conciliar; **~ o.s. to ...** hacerse a la idea de ...; **be ~d** *of two people* haberse reconciliado

rec·on·cil·i·a·tion [rekənsɪlɪ'eɪʃn] *of people* reconciliación *f*; *of differences, facts* conciliación *f*

re·con·di·tion [riːkən'dɪʃn] *v/t* reacondicionar

re·con·nais·sance [rɪ'kɑːnɪsns] MIL reconocimiento *m*

re·con·sid·er [riːkən'sɪdər] **1** *v/t offer, one's position* reconsiderar **2** *v/i*: **won't you please ~?** ¿por qué no lo reconsideras, por favor?

re·con·struct [riːkən'strʌkt] *v/t* reconstruir

rec·ord¹ ['rekɔːrd] *n* MUS disco *m*; SP *etc* récord *m*; *written document etc* registro *m*, documento *m*; *in database* registro *m*; **~s** archivos *mpl*; **say sth off the ~** decir algo oficiosamente; **have a criminal ~** tener antecedentes penales; **have a good ~ for sth** tener un buen historial en materia de algo

re·cord² [rɪ'kɔːrd] *v/t electronically* grabar; *in writing* anotar

'rec·ord-break·ing *adj* récord

re·cord·er [rɪ'kɔːrdər] MUS flauta *f* dulce

'rec·ord hold·er plusmarquista *m/f*

re·cord·ing [rɪ'kɔːrdɪŋ] grabación *f*

re'cord·ing stu·di·o estudio *m* de grabación

'rec·ord play·er tocadiscos *m inv*

re·count [rɪ'kaʊnt] *v/t (tell)* relatar

re-count ['riːkaʊnt] **1** *n of votes* segundo recuento *m* **2** *v/t (count again)* volver a contar

re·coup [rɪ'kuːp] *v/t financial losses* resarcirse de

re·cov·er [rɪ'kʌvər] **1** *v/t sth lost, stolen goods* recuperar; *composure* recobrar **2** *v/i from illness* recuperarse

re·cov·er·y [rɪ'kʌvərɪ] recuperación *f*; **he has made a good ~** se ha recuperado muy bien

rec·re·a·tion [rekrɪ'eɪʃn] ocio *m*

rec·re·a·tion·al [rekrɪ'eɪʃnl] *adj done for pleasure* recreativo

re·cruit [rɪ'kruːt] **1** *n* MIL recluta *m/f*; *to company* nuevo(-a) trabajador(a) **2** *v/t new staff* contratar

re·cruit·ment [rɪ'kruːtmənt] MIL reclutamiento *m*; *to company* contratación *f*

re'cruit·ment drive MIL campaña *f* de reclutamiento; *to company* campaña *f* de contratación

rec·tan·gle ['rektæŋgl] rectángulo *m*

rec·tan·gu·lar [rek'tæŋgjʊlər] *adj* rectangular

rec·ti·fy ['rektɪfaɪ] *v/t (pret & pp -ied)* rectificar

re·cu·pe·rate [rɪ'kuːpəreɪt] *v/i* recuperarse

re·cur [rɪ'kɜːr] *v/i (pret & pp -red) of error, event* repetirse; *of symptoms* reaparecer

re·cur·rent [rɪ'kʌrənt] *adj* recurrente

re·cy·cla·ble [riː'saɪkləbl] *adj* reciclable

re·cy·cle [riː'saɪkl] *v/t* reciclar

re·cy·cling [riː'saɪklɪŋ] reciclado *m*

red [red] **1** *adj* rojo **2** *n*: **in the ~** FIN en números rojos

Red 'Cross Cruz *f* Roja

red·den ['redn] *v/i (blush)* ponerse

colorado

re·dec·o·rate [riːˈdekəreɪt] v/t with paint volver a pintar; with paper volver a empapelar

re·deem [rɪˈdiːm] v/t debt amortizar; REL redimir

re·deem·ing fea·ture [rɪˈdiːmɪŋ]: his one ~ is that … lo único que lo salva es que …

re·demp·tion [rɪˈdempʃn] REL redención f

re·de·vel·op [riːdɪˈveləp] v/t part of town reedificar

red-hand·ed [red'hændɪd] adj: catch s.o. ~ coger a alguien con las manos en la masa; **'red·head** pelirrojo(-a) m(f); **red-'hot** adj al rojo vivo; **red-'let·ter day** día m señalado; **red 'light** at traffic light semáforo m (en) rojo; **red 'light dis·trict** zona f de prostitución; **red 'meat** carne f roja; **'red·neck** F individuo racista y reaccionario, normalmente de clase trabajadora

re·dou·ble [riːˈdʌbl] v/t: ~ one's efforts redoblar los esfuerzos

red 'pep·per vegetable pimiento m rojo

red 'tape F burocracia f, papeleo m

re·duce [rɪˈduːs] v/t reducir; price rebajar

re·duc·tion [rɪˈdʌkʃn] reducción f; in price rebaja f

re·dun·dant [rɪˈdʌndənt] adj (unnecessary) innecesario; be made ~ at work ser despedido

reed [riːd] BOT junco m

reef [riːf] in sea arrecife m

'reef knot nudo m de rizos

reek [riːk] v/i apestar (of a)

reel [riːl] n of film rollo m; of thread carrete m

♦ **reel off** v/t soltar

re·e'lect v/t reelegir

re·e'lec·tion reelección f

re·'en·try of spacecraft reentrada f

ref [ref] F árbitro(-a) m(f)

re·fer [rɪˈfɜːr] v/t (pret & pp -red): ~ a decision/ problem to s.o. remitir una decisión / un problema a alguien

♦ **refer to** v/t (allude to) referirse a; dictionary etc consultar

ref·er·ee [refəˈriː] SP árbitro(-a) m(f); (for job) persona que pueda dar referencias

ref·er·ence ['refərəns] referencia f; with ~ to con referencia a

'ref·er·ence book libro m de consulta; **'ref·er·ence li·bra·ry** biblioteca f de consulta; **'ref·er·ence num·ber** número m de referencia

ref·e·ren·dum [refəˈrendəm] referéndum m

re·fill ['riːfɪl] v/t tank, glass volver a llenar

re·fine [rɪˈfaɪn] v/t oil, sugar refinar; technique perfeccionar

re·fined [rɪˈfaɪnd] adj manners, language refinado

re·fine·ment [rɪˈfaɪnmənt] to process, machine mejora f

re·fin·e·ry [rɪˈfaɪnəri] refinería f

re·fla·tion ['riːfleɪʃn] reflación f

re·flect [rɪˈflekt] **1** v/t light reflejar; be ~ed in reflejarse en **2** v/i (think) reflexionar

re·flec·tion [rɪˈflekʃn] in water, glass etc reflejo m; (consideration) reflexión f

re·flex ['riːfleks] in body reflejo m

re·flex re'ac·tion acto m reflejo

re·form [rɪˈfɔːrm] **1** n reforma f **2** v/t reformar

re·form·er [rɪˈfɔːrmər] reformador(a) m(f)

re·frain¹ [rɪˈfreɪn] v/i fml abstenerse; please ~ from smoking se ruega no fumar

re·frain² [rɪˈfreɪn] n in song, poem estribillo m

re·fresh [rɪˈfreʃ] v/t person refrescar; feel ~ed sentirse fresco

re·fresh·er course [rɪˈfreʃər] curso m de actualización or reciclaje

re·fresh·ing [rɪˈfreʃɪŋ] adj drink refrescante; experience reconfortante

re·fresh·ments [rɪˈfreʃmənts] npl refrigerio m

re·fri·ge·rate [rɪˈfrɪdʒəreɪt] v/t refrigerar; keep ~d conservar refrigerado

re·fri·ge·ra·tor [rɪ'frɪdʒəreɪtər] frigorífico *m*, refrigerador *m*

re·fu·el [riː'fjuːəl] **1** *v/t airplane* reabastecer de combustible a **2** *v/i of airplane* repostar

ref·uge ['refjuːdʒ] refugio *m*; **take ~ from storm etc** refugiarse

ref·u·gee [refjʊ'dʒiː] refugiado(-a) *m(f)*

ref·u·gee camp campo *m* de refugiados

re·fund ['riːfʌnd] **1** *n* ['riːfʌnd] reembolso *m*; **give s.o. a ~** devolver el dinero a alguien **2** *v/t* [rɪ'fʌnd] reembolsar

re·fus·al [rɪ'fjuːzl] negativa *f*

re·fuse [rɪ'fjuːz] **1** *v/i* negarse **2** *v/t help, food* rechazar; **~ s.o. sth** negar algo a alguien; **~ to do sth** negarse a hacer algo

re·gain [rɪ'geɪn] *v/t* recuperar

re·gal ['riːgl] *adj* regio

re·gard [rɪ'gɑːrd] **1** *n*: **have great ~ for s.o.** sentir gran estima por alguien; **in this ~** en este sentido; **with ~ to** con respecto a; **(kind) ~s** saludos; **give my ~s to Paula** dale saludos *or* recuerdos a Paula de mi parte; **with no ~ for** sin tener en cuenta **2** *v/t*: **~ s.o./ sth as sth** considerar a alguien / algo como algo; **I ~ it as an honor** para mí es un honor; **as ~s** con respecto a

re·gard·ing [rɪ'gɑːrdɪŋ] *prep* con respecto a

re·gard·less [rɪ'gɑːrdlɪs] *adv* a pesar de todo; **~ of** sin tener en cuenta

re·gime [reɪ'ʒiːm] *(government)* régimen *m*

re·gi·ment ['redʒɪmənt] *n* regimiento *m*

re·gion ['riːdʒən] región *f*; **in the ~ of** del orden de

re·gion·al ['riːdʒənl] *adj* regional

re·gis·ter ['redʒɪstər] **1** *n* registro *m*; *at school* lista *f* **2** *v/t birth, death* registrar; *vehicle* matricular; *letter* certificar; *emotion* mostrar; **send a letter ~ed** enviar una carta por correo certificado **3** *v/i at university, for a course* matricularse; *with police* registrarse

re·gis·tered let·ter ['redʒɪstərd] carta *f* certificada

re·gis·tra·tion [redʒɪ'streɪʃn] registro *m*; *at university, for course* matriculación *f*

re·gis·tra·tion num·ber *Br* MOT (número *m* de) matrícula *f*

re·gret [rɪ'gret] **1** *v/t (pret & pp -ted)* lamentar, sentir **2** *n* arrepentimiento *m*, pesar *m*

re·gret·ful [rɪ'gretfəl] *adj* arrepentido

re·gret·ful·ly [rɪ'gretfəlɪ] *adv* lamentablemente

re·gret·ta·ble [rɪ'gretəbl] *adj* lamentable

re·gret·ta·bly [rɪ'gretəblɪ] *adv* lamentablemente

reg·u·lar ['regjʊlər] **1** *adj* regular; *(normal, ordinary)* normal **2** *n at bar etc* habitual *m/f*

reg·u·lar·i·ty [regjʊ'lærətɪ] regularidad *f*

reg·u·lar·ly ['regjʊlərlɪ] *adv* regularmente

reg·u·late ['regʊleɪt] *v/t* regular

reg·u·la·tion [regʊ'leɪʃn] *(rule)* regla *f*, norma *f*

re·hab ['riːhæb] F rehabilitación *f*

re·ha·bil·i·tate [riːhə'bɪlɪteɪt] *v/t ex-criminal* rehabilitar

re·hears·al [rɪ'hɜːrsl] ensayo *m*

re·hearse [rɪ'hɜːrs] *v/t & v/i* ensayar

reign [reɪn] **1** *n* reinado *m* **2** *v/i* reinar

re·im·burse [riːɪm'bɜːrs] *v/t* reembolsar

rein [reɪn] rienda *f*

re·in·car·na·tion [riːɪnkɑːr'neɪʃn] reencarnación *f*

re·in·force [riːɪn'fɔːrs] *v/t structure* reforzar; *beliefs* reafirmar

re·in·forced con·crete [riːɪn'fɔːrst] hormigón *m* armado

re·in·force·ments [riːɪn'fɔːrsmənts] *npl* MIL refuerzos *mpl*

re·in·state [riːɪn'steɪt] *v/t person in office* reincorporar; *paragraph in text* volver a colocar

re·it·e·rate [riː'ɪtəreɪt] *v/t fml* reiterar

re·ject [rɪ'dʒekt] *v/t* rechazar

R

re·jec·tion [rɪ'dʒekʃn] rechazo *m*; **he felt a sense of ~** se sintió rechazado

re·lapse ['riːlæps] *n* MED recaída *f*; **have a ~** sufrir una recaída

re·late [rɪ'leɪt] **1** *v/t story* relatar, narrar; **~ sth to sth** *connect* relacionar algo con algo **2** *v/i*: **~ to** *be connected with* estar relacionado con; **he doesn't ~ to people** no se relaciona fácilmente con la gente

re·lat·ed [rɪ'leɪtɪd] *adj by family* emparentado; *events, ideas etc* relacionado; **are you two ~?** ¿sois parientes?

re·la·tion [rɪ'leɪʃn] *in family* pariente *m/f*, *(connection)* relación *f*; **business / diplomatic ~s** relaciones *fpl* comerciales / diplomáticas

re·la·tion·ship [rɪ'leɪʃnʃɪp] relación *f*

rel·a·tive ['relətɪv] **1** *n* pariente *m/f* **2** *adj* relativo; **X is ~ to Y** X está relacionado con Y

rel·a·tive·ly ['relətɪvlɪ] *adv* relativamente

re·lax [rɪ'læks] **1** *v/i* relajarse; **~!, don't get angry** ¡tranquilízate!, no te enfades **2** *v/t muscle, pace* relajar

re·lax·a·tion [riːlæk'seɪʃn] relajación *f*; **what do you do for ~?** ¿qué haces para relajarte?

re·laxed [rɪ'lækst] *adj* relajado

re·lax·ing [rɪ'læksɪŋ] *adj* relajante

re·lay [riː'leɪ] **1** *v/t message* pasar; *radio, TV signals* retransmitir **2** *n*: **~ (race)** carrera *f* de relevos

re·lease [rɪ'liːs] **1** *n from prison* liberación *f*, puesta *f* en libertad; *of CD etc* lanzamiento *m*; *CD, record* trabajo *m* **2** *v/t prisoner* liberar, poner en libertad; *parking brake* soltar; *information* hacer público

rel·e·gate ['relɪgeɪt] *v/t* relegar

re·lent [rɪ'lent] *v/i* ablandarse, ceder

re·lent·less [rɪ'lentlɪs] *adj (determined)* implacable; *rain etc* que no cesa

re·lent·less·ly [rɪ'lentlɪslɪ] *adv* implacablemente; *rain* sin cesar

rel·e·vance ['relʌvəns] pertinencia *f*

rel·e·vant ['relʌvənt] *adj* pertinente

re·li·a·bil·i·ty [rɪlaɪə'bɪlətɪ] fiabilidad *f*

re·li·a·ble [rɪ'laɪəbl] *adj* fiable; *information* fiable, fidedigna

re·li·a·bly [rɪ'laɪəblɪ] *adv*: **I am ~ informed that** sé de buena fuente que

re·li·ance [rɪ'laɪəns] confianza *f*, dependencia *f*; **~ on s.o. / sth** confianza en alguien / algo, dependencia de alguien / algo

re·li·ant [rɪ'laɪənt] *adj*: **be ~ on** depender de

rel·ic ['relɪk] reliquia *f*

re·lief [rɪ'liːf] alivio *m*; **that's a ~** qué alivio; **in ~** *in art* en relieve

re·lieve [rɪ'liːv] *v/t pressure, pain* aliviar; *(take over from)* relevar; **be ~d** *at news etc* sentirse aliviado

re·li·gion [rɪ'lɪdʒən] religión *f*

re·li·gious [rɪ'lɪdʒəs] *adj* religioso

re·li·gious·ly [rɪ'lɪdʒəslɪ] *adv (conscientiously)* religiosamente

re·lin·quish [rɪ'lɪŋkwɪʃ] *v/t* renunciar a

rel·ish ['relɪʃ] **1** *n sauce* salsa *f*; *(enjoyment)* goce *m* **2** *v/t idea, prospect* gozar con; **I don't ~ the idea** la idea no me entusiasma

re·live [riː'lɪv] *v/t the past, an event* revivir

re·lo·cate [riːlə'keɪt] *v/i of business, employee* trasladarse

re·lo·ca·tion [riːlə'keɪʃn] *of business, employee* traslado *m*

re·luc·tance [rɪ'lʌktəns] reticencia *f*

re·luc·tant [rɪ'lʌktənt] *adj* reticente, reacio; **be ~ to do sth** ser reacio a hacer algo

re·luc·tant·ly [rɪ'lʌktəntlɪ] *adv* con reticencia

♦ **re·ly on** [rɪ'laɪ] *v/t (pret & pp -ied)* depender de; **rely on s.o. to do sth** contar con alguien para hacer algo

re·main [rɪ'meɪn] *v/i (be left)* quedar; *(stay)* permanecer

re·main·der [rɪ'meɪndər] **1** *n also* MATH resto *m* **2** *v/t* vender como saldo

re·main·ing [rɪ'meɪnɪŋ] *adj* restante

re·mains [rɪ'meɪnz] *npl of body* restos *mpl* (mortales)

re·make ['riːmeɪk] *n of movie* nueva versión *f*

re·mand [rɪ'mænd] **1** *v/t:* **~ s.o. in custody** poner a alguien en prisión preventiva **2** *n:* **be on ~ in prison** estar en prisión preventiva; **on bail** estar en libertad bajo fianza

re·mark [rɪ'maːrk] **1** *n* comentario *m*, observación *f* **2** *v/t* comentar, observar

re·mar·ka·ble [rɪ'maːrkəbl] *adj* notable, extraordinario

re·mar·ka·bly [rɪ'maːrkəblɪ] *adv* extraordinariamente

re·mar·ry [riː'mærɪ] *v/i* (*pret & pp* **-ied**) volver a casarse

rem·e·dy ['remədɪ] *n* MED, *fig* remedio *m*

re·mem·ber [rɪ'membər] **1** *v/t s.o., sth* recordar, acordarse de; **~ to lock the door** acuérdate de cerrar la puerta; **~ me to her** dale recuerdos de mi parte **2** *v/i* recordar, acordarse; **I don't ~** no recuerdo, no me acuerdo

re·mind [rɪ'maɪnd] *v/t:* **~ s.o. of sth** recordar algo a alguien; **~ s.o. of s.o.** recordar alguien a alguien; **you ~ me of your father** me recuerdas a tu padre

re·mind·er [rɪ'maɪndər] recordatorio *m*; *for payment* recordatorio *m* de pago

rem·i·nisce [remɪ'nɪs] *v/i* contar recuerdos

rem·i·nis·cent [remɪ'nɪsənt] *adj:* **be ~ of sth** recordar a algo, tener reminiscencias de algo

re·miss [rɪ'mɪs] *adj fml* negligente, descuidado

re·mis·sion [rɪ'mɪʃn] remisión *f*; **go into ~** MED remitir

rem·nant ['remnənt] resto *m*

re·morse [rɪ'mɔːrs] remordimientos *mpl*

re·morse·less [rɪ'mɔːrslɪs] *adj person* despiadado; *pace, demands* implacable

re·mote [rɪ'moʊt] *adj village, possibility* remoto; (*aloof*) distante; *ancestor* lejano

re·mote 'ac·cess COMPUT acceso *m* remoto

re·mote con'trol control *m* remoto; *for TV* mando *m* a distancia

re·mote·ly [rɪ'moʊtlɪ] *adv related, connected* remotamente; **it's just ~ possible** es una posibilidad muy remota

re·mote·ness [rɪ'moʊtnəs]: **the ~ of the house** la lejanía *or* lo aislado de la casa

re·mov·a·ble [rɪ'muːvəbl] *adj* de quita y pon

re·mov·al [rɪ'muːvl] eliminación *f*

re·move [rɪ'muːv] *v/t* eliminar; *top, lid* quitar; *coat etc* quitarse; *doubt, suspicion* despejar; *growth, organ* extirpar

re·mu·ner·a·tion [rɪmjuːnə'reɪʃn] remuneración *f*

re·mu·ner·a·tive [rɪ'mjuːnərətɪv] *adj* bien remunerado

re·name [riː'neɪm] *v/t* cambiar el nombre a

ren·der ['rendər] *v/t service* prestar; **~ s.o. helpless / unconscious** dejar a alguien indefenso / inconsciente

ren·der·ing ['rendərɪŋ] *of piece of music* interpretación *f*

ren·dez·vous ['raːndeɪvuː] *romantic* cita *f*; MIL encuentro *m*

re·new [rɪ'nuː] *v/t contract, license* renovar; *discussions* reanudar; **feel ~ed** sentirse como nuevo

re·new·al [rɪ'nuːəl] *of contract etc* renovación *f*; *of discussions* reanudación *f*

re·nounce [rɪ'naʊns] *v/t title, rights* renunciar a

ren·o·vate ['renəveɪt] *v/t* renovar

ren·o·va·tion [renə'veɪʃn] renovación *f*

re·nown [rɪ'naʊn] renombre *m*

re·nowned [rɪ'naʊnd] *adj* renombrado; **be ~ for sth** ser célebre por algo

rent [rent] **1** *n* alquiler *m*; **for ~** se alquila **2** *v/t apartment, car, equipment* alquilar, *Mex* rentar

rent·al ['rentl] *for apartment, TV* alquiler *m*, *Mex* renta *f*

'rent·al a·gree·ment acuerdo *m* de alquiler

R

'rent·al car coche *m* de alquiler

rent-'free *adv* sin pagar alquiler

re·o·pen [riːˈəʊpn] **1** *v/t* reabrir; *negotiations* reanudar **2** *v/i of theater etc* volver a abrir

re·or·gan·i·za·tion [riːɔːrgənaɪzˈeɪʃn] reorganización *f*

re·or·gan·ize [riːˈɔːrgənaɪz] *v/t* reorganizar

rep [rep] COM representante *m/f*, comercial *m/f*

re·paint [riːˈpeɪnt] *v/t* repintar

re·pair [rɪˈper] **1** *v/t fence, TV* reparar; *shoes* arreglar **2** *n to fence, TV* reparación *f*; *of shoes* arreglo *m*; **in a good/ bad state of ~** en buen/ mal estado

re'pair·man técnico *m*

re·pa·tri·ate [riːˈpætrɪeɪt] *v/t* repatriar

re·pa·tri·a·tion [riːpætrɪˈeɪʃn] repatriación *f*

re·pay [riːˈpeɪ] *v/t* (*pret & pp* **-paid**) *money* devolver; *person* pagar

re·pay·ment [riːˈpeɪmənt] devolución *f*; *installment* plazo *m*

re·peal [rɪˈpiːl] *v/t law* revocar

re·peat [rɪˈpiːt] **1** *v/t* repetir; **am I ~ing myself?** ¿me estoy repitiendo? **2** *n TV program etc* repetición *f*

re·peat 'busi·ness COM negocio *m* que se repite

re·peat·ed [rɪˈpiːtɪd] *adj* repetido

re·peat·ed·ly [rɪˈpiːtɪdlɪ] *adv* repetidamente, repetidas veces

re·peat 'or·der COM pedido *m* repetido

re·pel [rɪˈpel] *v/t* (*pret & pp* **-led**) *invaders, attack* rechazar; *insects* repeler, ahuyentar; (*disgust*) repeler, repugnar

re·pel·lent [rɪˈpelənt] **1** *n* (*insect ~*) repelente *m* **2** *adj* repelente, repugnante

re·pent [rɪˈpent] *v/i* arrepentirse

re·per·cus·sions [riːpərˈkʌʃnz] *npl* repercusiones *fpl*

rep·er·toire [ˈrepərtwɑːr] repertorio *m*

rep·e·ti·tion [repɪˈtɪʃn] repetición *f*

re·pet·i·tive [rɪˈpetɪtɪv] *adj* repetiti-

vo

re·place [rɪˈpleɪs] *v/t* (*put back*) volver a poner; (*take the place of*) reemplazar, sustituir

re·place·ment [rɪˈpleɪsmənt] *person* sustituto(-a) *m(f)*; *thing* recambio *m*, reemplazo *m*

re·place·ment 'part (pieza *f* de) recambio *m*

re·play [ˈriːpleɪ] **1** *n recording* repetición *f* (de la jugada); *match* repetición *f* (del partido) **2** *v/t match* repetir

re·plen·ish [rɪˈplenɪʃ] *v/t container* rellenar; *supplies* reaprovisionar

rep·li·ca [ˈreplɪkə] réplica *f*

re·ply [rɪˈplaɪ] **1** *n* respuesta *f*, contestación *f* **2** *v/t & v/i* (*pret & pp* **-ied**) responder, contestar

re·port [rɪˈpɔːrt] **1** *n* (*account*) informe *m*; *by journalist* reportaje *m* **2** *v/t facts* informar; *to authorities* informar de, dar parte de; **~ s.o. to the police** denunciar a alguien a la policía; **he is ~ed to be in Washington** se dice que está en Washington **3** *v/i of journalist* informar; (*present o.s.*) presentarse (**to** ante)

♦ **report to** *v/t in business* trabajar a las órdenes de

re'port card boletín *m* de evaluación

re·port·er [rɪˈpɔːrtər] reportero(-a) *m(f)*

re·pos·sess [riːpəˈzes] *v/t* COM embargar

rep·re·hen·si·ble [reprɪˈhensəbl] *adj* recriminable

rep·re·sent [reprɪˈzent] *v/t* representar

rep·re·sen·ta·tive [reprɪˈzentətɪv] **1** *n* representante *m/f*; POL representante *m/f*, diputado(-a) *m(f)* **2** *adj* (*typical*) representativo

re·press [rɪˈpres] *v/t revolt* reprimir; *feelings, laughter* reprimir, controlar

re·pres·sion [rɪˈpreʃn] POL represión *f*

re·pres·sive [rɪˈpresɪv] *adj* POL represivo

re·prieve [rɪˈpriːv] **1** *n* LAW indulto *m*; *fig* aplazamiento *m* **2** *v/t prisoner* indultar

rep·ri·mand ['reprɪmænd] *v/t* reprender

re·print ['riːprɪnt] **1** *n* reimpresión *f* **2** *v/t* reimprimir

re·pri·sal [rɪ'praɪzl] represalia *f*; **take ~s** tomar represalias; **in ~ for** en represalia por

re·proach [rɪ'prəʊtʃ] **1** *n* reproche *m*; **be beyond ~** ser irreprochable **2** *v/t*: **~ s.o. for sth** reprochar algo a alguien

re·proach·ful [rɪ'prəʊtʃfəl] *adj* de reproche

re·proach·ful·ly [rɪ'prəʊtʃfəlɪ] *adv* *look* con una mirada de reproche; *say* con tono de reproche

re·pro·duce [riːprə'djuːs] **1** *v/t atmosphere, mood* reproducir **2** *v/i* BIO reproducirse

re·pro·duc·tion [riːprə'dʌkʃn] reproducción *f*

re·pro·duc·tive [rɪprə'dʌktɪv] *adj* reproductivo

rep·tile ['reptaɪl] reptil *m*

re·pub·lic [rɪ'pʌblɪk] república *f*

re·pub·li·can [rɪ'pʌblɪkn] **1** *n* republicano(-a) *m(f)*; **Republican** POL Republicano(-a) *m(f)* **2** *adj* republicano

re·pu·di·ate [rɪ'pjuːdɪeɪt] *v/t* (*deny*) rechazar

re·pul·sive [rɪ'pʌlsɪv] *adj* repulsivo

rep·u·ta·ble ['repjʊtəbl] *adj* reputado, acreditado

rep·u·ta·tion [repjʊ'teɪʃn] reputación *f*; **have a good / bad ~** tener una buena / mala reputación

re·put·ed [rep'jʊtəd] *adj*: **be ~ to be** tener fama de ser

re·put·ed·ly [rep'jʊtədlɪ] *adv* según se dice

re·quest [rɪ'kwest] **1** *n* petición *f*, solicitud *f*; **on ~** por encargo **2** *v/t* pedir, solicitar

re·qui·em ['rekwɪəm] MUS réquiem *m*

re·quire [rɪ'kwaɪr] *v/t* (*need*) requerir, necesitar; **it ~s great care** se requiere mucho cuidado; **as ~d by law** como estipula la ley; **guests are ~d to …** se ruega a los invitados que …

re·quired [rɪ'kwaɪrd] *adj* (*necessary*) necesario

re·quire·ment [rɪ'kwaɪrmənt] (*need*) necesidad *f*; (*condition*) requisito *m*

req·ui·si·tion [rekwɪ'zɪʃn] *v/t* requisar

re·route [riː'ruːt] *v/t airplane etc* desviar

re·run ['riːrʌn] **1** *n of TV program* reposición *f* **2** *v/t* (*pret* **-ran**, *pp* **-run**) *tape* volver a poner

re·sched·ule [riː'ʃeduːl] *v/t* volver a programar

res·cue ['reskjuː] **1** *n* rescate *m*; **come to s.o.'s ~** acudir al rescate de alguien **2** *v/t* rescatar

'res·cue par·ty equipo *m* de rescate

re·search [rɪ'sɜːrtʃ] *n* investigación *f*
 ♦ **research into** *v/t* investigar

re·search and de·vel·op·ment investigación *f* y desarrollo

re'search as·sis·tant ayudante *m/f* de investigación

re·search·er [rɪ'sɜːrtʃər] investigador(a) *m(f)*

re'search proj·ect proyecto *m* de investigación

re·sem·blance [rɪ'zembləns] parecido *m*, semejanza *f*

re·sem·ble [rɪ'zembl] *v/t* parecerse a

re·sent [rɪ'zent] *v/t* estar molesto por

re·sent·ful [rɪ'zentfəl] *adj* resentido

re·sent·ful·ly [rɪ'zentfəlɪ] *adv* con resentimiento

re·sent·ment [rɪ'zentmənt] resentimiento *m*

res·er·va·tion [rezər'veɪʃn] reserva *f*; **I have a ~** *in hotel, restaurant* tengo una reserva

re·serve [rɪ'zɜːrv] **1** *n* reserva *f*; SP reserva *m/f*; **~s** FIN reservas *fpl*; **keep sth in ~** tener algo en la reserva **2** *v/t seat, table* reservar; *judgment* reservarse

re·served [rɪ'zɜːrvd] *adj table, manner* reservado

res·er·voir ['rezərvwɑːr] *for water* embalse *m*, pantano *m*

re·shuf·fle ['riːʃʌfl] **1** *n* POL remodelación *f* **2** *v/t* POL remodelar

R

re·side [rɪ'zaɪd] *v/i fml* residir

res·i·dence ['rezɪdəns] *fml: house etc* residencia *f*; *(stay)* estancia *f*

'res·i·dence per·mit permiso *m* de residencia

'res·i·dent ['rezɪdənt] **1** *n* residente *m/f* **2** *adj* *(living in a building)* residente

res·i·den·tial [rezɪ'denʃl] *adj district* residencial

res·i·due ['rezɪdju:] residuo *m*

re·sign [rɪ'zaɪn] **1** *v/t position* dimitir de; **~ o.s. to** resignarse a **2** *v/i from job* dimitir

res·ig·na·tion [rezɪg'neɪʃn] *from job* dimisión *f*; *mental* resignación *f*

re·signed [re'zaɪnd] *adj* resignado; **we have become ~ to the fact that ...** nos hemos resignado a aceptar que ...

re·sil·i·ent [rɪ'zɪliənt] *adj personality* fuerte; *material* resistente

res·in ['rezɪn] resina *f*

re·sist [rɪ'zɪst] **1** *v/t* resistir; *new measures* oponer resistencia a **2** *v/i* resistir

re·sist·ance [rɪ'zɪstəns] resistencia *f*

re·sis·tant [rɪ'zɪstənt] *adj material* resistente; **~ to heat/rust** resistente al calor/a la oxidación

res·o·lute ['rezəlu:t] *adj* resuelto

res·o·lu·tion [rezə'lu:ʃn] resolución *f*; *made at New Year etc* propósito *m*

re·solve [rɪ'zɑ:lv] *v/t problem, mystery* resolver; **~ to do sth** resolver hacer algo

re·sort [rɪ'zɔ:rt] *n place* centro *m* turístico; **as a last ~** como último recurso

♦ **resort to** *v/t violence, threats* recurrir a

♦ **re·sound with** [rɪ'zaʊnd] *v/t* resonar con

re·sound·ing [rɪ'zaʊndɪŋ] *adj success, victory* clamoroso

re·source [rɪ'sɔ:rs] recurso *m*

re·source·ful [rɪ'sɔ:rsfəl] *adj person* lleno de recursos; *attitude, approach* ingenioso

re·spect [rɪ'spekt] **1** *n* respeto *m*; **show ~ to** mostrar respeto hacia; **with ~ to** con respecto a; **in this/that ~** en cuanto a esto/eso; **in many ~s** en muchos aspectos; **pay one's last ~s to s.o.** decir el último adiós a alguien **2** *v/t* respetar

re·spect·a·bil·i·ty [rɪspektə'bɪlətɪ] respetabilidad *f*

re·spec·ta·ble [rɪ'spektəbl] *adj* respetable

re·spec·ta·bly [rɪ'spektəblɪ] *adv* respetablemente

re·spect·ful [rɪ'spektfəl] *adj* respetuoso

re·spect·ful·ly [rɪ'spektfəlɪ] *adv* respetuosamente, con respeto

re·spec·tive [rɪ'spektɪv] *adj* respectivo

re·spec·tive·ly [rɪ'spektɪvlɪ] *adv* respectivamente

res·pi·ra·tion [respɪ'reɪʃn] respiración *f*

res·pi·ra·tor [respɪ'reɪtər] MED respirador *m*

re·spite ['respaɪt] respiro *m*; **without ~** sin respiro

re·spond [rɪ'spɑ:nd] *v/i* responder

re·sponse [rɪ'spɑ:ns] respuesta *f*

re·spon·si·bil·i·ty [rɪspɑ:nsɪ'bɪlətɪ] responsabilidad *f*; **accept ~ for** aceptar responsabilidad de; **a job with more ~** un trabajo con más responsabilidad

re·spon·si·ble [rɪ'spɑ:nsəbl] *adj* responsable (*for* de); *job* de responsabilidad

re·spon·sive [rɪ'spɑ:nsɪv] *adj brakes* que responde bien; **a ~ audience** una audiencia que muestra interés

rest[1] [rest] **1** *n* descanso *m*; **he needs a ~** necesita descansar; **set s.o.'s mind at ~** tranquilizar a alguien **2** *v/i* descansar; **~ on** *of theory, box* apoyarse en; **it all ~s with him** todo depende de él **3** *v/t* (*lean, balance*) apoyar

rest[2] [rest]: **the ~** el resto

res·tau·rant ['restrɑ:nt] restaurante *m*

'res·tau·rant car vagón *m* or coche *m* restaurante

'rest cure cura *f* de reposo *or* descanso

rest·ful ['restfəl] *adj* tranquilo, relajante

'**rest home** residencia *f* de ancianos

rest·less ['restlɪs] *adj* inquieto; *have a ~ night* pasar una mala noche

rest·less·ly ['restlɪslɪ] *adv* sin descanso

res·to·ra·tion [restə'reɪʃn] restauración *f*

re·store [rɪ'stɔːr] *v/t building etc* restaurar; *(bring back)* devolver

re·strain [rɪ'streɪn] *v/t* contener; *~ o.s.* contenerse

re·straint [rɪ'streɪnt] *(moderation)* moderación *f*, comedimiento *m*

re·strict [rɪ'strɪkt] *v/t* restringir, limitar; *I'll ~ myself to …* me limitaré a …

re·strict·ed [rɪ'strɪktɪd] *adj view* limitado

re·strict·ed 'ar·e·a MIL zona *f* de acceso restringido

re·stric·tion [rɪ'strɪkʃn] restricción *f*, limitación *f*; *place ~s upon s.o.* imponer restricciones *or* limitaciones a alguien

'**rest room** aseo *m*, servicios *mpl*

re·sult [rɪ'zʌlt] *n* resultado *m*; *as a ~ of this* como resultado de esto

♦ **result from** *v/t* resultar de

♦ **result in** *v/t* tener como resultado

re·sume [rɪ'zjuːm] **1** *v/t* reanudar **2** *v/i* continuar

ré·su·mé ['rezʊmeɪ] currículum *m* (vitae)

re·sump·tion [rɪ'zʌmpʃn] reanudación *f*

re·sur·face [riː'sɜːfɪs] **1** *v/t roads* volver a asfaltar **2** *v/i (reappear)* reaparecer

res·ur·rec·tion [rezə'rekʃn] REL resurrección *f*

re·sus·ci·tate [rɪ'sʌsɪteɪt] *v/t* resucitar, revivir

re·sus·ci·ta·tion [rɪsʌsɪ'teɪʃn] resucitación *f*

re·tail ['riːteɪl] **1** *adv*: *sell sth ~* vender algo al por menor **2** *v/i*: *it ~s at …* su precio de venta al público es de …

re·tail·er ['riːteɪlər] minorista *m/f*

'**re·tail out·let** punto *m* de venta

'**re·tail price** precio *m* de venta al público

re·tain [rɪ'teɪn] *v/t* conservar; *heat* retener

re·tain·er [rɪ'teɪnər] FIN anticipo *m*

re·tal·i·ate [rɪ'tælɪeɪt] *v/i* tomar represalias

re·tal·i·a·tion [rɪtælɪ'eɪʃn] represalias *fpl*; *in ~ for* como represalia por

re·tard·ed [rɪ'tɑːrdɪd] *adj mentally* retrasado mental

re·think [riː'θɪŋk] *v/t (pret & pp -thought)* replantear

ret·i·cence ['retɪsns] reserva *f*

ret·i·cent ['retɪsnt] *adj* reservado

re·tire [rɪ'taɪr] *v/i from work* jubilarse

re·tired [rɪ'taɪrd] *adj* jubilado

re·tire·ment [rɪ'taɪrmənt] jubilación *f*

re'tire·ment age edad *f* de jubilación

re·tir·ing [rɪ'taɪrɪŋ] *adj* retraído, reservado

re·tort [rɪ'tɔːrt] **1** *n* réplica *f* **2** *v/t* replicar

re·trace [rɪ'treɪs] *v/t*: *they ~d their footsteps* volvieron sobre sus pasos

re·tract [rɪ'trækt] *v/t claws* retraer; *undercarriage* replegar; *statement* retirar

re·train [riː'treɪn] *v/i* reciclarse

re·treat [rɪ'triːt] **1** *v/i* retirarse **2** *n* MIL retirada *f*; *place* retiro *m*

re·trieve [rɪ'triːv] *v/t* recuperar

re·triev·er [rɪ'triːvər] *dog* perro *m* cobrador

ret·ro·ac·tive [retroʊ'æktɪv] *adj law etc* retroactivo

ret·ro·ac·tive·ly [retroʊ'æktɪvlɪ] *adv* con retroactividad

ret·ro·grade ['retrəgreɪd] *adj move, decision* retrógrado

ret·ro·spect ['retrəspekt]: *in ~* en retrospectiva

ret·ro·spec·tive [retrə'spektɪv] *n* retrospectiva *f*

re·turn [rɪ'tɜːrn] **1** *n to a place* vuelta *f*, regreso *m*; *(giving back)* devolución *f*; COMPUT retorno *m*; *in tennis* resto

R

m; (*profit*) rendimiento m; *Br ticket* billete m *or L.Am.* boleto m de ida y vuelta; **by ~ (of post)** a vuelta de correo; **many happy ~s (of the day)** feliz cumpleaños; **in ~ for** a cambio de **2** v/t devolver; (*put back*) volver a colocar **3** v/i (*go back, come back*) volver, regresar; *of good times, doubts etc* volver

re•turn 'flight vuelo m de vuelta

re•turn 'jour•ney viaje m de vuelta

re•u•ni•fi•ca•tion [riːjuːnɪfɪˈkeɪʃn] reunificación f

re•u•nion [riːˈjuːnjən] reunión f

re•u•nite [riːjuːˈnaɪt] v/t reunir

re•us•a•ble [riːˈjuːzəbl] *adj* reutilizable

re•use [riːˈjuːz] v/t reutilizar

rev [rev] n revolución f; **~s per minute** revoluciones por minuto

♦ rev up v/t (*pret & pp* **-ved**) *engine* revolucionar

re•val•u•a•tion [riːvæljʊˈeɪʃn] revaluación f

re•veal [rɪˈviːl] v/t (*make visible*) revelar; (*make known*) revelar, desvelar

re•veal•ing [rɪˈviːlɪŋ] *adj remark* revelador; *dress* insinuante, atrevido

♦ rev•el in ['revl] v/t (*pret & pp* **-ed**, *Br* **-led**) deleitarse con

rev•e•la•tion [revəˈleɪʃn] revelación f

re•venge [rɪˈvendʒ] n venganza f; **take one's ~** vengarse; **in ~ for** como venganza por

rev•e•nue ['revənuː] ingresos mpl

re•ver•be•rate [rɪˈvɜːrbəreɪt] v/i *of sound* reverberar

re•vere [rɪˈvɪr] v/t reverenciar

rev•e•rence ['revərəns] reverencia f

Rev•e•rend ['revərənd] REL Reverendo m

rev•e•rent ['revərənt] *adj* reverente

re•verse [rɪˈvɜːrs] **1** *adj sequence* inverso; **in ~ order** en orden inverso **2** n (*back*) dorso m; MOT marcha f atrás; **the ~** (*the opposite*) lo contrario **3** v/t *sequence* invertir; **~ a vehicle** hacer marcha atrás con un vehículo **4** v/i MOT hacer marcha atrás

re•vert [rɪˈvɜːrt] v/i: **~ to** volver a

re•view [rɪˈvjuː] **1** n *of book, movie* reseña f, crítica f; *of troops* revista f; *of situation etc* revisión f **2** v/t *book, movie* reseñar, hacer una crítica de; *troops* pasar revista a; *situation etc* revisar; EDU repasar

re•view•er [rɪˈvjuːər] *of book, movie* crítico(-a) m(f)

re•vise [rɪˈvaɪz] v/t *opinion, text* revisar

re•vi•sion [rɪˈvɪʒn] *of opinion, text* revisión f

re•viv•al [rɪˈvaɪvl] *of custom, old style etc* resurgimiento m; *of patient* reanimación f

re•vive [rɪˈvaɪv] **1** v/t *custom, old style etc* hacer resurgir; *patient* reanimar **2** v/i *of business, exchange rate etc* reactivarse

re•voke [rɪˈvoʊk] v/t *law* derogar; *license* revocar

re•volt [rɪˈvoʊlt] **1** n rebelión f **2** v/i rebelarse

re•volt•ing [rɪˈvoʊltɪŋ] *adj* (*disgusting*) repugnante

rev•o•lu•tion [revəˈluːʃn] POL revolución f; (*turn*) vuelta f, revolución f

rev•o•lu•tion•a•ry [revəˈluːʃn ərɪ] **1** n POL revolucionario(-a) m(f) **2** *adj* revolucionario

rev•o•lu•tion•ize [revəˈluːʃnaɪz] v/t revolucionar

re•volve [rɪˈvaːlv] v/i girar (**around** en torno a)

re•volv•er [rɪˈvaːlvər] revólver m

re•volv•ing 'door [rɪˈvaːlvɪŋ] puerta f giratoria

re•vue [rɪˈvjuː] THEA revista f

re•vul•sion [rɪˈvʌlʃn] repugnancia f

re•ward [rɪˈwɔːrd] **1** n recompensa f **2** v/t *financially* recompensar

re•ward•ing [rɪˈwɔːrdɪŋ] *adj experience* gratificante

re•wind [riːˈwaɪnd] v/t (*pret & pp* **-wound**) *film, tape* rebobinar

re•write [riːˈraɪt] v/t (*pret* **-wrote**, pp **-written**) reescribir

rhe•to•ric ['retərɪk] retórica f

rhe•to•ric•al 'ques•tion [rɪˈtɑːrɪkl] pregunta f retórica

rheu•ma•tism ['ruːmətɪzm] reumatismo *m*

rhi·no·ce·ros [raɪ'nɑːsərəs] rinoceronte *m*

rhu·barb |'ruːbɑːrb] ruibarbo *m*

rhyme [raɪm] **1** *n* rima *f* **2** *v/i* rimar

rhythm ['rɪðm] ritmo *m*

rib [rɪb] ANAT costilla *f*

rib·bon ['rɪbən] cinta *f*

rice [raɪs] arroz *m*

rich [rɪtʃ] **1** *adj* (*wealthy*) rico; *food* sabroso; *it's too ~* es muy pesado **2** *npl*: *the ~* los ricos

rich·ly ['rɪtʃlɪ] *adv*: *be ~ deserved* ser muy merecido

rick·et·y ['rɪkətɪ] *adj* desvencijado

ric·o·chet ['rɪkəʃeɪ] *v/i* rebotar

rid [rɪd]: *get ~ of* deshacerse de

rid·dance ['rɪdns] F: *good ~ to her!* ¡espero no volver a verla nunca!

rid·den ['rɪdn] *pp* → **ride**

rid·dle ['rɪdl] **1** *n* acertijo *m* **2** *v/t*: *be ~d with* estar lleno de

ride [raɪd] **1** *n* on horse, in vehicle paseo *m*, vuelta *f*; (*journey*) viaje *m*; *do you want a ~ into town?* ¿quieres que te lleve al centro? **2** *v/t* (*pret rode*, *pp ridden*) *horse* montar a; *bike* montar en **3** *v/i* (*pret rode*, *pp ridden*) *on horse* montar; *can you ~?* ¿sabes montar?; *those who were riding at the back of the bus* los que iban en la parte de atrás del autobús

rid·er ['raɪdər] *on horse* jinete *m*, amazona *f*; *on bicycle* ciclista *m/f*; *on motorbike* motorista *m/f*

ridge [rɪdʒ] *raised strip* borde *m*; *of mountain* cresta *f*, *of roof* caballete *m*

rid·i·cule ['rɪdɪkjuːl] **1** *n* burlas *fpl* **2** *v/t* ridiculizar, poner en ridículo

ri·dic·u·lous [rɪ'dɪkjʊləs] *adj* ridículo

ri·dic·u·lous·ly [rɪ'dɪkjʊləslɪ] *adv expensive, difficult* terriblemente; *it's ~ easy* es facilísimo

rid·ing ['raɪdɪŋ] *on horseback* equitación *f*

ri·fle ['raɪfl] *n* rifle *m*

rift [rɪft] *in earth* grieta *f*; *in party etc* escisión *f*

rig [rɪg] **1** *n* (*oil ~*) plataforma *f* petrolífera; (*truck*) camión *m* **2** *v/t* (*pret & pp -ged*) *elections* amañar

right [raɪt] **1** *adj* (*correct*) correcto; (*suitable*) adecuado, apropiado; (*not left*) derecho; *it's not ~ to treat people like that* no está bien tratar así a la gente; *it's the ~ thing to do* es lo que hay que hacer; *be ~ of answer* estar correcto; *of person* tener razón; *of clock* ir bien; *put things ~* arreglar las cosas; *that's ~!* ¡eso es!; *that's all ~ doesn't matter* no te preocupes; *when s.o. says thank you de nada*; *is quite good* está bastante bien; *I'm all ~ not hurt* estoy bien; *have got enough* no, gracias; *all ~, that's enough!* ¡ahora sí que ya está bien! **2** *adv* (*directly*) justo; (*correctly*) correctamente; (*not left*) a la derecha; *he broke it ~ off* lo rompió por completo; *~ back in 1982* allá en 1982; *~ now* ahora mismo **3** *n* civil, legal etc derecho *m*; *not left*, POL derecha *f*; *on the ~ also* POL a la derecha; *turn to the ~, take a ~* gira a la derecha; *be in the ~* tener razón; *know ~ from wrong* distinguir lo que está bien de lo que está mal

right-'an·gle ángulo *m* recto; *at ~s to* en *or* formando ángulo recto con

right·ful ['raɪtfəl] *adj heir, owner etc* legítimo

'right-hand *adj*: *on the ~ side* a mano derecha; **right-hand 'drive** *n* MOT vehículo *m* con el volante a la derecha; **right-hand·ed** [raɪt'hændɪd] *adj person* diestro; **right-hand 'man** mano *f* derecha; **right of 'way** *in traffic* preferencia *f*; *across land* derecho *m* de paso; **right 'wing** *n* POL derecha *f*; SP banda *f* derecha; **right-'wing** *adj* POL de derechas; **right-'wing·er** POL derechista *m/f*; **right-wing ex'trem·ism** POL extremismo *m* de derechas

rig·id ['rɪdʒɪd] *adj* rígido

rig·or ['rɪgər] *of discipline* rigor *m*; *the ~s of the winter* los rigores del invierno

rig·or·ous ['rɪgərəs] *adj* riguroso

R

rig·or·ous·ly [ˈrɪɡərəslɪ] *adv* check, *examine* rigurosamente

rig·our *Br* → *rigor*

rile [raɪl] *v/t* F fastidiar, *Span* mosquear F

rim [rɪm] *of wheel* llanta *f*; *of cup* borde *m*; *of eye glasses* montura *f*

ring¹ [rɪŋ] *n* (*circle*) círculo *m*; *on finger* anillo *m*; *in boxing* cuadrilátero *m*, ring *m*; *at circus* pista *f*

ring² [rɪŋ] **1** *n of bell* timbrazo *m*; *of voice* tono *m*; **give s.o. a ~** *Br* TELEC dar un telefonazo a alguien **2** *v/t* (*pret* **rang**, *pp* **rung**) *bell* hacer sonar **3** *v/i* (*pret* **rang**, *pp* **rung**) *of bell* sonar; **please ~ for attention** toque el timbre para que lo atiendan

ˈring·lead·er cabecilla *m/f*

ˈring-pull anilla *f*

rink [rɪŋk] pista *f* de patinaje

rinse [rɪns] **1** *n for hair color* reflejo *m* **2** *v/t* aclarar

ri·ot [ˈraɪət] **1** *n* disturbio *m* **2** *v/i* causar disturbios

ri·ot·er [ˈraɪətər] alborotador(a) *m(f)*

ˈri·ot po·lice policía *f* antidisturbios

rip [rɪp] **1** *n in cloth etc* rasgadura *f* **2** *v/t* (*pret & pp* **-ped**) *cloth* rasgar; **~ sth open** romper algo rasgándolo

♦ **rip off** *v/t* F *customers* robar F, clavar F; (*cheat*) timar

♦ **rip up** *v/t letter, sheet* hacer pedazos

ripe [raɪp] *adj fruit* maduro

rip·en [ˈraɪpn] *v/i of fruit* madurar

ripe·ness [ˈraɪpnɪs] *of fruit* madurez *f*

ˈrip-off *n* F robo *m* F

rip·ple [ˈrɪpl] *on water* onda *f*

rise [raɪz] **1** *v/i* (*pret* **rose**, *pp* **risen**) *from chair etc* levantarse; *of sun* salir; *of rocket* ascender, subir; *of price, temperature, water* subir **2** *n in price, temperature* subida *f*, aumento *m*; *in water level* subida *f*; *in salary* aumento *m*; **give ~ to** dar pie a

ris·en [ˈrɪzn] *pp* → *rise*

ris·er [ˈraɪzər]: **be an early ~** ser un madrugador; **be a late ~** levantarse tarde

risk [rɪsk] **1** *n* riesgo *m*, peligro *m*; **take a ~** arriesgarse **2** *v/t* arriesgar;

let's ~ it arriesguémonos

risk·y [ˈrɪskɪ] *adj* arriesgado

ris·qué [rɪˈskeɪ] *adj* subido de tono

rit·u·al [ˈrɪtʊəl] **1** *n* ritual *m* **2** *adj* ritual

ri·val [ˈraɪvl] **1** *n* rival *m/f* **2** *v/t* (*pret & pp* **-ed**, *Br* **-led**) rivalizar con; **I can't ~ that** no puedo rivalizar con eso

ri·val·ry [ˈraɪvlrɪ] rivalidad *f*

riv·er [ˈrɪvər] río *m*

ˈriv·er·bank ribera *f*; **ˈriv·er·bed** lecho *m*; **Riv·er 'Plate**: **the ~** el Río de la Plata; **ˈriv·er·side 1** *adj* a la orilla del río **2** *n* ribera *f*, orilla *f* del río

riv·et [ˈrɪvɪt] **1** *n* remache *m* **2** *v/t* remachar; **~ sth to sth** unir algo a algo con remaches

riv·et·ing [ˈrɪvɪtɪŋ] *adj* fascinante

road [roʊd] *in country* carretera *f*; *in city* calle *f*; **it's just down the ~** está muy cerca

ˈroad·block control *m* de carretera; **ˈroad hog** *conductor(a)* temerario(-a); **ˈroad-hold·ing** *of vehicle* adherencia *f*, agarre *m*; **ˈroad map** mapa *m* de carreteras; **road 'safe·ty** seguridad *f* vial; **ˈroad·side**: **at the ~** al borde de la carretera; **ˈroad-sign** señal *f* de tráfico; **ˈroad·way** calzada *f*; **ˈroad-wor·thy** *adj* en condiciones de circular

roam [roʊm] *v/i* vagar

roar [rɔːr] **1** *n of traffic, engine* estruendo *m*; *of lion* rugido *m*; *of person* grito *m*, bramido *m* **2** *v/i of engine, lion* rugir; *of person* gritar, bramar; **~ with laughter** reírse a carcajadas

roast [roʊst] **1** *n of beef etc* asado *m* **2** *v/t* asar **3** *v/i of food* asarse; **we're ~ing** nos estamos asando

roast 'beef rosbif *m*

roast 'pork cerdo *m* asado

rob [rɑːb] *v/t* (*pret & pp* **-bed**) *person* robar a; *bank* atracar, robar; **I've been ~bed** me han robado

rob·ber [ˈrɑːbər] atracador(a) *m(f)*

rob·ber·y [ˈrɑːbərɪ] atraco *m*, robo *m*

R *(margin tab)*

robe [roʊb] *of judge* toga *f; of priest* sotana *f; (bath~)* bata *f*

rob·in ['rɑːbɪn] petirrojo *m*

ro·bot ['roʊbɑːt] robot *m*

ro·bust [roʊ'bʌst] *adj person, structure* robusto; *material* resistente; **be in ~ health** tener una salud de hierro

rock [rɑːk] **1** *n* roca *f*; MUS rock *m*; **on the ~s** *of drink* con hielo; *their marriage is on the ~s* su matrimonio está en crisis **2** *v/t baby* acunar; *cradle* mecer; *(surprise)* sorprender, impactar **3** *v/i on chair* mecerse; *of boat* balancearse

'**rock band** grupo *m* de rock; **rock 'bot·tom**: *reach ~* tocar fondo; '**rock-bot·tom** *adj prices* mínimo; '**rock climb·er** escalador(a) *m(f)*; '**rock climb·ing** escalada *f* (en roca)

rock·et ['rɑːkɪt] **1** *n* cohete *m* **2** *v/i of prices etc* dispararse

rock·ing chair ['rɑːkɪŋ] mecedora *f*

'**rock·ing horse** caballito *m* de juguete

rock 'n' roll [rɑːkn'roʊl] rock and roll *m*

'**rock star** estrella *f* del rock

rock·y ['rɑːkɪ] *adj beach, path* pedregoso

rod [rɑːd] vara *f; for fishing* caña *f*

rode [roʊd] *pret* → **ride**

ro·dent ['roʊdnt] roedor *m*

rogue [roʊg] granuja *m/f*, bribón(-ona) *m(f)*

role [roʊl] papel *m*

'**role mod·el** ejemplo *m*

roll [roʊl] **1** *n (bread ~)* panecillo *m; of film* rollo *m; of thunder* retumbo *m; (list, register)* lista *f* **2** *v/i of ball etc* rodar; *of boat* balancearse **3** *v/t: ~ sth into a ball* hacer una bola con algo; *~ sth along the ground* hacer rodar algo por el suelo

♦ **roll over 1** *v/i* darse la vuelta **2** *v/t person, object* dar la vuelta a; *(renew)* renovar; *(extend)* refinanciar

♦ **roll up 1** *v/t sleeves* remangar **2** *v/i* F *(arrive)* llegar

'**roll-call** lista *f*

roll·er ['roʊlər] *for hair* rulo *m*

'**roll·er blade®** *n* patín *m* en línea; '**roll·er blind** *Br* persiana *f*; **roll·er coast·er** ['roʊlərkoʊstər] montaña *f* rusa; '**roll·er skate** *n* patín *m* (de ruedas)

'**roll·ing pin** ['roʊlɪŋ] rodillo *m* de cocina

ROM [rɑːm] COMPUT *abbr (= read only memory)* ROM *f* (= memoria *f* de sólo lectura)

Ro·man ['roʊmən] **1** *adj* romano **2** *n* romano(-a) *m(f)*

Ro·man 'Cath·o·lic 1 *n* REL católico(-a) *m(f)* romano(-a) *m(f)* **2** *adj* católico romano

ro·mance [rə'mæns] *n (affair)* aventura *f* (amorosa); *novel* novela *f* rosa; *movie* película *f* romántica

ro·man·tic [roʊ'mæntɪk] *adj* romántico

ro·man·tic·al·ly [roʊ'mæntɪklɪ] *adv*: **be ~ involved with s.o.** tener un romance con alguien

roof [ruːf] techo *m*, tejado *m*; **have a ~ over one's head** tener un techo donde dormir

'**roof-rack** MOT baca *f*

rook·ie ['rʊkɪ] F novato(-a) *m(f)*

room [ruːm] habitación *f; (space)* espacio *m*, sitio *m*; **there's no ~ for ...** no hay sitio para ..., no cabe ...

'**room clerk** recepcionista *m/f*; '**room·mate** *sharing room* compañero(-a) *m(f)* de habitación; *sharing apartment* compañero(-a) *m(f)* de apartamento; '**room ser·vice** servicio *m* de habitaciones; **room 'tem·per·a·ture** temperatura *f* ambiente

room·y ['ruːmɪ] *adj house, car etc* espacioso; *clothes* holgado

root [ruːt] *n* raíz *f*; **~s** *of person* raíces *fpl*

♦ **root for** *v/t* F apoyar

♦ **root out** *v/t (get rid of)* cortar de raíz; *(find)* encontrar

rope [roʊp] cuerda *f; thick* soga *f*; **show s.o. the ~s** F poner a alguien al tanto

♦ **rope off** *v/t* acordonar

R

ro·sa·ry ['rouzəri] REL rosario *m*
rose¹ [rouz] BOT rosa *f*
rose² [rouz] *pret → rise*
rose·ma·ry ['rouzmeri] romero *m*
ros·ter ['rɑːstər] turnos *mpl; actual document* calendario *m* con los turnos
ros·trum ['rɑːstrəm] estrado *m*
ros·y ['rouzi] *adj cheeks* sonrosado; *future* de color de rosa
rot [rɑːt] **1** *n in wood* putrefacción *f* **2** *v/i* (*pret & pp* **-ted**) *of food, wood* pudrirse; *of teeth* cariarse
ro·tate [rou'teit] **1** *v/i of blades, earth* girar **2** *v/t* hacer girar; *crops* rotar
ro·ta·tion [rou'teiʃn] *around the sun etc* rotación *f*; *do sth in ~* hacer algo por turnos rotatorios
rot·ten ['rɑːtn] *adj food, wood etc* podrido; F *weather, luck* horrible; *that was a ~ trick* F ¡qué mala idea!
rough [rʌf] **1** *adj surface, ground* accidentado; *hands, skin* áspero; *voice* ronco; (*violent*) bruto; *seas* bravo; (*approximate*) aproximado; *~ draft* borrador *m* **2** *adv: sleep ~* dormir a la intemperie **3** *n in golf* rough *m* **4** *v/t: ~ it* apañárselas
♦**rough up** *v/t* F dar una paliza a
rough·age ['rʌfidʒ] *in food* fibra *f*
rough·ly ['rʌfli] *adv* (*approximately*) aproximadamente; (*harshly*) brutalmente; *~ speaking* aproximadamente
rou·lette [ruː'let] ruleta *f*
round [raund] **1** *adj* redondo; *in ~ figures* en números redondos **2** *n of mailman, doctor, drinks, competition* ronda *f; of toast* rebanada *f; in boxing match* round *m*, asalto *m* **3** *v/t corner* doblar **4** *adv, prep → around*
♦**round off** *v/t edges* redondear; *meeting, night out* concluir
♦**round up** *v/t figure* redondear (hacia la cifra más alta); *suspects, criminals* detener
round·a·bout ['raundəbaut] **1** *adj route, way of saying sth* indirecto **2** *n Br on road* rotonda *f*, *Span* glorieta *f;*
'round-the-world *adj* alrededor

del mundo; **round 'trip** viaje *m* de ida y vuelta; **round trip 'tick·et** billete *m or L.Am.* boleto *m* de ida y vuelta; **'round-up** *of cattle* rodeo *m; of suspects, criminals* redada *f; of news* resumen *m*
rouse [rauz] *v/t from sleep* despertar; *interest, emotions* excitar, provocar
rous·ing ['rauzıŋ] *adj speech, finale* emocionante
route [ruːt] *n* ruta *f*, recorrido *m*
rou·tine [ruː'tiːn] **1** *adj* habitual **2** *n* rutina *f; as a matter of ~* como rutina
row¹ [rou] *n* (*line*) hilera *f*; *5 days in a ~* 5 días seguidos
row² [rou] **1** *v/t boat* llevar remando **2** *v/i* remar
row·boat ['roubout] bote *m* de remos
row·dy ['raudi] *adj* alborotador, *Span* follonero
roy·al ['rɔiəl] *adj* real
roy·al·ty ['rɔiəlti] *royal persons* realeza *f; on book, recording* derechos *mpl* de autor
rub [rʌb] *v/t* (*pret & pp* **-bed**) frotar
♦**rub down** *v/t to clean* lijar
♦**rub in** *v/t cream, ointment* extender, frotar; *don't rub it in! fig* ¡no me lo restriegues por las narices!
♦**rub off** *v/t dirt* limpiar frotando; *paint etc* borrar **2** *v/i: it rubs off on you* se te contagia
rub·ber ['rʌbər] **1** *n material* goma *f*, caucho *m;* P (*condom*) goma *f* P **2** *adj* de goma *or* caucho
rub·ber 'band goma *f* elástica
rub·ber 'gloves *npl* guantes *mpl* de goma
rub·ble ['rʌbl] escombros *mpl*
ru·by ['ruːbi] *jewel* rubí *m*
ruck·sack ['rʌksæk] mochila *f*
rud·der ['rʌdər] timón *m*
rud·dy ['rʌdi] *adj complexion* rubicundo
rude [ruːd] *adj person, behavior* maleducado, grosero; *language* grosero; *it is ~ to ...* es de mala educación ...; *I didn't mean to be ~* no pretendía faltar al respeto
rude·ly ['ruːdli] *adv* (*impolitely*) gro-

seramente

rude·ness ['ru:dnɪs] mala f educación, grosería f

ru·di·men·ta·ry [ru:dɪ'mentərɪ] *adj* rudimentario

ru·di·ments ['ru:dɪmənts] *npl* rudimentos *mpl*

rue·ful ['ru:fəl] *adj* arrepentido, compungido

rue·ful·ly ['ru:fəlɪ] *adv* con arrepentimiento

ruf·fi·an ['rʌfɪən] rufián *m*

ruf·fle ['rʌfl] **1** *n on dress* volante *m* **2** *v/t hair* despeinar; *clothes* arrugar; *person* alterar; **get ~d** alterarse

rug [rʌg] alfombra *f*; (*blanket*) manta *f* (*de viaje*)

rug·by ['rʌgbɪ] rugby *m*

'**rug·by match** partido *m* de rugby

'**rug·by play·er** jugador(a) *m(f)* de rugby

rug·ged ['rʌgɪd] *adj scenery, cliffs* escabroso, accidentado; *face* de rasgos duros; *resistance* decidido

ru·in ['ru:ɪn] **1** *n* ruina *f*; **~s** ruinas *fpl*; **in ~s** *city, building* en ruinas; *plans, marriage* arruinado **2** *v/t* arruinar; **be ~ed** *financially* estar arruinado *or* en la ruina

rule [ru:l] **1** *n of club, game* regla *f*, norma *f*; *of monarch* reinado *m*; *for measuring* regla *f*; **as a ~** por regla general **2** *v/t country* gobernar; **the judge ~d that ...** el juez dictaminó que ...; **3** *v/i of monarch* reinar

♦ **rule out** *v/t* descartar

rul·er ['ru:lər] *for measuring* regla *f*; *of state* gobernante *m/f*

rul·ing ['ru:lɪŋ] **1** *n* fallo *m*, decisión *f* **2** *adj party* gobernante, en el poder

rum [rʌm] *n drink* ron *m*

rum·ble ['rʌmbl] *v/i of stomach* gruñir; *of thunder* retumbar

♦ **rum·mage around** ['rʌmɪdʒ] *v/i* buscar revolviendo

'**rum·mage sale** rastrillo *m* benéfico

ru·mor, *Br* **ru·mour** ['ru:mər] **1** *n* rumor *m* **2** *v/t*: **it is ~ed that ...** se rumorea que ...

rump [rʌmp] *of animal* cuartos *mpl* traseros

rum·ple ['rʌmpl] *v/t clothes, paper* arrugar

rump'steak filete *m* de lomo

run [rʌn] **1** *n on foot, in pantyhose* carrera *f*; *Br: in car* viaje *m*; carrera *f*; THEA: *of play* temporada *f*; **it has had a three year ~** *of play* lleva tres años en cartel; **go for a ~** ir a correr; **make a ~ for it** salir corriendo; **a criminal on the ~** un criminal fugado; **in the short / long ~** a corto / largo plazo; **a ~ on the dollar** un movimiento especulativo contra el dólar **2** *v/i* (*pret* **ran**, *pp* **run**) *of person, animal* correr; *of river* correr, discurrir; *of paint, make-up* correrse; *of play* estar en cartel; *of engine, machine, software* funcionar; *in election* presentarse; **~ for President** presentarse a las elecciones presidenciales; **the trains ~ every ten minutes** pasan trenes cada diez minutos; **it doesn't ~ on Saturdays** *of bus, train* no funciona los sábados; **don't leave the water ~ning** no dejes el grifo abierto; **his nose is ~ning** le moquea la nariz; **her eyes are ~ning** le lloran los ojos **3** *v/t* (*pret* **ran**, *pp* **run**) *race* correr; *business, hotel, project etc* dirigir; *software* usar; *car* tener; (*use*) usar; **can I ~ you to the station?** ¿te puedo llevar hasta la estación?; **he ran his eye down the page** echó una ojeada a la página

♦ **run across** *v/t* (*meet*) encontrarse con; (*find*) encontrar

♦ **run away** *v/i* salir corriendo, huir; *from home* escaparse

♦ **run down 1** *v/t* (*knock down*) atropellar; (*criticize*) criticar; *stocks* reducir **2** *v/i of battery* agotarse

♦ **run into** *v/t* (*meet*) encontrarse con; *difficulties* tropezar con

♦ **run off 1** *v/i* salir corriendo **2** *v/t* (*print off*) tirar

♦ **run out** *v/i of contract* vencer; *of supplies* agotarse; **time has run out** se ha acabado el tiempo

♦ **run out of** *v/t time, supplies* quedarse sin; **I ran out of gas** me quedé sin

R

gasolina; *I'm running out of patience* se me está acabando la paciencia

♦ **run over 1** v/t (*knock down*) atropellar; *can we run over the details again?* ¿podríamos repasar los detalles otra vez? **2** v/i *of water etc* desbordarse

♦ **run through** v/t (*rehearse, go over*) repasar

♦ **run up** v/t *debts, large bill* acumular; *clothes* coser

run·a·way ['rʌnəweɪ] *n* persona que se ha fugado de casa

run-'down *adj person* débil, apagado; *part of town, building* ruinoso

rung[1] [rʌŋ] *of ladder* peldaño *m*

rung[2] [rʌŋ] *pp →* **ring**

run·ner ['rʌnər] *athlete* corredor(a) *m(f)*

run·ner 'beans *npl* judías *fpl* verdes, *L.Am.* porotos *mpl* verdes, *Mex* ejotes *mpl*

run·ner-'up subcampeón(-ona) *m(f)*

run·ning ['rʌnɪŋ] **1** *n* SP el correr; (*jogging*) footing *m*; *of business* gestión *f* **2** *adj: for two days ~* durante dos días seguidos

run·ning 'wa·ter agua *f* corriente

run·ny ['rʌnɪ] *adj mixture* fluido, líquido; *nose* que moquea

'run-up SP carrerilla *f*; *in the ~ to* en el periodo previo a

'run·way pista *f* (de aterrizaje / despegue)

rup·ture ['rʌptʃər] **1** *n* ruptura *f* **2** v/i *of pipe etc* romperse

ru·ral ['rʊrəl] *adj* rural

ruse [ruːz] artimaña *f*

rush [rʌʃ] **1** *n* prisa *f*; *do sth in a ~* hacer algo con prisas; *be in a ~* tener prisa; *what's the big ~?* ¿qué prisa tenemos? **2** v/t *person* meter prisa a; *meal* comer a toda prisa; *~ s.o. to the hospital* llevar a alguien al hospital a toda prisa **3** v/i darse prisa

'rush hour hora *f* punta

Rus·sia ['rʌʃə] Rusia

Rus·sian ['rʌʃən] **1** *adj* ruso **2** *n* ruso(-a) *m(f)*; *language* ruso *m*

rust [rʌst] **1** *n* óxido *m* **2** v/i oxidarse

rus·tle ['rʌsl] **1** *n of silk, leaves* susurro *m* **2** v/i *of silk, leaves* susurrar

♦ **rustle up** v/t F *meal* improvisar

'rust-proof *adj* inoxidable

rust re·mov·er ['rʌstrɪmuːvər] desoxidante *m*

rust·y ['rʌstɪ] *adj* oxidado; *my French is pretty ~* tengo el francés muy abandonado; *I'm a little ~* estoy un poco falto de forma

rut [rʌt] *in road* rodada *f*; *be in a ~ fig* estar estancado

ruth·less ['ruːθlɪs] *adj* implacable, despiadado

ruth·less·ly ['ruːθlɪslɪ] *adv* sin compasión, despiadadamente

ruth·less·ness ['ruːθlɪsnɪs] falta *f* de compasión

rye [raɪ] centeno *m*

'rye bread pan *m* de centeno

R

S

sab·bat·i·cal [sə'bætɪkl] *n year* año *m* sabático; *a 6 month ~* 6 meses de excedencia

sab·o·tage ['sæbətɑːʒ] **1** *n* sabotaje *m* **2** v/t sabotear

sab·o·teur [sæbə'tɜːr] saboteador(a) *m(f)*

sac·cha·rin ['sækərɪn] *n* sacarina *f*

sa·chet ['sæʃeɪ] *of shampoo, cream etc* sobrecito *m*

sack [sæk] **1** *n bag* saco *m*; *for groceries* bolsa *f* **2** v/t F echar

sa·cred ['seɪkrɪd] *adj* sagrado

sac·ri·fice ['sækrɪfaɪs] **1** *n* sacrificio *m*; **make ~s** *fig* hacer sacrificios **2** *v/t* sacrificar

sac·ri·lege ['sækrɪlɪdʒ] sacrilegio *m*

sad [sæd] *adj person, face, song* triste; *state of affairs* lamentable, desgraciado

sad·dle ['sædl] **1** *n* silla *f* de montar **2** *v/t horse* ensillar; **~ s.o. with sth** *fig* endilgar algo a alguien

sa·dism ['seɪdɪzm] sadismo *m*

sa·dist ['seɪdɪst] sádico(-a) *m(f)*

sa·dis·tic [sə'dɪstɪk] *adj* sádico

sad·ly ['sædlɪ] *adv look, say etc* con tristeza; *(regrettably)* lamentablemente

sad·ness ['sædnɪs] tristeza *f*

safe [seɪf] **1** *adj* seguro; *driver* prudente; *(not in danger)* a salvo; **is it - to walk here?** ¿se puede andar por aquí sin peligro? **2** *n* caja *f* fuerte

'safe·guard 1 *n* garantía *f*; **as a ~ against** como garantía contra **2** *v/t* salvaguardar

'safe·keep·ing: give sth to s.o. for ~ dar algo a alguien para que lo custodie

safe·ly ['seɪflɪ] *adv arrive* sin percances; *(successfully)* sin problemas; *drive* prudentemente; *assume* con certeza

safe·ty ['seɪftɪ] seguridad *f*

'safety belt cinturón *m* de seguridad; **'safe·ty-con·scious** *adj:* **be ~** tener en cuenta la seguridad; **safe·ty 'first** prevención *f* de accidentes; **'safe·ty pin** imperdible *m*

sag [sæg] **1** *n in ceiling etc* combadura *f* **2** *v/i (pret & pp -ged) of ceiling* combarse; *of rope* destensarse; *of tempo* disminuir

sa·ga ['sɑːgə] saga *f*

sage [seɪdʒ] *n herb* salvia *f*

Sa·git·tar·i·us [sædʒɪ'terɪəs] ASTR Sagitario *m/f inv*

said [sed] *pret & pp →* **say**

sail [seɪl] **1** *n of boat* vela *f*; *trip* viaje *m* (en barco); **go for a ~** salir a navegar **2** *v/t yacht* manejar **3** *v/i* navegar; *(depart)* zarpar, hacerse a la mar

'sail·board 1 *n* tabla *f* de windsurf **2** *v/i* hacer windsurf; **'sail·board·ing** windsurf *m*; **'sail·boat** barco *m* de vela, velero *m*

sail·ing ['seɪlɪŋ] SP vela *f*

'sail·ing ship barco de vela, velero *m*

sail·or ['seɪlər] *in the navy* marino *m/f*; *in the merchant navy*, SP marinero(-a) *m(f)*; **I'm a good/ bad ~** no me mareo/ me mareo con facilidad

saint [seɪnt] santo *m*

sake [seɪk]: **for my ~** por mí; **for the ~ of peace** por la paz

sal·ad ['sæləd] ensalada *f*

sal·ad 'dress·ing aliño *m or* aderezo *m* para ensalada

sal·a·ry ['sælərɪ] sueldo *m*, salario *m*

'sal·a·ry scale escala *f* salarial

sale [seɪl] venta *f*; *reduced prices* rebajas *fpl*; **for ~** *sign* se vende; **is this for ~?** ¿está a la venta?; **be on ~** estar a la venta; *at reduced prices* estar de rebajas

sales [seɪlz] *npl department* ventas *fpl*

'sales clerk *in store* vendedor(a) *m(f)*, dependiente(-a) *m(f)*; **'sales fig·ures** *npl* cifras *fpl* de ventas; **'sales·man** vendedor *m*; **sales 'man·ag·er** jefe(-a) *m(f)* de ventas; **'sales meet·ing** reunión *f* del departamento de ventas; **'sales·wo·man** vendedora *f*

sa·lient ['seɪlɪənt] *adj* sobresaliente, destacado

sa·li·va [sə'laɪvə] saliva *f*

salm·on ['sæmən] *(pl salmon)* salmón *m*

sa·loon [sə'luːn] *Br* MOT turismo *m*; *(bar)* bar *m*

salt [sɒːlt] **1** *n* sal *f* **2** *v/t food* salar

'salt·cel·lar salero *m*; **salt 'wa·ter** agua *f* salada; **'salt-wa·ter fish** pez *m* de agua salada

salt·y ['sɒːltɪ] *adj* salado

sal·u·tar·y ['sæljʊterɪ] *adj experience* beneficioso

sa·lute [sə'luːt] **1** *n* MIL saludo *m*; **take the ~** presidir un desfile **2** *v/t* saludar; *fig (hail)* elogiar **3** *v/i* MIL saludar

Sal·va·dor(e)·an [sælvə'dɔːrən]

1 *adj* salvadoreño **2** *n* salvadoreño(-a) *m(f)*

sal·vage ['sælvɪdʒ] *v/t from wreck* rescatar

sal·va·tion [sæl'veɪʃn] *also fig* salvación *f*

Sal·va·tion 'Ar·my Ejército *m* de Salvación

same [seɪm] **1** *adj* mismo **2** *pron*: **the** ~ lo mismo; *Happy New Year – the* ~ *to you* Feliz Año Nuevo – igualmente; *he's not the* ~ *any more* ya no es el mismo; *life isn't the* ~ *without you* la vida es distinta sin ti; *all the* ~ (*even so*) aun así; *men are all the* ~ todos los hombres son iguales; *it's all the* ~ *to me* me da lo mismo, me da igual **3** *adv*: **the** ~ igual

sam·ple ['sæmpl] *n* muestra *f*

sanc·ti·mo·ni·ous [sæŋktɪ'moʊnɪəs] *adj* mojigato

sanc·tion ['sæŋkʃn] **1** *n* (*approval*) consentimiento *m*, aprobación *f*; (*penalty*) sanción *f* **2** *v/t* (*approve*) sancionar

sanc·ti·ty ['sæŋktətɪ] carácter *m* sagrado

sanc·tu·a·ry ['sæŋktʃʊerɪ] santuario *m*

sand [sænd] **1** *n* arena *f* **2** *v/t with sandpaper* lijar

san·dal ['sændl] sandalia *f*

'sand·bag saco *m* de arena; **'sand·blast** *v/t* arenar; **'sand dune** duna *f*

sand·er ['sændər] *tool* lijadora *f*

'sand·pa·per 1 *n* lija *f* **2** *v/t* lijar

'sand·stone arenisca *f*

sand·wich ['sænwɪtʃ] **1** *n* Span bocadillo *m*, *L.Am.* sandwich *m* **2** *v/t*: *be ~ed between two …* estar encajonado entre dos …

sand·y ['sændɪ] *adj soil* arenoso; *feet, towel etc* lleno de arena; *hair* rubio oscuro; ~ *beach* playa *f* de arena

sane [seɪn] *adj* cuerdo

sang [sæŋ] *pret →* **sing**

san·i·tar·i·um [sænɪ'terɪəm] sanatorio *m*

san·i·ta·ry ['sænɪterɪ] *adj conditions* salubre, higiénico; ~ *installations* instalaciones *fpl* sanitarias

'san·i·ta·ry nap·kin compresa *f*

san·i·ta·tion [sænɪ'teɪʃn] (*sanitary installations*) instalaciones *fpl* sanitarias; (*removal of waste*) saneamiento *m*

san·i·ta·tion de·part·ment servicio *m* de limpieza

san·i·ty ['sænətɪ] razón *f*, juicio *m*

sank [sæŋk] *pret →* **sink**

San·ta Claus ['sæntəklɔːz] Papá Noel *m*, Santa Claus *m*

sap [sæp] **1** *n in tree* savia *f* **2** *v/t* (*pret & pp -ped*) *s.o.'s energy* consumir

sap·phire ['sæfaɪr] *n jewel* zafiro *m*

sar·cas·m ['sɑːrkæzm] sarcasmo *m*

sar·cas·tic [sɑːr'kæstɪk] *adj* sarcástico

sar·cas·ti·cal·ly [sɑːr'kæstɪklɪ] *adv* sarcásticamente

sar·dine [sɑːr'diːn] sardina *f*

sar·don·ic [sɑːr'dɑːnɪk] *adj* sardónico

sar·don·i·cal·ly [sɑːr'dɑːnɪklɪ] *adv* sardónicamente

sash [sæʃ] *on dress* faja *f*; *on uniform* fajín *m*

sat [sæt] *pret & pp →* **sit**

Sa·tan ['seɪtn] Satán, Satanás

sat·el·lite ['sætəlaɪt] satélite *m*

'sat·el·lite dish antena *f* parabólica

sat·el·lite T'V televisión *f* por satélite

sat·in ['sætɪn] **1** *adj* satinado **2** *n* satén *m*

sat·ire ['sætaɪr] sátira *f*

sa·tir·i·cal [sə'tɪrɪkl] *adj* satírico

sat·i·rist ['sætərɪst] escritor(a) *m(f)* de sátiras

sat·ir·ize ['sætəraɪz] *v/t* satirizar

sat·is·fac·tion [sætɪs'fækʃn] satisfacción *f*

sat·is·fac·to·ry [sætɪs'fæktərɪ] *adj* satisfactorio; (*just good enough*) suficiente

sat·is·fy ['sætɪsfaɪ] *v/t* (*pret & pp -ied*) satisfacer; *conditions* cumplir; *I am satisfied* (*had enough to eat*) estoy lleno; *I am satisfied that …* (*convinced*) estoy convencido *or* satisfecho de que …; *I hope you're*

satisfied! ¡estarás contento!

Sat·ur·day ['sætərdeɪ] sábado *m*

sauce [sɔːs] salsa *f*

'sauce·pan cacerola *f*

sau·cer ['sɔːsər] plato *m* (*de taza*)

sauc·y ['sɔːsɪ] *adj person, dress* descarado

Sa·u·di A·ra·bi·a [saʊdɪə'reɪbɪə] Arabia Saudí *or* Saudita

Sa·u·di A·ra·bi·an [saʊdɪə'reɪbɪən] **1** *adj* saudita, saudí **2** *n* saudita *m/f*, saudí *m/f*

sau·na ['sɔːnə] sauna *f*

saun·ter ['sɔːntər] *v/i* andar sin prisas

saus·age ['sɔːsɪdʒ] salchicha *f*

sav·age ['sævɪdʒ] **1** *adj animal, attack* salvaje; *criticism* feroz **2** *n* salvaje *m/f*

sav·age·ry ['sævɪdʒrɪ] crueldad *f*

save [seɪv] **1** *v/t* (*rescue*) rescatar, salvar; *money, time, effort* ahorrar; (*collect*), COMPUT guardar; *goal* parar; REL salvar **2** *v/i* (*put money aside*) ahorrar; SP hacer una parada **3** *n* SP parada *f*

♦ **save up for** *v/t* ahorrar para

sav·er ['seɪvər] *person* ahorrador(a) *m(f)*

sav·ing ['seɪvɪŋ] *amount saved, activity* ahorro *m*

sav·ings ['seɪvɪŋz] *npl* ahorros *mpl*

'sav·ings ac·count cuenta *f* de ahorros; **sav·ings and 'loan** caja *f* de ahorros; **'sav·ings bank** caja *f* de ahorros

sa·vior, *Br* **sa·viour** ['seɪvjər] REL salvador *m*

sa·vor ['seɪvər] *v/t* saborear

sa·vor·y ['seɪvərɪ] *adj not sweet* salado

sa·vour *etc Br* → **savor** *etc*

saw¹ [sɔː] **1** *n tool* serrucho *m*, sierra *f* **2** *v/t* aserrar

saw² [sɔː] *pret* → **see**

♦ **saw off** *v/t* cortar (con un serrucho)

'saw·dust serrín *m*, aserrín *m*

sax·o·phone ['sæksəfoʊn] saxofón *m*

say [seɪ] **1** *v/t* (*pret & pp* **said**) decir; *poem* recitar; *that is to* ~ es decir;

what do you ~ *to that?* ¿qué opinas de eso?; *what does the note* ~? ¿qué dice la nota?, ¿qué pone en la nota? **2** *n*: *have one's* ~ expresar una opinión

say·ing ['seɪɪŋ] dicho *m*

scab [skæb] *on skin* costra *f*

scaf·fold·ing ['skæfəldɪŋ] *on building* andamiaje *m*

scald [skɔːld] *v/t* escaldar

scale¹ [skeɪl] *on fish, reptile* escama *f*

scale² [skeɪl] **1** *n* (*size*) escala *f*, tamaño *m*; *on thermometer, map*, MUS escala *f*; *on a larger* ~ a gran escala; *on a smaller* ~ a pequeña escala **2** *v/t cliffs etc* escalar

♦ **scale down** *v/t* disminuir, reducir

scale 'draw·ing dibujo *m* a escala

scales [skeɪlz] *npl for weighing* báscula *f*, peso *m*

scal·lop ['skæləp] *n shellfish* vieira *f*

scalp [skælp] *n* cuero *m* cabelludo

scal·pel ['skælpl] bisturí *m*

scal·per ['skælpər] revendedor *m*

scam [skæm] F chanchullo *m* F

scam·pi ['skæmpɪ] gambas *fpl* rebozadas

scan [skæn] **1** *v/t* (*pret & pp* **-ned**) *horizon* otear; *page* ojear; COMPUT escanear **2** *n of brain* escáner *m*; *of fetus* ecografía *f*

♦ **scan in** *v/t* COMPUT escanear

scan·dal ['skændl] escándalo *m*

scan·dal·ize ['skændəlaɪz] *v/t* escandalizar

scan·dal·ous ['skændələs] *adj affair, prices* escandaloso

scan·ner ['skænər] MED, COMPUT escáner *m*; *for foetus* ecógrafo *m*

scant [skænt] *adj* escaso

scant·i·ly ['skæntɪlɪ] *adv*: *be* ~ *clad* andar ligero de ropa

scant·y ['skæntɪ] *adj skirt* cortísimo; *bikini* mínimo

scape·goat ['skeɪpgoʊt] cabeza *f* de turco, chivo *m* expiatorio

scar [skɑːr] **1** *n* cicatriz *f* **2** *v/t* (*pret & pp* **-red**) cicatrizar

scarce [skers] *adj in short supply* escaso; *make o.s.* ~ desaparecer

scarce·ly ['skerslɪ] *adv*: *he had* ~

S

said it when ... apenas lo había dicho cuando ...; **there was ~ anything left** no quedaba casi nada; **I ~ know her** apenas la conozco

scar·ci·ty ['skersɪtɪ] escasez *f*

scare [sker] **1** *v/t* asustar, atemorizar; **be ~d of** tener miedo de **2** *n* (*panic, alarm*) miedo *m*, temor *m*; **give s.o. a ~** dar a alguien un susto

♦ **scare away** *v/t* ahuyentar

'**scare·crow** espantapájaros *m inv*

scare·mon·ger ['skermʌŋgər] alarmista *m/f*

scarf [skɑːrf] *around neck, over head* pañuelo *m*; *woollen* bufanda *f*

scar·let ['skɑːrlət] *adj* escarlata

scar·let 'fe·ver escarlatina *f*

scar·y ['skerɪ] *adj sight* espeluznante; **~ music** música de miedo

scath·ing ['skeɪðɪŋ] *adj* feroz

scat·ter ['skætər] **1** *v/t leaflets* esparcir; *seeds* diseminar; **be ~ed all over the room** estar esparcido por toda la habitación **2** *v/i of people* dispersarse

scat·ter-brained ['skætərbreɪnd] *adj* despistado

scat·tered ['skætərd] *adj showers, family, villages* disperso

scav·enge ['skævɪndʒ] *v/i* rebuscar; **~ for sth** rebuscar en busca de algo

scav·eng·er ['skævɪndʒər] *animal, bird* carroñero *m*; (*person*) persona que busca comida entre la basura

sce·na·ri·o [sɪ'nɑːrɪoʊ] situación *f*

scene [siːn] escena *f*; *of accident, crime etc* lugar *m*; (*argument*) escena *f*, número *m*; **make a ~** hacer una escena, montar un número; **~s** THEA decorados *mpl*; **jazz/ rock ~** mundo del jazz/ rock; **behind the ~s** entre bastidores

sce·ne·ry ['siːnərɪ] THEA escenario *m*

scent [sent] *n* olor *m*; (*perfume*) perfume *m*, fragancia *f*

scep·tic *etc Br* → **skeptic** *etc*

sched·ule ['skedjuːl] **1** *n* of events, work programa *m*; *of exams* calendario *m*; *for train, work, of lessons* horario *m*; **be on ~** of work ir según lo

previsto; *of train* ir a la hora prevista; **be behind ~** *of work, train etc* ir con retraso **2** *v/t* (*put on ~*) programar; **it's ~d for completion next month** está previsto que se complete el próximo mes

sched·uled 'flight ['ʃedjuːld] vuelo *m* regular

scheme [skiːm] **1** *n* (*plan*) plan *m*, proyecto *m*; (*plot*) confabulación *f* **2** *v/i* (*plot*) confabularse

schem·ing ['skiːmɪŋ] *adj* maquinador

schiz·o·phre·ni·a [skɪtsə'friːnɪə] esquizofrenia *f*

schiz·o·phren·ic [skɪtsə'frenɪk] **1** *n* esquizofrénico(-a) *m(f)* **2** *adj* esquizofrénico

schol·ar ['skɑːlər] erudito(-a) *m(f)*

schol·ar·ly ['skɑːlərlɪ] *adj* erudito

schol·ar·ship ['skɑːlərʃɪp] (*scholarly work*) estudios *mpl*; *financial award* beca *f*

school [skuːl] *n* escuela *f*, colegio *m*; (*university*) universidad *f*

'**school bag** (*satchel*) cartera *f*; '**school·boy** escolar *m*; '**school·child·ren** *npl* escolares *mpl*; '**school days** *npl*; **do you remember your ~?** ¿te acuerdas de cuándo ibas al colegio?; '**school·girl** escolar *f*; '**school·mate** *Br* compañero *m* de colegio; '**school·teach·er** maestro(-a) *m(f)*, profesor(a) *m(f)*

sci·at·i·ca [saɪ'ætɪkə] ciática *f*

sci·ence ['saɪəns] ciencia *f*

sci·ence 'fic·tion ciencia *f* ficción

sci·en·tif·ic [saɪən'tɪfɪk] *adj* científico

sci·en·tist ['saɪəntɪst] científico(-a) *m(f)*

scis·sors ['sɪzərz] *npl* tijeras *fpl*

scoff[1] [skɑːf] *v/t* F (*eat fast*) zamparse F

scoff[2] [skɑːf] *v/i* (*mock*) burlarse, mofarse

♦ **scoff at** *v/t* burlarse de, mofarse de

scold [skoʊld] *v/t child, husband* regañar

scoop [skuːp] **1** *n implement* cuchara *f*; *of dredger* pala *f*; *story* exclusiva *f*

2 v/t: **~ sth into sth** recoger algo para meterlo en algo

♦ **scoop up** v/t recoger

scoot·er ['sku:tər] *with motor* escúter *m*; *child's* patinete *m*

scope [skoup] alcance *m*; (*freedom, opportunity*) oportunidad *f*; **he wants more ~ to do his own thing** quiere más libertad para hacer lo que quiere

scorch [skɔːrtʃ] v/t quemar

scorch·ing ['skɔːrtʃɪŋ] adj abrasador

score [skɔːr] **1** n SP resultado *m*; *in competition* puntuación *f*; (*written music*) partitura *f*; *of movie etc* banda *f* sonora, música *f*; **what's the ~?** SP ¿cómo van?; **have a ~ to settle with s.o.** tener una cuenta pendiente con alguien; **keep (the) ~** llevar el tanteo **2** v/t goal marcar; *point* anotar; (*cut: line*) marcar **3** v/i marcar; (*keep the ~*) llevar el tanteo; **that's where he ~s** ése es su punto fuerte

'**score·board** marcador *m*

scor·er ['skɔːrər] *of goal* goleador(a) *m(f)*; *of point* anotador(a) *m(f)*; (*official score-keeper*) encargado del marcador

scorn [skɔːrn] **1** n desprecio *m*; **pour ~ on sth** despreciar algo, menospreciar algo **2** v/t idea, suggestion despreciar

scorn·ful ['skɔːrnfəl] adj despreciativo

scorn·ful·ly ['skɔːrnfəlɪ] adv con desprecio

Scor·pi·o ['skɔːrpɪoʊ] ASTR Escorpio *m*/*f* inv

Scot [skɑːt] escocés(-esa) *m(f)*

Scotch [skɑːtʃ] (*whiskey*) whisky *m* escocés

Scotch 'tape® celo *m*, *L.Am.* Durex® *m*

scot-'free adv: **get off ~** salir impune

Scot·land ['skɑːtlənd] Escocia

Scots·man ['skɑːtsmən] escocés *m*

Scots·wom·an ['skɑːtswʊmən] escocesa *f*

Scot·tish ['skɑːtɪʃ] adj escocés

scoun·drel ['skaʊndrəl] canalla *m*/*f*

scour¹ ['skaʊər] v/t (*search*) rastrear, peinar

scour² ['skaʊər] v/t pans fregar

scout [skaʊt] n (*boy ~*) boy-scout *m*

scowl [skaʊl] **1** n ceño *m* **2** v/i fruncir el ceño

scram [skræm] v/i (pret & pp **-med**) F largarse F; **~!** ¡largo!

scram·ble ['skræmbl] **1** n (*rush*) prisa *f* **2** v/t message cifrar, codificar **3** v/i (*climb*) trepar; **he ~d to his feet** se levantó de un salto

scram·bled 'eggs ['skræmbld] npl huevos *mpl* revueltos

scrap [skræp] **1** n metal chatarra *f*; (*fight*) pelea *f*; *of food* trocito *m*; *of evidence* indicio *m*; *of common sense* pizca *f* **2** v/t (pret & pp **-ped**) plan, project abandonar; paragraph borrar

'**scrap·book** álbum *m* de recortes

scrape [skreɪp] **1** n on paintwork etc arañazo *m* **2** v/t paintwork rayar; **~ a living** apañarse

♦ **scrape through** v/i in exam aprobar por los pelos

'**scrap heap**: **be good for the ~** of person estar para el arrastre; of object estar para tirar; **scrap 'met·al** chatarra *f*; **scrap 'pa·per** papel *m* usado

scrap·py ['skræpɪ] adj work, play desorganizado

scratch [skrætʃ] **1** n mark marca *f*; **have a ~ to stop itching** rascarse; **start from ~** empezar desde cero; **your work isn't up to ~** tu trabajo es insuficiente **2** v/t (mark: skin) arañar; (mark: paint) rayar; because of itch rascarse **3** v/i of cat etc arañar; because of itch rascarse

scrawl [skrɔːl] **1** n garabato *m* **2** v/t garabatear

scraw·ny ['skrɔːnɪ] adj escuálido

scream [skriːm] **1** n grito *m*; **~s of laughter** carcajadas *fpl* **2** v/i gritar

screech [skriːtʃ] **1** n of tires chirrido *m*; (scream) chillido *m* **2** v/i of tires chirriar; (scream) chillar

screen [skriːn] **1** n in room, hospital mampara *f*; protective cortina *f*; in movie theater pantalla *f*; COMPUT

monitor *m*, pantalla *f* **2** *v/t* (*protect,
hide*) ocultar; *movie* proyectar; *for
security reasons* investigar
'**screen·play** guión *m*; '**screen
sav·er** COMPUT salvapantallas *m
inv*; '**screen test** *for movie* prueba *f*

screw [skruː] **1** *n* tornillo *m*; V (*sex*)
polvo *m* V **2** *v/t with a screwdriver*
atornillar (**to** a); V (*have sex with*)
echar un polvo con V; F (*cheat*) timar
F

♦ **screw up 1** *v/t eyes* cerrar; *piece of
paper* arrugar; F (*make a mess of*)
fastidiar F **2** *v/i* F (*make a bad
mistake*) meter la pata F
'**screw·driv·er** destornillador *m*
screwed 'up [skruːd'ʌp] *adj* F
psychologically acomplejado
'**screw top** *on bottle* tapón *m* de rosca
screw·y ['skruːɪ] *adj* F chiflado F; *idea,
film* descabellado F
scrib·ble ['skrɪbl] **1** *n* garabato *m*
2 *v/t & v/i* garabatear
scrimp [skrɪmp] *v/i*: **~ and scrape**
pasar apuros, pasar estrecheces
script [skrɪpt] *for movie, play* guión *m*;
form of writing caligrafía *f*
scrip·ture ['skrɪptʃər] escritura *f*; *the
(Holy) Scriptures* las Sagradas Escrituras
'**script·writ·er** guionista *m / f*
scroll [skroʊl] *n* (*manuscript*) manuscrito *m*
♦ **scroll down** *v/i* COMPUT avanzar
♦ **scroll up** *v/i* COMPUT retroceder
scrounge [skraʊndʒ] *v/t* gorronear
scroung·er ['skraʊndʒər] gorrón(-ona) *m(f)*
scrub [skrʌb] *v/t* (*pret & pp -bed*)
floors fregar; *hands* frotar
scrub·bing brush ['skrʌbɪŋ] *for floor*
cepillo *m* para fregar
scruff·y ['skrʌfɪ] *adj* andrajoso, desaliñado
scrum [skrʌm] *in rugby* melé *f*
♦ **scrunch up** [skrʌntʃ] *v/t plastic cup
etc* estrujar
scru·ples ['skruːplz] *npl* escrúpulos
mpl
scru·pu·lous ['skruːpjələs] *adj with
moral principles* escrupuloso;

(*thorough*) meticuloso; *attention to
detail* minucioso
scru·pu·lous·ly ['skruːpjələslɪ] *adv*
(*meticulously*) minuciosamente
scru·ti·nize ['skruːtɪnaɪz] *v/t* (*examine closely*) estudiar, examinar
scru·ti·ny ['skruːtɪnɪ] escrutinio *m*;
come under ~ ser objeto de investigación
scu·ba div·ing ['skuːbə] submarinismo *m*
scuff·le ['skʌfl] *n* riña *f*
sculp·tor ['skʌlptər] escultor(a)
m(f)
sculp·ture ['skʌlptʃər] escultura *f*
scum [skʌm] *on liquid* película *f* de
suciedad; *pej: people* escoria *f*
sea [siː] mar *m*; **by the ~** junto al mar
'**sea·bed** fondo *m* marino; '**sea·bird**
ave *f* marina; **sea·far·ing** ['siːferɪŋ]
adj nation marinero; '**sea·food** marisco *m*; '**sea·front** paseo *m* marítimo; '**sea·go·ing** *adj vessel* de altura;
'**sea·gull** gaviota *f*
seal[1] [siːl] *n animal* foca *f*
seal[2] [siːl] **1** *n on document* sello *m*;
TECH junta *f*, sello *m* **2** *v/t container*
sellar
♦ **seal off** *v/t area* aislar
'**sea lev·el**: **above ~** sobre el nivel del
mar; **below ~** bajo el nivel del mar
seam [siːm] *n on garment* costura *f*; *of
ore* filón *m*
'**sea·man** marinero *m*
seam·stress ['siːmstrɪs] modista *f*
'**sea·port** puerto *m* marítimo
'**sea pow·er** *nation* potencia *f* marítima
search [sɜːrtʃ] **1** *n* búsqueda *f*; **be in ~
of** estar en busca de **2** *v/t baggage,
person* registrar; **~ a place for s.o.**
buscar a alguien en un lugar
♦ **search for** *v/t* buscar
search·ing ['sɜːrtʃɪŋ] *adj look* escrutador; *question* difícil
'**search·light** reflector *m*; '**search
par·ty** grupo *m* de rescate; '**search
war·rant** orden *f* de registro
'**sea·shore** orilla *f*; '**sea·sick** *adj* mareado; **get ~** marearse; '**sea·side**
costa *f*, playa *f*; **~ resort** centro *m* de

veraneo costero

sea·son ['siːzn] *n* (*winter, spring etc*) estación *f*; *for tourism etc* temporada *f*; *plums aren't in ~ at the moment* ahora no es temporada de ciruelas

sea·son·al ['siːznl] *adj fruit, vegetables* del tiempo; *employment* temporal

sea·soned ['siːznd] *adj wood* seco; *traveler, campaigner* experimentado

sea·son·ing ['siːznɪŋ] condimento *m*

'sea·son tick·et abono *m*

seat [siːt] **1** *n in room, bus, plane* asiento *m*; *in theater* butaca *f*; *of pants* culera *f*; *please take a ~* por favor, siéntese **2** *v/t* (*have seating for*): *the hall can ~ 200 people* la sala tiene capacidad para 200 personas; *please remain ~ed* por favor, permanezcan sentados

'seat belt cinturón *m* de seguridad

'sea ur·chin erizo *m* de mar

'sea·weed alga(s) *f*(*pl*)

se·clud·ed [sɪ'kluːdɪd] *adj* apartado

se·clu·sion [sɪ'kluːʒn] aislamiento *m*

sec·ond¹ ['sekənd] **1** *n of time* segundo *m* **2** *adj* segundo **3** *adv* come in en segundo lugar **4** *v/t motion* apoyar

se·cond² [sɪ'kɑːnd] *v/t*: *be ~ed to* ser asignado a

sec·on·da·ry ['sekəndərɪ] *adj* secundario; *of ~ importance* de menor importancia

sec·on·da·ry ed·u·ca·tion educación *f* secundaria

se·cond 'best *adj*: *be ~* ser el segundo mejor; *inferior* ser un segundón; **sec·ond 'big·gest** *adj*: *it is the ~ company in the area* es la segunda empresa más grande de la zona; **sec·ond 'class** *adj ticket* de segunda clase; **sec·ond 'floor** primer piso *m*, *Br* segundo piso *m*; **'sec·ond hand** *n on clock* segundero *m*; **sec·ond-'hand 1** *adj* de segunda mano **2** *adv buy* de segunda mano

sec·ond·ly ['sekəndlɪ] *adv* en segundo lugar

sec·ond-'rate *adj* inferior

sec·ond 'thoughts: *I've had ~* he cambiado de idea

se·cre·cy ['siːkrəsɪ] secretismo *m*

se·cret ['siːkrət] **1** *n* secreto *m*; *in ~* en secreto **2** *adj* secreto

se·cret 'a·gent agente *m/f* secreto

sec·re·tar·i·al [sekrə'terɪəl] *adj tasks, job* de secretario

sec·re·tar·y ['sekrəterɪ] secretario(-a) *m*(*f*); POL ministro(-a) *m*(*f*)

Sec·re·tar·y of 'State *in USA* Secretario(-a) *m*(*f*) de Estado

se·crete [sɪ'kriːt] *v/t* (*give off*) segregar; (*hide away*) esconder

se·cre·tion [sɪ'kriːʃn] secreción *f*

se·cre·tive ['siːkrətɪv] *adj* reservado

se·cret·ly ['siːkrətlɪ] *adv* en secreto

se·cret po'lice policía *f* secreta

se·cret 'ser·vice servicio *m* secreto

sect [sekt] secta *f*

sec·tion ['sekʃn] *of book, company, text* sección *f*; *of building* zona *f*; *of apple* parte *f*

sec·tor ['sektər] sector *m*

sec·u·lar ['sekjələr] *adj* laico

se·cure [sɪ'kjʊr] **1** *adj shelf etc* seguro; *job, contract* fijo **2** *v/t shelf etc* asegurar; *help* conseguir

se'cu·ri·ties mar·ket FIN mercado *m* de valores

se·cu·ri·ty [sɪ'kjʊrətɪ] seguridad *f*; *for investment* garantía *f*

se'cu·ri·ty a·lert alerta *f*; **se'cu·ri·ty check** control *m* de seguridad; **se'cu·ri·ty-con·scious** *adj* consciente de la seguridad; **se'cu·ri·ty for·ces** *npl* fuerzas *fpl* de seguridad; **se'cu·ri·ty guard** guardia *m/f* de seguridad; **se'cu·ri·ty risk** *person* peligro *m* (para la seguridad)

se·dan [sɪ'dæn] MOT turismo *m*

se·date [sɪ'deɪt] *v/t* sedar

se·da·tion [sɪ'deɪʃn]: *be under ~* estar sedado

sed·a·tive ['sedətɪv] *n* sedante *m*

sed·en·ta·ry ['sedənterɪ] *adj job* sedentario

sed·i·ment ['sedɪmənt] sedimento *m*

se·duce [sɪ'duːs] *v/t* seducir

se·duc·tion [sɪ'dʌkʃn] seducción *f*

se·duc·tive [sɪ'dʌktɪv] *adj dress* seductor; *offer* tentador

see [siː] *v/t* (*pret saw*, *pp seen*) ver;

(*understand*) entender, ver; *romantically* ver, salir con; *I ~ ya veo*; *can I ~ the manager?* ¿puedo ver al encargado?; *you should ~ a doctor* deberías ir a que te viera un médico; *~ s.o. home* acompañar a alguien a casa; *you!* F ¡hasta la vista!, ¡chao! F

♦ **see about** *v/t* (*look into*): *I'll see about getting it repaired* me encargaré de que lo arreglen

♦ **see off** *v/t at airport etc* despedir; (*chase away*) espantar

♦ **see out** *v/t*: *see s.o. out* acompañar a alguien a la puerta

♦ **see to** *v/t*: *see to sth* ocuparse de algo; *see to it that sth gets done* asegurarse de que algo se haga

seed [siːd] semilla *f*; *in tennis* cabeza *f* de serie; *go to ~ of person* descuidarse; *of district* empeorarse

seed·ling ['siːdlɪŋ] planta *f* de semillero

seed·y ['siːdɪ] *adj bar, district* de mala calaña

see·ing 'eye dog ['siːɪŋ] perro *m* lazarillo

see·ing (that) ['siːɪŋ] *conj* dado que, ya que

seek [siːk] *v/t* (*pret & pp* **sought**) buscar

seem [siːm] *v/i* parecer; *it ~s that ...* parece que ...

seem·ing·ly ['siːmɪŋlɪ] *adv* aparentemente

seen [siːn] *pp* → **see**

seep [siːp] *v/i of liquid* filtrarse

♦ **seep out** *v/i of liquid* filtrarse

see·saw ['siːsɔː] *n* subibaja *m*

seethe [siːð] *v/i*: *be seething with anger* estar a punto de estallar (de cólera)

'see-through *adj dress, material* transparente

seg·ment ['segmənt] segmento *m*

seg·ment·ed [seg'məntɪd] *adj* segmentado, dividido

seg·re·gate ['segrɪgeɪt] *v/t* segregar

seg·re·ga·tion [segrɪ'geɪʃn] segregación *f*

seis·mol·o·gy [saɪz'mɑːlədʒɪ] sismología *f*

seize [siːz] *v/t s.o., s.o.'s arm* agarrar; *opportunity* aprovechar; *of Customs, police etc* incautarse de

♦ **seize up** *v/i of engine* atascarse

sei·zure ['siːʒər] MED ataque *m*; *of drugs etc* incautación *f*; *amount seized* alijo *m*

sel·dom ['seldəm] *adv* raramente, casi nunca

se·lect [sɪ'lekt] 1 *v/t* seleccionar 2 *adj* (*exclusive*) selecto

se·lec·tion [sɪ'lekʃn] selección *f*; (*choosing*) elección *f*

se·lec·tion pro·cess proceso *m* de selección

se·lec·tive [sɪ'lektɪv] *adj* selectivo

self [self] (*pl* **selves** [selvz]) ego *m*; *my other ~* mi otro yo

self-ad·dressed 'en·ve·lope [selfə'drest]: *send us a ~* envíenos un sobre con sus datos; **self-as'sur·ance** confianza *f* en sí mismo; **self-as·sured** [selfə'ʃʊrd] *adj* seguro de sí mismo; **self-ca·ter·ing a'part·ment** [self'keɪtərɪŋ] *Br* apartamento *m* or *Span* piso *m* sin servicio de comidas; **self-'cen·tered**, *Br* **self-'cen·tred** [self'sentərd] *adj* egoísta; **self-'clean·ing** *adj oven* con autolimpieza; **self-con'fessed** [selfkən'fest] *adj*: *he's a ~ megalomaniac* se confiesa megalómano; **self-'con·fi·dence** confianza *f* en sí mismo; **self-'con·fi·dent** *adj* seguro de sí mismo; **self-'con·scious** *adj* tímido; **self-'con·scious·ness** timidez *f*; **self-con·tained** [selfkən'teɪnd] *adj apartment* independiente; **self-con'trol** autocontrol *m*; **self-de'fence** *Br*, **self-de'fense** autodefensa *f*; *in ~* en defensa propia; **self-'dis·ci·pline** autodisciplina *f*; **self-'doubt** inseguridad *f*; **self-em·ployed** [selfɪm'plɔɪd] *adj* autónomo; **self-es'teem** autoestima *f*; **self-'ev·i·dent** *adj* obvio; **self-ex'pres·sion** autoexpresión *f*; **self-'gov·ern·ment** autogobierno *m*; **self-'in·ter·est** interés *m* propio

self·ish ['selfɪʃ] *adj* egoísta
self·less ['selflɪs] *adj* desinteresado
self-made 'man [self'meɪd] hombre *m* hecho a sí mismo; **self-'pit·y** autocompasión *f*; **self-'por·trait** autorretrato *m*; **self-pos·sessed** [selfpə'zest] *adj* sereno; **self-re'li·ant** *adj* autosuficiente; **self-re'spect** amor *m* propio; **self-right·eous** [self'raɪtʃəs] *adj pej* santurrón, intolerante; **self-sat·is·fied** [self'sætɪzfaɪd] *adj pej* pagado de sí mismo; **self-'ser·vice** *adj* de autoservicio; **self-ser·vice 'res·tau·rant** (restaurante *m*) autoservicio *m*; **self-taught** [self'tɒːt] *adj* autodidacta
sell [sel] *v/t & v/i* (*pret & pp* **sold**) vender
♦ **sell out** *v/i of product* agotarse; **we've sold out** se nos ha(n) agotado
♦ **sell out of** *v/t* agotar las existencias de
♦ **sell up** *v/i* vender todo
'sell-by date fecha *f* límite de venta; **be past its ~** haber pasado la fecha límite de venta
sell·er ['selər] vendedor(a) *m(f)*
sell·ing ['selɪŋ] COM ventas *fpl*
'sell·ing point COM ventaja *f*
Sel·lo·tape® ['seləteɪp] *Br* celo *m*, *L.Am.* Durex® *m*
se·men ['siːmən] semen *m*
se·mes·ter [sɪ'mestər] semestre *m*
sem·i ['semɪ] *n truck* camión *m* semirremolque
'sem·i·cir·cle semicírculo *m*; **sem·i·'cir·cu·lar** *adj* semicircular; **sem·i·'co·lon** punto *m* y coma; **sem·i·con'duc·tor** ELEC semiconductor *m*; **sem·i·fi·nal** semifinal *f*; **sem·i·fi·nal·ist** semifinalista *m/f*
sem·i·nar ['semɪnɑːr] seminario *m*
sem·i·skilled *adj* semicualificado
sen·ate ['senət] senado *m*
sen·a·tor ['senətər] senador(a) *m(f)*; **Senator George Schwarz** el Senador George Schwarz
send [send] *v/t* (*pret & pp* **sent**) enviar, mandar; **~ her my best wishes**

dale recuerdos de mi parte
♦ **send back** *v/t* devolver
♦ **send for** *v/t* mandar buscar
♦ **send in** *v/t troops, application* enviar, mandar; *next interviewee* hacer pasar
♦ **send off** *v/t letter, fax etc* enviar, mandar
send·er ['sendər] *of letter* remitente *m/f*
se·nile ['siːnaɪl] *adj* senil
se·nil·i·ty [sɪ'nɪlətɪ] senilidad *f*
se·ni·or ['siːnjər] *adj* (*older*) mayor; *in rank* superior
se·ni·or 'cit·i·zen persona *f* de la tercera edad
se·ni·or·i·ty [siːnj'ɑːrətɪ] *in job* antigüedad *f*
sen·sa·tion [sen'seɪʃn] sensación *f*
sen·sa·tion·al [sen'seɪʃnl] *adj news, discovery* sensacional
sense [sens] **1** *n* (*meaning, point, hearing etc*) sentido *m*; (*feeling*) sentimiento *m*; (*common sense*) sentido *m* común, sensatez *f*; **in a ~** en cierto sentido; **talk ~, man!** ¡no digas tonterías!; **come to one's ~s** entrar en razón; **it doesn't make ~** no tiene sentido; **there's no ~ in waiting** no tiene sentido que esperemos **2** *v/t s.o.'s presence* sentir, notar; **I could ~ that something was wrong** tenía la sensación de que no iba bien
sense·less ['senslɪs] *adj* (*pointless*) absurdo
sen·si·ble ['sensəbl] *adj* sensato; *clothes, shoes* práctico, apropiado
sen·si·bly ['sensəblɪ] *adv* con sensatez; **she wasn't ~ dressed** no llevaba ropa apropiada
sen·si·tive ['sensətɪv] *adj skin, person* sensible
sen·si·tiv·i·ty [sensə'tɪvətɪ] *of skin, person* sensibilidad *f*
sen·sor ['sensər] sensor *m*
sen·su·al ['senʃuəl] *adj* sensual
sen·su·al·i·ty [senʃu'ælətɪ] sensualidad *f*
sen·su·ous ['senʃuəs] *adj* sensual
sent [sent] *pret & pp* → **send**

S

sen·tence ['sentəns] **1** *n* GRAM oración *f*; LAW sentencia *f* **2** *v/t* LAW sentenciar, condenar

sen·ti·ment ['sentɪmənt] (*sentimentality*) sentimentalismo *m*; (*opinion*) opinión *f*

sen·ti·men·tal [sentɪ'mentl] *adj* sentimental

sen·ti·men·tal·i·ty [sentɪmen'tælətɪ] sentimentalismo *m*

sen·try ['sentrɪ] centinela *m*

sep·a·rate¹ ['sepərət] *adj* separado; **keep sth ~ from sth** guardar algo separado de algo

sep·a·rate² ['sepəreɪt] **1** *v/t* separar; **~ sth from sth** separar algo de algo **2** *v/i* of couple separarse

sep·a·rat·ed ['sepəreɪtɪd] *adj* couple separado

sep·a·rate·ly ['sepərətlɪ] *adv* pay, treat por separado

sep·a·ra·tion [sepə'reɪʃn] separación *f*

Sep·tem·ber [sep'tembər] septiembre *m*

sep·tic ['septɪk] *adj* séptico; **go ~** of wound infectarse

se·quel ['siːkwəl] continuación *f*

se·quence ['siːkwəns] *n* secuencia *f*; **in ~** en orden; **out of ~** en desorden; **the ~ of events** la secuencia de hechos

se·rene [sɪ'riːn] *adj* sereno

ser·geant ['sɑːrdʒənt] sargento *m*/*f*

se·ri·al ['sɪrɪəl] *n* on TV, radio serie *f*, serial *m*; in magazine novela *f* por entregas

se·ri·al·ize ['sɪrɪəlaɪz] *v/t* novel on TV emitir en forma de serie; in newspaper publicar por entregas

'se·ri·al kill·er asesino(-a) *m(f)* en serie; **'se·ri·al num·ber** número *m* de serie; **'se·ri·al port** COMPUT puerto *m* (en) serie

se·ries ['sɪriːz] *nsg* serie *f*

se·ri·ous ['sɪrɪəs] *adj* situation, damage, illness grave; (person: earnest) serio; (company) serio; **I'm ~** lo digo en serio; **we'd better take a ~ look at it** deberíamos examinarlo seriamente

se·ri·ous·ly ['sɪrɪəslɪ] *adv* injured gravemente; **~ intend to ...** tener intenciones firmes de ...; **~?** ¿en serio?; **take s.o. ~** tomar a alguien en serio

se·ri·ous·ness ['sɪrɪəsnɪs] of person seriedad *f*; of situation seriedad *f*, gravedad *f*; of illness gravedad *f*

ser·mon ['sɜːrmən] sermón *m*

ser·vant ['sɜːrvənt] sirviente(-a) *m(f)*

serve [sɜːrv] **1** *n* in tennis servicio *m*, saque *m* **2** *v/t* food, meal servir; customer in shop atender; one's country, the people servir a; **it ~s you right** ¡te lo mereces! **3** *v/i* servir; in tennis servir, sacar
♦ **serve up** *v/t* meal servir

serv·er ['sɜːrvər] in tennis jugador(a) *m(f)* al servicio; COMPUT servidor *m*

ser·vice ['sɜːrvɪs] **1** *n* to customers, community servicio *m*; for vehicle, machine revisión *f*; in tennis servicio *m*, saque *m*; **~s** (~ sector) el sector servicios; **the ~s** MIL las fuerzas armadas **2** *v/t* vehicle, machine revisar

'ser·vice ar·e·a área *f* de servicio; **'ser·vice charge** in restaurant servicio *m* (tarifa); **'ser·vice in·dus·try** industria *f* de servicios; **'ser·vice·man** MIL militar *m*; **'ser·vice pro·vid·er** COMPUT proveedor *m* de servicios; **'ser·vice sec·tor** sector *m* servicios; **'ser·vice sta·tion** estación *f* de servicio

ser·vile ['sɜːrvəl] *adj pej* servil

serv·ing ['sɜːrvɪŋ] *n* of food ración *f*

ses·sion ['seʃn] sesión *f*; with boss reunión *f*

set [set] **1** *n* of tools juego *m*; of books colección *f*; (group of people) grupo *m*; MATH conjunto *m*; (THEA: scenery) decorado *m*; where a movie is made plató *m*; in tennis set *m*; **television ~** televisor *m*; **a ~ of dishes** una vajilla; **a ~ of glasses** una cristalería **2** *v/t* (pret & pp **set**) (place) colocar; movie, novel etc ambientar; date, time, limit fijar; mechanism, alarm poner; clock poner en hora; broken limb recomponer; jewel engastar; (type~) componer; **~ the table** poner la mesa **3** *v/i* (*pret & pp* **set**) *of sun* ponerse; *of glue* solidificarse **4** *adj views, ideas* fijo; (*ready*) preparado; **be dead ~ on sth** estar empeñado en hacer algo; **be very ~ in one's ways** ser de ideas fijas; **~ meal** menú *m* (del día)

♦ **set apart** *v/t* distinguir

♦ **set aside** *v/t material, food* apartar; *money* ahorrar

♦ **set back** *v/t in plans etc* retrasar; *it set me back $400* me salió por 400 dólares

♦ **set off 1** *v/i on journey* salir **2** *v/t explosion* provocar; *bomb* hacer explotar; *chain reaction* desencadenar; *alarm* activar

♦ **set out 1** *v/i on journey* salir (**for** hacia) **2** *v/t ideas, goods* exponer; **set out to do sth** (*intend*) tener la intención de hacer algo

♦ **set to** *v/i* (*start on a task*) empezar a trabajar

♦ **set up 1** *v/t new company* establecer; *equipment, machine* instalar; *market stall* montar; *meeting* organizar; F (*frame*) tender una trampa a **2** *v/i in business* emprender un negocio

'**set·back** contratiempo *m*

set·tee [se'tiː] (*couch, sofa*) sofá *m*

set·ting ['setɪŋ] *n of novel etc* escenario *m*; *of house* ubicación *f*

set·tle ['setl] **1** *v/i of bird, dust* posarse; *of building* hundirse; *to live* establecerse **2** *v/t dispute, uncertainty* resolver, solucionar; *debts* saldar; *nerves, stomach* calmar; *that ~s it!* ¡está decidido!

♦ **settle down** *v/i* (*stop being noisy*) tranquilizarse; (*stop wild living*) sentar la cabeza; *in an area* establecerse

♦ **settle for** *v/t* (*take, accept*) conformarse con

♦ **settle up with** *v/t* (*pay*) ajustar cuentas con

set·tled ['setld] *adj weather* estable

set·tle·ment ['setlmənt] *of claim* resolución *f*; *of debt* liquidación *f*; *of dispute* acuerdo *m*; (*payment*) suma *f*; *of building* hundimiento *m*

set·tler ['setlər] *in new country* colono *m*

'**set-up** (*structure*) estructura *f*; (*relationship*) relación *f*; F (*frame-up*) trampa *f*

sev·en ['sevn] siete

sev·en·teen [sevn'tiːn] diecisiete

sev·en·teenth [sevn'tiːnθ] *n & adj* décimoséptimo

sev·enth ['sevnθ] *n & adj* séptimo

sev·en·ti·eth ['sevntɪɪθ] *n & adj* septuagésimo

sev·en·ty ['sevntɪ] setenta

sev·er ['sevər] *v/t* cortar; *relations* romper

sev·e·ral ['sevrl] **1** *adj* varios **2** *pron* varios(-as) *mpl* (*fpl*)

se·vere [sɪ'vɪr] *adj illness* grave; *penalty, winter, weather* severo; *teacher* estricto

se·vere·ly [sɪ'vɪrlɪ] *adv punish, speak* con severidad; *injured, disrupted* gravemente

se·ver·i·ty [sɪ'verətɪ] severidad *f*; *of illness* gravedad *f*

Se·ville [sə'vɪl] *n* Sevilla

sew [sou] *v/t & v/i* (*pret* **-ed**, *pp* **sewn**) coser

♦ **sew on** *v/t button* coser

sew·age ['suːɪdʒ] aguas *fpl* residuales

'**sew·age plant** planta *f* de tratamiento de aguas residuales, depuradora *f*

sew·er ['suːər] alcantarilla *f*, cloaca *f*

sew·ing ['souɪŋ] *skill* costura *f*; *that being sewn* labor *f*

'**sew·ing ma·chine** máquina *f* de coser

sewn [soun] *pp* → **sew**

sex [seks] (*act, gender*) sexo *m*; **have ~ with** tener relaciones sexuales con, acostarse con

sex·ist ['seksɪst] **1** *adj* sexista **2** *n* sexista *m/f*

sex·u·al ['sekʃuəl] *adj* sexual

sex·u·al as'sault agresión *f* sexual; **sex·u·al ha'rass·ment** acoso *m* sexual; **sex·u·al 'in·ter·course** relaciones *fpl* sexuales

sex·u·al·i·ty [sekʃʊˈæləti] sexualidad *f*

sex·u·al·ly [ˈsekʃʊli] *adv* sexualmente; **~ transmitted disease** enfermedad *f* de transmisión sexual

sex·y [ˈseksi] *adj* sexy *inv*

shab·bi·ly [ˈʃæbili] *adv* **dressed** con desaliño; **treat** muy mal, de manera muy injusta

shab·by [ˈʃæbi] *adj* **coat etc** desgastado, raído; **treatment** malo, muy injusto

shack [ʃæk] choza *f*

shade [ʃeid] **1** *n* for lamp pantalla *f*; of color tonalidad *f*; on window persiana *f*; **in the ~** a la sombra **2** *v/t* from sun, light proteger de la luz

shad·ow [ˈʃædou] *n* sombra *f*

shad·y [ˈʃeidi] *adj* **spot** umbrío; **character**, **dealings** sospechoso

shaft [ʃæft] TECH eje *m*, árbol *m*; of mine pozo *m*

shag·gy [ˈʃægi] *adj* **hair**, **dog** greñudo

shake [ʃeik] **1** *n* sacudida *f*; **give sth a good ~** agitar algo bien **2** *v/t* (*pret* **shook**, *pp* **shaken**) agitar; *emotionally* conmocionar; **he shook his head** negó con la cabeza; **~ hands** estrechar *or* darse la mano; **~ hands with s.o.** estrechar *or* dar la mano a alguien **3** *v/i* (*pret* **shook**, *pp* **shaken**) *of voice*, *building*, *person* temblar

shak·en [ˈʃeikən] **1** *adj* *emotionally* conmocionado **2** *pp* → **shake**

'shake-up reestructuración *f*

'shak·y [ˈʃeiki] *adj* **table etc** inestable; **after illness** débil; **after shock** conmocionado; **grasp of sth**, **grammar etc** flojo; **voice**, **hand** tembloroso

shall [ʃæl] *v/aux* ◊ *future*: **I ~ do my best** haré todo lo que pueda ◊ *suggesting*: **~ we go?** ¿nos vamos?

shal·low [ˈʃælou] *adj* **water** poco profundo; **person** superficial

sham·bles [ˈʃæmblz] *nsg* caos *m*

shame [ʃeim] **1** *n* vergüenza *f*, *Col*, *Mex*, *Ven* pena *f*; **bring ~ on** avergonzar a, *Col*, *Mex*, *Ven* apenar a; **~ on you!** ¡debería darte vergüenza!; **what a ~!** ¡qué pena *or* lástima! **2** *v/t*

avergonzar, *Col*, *Mex*, *Ven* apenar; **~ s.o. into doing sth** avergonzar a alguien para que haga algo

shame·ful [ˈʃeimfəl] *adj* vergonzoso

shame·ful·ly [ˈʃeimfəli] *adv* vergonzosamente

shame·less [ˈʃeimlis] *adj* desvergonzado

sham·poo [ʃæmˈpuː] **1** *n* champú *m* **2** *v/t* **customer** lavar la cabeza a; **hair** lavar

shan·ty town [ˈʃænti] *Span* barrio *m* de chabolas, *L.Am.* barriada *f*, *Arg* villa *f* miseria, *Chi* callampa *f*, *Mex* ciudad *f* perdida, *Urug* cantegril *m*

shape [ʃeip] **1** *n* forma *f* **2** *v/t* **clay** modelar; **person's life**, **character** determinar; **the future** dar forma a

shape·less [ˈʃeiplis] *adj* **dress etc** amorfo

shape·ly [ˈʃeipli] *adv* **figure** esbelto

share [ʃer] **1** *n* parte *f*; FIN acción *f*; **I did my ~ of the work** hice la parte del trabajo que me correspondía **2** *v/t* & *v/i* compartir

♦ **share out** *v/t* repartir

'share·hold·er [ʃɑːrk] accionista *m/f*

shark [ʃɑːrk] *fish* tiburón *m*

sharp [ʃɑːrp] **1** *adj* **knife** afilado; **mind** vivo; **pain** agudo; **taste** ácido **2** *adv* MUS demasiado alto; **at 3 o'clock ~** a las tres en punto

sharp·en [ˈʃɑːrpn] *v/t* **knife** afilar; **pencil** sacar punta a; **skills** perfeccionar

sharp 'prac·tice triquiñuelas *fpl*, tejemanejes *mpl*

shat [ʃæt] *pret* & *pp* → **shit**

shat·ter [ˈʃætər] **1** *v/t* **glass** hacer añicos; **illusions** destrozar **2** *v/i* of glass hacerse añicos

shat·tered [ˈʃætərd] *adj* F (*exhausted*) destrozado F, hecho polvo F; (*very upset*) destrozado F

shat·ter·ing [ˈʃætəriŋ] *adj* **news**, **experience** demoledor, sorprendente

shave [ʃeiv] **1** *v/t* afeitar **2** *v/i* afeitarse **3** *n* afeitado *m*; **have a ~** afeitarse; **that was a close ~!** ¡le faltó un pelo!

♦ **shave off** v/t *beard* afeitar; *from piece of wood* rebajar

shav·en ['ʃeɪvn] *adj head* afeitado

shav·er ['ʃeɪvər] *electric* máquinilla *f* de afeitar (eléctrica)

shav·ing brush ['ʃeɪvɪŋ] brocha *f* de afeitar

'**shav·ing soap** jabón *m* de afeitar

shawl [ʃɔːl] chal *m*

she [ʃiː] *pron* ella; *~ is German/a student* es alemana/estudiante; *you're funny, ~'s not* tú tienes gracia, ella no

shears [ʃɪrz] *npl for gardening* tijeras *fpl* (de podar); *for sewing* tijeras *fpl* (*grandes*)

sheath [ʃiːθ] *for knife* funda *f*; *contraceptive* condón *m*

shed[1] [ʃed] v/t (*pret & pp* **shed**) *blood, tears* derramar; *leaves* perder; *~ light on fig* arrojar luz sobre

shed[2] [ʃed] *n* cobertizo *m*

sheep [ʃiːp] (*pl* **sheep**) oveja *f*

'**sheep·dog** perro *m* pastor

sheep·herd·er ['ʃiːphɜːrdər] pastor *m*

sheep·ish ['ʃiːpɪʃ] *adj* avergonzado

'**sheep·skin** *adj lining* (de piel) de borrego

sheer [ʃɪr] *adj madness, luxury* puro, verdadero; *hell* verdadero; *drop, cliffs* escarpado

sheet [ʃiːt] *for bed* sábana *f*; *of paper* hoja *f*; *of metal* chapa *f*, plancha *f*; *of glass* hoja *f*, lámina *f*

shelf [ʃelf] (*pl* **shelves** [ʃelvz]) estante *m*; **shelves** estanterías *fpl*

shell [ʃel] **1** *n of mussel etc* concha *f*; *of egg* cáscara *f*; *of tortoise* caparazón *m*; MIL proyectil *m*; **come out of one's ~** *fig* salir del caparazón **2** v/t *peas* pelar; MIL bombardear (*con artillería*)

'**shell·fire** fuego *m* de artillería

'**shell·fish** marisco *m*

shel·ter ['ʃeltər] **1** *n* refugio *m*; (*bus ~*) marquesina *f* **2** v/i *from rain, bombing etc* refugiarse **3** v/t (*protect*) proteger

shel·tered ['ʃeltərd] *adj place* resguardado; *lead a ~ life* llevar una vida protegida

shelve [ʃelv] v/t *fig* posponer

shep·herd ['ʃepərd] *n* pastor *m*

sher·iff ['ʃerɪf] sheriff *m/f*

sher·ry ['ʃerɪ] jerez *m*

shield [ʃiːld] **1** *n* escudo *m*; *sports trophy* trofeo *m* (*en forma de escudo*); TECH placa *f* protectora; *of policeman* placa *f* **2** v/t (*protect*) proteger

shift [ʃɪft] **1** *n* cambio *m*; *period of work* turno *m* **2** v/t (*move*) mover; *stains etc* eliminar **3** v/i (*move*) moverse; (*change*) trasladarse, desplazarse; *of wind* cambiar; *he was ~ing!* F iba a toda mecha F

'**shift key** COMPUT tecla *f* de mayúsculas; '**shift work** trabajo *m* por turnos; '**shift work·er** trabajador(a) *m(f)* por turnos

shift·y ['ʃɪftɪ] *adj pej* sospechoso

shim·mer ['ʃɪmər] v/i brillar; *of roads in heat* reverberar

shin [ʃɪn] *n* espinilla *f*

shine [ʃaɪn] **1** v/i (*pret & pp* **shone**) brillar; *fig: of student etc* destacar (*at* en) **2** v/t (*pret & pp* **shone**): *could you ~ a light in here?* ¿podrías alumbrar aquí? **3** *n on shoes etc* brillo *m*

shin·gle ['ʃɪŋgl] *on beach* guijarros *mpl*

shin·gles ['ʃɪŋglz] *nsg* MED herpes *m*

shin·y ['ʃaɪnɪ] *adj surface* brillante

ship [ʃɪp] **1** *n* barco *m*, buque *m* **2** v/t (*pret & pp* **-ped**) (*send*) enviar; *by sea* enviar por barco

ship·ment ['ʃɪpmənt] (*consignment*) envío *m*

'**ship·own·er** naviero(-a) *m(f)*, armador(a) *m(f)*

ship·ping ['ʃɪpɪŋ] (*sea traffic*) navíos *mpl*, buques *mpl*; (*sending, dispatch*) envío *m*; (*sending by sea*) envío *m* por barco

'**ship·ping com·pa·ny** (*compañía f*) naviera *f*

ship·ping costs *npl* gastos *mpl* de envío

ship'shape *adj* ordenado, organiza-

S

do; '**ship·wreck 1** *n* naufragio *m*
2 *v/t*: *be ~ed* naufragar; '**ship·yard**
astillero *m*

shirk [ʃɜːrk] *v/t* eludir

shirk·er [ˈʃɜːrkər] vago(-a) *m(f)*

shirt [ʃɜːrt] camisa *f*; *in his ~ sleeves*
en mangas de camisa

shit [ʃɪt] **1** *n* P mierda *f* P; *I need a ~*
tengo que cagar P **2** *v/i* (*pret & pp*
shat) P cagar P **3** *int* P mierda P

shit·ty [ˈʃɪtɪ] *adj* F asqueroso F; *I feel*
~ me encuentro de pena F

shiv·er [ˈʃɪvər] *v/i* tiritar

shock [ʃɑːk] **1** *n* shock *m*, impresión
f; ELEC descarga *f*; *be in* – MED estar
en estado de shock **2** *v/t* impresionar, dejar boquiabierto; *I was ~ed*
by the news la noticia me impresio-
nó *or* dejó boquiabierto; *an artist*
who tries to ~ his public un artista
que intenta escandalizar a su público

'**shock ab·sorb·er** [əbˈsɔːrbər] MOT
amortiguador *m*

shock·ing [ˈʃɑːkɪŋ] *adj behavior*,
poverty impresionante, escandaloso; F *prices* escandaloso; F *weather*,
spelling terrible

shock·ing·ly [ˈʃɑːkɪŋlɪ] *adv behave*
escandalosamente

shod·dy [ˈʃɑːdɪ] *adj goods* de mala
calidad; *behavior* vergonzoso

shoe [ʃuː] zapato *m*

'**shoe·horn** calzador *m*; '**shoe·lace**
cordón *m*; '**shoe·mak·er** zapa-
tero(-a) *m(f)*; '**shoe mend·er**
zapatero(-a) *m(f)* remen-
dón(-ona); '**shoe·store** zapatería *f*;
'**shoe·string**: *do sth on a ~* hacer
algo con cuatro duros

shone [ʃɑːn] *pret & pp → shine*

♦**shoo away** [ʃuː] *v/t children*,
chicken espantar

shook [ʃʊk] *pret → shake*

shoot [ʃuːt] **1** *n* BOT brote *m* **2** *v/t*
(*pret & pp shot*) disparar; *and kill*
matar de un tiro; *movie* rodar; *~ s.o.*
in the leg disparar a alguien en la
pierna

♦**shoot down** *v/t airplane* derribar;
fig: suggestion echar por tierra

♦**shoot off** *v/i* (*rush off*) irse deprisa

♦**shoot up** *v/i of prices* dispararse; *of*
children crecer mucho; *of new*
suburbs, buildings etc aparecer de repente; F *of drug addict* chutarse F

shoot·ing star [ˈʃuːtɪŋ] estrella *f* fugaz

shop [ʃɑːp] **1** *n* tienda *f*; *talk ~* hablar
del trabajo **2** *v/i* (*pret & pp -ped*)
comprar; *go ~ping* ir de compras

shop·keep·er [ˈʃɑːkiːpər] tende-
ro(-a) *m(f)*; **shop·lift·er** [ˈʃɑːplɪft-
ər] ladrón(-ona) *m(f)* (*en tienda*);
shop·lift·ing [ˈʃɑːplɪftɪŋ] *n* hurtos
mpl (*en tiendas*)

shop·per [ˈʃɑːpər] *person* comprador(a)
m(f)

shop·ping [ˈʃɑːpɪŋ] *items* compra *f*; *I*
hate ~ odio hacer la compra; *do*
one's ~ hacer la compra

'**shop·ping bag** bolsa *f* de la compra;
'**shop·ping cen·ter**, *Br* '**shop·ping**
cen·tre centro *m* comercial;
'**shop·ping list** lista *f* de la compra;
'**shop·ping mall** centro *m* comercial

shop 'stew·ard representante *m/f*
sindical

shore [ʃɔːr] orilla *f*; *on ~* (*not at sea*)
en tierra

short [ʃɔːrt] **1** *adj* corto; *in height*
bajo; *it's just a ~ walk* está a poca
distancia a pie; *we're ~ of fuel* nos
queda poco combustible; *he's not ~*
of ideas no le faltan ideas; *time is ~*
hay poco tiempo **2** *adv*: *cut ~*
vacation, meeting interrumpir; *stop*
a person ~ hacer pararse a una persona; *go ~ of* pasar sin; *in ~* en resumen

short·age [ˈʃɔːrtɪdʒ] escasez *f*, falta *f*

short 'cir·cuit *n* cortocircuito *m*;
short·com·ing [ˈʃɔːrtkʌmɪŋ] defecto *m*; '**short·cut** atajo *m*

short·en [ˈʃɔːrtn] *v/t dress, hair,*
vacation acortar; *chapter, article*
abreviar; *work day* reducir

short·en·ing [ˈʃɔːrtnɪŋ] grasa utiliza-
da para hacer masa de pastelería

'**short·fall** déficit *m*; '**short·hand** *n*
taquigrafía *f*; **short·hand·ed**

[ʃɔːrt'hændɪd] *adj* falto de personal; **short-lived** ['ʃɔːrtlɪvd] *adj* efímero **short-ly** ['ʃɔːrtlɪ] *adv* (*soon*) pronto; ~ **before/after** justo antes/después **short-ness** ['ʃɔːrtnɪs] *of visit* brevedad *f*; *in height* baja *f* estatura

shorts [ʃɔːrts] *npl* pantalones *mpl* cortos, shorts *mpl*; *underwear* calzoncillos *mpl*

short-sight-ed [ʃɔːrt'saɪtɪd] *adj* miope; *fig* corto de miras; **short-sleeved** ['ʃɔːrtsliːvd] *adj* de manga corta; **short-staffed** [ʃɔːrt'stæft] *adj* falto de personal; **short 'sto-ry** relato *m or* cuento corto; **short-tem-pered** [ʃɔːrt'tempərd] *adj* irascible; **short time**: *be on ~ of workers* trabajar a jornada reducida; **'short wave** onda *f* corta

shot[1] [ʃɑːt] *from gun* disparo *m*; (*photograph*) fotografía *f*; (*injection*) inyección *f*; *be a good/poor ~* tirar bien/mal; *he accepted like a ~* aceptó al instante; *he ran off like a ~* se fue como una bala

shot[2] [ʃɑːt] *pret & pp* → **shoot** **'shot-gun** escopeta *f*

should [ʃʊd] *v/aux*: *what ~ I do?* ¿qué debería hacer?; *you ~n't do that* no deberías hacer eso; *that ~ be long enough* debería ser lo suficientemente largo; *you ~ have heard him!* ¡tendrías que haberle oído!

shoul-der ['ʃoʊldər] *n* ANAT hombro *m*

'shoul-der bag bolso *m* (de bandolera); **'shoul-der blade** omóplato *m*, omoplato; **'shoul-der strap** *of brassiere, dress* tirante *m*; *of bag* correa *f*

shout [ʃaʊt] **1** *n* grito *m* **2** *v/t & v/i* gritar
♦ **shout at** *v/t* gritar a

shout-ing ['ʃaʊtɪŋ] *n* griterío *m*

shove [ʃʌv] **1** *n* empujón *m* **2** *v/t & v/i* empujar
♦ **shove in** *v/i in line* meterse empujando
♦ **shove off** *v/i* F (*go away*) largarse F

shov-el ['ʃʌvl] **1** *n* pala *f* **2** *v/t* (*pret & pp* **-ed**, *Br* **-led**): *~ snow off the path* retirar a paladas la nieve del camino

show [ʃoʊ] **1** *n* THEA espectáculo *m*; *TV* programa *m*; *of emotion* muestra *f*; *on ~ at exhibition* expuesto, en exposición **2** *v/t* (*pret* **-ed**, *pp* **shown**) *passport, ticket* enseñar, mostrar; *interest, emotion* mostrar; *at exhibition* exponer; *movie* proyectar; *~ s.o. sth, ~ sth to s.o.* enseñar *or* mostrar algo a alguien **3** *v/i* (*pret* **-ed**, *pp* **shown**) (*be visible*) verse; *what's ~ing at ...?* *at movie theater* qué ponen en el ...?
♦ **show around** *v/t* enseñar; *he showed us around* nos enseñó la casa/el edificio *etc*
♦ **show in** *v/t* hacer pasar a
♦ **show off 1** *v/t skills* mostrar **2** *v/i pej* presumir, alardear
♦ **show up 1** *v/t shortcomings etc* poner de manifiesto; *don't show me up in public* (*embarrass*) no me avergüences en público **2** *v/i* (*be visible*) verse; F (*arrive*) aparecer

'show busi-ness el mundo del espectáculo; **'show-case** *n* vitrina *f*; *fig* escaparate *m*; **'show-down** enfrentamiento *m*

show-er ['ʃaʊər] **1** *n of rain* chaparrón *m*, chubasco *m*; *to wash* ducha *f*, *Mex* regadera *f*; (*party*) fiesta con motivo de un bautizo, una boda etc., en la que los invitados llevan obsequios; *take a ~* ducharse **2** *v/i* ducharse **3** *v/t*: *~ s.o. with compliments/praise* colmar a alguien de cumplidos/alabanzas

'show-er cap gorro *m* de baño; **'show-er cur-tain** cortina *f* de ducha; **'show-er-proof** *adj* impermeable

'show-jump-ing concurso *m* de saltos

shown [ʃoʊn] *pp* → **show**

'show-off *n pej* fanfarrón(-ona) *m(f)*

'show-room sala *f* de exposición *f*; *in ~ condition* como nuevo

S

show·y ['ʃoʊɪ] *adj* llamativo

shrank [ʃræŋk] *pret* → **shrink**

shred [ʃred] **1** *n of paper etc* trozo *m*; *of fabric* jirón *m*; **there isn't a ~ of evidence** no hay prueba alguna **2** *v/t* (*pret & pp* **-ded**) *paper* hacer trizas; *in cooking* cortar en tiras

shred·der ['ʃredər] *for documents* trituradora *f* (de documentos)

shrewd [ʃruːd] *adj person* astuto; *judgement, investment* inteligente

shrewd·ness ['ʃruːdnɪs] *of person* astucia *f*; *of decision* inteligencia *f*

shriek [ʃriːk] **1** *n* alarido *m*, chillido *m* **2** *v/i* chillar

shrill [ʃrɪl] *adj* estridente, agudo

shrimp [ʃrɪmp] *gamba f*; *larger Span* langostino *m*, *L.Am.* camarón *m*

shrine [ʃraɪn] santuario *m*

shrink¹ [ʃrɪŋk] *v/i* (*pret* **shrank**, *pp* **shrunk**) *of material* encoger(se); *of level of support etc* reducirse

shrink² [ʃrɪŋk] *n* F (*psychiatrist*) psiquiatra *m/f*

'**shrink-wrap** *v/t* (*pret & pp* **-ped**) envolver en plástico adherente

'**shrink-wrap·ping** *material plástico adherente para envolver*

shriv·el ['ʃrɪvl] *v/i* (*pret & pp* **-ed**, *Br* **-led**) *of skin* arrugarse; *of leaves* marchitarse

shrub [ʃrʌb] arbusto *m*

shrub·be·ry ['ʃrʌbərɪ] arbustos *mpl*

shrug [ʃrʌɡ] **1** *n*: **... he said with a ~** ... dijo encogiendo los hombros **2** *v/i* (*pret & pp* **-ged**) encoger los hombros **3** *v/t* (*pret & pp* **-ged**): **~ one's shoulders** encoger los hombros

shrunk [ʃrʌŋk] *pp* → **shrink**

shud·der ['ʃʌdər] **1** *n of fear, disgust* escalofrío *m*; *of earth, building* temblor *m* **2** *v/i with fear, disgust* estremecerse; *of earth, building* temblar

shuf·fle ['ʃʌfl] **1** *v/t cards* barajar **2** *v/i in walking* arrastrar los pies

shun [ʃʌn] *v/t* (*pret & pp* **-ned**) rechazar

shut [ʃʌt] *v/t & v/i* (*pret & pp* **shut**) cerrar

◆**shut down 1** *v/t business* cerrar; *computer* apagar **2** *v/i of business* cerrarse; *of computer* apagarse

◆**shut off** *v/t* cortar

◆**shut up** *v/i* F (*be quiet*) callarse; **shut up!** ¡cállate!

shut·ter ['ʃʌtər] *on window* contraventana *f*; PHOT obturador *m*

'**shut·ter speed** PHOT tiempo *m* de exposición

shut·tle ['ʃʌtl] *v/i*: **~ between** *of bus* conectar; *of airplane* hacer el puente aéreo entre

'**shut·tle·bus** *at airport* autobús *m* de conexión; '**shut·tle·cock** SP volante *m*; '**shut·tle ser·vice** servicio *m* de conexión

shy [ʃaɪ] *adj* tímido

shy·ness ['ʃaɪnɪs] timidez *f*

Si·a·mese 'twins [saɪə'miːz] *npl* siameses *mpl* (*fpl*)

sick [sɪk] *adj* enfermo; *sense of humor* morboso, macabro; *society* enfermo; **be ~** (*vomit*) vomitar; **be ~ of** (*fed up with*) estar harto de

sick·en ['sɪkn] **1** *v/t* (*disgust*) poner enfermo **2** *v/i*: **be ~ing for sth** estar incubando algo

sick·en·ing ['sɪknɪŋ] *adj stench* nauseabundo; *behavior, crime* repugnante

'**sick leave** baja *f* (por enfermedad); **be on ~** estar de baja

sick·ly ['sɪklɪ] *adj person* enfermizo; *color* pálido

sick·ness ['sɪknɪs] enfermedad *f*; (*vomiting*) vómitos *mpl*

side [saɪd] *n of box, house, field* lado *m*; *of mountain* ladera *f*, vertiente *f*; *of person* costado *m*; SP equipo *m*; **take ~s** (*favor one ~*) tomar partido (**with** por); **I'm on your ~** estoy de parte tuya; **~ by ~** uno al lado del otro; **at the ~ of the road** al lado de la carretera; **on the big/ small ~** un poco grande / pequeño

◆**side with** *v/t* tomar partido por

'**side·board** aparador *m*; '**side·burns** *npl* patillas *fpl*; '**side dish** plato *m* de acompañamiento; '**side ef·fect** efecto *m* secundario; '**side·light** MOT luz *f* de posición;

S

'side·line 1 *n* actividad *f* complementaria 2 *v/t*: *feel ~d* sentirse marginado; 'side·step *v/t* (*pret & pp -ped*) *fig* evadir; 'side street bocacalle *f*; 'side·track *v/t* distraer; *get ~ed* distraerse; 'side·walk acera *f*, *Rpl* vereda *f*, *Mex* banqueta *f*; side·walk 'caf·é terraza *f*; side·ways ['saɪdweɪz] *adv* de lado

siege [siːdʒ] sitio *m*; *lay ~ to* sitiar
sieve [sɪv] *n* tamiz *m*
sift [sɪft] *v/t flour* tamizar; *data* examinar a fondo

♦ sift through *v/t details*, *data* pasar por el tamiz

sigh [saɪ] 1 *n* suspiro *m*; *heave a ~ of relief* suspirar de alivio 2 *v/i* suspirar

sight [saɪt] *n* vista *f*; (*power of seeing*) vista *f*, visión *f*; *~s of city* lugares *mpl* de interés; *he can't stand the ~ of blood* no aguanta ver sangre; *I caught ~ of him just as ...* lo vi justo cuando ...; *know by ~* conocer de vista; *within ~ of* a la vista de; *as soon as the car was out of ~* en cuanto se dejó de ver el coche; *what a ~ you look!* ¡qué pintas llevas!; *lose ~ of objective etc* olvidarse de

sight·see·ing ['saɪtsiːɪŋ]: *we like ~* nos gusta hacer turismo; *go ~* hacer turismo

'sight·see·ing tour visita *f* turística
sight·seer ['saɪtsiːər] turista *m/f*
sign [saɪn] 1 *n* señal *f*; *outside shop, on building* cartel *m*, letrero *m*; *it's a ~ of the times* es un signo de los tiempos que corren 2 *v/t & v/i* firmar

♦ sign in *v/i* registrarse
♦ sign up *v/i* (*join the army*) alistarse
sig·nal ['sɪgnl] 1 *n* señal *f*; *send out all the wrong ~s* dar a una impresión equivocada 2 *v/i* (*pret & pp -ed*, *Br* -led*) *of driver* poner el intermitente
sig·na·to·ry ['sɪgnətɔːrɪ] *n* signatario(-a) *m(f)*, firmante *m/f*
sig·na·ture ['sɪgnətʃər] firma *f*
sig·na·ture 'tune sintonía *f*
sig·net ring ['sɪgnɪt] sello *m* (*anillo*)
sig·nif·i·cance [sɪg'nɪfɪkəns] impor-

tancia *f*, relevancia *f*
sig·nif·i·cant [sɪg'nɪfɪkənt] *adj event etc* importante, relevante; (*quite large*) considerable
sig·nif·i·cant·ly [sɪg'nɪfɪkəntlɪ] *adv larger, more expensive* considerablemente
sig·ni·fy ['sɪgnɪfaɪ] *v/t* (*pret & pp -ied*) significar, suponer
'sign lan·guage lenguaje *m* por señas
'sign·post señal *f*
si·lence ['saɪləns] 1 *n* silencio *m*; *in ~* en silencio 2 *v/t* hacer callar
si·lenc·er ['saɪlənsər] *on gun* silenciador *m*
si·lent ['saɪlənt] *adj* silencioso; *movie* mudo; *stay ~* (*not comment*) permanecer callado
sil·hou·ette [sɪluː'et] *n* silueta *f*
sil·i·con ['sɪlɪkən] silicio *m*
sil·i·con 'chip chip *m* de silicio
sil·i·cone ['sɪlɪkoʊn] silicona *f*
silk [sɪlk] 1 *n* seda *f* 2 *adj shirt etc* de seda
silk·y ['sɪlkɪ] *adj hair, texture* sedoso
sil·li·ness ['sɪlɪnɪs] tontería *f*, estupidez *f*
sil·ly ['sɪlɪ] *adj* tonto, estúpido
si·lo ['saɪloʊ] silo *m*
sil·ver ['sɪlvər] 1 *n metal, medal* plata *f*; (*~ objects*) (objetos *mpl* de) plata *f* 2 *adj ring* de plata; *hair* canoso
sil·ver med·al medalla *f* de plata;
sil·ver-plat·ed [sɪlvər'pleɪtɪd] *adj* plateado; sil·ver·ware ['sɪlvərwer] plata *f*; sil·ver 'wed·ding bodas *fpl* de plata
sim·i·lar ['sɪmɪlər] *adj* parecido, similar; *be ~ to* ser parecido a, parecerse a
sim·i·lar·i·ty [sɪmɪ'lærətɪ] parecido *m*, similitud *f*
sim·i·lar·ly ['sɪmɪlərlɪ] *adv* de la misma manera
sim·mer ['sɪmər] *v/i in cooking* cocer a fuego lento; *be ~ing* (*with rage*) estar a punto de explotar
♦ simmer down *v/i* tranquilizarse
sim·ple ['sɪmpl] *adj* (*easy, not fancy*) sencillo; *person* simple

S

simple-minded

sim·ple-mind·ed [sɪmpl'maɪndɪd] *adj pej* simplón

sim·pli·ci·ty [sɪm'plɪsətɪ] *of task, design* sencillez *f*, simplicidad *f*

sim·pli·fy ['sɪmplɪfaɪ] *v/t (pret & pp -ied)* simplificar

sim·plis·tic [sɪm'plɪstɪk] *adj* simplista

sim·ply ['sɪmplɪ] *adv* sencillamente; *it is ~ the best* es sin lugar a dudas el mejor

sim·u·late ['sɪmjʊleɪt] *v/t* simular

sim·ul·ta·ne·ous [saɪml'teɪnɪəs] *adj* simultáneo

sim·ul·ta·ne·ous·ly [saɪml'teɪnɪəslɪ] *adv* simultáneamente

sin [sɪn] **1** *n* pecado *m* **2** *v/i (pret & pp -ned)* pecar

since [sɪns] **1** *prep* desde; *~ last week* desde la semana pasada **2** *adv* desde entonces; *I haven't seen him ~* no lo he visto desde entonces **3** *conj in expressions of time* desde que; *(seeing that)* ya que, dado que; *~ you left* desde que te marchaste; *~ I have been living here* desde que vivo aquí; *~ you don't like it* ya que *or* dado que no te gusta

sin·cere [sɪn'sɪr] *adj* sincero

sin·cere·ly [sɪn'sɪrlɪ] *adv* sinceramente; *I ~ hope he appreciates it* espero de verdad que lo aprecie; *Yours ~* atentamente

sin·cer·i·ty [sɪn'serətɪ] sinceridad *f*

sin·ful ['sɪnfəl] *adj person* pecador; *things* pecaminoso; *it is ~ to ...* es pecado ...

sing [sɪŋ] *v/t & v/i (pret sang, pp sung)* cantar

singe [sɪndʒ] *v/t* chamuscar

sing·er ['sɪŋər] cantante *m/f*

sin·gle ['sɪŋgl] **1** *adj (sole)* único, solo; *(not double)* único; *(not married)* soltero *m*; *there wasn't a ~ mistake* no había ni un solo error; *in ~ file* en fila india **2** *n* MUS sencillo *m*; *(~ room)* habitación *f* individual; *person* soltero(-a) *m(f)*; *Br ticket* billete *m or L.Am.* boleto *m* de ida; *holidays for ~s* vacaciones para gente sin pareja; *~s in tennis* indivi-

duales *mpl*

◆ **single out** *v/t (choose)* seleccionar; *(distinguish)* distinguir

sin·gle-breast·ed [sɪŋgl'brestɪd] *adj* recto, con una fila de botones; **sin·gle-'hand·ed** [sɪŋgl'hændɪd] *adj & adv* en solitario; **sin·gle-mind·ed** [sɪŋgl'maɪndɪd] *adj* determinado, resuelto; **Sin·gle 'Mar·ket** *(in Europe)* Mercado *m* Único; **sin·gle 'moth·er** madre *f* soltera; **sin·gle 'pa·rent** padre *m* / madre *f* soltero(-a); **sin·gle pa·rent 'fam·i·ly** familia *f* monoparental; **sin·gle 'room** habitación *f* individual

sin·gu·lar ['sɪŋgjʊlər] **1** *adj* GRAM singular **2** *n* GRAM singular *m*; *in the ~* en singular

sin·is·ter ['sɪnɪstər] *adj* siniestro; *sky* amenazador

sink [sɪŋk] **1** *n in kitchen* fregadero *m*; *in bathroom* lavabo *m* **2** *v/i (pret sank, pp sunk) of ship, object* hundirse; *of sun* ponerse; *of interest rates, pressure etc* descender, bajar; *he sank onto the bed* se tiró a la cama **3** *v/t (pret sank, pp sunk) ship* hundir; *funds* invertir

◆ **sink in** *v/i of liquid* penetrar; *it still hasn't really sunk in of realization* todavía no lo he asumido

sin·ner ['sɪnər] pecador(a) *m(f)*

si·nus ['saɪnəs] seno *m (nasal)*

si·nus·i·tis [saɪnə'saɪtɪs] MED sinusitis *f*

sip [sɪp] **1** *n* sorbo *m* **2** *v/t (pret & pp -ped)* sorber

sir [sɜːr] señor *m*; *excuse me, ~* perdone, caballero

si·ren ['saɪrən] sirena *f*

sir·loin ['sɜːlɔɪn] solomillo *m*

sis·ter ['sɪstər] hermana *f*

'sis·ter-in-law *(pl sisters-in-law)* cuñada *f*

sit [sɪt] *v/i (pret & pp sat)* estar sentado; *(~ down)* sentarse

◆ **sit down** *v/i* sentarse

◆ **sit up** *v/i in bed* incorporarse; *(straighten one's back)* sentarse derecho; *(wait up at night)* esperar levantado

sit·com ['sɪtkɑːm] telecomedia f, comedia f de situación

site [saɪt] **1** n emplazamiento m; of battle lugar m **2** v/t new offices etc situar

sit·ting ['sɪtɪŋ] n of committee, court, for artist sesión f; for meals turno m

'sit·ting room sala f de estar, salón m

sit·u·at·ed ['sɪtʊeɪtɪd] adj situado

sit·u·a·tion [sɪtʊ'eɪʃn] situación f

six [sɪks] seis

six·teen [sɪks'tiːn] dieciséis

six·teenth [sɪks'tiːnθ] n & adj decimosexto

sixth [sɪksθ] n & adj sexto

six·ti·eth ['sɪkstɪɪθ] n & adj sexagésimo

six·ty ['sɪkstɪ] sesenta

size [saɪz] tamaño m; of loan importe m; of jacket talla f; of shoes número m
♦ **size up** v/t evaluar, examinar

size·a·ble ['saɪzəbl] adj house, order considerable; meal copioso

siz·zle ['sɪzl] v/i chisporrotear

skate [skeɪt] **1** n patín m **2** v/i patinar

skate·board ['skeɪtbɔːrd] n monopatín m

skate·board·er ['skeɪtbɔːrdər] persona que patina en monopatín

skate·board·ing ['skeɪtbɔːrdɪŋ] patinaje m en monopatín

skat·er ['skeɪtər] patinador(a) m(f)

skat·ing ['skeɪtɪŋ] patinaje m

'skat·ing rink pista f de patinaje

skel·e·ton ['skelɪtn] esqueleto m

'skel·e·ton key llave f maestra

skep·tic ['skeptɪk] escéptico(-a) m(f)

skep·ti·cal ['skeptɪkl] adj escéptico

skep·ti·cism ['skeptɪsɪzm] escepticismo m

sketch [sketʃ] **1** n boceto m, esbozo m; THEA sketch m **2** v/t bosquejar

'sketch·book cuaderno m de dibujo

sketch·y ['sketʃɪ] adj knowledge etc básico, superficial

skew·er ['skjʊər] n brocheta f

ski [skiː] **1** n esquí m **2** v/i esquiar

'ski boots npl botas fpl de esquí

skid [skɪd] **1** n of car patinazo m; of person resbalón m **2** v/i (pret & pp
-ded) of car patinar; of person resbalar

ski·er ['skiːər] esquiador(a) m(f)

ski·ing ['skiːɪŋ] esquí m

'ski in·struc·tor monitor(a) m(f) de esquí

skil·ful etc Br → **skillful** etc

'ski lift remonte m

skill [skɪl] destreza f, habilidad f

skilled [skɪld] adj capacitado, preparado

skilled 'work·er trabajador(a) m(f) cualificado

'skill·ful ['skɪlfəl] adj hábil, habilidoso

'skill·ful·ly ['skɪlfəlɪ] adv con habilidad or destreza

skim [skɪm] v/t (pret & pp -med) surface rozar; milk desnatar, descremar
♦ **skim off** v/t the best escoger
♦ **skim through** v/t text leer por encima

skimmed 'milk [skɪmd] leche f desnatada or descremada

skimp·y ['skɪmpɪ] adj account etc superficial; dress cortísimo; bikini mínimo

skin [skɪn] **1** n piel f **2** v/t (pret & pp -ned) despellejar, desollar

'skin div·ing buceo m (en bañador)

skin·flint ['skɪnflɪnt] F agarrado(a) m(f) F, roñoso(-a) m(f)

skin graft injerto m de piel

skin·ny ['skɪnɪ] adj escuálido

'skin-tight adj ajustado

skip [skɪp] **1** n (little jump) brinco m, saltito m **2** v/i (pret & pp -ped) brincar **3** v/t (pret & pp -ped) (omit) pasar por alto

'ski pole bastón m de esquí

skip·per ['skɪpər] NAUT patrón (-ona) m(f), capitán (-ana) m(f); of team capitán(-ana) m(f)

'ski re·sort estación f de esquí

skirt [skɜːrt] n falda f

'ski run pista f de esquí

'ski tow telesquí m

skull [skʌl] cráneo m

skunk [skʌŋk] mofeta f

sky [skaɪ] cielo m

'sky·light claraboya f; **'sky·line** horizonte *m*; **sky·scrap·er** ['skaɪ-skreɪpər] rascacielos *m inv*

slab [slæb] *of stone* losa *f*; *of cake etc* trozo *m* grande

slack [slæk] *adj rope* flojo; *work* descuidado; *period* tranquilo; **discipli-ne is very ~** no hay disciplina

slack·en ['slækn] *v/t rope, pace* aflojar

♦**slacken off** *v/i of trading, pace* disminuir

slacks [slæks] *npl* pantalones *mpl*

slain [sleɪn] *pp →* **slay**

slam [slæm] **1** *v/t (pret & pp -med) door* cerrar de un golpe **2** *v/i (pret & pp -med) of door* cerrarse de golpe

♦**slam down** *v/t* estampar

slan·der ['slændər] **1** *n* difamación *f* **2** *v/t* difamar

slan·der·ous ['slændərəs] *adj* difamatorio

slang [slæŋ] argot *m*, jerga *f*; *of a specific group* jerga *f*

slant [slænt] **1** *v/i* inclinarse **2** *n* inclinación *f*; *given to a story* enfoque *m*

slant·ing ['slæntɪŋ] *adj roof* inclinado; *eyes* rasgado

slap [slæp] **1** *n (blow)* bofetada *f*, cachete *m* **2** *v/t (pret & pp -ped)* dar una bofetada *or* un cachete a; **~ s.o. in the face** dar una bofetada a alguien **3** *adv* F de plano F

'slap-dash *adj* chapucero

slash [slæʃ] **1** *n cut* corte *m*, raja *f*; *in punctuation* barra *f* **2** *v/t skin etc* cortar; *prices, costs* recortar drásticamente; **~ one's wrists** cortarse las venas

slate [sleɪt] *n* pizarra *f*

slaugh·ter ['slɔːtər] **1** *n of animals* sacrificio *m*; *of people, troops* matanza *f* **2** *v/t animals* sacrificar; *people, troops* masacrar

'slaugh·ter·house *for animals* matadero *m*

Slav [slɑːv] *adj* eslavo

slave [sleɪv] *n* esclavo(-a) *m(f)*

'slave-driv·er F negrero(-a) *m(f)* F

slay [sleɪ] *v/t (pret slew, pp slain)* asesinar

slay·ing ['sleɪɪŋ] *(murder)* asesinato *m*

sleaze [sliːz] POL corrupción *f*

slea·zy ['sliːzɪ] *adj bar* sórdido; *person* de mala calaña

sled, sledge [sled, sledʒ] *n* trineo *m*

'sledge ham·mer mazo *m*

sleep [sliːp] **1** *n* sueño *m*; **go to ~** dormirse; **I need a good ~** necesito dormir bien; **I couldn't get to ~** no pude dormir **2** *v/i (pret & pp slept)* dormir; **~ late** dormir hasta tarde

♦**sleep on** *v/t:* **sleep on sth** *decision* consultar algo con la almohada

♦**sleep with** *v/t (have sex with)* acostarse con

sleep·i·ly ['sliːpɪlɪ] *adv:* **say sth ~** decir algo medio dormido

'sleep·ing bag ['sliːpɪŋ] saco *m* de dormir; **'sleep·ing car** RAIL coche *m* cama; **'sleep·ing pill** somnífero *m*, pastilla *f* para dormir

sleep·less ['sliːplɪs] *adj:* **have a ~ night** pasar la noche en blanco

'sleep·walk·er sonámbulo(-a) *m(f)*

'sleep·walk·ing sonambulismo *m*

sleep·y ['sliːpɪ] *adj* adormilado, somnoliento; *town* tranquilo; **I'm ~** tengo sueño

sleet [sliːt] *n* aguanieve *f*

sleeve [sliːv] *of jacket etc* manga *f*

sleeve·less ['sliːvlɪs] *adj* sin mangas

sleigh [sleɪ] *n* trineo *m*

sleight of 'hand [slaɪt] juegos *mpl* de manos

slen·der ['slendər] *adj figure, arms* esbelto; *income, margin* escaso; *chance* remoto

slept [slept] *pret & pp →* **sleep**

slew [sluː] *pret →* **slay**

slice [slaɪs] **1** *n of bread* rebanada *f*; *of cake* trozo *m*; *of salami, cheese* loncha *f*; *fig: of profits etc* parte *f* **2** *v/t loaf etc* cortar (en rebanadas)

sliced 'bread [slaɪst] pan *m* de molde en rebanadas

slick [slɪk] **1** *adj performance* muy logrado; *(pej: cunning)* con mucha labia **2** *n of oil* marea *f* negra

slid [slɪd] *pret & pp →* **slide**

slide [slaɪd] **1** *n for kids* tobogán *m*; PHOT diapositiva *f* **2** *v/i (pret & pp* *slid*) deslizarse; *of exchange rate etc* descender **3** *v/t* (*pret & pp* **slid**) deslizar

slid·ing 'door ['slaɪdɪŋ] puerta *f* corredera

slight [slaɪt] *adj person, figure* menudo; (*small*) pequeño; *accent* ligero; *I have a ~ headache* me duele un poco la cabeza; *no, not in the ~est* no, en absoluto

slight·ly ['slaɪtlɪ] *adv* un poco

slim [slɪm] **1** *adj* delgado; *chance* remoto **2** *v/i* (*pret & pp* **-med**): *I'm ~ming* estoy a dieta

slime [slaɪm] (*mud*) lodo *m*; *of slug etc* baba *f*

slim·y ['slaɪmɪ] *adj liquid* viscoso; *river bed* lleno de lodo

sling [slɪŋ] **1** *n for arm* cabestrillo *m* **2** *v/t* (*pret & pp* **slung**) F (*throw*) tirar

slip [slɪp] **1** *n on ice etc* resbalón *m*; (*mistake*) desliz *m*; *a ~ of paper* un trozo de papel; *a ~ of the tongue* un lapsus; *give s.o. the ~* dar esquinazo a alguien **2** *v/i* (*pret & pp* **-ped**) *on ice etc* resbalar; *of quality etc* empeorar; *he ~ped out of the room* se fue de la habitación sigilosamente **3** *v/t* (*pret & pp* **-ped**) (*put*): *he ~ped it into his briefcase* lo metió en su maletín sigilosamente; *it ~ped my mind* se me olvidó

♦ **slip away** *v/i of time* pasar; *of opportunity* esfumarse; (*die quietly*) morir tranquilamente

♦ **slip off** *v/t jacket etc* quitarse

♦ **slip on** *v/t jacket etc* ponerse

♦ **slip out** *v/i* (*go out*) salir (sigilosamente)

♦ **slip up** *v/i* (*make mistake*) equivocarse

slipped 'disc [slɪpt] hernia *f* discal

slip·per ['slɪpər] zapatilla *f* (*de estar por casa*)

slip·per·y ['slɪpərɪ] *adj surface, road* resbaladizo; *fish* escurridizo

slip·shod ['slɪpʃɑːd] *adj* chapucero

'slip-up (*mistake*) error *m*

slit [slɪt] **1** *n* (*tear*) raja *f*; (*hole*) rendija *f*; *in skirt* corte *m* **2** *v/t* (*pret & pp*

slit) abrir; *~ s.o.'s throat* degollar a alguien

slith·er ['slɪðər] *v/i* deslizarse

sliv·er ['slɪvər] trocito *m*, *of wood, glass* astilla *f*

slob [slɑːb] *pej* dejado(-a) *m/f*, guarro(-a) *m/f*

slob·ber ['slɑːbər] *v/i* babear

slog [slɑːg] *n* paliza *f*

slo·gan ['sloʊgən] eslogan *m*

slop [slɑːp] *v/t* (*pret & pp* **-ped**) derramar

slope [sloʊp] **1** *n of roof, handwriting* inclinación *f*; *of mountain* ladera *f*; *built on a ~* construido en una pendiente **2** *v/i* inclinarse; *the road ~s down to the sea* la carretera baja hasta el mar

slop·py ['slɑːpɪ] *adj* descuidado; *too sentimental* sensiblero

slot [slɑːt] *n* ranura *f*; *in schedule* hueco *m*

♦ **slot in 1** *v/t* (*pret & pp* **-ted**) introducir **2** *v/i* (*pret & pp* **-ted**) encajar

'slot ma·chine *for cigarettes, food* máquina *f* expendedora; *for gambling* máquina *f* tragaperras

slouch [slaʊtʃ] *v/i*: *don't ~* ponte derecho

slov·en·ly ['slʌvnlɪ] *adj* descuidado

slow [sloʊ] *adj* lento; *be ~ of clock* ir retrasado

♦ **slow down 1** *v/t work, progress* retrasar; *traffic, production* ralentizar **2** *v/i in walking, driving* reducir la velocidad; *of production etc* relantizarse; *you need to slow down in lifestyle* tienes que tomarte las cosas con calma

'slow·down *in production* ralentización *f*

slow·ly ['sloʊlɪ] *adv* despacio, lentamente

slow 'mo·tion: *in ~* a cámara lenta

slow·ness ['sloʊnɪs] lentitud *f*

'slow·poke F tortuga *f* F

slug [slʌg] *n animal* babosa *f*

slug·gish ['slʌgɪʃ] *adj* lento

slum [slʌm] *n* suburbio *m*, arrabal

slump [slʌmp] **1** *n in trade* desplome *m* **2** *v/i economically* desplomarse, hundirse; (*collapse: of person*) desplomarse

slung [slʌŋ] *pret* & *pp* → **sling**

slur [slɜːr] **1** *n on s.o.'s character* difamación *f* **2** *v/t* (*pret* & *pp* **-red**) *words* arrastrar

slurp [slɜːrp] *v/t* sorber

slurred [slɜːrd] *adj*: **his speech was ~** habló arrastrando las palabras

slush [slʌʃ] nieve *f* derretida; (*pej*: *sentimental stuff*) sensiblería *f*

'**slush fund** fondo *m* para corruptelas

slush·y ['slʌʃɪ] *adj snow* derretido; *movie*, *novel* sensiblero

slut [slʌt] *pej* fulana *f*

sly [slaɪ] *adj* ladino; **on the ~** a escondidas

smack [smæk] **1** *n*: **a ~ on the bottom** un azote; **a ~ in the face** una bofetada **2** *v/t child* pegar; *bottom* dar un azote en

small [smɒːl] *adj* pequeño, *L.Am.* chico

small 'change cambio *m*, suelto *m*, *L.Am.* sencillo *m*; **small 'hours** *npl* madrugada *f*; **small·pox** ['smɒːlpɑːks] viruela *f*; **small print** letra *f* pequeña; '**small talk**: **make ~** hablar de banalidades *or* trivialidades

smart¹ [smɑːrt] *adj* (*elegant*) elegante; (*intelligent*) inteligente; *pace* rápido; **get ~ with** hacerse el listillo con

smart² [smɑːrt] *v/i* (*hurt*) escocer

'**smart ass** F sabelotodo *m/f* F

'**smart card** tarjeta *f* inteligente

♦**smart·en up** ['smɑːrtn] *v/t appearance* mejorar; *room* arreglar

smart·ly ['smɑːrtlɪ] *adv dressed* con elegancia

smash [smæʃ] **1** *n noise* estruendo *m*; (*car crash*) choque *m*; *in tennis* smash *m*, mate *m* **2** *v/t break* hacer pedazos *or* añicos; **he ~ed the toys against the wall** estrelló los juguetes contra la pared; **~ sth to pieces** hacer algo añicos **3** *v/i break* romperse; **the driver ~ed into ...** el conductor se estrelló contra ...

♦**smash up** *v/t place* destrozar

smash 'hit F exitazo *m* F

smat·ter·ing ['smætərɪŋ] *of a language* nociones *fpl*

smear [smɪr] **1** *n of ink* borrón *m*; *of paint* mancha *f*; MED citología *f*; *on character* difamación *f* **2** *v/t character* difamar; **~ X over Y** untar *or* embadurnar Y de X

'**smear cam·paign** campaña *f* de difamación

smell [smel] **1** *n olor m*; **it has no ~** no huele a nada; **sense of ~** sentido *m* del olfato **2** *v/t* oler **3** *v/i unpleasantly* oler (mal); (*sniff*) olfatear; **you ~ of beer** hueles a cerveza; **it ~s good** huele bien

smell·y ['smelɪ] *adj* apestoso; **she had ~ feet** le olían los pies

smile [smaɪl] **1** *n* sonrisa *f* **2** *v/i* sonreír

♦**smile at** *v/t* sonreír a

smirk [smɜːrk] **1** *n* sonrisa *f* maligna **2** *v/i* sonreír malignamente

smog [smɑːg] niebla *f* tóxica

smoke [smoʊk] **1** *n* humo *m*; **have a ~** fumarse un cigarrillo **2** *v/t cigarettes* fumar; *bacon* ahumar **3** *v/i of person* fumar

smok·er ['smoʊkər] *person* fumador(-a) *m(f)*

smok·ing ['smoʊkɪŋ]: **~ is bad for you** fumar es malo; **no ~** prohibido fumar

'**smok·ing car** RAIL compartimento *m* de fumadores

smok·y ['smoʊkɪ] *adj room, air* lleno de humo

smol·der, *Br* **smoul·der** ['smoʊldər] *v/i with anger* arder de rabia; *with desire* arder en deseos; **the fire was still ~ing** todavía ardían los rescoldos

smooth [smuːð] **1** *adj surface, skin* liso, suave; *sea* en calma; (*peaceful*) tranquilo; *ride, drive* sin vibraciones; *transition* sin problemas; *pej: person* meloso **2** *v/t hair* alisar

♦**smooth down** *v/t with sandpaper etc* alisar

♦**smooth out** *v/t paper, cloth* alisar

♦**smooth over** *v/t*: **smooth things over** suavizar las cosas

smooth·ly ['smu:ðlɪ] *adv without any problems* sin incidentes

smoth·er ['smʌðər] *v/t flames* apagar, sofocar; *person* asfixiar; **~ s.o. with kisses** comerse a alguien a besos

smoul·der ['smoʊldər] *v/i Br* → **smolder**

smudge [smʌdʒ] **1** *n of paint* mancha *f*; *of ink* borrón *m* **2** *v/t ink* emborronar; *paint* difuminar

smug [smʌg] *adj* engreído

smug·gle ['smʌgl] *v/t* pasar de contrabando

smug·gler ['smʌglər] contrabandista *m/f*

smug·gling ['smʌglɪŋ] contrabando *m*

smug·ly ['smʌglɪ] *adv* con engreimiento *or* suficiencia

smut·ty ['smʌtɪ] *adj joke* obsceno

snack [snæk] *n* tentempié *m*, aperitivo *m*

'snack bar cafetería *f*

snag [snæg] *n (problem)* inconveniente *m*, pega *f*

snail [sneɪl] caracol *m*

snake [sneɪk] *n* serpiente *f*

snap [snæp] **1** *n* chasquido *m*; PHOT foto *f* **2** *v/t (pret & pp -ped) break* romper; *none of your business, she* ~*ped* no es asunto tuyo, saltó **3** *v/i (pret & pp -ped) break* romperse **4** *adj decision, judgement* rápido, súbito

♦ **snap up** *v/t bargains* llevarse

snap fast·en·er ['snæpfæsnər] automático *m*, corchete *m*

snap·py ['snæpɪ] *adj person, mood* irascible; *decision, response* rápido; *(elegant)* elegante

'snap·shot foto *f*

snarl [snɑːrl] **1** *n of dog* gruñido *m* **2** *v/i* gruñir

snatch [snætʃ] **1** *v/t* arrebatar; *(steal)* robar; *(kidnap)* secuestrar; **~ sth from s.o.** arrebatar algo a alguien **2** *v/i*: *don't* ~ no lo agarres

♦ **snatch at** *v/t* intentar agarrar

snaz·zy ['snæzɪ] *adj F* vistoso, *Span* chulo *F*

sneak [sniːk] **1** *v/t (remove, steal)* lle-

varse; **~ a glance at** mirar con disimulo a **2** *v/i*: **~ into the room** entrar a la habitación a hurtadillas

sneak·ers ['sniːkərz] *npl* zapatillas *fpl* de deporte

sneak·ing ['sniːkɪŋ] *adj*: **have a ~ suspicion that ...** sospechar que ...

sneak·y ['sniːkɪ] *adj F (crafty)* ladino, cuco *F*

sneer [snɪr] **1** *n* mueca *f* desdeñosa **2** *v/i* burlarse **(at** de)

sneeze [sniːz] **1** *n* estornudo *m* **2** *v/i* estornudar

snick·er ['snɪkər] **1** *n* risita *f* **2** *v/i* reírse *(en voz baja)*

sniff [snɪf] **1** *v/i to clear nose* sorberse los mocos; *of dog* olfatear **2** *v/t (smell)* oler; *of dog* olfatear

snip [snɪp] *n F (bargain)* ganga *f*

snip·er ['snaɪpər] francotirador(a) *m(f)*

snitch [snɪtʃ] *F* **1** *n (telltale)* chivato(-a) *m(f)* **2** *v/i* chivarse

sniv·el ['snɪvl] *v/i* gimotear

snob [snɑːb] presuntuoso(-a) *m(f)*

snob·ber·y ['snɑːbərɪ] presuntuosidad *f*

snob·bish ['snɑːbɪʃ] *adj* presuntuoso

snoop [snuːp] *n* fisgón(-ona) *m(f)*

♦ **snoop around** *v/i* fisgonear

snoot·y ['snuːtɪ] *adj* presuntuoso

snooze [snuːz] **1** *n* cabezada *f*; **have a ~** echar una cabezada **2** *v/i* echar una cabezada

snore [snɔːr] *v/i* roncar

snor·ing ['snɔːrɪŋ] ronquidos *mpl*

snor·kel ['snɔːrkl] *n* snorkel *m*, tubo *m* para bucear

snort [snɔːrt] *v/i of bull, person* bufar, resoplar

snout [snaʊt] *of pig, dog* hocico *m*

snow [snoʊ] **1** *n* nieve *f* **2** *v/i* nevar

♦ **snow under** *v/t*: **be snowed under** estar desbordado

'snow·ball bola *f* de nieve; **'snow·bound** *adj* aislado por la nieve; **'snow chains** *npl* MOT cadenas *fpl* para la nieve; **'snow·drift** nevero *m*; **'snow·drop** campanilla *f* de invierno; **'snow·flake** copo *m* de nieve; **'snow·man** muñeco *m* de

nieve; '**snow·plow** quitanieves *f
inv*; '**snow·storm** tormenta *f* de nieve

snow·y ['snoʊɪ] *adj weather* de nieve;
roads, hills nevado

snub [snʌb] **1** *n* desaire **2** *v/t* (*pret &
pp* **-bed**) desairar

snub-nosed ['snʌbnoʊzd] *adj* con la
nariz respingona

snug [snʌg] *adj* (*tight-fitting*) ajustado; *we are nice and ~ in here* aquí
se está muy a gusto

♦ **snug·gle down** ['snʌgl] *v/i* acurrucarse

♦ **snug·gle up to** *v/t* acurrucarse contra

so [soʊ] **1** *adv* tan; *it was ~ easy* fue
tan fácil; *I'm ~ cold* tengo tanto frío;
that was ~ kind of you fue muy
amable de tu parte; *not ~ much* no
tanto; *~ much easier* mucho más fácil; *you shouldn't eat/drink ~
much* no deberías comer/beber
tanto; *I miss you ~* te echo tanto de
menos; *~ am/do I* yo también; *~ is
she/does she* ella también; *and ~
on* etcétera **2** *pron: I hope/think ~*
eso espero/creo; *you didn't tell me
– I did* no me lo dijiste – sí que lo
hice; *50 or ~* unos 50 **3** *conj for that
reason* así que; *in order that* para que;
*I got up late and ~ I missed the
train* me levanté tarde y por eso per-
dí el tren; *~ (that) I could come too*
para que yo también pudiera venir;
~ what? F ¿y qué? F

soak [soʊk] *v/t* (*steep*) poner en remojo; *of water, rain* empapar

♦ **soak up** *v/t liquid* absorber; *soak
up the sun* tostarse al sol

soaked [soʊkt] *adj* empapado; *be ~
to the skin* estar calado hasta los
huesos

soak·ing (wet) ['soʊkɪŋ] *adj* empapado

so-and-so ['soʊənsoʊ] F (*unknown
person*) fulanito *m*; (*euph: annoying
person*) canalla *m/f*

soap [soʊp] *for washing* jabón *m*

'**soap** (**op·e·ra**) telenovela *f*

soap·y ['soʊpɪ] *adj water* jabonoso

soar [sɔːr] *v/i of rocket etc* elevarse; *of
prices* dispararse

sob [saːb] **1** *n* sollozo *m* **2** *v/i* (*pret &
pp* **-bed**) sollozar

so·ber ['soʊbər] *adj* (*not drunk*) sobrio; (*serious*) serio

♦ **sober up** *v/i: he sobered up* se le
pasó la borrachera

so-'called *adj* (*referred to as*) así llamado; (*incorrectly referred to as*) mal
llamado

soc·cer ['saːkər] fútbol *m*

'**soc·cer hoo·li·gan** hincha *m* violento

so·cia·ble ['soʊʃəbl] *adj* sociable

so·cial ['soʊʃl] *adj* social

so·cial 'dem·o·crat socialdemócra-
ta *m/f*

so·cial·ism ['soʊʃəlɪzm] socialismo
m

so·cial·ist ['soʊʃəlɪst] **1** *adj* socialista
2 *n* socialista *m/f*

so·cial·ize ['soʊʃəlaɪz] *v/i* socializar
(*with* con)

'**so·cial life** vida *f* social; **so·cial
'sci·ence** ciencia *f* social; '**so·cial
work** trabajo *m* social; '**so·cial
work·er** asistente(-a) *m(f)*

so·ci·e·ty [sə'saɪətɪ] sociedad *f*

so·ci·ol·o·gist [soʊsɪ'aːlədʒɪst]
sociólogo(-a) *m(f)*

so·ci·ol·o·gy [soʊsɪ'aːlədʒɪ] sociología *f*

sock[1] [saːk] *for wearing* calcetín *m*

sock[2] [saːk] **1** *n* (*punch*) puñetazo *m*
2 *v/t* (*punch*) dar un puñetazo a

sock·et ['saːkɪt] *for light bulb* casquillo *m*; *of arm* cavidad *f*; *of eye* cuenca
f; ELEC enchufe *m*

so·da ['soʊdə] (*~ water*) soda *f*; (*soft
drink*) refresco *m*; (*ice-cream ~*) refresco de soda con helado

sod·den ['saːdn] *adj* empapado

so·fa ['soʊfə] sofá *m*

'**so·fa-bed** sofá cama *m*

soft [saːft] *adj voice, light, color, skin*
suave; *pillow, attitude* blando; *have a
~ spot for* tener una debilidad por

'**soft drink** refresco *m*

'**soft drug** droga *f* blanda

soft·en ['saːfn] **1** *v/t position* ablandar; *impact, blow* amortiguar **2** *v/i of butter, ice cream* ablandarse, reblandecerse

soft·ly ['sɒftlɪ] *adv* suavemente

soft 'toy peluche *m*

soft·ware ['sɒftwer] software *m*

sog·gy ['sɒgɪ] *adj* empapado

soil [sɔɪl] **1** *n* (*earth*) tierra *f* **2** *v/t* ensuciar

so·lar 'en·er·gy ['soʊlər] energía *f* solar; **'so·lar pan·el** panel *m* solar; **'solar sys·tem** sistema *m* solar

sold [soʊld] *pret & pp →* **sell**

sol·dier ['soʊldʒər] soldado *m*

♦ **soldier on** *v/i* seguir adelante; **we'll have to soldier on without her** nos las tendremos que arreglar sin ella

sole[1] [soʊl] *n of foot* planta *f*; *of shoe* suela *f*

sole[2] [soʊl] *adj* único

sole·ly ['soʊlɪ] *adv* únicamente

sol·emn ['sɑːləm] *adj* solemne

so·lem·ni·ty [sə'lemnətɪ] solemnidad *f*

sol·emn·ly ['sɑːləmlɪ] *adv* solemnemente

so·lic·it [sə'lɪsɪt] *v/i of prostitute* abordar clientes

so·lic·i·tor [sə'lɪsɪtər] *Br* abogado(-a) *m(f)* (*que no aparece en tribunales*)

sol·id ['sɑːlɪd] *adj* sólido; (*without holes*) compacto; *gold, silver* macizo; **a ~ hour** una hora seguida

sol·i·dar·i·ty [sɑːlɪ'dærətɪ] solidaridad *f*

so·lid·i·fy [sə'lɪdɪfaɪ] *v/i* (*pret & pp -ied*) solidificarse

sol·id·ly ['sɑːlɪdlɪ] *adv* built sólidamente; *in favor of sth* unánimente

so·lil·o·quy [sə'lɪləkwɪ] soliloquio *m*

sol·i·taire [sɑːlɪ'ter] *card game* solitario *m*

sol·i·ta·ry ['sɑːlɪterɪ] *adj life, activity* solitario; (*single*) único

sol·i·ta·ry con'fine·ment prisión *f* incomunicada

sol·i·tude ['sɑːlɪtuːd] soledad *f*

so·lo ['soʊloʊ] **1** *n* MUS solo *m* **2** *adj* en solitario

so·lo·ist ['soʊloʊɪst] solista *m/f*

sol·u·ble ['sɑːljʊbl] *adj substance, problem* soluble

so·lu·tion [sə'luːʃn] (*also mixture*) solución *f*

solve [sɑːlv] *v/t problem* solucionar, resolver; *mystery* resolver; *crossword* resolver, sacar

sol·vent ['sɑːlvənt] *adj financially* solvente

som·ber, *Br* **som·bre** ['sɑːmbər] *adj* (*dark*) oscuro; (*serious*) sombrío

some [sʌm] **1** *adj:* **would you like ~ water/ cookies?** ¿quieres agua/ galletas?; **~ countries** algunos países; **I gave him ~ money** le di (algo de) dinero; **~ people say that ...** hay quien dice ... **2** *pron:* **~ of the group** parte del grupo; **would you like ~?** ¿quieres?; **milk? – no thanks, I already have ~** ¿leche? – gracias, ya tengo **3** *adv* (*a bit*): **we'll have to wait ~** tendremos que esperar algo *or* un poco

some·bod·y ['sʌmbədɪ] *pron* alguien; **'some·day** *adv* algún día; **'some·how** *adv* (*by one means or another*) de alguna manera; (*for some unknown reason*) por alguna razón; **I've never liked him ~** por alguna razón u otra nunca me cayó bien

'some·one *pron →* **somebody**

'some·place *adv →* **somewhere**

som·er·sault ['sʌmərsɒːlt] **1** *n* salto mortal **2** *v/i* dar un salto mortal

'some·thing *pron* algo; **would you like ~ to drink/ eat?** ¿te gustaría beber/ comer algo?; **is ~ wrong?** ¿pasa algo?

'some·time *adv:* **let's have lunch ~** quedemos para comer un día de éstos; **~ last year** en algún momento del año pasado

'some·times ['sʌmtaɪmz] *adv* a veces

'some·what *adv* un tanto

'some·where 1 *adv* en alguna parte *or* algún lugar **2** *pron:* **let's go to ~ quiet** vamos a algún sitio tranquilo; **I was looking for ~ to park** buscaba un sitio donde aparcar

S

son [sʌn] hijo *m*

so·na·ta [sə'nɑːtə] MUS sonata *f*

song [sɒŋ] canción *f*

'song·bird pájaro *m* cantor

'song·writ·er cantautor(a) *m(f)*

'son-in-law (*pl* **sons-in-law**) yerno *m*

'son·net ['sɑːnɪt] soneto *m*

son of a 'bitch n V hijo *m* de puta P

soon [suːn] *adv* pronto; *how ~ can you be ready to leave?* ¿cuándo estarás listo para salir?; *he left ~ after I arrived* se marchó al poco de llegar yo; *can't you get here any ~er?* ¿no podrías llegar antes?; *as ~ as* tan pronto como; *as ~ as possible* lo antes posible; *~er or later* tarde o temprano; *the ~er the better* cuanto antes mejor

soot [sʊt] hollín *m*

soothe [suːð] *v/t* calmar

so·phis·ti·cat·ed [sə'fɪstɪkeɪtɪd] *adj* sofisticado

so·phis·ti·ca·tion [sə'fɪstɪkeɪʃn] sofisticación *f*

soph·o·more ['sɑːfəmɔːr] estudiante *m/f* de segundo año

sop·py ['sɑːpɪ] *adj* F sensiblero

so·pra·no [sə'prænoʊ] *n singer* soprano *m/f*; *voice* voz *f* de soprano

sor·did ['sɔːrdɪd] *adj affair, business* sórdido

sore [sɔːr] **1** *adj* (*painful*) dolorido; F (*angry*) enojado, *Span* mosqueado F; *is it ~?* ¿duele?; *I'm ~ all over* me duele todo el cuerpo **2** *n* llaga *f*

sor·row ['sɑːroʊ] *n* pena *f*

sor·ry ['sɑːrɪ] *adj day, sight,* (*sad*) triste; (*I'm*) *~!* apologizing ¡lo siento!; *I'm ~ that I didn't tell you sooner* lamento no habértelo dicho antes; *I was so ~ to hear of her death* me dio mucha pena oír lo de su muerte; (*I'm*) *~ but I can't help* lo siento pero no puedo ayudar; *I won't be ~ to leave here* no me arrepentiré de irme de aquí; *I feel ~ for her* siento pena *or* lástima por ella; *be a ~ sight* ofrecer un espectáculo lamentable

sort [sɔːrt] **1** *n* clase *f*, tipo *m*; *~ of ...* F un poco, algo; *is it finished? – ~ of* F

¿está acabado? – más o menos **2** *v/t* ordenar, clasificar; COMPUT ordenar

♦ **sort out** *v/t papers* ordenar, clasificar; *problem* resolver, arreglar

SOS [esoʊ'es] SOS *m*; *fig* llamada *f* de auxilio

so-'so *adv* F así así F

sought [sɔːt] *pret & pp* → **seek**

soul [soʊl] REL, *fig: of a nation etc* alma *f*; *character* personalidad *f*; *the poor ~* el pobrecillo

sound[1] [saʊnd] **1** *adj* (*sensible*) sensato; (*healthy*) sano; *sleep* profundo **2** *adv:* *be ~ asleep* estar profundamente dormido

sound[2] [saʊnd] **1** *n* sonido *m*; (*noise*) ruido *m* **2** *v/t* (*pronounce*) pronunciar; MED auscultar; *~ one's horn* tocar la bocina **3** *v/i:* *that ~s interesting* parece interesante; *she ~ed unhappy* parecía triste

♦ **sound out** *v/t* sondear; *I sounded her out about the idea* sondeé a ver qué le parecía la idea

'sound card COMPUT tarjeta *f* de sonido

'sound ef·fects *npl* efectos *mpl* sonoros

sound·ly ['saʊndlɪ] *adv sleep* profundamente; *beaten* rotundamente

'sound·proof *adj* insonorizado

'sound·track banda *f* sonora

soup [suːp] sopa *f*

'soup bowl cuenco *m*; **souped-up** [suːpt'ʌp] *adj* F trucado; **'soup plate** plato *m* sopero; **'soup spoon** cuchara *f* sopera

sour [saʊr] *adj apple, orange* ácido, agrio; *milk* cortado; *comment* agrio

source [sɔːrs] *n* fuente *f*; *of river* nacimiento *m*

'sour cream nata *f* agria

south [saʊθ] **1** *adj* sur, del sur **2** *n* sur *m*; *to the ~ of* al sur de **3** *adv* al sur; *~ of* al sur de

South 'Af·ri·ca Sudáfrica; **South 'Af·ri·can 1** *adj* sudafricano **2** *n* sudafricano(-a) *m(f)*; **South A'mer·i·ca** Sudamérica, América del Sur; **South A'mer·i·can 1** *adj* sudamericano **2** *n* sudamericano(-a) *m*(*f*); **south-'east 1** *n* sudeste *m*, sureste *m* **2** *adj* sudeste, sureste **3** *adv* al sudeste *or* sureste; **~ of** al sudeste de; **south-'east·ern** *adj* del sudeste

south·er·ly ['sʌðərlɪ] *adj wind* sur, del sur; *direction* sur

south·ern ['sʌðərn] *adj* sureño

south·ern·er ['sʌðərnər] sureño(-a) *m*(*f*)

south·ern·most ['sʌðərnmoʊst] *adj* más al sur

South 'Pole Polo *m* Sur

south·ward ['saʊθwərd] *adv* hacia el sur

south'west 1 *n* sudoeste *m*, suroeste *m* **2** *adj* sudoeste, suroeste **3** *adv* al sudoeste *or* suroeste; **~ of** al sudoeste *or* suroeste de

south'west·ern *adj* del sudoeste *or* suroeste

sou·ve·nir [su:və'nɪr] recuerdo *m*

sove·reign ['sɑːvrɪn] *adj state* soberano

sove·reign·ty ['sɑːvrɪntɪ] *of state* soberanía *f*

So·vi·et ['soʊvɪət] *adj* soviético

So·vi·et 'U·nion Unión *f* Soviética

sow[1] [saʊ] *n* (*female pig*) cerda *f*, puerca *f*

sow[2] [soʊ] *v/t* (*pret* **sowed**, *pp* **sown**) *seeds* sembrar

sown [soʊn] *pp* → **sow**[2]

'soy bean [sɔɪ] semilla *f* de soja

soy 'sauce salsa *f* de soja

space [speɪs] *n* espacio *m*

♦ **space out** *v/t* espaciar

'space-bar COMPUT barra *f* espaciadora; **'space·craft** nave *f* espacial; **'space·ship** nave *f* espacial; **'space shut·tle** transbordador *m* espacial; **'space sta·tion** estación *f* espacial; **'space·suit** traje *m* espacial

spa·cious ['speɪʃəs] *adj* espacioso

spade [speɪd] *for digging* pala *f*; **~s** *in card game* picas *fpl*

'spade·work *fig* trabajo *m* preliminar

spa·ghet·ti [spə'getɪ] *nsg* espaguetis *mpl*

Spain [speɪn] España

span [spæn] *v/t* (*pret & pp* **-ned**) abarcar; *of bridge* cruzar

Span·iard ['spænjərd] español(a) *m*(*f*)

Span·ish ['spænɪʃ] **1** *adj* español **2** *n language* español *m*; **the ~** los españoles

spank [spæŋk] *v/t* azotar

spank·ing ['spæŋkɪŋ] *n* azotaina *f*

span·ner ['spænər] *Br* llave *f*

spare [sper] **1** *v/t*: **can you ~ me $50?** ¿me podrías dejar 50 dólares?; **we can't ~ a single employee** no podemos prescindir ni de un solo trabajador; **can you ~ the time?** ¿tienes tiempo?; **I have time to ~** me sobra el tiempo; **there were 5 to ~** sobraban cinco **2** *adj pair of glasses, set of keys* de repuesto; **do you have any ~ cash?** ¿no te sobrará algo de dinero? **3** *n* recambio *m*, repuesto *m*

spare 'part pieza *f* de recambio *or* repuesto; **spare 'ribs** *npl* costillas *fpl* de cerdo; **spare 'room** habitación *f* de invitados; **spare 'time** tiempo *m* libre; **spare 'tire**, *Br* **spare 'tyre** MOT rueda *f* de recambio *or* repuesto

spar·ing ['sperɪŋ] *adj* moderado; **be ~ with** no derrochar

spar·ing·ly ['sperɪŋlɪ] *adv* con moderación

spark [spɑːrk] *n* chispa *f*

spar·kle ['spɑːrkl] *v/i* destellar

spar·kling 'wine ['spɑːrklɪŋ] vino *m* espumoso

'spark plug bujía *f*

spar·row ['spæroʊ] gorrión *m*

sparse [spɑːrs] *adj vegetation* escaso

sparse·ly ['spɑːrslɪ] *adv*: **~ pop·ulated** poco poblado

spar·tan ['spɑːrtn] *adj room* espartano

spas·mod·ic [spæz'mɑːdɪk] *adj* intermitente

spat [spæt] *pret & pp* → **spit**

spate [speɪt] *fig* oleada *f*

spa·tial ['speɪʃl] *adj* espacial

spat·ter ['spætər] *v/t*: **the car ~ed mud all over me** el coche me salpicó de barro

speak [spi:k] **1** v/i (pret **spoke**, pp **spoken**) hablar (**to, with** con); (make a speech) dar una charla; **we're not ~ing** (**to each other**) (we've quarreled) no nos hablamos; **~ing** TELEC v/i **2** v/t (pret **spoke**, pp **spoken**) foreign language hablar; **she spoke her mind** dijo lo que pensaba
♦ **speak for** v/t hablar en nombre de
♦ **speak out** v/i: **speak out against injustice** denunciar la injusticia
♦ **speak up** v/i (speak louder) hablar más alto

speak·er ['spi:kər] at conference conferenciante m/f; (orator) orador(a) m(f); of sound system altavoz m, L.Am. altoparlante m; of language hablante m/f

spear [spɪr] lanza f

spear·mint ['spɪrmɪnt] hierbabuena f

spe·cial ['speʃl] adj especial; **be on ~** estar de oferta

spe·cial ef·fects npl efectos mpl especiales

spe·cial·ist ['speʃlɪst] especialista m/f

spe·cial·ize ['speʃəlaɪz] v/i especializarse (**in** en)

spe·cial·ly ['speʃlɪ] adv → **especially**

spe·cial·ty ['speʃəltɪ] especialidad f

spe·cies ['spi:ʃi:z] nsg especie f

spe·cif·ic [spə'sɪfɪk] adj específico

spe·cif·i·cal·ly [spə'sɪfɪklɪ] adv específicamente

spec·i·fi·ca·tions [spesɪfɪ'keɪʃnz] npl of machine etc especificaciones fpl

spe·ci·fy ['spesɪfaɪ] v/t (pret & pp **-ied**) especificar

spe·ci·men ['spesɪmən] muestra f

speck [spek] of dust, soot mota f

specs [speks] npl Br F (spectacles) gafas fpl, L.Am. lentes mpl

spec·ta·cle ['spektəkl] (impressive sight) espectáculo m

spec·tac·u·lar [spek'tækjulər] adj espectacular

spec·ta·tor [spek'teɪtər] espectador(a) m(f)

spec·ta·tor sport deporte m espectáculo

spec·trum ['spektrəm] fig espectro m

spec·u·late ['spekjuleɪt] v/i also FIN especular

spec·u·la·tion [spekju'leɪʃn] also FIN especulación f

spec·u·la·tor ['spekjuleɪtər] FIN especulador(a) m(f)

sped [sped] pret & pp → **speed**

speech [spi:tʃ] (address) discurso m; in play parlamento m; (ability to speak) habla f, dicción f; (way of speaking) forma f de hablar

'speech de·fect defecto m del habla

speech·less ['spi:tʃlɪs] adj with shock, surprise sin habla; **I was left ~** me quedé sin habla

'speech ther·a·pist logopeda m/f;
'speech ther·a·py logopedia f;
'speech writ·er redactor(a) m(f) de discursos

speed [spi:d] **1** n velocidad f; (promptness) rapidez f; **at a ~ of 150 mph** a una velocidad de 150 millas por hora **2** v/i (pret & pp **sped**) run correr; drive too quickly sobrepasar el límite de velocidad; **we were ~ing along** íbamos a toda velocidad
♦ **speed by** v/i pasar a toda velocidad
♦ **speed up 1** v/i of car, driver acelerar; when working apresurarse **2** v/t process acelerar

'speed·boat motora f, planeadora f

'speed bump resalto m (para reducir la velocidad del tráfico), Arg despertador m, Mex tope m

speed·i·ly ['spi:dɪlɪ] adv con rapidez

speed·ing ['spi:dɪŋ] n: **fined for ~** multado por exceso de velocidad

'speed·ing fine multa f por exceso de velocidad

'speed lim·it on roads límite m de velocidad

speed·om·e·ter [spi:'dɑ:mɪtər] velocímetro m

'speed trap control m de velocidad por radar

speed·y ['spi:dɪ] adj rápido

spell[1] [spel] **1** v/t word deletrear; **how**

do you ~ ...? ¿cómo se escribe ... ? **2** *v/i* deletrear

spell² [spel] *n* (*period of time*) periodo *m*, temporada *f*; **I'll take a ~ at the wheel** te relevaré un rato al volante

'**spell·bound** *adj* hechizado; '**spell·check** COMPUT: **do a ~ on** pasar el corrector ortográfico a; '**spell·check·er** COMPUT corrector *m* ortográfico

spell·ing ['spelɪŋ] ortografía *f*

spend [spend] *v/t* (*pret & pp* **spent**) *money* gastar; *time* pasar

'**spend·thrift** *n pej* derrochador(a) *m(f)*

spent [spent] *pret & pp* → **spend**

sperm [spɜːrm] espermatozoide *m*; (*semen*) esperma *f*

'**sperm bank** banco *m* de esperma

'**sperm count** recuento *m* espermático

sphere [sfɪr] *also fig* esfera *f*; **~ of influence** ámbito *m* de influencia

spice [spaɪs] *n* (*seasoning*) especia *f*

spic·y ['spaɪsɪ] *adj food* con especias; (*hot*) picante

spi·der ['spaɪdər] araña *f*

'**spi·der·web** telaraña *f*, tela *f* de araña

spike [spaɪk] *n* pincho *m*; *on running shoe* clavo *m*

spill [spɪl] **1** *v/t* derramar **2** *v/i* derramarse **3** *n* derrame *m*

spin¹ [spɪn] **1** *n* (*turn*) giro *m* **2** *v/t* (*pret & pp* **spun**) hacer girar **3** *v/i* (*pret & pp* **spun**) *of wheel* girar, dar vueltas; **my head is ~ning** me da vueltas la cabeza

spin² [spɪn] *v/t wool, cotton* hilar; *web* tejer

♦ **spin around** *v/i of person, car* darse la vuelta

♦ **spin out** *v/t* alargar

spin·ach ['spɪnɪdʒ] espinacas *fpl*

spin·al ['spaɪnl] *adj* de la columna vertebral

spin·al 'col·umn columna *f* vertebral

spin·al 'cord médula *f* espinal

'**spin doc·tor** F asesor encargado de dar la mejor prensa posible a un político o asunto; '**spin-dry** *v/t* centrifugar; **spin-'dry·er** centrifugadora *f*

spine [spaɪn] *of person, animal* columna *f* vertebral; *of book* lomo *m*; *on plant, hedgehog* espina *f*

spine·less ['spaɪnlɪs] *adj* (*cowardly*) débil

'**spin-off** producto *m* derivado

spin·ster ['spɪnstər] solterona *f*

spin·y ['spaɪnɪ] *adj* espinoso

spi·ral ['spaɪrəl] **1** *n* espiral *f* **2** *v/i* (*rise quickly*) subir vertiginosamente

spi·ral 'stair·case escalera *f* de caracol

spire [spaɪr] aguja *f*

spir·it ['spɪrɪt] *n* espíritu *m*; (*courage*) valor *m*; **in a ~ of cooperation** con espíritu de cooperación

spir·it·ed ['spɪrɪtɪd] *adj* (*energetic*) enérgico

'**spir·it lev·el** nivel *m* de burbuja

spir·its ['spɪrɪts] *npl* (*morale*) la moral; **be in good/ poor ~** tener la moral alta/ baja

spir·i·tu·al ['spɪrɪtʃuəl] *adj* espiritual

spir·i·tu·al·ism ['spɪrɪtʃəlɪzm] espiritismo *m*

spir·i·tu·al·ist ['spɪrɪtʃəlɪst] *n* espiritista *m/f*

spit [spɪt] *v/i* (*pret & pp* **spat**) *of person* escupir; **it's ~ting with rain** está chispeando

♦ **spit out** *v/t food, liquid* escupir

spite [spaɪt] *n* rencor *m*; **in ~ of** a pesar de

spite·ful ['spaɪtfəl] *adj* malo, malicioso

spite·ful·ly ['spaɪtfəlɪ] *adv* con maldad *or* malicia

spit·ting 'im·age ['spɪtɪŋ]: **be the ~ of s.o.** ser el vivo retrato de alguien

splash [splæʃ] **1** *n small amount of liquid* chorrito *m*; *of color* mancha *f* **2** *v/t person* salpicar **3** *v/i* chapotear; *of water* salpicar

♦ **splash down** *v/i of spacecraft* amerizar

♦ **splash out** *v/i in spending* gastarse una fortuna

splen·did ['splendɪd] *adj* espléndido

splen·dor, *Br* **splen·dour** ['splendər] esplendor *m*

splint [splɪnt] *n* MED tablilla *f*

splin·ter ['splɪntər] **1** *n* astilla *f* **2** *v/i* astillarse

'**splin·ter group** grupo *m* escindido

split [splɪt] **1** *n damage* raja *f*; (*disagreement*) escisión *f*; (*division, share*) reparto *m* **2** *v/t* (*pret & pp* **split**) *damage* rajar; *logs* partir en dos; (*cause disagreement in*) escindir; (*share*) repartir **3** *v/i* (*pret & pp* **split**) (*tear*) rajarse; (*disagree*) escindirse

♦ **split up** *v/i of couple* separarse

split per·son·al·i·ty PSYCH doble personalidad *f*

split·ting ['splɪtɪŋ] *adj*: ~ **headache** dolor *m* de cabeza atroz

splut·ter ['splʌtər] *v/i* farfullar

spoil [spɔɪl] *v/t* estropear, arruinar

'**spoil·sport** F aguafiestas *m/f inv* F

spoilt [spɔɪlt] *adj child* consentido, mimado; **be ~ for choice** tener mucho donde elegir

spoke[1] [spoʊk] *of wheel* radio *m*

spoke[2] [spoʊk] *pret* → **speak**

spo·ken ['spoʊkən] *pp* → **speak**

spokes·man ['spoʊksmən] portavoz *m*

spokes·per·son ['spoʊkspɜːrsən] portavoz *m/f*

spokes·wom·an ['spoʊkswʊmən] portavoz *f*

sponge [spʌndʒ] *n* esponja *f*

♦ **sponge off, sponge on** *v/t* F vivir a costa de

'**sponge cake** bizcocho *m*

spong·er ['spʌndʒər] F gorrón(-ona) *m(f)* F

spon·sor ['spɑːnsər] **1** *n* patrocinador *m* **2** *v/t* patrocinar

spon·sor·ship ['spɑːnsərʃɪp] patrocinio *m*

spon·ta·ne·ous [spɑːn'teɪnɪəs] *adj* espontáneo

spon·ta·ne·ous·ly [spɑːn'teɪnɪəslɪ] *adv* espontáneamente

spook·y ['spuːkɪ] *adj* F espeluznante, terrorífico

spool [spuːl] *n* carrete *m*

spoon [spuːn] *n* cuchara *f*

'**spoon-feed** *v/t* (*pret & pp* **-fed**) *fig* dar todo mascado a

spoon·ful ['spuːnfʊl] cucharada *f*

spo·rad·ic [spə'rædɪk] *adj* esporádico

sport [spɔːrt] *n* deporte *m*

sport·ing ['spɔːrtɪŋ] *adj* deportivo; **a ~ gesture** un gesto deportivo

'**sports car** [spɔːrts] (coche *m*) deportivo *m*; '**sports-coat** chaqueta *f* de sport; **sports 'jour·nal·ist** periodista *m/f* deportivo(-a); '**sports·man** deportista *m*; '**sports med·i·cine** medicina *f* deportiva; '**sports news** *nsg* noticias *fpl* deportivas; '**sports page** página *f* de deportes; '**sports·wear** ropa *f* de deporte; '**sports·wom·an** deportista *f*

sport·y ['spɔːrtɪ] *adj person* deportista; *clothes* deportivo

spot[1] [spɑːt] (*pimple etc*) grano *m*; (*part of pattern*) lunar *m*; **a ~ of ...** (*a little*) algo de ..., un poco de ...

spot[2] [spɑːt] (*place*) lugar *m*, sitio *m*; **on the ~** (*in the place in question*) en el lugar; (*immediately*) en ese momento; **put s.o. on the ~** poner a alguien en un aprieto

spot[3] [spɑːt] *v/t* (*pret & pp* **-ted**) (*notice*) ver; (*identify*) ver, darse cuenta de

spot 'check *n control m* al azar; **carry out spot checks** llevar a cabo controles al azar

spot·less ['spɑːtlɪs] *adj* inmaculado, impecable

'**spot·light** *n* foco *m*

spot·ted ['spɑːtɪd] *adj fabric* de lunares

spot·ty ['spɑːtɪ] *adj with pimples* con granos

spouse [spaʊs] *fml* cónyuge *m/f*

spout [spaʊt] **1** *n* pitorro *m* **2** *v/i of liquid* chorrear **3** *v/t* F soltar F

sprain [spreɪn] **1** *n* esguince *m* **2** *v/t* hacerse un esguince en

sprang [spræŋ] *pret* → **spring**

sprawl [sprɔːl] *v/i* despatarrarse; *of city* expandirse; **send s.o. ~ing** *of* *punch* derribar de un golpe

sprawl·ing ['sprɔ:lɪŋ] *adj city*, *suburbs* en expansión

spray [spreɪ] **1** *n of sea water, from fountain* rociada *f*; *for hair* spray *m*; *container* aerosol *m*, spray *m* **2** *v/t* rociar; **~ sth with sth** rociar algo con algo

'**spray·gun** pistola *f* pulverizadora

spread [spred] **1** *n of disease, religion etc* propagación *f*; F (*big meal*) comilona *f* F **2** *v/t* (*pret & pp* **spread**) (*lay*) extender; *butter, jelly* untar; *news, rumor* difundir; *disease* propagar; *arms, legs* extender **3** *v/i* (*pret & pp* **spread**) *of disease, fire* propagarse; *of rumor, news* difundirse; *of butter* extenderse, untarse

'**spread·sheet** COMPUT hoja *f* de cálculo

spree [spri:] F: **go (out) on a ~** ir de juerga; **go on a shopping ~** salir a comprar a lo loco

sprig [sprɪg] ramita *f*

spright·ly ['spraɪtlɪ] *adj* lleno de energía

spring[1] [sprɪŋ] *n season* primavera *f*

spring[2] [sprɪŋ] *n device* muelle *m*

spring[3] [sprɪŋ] **1** *n* (*jump*) brinco *m*, salto *m*; (*stream*) manantial *m* **2** *v/i* (*pret* **sprang**, *pp* **sprung**) brincar, saltar; **~ from** proceder de; **he sprang to his feet** se levantó de un salto

'**spring·board** trampolín *m*; **spring 'chick·en** *hum*: **she's no ~** no es ninguna niña; **spring-'clean·ing** limpieza *f* a fondo; '**spring·time** primavera *f*

spring·y ['sprɪŋɪ] *adj mattress, ground* mullido; *walk* ligero; *piece of elastic* elástico

sprin·kle ['sprɪŋkl] *v/t* espolvorear; **~ sth with sth** espolvorear algo con algo

sprin·kler ['sprɪŋklər] *for garden* aspersor *m*; *in ceiling* rociador *m* contra incendios

sprint [sprɪnt] **1** *n* esprint *m*; SP carrera *f* de velocidad **2** *v/i* (*run fast*) correr a toda velocidad; *of runner* esprintar

sprint·er ['sprɪntər] SP esprínter *m/f*, velocista *m/f*

sprout [spraʊt] **1** *v/i of seed* brotar **2** *n*: (*Brussels*) **~s** coles *fpl* de Bruselas

spruce [spru:s] *adj* pulcro

sprung [sprʌŋ] *pp* → **spring**

spry [spraɪ] *adj* lleno *m* de energía

spun [spʌn] *pret & pp* → **spin**

spur [spɜ:r] *n* espuela *f*; *fig* incentivo; **on the ~ of the moment** sin pararse a pensar

♦ **spur on** *v/t* (*pret & pp* **-red**) (*encourage*) espolear

spurt [spɜ:rt] **1** *n in race* arrancada *f*; **put on a ~** acelerar **2** *v/i of liquid* chorrear

sput·ter ['spʌtər] *v/i of engine* chisporrotear

spy [spaɪ] **1** *n* espía *m/f* **2** *v/i* (*pret & pp* **-ied**) espiar **3** *v/t* (*pret & pp* **-ied**) (*see*) ver

♦ **spy on** *v/t* espiar

squab·ble ['skwɑ:bl] **1** *n* riña *f* **2** *v/i* reñir

squal·id ['skwɑ:lɪd] *adj* inmundo, miserable

squal·or ['skwɑ:lər] inmundicia *f*

squan·der ['skwɑ:ndər] *v/t money* despilfarrar

square [skwer] **1** *adj in shape* cuadrado; **~ miles** millas cuadradas **2** *n also* MATH cuadrado *m*; *in town* plaza *f*; *in board game* casilla *f*; **we're back to ~ one** volvemos al punto de partida

♦ **square up** *v/i* hacer cuentas

square 'root raíz *f* cuadrada

squash[1] [skwɑ:ʃ] *n vegetable* calabacera *f*

squash[2] [skwɑ:ʃ] *n game* squash *m*

squash[3] [skwɑ:ʃ] *v/t* (*crush*) aplastar

squat [skwɑ:t] **1** *adj person, build* chaparro; *figure, buildings* bajo **2** *v/i* (*pret & pp* **-ted**) *sit* agacharse; **~ in a building** ocupar ilegalmente un edificio

squat·ter ['skwɑ:tər] ocupante *m/f* ilegal, *Span* okupa *m/f* F

squeak [skwi:k] **1** *n of mouse* chillido *m*; *of hinge* chirrido *m* **2** *v/i of mouse*

S

chillar; *of hinge* chirriar; *of shoes* crujir

squeak·y ['skwi:kɪ] *adj hinge* chirriante; *shoes* que crujen; *voice* chillón

'squeak·y clean *adj* F bien limpio

squeal [skwi:l] **1** *n* chillido; *there was a ~ of brakes* se oyó una frenada estruendosa **2** *v/i* chillar; *of brakes* armar un estruendo

squeam·ish ['skwi:mɪʃ] *adj* aprensivo

squeeze [skwi:z] **1** *n of hand, shoulder* apretón *m* **2** *v/t* (*press*) apretar; (*remove juice from*) exprimir

♦ **squeeze in 1** *v/i to a car etc* meterse a duras penas **2** *v/t* hacer hueco para

♦ **squeeze up** *v/i to make space* apretarse

squid [skwɪd] calamar *m*

squint [skwɪnt] *n*: *she has a ~* es estrábica, tiene estrabismo

squirm [skwɜːrm] *v/t* retorcerse

squir·rel ['skwɪrl] *n* ardilla *f*

squirt [skwɜːrt] **1** *v/t* lanzar un chorro de **2** *n* F *pej* canijo(-a) *m(f)* F, mequetrefe *m/f* F

St *abbr* (= *saint*) Sto; Sta (= santo *m*; santa *f*); (= *street*) c/ (= calle *f*)

stab [stæb] **1** *n* F intento *m*; *have a ~ at sth* intentar algo **2** *v/t* (*pret & pp -bed*) *person* apuñalar

sta·bil·i·ty [stə'bɪlətɪ] estabilidad *f*

sta·bil·ize ['steɪbɪlaɪz] **1** *v/t prices, boat* estabilizar **2** *v/i of prices etc* estabilizarse

sta·ble[1] ['steɪbl] *n for horses* establo *m*

sta·ble[2] ['steɪbl] *adj* estable; *patient's condition* estacionario

stack [stæk] **1** *n* (*pile*) pila *f*; (*smokestack*) chimenea *f*; *~s of* F montones de F **2** *v/t* apilar

sta·di·um ['steɪdɪəm] estadio *m*

staff [stæf] *npl* (*employees*) personal *m*; (*teachers*) profesorado *m*; *~ are not allowed to …* los empleados no tienen permitido …

staf·fer ['stæfər] empleado(-a) *m(f)*

'staff·room *in school* sala *f* de profesores

stag [stæg] ciervo *m*

stage[1] [steɪdʒ] *in life, project etc* etapa *f*

stage[2] [steɪdʒ] **1** *n* THEA escenario *m*; *go on the ~* hacerse actor / actriz **2** *v/t play* escenificar, llevar a escena; *demonstration* llevar a cabo

stage 'door entrada *f* de artistas; **'stage fright** miedo *m* escénico; **'stage hand** tramoyista *m/f*

stag·ger ['stægər] **1** *v/i* tambalearse **2** *v/t* (*amaze*) dejar anonadado; *coffee breaks etc* escalonar

stag·ger·ing ['stægərɪŋ] *adj* asombroso

stag·nant ['stægnənt] *adj also fig* estancado

stag·nate [stæg'neɪt] *v/i fig* estancarse

stag·na·tion [stæg'neɪʃn] estancamiento *m*

'stag par·ty despedida *f* de soltero

stain [steɪn] **1** *n* (*dirty mark*) mancha *f*; *for wood* tinte *m* **2** *v/t* (*dirty*) manchar; *wood* teñir **3** *v/i of wine etc* manchar, dejar mancha; *of fabric* mancharse

stained-glass 'win·dow [steɪnd] vidriera *f*

stain re·mov·er [rɪ'mu:vər] quitamanchas *m inv*

stain·less 'steel ['steɪnlɪs] *n* acero *m* inoxidable

stair [ster] escalón *m*; *the ~s* la(s) escalera(s)

'stair·case escalera(s) *f(/pl)*

stake [steɪk] **1** *n of wood* estaca *f*; *when gambling* apuesta *f*; (*investment*) participación *f*; *be at ~* estar en juego **2** *v/t tree* arrodrigar; *money* apostar; *reputation* jugarse; *person* ayudar (*económicamente*)

stale [steɪl] *adj bread* rancio; *air* viciado; *fig: news* viejo

'stale·mate *in chess* tablas *fpl* (*por rey ahogado*); *fig* punto *m* muerto

stalk[1] [stɒk] *n of fruit, plant* tallo *m*

stalk[2] [stɒk] *v/t* (*follow*) acechar; *person* seguir

stalk·er ['stɒkər] persona que sigue a

otra obsesivamente

stall¹ [stɔːl] *n at market* puesto *m*; *for cow, horse* casilla *f*

stall² [stɔːl] **1** *v/i of vehicle, engine* calarse; *of plane* entrar en pérdida; (*play for time*) intentar ganar tiempo **2** *v/t engine* calar; *person* retener

stal·li·on ['stæljən] semental *m*

stalls [stɔːlz] *npl* patio *m* de butacas

stal·wart ['stɔːlwərt] *adj support, supporter* incondicional

stam·i·na ['stæmɪnə] resistencia *f*

stam·mer ['stæmər] **1** *n* tartamudeo *m* **2** *v/i* tartamudear

stamp¹ [stæmp] **1** *n for letter* sello *m*, *L.Am.* estampilla *f*, *Mex* timbre *m*; *device* tampón *m*; *mark made with device* sello *m* **2** *v/t* sellar; *~ed addressed envelope* sobre *m* franqueado con la dirección

stamp² [stæmp] *v/t*: *~ one's feet* patear

♦ **stamp out** *v/t* (*eradicate*) terminar con

'**stamp col·lec·ting** filatelia *f*; '**stamp col·lec·tion** colección *f* de sellos *or L.Am.* estampillas *or Mex* timbres; '**stamp col·lec·tor** coleccionista *m/f* de sellos *or L.Am.* estampillas *or Mex* timbres

stam·pede [stæm'piːd] **1** *n of cattle etc* estampida *f*; *of people* desbandada *f* **2** *v/i of cattle etc* salir de estampida; *of people* salir en desbandada

stance [stæns] (*position*) postura *f*

stand [stænd] **1** *n at exhibition* puesto *m*, stand *m*; (*witness ~*) estrado *m*; (*support, base*) soporte *m*; *take the ~* LAW subir al estrado **2** *v/i* (*pret & pp* ***stood***) *of building* encontrarse, hallarse; *of people* estar, estar de pie; (*rise*) ponerse de pie; *did you notice two men ~ing near the window?* ¿viste a dos hombres al lado de la ventana?; *there was a large box ~ing in the middle of the floor* había una caja muy grande en mitad del suelo; *the house ~s at the corner of ...* la casa se encuentra en la esquina de ...; *~ still* quedarse quieto; *where do you ~ with Liz?*

¿cual es tu situación con Liz? **3** *v/t* (*pret & pp* ***stood***) (*tolerate*) aguantar, soportar; (*put*) colocar; *you don't ~ a chance* no tienes ninguna posibilidad; *~ one's ground* mantenerse firme

♦ **stand back** *v/i* echarse atrás

♦ **stand by 1** *v/i* (*not take action*) quedarse sin hacer nada; (*be ready*) estar preparado **2** *v/t person* apoyar; *decision* atenerse a

♦ **stand down** *v/i* (*withdraw*) retirarse

♦ **stand for** *v/t* (*tolerate*) aguantar; (*represent*) significar

♦ **stand in for** *v/t* sustituir

♦ **stand out** *v/i* destacar

♦ **stand up 1** *v/i* levantarse **2** *v/t* F plantar F

♦ **stand up for** *v/t* defender; *stand up for yourself!* ¡defiéndete!

♦ **stand up to** *v/t* hacer frente a

stan·dard ['stændərd] **1** *adj* (*usual*) habitual **2** *n* (*level of excellence*) nivel *m*; TECH estándar *m*; *be up to ~* cumplir el nivel exigido; *not be up to ~* estar por debajo del nivel exigido; *my parents set very high ~s* mis padres exigen mucho

stan·dard·ize ['stændərdaɪz] *v/t* normalizar

stan·dard of 'li·ving nivel *m* de vida

'**stand·by 1** *n ticket* billete *m* stand-by; *be on ~* estar en stand-by *or* en lista de espera **2** *adv fly* con un billete stand-by

'**stand·by pas·sen·ger** pasajero(-a) *m(f)* en stand-by *or* en lista de espera

stand·ing ['stændɪŋ] *n in society etc* posición *f*; (*repute*) reputación *f*; *a musician/ politician of some ~* un reputado músico / político; *a relationship of long ~* una relación establecida hace mucho tiempo

'**stand·ing room**: *~ only* no quedan asientos

stand·off·ish [stænd'ɑːfɪʃ] *adj* distante; '**stand·point** punto *m* de vista; '**stand·still**: *be at a ~* estar paralizado; *bring to a ~* paralizar

S

stank [stæŋk] *pret* → **stink**

stan·za ['stænzə] estrofa *f*

sta·ple¹ ['steɪpl] *n foodstuff* alimento *m* básico

sta·ple² ['steɪpl] **1** *n* (*fastener*) grapa *f* **2** *v/t* grapar

sta·ple 'di·et dieta *f* básica

'sta·ple gun grapadora *f* industrial

sta·pler ['steɪplər] grapadora *f*

star [stɑːr] **1** *n also person* estrella *f* **2** *v/t* (*pret & pp* **-red**) *of movie* estar protagonizado por **3** *v/i* (*pret & pp* **-red**) *in movie*: *Depardieu ~red in ...* Depardieu protagonizó ...

'star·board *adj* de estribor

starch [stɑːrtʃ] *in foodstuff* fécula *f*

stare [ster] **1** *n* mirada *f* fija **2** *v/i* mirar fijamente; *~ at* mirar fijamente

'star·fish estrella *f* de mar

stark [stɑːrk] **1** *adj landscape* desolado; *reminder, picture etc* desolador; *in ~ contrast to* en marcado contraste con **2** *adv*: *~ naked* completamente desnudo

star·ling ['stɑːrlɪŋ] estornino *m*

star·ry ['stɑːrɪ] *adj night* estrellado

star·ry-eyed [stɑːrɪ'aɪd]] *adj person* cándido, ingenuo

Stars and 'Stripes la bandera estadounidense

start [stɑːrt] **1** *n* (*beginning*) comienzo *m*, principio *m*; *of race* salida *f*; *get off to a good/bad ~* empezar bien/mal; *from the ~* desde el principio; *well, it's a ~!* bueno, ¡algo es algo! **2** *v/i* empezar, comenzar; *of engine, car* arrancar; *~ing from tomorrow* a partir de mañana **3** *v/t* empezar, comenzar; *engine, car* arrancar; *business* montar; *~ to do sth, ~ doing sth* empezar *or* comenzar a hacer algo; *he ~ed to cry* se puso a llorar

start·er ['stɑːrtər] (*part of meal*) entrada *f*, entrante *m*; *of car* motor *m* de arranque

'start·ing point punto *m* de partida

'start·ing sal·a·ry sueldo *m* inicial

start·le ['stɑːrtl] *v/t* sobresaltar

start·ling ['stɑːrtlɪŋ] *adj* sorprendente, asombroso

starv·a·tion [stɑːr'veɪʃn] inanición *f*, hambre *f*

starve [stɑːrv] *v/i* pasar hambre; *~ to death* morir de inanición *or* hambre; *I'm starving* F me muero de hambre F

state¹ [steɪt] **1** *n* (*condition, country*) estado *m*; *the States* (los) Estados Unidos **2** *adj capital etc* estatal, del estado; *banquet etc* de estado

state² [steɪt] *v/t* declarar

'State De·part·ment Departamento *m* de Estado, *Ministerio de Asuntos Exteriores*

state·ment ['steɪtmənt] declaración *f*; (*bank ~*) extracto *m*

state of e'mer·gen·cy estado *m* de emergencia

state-of-the-'art *adj* modernísimo

states·man ['steɪtsmən] hombre *m* de estado

state 'troop·er policía *m/f* estatal

state 'vis·it visita *f* de estado

stat·ic (e·lec'tric·i·ty) ['stætɪk] electricidad *f* estática

sta·tion ['steɪʃn] **1** *n* RAIL estación *f*; RAD emisora *f*; TV canal *m* **2** *v/t guard etc* apostar; *be ~ed in of soldier* estar destinado en

sta·tion·a·ry ['steɪʃnərɪ] *adj* parado

sta·tion·er ['steɪʃənər] papelería *f*

sta·tion·er·y ['steɪʃənerɪ] artículos *mpl* de papelería

sta·tion 'man·ag·er RAIL jefe *m* de estación

'sta·tion wag·on ranchera *f*

sta·tis·ti·cal [stə'tɪstɪkl] *adj* estadístico

sta·tis·ti·cal·ly [stə'tɪstɪklɪ] *adv* estadísticamente

sta·tis·ti·cian [stætɪs'tɪʃn] estadístico(-a) *m(f)*

sta·tis·tics [stə'tɪstɪks] (*nsg: science*) estadística *f*; (*npl: figures*) estadísticas *fpl*

stat·ue ['stætʃuː] estatua *f*

Stat·ue of 'Lib·er·ty Estatua *f* de la Libertad

sta·tus ['stætəs] categoría *f*, posición *f*; *women want equal ~ with men* las mujeres quieren igualdad con los hombres

'**sta·tus bar** COMPUT barra *f* de estado

'**sta·tus sym·bol** símbolo *m* de estatus

stat·ute ['stætu:t] estatuto *m*

staunch [stɒːntʃ] *adj supporter* incondicional; *friend* fiel

stay [steɪ] **1** *n* estancia *f*, *L.Am.* estadía *f* **2** *v/i in a place* quedarse; *in a condition* permanecer; ~ **in a hotel** alojarse en un hotel; ~ **right there!** ¡quédate ahí!; ~ **put** no moverse

♦ **stay away** *v/i*: **tell the children to stay away** diles a los niños que no se acerquen

♦ **stay away from** *v/t* no acercarse a

♦ **stay behind** *v/i* quedarse

♦ **stay up** *v/i (not go to bed)* quedarse levantado

stead·i·ly ['stedɪlɪ] *adv improve etc* constantemente

stead·y ['stedɪ] **1** *adj (not shaking)* firme; *(continuous)* continuo; *beat* regular; *boyfriend* estable **2** *adv*: **they've been going ~ for two years** llevan saliendo dos años; ~ **on!** ¡un momento! **3** *v/t (pret & pp -ied)* afianzar; *voice* calmar

steak [steɪk] filete *m*

steal [sti:l] **1** *v/t (pret stole, pp stolen) money etc* robar **2** *v/i (pret stole, pp stolen) (be a thief)* robar; **he stole into the bedroom** entró furtivamente en la habitación

'**stealth bomb·er** [stelθ] bombardero *m* invisible

stealth·y ['stelθɪ] *adj* sigiloso

steam [sti:m] **1** *n* vapor *m* **2** *v/t food* cocinar al vapor

♦ **steam up** *v/i of window* empañarse

steamed up [sti:md'ʌp] *adj* F *(angry)* enojado, *Span* mosqueado F

steam·er ['sti:mər] *for cooking* olla *f* para cocinar al vapor

'**steam i·ron** plancha *f* de vapor

steel [sti:l] **1** *n* acero *m* **2** *adj (made of* ~) de acero

'**steel·work·er** trabajador(a) *m(f)* del acero

'**steel·works** acería *f*

steep¹ [sti:p] *adj hill etc* empinado; F: *prices* caro

steep² [sti:p] *v/t (soak)* poner en remojo

stee·ple ['sti:pl] torre *f*

'**stee·ple·chase** *in athletics* carrera *f* de obstáculos

steep·ly ['sti:plɪ] *adv*: **climb ~ of path** subir pronunciadamente; *of prices* dispararse

steer¹ [stɪr] *n animal* buey *m*

steer² [stɪr] *v/t car* conducir, *L.Am.* manejar; *boat* gobernar; *person* guiar; *conversation* llevar

steer·ing ['stɪrɪŋ] *n* MOT dirección *f*

'**steer·ing wheel** volante *m*, *S.Am.* timón *m*

stem¹ [stem] *n of plant* tallo *m*; *of glass* pie *m*; *of pipe* tubo *m*; *of word* raíz *f*

♦ **stem from** *v/t (pret & pp -med)* derivarse de

stem² [stem] *v/t (block)* contener

'**stem·ware** [stemwer] cristalería *f*

stench [stentʃ] peste *f*, hedor *m*

sten·cil ['stensɪl] **1** *n* plantilla *f* **2** *v/t (pret & pp -ed, Br -led) pattern* estarcir

step [step] **1** *n (pace)* paso *m*; *(stair)* escalón *m*; *(measure)* medida *f*; ~ **by** ~ paso a paso **2** *v/i (pret & pp -ped)*: ~ **on sth** pisar algo; ~ **into a puddle** pisar un charco; **I ~ped back** di un paso atrás; ~ **forward** dar un paso adelante

♦ **step down** *v/i from post etc* dimitir

♦ **step out** *v/i (go out for a short time)* salir un momento

♦ **step up** *v/t (increase)* incrementar

'**step·broth·er** hermanastro *m*; '**step·daugh·ter** hijastra *f*; '**step·fa·ther** padrastro *m*; '**step·lad·der** escalera *f* de tijera; '**step·moth·er** madrastra *f*

step·ping stone ['stepɪŋ] pasadera *f*; *fig* trampolín *m*

'**step·sis·ter** hermanastra *f*

'**step·son** hijastro *m*

ster·e·o ['sterɪoʊ] *n (sound system)* equipo *m* de música

ster·e·o·type ['sterɪoʊtaɪp] *n* estereotipo *m*

S

ster·ile ['sterəl] *adj* estéril

ster·il·ize ['sterəlaɪz] *v/t woman, equipment* esterilizar

ster·ling ['stɜːrlɪŋ] *n* FIN libra *f* esterlina

stern[1] [stɜːrn] *adj* severo

stern[2] [stɜːrn] *n* NAUT popa *f*

stern·ly ['stɜːrnlɪ] *adv* con severidad

ster·oids ['sterɔɪdz] *npl* esteroides *mpl*

steth·o·scope ['steθəskoʊp] fonendoscopio *m*, estetoscopio *m*

Stet·son® ['stetsn] sombrero *m* de vaquero

ste·ve·dore ['stiːvədɔːr] estibador *m*

stew [stuː] *n* guiso *m*

stew·ard ['stuːərd] *n on plane* auxiliar *m* de vuelo; *on ship* camarero *m*; *at demonstration, meeting* miembro *m* de la organización

stew·ard·ess [stuːər'des] *on plane* auxiliar *f* de vuelo; *on ship* camarera *f*

stewed [stuːd] *adj apples, plums* en compota

stick[1] [stɪk] *n* palo *m*; *of policeman* porra *f*; *(walking ~)* bastón *m*; **live out in the ~s** F vivir en el quinto pino F, vivir en el campo

stick[2] [stɪk] **1** *v/t (pret & pp* **stuck**) *with adhesive* pegar; F *(put)* meter **2** *v/i (pret & pp* **stuck**) *(jam)* atascarse; *(adhere)* pegarse

♦ **stick around** *v/i* F quedarse

♦ **stick by** *v/t* F apoyar, no abandonar

♦ **stick out** *v/i (protrude)* sobresalir; *(be noticeable)* destacar; **his ears stick out** tiene las orejas salidas

♦ **stick to** *v/t of sth sticky* pegarse a; F *plan etc* seguir; F *(trail, follow)* pegarse a F

♦ **stick together** *v/i* mantenerse unidos

♦ **stick up** *v/t poster, leaflet* pegar

♦ **stick up for** *v/t* F defender

stick·er ['stɪkər] pegatina *f*

'stick-in-the-mud F aburrido(-a) *m(f)* F, soso(-a) *m(f)*

stick·y ['stɪkɪ] *adj hands, surface* pegajoso; *label* adhesivo

stiff [stɪf] **1** *adj cardboard, manner* rígido; *brush, penalty, competition* duro; *muscle, body* agarrotado; *mixture, paste* consistente; *drink* cargado **2** *adv*: **be scared ~** F estar muerto de miedo F; **be bored ~** F aburrirse como una ostra F

stiff·en ['stɪfn] *v/i of person* agarrotarse

♦ **stiffen up** *v/i of muscle* agarrotarse

stiff·ly ['stɪflɪ] *adv* con rigidez; *fig* forzadamente

stiff·ness ['stɪfnəs] *of muscles* agarrotamiento *m*; *fig: of manner* rigidez *f*

sti·fle ['staɪfl] *v/t yawn, laugh* reprimir, contener; *criticism, debate* reprimir

sti·fling ['staɪflɪŋ] *adj* sofocante; **it's ~ in here** hace un calor sofocante aquí dentro

stig·ma ['stɪgmə] estigma *m*

sti·let·tos [stɪ'letoʊz] *npl shoes* zapatos *mpl* de tacón de aguja

still[1] [stɪl] **1** *adj (not moving)* quieto; *with no wind* sin viento; **it was very ~** *no wind* no soplaba nada de viento **2** *adv*: **keep ~!** ¡estáte quieto!; **stand ~!** ¡no te muevas!

still[2] [stɪl] *adv (yet)* todavía, aún; *(nevertheless)* de todas formas; **do you ~ want it?** ¿todavía *or* aún lo quieres?; **she ~ hasn't finished** todavía *or* aún no ha acabado; **I ~ don't understand** sigo sin entenderlo; **she might ~ come** puede que aún venga; **they are ~ my parents** siguen siendo mis padres; **~ more** *(even more)* todavía más

'still·born *adj*: **be ~** nacer muerto

still 'life naturaleza *f* muerta, bodegón *m*

stilt·ed ['stɪltɪd] *adj* forzado

stim·u·lant ['stɪmjʊlənt] estimulante *m*

stim·u·late ['stɪmjʊleɪt] *v/t person* estimular; *growth, demand* estimular, provocar

stim·u·lat·ing ['stɪmjʊleɪtɪŋ] *adj* estimulante

stim·u·la·tion [stɪmjʊ'leɪʃn] estimulación *f*

stim·u·lus ['stɪmjʊləs] (*incentive*) estímulo *m*

sting [stɪŋ] **1** *n from bee, jellyfish* picadura *f* **2** *v/t* (*pret & pp* **stung**) *of bee, jellyfish* picar **3** *v/i* (*pret & pp* **stung**) *of eyes, scratch* escocer

sting·ing ['stɪŋɪŋ] *adj remark, criticism* punzante

sting·y ['stɪndʒɪ] *adj* F agarrado F, rácano F

stink [stɪŋk] **1** *n* (*bad smell*) peste *f*, hedor *m*; F (*fuss*) escándalo F; **make a ~** F armar un escándalo F **2** *v/i* (*pret* **stank**, *pp* **stunk**) (*smell bad*) apestar; F (*be very bad*) dar asco

stint [stɪnt] *n* temporada *f*; **do a ~ in the army** pasar una temporada en el ejército

♦ **stint on** *v/t* F racanear F

stip·u·late ['stɪpjʊleɪt] *v/t* estipular

stip·u·la·tion [stɪpjʊ'leɪʃn] estipulación *f*

stir [stɜːr] **1** *n:* **give the soup a ~** darle vueltas a la sopa; **cause a ~** causar revuelo **2** *v/t* (*pret & pp* **-red**) remover, dar vueltas a **3** *v/i* (*pret & pp* **-red**) *of sleeping person* moverse

♦ **stir up** *v/t crowd* agitar; *bad memories* traer a la memoria

stir·'cra·zy *adj* F majareta F

'stir-fry *v/t* (*pret & pp* **-ied**) freír rápidamente y dando vueltas

stir·ring ['stɜːrɪŋ] *adj music, speech* conmovedor

stir·rup ['stɪrəp] estribo *m*

stitch [stɪtʃ] **1** *n in sewing* puntada *f*; *in knitting* punto *m*; **~es** MED puntos *mpl*; **be in ~es** *laughing* partirse de risa; **have a ~** tener flato **2** *v/t sew* coser

♦ **stitch up** *v/t wound* coser, suturar

stitch·ing ['stɪtʃɪŋ] (*stitches*) cosido *m*

stock [stɑːk] **1** *n* (*reserves*) reservas *fpl*, COM *of store* existencias *fpl*; (*animals*) ganado *m*; FIN acciones *fpl*; *for soup etc* caldo *m*; **in ~** en existencias; **out of ~** agotado; **take ~** hacer balance **2** *v/t* COM (*have*) tener en existencias; COM (*sell*) vender

♦ **stock up on** *v/t* aprovisionarse de

'**stock·breed·er** ganadero(-a) *m*(*f*); '**stock·brok·er** corredor(a) *m*(*f*) de bolsa; '**stock cube** pastilla *f* de caldo concentrado; '**stock ex·change** bolsa *f* (de valores); '**stock·hold·er** accionista *m*/*f*

stock·ing ['stɑːkɪŋ] media *f*

stock·ist ['stɑːkɪst] distribuidor(a) *m*(*f*)

'**stock mar·ket** mercado *m* de valores; '**stock·mar·ket crash** crack *m* bursátil; '**stock·pile 1** *n of food, weapons* reservas *fpl* **2** *v/t* acumular; '**stock·room** almacén *m*; **stock-'still** *adv*: **stand ~** quedarse inmóvil; '**stock·tak·ing** inventario *m*

'**stock·y** ['stɑːkɪ] *adj* bajo y robusto

stodg·y ['stɑːdʒɪ] *adj food* pesado

sto·i·cal ['stoʊɪkl] *adj* estoico

sto·i·cism ['stoʊɪsɪzm] estoicismo *m*

stole [stoʊl] *pret* → **steal**

stol·en ['stoʊlən] *pp* → **steal**

stom·ach ['stʌmək] **1** *n* estómago *m*, tripa *f* **2** *v/t* (*tolerate*) soportar

'**stom·ach·ache** dolor *m* de estómago

stone [stoʊn] *n* piedra *f*

stoned [stoʊnd] *adj* F (*on drugs*) colocado F

stone-'deaf *adj*: **be ~** estar más sordo que una tapia

'**stone·wall** *v/i* F andarse con evasivas

ston·y ['stoʊnɪ] *adj ground, path* pedregoso

stood [stʊd] *pret & pp* → **stand**

stool [stuːl] (*seat*) taburete *m*

stoop[1] [stuːp] **1** *n:* **have a ~** estar encorvado **2** *v/i* (*bend down*) agacharse

stoop[2] [stuːp] *n* (*porch*) porche *m*

stop [stɑːp] **1** *n for train, bus* parada *f*; **come to a ~** detenerse; **put a ~ to** poner fin a **2** *v/t* (*pret & pp* **-ped**) (*put an end to*) poner fin a; (*prevent*) impedir; (*cease*), *person in street* parar; *car, bus, train, etc: of driver* detener; *check* bloquear; **~ doing sth** dejar de hacer algo; **it has ~ped raining** ha parado *or* dejado de llover; **I ~ped her from leaving** impedí que se fuera **3** v/i (*pret & pp* **-ped**) (*come to a halt*) pararse, detenerse; *in a particular place: of bus, train* parar

♦ **stop by** v/i (*visit*) pasarse
♦ **stop off** v/i hacer una parada
♦ **stop over** v/i hacer escala
♦ **stop up** v/t *sink* atascar

'**stop·gap** solución *f* intermedia; '**stop·light** (*traffic light*) semáforo *m*; (*brake light*) luz *m* de freno; '**stop·o·ver** *n* parada *f*; *in air travel* escala *f*

stop·per ['stɑːpər] *for bath, bottle* tapón *m*

stop·ping ['stɑːpɪŋ]: **no ~ sign** prohibido estacionar

'**stop sign** (señal *f* de) stop *m*
'**stop·watch** cronómetro *m*

stor·age ['stɔːrɪdʒ] almacenamiento *m*; **put sth in ~** almacenar algo; **be in ~** estar almacenado

'**stor·age ca·pac·i·ty** COMPUT capacidad *f* de almacenamiento

'**stor·age space** espacio *m* para guardar cosas

store [stɔːr] **1** *n* tienda *f*; (*stock*) reserva *f*; (*storehouse*) almacén *m* **2** v/t almacenar; COMPUT guardar

'**store·front** fachada *f* de tienda; '**store·house** almacén *m*; '**store·keep·er** tendero(-a) *m(f)*; '**store·room** almacén *m*; **store 'win·dow** escaparate *m*, *L.Am.* vidriera *f*, *Mex* aparador *m*

sto·rey *Br* → **story**[2]

stork [stɔːrk] cigüeña *f*

storm [stɔːrm] *n* tormenta *f*

'**storm drain** canal *m* de desagüe; '**storm warn·ing** aviso *m* de tormenta; **storm 'win·dow** contraventana *f*

storm·y ['stɔːrmɪ] *adj weather, relationship* tormentoso

sto·ry[1] ['stɔːrɪ] (*tale*) cuento *m*; (*account*) historia *f*; (*newspaper article*) artículo *m*; F (*lie*) cuento *m*

sto·ry[2] ['stɔːrɪ] *of building* piso *m*, planta *f*

stout [staʊt] *adj person* relleno, corpulento; *boots* resistente; *defender*

valiente

stove [stoʊv] *for cooking* cocina *f*, *Col, Mex, Ven* estufa *f*; *for heating* estufa *f*

stow [stoʊ] v/t guardar

♦ **stow away** v/i viajar de polizón
'**stow·a·way** *n* polizón *m*

strag·gler ['stræglər] rezagado(-a) *m(f)*

straight [streɪt] **1** *adj line, back* recto; *hair* liso; (*honest, direct*) franco; *whiskey* solo; (*tidy*) en orden; (*conservative*) serio; (*not homosexual*) heterosexual; **be a ~ A student** sacar sobresaliente en todas las asignaturas; **keep a ~ face** contener la risa **2** *adv* (*in a straight line*) recto; (*directly, immediately*) directamente; (*clearly*) con claridad; **stand up ~!** ¡ponte recto!; **look s.o. ~ in the eye** mirar a los ojos de alguien; **go ~** F *of criminal* reformarse; **give it to me ~** F dímelo sin rodeos; **~ ahead** *be situated* todo derecho; *walk, drive* todo recto; *look* hacia delante; **carry ~ on** *of driver etc* seguir recto; **~away, ~ off** en seguida; **~ out** directamente; **~ up** *without ice* solo

straight·en ['streɪtn] v/t enderezar

♦ **straighten out** v/t *situation* resolver; F *person* poner por el buen camino **2** v/i *of road* hacerse recto
♦ **straighten up** v/i ponerse derecho

straight'for·ward *adj* (*honest, direct*) franco; (*simple*) simple

strain[1] [streɪn] **1** *n on rope* tensión *f*; *on engine, heart* esfuerzo *m*; *on person* agobio *m* **2** v/t fig: *finances, budget* crear presión en; **~ one's back** hacerse daño en la espalda; **~ one's eyes** forzar la vista

strain[2] [streɪn] v/t *vegetables* escurrir; *oil, fat etc* colar

strain[3] [streɪn] *n of virus* cepa *f*

strained [streɪnd] *adj relations* tirante

strain·er ['streɪnər] *for vegetables etc* colador *m*

strait [streɪt] estrecho *m*

strait·laced [streɪt'leɪst] *adj* mojigato

strand[1] [strænd] *n of wool, thread* hebra *f*; *a ~ of hair* un pelo

strand² ['strænd] *v/t* abandonar; *be ~ed* quedarse atrapado *or* tirado

strange [streɪndʒ] *adj* (*odd, curious*) extraño, raro, (*unknown, foreign*) extraño

strange·ly ['streɪndʒlɪ] *adv* (*oddly*) de manera extraña; *~ enough* aunque parezca extraño

strang·er ['streɪndʒər] (*person you don't know*) extraño(-a) *m(f)*, desconocido(-a) *m(f)*; *I'm a ~ here myself* yo tampoco soy de aquí

stran·gle ['stræŋgl] *v/t person* estrangular

strap [stræp] *n of purse, watch* correa *f*; *of brassiere, dress* tirante *m*; *of shoe* tira *f*

♦ **strap in** *v/t* (*pret & pp -ped*) poner el cinturón de seguridad a

♦ **strap on** *v/t* ponerse

strap·less ['stræplɪs] *adj* sin tirantes

stra·te·gic [strə'tiːdʒɪk] *adj* estratégico

strat·e·gy ['strætədʒɪ] estrategia *f*

straw¹ [strɔː] *material* paja *f*; *that's the last ~!* ¡es la gota que colma el vaso!

straw² [strɔː] *for drink* pajita *f*

straw·ber·ry ['strɔːberɪ] *fruit* fresa *f*, *S.Am.* frutilla *f*

stray [streɪ] **1** *adj animal* callejero; *bullet* perdido **2** *n dog* perro *m* callejero; *cat* gato *m* callejero **3** *v/i of animal, child* extraviarse, perderse; *fig: of eyes, thoughts* desviarse

streak [striːk] **1** *n of dirt, paint* raya *f*; *in hair* mechón *m*; *fig: of nastiness etc* vena *f* **2** *v/i move quickly* pasar disparado

streak·y ['striːkɪ] *adj* veteado

stream [striːm] **1** *n* riachuelo *m*; *fig: of people, complaints* oleada *f*; *come on ~* entrar en funcionamiento **2** *v/i: there were tears ~ing down my face* me bajaban ríos de lágrimas por la cara; *people ~ed out of the building* la gente salía en masa

stream·er ['striːmər] serpentina *f*

stream·line *v/t fig* racionalizar

stream·lined *adj car, plane* aerodi-

námico; *fig: organization* racionalizado

street [striːt] calle *f*

'street·car tranvía *f*; **'street·light** farola *f*; **'street peo·ple** *npl* los sin techo; **'street val·ue** *of drugs* valor *m* en la calle; **'street·walk·er** *F* prostituta *f*; **'street·wise** *adj* espabilado

strength [streŋθ] fuerza *f*; *fig* (*strong point*) punto *m* fuerte; *of friendship etc* solidez *f*; *of emotion* intensidad *f*; *of currency* fortaleza *f*

strength·en ['streŋθn] **1** *v/t muscles, currency* fortalecer; *bridge* reforzar; *country, ties, relationship* consolidar **2** *v/i of bonds, ties* consolidarse; *of currency* fortalecerse

stren·u·ous ['strenjʊəs] *adj* agotador

stren·u·ous·ly ['strenjʊəslɪ] *adv deny* tajantemente

stress [stres] **1** *n* (*emphasis*) énfasis *m*; (*tension*) estrés *m*; *on syllable* acento *m*; *be under ~* estar estresado **2** *v/t* (*emphasize: syllable*) acentuar; *importance etc* hacer hincapié en; *I must ~ that ...* quiero hacer hincapié en que ...

stressed 'out [strest] *adj* F estresado

stress·ful ['stresfəl] *adj* estresante

stretch [stretʃ] **1** *n of land, water* extensión *f*; *of road* tramo *m*; *at a ~* (*non-stop*) de un tirón **2** *adj fabric* elástico **3** *v/t material, income* estirar; *F rules* ser flexible con; *he ~ed out his hand* estiró la mano; *my job ~es me* mi trabajo me obliga a esforzarme **4** *v/i to relax muscles, reach sth* estirarse; (*spread*) extenderse; *of fabric* estirarse, dar de sí

stretch·er ['stretʃər] camilla *f*

strict [strɪkt] *adj* estricto

strict·ly ['strɪktlɪ] *adv* con rigor; *it is ~ forbidden* está terminantemente prohibido

strid·den ['strɪdn] *pp* → **stride**

stride [straɪd] **1** *n* zancada *f*; *take sth in one's ~* tomarse algo con tranquilidad; *make great ~s fig* avanzar a pasos agigantados **2** *v/i* (*pret*

S

***strode**, pp **stridden*) caminar dando zancadas

stri·dent ['straɪdnt] adj also fig estridente

strike [straɪk] **1** n of workers huelga f; in baseball strike m; of oil descubrimiento m; **be on ~** estar en huelga; **go on ~** ir a la huelga **2** v/i (pret & pp **struck**) of workers hacer huelga; (attack) atacar; of disaster sobrevenir; of clock dar las horas; **the clock struck three** el reloj dio las tres **3** v/t (pret & pp **struck**) (hit) golpear; fig: of disaster sacudir; match encender; oil descubrir; **didn't it ever ~ you that ...?** ¿no se te ocurrió que ...?; **she struck me as being ...** me dio la impresión de ser ...

♦ **strike out 1** v/t (delete) tachar; in baseball eliminar a, L.Am. ponchar **2** v/i in baseball quedar eliminado, L.Am. poncharse

'**strike·break·er** esquirol(a) m(f)

strik·er ['straɪkər] (person on strike) huelguista m/f; in soccer delantero(-a) m(f)

strik·ing ['straɪkɪŋ] adj (marked) sorprendente, llamativo; (eye-catching) deslumbrante

string [strɪŋ] n also of violin, racket etc cuerda f; **~s musicians** la sección de cuerda; **pull ~s** mover hilos; **a ~ of** (series) una serie de

♦ **string along 1** v/i (pret & pp **strung**) F apuntarse F **2** v/t (pret & pp **strung**) F: **string s.o. along** dar falsas esperanzas a alguien

♦ **string up** v/t F colgar

stringed 'in·stru·ment [strɪŋd] instrumento m de cuerda

strin·gent ['strɪndʒnt] adj riguroso

'**string play·er** instrumentista m/f de cuerda

strip [strɪp] **1** n of land franja f; of cloth tira f; (comic ~) tira f cómica **2** v/t (pret & pp **-ped**) (remove) quitar; (undress) desnudar; **~ s.o. of sth** despojar a alguien de algo **3** v/i (pret & pp **-ped**) (undress) desnudarse; of stripper hacer striptease

'**strip club** club m de striptease

stripe [straɪp] raya f; indicating rank galón m

striped [straɪpt] adj a rayas

'**strip joint** F → **strip club**

strip·per ['strɪpər] artista m/f de striptease

'**strip show** espectáculo m de striptease

strip'tease striptease m

strive [straɪv] v/i (pret **strove**, pp **striven**) esforzarse; **~ to do sth** esforzarse por hacer algo; **~ for** luchar por

striv·en ['strɪvn] pp → **strive**

strobe (**light**) [stroʊb] luz f estroboscópica

strode [stroʊd] pret → **stride**

stroke [stroʊk] **1** n MED derrame m cerebral; when writing trazo m; when painting pincelada f; (style of swimming) estilo m; **~ of luck** golpe de suerte; **she never does a ~** (of **work**) no pega ni golpe **2** v/t acariciar

stroll [stroʊl] **1** n paseo m **2** v/i caminar

stroll·er ['stroʊlər] for baby silla f de paseo

strong [strɔːŋ] adj fuerte; structure resistente; candidate claro, con muchas posibilidades; support, supporter, views, objection firme; tea, coffee cargado, fuerte

'**strong·hold** fig baluarte m

strong·ly ['strɔːŋlɪ] adv fuertemente, rotundamente

strong-mind·ed [strɔːŋ'maɪndɪd] adj decidido; '**strong point** (punto m) fuerte m; '**strong·room** cámara f acorazada; **strong-willed** [strɔːŋ'wɪld] adj tenaz

strove [stroʊv] pret → **strive**

struck [strʌk] pret & pp → **strike**

struc·tur·al ['strʌktʃərl] adj estructural

struc·ture ['strʌktʃər] **1** n (something built) construcción f; of novel, society etc estructura f **2** v/t estructurar

strug·gle ['strʌgl] **1** n lucha f **2** v/i with a person forcejear; (have a hard time) luchar; **he was struggling**

with the door tenía problemas para abrir la puerta; **~ to do sth** luchar por hacer algo

strum [strʌm] *v/t* (*pret & pp* **-med**) *guitar* rasguear

strung [strʌŋ] *pret & pp* → **string**

strut [strʌt] *v/i* (*pret & pp* **-ted**) pavonearse

stub [stʌb] **1** *n of cigarette* colilla *f; of check* matriz *f; of ticket* resguardo *m* **2** *v/t* (*pret & pp* **-bed**): **~ one's toe** darse un golpe en el dedo (del pie)

♦ **stub out** *v/t* apagar (apretando)

stub·ble ['stʌbl] *on man's face* barba *f* incipiente

stub·born ['stʌbərn] *adj person* testarudo, terco; *defense, refusal, denial* tenaz, pertinaz

stub·by ['stʌbɪ] *adj* regordete

stuck [stʌk] **1** *pret & pp* → **stick 2** *adj* F: **be ~ on s.o.** estar colado por alguien F

stuck-'up *adj* F engreído

stu·dent ['stu:dnt] *at high school* alumno(-a) *m(f); at college, university* estudiante *m/f*

stu·dent 'nurse estudiante *m/f* de enfermería

stu·dent 'teach·er profesor(a) *m(f)* en prácticas

stu·di·o ['stu:dɪoʊ] *of artist, sculptor* estudio *m; (film ~, TV ~)* estudio *m*, plató *m*

stu·di·ous ['stu:dɪəs] *adj* estudioso

stud·y ['stʌdɪ] **1** *n* estudio *m* **2** *v/t & v/i* (*pret & pp* **-ied**) estudiar

stuff [stʌf] **1** *n* (*things*) cosas *fpl* **2** *v/t turkey* rellenar; **~ sth into sth** meter algo dentro de algo

stuffed 'toy [stʌft] muñeco *m* de peluche

stuff·ing ['stʌfɪŋ] relleno *m*

stuff·y ['stʌfɪ] *adj room* cargado; *person* anticuado, estirado

stum·ble ['stʌmbl] *v/i* tropezar

♦ **stumble across** *v/t* toparse con

♦ **stumble over** *v/t* tropezar con; *words* trastrabillarse con

stum·bling-block ['stʌmblɪŋ] escollo *m*

stump [stʌmp] **1** *n of tree* tocón *m*

2 *v/t of question, questioner* dejar perplejo

♦ **stump up** *v/t* F aflojar, *Span* apoquinar F

stun [stʌn] *v/t* (*pret & pp* **-ned**) *of blow* dejar sin sentido; *of news* dejar atónito *or* de piedra

stung [stʌŋ] *pret & pp* → **sting**

stunk [stʌŋk] *pp* → **stink**

stun·ning ['stʌnɪŋ] *adj* (*amazing*) increíble, sorprendente; (*very beautiful*) imponente

stunt [stʌnt] *n for publicity* truco *m; in movie* escena *f* peligrosa

'stunt·man *in movie* doble *m*, especialista *m*

stu·pe·fy ['stu:pɪfaɪ] *v/t* (*pret & pp* **-ied**) dejar perplejo

stu·pen·dous [stu:'pendəs] *adj* extraordinario

stu·pid ['stu:pɪd] *adj* estúpido; **what a ~ thing to say/ do!** ¡qué estupidez!

stu·pid·i·ty [stu:'pɪdətɪ] estupidez *f*

stu·por ['stu:pər] aturdimiento *m*

stur·dy ['stɜːrdɪ] *adj person* robusto; *table, plant* resistente

stut·ter ['stʌtər] *v/i* tartamudear

sty [staɪ] *for pig* pocilga *f*

style [staɪl] *n* estilo *m;* (*fashion*) moda *f;* **go out of ~** pasarse de moda

styl·ish ['staɪlɪʃ] *adj* elegante

styl·ist ['staɪlɪst] (*hair ~*) estilista *m/f*

sub·com·mit·tee ['sʌbkəmɪtɪ] subcomité *m*

sub·com·pact (car) [sʌb'kɑːmpækt] *utilitario de pequeño tamaño*

sub·con·scious [sʌb'kɑːnʃəs] *adj* subconsciente; **the ~** (*mind*) el subconsciente

sub·con·scious·ly [sʌb'kɑːnʃəslɪ] *adv* inconscientemente

sub·con·tract [sʌbkən'trækt] *v/t* subcontratar

sub·con·trac·tor [sʌbkən'træktər] subcontratista *m/f*

sub·di·vide [sʌbdɪ'vaɪd] *v/t* subdividir

sub·due [səb'du:] *v/t rebellion, mob* someter, contener

sub·dued [səb'du:d] *adj* apagado

S

sub·head·ing ['sʌbhedɪŋ] subtítulo *m*

sub·hu·man [sʌb'hjuːmən] *adj* inhumano

sub·ject 1 *n* ['sʌbdʒɪkt] (*topic*) tema *m*; (*branch of learning*) asignatura *f*, materia *f*; GRAM sujeto *m*; *of monarch* súbdito(-a) *m(f)*; ***change the ~*** cambiar de tema **2** *adj* ['sʌbdʒɪkt]: ***be ~ to*** have tendency to ser propenso a; *be regulated by* estar sujeto a; ***~ to availability*** goods promoción válida hasta la fin de existencias **3** *v/t* [səb'dʒekt] someter

sub·jec·tive [səb'dʒektɪv] *adj* subjetivo

sub·junc·tive [səb'dʒʌŋktɪv] *n* GRAM subjuntivo *m*

sub·let ['sʌblet] *v/t* (*pret & pp* **-let**) realquilar

sub·ma'chine gun metralleta *f*

sub·ma·rine ['sʌbməriːn] submarino *m*

sub·merge [səb'mɜːrdʒ] **1** *v/t* sumergir **2** *v/i of submarine* sumergirse

sub·mis·sion [səb'mɪʃn] (*surrender*) sumisión *f*; *to committee etc* propuesta *f*

sub·mis·sive [səb'mɪsɪv] *adj* sumiso

sub·mit [səb'mɪt] **1** *v/t* (*pret & pp* **-ted**) plan, proposal presentar **2** *v/i* (*pret & pp* **-ted**) someterse

sub·or·di·nate [sə'bɔːrdɪneɪt] **1** *adj* employee, position subordinado **2** *n* subordinado(-a) *m(f)*

sub·poe·na [sə'piːnə] **1** *n* citación *f* **2** *v/t person* citar

♦ **sub·scribe to** [səb'skraɪb] *v/t* magazine etc suscribirse a; theory suscribir

sub·scrib·er [səb'skraɪbər] *to magazine* suscriptor(a) *m(f)*

sub·scrip·tion [səb'skrɪpʃn] suscripción *f*

sub·se·quent ['sʌbsɪkwənt] *adj* posterior

sub·se·quent·ly ['sʌbsɪkwəntlɪ] *adv* posteriormente

sub·side [səb'saɪd] *v/i of flood waters* bajar; *of high winds* amainar; *of building* hundirse; *of fears, panic* calmarse

sub·sid·i·a·ry [səb'sɪdɪerɪ] *n* filial *f*

sub·si·dize ['sʌbsɪdaɪz] *v/t* subvencionar

sub·si·dy ['sʌbsɪdɪ] subvención *f*

♦ **sub·sist on** *v/t* subsistir a base de

sub·sis·tence 'farm·er [səb'sɪstəns] agricultor(a) *m(f)* de subsistencia

sub·sis·tence lev·el nivel *m* mínimo de subsistencia

sub·stance ['sʌbstəns] (*matter*) sustancia *f*

sub·stan·dard [sʌb'stændərd] *adj* performance deficiente; shoes, clothes con tara

sub·stan·tial [səb'stænʃl] *adj* sustancial, considerable

sub·stan·tial·ly [səb'stænʃlɪ] *adv* (*considerably*) considerablemente; (*in essence*) sustancialmente, esencialmente

sub·stan·ti·ate [səb'stænʃɪeɪt] *v/t* probar

sub·stan·tive [səb'stæntɪv] *adj* significativo

sub·sti·tute ['sʌbstɪtuːt] **1** *n for person* sustituto(-a) *m(f)*; *for commodity* sustituto *m*; SP suplente *m/f* **2** *v/t* sustituir, reemplazar; ***~ X for Y*** sustituir Y por X **3** *v/i*: ***~ for s.o.*** sustituir a alguien

sub·sti·tu·tion [sʌbstɪ'tuːʃn] (*act*) sustitución *f*; ***make a ~*** SP hacer un cambio *or* sustitución

sub·ti·tle ['sʌbtaɪtl] *n* subtítulo *m*

sub·tle ['sʌtl] *adj* sutil

sub·tract [səb'trækt] *v/t number* restar

sub·urb ['sʌbɜːrb] zona *f* residencial de la periferia

sub·ur·ban [sə'bɜːrbən] *adj* housing de la periferia; attitudes, lifestyle aburguesado

sub·ver·sive [səb'vɜːrsɪv] **1** *adj* subversivo **2** *n* subversivo(-a) *m(f)*

sub·way ['sʌbweɪ] metro *m*

sub 'ze·ro *adj* bajo cero

suc·ceed [sək'siːd] **1** *v/i* (*be successful*) tener éxito; *to throne* suceder en el trono; ***~ in doing sth*** conseguir hacer algo **2** *v/t* (*come* *after*) suceder

suc·ceed·ing [sək'siːdɪŋ] *adj* siguiente

suc·cess [sək'ses] éxito *m*; **be a ~ of** *book, play, idea* ser un éxito; *of person* tener éxito

suc·cess·ful [sək'sesfəl] *adj person* con éxito; **be ~ in business** tener éxito en los negocios; **be ~ in doing sth** lograr hacer algo

suc·cess·ful·ly [sək'sesfəlɪ] *adv* con éxito

suc·ces·sion [sək'seʃn] sucesión *f*; **three days in ~** tres días seguidos

suc·ces·sive [sək'sesɪv] *adj* sucesivo

suc·ces·sor [sək'sesər] sucesor(a) *m(f)*

suc·cinct [sək'sɪŋkt] *adj* sucinto

suc·cu·lent ['ʃʌkjulənt] *meat, fruit* suculento

suc·cumb [sə'kʌm] *v/i* (*give in*) sucumbir

such [sʌtʃ] **1** *adj* (*of that kind*) tal; **~ men are dangerous** los hombres así son peligrosos; **I know of many cases** conozco muchos casos así; **don't make ~ a fuss** no armes tanto alboroto; **I never thought it would be ~ a success** nunca imaginé que sería un éxito tal; **~ as** como; **there is no ~ word as ...** no existe la palabra ... **2** *adv* tan; **as ~** como tal

suck [sʌk] **1** *v/t candy etc* chupar; **~ one's thumb** chuparse el dedo **2** *v/i* P: **it ~s** (*is awful*) es una mierda P

♦ **suck up 1** *v/t* absorber **2** *v/i* F: **suck up to s.o.** hacer la pelota a alguien

suck·er ['sʌkər] F (*person*) primo(-a) *m/f* F, ingenuo(-a) *m/f*; F (*lollipop*) piruleta *f*

suc·tion ['sʌkʃn] succión *f*

sud·den ['sʌdn] *adj* repentino; **all of a ~** de repente

sud·den·ly ['sʌdnlɪ] *adv* de repente

suds [sʌdz] *npl* (*soap ~*) espuma *f*

sue [suː] *v/t* demandar

suede [sweɪd] *n* ante *m*

suf·fer ['sʌfər] **1** *v/i* (*be in great pain*) sufrir; (*deteriorate*) deteriorarse; **be ~ing from** sufrir **2** *v/t loss, setback, heart attack* sufrir

suf·fer·ing ['sʌfərɪŋ] *n* sufrimiento *m*

suf·fi·cient [sə'fɪʃnt] *adj* suficiente

suf·fi·cient·ly [sə'fɪʃntlɪ] *adv* suficientemente

suf·fo·cate ['sʌfəkeɪt] **1** *v/i* asfixiarse **2** *v/t* asfixiar

suf·fo·ca·tion [sʌfə'keɪʃn] asfixia *f*

sug·ar ['ʃugər] **1** *n* azúcar *m or f*; **how many ~s?** ¿cuántas cucharadas de azúcar? **2** *v/t* echar azúcar a; **is it ~ed?** ¿lleva azúcar?

'sug·ar bowl azucarero *m*

'sug·ar cane caña *f* de azúcar

sug·gest [sə'dʒest] *v/t* sugerir

sug·ges·tion [sə'dʒestʃən] sugerencia *f*

su·i·cide ['suːɪsaɪd] suicidio *m*; **commit ~** suicidarse

suit [suːt] **1** *n* traje *m*; *in cards* palo *m* **2** *v/t of clothes, color* sentar bien a; **~ yourself!** F ¡haz lo que quieras!; **be ~ed for sth** estar hecho para algo

sui·ta·ble ['suːtəbl] *adj partner, words, clothing* apropiado, adecuado; *time* apropiado

sui·ta·bly ['suːtəblɪ] *adv* apropiadamente, adecuadamente

'suit·case maleta *f*, *L.Am.* valija *f*

suite [swiːt] *of rooms*, MUS suite *f*; *furniture* tresillo *m*

sul·fur ['sʌlfər] azufre *m*

sul·fur·ic ac·id [sʌl'fjuːrɪk] ácido *m* sulfúrico

sulk [sʌlk] *v/i* enfurruñarse; **be ~ing** estar enfurruñado

sulk·y ['sʌlkɪ] *adj* enfurruñado

sul·len ['sʌlən] *adj* malhumorado, huraño

sul·phur *etc* Br → **sulfur** *etc*

sul·try ['sʌltrɪ] *adj climate* sofocante, bochornoso; *sexually* sensual

sum [sʌm] (*total*) total *m*, suma *f*; (*amount*) cantidad *f*; *in arithmetic* suma *f*; **a large ~ of money** una gran cantidad de dinero; **~ insured** suma *f* asegurada; **the ~ total of his efforts** la suma de sus esfuerzos

♦ **sum up 1** *v/t* (*pret & pp -med*) (*summarize*) resumir; (*assess*) catalogar **2** *v/i* (*pret & pp -med*) LAW recapitular

sum·mar·ize ['sʌməraɪz] *v/t* resumir

sum·ma·ry ['sʌmərɪ] *n* resumen *m*

sum·mer ['sʌmər] *n* verano *m*

sum·mit ['sʌmɪt] *of mountain* cumbre *f*, cima *f*; POL cumbre *f*

'**sum·mit meet·ing** → **summit**

sum·mon ['sʌmən] *v/t staff, ministers* llamar; *meeting* convocar

♦ **summon up** *v/t*: *he summoned up his strength* hizo acopio de fuerzas

sum·mons ['sʌmənz] *nsg* LAW citación *f*

sump [sʌmp] *for oil* cárter *m*

sun [sʌn] sol *m*; *in the* ~ al sol; *out of the* ~ a la sombra; *he has had too much* ~ le ha dado demasiado el sol

'**sun·bathe** *v/i* tomar el sol; '**sun·bed** cama *f* de rayos UVA; '**sun·block** crema *f* solar de alta protección; '**sun·burn** quemadura *f* (del sol); '**sun·burnt** *adj* quemado (por el sol)

Sun·day ['sʌndeɪ] domingo *m*

'**sun·dial** reloj *m* de sol

sun·dries ['sʌndrɪz] *npl* varios *mpl*

sung [sʌŋ] *pp* → **sing**

'**sun·glass·es** *npl* gafas *fpl or L.Am.* anteojos *mpl* de sol

sunk [sʌŋk] *pp* → **sink**

sunk·en ['sʌŋkn] *adj ship, cheeks* hundido

sun·ny ['sʌnɪ] *adj day* soleado; *disposition* radiante; *it is* ~ hace sol

'**sun·rise** amanecer *m*; '**sun·set** atardecer *m*, puesta *f* de sol; '**sun·shade** sombrilla *f*; '**sun·shine** sol *m*; '**sun·stroke** insolación *f*; '**sun·tan** bronceado *m*; *get a* ~ broncearse

su·per ['suːpər] **1** *adj* F genial F, estupendo F **2** *n* (*janitor*) portero(-a) *m(f)*

su·perb [suˈpɜːrb] *adj* excelente

su·per·fi·cial [suːpərˈfɪʃl] *adj* superficial

su·per·flu·ous [suˈpɜːrfluəs] *adj* superfluo

su·per·hu·man *adj efforts* sobrehumano

su·per·in·tend·ent [suːpərɪnˈtendənt] *of apartment block* portero(-a) *m(f)*

su·pe·ri·or [suːˈpɪrɪər] **1** *adj* (*better*) superior; *pej: attitude* arrogante **2** *n in organization* superior *m*

su·per·la·tive [suːˈpɜːrlətɪv] **1** *adj superb* excelente **2** *n* GRAM superlativo *m*

'**su·per·mar·ket** supermercado *m*

su·per·nat·u·ral 1 *adj powers* sobrenatural **2** *n*: *the* ~ lo sobrenatural

'**su·per·pow·er** POL superpotencia *f*

su·per·son·ic [suːpərˈsɑːnɪk] *adj flight, aircraft* supersónico

su·per·sti·tion [suːpərˈstɪʃn] superstición *f*

su·per·sti·tious [suːpərˈstɪʃəs] *adj person* supersticioso

su·per·vise ['suːpərvaɪz] *v/t class* vigilar; *workers* supervisar; *activities* dirigir

su·per·vi·sor [ˈsuːpərvaɪzər] *at work* supervisor(a) *m(f)*

sup·per ['sʌpər] cena *f*, *L.Am.* comida *f*

sup·ple ['sʌpl] *adj person* ágil; *limbs, material* flexible

sup·ple·ment ['sʌplɪmənt] (*extra payment*) suplemento *m*

sup·pli·er [səˈplaɪər] COM proveedor *m*

sup·ply [səˈplaɪ] **1** *n* suministro *m*, abastecimiento *m*; ~ *and demand* la oferta y la demanda; *supplies of food* provisiones *fpl*; *office supplies* material *f* de oficina **2** *v/t* (*pret & pp -ied*) *goods* suministrar; ~ *s.o. with sth* suministrar algo a alguien; *be supplied with ...* venir con ...

sup·port [səˈpɔːrt] **1** *n for structure* soporte *m*; (*backing*) apoyo *m* **2** *v/t building, structure* soportar, sostener; *financially* mantener; (*back*) apoyar

sup·port·er [səˈpɔːrtər] partidario(-a) *m(f)*; *of football team etc* seguidor(a) *m(f)*

sup·port·ive [səˈpɔːrtɪv] *adj* comprensivo; *be* ~ apoyar (*toward, of* a)

sup·pose [səˈpoʊz] *v/t* (*imagine*) suponer; *I* ~ *so* supongo (que sí); *you* *are not ~d to ...* (*not allowed to*) no deberías ...; *it is ~d to be delivered today* se supone que se lo van a entregar hoy; *it's ~d to be very beautiful* se supone que es hermosísimo

sup·pos·ed·ly [sə'pouzɪdlɪ] *adv* supuestamente

sup·pos·i·to·ry [sə'pɑːzɪtɔːrɪ] MED supositorio *m*

sup·press [sə'pres] *v/t rebellion etc* reprimir, sofocar

sup·pres·sion [sə'preʃn] represión *f*

su·prem·a·cy [suː'preməsɪ] supremacía *f*

su·preme [suː'priːm] *adj* supremo

Su'preme Court Tribunal *m* Supremo, *L.Am.* Corte *f* Suprema

sur·charge ['sɜːrtʃɑːrdʒ] *n* recargo *m*

sure [ʃʊr] **1** *adj* seguro; *I'm not ~* no estoy seguro; *be ~ about sth* estar seguro de algo; *make ~ that ...* asegurarse de que ... **2** *adv:* *~ enough* efectivamente; *it ~ is hot today* F vaya calor que hace F; *~!* F ¡claro!

sure·ly ['ʃʊrlɪ] *adv* (*gladly*) claro que sí; *~ you don't mean that!* ¡ no lo dirás en serio!; *~ somebody knows* alguien tiene que saberlo

sure·e·ty ['ʃʊrətɪ] *for loan* fianza *f*, depósito *m*

surf [sɜːrf] **1** *n on sea* surf *m* **2** *v/t:* *the Net* navegar por Internet

sur·face ['sɜːrfɪs] **1** *n of table, object, water* superficie *f*; *on the ~* *fig* a primera vista **2** *v/i of swimmer, submarine* salir a la superficie; (*appear*) aparecer

'sur·face mail correo *m* terrestre

'surf·board tabla *f* de surf

surf·er ['sɜːrfər] *on sea* surfista *m/f*

surf·ing ['sɜːrfɪŋ] surf *m*; *go ~* ir a hacer surf

surge [sɜːrdʒ] *n in electric current* sobrecarga *f*; *in demand etc* incremento *m* repentino

♦ **surge forward** *v/i of crowd* avanzar atropelladamente

sur·geon ['sɜːrdʒən] cirujano(-a) *m(f)*

sur·ge·ry ['sɜːrdʒərɪ] cirugía *f*; *undergo ~* ser intervenido quirúr-

gicamente

sur·gi·cal ['sɜːrdʒɪkl] *adj* quirúrgico

sur·gi·cal·ly ['sɜːrdʒɪklɪ] *adv* quirúrgicamente

sur·ly ['sɜːrlɪ] *adj* arisco, hosco

sur·mount [sər'maunt] *v/t difficulties* superar

sur·name ['sɜːrneɪm] apellido *m*

sur·pass [sər'pæs] *v/t* superar

sur·plus ['sɜːrpləs] **1** *n* excedente *m* **2** *adj* excedente

sur·prise [sər'praɪz] **1** *n* sorpresa *f*; *it came as no ~* no me sorprendió **2** *v/t* sorprender; *be/look ~d* estar / parecer sorprendido

sur·pris·ing [sər'praɪzɪŋ] *adj* sorprendente; *it's no ~ that ...* no me sorprende que ...

sur·pris·ing·ly [sər'praɪzɪŋlɪ] *adv* sorprendentemente

sur·ren·der [sə'rendər] **1** *v/i of army* rendirse **2** *v/t weapons etc* entregar **3** *n* rendición *f*; (*handing in*) entrega *f*

sur·ro·gate 'moth·er [ˈsʌrəgət] madre *f* de alquiler

sur·round [sə'raund] **1** *v/t* rodear; *~ed by* rodeado de *or* por **2** *n of picture etc* marco *m*

sur·round·ing [sə'raundɪŋ] *adj* circundante

sur·round·ings [sə'raundɪŋz] *npl of village* alrededores *mpl*; (*environment*) entorno *m*

sur·vey ['sɜːrveɪ] **1** *n* ['sɜːrveɪ] *of modern literature etc* estudio *m*; *of building* tasación *f*, peritaje; *poll* encuesta *f* **2** *v/t* [sər'veɪ] (*look at*) contemplar; *building* tasar, peritar

sur·vey·or [sɜːr'veɪr] tasador(a) *m(f)* or perito (-a) *m(f)* de la propiedad

sur·viv·al [sər'vaɪvl] supervivencia *f*

sur·vive [sər'vaɪv] **1** *v/i* sobrevivir; *how are you? – I'm surviving* ¿cómo estás? – voy tirando; *his two surviving daughters* las dos hijas que aún viven **2** *v/t accident, operation* sobrevivir a; (*outlive*) sobrevivir

sur·vi·vor [sər'vaɪvər] superviviente

S

m/f; **he's a ~** *fig* es incombustible

sus·cep·ti·ble [sə'septəbl] *adj* emotionally sensible, susceptible; **be ~ to the cold/heat** ser sensible al frío/calor

sus·pect **1** *n* ['sʌspekt] sospechoso(-a) *m(f)* **2** *v/t* [sə'spekt] *person* sospechar de; (*suppose*) sospechar

sus·pect·ed [sə'spektɪd] *adj murderer* presunto; *cause, heart attack etc* supuesto

sus·pend [sə'spend] *v/t* (*hang*) colgar; *from office, duties* suspender

sus·pend·ers [sə'spendərz] *npl for pants* tirantes *mpl*, *S.Am.* suspensores *mpl*

sus·pense [sə'spens] *Span* suspense *m*, *L.Am.* suspenso *m*

sus·pen·sion [sə'spenʃn] MOT, *from duty* suspensión *f*

sus'pen·sion bridge puente *m* colgante

sus·pi·cion [sə'spɪʃn] sospecha *f*

sus·pi·cious [sə'spɪʃəs] *adj* (*causing suspicion*) sospechoso; (*feeling suspicion*) receloso, desconfiado; **be ~ of** sospechar de

sus·pi·cious·ly [sə'spɪʃəslɪ] *adv behave* de manera sospechosa; *ask* con recelo *or* desconfianza

sus·tain [sə'steɪn] *v/t* sostener

sus·tain·a·ble [sə'steɪnəbl] *adj* sostenible

swab [swɑːb] *material* torunda *f*; *test* muestra *f*

swag·ger ['swægər] *n*: **walk with a ~** caminar pavoneándose

swal·low¹ ['swɑːloʊ] **1** *v/t liquid, food* tragar, tragarse **2** *v/i* tragar

swal·low² ['swɑːloʊ] *n bird* golondrina *f*

swam [swæm] *pret* → **swim**

swamp [swɑːmp] **1** *n* pantano *m* **2** *v/t*: **be ~ed with** estar inundado de

swamp·y ['swɑːmpɪ] *adj* pantanoso

swan [swɑːn] cisne *m*

swap [swɑːp] **1** *v/t* (*pret & pp* **-ped**) cambiar; **~ sth for sth** cambiar algo por algo **2** *v/i* (*pret & pp* **-ped**) hacer un cambio

swarm [swɔːrm] **1** *n of bees* enjambre

m **2** *v/i*: **the town was ~ing with ...** la ciudad estaba abarrotada de ...

swar·thy ['swɔːrðɪ] *adj face, complexion* moreno

swat [swɑːt] *v/t* (*pret & pp* **-ted**) *insect, fly* aplastar, matar

sway [sweɪ] **1** *n* (*influence, power*) dominio *m* **2** *v/i* tambalearse

swear [swer] **1** *v/i* (*pret* **swore**, *pp* **sworn**) (*use swearword*) decir palabrotas *or* tacos; **~ at s.o.** insultar a alguien; **I ~** lo juro **2** *v/t* (*pret* **swore**, *pp* **sworn**) (*promise*), LAW jurar

♦ **swear in** *v/t witnesses etc* tomar juramento a

'swear·word palabrota *f*, taco *m*

sweat [swet] **1** *n* sudor *m*; **covered in ~** empapado de sudor **2** *v/i* sudar

'sweat·band banda *f* (en la frente); *on wrist* muñequera *f*

sweat·er ['swetər] suéter *m*, *Span* jersey *m*

'sweat·shirt sudadera *f*

sweat·y ['swetɪ] *adj hands* sudoroso

Swede [swiːd] sueco(-a) *m(f)*

Swe·den ['swiːdn] Suecia *f*

Swe·dish ['swiːdɪʃ] **1** *adj* sueco **2** *n* sueco *m*

sweep [swiːp] **1** *v/t* (*pret & pp* **swept**) *floor, leaves* barrer **2** *n* (*long curve*) curva *f*

♦ **sweep up** *v/t mess, crumbs* barrer

sweep·ing ['swiːpɪŋ] *adj statement* demasiado generalizado; *changes* radical

sweet [swiːt] *adj taste, tea* dulce; F (*kind*) amable; F (*cute*) mono

sweet and 'sour *adj* agridulce

'sweet·corn maíz *m*, *S.Am.* choclo *m*

sweet·en ['swiːtn] *v/t drink, food* endulzar

sweet·en·er ['swiːtnər] *for drink* edulcorante *m*

'sweet·heart novio(-a) *m(f)*

swell [swel] **1** *v/i* (*pp* **swollen**) *of wound, limb* hincharse **2** *adj* F (*good*) genial F, fenomenal F **3** *n of the sea* oleaje *m*

swell·ing ['swelɪŋ] *n* MED hinchazón *f*

swel·ter·ing ['sweltərɪŋ] *adj heat, day*

sofocante

swept [swept] *pret* & *pp* → **sweep**

swerve [swɜːrv] *v/i of driver, car* girar bruscamente, *car* dar un volantazo

swift [swɪft] *adj* rápido

swim [swɪm] **1** *v/i* (*pret* **swam**, *pp* **swum**) nadar; **go ~ming** ir a nadar; **my head is ~ming** me da vueltas la cabeza **2** *n* baño *m*; **go for a ~** ir a darse un baño

swim·mer ['swɪmər] nadador(-a) *m(f)*

swim·ming ['swɪmɪŋ] natación *f*

'**swim·ming pool** piscina *f*, *Mex* alberca *f*, *Rpl* pileta *f*

'**swim·suit** traje *m* de baño, bañador *m*

swin·dle ['swɪndl] **1** *n* timo *m*, estafa *f* **2** *v/t* timar, estafar; **~ s.o. out of sth** estafar algo a alguien

swine [swaɪn] F (*person*) cerdo(-a) *m(f)* F

swing [swɪŋ] **1** *n* oscilación *f; for child* columpio *m*; **~ to the Democrats** giro favorable a los Demócratas **2** *v/t* (*pret* & *pp* **swung**) balancear; *hips* menear **3** *v/i* (*pret* & *pp* **swung**) balancearse; (*turn*) girar; *of public opinion etc* cambiar

swing-'door puerta *f* basculante *or* de vaivén

Swiss [swɪs] **1** *adj* suizo **2** *n person* suizo(-a) *m(f)*; **the ~** los suizos

switch [swɪtʃ] **1** *n for light* interruptor *m*; (*change*) cambio *m* **2** *v/t* (*change*) cambiar de **3** *v/i* (*change*) cambiar

♦ **switch off** *v/t lights, engine, PC, TV* apagar

♦ **switch on** *v/t lights, engine, PC, TV* encender, *L.Am.* prender

'**switch·board** centralita *f*, *L.Am.* conmutador *m*

'**switch·o·ver** cambio *m* (**to** a)

Swit·zer·land ['swɪtsərlənd] Suiza *f*

swiv·el ['swɪvl] *v/i* (*pret* & *pp* **-ed**, *Br* **-led**) *of chair, monitor* girar

swol·len ['swoʊlən] **1** *pp* → **swell** **2** *adj* hinchado

swoop [swuːp] *v/i of bird* volar en picado

♦ **swoop down on** *v/t prey* caer en picado sobre

♦ **swoop on** *v/t of police etc* hacer una redada contra

sword [sɔːrd] espada *f*

'**sword·fish** pez *f* espada

swore [swɔːr] *pret* → **swear**

sworn [swɔːrn] *pp* → **swear**

swum [swʌm] *pp* → **swim**

swung [swʌŋ] *pret* & *pp* → **swing**

syc·a·more ['sɪkəmɔːr] plátano *m* (árbol)

syl·la·ble ['sɪləbl] sílaba *f*

syl·la·bus ['sɪləbəs] plan *m* de estudios

sym·bol ['sɪmbəl] símbolo *m*

sym·bol·ic [sɪm'bɑːlɪk] *adj* simbólico

sym·bol·ism ['sɪmbəlɪzm] simbolismo *m*

sym·bol·ist ['sɪmbəlɪst] simbolista *m/f*

sym·bol·ize ['sɪmbəlaɪz] *v/t* simbolizar

sym·met·ri·cal [sɪ'metrɪkl] *adj* simétrico

sym·me·try ['sɪmətri] simetría *f*

sym·pa·thet·ic [sɪmpə'θetɪk] *adj* (*showing pity*) compasivo; (*understanding*) comprensivo; **be ~ toward a person/ an idea** simpatizar con una persona / una idea

♦ **sym·pa·thize with** ['sɪmpəθaɪz] *v/t person, views* comprender

sym·pa·thiz·er ['sɪmpəθaɪzər] POL simpatizante *m/f*

sym·pa·thy ['sɪmpəθɪ] (*pity*) compasión *f*; (*understanding*) comprensión *f*; **don't expect any ~ from me!** no esperes que te compadezca

sym·pho·ny ['sɪmfənɪ] sinfonía *f*

'**sym·pho·ny or·ches·tra** orquesta *f* sinfónica

symp·tom ['sɪmptəm] *also fig* síntoma *f*

symp·to·mat·ic [sɪmptə'mætɪk] *adj*: **be ~ of** *fig* ser sintomático de

syn·chro·nize ['sɪŋkrənaɪz] *v/t* sincronizar

syn·o·nym ['sɪnənɪm] sinónimo *m*

sy·non·y·mous [sɪ'nɑːnɪməs] *adj* sinónimo; **be ~ with** *fig* ser sinónimo de

S

syn·tax ['sɪntæks] sintaxis *f inv*
syn·the·siz·er ['sɪnθəsaɪzər] MUS sintetizador *m*
syn·thet·ic [sɪn'θetɪk] *adj* sintético
syph·i·lis ['sɪfɪlɪs] sífilis *f*
Syr·i·a ['sɪrɪə] Siria
Syr·i·an ['sɪrɪən] **1** *adj* sirio **2** *n* sirio(-a) *m(f)*
sy·ringe [sɪ'rɪndʒ] *n* jeringuilla *f*
syr·up ['sɪrəp] almíbar *m*

sys·tem ['sɪstəm] *also* COMPUT sistema *m*; *the braking* ~ el sistema de frenado; *the digestive* ~ el aparato digestivo
sys·te·mat·ic [sɪstə'mætɪk] *adj* sistemático
sys·tem·at·i·cal·ly [sɪstə'mætɪklɪ] *adv* sistemáticamente
sys·tems 'an·a·lyst ['sɪstəmz] COMPUT analista *m/f* de sistemas

T

tab [tæb] *n for pulling* lengüeta *f*; *in text* tabulador *m*; *bill* cuenta *f*; *pick up the* ~ pagar (la cuenta)
ta·ble ['teɪbl] *n* mesa *f*; *of figures* cuadro *m*
'ta·ble·cloth mantel *m*; **'table lamp** lámpara *f* de mesa; **ta·ble of 'contents** índice *m* (de contenidos); **'ta·ble·spoon** *object* cuchara *f* grande; *quantity* cucharada *f* grande
ta·blet ['tæblɪt] MED pastilla *f*
'ta·ble ten·nis tenis *m* de mesa
tab·loid ['tæblɔɪd] *n newspaper* periódico *m* sensacionalista (*de tamaño tabloide*)
ta·boo [tə'buː] *adj* tabú *inv*
ta·cit ['tæsɪt] *adj* tácito
ta·ci·turn ['tæsɪtɜːrn] *adj* taciturno
tack [tæk] **1** *n* (*nail*) tachuela *f* **2** *v/t* (*sew*) hilvanar **3** *v/i of yacht* dar bordadas
tack·le ['tækl] **1** *n* (*equipment*) equipo *m*; SP entrada *f*; *fishing* ~ aparejos *mpl* de pesca **2** *v/t* SP entrar a; *problem* abordar; *intruder* hacer frente a
tack·y ['tækɪ] *adj paint, glue* pegajoso; F (*cheap, poor quality*) chabacano, *Span* hortera F; *behavior* impresentable
tact [tækt] tacto *m*
tact·ful ['tæktfəl] *adj* diplomático

tact·ful·ly ['tæktfəlɪ] *adv* diplomáticamente
tac·tic·al ['tæktɪkl] *adj* táctico
tac·tics ['tæktɪks] *npl* táctica *f*
tact·less ['tæktlɪs] *adj* indiscreto
tad·pole ['tædpoʊl] renacuajo *m*
tag [tæg] *n* (*label*) etiqueta *f*
♦ **tag along** *v/i* (*pret & pp* **-ged**) pegarse
tail [teɪl] *n of bird, fish* cola *f*; *of mammal* cola *f*, rabo *m*
'tail light luz *f* trasera
tai·lor ['teɪlər] *n* sastre *m*
tai·lor-made [teɪlər'meɪd] *adj suit, solution* hecho a medida
'tail·pipe *of car* tubo *m* de escape
'tail·wind viento *m* de cola
taint·ed ['teɪntɪd] *adj food* contaminado; *reputation* empañado
Tai·wan [taɪ'wɑːn] Taiwán
Tai·wan·ese [taɪwɑːn'iːz] **1** *adj* taiwanés **2** *n* taiwanés(-esa) *m(f)*; *dialect* taiwanés *m*
take [teɪk] *v/t* (*pret* **took**, *pp* **taken**) (*remove*) llevarse, *Span* coger; (*steal*) llevarse; (*transport, accompany*) llevar; (*accept: money, gift, credit cards*) aceptar; (*study: maths, French*) hacer, estudiar; (*photograph, photocopy*) hacer, sacar; *exam, degree* hacer; *shower* darse; *stroll* dar; *medicine, s.o.'s temperature, taxi* tomar;

(*endure*) aguantar; *how long does it ~?* ¿cuánto tiempo lleva?; *I'll ~ it when shopping* me lo llevo; *it ~s a lot of courage* se necesita mucho valor

♦ **take after** v/t parecerse a

♦ **take apart** v/t (*dismantle*) desmontar; F (*criticize*) hacer pedazos; F (*reprimand*) echar una bronca a F; F *in physical fight* machacar F

♦ **take away** v/t *pain* hacer desaparecer; *object* quitar; MATH restar; *take sth away from s.o.* quitar algo a alguien

♦ **take back** v/t (*return: object*) devolver; *person* llevar de vuelta; (*accept back: husband etc*) dejar volver; *that takes me back of music, thought etc* me trae recuerdos

♦ **take down** v/t *from shelf* bajar; *scaffolding* desmontar; *trousers* bajarse; (*write down*) anotar, apuntar

♦ **take in** v/t (*take indoors*) recoger; (*give accommodation to*) acoger; (*make narrower*) meter; (*deceive*) engañar; (*include*) incluir

♦ **take off 1** v/t *clothes, hat* quitarse; *10% etc* descontar; (*mimic*) imitar; (*cut off*) cortar; *take a day / week off* tomarse un día / una semana de vacaciones **2** v/i *of airplane* despegar, L.Am. decolar; (*become popular*) empezar a cuajar

♦ **take on** v/t *job* aceptar; *staff* contratar

♦ **take out** v/t *from bag, money from bank* sacar; *tooth* sacar, extraer; *word from text* quitar, borrar; *insurance policy* suscribir; *he took her out to dinner* la llevó a cenar; *take the dog out* sacar al perro a pasear; *take the kids out to the park* llevar a los niños al parque; *don't take it out on me!* ¡no la pagues conmigo!

♦ **take over 1** v/t *company etc* absorber, adquirir; *tourists took over the town* los turistas invadieron la ciudad **2** v/i *of new management etc* asumir el cargo; *of new government* asumir el poder; (*do sth in s.o.'s place*) tomar el relevo

♦ **take to** v/t (*like*): *how did they take to the new idea?* ¿qué les pareció la nueva idea?; *I immediately took to him* me cayó bien de inmediato; *he has taken to getting up early* le ha dado por levantarse temprano; *she took to drink* se dio a la bebida

♦ **take up** v/t *carpet etc* levantar; (*carry up*) subir; (*shorten: dress etc*) acortar; *hobby* empezar a hacer; *subject* empezar a estudiar; *offer* aceptar; *new job* comenzar; *space, time* ocupar; *I'll take you up on your offer* aceptaré tu oferta

'take-home pay salario *m* neto

tak·en ['teɪkən] pp → **take**

'take-off *of airplane* despegue *m*, L.Am. decolaje *m*; (*impersonation*) imitación *f*; **'take·o·ver** COM absorción *f*, adquisición *f*; **'take·o·ver bid** oferta *f* pública de adquisición, OPA *f*

ta·kings ['teɪkɪŋz] npl recaudación *f*

tal·cum pow·der ['tælkəmpaʊdər] polvos *mpl* de talco

tale [teɪl] cuento *m*, historia *f*

tal·ent ['tælənt] talento *m*

tal·ent·ed ['tæləntɪd] adj con talento; *she's very ~* tiene mucho talento

'tal·ent scout cazatalentos *m inv*

talk [tɔːk] **1** v/i hablar; *can I talk to …?* ¿podría hablar con …?; *I'll ~ to him about it* hablaré del tema con él **2** v/t English etc hablar; *~ business / politics* hablar de negocios / de política; *~ s.o. into sth* persuadir a alguien para que haga algo **3** n (*conversation*) charla *f*, C.Am., Mex plática *f*; (*lecture*) conferencia *f*, *give a ~ on sth* dar una conferencia sobre algo; *~s* negociaciones *fpl*; *he's all ~ pej* habla mucho y no hace nada

♦ **talk back** v/i responder, contestar

♦ **talk down to** v/t hablar con aires de superioridad a

♦ **talk over** v/t hablar de, discutir

talk·a·tive ['tɔːkətɪv] adj hablador

talk·ing-to ['tɔːkɪŋtuː] sermón *m*, rapapolvo *m*; *give s.o. a good ~* echar a alguien un buen sermón or rapapolvo

T

'**talk show** programa *m* de entrevistas

tall [tɔːl] *adj* alto; *it is ten meters ~* mide diez metros de alto

tall 'or·der: *that's a ~* eso es muy difícil

tall 'sto·ry cuento *m* chino

tal·ly ['tælɪ] **1** *n* cuenta *f* **2** *v/i* (*pret & pp* **-ied**) cuadrar, encajar
♦ **tally with** *v/t* cuadrar con, encajar con

tame [teɪm] *adj animal* manso, domesticado; *joke etc* soso
♦ **tam·per with** ['tæmpər] *v/t lock* intentar forzar; *brakes* tocar

tam·pon ['tæmpɑːn] tampón *m*

tan [tæn] **1** *n from sun* bronceado *m*; (*color*) marrón *m* claro; *get a ~* ponerse moreno **2** *v/i* (*pret & pp* **-ned**) *in sun* broncearse **3** *v/t* (*pret & pp* **-ned**) *leather* curtir

tan·dem ['tændəm] (*bike*) tándem *m*

tan·gent ['tændʒənt] MATH tangente *f*

tan·ge·rine [tændʒə'riːn] mandarina *f*

tan·gi·ble ['tændʒɪbl] *adj* tangible

tan·gle ['tæŋgl] *n* lío *m*, maraña *f*
♦ **tangle up:** *get tangled up of string etc* quedarse enredado

tan·go ['tæŋgoʊ] *n* tango *m*

tank [tæŋk] *for water* depósito *m*, tanque *m*; *for fish* pecera *f*; MOT depósito *m*; MIL, *for skin diver* tanque *m*

tank·er ['tæŋkər] *truck* camión *m* cisterna; *ship* buque *m* cisterna; *for oil* petrolero *m*

'**tank top** camiseta *f* sin mangas

tanned [tænd] *adj* moreno, bronceado

Tan·noy® ['tænɔɪ] megafonía *f*

tan·ta·liz·ing ['tæntəlaɪzɪŋ] *adj* sugerente

tan·ta·mount ['tæntəmaʊnt] *adj:* *be ~ to* equivaler a

tan·trum ['tæntrəm] rabieta *f*

tap [tæp] **1** *n* (*faucet*) grifo *m*, *L.Am.* llave *f* **2** *v/t* (*pret & pp* **-ped**) (*knock*) dar un golpecito en; *phone* intervenir
♦ **tap into** *v/t resources* explotar

'**tap dance** *n* claqué *m*

tape [teɪp] **1** *n* cinta *f* **2** *v/t conversation etc* grabar; *with sticky tape* pegar con cinta adhesiva

'**tape deck** pletina *f*; '**tape drive** COMPUT unidad *f* de cinta; '**tape meas·ure** cinta *f* métrica

tap·er ['teɪpər] *v/i* estrecharse
♦ **taper off** *v/i of production, figures* disminuir

'**tape re·cor·der** magnetófon *m*, *L.Am.* grabador *m*

'**tape re·cor·ding** grabación *f* (magnetofónica)

ta·pes·try ['tæpɪstrɪ] *cloth* tapiz *m*; *art* tapicería *f*

'**tape·worm** tenia *f*, solitaria *f*

tar [tɑːr] *n* alquitrán *m*

tar·dy ['tɑːrdɪ] *adj* tardío

tar·get ['tɑːrgɪt] **1** *n in shooting* blanco *m*; *for sales, production* objetivo *m* **2** *v/t market* apuntar a

tar·get 'au·di·ence audiencia *f* a la que está orientado el programa; '**tar·get date** fecha *f* fijada; **tar·get 'fig·ure** cifra *f* objetivo; '**tar·get group** COM grupo *m* estratégico; '**tar·get mar·ket** mercado *m* objetivo

tar·iff ['tærɪf] (*price*) tarifa *f*; (*tax*) arancel *m*

tar·mac ['tɑːrmæk] *for road surface* asfalto *m*; *at airport* pista *f*

tar·nish ['tɑːrnɪʃ] *v/t metal* deslucir, deslustrar; *reputation* empañar

tar·pau·lin [tɑːr'pɔːlɪn] lona *f* (*impermeable*)

tart [tɑːrt] *n* tarta *f*, pastel *m*

tar·tan ['tɑːrtn] tartán *m*

task [tæsk] tarea *f*

'**task force** *for a special job* equipo *m* de trabajo; MIL destacamento *m*

tas·sel ['tæsl] borla *f*

taste [teɪst] **1** *n* gusto *m*; *of food etc* sabor *m*; *he has no ~* tiene mal gusto **2** *v/t also fig* probar

taste·ful ['teɪstfəl] *adj* de buen gusto

taste·ful·ly ['teɪstfəlɪ] *adv* con buen gusto

taste·less ['teɪstlɪs] *adj food* insípido; *remark* de mal gusto

tast·ing ['teɪstɪŋ] *of wine* cata *f*, degustación *f*

tast·y ['teɪstɪ] *adj* sabroso, rico

tat·tered ['tætərd] *adj clothes* andrajoso; *book* destrozado

tat·ters ['tætərz]: **in ~** *clothes* hecho jirones; *reputation, career* arruinado

tat·too [tə'tuː] *n* tatuaje *m*

tat·ty ['tætɪ] *adj* F sobado, gastado

taught [tɔːt] *pret & pp* → **teach**

taunt [tɔːnt] **1** *n* pulla *f* **2** *v/t* mofarse de

Taur·us ['tɔːrəs] ASTR Tauro *m/f inv*

taut [tɔːt] *adj* tenso

taw·dry ['tɔːdrɪ] *adj* barato, cursi

tax [tæks] **1** *n* impuesto *m*; **before/after ~** sin descontar / descontando impuestos **2** *v/t people* cobrar impuestos a; *product* gravar

tax·a·ble 'in·come ingresos *mpl* gravables

ta·x·ation [tæk'seɪʃn] *(act of taxing)* imposición *f* de impuestos; *(taxes)* fiscalidad *f*, impuestos *mpl*

'tax avoid·ance elusión *f* legal de impuestos; **'tax brack·et** banda *f* impositiva; **'tax-de·duct·i·ble** *adj* desgravable; **'tax eva·sion** evasión *f* fiscal; **'tax-free** *adj* libre de impuestos; **'tax haven** paraíso *m* fiscal

tax·i ['tæksɪ] *n* taxi *m*

'tax·i dri·ver taxista *m/f*

tax·ing ['tæksɪŋ] *adj* difícil, arduo

'tax in·spect·or inspector(a) *m(f)* de Hacienda

'tax·i rank parada *f* de taxis

'tax·pay·er contribuyente *m/f*; **'tax re·turn** *form* declaración *f* de la renta; **'tax year** año *m* fiscal

TB [tiː'biː]: *abbr* (= *tuberculosis*) tuberculosis *f*

tea [tiː] *drink* té *m*; *meal* merienda *f*

tea·bag ['tiːbæg] bolsita *f* de té

teach [tiːtʃ] **1** *v/t* (*pret & pp* **taught**) *person, subject* enseñar; **~ s.o. to do sth** enseñar a alguien a hacer algo **2** *v/i* (*pret & pp* **taught**): **I taught at that school** di clases en ese colegio; **he always wanted to ~** siempre quiso ser profesor

tea·cher ['tiːtʃər] *at primary school* maestro(-a) *m(f)*; *at secondary school, university* profesor(a) *m(f)*

tea·cher 'train·ing formación *f* pedagógica, magisterio *m*

tea·ching ['tiːtʃɪŋ] *profession* enseñanza *f*, docencia *f*

'tea·ching aid material *m* didáctico

'tea cloth paño *m* de cocina; **'tea·cup** taza *f* de té; **'tea drink·er** bebedor(a) *m(f)* de té

teak [tiːk] teca *f*

'tea leaf hoja *f* de té

team [tiːm] equipo *m*

'team-mate compañero(-a) *m(f)* de equipo

team 'spirit espíritu *m* de equipo

team·ster ['tiːmstər] camionero(-a) *m(f)*

'team·work trabajo *m* en equipo

'tea·pot tetera *f*

tear¹ [ter] **1** *n in cloth etc* desgarrón *m*, rotura *f* **2** *v/t* (*pret* **tore**, *pp* **torn**) *paper, cloth* rasgar; **be torn between two alternatives** debatirse entre dos alternativas **3** *v/i* (*pret* **tore**, *pp* **torn**) *(run fast, drive fast)* ir a toda velocidad

♦ **tear down** *v/t poster* arrancar; *building* derribar

♦ **tear out** *v/t* arrancar

♦ **tear up** *v/t paper* romper, rasgar; *agreement* romper

tear² [tɪr] *in eye* lágrima *f*; **burst into ~s** echarse a llorar; **be in ~s** estar llorando

tear·drop ['tɪrdrɑːp] lágrima *f*

tear·ful ['tɪrfəl] *adj* lloroso

'tear gas gas *m* lacrimógeno

tease [tiːz] *v/t person* tomar el pelo a, burlarse de; *animal* hacer rabiar

'tea·spoon *object* cucharilla *f*; *quantity* cucharadita *f*

teat [tiːt] teta *f*

tech·ni·cal ['teknɪkl] *adj* técnico

tech·ni·cal·i·ty [teknɪ'kælətɪ] *(technical nature)* tecnicismo *m*; LAW detalle *m* técnico

tech·ni·cal·ly ['teknɪklɪ] *adv* técnicamente

tech·ni·cian [tek'nɪʃn] técnico(-a) *m(f)*

T

tech·nique [tek'ni:k] técnica f
tech·no·log·i·cal [teknə'lɑ:dʒɪkl] adj tecnológico
tech·no·lo·gy [tek'nɑ:lədʒɪ] tecnología f
tech·no·phob·i·a [teknə'foʊbɪə] rechazo m de las nuevas tecnologías
ted·dy bear ['tedɪbr] osito m de peluche
te·di·ous ['ti:dɪəs] adj tedioso
tee [ti:] n in golf tee m
teem [ti:m] v/i: **be ~ing with rain** llover a cántaros; **be ~ing with tourists/ants** estar abarrotado de turistas/lleno de hormigas
teen·age ['ti:neɪdʒ] adj fashions adolescente, juvenil; **a ~ boy/girl** un adolescente/una adolescente
teen·ag·er ['ti:neɪdʒər] adolescente m/f
teens [ti:nz] npl adolescencia f; **be in one's ~** ser un adolescente; **reach one's ~** alcanzar la adolescencia
tee·ny ['ti:nɪ] adj F chiquitín F
teeth [ti:θ] pl → **tooth**
teethe [ti:ð] v/i echar los dientes
'teeth·ing prob·lems npl problemas mpl iniciales
tel·e·com·mu·ni·ca·tions [telɪkəmju:nɪ'keɪʃnz] telecomunicaciones fpl
tel·e·gram ['telɪgræm] telegrama m
tel·e·graph pole ['telɪgræf] poste m telegráfico
tel·e·path·ic [telɪ'pæθɪk] adj telepático; **you must be ~!** ¡debes tener telepatía!
te·lep·a·thy [tɪ'lepəθɪ] telepatía f
tel·e·phone ['telɪfoʊn] **1** n teléfono m; **be on the ~** (be speaking) estar hablando por teléfono; (possess a phone) tener teléfono **2** v/t person telefonear, llamar por teléfono a **3** v/i telefonear, llamar por teléfono
'tel·e·phone bill factura f del teléfono; **'tel·e·phone book** guía f telefónica, listín m telefónico; **'tel·e·phone booth** cabina f telefónica; **'tel·e·phone call** llamada f telefónica; **'tel·e·phone con·ver·sa·tion** conversación f por teléfono or telefónica; **'tel·e·phone di·rec·to·ry** guía f telefónica, listín m telefónico; **'tel·e·phone ex·change** central f telefónica, centralita f; **'tel·e·phone mes·sage** mensaje m telefónico; **'tel·e·phone num·ber** número m de teléfono

tel·e·pho·to lens [telɪ'foʊtoʊlenz] teleobjetivo m
tel·e·sales ['telɪseɪlz] televentas fpl
tel·e·scope ['telɪskoʊp] telescopio m
tel·e·thon ['telɪθɑːn] maratón m benéfico televisivo
tel·e·vise ['telɪvaɪz] v/t televisar
tel·e·vi·sion ['telɪvɪʒn] televisión f; set televisión f, televisor m; **on ~** en or por (la) televisión; **watch ~** ver la televisión
'tel·e·vi·sion au·di·ence audiencia f televisiva; **'tel·e·vi·sion pro·gram**, Br **'tel·e·vi·sion pro·gramme** programa m televisivo; **'tel·e·vi·sion set** televisión f, televisor m; **'tel·e·vi·sion stu·di·o** estudio m de televisión
tell [tel] **1** v/t (pret & pp told) story contar; lie decir, contar; **I can't ~ the difference** no veo la diferencia; **~ s.o. sth** decir algo a alguien; **don't ~ Mom** no se lo digas a mamá; **could you ~ me the way to …?** ¿me podría decir por dónde se va a …?; **~ s.o. to do sth** decir a alguien que haga algo; **you're ~ing me!** F ¡a mí me lo vas a contar! **2** v/i (pret & pp told) (have effect) hacerse notar; **the heat is ~ing on him** el calor está empezando a afectarle; **time will ~** el tiempo lo dirá
tell·er ['telər] cajero(-a) m(f)
tell·ing ['telɪŋ] adj contundente
tell·ing 'off regañina f
tell·tale ['telteɪl] **1** adj signs revelador f **2** n chivato(-a) m(f)
temp [temp] **1** n employee trabajador(a) m(f) temporal **2** v/i hacer trabajo temporal
tem·per ['tempər] (bad ~) mal humor m; **be in a ~** estar de mal humor; **keep one's ~** mantener la calma; **lose one's ~** perder los estribos

tem·pe·ra·ment ['tempramant] temperamento *m*

tem·pe·ra·men·tal [tempra'mentl] *adj (moody)* temperamental

tem·pe·rate ['temparat] *adj* templado

tem·pe·ra·ture ['tempratʃar] temperatura *f*; *(fever)* fiebre *f*; **have a ~** tener fiebre

tem·ple¹ ['templ] REL templo *m*

tem·ple² ['templ] ANAT sien *f*

tem·po ['tempou] tempo *m*

tem·po·rar·i·ly [tempa'rerɪlɪ] *adv* temporalmente

tem·po·ra·ry ['tempareri] *adj* temporal

tempt [tempt] *v/t* tentar

temp·ta·tion [temp'teɪʃn] tentación *f*

tempt·ing ['temptɪŋ] *adj* tentador

ten [ten] diez

te·na·cious [tɪ'neɪʃəs] *adj* tenaz

te·nac·i·ty [tɪ'næsɪtɪ] tenacidad *f*

ten·ant ['tenənt] *of building* inquilino(-a) *m(f)*; *of farm, land* arrendatario(-a) *m(f)*

tend¹ [tend] *v/t (look after)* cuidar (de)

tend² [tend]: **~ to do sth** soler hacer algo; **~ toward sth** tender hacia algo

ten·den·cy ['tendənsɪ] tendencia *f*

ten·der¹ ['tendər] *adj (sore)* sensible, delicado; *(affectionate)* cariñoso, tierno; *steak* tierno

ten·der² ['tendər] *n* COM oferta *f*

ten·der·ness ['tendərnɪs] *(soreness)* dolor *m*; *of kiss etc* cariño *m*, ternura *f*

ten·don ['tendən] tendón *m*

ten·nis ['tenɪs] tenis *m*

'**ten·nis ball** pelota *f* de tenis; '**ten·nis court** pista *f* de tenis, cancha *f* de tenis; '**ten·nis pla·yer** tenista *m/f*; '**ten·nis rack·et** raqueta *f* de tenis

ten·or ['tenər] MUS tenor *m*

tense¹ [tens] *n* GRAM tiempo *m*

tense² [tens] *adj muscle, moment* tenso; *voice, person* tenso, nervioso

♦ **tense up** *v/i* ponerse tenso

ten·sion ['tenʃn] *of rope, in movie, novel* tensión *f*; *in atmosphere, voice* tensión *f*, tirantez *f*

tent [tent] tienda *f*

ten·ta·cle ['tentəkl] tentáculo *m*

ten·ta·tive ['tentətɪv] *adj move, offer* provisional

ten·ter·hooks ['tentərhʊks]: **be on ~** estar sobre ascuas

tenth [tenθ] **1** *adj* décimo **2** *n* décimo *m*, décima parte *f*; *of second, degree* décima *f*

tep·id ['tepɪd] *adj water, reaction* tibio

term [tɜːrm] *in office etc* mandato *m*; *Br* EDU trimestre *m*; *(condition)* término *m*, condición *f*; *(word)* término *m*; **be on good / bad ~s with s.o.** llevarse bien / mal con alguien; **in the long / short ~** a largo / corto plazo; **come to ~s with sth** llegar a aceptar algo

ter·mi·nal ['tɜːrmɪnl] **1** *n at airport, for buses, containers* terminal *f*; ELEC, COMPUT terminal *m*; *of battery* polo *m* **2** *adj illness* terminal

ter·mi·nal·ly ['tɜːrmɪnəlɪ] *adv*: **~ ill** en la fase terminal de una enfermedad

ter·mi·nate ['tɜːrmɪneɪt] **1** *v/t contract* rescindir; *pregnancy* interrumpir **2** *v/i* finalizar

ter·mi·na·tion [tɜːrmɪ'neɪʃn] *of contract* rescisión *f*; *of pregnancy* interrupción *f*

ter·mi·nol·o·gy [tɜːrmɪ'nɑːlədʒɪ] terminología *f*

ter·mi·nus ['tɜːrmɪnəs] *for buses* final *m* de trayecto; *for trains* estación *f* terminal

ter·race ['terəs] terraza *f*

ter·ra cot·ta [terə'kɑːtə] *adj* de terracota

ter·rain [te'reɪn] terreno *m*

ter·res·tri·al [te'restrɪəl] **1** *n* terrestre *m* **2** *adj television* por vía terrestre

ter·ri·ble ['terəbl] *adj* terrible, horrible

ter·ri·bly ['terəblɪ] *adv (very)* tremendamente

ter·rif·ic [tə'rɪfɪk] *adj* estupendo

ter·rif·i·cal·ly [tə'rɪfɪklɪ] *adv (very)*

tremendamente

ter·ri·fy ['terɪfaɪ] *v/t* (*pret & pp* **-ied**) aterrorizar; **be terrified** estar aterrorizado

ter·ri·fy·ing ['terɪfaɪɪŋ] *adj* aterrador

ter·ri·to·ri·al [terɪ'tɔːrɪəl] *adj* territorial

ter·ri·to·ri·al 'wa·ters *npl* aguas *fpl* territoriales

ter·ri·to·ry ['terɪtɔːrɪ] territorio *m*; *fig* ámbito *m*, territorio *m*

ter·ror ['terər] terror *m*

ter·ror·ism ['terərɪzm] terrorismo *m*

ter·ror·ist ['terərɪst] terrorista *m/f*

'ter·ror·ist at·tack atentado *m* terrorista

'ter·ror·ist or·gan·i·za·tion organización *f* terrorista

ter·ror·ize ['terəraɪz] *v/t* aterrorizar

terse [tɜːrs] *adj* tajante, seco

test [test] **1** *n* prueba *f*; *academic, for driving* examen *m* **2** *v/t* probar, poner a prueba

tes·ta·ment ['testəmənt] *to s.o.'s life etc* testimonio *m*; **Old/ New Testament** REL Viejo / Nuevo Testamento *m*

'test-drive *v/t* (*pret* **-drove**, *pp* **-driven**) *car* probar en carretera

tes·ti·cle ['testɪkl] testículo *m*

tes·ti·fy ['testɪfaɪ] *v/i* (*pret & pp* **-ied**) LAW testificar, prestar declaración

tes·ti·mo·ni·al [testɪ'moʊnɪəl] *n* referencias *fpl*

tes·ti·mo·ny ['testɪmənɪ] LAW testimonio *m*

'test tube tubo *m* de ensayo, probeta *f*

'test-tube ba·by niño(-a) *m(f)* probeta

tes·ty ['testɪ] *adj* irritable

te·ta·nus ['tetənəs] tétanos *m*

teth·er ['teðər] **1** *v/t horse* atar **2** *n* correa *f*; **be at the end of one's ~** estar al punto de perder la paciencia

text [tekst] texto *m*

'text·book libro *m* de texto

tex·tile ['tekstəl] *n* textil *m*

tex·ture ['tekstʃər] textura *f*

Thai [taɪ] **1** *adj* tailandés **2** *n person*

tailandés(-esa) *m(f)*; *language* tailandés *m*

Thai·land ['taɪlænd] Tailandia

than [ðæn] *adv* que; **bigger/ faster ~ me** más grande / más rápido que yo; **more than 50** más de 50

thank [θæŋk] *v/t* dar las gracias a; **~ you** gracias; **no ~ you** no, gracias

thank·ful ['θæŋkfəl] *adj* agradecido; **we have to be ~ that ...** tenemos que dar gracias de que ...

thank·ful·ly ['θæŋkfəlɪ] *adv* (*luckily*) afortunadamente

thank·less ['θæŋklɪs] *adj task* ingrato

thanks [θæŋks] *npl* gracias *fpl*; **~!** ¡gracias!; **~ to** gracias a

Thanks·giv·ing (Day) [θæŋks'gɪvɪŋdeɪ] Día *m* de Acción de Gracias

that [ðæt] **1** *adj* ese *m*, esa *f*; *more remote* aquel *m*, aquella; **~ one** ése **2** *pron* ése *m*, ésa; *more remote* aquél *m*, aquella *f*; **what is ~?** ¿qué es eso?; **who is ~?** ¿quién es ése?; **~'s mine** ése es mío; **~'s tea** es té; **~'s very kind** qué amable **3** *rel pron* que; **the person/ car ~ you see** el coche / la persona que ves **4** *conj* que; **I think ~ ...** creo que ... **5** *adv* (*so*) tan; **~ big/ expensive** tan grande / caro

thaw [θɔː] *v/i of snow* derretirse, fundirse; *of frozen food* descongelarse

the [ðə] el, la; *plural* los, las; **~ sooner ~ better** cuanto antes, mejor

the·a·ter ['θɪətər] teatro *m*

'the·a·ter crit·ic crítico *m* teatral

the·a·tre *Br* → **theater**

the·at·ri·cal [θɪ'ætrɪkl] *adj also fig* teatral

theft [θeft] robo *m*

their [ðer] *adj* su; (*his or her*) su; **~ brother** su hermano; **~ books** sus libros

theirs [ðerz] *pron* el suyo, la suya; **~ are red** los suyos son rojos; **that book is ~** ese libro es suyo; **a friend of ~** un amigo suyo

them [ðem] *pron direct object* los *mpl*, las *fpl*; *indirect object* les; *after prep* ellos *mpl*, ellas *fpl*; **I know ~** los / las conozco; **I gave ~ the keys** les di las llaves; *I sold it to* ~ se lo vendí; *he lives with* ~ vive con ellos / ellas; *if a person asks for help, you should help* ~ si una persona pide ayuda, hay que ayudarla

theme [θiːm] tema *m*

'**theme park** parque *m* temático

'**theme song** tema *m* musical

them·selves [ðem'selvz] *pron reflexive* se; *emphatic* ellos mismos *mpl*, ellas mismas *fpl*; *they hurt* ~ se hicieron daño; *when they saw* ~ *in the mirror* cuando se vieron en el espejo; *they saw it* ~ lo vieron ellos mismos; *by* ~ *(alone)* solos; *(without help)* ellos solos, ellos mismos

then [ðen] *adv (at that time)* entonces; *(after that)* luego, después; *deducing* entonces; *by* ~ para entonces

the·o·lo·gian [θiːə'loʊdʒiən] teólogo *m*

the·ol·o·gy [θi'ɑːlədʒi] teología *f*

the·o·ret·i·cal [θiə'retikl] *adj* teórico

the·o·ret·i·cal·ly [θiə'retikli] *adv* en teoría

the·o·ry ['θiri] teoría *f*; *in* ~ en teoría

ther·a·peu·tic [θerə'pjuːtik] *adj* terapéutico

ther·a·pist ['θerəpist] terapeuta *m/f*

ther·a·py ['θerəpi] terapia *f*

there [ðer] *adv* allí, ahí, allá; *over* ~ allí, ahí, allá; *down* ~ allí *or* ahí *or* allá abajo; ~ *is / are …* hay …; ~ *is / are not* … no hay …; ~ *you are* aquí tienes; *finding sth* aquí está; *completing sth* ya está; ~ *and back* ida y vuelta; *it's 5 miles* ~ *and back* entre ida y vuelta hay cinco millas; ~ *he is!* ¡ahí está!; ~, ~! ¡venga!

there·a·bouts [ðerə'baʊts] *adv* aproximadamente

there·fore ['ðerfɔːr] *adv* por (lo) tanto

ther·mom·e·ter [θər'mɑːmitər] termómetro *m*

ther·mos flask ['θɜːrməs] termo *m*

ther·mo·stat ['θɜːrməstæt] termostato *m*

these [ðiːz] **1** *adj* estos(-as) **2** *pron* éstos *mpl*, éstas *fpl*

the·sis ['θiːsis] (*pl* **theses** ['θiːsiːz])

tesis *f inv*

they [ðeɪ] *pron* ellos *mpl*, ellas *fpl*; ~ *are Mexican* son mexicanos; ~*'re going, but we're not* ellos van, pero nosotros no; *if anyone looks at this,* ~ *will see that …* si alguien mira esto, verá que …; ~ *say that …* dicen que …; ~ *are going to change the law* van a cambiar la ley

thick [θik] *adj* soup espeso; *fog* denso; *wall, book* grueso; *hair* poblado; F *(stupid)* corto; *it's 3 cm* ~ tiene 3 cm de grosor

thick·en ['θikən] *v/t sauce* espesar

thick·set ['θikset] *adj* fornido

thick-skinned [θik'skind] *adj fig* insensible

thief [θiːf] (*pl* **thieves** [θiːvz]) ladrón(-ona) *m(f)*

thigh [θaɪ] muslo *m*

thim·ble ['θimbl] dedal *m*

thin [θin] *adj person* delgado; *hair* ralo, escaso; *soup* claro; *coat, line* fino

thing [θiŋ] cosa *f*; ~*s (belongings)* cosas *fpl*; *how are* ~*s?* ¿cómo te va?; *it's a good* ~ *you told me* menos mal que me lo dijiste; *what a* ~ *to do / say!* ¡qué barbaridad!

thing·um·a·jig ['θiŋʌmədʒig] F *object* chisme *m*; *person* fulano *m*

think [θiŋk] *v/t & v/i* (*pret & pp* **thought**) pensar; *hold an opinion* pensar, creer; *I* ~ *so* creo que sí; *I don't* ~ *so* creo que no; *I* ~ *so too* pienso lo mismo; *what do you* ~? ¿qué piensas *or* crees?; *what do you* ~ *of it?* ¿qué te parece?; *I can't* ~ *of anything more* no se me ocurre nada más; ~ *hard!* ¡piensa más!; *I'm* ~*ing about emigrating* estoy pensando en emigrar

♦ **think over** *v/t* reflexionar sobre

♦ **think through** *v/t* pensar bien

♦ **think up** *v/t plan* idear

'**think tank** grupo *m* de expertos

thin-skinned [θin'skind] *adj* sensible

third [θɜːrd] **1** *adj* tercero **2** *n* tercero(a) *m(f)*; *fraction* tercio *m*, tercera parte *f*

third·ly ['θɜːrdli] *adv* en tercer lugar

third 'par·ty tercero *m*; **third-par·ty**

in·sur·ance seguro *m* a terceros; **third 'per·son** GRAM tercera persona *f*; **'third-rate** *adj* de tercera, de pacotilla F; **Third 'World** Tercer Mundo *m*

thirst [θɜːrst] sed *f*

thirst·y ['θɜːrstɪ] *adj* sediento; **be ~** tener sed

thir·teen [θɜːr'tiːn] trece

thir·teenth [θɜːr'tiːnθ] *n & adj* decimotercero

thir·ti·eth ['θɜːrtɪɪθ] *n & adj* trigésimo

thir·ty ['θɜːrtɪ] treinta

this [ðɪs] **1** *adj* este *m*, esta *f*; **~ one** éste **2** *pron* esto *m*, esta *f*; **~ is good** esto es bueno; **~ is ...** *introducing s.o.* éste / ésta es ...; TELEC soy ... **3** *adv*: **~ big / high** así de grande / de alto

thorn [θɔːrn] espina *f*

thorn·y ['θɔːrnɪ] *adj also fig* espinoso

thor·ough ['θɜːroʊ] *adj search* minucioso; *knowledge* profundo; *person* concienzudo

thor·ough·bred ['θɜːroʊbred] *horse* purasangre *m*

thor·ough·ly ['θɜːroʊlɪ] *adv* completamente; *clean up* a fondo; *search* minuciosamente; **I'm ~ ashamed** estoy avergonzadísimo

those [ðoʊz] **1** *adj* esos *mpl*, esas *fpl*; *more remote* aquellos *mpl*, aquellas *fpl* **2** *pron* ésos *mpl*, ésas *fpl*; *more remote* aquéllos *mpl*, aquéllas *mpl*

though [ðoʊ] **1** *conj* (*although*) aunque; **as ~** como si **2** *adv* sin embargo; **it's not finished ~** pero no está acabado

thought[1] [θɒːt] *single* idea *f*; *collective* pensamiento *m*

thought[2] [θɒːt] *pret & pp → **think**

thought·ful ['θɒːtfəl] *adj* pensativo; *book* serio; (*considerate*) atento

thought·less ['θɒːtlɪs] *adj* desconsiderado

thou·sand ['θaʊznd] mil *m*; **~s of** miles de; **a ~ and ten** mil diez

thou·sandth ['θaʊzndθ] *n & adj* milésimo

thrash [θræʃ] *v/t* golpear, dar una paliza a; SP dar una paliza a

♦ **thrash around** *v/i with arms etc* revolverse

♦ **thrash out** *v/t solution* alcanzar

thrash·ing ['θræʃɪŋ] *also* SP paliza *f*

thread [θred] **1** *n* hilo *m*; *of screw* rosca *f* **2** *v/t needle* enhebrar; *beads* ensartar

thread·bare ['θredber] *adj* raído

threat [θret] amenaza *f*

threat·en ['θretn] *v/t* amenazar

threat·en·ing ['θretnɪŋ] *adj* amenazador

three [θriː] tres

three-'quart·ers tres cuartos *mpl*

thresh [θreʃ] *v/t corn* trillar

thresh·old ['θreʃhoʊld] *of house, new age* umbral *m*; **on the ~ of** en el umbral *or* en puertas de

threw [θruː] *pret → **throw**

thrift [θrɪft] ahorro *m*

thrift·y ['θrɪftɪ] *adj* ahorrativo

thrill [θrɪl] **1** *n* emoción *f*, estremecimiento *m* **2** *v/t*: **be ~ed** estar entusiasmado

thrill·er ['θrɪlər] *movie* película *f* de *Span* suspense *or* L.Am. suspenso; *novel* novela *f* de *Span* suspense *or* L.Am. suspenso

thrill·ing ['θrɪlɪŋ] *adj* emocionante

thrive [θraɪv] *v/i of plant* medrar, crecer bien; *of business, economy* prosperar

throat [θroʊt] garganta *f*

'throat loz·enge pastilla *f* para la garganta

throb [θrɑːb] **1** *n of heart* latido *m*; *of music* zumbido *m* **2** *v/i* (*pret & pp* **-bed**) *of heart* latir; *of music* zumbar

throm·bo·sis [θrɑːm'boʊsɪs] trombosis *f*

throne [θroʊn] trono *m*

throng [θrɑːŋ] *n* muchedumbre *f*

throt·tle ['θrɑːtl] **1** *n on motorbike* acelerador *m*; *on boat* palanca *f* del gas; *on motorbike* mango *m* del gas **2** *v/t* (*strangle*) estrangular

♦ **throttle back** *v/i* desacelerar

through [θruː] **1** *prep* ◊ (*across*) a través de; **go ~ the city** atravesar la ciudad ◊ (*during*) durante; **~ the winter / summer** durante el invierno / verano; **Monday ~ Friday** de lunes a viernes ◊ (*by means of*) a través de, por medio de; **arranged ~ him** acordado por él **2** *adv*: **wet ~** completamente mojado; **watch a movie ~** ver una película de principio a fin **3** *adj*: **be ~** *of couple* haber terminado; (*have arrived*: *of news etc*) haber llegado; **you're ~** TELEC ya puede hablar; **I'm ~ with ...** (*finished with*) he terminado con ...

'**through flight** vuelo *m* directo

through·out [θruːˈaʊt] **1** *prep* durante, a lo largo de **2** *adv* (*in all parts*) en su totalidad

'**through train** tren *m* directo

throw [θroʊ] **1** *v/t* (*pret* **threw**, *pp* **thrown**) tirar; *of horse* tirar, desmontar; (*disconcert*) desconcertar; *party* dar **2** *n* lanzamiento *m*; **it's your ~** te toca tirar

♦ **throw away** *v/t* tirar, *L.Am.* botar

♦ **throw off** *v/t jacket etc* quitarse rápidamente; *cold etc* deshacerse de

♦ **throw on** *v/t clothes* ponerse rápidamente

♦ **throw out** *v/t old things* tirar, *L.Am.* botar; *from bar, job, home* echar; *from country* expulsar; *plan* rechazar

♦ **throw up 1** *v/t ball* lanzar hacia arriba; **throw up one's hands** echarse las manos a la cabeza **2** *v/i* (*vomit*) vomitar

'**throw·a·way** *adj remark* insustancial, pasajero; (*disposable*) desechable

'**throw-in** SP saque *m* de banda

thrown [θroʊn] *pp* → **throw**

thru [θruː] → **through**

thrush [θrʌʃ] *bird* zorzal *m*

thrust [θrʌst] *v/t* (*pret & pp* **thrust**) (*push hard*) empujar; *knife* hundir; **~ sth into s.o.'s hands** poner algo en las manos de alguien; **~ one's way through the crowd** abrirse paso a empujones entre la multitud

thud [θʌd] *n* golpe *m* sordo

thug [θʌg] matón *m*

thumb [θʌm] **1** *n* pulgar *m* **2** *v/t*: **~ a ride** hacer autoestop

thumb·tack ['θʌmtæk] chincheta *f*

thump [θʌmp] **1** *n blow* porrazo *m*;

noise golpe *m* sordo **2** *v/t person* dar un porrazo a; **~ one's fist on the table** pegar un puñetazo en la mesa **3** *v/i of heart* latir con fuerza; **~ on the door** aporrear la puerta

thun·der ['θʌndər] *n* truenos *mpl*

thun·der·ous ['θʌndərəs] *adj applause* tormenta *f*

thun·der·storm ['θʌndərstɔːrm] tormenta *f* (*con truenos*)

thun·der·struck *adj* atónito

thun·der·y ['θʌndərɪ] *adj weather* tormentoso

Thurs·day ['θɜːrzdeɪ] jueves *m inv*

thus [ðʌs] *adv* (*in this way*) así

thwart [θwɔːrt] *v/t person, plans* frustrar

thyme [taɪm] tomillo *m*

thy·roid gland ['θaɪrɔɪdɡlænd] (glándula *f*) tiroides *m inv*

tick [tɪk] **1** *n of clock* tictac *m*; (*checkmark*) señal *f* de visto bueno **2** *v/i of clock* hacer tictac

tick·et ['tɪkɪt] *for bus, train, lottery* billete *m*, *L.Am.* boleto *m*; *for airplane* billete *m*, *L.Am.* pasaje *m*; *for theater, concert, museum* entrada *f*, *L.Am.* boleto *m*; *for speeding etc* multa *f*

'**tick·et col·lec·tor** revisor(a) *m(f)*; '**tick·et in·spec·tor** revisor(a) *m(f)*; '**tick·et ma·chine** máquina *f* expendedora de billetes; '**tick·et of·fice** *at station* mostrador *m* de venta de billetes; THEA taquilla *f*, *L.Am.* boletería *f*

tick·ing ['tɪkɪŋ] *noise* tictac *m*

tick·le ['tɪkl] **1** *v/t person* hacer cosquillas a **2** *v/i of material* hacer cosquillas; **stop that, you're tickling!** ¡para ya, me haces cosquillas!

tick·lish ['tɪklɪʃ] *adj*: **be ~** *of person* tener cosquillas

ti·dal wave ['taɪdlweɪv] maremoto *m* (*ola*)

tide [taɪd] marea *f*; **high ~** marea alta; **low ~** marea baja; **the ~ is in/out** la marea está alta/baja

♦ **tide over** *v/t*: **20 dollars will tide me over** 20 dólares me bastarán

ti·di·ness ['taɪdɪnɪs] orden *m*

ti·dy ['taɪdɪ] *adj* ordenado

♦ **tidy away** *v/t* (*pret & pp* **-ied**) guardar

♦ **tidy up 1** *v/t room, shelves* ordenar; **tidy o.s. up** arreglarse **2** *v/i* recoger

tie [taɪ] **1** *n* (*necktie*) corbata *f*; SP (*even result*) empate *m*; **he doesn't have any ~s** no está atado a nada **2** *v/t knot* hacer, atar; *hands* atar; **~ two ropes together** atar dos cuerdas **3** *v/i* SP empatar

♦ **tie down** *v/t also fig* atar

♦ **tie up** *v/t person, laces* atar; *boat* amarrar; *hair* recoger; **I'm tied up tomorrow** (*busy*) mañana estaré muy ocupado

tier [tɪr] *of hierarchy* nivel *m*; *in stadium* grada *f*

ti·ger ['taɪgər] tigre *m*

tight [taɪt] **1** *adj clothes* ajustado, estrecho; *security* estricto; (*hard to move*) apretado; (*properly shut*) cerrado; (*not leaving much time*) justo de tiempo; F (*drunk*) como una cuba **F 2** *adv hold* fuerte; *shut* bien

tight·en ['taɪtn] *v/t screw* apretar; *control* endurecer; *security* intensificar; **~ one's grip on sth** on rope *etc* asir algo con más fuerza; *on power etc* incrementar el control sobre algo

♦ **tighten up** *v/i in discipline, security* ser más estricto

tight-fist·ed [taɪt'fɪstɪd] *adj* agarrado

tight·ly ['taɪtlɪ] *adv* → **tight**

tight·rope ['taɪtroup] cuerda *f* floja

tights [taɪts] *npl Br* medias *fpl*, pantis *mpl*

tile [taɪl] *on floor* baldosa *f*; *on wall* azulejo *m*; *on roof* teja *f*

till[^1] [tɪl] → **until**

till[^2] [tɪl] *n* (*cash register*) caja *f* (registradora)

till[^3] [tɪl] *v/t soil* labrar

tilt [tɪlt] **1** *v/t* inclinar **2** *v/i* inclinarse

tim·ber ['tɪmbər] madera *f* (de construcción)

time [taɪm] tiempo *m*; (*occasion*) vez *f*; **~ is up** se acabó (el tiempo); **for the ~ being** por ahora, por el momento; **have a good ~** pasarlo bien; **have a good ~!** ¡que lo paséis bien!;

what's the ~?, do you have the ~? ¿qué hora es?; **the first ~** la primera vez; **four ~s** cuatro veces; **~ and again** una y otra vez; **all the ~** todo el rato; **two / three at a ~** de dos en dos / de tres en tres; **at the same ~** *speak, reply etc* a la vez; (*however*) al mismo tiempo; **in ~** con tiempo; **on ~** puntual; **in no ~** en un santiamén

'**time bomb** bomba *f* de relojería; '**time clock** *in factory* reloj *m* registrador; '**time-con·sum·ing** *adj* que lleva mucho tiempo; '**time dif·fer·ence** diferencia *f* horaria; '**time-lag** intervalo *m*; '**time lim·it** plazo *m*

time·ly ['taɪmlɪ] *adj* oportuno

'**time out** SP tiempo *m* muerto

tim·er ['taɪmər] *device* temporizador *m*; *person* cronometrador *m*

'**time-sav·ing** *n* ahorro *m* de tiempo; '**time·scale** *of project* plazo *m* (de tiempo); '**time switch** temporizador *m*; '**time-warp** salto *m* en el tiempo; '**time zone** huso *m* horario

tim·id ['tɪmɪd] *adj* tímido

tim·ing ['taɪmɪŋ] *of dancer* sincronización *f*; *of actor* utilización *f* de las pausas y del ritmo; **the ~ of the announcement was perfect** el anuncio fue realizado en el momento perfecto

tin [tɪn] *metal* estaño *m*; *Br* (*can*) lata *f*

tin·foil ['tɪnfɔɪl] papel *m* de aluminio

tinge [tɪndʒ] *n of color, sadness* matiz *m*

tin·gle ['tɪŋgl] *n* hormigueo *m*

♦ **tin·ker with** ['tɪŋkər] *v/t* enredar con

tin·kle ['tɪŋkl] *n of bell* tintineo *m*

tin·sel ['tɪnsl] espumillón *m*

tint [tɪnt] **1** *n of color* matiz *m*; *in hair* tinte *m* **2** *v/t hair* teñir

tint·ed ['tɪntɪd] *glasses* con un tinte; *paper* coloreado

ti·ny ['taɪnɪ] *adj* diminuto, minúsculo

tip[^1] [tɪp] *n of stick, finger* punta *f*; *of mountain* cumbre *f*; *of cigarette* filtro *m*

tip[^2] [tɪp] **1** *n advice* consejo *m*; *money* propina *f* **2** *v/t* (*pret & pp* **-ped**) *waiter etc* dar propina a

♦ **tip off** *v/t* avisar

♦ **tip over** *v/t jug* volcar; *liquid* derramar; *he tipped water all over me* derramó agua encima mío

'**tip-off** soplo *m*

tipped [tɪpt] *adj cigarettes* con filtro

tip·py·toe ['tɪpɪtou]: *on* ~ de puntillas

tip·sy ['tɪpsɪ] *adj* achispado

tire[1] [taɪr] *n* neumático *m, L.Am.* llanta *f*

tire[2] [taɪr] **1** *v/t* cansar, fatigar **2** *v/i* cansarse, fatigarse; *he never* ~*s of telling the story* nunca se cansa de contar la historia

tired [taɪrd] *adj* cansado, fatigado; *be* ~ *of s.o. / sth* estar cansado de algo / alguien

tired·ness ['taɪrdnɪs] cansancio *m*, fatiga *f*

tire·less ['taɪrlɪs] *adj efforts* incansable, infatigable

tire·some ['taɪrsəm] *adj* (*annoying*) pesado

tir·ing ['taɪrɪŋ] *adj* agotador

tis·sue ['tɪʃuː] ANAT tejido *m*; (*handkerchief*) pañuelo *m* de papel, Kleenex® *m*

'**tis·sue pa·per** papel *m* de seda

tit[1] [tɪt] *bird* herrerillo *m*

tit[2] [tɪt]: *give s.o.* ~ *for tat* pagar a alguien con la misma moneda

tit[3] [tɪt] ∨ (*breast*) teta *f* ∨

ti·tle ['taɪtl] *of novel, person etc* título *m*; LAW título *m* de propiedad

'**ti·tle·hold·er** SP campeón(-ona) *m(f)*

tit·ter ['tɪtər] *v/i* reírse tontamente

to [tuː] *unstressed* [tə] **1** *prep* a; ~ *Japan / Chicago* a Japón / Chicago; *let's go* ~ *my place* vamos a mi casa; *walk* ~ *the station* caminar a la estación; ~ *the north / south of* ... al norte / sur de ...; *give sth* ~ *s.o.* dar algo a alguien; *from Monday* ~ *Wednesday* de lunes a miércoles; *from 10* ~ *15 people* de 10 a 15 personas **2** *with verbs:* ~ *speak* hablar; *learn* ~ *swim* aprender a nadar; *nice* ~ *eat* sabroso; *too heavy* ~

carry demasiado pesado para llevarlo; ~ *be honest with you* ... para ser sincero ... **3** *adv:* ~ *and fro* de un lado para otro

toad [toud] sapo *m*

toad·stool ['toudstuːl] seta *f* venenosa

toast [toust] **1** *n* pan *m* tostado; *when drinking* brindis *m inv*; *propose a* ~ *to s.o.* proponer un brindis en honor de alguien **2** *v/t when drinking* brindar por

toast·er ['toustər] tostador(a) *m(f)*

to·bac·co [tə'bækou] tabaco *m*

to·bog·gan [tə'bɑːgən] *n* tobogán *m*

to·day [tə'deɪ] *adv* hoy

tod·dle ['tɑːdl] *v/i of child* dar los primeros pasos

tod·dler ['tɑːdlər] niño *m* pequeño

to-do [tə'duː] F revuelo *m*

toe [tou] **1** *n* dedo *m* del pie; *of shoe* puntera *f* **2** *v/t:* ~ *the line* acatar la disciplina

toe·nail ['touneɪl] uña *f* del pie

to·geth·er [tə'geðər] *adv* juntos(-as); *mix two drinks* ~ mezclar dos bebidas; *don't all talk* ~ no hablen todos a la vez

toil [tɔɪl] *n* esfuerzo *m*

toi·let ['tɔɪlɪt] *place* cuarto *m* de baño, servicio *m*; *equipment* retrete *m*; *go to the* ~ ir al baño

'**toi·let pa·per** papel *m* higiénico

toi·let·ries ['tɔɪlɪtrɪz] *npl* artículos *mpl* de tocador

'**toi·let roll** rollo *m* de papel higiénico

to·ken ['toukən] (*sign*) muestra *f*; (*gift* ~) vale *m*; (*disk*) ficha *f*

told [tould] *pret & pp* → **tell**

tol·e·ra·ble ['tɑːlərəbl] *adj pain etc* soportable; (*quite good*) aceptable

tol·e·rance ['tɑːlərəns] tolerancia *f*

tol·e·rant ['tɑːlərənt] *adj* tolerante

tol·e·rate ['tɑːləreɪt] *v/t noise, person* tolerar; *I won't* ~ *it!* ¡no lo toleraré!

toll[1] [toul] *v/i of bell* tañer

toll[2] [toul] *n* (*deaths*) mortandad *f*, número *m* de víctimas

toll[3] [toul] *n for bridge, road* peaje *m*; TELEC tarifa *f*

T

'toll booth cabina *f* de peaje; **'toll-free** *adj* TELEC gratuito; **'toll road** carretera *f* de peaje

to·ma·to [təˈmeɪtoʊ] tomate *m*, *Mex* jitomate *m*

to·ma·to 'ketch·up ketchup *m*

to·ma·to 'sauce *for pasta etc* salsa *f* de tomate

tomb [tuːm] tumba *f*

tom·boy [ˈtɑːmbɔɪ] niña *f* poco femenina

tomb·stone [ˈtuːmstoʊn] lápida *f*

tom·cat [ˈtɑːmkæt] gato *m*

to·mor·row [təˈmɔːroʊ] *adv* mañana; **the day after ~** pasado mañana; **~ morning** mañana por la mañana

ton [tʌn] tonelada *f* (*907 kg*)

tone [toʊn] *of color, conversation* tono *m*; *of musical instrument* timbre *m*; *of neighborhood* nivel *m*; **~ of voice** tono *m* de voz

♦ **tone down** *v/t demands, criticism* bajar el tono de

ton·er [ˈtoʊnər] tóner *m*

tongs [tɑːŋz] *npl* tenazas *fpl*; *for hair* tenacillas *fpl* de rizar

tongue [tʌŋ] *n* lengua *f*

ton·ic [ˈtɑːnɪk] MED tónico *m*

'ton·ic (wa·ter) (agua *f*) tónica *f*

to·night [təˈnaɪt] *adv* esta noche

ton·sil [ˈtɑːnsl] amígdala *f*

ton·sil·li·tis [tɑːnsəˈlaɪtɪs] amigdalitis *f*

too [tuː] *adv* (*also*) también; (*excessively*) demasiado; **me ~** yo también; **~ big / hot** demasiado grande / caliente; **~ much rice** demasiado arroz; **eat ~ much** comer demasiado

took [tuk] *pret* → **take**

tool [tuːl] herramienta *f*

toot [tuːt] *v/t* F tocar

tooth [tuːθ] (*pl teeth* [tiːθ]) diente *m*

'tooth·ache dolor *m* de muelas

'tooth·brush cepillo *m* de dientes

tooth·less [ˈtuːθlɪs] *adj* desdentado

'tooth·paste pasta *f* de dientes, dentífrico *m*

'tooth·pick palillo *m*

top [tɑːp] **1** *n of mountain* cima *f*; *of tree* copa *f*; *of wall, screen, page* parte *f* superior; (*lid: of bottle etc*) tapón *m*; *of pen* capucha *f*; *clothing* camiseta *f*, top *m*; (MOT: *gear*) directa *f*; **on ~ of** encima de, sobre; **at the ~ of the page** en la parte superior de la página; **at the ~ of the mountain** en la cumbre; **be ~ of the class / league** ser el primero de la clase / de la liga; **get to the ~** *of company, mountain* llegar a la cumbre; **be over the ~** (*exaggerated*) ser una exageración **2** *adj branches* superior; *floor* de arriba, último; *management, official* alto; *player* mejor; *speed, note* máximo **3** *v/t* (*pret & pp* **-ped**): **~ped with ...** *of cake etc* con una capa de ... por encima

♦ **top up** *v/t glass, tank* llenar

top 'hat sombrero *m* de copa

top 'heav·y *adj* sobrecargado en la parte superior

top·ic [ˈtɑːpɪk] tema *m*

top·i·cal [ˈtɑːpɪkl] *adj* de actualidad

top·less [ˈtɑːplɪs] *adj* en topless

top·most [ˈtɑːpmoʊst] *adj branches, floor* superior

top·ping [ˈtɑːpɪŋ] *on pizza* ingrediente *m*

top·ple [ˈtɑːpl] **1** *v/i* derrumbarse **2** *v/t government* derrocar

top 'se·cret *adj* altamente confidencial

top·sy-tur·vy [tɑːpsɪˈtɜːrvɪ] *adj* (*in disorder*) desordenado; *world* al revés

torch [tɔːrtʃ] *with flame* antorcha *f*

tore [tɔːr] *pret* → **tear**

tor·ment 1 *n* [ˈtɔːrment] tormento *m* **2** *v/t* [tɔːrˈment] *person, animal* atormentar; **~ed by doubt** atormentado por la duda

torn [tɔːrn] *pp* → **tear**

tor·na·do [tɔːrˈneɪdoʊ] tornado *m*

tor·pe·do [tɔːrˈpiːdoʊ] **1** *n* torpedo *m* **2** *v/t also fig* torpedear

tor·rent [ˈtɑːrənt] *also fig* torrente *m*; *of lava* colada *f*

tor·ren·tial [təˈrenʃl] *adj rain* torrencial

tor·toise [ˈtɔːrtəs] tortuga *f*

tor·ture [ˈtɔːrtʃər] **1** *n* tortura *f* **2** *v/t*

torturar

toss [tɑːs] **1** v/t ball lanzar, echar; rider desmontar; salad remover; **~ a coin** echar a cara o cruz **2** v/i; **~ and turn** dar vueltas

to·tal ['toutl] **1** n total m **2** adj sum, amount total; disaster rotundo, completo; idiot de tomo y lomo; stranger completo **3** v/t F car cargarse F; **the truck was ~ed** el camión quedó destrozado

to·tal·i·tar·i·an [toutælɪ'terɪən] adj totalitario

to·tal·ly ['toutəlɪ] adv totalmente

tote bag ['toutbæg] bolsa f grande

tot·ter ['tɑːtər] v/i of person tambalearse

touch [tʌtʃ] **1** n toque m; sense tacto m; **lose ~ with s.o.** perder el contacto con alguien; **keep in ~ with s.o.** mantenerse en contacto con alguien; **we kept in ~** seguimos en contacto; **be out of ~** no estar al corriente; **the leader was out of ~ with the people** el líder estaba desconectado de lo que pensaba la gente; **in ~** SP fuera **2** v/t tocar; emotionally conmover **3** v/i tocar; of two lines etc tocarse

♦ **touch down** v/i of airplane aterrizar; SP marcar un ensayo

♦ **touch on** v/t (mention) tocar, mencionar

♦ **touch up** v/t photo retocar; Br: sexually manosear

touch·down ['tʌtʃdaun] of airplane aterrizaje m; SP touchdown m, ensayo m

touch·ing ['tʌtʃɪŋ] adj conmovedor

touch·line ['tʌtʃlaɪn] SP línea f de banda

'**touch screen** pantalla f táctil

touch·y ['tʌtʃɪ] adj person susceptible

tough [tʌf] adj person, meat, punishment duro; question, exam difícil; material resistente, fuerte

♦ **tough·en up** v/t person hacer más fuerte

'**tough guy** F tipo m duro F

tour [tur] **1** n of museum etc recorrido m; of area viaje m (**of** por); of band etc gira f **2** v/t area recorrer **3** v/i of band etc estar de gira

'**tour guide** guía m/f turístico(-a)

tour·i·sm ['turɪzm] turismo m

tour·i·st ['turɪst] turista m/f

'**tour·ist at·trac·tion** atracción f turística; '**tour·ist in·dus·try** industria f turística; '**tour·ist (in·for-'ma·tion) of·fice** oficina f de turismo; '**tour·ist sea·son** temporada f turística

tour·na·ment ['turnəmənt] torneo m

'**tour op·er·a·tor** operador m turístico

tous·led ['tauzld] adj hair revuelto

tow [tou] **1** v/t car, boat remolcar **2** n: **give s.o. a ~** remolcar a alguien

♦ **tow away** v/t car llevarse

to·ward [tɔːrd] prep hacia; **we are working ~ a solution** estamos intentando encontrar una solución

tow·el ['tauəl] toalla f

tow·er ['tauər] n torre m

♦ **tower over** v/t of building elevarse por encima de; of person ser mucho más alto que

town [taun] ciudad f; small pueblo m

town 'cen·ter, Br **town 'cen·tre** centro m de la ciudad / del pueblo; **town 'coun·cil** ayuntamiento m; **town 'hall** ayuntamiento m

'**tow·rope** cuerda f para remolcar

tox·ic ['tɑːksɪk] adj tóxico

tox·ic 'waste residuos mpl tóxicos

tox·in ['tɑːksɪn] BIO toxina f

toy [tɔɪ] juguete m

'**toy store** juguetería f, tienda f de juguetes

♦ **toy with** v/t object juguetear con; idea darle vueltas a

trace [treɪs] **1** n of substance resto m **2** v/t (find) localizar; (follow: footsteps of) seguir el rastro a; (draw) trazar

track [træk] n (path) senda f, camino, for horses hipódromo m; for dogs canódromo m; for cars circuito m; for athletics pista f; on CD canción f, corte m; RAIL vía f; **~ 10** RAIL vía 10; **keep ~ of sth** llevar la cuenta de algo

♦ **track down** *v/t* localizar

'**track·suit** chándal *m*

trac·tor ['træktər] tractor *m*

trade [treɪd] **1** *n* (*commerce*) comercio *m*; (*profession, craft*) oficio *m* **2** *v/i* (*do business*) comerciar; **~ in sth** comerciar en algo **3** *v/t* (*exchange*) intercambiar; **~ sth for sth** intercambiar algo por algo

♦ **trade in** *v/t when buying* entregar como parte del pago

'**trade fair** feria *f* de muestras; '**trade·mark** marca *f* registrada; '**trade mis·sion** misión *f* comercial

trad·er ['treɪdər] comerciante *m*

trade 'se·cret secreto *m* de la casa, secreto *m* comercial

trades·man ['treɪdzmən] (*plumber etc*) electricista, fontanero / plomero *etc*

tra·di·tion [trə'dɪʃn] tradición *f*

tra·di·tion·al [trə'dɪʃnl] *adj* tradicional

tra·di·tion·al·ly [trə'dɪʃnlɪ] *adv* tradicionalmente

traf·fic ['træfɪk] *n on roads, in drugs* tráfico *m*

♦ **traffic in** *v/t* (*pret & pp* -**ked**) *drugs* traficar con

'**traf·fic cir·cle** rotonda *f*, *Span* glorieta; '**traf·fic cop** F poli *m* de tráfico F; '**traf·fic is·land** isleta *f*; '**traf·fic jam** atasco *m*; '**traf·fic light** semáforo *m*; '**traf·fic po·lice** policía *f* de tráfico; '**traf·fic sign** señal *f* de tráfico

tra·ge·dy ['trædʒədɪ] tragedia *f*

tra·gic ['trædʒɪk] *adj* trágico

trail [treɪl] **1** *n* (*path*) camino *m*, senda *f*; *of blood* rastro *m* **2** *v/t* (*follow*) seguir la pista de; (*tow*) arrastrar **3** *v/i* (*lag behind*) ir a la zaga

trail·er ['treɪlər] *pulled by vehicle* remolque *m*; (*mobile home*) caravana *f*; *of film* avance *m*, tráiler *m*

train[1] [treɪn] *n* tren *m*; **go by ~** ir en tren

train[2] [treɪn] **1** *v/t team, athlete* entrenar; *employee* formar; *dog* adiestrar **2** *v/i of team, athlete* entrenarse; *of teacher etc* formarse

train·ee [treɪ'niː] aprendiz(a) *m(f)*

train·er ['treɪnər] SP entrenador(a) *m(f)*; *of dog* adiestrador(a) *m(f)*

train·ers ['treɪnərz] *npl Br shoes* zapatillas *fpl* de deporte

train·ing ['treɪnɪŋ] *of new staff* formación *f*; SP entrenamiento *m*; **be in ~** SP estar entrenándose; **be out of ~** SP estar desentrenado

'**train·ing course** cursillo *m* de formación

'**train·ing scheme** plan *m* de formación

'**train sta·tion** estación *f* de tren

trait [treɪt] rasgo *m*

trai·tor ['treɪtər] traidor(a) *m(f)*

tram·ple ['træmpl] *v/t* pisotear; **be ~d to death** morir pisoteado; **be ~d underfoot** ser pisoteado

♦ **trample on** *v/t person, object* pisotear

tram·po·line ['træmpəliːn] cama *f* elástica

trance [træns] trance *m*; **go into a ~** entrar en trance

tran·quil ['træŋkwɪl] *adj* tranquilo

tran·quil·i·ty [træŋ'kwɪlətɪ] tranquilidad *f*

tran·quil·iz·er ['træŋkwɪlaɪzər] tranquilizante *m*

trans·act [træn'zækt] *v/t deal* negociar

trans·ac·tion [træn'zækʃn] *action* transacción *f*; *deal* negociación *f*

trans·at·lan·tic [trænzət'læntɪk] *adj* transatlántico

tran·scen·den·tal [trænsen'dentl] *adj* trascendental

tran·script ['trænskrɪpt] transcripción *f*

trans·fer 1 *v/t* [træns'fɜːr] (*pret & pp* -**red**) transferir **2** *v/i* (*pret & pp* -**red**) *in traveling* hacer transbordo; *from one language to another etc* pasar **3** *n* ['trænsfɜːr] *also of money* transferencia *f*; *in travel* transbordo *m*

trans·fer·a·ble [træns'fɜːrəbl] *adj ticket* transferible

'**trans·fer fee** *for football player* traspaso *m*

trans·form [træns'fɔːrm] v/t transformar

trans·form·a·tion [trænsfər'meɪʃn] transformación f

trans·form·er [træns'fɔːrmər] ELEC transformador m

trans·fu·sion [træns'fjuːʒn] transfusión f

tran·sis·tor [træn'zɪstər] transistor m; (radio) transistor m, radio m transistor

tran·sit ['trænzɪt]: **in ~** en tránsito

tran·si·tion [træn'sɪʒn] transición f

tran·si·tion·al [træn'sɪʒnl] adj de transición

'**tran·sit lounge** at airport sala f de tránsito

'**trans·it pas·sen·ger** pasajero m en tránsito

trans·late [træns'leɪt] v/t & v/i traducir

trans·la·tion [træns'leɪʃn] traducción f

trans·la·tor [træns'leɪtər] traductor(a) m(f)

trans·mis·sion [trænz'mɪʃn] of news, program emisión f; of disease, MOT transmisión f

trans·mit [trænz'mɪt] v/t (pret & pp -**ted**) news, program emitir; disease transmitir

trans·mit·ter [trænz'mɪtər] for radio, TV emisora f

trans·par·en·cy [træns'pærənsɪ] PHOT diapositiva f

trans·par·ent [træns'pærənt] adj transparente; (obvious) obvio

trans·plant MED **1** v/t [træns'plænt] transplantar **2** n ['trænsplænt] transplante m

trans·port 1 v/t [træn'spɔːrt] goods, people transportar **2** n ['trænspɔːrt] of goods, people transporte m

trans·por·ta·tion [trænspɔːr'teɪʃn] of goods, people transporte m; **means of ~** medio m de transporte; **public ~** transporte m público; **Department of Transportation** Ministerio m de Transporte

trans·ves·tite [træns'vestaɪt] travestí m, travestido m

trap [træp] **1** n trampa f; **set a ~ for s.o.** tender una trampa a alguien **2** v/t (pret & pp -**ped**) atrapar; **be ~ped** by enemy, flames, landslide etc quedar atrapado

'**trap·door** ['træpdɔːr] trampilla f

tra·peze [trə'piːz] trapecio m

trap·pings ['træpɪŋz] npl of power parafernalia f

trash [træʃ] (garbage) basura f; (poor product) bazofia f; (despicable person) escoria f

'**trash·can** [træʃkæn] cubo m de la basura

trash·y ['træʃɪ] adj goods barato

trau·mat·ic [trə'mætɪk] adj traumático

trau·ma·tize ['traʊmətaɪz] v/t traumatizar

trav·el ['trævl] **1** n viajes mpl; **do you like ~?** ¿te gusta viajar?; **on my ~s** en mis viajes **2** v/i (pret & pp -**ed**, Br -**led**) viajar **3** v/t miles viajar, recorrer

'**trav·el a·gen·cy** agencia f de viajes; '**trav·el a·gent** agente m de viajes; '**trav·el bag** bolsa f de viaje

trav·el·er, Br **trav·el·ler** ['trævələr] viajero(-a) m(f)

'**trav·el·er's check**, Br '**trav·el·ler's cheque** cheque m de viaje

'**trav·el ex·pens·es** npl gastos mpl de viaje; '**trav·el in·sur·ance** seguro m de asistencia en viaje; '**trav·el pro·gram**, Br '**trav·el pro·gramme** on TV etc programa m de viajes; '**trav·el·sick** adj mareado

trawl·er ['trɔːlər] (barco m) arrastrero m

tray [treɪ] bandeja f

treach·er·ous ['tretʃərəs] adj traicionero

treach·er·y ['tretʃərɪ] traición f

tread [tred] **1** n pasos mpl; of staircase huella f (del peldaño); of tire dibujo m **2** v/i (pret **trod**, pp **trodden**) andar; **mind where you ~** cuida dónde pisas

♦ **tread on** v/t s.o.'s foot pisar

trea·son ['triːzn] traición f

trea·sure ['treʒər] **1** n also person te-

T

soro *m* **2** *v/t gift etc* apreciar mucho

trea·sur·er ['treʒərər] tesorero(-a) *m(f)*

Trea·sur·y De·part·ment ['treʒərɪ] Ministerio *m* de Hacienda

treat [triːt] **1** *n* placer; *it was a real ~* fue un auténtico placer; *I have a ~ for you* tengo una sorpresa agradable para ti; *it's my ~* (*I'm paying*) yo invito **2** *v/t* tratar; *~ s.o. to sth* invitar a alguien a algo

treat·ment ['triːtmənt] tratamiento *m*

treat·y ['triːtɪ] tratado *m*

tre·ble¹ ['trebl] *n* MUS soprano *m*

tre·ble² ['trebl] **1** *adv*: *~ the price* el triple del precio **2** *v/i* triplicarse

tree [triː] árbol *m*

trem·ble ['trembl] *v/i* temblar

tre·men·dous [trɪ'mendəs] *adj* (*very good*) estupendo; (*enormous*) enorme

tre·men·dous·ly [trɪ'mendəslɪ] *adv* (*very*) tremendamente; (*a lot*) enormemente

trem·or ['tremər] *of earth* temblor *m*

trench [trentʃ] trinchera *f*

trend [trend] tendencia *f*; (*fashion*) moda *f*

trend·y ['trendɪ] *adj* de moda; *views* moderno

tres·pass ['trespæs] *v/i* entrar sin autorización; *no ~ing* prohibido el paso

♦ trespass on *v/t land* entrar sin autorización en; *privacy* entrometerse en

tres·pass·er ['trespæsər] intruso(-a) *m(f)*

tri·al ['traɪəl] LAW juicio *m*; *of equipment* prueba *f*; *be on ~* LAW estar siendo juzgado; *have sth on ~ equipment* tener algo a prueba

tri·al 'pe·ri·od periodo *m* de prueba

tri·an·gle ['traɪæŋgl] triángulo *m*

tri·an·gu·lar [traɪ'æŋgjʊlər] *adj* triangular

tribe [traɪb] tribu *f*

tri·bu·nal [traɪ'bjuːnl] tribunal *m*

tri·bu·ta·ry ['trɪbjətərɪ] *of river* afluente *m*

trick [trɪk] **1** *n* (*to deceive, knack*) truco *m*; *play a ~ on s.o.* gastar una broma a alguien **2** *v/t* engañar; *~ s.o. into doing sth* engañar a alguien para que haga algo

trick·e·ry ['trɪkərɪ] engaños *mpl*

trick·le ['trɪkl] **1** *n* hilo *m*, reguero *m*; *fig*: *of money* goteo *m* **2** *v/i* gotear, escurrir

trick·ster ['trɪkstər] embaucador(a) *m(f)*

trick·y ['trɪkɪ] *adj* (*difficult*) difícil

tri·cy·cle ['traɪsɪkl] triciclo *m*

tri·fle ['traɪfl] *n* (*triviality*) nadería *f*

tri·fling ['traɪflɪŋ] *adj* insignificante

trig·ger ['trɪgər] *n on gun* gatillo *m*; *on camcorder* disparador *m*

♦ trigger off *v/t* desencadenar

trim [trɪm] **1** *adj* (*neat*) muy cuidado; *figure* delgado **2** *v/t* (*pret & pp -med*) *hair, hedge* recortar; *budget, costs* recortar, reducir; (*decorate*: *dress*) adornar **3** *n* (*light cut*) recorte *m*; *just a ~, please* to hairdresser corte sólo las puntas, por favor; *in good ~* en buenas condiciones

trim·ming ['trɪmɪŋ] *on clothes* adorno *m*; *with all the ~s dish* con la guarnición clásica; *car* con todos los extras

trin·ket ['trɪŋkɪt] baratija *f*

tri·o ['triːoʊ] MUS trío *m*

trip [trɪp] **1** *n* (*journey*) viaje *m* **2** *v/i* (*pret & pp -ped*) (*stumble*) tropezar **3** *v/t* (*pret & pp -ped*) (*make fall*) poner la zancadilla a

♦ trip up 1 *v/t* (*make fall*) poner la zancadilla a; (*cause to go wrong*) confundir **2** *v/i* (*stumble*) tropezar; (*make a mistake*) equivocarse

tripe [traɪp] *to eat* mondongo *m*, *Span* callos *mpl*

trip·le ['trɪpl] → *treble*

trip·lets ['trɪplɪts] *npl* trillizos *mpl*

tri·pod ['traɪpɑːd] PHOT trípode *m*

trite [traɪt] *adj* manido

tri·umph ['traɪʌmf] *n* triunfo *m*

triv·i·al ['trɪvɪəl] *adj* trivial

triv·i·al·i·ty [trɪvɪ'ælətɪ] trivialidad *f*

trod [trɑːd] *pret* → *tread*

trod·den ['trɑːdn] *pp* → *tread*

trol·ley ['trɑːlɪ] (*streetcar*) tranvía *f*

trom·bone [trɑːmˈboʊn] trombón *m*

troops [truːps] *npl* tropas *fpl*

tro·phy [ˈtroʊfɪ] trofeo *m*

tro·pic [ˈtrɑːpɪk] trópico *m*

trop·i·cal [ˈtrɑːpɪkl] *adj* tropical

trop·ics [ˈtrɑːpɪks] *npl* trópicos *mpl*

trot [trɑːt] *v/i* (*pret & pp* **-ted**) trotar

trou·ble [ˈtrʌbl] **1** *n* (*difficulties*) problema *m*, problemas *mpl*; (*inconvenience*) molestia *f*; (*disturbance*) conflicto *m*, desorden *m*; **go to a lot of ~ to do sth** complicarse mucho la vida para hacer algo; **no ~!** no es molestia; **get into ~** meterse en líos **2** *v/t* (*worry*) preocupar, inquietar; (*bother, disturb*) molestar

trou·ble-free *adj* sin complicaciones; **trou·ble·mak·er** alborotador(a) *m(f)*; **trou·ble·shoot·er** persona encargada de resolver problemas; **trou·bleshoot·ing** resolución *f* de problemas

trou·ble·some [ˈtrʌblsəm] *adj* problemático

trou·sers [ˈtrauzərz] *npl Br* pantalones *mpl*

trout [traut] (*pl trout*) trucha *f*

tru·ant [ˈtruːənt]: *play ~* hacer novillos, *Mex* irse de pinta, *S.Am.* hacerse la rabona

truce [truːs] tregua *f*

truck [trʌk] camión *m*

truck driv·er camionero(-a) *m(f)*; **truck farm** huerta *f*; **truck farm·er** horticultor(a) *m(f)*; **truck stop** restaurante *m* de carretera

trudge [trʌdʒ] **1** *v/i* caminar fatigosamente **2** *n* caminata *f*

true [truː] *adj* verdadero, cierto; *friend, American* auténtico; **come ~** *of hopes, dream* hacerse realidad

trul·y [ˈtruːlɪ] *adv* verdaderamente, realmente; *Yours ~* le saluda muy atentamente

trum·pet [ˈtrʌmpɪt] *n* trompeta *f*

trum·pet·er [ˈtrʌmpɪtər] trompetista *m/f*

trunk [trʌŋk] *of tree, body* tronco *m*; *of elephant* trompa *f*; (*large case*) baúl *m*; *of car* maletero *m*, *C.Am.*, *Mex* cajuela *f*, *Rpl* baúl *m*

trust [trʌst] **1** *n* confianza *f*; FIN fondo *m* de inversión **2** *v/t* confiar en

trust·ed [ˈtrʌstɪd] *adj* de confianza

trust·ee [trʌsˈtiː] fideicomisario(-a) *m(f)*

trust·ful, trust·ing [ˈtrʌstful, ˈtrʌstɪŋ] *adj* confiado

trust·wor·thy [ˈtrʌstwɜːrðɪ] *adj* de confianza

truth [truːθ] verdad *f*

truth·ful [ˈtruːθfəl] *adj person* sincero; *account* verdadero

try [traɪ] **1** *v/t* (*pret & pp* **-ied**) probar; LAW juzgar; *~ to do sth* intentar hacer algo, tratar de hacer algo **2** *v/i* (*pret & pp* **-ied**): *he didn't even ~* ni siquiera lo intentó; *you must ~ harder* debes esforzarte más **3** *n* intento *m*; *can I have a ~?* *of food* ¿puedo probar?; *at doing sth* ¿puedo intentarlo?

♦ **try on** *v/t clothes* probar

♦ **try out** *v/t new machine, new method* probar

try·ing [ˈtraɪɪŋ] *adj* (*annoying*) molesto, duro

T-shirt [ˈtiːʃɜːrt] camiseta *f*

tub [tʌb] (*bath*) bañera *f*, *L.Am.* tina *f*; *for liquid* cuba *f*; *for yoghurt, ice cream* envase *m*

tub·by [ˈtʌbɪ] *adj* rechoncho

tube [tuːb] tubo *m*

tube·less [ˈtuːblɪs] *adj tire* sin cámara de aire

tu·ber·cu·lo·sis [tuːbɜːrkjəˈloʊsɪs] tuberculosis *f*

tuck [tʌk] **1** *n in dress* pinza *f* **2** *v/t* (*put*) meter

♦ **tuck away** *v/t* (*put away*) guardar; F (*eat quickly*) zamparse F

♦ **tuck in 1** *v/t children* arropar; *sheets* remeter **2** *v/i* (*start eating*) ponerse a comer

♦ **tuck up** *v/t sleeves etc* remangar; **tuck s.o. up in bed** meter a alguien en la cama

Tues·day [ˈtuːzdeɪ] martes *m inv*

tuft [tʌft] *of hair* mechón *m*; *of grass* mata *f*

tug [tʌg] **1** *n* (*pull*) tirón *m*; NAUT remolcador *m* **2** *v/t* (*pret & pp* **-ged**)

(*pull*) tirar de

tu·i·tion [tuː'ɪʃn] clases *fpl*

tu·lip ['tuːlɪp] tulipán *m*

tum·ble ['tʌmbl] *v/i* caer, caerse

tum·ble-down ['tʌmbldaʊn] *adj* destartalado

tum·bler ['tʌmblər] *for drink* vaso *m*; *in circus* acróbata *m/f*

tum·my ['tʌmɪ] F tripa *f* F, barriga *f* F

'tum·my ache dolor *m* de tripa *or* barriga

tu·mor, *Br* **tu·mour** ['tuːmər] tumor *m*

tu·mult ['tuːmʌlt] tumulto *m*

tu·mul·tu·ous [tuː'mʌltʊəs] *adj* tumultuoso

tu·na ['tuːnə] atún *m*

tune [tuːn] **1** *n* melodía *f*; **be in ~** *of instrument* estar afinado; **sing in ~** cantar sin desafinar; **be out of ~** *of singer* desafinar; *of instrument* estar desafinado **2** *v/t instrument* afinar

♦ **tune in** *v/i Radio, TV* sintonizar

♦ **tune in to** *v/t Radio, TV* sintonizar (con)

♦ **tune up 1** *v/i of orchestra, players* afinar **2** *v/t engine* poner a punto

tune·ful ['tuːnfəl] *adj* melodioso

tun·er ['tuːnər] *hi-fi* sintonizador *m*

tune-up ['tuːnʌp] *of engine* puesta *f* a punto

tun·nel ['tʌnl] *n* túnel *m*

tur·bine ['tɜːrbaɪn] turbina *f*

tur·bu·lence ['tɜːrbjələns] *in air travel* turbulencia *f*

tur·bu·lent ['tɜːrbjələnt] *adj* turbulento

turf [tɜːrf] césped *m*; *piece* tepe *m*

Turk [tɜːrk] turco(-a) *m(f)*

Tur·key ['tɜːrkɪ] Turquía

tur·key ['tɜːrkɪ] pavo *m*

Turk·ish ['tɜːrkɪʃ] **1** *adj* turco **2** *n language* turco *m*

tur·moil ['tɜːrmɔɪl] desorden *m*, agitación *f*

turn [tɜːrn] **1** *n* (*rotation*) vuelta *f*; *in road* curva *f*; *junction* giro *m*; *in vaudeville* número *m*; **take ~s in doing sth** turnarse para hacer algo; **it's my ~** me toca a mí; **it's not your ~ yet** no te toca todavía; **take a ~ at**

the wheel turnarse para conducir *or L.Am.* manejar; **do s.o. a good ~** hacer un favor a alguien **2** *v/t wheel* girar; *corner* dar la vuelta a; **~ one's back on s.o.** dar la espalda a alguien **3** *v/i of driver, car, wheel* girar; *of person: turn around* volverse; **~ left/right here** gira aquí a la izquierda/a la derecha; **it has ~ed sour/cold** se ha cortado/enfriado; **it ~ed blue** se volvió *or* puso azul; **he has ~ed 40** ha cumplido cuarenta años

♦ **turn around 1** *v/t object* dar la vuelta a; *company* dar un vuelco a; COM (*deal with*) procesar, preparar **2** *v/i of person* volverse, darse la vuelta; *of driver* dar la vuelta

♦ **turn away 1** *v/t* (*send away*) rechazar; **the doorman turned us away** el portero no nos dejó entrar **2** *v/i* (*walk away*) marcharse; (*look away*) desviar la mirada

♦ **turn back 1** *v/t edges, sheets* doblar **2** *v/i of walkers etc* volver; *in course of action* echarse atrás

♦ **turn down** *v/t offer, invitation* rechazar; *volume, TV, heating* bajar; *edge, collar* doblar

♦ **turn in 1** *v/i* (*go to bed*) irse a dormir **2** *v/t to police* entregar

♦ **turn off 1** *v/t TV, engine* apagar; *faucet* cerrar; *heater* apagar; **it turns me off** F *sexually* me quita las ganas F **2** *v/i of car, driver* doblar

♦ **turn on 1** *v/t TV, engine, heating* encender, *L.Am.* prender; *faucet* abrir; F *sexually* excitar **2** *v/i of machine* encenderse, *L.Am.* prenderse

♦ **turn out 1** *v/t lights* apagar **2** *v/i: it turned out well* salió bien; **as it turned out** al final; **he turned out to be ...** resultó ser ...

♦ **turn over 1** *v/i in bed* darse la vuelta; *of vehicle* volcar, dar una vuelta de campana **2** *v/t* (*put upside down*) dar la vuelta a; *page* pasar; FIN facturar

♦ **turn up 1** *v/t collar* subirse; *volume, heating* subir **2** *v/i* (*arrive*) aparecer

turn·ing ['tɜːrnɪŋ] giro *m*

'turn·ing point punto *m* de inflexión
tur·nip ['tɜːrnɪp] nabo *m*
'turn·out *of people* asistencia *f*;
'turn·o·ver FIN facturación *f*; *staff ~*
rotación *f* de personal; 'turn·pike
autopista *f* de peaje; 'turn sig·nal
on car intermitente *m*; 'turn·stile
torniquete *m* (*de entrada*); 'turn-
ta·ble *of record player* plato *m*,
tur·quoise ['tɜːrkwɔɪz] *adj* turquesa
tur·ret ['tʌrɪt] *of castle* torrecilla *f*; *of
tank* torreta *f*
tur·tle ['tɜːrtl] tortuga *f* (marina)
tur·tle·neck 'sweat·er suéter *m* de
cuello alto
tusk [tʌsk] colmillo *m*
tu·tor ['tuːtər] *at university* tutor *m*;
(*private*) ~ profesor(a) *m(f)* particular
tu·xe·do [tʌk'siːdoʊ] esmoquin *m*
TV [tiːˈviː] televisión *f*; *on ~* en la televisión
T'V din·ner menú *m* precocinado;
T'V guide guía *f* televisiva; T'V program, *Br* T'V pro·gramme programa *m* de televisión
twad·dle ['twɑːdl] F tonterías *fpl*
twang [twæŋ] 1 *n in voice* entonación
f nasal 2 *v/t guitar string* puntear
tweez·ers ['twiːzərz] *npl* pinzas *fpl*
twelfth [twelfθ] *n & adj* duodécimo
twelve [twelv] doce
twen·ti·eth ['twentɪɪθ] *n & adj* vigésimo
twen·ty ['twentɪ] veinte
twice [twaɪs] *adv* dos veces; *~ as
much* el doble
twid·dle ['twɪdl] *v/t* dar vueltas a; ~
one's thumbs holgazanear
twig [twɪg] *n* ramita *f*
twi·light ['twaɪlaɪt] crepúsculo *m*
twin [twɪn] gemelo *m*
'twin beds *npl* camas *fpl* gemelas
twinge [twɪndʒ] *of pain* punzada *f*
twin·kle ['twɪŋkl] *v/i of stars* parpa-

deo *m*; *of eyes* brillo *m*
twin 'room habitación *f* con camas
gemelas
'twin town ciudad *f* hermana
twirl [twɜːrl] 1 *v/t* hacer girar 2 *n of
cream etc* voluta *f*
twist [twɪst] 1 *v/t* retorcer; ~ *one's
ankle* torcerse el tobillo 2 *v/i of
road, river* serpentear 3 *n in rope,
road* vuelta *f*; *in plot, story* giro *m* inesperado
twist·y ['twɪstɪ] *adj road* serpenteante
twit [twɪt] F memo(-a) *m(f)* F
twitch [twɪtʃ] 1 *n nervous* tic *m* 2 *v/i*
(*jerk*) moverse (ligeramente)
twit·ter ['twɪtər] *v/i of birds* gorjear
two [tuː] dos; *the ~ of them* los dos,
ambos
two-faced ['tuːfeɪst] *adj* falso; 'two-
stroke *adj engine* de dos tiempos;
two-way 'traf·fic tráfico *m* en dos
direcciones
ty·coon [taɪˈkuːn] magnate *m*
type [taɪp] 1 *n* (*sort*) tipo *m*, clase *f*;
what ~ of ...? ¿qué tipo *or* clase de
...? 2 *v/i* (*use a keyboard*) escribir a
máquina 3 *v/t with a typewriter* mecanografiar, escribir a máquina
'type·set *v/t* componer
'type·writ·er máquina *f* de escribir
ty·phoid ['taɪfɔɪd] fiebre *f* tifoidea
ty·phoon [taɪˈfuːn] tifón *m*
ty·phus ['taɪfəs] tifus *m*
typ·i·cal ['tɪpɪkl] *adj* típico; *that's ~
of you*/ *him!* ¡típico tuyo / de él!
typ·i·cal·ly ['tɪpɪklɪ] *adv* típicamente;
~ *American* típicamente americano
typ·ist ['taɪpɪst] mecanógrafo(-a)
m(f)
ty·ran·ni·cal [tɪˈrænɪkl] *adj* tiránico
ty·ran·nize ['tɪrənaɪz] *v/t* tiranizar
ty·ran·ny ['tɪrənɪ] tiranía *f*
ty·rant ['taɪrənt] tirano(-a) *m(f)*
tyre *Br* → tire¹

T

U

ug·ly ['ʌglɪ] *adj* feo

UK [juː'keɪ] *abbr* (= ***United Kingdom***) RU *m* (= Reino *m* Unido)

ul·cer ['ʌlsər] úlcera *f*; *in mouth* llaga *f*

ul·ti·mate ['ʌltɪmət] *adj* (*final*) final; (*fundamental*) esencial; *the ~ car* (*best, definitive*) lo último en coches

ul·ti·mate·ly ['ʌltɪmətlɪ] *adv* (*in the end*) en última instancia

ul·ti·ma·tum [ʌltɪ'meɪtəm] ultimátum *m*

ul·tra·sound ['ʌltrəsaʊnd] MED ultrasonido *m*; (*scan*) ecografía *f*

ul·tra·vi·o·let [ʌltrə'vaɪələt] *adj* ultravioleta

um·bil·i·cal cord [ʌm'bɪlɪkl] cordón *m* umbilical

um·brel·la [ʌm'brelə] paraguas *m inv*

um·pire ['ʌmpaɪr] *n* árbitro *m*; *in tennis* juez *m/f* de silla

ump·teen [ʌmp'tiːn] *adj* F miles de F

UN [juː'en] *abbr* (= ***United Nations***) ONU *f* (= Organización *f* de las Naciones Unidas)

un·a·ble [ʌn'eɪbl] *adj*: *be ~ to do sth* (*not know how to*) no saber hacer algo; (*not be in a position to*) no poder hacer algo

un·ac·cept·a·ble [ʌnək'septəbl] *adj* inaceptable; *it is ~ that* es inaceptable que

un·ac·count·a·ble [ʌnə'kaʊntəbl] *adj* inexplicable

un·ac·cus·tomed [ʌnə'kʌstəmd] *adj*: *be ~ to sth* no estar acostumbrado a algo

un·a·dul·ter·at·ed [ʌnə'dʌltəreɪtɪd] *adj fig* (*absolute*) absoluto

un-A·mer·i·can [ʌnə'merɪkən] *adj* poco americano; *activities* antiamericano

u·nan·i·mous [juː'nænɪməs] *adj verdict* unánime; *be ~ on* ser unánime respecto a

u·nan·i·mous·ly [juː'nænɪməslɪ] *adv vote, decide* unánimemente

un·ap·proach·a·ble [ʌnə'proʊtʃəbl] *adj person* inaccesible

un·armed [ʌn'ɑːrmd] *adj person* desarmado; *~ combat* combate *m* sin armas

un·as·sum·ing [ʌnə'suːmɪŋ] *adj* sin pretensiones

un·at·tached [ʌnə'tætʃt] *adj* (*without a partner*) sin compromiso, sin pareja

un·at·tend·ed [ʌnə'tendɪd] *adj* desatendido; *leave sth ~* dejar algo desatendido

un·au·thor·ized [ʌn'ɔːθəraɪzd] *adj* no autorizado

un·a·void·a·ble [ʌnə'vɔɪdəbl] *adj* inevitable

un·a·void·a·bly [ʌnə'vɔɪdəblɪ] *adv*: *be ~ detained* entretenerse sin poder evitarlo

un·a·ware [ʌnə'wer] *adj*: *be ~ of* no ser consciente de

un·a·wares [ʌnə'werz] *adv* desprevenido; *catch s.o. ~* agarrar *or Span* coger a alguien desprevenido

un·bal·anced [ʌn'bælənst] *adj also* PSYCH desequilibrado

un·bear·a·ble [ʌn'berəbl] *adj* insoportable

un·beat·a·ble [ʌn'biːtəbl] *adj team* invencible; *quality* insuperable

un·beat·en [ʌn'biːtn] *adj team* invicto

un·be·knownst [ʌnbɪ'noʊnst] *adj*: *~ to her* sin que ella lo supiera

un·be·liev·a·ble [ʌnbɪ'liːvəbl] *adj also* F increíble; *he's ~* F (*very good / bad*) es increíble

un·bi·as(s)ed [ʌn'baɪəst] *adj* imparcial

un·block [ʌn'blɑːk] *v/t pipe* desatascar

un·born [ʌn'bɔːrn] *adj* no nacido

un·break·a·ble [ʌn'breɪkəbl] *adj* *plates* irrompible; *world record* inalcanzable

un·but·ton [ʌn'bʌtn] *v/t* desabotonar

un·called-for [ʌn'kɒːldfɔːr] *adj*: **be ~** estar fuera de lugar

un·can·ny [ʌn'kænɪ] *adj* *resemblance* increíble, asombroso; *skill* inexplicable; *(worrying: feeling)* extraño, raro

un·ceas·ing [ʌn'siːsɪŋ] *adj* incesante

un·cer·tain [ʌn'sɜːrtn] *adj* *future, origins* incierto; **be ~ about sth** no estar seguro de algo; *what will happen? – it's ~* ¿qué ocurrirá? – no se sabe

un·cer·tain·ty [ʌn'sɜːrtntɪ] incertidumbre *f*; *there is still ~ about his health* todavía hay incertidumbre en torno a su estado de salud

un·checked [ʌn'tʃekt] *adj*: *let sth go* **~** no controlar algo

un·cle ['ʌŋkl] tío *m*

un·com·for·ta·ble [ʌn'kʌmftəbl] *adj* *chair* incómodo; *feel ~ about sth about decision etc* sentirse incómodo con algo; *I feel ~ with him* me siento incómodo con él

un·com·mon [ʌn'kɑːmən] *adj* poco corriente, raro; *it's not ~* no es raro *or* extraño

un·com·pro·mis·ing [ʌn'kɑːprəmaɪzɪŋ] *adj* inflexible

un·con·cerned [ʌnkən'sɜːrnd] *adj* indiferente; *be ~ about s.o. / sth* no preocuparse por alguien / algo

un·con·di·tion·al [ʌnkən'dɪʃnl] *adj* incondicional

un·con·scious [ʌn'kɑːnʃəs] *adj* MED, PSYCH inconsciente; *knock ~* dejar inconsciente; *be ~ of sth (not aware)* no ser consciente de algo

un·con·trol·la·ble [ʌnkən'troʊləbl] *adj* *anger, children* incontrolable; *desire* incontrolable, irresistible

un·con·ven·tion·al [ʌnkən'venʃnl] *adj* poco convencional

un·co·op·er·a·tive [ʌnkoʊ'ɑːpərətɪv] *adj*: *be ~* no estar dispuesto a colaborar

un·cork [ʌn'kɔːrk] *v/t* *bottle* descorchar

un·cov·er [ʌn'kʌvər] *v/t* *remove cover from* destapar; *plot, ancient remains* descubrir

un·dam·aged [ʌn'dæmɪdʒd] *adj* intacto

un·daunt·ed [ʌn'dɒːntɪd] *adj* impertérrito; *carry on ~* seguir impertérrito

un·de·cid·ed [ʌndɪ'saɪdɪd] *adj* *question* sin resolver; *be ~ about s.o. / sth* estar indeciso sobre alguien / algo

un·de·ni·a·ble [ʌndɪ'naɪəbl] *adj* innegable

un·de·ni·a·bly [ʌndɪ'naɪəblɪ] *adv* innegablemente

un·der ['ʌndər] **1** *prep (beneath)* debajo de, bajo; *(less than)* menos de; **~ the water** bajo el agua; *it is ~ review / investigation* está siendo revisado / investigado **2** *adv (anesthetized)* anestesiado

un·der·age *adj*: *~ drinking* el consumo de alcohol por menores de edad

'**un·der·arm** *adv*: *throw a ball ~* lanzar una pelota soltándola por debajo de la altura del hombro

'**un·der·car·riage** tren *m* de aterrizaje

'**un·der·cov·er** *adj* *agent* secreto

un·der'cut *v/t (pret & pp -cut)* COM vender más barato que

'**un·der·dog** *n*: *support the ~* apoyar al más débil

un·der'done *adj* *meat* poco hecho

un·der'es·ti·mate *v/t* subestimar

un·der·ex'posed *adj* PHOT subexpuesto

un·der'fed *adj* malnutrido

un·der'go *v/t (pret -went, pp -gone)* *surgery, treatment* ser sometido a; *experiences* sufrir; *the hotel is ~ing refurbishment* se están efectuando renovaciones en el hotel

un·der·grad·u·ate estudiante *m/f* universitario(-a) *(todavía no licenciado(a))*

'**un·der·ground 1** *adj* *passages etc*

U

subterráneo; POL *resistance, newspaper etc* clandestino **2** *adv work* bajo tierra; *go* **~** POL pasar a la clandestinidad

'**un·der·growth** maleza *f*

un·der'hand *adj* (*devious*) poco honrado

un·der'lie *v/t* (*pret* **-lay**, *pp* **-lain**) (*form basis of*) sostener

un·der'line *v/t text* subrayar

un·der'ly·ing *adj causes, problems* subyacente

un·der'mine *v/t s.o.'s position, theory* minar, socavar

un·der·neath [ʌndər'niːθ] **1** *prep* debajo de, bajo **2** *adv* debajo

'**un·der·pants** *npl* calzoncillos *mpl*

'**un·der·pass** *for pedestrians* paso *m* subterráneo

un·der·priv·i·leged [ʌndər'prɪvɪlɪdʒd] *adj* desfavorecido

un·der'rate *v/t* subestimar, infravalorar

'**un·der·shirt** camiseta *f*

un·der·sized [ʌndər'saɪzd] *adj* demasiado pequeño

'**un·der·skirt** enaguas *fpl*

un·der·staffed [ʌndər'stæft] *adj* sin suficiente personal

un·der·stand [ʌndər'stænd] **1** *v/t* (*pret & pp* **-stood**) entender, comprender; *language* entender; *I* **~** *that you ...* tengo entendido que ...; *they are understood to be in Canada* se cree que están en Canadá **2** *v/i* (*pret & pp* **-stood**) entender, comprender

un·der·stand·a·ble [ʌndər'stændəbl] *adj* comprensible

un·der·stand·a·bly [ʌndər'stændəblɪ] *adv* comprensiblemente

un·der·stand·ing [ʌndər'stændɪŋ] **1** *adj person* comprensivo **2** *n of problem, situation* interpretación *f*; (*agreement*) acuerdo *m*; *on the* **~** *that ...* (*condition*) a condición de que ...

'**un·der·state·ment** *n*: *that's an* **~** ¡y te quedas corto!

un·der'take *v/t* (*pret* **-took**, *pp* **-taken**) *task* emprender; **~** *to do sth*

(*agree to*) encargarse de hacer algo

un·der·tak·er ['ʌndərteɪkər] *Br* encargado *m* de una funeraria

'**un·der·tak·ing** (*enterprise*) proyecto *m*, empresa *f*; *give an* **~** *to do sth* compreterse a hacer algo

un·der'val·ue *v/t* infravalorar

'**un·der·wear** ropa *f* interior

un·der'weight *adj*: *be* **~** pesar menos de lo normal

'**un·der·world** *criminal* hampa *f*; *in mythology* Hades *m*

un·der'write *v/t* (*pret* **-wrote**, *pp* **-written**) FIN asegurar, garantizar

un·de·served [ʌndɪ'zɜːrvd] *adj* inmerecido

un·de·sir·a·ble [ʌndɪ'zaɪrəbl] *adj features, changes* no deseado; *person* indeseable; **~** *element person* persona *f* problemática

un·dis·put·ed [ʌndɪ'spjuːtɪd] *adj champion, leader* indiscutible

un·do [ʌn'duː] *v/t* (*pret* **-did**, *pp* **-done**) *parcel, wrapping* abrir; *buttons, shirt* desabrochar; *shoelaces* desatar; *s.o. else's work* deshacer

un·doubt·ed·ly [ʌn'daʊtɪdlɪ] *adv* indudablemente

un·dreamt-of [ʌn'dremtəv] *adj riches* inimaginable

un·dress [ʌn'dres] **1** *v/t* desvestir, desnudar; *get* **~***ed* desvestirse, desnudarse **2** *v/i* desvestirse, desnudarse

un·due [ʌn'duː] *adj* (*excessive*) excesivo

un·du·ly [ʌn'duːlɪ] *adv punished, blamed* injustamente; (*excessively*) excesivamente

un·earth [ʌn'ɜːrθ] *v/t* descubrir; *ancient remains* desenterrar

un·earth·ly [ʌn'ɜːrθlɪ] *adv*: *at this* **~** *hour* a esta hora intempestiva

un·eas·y [ʌn'iːzɪ] *adj relationship, peace* tenso; *feel* **~** *about* estar inquieto por

un·eat·a·ble [ʌn'iːtəbl] *adj* incomible

un·e·co·nom·ic [ʌniːkə'nɑːmɪk] *adj* antieconómico, no rentable

un·ed·u·cat·ed [ʌn'edʒəkeɪtɪd] *adj*

inculto, sin educación

un·em·ployed [ʌnɪm'plɔɪd] *adj* desempleado, *Span* parado

un·em·ploy·ment [ʌnɪm'plɔɪmənt] desempleo *m*, *Span* paro *m*

un·end·ing [ʌn'endɪŋ] *adj* interminable

un·e·qual [ʌn'iːkwəl] *adj* desigual; **be ~ to the task** no estar a la altura de lo que requiere el trabajo

un·er·ring [ʌn'erɪŋ] *adj judgement, instinct* infalible

un·e·ven [ʌn'iːvn] *adj quality* desigual; *surface, ground* irregular

un·e·ven·ly [ʌn'iːvnlɪ] *adv distributed, applied* de forma desigual; **be ~ matched** *of two contestants* no estar en igualdad de condiciones

un·e·vent·ful [ʌnɪ'ventfəl] *adj day, journey* sin incidentes

un·ex·pec·ted [ʌnɪk'spektɪd] *adj* inesperado

un·ex·pec·ted·ly [ʌnɪk'spektɪdlɪ] *adv* inesperadamente, de forma inesperada

un·fair [ʌn'fer] *adj* injusto; **that's ~** eso no es justo

un·faith·ful [ʌn'feɪθfəl] *adj husband, wife* infiel; **be ~ to s.o.** ser infiel a alguien

un·fa·mil·i·ar [ʌnfə'mɪljər] *adj* desconocido, extraño; **be ~ with sth** desconocer algo

un·fas·ten [ʌn'fæsn] *v/t belt* desabrochar

un·fa·vo·ra·ble, *Br* **un·fa·vou·ra·ble** [ʌn'feɪvərəbl] *adj* desfavorable

un·feel·ing [ʌn'fiːlɪŋ] *adj person* insensible

un·fin·ished [ʌn'fɪnɪʃt] *adj* inacabado; **leave sth ~** dejar algo sin acabar

un·fit [ʌn'fɪt] *adj:* **be ~ physically** estar en baja forma; **be ~ to eat** no ser apto para el consumo; **be ~ to drink** no ser potable; **he's ~ to be a parent** no tiene lo que se necesita para ser padre

un·fix [ʌn'fɪks] *v/t part* soltar, desmontar

un·flap·pa·ble [ʌn'flæpəbl] *adj* impasible

un·fold [ʌn'fould] **1** *v/t sheets, letter* desdoblar; *one's arms* descruzar **2** *v/i of story etc* desarrollarse; *of view* abrirse

un·fore·seen [ʌnfɔːr'siːn] *adj* imprevisto

un·for·get·ta·ble [ʌnfər'getəbl] *adj* inolvidable

un·for·giv·a·ble [ʌnfər'gɪvəbl] *adj* imperdonable; **that was ~ of you** eso ha sido imperdonable

un·for·tu·nate [ʌn'fɔːrtʃənət] *adj people* desafortunado; *event* desgraciado; *choice of words* desafortunado, desacertado; **that's ~ for you** has tenido muy mala suerte

un·for·tu·nate·ly [ʌn'fɔːrtʃənətlɪ] *adv* desgraciadamente

un·found·ed [ʌn'faundɪd] *adj* infundado

un·friend·ly [ʌn'frendlɪ] *adj person* antipático; *place* desagradable; *welcome* hostil; *software* de difícil manejo

un·fur·nished [ʌn'fɜːrnɪʃt] *adj* sin amueblar

un·god·ly [ʌn'gɑːdlɪ] *adj:* **at this ~ hour** a esta hora intempestiva

un·grate·ful [ʌn'greɪtfəl] *adj* desagradecido

un·hap·pi·ness [ʌn'hæpɪnɪs] infelicidad *f*

un·hap·py [ʌn'hæpɪ] *adj person, look* infeliz; *day* triste; *customer etc* descontento

un·harmed [ʌn'hɑːrmd] *adj* ileso; **be ~** salir ileso

un·health·y [ʌn'helθɪ] *adj person* enfermizo; *conditions, food, economy* poco saludable

un·heard-of [ʌn'hɜːrdəv] *adj* inaudito

un·hurt [ʌn'hɜːrt] *adj:* **be ~** salir ileso

un·hy·gien·ic [ʌnhaɪ'dʒiːnɪk] *adj* antihigiénico

u·ni·fi·ca·tion [juːnɪfɪ'keɪʃn] unificación *f*

u·ni·form ['juːnɪfɔːrm] **1** *n* uniforme *m* **2** *adj* uniforme

u·ni·fy ['juːnɪfaɪ] *v/t* (*pret & pp* **-ied**) unificar

U

u·ni·lat·er·al [juːnɪˈlætərəl] *adj* unilateral

un·i·ma·gi·na·ble [ʌnɪˈmædʒɪnəbl] *adj* inimaginable

un·i·ma·gi·na·tive [ʌnɪˈmædʒɪnətɪv] *adj* sin imaginación

un·im·por·tant [ʌnɪmˈpɔːrtənt] *adj* poco importante

un·in·hab·i·ta·ble [ʌnɪnˈhæbɪtəbl] *adj* inhabitable

un·in·hab·it·ed [ʌnɪnˈhæbɪtɪd] *adj building* deshabitado; *region* desierto

un·in·jured [ʌnˈɪndʒərd] *adj*: **be ~** salir ileso

un·in·tel·li·gi·ble [ʌnɪnˈtelɪdʒəbl] *adj* ininteligible

un·in·ten·tion·al [ʌnɪnˈtenʃnl] *adj* no intencionado; *sorry, that was ~* lo siento, ha sido sin querer

un·in·ten·tion·al·ly [ʌnɪnˈtenʃnlɪ] *adv* sin querer

un·in·te·rest·ing [ʌnˈɪntrəstɪŋ] *adj* sin interés

un·in·ter·rupt·ed [ʌnɪntəˈrʌptɪd] *adj sleep, two hours' work* ininterrumpido

u·nion [ˈjuːnjən] POL unión *f*; (*labor ~*) sindicato *m*

u·nique [juːˈniːk] *adj* único

u·nit [ˈjuːnɪt] unidad *f*; **~ of measurement** unidad *f* de medida; **power ~** fuente *f* de alimentación

u·nit 'cost COM costo *m* or *Span* coste *m* unitario *or* por unidad

u·nite [juːˈnaɪt] **1** *v/t* unir **2** *v/i* unirse

u·nit·ed [juːˈnaɪtɪd] *adj* unido

U·nit·ed 'King·dom Reino *m* Unido; **U·nit·ed 'Na·tions** Naciones *fpl* Unidas; **U·nit·ed 'States (of A·mer·i·ca)** Estados *mpl* Unidos (de América)

u·ni·ty [ˈjuːnətɪ] unidad *f*

u·ni·ver·sal [juːnɪˈvɜːrsl] *adj* universal

u·ni·ver·sal·ly [juːnɪˈvɜːrsəlɪ] *adv* universalmente

u·ni·verse [ˈjuːnɪvɜːrs] universo *m*

u·ni·ver·si·ty [juːnɪˈvɜːrsətɪ] **1** *n* universidad *f*; **he is at ~** está en la universidad **2** *adj* universitario

un·just [ʌnˈdʒʌst] *adj* injusto

un·kempt [ʌnˈkempt] *adj appearance* descuidado; *hair* revuelto

un·kind [ʌnˈkaɪnd] *adj* desgradable, cruel

un·known [ʌnˈnoun] **1** *adj* desconocido **2** *n*: *a journey into the* **~** un viaje hacia lo desconocido

un·lead·ed [ʌnˈledɪd] *adj* sin plomo

un·less [ənˈles] *conj* a menos que, a no ser que; *don't say anything ~ you're sure* no digas nada a menos que *or* a no ser que estés seguro

un·like [ʌnˈlaɪk] *prep (not similar to)* diferente de; *it's ~ him to drink so much* él no suele beber tanto; *that photograph is so ~ you* has salido completamente diferente en esa fotografía

un·like·ly [ʌnˈlaɪklɪ] *adj (improbable)* improbable; *explanation* inverosímil; *he is ~ to win* es improbable *or* poco probable que gane

un·lim·it·ed [ʌnˈlɪmɪtɪd] *adj* ilimitado

un·list·ed [ʌnˈlɪstɪd] *adj*: **be ~** no aparecer en la guía telefónica

un·load [ʌnˈloud] *v/t* descargar

un·lock [ʌnˈlɑːk] *v/t* abrir

un·luck·i·ly [ʌnˈlʌkɪlɪ] *adv* desgraciadamente, por desgracia

un·luck·y [ʌnˈlʌkɪ] *adj day, choice* aciago, funesto; *person* sin suerte; *that was so ~ for you!* ¡qué mala suerte tuviste!

un·manned [ʌnˈmænd] *adj spacecraft* no tripulado

un·mar·ried [ʌnˈmærɪd] *adj* soltero

un·mis·ta·ka·ble [ʌnmɪˈsteɪkəbl] *adj* inconfundible

un·moved [ʌnˈmuːvd] *adj*: *he was ~ by her tears* sus lágrimas no lo conmovieron

un·mu·si·cal [ʌnˈmjuːzɪkl] *adj person* sin talento musical; *sounds* estridente

un·nat·u·ral [ʌnˈnætʃrəl] *adj* anormal; *it's not ~ to be annoyed* es normal estar enfadado

un·ne·ces·sa·ry [ʌnˈnesəserɪ] *adj* innecesario

un·nerv·ing [ʌnˈnɜːrvɪŋ] *adj* desconcertante

un·no·ticed [ʌnˈnoʊtɪst] *adj*: *it went ~* pasó desapercibido

un·ob·tain·a·ble [ʌnəbˈteɪnəbl] *adj goods* no disponible; TELEC desconectado

un·ob·tru·sive [ʌnəbˈtruːsɪv] *adj* discreto

un·oc·cu·pied [ʌnˈɑːkjʊpaɪd] *adj building, house* desocupado; *post* vacante

un·of·fi·cial [ʌnəˈfɪʃl] *adj* no oficial; *this is still ~ but ...* esto todavía no es oficial, pero ...

un·of·fi·cial·ly [ʌnəˈfɪʃlɪ] *adv* extraoficialmente

un·or·tho·dox [ʌnˈɔːrθədɑːks] *adj* poco ortodoxo

un·pack [ʌnˈpæk] **1** *v/t* deshacer **2** *v/i* deshacer el equipaje

un·paid [ʌnˈpeɪd] *adj work* no remunerado

un·pleas·ant [ʌnˈpleznt] *adj* desagradable; *he was very ~ to her* fue muy desagradable con ella

un·plug [ʌnˈplʌɡ] *v/t* (*pret & pp -ged*) *TV, computer* desenchufar

un·pop·u·lar [ʌnˈpɑːpjələr] *adj* impopular

un·pre·ce·dent·ed [ʌnˈpresɪdentɪd] *adj* sin precedentes; *it was ~ for a woman to ...* no tenía precedentes que una mujer ...

un·pre·dict·a·ble [ʌnprɪˈdɪktəbl] *adj person, weather* imprevisible, impredecible

un·pre·ten·tious [ʌnprɪˈtenʃəs] *adj person, style, hotel* modesto, sin pretensiones

un·prin·ci·pled [ʌnˈprɪnsɪpld] *adj* sin principios

un·pro·duc·tive [ʌnprəˈdʌktɪv] *adj meeting, discussion* infructuoso; *soil* improductivo

un·pro·fes·sion·al [ʌnprəˈfeʃnl] *adj* poco profesional

un·prof·it·a·ble [ʌnˈprɑːfɪtəbl] *adj* no rentable

un·pro·nounce·a·ble [ʌnprəˈnaʊnsəbl] *adj* impronunciable

un·pro·tect·ed [ʌnprəˈtektɪd] *adj borders* desprotegido, sin protección; *~ sex* sexo *m* sin preservativos

un·pro·voked [ʌnprəˈvoʊkt] *adj attack* no provocado

un·qual·i·fied [ʌnˈkwɑːlɪfaɪd] *adj worker, doctor etc* sin titulación

un·ques·tio·na·bly [ʌnˈkwestʃnəblɪ] *adv* (*without doubt*) indiscutiblemente

un·ques·tion·ing [ʌnˈkwestʃnɪŋ] *adj attitude, loyalty* incondicional

un·rav·el [ʌnˈrævl] *v/t* (*pret & pp -ed*, *Br* -led) *string, knitting* desenredar; *mystery, complexities* desentrañar

un·rea·da·ble [ʌnˈriːdəbl] *adj book* ilegible

un·re·al [ʌnˈrɪəl] *adj* irreal; *this is ~!* F ¡esto es increíble! F

un·re·al·is·tic [ʌnrɪəˈlɪstɪk] *adj* poco realista

un·rea·so·na·ble [ʌnˈriːznəbl] *adj person* poco razonable, irrazonable; *demand, expectation* excesivo, irrazonable; *you're being ~* no estás siendo razonable

un·re·lat·ed [ʌnrɪˈleɪtɪd] *adj issues* no relacionado; *people* no emparentado

un·re·lent·ing [ʌnrɪˈlentɪŋ] *adj* implacable

un·rel·i·able [ʌnrɪˈlaɪəbl] *adj car, machine* poco fiable; *person* informal

un·rest [ʌnˈrest] malestar *m*; (*rioting*) disturbios *mpl*

un·re·strained [ʌnrɪˈstreɪnd] *adj emotions* incontrolado

un·road·wor·thy [ʌnˈroʊdwɜːrðɪ] *adj* que no está en condiciones de circular

un·roll [ʌnˈroʊl] *v/t carpet, scroll* desenrollar

un·ru·ly [ʌnˈruːlɪ] *adj* revoltoso

un·safe [ʌnˈseɪf] *adj* peligroso; *it's ~ to drink/eat* no se puede beber/comer

un·san·i·tar·y [ʌnˈsænɪterɪ] *adj conditions, drains* insalubre

un·sat·is·fac·to·ry [ʌnsætɪsˈfæktərɪ] *adj* insatisfactorio

un·sa·vo·ry [ʌnˈseɪvərɪ] *adj person, reputation* indeseable; *district* desagradable

un·scathed [ʌnˈskeɪðd] *adj (not injured)* ileso; *(not damaged)* intacto

un·screw [ʌnˈskruː] *v/t top* desenroscar; *shelves, hooks* desatornillar

un·scru·pu·lous [ʌnˈskruːpjələs] *adj* sin escrúpulos

un·self·ish [ʌnˈselfɪʃ] *adj* generoso

un·set·tled [ʌnˈsetld] *adj issue* sin decidir; *weather, stock market, lifestyle* inestable; *bills* sin pagar

un·shav·en [ʌnˈʃeɪvn] *adj* sin afeitar

un·sight·ly [ʌnˈsaɪtlɪ] *adj* horrible, feo

un·skilled [ʌnˈskɪld] *adj* no cualificado

un·so·cia·ble [ʌnˈsoʊʃəbl] *adj* insociable

un·so·phis·ti·cat·ed [ʌnsəˈfɪstɪkeɪtɪd] *adj person, beliefs* sencillo; *equipment* simple

un·sta·ble [ʌnˈsteɪbl] *adj* inestable

un·stead·y [ʌnˈstedɪ] *adj hand* tembloroso; *ladder* inestable; *be ~ on one's feet* tamblearse

un·stint·ing [ʌnˈstɪntɪŋ] *adj* generoso; *be ~ in one's efforts / generosity* no escatimar esfuerzos / generosidad

un·suc·cess·ful [ʌnsəkˈsesfəl] *adj writer etc* fracasado; *candidate* perdedor; *party, attempt* fallido; *he tried but was ~* lo intentó sin éxito

un·suc·cess·ful·ly [ʌnsəkˈsesfəlɪ] *adv try, apply* sin éxito

un·suit·a·ble [ʌnˈsuːtəbl] *adj partner, film, clothing* inadecuado; *thing to say* inoportuno

un·sus·pect·ing [ʌnsəsˈpektɪŋ] *adj* confiado

un·swerv·ing [ʌnˈswɜːrvɪŋ] *adj loyalty, devotion* inquebrantable

un·think·a·ble [ʌnˈθɪŋkəbl] *adj* impensable

un·ti·dy [ʌnˈtaɪdɪ] *adj room, desk* desordenado; *hair* revuelto

un·tie [ʌnˈtaɪ] *v/t knot, laces, prisoner* desatar

un·til [ənˈtɪl] **1** *prep* hasta; *from Monday ~ Friday* desde el lunes hasta el viernes; *I can wait ~ tomorrow* puedo esperar hasta mañana; *not ~ Friday* no antes del viernes; *it won't be finished ~ July* no estará acabado hasta julio **2** *conj* hasta que; *can you wait ~ I'm ready?* ¿puedes esperar hasta que esté listo?; *they won't do anything ~ you say so* no harán nada hasta que (no) se lo digas

un·time·ly [ʌnˈtaɪmlɪ] *adj death* prematuro

un·tir·ing [ʌnˈtaɪrɪŋ] *adj efforts* incansable

un·told [ʌnˈtoʊld] *adj suffering* indecible; *riches* inconmensurable; *story* nunca contado

un·trans·lat·a·ble [ʌntrænsˈleɪtəbl] *adj* intraducible

un·true [ʌnˈtruː] *adj* falso

un·used¹ [ʌnˈjuːzd] *adj goods* sin usar

un·used² [ʌnˈjuːst] *adj*: *be ~ to sth* no estar acostumbrado a algo; *be ~ to doing sth* no estar acostumbrado a hacer algo

un·u·su·al [ʌnˈjuːʒl] *adj* poco corriente; *it is ~ ...* es raro *or* extraño ...

un·u·su·al·ly [ʌnˈjuːʒəlɪ] *adv* inusitadamente; *the weather's ~ cold* hace un frío inusual

un·veil [ʌnˈveɪl] *v/t memorial, statue etc* desvelar

un·well [ʌnˈwel] *adj* indispuesto, mal; *be ~* sentirse indispuesto *or* mal

un·will·ing [ʌnˈwɪlɪŋ] *adj* poco dispuesto, reacio; *be ~ to do sth* no estar dispuesto a hacer algo, ser reacio a hacer algo

un·will·ing·ly [ʌnˈwɪlɪŋlɪ] *adv* de mala gana, a regañadientes

un·wind [ʌnˈwaɪnd] **1** *v/t (pret & pp -wound) tape* desenrollar **2** *v/i (pret & pp -wound) of tape* desenrollarse; *of story* irse desarrollando; *(relax)* relajarse

un·wise [ʌnˈwaɪz] *adj* imprudente

un·wrap [ʌnˈræp] *v/t (pret & pp -ped) gift* desenvolver

un·writ·ten [ʌnˈrɪtn] *adj law*, *rule* no escrito

un·zip [ʌnˈzɪp] *v/t* (*pret* & *pp* **-ped**) *dress etc* abrir la cremallera de; COMPUT descomprimir

up [ʌp] **1** *adv position* arriba; *movement* hacia arriba; **~ in the sky / ~ on the roof** (arriba) en el cielo / tejado; **~ here / there** aquí / allí arriba; **be ~** (*out of bed*) estar levantado; *of sun* haber salido; (*be built*) haber sido construido, estar acabado; *of shelves* estar montado; *of prices, temperature* haber subido; (*have expired*) haberse acabado; **what's ~?** F ¿qué pasa?; **~ to the year 1989** hasta el año 1989; **he came ~ to me** se me acercó; **what are you ~ to these days?** ¿qué es de tu vida?; **what are those kids ~ to?** ¿qué están tramando esos niños?; **be ~ to something** (*bad*) estar tramando algo; **I don't feel ~ to it** no me siento en condiciones de hacerlo; **it's ~ to you** tú decides; **it is ~ to them to solve it** (*their duty*) les corresponde a ellos resolverlo; **be ~ and about** *after illness* estar recuperado **2** *prep*: **further ~ the mountain** más arriba de la montaña; **he climbed ~ a tree** se subió a un árbol; **they ran ~ the street** corrieron por la calle; **the water goes ~ this pipe** el agua sube por esta tubería; **we traveled ~ to Chicago** subimos hasta Chicago **3** *n*: **~s and downs** altibajos *mpl*

ˈup·bring·ing educación *f*

ˈup·com·ing *adj* (*forthcoming*) próximo

ˈup·date[1] *v/t file*, *records* actualizar; **~ s.o. on sth** poner a alguien al corriente de algo

ˈup·date[2] *n* actualización *f*; **can you give me an ~ on the situation?** ¿me puedes poner al corriente de la situación?

ˈup·grade *v/t computers etc* actualizar; (*replace with new versions*) modernizar; *product* modernizar; **~ s.o. to business class** cambiar a alguien a clase ejecutiva

up·heav·al [ʌpˈhiːvl] *emotional* conmoción *f*; *physical* trastorno *m*; *political, social* sacudida *f*

up·hill 1 *adv* [ʌpˈhɪl] *walk* cuesta arriba **2** *adj* [ˈʌphɪl] *struggle* arduo, difícil

up·hold *v/t* (*pret* & *pp* **-held**) *traditions, rights* defender, conservar; (*vindicate*) confirmar

up·hol·ster·y [ʌpˈhoʊlstərɪ] (*coverings*) tapicería *f*; (*padding*) relleno *m*

ˈup·keep *of buildings, parks etc* mantenimiento *m*

ˈup·load *v/t* COMPUT cargar

ˈup·mar·ket *adj restaurant*, *hotel* de categoría

up·on [əˈpɑːn] *prep* → **on**

up·per[ˈʌpər] *adj part of sth* superior; *stretches of a river* alto; *deck* superior, de arriba

up·per ˈclass *adj accent*, *family* de clase alta

up·per ˈclas·ses *npl* clases *fpl* altas

ˈup·right 1 *adj citizen* honrado **2** *adv sit* derecho

ˈup·right (**ˈpi·an·o**) piano *m* vertical

ˈup·ris·ing levantamiento *m*

ˈup·roar (*loud noise*) alboroto *m*; (*protest*) tumulto *m*

up·set 1 *v/t* (*pret* & *pp* **-set**) *drink*, *glass* tirar; *emotionally* disgustar **2** *adj emotionally* disgustado; **get ~ about sth** disgustarse por algo; **have an ~ stomach** tener el estómago mal

up·ˈset·ting *adj* triste

ˈup·shot (*result, outcome*) resultado *m*

up·side ˈdown *adv* boca abajo; **turn sth ~** *box etc* poner algo al revés *or* boca abajo

up·ˈstairs 1 *adv* arriba **2** *adj room* de arriba

ˈup·start advenedizo(-a) *m(f)*

up·ˈstream *adv* río arriba

ˈup·take FIN respuesta *f* (*of* a); **be quick / slow on the ~** F ser / no ser muy espabilado F

up·ˈtight*adj* F (*nervous*) tenso; (*inhib-*

ited) estrecho

up-to-'date *adj information* actualizado; *fashions* moderno

'**up·turn** *in economy* mejora *f*

up·ward ['ʌpwərd] *adv fly, move* hacia arriba; *~ of 10,000* más de 10.000

u·ra·ni·um [juˈreɪnɪəm] uranio *m*

ur·ban ['ɜːrbən] *adj* urbano

ur·ban·i·za·tion [ɜːrbənaɪˈzeɪʃn] urbanización *f*

ur·chin ['ɜːrtʃɪn] golfillo(-a) *m(f)*

urge [ɜːrdʒ] **1** *n* impulso *m; I felt an ~ to hit her* me entraron ganas de pegarle; *I have an ~ to do something new* siento la necesidad de hacer algo nuevo **2** *v/t: ~ s.o. to do sth* rogar a alguien que haga algo

♦ **urge on** *v/t* (*encourage*) animar

ur·gen·cy ['ɜːrdʒənsɪ] *of situation* urgencia *f*

ur·gent ['ɜːrdʒənt] *adj job, letter* urgente; *be in ~ need of sth* necesitar algo urgentemente; *is it ~?* ¿es urgente?

u·ri·nate ['jʊrəneɪt] *v/i* orinar

u·rine ['jʊrɪn] orina *f*

urn [ɜːrn] urna *f*

U·ru·guay ['jʊrəgwaɪ] Uruguay

U·ru·guay·an [jʊrəˈgwaɪən] **1** *adj* uruguayo **2** *n* uruguayo(-a) *m(f)*

US [juːˈes] *abbr* (= *United States*) EE.UU. *mpl* (= Estados *mpl* Unidos)

us [ʌs] *pron* nos; *after prep* nosotros(-as); *they love ~* nos quieren; *she gave ~ the keys* nos dio las llaves; *he sold it to ~* nos lo vendió; *that's for ~* eso es para nosotros; *who's that? – it's ~* ¿quién es? – ¡somos nosotros!

USA [juːesˈeɪ] *abbr* (= *United States of America*) EE.UU. *mpl* (= Estados *mpl* Unidos)

us·a·ble ['juːzəbl] *adj* utilizable; *it's not ~* no se puede utilizar

us·age ['juːzɪdʒ] uso *m*

use 1 *v/t* [juːz] *tool, word* utilizar, usar; *skills, knowledge, car* usar; *a lot of gas* consumir; *pej: person* utilizar; *I could ~ a drink* F no me vendría mal una copa **2** *n* [juːs] uso *m*, utilización

f; be of great ~ to s.o. ser de gran utilidad para alguien; *it's of no ~ to me* no me sirve; *is that of any ~?* ¿eso sirve para algo?; *it's no ~* no sirve de nada; *it's no ~ trying/ waiting* no sirve de nada intentarlo / esperar

♦ **use up** *v/t* agotar

used¹ [juːzd] *adj car etc* de segunda mano

used² [juːst] *adj: be ~ to s.o./ sth* estar acostumbrado a alguien / algo; *get ~ to s.o./ sth* acostumbrarse a alguien / algo; *be ~ to doing sth* estar acostumbrado a hacer algo; *get ~ to doing sth* acostumbrarse a hacer algo

used³ [juːst]: *I ~ to like him* antes me gustaba; *they ~ to meet every Saturday* solían verse todos los sábados

use·ful ['juːsfəl] *adj* útil

use·ful·ness ['juːsfʊlnɪs] utilidad *f*

use·less ['juːslɪs] *adj* inútil; *machine, computer* inservible; *be ~* F *person* ser un inútil F; *it's ~ trying* (*there's no point*) no vale la pena intentarlo

us·er ['juːzər] *of product* usuario(-a) *m(f)*

us·er-'friend·ly *adj* de fácil manejo

ush·er ['ʌʃər] *n* (*at wedding*) persona que se encarga de indicar a los asistentes dónde se deben sentar

♦ **usher in** *v/t new era* anunciar

u·su·al ['juːʒl] *adj* habitual, acostumbrado; *as ~* como de costumbre; *the ~, please* lo de siempre, por favor

u·su·al·ly ['juːʒəlɪ] *adv* normalmente; *I ~ start at 9* suelo empezar a las 9

u·ten·sil [juːˈtensl] utensilio *m*

u·te·rus ['juːtərəs] útero *m*

u·til·i·ty [juːˈtɪlətɪ] (*usefulness*) utilidad *f; public utilities* servicios *mpl* públicos

u·til·ize ['juːtɪlaɪz] *v/t* utilizar

ut·most ['ʌtmoʊst] **1** *adj* sumo **2** *n: do one's ~* hacer todo lo posible

ut·ter ['ʌtər] **1** *adj* completo, total **2** *v/t sound* decir, pronunciar

ut·ter·ly ['ʌtərlɪ] *adv* completamente,

totalmente
U-turn ['juːtɜːrn] cambio *m* de senti-do; ***do a ~*** *fig: in policy etc* dar un giro de 180 grados

V

va·cant ['veɪkənt] *adj building* vacío; *position* vacante; *look, expression* vago, distraído

va·cant·ly ['veɪkəntlɪ] *adv* distraída-mente

va·cate [veɪ'keɪt] *v/t room* desalojar

va·ca·tion [veɪ'keɪʃn] *n* vacaciones *fpl*; ***be on ~*** estar de vacaciones; ***go to ... on ~*** ir de vacaciones a ...

va·ca·tion·er [veɪ'keɪʃənər] turista *m/f*; *in summer* veraneante *m/f*

vac·cin·ate ['væksɪneɪt] *v/t* vacunar; ***be ~d against ...*** estar vacunado contra ...

vac·cin·a·tion [væksɪ'neɪʃn] *action* vacunación *f*; *(vaccine)* vacuna *f*

vac·cine ['væksiːn] vacuna *f*

vac·u·um ['vækjuəm] **1** *n* PHYS, *fig* vacío *m* **2** *v/t floors* pasar el aspira-dor por, aspirar

'vac·u·um clean·er aspirador *m*, aspiradora *f*; **'vac·u·um flask** termo *m*; **vac·u·um-'packed** *adj* envasa-do al vacío

vag·a·bond ['vægəbɑːnd] vagabun-do(-a) *m(f)*

va·gi·na [və'dʒaɪnə] vagina *f*

va·gi·nal ['vædʒɪnl] *adj* vaginal

va·grant ['veɪgrənt] vagabundo(-a) *m(f)*

vague [veɪg] *adj* vago; ***he was very ~ about it*** no fue muy preciso

vague·ly ['veɪglɪ] *adv answer*, *(slightly)* vagamente; *possible* muy poco

vain [veɪn] **1** *adj person* vanidoso; *hope* vano **2** *n*: ***in ~*** en vano

val·en·tine ['væləntaɪn] *card* tarjeta *f* del día de San Valentín; ***Valentine's Day*** día de San Valentín *or* de los enamorados

val·et 1 *n* ['væleɪ] *person* mozo *m* **2** *v/t* ['vælət] *car* lavar y limpiar

'val·et ser·vice *for clothes* servicio *m* de planchado; *for cars* servicio *m* de lavado y limpiado

val·iant ['væljənt] *adj* valiente, vale-roso

val·iant·ly ['væljəntlɪ] *adv* valiente-mente, valerosamente

val·id ['vælɪd] *adj* válido

val·i·date ['vælɪdeɪt] *v/t with official stamp* sellar; *s.o.'s alibi* dar validez a

va·lid·i·ty [və'lɪdətɪ] validez *f*

val·ley ['vælɪ] valle *m*

val·u·a·ble ['væljʊbl] **1** *adj* valioso **2** *n*: **~s** objetos *mpl* de valor

val·u·a·tion [væljʊ'eɪʃn] tasación *f*, valoración *f*

val·ue ['væljuː] **1** *n* valor *m*; ***be good ~*** ofrecer buena relación calidad-precio; ***get ~ for money*** recibir una buena relación calidad-precio; ***rise / fall in ~*** aumentar / disminuir de valor **2** *v/t s.o.'s friendship, one's freedom* valorar; ***I ~ your advice*** va-loro tus consejos; ***have an object ~d*** pedir la valoración *or* tasación de un objeto

valve [vælv] válvula *f*

van [væn] camioneta *f*, furgoneta *f*

van·dal ['vændl] vándalo *m*, gambe-rro(-a) *m(f)*

van·dal·ism ['vændəlɪzm] vandalis-mo *m*

van·dal·ize ['vændəlaɪz] *v/t* destro-zar *(intencionadamente)*

van·guard ['væŋgɑːrd] vanguardia *f*; ***be in the ~ of*** *fig* estar a la vanguar-dia de

va·nil·la [vəˈnɪlə] **1** *n* vainilla *f* **2** *adj* de vainilla

van·ish [ˈvænɪʃ] *v/i* desaparecer

van·i·ty [ˈvænətɪ] *of person* vanidad *f*

'van·i·ty case néceser *m*

van·tage point [ˈvæntɪdʒ] *on hill etc* posición *f* aventajada

va·por [ˈveɪpər] vapor *m*

va·por·ize [ˈveɪpəraɪz] *v/t of atomic bomb, explosion* vaporizar

'va·por trail *of airplane* estela *f*

va·pour *Br* → *vapor*

var·i·a·ble [ˈverɪəbl] **1** *adj* variable **2** *n* MATH, COMPUT variable *f*

var·i·ant [ˈverɪənt] *n* variante *f*

var·i·a·tion [verɪˈeɪʃn] variación *f*

var·i·cose 'vein [ˈværɪkoʊs] variz *f*

var·ied [ˈverɪd] *adj* variado

var·i·e·ty [vəˈraɪətɪ] (*variedness, type*) variedad *f*; *a ~ of things to do* (*range, mixture*) muchas cosas para hacer

var·i·ous [ˈverɪəs] *adj* (*several*) varios; (*different*) diversos

var·nish [ˈvɑːrnɪʃ] **1** *n for wood* barniz *m*; *for fingernails* esmalte *m* **2** *v/t wood* barnizar; *fingernails* poner esmalte a, pintar

var·y [ˈverɪ] **1** *v/i* (*pret & pp -ied*) variar; *it varies* depende **2** *v/t* (*pret & pp -ied*) variar

vase [veɪz] jarrón *m*

vas·ec·to·my [vəˈsektəmɪ] vasectomía *f*

vast [væst] *adj desert, knowledge* vasto; *number, improvement* enorme

vast·ly [ˈvæstlɪ] *adv* enormemente

VAT [viːeɪˈtiː, væt] *Br abbr* (= *value-added tax*) IVA *m* (= impuesto *m* sobre el valor añanido)

Vat·i·can [ˈvætɪkən]: *the ~* el Vaticano

vau·de·ville [ˈvɒːdvɪl] vodevil *m*

vault¹ [vɒːlt] *n in roof* bóveda *f*; *~s* (*cellar*) sótano *m*; *of bank* cámara *f* acorazada

vault² [vɒːlt] **1** *n* SP salto *m* **2** *v/t beam etc* saltar

VCR [viːsiːˈɑːr] *abbr* (= *video cassette recorder*) aparato *m* de vídeo *or L.Am.* video *Span*

VDU [viːdiːˈjuː] *abbr* (= *visual display unit*) monitor *m*

veal [viːl] ternera *f*

veer [vɪr] *v/i* girar, torcer

ve·gan [ˈviːgn] **1** *n* vegetariano(-a) *m(f)* estricto (-a) (*que no come ningún producto de origen animal*) **2** *adj* vegetariano estricto

vege·ta·ble [ˈvedʒtəbl] hortaliza *f*; *~s* verduras *fpl*

ve·ge·tar·i·an [vedʒɪˈterɪən] **1** *n* vegetariano(-a) *m(f)* **2** *adj* vegetariano

ve·ge·tar·i·an·ism [vedʒɪˈterɪənɪzm] vegetarianismo *m*

vege·ta·tion [vedʒɪˈteɪʃn] vegetación *f*

ve·he·mence [ˈviːəməns] vehemencia *f*

ve·he·ment [ˈviːəmənt] *adj* vehemente

ve·he·ment·ly [ˈviːəməntlɪ] *adv* vehementemente

ve·hi·cle [ˈviːɪkl] *also fig* vehículo *m*

veil [veɪl] **1** *n* velo *m* **2** *v/t* cubrir con un velo

vein [veɪn] ANAT vena *f*; *in this ~ fig* en este tono

Vel·cro® [ˈvelkroʊ] velcro *m*

ve·loc·i·ty [vɪˈlɑːsətɪ] velocidad *f*

vel·vet [ˈvelvɪt] *n* terciopelo *m*

vel·vet·y [ˈvelvɪtɪ] *adj* aterciopelado

ven·det·ta [venˈdetə] vendetta *f*

vend·ing ma·chine [ˈvendɪŋ] máquina *f* expendedora

vend·or [ˈvendər] LAW parte *f* vendedora

ve·neer [vəˈnɪr] *on wood* chapa *f*; *of politeness etc* apariencia *f*, fachada *f*

ven·e·ra·ble [ˈvenərəbl] *adj* venerable

ven·e·rate [ˈvenəreɪt] *v/t* venerar

ven·e·ra·tion [venəˈreɪʃn] veneración *f*

ven·e·re·al dis·ease [vɪˈnɪrɪəl] enfermedad *f* venérea

ve·ne·tian 'blind persiana *f* veneciana

Ven·e·zue·la [venɪzˈweɪlə] Venezuela

Ven·e·zue·lan [venɪzˈweɪlən] **1** *adj*

venezolano **2** *n* venezolano(-a) *m(f)*

ven·geance ['vendʒəns] venganza *f*; *with a* ~ con ganas

ven·i·son ['venɪsn] venado *m*

ven·om ['venəm] *also fig* veneno *m*

ven·om·ous ['venəməs] *adj snake* venenoso; *fig* envenenado

vent [vent] *n for air* respiradero *m*; *give ~ to feelings* dar rienda suelta a

ven·ti·late ['ventɪleɪt] *v/t* ventilar

ven·ti·la·tion [ventɪ'leɪʃn] ventilación *f*

ven·ti·la·tion shaft pozo *m* de ventilación

ven·ti·la·tor ['ventɪleɪtər] ventilador *m*; MED respirador *m*

ven·tril·o·quist [ven'trɪləkwɪst] ventrílocuo(-a) *m(f)*

ven·ture ['ventʃər] **1** *n (undertaking)* iniciativa *f*; COM empresa *f* **2** *v/i* aventurarse

ven·ue ['venjuː] *for meeting* lugar *m*; *for concert* local *m*, sala *f*

ve·ran·da [vəˈrændə] porche *m*

verb [vɜːrb] verbo *m*

verb·al ['vɜːrbl] *adj (spoken)* verbal

verb·al·ly ['vɜːrbəli] *adv* de palabra

ver·ba·tim [vɜːrˈbeɪtɪm] *adv* literalmente

ver·dict ['vɜːrdɪkt] LAW veredicto *m*; *what's your ~?* ¿qué te parece?, ¿qué opinas?

verge [vɜːrdʒ] *n of road* arcén *m*; *be on the ~ of ruin* estar al borde de; *tears* estar a punto de

♦ **verge on** *v/t* rayar en

ver·i·fi·ca·tion [verɪfɪ'keɪʃn] *(checking)* verificación *f*; *(confirmation)* confirmación *f*

ver·i·fy ['verɪfaɪ] *v/t (pret & pp -ied) (check)* verificar; *(confirm)* confirmar

ver·mi·cel·li [vɜːrmɪ'tʃeli] *nsg* fideos *mpl*

ver·min ['vɜːrmɪn] *npl* bichos *mpl*, alimañas *fpl*

ver·mouth [vɜːrˈmuːθ] vermut *m*

ver·nac·u·lar [vərˈnækjələr] *n* lenguaje *m* de la calle

ver·sa·tile ['vɜːrsətəl] *adj* polifacético, versátil

ver·sa·til·i·ty [vɜːrsə'tɪlətɪ] polivalencia *f*, versatilidad *f*

verse [vɜːrs] verso *m*

versed [vɜːrst] *adj*: *be well ~ in a subject* estar muy versado en una materia

ver·sion ['vɜːrʃn] versión *f*

ver·sus ['vɜːrsəs] *prep* SP, LAW contra

ver·te·bra ['vɜːrtɪbrə] vértebra *f*

ver·te·brate ['vɜːrtɪbreɪt] *n* vertebrado(-a) *m(f)*

ver·ti·cal ['vɜːrtɪkl] *adj* vertical

ver·ti·go ['vɜːrtɪgoʊ] vértigo *m*

ver·y ['veri] **1** *adv* muy; *was it cold? – not* ~ ¿hizo frío? – no mucho; *the ~ best* el mejor de todos **2** *adj*: *at that ~ moment* en ese mismo momento; *that's the ~ thing I need (exact)* eso es precisamente lo que necesito; *the ~ thought of* sólo de pensar en; *right at the ~ top/bottom* arriba/al fondo del todo

ves·sel ['vesl] NAUT buque *m*

vest [vest] chaleco *m*

ves·tige ['vestɪdʒ] vestigio *m*

vet¹ [vet] *n (veterinary surgeon)* veterinario(-a) *m(f)*

vet² [vet] *v/t (pret & pp -ted) applicants etc* examinar, investigar

vet³ [vet] MIL veterano(-a) *m(f)*

vet·e·ran ['vetərən] **1** *n* veterano(-a) *m(f)* **2** *adj* veterano

vet·e·ri·nar·i·an [vetərə'neriən] veterinario(-a) *m(f)*

ve·to ['viːtoʊ] **1** *n* veto *m* **2** *v/t* vetar

vex [veks] *v/t (concern, worry)* molestar, irritar

vexed [vekst] *adj (worried)* molesto, irritado; *the ~ question of* la polémica cuestión de

vi·a ['vaɪə] *prep* vía

vi·a·ble ['vaɪəbl] *adj* viable

vi·brate [vaɪ'breɪt] *v/i* vibrar

vi·bra·tion [vaɪ'breɪʃn] vibración *f*

vic·ar ['vɪkər] *Br* vicario *m*

vice¹ [vaɪs] vicio *m*; *the problem of* ~ el problema del vicio

vice² *Br* → *vise*

V

vice 'pres·i·dent vicepresidente(-a) *m(f)*

'vice squad brigada *f* antivicio

vi·ce ver·sa [vaɪs'vɜːrsə] *adv* viceversa

vi·cin·i·ty [vɪ'sɪnɪtɪ] zona *f*; *in the ~ of ...* the church etc en las cercanías de ...; *$500 etc* rondando ...

vi·cious ['vɪʃəs] *adj* fiero; *attack, temper, criticism* feroz

vi·cious 'cir·cle círculo *m* vicioso

vi·cious·ly ['vɪʃəslɪ] *adv* con brutalidad

vic·tim ['vɪktɪm] víctima *f*

vic·tim·ize ['vɪktɪmaɪz] *v/t* tratar injustamente

vic·tor ['vɪktər] vencedor(a) *m(f)*

vic·to·ri·ous [vɪk'tɔːrɪəs] *adj* victorioso

vic·to·ry ['vɪktərɪ] victoria *f*; *win a ~ over ...* obtener una victoria sobre ...

vid·e·o ['vɪdɪoʊ] **1** *n Span* vídeo *m*, *L.Am.* video *m*; *have X on ~* tener a X en *Span* vídeo *or L.Am.* video **2** *v/t* grabar en *Span* vídeo *or L.Am.* video

'vid·e·o cam·e·ra videocámara *f*; **vid·e·o cas'sette** videocasete *m*; **'vid·e·o con·fer·ence** TELEC videoconferencia *f*; **'vid·e·o game** videojuego *m*; **'vid·e·o·phone** videoteléfono *m*; **'vid·e·o re·cord·er** aparato *m* de *Span* vídeo *or L.Am.* video; **'vid·e·o re·cord·ing** grabación *f* en *Span* vídeo *or L.Am.* video; **'vid·e·o·tape** cinta *f* de *Span* vídeo *or L.Am.* video

vie [vaɪ] *v/i* competir

Vi·et·nam [vɪet'nɑːm] Vietnam

Vi·et·nam·ese [vɪetnɑ'miːz] **1** *adj* vietnamita **2** *n* vietnamita *m/f*; *language* vietnamita *m*

view [vjuː] **1** *n* vista *f*; *of situation* opinión *f*; *in ~ of* teniendo en cuenta; *be on ~ of paintings* estar expuesto al público; *with a ~ to* con vistas a **2** *v/t events, situation* ver, considerar; *TV program, house* ver **3** *v/i* (*watch TV*) ver la televisión

view·er ['vjuːər] TV telespectador(a) *m(f)*

'view·find·er PHOT visor *m*

'view·point punto *m* de vista

vig·or ['vɪgər] (*energy*) vigor *m*

vig·or·ous ['vɪgərəs] *adj shake* vigoroso; *person* enérgico; *denial* rotundo

vig·or·ous·ly ['vɪgərəslɪ] *adv shake* con vigor; *deny, defend* rotundamente

vig·our *Br* → **vigor**

vile [vaɪl] *adj smell* asqueroso; *thing to do* vil

vil·la ['vɪlə] chalet *m*; *in the country* villa *f*

vil·lage ['vɪlɪdʒ] pueblo *m*

vil·lag·er ['vɪlɪdʒər] aldeano(-a) *m(f)*

vil·lain ['vɪlən] malo(a) *m(f)*

vin·di·cate ['vɪndɪkeɪt] *v/t* (*show to be correct*) dar la razón a; (*show to be innocent*) vindicar; *I feel ~d* los hechos me dan ahora la razón

vin·dic·tive [vɪn'dɪktɪv] *adj* vengativo

vin·dic·tive·ly [vɪn'dɪktɪvlɪ] *adv* vengativamente

vine [vaɪn] vid *f*

vin·e·gar ['vɪnɪgər] vinagre *m*

vine·yard ['vɪnjɑːrd] viñedo *m*

vin·tage ['vɪntɪdʒ] **1** *n of wine* cosecha *f* **2** *adj* (*classic*) clásico *m*

vi·o·la [vɪ'oʊlə] MUS viola *f*

vi·o·late ['vaɪəleɪt] *v/t* violar

vi·o·la·tion [vaɪə'leɪʃn] violación *f*; (*traffic ~*) infracción *f*

vi·o·lence ['vaɪələns] violencia *f*; *outbreak of ~* estallido de violencia

vi·o·lent ['vaɪələnt] *adj* violento; *have a ~ temper* tener muy mal genio

vi·o·lent·ly ['vaɪələntlɪ] *adv react* violentamente; *object* rotundamente; *fall ~ in love with s.o.* enamorarse perdidamente de alguien

vi·o·let ['vaɪələt] *n color* violeta *m*; *plant* violeta *f*

vi·o·lin [vaɪə'lɪn] violín *m*

vi·o·lin·ist [vaɪə'lɪnɪst] violinista *m/f*

VIP [viːaɪ'piː] *abbr* (= *very important person*) VIP *m*

V

vi·per ['vaɪpər] *snake* víbora *f*

vi·ral ['vaɪrəl] *adj infection* vírico, viral

vir·gin ['vɜːrdʒɪn] virgen *m/f*

vir·gin·i·ty [vɜːr'dʒɪnətɪ] virginidad *f*; *lose one's ~* perder la virginidad

Vir·go ['vɜːrgoʊ] ASTR Virgo *m/f inv*

vir·ile ['vɪrəl] *adj man* viril; *prose* vigoroso

vi·ril·i·ty [vɪ'rɪlətɪ] virilidad *f*

vir·tu·al ['vɜːrtʃʊəl] *adj* virtual

vir·tu·al·ly ['vɜːrtʃʊəlɪ] *adv* (*almost*) virtualmente, casi

virtual re'al·i·ty realidad *f* virtual

vir·tue ['vɜːrʃtuː] virtud *f*; *in ~ of* en virtud de

vir·tu·o·so [vɜːrtʃu'oʊzoʊ] MUS virtuoso(-a) *m(f)*

vir·tu·ous ['vɜːrtʃʊəs] *adj* virtuoso

vir·u·lent ['vɪrʊlənt] *adj* virulento

vi·rus ['vaɪrəs] MED, COMPUT virus *m inv*

vi·sa ['viːzə] visa *f*, visado *m*

vise [vaɪs] torno *m* de banco

vis·i·bil·i·ty [vɪzə'bɪlətɪ] visibilidad *f*

vis·i·ble ['vɪzəbl] *adj object, difference* visible; *anger* evidente; *not be ~ to the naked eye* no ser visible a simple vista

vis·i·bly ['vɪzəblɪ] *adv different* visiblemente; *he was ~ moved* estaba visiblemente conmovido

vi·sion ['vɪʒn] *also* REL visión *f*

vis·it ['vɪzɪt] **1** *n* visita *f*; *pay a ~ to the doctor/dentist* visitar al doctor/dentista; *pay s.o. a ~* hacer una visita a alguien **2** *v/t* visitar

vis·it·ing card ['vɪzɪtɪŋ] tarjeta *f* de visita

'vis·it·ing hours *npl at hospital* horas *fpl* de visita

vis·it·or ['vɪzɪtər] (*guest*) visita *f*; (*tourist*), *to museum etc* visitante *m/f*

vi·sor ['vaɪzər] visera *f*

vis·u·al ['vɪʒʊəl] *adj* visual

visual 'aid medio *m* visuale

visual dis'play u·nit monitor *m*

vis·u·al·ize ['vɪʒʊəlaɪz] *v/t* visualizar; (*foresee*) prever

vis·u·al·ly ['vɪʒʊlɪ] *adv* visualmente

vis·u·al·ly im'paired *adj* con discapacidad visual

vi·tal ['vaɪtl] *adj* (*essential*) vital; *it is ~ that …* es vital que …

vi·tal·i·ty [vaɪ'tælətɪ] *of person, city etc* vitalidad *f*

vi·tal·ly ['vaɪtəlɪ] *adv*: *~ important* de importancia vital

vital 'or·gans *npl* órganos *mpl* vitales

vital sta'tis·tics *npl of woman* medidas *fpl*

vit·a·min ['vaɪtəmɪn] vitamina *f*

'vit·a·min pill pastilla *f* vitamínica

vit·ri·ol·ic [vɪtrɪ'ɑːlɪk] *adj* virulento

vi·va·cious [vɪ'veɪʃəs] *adj* vivaz

vi·vac·i·ty [vɪ'væsətɪ] vivacidad *f*

viv·id ['vɪvɪd] *adj color* vivo; *memory, imagination* vívido

viv·id·ly ['vɪvɪdlɪ] *adv* (*brightly*) vivamente; (*clearly*) vívidamente

V-neck ['viːnek] cuello *m* de pico

vo·cab·u·la·ry [voʊ'kæbjʊlərɪ] vocabulario *m*

vo·cal ['voʊkl] *adj to do with the voice* vocal; *expressing opinions* ruidoso; *a ~ opponent* un declarado adversario

'vo·cal cords *npl* cuerdas *fpl* vocales

'vo·cal group MUS grupo *m* vocal

vo·cal·ist ['voʊkəlɪst] MUS vocalista *m/f*

vo·ca·tion [və'keɪʃn] (*calling*) vocación *f*; (*profession*) profesión *f*

vo·ca·tion·al [və'keɪʃnl] *adj guidance* profesional

vod·ka ['vɑːdkə] vodka *m*

vogue [voʊg] moda *f*; *be in ~* estar en boga

voice [vɔɪs] **1** *n* voz *f* **2** *v/t opinions* expresar

'voice·mail correo *m* de voz

void [vɔɪd] **1** *n* vacío *m* **2** *adj*: *~ of* carente de

vol·a·tile ['vɑːlətəl] *adj personality, moods* cambiante; *markets* inestable

vol·ca·no [vɑːl'keɪnoʊ] volcán *m*

vol·ley ['vɑːlɪ] *n of shots* ráfaga *f*; *in tennis* volea *f*

'vol·ley·ball voleibol *m*

volt [voʊlt] voltio *m*

volt·age ['voʊltɪdʒ] voltaje *m*

vol·ume ['vɑːljəm] volumen *m*; *of*

V

container capacidad *f*; *of book* volumen *m*, tomo *m*

vol·ume con'trol control *m* del volumen

vol·un·tar·i·ly [vɑːlənˈterɪlɪ] *adv* voluntariamente

vol·un·ta·ry [ˈvɑːləntrɪ] *adj* voluntario

vol·un·teer [vɑːlənˈtɪr] **1** *n* voluntario(-a) *m(f)* **2** *v/i* ofrecerse voluntariamente

vo·lup·tu·ous [vəˈlʌptʃʊəs] *adj figure* voluptuoso

vom·it [ˈvɑːmət] **1** *n* vómito *m* **2** *v/i* vomitar

♦ **vomit up** *v/t* vomitar

vo·ra·cious [vəˈreɪʃəs] *adj appetite* voraz

vo·ra·cious·ly [vəˈreɪʃəslɪ] *also fig* vorazmente

vote [voʊt] **1** *n* voto *m*; **have the ~** (*be entitled to vote*) tener el derecho al voto **2** *v/i* POL votar; ~ **for**/**against** votar a favor/en contra **3** *v/t*: **they**

~d him President lo votaron presidente; **they ~d to stay behind** votaron (a favor de) quedarse atrás

♦ **vote in** *v/t new member* elegir en votación

♦ **vote on** *v/t issue* someter a votación

♦ **vote out** *v/t of office* rechazar en votación

vot·er [ˈvoʊtər] POL votante *m/f*

vot·ing [ˈvoʊtɪŋ] POL votación *f*

'vot·ing booth cabina *f* electoral

♦ **vouch for** [vaʊtʃ] *v/t truth of sth* dar fe de; *person* responder por

vouch·er [ˈvaʊtʃər] vale *m*

vow [vaʊ] **1** *n* voto *m* **2** *v/t*: ~ **to do sth** prometer hacer algo

vow·el [vaʊl] vocal *f*

voy·age [ˈvɔɪɪdʒ] *n* viaje *m*

vul·gar [ˈvʌlgər] *adj person, language* vulgar, grosero

vul·ne·ra·ble [ˈvʌlnərəbl] *adj to attack, criticism* vulnerable

vul·ture [ˈvʌltʃər] buitre *m*

W

wad [wɑːd] *n of paper, absorbent cotton etc* bola *f*; **a ~ of $100 bills** un fajo de billetes de 100 dólares

wad·dle [ˈwɑːdl] *v/i of duck* caminar; *of person* anadear

wade [weɪd] *v/i* caminar en el agua

♦ **wade through** *v/t book, documents* leerse

wa·fer [ˈweɪfər] *cookie* barquillo *m*; REL hostia *f*

'wa·fer-thin *adj* muy fino

waf·fle[1] [ˈwɑːfl] *n to eat* gofre *m*

waf·fle[2] [ˈwɑːfl] *v/i* andarse con rodeos

wag [wæg] **1** *v/t* (*pret & pp* **-ged**) *tail, finger* menear **2** *v/i* (*pret & pp* **-ged**) *of tail* menearse

wage[1] [weɪdʒ] *v/t*: ~ **war** hacer la guerra

wage[2] [weɪdʒ] *n* salario *m*, sueldo *m*; ~**s** salario *m*, sueldo *m*

'wage earn·er asalariado(-a) *m(f)*; **'wage freeze** congelación *f* salarial; **'wage ne·go·ti·a·tions** *npl* negociación *f* salarial; **'wage pack·et** *fig* salario *m*, sueldo *m*

wag·gle [ˈwægl] *v/t hips* menear; *ears, loose screw etc* mover

wag·on [ˈwægən] *Br* RAIL vagón *m*; **be on the ~** F haber dejado la bebida

wail [weɪl] **1** *n of person, baby* gemido *m*; *of siren* sonido *m*, aullido *m* **2** *v/i of person, baby* gemir; *of siren* sonar, aullar

waist [weɪst] cintura f
'waist·coat Br chaleco m
'waist·line cintura f
wait [weɪt] **1** n espera f; *I had a long ~ for a train* esperé mucho rato el tren **2** v/i esperar; *have you been ~ing long?* ¿llevan mucho rato esperando? **3** v/t: *don't ~ supper for me* no me esperéis a cenar; *~ table* trabajar de camarero(-a)
♦ **wait for** v/t esperar; *wait for me!* ¡esperame!
♦ **wait on** v/t (*serve*) servir; (*wait for*) esperar
♦ **wait up** v/i esperar levantado
wait·er ['weɪtər] camarero m
wait·ing ['weɪtɪŋ] n espera f; *no ~ sign* señal f de prohibido estacionar
'wait·ing list lista f de espera
'wait·ing room sala f de espera
wait·ress ['weɪtrɪs] camarera f
waive [weɪv] v/t *right* renunciar; *requirement* no aplicar
wake¹ [weɪk] **1** v/i (*pret woke*, *pp woken*): *~ (up)* despertarse **2** v/t (*pret woke*, *pp woken*): *~ (up)* despertar
wake² [weɪk] n of ship estela f; *in the ~ of fig* tras; *missionaries followed in the ~ of the explorers* a los exploradores siguieron los misioneros
'wake-up call: *could I have a ~ at 6.30?* ¿me podrían despertar a las 6.30?
Wales [weɪlz] Gales
walk [wɔːk] **1** n paseo m; *longer* caminata f; (*path*) camino m; *it's a long / short ~ to the office* hay una caminata / un paseo hasta la oficina; *go for a ~* salir a dar un paseo, salir de paseo; *it's a five-minute ~* está a cinco minutos a pie **2** v/i caminar, andar; *as opposed to driving* ir a pie; *she ~ed over to the window* se acercó a la ventana **3** v/t *dog* sacar a pasear; *~ the streets* (*walk around*) caminar por las calles
♦ **walk out** v/i of spouse marcharse; *from theater etc* salir; (*go on strike*) declararse en huelga
♦ **walk out on** v/t: *walk out on s.o.* abandonar a alguien
walk·er ['wɔːkər] (*hiker*) excursionista m/f; *for baby, old person* andador m; *be a slow / fast ~* caminar or andar despacio / rápido
walk-in 'clos·et vestidor m, armario m empotrado
walk·ing ['wɔːkɪŋ] n (*hiking*) excursionismo m; *~ is one of the best forms of exercise* caminar es uno de los mejores ejercicios; *it's within ~ distance* se puede ir caminando or andando
'walk·ing stick bastón m
'walk·ing tour visita f a pie
'Walk·man® walkman m; **'walk·out** (*strike*) huelga f; **'walk·over** (*easy win*) paseo m; **'walk-up** n apartamento or un edificio sin ascensor
wall [wɔːl] *external, fig* muro m; *of room* pared f; *go to the ~ of company* quebrar; *drive s.o. up the ~ F* hacer que alguien se suba por las paredes
wal·let ['wɑːlɪt] (*billfold*) cartera f
wal·lop ['wɑːləp] **1** n F *blow* tortazo m F, galletazo m F **2** v/t F dar un golpetazo a F; *opponent* dar una paliza a F
'wall·pa·per 1 n papel m pintado **2** v/t empapelar
wall-to-wall 'car·pet *Span* moqueta f, *L.Am.* alfombra f
wal·nut ['wɔːlnʌt] nuez f; *tree, wood* nogal m
waltz [wɔːlts] n vals m
wan [wɑːn] adj face pálido m
wan·der ['wɑːndər] v/i (*roam*) vagar, deambular; (*stray*) extraviarse; *my attention began to ~* empecé a distraerme
♦ **wander around** v/i deambular, pasear
wane [weɪn] v/i of interest, enthusiasm decaer, menguar
wan·gle ['wæŋgl] v/t F agenciarse F
want [wɑːnt] **1** n: *for ~ of* por falta de **2** v/t querer; (*need*) necesitar; *~ to do sth* querer hacer algo; *I ~ to stay here* quiero quedarme aquí; *do you ~ to come too? – no, I don't ~ to*

W

¿quieres venir tú también? – no, no quiero; *you can have whatever you ~* toma lo que quieras; *it's not what I ~ed* no es lo que quería; *she ~s you to go back* quiere que vuelvas; *he ~s a haircut* necesita un corte de pelo **3** *v/i*: *he ~s for nothing* no le falta nada

'**want ad** anuncio *m* por palabras (*buscando algo*)

want·ed ['wɑːntɪd] *adj by police* buscado por la policía

want·ing ['wɑːntɪŋ] *adj*: *the team is ~ in experience* al equipo le falta experiencia

wan·ton ['wɑːntən] *adj* gratuito

war [wɔːr] *n also fig* guerra *f*; *be at ~* estar en guerra

war·ble ['wɔːrbl] *v/i of bird* trinar

ward [wɔːrd] *n in hospital* sala *f*; *child* pupilo(-a) *m(f)*

♦ **ward off** *v/t blow* parar; *attacker* rechazar; *cold* evitar

war·den ['wɔːrdn] *of prison* director(-a) *m(f)*, alcaide(sa) *m(f)*; *Br of hostel* vigilante *m/f*

'**ward·robe** *for clothes* armario *m*; (*clothes*) guardarropa *m*

'**ware·house** ['werhaʊs] almacén *m*

'**war·fare** guerra *f*

'**war·head** ojiva *f*

war·i·ly ['werɪlɪ] *adv* cautelosamente

warm [wɔːrm] *adj hands, room, water* caliente; *weather, welcome* cálido; *coat* de abrigo; *it's ~er than yesterday* hace más calor que ayer

♦ **warm up 1** *v/t* calentar **2** *v/i* calentarse; *of athlete etc* calentar

warm-heart·ed ['wɔːrmhɑːrtɪd] *adj* cariñoso, simpático

warm·ly ['wɔːrmlɪ] *adv welcome, smile* calurosamente; *~ dressed* abrigado

warmth [wɔːrmθ] calor *m*; *of welcome, smile* calor *m*, calidez *m*

'**warm-up** SP calentamiento *m*

warn [wɔːrn] *v/t* advertir, avisar

warn·ing ['wɔːrnɪŋ] *n* advertencia *f*, aviso *m*; *without ~* sin previo aviso

warp [wɔːrp] **1** *v/t wood* combar;

character corromper **2** *v/i of wood* combarse

warped [wɔːrpt] *adj fig* retorcido

'**war·plane** avión *m* de guerra

war·rant ['wɔːrənt] **1** *n* orden *f* judicial **2** *v/t* (*deserve, call for*) justificar

war·ran·ty ['wɔːrəntɪ] (*guarantee*) garantía *f*; *be under ~* estar en garantía

war·ri·or ['wɔːrɪər] guerrero(-a) *m(f)*

'**war·ship** buque *m* de guerra

wart [wɔːrt] verruga *f*

'**war·time** tiempos *mpl* de guerra

war·y ['werɪ] *adj* cauto, precavido; *be ~ of* desconfiar de

was [wʌz] *pret* → **be**

wash [wɑːʃ] **1** *n* lavado *m*; *have a ~* lavarse; *that shirt needs a ~* hay que lavar esa camisa **2** *v/t* lavar **3** *v/i* lavarse

♦ **wash up** *v/i* (*wash one's hands and face*) lavarse

wash·a·ble ['wɑːʃəbl] *adj* lavable

'**wash·ba·sin**, '**wash·bowl** lavabo *m*

'**wash·cloth** toallita *f*

washed out [wɑːʃt'aʊt] *adj* agotado

wash·er ['wɑːʃər] *for faucet etc* arandela *f*; → **washing machine**

wash·ing ['wɑːʃɪŋ] (*clothes washed*) ropa *f* limpia; (*dirty clothes*) ropa *f* sucia; *do the ~* lavar la ropa, hacer la colada

'**wash·ing ma·chine** lavadora *f*

'**wash·room** lavabo *m*, aseo *m*

wasp [wɑːsp] *insect* avispa *f*

waste [weɪst] **1** *n* desperdicio *m*; *from industrial process* desechos *mpl*; *it's a ~ of time / money* es una pérdida de tiempo / dinero **2** *adj* residual **3** *v/t* derrochar; *money* gastar; *time* perder

♦ **waste away** *v/i* consumirse

'**waste dis·pos·al** (**unit**) trituradora *f* de basuras

waste·ful ['weɪstfəl] *adj* despilfarrador, derrochador

'**waste·land** erial *m*; **waste·pa·per** papel *m* usado; **waste·pa·per bas·ket** papelera *f*; '**waste pipe** tubería *f* de desagüe; '**waste**

prod·uct desecho *m*

watch [wɑːtʃ] **1** *n timepiece* reloj *m*; **keep ~** hacer la guardia, vigilar **2** *v/t film, TV* ver; (*look after*) vigilar **3** *v/i* mirar, observar

♦ **watch for** *v/t* esperar

♦ **watch out** *v/i* (*be wary of*) tener cuidado; **watch out!** ¡cuidado!

♦ **watch out for** *v/t* tener cuidado con

watch·ful ['wɑːtʃfəl] *adj* vigilante

'watch·mak·er relojero(-a) *m(f)*

wa·ter ['wɔːtər] **1** *n* agua *f*; **~s** NAUT aguas *fpl* **2** *v/t plant* regar **3** *v/i*: **my eyes are ~ing** me lloran los ojos; **my mouth is ~ing** se me hace la boca agua

♦ **water down** *v/t drink* aguar, diluir

'wa·ter can·non cañón *m* de agua; **'wa·ter·col·or,** *Br* **'wa·ter·col·our** acuarela *f*; **'wa·ter·cress** berro *m*

wa·tered 'down ['wɔːtərd] *adj fig* dulcificado

'wa·ter·fall cascada *f*, catarata *f*

wa·ter·ing can ['wɔːtərɪŋ] regadera *f*

'wa·ter·ing hole *hum* bar *m*

'wa·ter lev·el nivel *m* del agua; **'wa·ter lil·y** nenúfar *m*; **'wa·ter·line** línea *f* de flotación; **wa·ter·logged** ['wɔːtərlɑːgd] *adj earth, field* anegado; *boat* lleno de agua; **'wa·ter main** tubería *f* principal; **'wa·ter·mark** filigrana *f*; **'wa·ter·mel·on** sandía *f*; **'wa·ter pol·lu·tion** contaminación *f* del agua; **'wa·ter po·lo** waterpolo *m*; **'wa·ter·proof** *adj* impermeable; **'wa·ter·shed** *fig* momento *m* clave; **'wa·ter·side** *n* orilla *f*; **at the ~** en la orilla; **'wa·ter·ski·ing** esquí *m* acuático; **'wa·ter·tight** *adj compartment* estanco; *fig* irrefutable; **'wa·ter·way** curso *m* de agua navegable; **'wa·ter·wings** *npl* flotadores *mpl* (*para los brazos*); **wa·ter·works** F: **turn on the ~** ponerse a llorar como una magdalena F

wa·ter·y ['wɔːtərɪ] *adj* aguado

watt [wɑːt] *n* vatio *m*

wave[1] [weɪv] *n in sea* ola *f*

wave[2] [weɪv] **1** *n of hand* saludo *m*

2 *v/i with hand* saludar con la mano; **~ to s.o.** saludar con la mano a alguien **3** *v/t flag etc* agitar

'wave·length RAD longitud *f* de onda, **be on the same ~** *fig* estar en la misma onda

wa·ver ['weɪvər] *v/i* vacilar, titubear

wav·y ['weɪvɪ] *adj hair, line* ondulado

wax [wæks] *n for floor, furniture* cera *f*; *in ear* cera *f*, cerumen

way [weɪ] **1** *n* (*method*) manera *f*, forma *f*; (*manner*) manera *f*, modo *m*; (*route*) camino *m*; **I don't like the ~ he behaves** no me gusta cómo se comporta; **can you tell me the ~ to …?** ¿me podría decir cómo se va a …?; **this ~** (*like this*) así; (*in this direction*) por aquí; **by the ~** (*incidentally*) por cierto, a propósito; **by ~ of** (*via*) por; (*in the form of*) a modo de; **in a ~** (*in certain respects*) en cierto sentido; **be under ~** haber comenzado, estar en marcha; **give ~** MOT ceder el paso; (*collapse*) ceder; **give ~ to** (*be replaced by*) ser reemplazado por; **have one's (own) ~** salirse con la suya; **OK, we'll do it your ~** de acuerdo, lo haremos a tu manera; **lead the ~** abrir el (el) camino; *fig* marcar la pauta; **lose one's ~** perderse; **be in the ~** (*be an obstruction*) estar en medio; **it's on the ~ to the station** está camino de la estación; **I was on my ~ to the station** iba camino de la estación; **no ~!** ¡ni hablar!, ¡de ninguna manera!; **there's no ~ he can do it** es imposible que lo haga **2** *adv* F (*much*): **it's ~ too soon to decide** es demasiado pronto como para decidir; **they are ~ behind with their work** van atrasadísimos en el trabajo

way 'in entrada *f*; **way of 'life** modo *m* de vida; **way 'out** *n also fig*: *from situation* salida *f*

we [wiː] *pron* nosotros *mpl*, nosotras *fpl*; **~ are the best** somos los mejores; **they're going, but ~'re not** ellos van, pero nosotros no

weak [wiːk] *adj* débil; *tea, coffee* poco cargado

W

weak·en ['wi:kn] **1** *v/t* debilitar **2** *v/i* debilitarse

weak·ling ['wi:klɪŋ] *morally* cobarde *m/f*; *physically* enclenque *m/f*

weak·ness ['wi:knɪs] debilidad *f*; *have a ~ for sth* (*liking*) sentir debilidad por algo

wealth [welθ] riqueza *f*; *a ~ of* abundancia de

wealth·y ['welθɪ] *adj* rico

wean [wi:n] *v/t* destetar

weap·on ['wepən] arma *f*

wear [wer] **1** *n*: *~ (and tear)* desgaste *m*; *clothes for everyday / evening ~* ropa *f* de diario / de noche **2** *v/t* (*pret* **wore**, *pp* **worn**) (*have on*) llevar; (*damage*) desgastar **3** *v/i* (*pret* **wore**, *pp* **worn**) (*wear out*) desgastarse; (*last*) durar

♦ **wear away 1** *v/i* desgastarse **2** *v/t* desgastar

♦ **wear down** *v/t* agotar

♦ **wear off** *v/i of effect, feeling* pasar

♦ **wear out 1** *v/t* (*tire*) agotar; *shoes* desgastar **2** *v/i of shoes, carpet* desgastarse

wea·ri·ly ['wɪrɪlɪ] *adv* cansinamente

wear·ing ['werɪŋ] *adj* (*tiring*) agotador

wea·ry ['wɪrɪ] *adj* cansado

weath·er ['weðər] **1** *n* tiempo *m*; *what's the ~ like?* ¿qué tiempo hace?; *be feeling under the ~* estar pachucho **2** *v/t crisis* capear, superar

'**weath·er-beat·en** *adj* curtido; '**weath·er chart** mapa *m* del tiempo; '**weath·er fore·cast** pronóstico *m* del tiempo; '**weath·er·man** hombre *m* del tiempo

weave [wi:v] **1** *v/t* (*pret* **wove**, *pp* **woven**) tejer **2** *v/i* (*pret* **wove**, *pp* **woven**) *move* zigzaguear

web [web] *of spider* tela *f*; *the Web* COMPUT la Web

webbed '**feet** patas *fpl* palmeadas

'**web page** página *f* web

'**web site** sitio *m* web

wed·ding ['wedɪŋ] boda *f*

'**wed·ding an·ni·ver·sa·ry** aniversario *m* de boda; '**wed·ding cake** pastel *m or* tarta *f* de boda; '**wed·ding**

day día *f* de la boda; '**wed·ding dress** vestido *m* de boda *or* novia; '**wed·ding ring** anillo *m* de boda

wedge [wedʒ] **1** *n to hold sth in place* cuña *f*; *of cheese etc* trozo *m* **2** *v/t*: *~ a door open* calzar una puerta para que se quede abierta

Wed·nes·day ['wenzdeɪ] miércoles *m inv*

weed [wi:d] **1** *n* mala hierba **2** *v/t* escardar

♦ **weed out** *v/t* (*remove*) eliminar; *candidates* descartar

'**weed-kill·er** herbicida *m*

weed·y ['wi:dɪ] *adj* F esmirriado, enclenque

week [wi:k] semana *f*; *a ~ tomorrow* dentro de una semana

'**week·day** día *m* de la semana

week'end fin *m* de semana; *on the ~* el fin de semana

week·ly ['wi:klɪ] **1** *adj* semanal **2** *n magazine* semanario *m* **3** *adv* semanalmente

weep [wi:p] *v/i* (*pret & pp* **wept**) llorar

'**weep·ing wil·low** sauce *m* llorón

weep·y ['wi:pɪ] *adj*: *be ~* estar lloroso

wee-wee 1 *n* F pipí *m*; *do a ~* hacer pipí **2** *v/i* F hacer pipí

weigh¹ [weɪ] **1** *v/t* pesar **2** *v/i* pesar; *how much do you ~?* ¿cuánto pesas?

weigh² [weɪ] *v/t*: *~ anchor* levar anclas

♦ **weigh down** *v/t* cargar; *be weighed down with bags* ir cargado con; *worries* estar abrumado por

♦ **weigh on** *v/t* preocupar

♦ **weigh up** *v/t* (*assess*) sopesar

weight [weɪt] peso *m*; *put on ~* engordar, ganar peso; *lose ~* adelgazar, perder peso

♦ **weight down** *v/t* sujetar (*con pesos*)

'**weight·less** ['weɪtləs] *adj* ingrávido

'**weight·less·ness** ['weɪtləsnəs] ingravidez *f*

'**weight-lift·er** levantador(a) *m(f)* de pesas

'**weight-lift·ing** halterofilia *f*, levantamiento *m* de pesas

weight·y ['weɪtɪ] *adj fig (important)* serio

weir [wɪr] presa *f (rebasadero)*

weird [wɪrd] *adj* extraño, raro

weird·ly ['wɪrdlɪ] *adv* extrañamente

weird·o ['wɪrdou] *n* F bicho *m* raro F

wel·come ['welkəm] **1** *adj* bienvenido; *you're ~!* ¡de nada!; *you're ~ to try some* prueba algunos, por favor **2** *n* bienvenida *f* **3** *v/t guests etc* dar la bienvenida a; *fig: decision etc* acoger positivamente

weld [weld] *v/t* soldar

weld·er ['weldər] soldador(a) *m(f)*

wel·fare ['welfer] bienestar *m*; *financial assistance* subsidio *m* estatal; *be on ~* estar recibiendo subsidios del Estado

'wel·fare check *cheque con el importe del subsidio estatal*; **wel·fare 'state** estado *m* del bienestar; **'wel·fare work** trabajo *m* social; **'wel·fare work·er** asistente *m/f* social

well[1] [wel] *n for water, oil* pozo *m*

well[2] **1** *adv* bien; *as ~ (too)* también; *as ~ as (in addition to)* así como; *it's just as ~ you told me* menos mal que me lo dijiste; *very ~* muy bien; *~, ~!* I surprise ¡caramba!; *~ ...* *uncertainty, thinking* bueno ...; *you might as ~ spend the night here* ya puestos quédate a pasar la noche aquí; *you might as ~ throw it out* yo de ti lo tiraría **2** *adj: be ~* estar bien; *how are you? – I'm very ~* ¿cómo estás? – muy bien; *feel ~* sentirse bien; *get ~ soon!* ¡ponte bueno!, ¡que te mejores!

well·'bal·anced *adj person, diet* equilibrado; **well·be'haved** *adj* educado; **well·'be·ing** bienestar *m*; **well·'built** *adj also euph* fornido; **well·'done** *adj meat* muy hecho; **well·'dressed** *adj* bien vestido; **well·'earned** *adj* merecido; **well·'heeled** *adj* F adinerado, *Span* con pasta F; **well·in'formed** *adj* bien informado; **well·'known** *adj fact* conocido; *person* conocido, famoso; **well·'made** *adj* bien hecho; **well·'man·nered** *adj* bien educado; **well·'mean·ing** *adj* bienintencionado; **well·'off** *adj* acomodado; **well·'paid** *adj* bien pagado; **well·'read** *adj:* *be ~* haber leído mucho; **well·'timed** *adj* oportuno; **well·to·'do** *adj* acomodado; **'well·wish·er** admirador(a) *m(f)*; **well·'worn** *adj* gastado

Welsh [welʃ] **1** *adj* galés **2** *n language* galés; *the ~* los galeses

went [went] *pret →* **go**

wept [wept] *pret & pp →* **weep**

were [wer] *pret →* **be**

west [west] **1** *n* oeste *m*; *the West (Western nations)* el Occidente; *(western part of a country)* el oeste **2** *adj* del oeste; *~ Africa* África occidental **3** *adv travel* hacia el oeste; *~ of* al oeste de

West 'Coast *of USA* Costa *f* Oeste

west·er·ly ['westərlɪ] *adj wind* del oeste; *direction* hacia el oeste

west·ern ['westərn] **1** *adj* occidental; *Western* occidental **2** *n movie* western *m*, película *f* del oeste

West·ern·er ['westərnər] occidental *m/f*

west·ern·ized ['westərnaɪzd] *adj* occidentalizado

West 'In·di·an 1 *adj* antillano **2** *n* antillano(-a) *m(f)*

West In·dies ['ɪndiːz] *npl: the ~* las Antillas

west·ward ['westwərd] *adv* hacia el oeste

wet [wet] *adj* mojado; *(damp)* húmedo; *(rainy)* lluvioso; *get ~* mojarse; *~ paint as sign* recién pintado; *be ~ through* estar empapado

wet 'blan·ket F aguafiestas *m/f inv*

'wet suit *for diving* traje *m* de neopreno

whack [wæk] **1** *n* F *(blow)* porrazo *m* F; F *(share)* parte *f* **2** *v/t* F dar un porrazo a F

whacked [wækt] *adj* F hecho polvo F

whale [weɪl] ballena *f*

whal·ing ['weɪlɪŋ] caza *f* de ballenas

wharf [wɔːrf] *n* embarcadero *m*

what [wɑːt] **1** *pron* qué; *~ is that?* ¿qué es eso?; *~ is it?* *(what do you*

W

want) ¿qué quieres?; **~?** (*what do you want*) ¿qué?; (*what did you say*) ¿qué?, ¿cómo?; *astonishment* ¿qué?; **~ about some dinner?** ¿os apetece cenar?; **~ about heading home?** ¿y si nos fuéramos a casa?; **~ for?** (*why*) ¿para qué?; **so ~?** ¿y qué?; **~ is the book about?** ¿de qué trata el libro?; **take ~ you need** toma lo que te haga falta **2** *adj* qué; **~ university are you at?** ¿en qué universidad estás?; **~ color is the car?** ¿de qué color es el coche?

what·ev·er [wɑːt'evər] **1** *pron*: **I'll do ~ you want** haré lo que quieras; **~ gave you that idea?** ¿se puede saber qué te ha dado esa idea?; **~ the season** en cualquier estación; **~ people say** diga lo que diga la gente **2** *adj* cualquier; **you have no reason ~ to worry** no tienes por qué preocuparte en absoluto

wheat [wiːt] trigo *m*

whee·dle ['wiːdl] *v/t*: **~ sth out of s.o.** camelar algo a alguien

wheel [wiːl] **1** *n* rueda *f*; (*steering ~*) volante *m* **2** *v/t bicycle* empujar **3** *v/i of birds* volar en círculo

♦ **wheel around** *v/i* darse la vuelta

'**wheel·bar·row** carretilla *f*; '**wheel·chair** silla *f* de ruedas; '**wheel clamp** cepo *m*

wheeze [wiːz] *n* resoplido *m*

when [wen] **1** *adv* cuándo; **~ do you open?** ¿a qué hora abren? **2** *conj* cuando; **~ I was a child** cuando era niño

when·ev·er [wen'evər] *adv* (*each time*) cada vez que; **call me ~ you like** llámame cuando quieras; **I go to Paris ~ I can afford it** voy a París siempre que me lo pueda permitir

where [wer] **1** *adv* dónde; **~ from?** ¿de dónde?; **~ to?** ¿a dónde? **2** *conj* donde; **this is ~ I used to live** aquí es donde vivía antes

where·a·bouts [werə'bauts] **1** *adv* dónde **2** *npl*: **nothing is known of his ~** está en paradero desconocido

where·as *conj* mientras que

wher·ev·er [wer'evər] **1** *conj* donde-

quiera que; **sit ~ you like** siéntate donde prefieras **2** *adv* dónde

whet [wet] *v/t* (*pret & pp* **-ted**) *appetite* abrir

wheth·er ['weðər] *conj* si; **I don't know ~ to tell him or not** no sé si decírselo o no; **~ you approve or not** te parezca bien o no

which [wɪtʃ] **1** *adj* qué; **~ one is yours?** ¿cuál es tuyo? **2** *pron interrogative* cuál; *relative* que; **take one, it doesn't matter ~** toma uno, no importa cuál

which·ev·er [wɪtʃ'evər] **1** *adj*: **~ color you choose** elijas el color que elijas **2** *pron*: **~ you like** el que quieras; **use ~ of the methods you prefer** utiliza el método que prefieras

whiff [wɪf] (*smell*) olorcillo *m*

while [waɪl] **1** *conj* mientras; (*although*) si bien **2** *n* rato *m*; **a long ~** un rato largo; **for a ~** durante un tiempo; **I lived in Tokyo for a ~** viví en Tokio una temporada; **I'll wait a ~ longer** esperaré un rato más

♦ **while away** *v/t* pasar

whim [wɪm] capricho *m*

whim·per ['wɪmpər] **1** *n* gimoteo *m* **2** *v/i* gimotear

whine [waɪn] *v/i of dog* gimotear; F (*complain*) quejarse

whip [wɪp] **1** *n* látigo *m* **2** *v/t* (*pret & pp* **-ped**) (*beat*) azotar; *cream* batir, montar; F (*defeat*) dar una paliza a F

♦ **whip up** *v/t* (*arouse*) agitar

'**whipped cream** [wɪpt] nata *f* montada

whip·ping ['wɪpɪŋ] (*beating*) azotes *mpl*; F (*defeat*) paliza *f* F

'**whip·round** F colecta *f*; **have a ~** hacer una colecta

whirl [wɜːrl] **1** *n*: **my mind is in a ~** me da vueltas la cabeza **2** *v/i* dar vueltas

'**whirl·pool** *in river* remolino *m*; *for relaxation* bañera *f* de hidromasaje

whirr [wɜːr] *v/i* zumbar

whisk [wɪsk] **1** *n kitchen implement* **2** *v/t eggs* batir

♦ **whisk away** *v/t* retirar rápidamente

whis·kers ['wɪskərz] *npl of man* patillas *fpl*; *of animal* bigotes *mpl*

whis·key ['wɪskɪ] whisky *m*

whis·per ['wɪspər] **1** *n* susurro *m*; (*rumor*) rumor *m* **2** *v/i* susurrar **3** *v/t* susurrar

whis·tle ['wɪsl] **1** *n sound* silbido *m*; *device* silbato *m* **2** *v/t* & *v/i* silbar

white [waɪt] **1** *n color* blanco *m*; *of egg* clara *f*; *person* blanco(-a) *m(f)* **2** *adj* blanco; *her face went* ~ se puso blanca

white 'Christ·mas Navidades *fpl* blancas; **white 'cof·fee** *Br* café *m* con leche; **white-col·lar 'work·er** *persona que trabaja en una oficina*; **'White House** Casa *f* Blanca; **white 'lie** mentira *f* piadosa; **white 'meat** carne *f* blanca; **'white-out** (*for text*) Tipp-Ex® *m*; **'white·wash 1** *n* cal *f*; *fig* encubrimiento *m* **2** *v/t* encalar; **white 'wine** vino *m* blanco

whit·tle ['wɪtl] *v/t wood* tallar

♦ **whittle down** *v/t* reducir

whiz(z) [wɪz] *n*: *be a* ~ *at* F ser un genio de

♦ **whizz by, whizz past** *v/i of time, car* pasar zumbando

'whizz-kid F joven *m/f* prodigio

who [huː] *pron interrogative* ¿quién?; *relative* que; ~ *do you want to speak to?* ¿con quién quieres hablar?; *I don't know* ~ *to believe* no sé a quién creer

who·dun·(n)it [huː'dʌnɪt] *libro o película centrados en la resolución de un caso*

who·ev·er [huː'evər] *pron* quienquiera; ~ *can that be calling at this time of night?* ¿pero quién llama a estas horas de la noche?

whole [hoʊl] **1** *adj* entero; *the* ~ *town/country* toda la ciudad / todo el país; *it's a* ~ *lot easier/better* es mucho más fácil / mucho mejor **2** *n* totalidad *f*; *the* ~ *of the United States* la totalidad de los Estados Unidos; *on the* ~ en general

whole-heart·ed [hoʊl'hɑːrtɪd] *adj* incondicional; **whole-heart·ed·ly** [hoʊl'hɑːrtɪdlɪ] *adv* incondicionalmente; **whole·meal 'bread** pan *m*

integral; **'whole·sale 1** *adj* al por mayor; *fig* indiscriminado **2** *adv* al por mayor; **whole·sal·er** ['hoʊlseɪlər] mayorista *m/f*; **whole·some** ['hoʊlsəm] *adj* saludable, sano

whol·ly ['hoʊlɪ] *adv* completamente

whol·ly owned 'sub·sid·i·ar·y subsidiaria *f* en propiedad absoluta

whom [huːm] *pron fml* quién; ~ *did you see?* ¿a quién vio?; *the person to* ~ *I was speaking* la persona con la que estaba hablando

whoop·ing cough ['huːpɪŋ] tos *f* ferina

whop·ping ['wɑːpɪŋ] *adj* F enorme

whore [hɔːr] *n* prostituta *f*

whose [huːz] **1** *pron interrogative* de quién; *relative* cuyo(-a); ~ *is this?* ¿de quién es esto?; *a country* ~ *economy is booming* un país cuya economía está experimentando un boom **2** *adj* de quién; ~ *bike is that?* ¿de quién es esa bici?

why [waɪ] *adv interrogative, relative* por qué; *that's* ~ por eso; ~ *not?* ¿por qué no?

wick [wɪk] pabilo *m*

wick·ed ['wɪkɪd] *adj* malvado, perverso

wick·er ['wɪkər] *adj* de mimbre

wick·er 'chair silla *f* de mimbre

wick·et ['wɪkɪt] *in station, bank etc* ventanilla *f*

wide [waɪd] *adj* ancho; *experience, range* amplio; *be 12 feet* ~ tener 12 pies de ancho

wide a'wake *adj* completamente despierto

wide·ly ['waɪdlɪ] *adv used, known* ampliamente

wid·en ['waɪdn] **1** *v/t* ensanchar **2** *v/i* ensancharse

wide-'o·pen *adj* abierto de par en par; **wide-'rang·ing** *adj* amplio; **'wide·spread** *adj* extendido, muy difundido

wid·ow ['wɪdoʊ] *n* viuda *f*

wid·ow·er ['wɪdoʊər] viudo *m*

width [wɪdθ] anchura *f*, ancho *m*

wield [wiːld] *v/t weapon* empuñar; *power* detentar

wife [waɪf] (*pl* **wives** [waɪvz]) mujer *f*, esposa *f*

wig [wɪg] peluca *f*

wig·gle ['wɪgl] *v/t* menear

wild [waɪld] **1** *adj animal* salvaje; *flower* silvestre; *teenager, party* descontrolado; (*crazy: scheme*) descabellado; *applause* arrebatado; **be ~ about ...** (*enthusiastic*) estar loco por ...; **go ~** (*express enthusiasm*) volverse loco; (*become angry*) ponerse hecho una furia; **run ~** *of children* desahogarse **2** *n:* **the ~s** los parajes remotos

wil·der·ness ['wɪldərnɪs] desierto *m*, yermo *m*

'**wild·fire**: **spread like ~** extenderse como un reguero de pólvora; **wild·'goose chase** búsqueda *f* infructuosa; '**wild·life** flora *f* y fauna; **~ program** TV documental *f* sobre la naturaleza

wild·ly ['waɪldlɪ] *adv applaud* enfervorizadamente; *I'm not ~ enthusiastic about the idea* la idea no me emociona demasiado

wil·ful *Br* → **willful**

will[1] [wɪl] *n* LAW testamento *m*

will[2] [wɪl] *n* (*willpower*) voluntad *f*

will[3] [wɪl] *v/aux*: *I ~ let you know tomorrow* te lo diré mañana; **~ you be there?** ¿estarás allí?; *I won't be back until late* volveré tarde; *you ~ call me, won't you?* me llamarás, ¿verdad?; *I'll pay for this – no you won't* esto lo pago yo – no, ni hablar; *the car won't start* el coche no arranca; **~ you tell her that ...?** ¿le quieres decir que ...?; **~ you have some more tea?** ¿quiere más té?; **~ you stop that!** ¡basta ya!

will·ful ['wɪlfəl] *adj person* tozudo, obstinado; *action* deliberado, intencionado

will·ing ['wɪlɪŋ] *adj* dispuesto

will·ing·ly ['wɪlɪŋlɪ] *adv* gustosamente

will·ing·ness ['wɪlɪŋnɪs] buena disposición *f*

will·low ['wɪləʊ] sauce *m*

'**will·pow·er** fuerza *f* de voluntad

wil·ly-nil·ly [wɪlɪ'nɪlɪ] *adv* (*at random*) a la buena de Dios

wilt [wɪlt] *v/i of plant* marchitarse

wi·ly ['waɪlɪ] *adj* astuto

wimp [wɪmp] F enclenque *m/f* F, blandengue *m/f* F

win [wɪn] **1** *n* victoria *f*, triunfo *m* **2** *v/t & v/i* (*pret & pp* **won**) ganar

♦ **win back** *v/t* recuperar

wince [wɪns] *v/i* hacer una mueca de dolor

winch [wɪntʃ] *n* torno *m*, cabestrante *m*

wind[1] [wɪnd] **1** *n* viento *m*; (*flatulence*) gases *mpl*; **get ~ of ...** enterarse de ... **2** *v/t*: **be ~ed** quedarse sin respiración

wind[2] [waɪnd] **1** *v/i* (*pret & pp wound*) zigzaguear, serpentear; **~ around** enrollarse en **2** *v/t* (*pret & pp wound*) enrollar

♦ **wind down 1** *v/i of party etc* ir finalizando **2** *v/t car window* bajar, abrir; *business* ir reduciendo

♦ **wind up 1** *v/t clock* dar cuerda a; *car window* subir, cerrar; *speech, presentation* finalizar; *business, affairs* concluir; *company* cerrar **2** *v/i* (*finish*) concluir; **wind up in hospital** acabar en el hospital

'**wind·bag** F cotorra *f* F

'**wind·fall** *fig* dinero *m* inesperado

wind·ing ['waɪndɪŋ] *adj* zigzagueante, serpenteante

'**wind in·stru·ment** instrumento *m* de viento

'**wind·mill** molino *m* de viento

win·dow ['wɪndəʊ] *also* COMPUT ventana *f*; *of car* ventana *f*, ventanilla *f*; **in the ~** *of store* en el escaparate *or L.Am.* la vidriera

'**win·dow box** jardinera *f*; '**win·dow clean·er** *person* limpiacristales *m/f inv*; '**win·dow·pane** cristal *f* (*de una ventana*); '**win·dow seat** *on plane, train* asiento *m* de ventana; '**win·dow-shop** *v/i* (*pret & pp -ped*): **go ~ping** ir de escaparates *or L.Am.* vidrieras; **win·dow·sill** ['wɪndəʊsɪl] alféizar *m*

'**wind·pipe** tráquea *f*; '**wind·screen**

Br, '**wind·shield** parabrisas *m inv*; '**wind·shield wip·er** limpiaparabrisas *m inv*; '**wind·surf·er** *person* windsurfista *m/f*; *board* tabla *f* de windsurf; '**wind·surf·ing** el windsurf

wind·y ['wɪndɪ] *adj* ventoso; *a ~ day* un día de mucho viento; *it's very ~ today* hoy hace mucho viento; *it's getting ~* está empezando a soplar el viento

wine [waɪn] vino *m*

'**wine bar** *bar especializado en vinos*; '**wine cel·lar** bodega *f*; '**wine glass** copa *f* de vino; '**wine list** lista *f* de vinos; '**wine mak·er** viticultor(a) *m(f)*; '**wine mer·chant** comerciante *m/f* de vinos

win·ery ['waɪnərɪ] bodega *f*

wing [wɪŋ] *n* ala *f*; SP lateral *m/f*, extremo *m/f*

'**wing·span** envergadura *f*

wink [wɪŋk] **1** *n* guiño *m*; *I didn't sleep a ~* F no pegué ojo **2** *v/i of person* guiñar, hacer un guiño; *~ at s.o.* guiñar *or* hacer un guiño a alguien

win·ner ['wɪnər] ganador(a) *m(f)*, vencedor(a) *m(f)*; *of lottery* acertante *m/f*

win·ning ['wɪnɪŋ] *adj* ganador

'**win·ning post** meta *f*

win·nings ['wɪnɪŋz] *npl* ganancias *fpl*

win·ter ['wɪntər] *n* invierno *m*

win·ter 'sports *npl* deportes *mpl* de invierno

win·try ['wɪntrɪ] *adj* invernal

wipe [waɪp] *v/t* limpiar; *tape* borrar

♦ **wipe out** *v/t* (*kill, destroy*) eliminar; *debt* saldar

wip·er ['waɪpər] → *windshield wiper*

wire [waɪr] *n* alambre *m*; ELEC cable *m*

wire·less ['waɪrlɪs] radio *f*

wire 'net·ting tela *f* metálica

wir·ing ['waɪrɪŋ] *n* ELEC cableado *m*

wir·y ['waɪrɪ] *adj person* fibroso

wis·dom ['wɪzdəm] *of person* sabiduría *f*; *of action* prudencia *f*, sensatez *f*

'**wis·dom tooth** muela *f* del juicio

wise [waɪz] *adj* sabio; *action, decision* prudente, sensato

'**wise·crack** *n* F chiste *m*, comentario *m* gracioso

'**wise guy** *pej* sabelotodo *m*

wise·ly ['waɪzlɪ] *adv act* prudentemente, sensatamente

wish [wɪʃ] **1** *n* deseo *m*; *best ~es* un saludo cordial; *make a ~* pedir un deseo **2** *v/t* desear; *I ~ that you could stay* ojalá te pudieras quedar; *~ s.o. well* desear a alguien lo mejor; *I ~ed him good luck* le deseé buena suerte **3** *v/i*: *~ for* desear

'**wish·bone** espoleta *f*

wish·ful '**think·ing** ['wɪʃfəl] ilusiones *fpl*; *that's ~ on her part* que no se haga ilusiones

wish·y-wash·y ['wɪʃɪwɑːʃɪ] *adj person* anodino; *color* pálido

wisp [wɪsp] *of hair* mechón *m*; *of smoke* voluta *f*

wist·ful ['wɪstfəl] *adj* nostálgico

wist·ful·ly ['wɪstfəlɪ] *adv* con nostalgia

wit [wɪt] (*humor*) ingenio *m*; *person* ingenioso(-a) *m(f)*; *be at one's ~'s end* estar desesperado; *keep one's ~s about one* mantener la calma; *be scared out of one's ~s* estar aterrorizado

witch [wɪtʃ] bruja *f*

'**witch-hunt** *fig* caza *f* de brujas

with [wɪð] *prep* con; *shivering ~ fear* temblando de miedo; *a girl ~ brown eyes* una chica de ojos castaños; *are you ~ me?* (*do you understand*) ¿me sigues?; *~ no money* sin dinero

with·draw [wɪð'drɔː] **1** *v/t* (*pret -drew, pp -drawn*) *complaint, money, troops* retirar **2** *v/i* (*pret -drew, pp -drawn*) *of competitor, troops* retirarse

with·draw·al [wɪð'drɔːəl] *of complaint, application, troops* retirada *f*; *of money* reintegro *m*

with·draw·al symp·toms *npl* síndrome *m* de abstinencia

with·drawn [wɪð'drɔːn] *adj person* retraído

with·er ['wɪðər] *v/i* marchitarse

W

with·hold v/t (pret & pp **-held**) information ocultar; payment retener; consent negar

with·in prep (inside) dentro de; in expressions of time en menos de; **~ five miles of home** a cinco millas de casa; **we kept ~ the budget** no superamos el presupuesto; **it is well ~ your capabilities** lo puedes conseguir perfectamente; **~ reach** al alcance de la mano

with·out prep sin; **~ looking / asking** sin mirar / preguntar

with·stand v/t (pret & pp **-stood**) resistir, soportar

wit·ness ['wɪtnɪs] **1** n testigo m/f **2** v/t ser testigo de; **I ~ed his signature** firmé en calidad de testigo

'wit·ness stand estrado m del testigo

wit·ti·cism ['wɪtɪsɪzm] comentario m gracioso or agudo

wit·ty ['wɪtɪ] adj ingenioso, agudo

wob·ble ['wɑːbl] v/i tambalearse

wob·bly ['wɑːblɪ] adj tambaleante

wok [wɑːk] wok m, sartén típica de la cocina china

woke [woʊk] pret → **wake**

wok·en ['woʊkn] pp → **wake**

wolf [wʊlf] **1** n (pl **wolves** [wʊlvz]) animal lobo m; fig (womanizer) don juan m **2** v/t: **~ (down)** engullir

'wolf whis·tle n silbido m

'wolf-whis·tle v/i: **~ at s.o.** silbar a alguien (como piropo)

wom·an ['wʊmən] (pl **women** ['wɪmɪn]) mujer f

wom·an 'doc·tor médica f

wom·an 'driv·er conductora f

wom·an·iz·er ['wʊmənaɪzər] mujeriego(-a) m(f)

wom·an·ly ['wʊmənlɪ] adj femenino

wom·an 'priest mujer f sacerdote

womb [wuːm] matriz f, útero m

wom·en ['wɪmɪn] pl → **woman**

wom·en's lib [wɪmɪnz'lɪb] la liberación de la mujer

wom·en's lib·ber [wɪmɪnz'lɪbər] partidario(-a) m(f) de la liberación de la mujer

won [wʌn] pret & pp → **win**

won·der ['wʌndər] **1** n (amazement) asombro m; **no ~!** ¡no me sorprende!; **it's a ~ that ...** es increíble que ... **2** v/i preguntarse; **I've often ~ed about that** me he preguntado eso a menudo **3** v/t preguntarse; **I ~ if you could help** ¿le importaría ayudarme?

won·der·ful ['wʌndərfəl] adj maravilloso

won·der·ful·ly ['wʌndərfəlɪ] adv (extremely) maravillosamente

won't [woʊnt] → **will**

wood [wʊd] n madera f; for fire leña f; (forest) bosque m

wood·ed ['wʊdɪd] adj arbolado

wood·en ['wʊdn] adj (made of wood) de madera

wood·peck·er ['wʊdpekər] pájaro m carpintero

'wood·wind MUS sección f de viento de madera

'wood·work carpintería f

wool [wʊl] lana f

wool·en, Br **wool·len** ['wʊlən] **1** adj de lana **2** n prenda f de lana

word [wɜːrd] **1** n palabra f; **I didn't understand a ~ of what she said** no entendí nada de lo que dijo; **is there any ~ from ...?** ¿se sabe algo de ...?; **I've had ~ from my daughter** (news) he recibido noticias de mi hija; **you have my ~** tienes mi palabra; **have ~s** (argue) discutir; **have a ~ with s.o.** hablar con alguien; **the ~s** of song la letra **2** v/t article, letter redactar

word·ing ['wɜːrdɪŋ]: **the ~ of a letter** la redacción de una carta

word 'pro·cess·ing procesamiento m de textos

word 'pro·ces·sor software procesador m de textos

wore [wɔːr] pret → **wear**

work [wɜːrk] **1** n (job) trabajo m; (employment) trabajo m, empleo m; **out of ~** desempleado, Span en el paro; **be at ~** estar en el trabajo; **I go to ~ by bus** voy al trabajo en autobús **2** v/i of person trabajar; of machine, (succeed) funcionar; **how**

does it ~? *of device* ¿cómo funciona? **3** *v/t employee* hacer trabajar; *machine* hacer funcionar, utilizar

♦ **work off** *v/t bad mood, anger* desahogarse de; *flab* perder haciendo ejercicio

♦ **work out 1** *v/t problem, puzzle* resolver; *solution* encontrar, hallar **2** *v/i at gym* hacer ejercicios; *of relationship etc* funcionar, ir bien

♦ **work out to** *v/t (add up to)* sumar

♦ **work up** *v/t appetite* abrir; **work up enthusiasm** entusiasmarse; **get worked up** *(get angry)* alterarse; *(get nervous)* ponerse nervioso

work·a·ble ['wɜːrkəbl] *adj solution* viable

work·a·hol·ic [wɜːrkə'hɑːlɪk] *n* F *persona adicta al trabajo*

'work·day *(hours of work)* jornada *f* laboral; *(not a holiday)* día *f* de trabajo

work·er ['wɜːrkər] trabajador/a *m(f)*; **she's a good ~** trabaja bien

'work·force trabajadores *mpl*

'work hours *npl* horas *fpl* de trabajo

work·ing ['wɜːrkɪŋ] *n* funcionamiento *m*

'work·ing class clase *f* trabajadora; **'work·ing-class** *adj* de clase trabajadora; **'work·ing con·di·tions** *npl* condiciones *fpl* de trabajo; **work·ing 'day** → **workday**; **'work·ing hours** → **workhours**; **work·ing 'know·ledge** conocimientos *mpl* básicos; **work·ing 'moth·er** madre *f* que trabaja

'work·load cantidad *f* de trabajo; **'work·man** obrero *m*; **'work·man·like** *adj* competente; **'work·man·ship** factura *f*, confección *f*; **work of 'art** obra *f* de arte; **'work·out** sesión *f* de ejercicios; **'work per·mit** permiso *m* de trabajo; **'work·shop** *also seminar* taller *m*; **'work sta·tion** estación *f* de trabajo; **'work·top** encimera *f*

world [wɜːrld] mundo *m*; **the ~ of computers/ the theater** el mundo de la informática / del teatro; **out of this ~** F sensacional

world-'class *adj* de categoría mundial; **World 'Cup** Mundial *m*, Copa *f* del Mundo; **world-'fa·mous** *adj* mundialmente famoso

world·ly ['wɜːrldlɪ] *adj* mundano

world 'pow·er potencia *f* mundial; **world 're·cord** récord *m* mundial *or* del mundo; **world 'war** guerra *f* mundial; **'world·wide 1** *adj* mundial **2** *adv* en todo el mundo

worm [wɜːrm] *n* gusano *m*

worn [wɔːrn] *pp* → **wear**

worn-'out *adj shoes, carpet, part* gastado; *person* agotado

wor·ried ['wʌrɪd] *adj* preocupado

wor·ried·ly ['wʌrɪdlɪ] *adv* con preocupación

wor·ry ['wʌrɪ] **1** *n* preocupación *f* **2** *v/t (pret & pp **-ied**)* preocupar **3** *v/i (pret & pp **-ied**)* preocuparse; **don't ~, I'll get it!** ¡no te molestes, ya respondo yo!

wor·ry·ing ['wʌrɪɪŋ] *adj* preocupante

worse [wɜːrs] **1** *adj* peor; **get ~** empeorar **2** *adv* peor

wors·en ['wɜːrsn] *v/i* empeorar

wor·ship ['wɜːrʃɪp] **1** *n* culto *m* **2** *v/t (pret & pp **-ped**)* adorar, rendir culto a; *fig* adorar

worst [wɜːrst] **1** *adj & adv* peor **2** *n*: **the ~** lo peor; **if the ~ comes to ~** en el peor de los casos

worst-case scen'a·ri·o el peor de los casos

worth [wɜːrθ] *adj:* **$20 ~ of gas** 20 dólares de gasolina; **be ~ ... in** *monetary terms* valer ...; **the book's ~ reading** valer la pena leer el libro; **be ~ it** valer la pena

worth·less ['wɜːrθlɪs] *adj person* inútil; **be ~** *of object* no valer nada

worth'while *adj* que vale la pena; **be ~** valer la pena

wor·thy ['wɜːrðɪ] *adj* digno; *cause* justo; **be ~ of** *(deserve)* merecer

would [wʊd] *v/aux:* **I ~ help if I could** te ayudaría si pudiera; **I said that I ~ go** dije que iría; **I told him I ~ not leave unless ....** le dije que no me iría a no ser que ...; **~ you like to go to the movies?** ¿te gustaría ir al cine?; **~ you mind if I smoked?** ¿le importa si fumo?; **~ you tell her that ...?** ¿le podrías decir que ...?; **~ you close the door?** ¿podrías cerrar la puerta?; **I ~ have told you but ...** te lo habría dicho pero ...; **I ~ not have been so angry if ...** no me habría enfadado tanto si ...

wound¹ [wuːnd] **1** *n* herida *f* **2** *v/t with weapon, remark* herir

wound² [waund] *pret & pp* → **wind**²

wove [wouv] *pret* → **weave**

wov·en ['wouvn] *pp* → **weave**

wow [wau] *int* ¡hala!

wrap [ræp] *v/t* (*pret & pp* **-ped**) *parcel, gift* envolver; **he ~ped a scarf around his neck** se puso una bufanda al cuello

♦ **wrap up** *v/i against the cold* abrigarse

wrap·per ['ræpər] *for candy etc* envoltorio *m*

wrap·ping ['ræpɪŋ] envoltorio *m*

'**wrap·ping pa·per** papel *m* de envolver

wrath [ræθ] ira *f*

wreath [riːθ] corona *f* de flores

wreck [rek] **1** *n* restos *mpl*; **be a nervous ~** ser un manojo de nervios **2** *v/t ship* hundir; *car* destrozar; *plans, marriage* arruinar

wreck·age ['rekɪdʒ] *of car, plane* restos *mpl*; *of marriage, career* ruina *f*

wreck·er ['rekər] grúa *f*

wreck·ing com·pa·ny ['rekɪŋ] empresa *f* de auxilio en carretera

wrench [renʧ] **1** *n tool* llave *f* **2** *v/t* (*pull*) arrebatar; **~ one's wrist** hacerse un esguince en la muñeca

wres·tle ['resl] *v/i* luchar

♦ **wrestle with** *v/t problems* combatir

wres·tler ['reslər] luchador(a) *m(f)* (de lucha libre)

wres·tling ['reslɪŋ] lucha *f* libre

'**wres·tling contest** combate *m* de lucha libre

wrig·gle ['rɪgl] *v/i* (*squirm*) menearse; *along the ground* arrastrarse; *into small space* escurrirse

♦ **wriggle out of** *v/t* librarse de

♦ **wring** out *v/t* (*pret & pp* **wrung**) *cloth* escurrir

wrin·kle ['rɪŋkl] **1** *n* arruga *f* **2** *v/t clothes* arrugar **3** *v/i of clothes* arrugarse

wrist [rɪst] muñeca *f*

'**wrist·watch** reloj *m* de pulsera

writ [rɪt] LAW mandato *m* judicial

write [raɪt] **1** *v/t* (*pret* **wrote**, *pp* **written**) escribir; *check* extender **2** *v/i* (*pret* **wrote**, *pp* **written**) escribir

♦ **write down** *v/t* escribir, tomar nota de

♦ **write off** *v/t debt* cancelar, anular; *car* destrozar

writ·er ['raɪtər] escritor(a) *m(f)*; *of book, song* autor(a) *m(f)*

'**write-up** reseña *f*

writhe [raɪð] *v/i* retorcerse

writ·ing ['raɪtɪŋ] *words, text* escritura *f*; (*hand-~*) letra *f*; **in ~** por escrito

'**writ·ing desk** escritorio *m*

'**writ·ing pa·per** papel *m* de escribir

writ·ten ['rɪtn] *pp* → **write**

wrong [rɔːŋ] **1** *adj answer, information* equivocado; *decision, choice* erróneo; **be ~ of person** estar equivocado; *of answer* ser incorrecto; *morally* ser injusto; **what's ~?** ¿qué pasa?; **there is something ~ with the car** al coche le pasa algo; **you have the ~ number** TELEC se ha equivocado **2** *adv* mal; **go ~ of person** equivocarse; *of marriage, plan etc* fallar **3** *n* mal *m*; **right a ~** deshacer un entuerto; **he knows right from ~** sabe distinguir entre el bien y el mal; **be in the ~** tener la culpa

wrong·ful ['rɔːŋfəl] *adj* ilegal

wrong·ly ['rɔːŋlɪ] *adv* erróneamente

wrote [rout] *pret* → **write**

wrought 'i·ron [rɔːt] hierro *m* forjado

wrung [rʌŋ] *pret & pp* → **wring**

wry [raɪ] *adj* socarrón

xen·o·pho·bi·a [zenou'foubɪə] xenofobia *f*

X

X-ray ['eksreɪ] **1** *n* rayo *m* X; *picture* radiografía *f* **2** *v/t* radiografiar, sacar un radiografía de

xy·lo·phone ['zaɪləfoʊn] xilofón *m*

Y

yacht [jɑːt] yate *m*

yacht·ing ['jɑːtɪŋ] vela *f*

yachts·man ['jɑːtsmən] navegante *m/f* (*en embarcación de vela*)

Yank [jæŋk] F yanqui *m/f*

yank [jæŋk] *v/t* tirar de

yap [jæp] *v/i* (*pret & pp -ped*) *of small dog* ladrar (*con ladridos agudos*); F (*talk a lot*) parlotear F, largar F

yard¹ [jɑːrd] *of prison, institution etc* patio *m*; *behind house* jardín *m*; *for storage* almacén *m* (*al aire libre*)

yard² [jɑːrd] *measurement* yarda *f*

'yard·stick patrón *m*

yarn [jɑːrn] *n* (*thread*) hilo *m*; F (*story*) batallita *f* F

yawn [jɔːn] **1** *n* bostezo *m* **2** *v/i* bostezar

year [jɪr] año *m*; *I've known her for ~s* la conozco desde hace años; *be six ~s old* tener seis años (*de edad*)

year·ly ['jɪrlɪ] **1** *adj* anual **2** *adv* anualmente

yearn [jɜːrn] *v/i* anhelar

♦ **yearn for** *v/t* ansiar

yearn·ing ['jɜːrnɪŋ] *n* anhelo *m*

yeast [jiːst] levadura *f*

yell [jel] **1** *n* grito *m* **2** *v/t & v/i* gritar

yel·low ['jeloʊ] **1** *n* amarillo *m* **2** *adj* amarillo

yel·low 'pag·es *npl* páginas *fpl* amarillas

yelp [jelp] **1** *n* aullido *m* **2** *v/i* aullar

yes [jes] *int* sí; *she said* ~ dijo que sí

'yes·man *pej* pelotillero *m*

yes·ter·day ['jestərdeɪ] **1** *adv* ayer; *the day before* ~ anteayer; ~ *afternoon* ayer por la tarde **2** *n* ayer *m*

yet [jet] **1** *adv* todavía, aún; *as* ~ aún, todavía; *have you finished* ~? ¿has acabado ya?; *he hasn't arrived* ~ todavía *or* aún no ha llegado; *is he here* ~? – *not* ~ ¿ha llegado ya? – todavía *or* aún no; ~ *bigger / longer* aún más grande / largo; *the fastest one* ~ el más rápido hasta el momento **2** *conj* sin embargo; ~ *I'm not sure* sin embargo no estoy seguro

yield [jiːld] **1** *n from fields etc* cosecha *f*; *from investment* rendimiento *m* **2** *v/t fruit, good harvest* proporcionar; *interest* rendir, devengar **3** *v/i* (*give way*) ceder; *of driver* ceder el paso

yo·ga ['joʊɡə] yoga *m*

yog·hurt ['joʊɡərt] yogur *m*

yolk [joʊk] yema *f*

you [juː] *pron singular* tú, *L.Am.* usted, *Rpl, C.Am.* vos; *formal* usted; *plural: Span* vosotros, vosotras, *L.Am.* ustedes; *formal* ustedes; ~ *are clever* eres / es inteligente; *do* ~ *know him?* ¿lo conoces / conoce?; ~

go, I'll stay tú ve / usted vaya, yo me quedo; **~ never know** nunca se sabe; **~ have to pay** hay que pagar; **exercise is good for ~** es bueno hacer ejercicio

young [jʌŋ] *adj* joven

young·ster ['jʌŋstər] joven *m/f*

your [jʊr] *adj singular* tu, *L.Am.* su; *formal* su; *plural: Span* vuestro, *L.Am.* su; *formal* su; **~ house** tu / su casa; **~ books** tus / sus libros

yours [jʊrz] *pron singular* el tuyo, la tuya, *L.Am.* el suyo, la suya; *formal* el suyo, la suya; *plural* el vuestro, la vuestra, *L.Am.* el suyo, la suya; *formal* el suyo, la suya; **a friend of ~** un amigo tuyo / suyo / vuestro; **~ ... at end of letter** un saludo

your·self [jʊr'self] *pron reflexive* te, *L.Am.* se; *formal* se; *emphatic* tú mismo *m*, tú misma *f*, *L.Am.* usted mismo, usted misma; *Rpl, C.Am.* vos mismo, vos misma; *formal* usted mismo, usted misma; **did you hurt ~?** ¿te hiciste / se hizo daño?; **when you see ~ in the mirror** cuando te ves / se ve en el espejo; **by ~** *(alone)* solo; *(without help)* tú solo, tú mis-

mo, *Rpl, C.Am.* vos solo, vos mismo, *L.Am.* usted solo, usted mismo; *formal* usted solo, usted mismo

your·selves [jʊr'selvz] *pron reflexive* os, *L.Am.* se; *formal* se; *emphatic* vosotros mismos *mpl*, vosotras mismas *fpl*, *L.Am.* ustedes mismos, ustedes mismas; *formal* ustedes mismos, ustedes mismas; **did you hurt ~?** ¿os hicisteis / se hicieron daño?; **when you see ~ in the mirror** cuando os veis / se ven en el espejo; **by ~** *(alone)* solos; *(without help)* vosotros solos, *L.Am.* ustedes solos, ustedes mismos; *formal* ustedes solos, ustedes mismos

youth [ju:θ] *n* juventud *f*; *(young man)* joven *m/f*

'youth club club *m* juvenil

youth·ful ['ju:θfəl] *adj* joven; *fashion, idealism* juvenil

'youth hos·tel albergue *m* juvenil

Yu·go·sla·vi·a [ju:gə'slɑ:vɪə] Yugoslavia

Yu·go·sla·vi·an [ju:gə'slɑ:vɪən] **1** *adj* yugoslavo **2** *n* yugoslavo(-a) *m(f)*

yup·pie ['jʌpɪ] F yupi *m/f*

Z

zap [zæp] *v/t (pret & pp* **-ped***)* F *(*COMPUT*: delete)* borrar; *(kill)* liquidar F; *(hit)* golpear; *(send)* enviar

♦ **zap along** *v/i* F *(move fast)* volar F

zapped [zæpt] *adj* F *(exhausted)* hecho polvo F

zap·per ['zæpər] *for changing TV channels* telemando *m*, mando *m* a distancia

zap·py ['zæpɪ] *adj* F *car, pace* rápido; *(lively, energetic)* vivo

zeal [zi:l] celo *m*

ze·bra ['zebrə] cebra *f*

ze·ro ['zɪrou] cero *m*; **10 degrees**

below ~ 10 bajo cero

♦ **zero in on** *v/t (identify)* centrarse en

ze·ro 'growth crecimiento *m* cero

zest [zest] entusiasmo *m*

zig·zag ['zɪgzæg] **1** *n* zigzag *m* **2** *v/i (pret & pp* **-ged***)* zigzaguear

zilch [zɪltʃ] F nada de nada

zinc [zɪŋk] cinc *m*

zip [zɪp] *Br* cremallera *f*

♦ **zip up** *v/t (pret & pp* **-ped***)* *dress, jacket* cerrar la cremallera de; COMPUT compactar

'zip code código *m* postal

zip·per ['zɪpər] cremallera *f*

zucchini

zit [zɪt] F *on face* grano *m*

zo·di·ac [ˈzoʊdɪæk] zodiaco *m*; *signs of the* ~ signos *mpl* del zodiaco

zom·bie [ˈzɑːmbɪ] F (*idiot*) estúpi-do(-a) *m(f)* F, *feel like a* ~ (*exhausted*) sentirse como un zombi

zone [zoʊn] zona *f*

zonked [zɑːŋkt] *adj* P (*exhausted*) molido P

zoo [zuː] zoo *m*

zo·o·log·i·cal [zuːəˈlɑːdʒɪkl] *adj* zoo-lógico

zo·ol·o·gist [zuːˈɑːlədʒɪst] zoólo-go(-a) *m(f)*

zo·ol·o·gy [zuːˈɑːlədʒɪ] zoología *f*

zoom [zuːm] *v/i* F (*move fast*) ir zum-bando F

♦ **zoom in on** *v/t* PHOT hacer un zoom sobre

zoom 'lens zoom *m*

zuc·chi·ni [zuːˈkiːnɪ] calabacín *m*

Z

Spanish verb conjugations

In the following conjugation patterns verb stems are shown in normal type and verb endings in *italic* type. Irregular forms are indicated by **bold** type.

Notes on the formation of tenses.

The following stems can be used to generate derived forms.

Stem forms	Derived forms
I. From the **Present indicative**, *3rd pers sg* (mand*a*, vend*e*, recib*e*)	**Imperative** *2nd pers. sg* (¡mand*a*! ¡vend*e*! ¡recib*e*!)
II. From the **Present subjunctive**, *2nd* and *3rd pers sg* and all plural forms (mand*es*, mand*e*, mand*emos*, mand*éis*, mand*en* – vend*as*, vend*a*, vend*amos*, vend*áis*, vend*an* – recib*as*, recib*a*, recib*amos*, recib*áis*, recib*an*)	**Imperative** *1st pers pl, 3rd pers sg* and *pl* as well as the negative imperative of the *2nd pers sg* and *pl* (no mand*es*, mand*e* Vd., mand*emos*, no mand*éis*, mand*en* Vds. – no vend*as*, vend*a* Vd., vend*amos*, no vend*áis*, vend*an* Vds. – no recib*as etc*)
III. From the **Preterite**, *3rd pers pl* (mand*aron*, vend*ieron*, recib*ieron*)	a) **Imperfect Subjunctive I** by changing ...ron to ...*ra* (mand*ara*, vend*iera*, recib*iera*) b) **Imperfect Subjunctive II** by changing ...ron to ...*se* (mand*ase*, vend*iese*, recib*iese*) c) **Future Subjunctive** by changing ...ron to ...*re* (mand*are*, vend*iere*, recib*iere*)
IV. From the **Infinitive** (mand*ar*, vend*er*, recib*ir*)	a) **Imperative** *2nd pers pl* by changing ...r to ...*d* (mand*ad*, vend*ed*, recib*id*) b) **Present participle** by changing ...ar to ...*ando*, ...er and ...ir to ...*iendo* (or sometimes ...*yendo*) (mand*ando*, vend*iendo*, recib*iendo*) c) **Future** by adding the *Present* tense endings of **haber** (mandar*é*, vender*é*, recibir*é*) d) **Conditional** by adding the *Imperfect* endings of **haber** (mandar*ía*, vender*ía*, recibir*ía*)
V. From the **Past participle** (mand*ado*, vend*ido*, recib*ido*)	all **compound tenses** by placing a form of **haber** or **ser** in front of the participle.

First Conjugation

<1a> mandar. No change to the written or spoken form of the stem.

Simple tenses

Indicative

	Present	Imperfect	Preterite
sg	mando	mandaba	mandé
	mandas	mandabas	mandaste
	manda	mandaba	mandó
pl	mandamos	mandábamos	mandamos
	mandáis	mandabais	mandasteis
	mandan	mandaban	mandaron

	Future	Conditional
sg	mandaré	mandaría
	mandarás	mandarías
	mandará	mandaría
pl	mandaremos	mandaríamos
	mandaréis	mandaríais
	mandarán	mandarían

Subjunctive

	Present	Imperfect I	Imperfect II
sg	mande	mandara	mandase
	mandes	mandaras	mandases
	mande	mandara	mandase
pl	mandemos	mandáramos	mandásemos
	mandéis	mandarais	mandaseis
	manden	mandaran	mandasen

	Future	Imperative
sg	mandare	—
	mandares	manda (no mandes)
	mandare	mande Vd.
pl	mandáremos	mandemos
	mandareis	mandad (no mandéis)
	mandaren	manden Vds.

Infinitive: mandar
Present participle: mandando
Past participle: mandado

Compound tenses

1. **Active forms:** the conjugated form of **_haber_** is placed before the *Past participle* (which does not change):

Indicative

Perfect	*he* mand*ado*	**Future perfect**	*habré* mand*ado*
Pluperfect	*había* mand*ado*	**Past conditional**	*habría* mand*ado*
Past anterior	*hube* mand*ado*		
Past infinitive	*haber* mand*ado*	**Past gerundive**	*habiendo* mand*ado*

Subjunctive

Perfect	*haya* mand*ado*	**Future perfect**	*hubiere* mand*ado*
Pluperfect	*hubiera* mand*ado*		
	hubiese mand*ado*		

2. **Passive forms:** the conjugated form of **_ser_** (or **_haber_**) is placed before the *Past participle* (which does not change):

Indicative

Present	*soy* mand*ado*	**Past anterior**	*hube sido* mand*ado*
Imperfect	*era* mand*ado*	**Future**	*seré* mand*ado*
Preterite	*fui* mand*ado*	**Future perfect**	*habré sido* mand*ado*
Perfect	*he sido* mand*ado*	**Conditional**	*sería* mand*ado*
Pluperfect	*había sido* mand*ado*	**Past conditional**	*habría sido* mand*ado*

Infinitive		Gerundive	
Present	*ser* mand*ado etc*	**Present**	*siendo* mand*ado*
Past	*haber sido* mand*ado*	**Past**	*habiendo sido* mand*ado*

Subjunctive

Present	*sea* mand*ado*	**Pluperfect**	*hubiera sido* mand*ado*
			hubiese sido mand*ado*
Imperfect	*fuera* mand*ado*		
	fuese mand*ado*		
Future	*fuere* mand*ado*	**Future perfect**	*hubiere sido* mand*ado*
Past	*haya sido* mand*ado*		

	Infinitive	Present Indicative	Present Subjunctive	Preterite
\<1b\>	**cambiar.** Model for all ...*iar* verbs, unless formed like *variar* \<1c\>.			
		camb*io*	camb*ie*	camb*ié*
		camb*ias*	camb*ies*	camb*iaste*
		camb*ia*	camb*ie*	camb*ió*
		camb*iamos*	camb*iemos*	camb*iamos*
		camb*iáis*	camb*iéis*	camb*iasteis*
		camb*ian*	camb*ien*	camb*iaron*

	Infinitive	Present Indicative	Present Subjunctive	Preterite
\<1c\>	**variar.** *i* becomes *í* when the stem is stressed.			
		varío	varíe	varié
		varías	varíes	variaste
		varía	varíe	varió
		variamos	variemos	variamos
		variáis	variéis	variasteis
		varían	varíen	variaron
\<1d\>	**evacuar.** Model for all ...*uar* verbs, unless formed like *acentuar* \<1e\>.			
		evacuo	evacue	evacué
		evacuas	evacues	evacuaste
		evacua	evacue	evacuó
		evacuamos	evacuemos	evacuamos
		evacuáis	evacuéis	evacuasteis
		evacuan	evacuen	evacuaron
\<1e\>	**acentuar.** *u* becomes *ú* when the stem is stressed.			
		acentúo	acentúe	acentué
		acentúas	acentúes	acentuaste
		acentúa	acentúe	acentuó
		acentuamos	acentuemos	acentuamos
		acentuáis	acentuéis	acentuasteis
		acentúan	acentúen	acentuaron
\<1f\>	**cruzar.** Final *z* in the stem becomes *c* before *e*. Model for all ...*zar* verbs.			
		cruzo	cruce	crucé
		cruzas	cruces	cruzaste
		cruza	cruce	cruzó
		cruzamos	crucemos	cruzamos
		cruzáis	crucéis	cruzasteis
		cruzan	crucen	cruzaron
\<1g\>	**tocar.** Final *c* in the stem becomes *qu* before *e*. Model for all ...*car* verbs.			
		toco	toque	toqué
		tocas	toques	tocaste
		toca	toque	tocó
		tocamos	toquemos	tocamos
		tocáis	toquéis	tocasteis
		tocan	toquen	tocaron

	Infinitive	Present Indicative	Present Subjunctive	Preterite

<1h> **pagar.** Final *g* in the stem becomes *gu* (*u* is silent) before *e*. Model for all ...*gar* verbs.

		pago	pague	pagué
		pagas	pagues	pagaste
		paga	pague	pagó
		pagamos	paguemos	pagamos
		pagáis	paguéis	pagasteis
		pagan	paguen	pagaron

<1i> **fraguar.** Final *gu* in the stem becomes *gü* before *e* (*u* with dieresis is pronounced). Model for all ...*guar* verbs.

		fraguo	fragüe	fragüé
		fraguas	fragües	fraguaste
		fragua	fragüe	fraguó
		fraguamos	fragüemos	fraguamos
		fraguáis	fragüéis	fraguasteis
		fraguan	fragüen	fraguaron

<1k> **pensar.** Stressed *e* in the stem becomes *ie*.

		pienso	piense	pensé
		piensas	pienses	pensaste
		piensa	piense	pensó
		pensamos	pensemos	pensamos
		pensáis	penséis	pensasteis
		piensan	piensen	pensaron

<1l> **errar.** Stressed *e* in the stem becomes *ye* (because it comes at the beginning of the word).

		yerro	yerre	erré
		yerras	yerres	erraste
		yerra	yerre	erró
		erramos	erremos	erramos
		erráis	erréis	errasteis
		yerran	yerren	erraron

<1m> **contar.** Stressed *o* of the stem becomes *ue* (*u* is pronounced).

		cuento	cuente	conté
		cuentas	cuentes	contaste
		cuenta	cuente	contó
		contamos	contemos	contamos
		contáis	contéis	contasteis
		cuentan	cuenten	contaron

	Infinitive	Present Indicative	Present Subjunctive	Preterite

<1n> **agorar.** Stressed *o* of the stem becomes *üe* (*u* with dieresis is pronounced).

	ag*ü*e*ro*	ag*ü*e*re*	ago*ré*
	ag*ü*e*ras*	ag*ü*e*res*	ago*raste*
	ag*ü*e*ra*	ag*ü*e*re*	ago*ró*
	ago*ramos*	ago*remos*	ago*ramos*
	ago*ráis*	ago*réis*	ago*rasteis*
	ag*ü*e*ran*	ag*ü*e*ren*	ago*raron*

<1o> **jugar.** Stressed *u* in the stem becomes *ue*; final *g* of the stem becomes *gu* before *e*: (see <1h>); *conjugar*, *enjugar* and *enjugarse* are regular.

	j*ue*g*o*	j*ue*g*ue*	jug*ué*
	j*ue*g*as*	j*ue*g*ues*	jug*aste*
	j*ue*g*a*	j*ue*g*ue*	jug*ó*
	jug*amos*	jug*uemos*	jug*amos*
	jug*áis*	jug*uéis*	jug*asteis*
	j*ue*g*an*	j*ue*g*uen*	jug*aron*

<1p> **estar.** *Present indicative 1st pers sg in ...oy, otherwise regular, but note the stressed a; the Present subjunctive has a stress on the e in the endings (apart from 1st pers pl); Preterite etc as <21>. Otherwise regular.*

	esto*y*	est*é*	est*uve*
	est*ás*	est*és*	est*uviste*
	est*á*	est*é*	est*uvo*
	est*amos*	est*emos*	est*uvimos*
	est*áis*	est*éis*	est*uvisteis*
	est*án*	est*én*	est*uvieron*

<1q> **andar.** *Preterite and derived forms like estar as in <21>. Otherwise regular.*

	and*o*	and*e*	and*uve*
	and*as*	and*es*	and*uviste*
	and*a*	and*e*	and*uvo*
	and*amos*	and*emos*	and*uvimos*
	and*áis*	and*éis*	and*uvisteis*
	and*an*	and*en*	and*uvieron*

<1r> **dar.** *Present indicative 1st pers sg in ...oy, otherwise regular. Present subjunctive 1st and 3rd pers sg takes an accent. Preterite etc follow the regular second conjugation. Otherwise regular.*

	do*y*	d*é*	d*i*
	d*as*	d*es*	d*iste*
	d*a*	d*é*	d*io*
	d*amos*	d*emos*	d*imos*
	d*áis*	d*eis*	d*isteis*
	d*an*	d*en*	d*ieron*

Second Conjugation

<2a> **vender.** No change to the written or spoken form of the stem.

Simple tenses

Indicative

	Present	**Imperfect**	**Preterite**
sg	vendo	vendía	vendí
	vendes	vendías	vendiste
	vende	vendía	vendió
pl	vendemos	vendíamos	vendimos
	vendéis	vendíais	vendisteis
	venden	vendían	vendieron

	Future	**Conditional**
sg	venderé	vendería
	venderás	venderías
	venderá	vendería
pl	venderemos	venderíamos
	venderéis	venderíais
	venderán	venderían

Subjunctive

	Present	**Imperfect I**	**Imperfect II**
sg	venda	vendiera	vendiese
	vendas	vendieras	vendieses
	venda	vendiera	vendiese
pl	vendamos	vendiéramos	vendiésemos
	vendáis	vendierais	vendieseis
	vendan	vendieran	vendiesen

	Future	**Imperative**
sg	vendiere	—
	vendieres	vende (no vendas)
	vendiere	venda Vd.
pl	vendiéremos	vendamos
	vendiereis	vended (no vendáis)
	vendieren	vendan Vds.

Infinitive: vender
Present participle: vendiendo
Past participle: vendido

Compound tenses

Formed with the *Past participle* together with **haber** and **ser**, see <1a>.

	Infinitive	Present Indicative	Present Subjunctive	Preterite

<2b> **vencer.** Final *c* of the stem becomes *z* before *a* and *o*. Model for all ...*cer* verbs where the ...*cer* is preceded by a consonant.

		Present Indicative	Present Subjunctive	Preterite
		venzo	venza	vencí
		vences	venzas	venciste
		vence	venza	venció
		vencemos	venzamos	vencimos
		vencéis	venzáis	vencisteis
		vencen	venzan	vencieron

<2c> **coger.** Final *g* of the stem becomes *j* before *a* and *o*. Model for all ...*ger* verbs.

cojo	coja	cogí
coges	cojas	cogiste
coge	coja	cogió
cogemos	cojamos	cogimos
cogéis	cojáis	cogisteis
cogen	cojan	cogieron

<2d> **merecer.** Final *c* of the stem becomes *zc* before *a* and *o*.

merezco	merezca	merecí
mereces	merezcas	mereciste
merece	merezca	mereció
merecemos	merezcamos	merecimos
merecéis	merezcáis	merecisteis
merecen	merezcan	merecieron

<2e> **creer.** Unstressed *i* between two vowels becomes *y*. Past participle: *creído*. Present participle: *creyendo*.

creo	crea	creí
crees	creas	creíste
cree	crea	creyó
creemos	creamos	creímos
creéis	creáis	creísteis
creen	crean	creyeron

<2f> **tañer.** Unstressed *i* is omitted after *ñ* and *ll*; compare <3h> Present participle: *tañendo*.

taño	taña	tañí
tañes	tañas	tañiste
tañe	taña	tañó
tañemos	tañamos	tañimos
tañéis	tañáis	tañisteis
tañen	tañan	tañeron

	Infinitive	Present Indicative	Present Subjunctive	Preterite

<2g> perder. Stressed *e* in the stem becomes *ie*; model for many other verbs.

		pierdo	pierda	perdí
		pierdes	pierdas	perdiste
		pierde	pierda	perdió
		perdemos	perdamos	perdimos
		perdéis	perdáis	perdisteis
		pierden	pierdan	perdieron

<2h> mover. Stressed *o* in the stem becomes *ue*. ...*olver* verbs form their *Past participle* with ...*uelto*.

		muevo	mueva	moví
		mueves	muevas	moviste
		mueve	mueva	movió
		movemos	movamos	movimos
		movéis	mováis	movisteis
		mueven	muevan	movieron

<2i> oler. Stressed *o* in the stem becomes *hue*... (when it comes at the beginning of the word).

		huelo	huela	olí
		hueles	huelas	oliste
		huele	huela	olió
		olemos	olamos	olimos
		oléis	oláis	olisteis
		huelen	huelan	olieron

<2k> haber. Many irregular forms. In the *Future* and *Conditional* the *e* after the stem *hab*... is dropped. Future: *habré.* Imperative *2nd pers sg: he.*

		he	haya	hube
		has	hayas	hubiste
		ha	haya	hubo
		hemos	hayamos	hubimos
		habéis	hayáis	hubisteis
		han	hayan	hubieron

<2l> tener. Irregular in most forms. In the *Future* and *Conditional* the *e* coming after the stem is dropped and a *d* is inserted. Future: *tendré.* Imperative *2nd pers sg: ten.*

		tengo	tenga	tuve
		tienes	tengas	tuviste
		tiene	tenga	tuvo
		tenemos	tengamos	tuvimos
		tenéis	tengáis	tuvisteis
		tienen	tengan	tuvieron

	Infinitive	Present Indicative	Present Subjunctive	Preterite

\<2m\> caber. Irregular in many forms. In the *Future* and *Conditional* the *e* coming after the stem is dropped. Future: *cabré*.

	quep*o*	quep*a*	*cupe*
	cab*es*	quep*as*	*cupiste*
	cab*e*	quep*a*	*cupo*
	cab*emos*	quep*amos*	*cupimos*
	cab*éis*	quep*áis*	*cupisteis*
	cab*en*	quep*an*	*cupieron*

\<2n\> saber. Irregular in many forms. In the *Future* and *Conditional* the *e* coming after the stem is dropped. Future: *sabré*.

	s*é*	sep*a*	*supe*
	sab*es*	sep*as*	*supiste*
	sab*e*	sep*a*	*supo*
	sab*emos*	sep*amos*	*supimos*
	sab*éis*	sep*áis*	*supisteis*
	sab*en*	sep*an*	*supieron*

\<2o\> caer. In the *Present* ...ig... is inserted after the stem. Unstressed *i* between vowels changes to *y* as with \<2e\>. Past participle: *caído*. Present participle: *cayendo*.

	cai*go*	cai*ga*	*caí*
	ca*es*	cai*gas*	*caíste*
	ca*e*	cai*ga*	*cayó*
	ca*emos*	cai*gamos*	*caímos*
	ca*éis*	cai*gáis*	*caísteis*
	ca*en*	cai*gan*	*cayeron*

\<2p\> traer. In the *Present* ...ig... is inserted after the stem. The *Preterite* ends in ...je. In the *Present participle* i changes to *y*. Past participle: *traído*. Present participle: *trayendo*.

	trai*go*	trai*ga*	*traje*
	tra*es*	trai*gas*	*trajiste*
	tra*e*	trai*ga*	*trajo*
	tra*emos*	trai*gamos*	*trajimos*
	tra*éis*	trai*gáis*	*trajisteis*
	tra*en*	trai*gan*	*trajeron*

\<2q\> valer. In the *Present* ...g... is inserted after the stem. In the *Future* and *Conditional* the *e* coming after the stem is dropped and a ...d... inserted. Future: *valdré*.

	val*go*	val*ga*	*valí*
	val*es*	val*gas*	*valiste*
	val*e*	val*ga*	*valió*
	val*emos*	val*gamos*	*valimos*
	val*éis*	val*gáis*	*valisteis*
	val*en*	val*gan*	*valieron*

	Infinitive	Present Indicative	Present Subjunctive	Preterite

<2r> **poner.** ...*g*... is inserted in the *Present*. Irregular in the *Preterite* and *Past participle*. In the *Future* and *Conditional* the *e* coming after the stem is dropped and a ...*d*... inserted. Future: *pondré*. Past participle: *puesto*. Imperative *2nd pers sg*: *pon*.

	pon*g*o	pon*g*a	*pus*e
	pon*es*	pon*g*as	*pus*iste
	pon*e*	pon*g*a	*pus*o
	pon*emos*	pon*g*amos	*pus*imos
	pon*éis*	pon*g*áis	*pus*isteis
	pon*en*	pon*g*an	*pus*ieron

<2s> **hacer.** In the *1st* person of the *Present Indicative* and *Subjunctive* g replaces c. Irregular in the *Preterite* and *Past participle*. In the *Future* and *Conditional* the *ce* is dropped. In the *Imperative sg* just the stem is used with ...*c* changing to ...*z*. Future: *haré*. Imperative *2nd pers sg*: *haz*. Past participle: *hecho*.

	ha*g*o	ha*g*a	*hic*e
	ha*ces*	ha*g*as	*hic*iste
	ha*ce*	ha*g*a	*hiz*o
	ha*cemos*	ha*g*amos	*hic*imos
	ha*céis*	ha*g*áis	*hic*isteis
	ha*cen*	ha*g*an	*hic*ieron

<2t> **poder.** Stressed *o* in the stem changes to ...*ue*... in the *Present* and the *Imperative*. Irregular in the *Preterite* and *Present participle*. In the *Future* and *Conditional* the *e* coming after the stem is dropped. Future: *podré*. Present participle: *pudiendo*.

	pu*e*do	pu*e*da	*pud*e
	pu*e*des	pu*e*das	*pud*iste
	pu*e*de	pu*e*da	*pud*o
	pod*emos*	pod*amos*	*pud*imos
	pod*éis*	pod*áis*	*pud*isteis
	pu*e*den	pu*e*dan	*pud*ieron

<2u> **querer.** Stressed *e* in the stem changes to *ie* in the *Present* and *Imperative*. Irregular in the *Preterite*. In the *Future* and *Conditional* the *e* coming after the stem is dropped. Future: *querré*.

	qui*e*ro	qui*e*ra	*quis*e
	qui*e*res	qui*e*ras	*quis*iste
	qui*e*re	qui*e*ra	*quis*o
	quer*emos*	quer*amos*	*quis*imos
	quer*éis*	quer*áis*	*quis*isteis
	qui*e*ren	qui*e*ran	*quis*ieron

Infinitive	Present Indicative	Present Subjunctive	Preterite

<2v> **ver.** *Present indicative 1st pers sg, Present subjunctive* and *Imperfect* are formed on the stem *ve...,* otherwise formation is regular using the shortened stem *v...* Irregular in the *Past participle*. Past participle: *visto.*

veo	vea	vi
ves	veas	viste
ve	vea	vio
vemos	veamos	vimos
veis	veáis	visteis
ven	vean	vieron

Infinitive	Present Indicative	Present Subjunctive	Imperfect Indicative	Preterite

<2w> **ser.** Totally irregular with several different stems being used. Past participle: *sido.* Imperative *2nd pers sg: sé. 2nd pers pl: sed.*

soy	sea	era	fui
eres	seas	eras	fuiste
es	sea	era	fue
somos	seamos	éramos	fuimos
sois	seáis	erais	fuisteis
son	sean	eran	fueron

<2x> **placer.** Used almost exclusively in the *3rd pers sg.* Irregular forms: *Present subjunctive* ple*ga* and ple*gue* as well as plazca; *Preterite* plu*go* (or plació), plu*guieron* (or placieron); *Imperfect subjunctive* plu*guiera,* plu*guiese* (or placiera, placiese); *Future subjunctive* plu*guiere* (or placiere).

<2y> **yacer.** Used mainly on gravestones and so used primarily in the *3rd pers.* The *Present indicative 1st pers sg* and *Present subjunctive* have three forms. The *Imperative* is regular; just the stem with *c* changing to *z. Present indicative:* ya*zco,* ya*zgo,* ya*go,* yaces etc; *Present subjunctive:* ya*zca,* ya*zga,* ya*ga* etc; *Imperative* yace and ya*z.*

<2z> **raer.** The regular forms of the *Present indicative 1st pers sg* and *Present subjunctive* are less common that the forms with inserted ...*ig...* as in <2o>: ra*igo,* ra*iga;* but also rayo, raya (less common). Otherwise regular.

<2za> **roer.** As well as their regular forms the *Present indicative 1st pers sg* and *Present subjunctive* have the less common forms: ro*igo,* ro*iga,* royo, roya.

Third Conjugation

<3a> recibir. No change to the written or spoken form of the stem.

Simple tenses

Indicative

	Present	**Imperfect**	**Preterite**
sg	recibo	recibía	recibí
	recibes	recibías	recibiste
	recibe	recibía	recibió
pl	recibimos	recibíamos	recibimos
	recibís	recibíais	recibisteis
	reciben	recibían	recibieron

	Future	**Conditional**
sg	recibiré	recibiría
	recibirás	recibirías
	recibirá	recibiría
pl	recibiremos	recibiríamos
	recibiréis	recibiríais
	recibirán	recibirían

Subjunctive

	Present	**Imperfect I**	**Imperfect II**
sg	reciba	recibiera	recibiese
	recibas	recibieras	recibieses
	reciba	recibiera	recibiese
pl	recibamos	recibiéramos	recibiésemos
	recibáis	recibierais	recibieseis
	reciban	recibieran	recibiesen

	Future	**Imperative**
sg	recibiere	—
	recibieres	recibe (no recibas)
	recibiere	reciba Vd.
pl	recibiéremos	recibamos
	recibiereis	recibid (no recibáis)
	recibieren	reciban Vds.

Infinitive: recibir
Present participle: recibiendo
Past participle: recibido

Compound tenses

Formed with the *Past participle* together with **haber** and **ser**, see <1a>.

	Infinitive	Present Indicative	Present Subjunctive	Preterite

<3b> **esparcir.** Final *c* of the stem becomes *z* before *a* and *o*.

	esparzo	esparza	esparcí
	esparces	esparzas	esparciste
	esparce	esparza	esparció
	esparcimos	esparzamos	esparcimos
	esparcís	esparzáis	esparcisteis
	esparcen	esparzan	esparcieron

<3c> **dirigir.** Final *g* of the stem becomes *j* before *a* and *o*.

	dirijo	dirija	dirigí
	diriges	dirijas	dirigiste
	dirige	dirija	dirigió
	dirigimos	dirijamos	dirigimos
	dirigís	dirijáis	dirigisteis
	dirigen	dirijan	dirigieron

<3d> **distinguir.** Final *gu* of the stem becomes *g* before *a* and *o*.

	distingo	distinga	distinguí
	distingues	distingas	distinguiste
	distingue	distinga	distinguió
	distinguimos	distingamos	distinguimos
	distinguís	distingáis	distinguisteis
	distinguen	distingan	distinguieron

<3e> **delinquir.** Final *qu* of the stem becomes *c* before *a* and *o*.

	delinco	delinca	delinquí
	delinques	delincas	delinquiste
	delinque	delinca	delinquió
	delinquimos	delincamos	delinquimos
	delinquís	delincáis	delinquisteis
	delinquen	delincan	delinquieron

<3f> **lucir.** Final *c* of the stem becomes *zc* before *a* and *o*.

	luzco	luzca	lucí
	luces	luzcas	luciste
	luce	luzca	lució
	lucimos	luzcamos	lucimos
	lucís	luzcáis	lucisteis
	lucen	luzcan	lucieron

<3g> **concluir.** A *y* is inserted after the stem unless the ending begins with *i*. Past participle: *concluido*. Present participle: *concluyendo*.

	concluyo	concluya	concluí
	concluyes	concluyas	concluiste
	concluye	concluya	concluyó
	concluimos	concluyamos	concluimos
	concluís	concluyáis	concluisteis
	concluyen	concluyan	concluyeron

	Infinitive	Present Indicative	Present Subjunctive	Preterite

<3h> **gruñir.** Unstressed *i* is dropped after *ñ*, *ll* and *ch*. Likewise *mullir*: *mulló*, *mulleron*, *mullendo*; *henchir*: *hinchó*, *hincheron*, *hinchendo* Present participle: *gruñendo*.

	gruño	gruña	gruñí
	gruñes	gruñas	gruñiste
	gruñe	gruña	gruñó
	gruñimos	gruñamos	gruñimos
	gruñís	gruñáis	gruñisteis
	gruñen	gruñan	gruñeron

<3i> **sentir.** Stressed *e* of the stem becomes *ie*; unstressed *e* remains unchanged before endings starting with *i*, but before other endings it changes to ...*i*...; likewise *adquirir*: stressed *i* of the stem becomes *ie*; unstressed *i* remains unchanged in all forms. Present participle: *sintiendo*.

	siento	sienta	sentí
	sientes	sientas	sentiste
	siente	sienta	sintió
	sentimos	sintamos	sentimos
	sentís	sintáis	sentisteis
	sienten	sientan	sintieron

<3k> **dormir.** Stressed *o* of the stem becomes *ue*; unstressed *o* is unchanged when the ending starts with *i*; otherwise it changes to ...*u*... Present participle: *durmiendo*.

	duermo	duerma	dormí
	duermes	duermas	dormiste
	duerme	duerma	durmió
	dormimos	durmamos	dormimos
	dormís	durmáis	dormisteis
	duermen	duerman	durmieron

<3l> **medir.** The *e* of the stem is kept if the ending contains an *i*. Otherwise it changes to ...*i*... whether stressed or unstressed. Present participle: *midiendo*.

	mido	mida	medí
	mides	midas	mediste
	mide	mida	midió
	medimos	midamos	medimos
	medís	midáis	medisteis
	miden	midan	midieron

	Infinitive	Present Indicative	Present Subjunctive	Preterite

\<3m\> reír. As *medir* \<3l\>; when *e* changes to *i* any second *i* belonging to the ending is dropped. Past participle: *reído*. Present participle: *riendo*.

r*í*o	r*í*a	re*í*
r*í*es	r*í*as	re*í*ste
r*í*e	r*í*a	ri*ó*
re*í*mos	r*í*amos	re*í*mos
re*í*s	ri*á*is	re*í*steis
r*í*en	r*í*an	rieron

\<3n\> erguir. As *medir* in the *Present indicative, Subjunctive* and *Imperative.* Other forms follow *sentir* with initial *ie...* changing to *ye...* Present participle: *irguiendo*. Imperative: *irgue, yergue*.

irg*o*, yerg*o*	irg*a*, yerg*a*	ergu*í*
irgu*es*, yergu*es*	irg*as*, yerg*as*	erguiste
irgu*e*, yergu*e*	irg*a*, yerg*a*	irgui*ó*
ergu*i*mos	irg*amos*, yerg*amos*	erguimos
ergu*í*s	irg*áis*, yerg*áis*	erguisteis
irgu*en*, yergu*en*	irg*an*, yerg*an*	irgu*i*eron

\<3o\> conducir. Final *c* of the stem, as with *lucir* (3f), becomes *zc* before *a* and *o*. *Preterite* is irregular with *...je*.

conduz*c*o	conduz*c*a	conduje
conduces	conduz*c*as	conduj*i*ste
conduce	conduz*c*a	conduj*o*
conduc*i*mos	conduz*c*amos	conduj*i*mos
conduc*í*s	conduz*c*áis	conduj*i*steis
conducen	conduz*c*an	conduj*e*ron

\<3p\> decir. In the *Present* and *Imperative e* and *i* are changed, as with *medir*; in the *Present indicative 1st pers sg* and in the *Present subjunctive c* becomes *g*. Irregular *Future* and *Conditional* based on a shortened *Infinitive. Preterite* has *je.* Future: *diré*. Past participle: *dicho*. Present participle: *diciendo*. Imperative *2nd pers sg: di*.

dig*o*	dig*a*	dije
dices	dig*as*	dij*i*ste
dice	dig*a*	dij*o*
dec*i*mos	dig*amos*	dij*i*mos
dec*í*s	dig*áis*	dij*i*steis
dicen	dig*an*	dij*e*ron

	Infinitive	Present Indicative	Present Subjunctive	Preterite

<3q> **oír.** In the *Present indicative 1st pers sg* and *Present subjunctive ...ig...* is inserted after the *o...* of the stem. Unstressed *...i...* changes to *...y...* when coming between two vowels. Past participle: *oído*. Present participle: *oyendo*.

oigo	oiga	oí
oyes	oigas	oíste
oye	oiga	oyó
oímos	oigamos	oímos
oís	oigáis	oísteis
oyen	oigan	oyeron

<3r> **salir.** In the *Present indicative 1st pers sg* and the *Present subjunctive* a *...g...* is inserted after the stem. In the *Future* and *Conditional* the *i* is replaced by *d*. Future: *saldré*. Imperative: *2nd pers sg: sal*.

salgo	salga	salí
sales	salgas	saliste
sale	salga	salió
salimos	salgamos	salimos
salís	salgáis	salisteis
salen	salgan	salieron

	Infinitive	Present Indicative	Subjunctive	Imperfect Indicative	Preterite

<3s> **venir.** In the *Present* two changes: either a *...g...* is inserted after the stem or *e, ie* and *i* follow the same changes as *sentir*. In the *Future* and *Conditional* the *i* is dropped and replaced by *d*. Future: *vendré*. Present participle: *viniendo*. Imperative *2nd pers sg: ven*.

vengo	venga	venía	vine
vienes	vengas	venías	viniste
viene	venga	venía	vino
venimos	vengamos	veníamos	vinimos
venís	vengáis	veníais	vinisteis
vienen	vengan	venían	vinieron

<3t> **ir.** Totally irregular with several different stems being used. Present participle: *yendo*

voy	vaya	iba	fui
vas	vayas	ibas	fuiste
va	vaya	iba	fue
vamos	vayamos	íbamos	fuimos
vais	vayáis	ibais	fuisteis
van	vayan	iban	fueron

Imperative: **ve** (no **vayas**), **vaya** Vd, **vamos**, **id** (no **vayáis**), **vayan** Vds.

Notas sobre el verbo inglés

a) Conjugación

1. **El tiempo presente** tiene la misma forma que el infinitivo en todas las personas menos la **3ª** del singular; en ésta, se añade una *-s* al infinitivo, p.ej. *he brings*, o se añade *-es* si el infinitivo termina en sibilante (ch, sh, ss, zz), p.ej. *he passes*. Esta *s* tiene dos pronunciaciones distintas: tras consonante sorda se pronuncia sorda, p.ej. *he paints* [peɪnts]; tras consonante sonora se pronuncia sonora, *he sends* [sendz]; *-es* se pronuncia también sonora, sea la *e* parte de la desinencia o letra final del infinitivo, p.ej. *he washes* ['wɑːʃɪz], *he urges* ['ɜːrdʒɪz]. Los verbos que terminan en *-y* la cambian en *-ies* en la tercera persona, p.ej. *he worries, he tries*, pero son regulares los verbos que en el infinitivo tienen una vocal delante de la *-y*, p.ej. *he plays*. El verbo *to be* es irregular en todas las personas: *I am, you are, he is, we are, you are, they are*. Tres verbos más tienen forma especial para la tercera persona del singular: *do-he does, go-he goes, have-he has*.

   En los demás tiempos, todas las personas son iguales. **El pretérito** y **el participio del pasado** se forman añadiendo *-ed* al infinitivo, p.ej. *I passed, passed*, o añadiendo *-d* a los infinitivos que terminan en *-e*, p.ej. *I faced, faced*. (Hay muchos verbos irregulares: v. abajo). Esta *-(e)d* se pronuncia generalmente como [t]: *passed* [pæst], *faced* [feɪst]; pero cuando se añade a un infinitivo que termina en consonante sonora o en sonido consonántico sonoro o en *r*, se pronuncia como [d]: *warmed* [wɔːrmd], *moved* [muːvd], *feared* [fɪrd]. Si el infinitivo termina en *-d* o *-t*, la desinencia *-ed* se pronuncia [ɪd]. Si el infinitivo termina en *-y*, ésta se cambia en *-ie*, antes de añadirse la *-d*: *try-tried* [traɪd], *pity-pitied* ['pɪtiːd]. **Los tiempos compuestos del pasado** se forman con el verbo auxiliar *have* y el participio del pasado, como en español: **perfecto** *I have faced*, **pluscuamperfecto** *I had faced*. Con el verbo auxiliar *will* (*shall*) y el infinitivo se forma **el futuro**, p.ej. *I shall face*; y con el verbo auxiliar *would* (*should*) y el infinitivo se forma **el condicional**, p.ej. *I should face*. En cada tiempo existe además una forma continua que se forma con el verbo *be* (= estar) y el participio del presente (v. abajo): *I am going, I was writing, I had been staying, I shall be waiting*, etc.

2. **El subjuntivo** ha dejado casi de existir en inglés, salvo en algún caso especial (*if I were you, so be it, it is proposed that a vote be taken*, etc.). En el presente, tiene en todas las personas la misma forma que el infinitivo, *that I go, that he go*, etc.

3. **El participio del presente** y **el gerundio** tienen la misma forma en inglés, añadiéndose al infinitivo la desinencia *-ing*: *painting, sending*. Pero **1)** Los verbos cuyo infinitivo termina en *-e* muda la pierden al añadir *-ing*, p.ej. *love-loving, write-writing* (excepciones que conservan la *-e*: *dye-dyeing, singe-singeing*); **2)** El participio del presente de los verbos *die, lie, vie*, etc. se escribe *dying, lying, vying*, etc.

4. Existe una clase de verbos ligeramente irregulares, que terminan en consonante simple precedida de vocal simple acentuada; en éstos, antes de añadir la desinencia *-ing* o *-ed*, se dobla la consonante:

lob	lob*bed*	lob*bing*	compel	compel*led*	compel*ling*
wed	wed*ded*	wed*ding*	control	control*led*	cont*rolling*
beg	beg*ged*	beg*ging*	bar	bar*red*	bar*ring*
step	step*ped*	step*ping*	stir	stir*red*	stir*ring*
quit	quit*ted*	quit*ting*			

Los verbos que terminan en *-l*, *-p*, aunque precedida de vocal átona, tienen doblada la consonante en los dos participios en el inglés escrito en Gran Bretaña, aunque no en el de Estados Unidos:

travel traveled, traveling,
Br travel*led*, *Br* travel*led*

Los verbos que terminan en *-c* la cambian en *-ck* al añadirse las desinencias *-ed*, *-ing*:

traffic traffi*cked* traffi*cking*

5. **La voz pasiva** se forma exactamente como en español, con el verbo *be* y el participio del pasado: *I am obliged*, *he was fined*, *they will be moved*, etc.

6. Cuando se dirige uno directamente a otra(s) persona(s) en inglés se emplea únicamente el pronombre *you*. *You* se traduce por el *tú*, *vosotros*, *usted* y *ustedes* del español.

b) Los verbos irregulares ingleses

Se citan las tres partes principales de cada verbo: infinitivo, pretérito, participio del pasado.

alight - alighted, alit - alighted, alit
arise - arose - arisen
awake - awoke - awoken, awaked
be (am, is, are) - was (were) - been
bear - bore - borne
beat - beat - beaten
become - became - become
begin - began - begun
behold - beheld - beheld
bend - bent - bent
beseech - besought, beseeched - besought, beseeched
bet - bet, betted - bet, betted
bid - bid - bid

bind - bound - bound
bite - bit - bitten
bleed - bled - bled
blow - blew - blown
break - broke - broken
breed - bred - bred
bring - brought - brought
broadcast - broadcast - broadcast
build - built - built
burn - burnt, burned - burnt, burned
burst - burst - burst
bust - bust(ed) - bust(ed)
buy - bought - bought
cast - cast - cast
catch - caught - caught

choose - chose - chosen
cleave (*cut*) - clove, cleft - cloven, cleft
cleave (*adhere*) - cleaved - cleaved
cling - clung - clung
come - came - come
cost (*v/i*) - cost - cost
creep - crept - crept
crow - crowed, crew - crowed
cut - cut - cut
deal - dealt - dealt
dig - dug - dug
do - did - done
draw - drew - drawn
dream - dreamt, dreamed - dreamt, dreamed
drink - drank - drunk
drive - drove - driven
dwell - dwelt, dwelled - dwelt, dwelled
eat - ate - eaten
fall - fell - fallen
feed - fed - fed
feel - felt - felt
fight - fought - fought
find - found - found
flee - fled - fled
fling - flung - flung
fly - flew - flown
forbear - forbore - forborne
forbid - forbad(e) - forbidden
forecast - forecast(ed) - forecast(ed)
forget - forgot - forgotten
forgive - forgave - forgiven
forsake - forsook - forsaken
freeze - froze - frozen
get - got - got, gotten
give - gave - given
go - went - gone
grind - ground - ground
grow - grew - grown
hang - hung, (*v/t*) hanged - hung, (*v/t*) hanged
have - had - had
hear - heard - heard

heave - heaved, NAUT hove - heaved, NAUT hove
hew - hewed - hewed, hewn
hide - hid - hidden
hit - hit - hit
hold - held - held
hurt - hurt - hurt
keep - kept - kept
kneel - knelt, kneeled - knelt, kneeled
know - knew - known
lay - laid - laid
lead - led - led
lean - leaned, leant - leaned, leant
leap - leaped, leapt - leaped, leapt
learn - learned, learnt - learned, learnt
leave - left - left
lend - lent - lent
let - let - let
lie - lay - lain
light - lighted, lit - lighted, lit
lose - lost - lost
make - made - made
mean - meant - meant
meet - met - met
mow - mowed - mowed, mown
pay - paid - paid
plead - pleaded, pled - pleaded, pled
prove - proved - proved, proven
put - put - put
quit - quit(ted) - quit(ted)
read - read [red] - read [red]
rend - rent - rent
rid - rid - rid
ride - rode - ridden
ring - rang - rung
rise - rose - risen
run - ran - run
saw - sawed - sawn, sawed
say - said - said
see - saw - seen
seek - sought - sought
sell - sold - sold
send - sent - sent
set - set - set

sew - sewed - sewed, sewn
shake - shook - shaken
shear - sheared - sheared, shorn
shed - shed - shed
shine - shone - shone
shit - shit(ted), shat - shit(ted), shat
shoe - shod - shod
shoot - shot - shot
show - showed - shown
shrink - shrank - shrunk
shut - shut - shut
sing - sang - sung
sink - sank - sunk
sit - sat - sat
slay - slew - slain
sleep - slept - slept
slide - slid - slid
sling - slung - slung
slink - slunk - slunk
slit - slit - slit
smell - smelt, smelled - smelt, smelled
smite - smote - smitten
sow - sowed - sown, sowed
speak - spoke - spoken
speed - sped, speeded - sped, speeded
spell - spelt, spelled - spelt, spelled
spend - spent - spent
spill - spilt, spilled - spilt, spilled
spin - spun, span - spun
spit - spat - spat
split - split - split
spoil - spoiled, spoilt - spoiled, spoilt
spread - spread - spread
spring - sprang, sprung - sprung

stand - stood - stood
stave - staved, stove - staved, stove
steal - stole - stolen
stick - stuck - stuck
sting - stung - stung
stink - stunk, stank - stunk
strew - strewed - strewed, strewn
stride - strode - stridden
strike - struck - struck
string - strung - strung
strive - strove - striven
swear - swore - sworn
sweep - swept - swept
swell - swelled - swollen
swim - swam - swum
swing - swung - swung
take - took - taken
teach - taught - taught
tear - tore - torn
tell - told - told
think - thought - thought
thrive - throve - thriven
throw - threw - thrown
thrust - thrust - thrust
tread - trod - trodden
understand - understood - understood
wake - woke, waked - woken, waked
wear - wore - worn
weave - wove - woven
wed - wed(ded) - wed(ded)
weep - wept - wept
wet - wet(ted) - wet(ted)
win - won - won
wind - wound - wound
wring - wrung - wrung
write - wrote - written

Numerales – Numbers

Números cardinales – Cardinal Numbers

0	zero, *Br tb* nought *cero*	90	ninety *noventa*
1	one *uno, una*	100	a hundred, one hundred *cien(to)*
2	two *dos*	101	a hundred and one *ciento uno*
3	three *tres*	110	a hundred and ten *ciento diez*
4	four *cuatro*	200	two hundred *doscientos, -as*
5	five *cinco*	300	three hundred *trescientos, -as*
6	six *seis*	400	four hundred *cuatrocientos, -as*
7	seven *siete*	500	five hundred *quinientos, -as*
8	eight *ocho*	600	six hundred *seiscientos, -as*
9	nine *nueve*	700	seven hundred *setecientos, -as*
10	ten *diez*	800	eight hundred *ochocientos, -as*
11	eleven *once*	900	nine hundred *novecientos, -as*
12	twelve *doce*	1000	a thousand, one thousand *mil*
13	thirteen *trece*		
14	fourteen *catorce*	1959	one thousand nine hundred and fifty-nine *mil novecientos cincuenta y nueve*
15	fifteen *quince*		
16	sixteen *dieciséis*		
17	seventeen *diecisiete*		
18	eighteen *dieciocho*		
19	nineteen *diecinueve*	2000	two thousand *dos mil*
20	twenty *veinte*	1 000 000	a million, one million *un millón*
21	twenty-one *veintiuno*		
22	twenty-two *veintidós*	2 000 000	two million *dos millones*
30	thirty *treinta*		
31	thirty-one *treinta y uno*		
40	forty *cuarenta*		
50	fifty *cincuenta*		
60	sixty *sesenta*		
70	seventy *setenta*		
80	eighty *ochenta*		

Notas:

i) En los números ingleses se utiliza un punto para separar los decimales:

1.25   **uno coma veinticinco**   one point two five

ii) Se usa coma en los lugares en los que en español utilizaríamos un punto:

1,000,000 = 1.000.000 o 1 000 000

Números ordinales – Ordinal Numbers

1st	first	1°	*primero*
2nd	second	2°	*segundo*
3rd	third	3°	*tercero*
4th	fourth	4°	*cuarto*
5th	fifth	5°	*quinto*
6th	sixth	6°	*sexto*
7th	seventh	7°	*séptimo*
8th	eighth	8°	*octavo*
9th	ninth	9°	*noveno, nono*
10th	tenth	10°	*décimo*
11th	eleventh	11°	*undécimo*
12th	twelfth	12°	*duodécimo*
13th	thirteenth	13°	*decimotercero*
14th	fourteenth	14°	*decimocuarto*
15th	fifteenth	15°	*decimoquinto*
16th	sixteenth	16°	*decimosexto*
17th	seventeenth	17°	*decimoséptimo*
18th	eighteenth	18°	*decimoctavo*
19th	nineteenth	19°	*decimonoveno, decimonono*
20th	twentieth	20°	*vigésimo*
21st	twenty-first	21°	*vigésimo prim(er)o*
22nd	twenty-second	22°	*vigésimo segundo*
30th	thirtieth	30°	*trigésimo*
31st	thirty-first	31°	*trigésimo prim(er)o*
40th	fortieth	40°	*cuadragésimo*
50th	fiftieth	50°	*quincuagésimo*
60th	sixtieth	60°	*sexagésimo*
70th	seventieth	70°	*septuagésimo*
80th	eightieth	80°	*octogésimo*
90th	ninetieth	90°	*nonagésimo*
100th	hundredth	10°	*centésimo*
101st	hundred and first	101°	*centésimo primero*
110th	hundred and tenth	110°	*centésimo décimo*
200th	two hundredth	200°	*ducentésimo*
300th	three hundredth	300°	*trecentésimo*
400th	four hundredth	400°	*cuadringentésimo*
500th	five hundredth	500°	*quingentésimo*
600th	six hundredth	600°	*sexcentésimo*
700th	seven hundredth	700°	*septingentésimo*
800th	eight hundredth	800°	*octingentésimo*
900th	nine hundredth	900°	*noningentésimo*
1000th	thousandth	1000°	*milésimo*
2000th	two thousandth	2000°	*dos milésimo*
1,000,100th	millionth	1 000 100°	*millonésimo*
2,000,000th	two millionth	2 000 000°	*dos millonésimo*

Números quebrados y otros – Fractions and other Numerals

½	one half, a half	*medio, media*
1½	one and a half	*uno y medio*
2½	two and a half	*dos y medio*
⅓	one third, a third	*un tercio, la tercera parte*
⅔	two thirds	*dos tercios, las dos terceras partes*
¼	one quarter, a quarter	*un cuarto, la cuarta parte*
¾	three quarters	*tres cuartos, las tres cuartas partes*
⅕	one fifth, a fifth	*un quinto*
3⅘	three and four fifths	*tres y cuatro quintos*
1/11	one eleventh, an eleventh	*un onzavo*
5/12	five twelfths	*cinco dozavos*
1/1000	one thousandth, a thousandth	*un milésimo*
	seven times as big, seven times bigger	*siete veces más grande*
	twelve times more	*doce veces más*
	first(ly)	*en primer lugar*
	second(ly) etc	*en segundo lugar*
7 + 8 = 15	seven and (*or* plus) eight are (*or* is) fifteen	*siete y (or más) ocho son quince*
10 − 3 = 7	ten minus three is seven, three from ten leaves seven	*diez menos tres resta siete, de tres a diez van siete*
2 x 3 = 6	two times three is six	*dos por tres son seis*
20 ÷ 4 = 5	twenty divided by four is five	*veinte dividido por cuatro es cinco*

Fechas – Dates

1996	nineteen ninety-six	*mil novecientos noventa y seis*
2005	two thousand (and) five	*dos mil cinco*

the 10th of November, November 10 (ten)
el diez de noviembre, el 10 de noviembre

the 1st of March, March 1 (first)
el uno de marzo, *L.Am.* el primero de marzo, el 1º de marzo